To the frontline workers in the field of addiction, to the men and women for whom substance abuse treatment is not only a profession but a mission, who so often "have been there" themselves, persons who care so much that they may even burn out eventually, but who in the meantime will help save people from the demon that is addiction. We need to keep in mind that for every individual helped, one whole family is spared—from child abuse, violence, bankruptcy. Therefore, with gratitude to the professional helpers and AA/NA sponsors alike, I dedicate my contribution to this book to you.

And, in particular, to my son, Rupert van Wormer, MSW, with extensive experience as a mental health case manager and harm reduction specialist who is now a medical social worker at Harborview Medical Center, Seattle.
—Katherine van Wormer

To my family, who support me no matter what with their love—Zach, Andy, John, Jayne, Mike, and Donna—and to the men and women who are taking their lives back from addiction.

—Diane Rae Davis

CONTENTS

ADDICTION TREATMENT

A Strengths Perspective

THIRD EDI

Wormer
Iowa

vis
niversity

BROOKS/COLE
CENGAGE Learning·

Australia · Brazil · Japan · Korea · Mexico · Singapore · Spain · United Kingdom · United States

BROOKS/COLE
CENGAGE Learning

**Addiction Treatment:
A Strengths Perspective,
Third Edition**
Katherine van Wormer and
Diane Rae Davis

Publisher: Jon-David Hague

Acquisitions Editor: Seth Dobrin

Assistant Editor: Suzanna Kincaid

Media Editor: Elizabeth Momb

Marketing Program Manager: Tami Strang

Cover Direction, Production Management and Composition: PreMediaGlobal

Art Director: Brenda Carmichael

Manufacturing Planner: Judy Inouye

Rights Acquisition Specialist: Roberta Broyer

Cover Image: © Sander van der Werf/Shutterstock

For product information and technology assistance, contact us at **Cengage Learning Customer & Sales Support, 1-800-354-9706.**

For permission to use material from this text or product, submit all requests online at **www.cengage.com/permissions.** Further permissions questions can be e-mailed to **permissionrequest@cengage.com.**

Library of Congress Control Number: 2011943253

ISBN-13: 978-0-8400-2916-4

ISBN-10: 0-8400-2916-0

Brooks/Cole
20 Davis Drive
Belmont, CA 94002-3098
USA

Cengage Learning is a leading provider of customized learning solutions with office locations around the globe, including Singapore, the United Kingdom, Australia, Mexico, Brazil, and Japan. Locate your local office at **www.cengage.com/global.**

Cengage Learning products are represented in Canada by Nelson Education, Ltd.

To learn more about Brooks/Cole, visit **www.cengage.com/brookscole.**

Purchase any of our products at your local college store or at our preferred online store **www.cengagebrain.com**

Printed in the United States of America
3 4 5 6 15 14 13 12

PART 2 | THE BIOLOGY OF ADDICTION   107

PREFACE

There is nothing so practical as good theory.
—Kurt Lewin

In the nine years since the publication of the first edition and the four years since the publication of the second edition of this book, the interest in the development and refinement of a strengths-based approach to work with addicted populations has continued to impact the field. Strengths-based practices increasingly are being adapted by mental health agencies and other fields of practice (Gray, 2011; Rapp & Goscha, 2006). Even more striking is the parallel growth and heightened attention devoted to harm reduction as a goal and as a process. Books have been published, conferences held, articles written in mainstream journals, and university courses shaped to focus on or at least incorporate principles of harm reduction. Workshops and lectures on the related principles of motivational interviewing and on treatment interventions tailored for the individual's stage of motivation to change have proliferated exponentially.

At the same time, and quite recently, the Twelve-Step approach to treatment has received a new respectability in research circles thanks to improved research findings on treatment effectiveness that can no longer be ignored. We have not gotten there yet, but the ideal arrangement would be to tailor the treatment philosophy to the special needs of the client. Note the bridge chosen for the cover design of this text. Our choice was a bridge to signify our attempt in this book to bridge the gap between the traditional Twelve-Step approach and the teachings of harm reduction. The bridge also symbolizes a way to cross over water (as in a "Bridge over Troubled Water") or a swamp or a steep decline, as a way of easing or expediting one's travels. In this sense, we can think of a bridge to recovery.

The response to the first edition of *Addiction Treatment: A Strengths Perspective,* both by readers of the book and by critics, was gratifying. In fact, the only criticism was that the theoretical framework of harm reduction was not emphasized to a greater degree than it was. Because of the consistently positive response to the book's theme of harm reduction, in the second edition we bolstered our harm reduction emphasis both in terms of policy and practice through a motivational enhancement model.

Critics of the second edition also responded highly favorably to the harm reduction approach. The major suggestion was to provide more information on assessment, especially strengths-based assessment for clients with alcohol and other drug problems. Taking this suggestion to heart, we have added a chapter to focus primarily on assessment and other interventions. To make more space for the new chapter, we combined the biology chapters into one and moved two other chapters that focus on biology-related addictive behavior—the chapters on gender issues and behavior disorders, such as gambling addiction and binge eating disorders—into the biological section of the book. Another substantial addition to this text is the inclusion in Chapter 6, Addiction across the Life Span, of a section on treatment needs of middle aged persons, or the "baby boom" generation, some members of whom are now paying the price for some of the indulgences of their youth, while others continue to engage in habits that are potentially life threatening.

All the content of the text has been carefully updated to reflect scientific advances in the field and in research as well as advances in the conceptualization of the nature of addiction itself. Exciting developments are underway: We are referring to calls from the government for a public health approach to substance use problems and trends favoring treatment over incarceration for people in trouble with the law over their drug use. At the same time, and this represents another major development enacted by the authorities, *The Diagnostic and Statistical Manual of Mental Disorders* in its fifth edition (*DSM-5*) is changing its diagnostic treatment of alcohol and other drug use disorders (APA, 2010). The first major change concerns the use of the term *addiction*, which was vigorously avoided in the fourth edition, and the second, which is even more far-reaching, is the conceptualization of addiction as existing along a continuum of severity. Now, with these modifications, the basic assumptions of the APA are more compatible with those of this text than they were before.

In this third edition, we continue to stress the prominence of co-occurring disorders in the substance use disorder population as in the population of persons with mental illness. Hence, this edition continues to infuse content throughout the chapters on the treatment needs of substance using persons with mental health disorders.

War-related trauma increasingly is an issue at all treatment centers due to the legacy of the wars in Iraq and Afghanistan, and even more so at Veterans Affairs (VA) hospitals. Facts concerning the treatment needs of returning soldiers, accordingly, have been incorporated in this text.

The criminal justice system is swelling. More than 1 million inmates incarcerated today are serving time for drug-related crimes. Substance abuse agencies and their staff are far more involved than in previous years in providing services to incarcerated men and women and to persons on probation and parole. This new edition, therefore, includes extensive material on the treatment needs of clients involved in the criminal justice system, including specialized drug courts and mental health courts.

Is cutting down on drinking and drug use a realistic option for alcoholics and addicts? Or is total abstinence the only path to recovery? The moderation versus abstinence controversy is easily the most hotly contested issue in substance abuse treatment today. Each position has its strengths, and each carries inherent risks. Addiction counselors who help clients merely moderate their destructive behavior run the risk of giving some of their clients false hopes and setting them up for failure. Proponents of immediate and total abstinence, on the other hand, can rest assured that they will drive away the majority of people who might otherwise come to them for help. Opponents on one side or the other of this controversy are discussing the issue both behind closed doors at treatment centers and openly on TV talk shows, in newspaper editorials, and on social work and counseling listservs. This debate—moderation versus abstinence—which has been part of the European scene for decades, has now reached American shores. Unfortunately, the debate in the United States sometimes resembles a feud. How addiction treatment providers and their political allies resolve this dilemma will largely determine the shape of addiction treatment in the 21st century.

As recently as 2000, the chief of an addiction treatment center in Manhattan, Dr. Alex De Luca, was forced to resign after he announced a plan to include a moderation management option for problem drinkers. "I was merely suggesting that you could engage people in a kinder, gentler manner," Dr. De Luca explained, "rather than telling them that they had to sign up for a goal achieving abstinence from the beginning" (Steinhaver, 2000, p. A26). So who would have anticipated a major paradigm shift a mere 9 years later? Yet, no other organization than the National Institute of Alcohol Abuse and Alcoholism (NIAAA) itself has discovered what addiction researchers have been saying for some time, that many people with alcohol use disorders at one point in time can learn to control their drinking or likely will do so, on their own, later in life (Peele, 2009). "Alcoholism Isn't What It Used To Be," according to NIAAA (2011).

Addiction treatment in the United States today is at a crossroads. Increasingly, the Twelve-Step–total abstinence model and, more broadly, the disease concept are being subjected to public and professional scrutiny (see, e.g., Carroll & Miller, 2006; Mancini & Linhorst, 2011; Peele, 2009; Wallace, 2005). This very questioning by commentators, and even the vociferous counter-response by representatives of mainstream organizations, is testimony to the fact that change is in the wind. Why shouldn't counselors, as some commentators and even some substance abuse counselors are asking, be available to help people just cut down on their drinking and other drug use, protect themselves, even in small ways, from harm, and thereby enhance their motivation for change? Why not keep our treatment options open?

Granted there have been attacks on the "one-size-fits-all" approach from the beginning. What is new today is, first, that the attacks have been widely publicized and, second, that much of the questioning of the orthodox position is coming from within the treatment field itself, as mentioned previously, from the federal government. Additionally, some viable alternative models are being used—and used successfully—for example, providing homeless people with co-occurring disorders with permanent rather than transitional housing.

The favorable mass media coverage of moderation efforts, the volume of professional critiques of the disease-model premises, and the slew of harm reduction workshops are all signals of impending change and a paradigm shift of sorts. Central to this shift is the realization that so many people in desperate need of treatment—with binge drinking, compulsive cocaine use, and other high-risk behaviors—will never seek help under present circumstances and that many literally will die as a result.

Hence, this book: a new book for a new day. Consistent with the strengths approach, this is not a book that lambastes, denigrates, or ridicules contributions of pioneers who have charted the course in substance abuse treatment. Indeed, many thought-provoking and volatile critiques of the addiction-as-disease model have already been written. Much that needed to be said has been said. Now is the time to move forward, to reconcile differences, and to get on with the task of helping people in the throes of addiction. So, no, this is not a book to tear down methods that have a history of success, methods in the promotion of which both authors have been personally involved. In our fascination in determining which faction is correct and who owns the soul of chemical dependence treatment—the abstinence or individual responsibility folk—we lose sight of the complete picture.

Tearing down is simple. The primary task of *Addiction Treatment* is more complicated than that; the task is to shape a text grounded in a strengths or empowerment perspective, a theoretical framework that is inclusive and holistic. We hope to achieve this task by providing a digest of the theory, facts, and guidelines necessary for direct practice in a field whose practitioners and administrators have been traditionally resistant to change.

Sociologically speaking, the addictions field is characterized by fierce loyalties and a devotion to principle not seen in any other comparable profession. Interventions flow logically from the basic premises. Two types of bias are common in the field of addictions. First is the tendency to see disease where there may be only bad habits or even emotionally dependent behavior. Second, there is the countertendency of these doctrinaire positions to see only bad habits where there is great personal pain, illness, and suffering.

The addiction-as-disease bias, a carryover from the anti-professionalism in the alcoholism treatment field of the 1980s, demands immediate and total abstinence from all mood-altering substances, with the usual exception of to-bacco. For persons with mental disorders, who often use alcohol and other drugs to relieve their symptoms, conformity to strict abstinence-only policies is extremely difficult (Mancini & Linhorst, 2011). And despite the fact that Twelve-Step groups operate on the principle that attendance is strictly volun-tary and anonymous, this model generally requires regular attendance at meetings of an Alcoholics Anonymous– or Narcotics Anonymous–type of group. Bolstered at the societal level by government policies of zero tolerance for illegal drug use, this treatment approach, in its attention to structure and mandates, is a natural fit for work with criminal justice referrals. And today, according to the Substance Abuse and Mental Health Services Administration (SAMHSA) (2009), in the United States, most treatment referrals come from the criminal justice system. (To read the tenets of the Twelve-Step movement, see *Alcoholics Anonymous: The Big Book* [2002].)

At the other extreme is the school of thought bent on tearing down the basic precepts of the disease model. This "rational," highly critical orientation focuses on individual responsibility for ending the bad habits that have erro-neously been labeled a disease. This approach is probably as blaming in its way as the predominant approach that it seeks to replace. Placing complete responsibility on individuals for their bad habits, this rational model expects people simply to control their excessive urges. As in the era before the disease model, emphasis is on will power and self-control; this treatment, approach (voiced most articulately by Fingarette [1988] and Peele [2004]) is reflected in government and insurance policies that deny funding for therapy alto-gether. People, the reasoning goes, should be able to alter their bad habits on their own or at least with nominal intervention.

In truth, these seemingly polarized positions have rather more in common than their proponents would care to admit. Central to both approaches is a moralism and even, at times, a blaming that is characteristically American. This culturally based moralism will be explored from a historical standpoint in Chapter 2.

In contrast to the extreme positions of these rival camps of "true believ-ers," both of whom are apt to hold their views intransigently, passionately, against accusations from the other side, comes the harm reduction model. The *harm reduction model* is a grassroots movement that originated in Europe as a realistic response to serious public health problems, including the rapid spread of AIDS/HIV. A holistic approach, harm reduction is client-centered and is capable of absorbing elements from the disease model, de-pending on client preferences as revealed through dialogue. Contrary to a popular misconception, this model does not preclude eventual abstinence for persons seeking help with substance misuse problems. We seek, in this book, to integrate rather than reject truths that, whether based on science or not, have been a godsend to so many. So instead of "tossing out the baby with the bathwater," for example, throwing out the Twelve Steps, we recognize Twelve-Step programs as a valuable contribution to individuals and society.

Clearly, however, one size does not fit all. What this text will focus on is how to skillfully help people find the treatment they need to get well. The basic organizing framework of this textbook—harm reduction—is consistent with the National Association of Social Work's (NASW's) (2009) policy statement that "All reasonable avenues to address ATOD (alcohol, tobacco, and other drugs) problems must be considered, including psychosocial treatments, medications, alternatives to incarceration, and harm-reduction approaches" (p. 28). Adopting such a comprehensive public health approach should enable social workers to focus on the prevention and treatment of alcohol, tobacco, and other drug problems.

ORGANIZATION AND FRAMEWORK

In common with the disease model, this text puts an emphasis on biology as a key factor in understanding the nature of addiction. It is our belief that human behavior can be understood only in terms of its biological, psychological, social, and spiritual components. The biopsychosocial framework, accordingly, has been chosen as the organizing framework for this book. *Biologically,* we will be looking at recent developments in neurobiological and pharmaceutical research related to addictive behavior. From a *psychological* standpoint, we will want to consider motivational and cognitive-based treatment innovations and evidence-based research on treatment effectiveness. And *sociologically,* we always consider the fact that any specific individual who enters into treatment does not live in a vacuum but is both shaped by and a shaper of his or her social and political environment.

The organization of the book, in short, reflects the biopsychosocial roots of its subject, which is addiction. Divided into four parts, the first of which is introductory, *Addiction Treatment* includes three core sections that cover the biology, psychology, and social aspects of addiction, respectively. The spiritual dimension is included in the psychological and social parts of the book.

STRENGTHS-BASED THERAPY

The terminology, ideology, and conceptual framework for this undertaking derive from the strengths perspective. This client-centered approach is compatible with the harm reduction model in that the overriding purpose is to help the client reduce the harm to himself or herself or others. Harm reduction therapy allows for creativity in the design of treatment strategies. Total abstinence from dangerous drug use is certainly not discouraged, nor is total abstinence from alcoholic beverages by those with a genetic predisposition to get "hooked." But starting with "where the client is" rather than where we think the client should be is the basic principle underlying harm reduction. Placing faith in the client's ability to make choices is a related concept.

Our aim in writing this book is, above all, to be pragmatic. The word *pragmatic* is used here in the dual sense of being realistic and having relevance to direct practice. Of what use is theory, after all, without practical application? The focus on the strengths perspective in the treatment of addicts and alcoholics, accordingly, is not chosen because of some ideology of "looking at the bright side of things." Rather, it comes from the practical understanding that a focus on capabilities rather than defects fosters hope (where there is despair), options (where there is a perceived dead end), and increased self-efficacy (where there is a feeling of helplessness). Chapters 1 and 8 will address the specifics of strengths-based therapy with addictive populations. Interventions will be directed at the individual, group, and community levels.

Social work and mental health counseling with clients suffering from alcoholism and other addictions must be performed within the constraints of political and economic realities. Economically, constraints on the form and length of treatment can be expected to continue under the dictates of managed care cost-saving restrictions. Largely because of the war on drugs, with the arrests and sentencing of so many drug users, much of treatment undoubtedly will continue to be provided under the auspices of departments of correction. In such a climate of oppression and mean spiritedness, it is imperative that those of us who are in the helping professions work through political advocacy to improve treatment offerings for some of our most vulnerable citizens and their families.

BASIC ASSUMPTIONS

Congruent with the biopsychosocial, ecosystems configuration, the perspective advanced in this book is that addiction, to be a viable concept, must be viewed interactionally. Each component of the system, in other words, is seen in constant and dynamic interaction with every other component; reality is rarely linear; cause and effect are intertwined. Related to addiction, the nature versus nurture controversy is resolved through an understanding that steers away from a dichotomized "either–or" type of logic, as seen in the pointless is it nature or nurture arguments, for example. Our preference is for logic of the "both–and" variety. Consistent with this perspective, addiction is viewed as both a biological and a psychosocial phenomenon. There is, further, a spiritual dimension as well. The simplistic, adversarial view of human phenomena leaves us with only partial truths and fierce loyalties that hinder us in our understanding of complexity. To advance knowledge, we need to hear from a multiplicity of voices. That the nature of addiction is infinitely complex will be revealed in the pages of this book. Essential to the study of addiction is a theoretical approach that is eclectic; such an approach is inclusive and broadening. One might even say that it is friendly rather than antagonistic toward diverse models.

To summarize, a major theoretical assumption of this book is that in our pursuit of knowledge concerning addiction and its treatment, our goal is to build upon the professional literature in the United States, Canada, and abroad and from old models and new models, whether psychodynamic or sociological, abstinence-based or experimental in nature. Some other basic assumptions that underlie this presentation are:

- Addiction exists along a continuum; many people may be addicted to one substance or product; one person may be addicted to multiple substances or activities involving risk (in relationships).
- Much of the criticism concerning various models of addiction (e.g., the disease model and individual responsibility theory) is valid; these models do tend to be unidimensional and narrow, but then, much of the criticism itself is unidimensional and narrow.
- There are hereditary tendencies toward addiction, but with work, these tendencies can usually be controlled.
- Better than forbidding adolescents from drinking is to have them learn moderate drinking from parents who drink moderately in the home.
- Whether alcoholism or addiction is regarded as a disease depends on the definition of disease; that addiction can be regarded as *like* a disease is a fact to which we can all agree.
- Involvement in mutual-help groups such as Alcoholics Anonymous can be invaluable in enhancing recovery and providing support to family members.
- When the focus is on promoting healthy lifestyles and on becoming motivated to change rather than on the substance misuse per se, many clients can be reached who would otherwise stay away.
- The war on drugs is politically and ethically misguided; issues of race, class, and gender define the parameters of this "war."
- Because there will never be a drug-free society, the only pragmatic approach is a public health or harm reduction approach.
- Addiction counselors who are themselves recovering have some advantages over counselors who "have not been there"; however, this kind of personal involvement is no more essential in this field than in related fields such as health and mental health. A continuously self-reflective stance is necessary for all counselors to be effective.
- Addictive behaviors are highly destructive to the family as a system and to each family member within that system; treatment, therefore, needs to include strong family counseling components.
- Professional training in counseling skills and neurobiological and psychosocial knowledge is just as essential for work in this field as it is for comparable fields of practice.
- Specialized training in substance misuse and the various addictions should be a requirement for practitioners in this field; such training should take place outside the treatment center and be scientifically based.
- Treatment must be tailored to the needs of the individual seeking help and include family and community support for recovery.

- Treatment ideally should be offered in all systems across health and human services and juvenile justice systems, not only in specialized substance abuse treatment centers.
- Treatment effectiveness is most accurately measured in terms of the reduction of harmful health-related practices rather than by total abstinence from drinking and drug use.

Addiction Treatment: A Strengths Perspective is intended for use as a primary text in courses related to substance misuse or as a secondary text in courses, graduate or undergraduate, related to health, social work, mental health, offender rehabilitation, and family counseling. Suffused with case examples and summaries of the latest scientific research, this book is directed to many types of practitioners in the addictions or related fields—from those who work with addicts and their families on a day-to-day basis to those who rarely see an addict but who are in positions of supervision, management, and policymaking related to addiction issues.

In the same way that hope is offered by counselors to even the most down-and-out addicts, we wish to offer hope (and appreciation) to the practitioners who dedicate their lives to work with those for whom other practitioners have little empathy or use. The hope that we would offer is ingrained in the strengths perspective itself. An approach that seeks resilience in clients and encourages workers to focus on possibilities rather than problems should go a long way toward preventing exhaustion and burnout in a field that is often characterized by both. The strengths perspective is not new to the chemical dependence field; in fact, as we argue in Chapter 1, empowerment has been inadvertently used by caring counselors for years. What we are providing here is its formulation and, ideally, reinforcement. In any case, working with addicts on the verge of self-destruction is a tough assignment. We constantly have to remember that the phoenix rose from a pyre of ashes, not a soft pillow, and that it is in those ashes that we find the embers of hope and change. That is what this book is about.

A Word from Katherine van Wormer, MSSW, PhD, Professor of Social Work, University of Northern Iowa, Cedar Falls. Website: www.katherine-vanwormer.com

Being from an alcoholic background (my father) and an alcoholic city (New Orleans), I had no desire to do substance abuse counseling initially. But then in the 1980s, equipped with a brand new degree in social work, I ventured to Washington State in search of scenery and a job. After an inauspicious beginning in community home health and hospice, I found myself working at the community alcohol center in Longview, Washington. This treatment center was fairly laid back as far as substance abuse treatment centers go. Unlike my previous job, the work was fun and highly creative, and the clients got progressively better instead of progressively worse. The two-year outpatient program brought palpable results that were gratifying to see.

About five years later, I found myself in another scenic part of the world, Norway. As part of a mini-migration of Americans to Norway and Sweden to bring the Minnesota Model or Twelve-Step–based treatment, I trained counselors in group skills and actually learned the rudiments of the American disease model from a fellow American in Norway. Although the inevitable personnel crises abounded in a program that was run by ex-clients with limited periods of sobriety, I again witnessed the miracles of recovery and experienced the joy of seeing lives on the mend. In my public relations capacity, I spoke through translators to various community groups about alcoholism as a personal disease and as a family disease. Today, I coordinate the substance abuse certificate for social work students at the University of Northern Iowa. Relevant books I have written include *Alcoholism Treatment: A Social Work Perspective* (1995) and *Introduction to Social Welfare and Social Work: The U.S. in Global Perspective* (2006), both published by Cengage Publishing Company. I have coauthored *Social Work with Lesbians, Gays, and Bisexuals: A Strengths Perspective* (2000) and *Women and the Criminal Justice System* (3rd ed.) (2010), both published by Allyn & Bacon/Pearson, and *Working with Female Offenders: A Gender-Sensitive Approach* (2010), published by Wiley & Sons. My most recent book is a two-volume set, *Human Behavior and the Social Environment: Micro Level* and *Macro Level,* published by Oxford University Press (2011).

A Word from Diane Rae Davis, MSW, PhD, Professor of Social Work, Eastern Washington University, Cheney

It seems that my entire life has been intertwined with one addiction or another. If you looked at my genogram, you would see addiction all over it and the subsequent deaths, illnesses, and divorces that follow. You would also see pockets of recovery. My own recovery from alcoholism was a terrible struggle. It took 3 years to get clean and sober from the time I was absolutely convinced I was an alcoholic. When I finally did, I had no job, no husband, no home to live in, and a son in my care. Yet my middle-class background had protected me from many of the consequences that women who are addicted face: jail or prison, prostitution, bankruptcy, infectious disease, and so on.

During the years of my own recovery, I have witnessed hundreds of men and women recover from the direst circumstances, and I have also witnessed the death or suicide of others who didn't make it. The effect of all this history may seem contradictory. On the one hand, I have a strong conviction to "never to give up" on even the worst scenarios—I have seen way too many miracles to ever "close the case" on anyone. On the other hand, I have learned the hard way the futility of hanging on to my own agenda regarding someone else's recovery. People make changes on their own timing, doing the best they can and surviving how they can. Behaviors that look like "resistance" and "noncompliance" from the outside may have completely different meanings when viewed from the inside. I have learned about "letting go." And finally, I've learned that there are many paths to recovery and that "recovery" means different things to different people. It took a while for me to give up the idea that what saved *my* life is the path for everyone. Having given that up, I find I have increased my capacity to help others. I have a profound belief in the strengths perspective and the possibilities of change. Similarly, I support the harm reduction model because of its many paths to sobriety, including abstinence, and because it honors a person's dignity by offering choices over and over again, no matter what.

Professionally, I have stayed close to the addiction field in social work practice and academic teaching, publishing, and research. In 1992, I received my PhD at the University of Texas at Austin under the mentorship of Dr. Diana DiNitto. I now teach a variety of courses at the School of Social Work and Human Services at Eastern Washington University, including Addiction Treatment and Motivational Interviewing for MSW students. The publication of my article (with Golie Jansen) "Making Meaning of Alcoholics Anonymous" in *Social Work* (1998) allowed me to fulfill a personal mission to address the massive misunderstandings about mutual-help organizations among professional helpers. One of my most interesting research projects was "Women Who Have Taken Their Lives Back from Compulsive Gambling." This project involved an online research survey and qualitative interviews from women around the United States who are recovering from compulsive gambling. The result of this effort was several scholarly articles and the book *Taking back Your Life: Women and Problem Gambling* (2009), which was written for women who are currently experiencing gambling as a problem. My current mission is to help bring the problems of compulsive gambling to the attention of social workers and other helping professionals.

My other areas of research and publications include women's addiction and recovery, rural substance abuse treatment, ropes course treatment, harm reduction, alternative "sobriety" schools, and methadone maintenance.

NOTE

We both share responsibility for this book as a whole, and each chapter is a collaborative effort by both of us. However, the Preface; Chapters 1, 2, 3, 5, 6, 10, and 13; and the Epilogue were the primary responsibility of Katherine van Wormer. Chapters 4, 7, 8, 11, and 12, were the primary responsibility of Diane Rae Davis.

ACKNOWLEDGMENTS

The authors' appreciation goes to the following reviewers for their helpful critiques of the manuscript:

Both authors extend thanks to those people in recovery, family members of persons with addiction problems, and substance abuse professionals who provided case histories and boxed readings for this edition. Diane Rae Davis thanks her Chair, Martha Raske, PhD, School of Social Work, Eastern Washington University, for supporting her in completing the third edition. The authors would like to recognize the publisher's social work acquisitons editor, Seth Dobrin and his former assistant editor, Alicia McLaughlin, for their personal support in directing this project; Project Manager Sharmila Krishnamurthy, and the copy editor, whose meticulous attention to detail has improved the final product.

REFERENCES

Alcoholics Anonymous. (2002). *Alcoholics Anonymous: The big book*. Center City, MN: Hazelden.

American Psychiatric Association (APA). (2010). *Diagnostic and statistical manual of mental disorders (DSM-5.)* Proposed revision: addiction. Washington, DC: Author.

Carroll, K. M., & Miller, W. R. (2006). Defining and addressing the problem. In W. R. Miller & K. M. Carroll (Eds.), *Rethinking substance abuse: What the science shows* (pp. 3–7). New York: Guilford Press.

Fingarette, H. (1988). *Heavy drinking: The myth of alcoholism as a disease*. Los Angeles: University of California Press.

Gray, M. (2011). Back to basics: A critique of the strengths perspective in social work. *Families in Society, 92*(1), 5–11.

Mancini, M. A., & Linhorst, D. M. (2011). Harm reduction in community mental health settings. *Journal of Social Work in Disability and Rehabilitation, 9*(2), 130–147.

National Association of Social Workers (NASW). (2009). *Social work speaks: NASW policy statements, 2009–2012* (8th ed.) Washington, DC: Author.

National Institute on Alcohol Abuse and Alcoholism (NIAAA). (2011). Alcoholism isn't what it used to be. *NIAAA Spectrum, 3*(1). Retrieved from http://www.spectrum.niaaa.nih.gov/features/alcoholism.aspx

Peele, S. (2004). *Seven tools to beat addiction*. New York: Three Rivers Press.

Peele, S. (2009). United States changes its mind on addiction: It's not a chronic brain disease after all. *Psychology Today*. Retrieved from http://www.psychologytoday.com

Rapp, C. A., & Goscha, R. (2006). *The strengths model: Case management with people with psychiatric disabilities* (2nd ed.). New York: Oxford University Press.

Steinhaver, J. (2000, July 11). Chief of addiction center quits over policy. *New York Times*, p. A26.

Wallace, B. C. (2005). *Making mandated treatment work*. Lanham, MD: Jason Aronson.

INTRODUCTION

On the surface, our application of the strengths perspective to the field of addiction treatment marks a dramatic departure from the past. Our notion of reinforcing strengths in a self-directed program of harm reduction is seemingly a more extreme departure still. And yet the tone of this writing is intended to be conciliatory rather than adversarial; the focus is "building upon" rather than "tearing down."

Part I of this text, comprising Chapters 1 and 2, summarizes the current state of knowledge concerning the nature of addiction. A major task of the first chapter is definitional: to offer a conceptualization of addiction specific enough to be usable yet broad enough to encompass seemingly disparate behaviors such as compulsive overeating, disordered gambling, excessive devotion to work, and out-of-control spending. In these chapters and throughout the book, attention is paid to the biological, psychological, social, and spiritual aspects of addictive behavior.

The nature of addiction is complex. Its assessment and treatment represent such an inexact science that numerous theories exist, each one convincing in its own right, each with a school of followers, and each explaining only a part of the whole. The questions in the field run deep: What is addiction? Why are some people more addictive than others? How can addiction be controlled? Our perspectives—moralistic, scientific, and just plain oppositional—help shape our answers concerning the nature and treatment of addiction.

The nature of public policy is complex as well. Despite spending billions of dollars and arresting millions of Americans, the U.S. government has been unable to stop the flow of illegal drugs. Meanwhile, the harms associated with substance misuse—addiction, drug overdose, drug-related crime, the spread of HIV/AIDS—continue to mount. Add to this the casualties of the war on drugs—the broken families, children in foster care, lost worker productivity, homelessness, overcrowded prisons—and it is easy to see why so many of us are calling for change to reduce the social and psychological harm. We are calling for harm reduction and treatment availability and advocating for counseling techniques that motivate people to get help when they need it.

To learn where we are going, we need to look back to our cultural and historical roots. The purpose of Chapter 2 is to trace the roots of today's policies concerning drug use and society's attempts to control it. Two basic themes are central to this historical review. The first theme is technology, and the second is ideology. In Prohibition, as we will see, these themes converged. (Technologies such as alcohol distillation created a climate for change in public opinion about drinking.) Other forces, such as the Puritan legacy of the New England colonies, were involved as well. That there is a new prohibition movement today in the form of a war on drugs is a major argument of this chapter. That the drugs of choice that are most harshly punished and apt to be outlawed are those associated with poor minority groups is a second major argument.

The political and historical context of addiction treatment are among the issues tackled in the first two introductory chapters. Our journey to exploring these dimensions begins with Chapter 1, The Nature of Addiction. The first task of this book, in short, is to explore the nature of addiction and its conceptualization. The second task, which is the subject of Chapter 2, is to put today's conceptualizations in historical and theoretical context.

THE NATURE OF ADDICTION

CHAPTER I

*"We have three words to define what harm reduction expects
from an addict,"* says Dan Bigg of the Chicago Recovery Alliance.
"Any positive change."
—Shavelson (2001)

"The suffering of a soul that can suffer greatly—that and only that, is tragedy." So wrote Edith Hamilton (1948, p. 131), the foremost authority on ancient Greek culture of her day. She was talking about Greek tragedy. The purpose of classical Greek tragedy as acted out on the stage was to explore human psychology and to dramatize situations in which the hero met his or her fate. The hero in classical Greek tragedy possessed a tragic flaw, *hubris*, that ultimately would be his or her undoing (Walters, 2006). Today, in real life as in drama, the source of personal tragedy is often some sort of human flaw in the form of a harmful compulsion or obsession. The "fatal attraction" may involve a person, an activity, or a substance.

Thus, when we hear of the compulsive gambler who leads his or her family down the path of financial ruin, of the Internet whiz who, like the workaholic, sacrifices family life for an "affair" with Cyberspace, the kid who can't get off of Facebook, or of the drug addict who deals drugs or prostitutes herself to support her habit, we may find in us a sense of pity and awe, the essence of all great tragedy.

The effects of addiction are everywhere and nowhere—everywhere because they are in every family and workplace, nowhere because so much of the behavior is hidden from public view. Sometimes, as with Internet gambling or pill addiction, even family members are unaware of the problem until a major crisis ensues.

In contrast to the tales of classic literature, in real life there may be a way out of the pain, a way for the individual to get beyond the tragic flaw. The way out is called *recovery*. "I'm in recovery," says the proud member of Alcoholics Anonymous (AA). Similarly, the person who has gotten some personal counseling in reducing the harm announces that now his or her own life has gotten under control.

In our jails, hospitals, women's shelters, and child welfare departments, all places where professional counselors and social workers are employed, the impact of substance misuse and addiction is a given. Where there is assault, incest, rape, child neglect, or attempted suicide, more often than not some form of substance misuse is involved. The effects may be immediate—for example, the neglectful parent so strung out on methamphetamines (meth) that he or she has lost all sense of time and all sense of responsibility. The effects may be lifelong—for example, the woman who suffered sexual abuse by a male predator early in childhood and who has taken to using prescription drugs and alcohol for self-medication, to dull a pain the cause of which may or may not be remembered.

Members of other professions encounter the impact of addictive behavior as well. A police officer (personal communication, May 2010), for example, describes his daily experience in small town Iowa:

> Professionally, I see addicts every day. Whether it is the alcoholic who wanders the streets collecting cans to buy his bottle of wine, or the thief who steals the Texas fifth of vodka from the grocery store, I deal with meth addicts that cannot quit using even though they no longer work, lost their home, friends die of an overdose, yet the same day they shoot up, knowing they may be next.... It is these same addicted individuals who cause a good portion of the crime in society. It is this crime that I am left cleaning up after.

The impact of addiction, we should note, is seen in the suites as well as on the streets. This chapter explores the nature of addiction and contemporary trends in its treatment. Each section covers a different facet of drug and alcohol addiction, including definitional issues; an overview of the biological, psychological, and social aspects; various treatment approaches and trends; and a look at the politics of addiction treatment. Two concepts that form a theme of this book—the biopsychosocial-spiritual model and the strengths perspective—are introduced in this chapter. Subsequent sections of the chapter present an introduction to the art and science of addiction treatment and contemporary trends in treatment. (The intimate experience of substance misuse is shared by the addicts themselves, their children, and professionals in the field.)

WHAT IS ADDICTION?

Addiction is seen in the man in the detox unit of a hospital who is cringing from the pain of pancreatitis. He has no plans to quit drinking, his wife says. Addiction is evidenced in the two-pack-a-day smoker who coughs steadily from emphysema. Addiction is implicated in the actions of the trusted employee who was imprisoned for embezzlement; she needed more money to gamble.

The economic cost of addiction is incalculable. Certainly, billions of dollars are involved. There is the health toll of alcohol and drug misuse, the astronomical expenditures in running the war on drugs and in incarcerating the over 1 million persons whose crime was related to alcohol or some other drug. Catering to people's addictions is big business that ranges from marketing tobacco to special populations, to setting up state lotteries, to organized crime. So, what is addiction? According to the *Dictionary of Word Origins* (Ayto, 1990), the roots of the word *addiction* are in the Latin past participle *addictus*, meaning "having given over or awarded to someone or being attached to a person or cause." The original connotations were highly positive. Originally used as an adjective in English, its meaning has become increasingly negative over time.

The way in which substance misuse is perceived has important practical implications for how individuals with drinking and drug problems are treated—by their families, by medical and mental health professionals, and by the state. In the substance misuse literature, addiction is variously defined as a sin (Rosin, 2000); a sense of helplessness (Dodes, 2003); excessive behavior (Orford, 2001); a bad habit (Peele, 2004); a personal choice (Schaler, 1999); an expression of self-determination (Szasz, 2003); a moral and spiritual deficiency (Dalrymple, 2006; Morell, 1996); a disorder of choice (Heyman, 2009); and, more compassionately, as a brain disease (Leshner, 2006) and "a chronic relapsing brain disease" (Volkow, 2010, p. 5). And to William Miller (2006), addiction is fundamentally a problem of motivation.

For an official definition, we first turn to the *Diagnostic and Statistical Manual of Mental Disorders, Text Revision (DSM–IV–TR)* (American Psychiatric Association (APA), 2000) and to proposed changes that are underway for *DSM-5*, which is set for publication in May 2013. Because the first draft has already been written, we can include the revised conceptualizations in this book. The significance of the *DSM* cannot be exaggerated; the diagnoses that are finally agreed upon by the panel of experts are used almost universally by mental health professionals to diagnose and receive insurance reimbursement for treatment for behavioral disorders.

The starting point for conceptualizing and treating substance use disorders is terminology. The *DSM–IV–TR* avoided use of the term *addiction* in favor of the seemingly more scientific term *dependence*. We disagree with this terminology, as shown in our choice of *Addiction Treatment* as the title for our book. Now the members of the *DSM-5* substance-related work group have come around to the same conclusion. The term *dependence* will now be reserved for physiological dependence on a drug, for example, withdrawal symptoms. Along these lines, a decision has been made to include cannabis withdrawal in the fifth edition.

"Addictions and Related Disorders" is the heading to be used for this section of the manual. The *DSM-IV* differentiated substance use disorders into substance dependence and substance abuse. As denoted by the APA (2000), the major difference between them was the presence of tolerance and withdrawal problems. We, in previous editions of this text, disagreed with this dichotomization and conceptualized addiction as occurring along a continuum of severity. Now *DSM-5* is moving in this direction as well (see Curley, 2010). The drawback, however, is that, as Allen Frances, MD, indicates, the expanded definition of addiction, might result in pinning the "addict" label on persons who deliberately drink to get drunk, for example, or take other drugs to get high, but who are not on the road to addiction. Addiction, according to our understanding of the term, denotes loss of control over a substance or behavior. Although intervention may be required for reckless and potentially harmful behavior, the diagnosis of addiction disorder may not be helpful or accurate for many acting-out youths. How practitioners handle this diagnostic change in the *DSM* remains to be seen. In any case, substance use disorder now joins the abuse and dependence criteria into one unitary diagnosis. As provided by the APA (2010), these criteria are:

Substance Use Disorder

A. A maladaptive pattern of substance use leading to clinically significant impairment or distress, as manifested by 2 (or more) of the following, occurring within a 12-month period:
   1. recurrent substance use resulting in a failure to fulfill major role obligations at work, school, or home (e.g., repeated absences or poor work performance related to substance use; substance-related absences, suspensions, or expulsions from school; neglect of children or household)
   2. recurrent substance use in situations in which it is physically hazardous (e.g., driving an automobile or operating a machine when impaired by substance use)
   3. continued substance use despite having persistent or recurrent social or interpersonal problems caused or exacerbated by the effects of the substance (e.g., arguments with spouse about consequences of intoxication, physical fights)
   4. tolerance, as defined by either of the following:
      a. a need for markedly increased amounts of the substance to achieve intoxication or desired effect
      b. markedly diminished effect with continued use of the same amount of the substance *(Note: Tolerance is not counted for those taking medications under medical supervision such as analgesics, antidepressants, anti-anxiety medications or beta-blockers.)*
   5. withdrawal, as manifested by either of the following:
      a. the characteristic withdrawal syndrome for the substance (refer to criteria A and B of the criteria sets for withdrawal from the specific substances)
      b. the same (or a closely related) substance is taken to relieve or avoid withdrawal symptoms *(Note: Withdrawal is not counted for those taking medications under medical supervision such as analgesics, antidepressants, anti-anxiety medications or beta-blockers.)*

6. the substance is often taken in larger amounts or over a longer period than was intended
7. there is a persistent desire or unsuccessful efforts to cut down or control substance use
8. a great deal of time is spent in activities necessary to obtain the substance, use the substance, or recover from its effects
9. important social, occupational, or recreational activities are given up or reduced because of substance use
10. the substance use is continued despite knowledge of having a persistent or recurrent physical or psychological problem that is likely to have been caused or exacerbated by the substance
11. Craving or a strong desire or urge to use a specific substance.

(criteria available at http://www.dsm5.org)

According to the APA (2010) on the *DSM-5* Development website, in recognition of the similarity of gambling addictive behavior to substance use disorders, gambling disorder is now to be reclassified and placed under the category Addictions and Related Disorders as a behavioral disorder. Previously pathological gambling was listed as an Impulse Control Disorder and not considered as a form of dependence. Nevertheless, the diagnostic criteria for gambling disorder are relatively similar in the earlier and later versions of the *DSM*. The new standards are listed here:

GAMBLING DISORDER

A. Persistent and recurrent maladaptive gambling behavior as indicated by five (or more) of the following:
   1. is preoccupied with gambling (e.g., preoccupied with reliving past gambling experiences, handicapping or planning the next venture, or thinking of ways to get money with which to gamble)
   2. needs to gamble with increasing amounts of money in order to achieve the desired excitement
   3. has repeated unsuccessful efforts to control, cut back, or stop gambling
   4. is restless or irritable when attempting to cut down or stop gambling
   5. gambles as a way of escaping from problems or of relieving a dysphoric mood (e.g., feelings of helplessness, guilt, anxiety, depression)
   6. after losing money gambling, often returns another day to get even ("chasing" one's losses)
   7. lies to family members, therapist, or others to conceal the extent of involvement with gambling
   8. has jeopardized or lost a significant relationship, job, or educational or career opportunity because of gambling
   9. relies on others to provide money to relieve a desperate financial situation caused by gambling

(APA, 2010)

Box 1.1	A Social Work Major Working in a Casino
	Julie Taylor

As gambling fever makes its way across the United States, we hear different views and opinions expressed in the media on what seems like a daily basis. Especially here in Iowa, where there is a constant controversy over issues such as the morality of gambling, how casinos affect the economy, the legality of gambling, and other pertinent issues. There are specials on television about addiction and how it has affected the Native American peoples, about the glamour and glitz of casinos, and about the money made and lost. I have talked with different customers about their winning or losing streaks. One night while I was working, I saw a middle-aged man dressed in a very nice business suit playing a $5 slot machine. He kept putting in one $100 bill after another. I counted four times that he went to either the automatic teller machine (ATM) or the credit card machine. He was losing what I call a ton of money. He literally had sweat running down his head and had a look of sheer panic on his face. He looked up at me at one point and said, "I'm dead. I am just dead." I just stood there and with a look of sorrow on my face said, "As much money as you've put in it, I can't believe it hasn't paid out yet." What I really wanted to say was, "Why don't you just go home before you lose more money?" I will never forget the look on that man's face. It was obvious to me that he had a serious gambling problem. I see a lot of this at the casino.

One thing that you hear almost nothing about is what it is like to work at a casino. That's something I can tell you about. My husband, Dave, and I have worked at our local casino (Meskwaki Bingo, Casino, & Hotel) for just about 2 years, and I can tell you that there is certainly nothing glamorous about it. It is hard work not only from a physical point of view but more so from an emotional point of view.

Let's begin with the atmosphere in which we work. Customers, unless they are "regulars," don't really realize that they are being watched the entire time they are in there. There are literally hundreds of cameras rolling 24 hours a day from every angle. As the song goes, every move we make, every step we take, every single day, every single way, I'll be watching you. Why? It's not necessarily to watch the customers as it is to watch us employees! The assumption made by owners is that every employee is a thief. There is more truth in this than I like to imagine. The slightest mistake, the smallest unexplained movement, a sneeze, scratching your head, or touching another person can draw an instant call from "upstairs" surveillance and quite possibly a write-up, suspension, or being fired on the spot if they don't like what you did or how you did it. This atmosphere pervades every moment of your working life. To say the least, it is incredibly degrading. The joke in the employee break room is that the next thing we know, there will be cameras in the restrooms. Believe it or not, at one time there were microphones placed in the ceiling tiles in the break rooms so they could record what was being said by the employees. Swear, a true story.

Speaking of degrading, imagine what it is like to have customers screaming at you, swearing at you, doing everything short of physically attacking you because they are losing money (or, for that matter, winning money) or not getting the immediate service they feel is due them. One constant at the casino is they cannot keep enough people employed to service the enormous number of customers they deal with on a daily basis. The turnover rate of employees is phenomenal. In some departments, such as the pit (this is where the card games are played), we are 60 dealers short of being full staffed. The turnover rate is more than 70% per year. I love dealing cards to people. It is fun because I enjoy interacting with people and I know that this work isn't my lifetime career. I also attend college at the University of Northern Iowa full time.

Now let us move on to some things that people may not realize about casinos. For instance, when you see pictures in movies and on television of casinos, it appears that the customers are young, excited, partying people, when in reality, most customers are elderly folks living on Social Security and pensions. It is so sad to have an elderly woman crying to you about having lost her entire Social Security check and now having to go home and explain what happened to all the money that she had in the world. It tears your heart out and at the same time makes you realize why some people feel gambling should be illegal.

Another interesting thing about the casino life is that it is much like life in a bar. The customers are the same people day after day, night after night. Sometimes you wonder if they have any other life! Their whole existence seems to be gambling. Like the bartender, we know their names, we learn their lives, we hear about their problems, their families, and their spouses. After a while I find myself offering advice just like a bartender does. (I also was a bartender for 8 years.) However, because we are employees of the casino (and you never know who is listening), we have to say stupid things like, "That machine should hit anytime now," "Keep going, it has to pay off soon," or "At least you haven't lost as much as that person has." What you really want to say is, "Don't you people have homes you can go to?" or "Do you realize how many groceries you could have bought with the money you put in there?" I talked to a lady once who told me that she brought her rent money to try and win enough to pay her rent and light bill; she lost it all and left crying!

Something I learned about casinos: Until the last 20 years or so, casinos were the major way of laundering money for the mob and for drug dealers. This was accomplished simply by buying poker chips to gamble with, or placing cash in the casino's vault, or even exchanging $100 bills for smaller ones. This actually doesn't happen as much since the change in federal law requiring casinos to report all transactions over $1,200 to the IRS.

One more tidbit of information: Slot machines at casinos actually pay out 94–96%. That means that the casino actually only makes about 5 or 6% profit on slot machines. That doesn't seem like a lot, does it? In fact, you might consider if you're a player that this means that if you play a machine long enough, the most you could lose would be 5–6% of the money you put into it. That would be true if the customer knew which machines were paying off and which ones weren't. Casinos make millions off of the 6% they take in on slot machines. Can you imagine the total money spent on them to get them to pay out? It boggles the mind.

In this politically correct decade, the most horrific politically correct term ever created is the one that the gambling industry has made into an everyday word: *gaming*. There is no game here. You pay and you lose; that is the game.

Printed by permission of Julie Taylor.

Gambling disorder is listed as a behavioral disorder. Internet and sex addiction are not included, however, but are placed in the appendix as in need of further study. Another proposed change of relevance to our addiction book is that binge eating disorder is now included under eating disorders (see Chapter 5 on behavioral addictions).

Before we progress any further into the maze of classification and word usage, let us consider just how far into the depths of madness the addictive urge can lead us. Box 1.1, "A Social Work Major Working in a Casino," takes us behind the scenes into a work environment that preys on the vulnerable ones—compulsive gamblers.

In his book on lifestyle theory, Glenn Walters (2006) strenuously objects to the use of such criteria that relate to a loss of control over a substance; to the disease model of Alcoholics Anonymous, which he finds disempowering; and to the word *addiction* itself. He proposes an alternative concept—the lifestyle concept—that allows for an emphasis on personal choice. The lifestyle concept, however, in our opinion, has problems of its own, chiefly in its rejection of the biological component in behavior that impedes the ability of many individuals to make healthy choices. A too-heavy emphasis on individual responsibility in the use of mood-altering substances can play into the punitive response so much in evidence regarding drug use in U.S. society. (We delve into this matter more in a later section, Treatment Trends.)

To define addictive behavior in terms of a lack of responsibility is fraught with political and treatment difficulties, as Joranby, Pineda, and Gold (2005) suggest. If eating disorders, for example, are viewed as stemming from a lack of self-control, treatment resources will be hard to come by. And there is every indication of a close similarity between dependence on drugs and dependence on food. That food is a powerful mood-altering substance is borne out in scientific findings about brain reward systems and neurotransmitter aberrations, as, for example, among bulimics. Classification of eating disorders as an addiction, as these authors further argue, would help in our prevention and educational efforts. Many of the addictive chronic disorders, such as compulsive overeating and pathological gambling, are characterized by loss of control, relapse, compulsiveness, and continuation despite negative consequences.

The addiction concept, as stated previously, perceives addiction as occurring along a continuum. Severe life-threatening dependence may be placed at one end, the misuse of substances somewhere in the center, and a use of substances without problems at the other end. Individuals or their behaviors can be placed along a continuum according to levels of misuse or addiction at various points in their lives. The revised version of the *DSM* promises to discard the either–or categories of substance use that existed in the previous edition and to now help us appreciate the individual dimensions of human behavior. From this perspective, as Frances (2010) suggests, there are no rigid boundaries between normal and pathological populations or between common diagnostic categories.

From a contemporary perspective, in marked contrast to the earlier view of alcohol dependence as a progressive and irreversible disease, most problem drinkers move in and out of periods of dependent drinking. And we know that the majority of people who meet the criteria for addiction in their teens and 20s have become moderate drinkers or drug users by their 30s, as Harvard psychologist Gene Heyman (2009) informs us. And most of them will never set foot in a treatment center. We need to keep in mind, of course, that persons who present themselves at specialist treatment agencies (often by court order, as is typical in the United States) are apt to have severe problems and represent the extreme end of the continuum. For this reason, we should refrain from generalizing about addiction and recovery to the general population based on the biased sample from the treatment population when more than three-fourths of all persons with addiction problems, as Heyman estimates, never enter treatment and recover on their own.

We can take issue with the *DSM,* even in its improved format, for one other reason as well: the incompatibility of such labeling and diagnosis with the tenets of the strengths perspective. As the name would indicate, the *strengths perspective* is an approach geared to look for strengths rather than liabilities, not because they are "truer" but because an approach geared toward a person's possibilities is more effective than an approach focusing on a person's problems. The entire mental health field, as strengths-based theorists Rapp and Goscha (2012) indicate, is "dominated by assessment protocols and devices that seek to identify all that is wrong, problematic, deficient, or pathological in the client" (p. 93). Still, in the United States, mental health practitioners, rehabilitation counselors, and social workers in many fields use APA criteria for substance use disorders as a means of obtaining insurance reimbursement and vocational rehabilitation services for their clients (Heyman, 2009). The physical, psychological, and social aspects of addiction disorders, as spelled out in this diagnostic manual, can be helpful in assessment and communication among professionals and in giving testimony before the court.

A welcome change to the *DSM* is the proposed use of the term *substance use* in place of *substance abuse.* A problem semantically with the term *substance abuse* is that the substance is not being abused. The individual may be committing self-abuse, but the substance is merely consumed or otherwise ingested; it is hard to abuse an inanimate object, after all. The terms *substance use* and *substance misuse* are more accurate and even more sensible, and they are used in this text to refer more specifically to general and harmful drug use, respectively. The terms *substance abuse treatment* and *substance abuse counseling* are used because of their familiarity rather than due to any descriptive accuracy. *Addiction treatment,* however, is our preferred term.

The concept of addiction offers us the flexibility to cover various forms of problematic behavior. It also is highly compatible with the biopsychosocial model, which attends to the *subjective* as well as objective factors in human behavior. Addiction can be defined as a pattern of compulsive substance use or behavior. *The Social Work Dictionary* (Barker, 2003) defines addiction as follows:

ADDICTION: Physiological and psychological dependence on a behavior or substance. Behavioral addictions (sex, gambling, spending, obsessive internet use) and consumptive addictions (alcohol, drugs, food) often have similar etiologies, prognoses, and treatment procedures. Most professionals now use the term "substance dependence" for consumptive addictions. (p. 7)

Although the tendency is to equate addiction with loss of control, the extent to which the individual is truly beyond self-control cannot be proven but can be inferred only from external behavior or from an individual's self-reporting of this phenomenon. To what extent addiction is an involuntary disease is open to question. Heyman (2009), for example, argues that addiction is not an illness; the individual's decision to continue to use a harmful drug or to abstain depends on what the stakes are. People who have incentives to remain drug free, such as a good job, are more likely to do so than are people who have less to lose. Most addictions experts would agree with this supposition; what they would disagree with is the presupposition stated in the title of Heyman's book, *Addiction: A Disorder of Choice*. Few people, in fact, would choose to have any disorder, much less to be addicted to a substance or behavior. What's missing but needed in scientific research is a way to determine the point at which self control over a craving for an addictive substance has gone beyond the level that it can be controlled. Without getting inside the mind of a drug user, compulsive gambler, or chain smoker, we do not know how hard it is to resist temptation. We will never be able to read people's minds, but we can gain a great deal of insight into this dimension from the recent advances in brain research. Through newer technologies such as magnetic resonance imaging (MRI), neurologists can now observe, for example, the impact that gambling has on neurotransmitters in the brains of pathological gamblers. Research on biogenetic vulnerabilities in gamblers is showing promising results as well. "Brain imaging studies from drug-addicted individuals," according to psychiatric researcher Nora Volkow (2010), "show physical changes in areas of the brain that are critical to judgment, decision making, learning and memory, and behavior control. Scientists believe that these changes alter the way the brain works and may help explain the compulsive and destructive behaviors" (p. 7).

To understand the pain connected with addictive and compulsive behavior, one must first understand the *pleasure* side of these activities (i.e., their attractiveness). Pete Hamill (1994) captured this attractiveness very well in his autobiography, *A Drinking Life*. "The culture of drink endures," he wrote, "because it offers so many rewards: confidence for the shy, clarity for the uncertain, solace to the wounded and lonely" (Introduction). Books on treatment, whether written by scholars or by self-help authors, focus almost exclusively on the harm of substance use, a harm inherent in the substances themselves. Yet, according to Volpicelli and Szalavitz (2000), it is crucial to learn why substances such as alcohol and licit or illicit drugs are useful as well as attractive. Volkow (2010) lists three major uses or attractions of intoxicating substances in answer to the question, Why do people take drugs? First, they take drugs to feel good, to enhance their sense of pleasure. "For example, with stimulants such as cocaine," she states, "the 'high' is followed by feelings of power, self-confidence, and increased energy. In contrast, the euphoria caused by opiates such as heroin is followed by feelings of relaxation and satisfaction" (p. 6). Second, people who suffer from anxiety and stress-related disorders may be attracted to intoxicants to feel better. The third temptation to use drugs is to do better, such as to enhance athletic or work performance.

Then we also need to take into account the fact that substance use in itself is not always wrong or harmful, despite attempts by various factors to convince us otherwise. Alcohol, for example, when used in moderation, has many health-giving properties and, like the opiates, has been used for centuries to relieve pain. Apart from nicotine, which is highly addictive, as Volpicelli and Szalavitz (2000) indicate, only a small percentage of drinkers, marijuana users, or heroin users exhibit the kind of problems that would define them as sick or in need of treatment. Few areas of human life exist where individual differences are more pronounced than in regard to people's taste (or distaste) for mood-altering substances, including food. Some crave uppers, ranging from caffeine to methamphetamines; others go to incredible lengths to obtain downers, such as alcohol and diazepam (Valium). Still others use such substances to enhance their sensual pleasures, but then only occasionally. Medical science is rapidly uncovering clues to these individual differences, clues that go beyond pharmacology or even environmental circumstances and into the realm of brain chemistry. But that is the topic of another chapter.

Of all the addictions, *alcoholism* is the most studied and the most common, next to nicotine addiction. The American Medical Association (AMA) (1956) declared that alcoholism was an illness. In 1968, the AMA offered the following definition, which is still widely used:

> Alcoholism is an illness characterized by preoccupation with alcohol and loss of control over its consumption such as to lead usually to intoxication if drinking is begun; by chronicity; by progression; and by tendency toward relapse. It is typically associated with physical disability and impaired emotional, occupational, and/or social adjustments as a direct consequence of persistent and excessive use of alcohol. (p. 6)

The AMA definition identifies the three basic areas of ecological concern: the physical, the psychological, and the social. Thus, it is the definition chosen for this text. The selection of the word *illness* to describe alcoholism provides a clear acknowledgment of alcoholism as a medical problem with widespread ramifications (social and moral). Illness is a nonjudgmental, non-victim-blaming term.

At the present time, on their website, the AMA (2011) "endorses the proposition that drug dependencies, including alcoholism, are diseases and that their treatment is a legitimate part of medical practice" (Definition H-95.983: Drug Dependencies as Diseases H-95.983). The word *disease* originally was applied to alcoholism by Jellinek (1960), who said that alcoholism was *like* a disease. It was a short road from "like a disease" to "a disease," one with vast political and medical connotations. In the United States in recent years, a trend toward the "diseasing" of behavior not ordinarily considered pathological (e.g., codependence) has been pronounced.

Simultaneously, there has been a countertrend stressing individual responsibility for a range of addictive behaviors, now labeled "bad habits." This movement away from the disease models carries some risk of "throwing the baby out with the bath water," of turning the clock back on treatment availability. Disregarding the political aspects for the moment, let us draw upon the dictionary definition of disease.

Disease

1. (Middle English) A pathological condition of a part, organ, or system of an organism resulting from various causes, such as infections, genetic defect.
2. A condition or tendency, as of society, regarded as abnormal or harmful.
3. Obsolete, lack of ease, trouble.

(American Heritage Dictionary, 2000, p. 517)

Similarly, the *Shorter Oxford English Dictionary* (2007, p.702) defines disease as

1. Absence of ease; inconvenience; trouble.
2. [A] disorder of structure or function in an animal or plant of such a degree as to produce or threaten to produce detectable illness or disorder; a definable variety of such a disorder, usually with specific signs or symptoms or affecting a specific location; (an) illness, (a) sickness.

According to this, as in most dictionary definitions, alcoholism certainly qualifies, along with diabetes and certain heart conditions, for consideration as a disease. McNeece and DiNitto (2005), however, warn against use of the term *disease* for two reasons. The first is that the word is generally used as simply a metaphor and not in a literal sense. The second reason is because "if a phenomenon is a *disease,* then we expect a cure in the form of a drug or other medical treatment" (p. 7). Alcohol and drug dependence are viewed by McNeece and DiNitto as addictions but not diseases, except when discussing the consequences of alcoholism, such as pancreatitis.

To denote the extensive pain and suffering wrought by the condition of alcoholism, we have chosen, as in the AMA definition, to favor use of the word *illness* over *disease*. Illness, in medical terminology, is the experience of being sick or diseased; it is a social psychological state caused by the disease (Larsen & Lubkin, 2009). Thus, pathologists treat disease, whereas patients experience illness. The subjective level of illness, as previously suggested, makes this term more relevant to helping professions' focus on the person in the environment and on the interaction between the person and the world outside. Understanding the illness experience is essential when providing holistic care.

The concept of addiction as an illness of body, mind, and soul is part and parcel of the biopsychosocial-spiritual understanding of this phenomenon. Through the initial act of drinking or drug ingestion, the body adapts remarkably, sometimes to the extent of permanent biochemical and psychological changes. As thought processes in the brain are altered, one's ability to adapt to stress may be weakened. Socially, the hard-drinking, drug-using life determines the company one keeps (and the company one loses); one's family members are affected in dramatic and devastating ways. The consequences of substance misuse raise stress levels; this, in combination with the physiological craving associated with heavy use, reinforces the urge to partake.

BIOPSYCHOSOCIAL-SPIRITUAL MODEL

Social work and other counseling professions conceive of addiction holistically, with attention to biological, psychological, and social components in its causation and consequences. The advantage of the biopsychosocial-spiritual model is in being able to address more than one problem at a time (Miller, 2005). Note that this model is a mere framework, as widely used in texts in the field to organize material. The biopsychosocial-spiritual model is atheoretical in that it doesn't explain anything, so it can be used with any philosophical approach, such as the traditional disease model or harm reduction model.

The pain and suffering of alcoholism and other addictions constitute the biopsychosocial reality. The *biology* of chemical use relates to the formidable hereditary components in the etiology of this illness and the physical problems that may arise with extended use. A growing literature documents the many ways in which addiction is a complex brain disease (Washton & Zweben, 2006). Predisposing characteristics such as endorphin deficiency can set the stage for future problems long before the use of any addictive substances. Thus, we hear from a man who is serving a long prison term for manslaughter following a drunken driving crash:

> My father has had a few DWIs (driving while intoxicated convictions), my sister one, and I've gotten two. I've never done drugs; alcohol is my drug of choice. I am also bulimic. I've struggled with my eating disorder for about eighteen years now. My problems with alcohol and bulimia along with depression just feed each other. (personal communication; June 13, 2006)

The *psychological* concept encompasses the thinking that leads to the drinking, injecting, or snorting of the substance. These irrational or unhealthy thought processes may be associated with depression or anxiety, which in turn may encourage escape through drug use or other compulsive behaviors.

That the high has a psychological as well as a biological basis is revealed in this description from a male compulsive shopper (Anderson, 1994):

> It was like, it was almost like my heart was palpitating.... I couldn't wait to see what was there. It was such a sensation. In the store, the lights, the people; they were playing Christmas music. I was hyperventilating and my hands were beginning to sweat, and all of a sudden I was touching sweaters and the whole feel of it was beckoning to me. And if they had a SALE sign up, forget it; I was gone. You never know when you're going to need it. (p. 223)

Leshner (2006) concurs that the traditional dichotomization into psychological and physical addictions has been shown to be faulty. Physical dependence to a drug, he says, is not that important. Withdrawal symptoms can be offset today through medication. And the most dangerously addictive drugs—meth and crack cocaine—do not produce severe withdrawal symptoms.

"What really matters most," continues Leshner (2006), "is whether or not a drug causes what we now know to be the essence of addiction, namely, the uncontrollable compulsive drug craving, seeking, and use, even in the face of negative health and social consequences" (pp. 2–3).

The *social* component in addiction relates to *where* as opposed to *why* or *how*. Where does the addictive activity take place and where is the impact felt? The peer group and family may be involved. One factor we should never lose sight of is social class. Economically disadvantaged persons are more likely to suffer alcohol-related problems, even when drinking at the same level as more economically privileged groups, because they lack the material resources and often the social supports available to others.

The *spiritual* dimension is a key component in the illness of addiction. Spirituality is crucial in recovery because it is related to one's sense of meaning and interconnectedness. A shift from negative punishing to positive forgiving views of spirituality often accompanies recovery (Neff & MacMaster, 2005). This is what David Carr (2008), a *New York Times* reporter, experienced after many years of drinking and drugging:

> It was hard to avoid a spiritual dimension in my own recovery. I woke up to a miracle every day that I was clean and crawled into bed each night grateful. (p. 250)

The closely related concepts of healing and forgiveness (of the self and others) enhance interpersonal relationships. A major component of the biopsychosocial-spiritual model of addiction is interactiveness. In the language of systems theory, the basic principle of interactionism is that cause and effect are intertwined. In the words of McLellan (2010), Deputy Director of the White House Office of National Drug Control Policy: "Some problems cause substance use; some problems result from substance use; and some simply emerge along with substance use as the result of genetic, personality or environmental conditions" (p. 3).

In the language of ordinary conversation, we talk of a vicious cycle. The expression "what goes around comes around" is another way of saying the same thing. Any member of an alcoholic family becomes aware of how pain and substance misuse feed into each other until the two become almost one and the same. As suffering induces the wish to escape unpleasant feelings through the use of chemicals, this indulgence in turn leads to pain at all four levels of the biopsychosocial-spiritual model. The resultant pain exacerbates the urge to drown the feelings—physically, in the bottle.

A second major principle of interactionism concerns the overlap among the four aforementioned components. Body, mind, society, and spirituality are all furiously intertwined in the cycle that is addiction. Cocaine may be used as an upper, for example, to dull the pain of organic or situational depression. The social costs of alternatively acting depressed and engaging in illicit drug use may be enormous.

Another form of interaction that figures in addiction is that between stress and individual responses to that stress. Consider, for example, how persons under severe stress tend to use alcohol and/or tranquilizers to reduce their anxiety levels. According to a study by the National Center on Addiction and Substance Abuse (CASA) at Columbia University, substance abuse treatment admissions increased 10–12% nationally after the events of September 11 ("Terrorist Attacks Cause Spike," 2001). This phenomenon was reminiscent, according to the same article, of the heightened demand for treatment in Oklahoma following the Oklahoma City bombing.

Interactionism is seen most vividly in the dynamics of the family system. Much has been written about "the alcoholic family." The set of demands imposed on the family members of persons with alcohol, drug use, and other addiction problems can be awesome, both emotionally and financially. Each family will have its own particular style of adaptation and coping, whether through blaming, denial, and/or overprotecting. Because the family is a system, one member's malfunctioning throws the whole family's functioning awry. While the individual addict remains to some extent "out of things," family members may take the tension out on each other. (See Chapter 10 for a study of addict/alcoholic family dynamics.) In personal correspondence of September 8, 2000, a woman who identifies herself only as Sue shares a childhood memory:

> During the week, he was a Grandpa/"Poppy"/teacher/best friend. On the weekends, he was this stranger who stumbled home late at night long after the corner bar had closed. And, to mollify Grandma and me, he'd carefully carry two fish fry dinners home for us. But he never understood why greasy French fries at 3 A.M. never appealed to me.
>
> After school on Friday afternoon, he volunteered to drive me to a doctor's appointment. But he had started an early weekend and so had a bottle of brandy in the car. I guess no one in the family had seen it before he left the house. We never made it to the appointment. He totaled the car on a downtown bridge. I wound up in the hospital with four fractured limbs.
>
> My father threatened to kill him; my mother threatened to leave my father for threatening her father; my grandma threatened divorce. I was crying as if my heart would break, and Grandpa fell asleep in the hospital room visitors' lounge, oblivious to the turmoil and heart-rending aftereffects of "a few early nips."

Interactionism is a concept with special significance in a treatment book of this sort, where the focus is on effecting interpersonal change and motivation. In the chapters ahead, we will be dealing with strategies to enhance motivation. Motivation is one of the most consistent predictors of how clients will perform in addiction treatment (Miller, Forcehimes, & Zweben, 2011). Therefore, counselors want to do what they can to help their clients become motivated to move in a health-inducing direction.

PREVALENCE OF SUBSTANCE MISUSE

Mental health professionals can expect approximately 50% of their clients to have problems stemming from their own or a family member's alcoholism (Corrigan, Mueser, Bond, Drake, & Solomon, 2008). Alcohol misuse also figures widely in family and marital counseling. Workers in child welfare observe firsthand the toll on the victims of neglect and abuse due to parental drinking problems.

The majority of addiction counselors' clients are court ordered to treatment; that is, they are persons who were convicted of drug-related crimes, or they are otherwise coerced in some way into treatment, perhaps before they make their court appearance. As Wallace (2005) suggests, in her study of mandated addiction treatment, the tremendous influx of clients from criminal justice systems referrals parallels the societal shift toward conservatism, moralism, and intolerance. The number of inmates has continued to climb to 2.3 million, 1.5 million of which meet the DSM IV medical criteria for substance abuse or addiction (CASA, 2010). Since 1970, incarceration rates have quadrupled in the United States, leaving over 2 million people behind bars, almost half of whom are minorities. As of 2009, nearly 1 in 20 Black men is incarcerated. Black males are 6 times more likely to be imprisoned than White males, and more than 2.5 times more likely to be incarcerated than Hispanic males, according to the Bureau of Justice Statistics (2010).

Diane Young (2003) reviewed the medical records of 359 mentally ill jail inmates. She found that 67% of this sample had a substance-related disorder in addition to the mental disorder. In a comparison of Canadian and U.S. policies of harm reduction, Judith Grant (2009) concluded that the social climates of the neighboring countries are strikingly different. The climate of domestic drug policy in the United States is the criminalization mode of regulation—a mode that is based on the model of addiction as a crime and one designed to prohibit the use of illegal drugs. Canada, in contrast, has a drug policy based mainly on the harm reduction model, which is directed toward decreasing the adverse health, social, and economic consequences of drug misuse without requiring abstinence from such use.

Correctional counselors constantly encounter the effects of drug use and addiction as they treat clients in the correctional system. Over 80% of persons incarcerated in the United States have a substance use problem upon admission into prison; 79% of all inmates in Canada have alcohol and/or other drug problems upon entry into prison; and 70% of prisoners in England and Wales reported use of illegal substances during the 12 months before their incarceration (Jolley & Kerbs, 2010). Many inmates have co-occurring disorders as well. When drug offenders reenter society after serving lengthy sentences, they are often unprepared to resume community and family life. The temptation to return to the world of drugs can be formidable. And so is the challenge facing social service providers. The need, according to Bina, Hall, Mollette, and colleagues (2008), is for more extensive training of social work students in substance abuse prevention and treatment, regardless of the area of specialization they choose, because addiction problems are rampant across all areas in which social services are provided.

According to a random survey of 2,000 National Association of Social Work (NASW) members, 71% of social workers had taken one or more actions with clients with substance abuse disorders in the past year (O'Neil, 2001). Citing this research, Bina and colleagues (2008) conducted a smaller survey of hundreds of master's level students to determine their sense of competence in handling the substance-related issues they undoubtedly would encounter in the field. These researchers found an overall low level of perceived preparation to work with clients with addiction problems, and they recommended that related courses be required for all social work students.

Social work practice with persons who have alcohol and other drug problems takes place in a wide range of settings. Hospital social workers, for instance, encounter both the early- and late-stage effects of heavy drinking in patients. The estimate is that one hospital bed in four is occupied by a patient whose ailment is related to alcohol. Alcohol misuse is the third leading cause of death, after heart disease and cancer.

THE GRIP OF ADDICTION

- "Help! I'm Addicted to Facebook" (Stiles, 2009)
- "Life after Meth: 'Methland' Author Explores How Drug Affects Entire Towns" (Kilen, 2009)
- "Second Rail-Equipped Drug Tunnel Found at Mexican Border" (Cathcart, 2010)
- "When Tanning Turns into an Addiction" (Brody, 2010)
- "U.S. Students Suffering from Internet Addiction: Study" (Siew, 2010).
- "Drugs in Ozarks Town Infect even Sheriff's Department" (Sulzberger, 2011)
- "Deputies Say Mom Eating Meth with Child on Her Lap" (Associated Press, 2011)

Such are the typical headlines in regional and national newspapers on any given day. The concern with addiction is as universal as the battle to control it. Some stories focus on individuals, with celebrities of course drawing the most attention. Numerous articles highlighted Robert Downey Jr.'s re-arrest due to continued drug problems. "If anyone ever had good reason to say no to drugs, it was surely Robert Downey, Jr." begins *Time* magazine's version (Lemonick, 2000, p. 97). This statement referred to the fact that this actor had recently completed treatment for cocaine and heroin use following an earlier arrest and had returned to a promising career, including a starring role in a Hollywood film with Julia Roberts, only to get caught possessing cocaine and speed shortly thereafter. Later, Mel Gibson attracted much negative attention in the media when he drunkenly blurted out a series of anti-Semitic remarks (Maugh, 2006). He quickly turned himself in to a rehab center for help with his alcohol problem and probably to appease the general public. Then during the following years, even more extensive news coverage was given to the drug-related antics of celebrities Britney Spears, Lesley Lohan, and Charlie Sheen (Sosnoff, 2011).

Although to explain these behaviors the traditional psychologist might look to a pattern of self-destructiveness and the sociologist to professional stress, a multidimensional analysis would certainly take biological factors into account. Aided by powerful new diagnostic tools that can document changes in the brain as a result of drug use, researchers can now fathom the relentless craving that accompanies depletion of endorphins, or "feel-good" chemicals, in the brain. The brain of the drug user is physically altered in ways that make resistance to further drug use difficult (Volkow, 2011). More will be said about this in Chapter 3.

Hereditary factors are involved in addiction as well. In a presentation at the University of Northern Iowa on April 25, 2008, a substance abuse counselor with 20 years of sobriety, Ralph Campbell, described his family background:

> My mother was an officer in the U.S. Navy who drank herself to death at age 58. My aunt died of the same thing at age 39. My father developed alcohol-related dementia. At age 12, I would check to see if my mother was breathing. Once I put a kitchen knife to her throat. This was a sort of an intervention, but it didn't work. Then I started drinking Scotch. Alcohol worked beautifully for me. When I drank, everything got better, felt better.

An excellent portrayal of the grip of addiction and the harrowing process of recovery is given in the 2000 Hollywood movie *28 Days*. Gwen, the alcoholic who goes into inpatient treatment to avoid a jail term for a drunken driving episode, lost her mother to alcoholism as a child. In treatment, Gwen injures her ankle climbing out of a window to retrieve some pills. "The definition of insanity," says her counselor, "is repeating the same behavior over and over and getting the same results."

Perhaps the most honest representation of an addict's surrender and recovery ever put on film is in the 1988 movie *Clean and Sober,* starring Michael Keaton. A cocaine-addicted real estate executive in deep financial trouble, Keaton's character hides out in a rehab center. The transformation he undergoes is moving and informative at the same time. Another noteworthy portrayal is provided in the European-produced film *Clean*. This 2004 movie depicts the emotionally charged struggle of a heroin-addicted mother to get her life and child back after serving time in a Canadian prison.

And then there is *Traffic*. Addictive behavior is woven through every generation in this powerful 2001 film portrayal of a family and other persons caught up in the war on drugs. As the leading character, played by Michael Douglas, prepares to become the nation's new drug czar, his 16-year-old daughter sinks ever more deeply into the mire of drug addiction. To learn of Johnny Cash, the legendary country music star's, long struggle with addiction and related relationship issues, see *Walk the Line*, which was made available on DVD in 2006.

Whereas celebrities and other rich people are more apt to use cocaine as a drug of choice, methamphetamines are more commonly associated with the poor. This is especially true in the Midwest. An Iowa police officer (personal communication, May 2010) graphically describes the hold this drug has on people:

> You will find few drugs that cause as much physical and mental damage to an individual. A user of meth will lose interest in personal hygiene and will not eat

properly, leading to substantial weight loss. Sustained users often believe that there is something under their skin and will pick at it until they develop awful sores. Tooth decay occurs under such use; users slowly lose all their teeth. Uncontrollable twitching and moving is noticeable. Since meth is a powerful stimulant, users will be up for days on end and not sleep.... Users in time become solely interested in only one thing, and that is using meth.

Marriages disrupted, kids getting into trouble, people committing illegal acts—the pattern is the same with nonsubstance addictions, sometimes called behavioral addictions, such as with compulsive gambling. Compulsive shoppers, for example, have obsessive buying urges that lead them to have closets full of never-worn clothing and then go out the next day and buy more. Medication seems to help reduce the strange cravings in many cases (see Chapter 3). Eating can present problems for persons who seem predisposed to addictive behavior, such as Wanda Haban (1999), who told her story to an addiction treatment class:

> I was a chronic dieter for 25 years. Today I try to have a healthy diet, but to change habits is a forever process. My father is an alcoholic, so genetically or psychologically those addictive traits are instilled in me. The first time I had a few drinks, I had a blackout. So I knew there was a problem there. I had hangovers, so I didn't choose that drug as my choice. I chose food as my choice. Once I ate beyond a certain point, I couldn't stop.
>
> My ex-husband said, "Don't ever get fat." My dieting was starvation and bingeing, yo-yo dieting. I am still obsessed with dieting.

THE STRENGTHS PERSPECTIVE

The strengths perspective, which cannot be considered a theory because it lacks explanatory power, is a way of perceiving people in their struggles to rise above difficult circumstances. In combination with the empowerment theoretical perspective, the strengths approach is the predominant approach in social work today. Positive psychology that focuses on well-being and resilience is a parallel perspective that is achieving a large following in psychology. Positive psychologists such as Biswas-Diener (2010) focus on mental health rather than mental illness and working with clients collaboratively to recognize and reinforce strengths and in so doing "to promote energy, effectiveness, productivity, and a sense of meaning" (p.38). Motivational psychologists such as William Miller and his colleagues write from a perspective of strengths as well. For working with people with addiction problems, their emphasis is on bolstering client self-efficacy. This is done, they inform us, in normal conversation through exploring successful changes the clients have made in the past. Mobilizing clients' own strengths and social support systems are important, Miller, Forcehimes, and Zweben (2011) suggest, in promoting rehabilitation and recovery maintenance.

One other discipline turning toward the use of strengths-based concepts to help people turn their lives around is criminology. Admittedly in its infancy, a form of positive criminology is being developed, according to Israeli social scientists Ronel and Elisha (2010). A new conceptual approach, positive criminology is geared to the study of "factors that may help at-risk individuals desist from deviance and crime" through positive experiences and connections (Ronel & Elisha, 2010, p. 306).

In all these disciplines, the strengths perspective is primarily a philosophy or way of interpreting information about bio-, psycho-, and social factors in people's lives that are forces for the good. These belief systems link human flourishing to following humanistic values and are rooted in Aristotle's writings on human striving to reach one's potential (Gray, 2011). In therapy, Carl Rogers operated from the premise that a nondirective, nurturing relationship would bring out the best in people. Similarly, the strengths perspective in social work favors an inductive approach whereby insights emerge through relationships with clients and the stories they tell (Gray). This approach to client treatment was pioneered and popularized through the writings of Dennis Saleebey (1992) and Charles Rapp (1998) in their books *The Strengths Perspective in Social Work Practice* and *The Strengths Model: Case Management with People Suffering from Severe and Persistent Mental Illness,* respectively.

Although there is much overlap between traditional and strengths-based approaches to the conceptualization of substance disorders and the treatment thereof, for the sake of distinction, we have constructed Table 1-1. Concepts from traditionally-based treatment are derived from van Wormer's alcoholism treatment practice experience with this 12-Step approach, from White's (1998) history of substance abuse treatment, and from Peele and Bufe's (2000) critique. On the opposite side of the table, we list concepts central to the strengths perspective as drawn from the writings of Saleebey (1992, 2009, 2011) and Miller, Forcehimes, and Zweben (2011).

As an inclusive approach, the biopsychosocial framework allows us to use the learning developed across disciplines and to employ a strengths-based approach to work with addicted individuals, their families, and communities (Corrigan, Bill, & Slater, 2009). Whereas the biopsychosocial-spiritual model helps us gain a holistic understanding of the roots and intransigence of addiction, the strengths perspective is geared toward direct practice, although it can shape our appreciation of particular treatment modalities (or aspects of these modalities) as well. This perspective represents a paradigm shift away from the treatment industry's emphasis on psychopathology, disease, and disorder, a focus on personal deficits rather than resilience. Harm reduction alone is not enough; the client caught in the mire of addiction and personal pain needs help in developing a healthy outlook on life and even a dramatically altered lifestyle.

Given the horrendous grip of addiction for certain individuals—the self-defeating behavior, guilt feelings, broken relationships—it is clear that the treatment modality used must offer hope and a way out of the morass of the addiction cycle. Hope, guidance, and relationships are three key ingredients in

TABLE 1.1 | COMPARATIVE APPROACHES TO ADDICTION

Traditional Counseling Approach	Strengths-Based Therapy
Biological	**Biological**
Looks to the individual for specific causes of disease	Stress on multiple, interactive levels of influence
Dichotomizes reality, for example, alcoholic vs. nonalcoholic	Addiction-like behaviors seen as existing along continuum
Psychological	**Psychological**
Problem focused	Strengths focused, looks to possibilities
Uses labels such as alcoholic, codependent	Tries to avoid use of negative labels
Assesses problems and losses	Assesses and builds on strengths
Client seen as typically resistant, in denial	Client seen as active participant in collaborative, health-seeking effort
Client motivation unimportant	Intervention geared to level of client motivation to change
Focus to prevent slip or relapse	Focus to maintain moderation or abstinence as client wishes
Expulsion from treatment for relapse	Client self-determination stressed; meet the client where he or she is
Uses confrontation to elicit change	Rolls with the resistance; redefines resistance as challenge
One size fits all	Individualized treatment; stresses client choice
Social	**Social**
Encourages identity as member of self-help group	Holistic approach
Identifies pathologies from upbringing in chemically dependent home	Seeks strengths in upbringing
Looks for codependence in family members	Perceives family as potential resource

successful recovery. Finding a spiritual connection can help tremendously as well.

Although most recovery does not stem from formal treatment, the incentive for sobriety can very well be an outgrowth of a treatment experience. And for the family of the person with an alcohol or other drug problem, family counseling can be a lifesaver.

The strengths approach, as its name implies, builds on clients' strengths and resources. This is "a versatile practice approach, relying heavily on ingenuity and creativity, the courage and common sense of both clients and their social workers" (Saleebey, 2009, p. 1). The root principles of strengths-based practice are disarmingly simple, as Saleebey (2011) indicates, but they are difficult to put into practice "because they run counter to some of the thinking that characterizes some practices and agency mandates today" (p. 482). Traditionally, work in the substance abuse field has focused on *breaking* client resistance and denial (Rapp & Goscha, 2012). According to this more positive framework, however, client resistance and denial can be viewed as healthy, intelligent responses to a situation that might involve unwelcome court mandates and other intrusive practices.

THEMES IN RECOVERY

A study of recovery is vital to treatment research so that we can discover what works. Because we now recognize, based on studies such as the comprehensive National Epidemiologic Survey on Alcohol and Related Conditions, that most recovery is natural recovery, the people we need to study are those whose recovery took place without any formal treatment or membership in a self-help group (Grant & Dawson, 2006). Perhaps from them, we can learn about them the process by which they managed to control their consumption. We can ask the same research question of former smokers: What is the secret of their success? In the past, research has focused on the most severely addicted populations—people who sometimes went through treatment programs several times before they could shake the destructive habit.

Here is a summary of the findings of the National Epidemiologic Survey. Factors associated with recovery included marriage, level of education, addiction severity, age at onset of dependence, tobacco and other drug use, and having a co-occurring personality disorder (Grant & Dawson, 2006). The analysis revealed that there are substantial levels of recovery from alcohol dependence. Information on such factors associated with what is sometimes termed *natural recovery* can be used to improve the prospects for treatment. From the reverse standpoint, through identifying those subpopulations at greatest risk for a particular alcohol-related problem, public health professionals can target prevention strategies to intervene early to prevent more serious problems from developing. But we still have a lot to learn for more effective preventative work.

Researchers at the Center for Addiction and Mental Health in Toronto, in a review of the findings in the treatment literature on the prevalence of self-change efforts, concluded that most of the people who are in trouble with alcohol and other drug use can successfully reduce their consumption to much more acceptable levels and do this on their own (see Arkowitz & Lilienfeld, 2008).

The strengths perspective is highly consistent with such a research approach, which is geared toward an investigation of what people do right—how they protect themselves—rather than what they do wrong. This approach, moreover, does not entail set rituals or dogma but is informed by certain basic principles that transcend treatment modality or style. To learn about how recovery is conceptualized from this perspective, we can turn to Rapp and Goscha's (2012) text on the strengths model for case management. Six critical elements are singled out by these authors as conducive to recovery. These are (1) identity as a competent human being; (2) the need for personal control or choice; (3) the need for hope; (4) the need for purpose; (5) the need for a sense of achievement; (6) and the presence of at least one key supportive person. The experience of illness and recovery is unique to each person, but these common themes emerge in the stories of recovery. Although Rapp and Goscha's focus was on mental illness, these recovery themes pertain equally well to all biochemical disorders. In the following pages, we draw on firsthand narrative accounts to illustrate each of these strengths-based recovery themes.

The first critical element of recovery, which has important implications for treatment, occurs when the person moves from an all-consuming identification with the illness to a *position of managing the symptoms of the disorder*. From a harm reduction perspective, Brad Karoll (2010) contends that for many seeking recovery, "labeling oneself only continues to erode one's self-esteem, self-confidence, and self-efficacy" (p. 275). Accordingly, Karoll recommends that clinicians and persons affected focus on the premise that one has an alcohol or drug disorder rather than that they *are* the disorder; terms such as *addict* and *alcoholic*, therefore, should be avoided in favor of terminology indicating a person has a particular disorder. The National Association of Social Workers (NASW) has issued a strong policy statement on the subject: "'Disease first' language, as opposed to 'people first' language, obliterates individual differences and depersonalizes those to whom the label is applied" (p. 25).

Sometimes sobriety brings with it a change in identity that can be inferred through one's behavioral changes. Consider this description of John Cheever, a famous writer, by his daughter Susan Cheever (1999), who observed the following change in her father upon his return from treatment:

> He went from being an alcoholic with a drug problem who smoked two packs of Marlboros a day to being a man so abstemious that his principal drugs were the sugar in desserts. ...
>
> Although he knew too well how easily he could slip, the change in him made it seem less likely than ever that he would. His self-pitying bombast was gone. There were apologies instead of accusations. He was a man who seemed involved with life again. (pp. 198–199)

The second theme concerns the need for personal control, or *choice*. As we hear from a former methamphetamine addict, "four years clean and sober," whose family had earlier disowned her:

My mother took my daughter while I served the 36 days in jail. NA (Narcotics Anonymous) didn't work—all that "powerlessness" got to me. I still have a few beers—I'm cursed by my counselor for this. But by the grace of my mother and my daughter, I'm not going back. ... Group therapy was really helpful for me. (personal communication, September 2000)

Michael Beechem (1996), a social work professor who had tried AA to no avail and then was referred by his college administrator for treatment, shares the secret of his success:

I find myself actively engaged in the recovery process, aware of the insidious nature of alcoholism and how a small voice within me can threaten to coax me into indulging in "just one drink" to help during a stressful situation. (p. 48)

Choice is the hallmark of the harm reduction model; its task is to help clients find their own way and to carve out their own paths to sobriety. In Britain, this is the predominant model for treatment, considered to be the most effective with young persons who express willingness to work on controlling their drinking and other drug use. The focus is on prevention, not cure. In his textbook, *Understanding and Working with Substance Misusers*, Aaron Pycroft (2010) of the University of Portsmouth in England discusses how a client-centered strategy would work. In practice, we must be agents of hope. In the early stages of treatment, a harm reduction approach is more appropriate than a requirement for abstinence, Pycroft suggests, as the latter may deter people from seeking help. "The client centered approach is obviously in keeping with a working relationship that seeks to build motivation rather than impose it" (p. 113).

Ralph Campbell, a substance abuse counselor from Minnesota, similarly tells us:

I received my substance abuse certification at the university. Half of my cohort is still working in the field, and others in the prison system. They were of a certain mind set. In Minnesota, where I work, we are not abstinence-based but use a harm reduction approach. The number one predictor of success is the therapeutic relationship with the client. I seek to establish a sense of trust with the clients. Then I try to discover, What do they do well? I will say to the clients, "Tell me about a time in your life when you were filled with awe and wonder."

(speech given at the University of Northern Iowa, April 25, 2008)

The third theme, *hope*, is a quality emphasized throughout the literature on substance abuse counseling. Without hope, of course, there can be no effort on working toward a meaningful goal. At the societal level, as Saleebey (2009, 2011) informs us, the strengths-based counselor's goal is forever searching the environment for forces that enhance human possibilities and resiliencies. Rather than focusing on problems, your eye turns toward possibility. "Like social caretaking and social work, the strengths perspective is about the revolutionary possibility of hope: hope realized through the strengthened sinew of social relationships in family, neighborhood, community, culture, and country" (Saleebey, 2009, p. 19). Saleebey stresses the power that stems from membership in community organizations. Membership in mutual support groups such as AA offers hope to alcoholics through the fellowship of shared experience. Sayings such as "I can't do it alone, but together we can" reinforce the strength of mutual help.

A sense of *purpose* is the next critical ingredient in recovery. Many of van Wormer's clients expressed a sense of purpose or meaning, saying, in essence, "Now I know this all happened for a reason. So I could help people who are going through the same thing." The Twelfth Step of AA involves taking the message of what has been learned to others. As people hear personal stories from others who have achieved sobriety and a happy outlook on life, they too may think change is possible.

Spirituality is a cornerstone of the many mutual-support groups, a connection with a Higher Power that gives life meaning. Pat Coughlin, a substance abuse counselor from Marshalltown, Iowa, who once suffered from multiple drug addictions (including meth and cocaine), describes the change that came over his life following a bar fight. In inpatient treatment for the third time, Coughlin says:

> I knew the game, knew it wouldn't work. I had a spiritual awakening. I got on my knees and prayed, and things began to change. I felt God was answering my prayers. Exactly what I prayed for came to be in the form of my 6-months stay at the Recovery House. There I formed the habit of attending AA, the habit of praying, and work with a personal sponsor. Then after 9 months sober, I started college. (speech, November 28, 2000)

A *sense of achievement* is a healthy counterpart to wrestling with the feelings of grief and loss that accompany the early period of recovery. Common types of achievement listed by Rapp and Goscha (2012) are helping others, personal success at work, and self-expression through hobbies and/or the arts. In reflecting on his life, Coughlin, the speaker in the preceding passage, described how his sister, so estranged from him in the past, now has turned to requesting help with her daughter who has started to drink. "To go from a drug-dealing nothing to being called to help with a drinking child—that is the miracle of AA, the power of The Program."

The final element in recovery delineated by Rapp and Goscha is the *presence of at least one key person*—a friend, professional helper, teacher, or family member. This element parallels the focus on relationship in all client-centered therapies (see Carl Rogers, 1931, for the classical formulation). Genuineness, empathy, and nonpossessive warmth are the key components of the effective therapeutic relationship. Through warmth (and caring), many a tough-minded personal spokesperson from AA, NA, or GA (Gamblers Anonymous) has guided the seemingly most recalcitrant addict through the rough periods of early sobriety. Whatever the personal style of the helper, it is sincerity and caring that are key. Witness this account from Tinia Holder, who at the time of writing was an inmate at the federal prison in Danbury,

Connecticut. Here she comments on the help she received from a dedicated psychologist:

> They have yet to financially fund the Bridge Program for substance abuse treatment. Dr. Onorato is the sole staff who renders countless hours trying to assist with the plight of abused women. He always treats each of us as individuals. He is a kind soul. Without him, I firmly believe that I would have ended my own life. I have learned a great deal from the trauma program. Dr. Onorato, through his hours of counseling, has shown me that I am a strong, capable woman who is realizing that I don't have just arms and legs but that I am able to run and fight, give and take. I can reclaim all the pieces of myself that had been stolen by stronger, cruel people who did whatever they wanted. I have learned that I have not only a voice, but a strong voice that can shout the word NO! (personal communication; July 7, 1998)

Central to all these stories of recovery is the theme of personal empowerment. Both harm reduction and mutual-help programs are based on a voluntary commitment to change. The greatest weakness of The Program—its dogmatism—is possibly also its greatest strength. The Program gives people who are highly vulnerable and clutching for support something concrete, something more faith-based than scientific, to latch on to. One is hard put to fault the kind of personal support that so many recovering alcoholics and other drug addicts have derived from what is commonly referred to as The Program (see Chapter 11 on mutual-help groups for an in-depth analysis).

For persons with co-occurring disorders—those with both substance use and mental health disorders—a more flexible approach than one based on total abstinence may be required (Mancini, Linhorst, Broderick, & Bayliff, 2008). Many persons with co-occurring disorders are unable to negotiate the demands of highly structured, abstinence-only programs, a fact that results in low retention rates in such programs. Harm reduction approaches are therefore essential for persons of such high vulnerability. Still, more than half of persons who have both a mental and a substance use disorder don't receive any treatment (CSAT, 2005). And we know from surveys that around one in four people in the general population who have a serious mental illness also have problems with substance use (SAMHSA, 2010), so the presence of co-occurring disorders is common. Of those who do get treatment, most receive mental health treatment only, and only a fraction receive integrated treatment geared to their special needs.

Within this context, the work of clinicians such as Catherine Crisp (2005) is rare. Crisp differentiates chemical dependence theory, which takes "a hard-lined approach," from mental illness theory, which stresses client nurturance. The following passage describes the approach that she has found most effective when working with clients with co-occurring disorders:

> Much of the work I do with clients individually is based on a strengths perspective and motivational therapy techniques. Many clients have tried and failed many times in their sobriety and have little hope in their ability to recover from their addiction. I attempt to educate them about the process of relapse, help them identify individual strengths and resources that may be helpful in their recovery, confront them on their denial, and assist them in understanding elements of their

substance abuse and their mental illness or depression. The most valuable thing I think I offer clients is a belief that if they are willing to do the work, they can recover. I let them know that they have the abilities to recover, but ultimately, they must complete the task themselves. (p. 207)

ADDICTION RECOVERY MANAGEMENT

The previously mentioned recovery themes are the cornerstone of a new movement, *addiction recovery management* (sometimes called *sustainable recovery management)*, a strengths-based approach that seeks to merge the best of the old and the new with a focus on recovery from alcohol and drug addiction. Proponents of this model stress the importance of case management to provide direct links to community resources for long-term care. They argue that the present model, an acute care model marked by treatment failure at a great cost, is economically and politically unsustainable (White & Kelly, 2010). Because of the recognition of the need for systemic change, nationally and internationally, these proponents go so far as to make the claim that "there is a revolution underway in the design and delivery of addiction treatment in the United States" (p. 2).

So what is addiction recovery management, and how does it operate?

The most complete discussion of this concept is found in the United Nations report by the UN Office on Drugs and Crime: Drug Dependence Treatment (UNODC) (2008). The UNODC manual on addiction recovery management provides a 124-page blueprint for policy programming that can be used by governments internationally. The starting point is the definition of recovery adapted by White (2007):

> Recovery is continuous process and experience through which individuals, families, and communities utilize internal and external resources to address drug dependence and substance abuse problems, actively manage their continued vulnerability to such problems, and develop a healthy, productive and meaningful life. (UNODC, 2008, p. 14)

The United Nations' manual provides a wealth of case reports of effective treatment strategies from across the world. These strategies utilize a strengths perspective, which is central to the recovery management approach. The focus is on linking individuals with systems of support in the community. The treatment scheme endorsed by the UNODC consists of the following components:

- Treatment provided by recovery coaches trained in strengths-based case management practices, behavioral technologies, and motivational interviewing in the treatment of drug and alcohol problems
- A holistic approach geared toward the elimination of stress factors in the macro environment, for example, job loss, the impact of natural disasters, and conflict
- Attention to micro environmental factors such as illness, divorce, and death of loved ones
- Interventions related to survival needs such as physical and mental health care, housing, employment, and family supports
- Success is measured in a reduction of drug/alcohol use as well as in abstinence

Addiction recovery management is an important conceptual development in that it integrates addiction treatment with mutual aid supports. At the same time, harm reduction elements are incorporated into the model as well. This brings us to a consideration of the strengths that can be found in diversity. We are talking here of the diversity of conceptual teachings and models.

FINDING THE STRENGTHS IN DIVERGENT MODELS

The strengths perspective is essentially an approach rather than a well-integrated therapy or, as Saleebey (2009) describes it, an approach to practice that directs us to "an appreciation of the assets of individuals, families, and communities" (p. 9). Because this is basically a focus, an outlook, there is no reason we cannot apply it to the macro level as well and look to the positives with an attitude of appreciation rather than devaluation.

As recreational therapist Angie Woods states concerning practices at her Iowa agency:

> The newer models are beginning to be utilized, especially with populations requiring special needs. Harm reduction models are being utilized primarily with the dually diagnosed because of the increased recidivism rate with this population. Confrontation and the breaking of denial are slowly being replaced by interventions designed to assist the consumer to evaluate behavior associated with chemical usage. Change, however, is a slow process. Some professionals are reluctant to truly embrace harm reduction as the goal of abstinence is clung to as the best solution. (personal communication; July 10, 2006)

In light of policy changes allowing increasing flexibility in the provision of treatment, the time is ripe for a comprehensive approach to the field of addiction treatment. This approach is about the acceptance of differences rather than one that takes sides among the various camps. As a highly adaptable and effective approach, the strengths perspective can serve to shape our conceptualization of client-centered policies, such as drug courts that favor treatment over punishment. This perspective also leads us to an appreciation for the high-quality work done by men and women whose devotion to their multiply addicted clients is almost heroic, as well as to an appreciation for the many effective treatment strategies being used. Instead of asking the question "What is wrong with this or that approach?" a framework based on strengths seeks to find the strong points in diverse frameworks such as the Twelve-Step approach and the harm reduction alternative. For an unabashedly negative point of view, consider the title of Peele and Bufe's almost blasphemous 2000 book, *Resisting 12-Step Coercion: How to Fight Forced Participation in AA, NA, or 12-Step Treatment.*

Granted, Peele and Bufe's attack is directed more at the courts for coercing individuals in trouble with the law into attending such groups and at Twelve-Step–based treatment programs than it is against the "once proudly voluntaristic religions' healing programs" (p. 14). Even nonaddicted drug users (of illegal drugs), as Peele and Bufe suggest, are being forced to say in treatment that they are "powerless" over the substance in question. This requirement is made in the belief that "according to drug war dogma there is no such thing as, for instance, moderate marijuana use" (p. 28).

Resisting 12-Step Coercion is well documented and thought provoking. Missing in all its 200-plus pages, however, is any acknowledgment of a program that has clearly saved so many lives. We who know firsthand of many apparent miracles of recovery from membership in a mutual-help group such as AA or from participation in a professionally run Minnesota Model program regret this omission.

Today, there are more than 1 million members of AA in the United States and just over 2 million members worldwide; AA is the most prominent of the Twelve-Step groups (AA website, 2011). When all the self-help groups are included, as in a national survey by Substance Abuse and Mental Health Services Administration (SAMHSA) (2009), the number rises to 5 million or 2% of the U.S. population who reported attending a self-help group because of alcohol and other drugs over the past year. About one-third who attended also reported undergoing treatment for addiction during that period. This high attendance undoubtedly reflects the fact that a large majority of residential and outpatient treatment programs in the United States draw directly on the principles of Twelve-Step groups and encourage if not require attendance at these groups. This approach is often called the Minnesota Model, and in this text we refer to the approach as the *traditional disease model*.

If anything, the critics of harm reduction are more vociferous than are the critics of the Minnesota Model. Let us consider what happened when the first program shown on a major U.S. television network that questioned the lack of alternatives to treatment in the United States was broadcast. *Drinking: Are You in Control?* aired in May 2000 on ABC's 20/20 to present alternatives to the Twelve-Step total abstinence approach. From the start, the reaction in the press and on the Internet was palpable. For example, here's how Bob Eck addressed subscribers to the NASW-ATOD (Alcohol Tobacco and Other Drugs) section LISTSERV:

> To mislead thousands of actively using alcoholics and addicts that it is indeed possible for them to "control drink" or use again is cruel, and then to attempt to support that opinion by the use of some unknown, backyard research on some chimps is truly an attempt to put one over on all of us. It looks like it worked, because I am sure there are those out there who will latch onto any potentially good reason to return to using their drug of choice. Believe me folks, there is no such thing as controlled use for the chemically dependent. The chemically abusive? Possibly so, but be careful here also. Go to the *DSM–IV* for the definition of the difference. Every so often someone comes along with this theory and some people line up behind the pied piper. Not possible, folks. (personal communication; June 16, 2000)

In fact, studies reveal the effectiveness of both traditional disease-model–based treatment and motivational enhancement therapy, the therapy favored in harm reduction programs (see Miller, Forcehimes, & Zweben,

2011; Project MATCH Research Group, 1997). Bob Eck does have a point, however. Moderate drinking is a possibility for some but not for all. The difficulty is in identifying who will be able to adopt this strategy.

A primary purpose of this text is to explore such dilemmas, adopt a wider vision, and find even more ways to help individuals who want to reduce risks, improve their health, and/or stop practicing their addiction. As a starting point, let us explore the harm reduction model in greater depth.

HARM REDUCTION AND THE STRENGTHS APPROACH

Consider the following scenarios:

- Street social workers distribute literature on safe sex and drug treatment in a notoriously crime-ridden neighborhood.
- A social worker receives training in drug screening to volunteer his or her services at a first-aid station at a secretly located rave; the drug screening is to protect youth from taking Ecstasy pills laced with life-threatening adulterants.
- A worker at a women's shelter helps clients develop a personal safety plan for themselves and their children, but she does not counsel them to leave their violent relationships.
- A college program to prevent binge drinking targets youth with problems and works with them to reduce their alcohol consumption and decrease the risks associated with intoxication.
- A school social worker conducts an after school group to help kids with gender identity issues talk through problems of internalized homophobia that might otherwise lead them to seek self-destructive channels of expression.

All of these situations are high risk for the individuals involved; yet, except for volunteering at the rave, they are typical of the ones social workers encounter regularly. Common to all these interventions is the theme of pragmatism, or helping people choose from options they are willing to take, rather than trying to push on them changes that they are unprepared to make. Harm reduction is not about doing what is best; it is about doing whatever works at whatever level makes sense to the client.

What is harm reduction? Irish social work educator Shane Butler (2002) describes it best:

> The new view of drug users as health service consumers was one which ideally saw them as having strengths and competence, and as being uniquely well placed to advise on how risk might be reduced; they were to be seen as active collaborators with healthcare professionals ... rather than as passive recipients of services delivered by professionals, on terms dictated by professionals. (p. 190)

"Meet the client where the client is" is a popular slogan of social work practice that sums up the harm reduction philosophy. Harm reduction joins client and therapist in the realistic pursuit of survival. Typical strategies include:

- Helping clients substitute a less harmful drug for a life-threatening drug; a controversial example is that of Brazil, where researchers help clients overcome crack cocaine addiction by providing marijuana.
- Recruiting heroin addicts into methadone-maintenance and needle exchange programs.
- Providing women returning to their battering partners a plan for self-protection.

Social work and the harm reduction approach are a natural fit: Both start where the client is and strive to help people improve their levels of functioning. This natural affinity is widely recognized by policymakers and social workers in Europe, Australia, and Canada. In the United States, in contrast, this realization is in its infancy. A search of Social Work Abstracts as of May 2011 revealed a mere 39 listings for harm reduction, practically all of which appeared after 2000; Criminal Justice Abstracts contain 1,044 listings, and PsycInfo has 2,024. The increases were more than doubled from a search we conducted several years ago. The latter two search engines contain a high percentage of references before the year 2000. Although social work got a relatively late start, we can conclude there is increasing interest today in harm reduction policies and practice. In an article in the *Journal of Social Work,* for example, Brad Karoll (2010) discussed his application of social work approaches to serve persons with alcohol and drug use disorders. In his literature review, he notes a recent upsurge in social work writings utilizing a harm reduction approach. And the National Association of Social Workers (NASW) (2009) has officially endorsed a policy statement, as mentioned in the preface to this book, favoring the development of harm reduction approaches to substance use disorders. Social workers are urged to advocate for the elimination of stigmatizing language and to "promote a more respectful, non-stigmatizing strengths-based language" (p. 26). For the first time, the NASW *Encyclopedia of Social Work,* now in its twentieth edition, includes an entry on harm reduction. This entry by Davis (2008) describes policies that are considered controversial but that are highly pragmatic and geared toward recognized social work values, including social justice.

To further define harm reduction, we need to take into account the two aspects of the term that are often poorly differentiated in the literature: policy and practice. As *policy,* harm reduction is an outgrowth of the international public health movement, a philosophy that opposes the criminalization of drug use and views substance misuse as a public health rather than a criminal justice concern. The goal of the harm reduction movement is to reduce the harm to users and misusers and to the communities in which they live, including the harm caused by the criminalization of the substances. A pragmatic approach, harm reduction seeks to control the risks in drug-taking behavior (Karoll, 2010). From this perspective, punitive laws against drinking by young adults under age 21 and possessing or using certain substances are opposed as a new form of Prohibition. The war on drugs is seen as exacting a toll in terms of deaths generated by the use of contaminated, unregulated chemicals; the spread of hepatitis, tuberculosis, and HIV/AIDS through the sharing of dirty needles; the social breakdown in America's inner cities; and political corruption elsewhere. In several European countries, it was the AIDS epidemic of the 1980s that catapulted harm reduction policies into prominence. Drug use was medicalized, and the behavior of drug use was closely monitored at methadone and other clinics, where a safe drug supply was provided under medical supervision. Several U.S. cities, including Baltimore, have moved in the direction of such progressive policies.

At the *practitioner* level, harm reduction is an umbrella term for a set of practical strategies based on motivational interviewing and other strengths-based approaches to help people help themselves by moving from safer use, to managed use, to abstinence, if so desired. The labeling of clients, as is the custom in mental health circles ("He has an antisocial personality," "She is borderline") or in treatment circles ("He's an alcoholic," "She has an eating disorder"), is avoided; clients provide the definition of the situation as they see it. Clients who wish it are given advice on how to reduce the harm in drug use, such as, "Don't drink on an empty stomach," or "Always make sure to use a clean needle." Most of the advice, however, is provided in a less direct fashion, such as, "Here are some options you might want to consider." Consistent with the strengths perspective, the counselor and client collaborate to consider a broad range of solutions to the client-defined problem; resources are gathered or located to meet the individual needs of the client. Above all, clients are viewed as amenable to change.

The harm reduction approach recognizes the importance of giving equal emphasis to each of the biopsychosocial and spiritual factors in drug use. In collaboration, the counselor and client consider a broad range of solutions to the consequences of drug misuse, abstinence being only one. Forcing the client to admit to a substance addiction as a way of breaking through "denial," according to proponents of this approach, can lead to resistance and a battle of wills between worker and client. When the focus of the professional relationship, however, is on promoting healthy lifestyles and on reducing problems that the client defines as important rather than on the substance use per se, many clients can be reached who would otherwise stay away (Denning & Little (2012); Miller et al., 2011). Seeking help is rare among substance misusers until the problems are overwhelming, probably due to the stringent and off-putting requirements of traditional substance abuse treatment. All of these arguments, pragmatic as opposed to dogmatic, have been introduced to America through international conferences and exchanges. Similarly, the Twelve-Step–based treatment program has made inroads in Europe, especially in private clinics, where its success with a certain type of client—extraverted, severely addicted, structure seeking—is reminiscent of the American experience. Common to all these treatments, especially in the United States, is the recognition that problems with alcohol, other drugs, and compulsive behaviors such as gambling affect not only individuals but whole families and communities as well.

This more flexible, harm reduction approach would appear more relevant to community-based treatment and prevention work than to counseling inmates sentenced for drug violations. Yet, in Scotland unlike in the United States, the drug court system operates on harm reduction principles; success is measured in reduction in drug use and in criminal activity to support the habit (McIvor et al., 2006). In Canada too, within the correctional system no less, these pragmatic principles are being adapted to substance abuse treatment. This move parallels an advance from the old punishment paradigm into a paradigm of healing (Thomas, 2005). Although needle exchanges are not allowed in prison, bleach is made available to sanitize the needles often used in tattooing. Total abstinence is not required for postprison treatment. Inmates ready to leave the system with no parole restrictions can choose either an abstinence- or a moderation-based goal.

EMPIRICAL RESEARCH

The substance abuse treatment field, even more than most other practice disciplines, has been characterized by an ideology, folk wisdom, and occasional brilliance that is impossible to quantify. Moreover, the gap between treatment practices that research has shown effective and what is actually done in treatment agencies is immense. Within a climate of pressure to implement evidence-based treatment practices, increase performance standards, and prove the cost-effectiveness of treatment programs, access to scientifically proven studies on treatment effectiveness is vital. But how can treatment effectiveness, under the circumstances, be measured?

Understandings about how addiction is conceptualized have much to do with the treatment modalities utilized and even the professional and personal qualifications of the treatment staff. Treatment effectiveness can be measured through the evaluation of improvement in terms of reduced healthcare needs, less dependence, lowered crime rates, success in employment, and so on of a group of individuals who had major economic and social problems before treatment. When measured this way, the cost-effectiveness of substance abuse treatment can be seen to pay for itself multiple times over. Keep in mind that, unlike traditional healthcare interventions that focus on one specific outcome (e.g., weight loss, reduced blood pressure), substance abuse treatment can achieve effects on a number of outcome measures, including health status, criminal behavior, family functioning, mental health, and employment (Belenko, Patapis, & French, 2005).

The California Treatment Outcome Project, a rigorously designed study of the effectiveness of alcohol abuse and other drug abuse treatment, showed that the state received a $7 return for every $1 invested, the largest savings of which were from reductions in crime (Ettner et al., 2006). More than 43 substance abuse treatment providers participated in the study. Similar reports have come from virtually every state. Even more cost-effective than treatment after the fact of addiction are public health programs of prevention. Researchers from Iowa State University conducted a cost-effectiveness analysis of two prevention programs—the Iowa Strengthening Families Program and the Life Skills Training Program, which operates in the local school system. The return was approximately a $10 savings for every dollar invested in prevention (Iowa State University News Service, 2009).

Despite the emphasis by the state and federal governments on reducing substance misuse, treatment needs are far from being met. According to the most recent National Survey on Drug Use and Health, around 3% of persons in the United States are in trouble with their drug use and in need of treatment (DHHS, 2008). Of these, only 17.8% of those who stated they needed treatment in the past year received the help they needed. Other respondents who did not receive treatment when they needed it pointed to the lack of access to affordable health care as a key reason. The rate of persons in need of treatment for problems with alcohol was three times that of those who needed treatment for other drug use. There is generous spending in another regard, however; this is for international efforts through military operations aimed at the destruction of the supply side of drugs and for national efforts through law enforcement to arrest and prosecute drug dealers and users.

Once behind bars, inmates with substance use disorders cannot count on receiving the psychological help they need to prepare for a successful return to the community. In the state system, only a fraction (11%) of the 80% of state prison inmates with substance use problems receive the treatment they need (CASA, 2010). The state budgets are simply too small to accommodate the need. Spending priorities, however, continue to be placed on cleaning up the wreckage of substance misuse rather than on treatment and prevention. Over 15% of total state budgets, in fact, goes to "shoveling up" the damage caused by substance use. This impact has been measured by an extensive study of the economics of substance misuse conducted by researchers at Columbia University (CASA, 2009). According to their calculations, of every dollar federal and state governments spent on substance abuse and addiction in 2005, 95.6 cents went to shoveling up the wreckage; and only 1.9 cents to prevention and treatment, 0.4 cents to research, 1.4 cents to taxation or regulation, and 0.7 cents to interdiction.

Fortunately, recent changes in federal Medicaid and Medicare programs provide for screening and brief intervention programs for alcohol and other drug addiction, so these statistics might improve in the future. At the same time, drug czar ex-police chief Gil Kerlikowske has placed the emphasis on rehabilitation and treatment for nonviolent drug offenders rather than on imprisonment and jail (Johnson and Goldstein, 2009).

For years, researchers have argued over what scientific research says about the various treatments and their clinical recovery rates. Because virtually all U.S. programming relies on attendance at AA or NA as a supplement to treatment, solid studies comparing the disease-model abstinence-based approach and alternative approaches without AA and NA referrals have been few and far between.

Earlier Studies of Note

Directed by the National Institute on Alcohol Abuse and Alcoholism, the multisite, 8-year comparison study, Project MATCH (1997), involved almost 2,000 patients in the largest trial of psychotherapies ever undertaken. The goal of this $28 million project was not to measure treatment effectiveness but rather to study which types of treatments worked for which types of people.

The three treatment designs chosen for this extensive study were based on the principles of the three most popular treatment designs: conventional Twelve-Step–based treatment, cognitive strategies, and motivational enhancement therapy (MET). One unique aspect of the interventions offered under the umbrella of Project MATCH is that all treatment was one-on-one; no group therapy was provided. Attendance at AA meetings, which was stressed more by the therapists of the traditional disease-model school, was the only group contact that clients received. Any conclusion concerning treatment outcomes, accordingly, needs to take into account that Project MATCH, in contrast to the usual treatment practice in North America, provided individually delivered counseling.

The first of three treatment philosophies employed in Project MATCH was the Twelve-Step facilitation design. Counselors using this design explained to their clients the basic principles of Alcoholics Anonymous. In short: Alcoholism is a disease that is primary, progressive, chronic, and fatal if not arrested. Alcoholics need to acknowledge that they are powerless over alcohol and that only through turning to a power greater than themselves can they be restored to sanity. Recovering comes through regular attendance at mutual-help groups and through humility and surrender to a Higher Power.

Cognitively based treatment, as offered by the practitioners participating in Project MATCH, focused on relapse prevention. The underlying premise of this approach is the belief that people's cognitions, or the way they view the world, and their self-destructive behavior are intertwined. Social skills training and stress management are basic strategies used by cognitive therapists to help clients find ways of reducing stress as an alternative to alcohol misuse.

The third model selected by Project MATCH for scrutiny, motivational enhancement, is the pragmatic approach most closely associated with the harm reduction model. Motivational techniques are client-centered; the therapist assesses the level of the client's motivation for change and never fights the client but rather rolls with resistance. Such techniques are geared to help people find their own path to change; feedback is offered by reflecting back to the client what he or she seems to be saying about the need to reduce or eliminate self-destructive behaviors.

Although Project MATCH was designed to test the general assumption that matching could improve treatment outcomes, individuals were assigned randomly to three varieties of treatment so that researchers could determine which modality worked best for whom. The results were that 1 year and 3 years after treatment, clients showed substantial improvement regardless of the modality used.

To the surprise of the research team, outcome evaluations showed that patient-treatment matching is not necessary for satisfactory results and that participants in the intensive Twelve-Step format did as well on follow-up as those in the cognitive-behavioral therapy and motivational enhancement designs. Treatments were provided over 8- and 9-week periods, with motivational therapy offered only four times and the other two designs offered for 12 sessions. All participants showed significant and sustained improvements in the increased percentage of days they remained abstinent and the decreased number of drinks per drinking day, the researchers said. However, they noted that outpatients who received the Twelve-Step facilitation program were more likely to remain completely abstinent in the year following treatment than outpatients who received the other treatments. An important lesson that emerged from the experiment is that the most seriously addicted clients did best with a total abstinence approach; moderate drinking was not something they could handle, apparently (Miller et al., 2011). Individuals with strong religious beliefs and those who indicated they were seeking meaning in life generally did better with the Twelve-Step, disease-model focus, while clients with high levels of psychopathology did not do better with this approach. Clients low in motivation did best ultimately with the design tailored to their level of motivation (see Miller et al., 2011). A concentration on developing cognitive skills seemed to be the most effective treatment design for persons with evidence of psychopathology.

In subjects who were followed up for long-term aftercare, less successful outcomes were associated with male gender, psychiatric problems, and peer group support for drinking. The Twelve-Step approach had a major advantage for people whose drinking was closely connected to peer group support in that it provided the opportunity for replacement of the drinking peer group with a reference group composed of members who were in recovery.

Because there was no control group deprived of treatment, generalizations concerning the efficacy of treatment cannot be made, a fact that has brought this massive project considerable criticism (Wallace, 2005). Another major criticism is that of selection bias in study recruitment. Clients were barred from the experimental treatment if they were dependent on heroin or cocaine, used intravenous (IV) drugs, were suicidal, or had acute psychoses. Because the clients that counselors typically see are not so homogeneous and carefully screened, such restrictions affect generalization of the findings (Wallace, 2005). What this extensive and long-term study does show, however, is that all three individually delivered treatment approaches are relatively comparable in their results; treatment that is not abstinence based (motivational enhancement) is as helpful in getting clients to reduce their alcohol consumption as the more intensive treatment designs. These findings provide support for the guiding principle of this book, which is to find what works in seemingly diverse treatment designs.

Keep in mind that Project MATCH was concerned with diagnosable alcohol-dependent individuals only. The treatment needs of persons with alcohol and other drug problems in general, most of whom never come to the attention of specialized treatment centers, are clearly different from the needs of chronic alcoholics and addicts coerced into treatment (CSAT, 2005). Those other more typical persons with addiction problems are often seen in general social service and counseling settings for issues such as marital conflict and employment problems. An overreliance on medical models for diagnostic criteria often misses these problem substance misusers. Certainly, the conventional techniques of "breaking down denial" and forcing such individuals to abstain totally from drinking and drug using are counterproductive. When clients who enter treatment for personal problems seemingly unrelated to substance misuse are referred to a specialized chemical dependence treatment center, they often are lost to treatment altogether. A far more effective approach is to treat them for the issue at hand but to keep the channels of communication open.

We have described Project MATCH in detail not because it provides proof of treatment effectiveness—it does not, in the absence of a control group, nor did it intend to—but because it confirms the viability of diverse approaches. This finding that clients do well when treatment is steeped in Twelve-Step principles, cognitive skills training, or an approach geared for individual motivation for change validates the basic thesis of this book—the strengths inherent in each of the various standard treatment options.

Also worth noting is the manner in which treatment effectiveness was measured by Project MATCH researchers. No longer is government-funded research using subjects' ability to obtain abstinence as the standard for recovery (as in the follow-up surveys asking, "When did you have your last drink?"). Instead, the impact of treatment strategies is now being measured in terms of improvement in drinking and drug-taking habits. Retention in treatment itself is used in some evaluations as an outcome measure of success. Harm reduction models, much more commonly used in Europe than in the United States, measure success simply by whether harm was reduced. For example, a person who injects heroin might be reducing the harm of becoming HIV positive by using clean syringes. Rigid adherence to the traditional, total abstinence standard in the past is the myth of its effectiveness persists. Box 1.2 describes a classroom discussion that contrasts the all-or-nothing approach to measuring recovery in terms of a number of criteria related to a reduction in harmful pursuits.

In summary, the standard for "What is recovery?" is beginning to change in the United States, making room for broader definitions that include such variables as improvements in health, social, and legal status. It is important

Box 1.2   TREATMENT EFFECTIVENESS: DOES IMPROVEMENT COUNT?

Diane Rae Davis

I will never forget the day I first presented the results of Project MATCH to a group of first-year MSW (Master of Social Work) students. I put the overheads up showing graphs of the different treatment groups and the number of days of abstinence at 6 months and 15 months. As I was describing these results, trying to make it interesting by noting how few persons maintained 100% abstinence by the end of 15 months but how many had improved in number of days of abstinence, I noticed the visible agitation of a student near the back of the room. I knew she had come to the MSW program after several years of practice in the alcohol and drug treatment field, and I wondered what in the world could be upsetting her.

I finally asked if she wanted to comment on anything. She blurted out that "improvement doesn't cut it" in treatment. The idea of presenting improvement as a "success" was totally foreign to her. In fact, she suspected the information as it was presented on the graphs might be some kind of attempt to erode the recognized standard of recovery, which is "abstinence." As she talked further, it became clear that her concern was for clients who might hear the "improvement" message and take that as permission to relapse.

I am forever grateful to this student for launching a much deeper (than I had planned) discussion on what "recovery" means and who has the power to decide the meaning. The class concluded, as we all know in our hearts, that there is no "right" answer to these two questions. The reality is that it depends on which group is valued and powerful enough to determine goals and outcomes. The MATCH outcomes were "value-free" on the surface in that they just presented "the facts." However, by defining success as maintaining 80–90% days of abstinence over the follow-up period, this very expensive and high-profile study in essence "legitimized" that improvement does count. At a later date, the student told me she was glad her "blinders had been taken off," although this was a painful experience. She felt more prepared to deal with the complexities and ambiguities of the treatment world that are too often presented as if all answers are known. Sometimes, my biggest job as a teacher is to instill doubt.

to note, moreover, that recovery from alcohol dependence or other drug use most often occurs outside the confines of hospitals, substance abuse clinics, or Twelve-Step groups.

Vaillant (1983) discovered as much in his classic longitudinal study of boys growing up and growing old. Vaillant's extensive study, covering a low socioeconomic status (SES) population of males for over a 40-year period, is widely cited by supporters and detractors alike of the traditional Twelve-Step approach as the study par excellence in the literature. Tracking a large contingent of adult alcoholics identified from a community sample, Vaillant (1983) concluded that factors associated with recovery in middle age were personal will power, active church membership or other group membership such as

AA, stable marital relationships, and hobbies. He found that having a relative with a drinking problem significantly increased the risk of alcohol abuse irrespective of whether the individual lived with the problem drinker. More than half of the subjects in Vaillant's inner-city sample recovered at some point in their lives. In his more recent 50-year study of the same alcoholic cohorts, Vaillant (1995) found that over a lifetime, sustained recovery requires at least two of the following experiences: some sort of compulsory supervision or a painful alcohol-related event, finding a substitute dependence such as AA, a new stable relationship, and religious conversion. We learn from Vaillant's over-the-life-course study that many people recover through maturity or by other means and that alcoholism is not always progressive and fatal, as is commonly thought.

MORE RECENT RESEARCH FINDINGS

Using a different methodology from Vaillant—interview data—Dawson and colleagues (2005) at the National Institute on Alcohol Abuse and Alcoholism (NIAAA) found, similarly, that about one-third of the previously diagnosable alcoholics matured out of their dependence; about one-sixth abstained and another sixth became moderate drinkers. The greater the amount of alcohol that was consumed, the lower was the likelihood of either type of recovery. The significance of this study was in showing that many young people mature out of alcoholism and that individuals who were diagnosable alcoholics at one period in life could indeed become moderate drinkers at a later stage.

Hester and Miller's (2003) *Handbook of Alcohol Treatment Approaches* was highly skeptical of the fact that treatment providers in the United States were using a treatment model that was without any scientific foundation and overlooking treatment methods of documented effectiveness. Based on their review of hundreds of empirically based clinical trials, the authors reached two major conclusions: (1) there is no single superior approach to treatment for all individuals, and (2) treatment programs and systems should be constructed to include a variety of approaches inasmuch as different individuals respond best to different approaches.

Of the 47 different treatment modalities that were tested in the literature, the top scores for effectiveness were received for brief intervention motivational enhancement, the use of medications such as hydrochloride (Naltrexone), and cognitive therapy. The lowest rankings were found for the use of education tapes, lectures and films, confrontational counseling, and Twelve-Step facilitation. We should take into account, as Hester and Miller acknowledge, the fact that some modalities such as brief intervention and motivational enhancement generally have been conducted with less seriously addicted populations than some of the others. Also at the time that Hester and Miller examined the literature, very few scientifically based studies using a Twelve-Step facilitated approach were available. More recent research does confirm the effectiveness of this model, especially for clients who favor a highly structured approach (Miller et al., 2011; Norcross, Krebs, & Prochaska, 2011). In their re-analysis of the Project MATCH data, Wu and Witkiewitz (2008) found in a follow-up that clients who had been members of heavy drinking peer groups had more favorable results from therapy that focused on engagement with Twelve-Step groups (typically AA) than they did from therapies without this focus. Interestingly, this effect emerged 3 years after therapy, but not in the first year.

A special issue of the *Journal of Clinical Psychology* edited by Norcross, Krebs, and Prochaska (2011) devoted to evidence-based means of adapting psychotherapy to the client's characteristics drew on studies that use meta-analyses from empirically based literature. Research articles included in this collection documented the effectiveness of adapting psychotherapy to clients based on four client characteristics (preferences for type of treatment modality used, resistance, culture, and religion/spirituality). Taken as a whole, we can summarize the significant findings from this journal issue as follows. Clients who were matched to their preferred therapy conditions were less likely to drop out of therapy prematurely and showed greater improvements in treatment outcomes. Tailoring therapies to the cultural characteristics of clients increased the effectiveness of the interventions and especially regarding work with Asian American clients. For clients who showed resistance to treatment, a nondirective approach was superior to a more directive, confrontational approach, but the latter was more effective for work with clients who were cooperative from the start. This study confirms research from Project MATCH on one major advantage of motivational interviewing over other therapies.

Finally, Belenko and colleagues (2005) provide useful information for policy-makers in their survey of evidence provided from 51 published and 19 unpublished cost–benefit analyses of substance abuse interventions. Readers are referred to this 68-page reprint on the Treatment Research Institute website. Evidence provided there confirms the cost-effectiveness of drug courts (see the later section on drug courts) with typical savings of thousands of dollars per client saved over a 2-year period. The cost savings were driven largely by reductions in costs of jail, Medicaid, victim costs from crime, and drug-exposed infants. Also noteworthy were the prison treatment studies that showed greatly reduced reoffending rates.

TREATMENT TRENDS

The field of substance abuse or addiction treatment, as Straussner and Isralowitz (2008) point out, is constantly "evolving with new substances of abuse, new populations to treat, new treatment approaches, and changing policies" (p. 128). Treatment trends often are highly political, though, and are apt to lag behind contemporary attitudes and needs. At times, however, the government and other funding sources do take notice and open up new funding possibilities, and then treatment providers follow suit.

New Substances of Misuse

In response to a national survey showing a huge increase in the misuse of prescription drugs, the White House Office of the National Drug Control Policy (2011) issued a call for action. The sense of urgency of the situation regarding prescription drug misuse, especially of opiates, is reflected in national media reports such as those by the *New York Times* (see Hartocollis, 2011) concerning major problems in New York City. From the state of Florida are press reports of a major crackdown of nonmedical use of prescription medication, often of somebody else's (Gluck, 2011). To address this epidemic, in prescription pill misuse, the Prescription Drug Abuse Prevention Plan includes action in four major areas to reduce prescription drug abuse: education, monitoring, proper disposal, and enforcement.

One can expect that in light of this upsurge in prescription drug misuse, across the states the number of methadone clinics will increase. Methadone is a synthetic drug used in opiate replacement therapy. Long linked in popular culture to a drug replacement for heroin users, methadone has emerged as a key weapon in Florida's war against prescription drug abuse (Gluck, 2011). Methadone treatment is a harm reduction strategy provided in over 1,000 clinics nationwide; financing is through state and federal funding. This monetary support is provided in the interests of reducing the crime associated with opiate drug addiction and also the contraction of HIV/AIDS through the sharing of dirty needles among persons addicted to heroin.

Most of the treatment provided in the 11,000 or so substance abuse facilities in the United States are more traditional (SAMHSA, 2011); total abstinence is a tightly enforced goal for all clients. Because of funding considerations, outpatient services are strongly favored, although sometimes residential treatment is available on a short-term basis.

Calls for a Paradigm Shift

The treatment system faces many challenges that affect the utilization of services. In addition to the inadequate federal, state, and private insurance funding, the high staff turnover, relatively low pay, and use of outdated techniques and attitudes are issues that negatively impact services and in turn the attractiveness of treatment to voluntary clients (McLellan, 2010).

And yet the realization that no single substance abuse treatment approach is effective for everyone represents a major step forward today. We might even say that a revolution of sorts is brewing in substance abuse treatment circles, a paradigm shift in our understanding of the nature of addiction. Bolstered by extraordinary brain research showing the physiological basis in addiction, substance abuse treatment is moving slowly toward a more scientific, empirically based approach. Much of the impetus for change is economic. After expanding wildly in the 1980s, residential Twelve-Step–oriented treatment programs are falling on hard times; insurers and employers are seeking cheaper, less intensive alternatives (Belenko et al., 2005). There is simultaneously a trend, for prevention purposes, to treat alcohol and drug users with only mild problems (e.g., problem drinkers) (McLellan, 2010). Nonabstinence-based treatment programs, such as Moderation Management, which allow problem drinkers a set number of drinks, are becoming increasingly more acceptable (see the website at http://www.moderation.org). Extensive empirical data on the success of this program are not available, but researchers regard this approach as most appropriate for people with less severe drinking problems (Miller et al., 2011).

The Deputy Director of the White House Office of National Drug Policy, Tom McLellan (2010), addressed the state of addiction treatment today: "In this policy environment that I'm in now," he said, "one of the emerging themes is integrating addiction treatment into mainstream healthcare" (p. 4). He was referring to early intervention and screening by physicians, social workers, and nurses, among others, in the attempt to reach people with less severe and less chronic forms of substance use. The demand for brief interventions is compatible with managed healthcare requirements in both commercial markets and public systems. "We're trying to develop more and more varied kinds of treatments," McLellan further stated, "treatments that will involve medications, treatments that will involve families, treatments that will involve whole communities" (p. 4).

Clinicians must be innovative in treating the range of severity presented by persons with substance use problems, as McLellan (2010) suggests. Tomorrow's counselor is going to need to know a lot more about medicine, genetics, and case management to suit the treatment to the individual's needs. The premium today is on flexibility and individualized treatment. We need to suit the treatment to the client, not force the client into a standardized world. Just as new scientific discoveries are shaping knowledge about the biology of addiction, so political developments are changing the manner in which substance abuse treatment is provided. Until recently in the United States, for example, nonabstinence treatment programs were virtually unheard of. Today, at many progressive treatment centers, never-before-questioned traditions are being turned around. Chain smoking, which was previously taken for granted in treatment circles, is now correctly regarded as an addiction similar to any other. Clients are counseled in moderate drinking and not terminated if they can't quit taking drugs altogether at once. Meanwhile, for the first time ever, television programs on the major networks discuss moderation treatment as a viable alternative to traditional treatments requiring immediate abstinence from all mood-altering substances (and activities). The recent reporting in the mainstream media and medical journals on the practicality of a harm reduction philosophy is perhaps a harbinger of future advances.

As registered in opinion polls in recent years, public opinion is changing in the direction of increased optimism concerning recovery from addiction problems. A national opinion poll conducted by the SAMHSA (2008) found that 50% of Americans know someone in recovery from alcohol or other drug addiction, and furthermore, that more than two-thirds of respondents said they believe that recovery is possible and that people in recovery have a contribution to make to society. The most favorable responses came from younger adults and from women. The adults in the survey were more positive regarding recovery from problems related to alcohol than from those related to other illicit drugs, however.

These figures represent increases from earlier surveys. A shift in public opinion is evidenced today against continuing prison expansion and in favor of approval for rehabilitation, education, and prevention strategies.

IMPACT OF BUDGET CUTS

Given the drastic budget cuts across states in funding for social service programming including substance abuse treatment—for example, Illinois cut its $54 million budget for substance abuse treatment to zero, and Maine and Texas have seriously reduced their treatment options—states are turning to treatment options that are of proven cost effectiveness (Chambers 2011). Competition over the awarding of federal grants is now greater than ever. However, following the economic crisis of 2008 and the continuing economic and political fallout, substantial budget cuts are underway in Medicaid funding for mental health treatment and in block grants to the states for mental health and substance abuse treatment programming. According to a recent article in the *Psychiatric Times*, "A political tsunami threatens access to mental health care for individuals who depend on community programs" (Barlas, 2011, p. 1). Many states are drastically cutting Medicaid funding to community mental health centers. Only those programs that are demonstrably cost-saving in the short-term can be expected to survive under the circumstances, such as programs where community treatment is provided *in lieu of* more expensive incarceration or programs to provide housing for homeless persons with serious substance use problems as a means of keeping them out of jail and hospital emergency rooms.

At the international level, a rethinking on global drug strategy is in evidence, with an emphasis today on the demand rather than the supply side of drug use. The UN Office on Drugs and Crime (UNODC) is moving to a health-centered and evidence-based approach to help people affected by drugs (United Nations News Service, 2011). The agency says that drug and alcohol misuse is a public health issue with a serious impact on public health, development, and security. The ultimate goal is for universal access to drug dependence treatment and care for all those affected by addiction.

RESISTANCE TO CHANGE

In any period of paradigm change, however, there is always resistance as entrenched beliefs hang on from an earlier time. McLellan (2010) comments:

> Like many of the people I meet in my current job, I too thought that if you just reduce the drug use, all the other drug-related problems would disappear. This

was, and still is, a very naïve view. Worse, it has been a very big force in the way the original—and some of the existing—treatment programs were conceptualized, designed, funded and evaluated. (p. 3)

Some years back, this intransigence was brought home to Ron Schauer, who was called to return to the directorship of an agency in Washington State after a 15-year absence. In his own words:

> My brief story of returning as a temporary director back in the "field" was so surreal. A few talk about things that they see as cutting edge, which are things we thought, 15 years ago, were about to become commonplace: family treatment, etc., etc. But the old guard re-established control. Not unexpected in a reactionary, Puritan, and cost-cutting time. Two-year-degreed people, most of whom lack professional skills come for much less.
>
> I was daily amazed at what my staff didn't know, think, or even see in the definition of treatment. All but three were *heavy* smokers; all had disastrous personal lives, just like in 1977, when I first began.
>
> Managed care itself is, in my view, something of an evil. Yet it has served to push CD [chemical dependency] treatment off center and demanded some innovation, even in the name of greater profits and competitiveness. (personal communication; November 8, 1998)

The fact that this poorly functioning treatment center as described by Schauer has folded is perhaps a sign of a tightening up by external funding sources that began in the 1990s. The demise of this center (where van Wormer once worked) gives credence to the view that, as virtually all contemporary writers in the area of addiction treatment now contend, the field is reinventing itself to meet today's needs. The new addiction therapist must be prepared to meet the needs of polydrug-addicted clients, clients with mental health and addiction problems both, and persons referred from the criminal justice system (see, e.g., Belenko et al., 2005; Springer, McNeece, & Arnold, 2003; van Wormer & Bartollas, 2010; Wallace, 2005).

CHANGES AT THE GOVERNMENT LEVEL

Two additional developments that are being watched closely by addiction treatment professionals relate to the federal research organizations the National Institute of Alcoholis and Alcohol Abuse (NIAAA) and the National Institute of Drug Abuse (NIDA). The first development is more theoretical, and the second more political. NIAAA (2011), influenced by a wealth of research findings concerning the nature of addiction and especially alcohol addiction, has now published an editorial in *NIAAA Spectrum* acknowledging the research findings of a groundbreaking, longitudinal National Epidemiologic Survey on Drug and Related Conditions. This survey of 43,000 Americans conducted first in 2001 and 2002 and then again in 2004 and 2005 was largely overlooked until NIAAA recently reanalyzed the data. Around 30% of this sample experienced an alcohol use disorder, and about 70% of this group quit drinking or cut down to safe consumption levels on their own within four years. Only a small minority of heavy drinkers developed what is recognized as full-blown alcoholism. These realizations, according to the director of NIAAA's Division of Treatment and Recovery Research, "turn on its head much of what we thought we knew about alcoholism" and "call for a public health approach that targets at-risk drinkers and persons with mild alcohol disorder to prevent or arrest problems before they progress" (p. 2).

The second major development relevant to NIAAA and NIDA is the plan to abolish these parallel organizations, one focusing on one kind of drug—alcohol—and the other focusing on illicit drugs. Plans are underway to form a new National Institute of Substance Use and Addiction Disorders (Curley, 2010). This merger should provide more funding for alcohol addiction and give the agency more leverage in appeals for funding before Congress. To what extent this merger would advance the public health approach endorsed previously in this chapter is questionable, however, as an addictions institute would be geared only to the scientific study of treatment as opposed to prevention efforts. A medical approach to addiction research will be the likely outcome of such a merger.

LESS RELIANCE ON IMPRISONMENT

Among the most significant developments in recent times are the twin movements to incarcerate and decarcerate. We are referring to the impact of America's war on drugs, a war that has been driven by moral and political rhetoric but that is clearly racist and classist in practice (see Chapter 13). Despite the thrust toward rehabilitation today, many Americans still support harsh sentencing practices. Lee and Rasinski (2006) set out to discover why.

Lee and Rasinski's empirically based research drew on a representative survey that found that one-quarter of White Americans prefer drug treatment or probation for persons caught for the first time with five or more grams of cocaine. The same survey also found that those who supported prison sentences were likely to be extremely moralistic, blaming of addicts, and lacking in awareness of the extent of racism in the United States. Racism and the tendency to blame were related to support for harsh sanctions. A conclusion we can draw from this research is that the association of a drug with a minority population in high poverty areas of the cities leads to exaggerated fears of the drug (see Chapter 2). The states continue to be burdened by high costs of prison construction and incarceration; yet they continue to spend public funds that could be saved through stepped up prison substance abuse treatment and the use of drug courts and other alternative-to-prison programs (CASA, 2010). Unfortunately in a time of shrinking state revenues, mental health and addiction treatment funding is being cut and cut drastically (Velardo, 2010).

Far better than treatment behind bars for addiction problems is treatment in the community. The drug court movement, which has received considerable government support, is one of the most promising developments of the present time. Drug courts, mental health courts, and veterans courts are all specialty courts that offer intensively supervised treatment opportunities to members of the community who have gotten into trouble with the law. This almost paradoxical joining of the criminal justice system with mental health therapy is part of the therapeutic justice movement that has gathered momentum in the United States and Europe. Keeping people with substance and mental health disorders out of prison and in the community as productive citizens is the overriding goal of these specialty courts. They are described in more detail in Chapter 8 on strengths-based interventions.

Other Promising Initiatives

Quietly, in September 2001, San Francisco became the first U.S. city to adopt harm reduction as its official policy. The new philosophy is apparent at the Department of Public Health's needle exchange sites, in a media campaign to teach addicts how to reduce deaths from heroin overdose, and in the training of workers at dozens of agencies in harm reduction strategies (Torassa, 2001). Today, San Francisco is considering adopting a policy that has been highly cost-effective in other cities such as Seattle and Minneapolis (Prettyman, 2011). This is the setting up of wet houses or apartments for formerly homeless people with serious alcohol problems. They can drink in these establishments. To understand how great the cost savings are to the community in housing these homeless people, we can consider findings from a University of Washington–led research team whose research is cited in the article. The group of 95 chronically homeless people with drinking problems cost taxpayers more than $8 million in hospitalizations, detox center treatments, and incarcerations. These costs were reduced to around $1,000 per month per person after they were moved off the streets and into the apartments. An unexpected finding was that drinking levels declined significantly for the individuals when these attractive accommodations were provided.

When the state of California passed Proposition 36 in 2000, this treatment-over-incarceration law, which sends low-level drug offenders to treatment rather than prison, was a groundbreaking initiative. Despite the fact that the program was seriously underfunded from the beginning and that its existence is seriously threatened today, a follow-up evaluation proved its effectiveness (*New York Times,* 2006). Based on data from nearly 130,000 individuals who participated in the program, the University of California–Los Angeles study conducted by Longshore, Hawken, Vrada, and Anglin (2006) found that over 60,000 people completed the program by the fourth year, thereby avoiding a prison term and thereby helping to keep their families intact. Over the 5-year period of the study, California saved $1.4 billion. If any proof is needed that addiction treatment is both humane and cost-effective for drug users, this evaluation provides it.

Restorative justice, an exciting development with roots in the rituals of indigenous populations and Canadian Mennonites, advocates nonadversarial forms of settling disputes and strives to restore individual lawbreakers to the community rather than isolating them from it. Restorative justice, like harm reduction, is a philosophy that can encompass a wide range of treatment initiatives such as the substance abuse treatment program that is actually a high school—PEASE Academy (Peers Enjoying a Sober Education).

PEASE Academy is located in a church in Minneapolis (Riestenberg, 2003). The school has incorporated the circle process in which decisions are made by all participants and other restorative principles into its program. The circle process is used to repair harms such as angry words, bullying, or healing following a relapse by one of the students. Restorative justice and harm reduction thus come together as the circle process helps restore justice or balance to the situation (see van Wormer, 2004). A visit to the PEASE Academy website at www.peaseacademy.org reveals that as of 2011, this recovery high school (the oldest in the United States) is still going strong.

One significant change little noted in the literature or elsewhere is revealed in treatment effectiveness studies (refer back to Box 1.2). Whereas formerly the standard for a successful treatment outcome was based on total abstinence—the length of time a former client abstained from the use of all psychoactive substances—today much more flexible and realistic measures of treatment success are applied. Not surprisingly, these holistic measures of improvement in social and physical functioning are bringing much more positive results than measures recording a change from chronic binge drinking to drinking three glasses of wine a week as treatment failure. The use of an improvement standard in contemporary research is entirely consistent with the harm reduction approach and is bound to have an impact at the treatment delivery end.

To help bridge the gap between research and practice, the National Institute on Drug Abuse (NIDA) and other government agencies are currently funding several studies that aim to use neural imaging technology to observe how various therapies affect addicted brains (Koerner, 2010). The hope is to discover whether neurobiology can be used to predict a person's odds of benefiting from one treatment over another. A person's openness to the concept of spiritual rebirth, as determined by their neural makeup, for example, could predict how well he or she relates to a Twelve-Step program. It might be simpler, however, just to ask people to select the type of treatment programs they prefer. Another simpler possibility for effective client treatment matching would be to administer a personality-type questionnaire to gauge individuals' tolerance for ambiguity or preference for highly structured situations, for example. Measures of introversion and extraversion could be used as well.

In any case, despite threatened budget cuts, SAMHSA presently provides millions of dollars in funding opportunities for the development of comprehensive drug/alcohol and mental health treatment systems and for their evaluation. Because 97% of all incarcerated offenders eventually return to their communities, and the barriers to successful reintegration into society are many, one can expect that the bulk of the funding for treatment initiatives will be directed toward reentry. The Reentry Court Solutions (2010) website lists numerous grant possibilities to help meet the needs of ex-prisoners upon their release.

One area of substance abuse treatment desperately in need of research is the study of effective interventions to reduce intimate partner violence committed by clients in treatment for substance abuse. Fals-Stewart and Kennedy (2005) examine studies that indicate about half of married or cohabiting substance using clients report episodes of partner aggression in the year preceding entry into treatment. Intimate partner violence research, they note, is fundamentally research about harm reduction, attempting to ascertain which treatments result in the greatest reduction in partner aggression. Concerted efforts to develop and evaluate new integrated treatments that combine substance abuse treatment and batterers' education are long overdue. One promising experimental research design conducted by Scott, King, and colleagues (2011) that used a traditional control group found that resistant batterers who attended a 6-week-long motivation enhancing group completed the intervention at significantly higher rates than did either resistant or non-resistant clients who attended the control group.

In light of new developments, there is no need to abandon the disease conception of addiction or the Twelve-Step–based treatment strategies in favor of harm reduction. Clearly, those who follow the Program and abstain from alcohol or drug use reduce the harm to themselves and their families. So the apparent dichotomy between the disease model and an alternative model geared toward public health is a false one. We may all have different allegiances, but in the end, we all have the same allegiance to the pursuit of health. The basic thesis of this chapter and book, then, follows the principle of both–and, not either–or. The results of Project MATCH, the most extensive and expensive comparative research in this area performed to date, confirm the viability of three internally consistent models of treatment: the conventional Twelve-Step–based approach (albeit without the group work), cognitively oriented therapy, and motivational enhancement strategies. This last is the preferred framework for treatment offered by harm reduction proponents. From the strengths perspective, we would be remiss not to extend our appreciation and gratitude to those pioneers in the field, without whom there might be no profession known as substance abuse treatment today.

SUMMARY AND CONCLUSION

While the United States seemingly has unlimited resources for the imprisonment of drug users, managed care constraints and federal funding cutbacks have led to a shift from a clinical approach to a criminal justice approach—from a call for treatment to a call for punishment. As we enter the second decade of the new century, however, two countertrends are evident. The first is the impetus under drug court and restorative justice initiatives for offenders to serve time in the community rather than behind bars; the second is the continuous call at the highest levels for the provision of more prevention and treatment dollars. Meanwhile, state after state, in economic crisis, is cutting back on funding for substance abuse treatment. If present trends continue, much of the treatment provided by substance abuse treatment centers in the future is likely to be connected to the drug courts. Recent survey results show that the general public is open to a shift away from the earlier punitive stance involving locking up people for drug-related crime.

Across the states, studies on the cost-effectiveness of drug treatment confirm tremendous savings to taxpayers and reduced crime rates. The punitive response to substance-related problems at the federal level is countered in part by more realistic and cost-effective policies at the state level. Increasingly, treatment is seen as a cost-effective alternative to incarceration. More and more, it is realized as well that for those illicit drug users who do have to serve time in prison, prison is only a revolving door if they don't get the help they need before their release back into society. Protecting the health of the community as a whole requires protecting the health of drug users, and this requires providing adequate and diversified treatment for persons with substance abuse and dependence problems. A wide range of interventions is needed to meet the client where he or she is, at the client's individual moment of motivation.

Despite the economic constraints caused by managed care and federal cutbacks, this is an exciting time to be in the addiction treatment field. The horizons of this field have expanded considerably to include attention to a broad range of addictive problems (e.g., gambling, shopping, and sex addiction) as well as the substance use disorders (e.g., alcoholism and cocaine addiction). As we move away from the doctrinaire views that have so stifled innovation and experimentation in this field in the past, the door has opened to greater professionalism by staff and more emphasis on client self-determination and empowerment. Meanwhile, advances in the scientific study of addiction as a "brain disease" continue to enrich our knowledge of the causes and consequences of addiction (see Leshner, 2006; and Volkow, 2010).

Central to sound policy and treatment is an understanding of the nature of addiction as a complex biological, psychological, and sociological phenomenon. Addiction is a personal issue, a family issue, a state policy issue, and a health issue. Recent scientific discoveries, such as information about unraveling the DNA code as a blueprint for behavior and the availability of brain scan images that can show the extent of brain damage from drugs, have important implications for the addictions field. The connection between these discoveries and one's susceptibility to substance abuse is the subject of Chapter 3. Given the creation of an array of effective behavioral and pharmacological interventions, addiction treatment can now be as effective as treatment for other long-term, relapsing illnesses, such as diabetes and hypertension, when professional treatment is tailored to the needs of particular clients (Leshner, 2000). Promising developments in providing a gender-specific treatment curriculum for female alcoholics and addicts, such as that presented by Covington (2008), should do much to enhance treatment offerings for women. The new specialty courts for persons convicted of drug-related crimes are receiving much praise for the intensity of supervision provided and the positive outcomes in terms of cost-effectiveness and reduction in drug use. Overall, the increasing acceptance of alternative treatment options and approaches is a significant advance over the days when one and only one standardized treatment model was offered. This willingness to think more creatively and pragmatically is the most encouraging development of all.

REFERENCES

Alcoholics Anonymous (AA). (2011). Welcome to Alcoholics Anonymous. Retrieved from www.aa.org

American Heritage Dictionary of the English Language (4th ed.) (2000). Boston: Houghton-Mifflin.

American Medical Association (AMA). (1956). *AMA history: 1941 to 1960.* Retrieved June 2006 from http://ama-assn.org

American Medical Association (AMA). (1968). *Manual on alcohol.* Committee on alcoholism and drug dependency. Chicago: AMA.

American Medical Association (AMA). (2011). *AMA policies on alcohol.* Retrieved from http://www.ama-assn.org/resources/doc/alcohol/alcoholism_treatable.pdf

American Psychiatric Association. (2000). *Diagnostic and statistical manual of mental disorders, text revision (DSM-IV-TR)* (4th ed.). Washington, DC: Author.

American Psychiatric Association. (2010). *Diagnostic and statistical manual of mental disorders (DSM-5.)* Proposed revision: addiction. Washington, DC: Author. Retrieved from http://www.dsm5.org/Search/default.aspx?k=addiction

Anderson, J. (1994, July 15). Shop till you drop. *Chicago Tribune*, pp. 1, 6.

Arkowitz, H., & Lilienfeld, S. (2008). D.I.Y. addiction cures? *Scientific American Mind*, 19 (4), 78–79.

Associated Press. (2011, May 13). Deputies say mom eating meth with child on her lap. *New York Times*. Retrieved from http://www.nytimes.com/aponline/2011/05/13/us/AP-US-Meth-Mom.html

Ayto, J. (1990). *Dictionary of word origins.* New York: Little, Brown.

Beechem, M. (1996). Chained open. *Reflections: Narratives of Professional Helping*, 2(2), 42–48.

Barker, R. (2003). *The social work dictionary*, Washington, DC: NASW Press.

Barlas, S. (2011, May 4). Severe state and federal funding shortfalls likely for local mental health programs. *Psychiatric Times*. Retrieved from http://www.psychiatric-times.com

Belenko, S., Patapis, N., & French, M. T. (2005). *The economic benefits of drug treatment: A critical review of the evidence for policy makers.* Washington, DC: National Rural Institute on Drug and Alcohol Abuse.

Bina, R., Hall, D. M. H., Mollette, A. M., Smith-Osborne, A., & Yum, A. J., Sowbel, L., & Jani, I. (2008). Substance abuse training and perceived knowledge: Predictors of perceived preparedness to work in substance abuse. *Journal of Social Work Education*, 44(3), 7–20.

Biswas-Diener, R. (2010). *Practicing positive psychology coaching: Assessment, activities, and strategies for success.* Hoboken, NJ: Wiley.

Brody, J. (2010, June 21). When tanning turns into addiction. *New York Times*, p. D7.

Bureau of Justice Statistics (2010, June 23). Press release: *Number of state prisoners declined by almost 3,000 during 2009*. Washington, DC: Office of Justice Programs. Retrieved from http://bjs.ojp.usdoj.gov

Butler, S. (2002). *Alcohol, drugs, and health promotion in modern Ireland*. Dublin: Institute of Public Administration.

Campbell, R. (2008, April 25). Substance abuse treatment today. Presentation given before students at the department of social work. Cedar Falls, IA: University of Northern Iowa.

Cathcart, R. (2010, November 26). Second rail-equipped drug tunnel found at Mexican border. *New York Times*, p. A12.

Center for Substance Abuse Treatment (CSAT). (2005). *Substance abuse treatment for persons with co-occurring disorders*. Treatment Improvement Protocol (TIP) Series, No. 42. Washington, DC: Substance Abuse and Mental Health Services Administration.

Chambers, B. (2011, March 23). Illinois to cut all alcohol and drug treatment spending. *Reclaiming Futures*. Retrieved from http://blog.reclaimingfutures.org/adolescent-substance-abuse-treatment-Illinois-cuts-all-treatment-funding

Cheever, S. (1999). *Not found in a bottle: My life as a drinker*. New York: Simon & Schuster.

Corrigan, M., Bill, M., & Slater, J. (2009). The development of a substance abuse curriculum in a master's of social work program. *Journal of Social Work Education*, 45(3), 513–521.

Corrigan, P., Mueser, K., Bond, G., Drake, R., & Solomon, P. (2008). *Principles and practice of psychiatric rehabilitation: An empirical approach*. New York: Guilford.

Covington, S. (2008). *A woman's journal: A program for treating substance abuse*. San Francisco: Jossey-Bass.

Crisp, C. (2005). Dual diagnosis: Substance abuse and mental health in an inpatient setting. In L. M.Grobman (Ed.), *Days in the lives of social workers* (3rd ed., pp. 205–210). Harrisburg, PA: White Hat Communications.

Curley, B. (2010, October 6). Experts mull impact of proposed National Institute on Addictions. *Join Together Online*. Retrieved from http://www.drugfree.org

Dalrymple, T. (2006). *Romancing opiates: Pharmaceutical lies and the addiction bureaucracy*. New York: Encounter Books.

Davis, D. R. (2008). Harm reduction. In National Association of Social Workers (NASW) (Ed.), *Encyclopedia of social work* (20th ed.) (Vol.2, pp. 312–314). New York: Oxford University Press.

Dawson, D. A., Grant, B. F., Stinson, F. S., Chou, P. S., Huang, B., & Ruan, W. J. (2005). Recovery from *DSM–IV* alcohol dependence: United States, 2001–2002. *Addiction*, 100, 281–292.

Denning, P. & Little, J. (2012). Practicing harm reduction psychotherapy: An alternative approach to addictions (2nd ed.). New York: Guilford Press.

Dodes, L. (2003). *The heart of addiction: A new approach to understanding and managing alcoholism and other addictive behaviors*. New York: Harper Paperbacks.

Ettner, S. L., Huang, D., Evans, E., Ash, D. R., Hardy, M., Jourabchi, M., et al. (2006). Benefit–cost in the California treatment outcome project: Does substance abuse treatment pay for itself? *Health Services Research*, 41(1), 192–213.

Fals-Stewart, W., & Kennedy, C. (2005). Addressing intimate partner violence in substance-abuse treatment. *Journal of Substance Abuse Treatment*, 29(1), 5–17.

Frances, A. (2010, March 30). DSM-5: "Addiction" swallows substance abuse. *Psychiatric Times*. Retrieved from www.psychiatrictimes.com

Gluck, F. (2011, May 22). Use of anti-drug methadone prevalent, but controversial. *News Press*, pp.1–5.. Retrieved from http://www.news-press.com/

Grant, B. F., & Dawson, D. (2006). Introduction to the national epidemiologic survey on alcohol and related conditions. *Alcohol Research and Health*, 29(2), 74–78.

Grant, J. (2009). A profile of substance abuse, gender, crime and drug policy in the United States and Canada. *Journal of Offender Rehabilitation*, 8, 654–668.

Gray, M. (2011). Back to basics: A critique of the strengths perspective in social work. *Families in Society*, 92(1), 5–11.

Haban, W. (1999, February 9). *Eating disorders*. Presentation given at the University of Northern Iowa, Cedar Falls.

Hamill, P. (1994). *A drinking life*. New York: Deidre Enterprises.

Hamilton, E. (1948). *The Greek Way to Western civilization*. New York: Norton.

Hartocollis, A. (2011, May 6). 40 percent increase in prescription drug misuse, study finds. *New York Times*. Retrieved from http://cityroom.blogs.nytimes.com/2011/05/06/40-percent-increase-in-prescription-drug-misuse-study-finds/

Hester, R. K., & Miller, W. R. (2003). *Handbook of alcoholism treatment approaches: Effective alternatives* (3rd ed.). Boston: Allyn & Bacon.

Heyman, G. (2009). *Addiction: A disorder of choice*. Cambridge, MA: Harvard University Press.

Iowa State University News Service. (2009, January 20). ISU report to United Nations conference says drug prevention programs help the economy. Ames: Iowa State University. Retrieved from http://www2.iastate.edu/~nscentral/news/2009/jan/prevention.shtml

Jellinek, E. M. (1960). *The disease concept of alcoholism*. New Haven, CT: Yale Center for Alcoholic Studies.

Johnson, C., & Goldstein, A. (2009, March 12). Choice of drug czar indicates focus on treatment, not jail. *Washington Post*, p. A4.

Jolley, J., & Kerbs, J. (2010). Risk, need, and responsibility: Unrealized potential for the international delivery of substance abuse treatment in prison. *International Criminal Justice Review*, 20(3), 280–301.

Joranby, L., Pineda, K., & Gold, M. (2005). Addiction to food and brain reward systems. *Sexual Addiction and Compulsivity*, 12(2/3), 201–217.

Karoll, B. (2010). Applying social work approaches, harm reduction, and practice wisdom to better serve those with alcohol and drug use disorders. *Journal of Social Work*, 10(3), 263–281.

Kilen, M. (2009, July 19). Life after meth: "Methland" author explores how drug affects entire towns. *Des Moines Register*, pp. 1E–2E.

Koerner, B. (2010, June 23). Secret of AA: After 75 years, we don't know how it works. *Wired*. Retrieved from http://www.wired.com/magazine/2010

Larsen, P., & Lubkin, I. (2009). *Chronic illness: Impact and intervention* (7th ed.). Sudbury, MA: Jones and Bartlett Publications.

Lee, R. D., & Rasinski, K. (2006). Five grams of coke: Racism, moralism, and White public opinion on sanctions for first time possession. *International Journal of Drug Policy*, 17(3), 183–191.

Lemonick, M. D. (2000, December 11). Downey's downfall. *Time*, p. 97.

Leshner, A. I. (2000, June 17). Cited in M. Massey, Seeing drugs as a choice or as a brain anomaly. *New York Times*, p. A17.

Leshner, A. I. (2006). The addiction recovery guide: Your Internet guide to drug and alcohol addiction recovery. Retrieved from http://www.addictionrecoveryguide.com.

Longshore, D., Hawken, A., Vrada, D., & Anglin, M. D. (2006, April 5). *Evaluation of the substance abuse and crime prevention act: Cost analysis report.* Los Angeles, CA: University of California. Retrieved from http://www.uclaisap.org/prop36

Mancini, M. A., Linhorst, D. M., Broderick, F., & Bayliff, S. (2008). Challenges to implementing the harm reduction approach. *Journal of Social Work in the Addictions*, 8(3), 380–408.

Maugh, T. (2006, August 1). Was it alcohol or anti-Semitism talking? Doctors disagree. *Los Angeles Times*. Retrieved January 2007 from http://www.latimes.com/news

McIvor, G., Barnsdale, L., Eley, S., Malloch, M., Yates, R., & Brown, A. (2006). *The operation and effectiveness of the Scottish drug court pilots.* Edinburgh: Scottish Executive Social Research, http://www.scotland.gov.uk

McLellan, T. (2010, August). Interviewed by William L. White. On science and service: An interview with Tom McLellan, Ph.D. *Counselor Magazine*, 11(4). Retrieved from http://www.counselormagazine.com

McNeece, C. A., & DiNitto, D. (2005). *Chemical dependency: A systems approach* (3rd ed.). Boston: Allyn & Bacon.

Miller, G. (2005). *Learning the language of addiction counseling* (2nd ed.) Hoboken, NJ: Wiley.

Miller, W. R. (2006). Motivational factors in addictive behaviors. In W. R.Miller & K. M. Carroll (Eds.), *Rethinking substance abuse: What the science shows* (pp. 136–150). New York: Guilford Press.

Miller, W. R., Forcehimes, A., & Zweben, A. (2011). *Treating addiction: A guide for professionals.* New York: Guilford.

Morell, C. (1996). Radicalizing recovery: Addiction, spirituality, and politics. *Social Work*, 41(3), 306–312.

National Association of Social Workers (NASW). (2009). *Social work speaks: NASW policy statements, 2009–2012* (8th ed.) Washington, DC: Author.

National Center on Addiction and Substance Abuse (CASA). (2009, May 28). Shoveling up II: The impact of substance abuse on federal, state and local budgets. New York: Columbia University. Retrieved from http://www.casacolumbia.org

National Center on Addiction and Substance Abuse (CASA). (2010). *Behind bars II: Substance abuse and America's prison population.* New York: Columbia University.

National Institute on Alcohol Abuse and Alcoholism (NIAAA). (2011). Alcoholism isn't what it used to be. *NIAAA Spectrum*, 3(1). Retrieved from http://www.spectrum.niaaa.nih.gov/features/alcoholism.aspx

Neff, J. A., & MacMaster, S. A. (2005). Spiritual mechanisms underlying substance abuse behavioral change in faith-based substance abuse treatment. *Journal of Social Work Practice in the Addictions*, 5(3), 33–54.

New York Times. (2006, April 10). A victory for California [Editorial]. *New York Times*, p. 22A.

Norcross, J., Krebs, P., & Prochaska, J. (2011). What works for whom? Tailoring psychotherapy to the person. *Journal of Clinical Psychology*, 67(2), 127–132.

O'Neil, J. V. (2001, January). Expertise in addictions said crucial. *NASW News*, p. 10.

Orford, J. (2001). *Excessive appetites: A psychological view of addictions* (2nd ed.). Chichester, England: Wiley.

Peele, S. (2004). *Seven tools to beat addiction.* New York: Three Rivers Press.

Peele, S., & Bufe, C. (2000). *Resisting 12-Step coercion: How to fight forced participation in AA, NA, or 12-Step treatment.* Tucson, AZ: Sharp Press.

Prettyman, K. (2011, May 11). *Wet houses offer some hope for all.* Deseret News. Retrieved from http://www.deseretnews.com/article/700134453/Wet-houses-offer-some-hope-for-all.html

Project MATCH Research Group. (1997, January). Matching alcoholism treatment to client heterogeneity: Project MATCH post-treatment outcomes. *Journal of Studies on Alcohol, 58,* 7–28.

Pycroft, A. (2010). *Understanding and working with substance misusers.* London: Sage.

Rapp, C. A. (1998). *The strengths model: Case management with people suffering from severe and persistent mental illness.* New York: Oxford University Press.

Rapp, C., & Goscha, R. J. (2012). *The strengths model: A recovery-oriented approach to mental health services* (3rd ed.). New York: Oxford University Press.

Reentry Court Solutions. (2010, January 5). $20 million SAMHSA/BJA grant for joint drug court strategies. Retrieved from http://www.reentrycourtsolutions.com/tag/20-million-drug-court-funding/

Riestenberg, N. (2003). *PEASE Academy: The recovery school.* Minnesota Department of Education. Retrieved June 2006 from http://education.state.mn.us/mde/

Rogers, C. R. (1931). *Client-centered therapy.* Boston: Houghton-Mifflin.

Ronel, N., & Elisha, E. (2010). A different perspective: Introducing positive criminology. *International Journal of Offender Therapy and Comparative Criminology, 55*(2), 305–325.

Rosin, H. (2000, May 5). Bush puts faith in a social service rule. *Washington Post,* p. A1.

Saleebey, D. (Ed.). (1992). *The strengths perspective in social work practice.* Boston: Allyn & Bacon.

Saleebey, D. (2009). Introduction: Power to the people. In D.Saleebey (Ed.), *The strengths perspective in social work* (5th ed., pp. 1–23) Boston: Pearson.

Saleebey, D. (2011). Some basic ideas about the strengths perspective. In F.Turner (Ed.), *Social work treatment: Interlocking theoretical approaches* (5th ed., pp. 477–485). New York: Oxford University Press.

Schaler, J. (1999). *Addiction is a choice.* Chicago: Open Court.

Scott, K., King, C., McGinn, H., & Hosseini, N. (2011). Effects of motivational enhancement on immediate outcomes of batterer intervention. *Journal of Family Violence, 26*(2), 139–149.

Shorter Oxford English Dictionary (6th ed.). New York: Oxford University Press.

Siew, W. (2010, April 23). *U.S. students suffering from Internet addiction: Study.* Reuters. Retrieved from http://www.reuters.com/article/2010/04/23/us-internet-addicts-life-idUSTRE63M4QN20100423

Sosnoff, M. (2011, April 19). Open season on icons: From Apple and Google to Charlie Sheen. *Forbes.* Retrieved from http://blogs.forbes.com/martinsosnoff/2011/04/19/open-season-on-icons-from-apple-and-google-to-charlie-sheen/

Springer, D. W., McNeece, C. A., & Arnold, E. M. (2003). *Substance abuse treatment for criminal offenders: An evidence-based guide for practitioners.* Washington, DC: American Psychological Association.

Stiles, T. (2009, February 15). *Help! I'm addicted to facebook*. Huffington Post. Retrieved from http://www.huffingtonpost.com

Straussner, S. L. & Isralowitz, R. (2008). Alcohol and drug problems. In National Association of Social Workers (NASW) (Ed.), *Encyclopedia of Social Work* (20th ed., pp.121–130). New York: Oxford University Press.

Substance Abuse and Mental Health Services Administration (SAMHSA). (2008, September 30). *New national poll reveals public attitudes on substance abuse, treatment and the prospects of recovery*. Retrieved from http://www.samhsa.gov/newsroom/advisories/0809295133.aspx

Substance Abuse and Mental Health Services Administration (SAMHSA). (2009, January/February). *Self-help groups and recovery*. Newsletter. Retrieved from http://www.samhsa.gov/samhsanewsletter

Substance Abuse and Mental Health Services Administration (SAMHSA). (2010). *Results from the 2009 National Survey on Drug Use and Health: Volume I. Summary of National Findings*. Rockville, MD: Office of Applied Studies.

Substance Abuse and Mental Health Services Administration (SAMHSA). (2011). *Substance abuse treatment facility locator*. Retrieved from http://findtreatment.samhsa.gov

Sulzberger, A. (2011, April 30). Drugs in Ozarks town infect even sheriff's department. *New York Times*, p. A1.

Szasz, T. (2003). *Ceremonial chemistry: The ritual persecution of drugs, addicts, and pushers* (Rev. ed.). Syracuse, NY: Syracuse University Press.

Terrorist attacks cause spike in treatment requests. (2001, December 6). Join Together staff. Retrieved from http://www.jointogether.org

Thomas, G. (2005, May). *Harm reduction policies and programs for persons involved in the criminal justice system*. Canadian Centre on substance abuse. Retrieved from http://www.ccsa.ca/ccsa

Torassa, V. (2001, January 15). Changing method of treatment for drug addiction. *San Francisco Chronicle*. Retrieved January 2007 from http://www.cannabisnews.com/news/thread8324.shtml

United Nations News Service. (2011, March 22). *UN names goodwill ambassador to focus on drug treatment issues*. UN News Centre. Retrieved from http://www.un.org/apps/news/story.asp?NewsID=37853&Cr=drugs&Cr1

U.S. Department of Health and Human Services. (2008). *Results from the 2007 National Household Survey on Drug Abuse*. Washington, DC: U.S. Government Printing Office. Retrieved from http://oas.samhsa.gov

Vaillant, G. E. (1983). *The natural history of alcoholism*. Cambridge, MA: Harvard University Press.

Vaillant, G. E. (1995). *The natural history of alcoholism revisited*. Cambridge, MA: Harvard University Press.

van Wormer, K. (2004). *Confronting oppression, restoring justice: From policy analysis to social action*. Alexandria, VA: Council on Social Work Education (CSWE) Press.

van Wormer, K., & Bartollas, C. (2010). *Women and the criminal justice system* (3rd ed.). Boston: Allyn & Bacon.

Verlardo, M. (2010, April 16). Prison programs that help inmates being cut by states. *Detroit Substance Abuse Examiner*. Retrieved from http://www.examiner.com

Volkow, N. (2010, August). *The science of addiction: Drugs, brains, and behavior*. Washington, DC: National Institute on Drug Abuse (NIDA).

Volpicelli, J., & Szalavitz, M. (2000). *Recovery options: The complete guide*. New York: Wiley.

Wallace, B. C. (2005). *Making mandated treatment work*. Lantham, MD: Jason Aronson.

Walters, G. (2006). *Lifestyle theory: Past, present and future*. New York: Nova Science Publication.

Washton, A. M., & Zweben, J. E. (2006). *Treating alcohol and drug problems in psychotherapy practice: Doing what works*. New York: Guilford Press.

White, W. L. (1998). *Slaying the dragon: The history of addiction treatment and recovery in America*. Bloomington, IL: Chestnut Health Systems.

White, W. L. (2007) Addiction recovery: Its definition and conceptual boundaries. *Journal of Substance Abuse Treatment*, 33, 229–241.

White, W. L. & Kelly, J. (2010). Introduction: The theory, science, and practice of recovery management. In J. Kelly and W. L. White (Eds.), *Addiction recovery management: Theory, research, and practice* (pp. 1–8). New York: Humana Press.

White House Office of the National Drug Control Policy (ONDCP). (2011). *Epidemic: Responding to America's prescription drug abuse crisis*. Washington, DC: ONDCP.

Wu, J., & Witkiewitz, K. (2008). Network support for drinking: An application of multiple groups growth mixture modeling to examine client treatment matching. *Journal of Studies on Alcohol and Drugs*, 69(1), 21–29.

Young, D. (2003). Co-occurring disorders among jail inmates: Bridging the treatment gap. *Journal of Social Work Practice in the Addictions*, 3(3), 63–85.

HISTORICAL PERSPECTIVES

CHAPTER **2**

*What experiences and history teach is this—that people and governments
never have learned anything from history.*

—Hegel (1837)

INTRODUCTION

What role do our drugs of choice play in society? In what ways has society tried
to curb the use of drugs? Whether it is alcohol, nicotine, opium, or cocaine, our
drugs of choice have been alternatively glorified and vilified. Other excesses
with the power to be self-destructive—for example, gambling—have been
regarded with a great deal of ambivalence as well. This chapter focuses on the
history of America's, Canada's, and Europe's drug use and misuse, and on
economic and legal history from the earliest days to the present time. The problems we see today are hardly new; they have existed in other forms and with
other drugs throughout our history.

In the ancient Greek legend of Ulysses (Odysseus), Ulysses has his men tie
him to the mast so he won't jump into the sea when he's lured by the song of the
Sirens (Homer, circa 850 BCE). As far back as is known, there was a sense of
people being swept away from their senses through harmful passions of one
sort or another. The use of all kinds of intoxicants, derived mostly from plants.
There has been no civilization, as Zeldin (1994) suggests, whose citizens have
not tried to escape from stress or tedium to alter their consciousness, with the
help of alcohol, tobacco, tea, coffee, or plants of various sorts. The Aztecs, for
example, had 400 gods of drink and drunkenness to help them escape into
semiconscious bliss; the cacti and mushrooms they ate gave them hallucinations
and courage for battle. Every place in the world where apples, grapes, and
wheat grew, there was a good chance humans discovered uses for them that

went beyond mere satisfaction of hunger pangs. Because even various animals have been known to seek out fermented berries, it seems obvious that the earliest humans would have done the same. The human uniqueness comes with the rituals surrounding the use of mood-altering substances, the planning entailed in their acquisition, and ultimately, the social regulation pertaining to them.

In this chapter, in the first major section, we trace how the use of drugs, including alcohol, became defined and over time redefined. From evangelism to criminalization to medicalization, the road has been paved with many ill-fated attempts at social control. Starting with a look at the earliest civilizations, through the Middle Ages, to the modern world as represented by the United States and Europe (each taking divergent paths), we will study the policy aspect of drug manufacture and use. In our overview, we see that at times the technological advances—the ability to distill alcohol and produce smokable cocaine, for example—have exceeded our human capacity to absorb them. And the availability of the neighborhood slot machine or nearby casino can lead to all kinds of temptation.

The second portion of this history chapter reviews the modern history of substance use treatment itself, from its early beginnings in Minnesota. A proliferation of for-profit Twelve-Step–based programs occurred in the 1980s, and we will briefly examine that trend as well as more recent developments in the 21st century.

Four major themes will become apparent as we survey the history of substance use and addiction in modern society. One theme is the *ambivalence* accorded the role of intoxicants in society and the pleasure and pain associated with their use. This theme is reflected in a combination of heavy alcohol or drug use coupled with strict social control policies.

The second major theme concerns the different reactions to the same drug over time, as when the health-inducing potion of one period of time is banned as a dangerous substance (associated with dangerous people) some years later. The road from medicalization to criminalization, as we will see, is influenced less by the harmful nature of a particular activity than by considerations of *race, class, and gender*.

Third is the fact of the *rising potency of drugs* that has resulted whenever they have been banned. Even as the sale of alcohol was outlawed in the 1920s, the consumption of spirits replaced the consumption of beer and wine. One striking parallel today is seen in the increasing purity and potency of cocaine and heroin, drugs that have the advantage of being easier to smuggle across borders than bulky marijuana.

Fourth, as any familiarity with American history will show, legal prohibition of a popular substance or activity is fraught with *difficulties in enforcement* and is apt to lead to many unintended consequences. In some cases, legal restrictions even seem to increase the appeal of the product, especially among the young. The solution may thus become a problem in itself. Think of all the arrests and mass incarcerations and the human consequences of these actions while the original problem still persists.

EARLY USE AND MISUSE OF INTOXICANTS

Historical accounts from ancient Greece and Rome and other early civilizations describe the systematic doling out of alcoholic beverages to soldiers, along with food, weapons, and other military rations (Gately, 2008). Excavations in 1996 provided evidence of early alcohol use in the form of a yellowish residue preserved in a pottery jar for wine making by early settlers of northern Iran (McGovern, 2003). Archeologists date the pottery jar as having been produced over 7,000 years ago. Through chemical testing, archeologists were able to establish that a substance found only in large quantities of grapes had been preserved in the residue. Additionally, the residue contained a substance used in antiquity to keep wine from turning to vinegar. The significance is that we now know that wine was being made in the Middle East as early as 5000 B.C., which was about the time people were establishing the first permanent settlements and domesticating plants and animals. That special wine gods were worshipped by ancient people is testimony to the special place that alcohol came to assume in early civilization. Ancient Romans had their god of drink, Bacchus, and the Greeks had their Dionysus. As we know from papyri, Egyptian doctors included beer or wine in their prescriptions. Long before vineyards flourished in Bordeaux, a sophisticated wine industry arose along the banks of the Nile (Nash, 2003). In ancient Egypt, both beer and wine were deified and offered to the gods.

In *A History of the World in Six Glasses*, economist Tom Standage (2005) signifies each historical epoch as characterized by its signature beverage. Beer, according to Standage, was first made from fermenting grain in the Fertile Crescent. By 3000 B.C., it was used to pay wages, and later it became the main export of ancient Greece.

In China, a variety of alcoholic beverages have been used since prehistoric times and in all segments of society. Scientific evidence from northern China indicates that alcoholic consumption goes back even further than previously known (Gately, 2008). Chemical analysis of the residues found inside pottery jars in a grave in northern China provides proof that the Chinese were converting their produce (rice, grapes, and honey) into alcoholic beverages as early as 7000–6600 BCE.

Evidence attests (Gifford, 2009) that in the past, alcohol played an important role in religious life and that the use of alcohol in moderation was the norm. In what is now Greece, wine making was commonplace. The ancient Greeks were known for the temperance of their culture and their avoidance of excess in all things. Traditional Roman values of temperance and simplicity resembled the Greek ways of being. Gradually, however, these values were replaced by practices related to degeneracy.

From the Old Testament of the Bible, we learn of drinking practices of the Hebrews. Abundant wine made from grapes was regarded as a blessing that could "gladden the heart of man" (Psalm 105:15, King James Version). That it also had the property to wreak some havoc is revealed in Genesis 9:20:

> And Noah began to be a husbandman, and he planted a vineyard: And he drank of the wine and was drunken; and he was uncovered within his tent.

Later, we learn that the daughters of Lot got their father drunk to continue the family line (Genesis 19:32–36). Although there is a lot of drinking mentioned in the Bible, both the Old and New Testaments condemn drunkenness. Indeed, the dangers inherent in strong drink have been known at least since biblical times. Proverbs 33:29–30 provides a strong cautionary note:

> Who hath woe? Who hath sorrow? Who hath contentions? Who hath babbling? Who hath wounds without cause? Who hath redness of eyes? They that tarry long at the wine; they that go to seek mixed wine.

Whereas the large majority of the Hebrews rejoiced in wine and used it for medicinal and nutritional purposes, wine was relegated to a sacred and symbolic role. The New Testament depicts this common association. While the Hebrews condoned drinking but not drunkenness, a different kind of religious control was adopted later in the 7th century by Islam. The Koran simply condemned wine altogether, and an effective prohibition against all alcoholic beverages prevailed. In East Asia, India, and China, there were no religious restrictions on the consumption of alcohol.

The long road from the sacred to the profane was shortened by a 10th century discovery by Zakariya Razi (Rhazes), a noted Iranian physician and pharmacist (Kinney, 2011). The alcohol he used as a medicine in the way that we use rubbing alcohol today. Centuries later his discovery spread to Europe when his writings were translated. The word *alcohol* itself is derived from the Arabic *al-kuhul* (*Shorter Oxford English Dictionary*, 2007). Originally, in the Middle East, this distilled alcohol was used as a cosmetic to darken the eyelids as well as a medical cure. The process of distillation, according to Standage (2005), eventually fueled the age of exploration as seafaring European explorers established colonies, and then empires around the world. The Arabs may have viewed this strong substance as a kind of medicine, but it took on a whole different cast when the discovery reached European shores. This discovery of distilled spirits, which made possible the manufacture of much stronger alcoholic concoctions, is an instance of technology's reach exceeding its grasp. The devastation unleashed with this new development, however, did not occur suddenly but took place over centuries of use. Use of distilled liquors gradually become common in Europe from around the 16th century.

Self-indulgence in connection with food is demonstrated by the presence of the vomitorium in ancient Rome. The practices of feasting and drinking included vomiting so that people could keep repeating these processes. This was the forerunner of the binge–purge cycle known today as bulimia. Anorexia has its roots in holy fasting practices of 13th century women whose self-denial provided them with praise and admiration. Some of the "holy anorexics" were canonized as saints for their troubles (Bell, 1987).

Like alcohol, the use of opium goes far back in time as well, to about 5000 B.C. (Szasz, 2003). Extracted from the white juice of certain species of poppy, opium is believed to have been used by the Sumerians, an ancient

Middle Eastern people, to enhance their feelings of pleasure and by later civilizations for its medical properties.

Moving to the Americas, we find that while most of the pre-Columbian Native peoples lacked knowledge of alcohol, several of the cultures of northern Mexico and the southwestern United States consumed wine and beer. Columbus found indigenous peoples of the Caribbean drinking beer made from fermented maize. Drunkeness was limited to communal fiestas or preparations for war, was negatively sanctioned and therefore not disruptive. Significantly, the alcohol content was relatively low (Collins & McNair, 2003). Hard-drinking Europeans, such as traders and soldiers, promoted alcohol use among Native Americans by making high-alcohol–content distilled liquor increasingly available to them and by using it as payment in trade and negotiations.

For more than 2,000 years, indigenous societies have utilized various naturally occurring plants such as the "sacred" mushroom of Mexico and the peyote cactus (*Encyclopaedia Britannica,* 2005). There is evidence that a mushroom cult existed in the Mayan culture of Central America. Reports from Spanish explorers tell of the cultic use of peyote. Later, missionaries and government agents fought hard against these practices. Peyote has been used across the centuries in religious ceremonies and is not associated with compulsive use. The peyote-using American Indians are reported to have been more successful in leading productive and healthy lives than tribes that did not use peyote (*Encyclopaedia Britannica,* 2005).

The Spaniards introduced marijuana to the New World; the word *marijuana* comes from a Spanish word meaning a substance causing intoxication. Marijuana use can be traced back to cultivation by the ancient Greeks, Persians, and Chinese. As early as 3000 B.C.E., it was known in China. In Islamic nations, which prohibit use of alcohol, there has been much more general use of cannabis; the term *cannibis* is of Persian origin, and *hashish* is derived from an Arabic word for grass (Kinney, 2011). Marco Polo told sensational stories of the use of the highly potent form of cannabis known as hashish by a fanatical, brutal sect of Persians. Eventually, in the 17th century, Islamic scholars prohibited its use due to its psychoactive properties, which resembled those of wine, which is forbidden in the Koran.

Cocaine use as coca leaf chewing among South American indigenous peoples dates back centuries (Kinney, 2011). The Spanish conquerors made the drug available to slaves to boost their stamina. This form of cocaine use was not culturally destructive and not associated with addiction.

The history of nicotine addiction goes back to when Columbus and his men discovered dried tobacco leaves in Central America. It was introduced to Europe in 1493 (Szasz, 2003). By the 1600s, tobacco was a permanent European commodity and used by all social classes.

Later, in British America, however, exchanging liquor for furs was culturally and economically devastating to a people who, with the exception of those who lived in modern-day Mexico and the American Southwest, had no chance to develop a familiarity with alcohol's powers and in so knowing these powers be able to resist them. The Catawba tribal leader's plea to the colonists to cease supplying spirits to his people is one of many Native American voices for restraint described by Peter Mancall (2004).

THE EUROPEAN CONTEXT

In the *History of Intoxication,* Norwegian author Bjorn Qviller (1996) argues that from Viking drinking guilds to wine-soaked symposia in ancient Greece, alcohol played a central role in the political life of western Europe. People drank together to knit friendships and make political allies. Not much is known about the role of alcohol in women's lives in ancient history. We do know from ancient records that women's misuse of alcohol was linked to its harmful effects on unborn children (e.g., see the admonition in the Old Testament, Judges 13:7).

In the days before purification, alcohol was often safer than water, so Europeans consumed large quantities. Opium was used by physicians in classical Greece and Rome, and it was known to the Arab world as well. During the time of the Crusades, the Crusaders were introduced to this product and brought it back to Europe (Abadinsky, 2011). Later, in Europe, the opium was mixed with alcohol as a fashionable way to escape from pain and boredom (Zeldin, 1994). By 1854, opium was the most valued remedy for everyday maladies such as indigestion. In a reverse of today's war on international drug trafficking in which Britain is the recipient of drugs from abroad, the British began illegally smuggling opium into China in the early 18th century to exchange with Chinese traders for tea (Hart, Ksir, & Ray, 2010). The opium in Britain had been transported from India. Opium smoking became rampant among Chinese peasants. The Chinese were forced through a series of wars, known historically as the Opium Wars, which broke out in 1839, to keep their markets open to the opium trade (Abadinsky, 2011).

Sometimes, technological advance exceeds a people's ability to handle it. So it was with the invention of the distillation process for making alcohol stronger. And so it was with the discovery by German scientists of how to isolate cocaine from the coca bush (Benshoff & Janikowski, 2000). The process of distillation was widely used in the 15th century as a way of removing water from the fermented product, thereby increasing the concentration of alcohol. In 1575, a distillery was founded in Amsterdam, which is still in operation today. From a concoction of grains, herbs, and juniper berries, *jenever,* or gin, was produced. The availability of cheap gin, combined with the population displacement caused by industrialization and associated with the growth of an urban proletariat, contributed to an epidemic of drunkenness that was notorious in England (Levinthal, 2009). The devastation was so great that a staggering infant mortality rate and child starvation rate combined to prevent a growth in population from 1700 to 1750.

Public outrage at the drunken woman and neglectful mother may have reached its height, as Skinner (2007) indicates, during the infamous gin epidemics of London. Drinking women alarmed reformers because they associated drunkenness with lust, the spread of venereal disease, and failed motherhood. Crimes of violence and immorality among all social classes, but most evident among the poor, gave the age a debauched character, preserved in political commentary and the early novel. Parliament, which earlier had actively promoted gin production to utilize surplus grain and to raise revenue, now passed legislation to discourage its use. Gradually, a change in attitudes, probably related to the Industrial Revolution and the need for a hardworking, sober work force, coalesced to reduce the use of spirits considerably. The availability of higher-quality and more affordable beer was an additional factor in gin's decline.

COLONIAL AMERICA

We begin this section with a thought-provoking question, one commonly asked and best articulated by social work educator Ogden Rogers:

> Gathering people's thoughts on "non–12-steps" programs such as Rational Recovery, or Harm Reduction, or work by Stanton Peele on addictive behavior is often met either by anger on one end of the pole, or marginalization-almost-without-comment at the other. Whenever I encounter so much emotion about something I want to explore dispassionately, I ask myself "why?" Why is it that the subject of "use, abuse, and addiction" raises such passions? I suspect there must be deep values and/or fears enmeshed in the fabric of the issues surrounding treatment. The very use of consciousness altering substances provokes threat at some larger ideal of what is the "norm." Threat provokes fear, which tends to polarize thinking. I'm impressed with how much of the social conversation about drugs is focused in extreme ways: from libertarian abandon to "Just-Say-No" to everything. What makes it so difficult to find middle paths? (personal communication; April 16, 2011)

For an answer, we must look back to the holy experiment known to the world as Puritanism—that band of relatively humorless religious zealots who started things off in the Massachusetts Bay. Like the very language that Americans speak, the present-day American value system is rooted in that New England experience. To Puritans who sought guidance for all daily activities in Scripture, the truth was perfectly clear: God had chosen an elite few to represent Him on Earth (Erikson, 1966).

This is not to say, however, that sexual prudery or enforced abstinence from drink was a part of the Puritan scene. What these religious dissenters did was set the tone for all that took place then and was to come later—the rigidity and punitiveness but, above all, the moralism that was to become pervasive in American life.

The history of addiction in the United States begins but does not end, therefore, with alcohol. An article in the *Chicago Tribune* ("Documentary

Looks at Drinking in America," 1999) puts the American experience with mood-altering substances into perspective:

> Most students of popular culture already are well aware that cocaine began insin-uating itself into our society through the use of patent medicines and soft drinks; Bayer once marketed heroin alongside its aspirin products; and military service has turned more people into smokers than Humphrey Bogart, Lauren Bacall, and Joe Camel combined. What isn't well known, however, is how much booze was imbibed by our founding fathers … and mothers.

More beer than water was carried on the Mayflower. The Puritans saw alcohol as a blessing from God and as a good and healthy beverage (Gately, 2008). Colonial Americans of all ages drank daily; pregnant women and chil-dren, along with men, consumed a lot of beer. Punishments were reserved for drunkards who made nuisances of themselves. Still, the tavern was the center of much family, social, and economic activity.

Native Americans adopted the drug alcohol within their cultural context. They drank not for conviviality but to alter their mood and achieve a different state of consciousness (Murrin et al., 2001). Native Americans assumed that alcoholic drinks served the same purpose as hallucinogenic plants and tobacco and treated them in the same way. To drink small quantities was considered pointless. Europeans, as mentioned earlier, took advantage of the Native American propensity to drink to the point of insensibility and cheated them out of furs and other goods. Heavy alcohol use for Native Americans became a major cause of social problems that have continued until the present day.

With the passage of time, liquor came to be valued by the early settlers for both its high alcohol content and its shipping advantages. Besides, as we learn in *Ambitious Brew: The Story of American Beer,* growing hops and barley was too much work; it was easier to plant fruit trees and make alcoholic cider or fruit liqueurs (Ogle, 2005). The Puritans regarded rum as "God's good creature." Although an occasional drunk was placed in the stocks, the tavern was the center of social, economic, and political activity (Hart, Ksir, & Ray, 2010).

As the colonists turned to distilling alcohol, they proved as adaptable as they had earlier in producing passable beer. Honey, corn, rye, berries, and apples were used in domestic production. A general lack of concern about alcoholism and its problems was one of the most significant features of the Colonial era (Burns, 2004). Strong drink was thought to protect against dis-ease and be conducive to good health. Alcohol was used as a solvent, antisep-tic, and of course, as a painkiller. Because good drinking water was not always available, there was some substance to this argument that alcohol was a source of good health. And as long as the social norms were followed, drinking excesses could be tolerated. Rum, made from molasses that was imported in large quantities from Jamaica, figured prominently in the econ-omy of the new nation. For the sake of rum, New Englanders became the bankers of the slave trade that supplied the molasses needed to produce rum (Kinney, 2011). Rum was transported abroad on the same ships that went to

Africa to carry the slaves back to America. The rum was traded with Europeans for slaves. According to another version of history, however, the New Englanders' role in the business aspect of the slave trade, although prominent, was more limited than is commonly believed (Barr, 1999; Burns, 2004). The early Americans loved the rum they distilled from Jamaican molasses; they consumed it themselves and made large profits through exports (Barr, 1999). About half of the molasses brought to the New World from the West Indies went to the distilleries that produced the American national beverage--rum (Burns, 2004).

Consumption of copious amounts of alcohol was the norm among early European Americans, and alcohol was measured in barrels. Although severe restrictions were placed on drinking by slaves, laborers digging the Erie Canal were allotted a quart of whiskey a day (Kinney, 2011). When Congress passed an excise tax on whiskey in 1791, farmers and distillers staged the notorious Whiskey Rebellion, which was crushed by federal troops.

From 1785 to 1835, however, attitudes concerning alcohol began to change dramatically. During this period, drinking became a disruptive force for many Americans. As farmers turned surplus grain into whiskey, the old pattern of communal drinking began to break down; new patterns of solitary and binge drinking developed. The availability of cheap spirits, alcohol misuse, and family breakdown were all intertwined (Fletcher, 2008). For a dramatic description of the kind of havoc that could be wreaked on a population by access to vast quantities of rum, consider what Robert Hughes (1987) had to say of an early convict settlement in Australia:

> The most sought-after commodity of all was rum, a word which stood for spirits of all kinds.... In this little community (of about 10,000) nearly all the men and most of the women were addicted to alcohol. In Australia, especially between 1790 and 1820, rum became an overriding social obsession. Families were wrecked by it, ambitions destroyed, an iron chain of dependency forged. (p. 290)

Excessive drinking was the norm during the time that the English governors of Australia limited the liquor supplies by outlawing the barter of rum. But from 1821, once the anxiety over supply had been removed, Australian drinking habits changed (Gately, 2008). Wild drunkenness and the debauchery that had gone with it came to be associated with a part of their history that ex-convicts wanted to forget. Breweries were established, and the younger generations turned to beer as the favored alcoholic beverage.

Dr. Benjamin Rush, surgeon general during the American Revolution, had observed firsthand the devastation wrought by rum rations on soldiers. In his pamphlet recording his observations, Rush pinpointed the dangers of potent alcohol. Through such writings and his personal influence, Rush provided a scientific voice to the call for an end to the distillation and drinking of whiskey and other spirits. This call was echoed by concerned family members and members of the clergy, especially the descendants of Puritans, who aligned themselves with concerned citizens to condemn the wasteful behavior and debauchery that were characteristic of the day. The new focus was on saving the family. Denning, Little, and Glickman (2004) bring our attention to two facts: (1) Rush did not declare alcohol addiction a disease but, rather, said that the signs and symptoms were like those of a disease, and (2) he advocated moderation.

Two currents of thought, the temperance and the medical approaches, were inextricably interwoven in the 19th century, as in recent times. At the time, these views—one stressing evil and the other illness—appeared in opposition. While one stressed the supply side of alcohol, the other focused on reducing the need for the drug. Unity came because of awareness of a major social problem and the urgent need to address it.

A point worth underscoring: The temperance movement was about moderation, as the word implies. It was about control of "spirits," the distilled beverages, not of beer and wine. Another point worth noting concerns African traditions. The Africans brought to America as slaves came primarily from West African cultures. These cultures, as White (1998) indicates, had blended alcohol into economic, social, and religious customs since antiquity. Under the institution of slavery, slave masters came to promote excessive alcohol use on festive occasions such as Christmas and July 4. But the major problem for early African Americans was the risk they faced when White people were inebriated.

Following the mid-1800s, alcohol consumption was cut in half, and from then on, a minority of the population was dependent on alcohol (Zeldin, 1994). But later in the 19th century, a craze developed for patent medicines with a high opiate content. Morphine, which originally had been used for pain relief from battle wounds as far back as the Civil War, was now heralded as a treatment for chronic drinking problems (Gifford, 2009). Often prescribed to older White women of high socioeconomic class, morphine frequently resulted in iatrogenic, or medically induced, addiction.

The year 1900 marked a prohibition many find surprising: the prohibition of tobacco and lottery tickets. It was illegal to sell cigarettes in 14 states, and selling a lottery ticket was a federal crime (Savage, 1999). By that year, the modern tobacco industry was already under way. A ruthless businessman from North Carolina named James Buchanan Duke successfully used a cigarette-rolling machine that made mass production possible (McGinn, 1997). Millions of male immigrants who stepped off the boat onto U.S. soil were presented with a free bag of cigarettes. Many became hooked right from the start. The U.S. Supreme Court upheld Tennessee's tobacco prohibition in the belief that cigarettes were a noxious product and because of their deleterious effects on young people. All the while, opium, morphine, and heroin were being sold over the counter. Chewing tobacco, similarly, was acceptable, presumably only for men.

Smoking opium was associated with Chinese immigrant laborers; their foreign ways were feared and resented, as was their drug use (Hart, Ksir, & Ray, 2010). Labor unions resented that these exceptionally hardworking people were willing to work for low wages. Americans thus defamed not only the

Chinese but opium as well (Szasz, 2003). The invention of the hypodermic needle and the synthesis of heroin from morphine at the end of the 19th century further exacerbated the problem. Inevitably, there was a national outcry for legislation to curb what was seen as the moral degeneracy associated with drug use. The same xenophobia aroused by heavy drinking among the poor, Catholic, and European immigrants was a factor in the outcry against narcotic use as well.

Warnings of addiction as a result of morphine use began to appear in medical textbooks around 1900. In 1909, the import of opium was banned. Opium itself then became increasingly scarce at the consumer level, and heroin, a far more potent substance that was not smoked but injected, became the popular form of this drug. In banning such drugs as opium and later alcohol, governments actually were pressing users toward more dangerous methods or levels of consumption.

Meanwhile, the intolerance for smoking cigarettes began to dissolve. The popularity of cigarettes was boosted tremendously with their free distribution to World War I troops in France (Fishbein & Pease, 1996). The United States population, as Zeldin (1994) argues, was remarkable for the suddenness with which it moved from drug to drug, "from one escape to another" (p. 231). And when prohibition of alcohol spread throughout the country, drinks laced with cocaine, as Zeldin further indicates, stepped in as the savior. Cocaine, in fact, was considered the remedy for addiction to other substances. In fact, Coca-Cola had contained cocaine until 1903 and, not surprisingly, was an extremely popular "pick-me-upper."

Let's backtrack a moment to consider cocaine, a drug with effects that have been much more pronounced on society than the sedating opiates could ever be. Cocaine, which was particularly popular in literary and intellectual circles, was widely used for everything from sinus troubles to hysteria (Abadinsky, 2011). It began to get a bad name, however, because of its association with bizarre behavior, including violence. After the turn of the 20th century, cocaine became identified with the urban underworld, and southern Blacks according to Abadinsky. Fear of the effects of cocaine intensified until official regulation was inevitable.

The culmination of the fear of addiction and the association of the use of narcotics with the lower classes and foreigners culminated in the Harrison Act, which became law in 1914. The Harrison Act severely restricted the amount of opioids or cocaine in any remedy sold without a prescription (Maisto, Galizio, & Connors, 2011). It is important to note that this legislation related to the payment of taxes on the sale of these products only; it was not a punitive law. Enforcement was through the Treasury Department (Hart, Ksir, & Ray, 2010). Nevertheless, with the passage of this legislation, the criminalization process began in earnest (Robinson & Scherlen, 2007). Several years later physicians and pharmacists were arrested for providing drugs to addicted persons for the purposes of maintenance. Following this crackdown, doctors no longer would prescribe these drugs.

Szasz's (2003) insights are relevant here. Opium is organic, coming from the dried juice of the poppy. "No chemist, no pharmaceutical industry, no physician is needed to produce it or to administer it" (p. 65). This is the point, argues Szasz. Illicit drugs are those that can't be marketed; the medical community has embraced synthetic painkillers and mood changers instead. These drugs have become the licit or legal drug remedies.

Paradoxically, after restrictive laws such as the Harrison Act were passed, doctors became reluctant to prescribe drugs to addicts, and the street cost of heroin rose astronomically (Maisto, Galizio, & Connors, 2011). The drug problem grew more prominent, accordingly, than it ever was before. Public fear of dope peddlers grew with the increase in arrests. The same progression seen with other drugs that were banned was seen with cocaine. Fairly benign forms of consuming cocaine gave way to much more dangerous practices through drug interdiction. Addicts, bankrupted by the inflated cost of illegal drugs, sought out drugs that gave the most "bang for the buck" and proceeded to use those drugs in the most cost-efficient way.

Marijuana was associated with Mexican immigrants in the southwestern United States. *Marijuana* is the Mexican colloquial term for a plant that has been cultivated throughout the world and known in Central Asia and China for approximately 3,000 years (*Encyclopaedia Britannica,* 2005). Cannabis has long been considered to have medicinal value as an analgesic, anesthetic, and depressant. In the early 20th century in the United States, when anti-immigrant sentiment grew (associated with a wave of emigration to the American Southwest following the Mexican Revolution of 1910), rumors began to spread that Mexicans were distributing the "killer weed" to American schoolchildren (Schlosser, 1994). The drug was also associated with jazz musicians in New Orleans. Between 1914 and 1931, 29 states outlawed marijuana. The Marijuana Tax Act of 1937 essentially criminalized the possession of marijuana throughout the United States.

Then as now, seeking to influence international policies in other nations, the United States organized international conferences on the "drug menace." In response to this pressure, Britain passed the Dangerous Drug Act, which, like the Harrison Act, was intended to limit legal distribution of addictive drugs. Unlike in the United States, however, the new law was interpreted in favor of physicians to give them final authority in providing drugs to addicts as a legitimate form of treatment (King, 2009).

PROHIBITION OF ALCOHOL

Just as technological advances relevant to the drugs heroin and cocaine led to the creation of products that it seemed humans could not control, so it was with alcohol. The distillation process mentioned earlier carried the seeds of destruction. The temperance women, for this reason following the teachings of Dr. Rush, targeted strong liquor as the source of the evils they saw around them—chronic drunkenness, violence, and family poverty.

The temperance woman represented the Victorian ideal of purity; she fought alcohol as a rude intrusion upon the family and a threat to the family's very survival. By attacking "Demon Rum" as the root cause of family disintegration, temperance advocates viewed alcohol-related domestic problems as social problems requiring legal solutions (Rotskoff, 2004). The drunkard was scorned, and the drunkard's wife was pitied. The temperance woman was thus a crusader for traditional moral values. Yet as the historical record indicates, the temperance woman was in fact more radical than her image suggests. She fought against men's drunkenness and for the liberation of women from the tyranny of this form of indulgence (Fletcher, 2008). Eventually, this volunteer army of churchwomen led into another movement of renown, the women's suffrage movement. The two movements were interconnected in that men feared women's moral fervor and independence and that they would restrict men's drinking (Burns, 2004). As it was, however, the *men* were to outlaw the sale of alcoholic beverages themselves; only shortly thereafter did the women win the right to vote.

To understand how the women's suffrage movement and prohibition came together, let us examine the historical record in the nation's heartland. In Iowa, the legislature's plan to make Iowa the first state to give women the right to vote was destroyed by a confluence of volatile issues, chief among which was liquor. In tracing the history of the male resistance to women's suffrage, Fruhling (1996) cites the stated fear that if women were permitted to vote, they might use that political clout to close the saloons where men squandered their time and the family's money. Iowa's native thirst, as Fruhling further indicates, grew even larger with the tide of German and Irish immigrants that began arriving in the 1840s; the neighborhood saloon was a hallowed tradition.

"The modern drunk is 100-fold worse than the ancient drunk." So said the most renowned preacher of his day, the Reverend T. DeWitt Talmage (1887, p. 599). His comment was in reference to the impact on some people of the more potent forms of alcohol that were popular in his day. Talmage, like other Protestants, called for the politicians of his day to take a stand "in the battle between drunkenness and sobriety, God and the devil" (p. 604).

The temperance proponents, to reduce habitual drunkenness, promoted taking an abstinence pledge. Public confession figured in the decision to take this pledge. In Ireland, a religious-based temperance movement acquired a following under the leadership of a charismatic priest, Father Matthew, who was influenced by Protestant reformers. Ireland was temporarily transformed into a nation of teetotalers during the late 1800s. (Butler, 2010). (The word *teetotaler* came from the letter *T* for total abstinence, which was put next to a man's name on the society's rolls when he took the pledge.) Father Matthew, whose astonishingly successful temperance crusade swept across Ireland, converted millions of men and women to total abstinence (Townend, 2005). In a series of hundreds of emotional open-air meetings beginning in 1839, the priest addressed massive crowds for days on end until he got the people to make the sign of the cross, which was the letter T. In Scotland, the Presbyterian ministry led the way toward total abstinence, which became common among the middle classes in the early 1900s. Father Matthew's well-publicized work had a large following in North America, especially among the Irish. In Norway, strong anti-alcoholic measures were put into effect; distilling at home was outlawed.

In his history of the philosophy and policies of alcohol and then drug treatment in Ireland, Shane Butler (2002) recalls the story of the Irish struggle with the forces of moralism and pragmatism. The two most significant developments in Irish treatment history were (1) the introduction and the enthusiastic adoption of the disease model of Alcoholics Anonymous (AA)—a model with roots in the Protestant evangelical tradition—into Ireland, a Catholic country in the strictest sense of the word and (2) the adoption of harm reduction strategies such as needle exchange and methadone maintenance but without any large-scale adoption of harm reduction principles or philosophy. "Attitudes of staff," as Butler (2002) observes, "were still moralistic and authoritarian" (p. 190). Accordingly, methadone and other practices appeared to become a source of conflict between service users and service providers. The lesson that we can learn from Butler's insightful analysis is the need for compatibility between society's belief system and publicly instituted policy and for underlying integration of theory and practice. One could predict that change efforts that are congruent with cultural beliefs and norms will be more readily accepted than change efforts that are culturally alien.

Once under way, the American temperance movement, like any social movement, went to extremes. Therefore, what had begun as an effort to protect people from strong liquor became to some extent an attack on the people themselves and on the sorts of people who were the most prone to heavy drinking—the thousands upon thousands of immigrants to the United States from countries with diverse drinking practices (Abadinsky, 2011). Large numbers of German immigrants consumed a tremendous amount of beer. Many Irish immigrants also brought their drinking habits with them. Unlike the Germans, the many Irish tolerated a pattern of regular intoxication.

The Germans introduced lager beer to their adopted nation, thus providing, according to Murrin and colleagues (2001), a "wholesome alternative for Americans who wanted to give up spirits without joining the teetotalers" (p. 315). The Germans built old-country beer halls complete with sausage counters, group singing, and family attractions. The Irish, as Murrin and colleagues further note, reaffirmed their love of whiskey. The term *whiskey* is actually Gaelic, meaning "water of life" (Ayto, 2008).

The anti-immigrant and anti-Catholic nativism in the United States combined to give the temperance movement a new and fierce momentum. Saloons, which were frequented by the working class and immigrants, were feared as threats to the middle-class home and as forums for labor union organizers. The Anti-Saloon League grew out of these sentiments and became a strong lobbying group.

Ironically, as American society became more industrialized and disciplined, saloon life grew more civilized. Food was now served, and women began to accompany their menfolk to these establishments. Drunkenness became socially disapproved. With the arrival of Gerrmans, breweries popped up in the Midwest, more than 2,000 of them, especially in the towns where Germans settled—in Milwaukee, St. Louis, and Chicago (Ogle, 2005). Saloons opened on every corner, selling American beer, which was lighter in texture than the European variety. Unfortunately for the beer manufacturers, the anti-drinking groups were able to take advantage of the anti-German sentiment that sprang up in connection with World War I. By the time World War I broke out, anti-German prejudice was overwhelming. The support of the corporate world, which had an interest in promoting sober worker habits and reducing spending on alcohol, was instrumental in the passage of the Eighteenth Amendment to the Constitution, establishing national Prohibition in 1919 (to begin in 1920). The shift from a temperance, controlled-use philosophy to a total-abstinence model marked a shift in public perception of alcoholism as a moral failing to that of a socially proscribed behavior (Benshoff & Janikowski, 2000).

Of attempts throughout the world to control the use of alcohol, the most resounding failure was that of the United States from 1920 to 1933 (*Encyclopaedia Britannica,* 2005). The American experiment with Prohibition—the "noble experiment"—gave drinking the allure of the forbidden and led to the burgeoning and glamorizing of general crime, the growth of organized crime, the corruption of police and politicians, and the criminalization of ordinary citizens.

Before Prohibition, the Kennedy family had traded in alcoholic beverages and decided to stay with what they knew best. Joseph Kennedy, father to President John Kennedy and two U.S. senators, did not sell liquor directly to consumers but to figures at the highest levels of organized crime such as Frank Costello and Lucky Luciano (Burns, 2004). Kennedy was responsible for shipping huge quantities of Canadian whiskey and scotch into the United States. In his earlier best-selling and controversial *Double Cross* (1992), Chuck Giancana, the brother of Chicago Mafia godfather Sam Giancana, gives a graphic account of the Kennedy connection and ultimate refutation of organized crime. The title, *Double Cross,* refers to Attorney General Robert Kennedy's prosecution of some key Mafia leaders, which, as Giancana claims, played into the assassinations of the two Kennedy brothers (see Giancana & Giancana, 1992). In his recent history of Prohibition, Daniel Okrent (2010), however, decisively refutes this account, including the claimed connection of the Kennedy patriarch to organized crime.

As with the Harrison Act and its aftermath, previously legal activities became illegal at the stroke of a pen. And while these substances—some drugs, including alcohol—were banned, the tides had reversed. The cigarette bans were lifted. Smoking was on the road to becoming a glamorous all-American habit (Savage, 1999). Today Americans accept, or at least do not outlaw, sales of alcohol and tobacco, although these substances are no less potentially destructive than the ones they have outlawed.

Despite the restrictions on alcohol, people still drank during Prohibition, often consuming home-brewed alcohol that was legal (moonshine) or alcohol that was from questionable sources and likely to contain adulterants. During Prohibition, drinking patterns shifted from beer to more potent liquor because the latter was easier for bootleggers to transport (Benshoff & Janikowski, 2000). Marijuana became increasingly popular. During the 1920s, moreover, women began to drink openly. Their drinking, as Carter (1997) argues, accelerated because of the greater freedom women experienced following World War I, the right to vote, and the relaxed sexual mores of the day. Women who drank publicly, however, remained linked in the public eye to promiscuity and bad motherhood.

With the widespread disrespect for the law that developed during Prohibition's attempt to regulate what could not be regulated, the growth of organized crime became linked with police and political corruption (Okrent, 2010). Although the overall quantity of alcohol consumed did go down during this time, and the rate of cirrhosis of the liver and the death rate from poisoned liquor was appallingly high (Burns, 2004). Homicide rates in large cities almost doubled. Prohibition proved counterproductive not only because it encouraged beer drinkers to convert to spirits but also because it made drinking synonymous with drunkenness.

Economic interests coupled with disillusionment combined to put an end to the "noble experiment." The Depression created a desperate need for more jobs and government revenue through taxes (Ogle, 2005). Couldn't the re-establishment of the liquor industry help in this regard? In 1933, the Eighteenth Amendment was repealed.

Today, the legacy of Prohibition remains. Age-restrictive laws have been instituted. Young people often state that they see no difference between drinking and taking drugs (Barr, 1999). In contrast to the United States, which passed the National Minimum Drinking Age Act in 1984, which restricts drinking in public places to age 21, Canada has not raised the age, which remains at 18 or 19 depending on the province. What is surprising is the lack of controversy over the age-21 laws, even in light of the surge in binge drinking by the young (see Chapter 6). Although several states have considered lowering the drinking age for members of the military, and in many states young people can drink freely in the home, the age 21 drinking laws persist (Minton, 2011). In parts of the South and on many Native American reservations, dry counties and townships still outlaw the sale of alcohol, and Sunday sales of alcohol are illegal in many places.

The United States was not the only country to experience the ramifications of a temperance movement. After World War I began, support for prohibition increased in Canada. By 1918, every Canadian province except Quebec had adopted a prohibition law. Economic incentives were influential, however, in dimming Canadian enthusiasm for the restrictions. Great profits were to be made from sales to persons south of the border. The prohibition laws in Canada were therefore rescinded in most provinces. In Ireland, due to the temperance crusade described previously, a high percentage of people were teetotalers (McGoldrick, 2005).

Binge drinking in Ireland became an enormous problem during the economic boom of the 1980s and 1990s; Irish street violence increased significantly, as did alcohol-related mortality rates (Elkin, 2004). But then during the recent recession, the consumption rate dropped drastically and many pubs went out of business. Yet for those who lost their jobs, heavy drinking and suicide were common outcomes. (McGreevy, 2010).

Iceland, Norway, and Finland also outlawed the sale of alcohol for a period in the early 20th century. This attempt to control the consumption of alcohol was followed by alcohol taxation policies. Until recently, Sweden and Finland had high alcohol taxes by European standards, and sales were restricted to state-owned shops. Now that Sweden and Finland have joined the European Union, however, the days of state-sponsored temperance are over. Because of their integration into the global market, the Nordic means of alcohol control, the traditional form of harm reduction through high taxation, no longer can be relied on in this region. According to media reports, Swedes drink about 20% more per year than do Norwegians, who still have a high tax but can easily drive to Sweden for cheap alcohol. The effectiveness of heavy alcohol taxation such as exists in Norway was confirmed in an empirically based study by Wagenaar, Tobler, and Komro (2010) that studied the findings of 50 research papers. Their research confirmed a link between the availability of cheap alcohol and heavy drinking by the population. Elevated rates of death were also correlated with low-priced alcohol.

After the Communist Revolution swept Russia, the temperance movement was replaced with a belief that the answer to the serious vodka consumption problem would be found in the socialist way of life (White, 1996). Communism was incompatible with alcoholism, or so it was thought. Yet vodka played an important role in Russian cultural life and had been a significant source of government revenue through taxation since the 16th century. For a brief period in 1985 under Gorbachev, directives against the use of alcohol at public banquets and receptions were issued, the sale of alcohol to persons under age 21 was forbidden, and public drunkenness was severely punished.

In sharp contrast to the American ambivalence toward drinking and the Russian overindulgence, Italians are a national group that can be singled out for their healthy enjoyment of good wine. Unlike the Irish, who avoid eating with alcohol because food diminishes the effect, Italians tend to drink primarily when eating (McGoldrick, 2005). An Italian woman from Naples, Florida, for example, provides this description of her upbringing:

> In our large, traditional Italian family, gathering together in a large group is an event of great importance. Food, talk, and wine go hand in hand at these gatherings. Talk, of course, is the most important of these. (Contrary to what most movies depict, conversation is not necessarily loud and boisterous, and not everyone talks at once.) But talking and eating together is definitely the way to keep bonds tight. At the dinner table, there is always wine. Some people choose to

have a glass, or more, and others do not. No one's behavior or attitude changes because of the wine, and the only way to discern who is or is not drinking is by looking at their glasses.

It is not unusual for someone to give a sip of wine, or even a small amount in a glass, to one of their children. It's just no big deal. This is similar to when I was a preteen and felt privileged, and very grown up, on the occasions I was allowed to have a small cup of coffee with my mother and aunts. It wasn't the coffee; it was the conversation and the belonging! By the same token it's not just the wine. I think wine would be nothing without conversation and a sense of belonging. By "be-longing," I mean simply being welcomed by loved ones, and this extends, too, to people not in our family. It is not unusual for a family member to invite a neighbor, friend, or co-worker for dinner, or even a holiday meal. We always set a few extra places at the table on Sundays or holidays—"just in case."

I have talked about wine because it is the alcohol most commonly used by Italians, and it's placed on the dinner table. But I think distilled alcohol is also perceived in a similar way. My feeling, though, is that distilled alcohol is not associated with that warm leisurely experience of just sipping the wine with food and family. I think that, also in this context, the Italian people I know do not use alcohol for the mood-altering effect; they are drinking for relaxation and sociability. Another advantage of wine over distilled alcohol is that distilled alcohol doesn't taste as good (in my opinion), and surely is not credited with the health benefits of wine. When Italian immigrants were poor, they could have wine regardless of finances; my grandfather was one who had a tradition of making his own wine, and storing it in the cellar.

(Catherine Studiale Lusk, personal communication; July 7, 2005).

MARIJUANA CONTROL EFFORTS

During the 1920s and 1930s, most U.S. states with large Mexican populations enacted anti-marijuana legislation. Because marijuana smoking was common among Mexican migrant workers and other marginalized groups, racism seemingly was the key factor in the passage of the restrictive legislation. Hysterical literature of the day portrayed the marijuana user as more or less deranged and as engaging in drug-induced acts of sadistic violence (Abadinsky, 2011). In 1937, influenced by media propaganda such as the 1936 motion picture *Reefer Madness* (a film that is a great source of amusement today), Congress passed the Marijuana Tax Act. A series of harsh anti-drug laws that carried severe penalties were enacted in the 1950s.

Each of the periods following the world wars was a time of fear and suspicion that led to scapegoating (Abadinsky, 2011). Hence, strict laws carrying mandatory sentences were passed at these times. The American Bar Association and the American Medical Association voiced strong opposition to these harsh sentencing laws. The pendulum of drug policy began to shift in peacetime, accordingly, from a law enforcement model toward a treatment model in the 1970s with the drug penalties being reduced for all drugs, but especially for possession of marijuana, which had by that time become associated with middle-class youth. The leniency was not long lasting, however, as politicians capitalized on an association between drug use and crime, with an emphasis on inner-city violent crime. Sentences for marijuana were lengthened as well in the 1980s. Under the George W. Bush administration, an extravagant anti-marijuana advertising campaign was conducted along with a fight against medical marijuana providers (Abramsky, 2003). At the same time, possession of marijuana was being decriminalized in some states, and there was much discussion of taxation of the sale of this drug as a means of raising state revenues. At the present time, marijuana is no longer the focus of anti-drug campaigns; the government has deemphasized marijuana as a source of problems in favor of a focus on misuse of prescription medications (Sprague, 2009). Still, arrests for marijuana possession continue at the rate of roughly 800,000 annually, and they now represent nearly half of all drug arrests nationwide (Lacey, 2009).

The public attitude toward marijuana increasingly has grown sympathetic, however, and by 2010, 14 states passed laws permitting medical use of marijuana (Abadinsky, 2011). Growers can cultivate this crop for sale to bona fide patients for whom the drug has been prescribed. Recognized medical uses of marijuana are treating persons living with AIDS to help them gain weight and cancer patients receiving chemotherapy to reduce their nausea. Although the federal government still has the power to enforce prohibitions against the sale and use of marijuana for medical purposes, the Obama administration has made clear that prosecutions will be only for trafficking of the drug.

MODERN WAR ON DRUGS

Presidential access to the media, in conjunction with the media's capacity to make or break a politician, is a dynamic not to be overlooked in setting the stage for a mobilization of public opinion. So even though drug use was on the decline in the 1980s, political leaders moved to place illegal drugs on the public agenda (Robinson & Scherlen, 2007). The war against other drugs was waged on legal fronts, sometimes by means of well-publicized semi-military–style operations.

Controlling drug use was an attractive political issue for conservatives because it drew attention to individual deviance and immorality and away from questions of economic inequality and injustice. The drug scare was played up in the media with an orgy of news coverage to create an image of inner-city explosion centering on crack cocaine (Robinson & Scherlen, 2007). Public opinion changed dramatically following the barrage of news "exposés." Richard Nixon was the first American president to declare what he metaphorically called a "war on drugs," a strategy he devised to separate himself from Lyndon Johnson's liberal "war on poverty." His metaphor grew into a reality as the Reagan, the elder Bush, and Clinton administrations poured billions of dollars into a massive military operation to fight the enemy (drug suppliers) at home and on foreign soil. The political rhetoric connecting youth, violence, minorities, and crime has persisted in the minds of Americans for two decades since the Reagan administration, largely due to the crusading efforts of politicians. A lesson we can learn from the drug wars is that many of them have been inspired by racist sentiment and ethnocentrism because they are directed at marginalized groups; they are not based on empirical evidence from scientists concerning harms caused by drug use (Robinson & Scherlen, 2007) (see Chapter 13).

Media campaigns often follow government pronouncements concerning surging drug epidemics. According to Robinson and Scherlen, there have been only three times in history when there was anything like an epidemic of drug use. These were the popularity of heroin in the 1960s, the heavy use of powder cocaine in the 1970s and early 1980s, and crack cocaine use in the 1980s. Compared to outbreaks of physical disease, these epidemics in U.S. history, these drug use epidemics, according to Robinson and Scherlen, are not alarming. Yet, media anti-drug campaigns can lead to public panics. As the media campaign under President Reagan really got underway, for example, surveys taken in 1986 showed that the American public saw drugs as the most important problem facing the American nation.

In the 1960s, the horror stories concerned heroin; in the 1980s, crack cocaine was the focus. Concern about crack cocaine led Congress to write the anti-drug statutes of 1986 and 1988, which legislated everything from mandatory drug testing to funding international interdiction and domestic treatment (Stern, 2006). These statutes continue to dominate the way the federal law books address drug-related crime.

In the 1990s, the drug scare was about designer drugs such as Ecstasy and later the focus was on methamphetamine (meth). Although there may be a growing problem with the drugs of the day, and the media and political campaigns against them, the choice of which drugs are the focus of the anti-drug campaigns are often prompted by a shift in political priorities rather than an increase in drug misuse (*Encyclopaedia Britannica,* 2005).

Like its predecessor, Prohibition, America's war on drugs is directed toward the poor, especially those associated with urban social disorder. Also as with the criminalization of alcohol, criminalization of these drugs represents a desperate attempt to curb the unstoppable desire for mood-altering substances. Harsh laws that require lengthy minimum sentences for the possession of even small amounts of drugs have created a boom in prison construction. With two-thirds of the federal government's $15.5 billion expenditure on the drug problem going to law enforcement agencies and just one-third to prevention and treatment (Landers, 2011), the focus is clearly not on rehabilitation but on punishment. And like anti-drug legislation in the past, much of the blame is aimed at foreign forces, namely, the drug suppliers. If the supply can be stopped, whether through the use of weaponry or economic sanctioning, so the reasoning goes, illegal drug use on the streets can be curbed. Media accounts focus on foreign governments—for example, Mexico—to increase their commitment to work with the United States to eradicate the problem. Recently, Mexico has complied with mixed results. The battle against drug suppliers in Mexico, which is largely financed by the United States, has resulted in over 34,000 deaths and has greatly affected the tourist trade ("Mexican Drug Trafficking," 2011). The Mexican government has decriminalized personal use of small quantities of marijuana, methamphetamine, heroin, and LSD in order to focus on drug trafficking (Lacey, 2009). Mexican political leaders have repeatedly urged the United States to decriminalize marijuana to reduce the Mexican drug cartels' profits. They also urge a tightening of U.S. gun control laws to clamp down on the flow of weapons into Mexico.

Billions of dollars have been spent in drug eradication projects in other parts of Latin America as well. The U.S. government poured some $4 billion over the years into fumigating coca crops and arming the military in Colombia (Stokes, 2005). Colombia is the world's leading exporter of cocaine. Because the coca fields are far apart, aerial spraying when applied to a wide surface area harms crops and all other life in the region. Warning labels on the chemicals used in these spraying efforts explicitly caution against the health risks to human life (Mosher & Akins, 2007).

One of the most disturbing aspects of the war on drugs is the undeniable racism seen in the discrepancy between the sentences mandated for possession of the cheaper variety of cocaine (crack) and for the more expensive variety (powder cocaine). Until recently, trafficking in 500 grams of powder cocaine draws the same 5-year sentence as trafficking in 5 grams of crack—the infamous 100-to-1 ratio.

To learn the extent that race figures into anti-drug legislation, a comparison can be drawn between the congressional response to the crack and meth scares. Both, according to a *Congressional Quarterly Weekly* report, have been called by members of Congress a "plague on our nation" and associated with crime and community breakdown (Stern, 2006, p. 1548). But the users of crack cocaine are predominately Black, inner-city residents, while the users of meth tend to be White, rural residents. Yet meth, which is sometimes called "the poor person's cocaine," like crack, is associated with low-income drug users.

Meth use after 2006 exceeded crack use in popularity and has become the major law enforcement problem of today. Lawmakers increasingly have targeted meth users and suppliers. According to an analysis of racial sentencing disparities, the racial dynamics have changed drastically as more and more whites and fewer blacks are being incarcerated (Mauer, 2009). Harm reduction measures have been imposed to secure restrictions on the sale of pseudo-ephedrine, (commonly contained in cold medication), the key ingredient in the manufacture of meth.

Crack cocaine and meth are relatively inexpensive compared to other illicit drugs and associated with minorities and poor Whites. The war on drugs has thus become a war on minorities and the poor. Laws allowing law enforcement to seize drug-related assets at the time of arrest of a drug-dealing suspect. This loss of property has brought a lot of pain to poor families while it has created a bonanza for drug enforcement enterprises. Seizing drug-related assets has become more rewarding to police departments than the arrest itself. The profit side of property seizures is paralleled in the prison industry, now often privatized to meet the burgeoning demand for prison cells for persons convicted of drug offenses. The present policies have an extremely negative effect on high-crime areas; these policies have dramatically increased the profits of drug dealers and at the same time placed economic burdens on big cities to provide more law enforcement protection (McNeece & DiNitto, 2011).

Many strategies in the war on drugs backfire. As the supply of drugs is reduced, the street market value of the drug increases. Often, drug users turn to a cheaper, more harmful drug. Restrictions on the synthetic, psychoactive drug Ecstasy (MDMA), are a case in point. The U.S. Drug Enforcement Administration (DEA), in reaction to researchers' findings regarding whether or not the drug has therapeutic value, banned the drug and placed it on Schedule 1, the most severe listing in the Controlled Substances Act. This overscheduling of the drug led to a controversy, much publicity, and an escalation in its use (Harris, 2004). Today, teenagers and young adults across the United States experiment with this "club drug" at rock concerts and "raves."

Abramsky (2003) was optimistic that, because of a shift in public opinion against extremely harsh and counterproductive drug policies and because states wanted to adopt more cost-effective policies, true drug-law reform would gain ground. And improvements did come about in 2010, when, under the Obama administration, the Fair Sentencing Act was signed in an attempt to fix the 100-to-1 sentencing disparity between crack and powder cocaine offenses (Gilmore, 2010). Because crack cocaine is associated more often with Black than with White drug users, the sentencing disparity has had huge consequences for minority communities, as it has filled our prisons with young Black males. Under the Fair Sentencing Act, the ratio is now down to 18 to 1. The disparity still exists, although to a lesser degree than before, and the new law is not retroactive. The elimination of the mandatory sentencing aspect of this law was a major advance.

From 2000 to 2008, many states such as New York, North and South Carolina, and Mississippi introduced various sentencing reforms to help reduce the prison population. In other states such as Arizona, for example, the prison population actually grew at a rate of 5.1%, mostly related to drug convictions, even while the violent crime rate declined (Pratt, 2011).

Relentless pressure by the U.S. government has been exerted on Afghanistan to crack down on farmers who are cultivating opium. About 90% of the world's heroin comes from this war-wracked nation, which has a rugged terrain that is ideally suited for the cultivation of opium poppy plants. In recent years mass eradication efforts coupled with government subsidies to plant standard agricultural crops, have significantly reduced poppy cultivation. After many years of decreasing cultivation, however, the opium price sharply increased in 2010, making opium more attractive to farmers United Nations

Office of Drugs and Crime (UNODC) (2011). Even farmers who harvest opium, however, generally cultivate other crops twice a year in irrigated areas, typically growing maize, rice, vegetables, or cotton. Some farmers grow cannabis after the first summer harvest. None of Afghanistan's licit agricultural products currently match the gross income per hectare from opium, according to the UNODC.

International pressure has been exerted on European as well as Latin American countries. Much of this pressure is aimed at encouraging the United Nations World Health Organization to present drug use as a crime problem, not a health problem, and to reinforce drug control policies (Mosher & Akins, 2007). In the recent past, the United States has exerted economic pressure on Canadian, European, and Australian governments to pursue a global anti-drug military operation. European ideology, however, is geared toward a pragmatic, public health approach that is clearly at loggerheads with American moralism and inflexibility (see Chapter 13 on public policy).

HISTORY OF GAMBLING AND TREATMENT

Gambling is an activity that has appealed to human beings since ancient times. Archeological evidence indicates that ancient cave dwellers had their own versions of dice made of the bones of sheep or dogs, and 40,000-year-old cave drawings depict gambling activities. Gambling is featured in important events in legend and history. For example, the universe of heaven, hell, and the sea was divided up by the Greek gods Zeus, Hades, and Poseidon by a throw of the dice; and Roman soldiers "threw lots" for the clothes of Christ on the cross. All cultures have developed their own gambling variations through the centuries, from the Chinese games of chance using tiles, to the complicated dice games of Greek soldiers, to the stick games of Native Americans.

The very beginning of the United States of America was financed by lotteries during the Revolutionary War, and lotteries remained a popular and legal fund-raising activity in most states throughout the 18th and 19th centuries. The accessibility and legality of gambling venues has waxed and waned depending on prevailing social mores. In the reformist era after the Civil War, and again during Prohibition, lotteries were banned and gambling went underground. (In 1910, gambling was actually made a felony in Nevada). However, by 1931, casino gambling was legal in Nevada and horseracing venues had become popular again. As state governments were pressured to find more money without raising taxes, state-run lotteries again looked attractive, and New Hampshire (1964), New York (1967), and New Jersey (1971) began a national trend. Today, 37 states and the District of Columbia operate lotteries. It is the only form of commercial gambling in the United States that is a government monopoly.

Legal casino gambling gained in acceptability in the 1970s and 1980s, beginning with New Jersey's Atlantic City, which was a rundown resort facility "revitalized" by legalizing casino gambling in 1978. Native American tribal casinos became legal after the 1987 U.S. Supreme Court decision

California v. Cabazon Band of Mission Indians ruled that states could not regulate commercial gambling on Native American reservations. This decision spawned the Indian Gaming Regulatory Act, which requires tribes to negotiate a gambling compact with the state they reside in. Native American casinos developed rapidly and expanded to the unprecedented level of casino gambling that we have today.

Another boost that increased the popularity of gambling was provided by the development of riverboat casinos on the Mississippi River, designed to be strategically placed on the water and not on state land in order to circumvent state law. Today most people in the United States live within a 2-hour's drive of some sort of gambling, and the numbers of individuals with gambling problems has expanded commensurately. In the 1970s, casinos were legal in just one state, Nevada. Today, legalized gambling has morphed into a $92 billion industry established in all but two states as politicians assert that gambling is an effective way to raise revenue and create jobs (Skolnik, 2011). It is easy to conclude, therefore, that we have more persons with gambling addiction problems today than at any other time in our history. We also have states addicted to the gambling revenue.

The fastest growing segment of the gambling market is Internet gambling. An estimated 10 million poker players in the United States have turned to Internet sites where they can place bets through use of their credit cards. This enterprise has helped to generate as much as $5 billion in annual revenues for the companies involved. (Lipton, 2011). Washington, DC has become the first city in the United States to legalize online gambling, and several states plan to follow suit. The purpose is to earn large profits for the city by tapping into the proceeds that are now going to offshore Internet gambling (Richards, 2011).

Gambling excess has historically been "treated" by admonitions, punishment (lynching was popular in the Wild West), and declaring it illegal. To go back even further in Anglo-American history, we find in the 1667 Leathermore's *Advice on Gaming* a strong warning that gambling, more than any other vice, "renders a man incapable of prosecuting any serious action, and makes him always unsatisfied with his own condition" (Anonymous, p. 3). Due to this social attitude toward gambling, punishment was harsh.

The advent of alcohol treatment programs paved the way for a new conceptualization of gambling problems as sometimes stemming from an addiction. A corresponding remedy for gambling addiction was formal treatment programs. The first gambling treatment inpatient program started in 1972 (and continues today—information at http://www.cleveland.va.gov/about/) at the VA (Veterans Affairs) Hospital in Brecksville, Ohio. It was patterned after the existing disease-model program for alcoholics. Dr. Robert Custer, a psychiatrist, is widely recognized as a pioneer in establishing professional treatment, as well as setting up the VA treatment program in Brecksville. Inspired by Jellinek's U-curve depiction of the stages of alcoholism, Custer applied the downward spiral to gambling addiction (Ciarrocchi,

2001). One of his primary contributions was to reject prevailing Freudian theory that gambling compulsively was a substitute for sex; instead, he maintained that gambling addiction is what he called "the pain-avoidance mechanism," that is, the gambler continues gambling whether winning or losing to avoid psychic pain. From this beginning, gambling treatment has spread from inpatient to out-patient centers all over the country, funded by states as well as casinos, and featuring cognitive-behavioral interventions as well as disease-model treatments.

HISTORY OF ADDICTION TREATMENT

Our focus now turns from the control of drug use and sales to the treatment of individuals with substance misuse problems. Substance use treatment data released in 2010 from the Substance Abuse and Mental Health Services Administration (SAMHSA) shows a large increase in middle-aged and older adult clients over the past 10 years and a steady decline in the proportion of client admissions attributed to alcohol use as compared to other substance use. Especially notable is the increase in the proportion of treatment admissions involving misuse of prescription medication, an increase of over 400% during this period. The rise has been the most striking among women (Hartman, 2010).

In any given year, about 2–3% of the U.S. population has a gambling problem, but only a small fraction are getting or seeking help (National Council of Problem Gambling, 2010). Nearly 44% of all clients in substance abuse treatment were in treatment for both alcohol and substance abuse, about 23% for misuse of alcohol alone, and 37% for drug use alone, a striking increase from the first decade of the 21st century (SAMHSA, 2010). A comparison between the year 1998 and 2008, shows that alcohol as the primary problem went from 27% to 23% 10 years later, marijuana as the primary problem increased from 13% to 17%, opiate admissions rose from 16% to 20%, cocaine declined from 15% to 11%, and meth and other stimulant admissions rose from 4% to 6% (SAMHSA, 2010).

Throughout most of American history, as we have seen, religious institutions with a Protestant affiliation have viewed alcohol, gambling, and drug addiction as sinful or irresponsible behavior. Only after Philadelphia physician Benjamin Rush authored his influential pamphlet *An Inquiry into the Effects of Ardent Spirits on the Human Mind and Body* (1785) did a paradigm shift begin to emerge (Hart, Ksir, & Ray, 2010). In his notion of alcohol, especially distilled alcohol, as highly addictive and the compulsion to drink as extremely powerful in some individuals, Rush anticipated much of the modern, post-Prohibition thinking about alcoholism and other addictions. Rush was also the first American medical practitioner to recommend medical treatment for chronic "inebriates." When Prohibition—the attempt to control the supply side of alcohol—was revealed as a dismal failure, the emphasis shifted from the production of the beverage alcohol to characteristics of the individual drinker. The focus on the substance was replaced by a focus on the person (Barber, 2002). During the second half of the 19th century, there was an increased medical awareness of health problems associated with alcohol misuse, accompanied by a rapid growth in the number of institutions specializing in the treatment of addiction. This awareness of the medical aspects of alcohol misuse seems relatively modern, but as William White (1998), author of the definitive study *Slaying the Dragon: The History of Addiction Treatment and Recovery in America,* suggests, the notion of providing care for persons afflicted with alcoholic disorders goes back to ancient Egypt. And in America, mutual-aid societies were formed, often by groups of recovering alcoholics, some as early as 1750.

With the end of Prohibition in 1933, the population at large began to move toward the view that alcoholics were sick, not sinful. In fact, the social work profession had maintained this view for some time and had been actively working with alcoholics and their families from early on. Roiblatt and Dinis (2004) provide a history that is little known. Social work pioneers, they point out, had authored legislation, established institutions for the care and control of "inebriates," and supported the temperance movement that resulted in Prohibition. Caseworkers and settlement residents such as Jane Addams, who stated her belief that alcoholism was a disease as early as 1909, remained involved with alcohol issues through the era of repeal. These social work pioneers were to see their influence wane, however, after 1935. The fields of alcoholism treatment and social work diverged during this time, as Roiblatt and Dinis suggest, due to the fact that social workers had their own priorities and for various other reasons. Accordingly, the impact of social workers in the shaping of modern alcohol policy and treatment programming from this period to the start of the 21st century was considerably less than it had been previously. Instead of turning to the social work profession for leadership in treatment development, alcoholism treatment looked elsewhere. There were new forces afoot.

The creation of Alcoholics Anonymous was instrumental in reducing some of the stigma associated with alcoholism and in offering a highly structured program for recovery (Roizen, 2004). After the Twenty-First Amendment to the Constitution was passed, a new approach to viewing the problems related to alcohol was needed. The remarkable contribution of two alcoholics, Bill W. and Dr. Bob, was to join the new disease conception of alcoholism emerging out of academic research institutes with a remarkable organizational network of supporters united by a set of simply formulated principles of sobriety: the Twelve Steps. Although to stay out of medical controversy Bill W. himself avoided referring to alcoholism as a disease, he did use terms such as *malady, illness,* and *allergy* to depict the condition of active alcoholism (Davis & Jansen, 1998). Both members of the Oxford Group, an evangelical Protestant organization, Bill W. and Dr. Bob adopted the principles of the movement and, when many of the AA groups began to diverge from the original course, Bill W. codified the central principles into the Twelve

Steps. The notions of powerlessness, seeking divine guidance, making confession and restitution, and carrying the message to other persons were among the concepts borrowed. So influential was Bill W that he was selected by *Time* magazine as one of the 100 most influential people of the 20th century, a trailblazer who helped shape the century. "From the rubble of a wasted life, he overcame alcoholism and cofounded the Twelve-Step program that has helped millions of others do the same" begins the *Time* article about Bill W. (Cheever, 1999, p. 201). Publication of the book *Alcoholics Anonymous* (affectionately known as The Big Book) in 1939 marked a milestone in substance abuse treatment history. When an article on AA appeared in the *Saturday Evening Post* in 1941, the effect was stunning (White, 1998). Growth of AA groups skyrocketed from that point on. Narcotics Anonymous (NA) was officially launched in 1949 (see Chapter 12 for a detailed discussion of mutual-help groups).

Today, as Koerner (2010) indicates, more than 2 million members in 150 countries hold meetings in church basements, school gyms, and hospital conference rooms. Although the original members of AA created the Twelve Steps as a guide for alcoholics, other self-help programs have borrowed them and adapted them to help people struggling with eating disorders, gambling addiction, cocaine and heroin addiction, and sexual compulsions, to name a few.

Not only was the AA influence felt at the level of self-help groups, but the reduction in stigmatization of alcoholics revolutionized professional treatment as well. Keep in mind that before AA was founded, treatment for alcoholics was at a primitive level (Koerner, 2010). The period is known today as the "snake pit" era of alcohol treatment. Inebriates, as they were called, when hospitalized, were usually locked up with the mentally ill and considered hopeless. The conventional belief was that alcoholics simply lacked moral fortitude.

As the Hazelden (2011) information website indicates, nonalcoholic addicts or alcoholics with drug problems have not been made to feel welcome by AA groups from the beginning. Because AA's set of guidelines, the Twelve Traditions, directs that the primary purpose of AA is to help the alcoholic and that the only requirement for membership is a desire to stop drinking, participants are often sanctioned for speaking of problems with other drugs. On its member discussion page, The Hazelden (2011) website very openly contrasts NA and AA:

> Members of NA still struggle with stereotypes, something experienced by nearly all recovering people, but especially felt by nonalcoholic addicts. "NA is not dominated by dope-shooting criminals and burly, tattooed bikers," notes John, an NA member. "However, we are still a generation or more away from attracting and holding large numbers of mainstream professionals."
>
> As a counselor in Hazelden's Tiebout Unit, Keith Jensen acknowledges that NA "draws some of the people who feel a little bit more disenfranchised from society." He praises NA for an open-door policy that welcomes people addicted to any drug, including alcohol. "Most NA meetings are pretty open-minded in terms of admitting anybody who wants to quit using," says Jensen.

AA is more rigid about its participants. Official AA policy states that drug addicts are welcome at open AA meetings, but not at closed meetings. However, many closed AA groups do accept people "purely on drugs," and addicts cross-addicted to alcohol and another drug are always welcome (found at http://www.hazelden.org/web/public/namembers.page).

Because NA meetings are less commonly available than AA meetings, and judges often recommend addicted persons to AA, AA's nonacceptance of drug addicts is not without consequences. NA deserves credit for more holistically accepting all addicts regardless of their drug of choice and for stressing listening for similarities rather than differences among people.

A major criticism of AA and other Twelve-Step groups is their refusal to change with the times, even to modernize the wording of the steps and traditions. Many group members still oppose the use of mood-altering prescription medications that are geared toward the reduction of cravings (Koerner, 2010). On the other hand, this weakness of AA, its refusal to modernize, is also, in a real sense, a strength—the strength that comes from stability and structure. Milo Mead (2005), who can recite a whole chapter of The Big Book with ease, explains AA from his personal experience:

> Alcohol is only mentioned one time in the 12 steps. The concept of surrender is important—to win you have to surrender; the person has to be surrendered to a power greater than the self. This is a paradox. Another paradox is the saying of AA, "The only way I can keep this (peace of mind or serenity) is to give it away." This refers to Step 12, which is to spread the message and help others find the way to sobriety.

The sense of camaraderie and acceptance that prevails at a typical AA meeting is well captured in Augusten Burroughs's (2003) personal narrative of recovery, Dry:

> My feeling at the end is that AA is utterly amazing. Complete strangers getting together in rooms at all hours and saying things that are so personal, so incredibly intimate. This is the kind of stuff that happens in a relationship after a few months. But people here open up right away, with everyone. It's like some sort of love affair, stripped of the courtship phase. (p. 110)

And an anonymous writer, a social work student familiar with AA meetings, (personal communication; November 2008) describes her observational visit to an NA meeting:

> I was expecting the NA meeting to be similar to an AA meeting, but it was most definitely a different atmosphere. My first impression was that everyone felt very tense, and I did not get the same welcome as what an AA meeting would offer. But when others introduced themselves as newcomers, I didn't feel so out of place. The chairs and tables were arranged in a circular manner so that everyone talked face to face. There were free cookies and an abundance of coffee.
>
> When the meeting started, the stories were so enlightening that it was really the only thing I could focus on. It was obvious that these stories held a lot of pain and that these people had burned many bridges with family and friends.

The theme of this meeting was on Step 4, taking a moral inventory. One man took out a pamphlet titled "Just for Today" and started reading about the moral inventory. Participants focused on the damage they had caused by their addiction and the steps they needed to take to correct things in their lives. Later, at the end of the meeting, persons who had achieved long periods of sobriety were given token key chains.

The Twelve-Step influence is pronounced, although not dominant, in Europe. Disease-model programs designed along American lines generally are relegated to the private treatment sector and can be expensive. Ireland, perhaps because of its strong religious traditions, has embraced the Minnesota Model, which teaches the principle of powerlessness and the need to surrender oneself to a Higher Power. Both principles are derived from the Twelve Steps of recovery. Because of the compatibility between the precepts of this program and Irish cultural norms, the Minnesota Model has come to exert a major influence on Irish services for problem drinkers (Butler & Maycock, 2005; McGoldrick, 2005). Not hiring social workers for these programs has resulted in the exclusion of approaches such as motivational interviewing and solution-focused therapy, which as Butler and Maycock note, are favored by Irish social workers.

Norway, which is in contrast is a more secular country (although Norwegians often find a spiritual presence in nature), officially has resisted incorporating treatment based on Twelve-Step principles in its social welfare system. Extensive media coverage of scandalous practices at one Norwegian Minnesota Model-based treatment center (Vangseter) did not help matters. However, the 12-Step treatment model, as adapted for Norwegian consumption, thrives today in a small disease-model program in rural Norway, the only such program in that country that receives extensive county, as opposed to private, funding. Box 2.1, presented later in the chapter, provides a rare look at this program.

Jellinek's Pioneering Study

In many ways, Jellinek's book *The Disease Concept of Alcoholism,* written in 1960, is more progressive and up to date than much of the writing from the past two decades, much of which paradoxically cites Jellinek on the disease model. E. M. Jellinek was a statistician who conducted systematic research on male AA members. His goal was to study alcoholism in its many varieties. Jellinek's worldwide travels for the World Health Organization helped provide him with an international perspective for research that provided the basis for his typology of alcoholics.

The cultural patterns that differentiate one country from another, according to Jellinek, help account for the drinking patterns. Thus, the Italian contempt for alcohol intoxication is in contrast to the French tolerance for intoxication, accompanied by an insistence that most people take a drink. Furthermore, as Jellinek observed, the drinking patterns are to a large extent ascribable to the beverages that contain the alcohol; that is, wine or beer are associated with continual use and distilled spirits with concentrated consumption over short periods.

Using letters of the Greek alphabet, Jellinek singled out five "species of alcoholism" that he considered disease-related:

- *Alpha alcoholism* represents an undisciplined use of alcoholic beverages. Drinking may relieve emotional disturbance, but relationship problems are caused thereby. There is psychological dependence but no progression.
- *Beta alcoholism* involves heavy drinking, causing physical complications such as gastritis and cirrhosis of the liver, yet without physical or psychological dependence on alcohol.
- *Gamma alcoholism* is characterized by increased tissue tolerance, withdrawal symptoms when drinking is discontinued, and loss of control. A marked progression occurs, with interpersonal relations impaired to the highest degree. This variety predominates in Great Britain and northern Europe. Most AA members have experienced this kind of alcoholism.
- *Delta alcoholism* is similar to gamma alcoholism but without the loss of control over the amount consumed, only an inability to abstain for even one day. There are no distressing social problems over the quantity consumed, though health problems may result. This is the predominant pattern in France.
- *Epsilon alcoholism* is periodic alcoholism. In their periodic bouts, binge drinkers suffer a great deal of physical and emotional damage.

Of all the types of alcoholism, according to Jellinek, only the gamma and delta varieties can be considered addictions and/or diseases. The significance of Jellinek's writings is his conception of varieties of alcohol problems, as opposed to a conceptualization of alcoholism as one monolithic drinking disorder. Many former clients of substance abuse treatment centers are familiar with the so-called Jellinek curve. This U-shaped depiction of the progression of alcoholism from social drinking to the development of high tolerance to full-blown loss of control, and loss of family, job, and friends was a contribution of German-born psychiatrist G. Maxwell Glatt who filled in the design with the traits Jellinek had assigned to the gamma variety of alcoholism. It is perhaps unfortunate that only one part of his theory has been immortalized in the form of the Jellinek curve because this representation depicted only to the gamma type of alcoholism, which viewed alcoholism as primary, chronic, progressive, and if untreated, fatal. Virtually every treatment center in the United States has adopted this formulation, which is often presented to their clients in the form of a lecture. The model of gradual progression into heavier and heavier drinking and to high tolerance as well as to physical, mental, and moral destruction applies to many but not to all, and not very well to polydrug or amphetamine misusers.

ITEM CHARGED

Patron: Kassandra Lynn Marsala

Patron Barcode:

2 0 5 0 1 0 0 0 1 8 7 1 6 9

Patron Group: Undergraduate

Due Date: 2/8/2016 10:30 PM

Title: Addiction treatment : a strengths perspective / Katherine van Wormer, Diane Rae Davis

Author: Van Wormer, Katherine S

Call Number: RC564 .V35 2013

Enumeration:

Chronology:

Copy:

Item Barcode:

3 1 6 1 1 0 0 3 3 9 2 0 9 6

1

The Disease Concept of Alcoholism, as White (1998) notes, remains one of the most frequently cited and least read books in the alcoholism field. If more people did read the original, they might be surprised at what Jellinek actually said. He never said alcoholism was a disease; what he said was that alcoholism is *like* a disease. "The problem that I had all along in the field of addiction," notes Gorski (1998), "is that most people treating alcoholics never went back to this original source document, which very clearly presented an understanding of alcoholism and divided it into five subtypes" (p. 100). Gorski wisely warns his colleagues in the field against making one of two biased overgeneralizations—thinking everyone with a drinking problem has a progressive, fatal disease requiring treatment or, conversely, throwing out the disease model altogether and seeing only alcohol problems when the alcoholism may exist as a devastating illness.

From a sociological viewpoint, according to Barber (2002), it is interesting that the modern disease concept of addiction should have emanated from the principles of AA rather than from medical research. But with the publication of Jellinek's landmark work, the modern disease approach to alcoholism was to provide a scientifically acceptable foundation for later articulation by the medical profession itself.

The Disease Concept of Alcoholism, in short, had a profound impact on the state of the art in addiction treatment. This work provided just the sort of data and analysis needed at the time to convince members of Congress and the medical community alike that alcoholics are not immoral but persons with a disease (or a disease-like condition) and that, once addicted, the problem drinker is no longer able to control his or her behavior. The basic conclusions of Jellinek's work corresponded with the basic premises of AA and gave the rapidly growing organization a considerable boost.

The political implications of the disease concept should not be underestimated. The assumption that alcoholism is a pathology that lies within the individual and that the pathology can be measured and treated are basic to the medical or disease model. Central to the disease concept is the notion of irreversibility by which alcoholism inevitably became a progressive disease that could be arrested but never cured. The AA view begins with a crucial distinction between the alcoholic and other types of drinkers. For the alcoholic, it is a case of "one drink, one drunk," as the saying goes (Barber, 2002). The liquor industry was amenable to this reconstruction of the alcoholism concept because only a small minority could not drink, and the industry had no desire to take alcohol away from ordinary drinkers.

When the World Health Organization acknowledged alcoholism as a medical problem in 1951 and the American Medical Association declared alcoholism an illness in 1956 and a disease in 1966, the transformation to the medicalization of alcoholism was complete. The hospital replaced the church and legislators as the center of social control of a newly designated disease. Rather than punitive, the social response to alcoholism became therapeutic. The new ideology provided a rationale for costly complex medical approaches and for an extensive treatment apparatus. It absolved persons with alcohol problems of responsibility for the etiology of the disease but gave them the responsibility to seek treatment. Moreover, the disease model appealed to moderate drinkers in its implication that only some individuals are at risk of addiction. Finally, the American disease model was promoted by the alcohol beverage industry because it removed the blame from the alcohol and its sale and distribution (Barr, 1999).

MORE RECENT DEVELOPMENTS

In 1970, the Hughes Act was passed. This act, which was named after its primary sponsor, Senator Harold Hughes, provided for major research funding by the federal government and emphasized improved services for alcoholics (McNeece & DiNitto, 2011). Known officially as the Comprehensive Alcoholism Prevention and Treatment Act, this statute created the National Institute on Alcohol Abuse and Alcoholism (NIAAA). The federal seed money spawned the growth of alcoholism treatment centers across the United States, a growth that, as White (1998) observes, was almost explosive in its intensity.

And what about treatment of other drug addictions? Public concern over drug use and dependence among returning Vietnam veterans and the whole baby boom generation led President Nixon to declare drug abuse "America's Public Enemy Number One" (White, 1998, p. 266). The National Institute on Drug Abuse (NIDA) was established as a research institute, along with federally funded drug abuse treatment programs in what was to be the first national system of addictions treatment. Although alcoholism treatment centers and drug abuse treatment centers are no longer separate, NIAAA and NIDA have continued for years as separate research entities. This artificial separation is inconsistent with modern scientific research on the brain and the nature of addiction. At the present time, in recognition that alcoholism and drug dependence are both addictions, plans are underway to merge these entities under the auspices of a new addictions institute.

When the Hazelden Treatment Center opened in a farmhouse in Minnesota in 1949, drug and alcohol sanitaria were popularly conceived as snake pits run by quacks (Yee, 2008). The medical profession, like the general public, had little faith that alcoholics, once hooked, could recover. As developed at Willmar State Hospital and later at Hazelden, the Minnesota Model took a multidisciplinary approach (White, 1998). From psychology, therapy was borrowed; from the clergy (usually Lutherans), spirituality; and from the mutual-help group of Alcoholics Anonymous, group-based treatment and the Twelve Steps. The integration of recovering, nonprofessionally trained counselors as a legitimate component of the alcoholism treatment team was the key innovation of this model. In the early days, there was harsh confrontation in group settings; today, the regime is a pale replica of some of the antics that went on before. Gender-specific programs are offered for men and women. The sexes are kept completely separate at all times to prevent what Norwegian

Minnesota Model counselors call "abstinence romance." So much treatment takes place in the state today that Minnesota sometimes is facetiously called the land of 10,000 treatment centers. Thousands of former clients of this and the dozens of other similar treatment centers in Minnesota, many of whom come from cities on the East and West Coasts, have stayed on in nearby Minneapolis for the group support that is provided there.

By the early 1970s, more than 30 separate agencies and departments of the federal government were involved in some aspect of substance abuse treatment. A new trend was the integration of drug treatment and alcoholism treatment, fields that had been totally separate previously. The thinking had been that these addictions were unrelated. Sometimes as a result, as White indicates, residential drug abuse treatment centers focused entirely on drinking, which left alcoholic clients open to switch to other sedatives, such as prescription medications. Awareness of the reality of cross-addiction and, later, of facts about the brain chemistry of addiction-prone people, encouraged a merging of the two specializations: alcoholism treatment and drug abuse treatment. With the growing use of terms such as *addiction, substance abuse,* and *chemical dependence,* the professional literature reflected this merger.

In the late 1970s, when Betty Ford went public with her alcoholism, 28 inpatient days of treatment was the norm. Insurance coverage was readily available, and mass media accounts of celebrities in recovery following treatment were positive. The cumulative effect of two decades of public education on alcoholism, coupled with growing concerns about a youthful polydrug epidemic, had borne legislative fruit (White, 1998). During this time, a parallel big business had emerged—the substance abuse treatment industry. Many faltering hospitals' finances were bolstered by filling many hospital beds with recovering alcoholics. Beginning in the 1990s, however, third-party payers balked; many patients in need of extended treatment were denied it. Sadly, the building of prisons to house persons in trouble because of their substance misuse seems to have become the current ideological focus.

THE ANTI-TREATMENT BACKLASH

In his sweeping history of addiction treatment, *Slaying the Dragon,* William White provides the best account that we have come across in the literature of the ideological and cultural backlash against addiction treatment that took place in the 1980s and 1990s. In some ways, the climate for the backlash was set under the Reagan era, when zero tolerance of drug users dominated the airwaves. In some ways, too, the new ideology was promoted at the level of popular culture. A deluge of articles and books were published at this time, including Peele's (1989/1995) *The Diseasing of America* and Fingarette's (1988) *Heavy Drinking: The Myth of Alcoholism as a Disease.* Although these writings said a lot that needed to be said concerning the multimillion-dollar substance abuse treatment industry and the oversimplified alcoholism-as-disease model that was its raison d'être, the impact of this intellectual denigration of mainstream treatment was profound. Book reviews were exclamatory and, at times, laudatory. From the back cover of *Heavy Drinking: The Myth of Alcoholism as a Disease,* we read, for example, "Herbert Fingarette is at the forefront of a social counterrevolution that could redefine how the United States views alcoholism (*Christian Science Monitor*)."

Such a counterrevolution was evidenced in the growing number of court decisions upholding denials of benefits on the grounds that alcoholism results not from a disease but from "willful misconduct" (White, 1998, p. 28). Moreover, in light of what the court saw as the religious aspect of AA and NA, court-mandated attendance at such meetings was determined to be a violation of the First-Amendment requirement of separation of church and state. Uniformly, four higher courts ruled on this matter (for details, see Peele & Bufe, 2000). This ruling became an issue within some U.S. prisons because substance abuse treatment was usually based on the Twelve Steps and AA/NA attendance. In some states then, for example, in Iowa and New York State, substance abuse counselors, have been instructed to seek alternative treatment models. Significantly, Stephanie Covington's (2008) *A Woman's Journal: A Program for Treating Substance Abuse* is a workbook especially designed for use in the correctional system. This multidimensional manual is holistic in focus. The four modules of this gender-specific program are devoted to work on self, relationships, sexuality, and spirituality. A holistic rather than traditional disease model is the underlying philosophy of this program.

The available funding for treatment increasingly is connected to the criminal justice system rather than to medically based services. And many treatment facilities have managed care agreements or contracts (SAMHSA, 2004). Managed care treatment options, including generous reimbursement for inpatient and extended outpatient programs, have been severely curtailed (Wallace, 2005). Typically, managed care companies accept as providers only traditional mental health professionals.

The impact has been positive in terms of furthering the professionalization of the substance abuse field. Insurance companies stress that counselors have academic qualifications and that evidence-based treatment methods be applied. The influence of the third-party payers, however, has been negative in terms of the bureaucratic restraints. In a country (alone among industrialized nations) without nationalized healthcare, comprehensive insurance coverage for alcoholism and other drug addiction treatment must be mandated for all insurance and public welfare policies. To exchange the disease model for a punitive focus on individual responsibility may be less a step forward than two steps back.

Meanwhile, the rate of closure among U.S. substance abuse treatment facilities in the rest of the private sector is considerable, further reducing access to treatments that are already in short supply in many locales. This reduction in services was well underway at the end of the 20th century. By 1992, managed-care companies had seriously cut funding for long-term inpatient treatment and stressed short, outpatient programming (Koerner, 2010).

Research by Knudsen, Roman, and Ducharme (2005) analyzed the trends. Over the period of their research on treatment offerings in a representative sample of 450 substance abuse treatment centers, 26.4% of the centers ceased to offer substance abuse treatment services. Knudsen and colleagues concluded that centers offering a more diversified array of services had a lower likelihood of closure. Curiously, programs that added psychiatric programming for co-occurring disorders often closed down the substance abuse portion of the treatment. This development, as the authors speculate, is probably because mental health treatment receives far better financial reimbursement than does treatment for substance-related problems. One disappointing development Knudsen and colleagues (2005) found is the increasing reliance on federally approved medication to reduce craving (e.g., naltrexone hydrochloride [Naltrexone]) with a de-emphasis on personal counseling. The medical emphasis is apparent even in traditional treatment centers. Hazelden, for example, operates under a new vision that corresponds to a 21st century corporate model (Yee, 2008). One major change is the use of pharmaceuticals to treat addiction. Also today, simply being "in recovery" is no longer acceptable as a credential for counselors; professional qualifications now are stressed.

Meanwhile, the demand is for expanding services to treat other problems such as gambling, prescription drug, sex, and Internet addictions. Yet, following the recession of 2008, state funding for substance abuse treatment was reduced considerably. Across the United States residential programming is being seriously reduced as in Maine, Illinois, Texas, and Oregon (Chambers, 2011). The best hope for renewed funding comes from initiatives such as are presently being offered in the form of grants from the federal government for expanded treatment options (Landers, 2011).

This documentation of the new directions that the substance treatment field is taking (and should take) today has important implications for counselor and social work education. A comprehensive approach is required, as is a familiarity with motivational interviewing techniques. Box 2.1 discusses substance abuse treatment based on a U.S. model but within a social welfare system that clearly deserves its ranking as number one on the UN Human Development Index (see http://hdr.undp.org) (United Nations Human Development Index, 2011).

THE INTRODUCTION OF HARM REDUCTION

The history of substance abuse treatment is still being written. The concept of harm reduction originated first in the 1920s in the United Kingdom as a medical approach that called for prescribing heroin and cocaine to patients who were dependent on these drugs. The goal was to reduce the harm associated with their obtainment and use (Karoll, 2010). This policy continued until the 1960s when a scandal caused by a few doctors who diverted heroin onto a black market and a significant increase in the numbers of heroin addicts brought inevitable restrictions (Abadinsky, 2011). The political pendulum

Box 2.1	SUBSTANCE ABUSE TREATMENT THRIVES IN NORWAY
	Katherine van Wormer

Imagine a treatment center with little paperwork and no insurance reimburse-ment forms in a country where workers get paid leave as needed, even for family counseling sessions ("Family Weeks"). Literacy is 100%, and most alcoholism is still of the "pure" variety (meaning the alcoholics rarely have other drug pro-blems except for pill misuse). This is the reality in Norway, an American sub-stance abuse counselor's dream. It wasn't always this way, however.

The first time I went to Norway (I worked there from 1988 to 1990), I was hired to train alcoholism counselors about the basics of the Minnesota Model. My personal reasons for going had more to do with seeing the scenery and a desire to experience firsthand a truly benevolent social welfare state. This was just as well, given the way things turned out, because the treatment center was straight out of Schaef's *The Addictive Organization*. (To learn of the bizarre goings-on there, see van Wormer, 1997.)

I was back in Norway in the summer of 1997, less than 100 miles from where I had lived and worked before. Once again, I found myself in the land of sculptured trolls and Vikings, snow-streaked mountaintops, log cabins, and pine-finished houses, purple wildflowers, perpetual summer light, and dark-green landscapes dotted with pale birch trees. And once again, I was enjoying meals of moose meat with *tyttebaer* jam and baked salmon. But I wasn't here for the scenery or the meals. This time I was here for professional reasons.

I never expected to return to Norway, much less to an alcoholism treatment center where I would teach a workshop on the nature of addiction. But here I was in the company of two of the strongest personalities from my earlier work: Randi Isdahl, now the director of the clinic she founded, and Kirsten Male, a social worker and my personal translator. Isdahl, the director of *ValdresKlinik-ken* (Valdres Clinic), had been the assistant director and my supervisor previ-ously at the other clinical position she had held with the fierce loyalty of the "true believer." But one day when the owner-director's antisocial behavior became apparent to her, she simply walked out.

Following a period of utter disillusionment and depression, Isdahl saw that her only chance to help fellow alcoholics as she had been helped would be through opening her own inpatient treatment center. Following a course of train-ing in Sweden and at Hazelden in Minnesota, Isdahl assembled a group of talented people. Together they opened Valdres Clinic, a private, nonprofit, Twelve-Step inpatient program, the first treatment center of its kind in this part of Norway. Gradually, word spread about lives that were "turned around," and credibility with the local authorities followed. Male, my translator and political ally from previous days, had, like me, been fired for revealing the truth about client and staff abuse at the first treatment center.

Now happily working at a nearby social office (the equivalent of the Depart-ment of Health and Human Services in the United States), Male was a source of support and referral to the clinic. She and Isdahl, who had been on opposite sides of the earlier staff dispute, had become friends. Finding myself in Norway again, I marveled at the growing friendship and professional growth of these two extraordinary women, whose experience with life and addiction had instilled in them an almost religious calling to serve.

I expected the treatment center to be a small replica of Hazelden transplanted among fjords and cliffs. So I was not surprised that the basic program included group therapy, lectures, films, Alcoholics Anonymous meetings, and workbook assignments tied to the Twelve Steps of recovery. What did surprise me were certain innovations in treatment drawn not from Minnesota but from the East—from China and India.

Today, Valdres Clinic offers a comprehensive program built on the following elements:

- *From the West:* The concept of alcoholism as a disease—a personal and family disease—the treatment of which looks to extensive feeling work, communication emphasis, spirituality, and personal sharing.
- *From the East:* Detoxification of all clients, not through drugs but through acupuncture under medical supervision. This involves the application of needles to five points in the ear for 40 minutes a day in early treatment (ear points relate to the endorphins in the brain, liver, lungs, and kidneys); meditation with music; and a highly nutritious diet. (Isdahl brought these aspects of the program back from India, where she had visited an amazing treatment center for opium addicts on the upper floors of a New Delhi police station.)
- *From the welfare state:* The generous Norwegian social welfare system provides complete funding for 5 weeks of inpatient treatment, including an extensive family-week program. Aftercare is provided through the government-sponsored *Rusteam,* with its extensive network of clinics throughout the country. These state-run offices provide follow-up psychological work for trauma and mental disorders.

In the 7 years I was away, Norway's alcoholism treatment program has improved, providing enhanced funding and greater options. Meanwhile, in the United States, treatment options are dictated more by reimbursement policies than by client need, and the extravagance of the war on drugs charade ties up badly needed resources. In my return visit to Norway, I did not know how to explain what had happened to treatment in the United States in the past 7 years. I didn't even try.

(Update, July 2011: In response to my request for an update, Randi Isdahl, director of Valdres Clinic said: "This summer we are having our twentieth anniversary celebration. We have a whole new building which is very beautiful. In 2000, the government took over the treatment, which means they pay the total cost. But then there are whole new standards and a great deal of paperwork, just like in America. It's hard for me to do the therapy now; I'm so busy running the clinic. Many of the private clinics using the 12-Step Program had to close. The government requires that the staff have professional training. Today we have nurses, social workers, a psychologist, and a psychiatrist. Some of the counselors who have been here from the start received their training in the 12-Step Programming in Sweden. They are all in recovery and do the best work, but their credentials no longer count.

"For the clients, the inpatient program lasts from 6 weeks to 3 months, sometimes longer; relapse prevention programming follows for 6 weekends.... Today clients come from all over Norway; we have clients with all the drug problems but not mental illness. Assessments are done and detoxification happens before the clients come here; they are all motivated for treatment.")

(continued)

Box 2.1	Substance abuse Treatment Thrives in Norway *(continued)* Katherine van Wormer

References

Stenius, K. (1991). The most successful treatment model in the world: Introduction of the Minnesota Model in Nordic countries. *Contemporary Drug Problems, 18*(Spring), 151–179.

van Wormer, K. (1995). Whistleblowing against the company: A case of ethical violations at a Norwegian treatment center. *International Journal of Drug Abuse, 6*(1), 8–15.

van Wormer, K. (1997). Doing alcoholism treatment in Norway: A personal reminiscence. *Reflections, 3*(3), 67–71.

swung back again in the 1980s, however, when a grassroots movement called *harm reduction* emerged in the Netherlands and spread to northern England; it developed somewhat later in Australia (Inciardi & Harrison, 2000; Pycroft, 2010). The spread of AIDS at this time was seen as a bigger threat than illegal drugs, and the prospect of a plague of deaths was more compelling than addiction. The focus therefore is pragmatic: To save lives, help drug users modify their behavior.

At the same time Nancy Reagan launched her Just Say No campaign in the United States, the British government opened a program in Liverpool in response to the AIDS epidemic and started using the term *harm reduction* (Denning, Little, & Glickman, 2004). Britain and other countries modeled their programming on what had been provided in the Netherlands almost a decade prior to the identification of HIV/AIDS (Butler & Maycock, 2005). With the AIDS panic, countries that originally had been skeptical began in the HIV era to show a new interest in the Dutch experience. Accordingly, the Liverpool public health department and others in northern England began offering medical care, clean drugs (methadone, morphine, or heroin), clean needles, and safe injection education to injection users. As the program got underway, the HIV infection rate declined greatly in Britain. Compared to injection drug users in New York City who had an HIV infection rate of 60%, for example (Denning et al., 2004), the infection rate in Liverpool was reduced to 0.1%. Today in Britain, specially licensed doctors can provide heroin or cocaine to persons whose addiction to those substances is verified (Pycroft, 2010).

The first medically supervised injecting facility in North America opened in Vancouver, Canada in 2003 to prevent fatal overdoses of heroin. Recent empirically based research published in the British medical journal the *Lancet* indicates that the rate of fatal overdoses at this facility has decreased by 35% as a result of the supervision that is provided to these high-risk drug users (Marshall, Milloy, Wood, et al., 2011).

In the context of the public health crisis, harm reduction refers to strategies for drug users who are either unwilling or unable to stop using drugs (Pycroft, 2010). Such strategies are aimed at reducing a wide range of drug-related harms while not necessarily reducing drug use per se. This approach is decidedly optimistic and strengths-based because it draws on positive possibility and hope. The underlying belief in the predominant Western European approaches is that through effective therapy techniques, the counselor can help people tap into their inner strengths and natural resources.

In the United States, by the late 1990s, about 150 needle exchange programs had been set up in urban areas with the aim of preventing the contraction of HIV/AIDS and the hepatitis C virus (Centers for Disease Control and Prevention, CDC) (2002). For political reasons, however, federal funding was denied until 2009 when the Congress and the Obama administration lifted the ban on such funding in the interest of public health (Martin, 2010). Along with methadone and heroin maintenance, needle exchange is the approach most closely associated with the principles of harm reduction. Whereas the British approach and that of Vancouver, Canada, are to provide carefully monitored doses of heroin to heroin addicts (in heroin maintenance programs), the substitution of the synthetic drug methadone for heroin is the only legal recourse on this side of the Atlantic and below the 49th parallel (see Pycroft, 2010).

With regard to alcohol use, harm reduction similarly focuses on preventive measures, the best known of which are designated driver programs and the promotion of moderate drinking among youth as an alternative to secretive binge drinking. Regarding treatment for alcohol addiction, NIAAA is calling for the first time for a public health approach, based on new understandings about the transitory nature of alcohol dependence. This is a belated recognition that recovery from alcohol dependence is not only possible but even likely across the life span; people who are seemingly incapable of controlling their drinking at one point in time often can drink at low-risk levels at a later stage of life (see "Alcoholism Isn't What It Used to Be," 2011). The issuance of this statement of a changed concept of alcoholism from the acting director of NIAAA marks a major paradigm shift in research history, a shift toward acceptance of a public health rather than a total abstinence model. The individual whose name is most closely associated with harm reduction research is clinical psychologist G. Alan Marlatt. Marlatt died recently at the age of 69 (see Box 2.2).

One of the most significant developments in substance abuse treatment is the growing popularity of motivational therapy, an approach introduced by American psychologist William Miller and his associates to European audiences (see Miller, 1999; and Miller & Rollnick, 2002). Miller's motivational theory has been hailed as the most important advance in the treatment of addiction since the introduction of the disease model. Much of his theory, however, as Barber (2002) indicates, will be familiar to social workers already schooled in the nondirective counseling techniques he advocates. What is new about this philosophical approach that brings to substance abuse treatment an

Box 2.2	G. Alan Marlatt, 1942–2011: Harm Reduction Pioneer

A long-time member of the faculty at the University of Washington, Marlatt was the director of the Addictive Behaviors Research Center. Perhaps because of his Canadian upbringing, he had a perspective on the control of alcohol misuse that set him apart from his American peers. He was also greatly influenced by the pragmatic policies he learned about during his sabbaticals in Europe. According to an article in the *Seattle Times*, his ideas were considered heretical as late as the 1990s. In fact, when he gave public talks, he was sometimes warned that his teachings would kill alcoholics, a common accusation directed against those who advocated the teaching of moderate drinking to such individuals (Brunner, 2011).

As the director of the research center, Marlatt conducted studies on high school and college students, and demonstrated with empirical research that young people with potential drinking problems could be helped via a harm reduction approach to drink moderately. Opposed to a total abstinence focus, Marlatt conceived of harm reduction as a "one-step-at-a-time" approach. His writings and workshops on relapse prevention helped practitioners reframe this concept as a normal part of recovery, and his text, *Harm Reduction: Pragmatic Strategies for Managing High-Risk Behaviors* (Marlatt, 2002), is the best known book in this field. In later years, he was a strong advocate of the housing-first policy adopted by the city of Seattle to remove hard-drinking homeless people from the streets. This controversial program furnishes apartments for such individuals, who are allowed to drink as they wish. According to research directed by Marlatt, this housing-first policy is highly cost-effective for the city. College students might be more familiar with the counseling program he developed called BASICS—Brief Alcohol Screening and Intervention for College Students—which uses harm reduction principles to prevent binge drinking and is in place at 1,800 colleges (Hevesi, 2011).

entirely different way of viewing motivation? Under the traditional paradigm, according to Barber, motivation to use addictive substances or to abstain was seen as a characteristic of the user. Only when the stress had become overwhelming, when they had "hit bottom," could these motivationally deficient people seek help. Until then, there would be only denial and minimization of substance misuse.

Motivational theory de-emphasizes the use of negative labels and views substance misusers as being as susceptible to change as the rest of the population. Significantly, therapist characteristics and behavior are seen as playing a major role in treatment outcome. Such denial and resistance as there are, or have been, in treatment often say more about the therapist than the client and can be viewed as products of the interaction. The beauty of this approach is that it is decidedly optimistic and strengths-based in drawing on positive possibility and hope. The underlying belief here is that through effective therapy techniques, the counselor can help people tap into their inner strengths and natural resources.

By itself, Miller's theory is somewhat amorphous and vague. What was required was a step-by-step protocol for the training of therapists to help elicit a readiness to change in a previously unmotivated client. The missing ingredient was supplied in the empirical work of Prochaska and DiClemente, which was introduced in 1982. From their follow-up research with cigarette smokers who had experienced what is viewed as natural recovery and had successfully quit on their own, these researchers were able to delineate from this research (including interviews with successful changers) key factors in the process of self-change. The idea is that we change in stages, not all at once. The path to recovery or resolution from problematic use of substances involves a series of tasks that have been identified in a sequence of stages of change (DiClemente, 2006). This sequence is referred to as the *transtheoretical model* to refer to the fact that it is not derived from one particular school of thought. The transtheoretical model identified particular interventions tailored to the client's readiness to change. A form of consciousness raising to increase the user's awareness of the need for change was the recommended focus in therapy with someone who was only barely ready to contemplate change (Barber, 2002). Behavioral techniques were thought appropriate to the action stage in the change process.

Historically, this joining of motivational theory with stages-of-change intervention has provided the substance abuse treatment field with a pragmatic approach to serve as the practice component of harm reduction. Harm reduction is the goal: Motivational enhancement strategies teach the counselor how best to achieve that goal. Thus, in the interests of public health, interventions such as needle exchanges—the exchange of dirty needles for clean ones—methadone maintenance, the teaching of controlled drinking and of less harmful drug-taking practices than those the client has adopted, and above all, treatment instead of incarceration, are applied.

Immediately popular in Europe, where harsh confrontation of addicts was never popular, this client-centered approach is increasingly favored by insurance companies because of its cost-effectiveness, as was revealed in Project MATCH (see Chapter 1).

SUMMARY AND CONCLUSION

Professional addictions treatment arrived on the scene late. Long before there was professional treatment, there was the enjoyment of a variety of mood-altering substances. Whether deriving their pleasure from fermented fruit, coca leaves, or poppy flowers, people have always and will always seek refuge through the means available to them. In this chapter, we have seen how the drug of choice during one era was the substance most vile in the next. The way a particular drug was regarded depended on the circumstances of its use, on the political climate, and especially on what sorts of people were associated with its use (e.g., war heroes, "down-and-outs," genteel ladies). The decision pertaining to which drug or drugs to outlaw clearly had little to do with public health considerations.

In the days before water purification, alcohol was often safer than water. Although the Puritans who set up their theocracy in early America set the climate for a kind of moralism that would long outlast its religious bearings, they and their earliest descendants consumed vast quantities of beer and cider. There were few problems associated with this drinking; drunkenness was frowned upon, punished through public ridicule, and for the most part, avoided.

The switch from wine to beer to more potent liquor was associated with public drunkenness and violent behavior. In Britain, the infant mortality rate soared; on American shores, male drinking cults disrupted family life. Thus, the stage was set for a temperance movement with international consequences. Because excessive drinking in America came to be associated with newly arrived immigrant groups, a politically charged call for abstinence was in order.

Throughout this chapter, we have seen the pendulum swing from prohibition of one substance to prohibition of another. Zero tolerance of certain drugs has culminated in a war on drugs of vast proportions: A military crusade in drug-supplying countries is matched on the home front by the incarceration of more than 1 million people for drug-related crimes. Meanwhile, the sale of illegal drugs has become an underground enterprise of unbelievable proportions. Not only are individual and family economies affected but also the economies of entire nations.

Economics, too, has played a role in the sale and distribution of legal drugs. On the North American continent, as this brief historical review shows, products with addictive properties assumed great economic importance. Tobacco was a commodity that, as the early settlers realized, could sustain the economic life of a colony both in terms of exports and in the money raised from taxes. The sale and consumption of alcohol likewise played a major role in American economic history. Economics determined the manner in which alcohol was consumed, whether as wine from cultivated vines or in the form of distilled spirits, such as rum, which could be produced cheaply from molasses and transported cheaply as well. During Prohibition, the price of liquor shot up, and many working-class people could no longer afford to drink. For those who could afford to buy it, distilled alcohol became much preferred over beer. Liquor was easier to conceal, and people who were now breaking the law anyway were inclined to go all out, gulping down drink after drink with the abandon that often accompanies lawbreaking.

In addition to the obvious harms caused by Prohibition, including personal and political corruption, the economic incentive to get people back to work following the Great Depression was a key factor in the legalization of alcohol (Okrent, 2010). Once the distilleries and breweries were humming again, tax revenues were pouring in, and people's drinking habits could be to some extent controlled. The quality of the alcohol sold could be controlled as well.

Gambling, similarly, has gone from the underground economy to being a big moneymaker for the states and Indian reservations. Some form of legalized gambling is available in all but two U.S. states (Utah and Hawaii), and most states have become absolutely dependent on this form of entertainment as a major source of revenue.

Economic interests and ideology came together as the disease model began to gain currency in the public mind. Although temperance leaders had blamed both the drinker and the drug itself for drug-related problems, AA proponents later shifted the focus to *individual* susceptibilities. This shift in focus away from placing the blame on the drug alcohol was of course highly acceptable to the liquor industry. Ideologically, the strong punitive slant evidenced in the United States today has its roots in the moralism of an earlier time. The story of substance abuse treatment in this and other countries is a story of the wrestling between the forces of moralism and diseases, forces that philosophically are often hard to separate.

Starting in the 1950s, as we have seen, the treatment for alcoholism took a progressive turn in its conceptualization of addiction as a disease rather than a sin. What we now sometimes call the Minnesota Model adopted many of the precepts of Alcoholics Anonymous. Harsh confrontation of alcoholics "in denial" has given way in recent years to a more client-friendly approach. Today, Alcoholics Anonymous, Narcotics Anonymous, and family member self-help groups have brought help and guidance to millions across the world. As the addictions field has matured, it has moved away from the dogmatic authoritarianism of the early days to the use of motivational strategies geared to clients' individual needs. Still, much disagreement and confusion remain about the nature of addiction; this confusion spurs acrimonious debates about public drug control policy. Issues that need to be resolved in the future relevant to addictions treatment are inequities in the sentencing laws; the war on drugs, which has become a war on poor people of color; the need for a return to judicial discretion (as opposed to mandatory minimum sentencing of drug users); and more treatment and prevention options for people with chemical dependence problems.

The opposite of the war on drugs, which in effect is a war on people with problems, is a model to reduce harm to people and society. The war on drugs is an extension of the temperance-prohibition model in its focus on the destructive power of the agent of addiction itself. Psychodynamic approaches emphasize the self in terms of ego and memory. Moral and spiritual models place strong emphasis on factors within the person (Miller & Hester, 2003). Biological models stress the physiological impact of the substance. Ecological approaches look toward the person-environment interaction. A hallmark of harm reduction in a strengths-based formulation is its ability to address all these components—the availability of agent, which is the drug or behavior; a recognition of individual psychological and biological differences in responding to the agent of choice; and an understanding of the person-in-environment configuration as it applies to substance abuse. A harm reduction model provides the opportunity to integrate these components, each one representing a part of the whole, into a holistic framework. The time to involve social workers and other professionals schooled in motivational interviewing techniques and a harm reduction philosophy is now.

REFERENCES

Abadinsky, H. (2011). *Drugs: An introduction* (7th ed.). Belmont, CA: Cengage.

Abramsky, S. (2003, August 18). The drug war goes up in smoke. *Nation*, pp. 25–28.

Alcoholism Isn't What It Used to Be. (2011, February). *NIAAA Spectrum.* National Institute on Alcohol Abuse and Alcoholism. Retrieved from http://www.spectrum.niaaa.nih.gov/features/alcoholism.aspx

Anonymous. (1667). *Leather-more or advice concerning gambling* (2nd ed.). London: Wing.

Ayto, J. (2008). *Word origins* (2nd ed.). London: A & C Black.

Barber, J. G. (2002). *Social work with addictions* (2nd ed.). Hampshire, England: Palgrave.

Barr, A. (1999). *Drink: A social history of America.* New York: Carroll & Graf.

Bell, R. (1987). *Holy anorexia.* Chicago: University of Chicago Press.

Benshoff, J., & Janikowski, T. (2000). *Rehabilitation model of substance abuse counseling.* Belmont, CA: Wadsworth.

Brunner, J. (2011, March 17). Alan Marlatt, UW researcher respected worldwide, dies at 69. *Seattle Times.* Retrieved from http://seattletimes.nwsource.com/html/local-news/2014528623_marlattobit18m.html

Burns, E. (2004). *The spirits of America: The social history of alcohol.* Philadelphia: Temple University Press.

Burroughs, A. (2003). *Dry: A memoir.* New York: Picador.

Butler, S. (2002). *Alcohol, drugs, and health promotion in modern Ireland.* Dublin: Institute of Public Administration.

Butler, S. (2010). *Benign anarchy: Alcoholics Anonymous in Ireland.* Dublin: Academic Press.

Butler, S., & Maycock, P. (2005). An Irish solution to an Irish problem: Harm reduction and ambiguity in the drug policy of the Republic of Ireland. *International Journal of Drug Policy, 16,* 415–422.

Carter, C. S. (1997). Ladies don't: A historical perspective on attitudes toward alcoholic women. *Affilia, 12*(4), 471–485.

Centers for Disease Control and Prevention (CDC). (2002). Update: Syringe exchange programs. *Morbidity and Mortality Weekly Report, 54*(27), 673–676.

Chambers, B. (2011, March 23). *Illinois to cut all alcohol and drug treatment spending. Reclaiming Futures.* Retrieved from http://blog.reclaimingfutures.org/adolescent-substance-abuse-treatment-Illinois-cuts-all-treatment-funding

Cheever, S. (1999, June 14). Bill W.: The healer. *Time,* pp. 201–204.

Collins, R. L., & McNair, L. D. (2003). *Minority women and alcohol use.* National Institute on Alcohol Abuse and Alcoholism. Retrieved from http://niaaa.com/nih/gov/publications.

Covington, S. (2008). *A woman's journal: A program for treating substance abuse, special criminal justice edition.* San Francisco: Jossey-Bass.

Davis, D. R., & Jansen, G. G. (1998). Making meaning of Alcoholics Anonymous for social workers: Myths, metaphors, and realities. *Social Work, 43*(2), 169–183.

Denning, P., Little, J., & Glickman, A. (2004). *Over the influence: The harm reduction guide for managing drugs and alcohol.* New York: Guilford Press.

DiClemente, C. (2006). *Addiction and change: How addictions develop and addicted people recover.* New York: Guilford Press.

Documentary looks at drinking in America. (1999, September 13). *Waterloo-Cedar Falls Courier*, p. C8.

Elkin, M. (2004, March 11). Irish take a sober look at binge-drinking habits. *Christian Science Monitor*, p. 12.

Encyclopaedia Britannica. (2005). Alcohol and drug consumption. *Macropaedia* (15th ed., pp. 195–223). Chicago: Encyclopaedia Britannica.

Erickson (1966). *Wayward Puritans: A study in the sociology of deviance.* New York: Wiley.

Fingarette, H. (1988). *Heavy drinking: The myth of alcoholism as a disease.* Berkeley: University of California Press.

Fishbein, D. H., & Pease, S. E. (1996). *The dynamics of drug abuse.* Boston: Allyn & Bacon.

Fruhling, L. (1996, September 29). Allow women to vote? Ha! *Des Moines Register*, p. 10A.

Gately, I. (2008). *Drink: A cultural history.* London: Penguin.

Gilmore, B. (2010, August). Drug sentencing reform does not go far enough. *Progressive.* Retrieved from http://www.progressive.org/mpgilmore081010.html

Giancana, S., & Giancana, C. (1992). *Double cross.* New York: Warner.

Gifford, M. (2009). *Alcoholism: Biographies of disease.* Santa Barbara, CA: ABC-CLIO.

Gorski, T. T. (1998). Alcoholism should be treated as a disease. In S.Barber (Ed.), *Alcohol: Opposing viewpoints* (pp. 98–104). San Diego, CA: Greenhaven Press.

Harris, G. (2004). What all social workers should know about MDMA (Ecstasy). *Journal of Social Work Practice in the Addictions, 4*(1), 23–37.

Hartman, V. (2010, July/August). Treatment admissions: Dramatic rise in abuse of pain relievers. *SAMHSA News*, p. 5.

Hazelden (2011). Narcotics Anonymous members discover unity in powerlessness over addiction. Retrieved from http://www.hazelden.org/web/public/namembers.page

Hegel, G. W. (1837). *Philosophy of history* (Vol. *10*) (J.Sibree, Trans.). New York: Dover.

Hevesi, D. (2011, March 22). G. A. Marlatt, advocate of shift in treating addicts, dies at 69. *New York Times*, p. A25.

Homer (circa 850 BCE). *The Odyssey.* Translated from Greek by Robert Fitzgerald, 1961. New York: Doubleday.

Hughes, R. (1987). *The fatal shore: The epic of Australia's founding.* New York: Knopf.

Inciardi, J. A., & Harrison, L. D. (2000). Introduction: The concept of harm reduction. In J. A.Inciardi & L.Harrison (Eds.), *Harm reduction* (pp. vii–xviii). Thousand Oaks, CA: Sage.

Jellinek, E. M. (1960). *The disease concept of alcoholism.* New Haven, CT: Yale Center for Alcoholic Studies.

Karoll, B. R. (2010). Applying social work approaches, harm reduction, and practice wisdom to better serve those with alcohol and drug use disorders. *Journal of Social Work, 10*(3), 263–281.

King, L. (2009). *Forensic chemistry of substance misuse: A guide to drug control.* Cambridge, UK: Royal Society of Chemistry.

Kinney, J. (2011). *Loosening the grip: A handbook of alcohol information* (10th ed.). Boston: McGraw-Hill.

Knudsen, H. K., Roman, P. M., & Ducharme, L. J. (2005) Does service diversification embrace organizational survival? Evidence from the private substance abuse treatment system. *Journal of Behavioral Health Services and Research, 32*(3), 241–253.

Koerner, B. (2010, June 23). Secret of AA: After 75 years, we don't know how it works. *Wired.* Retrieved from http://www.wired.com/magazine/2010

Lacey, M. (2009, August 23). In Mexico, ambivalence on a drug law. *New York Times,* p. A4.

Landers, J. (2011, April 28). In policy shift, Obama administration emphasizes reducing demand for drugs. *Dallas Morning News.* Retrieved from http://www.dallasnews.com

Lipton, E. (2011, April 19). Foreign money fuels faltering bid to push online poker. *New York Times,* p. A16.

Maisto, S., Galizio, M., & Connors, G. (2011). *Drug use and abuse* (6th ed.). Belmont, CA: Cengage.

Mancall, P. (2004). "I was addicted to drinking rum": Four centuries of alcohol consumption in Indian country. In S.Tracy & C.Acken (Eds.), *Altering American consciousness* (pp. 91–107). Amherst: University of Massachusetts Press.

Marshall, B., Milloy, M., Wood, E., Montaner, J., & Kerr, T. (2011). Reduction in overdose mortality after the opening of North America's first medically supervised safer injecting facility: a retrospective population-based study. *Lancet, 377* (9775), 1429–1437.

Martin, W. (2010, January 8). *Time for Texas to support needle exchange.* Baker Institute. Retrieved from http://blogs.chron.com/bakerblog/2010/01/time_for_texas_to_support_needle_exchange.html

Mauer, M. (2009, April). *The changing racial dynamics of the war on drugs.* Washington, DC: The Sentencing Project.

McGinn, A. P. (1997, July/August). The nicotine control. *World Watch,* pp. 18–27.

McGoldrick, M. (2005). Irish families. In M.McGoldrick, J. Giordano, & N. Garcia-Preto (Eds.), *Ethnicity and family therapy* (3rd ed., pp. 595–615). New York: Guilford Press.

McGovern, P. E. (2003). *Ancient wine: The search for the origins of viniculture.* Princeton, NJ: Princeton University Press.

McGreevy, R. (2010, October 12). Rise in suicides related to recession. *Irish Times.* Retrieved from http://alcoholireland.ie

McNeece, C. A., & DiNitto, D. M. (2011). *Chemical dependence: A systems approach* (4th ed.). Boston: Allyn & Bacon.

Mead, M. (2005, February 21). Presentation to social work students. University of Northern Iowa: Cedar Falls.

Mexican drug trafficking. (2011, February 1). *New York Times.* Retrieved from http://topics.nytimes.com/top/news/international

Miller, W. R. (1999). *TIP 35. Treatment improvement protocol series.* Rockville, MD: Substance Abuse and Mental Health Service Administration.

Miller, W. R., & Hester, R. K. (2003). Treating alcohol problems: Towards an informed eclecticism. In R. K. Hester & W. R. Miller (Eds.), *Handbook of alcoholism treatment approaches: Effective alternatives* (3rd ed., pp. 1–12). Boston: Allyn & Bacon.

Miller, W. R., & Rollnick, S. (2002). *Enhancing motivation for change in substance abuse treatment* (2nd ed.). New York: Guilford Press.

Minton, M. (2011, April 20). Lower the drinking age for everyone. *National Review Online*. Retrieved from http://www.nationalreview.com/articles/264916/lower-drinking-age-everyone-michelle-minton

Mosher, C. J., & Akins, S. (2007). *Drug and drug control policy: The control of consciousness alteration*. Thousand Oaks, CA: Sage.

Murrin, J., Johnson, P., McPherson, J., Gersle, G., Rosenberg, E., & Rosenberg, N. (2001). *Liberty, equality, power: A history of the American people*. Fort Worth, TX: Harcourt, Brace, Jovanovich.

Nash, J. (2003, November 24). The first vintage. *Time*, pp. 60–61.

National Council of Problem Gambling. (2010). *National problem gambling awareness rises to the next level: Press release*. Retrieved from http://www.ncpgambling.org/files/Press/2010NCPGPressRelease.pdf

Ogle, M. (2005). *Ambitious brew: The story of American beer*. New York: Harcourt.

Okrent, D. (2010) *The last call: The rise and fall of Prohibition*. New York: Scribner.

Pratt, G. (2011, February 1). Arizona attorneys for criminal justice release new report on sentencing reform. *Phoenix New Times*. Retrieved from http://blogs.phoenixnewtimes.com/valleyfever/2011/02/arizona_attorneys_for_criminal.php

Prochaska, J. O., & DiClemente, C. C. (1982). Transtheoretical theory: Toward a more integrative model of change. *Psychotherapy: Theory, Research and Practice, 19*, 276–278.

Pycroft, A. (2010). *Understanding and working with substance misuse*. London: Sage.

Qviller, B. (1996). *Rusens historie (History of intoxication)*. Oslo: Det Norske Samlaget.

Richards, A. (2011, April 18). Washington DC to offer online gambling. *Casino Advisor*. Retrieved from http://www.casinoadvisor.com/

Robinson, M., & Scherlen, R. (2007). *Lies, damned lies, and drug war statistics: A critical analysis of claims made by the Office of National Drug Control Policy*. Albany: State University of New York Press.

Roiblatt, R., & Dinis, R. (2004). The lost link: Social work in the early 20th century alcohol policy. *Social Service Review, 78*(4), 652–674.

Roizen, R. (2004). How does the nation's "alcohol problem" change from era to era? In S. Tracy & C. Acken (Eds.), *Altering American consciousness: The history of alcohol and drug use in the United States, 1800–2000* (pp. 61–87). Amherst: University of Massachusetts Press.

Rotskoff, L. E. (2004). Sober husbands and supportive wives: Marital dramas of alcoholism in post–World War II America. In S.Tracy & C.Acker (Eds.) *Altering American consciousness: The history of alcohol and drug use in the United States, 1800–2000* (pp. 298–326). Amherst: University of Massachusetts Press.

Rush, B. (1785/1943). An inquiry into the effects of ardent spirits upon the human mind and body. Reprinted in *Quarterly Journal of Studies on Alcohol, 4* [Entire issue].

Savage, D. G. (1999, December 27). U.S. law has come full circle on personal vices in the last century. *Los Angeles Times*, p. 24A.

Schlosser, E. (1994, August). Reefer madness. *Atlantic Monthly, 274*(2), 45–59.

Shorter Oxford English Dictionary. (2007). New York: Oxford University Press.

Skinner, E. (2007, November 30). The gin craze: Drink, crime and women in 18th century London. *Cultural Shifts.* Retrieved from http://www.culturalshifts.vom/archives/168

Skolnik, S. (2011). *High stakes: The rising cost of America's gambling addiction.* New York: Beacon Press.

Sprague, E. (2009, July 15). Pot no longer focus of anti-drug campaigns. CBS News. Retrieved from http://www.cbsnews.com/stories

Standage, T. (2005). *A history of the world in six glasses.* New York: Walker.

Stern, S. (2006, June 5). Meth vs. crack: Different legislative approaches. *Congressional Quarterly Weekly*, p. 1548.

Stokes, D. (2005). *America's other war: Terrorizing Colombia.* New York: Zed Books.

Substance Abuse and Mental Health Services Administration (SAMHSA). (2004). *National survey of substance abuse treatment services.* Rockville, MD: Author.

Substance Abuse and Mental Health Services Administration (SAMHSA) (2010, July/August). Changes in admission patterns over a decade. *SAMHSA News*, p. 6.

Szasz, T. (2003). *Ceremonial chemistry: The ritual persecution of drugs, addicts, and pushers* (Rev. ed.). Syracuse, NY: Syracuse University Press.

Talmage, T. D. (1887). *Live coals.* Chicago: Fairbanks and Palmer.

Townend, P. (2005). Heretical plants of Irish growth: Catholic critics of Matthewite temperance. *Catholic Historical Review, 91*(4), 611–632.

United Nations Human Development Index (2011). *Regional and national trends in human development index.* Retrieved from http://hdr.undp.org/en/data/trends.

United Nations Office on Drugs and Crime (UNODC) (2011, April). *Afghanistan opium survey 2011: Winter rapid assessment in all regions.* Retrieved from http://www.unodc.org/documents/afghanistan//Opium_Surveys/Winter_Rapid_Assessment/Winter_assessment_Phase_12_FINAL.pdf

van Wormer, K. (1997). Doing alcoholism treatment in Norway: A personal reminiscence. *Reflections: Narratives of professional helping, 3*(3), 37–71.

Wagenaar, A. C., Tobler, A. L., & Komro, K. (2010). Effects of alcohol tax and price policies on morbidity and mortality: A systematic review. *American Journal of Public Health, 100*(11), 2270–2278.

Wallace, B. C. (2005). *Making mandated addiction treatment work.* Lanham, MD: Jason Aronson.

White, S. (1996). Russia goes dry: Alcohol, state, and society. Cambridge, England: Cambridge University Press.

White, W. L. (1998). *Slaying the dragon: The history of addiction treatment and recovery in America.* Bloomington, IL: Chestnut Health Systems.

Yee, C. M. (2008, May 11). If Hazelden is healthy, why have almost all execs left? *Minneapolis-St.Paul, Star Tribune.* Retrieved from http://www.startribune.com/business/18831544.html

Zeldin, T. (1994). *An intimate history of humanity.* New York: HarperCollins.

THE BIOLOGY OF ADDICTION

Despite lip service to the biopsychosocial-spiritual model of human behavior, substance abuse counselors often overlook the *bio* piece of the equation. Yet knowledge of the biology of addiction is crucial for an understanding of the hold that certain chemicals or behaviors have on people, the cravings that grip them, and the health problems associated with substance misuse. An awareness of the genetic features in addiction is also important. Thanks to advances in technology—namely, the development of positron emission tomography (PET) and functional magnetic resonance imaging (fMRI)—scientists can capture chemical images of the brain at work; they can also observe not only structures but also actual functions or processes of the living brain. The ability to observe directly the effects of neurological damage caused by long-term substance abuse is a significant accomplishment in itself; the ability to demonstrate the impact of craving itself on the pleasure circuits of the brain is even more remarkable. Due to neuroimaging technology, things can be known today that in previous decades could only be guessed at or only inferred from behavior. To see, as we can today, a slide of the serotonin-depleted brain is to bring us face-to-face with the clear insanity of addiction. In providing this glimpse into the inner workings of the mind, modern technology is truly revolutionary. Chapter 3 summarizes ground-breaking research on the addicted brain.

Why can one person drink and use drugs moderately over a lifetime while another person gets "hooked" after a short period of time? Why does the alcoholic tend to smoke and have a high tolerance for many depressant drugs? If the answers were simple, this part of the book would be a good deal shorter.

The three chapters that comprise Part II on biology are concerned with the physiological and pharmaceutical aspects of drug misuse, gender differences in substance use and addiction, and risks for the development of substance use disorders across the life span. Moe specifically, Chapter 3 provides an overview of the addictive properties of various drugs, the metabolizing process, and the effect of chronic use on the major organs of the body. Major emphasis is placed on the most complex organ of the body—the brain. We will see, through a review of the latest research from neuroscience and with the help of diagnosis, how addicting drugs work in the brain and on the brain. We conclude Chapter 3 with a presentation of biologically based interventions. Included under the rubric of biologically based interventions are aversion therapy, pharmaceutical remedies, assessment, and early-stage, highly structural group work. Perhaps the most intriguing part of this chapter is the description of experiments in altering brain chemistry through behavior therapy.

The term *gender* is used in the broad sense in Chapter 4 to encompass gender nonconformity as well as conformity in sex-role behavior. Because they do not conform to society's definition of sexuality, gays, lesbians, bisexuals, and transgender persons are highly vulnerable to drug use and misuse.

Chapter 5, Gambling, Eating Disorders, Shopping, and Other Behavioral Addictions, is at the intersection of biology and psychology. Biological aspects of the various disorders are discussed, and a motivational interviewing focus is adapted from psychology as the intervention of choice.

SUBSTANCE MISUSE, DEPENDENCE, AND THE BODY

CHAPTER 3

The golden age of brain research is right now.
—David Linden (2011, p. 5)

Drugs to get us off drugs? Just imagine—a generation of Americans trading in martinis for meds!

If you down a scotch and soda, take a drag of a cigarette, or snort cocaine, trillions of potent molecules surge through your bloodstream and into your brain. If you inject a drug such as heroin or meth directly into the veins, you get a rush within 30 seconds. Whatever the chosen method of ingestion—swallowing, inhaling, or injecting—psychoactive drugs are absorbed into the bloodstream and carried to the central nervous system. Unlike many other drugs, such as penicillin, these kinds of drugs pass the blood–brain barrier and cause the release of neurotransmitters (feel-good chemicals) in the brain (Abadinsky, 2011). Eventually, drugs are detoxified by metabolic processes or eliminated from the body as waste material (Jung, 2010).

The result of experimentation with drugs ranges from benign to seriously destructive. One purpose of this chapter is to show what happens to the mind and body after drugs enter the system and to present facts concerning the chemical properties of the various drugs—depressants, stimulants, hallucinogens, and cannabis. This knowledge is basic for working with people with problems that are related to urges, compulsions, and cravings because those urges, compulsions, and cravings often have biochemical roots. Another purpose of this chapter is to explore genetic factors in the etiology of addiction. Chapter highlights include a study of states of euphoria as registered in the brain and brain changes as pathways to addiction, shown in the graphic diagrams courtesy of the National Institute on Alcohol Abuse and Alcoholism (NIAAA) and the National Institute on Drug Abuse (NIDA). A boxed reading, "To Die for a Cigarette," helps us get into the mind of someone wrestling with life-threatening addiction. The concern of the central portion of the chapter is with genetic factors in susceptibility to addiction. The basic physiological effects of drugs on the brain, heart, liver, and reproductive system, and the developing fetus, are described.

One important core competency of addiction counselors, as indicated by Miller, Forcehimes, and Zweben (2011) is to have at least a working knowledge of psychoactive drugs and their effects. This includes not just illicit drugs but the array of pharmaceutical products that are being researched and used today to curb cravings and prevent relapse for clients in treatment. Accordingly, the second portion of this chapter looks at medical interventions that are viewed as a supplement to talking therapy. We consider not only pharmacological solutions but other interventions such as cognitive work to change the brain, meditation, and the use of herbal remedies.

The information of relevant biological processes provided in this chapter should enhance the counseling function regarding the standard tasks of assessment, problem formulation, and intervention as well as contribute to a more comprehensive understanding of the visceral aspects and power of addiction.

PROPERTIES OF ALCOHOL AND OTHER DRUGS

A *drug* is (1) any substance that affects the physical or mental functioning of a living organism, especially one used for the treatment or prevention of an ailment or disease or (2) a stimulant or narcotic taken otherwise than medically (*Shorter Oxford English Dictionary*, 2007). Psychoactive drugs are mood altering and used for purposes of recreation or self-medication. Such drugs can be categorized in various ways, but the usual division is into depressants (or downers), opiates, stimulants (or uppers), and hallucinogens. These substances all affect the central nervous system and therefore alter the user's mood and even sensory perceptions in some cases. The major drugs of misuse, whether uppers or downers, imitate the structure of neurotransmitters, the chemicals in the brain that give us pleasure.

DEPRESSANTS

This category of drugs includes alcohol, barbiturates, and tranquilizers. Narcotics may be natural (opium derivatives, e.g., morphine and codeine), semi-synthetic (e.g., heroin), or synthetic (e.g., methadone, oxycodone [OxyContin], and pethidine [Demerol]) (Abadinsky, 2011). Morphine, codeine, methadone, OxyContin, barbiturates, and tranquilizers all have some medical use. These drugs depress the central nervous system, reduce anxiety at low dosages, and can induce anesthesia and death at high dosages.

"Cunning, baffling, powerful!" These are the descriptive words used for alcohol in an oft-cited passage from *The Big Book* (Alcoholics Anonymous World Services, 1976/1939, pp. 58–59). Alcohol is a chemical and a drug; the kind that people drink is ethyl alcohol, or ethanol (C_2H_5OH), popularly abbreviated as ETOH. Ethyl alcohol is a colorless, flammable, volatile liquid with a burning taste (Abadinsky, 2011; Perkinson, 2012).

Alcohol is widely used as a solvent in industry, where it is denatured by adding a toxin to make it unpalatable (Maisto, Galizio, & Connors, 2010). The kind of alcohol we drink is produced by the fermentation of substances, such as fruit, containing sugar and by enzymes that are produced by a microorganism, yeast (Kinney, 2011). Through the process of distillation, the solution containing the alcohol is heated and the vapors are collected and condensed into liquid form again. This process, as we saw in Chapter 2, increases its potency considerably.

Whatever form of alcohol is consumed, when taken to excess, different levels of intoxication are likely to be observed with different individuals and at different time points. Early in the drinking period, as the *Diagnostic and Statistical Manual of Mental Disorders, Text Revision* (*DSM–IV–TR*) (APA, 2000) indicates, when blood alcohol levels are rising, symptoms often include talkativeness, a sensation of well-being, and a bright, expansive mood. Later, when blood alcohol levels are falling, the individual is likely to become depressed, less rational, and withdrawn. At very high blood alcohol levels, an individual who has not built up tolerance is likely to become sleepy.

Individual differences in brain chemistry may explain the observation that excessive alcohol intake consistently promotes aggression in some persons but not in others, and different genetic histories can make some people unduly sensitive to the effects of alcohol (Fisher, 2009; Gordh & Söderpalm, 2011). Father Martin (1972), in his charismatic lecture-film *Chalk Talk,* which is still widely shown in treatment centers, semi-humorously depicts four categories of drunks. Each category can represent a progressive stage in the course of an evening, or each can represent the drug-induced behavior of a particular individual. The types are:

- The *jocose* drunk, who is a barrel of laughs
- The *amorose* drunk, who can't keep his hands to himself
- The *bellicose* drunk, "the new man with the new teeth"
- The *lachrymose,* or crying, drunk, full of self-pity

To these, we have a few additions of our own:

- The *somnos,* or sleepy, drunk
- The *clamorose,* or loud, drunk
- The *scientose,* or "know-it-all," drunk

The toll that alcohol takes on U.S. society can be seen as summarized in Figure 3.1. Domestic violence, child abuse, rape, other crimes (including, of course, driving while intoxicated), serious illness, and accidents requiring hospitalization are all linked to alcohol misuse (only some to alcoholism). The

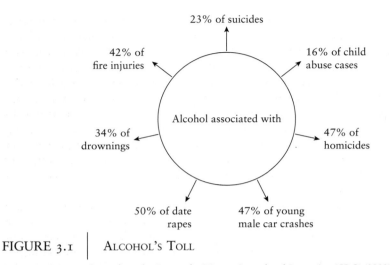

FIGURE 3.1 | ALCOHOL'S TOLL

Source: Statistics are drawn from the Centers for Disease Control and Prevention (CDC) (2008) and NIAAA, *College Drinking* at http://www.collegedrinkingprevention.gov.

large majority of drunk drivers in fatal motor vehicle accidents, for example, are casual or binge drinkers (Sharman, 2005). We need to keep in mind that most public health problems related to drinking come from acute intoxication, not dependence. Unfortunately, in many parts of Europe (especially the United Kingdom and Ireland) and North America, binge drinking is the predominant pattern. In Russia and nearby countries, one in five men die from alcohol-related causes (WHO, 2011a).

The highest level of alcohol use in the United States is among 21-year-olds (see Chapter 6). Alcohol use is the leading risk factor in three leading causes of deaths among youth: unintentional injuries (including motor vehicle accidents and drownings), suicides, and homicides (CDC, 2010b). Among young males, alcohol is a significant factor in about 50% of all drownings (CDC, 2011).

As we learn from the NIAAA (2010b) Surveillance Report #89, which provides statistics on discharges from community hospitals in the United States, over 27% of these discharges involved alcohol-related problems. The most common were persons with both psychoses and alcohol abuse, the second most frequent alcohol-related reason people were treated at the hospital was alcohol dependence problems, and 4.1% of those with alcohol-related problems had cirrhosis of the liver. Figure 3.1 shows a high percentage of hospital admissions that involve alcohol use.

Another economic consideration to bear in mind is that legal substances (alcohol and tobacco) account for most of the total cost of substance use. In Canada, for example, legal substances (alcohol and tobacco) account for about 80% of the total cost of substance use damage to the economy, and illegal drug use makes up the remaining 20% (Canadian Centre on Substance Abuse, 2006).

Partner violence, also as indicated in Figure 3.1, is commonly associated with alcohol. The most common pattern is drinking by both offender and victim. According to the *Global Status Report on Alcohol and Health* produced by the World Health Organization (WHO) (2004), the connection between alcohol and domestic partner violence is seen in nations in which drinking is common. A study of police reports in Zurich, Switzerland, for example, found evidence of alcohol use in 40% of investigated domestic violence situations. In Nigeria, alcohol use was involved in over half of husband–wife knifing incidents. In South Africa, violence was found to rise as the couple fought over the wife's drinking. Even in South India, in a region with an extremely low drinking rate, more than half of spousal abuse was reported to occur during a period of intoxication.

A U.S. investigation of almost 200 felony domestic violence cases found that around two-thirds involved same day alcohol or other drug use by the perpetrators (Friend, Langhinrichsen-Rohling, & Eichold, 2011). The commonly found correlation between alcohol and domestic violence in the literature, as Clements and Schumacher (2010) suggest, may be related to the cognitive impairment and social perception deficits associated with heavy drinking.

The number of deaths attributed to alcohol by health conditions such as pancreatitis, liver disease, and alcohol poisoning is considerable. In addition to the many adverse health effects that result directly from alcohol misuse, alcohol misuse and addiction often accompany other disorders such as depression, anxiety, and other substance use. For example, an estimated 90% of cocaine addicts have alcohol problems, and an estimated 60% of patients treated at mental health centers have problems with alcohol and other drugs (NIAAA, 2009). Excessive drinking is closely associated with a disregard for safe-sex precautions. Research shows that between 30 and 60% of people with HIV/AIDS also have alcohol use disorders (NIAAA, 2009).

According to the new National Institute on Alcohol Abuse and Alcoholism (NIAAA, 2010a) information on college drinking, drinking by college students aged 18 to 24 contributes to an estimated 1,825 student deaths a year, almost 600,000 injuries, and 97,000 of date rape cases each year. (For more statistics, visit www.collegedrinkingprevention.gov and see Chapter 6.)

CONSUMPTION LEVELS WORLDWIDE

We learn from the *Global Status Report on Alcohol and Health* (WHO, 2011a) facts of interest about international levels of consumption. Whereas alcohol consumption in many Muslim nations is close to zero, the level of drinking in the nations of the former Soviet Union is quite high. Moldova has the highest alcohol consumption in the world at 18.2 liters per capita per year, with the Czech Republic a close second. Table 3.1 gives some examples of alcohol consumption by region. When reading these statistics, it is important to take into account the fact that almost half of all men and two-thirds of women do

TABLE 3.1 | INTERNATIONAL CONSUMPTION RATES

Regions of the World	Total Annual per Capita Consumption in Liters of Pure Alcohol (a standard drink is .6 ounces of pure alcohol)
The Americas	8.67
Europe	12.18
Africa	6.15
Southeast Asia	2.2

Information from *Global Status Report on Alcohol*, World Health Organization, 2011a, p. 5.

not drink at all. Another important fact to consider is that much of the alcohol is homemade or illegally produced.

The drinking patterns in the various nations, in terms of preferred beverages, as the *Global Status Report* further indicates, are different. Eastern Europeans tend to prefer to take their alcohol as hard liquor or spirits, the British and Irish prefer beer, the French and Italians prefer wine, and the Russians prefer spirits. Globally, more than 45% of the total alcohol consumed is in the form of spirits, especially in Southeast Asia.

In Australia, the toll of alcohol misuse has received considerable attention. The WHO (2011a) refers to the heavy consumption of alcohol in Australia and singles out this country of 21 million as a land where more than 10 million people have been negatively impacted in some way by a stranger's drinking, according to surveys. An information paper published by the Australian Medical Association (2009) indicates that heavy drinking in children is on the rise and that alcohol accounts for 13% of all deaths among people 14–17 years of age. According to estimates, one Australian teenager dies and more than 60 are hospitalized every week from alcohol-related causes. And deaths from alcohol-related causes among indigenous Australians compared to non-indigenous Australians are almost eight times greater for males and 16 times greater for females

Swedish research has also shown high rates of substance use by members of its indigenous population. A recent investigation of unnatural deaths in Sweden's far North by Ahlm, Hassler, and colleagues (2010) analyzed government data on almost 7,500 Sami reindeer people. The term *unnatural deaths* refers to non–disease-related deaths, such as accidents, suicides, falls, traffic injuries, and homicides. Researchers found that half of the victims of these deaths at autopsy tested positive for alcohol. Many showed evidence of advanced liver disease. Their findings concerning high alcohol involvement by this indigenous population are consistent with other research on people who live in the Arctic regions of the world, areas where alcohol was not used until several hundred years ago. According to Ahlm and colleagues, one of the most serious problems affecting indigenous populations is excessive mortality caused by injuries. In Nunavut in northern Canada, as they further inform us, injuries accounted for 34% of all deaths during 2001–2003 compared to only 6% in the whole of Canada. Similar mortality data also have been reported from Greenland and Finnish Lapland.

In the interests of public health and as part of a global health strategy, the World Health Organization (WHO) (2011a) has produced a comprehensive report, the *Global Status Report on Alcohol and Health*. Among the facts revealed in this report are that alcohol consumption is the world's third leading risk factor for disease and disability, and in middle-income countries, it is the greatest risk. Alcohol is a causal factor in 60 types of diseases and injuries and a component cause in 200 others. Almost 4% of all deaths worldwide are attributed to alcohol, which is more than deaths caused by HIV/AIDS, violence, or tuberculosis. And yet despite these grim statistics, according to the WHO, "the harmful use of alcohol remains a low priority in public policy, including in health policy" (p. x).

The WHO report discusses several means of harm reduction policies that are being adopted by nations, including alcohol taxation and controls on advertising. The excise duty in the price of a liter of pure alcohol ranges from as much as 44.9% in Norway to as little as 0.3% in Kyrgyzstan. As far as advertising controls are concerned, a few examples are France's *Loi Évin*, which ·bans the advertising of alcoholic beverages containing over 1.2 % alcohol by volume on television or in cinemas and prohibits the targeting of young people; Belarus's move from a partial to a full ban on advertising of wine and spirits; Estonia's shift from a partial to a full ban on television advertising of all three beverages—wine, spirits, and beer; and Kenya's enactment of partial restrictions on sponsorship of sports or cultural events by alcohol companies.

A major concern of the Swedish government when the country joined the EU was that alcohol would be more readily available and that the country's high taxes on alcohol would have to be lowered to comply with EU regulations. In fact, Sweden has managed to retain high alcohol taxes but has been required to ease restrictions on private imports from Germany and Denmark (Eriksson & Fotina, 2010). Wine sales have increased as a result.

Throughout Latin America, alcohol intoxication ranks as the number one risk to health, according to an article in the Pan American Health Organization publication *Perspectives* (Sharman, 2005). The secret to prevention, therefore, argues Sharman, is to view alcohol misuse less as an individual malady and more as a problem of public health. Costa Rica is taking such measures today to reduce excessive consumption. These measures include restricting advertising, increasing taxes, imposing licensing laws, controlling the hours alcohol can be served, and banning drinking in parks and on the street. Other measures include tough drinking-and-driving limits and the use of screening at health centers and brief interventions with people who manifest problems with alcohol.

As McNeece and DiNitto (2005) suggest, "almost nothing good can be said about the effects of alcohol on the human body, except that moderate drinkers may have slightly lower risk of atherosclerosis and coronary heart disease" (p. 68). True, there are substantial health risks linked to alcohol, as we will see presently when we consider the damage to the various organs of the body through long-term alcohol misuse. Researchers, however, have long reported the health benefits of moderate drinking, namely, in preventing coronary heart disease and stroke. Because they are less prone to coronary artery disease—the leading killer of men and women in the United States—moderate drinkers tend to live longer than abstainers (Holahan, Schutte, et al., 2010; Raloff, 2003). Moderate drinking is defined as up to two drinks per day for men and one for women.

An article in *Science News* (Raloff, 2003) summarizes the research comparing abstainers with moderate drinkers. One problem with such research, she warns, is that surveys are often used. The surveys that ask about weekly consumption patterns compromise data by including as moderate drinkers people who consume all their alcohol only over the weekend. This is why carefully controlled experimental studies are best. In one such study, postmenopausal women drank a little over one standard drink or 15 grams of alcohol each night before bed. Results showed that their insulin levels, blood sugar, and cholesterol were healthiest during this two-drink period. Rat experiments show similar results. Other studies show benefits in humans of moderate drinking in terms of reasoning, memory, and decision making. On the whole, moderate drinking effects relate to diseases that emerge in middle age and after; there seems to be little health justification, therefore, for drinking in youth except to develop healthy habits such as learning when to stop. One benefit unrelated to age reported by Shapiro (1996) was the prevention of colds and protection of the stomach from tainted or unsanitary food. And an empirically based Mayo Clinic study found, curiously, that moderate drinkers have less tendency toward obesity than do abstainers or binge drinkers (Arif & Rohrer, 2005).

Holahan, Schutte, and colleagues (2010) studied 1,824 subjects who were ages 55 to 65 at the beginning of the study and 20 years older at the study's end. Death rates were 69% of the teetotalers, 60% of the heavy drinkers, and 41% of the moderate drinkers. The reasons for the striking findings are not clear, but the researchers reasoned that the moderate drinkers were more involved in social activities, and the activity helped sustain their lives. An even more massive study of 84,000 nurses over a 20-year period indicated that women who drank approximately one or two drinks daily were more likely to live to age 70 than were those who drank far less or those who drank in occasional binges (reported by Allday, 2010).

Years ago when research findings on the benefits of moderate drinking began to come out, Peele (1999) stated that because of the fear by American public health officials that word of the documented benefits of alcohol would encourage alcohol misuse, public proclamations tended to stress only the negative aspects of alcohol consumption. To such negative aspects, we now turn our attention.

One property of alcohol not usually considered is its addictiveness. The mechanisms that promote addiction occur primarily in the brain and relate to the effect of the chemical on the brain over time. Although researchers are only at the threshold of uncovering the mysteries of addiction, it is known that about 7–10% of drinkers develop dependence. Those psychoactive drugs that strongly activate the dopamine-using pleasure circuit of the brain (e.g., heroin, cocaine, and amphetamines) are the very ones that carry a substantial risk of addiction, while the drugs that weakly activate the pleasure circuit (e.g., alcohol and cannabis) carry a smaller risk of addiction (Linden, 2011). Estimates are that only around one-third of people who have injected heroin become addicted, compared to 22% for cocaine and 8% for marijuana. Only one drug causes addiction among a majority of its users—nicotine. Linden explains that whereas a heroin user needs only a fix that will last perhaps half a day with one injection, the average cigarette smoker will take at least ten puffs from one cigarette and smoke many in one day. The marketers of alcohol, like the marketers of tobacco products, focus their efforts where use is the strongest—on the young to encourage their drinking and on heavy drinkers. Excessive drinkers, according to a report by the National Center on Addiction and Substance Abuse (2003), account for 9% of drinkers but 46% of the total alcohol consumed. A scan of magazine and TV ads reveals heavy use of images that relate to unquenchable thirst, women as sex object, and sports.

Tolerance, Withdrawal, and Blackouts   Most heavy drinkers are proud of their high tolerance for alcohol; they can drink their friends "under the table." Some people have a high tolerance by nature; others develop an ability to handle large quantities of alcohol as the nervous system accommodates to its effects and the liver gets more efficient at metabolizing alcohol. Such individuals may drive fairly well, even though legally intoxicated. *Behavioral tolerance* refers to the process of learning to adapt one's behavior to the presence of the drug. People with this level of tolerance may be only moderately drunk at the blood alcohol level of 0.4, a level at which a normal drinker might be comatose. Many individuals, similarly, smoke a pack of cigarettes a day, a feat that would be highly unlikely for novice smokers who have not yet developed that tolerance.

Gmel and colleagues (2006), in their empirical investigation of emergency room injuries in a Swiss hospital, provide relevant documentation on the paradoxical benefits of tolerance. Chronic heavy drinkers who were admitted to the hospital experienced a lower rate of serious injury than did intoxicated persons who rarely drank heavily. Low-volume drinking women had a high rate of alcohol-related injuries. Prevention efforts, as the researchers recommend, should target heavy drinking occasions.

Low sensitivity to modest amounts of alcohol—as indicated by good performance on a test of coordination and balance—shows a strong link to future alcoholism among the sons of both alcoholic and nonalcoholic fathers, according to longitudinal research undertaken by Schuckit (2009). Earlier research on the original sample established a relationship between high tolerance in youth and the later development of alcoholism.

Tolerance levels are subject to alteration following a period of abstinence. Practitioners in Seattle, Washington, working from a harm reduction model, go to great pains to warn their clients immediately on their release from jail, "Don't take your usual level of drugs. Your body won't be able to handle it." Clients have died or nearly died in the past as they rush from jail to take their usual drug dose. (personal communication; May 12, 2008.)

Tolerance reversal is the phenomenon associated with aging in which the drinker loses his or her ability to handle alcohol. The liver is no longer efficient, and the experienced drinker now gets drunk on the first drink.

Cross-tolerance occurs as the tolerance developed for one drug generalizes to another drug in the same pharmaceutical class. Cross-tolerance also can be understood as tolerance to a substance to which the individual had not previously been exposed (WHO, 2011b). Barbiturates, general anesthetics, and alcohol are all sedative-hypnotic drugs, so tolerance for one is tolerance for all.

Withdrawal is defined by the *DSM–IV–TR* (APA, 2000) as "a maladaptive behavioral change, with physiological and cognitive concomitants" related to a reduction of intake following prolonged use of a substance. When the depressant effects of a sedative drug such as alcohol are removed, there is a rebound effect, and the central nervous system becomes hyperactive. This is because if the drug causes one effect, the body adapts, and removal of the drug brings the opposite reaction. (e.g., opioids may produce constipation, whereas withdrawal produces diarrhea.)

For stimulants such as cocaine and crack, the visible withdrawal reaction is relatively mild (APA, 2000; Linden, 2011). Depression following the discontinued use of stimulants is common, however, as the person's body crashes from the artificially induced high. The craving for more of the drug can be relentless during this period. There are no withdrawal symptoms with LSD, however.

Withdrawal symptoms usually start within 24 hours and can last up to several days. The typical medical treatment for alcohol withdrawal involves the use of another drug from the same class. The use of newer drugs such as Topamax, which helps restore neurotransmitter balance; beta blockers, which reduce anxiety; and naltrexone, which blocks the pleasurable effects of alcohol and reduces cravings have been successful (Jung, 2010). Black coffee and other lay remedies do nothing to speed up the brain's recovery from a night or weekend of indulgence. Caffeine plus alcohol creates a wide-awake drunk; reaction time is still impaired. Experiments with mice show that even when caffeine is administered, cognitive impairment persists (Highfield, 2011). Even the day following a binge, functions involving coordination and concentration are seriously altered. The most common and least debilitating of the postintoxication withdrawal syndromes is the *hangover*. A hangover simply has to be lived through; the condition is unpleasant but not dangerous. People who do not get hangovers after a hard night of drinking should realize this lack of aftereffects could signal addiction. Advice to prevent a hangover is to drink on a full stomach; avoid darker drinks, such as brandy, red wine, tequila, and whiskey, which have a higher content of congeners (toxic byproducts of alcohol fermentation); and drink a lot of non-alcoholic liquids, such as water (Lee, 2001). Better yet, drink moderately in the first place.

About 50% of alcohol-dependent patients develop at least some clinical symptoms of withdrawal. Yet, fewer than 5% of alcohol-dependent people ever have a grand mal seizure during withdrawal (usually on day two) or develop the DTs (delirium tremens) (Schuckit, 2009). Withdrawal from alcohol for seriously addicted persons consists of such symptoms as tremor of the hands, tongue, or eyelids; nausea or vomiting; anxiety, depressed mood, or irritability; illusions; headache; and insomnia. For several months after the last drink has been consumed, insomnia may be a problem (Schuckit, 2009). Seizures may occur. Patients who have gotten into serious trouble with alcohol may be found in the detoxification wings of local hospitals. Of those who develop withdrawal symptoms, fewer than 10% will develop severe symptoms such as tremors (APA, 2000). Seizures are experienced by up to 15% of persons with alcoholism during withdrawal. Structural brain imaging shows brain shrinkage in the frontal lobes of persons who have had seizures. DTs, which are rare but life threatening, involve visual and auditory hallucinations. DTs can be avoided by coming off the alcohol gradually or by using a depressant medication such as diazepam (Valium) or chlordiazepoxide (Librium) (Schuckit, 2009).

Different drugs bring different withdrawal symptoms. Withdrawal from heroin or other opiates causes diarrhea, chills, fever, and a runny nose (Maisto et al., 2010). Caffeine withdrawal produces frontal headaches, as many coffee drinkers know. Valium withdrawal produces seizures that may occur two or more weeks after cessation of drug use. Because persons who are addicted to alcohol are sometimes prescription drug misusers too, which is a big problem in Norway, clients in inpatient treatment commonly have seizures long after their bodies are clear of the alcohol.

The most powerful portrayal of the throes of withdrawal is given in the classic movie *The Lost Weekend,* produced by Billy Wilder in 1945. Starring Ray Milland and Jane Wyman, this movie marked a milestone in viewing alcoholism as a progressive and chronic disease. The long, lonely weekend contains one unforgettable scene as the hero, locked in a mental ward, suffers extremely gross hallucinations.

Blackouts are perhaps the most intriguing phenomenon associated with alcohol use and the one about which the least is known neurologically. *Blackout* is a term used by both habitual heavy drinkers and health researchers to describe the total inability to recall events that occurred while the person was drunk, even though the person appeared in a normal state of mind at the time. There is no lapse of consciousness with a blackout. The inability to store knowledge in long-term memory is attributed to a high blood alcohol level, usually over 0.15 blood alcohol concentration (BAC) (White, 2004). As more alcohol is consumed, larger sections of the brain are turned off, preventing cells from firing and new memories from being laid down (NIAAA, 2004). When scientists study states of intoxication in the laboratory in order to better understand the phenomena of blackouts, they find that these states are neither selective nor predictable, nor can they be anticipated by observed behavior. Blackouts are much more common among social drinkers than previously believed. About half of college students report they have experienced blackouts at some point (NIAAA, 2004). Females appear to be especially susceptible to this condition after a bout of heavy drinking. The exact neurological process of this loss of memory is not fully understood. Research shows that college students are at special risks for blackouts as they often drink too much too fast. Fragmentary blackouts are commonly reported by students. Such partial memory blackouts can contribute to greater alcohol misuse in the future as drinkers may fill in the memory gaps with false positive recollections (Bhattacharya, 2003).

The casualness with which persons in recovery discuss blackout episodes can be daunting. Often, the blackout is a source of amusement, if not amazement. Women may tell of waking up in bed in a strange place with a strange man; men may speak of having to search endlessly for a "lost" car. One man proposed marriage, which led to a later altercation. Afterword, friends said these people seemed to be acting normally. A typical difficulty encountered by the alcoholic person is hiding liquor and then searching high and low for it, to no avail. Another memorable scene in *The Lost Weekend* graphically depicts the alcoholic hero's utter joy on leaning far back in a chair and spotting his coveted bottle directly overhead in the ceiling lamp.

When experiencing a blackout, it is said, one can remember something for perhaps 15 minutes, long enough to drive a car to a nearby destination. One can think and plan. But nothing is stored in the memory; there is no way to retrieve the memory once lost. This is in contradistinction to repression, in which the memory is buried in the unconscious. The following story provided, by Lisa L. (2001), is typical:

> The blackout, as explained to me by an RN, is a chemical amnesia. It won't ever come back. There is stuff I did that I had no awareness of later. Many times I'd wake up and wouldn't know how I got home. Sometimes my car was there and sometimes not; "Where did I leave that damn car?" No matter how much I tried, I couldn't get that memory back.

Legally, the implications of a blackout are significant. Around any courtroom you will commonly hear the accused say, "I don't remember, I don't remember." In one case that van Wormer attended, the prosecutor told the jury, "Isn't that convenient? He killed his wife and he says he doesn't remember." In fact, even the defense attorney (who thought her client had repressed the memory) did not realize that the defendant, who had consumed a case of beer, had experienced a blackout. Being in a blackout does not exonerate a person from responsibility for crime—the person was thoroughly conscious at the time and probably knew right from wrong—but it does relate to the truthfulness of a witness with a blocked memory.

Because of the memory problem, a major risk in criminal investigations is that the accused will have been "turned in" by the actual culprit for a crime that the accused did not commit. Then, on the assumption of guilt, the accused will sign a confession. Mark Twain (1876) presented a fictional rendition of this happenstance in *Tom Sawyer*. Fortunately, Tom Sawyer and Huckleberry Finn, who were witnesses, were able to save the falsely accused man shortly before he was to be hanged.

In real life, Joe Giarratano was placed on Virginia's death row after confessing to a murder committed by a right-handed person. Giarratano is left-handed. He was also in an alcohol- and drug-induced blackout at the time the crimes were committed. Because of questions raised in the case, Giarratano's sentence was commuted to life in prison (McCarthy, 2000). A team of supporters continues to work for his release. A second case that has come to light is included in a collection by the Northwestern Law Center on Wrongful Convictions (2002). This case involved Gary Gauger, who was sentenced to death for the murder of his parents. The police coerced a confession by telling him he was in a blackout when he committed the crimes. Eventually, lawyers got the case overturned, and after that, another man confessed to the double murders.

Youth are the most likely age group to experience a blackout; and blackout is even stronger when alcohol is combined with Valium, sleeping pills, or muscle relaxants (White, 2004). Table 3.2 compares commonly used drugs in terms of their modes of administration and addictive qualities. This classification is provided by NIDA.

Opiates or Narcotics *Opiates* are naturally occurring chemicals (derived from the opium poppy) and similar synthetic drugs. Afghanistan has emerged as the global source of opium poppy and is associated with 90% of the world's illicit production (Kinney, 2011). Opiates or narcotics are commonly prescribed by physicians to supplement endorphins in the brain, which prevent the release of pain neurotransmitters (Maisto et al., 2010).

Because there is a constipation effect to this drug, opium originally was used by early Egyptian, Greek, and Arab cultures for the treatment of diarrhea (Fisher & Harrison, 2008). Because opium is not easily absorbed in the digestive tract, oral ingestion produces little effect (Jung, 2010). Opiate users, therefore, inject, smoke, or snort the substance for maximum effect. Some mix heroin and cocaine and shoot it. This extremely dangerous practice is called speedballing (APA, 2000). The even more dangerous combination of heroin and crack is practiced by some older injectors.

Heroin is cheaper and purer than in the past and is therefore more accessible to young people, who can now smoke or snort it. Opiates produce a powerful rush accompanied by feelings of contentment. The rush results because these drugs bind into endorphin receptor sites located in the pleasure centers of the brain (Johnson, 2004). Although used for physical pain, their appeal is in alleviating psychological pain. Morphine, an extract of opium,

TABLE 3.2 | DRUGS OF MISUSE

Substances: Category and Name	Examples of Commercial and Street Names	DEA Schedule*/How Administered**	Acute Effects/Health Risks
Tobacco			
Nicotine	Found in cigarettes, cigars, bidis, and smokeless tobacco (snuff, spit tobacco, chew)	Not scheduled/smoked, snorted, chewed	*Increased blood pressure, and heart rate/chronic lung disease; cardiovascular disease; stroke; cancers of the mouth, pharynx, larynx, esophagus, stomach, pancreas, cervix, kidney, bladder, and acute myeloid leukemia; adverse pregnancy outcomes; addiction*
Alcohol			
Alcohol (ethyl alcohol)	Found in liquor, beer, and wine	Not scheduled/swallowed	*In low doses, euphoria, mild stimulation, relaxation, lowered inhibitions; in higher doses, drowsiness, slurred speech, nausea, emotional volatility, loss of coordination, visual distortions, impaired memory, sexual dysfunction, loss of consciousness/ increased risk of injuries, violence, fetal damage (in pregnant women); depression; neurologic deficits; hypertension; liver and heart disease; addiction; fatal overdose*
Cannabinoids			
Marijuana	Blunt, dope, ganja, grass, herb, joint, bud, Mary Jane, pot, reefer, green, trees, smoke, sinsemilla, skunk, weed	I/smoked, swallowed	*Euphoria; relaxation; slowed reaction time; distorted sensory perception; impaired balance and coordination; increased heart rate and appetite; impaired learning, memory; anxiety; panic attacks; psychosis/cough, frequent respiratory infections; possible mental health decline; addiction*
Hashish	Boom, gangster, hash, hash oil, hemp	I/smoked, swallowed	
Opioids			
Heroin	*Diacetylmorphine:* smack, horse, brown sugar, dope, H, junk, skag, skunk, white horse, China white; cheese (with OTC cold medicine and antihistamine)	I/injected, smoked, snorted	*Euphoria; drowsiness; impaired coordination; dizziness; confusion; nausea; sedation; feeling of heaviness in the body; slowed or arrested breathing/constipation; endocarditis; hepatitis; HIV; addiction; fatal overdose*
Opium	*Laudanum, paregoric:* big O, black stuff, block, gum, hop	II, III, V/swallowed, smoked	
Stimulants			
Cocaine	*Cocaine hydrochloride:* blow, bump, C, candy, Charlie, coke, crack, flake, rock, snow, toot	II/snorted, smoked, injected	*Increased heart rate, blood pressure, body temperature, metabolism; feelings of exhilaration; increased energy, mental alertness; tremors; reduced appetite; irritability; anxiety; panic; paranoia; violent behavior; psychosis/weight loss, insomnia; cardiac or cardiovascular complications; stroke; seizures; addiction*

122

Substance	Examples of Commercial and Street Names	DEA Schedule*/How Administered	Acute Effects/Health Risks
Amphetamine	Biphetamine, Dexedrine: bennies, black beauties, crosses, hearts, LA turnaround, speed, truck drivers, uppers	II/swallowed, snorted, smoked, injected	
Methamphetamine	Desoxyn: meth, ice, crank, chalk, crystal, fire, glass, go fast, speed	II/swallowed, snorted, smoked, injected	Also, for cocaine—nasal damage from snorting; Also, for methamphetamine—severe dental problems
Club Drugs			
MDMA (methylenedioxy-methamphetamine)	Ecstasy, Adam, clarity, Eve, lover's speed, peace, uppers	I/swallowed, snorted, injected	MDMA—mild hallucinogenic effects; increased tactile sensitivity; empathic feelings; lowered inhibition; anxiety; chills; sweating; teeth clenching; muscle cramping/sleep disturbances; depression; impaired memory; hyperthermia; addiction
Flunitrazepam***	Rohypnol: forget-me pill, Mexican Valium, R2, roach, Roche, roofies, roofinol, rope, rophies	IV/swallowed, snorted	Flunitrazepam—sedation; muscle relaxation; confusion; memory loss; dizziness; impaired coordination/addiction
GHB***	Gamma-hydroxybutyrate: G, Georgia home boy, grievous bodily harm, liquid ecstasy, soap, scoop, goop, liquid X	I/swallowed	GHB—drowsiness; nausea; headache; disorientation; loss of coordination; memory loss/unconsciousness; seizures; coma
Dissociative Drugs			
Ketamine	Ketalar SV: cat Valium, K, Special K, vitamin K	III/injected, snorted, smoked	Feelings of being separate from one's body and environment; impaired motor function/anxiety; tremors; numbness; memory loss; nausea
PCP and analogs	Phencyclidine: angel dust, boat, hog, love boat, peace pill	I, II/swallowed, smoked, injected	Also, for ketamine—analgesia; impaired memory; delirium; respiratory depression and arrest; death
Salvia divinorum	Salvia, Shepherdess's Herb, Maria Pastora, magic mint, Sally-D	Not scheduled/chewed, swallowed, smoked	Also, for PCP and analogs—analgesia; psychosis; aggression; violence; slurred speech; loss of coordination; hallucinations
Dextromethorphan (DXM)	Found in some cough and cold medications: Robotripping, Robo, Triple C	Not scheduled/swallowed	Also, for DXM—euphoria; slurred speech; confusion; dizziness; distorted visual perceptions
Hallucinogens			
LSD	Lysergic acid diethylamide: acid, blotter, cubes, microdot yellow sunshine, blue heaven	I/swallowed, absorbed through mouth tissues	Altered states of perception and feeling; hallucinations; nausea
Mescaline	Buttons, cactus, mesc, peyote	I/swallowed, smoked	Also, LSD and mescaline—increased body temperature, heart rate, blood pressure; loss of appetite; sweating; sleeplessness; numbness, dizziness, weakness, tremors; impulsive behavior; rapid shifts in emotion
Psilocybin	Magic mushrooms, purple passion, shrooms, little smoke	I/swallowed	Also, for LSD—Flashbacks, Hallucinogen Persisting Perception Disorder; Also, for psilocybin—nervousness; paranoia; panic

123

TABLE 3.2 | CONTINUED

Substances: Category and Name	Examples of Commercial and Street Names	DEA Schedule*/How Administered**	Acute Effects/Health Risks
Other Compounds			
Anabolic Steroids	Anadrol, Oxandrin, Durabolin, Depo-Testosterone, Equipoise: roids, juice, gym candy, pumpers	III/injected, swallowed, applied to skin	**Steroids**—*no intoxication effects*/hypertension; blood clotting and cholesterol changes; liver cysts; hostility and aggression; acne; in adolescents—premature stoppage of growth; in males—prostate cancer, reduced sperm production, shrunken testicles, breast enlargement; in females—menstrual irregularities, development of beard and other masculine characteristics
Inhalants	Solvents (paint thinners, gasoline, glues); gases (butane, propane, aerosol propellants, nitrous oxide); nitrites (isoamyl, isobutyl, cyclohexyl): laughing gas, poppers, snappers, whippets	Not scheduled/inhaled through nose or mouth	**Inhalants** (varies by chemical)—*stimulation; loss of inhibition; headache; nausea or vomiting; slurred speech; loss of motor coordination; wheezing/cramps;* muscle weakness; depression; memory impairment; damage to cardiovascular and nervous systems; unconsciousness; sudden death
Prescription Medications			
CNS Depressants			
Stimulants	For more information on prescription medications, please visit http://www.nida.nih.gov/DrugPages/PrescripDrugsChart.html		
Opioid Pain Relievers			

*The Roman numerals beside the drugs indicate their classification by the DEA. Schedule I and II drugs have a high potential for abuse. They require greater storage security and have a quota on manufacturing, among other restrictions. Schedule I drugs are available for research only and have no approved medical use; Schedule II drugs are available only by prescription (unrefillable) and require a form for ordering. Schedule III and IV drugs are available by prescription, may have five refills in 6 months, and may be ordered orally. Some Schedule V drugs are available over the counter.

**Some of the health risks are directly related to the route of drug administration. For example, injection drug use can increase the risk of infection through needle contamination with staphylococci, HIV, hepatitis, and other organisms.

***Associated with sexual assaults.

Source: NIDA (2010): *Commonly Abused Drugs.* Retrieved from http://www.drugabuse.gov/DrugPages/DrugsofAbuse.html.

was isolated from opium in the early 1800s and was widely available until the 1900s when its nonmedical use was banned (Fisher & Harrison, 2008). Morphine is a powerful pain reliever and antidiarrhetic agent. It effectively blocks pain signals at the spine, a practice that is revolutionizing surgery.

Heroin usually appears as a white or brown powder and is a synthetic derivative of morphine. It was originally developed to treat opium and morphine addiction. The short-term effects of heroin use appear soon after a single dose, such as by injection. The effect, which is a surge of euphoria, or "rush," is accompanied by a warm flushing of the skin and a sense of heaviness (NIDA, 2010). Then the user typically nods off.

Associated with older drug addicts, heroin has experienced a resurgence in popularity with young street sellers, who often market heroin and cocaine together. As the drug is increasingly pure today, it can be snorted as well as smoked (chasing the dragon) (Kinney, 2011).

Morphine and heroin are rapidly metabolized by the liver and excreted by the kidneys, and they disappear from the body in 4 to 5 hours. Tolerance is incredibly strong for this drug, with users continually chasing that first high. The user must use more and more of the drug to get high as tolerance develops. Withdrawal in regular users may occur after a few hours; drug craving, muscle pain, restlessness, cold flashes, diarrhea, and vomiting may occur (NIDA, 2010). Withdrawal is painful and characterized by hyperexcitability, but this withdrawal is not dangerous compared to alcohol withdrawal, as Kinney (2011) suggests. The horrible agony of heroin withdrawal was presented in the wrenching bedroom scene in the British film *Trainspotting,* based on Welsh's (1996) novel of the same title.

Heroin overdose occurs due to a reaction to impurities present in this street drug. In Britain, where heroin may be prescribed directly under the close supervision of a registered physician, there are no such dangers accompanying its use. Probably the best-known opioid to treat addicts, methadone, is used in Britain, as in the United States, to block withdrawal symptoms and reduce cravings. Addictive and euphoric for nonaddicts, its euphoric effects are much less than those of heroin (Perkinson, 2012). The effect of orally administered methadone lasts up to 72 hours. Heroin and methadone maintenance treatment are provided in Britain, the United States, and many other countries to reduce contraction of HIV/AIDS, to reduce the patient's temptation to engage in crime to support the habit, and to monitor other drug use. The forms of treatment are a major component in the harm reduction philosophy geared to helping the addict live a stable and normal life.

OxyContin, a morphine-like substance, was introduced as a painkiller for terminally ill cancer patients. The advantage of this drug is that it is time released and effective over a long period (Maisto et al., 2010). Unfortunately, this drug is in big demand in the underground drug market. Illegal drug prescriptions and pharmacy robberies have escalated. Numerous deaths from overdoses have been reported in Kentucky and Ohio. Drug users crush the tiny white tablets to remove the time-release coating and then snort or boil them to inject the drug to get their high. Hospitalizations related to prescription drugs are up fivefold in the last decade, and overdose deaths have increased fourfold. More high school seniors report recreational use of tranquilizers or prescription narcotics, like OxyContin and acetominphen and amphetamine (Vicodin), than heroin and cocaine combined (Zuger, 2011).

To curb the problem, new restrictions are being placed on the way this drug is prescribed, and physicians and other prescribers are being more cautious. The pharmaceutical companies have now altered the formula to produce a harder casing so that people can't crush the tablet to produce a powder to inject or snort (Goodenough and Zezima, 2011). Unfortunately, people in need of pain relief from cancer and other diseases may be deprived of the help they need due to the tighter restrictions.

Opioids, including OxyContin, Darvon, and Vicodin, are the most commonly abused prescription drugs. Because these drugs are legal, doctor shopping is the means by which people often gain access to them. In 2003, Rush Limbaugh, whose earlier tirades against drug users are well known, was arrested and convicted of illegally obtaining large quantities of painkilling medications, including OxyContin (Thomas, 2003).

Misuse of pain medication is a growing problem today. According to Gil Kerlikowske (2011), Director of National Drug Control Policy, "Prescription drug abuse is our nation's fastest-growing drug problem, with shocking consequences measured by overdose deaths, emergency room visits, treatment admissions, and increases in youth drug use" (p. 1). He was referring in part to data stemming from a survey on emergency room visits. The data showed that in 2009, there were approximately 1.2 million visits to emergency rooms for causes related to pharmaceutical drugs, compared to 627,000 in 2004. These statistics do not include adverse reactions to pharmaceuticals taken as prescribed.

Other statistics from the same source—the Drug Abuse Warning Network's (2011), *The DAWN Report*—reveal a significant increase in male suicide rates in which prescription medication was used. The increase was over 50% from 2005 to 2009 for males aged 21 to 34, and the rate was more than doubled for older age groups. Three prescription opiate medications were the medications that were the most frequently involved in these emergencies—oxycodone, hydrocodone, and methadone. From school surveys, we know that experimentation with these prescription medications and with Oxycontin, Vicodin, and methylphenidate (Ritalin) is rampant. One in five high school students report taking a prescription drug for nonmedical reasons. They get these drugs from friends and from their home medicine cabinets (see Chapter 6). In Florida, deaths related to prescription drug abuse are so common that the state has become infamous for the "pill mills" that distribute pain pills onsite without any tracking. Legislation was recently passed to make it harder for these clinics to operate (Editor, 2010). Florida has a high population of older adults, some of whom consume large quantities of pain medication. Unlike young pill misusers, they start taking them for legitimate reasons, but like the young pill misusers, some become addicted.

Persons of all ages are not just getting prescriptions from their doctors but are ordering such medications over the Internet without a prescription. One of the impacts of the availability of these dangerous mood-altering drugs is seen in driving incidents, some of which are fatal (Goodenough & Zezima, 2010). This issue is creating a major problem for law enforcement because there is no agreement on what level of drugs in the blood impairs driving. Prosecution creates difficulties as well for the same reason.

INHALANTS

Used almost exclusively by children and teens, inhalants are a group of volatile chemicals that easily evaporate and can be inhaled, often directly from their container. These gaseous substances, which were never intended for human consumption, are primarily nervous system depressants (McNeece & DiNitto, 2005). Most of the inhalants ingested today are common household products found in the kitchen or garage: aerosols, paint, gasoline, glue, and lighter fluid. Users sniff, or "huff," these substances, sometimes by putting their heads in a paper bag to inhale the vapors. The intoxication produced by most inhalants is comparable to that produced by alcohol and includes a light headache (NIDA, 2010). At high levels, permanent damage can be done to the central and peripheral nervous systems (APA, 2000). With repeated inhalations, some may feel drowsy for several hours and experience a lingering headache (NIDA, 2010). An overdose can lead to coma. Sniffing highly concentrated amounts of the chemicals can directly induce heart failure or death within minutes of repeated inhalations.

In Toronto, a study of homeless youths found that 10% had inhaled solvents (e.g., paint thinners or removers, gasoline, or glue) in the past month. A Manitoba report revealed that half the children who lived on a First Nations reserve had inhaled solvents (Dell, 2005).

STIMULANTS

Substances in this category stimulate the central nervous system, increasing alertness and relieving fatigue. Stimulants range from mild, such as caffeine and nicotine, to the more powerful cocaine and methamphetamines. Stimulants may be sniffed, smoked, injected, or swallowed. Physiological reactions to stimulants include increased pulse and blood pressure rates, dilated pupils, insomnia, and loss of appetite. Usage may be chronic or episodic, with binges punctuated by brief drug-free periods. As with alcohol misuse, aggressive or violent behavior is associated with amphetamine dependence (APA, 2000). As tolerance develops, substantial escalation of the dose is common.

COCAINE The South American coca plant can be used to provide energy and stave off hunger. When chewed, it rarely creates social or medical problems. When the leaves are soaked and mashed, however, the more potent drug, cocaine, is then extracted from a coca paste as a white powder (Fisher &

Harrison, 2008). In its powder form, cocaine is usually snorted. It may also be dissolved in water and injected or smoked as freebase cocaine or crack.

Today, some users convert cocaine into crack (named for the cracking sound heard when the mixture is smoked), which involves cooking cocaine in a mixture of water, ammonia, and baking soda. Whereas snorted cocaine takes several minutes to reach the brain, the cooked crack delivers the same effect in seconds. Developed in the mid-1980s, crack is more concentrated than other forms of cocaine because the water base is boiled out through the heating process. The product is a crystal, or rock (Jung, 2010). Almost 15% of Americans have tried cocaine, with 6% having tried it by their senior year of high school (Volkow, 2010a). Though the effect is much more immediate when it is smoked or injected than when snorted, cocaine's behavioral effects do not differ much with the means by which this drug is delivered. Feelings of sexual arousal often accompany cocaine use, probably because of an increase in blood flow to the genitals (Stevens & Smith, 2004). Cocaine is associated with violence; today, crack use is down and heroin use is up in inner cities. Researchers generally attribute the decreased homicide rate to this decline in the popularity of crack cocaine and the turf wars associated with its sales (Finkelhor & Jones, 2006).

Cocaine is rapidly metabolized by the brain from the bloodstream and then travels back to the blood. Positron emission tomography (PET) scanners show that cocaine works by blocking dopamine transporter sites, preventing the reuptake of dopamine. The drug can be found in the urine up to 8 hours after ingestion. The high lasts only about 15 to 20 minutes (Perkinson, 2012). Short-acting drugs such as cocaine wear off quickly and leave an unpleasant crash in the wake. The addictive nature of cocaine is revealed in rat and primate studies; addicted rats will continue to press a lever administering cocaine, to the neglect of food and water. Eventually, they die of seizures or dehydration. Given a choice between food and cocaine, monkeys consistently choose cocaine (Perkinson, 2012). Because it is easy to develop a tolerance for cocaine, the frequency and dosage must be increased to maintain the same effect. In heavy cocaine users, dopamine levels are quickly depleted, which leads to severe depression, aggressive behavior, anxiety, and intense craving. Cocaine abusers can also experience severe paranoia—a temporary state of full-blown paranoid psychosis in which they lose touch with reality and experience auditory hallucinations (NIDA, 2010). Damage to the heart is another major consequence of regular cocaine use. Acting directly on the heart muscle, cocaine causes the heart to beat inefficiently. The most common causes of death from cocaine are heart attacks, strokes, and respiratory failure (NIDA, 2010).

Scientists have found that cocaine misuse coupled with the use of alcohol leads to poorer performance on tests of learning and memory than does the ingestion of either cocaine or alcohol alone. The negative effects on thinking persist for at least a month after the substance has been uses. The mixture of cocaine and alcohol is probably the most lethal of any two-drug combinations known (NIDA, 2010).

AMPHETAMINES AND METHAMPHETAMINES Unlike cocaine, amphetamines are synthetic drugs, yet many of the physiological effects are the same. Amphetamines in nonhyperactive people increase their adrenaline level and suppress the appetite. Hence, they are widely used as diet pills. Tolerance develops quickly, however, so the dosage must be increased. Ritalin is an example of an amphetamine; it is a prescription drug used to treat hyperactivity. Ritalin increases dopamine levels, enabling kids with ADHD to focus, filter out distractions, and make decisions based on reason rather than emotion. Although generally considered relatively harmless, recent research with gene expression in an animal model suggests that Ritalin has the potential for causing long-term changes in brain cell structure and function ("Ritalin and Cocaine," 2011). There is some indication as well that children who have been prescribed Ritalin over a long period of time are attracted to cocaine as a replacement drug because of a chemical similarity.

Methamphetamines (meth or crank) are usually available in powdered (crystal meth) form and can be snorted, injected, or smoked to produce a 4- to 16-hour high (Abadinsky, 2011). Smoking is the popular form of ingestion in San Diego, while in Texas most users inject it (NIDA, 2002). When smoked, the meth high can last 8 to 24 hours, compared to only a fraction of that time for cocaine (Perkinson, 2012).

This drug is hardly new. Nazi troops used methamphetamines to stay awake during World War II battles, and it was later associated with Hell's Angels motorcycle gangs (Stewart & Sitaramiah, 1997). Today, a far more potent formula using common chemicals has been developed. This drug is cheap to make and can be manufactured easily in local laboratories because the ingredients are readily available. Meth is sometimes referred to as the poor person's cocaine. It is also popularly said that compared to cocaine, meth gives more "bang for the buck."

Animal research consistently shows that high doses of meth damage neuron cell endings (NIDA, 2010). And in humans, over time, this drug appears to cause reduced levels of dopamine, which can result in uncontrollable shaking, symptoms like those of Parkinson's disease. The active ingredient is either ephedrine or pseudoephedrine, both of which are found in over-the-counter cold medicines. (In 2006, Congress passed a law restricting open sales of cold medicine, for example pseudoephedrine [Sudafed], containing these ingredients.) In meth labs, products such as drain cleaners are used to transform ephedrine or pseudoephedrine into a powder that can be ingested. Compared to cocaine, meth has a much longer duration, although the rush is not as strong when the drug is snorted. National surveys show a welcome decline in the percentage of teens who have tried this drug from, over 4.7% to around 1% (NIDA, 2010). Because of its energizing properties and relatively low cost, meth remains popular among blue-collar workers in the Midwest, many of whom have more than one job. Its manufacture is extremely hazardous because of the toxic fumes and possible explosions during the cooking process.

The new restrictions on the sale of products containing pseudoephedrine and ephedrine have successfully reduced home production of meth. Meth use has remained fairly constant, however, as supplies continue to be imported from Mexico. A purer form of the drug, called ice, is smoked today at alarming rates, triggering a rise in meth addiction and treatment admissions. Ice can cause convulsions, and an overdose can cause coma and death (Perkinson, 2012).

Burn units in Michigan have experienced a recent increase in cases due to changes in the production of these drugs that has paralleled a statewide crackdown. Today's meth cooks favor small batches, made in 2-liter soda pop bottles, often in cars or outbuildings, according to a news story in the *Kalamazoo Gazette* (Parker, 2011). These small operations are more common and more deadly: In 2010, there were 37 confirmed lab fires, with 32 people injured and three deaths. Five years after Congress passed restrictions on the sales of pseudoephedrine drugs to keep them behind sales counters and required pharmacists to keep records on the sales, there is a rise in meth lab seizures, concentrated in the South and Midwest (Goodenough, 2011) as drug users find new ways to get around the laws. A woman interviewed for the *Kalamazoo Gazette* article about the restrictions on buying cold medicine said of the limits and the requirement to show identification whenever she buys Zyrtec-D: "It's very irritating. I'm 77 years old with a head full of white hair, so they should look at me and know I'm not making meth" (p. A19). The toll on local governments in terms of cleanups of toxic waste left by home labs, the care for neglected children of heavy drug users, domestic violence, and criminal justice has been enormous. Associated with rough sex, meth sometimes causes physical injury in the partner of a meth user. The sex drive is tremendously enhanced under the influence of meth. This fact, as Reding (2009) suggests, may explain why meth use in gay communities is linked to huge increases in AIDS and hepatitis C.

Following publication of *Methland,* by Nick Reding (2009), a news story in the Sunday edition of the *Des Moines Register* highlighted the nonfiction book and the town of Oelwein, Iowa, on which it was based. Reding selected Olwein as the focus of his meth study, as we learn in the news account, because of the high number of burn victims of meth lab explosions that occurred there (Kilen, 2009). This fact drew Reding to set up residence in the town and to interview people whose lives were forever changed because of the meth epidemic. One of the book's burn victims interviewed for the newspaper story, who had spent months in the hospital and then served time in prison, had this to say: "I had always just thought of drugs as recreational. But when you look at the science of meth, it lends itself to being a working man's drug. You don't need to stop to eat, drink or sleep…. It's the devil inside you. I wished I never did it. After the fire I couldn't walk, see or go to the bathroom. I had to drink through a straw" (p. 2E).

Use of methamphetamines is linked to several serious medical complications, such as heart damage, stroke, and psychosis. Long-term neurological damage can result. A response to heavy meth use familiar to medical professionals is the sensation of insects creeping under the skin. Users often scratch their skin to the point of bleeding. Users stay awake for days, often weeks, at a time. Paranoia, aggression, and a breakdown in the immune system often occur with regular use of this drug. Heavy meth users, like cocaine users, are often thin and even emaciated. *Methland* clearly documents these dramatic changes. As we hear from the story of the owner of a beauty salon:

> Her husband accused his wife of having sex with a stranger in the bed next to him (she was hiding with her daughter in an adjourning room at the time), and then he tried to kill her. (p. 31)

For recovery, physical withdrawal is not the problem but, rather, anhedonia. *Anhedonia* is an inability to experience pleasure at the normal joys of life. As an informant describes the phenomenon in *Methland*:

> When you take away meth, nothing natural—sex, a glass of water, a good meal, anything for which we are supposed to be rewarded—feels good. The only thing that feels good is more meth." (pp. 48–49)

Lisa Kuennen (in a talk before a social work class of September 11, 2006) shared how after years on meth, she was unable to experience pleasure in any normal way:

> It took me 3 years to get out of that funk. I was down, unable to enjoy anything. I could go outside and feel the sun but it wouldn't warm me. This last year was the first time I felt the sun—I felt alive for the first time. Sometimes I just enjoy looking at the trees and flowers or the cloud formations in the sky.

NICOTINE   Nicotine, a highly toxic central nervous system stimulant, comes from the dried tobacco plant, which is native to North America. Nicotine is a natural insecticide. Native Americans have known about tobacco for centuries; documented use by the Mayan culture goes back more than 2,000 years (*Encyclopedia of Drugs and Addictive Substances*, 2011). Dependence on nicotine resembles that of the other drugs discussed in this chapter in that it produces compulsive patterns of use, craving, tolerance, and physical dependence. Tobacco use kills approximately 440,000 Americans each year; one in every five U.S. deaths can be blamed on smoking (Volkow, 2009). Smoking is directly responsible for approximately 90% of lung cancer deaths and 80–90% of emphysema and chronic bronchitis deaths (American Lung Association, 2006). Smoking harms nearly every organ in the body, causes many diseases, and compromises smokers' health in general (Volkow, 2009). Tobacco smoke contains many toxic compounds, including the highly addictive nicotine, tar, and carbon monoxide (Volkow, 2009). Alone or in combination, these compounds are responsible for most smoking-related diseases. A major cause of stroke, tobacco use is the leading cause of preventable death in the United States (NIDA, 2010).

Although far less serious than lung or heart disease, premature wrinkling of the skin has long been associated with smoking. Researchers are learning how smoking causes wrinkling by reducing the skin's elasticity. In a report from the Mayo Clinic, Hurt (2010) explains that the over 4,000 chemicals in tobacco smoke damage collagen and elastin, which are fibers that give the skin its strength and elasticity. As a result, skin begins to sag and wrinkle prematurely. In an earlier study, London dermatologists discovered that a gene implicated in wrinkles caused by sunbathing is also highly active in smokers ("Wrinkles Are Traced," 2001).

Cigarette and cigar smoking, pipe smoking, and tobacco chewing are the favorite methods of tobacco use. (The nicotine patch is a modern means of helping wean smokers from their habit.) After inhalation, it takes about 7 seconds for nicotine to reach the brain. One of the effects is to elevate blood and brain levels of serotonin, producing a calming effect. Uniquely, this drug can stimulate or relax the user depending on his or her emotional state and expectations. In light of this fact, combat troops often use tobacco as a stimulant to stay alert, as a stress reliever, a reward during a long day, and a way to ease the boredom of long periods of inactivity (Neale, 2008). A major feature of cigarette smoking is its ability to help the smoker lose weight through the release of specific neurotransmitters and the chronic stimulation that increases metabolism (APA, 2000).

Among the facts known about tobacco use from the extensive research on this product and on smokers is that a high percentage of persons addicted to alcohol also smoke cigarettes, with many smoking over one pack a day (NIAAA, 2007). Around 60–75% of people in substance abuse treatment programs smoke cigarettes ("Struggling with Alcohol," 2008). The reason for the co-occurrence of alcoholism and smoking is not entirely clear but may relate to the general tendency for addictive people to be highly susceptible to dependence on whichever drugs are readily available to them.

Studies show that rats bred for alcohol addiction have a high susceptibility for nicotine addiction compared to other rats even before they are ever exposed to alcohol (Lê, Li, et al., 2006). Interestingly, these highly addictive rats show little interest in cocaine when it is made available.

Another significant rat study highlights the effects of polydrug interactions. Parnell, West, and Chen (2006) showed that the presence of nicotine decreases BAC levels. This means drinkers who smoke have to consume more alcohol for the same effect as nonsmokers. This in turn causes more physiological damage. Compounding this innate tendency toward alcohol-nicotine addiction is another factor: cross-tolerance. Cross-tolerance is thought to occur through an interaction between alcohol and tobacco at nicotine receptors in the brain at the point where dopamine is released (NIAAA, 2007). This cross-tolerance is further revealed in the fact that to achieve the desired effect, alcoholic smokers may require higher doses of nicotine in their nicotine patches than people less accustomed to drinking heavily. Taken together, alcohol and tobacco greatly increase one's risk of getting cardiovascular and lung diseases, along with various forms of cancer. The risk involved in both smoking and drinking, according to the NIAAA report, is much higher than the sum of the risks for use of each drug individually. Changes in the liver, coupled with the breakdown of the immune system caused by long-term alcohol misuse, create a heightened susceptibility to the toxic chemicals released in the burning cigarette. An examination of the brains of alcoholic smokers found more severe brain damage had occurred than was the case in the brains of persons with alcoholism or smoking addiction alone (Durazzo, Gazdzinski, Banys, & Meyerhoff, 2004). A related fact is that nicotine dependence is common among individuals with mental disorders such as schizophrenia or bipolar disorder; 50–90% of individuals with serious mental disorders smoke (NIAAA, 2007).

When smokers are in treatment for alcohol use disorders, a question raised is: Should they abstain from all addictive behaviors at once, or should they focus only on the alcohol addiction? Because clients often use nicotine to deal with stress, many who are at a substance abuse treatment center are naturally reluctant to give up this second drug. A study using brain scans to discover how cognitive function changes with substance abuse treatment over a 9-month period found that the nonsmokers' brains recovered better as determined by performance on memory tests than did those who smoked regularly ("Struggling with alcohol?" 2008). As a result of such research and because tobacco dependence is a life-threatening addiction, many treatment programs now talk about nicotine and encourage patients (and staff) to quit smoking and refer them to a physician for nicotine-replacement therapy or prescription medication.

Cigarette smoking declined in the United States more than 50% between 1965 and 2009 (American Lung Association, 2011). In 2009, 20.6% of adults (over the age of 18) were current smokers. Males tend to have significantly higher rates of smoking prevalence than females. In 2009, 23.5% percent of males were current smokers compared to 17.9% of females.

The WHO (2011c) has declared tobacco use one of the biggest public health threats the world has ever faced. This United Nations organization urged all nations to conduct campaigns against smoking and to sign the Framework Convention on Tobacco Control, which obliges them to work to cut smoking rates and to protect citizens from secondhand smoke. Over 170 countries have signed up. China, a nation with 300 million smokers, has imposed a ban on smoking in restaurants and other public places (Haas, 2011). However, the ban is thought to have little chance of success due to the deeply entrenched smoking culture that is dominant there. Business deals are sealed with gifts of expensive tobacco, and cigarettes are exchanged in businessmen's greetings. Public health campaigns have been lacking, so few accept the connection between smoking and lung disease.

At the invitation of van Wormer, an American businessman who works in China agreed to share his experience related to the smoking culture:

> A few months ago, I was sitting in the office of my business partner's house and I noticed five or six cartons of high quality cigarettes in the closet. These were the kind that our governor's friends always smoked; they retail for about $9.50 a pack. I asked my friend why he had so many, and his response was that a friend of his that works for the government in a different city sold them to him. When

I asked him how this governor got ahold of so many cigarettes, he explained they were "gifts" from various acquaintances. Money moves everything in China, but these government officials are deathly afraid to take any cash bribes from people in exchange for special treatment. So my partner explained that they use things like cigarettes and expensive liquor in place of money. They are simply innocent gifts, so nobody really pays attention to it. I then asked him what he planned to do with them. He let me know that if we ever needed to win favor with any local government officials here, we would use them. This is, however, a smaller-sized city and things are a little bit different in the major cities.

Anytime I reach for a cigarette for myself, I *always* look at my surroundings. I have to judge who is around and decide whether to offer someone a cigarette. At a bar with friends or even when meeting people the first time it's a way to show respect and friendliness. Not offering another person a cigarette doesn't always necessarily mean you're being rude, but the gesture is often a very important step in connecting with people. For instance, every day when I walk out of my apartment and go past the security guards at the front gate, I will usually hand each of them a cigarette and say hello. My friends here taught me a long time ago that doing this will ensure that you or your guests will never be hassled by whatever regulations the guards are supposed to enforce. I even instinctively handed out cigarettes to the health inspector and the officers with him when they came to collect some information from my restaurant. And of course, depending where I am at, I may constantly be handed cigarettes, almost to the point where I gain a surplus at the end of the night. Due to this, it is very hard to estimate how many packs a week I smoke; sometimes a pack of cigarettes may last three days and sometimes they can disappear in 30 minutes. One last, kind of funny thing is that people still smoke *everywhere* in China. It's different in major cities, but it's not uncommon to see even a bank teller or postal clerk smoking behind their desks.

In a trip to the hospital to see my recovering friend, we all smoked together with an orderly standing right next to us. Our friend still even had an IV in his arm. The most extreme example was the last time I had to buy fireworks. We just finished purchasing them and the owner of the shop offers us a smoke as a friendly gesture. I instinctively went to walk out of the shop to the street before the owner called me back in to have a seat with him. It was definitely a funny feeling to be sitting 40 cm away from about 3–4 metric tons of explosives, smoking a cigarette. (personal communication by Levi Wallace; May 25, 2011)

Manufacturers are reaping tremendous profits from tobacco sales worldwide. Investigative research has revealed that manufacturers have known for a long time that smokers get hooked on cigarettes because of the nicotine they contain. Presumably to increase sales, manufacturers increased the level of nicotine that could be inhaled from cigarettes, according to data supplied by tobacco companies (as required by Massachusetts state law) and analyzed by the Harvard School of Public Health for the years 1998 through 2004 (Smith, 2007). The Harvard researchers have called for regulation of tobacco in much the same way that pharmaceutical products are regulated. Interestingly, Philip Morris issued a report that was used in a lobbying effort to influence politicians in the Czech Republic who had complained that the tobacco industry was saddling the country with huge healthcare expenses ("Philip Morris' Spin," 2001). The report refuted those claims by showing that inasmuch as smokers die sooner than nonsmokers by over 5 years, smokers saved the government millions of dollars from reduced costs in healthcare, pensions, and housing for the elderly. Not surprisingly, a storm of protest emerged from these findings not only in the Czech Republic but also throughout the world. More recently, Philip Morris's profits have suffered a serious decline throughout this part of Europe due to the European Union's requirement for heavy taxation on tobacco products. This has led to much illegal cigarette smuggling and the production of counterfeit cigarette brands ("Cigarette Tax Unbalances Profits," 2009).

As smoking declines in the United States among the non-Hispanic white population, tobacco companies have targeted both non-Hispanic Blacks and Hispanics with intensive merchandising, which includes advertising in media targeted to those communities and sponsorship of civic groups and athletic, cultural, and entertainment events (American Lung Association, 2011). Over $12.5 billion was spent on cigarette advertising and promotion by the five major tobacco companies in 2006. Because most smokers get started before the age of 18, the companies target youths in their advertisements.

Due to nicotine craving, prevention works far better than treatment in curbing tobacco use. No one who smokes, of course, sets out to get addicted. One wonders how many actors, when forced to smoke in the movies, get turned on to nicotine. Malachy McCourt (2000), in his autobiographical *Singing My Him Song*, describes his romance with cigarettes:

> Of the bad habits available, I missed very few. I drank too much, ate too much, philandered too much. I had managed, though, to somehow remain a nonsmoker, a state I remedied at about that time. I really disliked the damn things, but in the course of the commercial (for TV and for Lark cigarettes), I got hooked. I got paid around $300 for the day's work and proceeded to spend thousands of dollars to maintain my new habit, not to mention my damaged health and yellowed teeth and the hundreds of little burn holes I put in various garments (my own and others') over the years. (pp. 33–34)

Quitting smoking, as everyone knows, is immensely difficult; although 80% of smokers desire to quit, only 45% can eventually do so (APA, 2000). Withdrawal effects take place within hours of the last cigarette; one's craving subsides in 3 to 4 weeks. But before then, research shows that former chronic smokers suffer increased feelings of anger, hostility, and aggression (NIDA, 2010). A serendipitous discovery emerged recently when a stroke victim told his doctor his craving for cigarettes had disappeared. Further investigation revealed that smokers with brain damage involving the insula, a region implicated in conscious urges, were more likely than smokers with brain damage not involving the insula to discontinue smoking immediately with no withdrawal problems (Naqvi, Rudrauf, Damasio, & Bechara, 2007). This finding is likely to point researchers in new directions regarding therapies for addictive craving.

Box 3.1	To Die for a Cigarette
	Tammy Pearson, MSW

I have quit smoking. Finally. As an adult, I'd think, "I'm not hooked, I can quit any time." Until the day I said, "I need help." I'm a responsible person; everything else I did was in moderation. Everybody smoked. In elevators, in hospitals as employees, the grocery stores. In those days you just stomped it out in the floor. Those were the days when you'd ride in the car with smoking parents, the windows up, the car going 80 m.p.h. and no seatbelts.

Once I witnessed an outstanding example of a man exhibiting the helplessness of a nicotine addiction. I was living in Washington State and was shopping with my mother. We had just come outside to the parking lot when a man drove past, very aggressive in his hurry. When he got to his selected parking space he quickly lit a cigarette, and began an extreme act of deliberate and desperate smoking. We stayed to observe this whole ordeal. The car windows were up and he was dragging on this cigarette so hard and long that I almost expected him to just rumple it up and stuff it in his mouth, eating it. He smoked it down to where it was burning his fingers, then lit another off of the end. Now, I have also chain-smoked, but when this guy finished the first butt he cracked his car window just barely enough to stuff the butt out. He didn't even want the smoke to escape the car. My mom and I watched the rest of this in disbelief; both of us agreed to never let the other get "that bad" and we went on our way. ...

I remember when the doctor told me I was pregnant. "Now you're going to quit smoking," he said. I made it one-half hour. My son's father's smoke made me sick. I did everything to stop—threw the car ashtray out of the car. Once I went on crutches to the 7–11 at 2 A.M.! I had to have a cigarette. I busted out the stitches in my foot, undoing the recent surgery.

My parents had smoked for years. My dad had a cardiac arrest. He woke up from a coma in a hospital where no smoking was allowed. He woke up totally disoriented. We moved him to the V.A. hospital so he could get a cigarette. He

Box 3.1, "To Die for a Cigarette," presents Tammy Pearson's account of nicotine addiction, an account as gripping as that of any person trying to overcome alcohol or heroin addiction.

CHEWING TOBACCO Also devastating in its effects on the body is chewing tobacco, or snuff. When tobacco is chewed, the nicotine is absorbed into the bloodstream and travels to the brain. In 30 minutes of chewing, the individual intakes as much nicotine as from three cigarettes (National Cancer Institute, 2003). The American Lung Association (2011) provides the following key facts about smokeless (chewing) tobacco.

In the United States, an estimated 3.3% of adults are current smokeless tobacco users; use is much higher among males than females (6.5% vs. 0.4%). Among specific populations, American Indian/Alaska Natives have the highest use (7%), followed by white males (4.3%).

calmed down immediately and came back to himself. There I saw all those veterans—one man had smoked in the navy; he was smoking through his trachea. Later I became Dad's caregiver. Dad had a bubble on his lung that could burst at any time. I would rub his back so that he could breathe and it was horrible. 1988 was the last time I performed CPR on him. Mom and I were still smoking all this time.

In Washington State there was an ad on TV—people were throwing dirt on a grave. "Eventually everybody stops smoking," the ad said. Mom developed respiratory problems; she was on oxygen 24 hours a day. She had to go on Prednisone, a drug that causes your bones to break. I got a job at the National Jewish Medical Center in Denver, where she became a patient. I learned so much. Some of my friends there were world-famous scientists. To try to save my mother they even brought in drugs from foreign countries. Mom was deeply loved by everyone. But no one could save her. She suffered so much. I eventually became her primary caregiver. In April of 2000 we lost her to lung cancer.

For myself, I tried patches. I thought I needed a patch over my mouth! Oh God, that's me. Nobody was more addicted than me.

How did I quit? I didn't quit watching my son get sick from secondhand smoke, my mother dying, all the shameful things I did—smelling like smoke, going around feeling dirty like a salamander. I wished someone would just lock me up!

No, there was never a good time to quit. I worked at the number-one respiratory hospital in the world but I was going to have my cigarette! By now I had scar tissue on my lungs; my lungs were so shot. There never was a good time to quit, certainly not when I was happy; quitting would ruin my whole day. Finally, a bad day came. I was so miserable that any more pain wouldn't matter—"kick me while I'm down." Now is a good time. "I'll use this as a marker," I thought. And I did, and I died a thousand deaths but I did it.

Source: Speech given at the University of Northern Iowa, Cedar Falls, February 13, 2001. Printed with permission of Tammy Pearson.

- Smokeless tobacco contains 28 cancer-causing agents (carcinogens). It also increases the risk of developing cancer of the oral cavity and pancreas.
- Chewing tobacco comes in loose leaf, plug, and twist form. Snuff is finely ground tobacco that can be dry, moist, or in bag-like pouches. Most smokeless tobacco users place the product in the cheek or between their gum and cheek, suck on the tobacco, and spit out or swallow the juices.
- New smokeless tobacco products such as snus and tobacco products that dissolve when put into the mouth do not require the user to spit.
- In 2006, the five largest smokeless tobacco manufacturers spent over $354 million on advertising and promotion, the highest amount ever recorded. The majority of these dollars (57.5%) were spent on price discounts to smokeless tobacco retailers or wholesalers to reduce the price to consumers.

A former snuff user who is also in recovery from alcoholism shares his experience with chewing tobacco:

> When I was 18 years old (I refuse to tell how long ago), I saw an advertisement for Skoal chewing tobacco. It featured an ad with Walt Garrison, who was a football star with the Dallas Cowboys and in rodeos. It featured the phrase "Just a pinch between the cheek and gums." If you sent in the ad, you got a free can of tobacco. I thought it looked cool, so I did. We males are attracted to the use of spit tobacco at an early age (I was floored by the average age of 9) because we think it makes us look macho. I thought I was grown up and had a mystique about me when I first used it. I was hooked for the next 17 years of my life. I burnt my lower lip from chewing, so I switched to my upper lip. I finally said, "Enough is enough!" and quit cold-turkey 26 months ago. But as I thought about it, I had a huge urge to chew again that I did not act on. I have so many friends who use chewing tobacco that started when they were kids years ago, I can imagine the oral cancer epidemic that is forthcoming in the near future. What kids don't realize and tobacco companies don't tell you is that the nicotine is absorbed into the bloodstream very quickly through the lip and has a very short trip to begin its effects on the brain. (Larry Cranston, personal communication, 2000)

Major U.S. tobacco companies are rolling out smokeless tobacco products as a less dangerous alternative to smoking. According to the National Cancer Institute (2003), smokeless tobacco is not a safe alternative and carries many dangers of its own.

Hallucinogens

Hallucinogenic plants have been used for centuries as medicines, to cause an altered sense of reality, and for spiritual or religious purposes. *Psychedelic* is a term employed by users of hallucinogenic chemicals. Such substances occur in the natural world and can be produced synthetically. These drugs overwhelm the central nervous system and produce such desired outcomes as "out-of-body" experiences, sensory illusions, strange tactile sensations, an altered sense of time, and hallucinations (Abadinsky, 2011).

LSD AND PCP   Perhaps the best-known hallucinogen is LSD (lysergic acid diethylamide). This synthetic drug achieved great popularity during the late 1960s and 1970s as youth sought a different level of reality and consciousness along with the collective bonding experiences of "taking a trip." This drug, taken orally, is odorless, colorless, and tasteless; it is often squirted onto a small sugar cube. (A unique property of LSD is that it can be absorbed directly through the skin.) Effects take place approximately 1 hour after use and can last up to 8 hours. Heavy users sometimes experience flashbacks, even years after use; the effect is an involuntary return to the drugged state (Fisher & Harrison, 2008). A key danger in the use of LSD is the drug-induced psychosis that can lead users to think they can, for example, fly out the window or walk on water. Such illusions led to many well-publicized deaths in the late 1960s. "Bad trips" were also commonly reported as the drugged state turned nightmarish for some individuals. The long-term effects of LSD use are not known; this drug is not addictive, but tolerance does develop (APA, 2000).

Phencyclidine (PCP, angel dust), another synthetic drug, became a street drug in the 1970s because of its ability to produce trancelike states. Developed as an anesthetic for humans, it was later used as an animal tranquilizer. It was associated with drug-induced psychosis and violence (Perkinson, 2012). PCP can be swallowed, smoked, snorted, or injected for a high that peaks after 30 minutes and can last for 4 to 6 hours.

PEYOTE AND MESCALINE   The peyote cactus is native to Mexico and the southwestern United States. This psychoactive plant, dried to form a hard button, may be chewed directly or ingested in powder form (Fishbein & Pease, 1996). Native Americans have ritualistically harvested and eaten these plants in ceremonial fashion without ill effects (*Encyclopaedia Britannica*, 2006).

Mescaline, another psychedelic drug, occurs naturally in mushrooms. Less potent than LSD, it was popular during the 1960s. Psilocybin mushrooms, which can be found growing wild throughout the world, produce an intense religious experience in many people and feelings of fear and paranoia in others. Now, for the first time in over 40 years, Johns Hopkins medical researchers are assessing the effects of hallucinogenic substances on human subjects in the laboratory (Tierney, 2010). Researchers hope this study will revive interest in the effects psychedelic drugs such as "magic" mushrooms have on the human brain. These special mushrooms are associated in some parts of the world with religious experiences. The "sacred mushrooms" of Mexico were called God's Flesh by the Aztecs (*Encyclopaedia Britannica*, 2006).

CLUB DRUGS: ECSTASY, ROHYPOL, AND GHB   Developed by a German pharmaceutical firm as an appetite suppressant, MDMA (methylenedioxymethamphetamine), or Ecstasy, which was rediscovered in the 1980s, is sometimes known as a designer drug. Although consumption of drugs like cocaine and marijuana among American teens has stabilized, Ecstasy's popularity has increased exponentially. Churned out from underground factories run by international crime syndicates, Ecstasy can produce both stimulant and psychedelic effects (NIDA, 2010). Chemically, MDMA is similar to amphetamines and to the hallucinogen mescaline. MDMA releases the brain chemical serotonin, elevating mood and acting as a short-term antidepressant. In low doses, Ecstasy produces no hallucinogens but, instead, heightens one's sensory experiences and awareness of self.

MDMA is taken orally, usually as a capsule or tablet. It was initially popular among white adolescents and young adults in the nightclub scene or at weekend-long dance parties known as raves. More recently, the profile of the typical MDMA user has changed, with the drug now affecting a broader range of ethnic groups. MDMA is also popular among urban gay males—some report using MDMA as part of a multiple-drug experience that includes marijuana, cocaine, methamphetamine, ketamine, sildenafil (Viagra), and other legal and illegal substances (NIDA, 2010).

The loud music played at raves is thought to intensify the drug's effect. Ecstasy is relatively inexpensive ($10–$20 per tablet) and long lasting (Fisher & Harrison, 2008). Read the following description from the teenage scene in Fort Worth, Texas (Collier, 2010):

> The kandi kid is rolling hard. His sweaty teenage face is bathed in a supernaturally bright light, even though the surrounding rave is lit only by colored lasers and black lights. The kid is obviously in a rapturous trance. His face is full of awe and gratitude, his eyes gigantic, his body completely void of tension. His wrists, ringed by the fluorescent plastic bracelets that unofficially mark him as a member of the kandi gang, hang tranquilly at his sides. He wants to hug the whole world, and that tangible vibe seems to stretch out before him infinitely. He is a perfect picture of Ecstasy.
>
> The source of this young man's total devotion? Another kid, his white clothes incandescent in the black lights, waving gloved hands in his friend's face, the fingers tipped with multicolored LED lights.
>
> This is not a scene from the famous Dallas clubs in the 1980s, but from an August weekend in a warehouse party in the shadow of downtown Fort Worth. And the new chemical-tribal ritual wasn't connecting only these two kids. They were surrounded by hundreds of their peers. (p. 1)

Although MDMA is often thought of as a nonaddictive, harmless substance, emerging scientific evidence indicates that long-term use of the drug causes brain damage (Harris, 2004). Use of this drug may also lead to dehydration, hypertension, and heart or kidney failure (NIDA, 2010). In fact, as Harris (2004) reports, there have been deaths due to hyponatremia, or low plasma sodium, caused by the consumption of large quantities of water to offset dehydration.

Although users consistently describe that initial high as one of life's greatest experiences, due no doubt to chemical changes in the brain, replicating that original high is close to impossible. Many of the problems associated with this drug stem from the fact that dangerous chemicals are sometimes added. According to information distributed by the harm reduction network DanceSafe (2010), much of what is sold as Ecstasy on the black market actually contains other drugs, such as cocaine, speed, and PCP. Youth who consume Ecstasy tablets are advised to have the tablets chemically tested for foreign substances by DanceSafe representatives. Users are also advised to drink water but not an excessive amount. The deaths associated with Ecstasy use, according to DanceSafe, usually occur as a result of the heat stroke connected with dehydration. In high doses, MDMA can interfere with the body's ability to regulate temperature. On rare but unpredictable occasions, this can lead to a sharp increase in body temperature (NIDA, 2010). Mixing Ecstasy with alcohol or other drugs increases the risk of adverse reactions.

No club drug is benign, as NIDA Director Nora Volkow (2005) notes. Chronic misuse of MDMA appears to produce long-term damage to serotonin-containing neurons in the brain. Damage is most likely associated with depression, sleep abnormalities, and memory disturbances. Despite the damaging aspects, government-approved studies are taking place in Israel, Canada, and Jordan using Ecstasy to treat people with posttraumatic stress disorder (PTSD) and rape victims for whom no other treatment has worked (Drummond, 2010). This treatment is promoted because of the ability of MDMA to reduce the fear response to stimuli and because of anecdotal reports of success in reducing the impact of past trauma. In the United States, MDMA received approval from the Food and Drug Administration (FDA) to be tested on advanced cancer patients suffering from severe anxiety (Weiss, 2005). These compounds have the uncanny ability to induce spiritual or religious experiences.

In the United States, a research grant–funded study is underway that is entirely devoted to former members of the military (Drummond, 2010). Most of the veterans served in Iraq and Afghanistan and have PTSD. The study began with 16 male and female veterans. Earlier research with veterans brought promising results. The veterans receive intensive psychotherapy while they are under the influence of Ecstasy.

Rohypnol, better known as the date rape drug or roofies, is a sedative manufactured in Europe as a sleeping pill. Although it is chemically similar to Valium, it is included here as a newer drug and a partying drug. Rohypnol is cheap, which makes it popular on college campuses and in gay and lesbian bars. Many of the roofies used in the United States are obtained by prescription in Mexico. Although this drug is reportedly used by date rapists, usually dropped surreptitiously into a woman's drink, women are also known to use this drug purposely for its intoxicating effects. Roofies are often used to moderate the effects of a cocaine binge or to enhance the effects of alcohol or heroin. This drug causes amnesia of events that happened while under its influence. Blackouts can last up to 24 hours (Center for Substance Abuse Research, 2004).

GHB (gamma-hydroxybutyrate) is a substance currently circulating within the dance music scene as an alternative to Ecstasy or speed. An odorless, colorless, and nearly tasteless liquid, GHB is misused for bodybuilding effects and, like Rohypnol, is associated with sexual assaults, especially on university campuses (NIDA, 2010).

New Synthetic Substances

Consider these 2011 headlines:

"'Spice'" Traps Troops" (*Star Adviser*)

"'Bath Salts'" Have Dangerous and Long-Lasting Effects, Doctors Say" (Join Together Staff)

"The Drug Is Fake: The High Is Real" (Paynter, *Bloomberg Business Week*)

"Study of Hallucinogen Salvia Shows Intense, Novel Effects" (Desmon, *Johns Hopkins Gazette*)

Some of the reports are frightening, others not. Paynter (2011) refers to "the unlicensed, ingenious, and increasingly scary world of synthetic drugs" (p. 20). There are so many of these products on the market, being used for purposes not originally intended, that it is impossible to keep up with them. Drug tests and sniffing dogs cannot detect their presence. As the states pass legislation outlawing various types of synthetic substances, manufacturers and packagers create or find new variations. There are at least 1,000 synthetic drug makers in the U.S., according to Paynter; this is a quasi-legal industry worth billions. Marketed with warning labels "Not for human consumption," the products are sold in coffee houses and small shops, often as a form of incense.

As a warning to addiction specialists, Volkow (2011) provides basic information on a powdery stimulant drug that is sold in a small can, called bath salts. These chemicals act in the brain like stimulant drugs (indeed they are sometimes touted as cocaine substitutes); thus they present a high abuse and addiction liability. These products, as Volkow warns, have been reported to trigger intense cravings. They can also confer a high risk for other medical adverse effects. Some of these may be linked to the fact that, beyond their known psychoactive ingredients, the contents of these bath salts are largely unknown, which makes the practice of abusing them, by any route, that much more dangerous.

Bath salts have already been linked to an alarming number of emergency room (ER) visits across the country (Join Together Staff, 2011). Doctors and clinicians at U.S. poison centers have indicated that ingesting or snorting bath salts can cause chest pains, increased blood pressure, increased heart rate, agitation, hallucinations, extreme paranoia, and delusions (Volkow, 2011).

The Navy and Air Force are increasingly worried about the impact on military personnel of synthetic substances such as bath salts and others with names such as Spice and K2. These drugs are often referred to as synthetic marijuana; they consist of plant material coated with synthetic chemicals designed to produce an immediate high. Incidents including suicide and serious assaults have taken place in connection with these drugs. The Air Force is now able to detect five of the compounds contained in Spice. All branches of the military are working to develop testing for the new substances ("'Spice' Traps Troops," 2011).

One empirically based laboratory study is now available on another of these popular substances. Salvia is an organic herb that is often smoked like marijuana. Johns Hopkins researchers monitored two men and two women who had taken hallucinogens in the past for 20 sessions during which they inhaled a wide range of doses of the drug in its pure form (reported by Desmon, 2011). The researchers and subjects found that the effects were surprisingly strong, brief, and intensely disorienting but without apparent short-term adverse effects.

CANNABIS (MARIJUANA)

Although cannabis at high doses possesses some of the properties of hallucinogens and at low doses some of the properties of depressants, the *DSM–IV–TR*

(APA, 2000) recommends a separate category for this drug due to its unique behavioral effects. The plant *Cannabis sativa* (Latin for "cultivated hemp") grows wild throughout much of the tropical and temperate zones of the world (Abadinsky, 2011). *Cannabis sativa* is the hemp plant and has varying potency depending on the type of plant, the climate, and the soil. There is evidence that cannabis was cultivated at Jamestown by the early settlers for the hemp fibers used in rope (Doweiko, 2009). Known variously as Indian hemp, reefer, marijuana, pot, or grass, cannabis can be smoked in pipes or in a cigarette called a joint, eaten (as in brownies), or drunk. As the older generation tells the younger generation, the potency of marijuana has drastically increased in the United States. To what extent the marijuana of today is more potent than yesterday is debatable. In fact, according to Greenberg (2006) of the Marijuana Policy Project, the higher delta-9-tetrahydrocannabinol (THC) marijuana used today is only somewhat more potent than earlier varieties. More important, as she states, there is no scientific evidence to demonstrate greater risks of health problems from the modern-day marijuana. A more objective source, the European Monitoring Centre for Drugs and Drug Addiction (King, 2004) reviewed scientific data on the higher potency claims and found them largely unsubstantiated. Media accounts in the United States, however, relying on statements from NIDA, say that the cannabis of today is up to five times more potent than the cannabis in the 1970s (Kershaw & Cathcart, 2009).

Volkow (interviewed by Kershaw and Cathcart, 2009 concerning the risks of today's cannabis) stated, "If you only have access to whiskey, your risk is going to be higher for addiction. Now that people have access to very high potency marijuana, the game is different" (p. ST1). The situation may be too political to determine the truth about marijuana's potency. Another problem, as indicated by Room, Fischer, and colleagues (2010), who believe that the average potency has increased, is the variation internationally and locally in the product and the lack of a valid data set.

Hashish is the resin obtained from the flowering tops of the female plant; it is considerably more potent than marijuana (Room, Fischer, et al., 2010). Tetrahydro-cannabinol (THC), the psychoactive ingredient in marijuana, has been found, in large amounts, in imported products as well. After marijuana is smoked, the THC is absorbed by the lungs; the longer the smoke is held in the lungs, the higher the dose (Maisto et al., 2010). Smoking marijuana provides a more immediate high than eating food laced with marijuana. The effect is a state of relaxation, well-being, much gaiety, and laughter. Because THC lowers blood glucose levels, pot smokers often develop voracious appetites. Many animal studies confirm that marijuana activates the very receptors in the brain that are involved in the increase of appetite (National Cancer Institute, 2011). Many anecdotal stories confirm this: People who are "stoned" are inclined to eat voraciously. This attribute has a medicinal value in the treatment of cancer and AIDS patients; and marijuana is legally available in some places for this purpose. THC is fat-soluble and is readily stored in the body's fat cells and organs; its presence can be detected for long periods. No physical tolerance or withdrawal has been clearly documented with marijuana use. The long-term effects on the brain are not well known, although with chronic use there is some indication of diminished brain activity with possible implications for brain functioning (Room, Fischer, et al., 2010). Several studies, according to NIDA (2010), associate workers' marijuana smoking with increased absences, tardiness, accidents, workers' compensation claims, and job turnover.

On the other hand, this drug does not lead to fatal overdose, and its hazards pale beside those of alcohol. Nor is it associated—as are alcohol, cocaine, and methamphetamine—with violence. One recent worry is whether breathing this foreign substance into the lungs can lead to lung cancer. The NIDA (2010) report on marijuana suggests that this drug may be carcinogenic. However, NIDA researchers have backed down from claims made in a previous report that lung cancer was a risk factor for marijuana smokers. NIDA modified its original statement in light of research findings refuting the cancer-marijuana link. One such study was conducted at the University of California, Los Angeles, and widely publicized in the media (Kaufman, 2006). In the largest study of its kind, over 1,000 persons with lung cancer were interviewed along with a matched sample. The evidence implicated a background of smoking tobacco but not of marijuana in the development of the cancer. The researchers believe that the reason cancer-causing ingredients contained in marijuana did not raise cancer risks is because THC may have a protective effect on the body organs in the presence of toxins. Ironically, Donald Tashkin, the scientist who conducted the study, was the very researcher whose previous research was used by the federal government to show that marijuana was a life-threatening drug in the first place. Some exciting recent research funded by the National Institutes of Health has determined that when treated with THC, mice who were bred to develop cancer tumors were protected against the growth of tumors. For those who had tumors, the tumors shrank when given this treatment. The researchers stated: "Cannabinoids may cause antitumor effects by various mechanisms, including induction of cell death" (National Cancer Institute, 2011, p. 1).

In New Mexico and Delaware, medical marijuana is approved for patients who have been diagnosed with PTSD (Frosch, 2011). The situation is legally complicated, however, due to a U.S. Supreme Court ruling that the federal government can prosecute medical marijuana users even when state laws allow doctors to prescribe the drug (Lee, 2006). Today, the Justice Department is committed to prosecuting commercial growers of this plant, although they do not plan to prosecute individuals who are in compliance with state laws. Therefore, the situation remains legally complex (Pérez-Peña, 2011). New Jersey has legalized the use of marijuana for people with chronic medical conditions who are in need of pain relief. To comply with federal guidelines, the state has made arrangements for six nonprofit agencies to grow the marijuana.

Researchers are seeking federal approval for what is believed to be the first study to examine the effects of marijuana on veterans with PTSD (Frosch,

2011). If the proposal is approved, the researchers will use marijuana grown by the University of Mississippi under a contract with NIDA. Researchers plan to use different strains of marijuana and conduct an empirically-based study including a control group to determine the effectiveness of the treatment.

It is paradoxical that with all these medical possibilities, marijuana is classified by the Drug Enforcement Administration (DEA) along with heroin as a Schedule 1 drug. This category is reserved for the most dangerous drugs, those with no approved medical use (see Table 3.2 earlier in this chapter). Cocaine is given a Schedule II classification. The American Medical Association urged the government to review its classification of marijuana to facilitate its use in clinical research. However, recently the DEA decreed that marijuana has no accepted medical value and ruled to keep it as a Schedule 1 drug (Hoeffel, 2011).

METABOLISM

Metabolism is the sum total of the chemical processes and energy exchanges that take place within an organism. Alcohol metabolism is controlled by genetic factors, such as variations in the enzymes that break down alcohol; and environmental factors, such as the amount of alcohol an individual consumes and his or her overall nutrition (NIAAA, 2007). Metabolic processes in which complex substances, including food, are broken down into smaller ones for elimination from the body as waste, take place in every cell and tissue of the human body. But the liver is the major organ that metabolizes larger amounts of alcohol and other drugs. When ingested, alcohol passes from the stomach into the small intestine, where it is rapidly absorbed into the bloodstream due to the small size of its molecules. The body reacts to drugs as though they were toxins and attempts to eliminate the drugs by metabolizing and neutralizing them. If a drug is water soluble, like alcohol, it will mix freely with the blood plasma and travel throughout the entire body, including the brain. A minute amount (2–19%) of alcohol escapes metabolism and is excreted unchanged through the lungs, urine, and sweat (Schuckit, 2009). Because alcohol is distributed so quickly and thoroughly, it affects the central nervous system. No digestion is required; alcohol is simply absorbed through the bloodstream mainly by the small intestine. The absorption of alcohol from the stomach is quick, especially when there is little food in the stomach and when the alcohol is at a relatively high concentration. Absorbed alcohol is rapidly carried throughout the body in the blood until an equilibrium is reached such that blood at all points in the system as well as the breath and urine contains approximately the same concentration. Consumed with carbonated beverages, alcohol has an increased intoxicating effect (Highfield, 2011).

Once alcohol enters the bloodstream, it is transported to every cell in the body. Alcohol is diffused in the body in proportion to the water content of the various tissues and organs. Alcohol's small molecules and its solubility in water make it readily transportable across cell membranes, with the effect of harm to many different organs (NIAAA, 2009).

Because this metabolic activity in the liver takes place at a fixed rate, only part of the alcohol being pumped through the liver is metabolized at a time, while the rest continues to circulate. Alcohol is metabolized by enzymes, which are body chemicals that break down other chemicals. In the liver, an enzyme called alcohol dehydrogenase (ADH) mediates the conversion of alcohol to acetaldehyde (Maisto et al., 2010; NIAAA, 2007). The formation of this poison is the first step in the process. The chain of events involved in metabolism is as follows:

alcohol > acetaldehyde > acedic acid > carbon dioxide and water

The breakdown of alcohol that occurs in the stomach differs significantly in men and women. In chronic alcoholic men and in all women, the amount of alcohol metabolized by ADH is lower than in nonalcoholic men. For nonalcoholic men, the amount of alcohol that can be metabolized by the stomach may be as great as 30% (Kinney, 2011; NIAAA, 2005). Women get drunk faster than men not only because they are generally smaller and their bodies contain less water and more fatty tissue, but also because alcohol-destroying enzymes in the stomach work better in men.

Women Under the Influence, a book produced by the National Center on Addiction and Substance Abuse (CASA) (2006), states that at lower levels of alcohol use than men, women more rapidly develop alcohol-related diseases like cirrhosis and hypertension, brain damage from drinking and taking Ecstasy, and lung cancer and emphysema from smoking. Additionally, women who use sedatives and anti-anxiety drugs are almost twice as likely as men to become addicted to these products. Even nicotine dependence proceeds more rapidly in females than in males.

Sometimes, however, combinations are beneficial. One recent example is the finding that consumption of large quantities of coffee helps protect heavy alcohol drinkers against cirrhosis of the liver, liver cancer, Parkinson's disease, and type 2 diabetes mellitus (Hensrud, 2010).

The toxicity of acetaldehyde is not usually a problem. However, there is a prescription drug, Antabuse (disulfiram), that stops the breakdown of acetaldehyde by blocking ADH. The usefulness of this medication is in the prevention of drinking alcohol. Once Antabuse is ingested, drinking produces a severe physical reaction: nausea, flushing, and shortness of breath. Even if alcohol is placed on the skin, such as with perfume, a strong reaction occurs. Although consumption of alcohol is dangerous to most clients who have ingested Antabuse, some who are in an advanced stage of alcoholism will "brag" that they can take Antabuse and then drink freely with no negative consequences. There is as yet no substantiation of these claims, however, in the literature. For many individuals, Antabuse has a high risk of serious side effects (Perkinson, 2012).

The flushing response of some Asians and a minority of Caucasians to drinking is thought to derive from a low ADH level, which insulates them from ingesting an excess of alcoholic beverages. Around 40% of Japanese, Chinese, and Korean people have been found to have an inactive mutation of the gene that results in much more acetaldehyde after drinking than normal (Schuckit, 2009).

Healthy people metabolize alcohol at a fairly consistent rate, usually eliminating on average 0.25 to 0.5 ounces of alcohol per hour. One-half ounce of pure alcohol can be found in a 12-ounce can of beer, a 6-ounce glass of wine, or a 1-ounce shot of whiskey. The same alcohol is found in beer, wine, and spirits distilled from wine or beer. Most U.S. beer contains between 4 and 5% alcohol; European beer is stronger. Natural wines contain between 8 and 12% alcohol. Fortified wines have had alcohol or brandy added for a higher alcohol content. Spirits, including vodka, gin, whiskeys, and rum, usually contain between 40 and 50% alcohol. The word *proof* in the United States refers to twice the percentage of alcohol: 100-proof liquor is 50% ethanol. In Canada and Britain, 100-proof liquor is 57% ethanol. Beverage alcohol consists of ethanol, various byproducts of fermentation known as congeners, flavoring, coloring, and water. Table 3.3 shows the amount of alcohol in various drinks, along with facts concerning blood alcohol concentration.

One's blood alcohol concentration (BAC) is of special interest because of the laws regarding drinking and driving. A BAC of 0.1 is a ratio of 1 part alcohol to 1,000 parts blood. All states in the United States now use a 0.08 BAC cutoff point, reinforced by a law passed by Congress withholding millions of dollars in federal highway money from states that did not adopt the lower standard. In Scandinavia, the legal limit ranges from 0.02 to 0.05, in Canada it is 0.08 in some provinces and 0.05 in others, in Britain the limit is 0.08, in Japan it is 0.03, and in Russia and Iran it is 0.0 (WHO, 2011a). For youths, eight countries forbid young drivers from having any detectable alcohol in their blood. Austria permits only 0.01 BAC for young drivers. Bulgaria, Greece, Latvia, Lithuania, the Netherlands and the United States set the maximum BAC at 0.02

Because of the known dangers of drinking and driving, an effective means of measuring one's blood alcohol level is essential. The most effective is a blood test. However, drawing blood is an invasive and expensive procedure and therefore cannot be required. Urine alcohol testing indicates the presence of alcohol in a person's system but not the current condition (see Breathalyzer, 2007). After 1.5 to 2 hours, the alcohol shows up in the urine, so this is a measure of the drinker's condition from several hours before. A dehydrated person, moreover, will have a higher BAC than one with a normal level of fluid in his or her system. This information is crucial in contested driving while intoxicated (DWI) cases. The Breathalyzer is the next most accurate measure.

TABLE 3.3 | KNOW YOUR PERSONAL LIMIT

One Drink = One bottle of beer (12 oz.)
= One glass of wine (6 oz.)
= One "single" drink (1¼ oz. of liquor)

Number of Drinks Per Hours	100 lbs M / F	120 lbs M / F	140 lbs M / F	160 lbs M / F	180 lbs M / F	200 lbs M / F	220 lbs M / F	240 lbs M / F
1 drink in 1 hour	.02/.03	.02/.02	.01/.02	.01/.01	.00/.01	.00/.01	.00/.00	.00/.00
1 drink in 2 hours	.01/.02	.00/.01	.00/.00	.00/.00	.00/.00	.00/.00	.00/.00	.00/.00
1 drink in 3 hours	.00/.01	.00/.00	.00/.00	.00/.00	.00/.00	.00/.00	.00/.00	.00/.00
2 drinks in 2 hours	.03/.04	.03/.04	.02/.03	.01/.02	.01/.02	.00/.01	.00/.00	.00/.00
2 drinks in 3 hours	.02/.03	.01/.03	.00/.01	.00/.01	.00/.00	.00/.00	.00/.00	.00/.00
2 drinks in 1 hour	.06/.07	.05/.06	.04/.05	.03/.04	.03/.03	.02/.03	.02/.02	.02/.02
3 drinks in 3 hours	.06/.09	.05/.06	.03/.05	.02/.03	.01/.03	.01/.02	.00/.01	.00/.01
3 drinks in 2 hours	.08/.10	.07/.09	.05/.06	.04/.05	.03/.04	.02/.03	.02/.03	.01/.02
4 drinks in 4 hours	.09/.11	.06/.08	.04/.06	.03/.05	.02/.03	.01/.02	.00/.02	.00/.01
4 drinks in 3 hours	.10/.13	.08/.10	.06/.08	.05/.06	.03/.05	.03/.04	.02/.03	.01/.03
5 drinks in 5 hours	.11/.14	.08/.11	.05/.08	.04/.06	.02/.04	.01/.03	.00/.02	.00/.00
3 drinks in 1 hours	.10/.12	.08/.10	.07/.08	.06/.07	.05/.06	.04/.05	.04/.05	.03/.04
5 drinks in 4 hours	.13/.16	.09/.12	.09/.10	.05/.07	.04/.06	.03/.05	.02/.04	.01/.03
4 drinks in 2 hours	.12/.15	.09/.12	.08/.10	.06/.08	.05/.07	.04/.06	.04/.05	.03/.04
5 drinks in 3 hours	.14/.18	.11/.14	.09/.11	.07/.09	.06/.08	.05/.06	.04/.05	.03/.04
5 drink in 2 hours	.16/.19	.13/.16	.10/.13	.09/.11	.07/.09	.06/.08	.05/.07	.05/.06

Low Risk Drinking Guidelines:
Men: 3 drinks per day, *max,* and 14 drinks per week, *max.*
Women: 2 drinks per day, *max,* and 9 drinks per week, *max.*

NO AMOUNT OF ALCOHOL IS SAFE IF YOU ARE DRIVING.
YOUR RISK OF CRASHING GOES UP, *EVEN WITH VERY SMALL AMOUNTS.*
NO AMOUNT IS SAFE IF YOU ARE PREGNANT OR TRYING TO GET
PREGNANT.

Source: National Highway Traffic Safety Administration, 2007. Appendix. Available at http://www.nhtsa.gov/people/injury/alcohol/impaired_driving/appendix.htm.

Most people are quite intoxicated at 0.15 and comatose at 0.4, depending on their level of tolerance. When alcohol levels are between 0.5 and 1.0, the breathing center in the brain or the action of the heart may be anesthetized. If vomiting does not prevent intoxication at this level, death will swiftly follow. For a better understanding of what alcohol does to the body, let us look more closely at the metabolization process. Alcohol, as we have seen, is metabolized more slowly than it is absorbed. The BAC peaks 30 to 45 minutes after the consumption of one standard drink. After a night of hard drinking, therefore, a person may still be legally intoxicated when driving to work the next morning.

Because it enters the body by being swallowed, alcohol can be readily metabolized. Other drugs, such as Valium and amphetamines, tend to be swallowed as well. Swallowing drugs is a relatively slow form of delivery, so the effects are not felt for a few minutes to an hour. Other methods of drug delivery are more direct, such as inhalation, as in the case of cocaine snorting, snuff or smokeless tobacco, or glue sniffing. These drugs, like those that are injected, reach the brain quickly and so have a rapid intoxicating effect (Jung, 2010).

Valium, unlike alcohol, is transformed by the liver's enzymes into various compounds that have greater, rather than fewer, effects on the user. Whereas Valium is only gradually eliminated from the body, amphetamines are completely eliminated about two days after the last use. Their peak effect occurs about 2 to 3 hours after use. Caffeine is absorbed into the body in about 30 minutes, with the maximum impact occurring about 2 hours later. Cocaine, unlike alcohol which is detectable in the blood and urine, cannot be so easily detected due to its rapid metabolism (Jung, 2010).

Cannabis, or marijuana, which is fat soluble but not water soluble, is metabolized by the liver and distributed throughout the body much more slowly than alcohol. Cannabis enters readily through cell membranes and is retained in the body for long periods of time (Jung, 2010). Drugs that are fat-soluble leave long-lasting traces due to their slow release from fat stores For this reason, some persons on parole have been returned to prison for drug use even though they were tested a month after ingesting marijuana.

Drugs tend to be used in combination rather than singly. Many deaths caused by drug taking occur because the impact of drugs in combination is far greater than the potency of each drug singly. The chemical reaction of two drugs together often has a multiplying or synergistic effect. Among older Americans, drinking can be especially dangerous because of the interactions of alcohol with medications they are likely to be taking (Doweiko, 2009). The prevalence of polydrug use is often overlooked in research and surveys. The combination of alcohol and tobacco is common, as is the use of illicit drugs and alcohol. Sometimes the user combines drugs to maximize the effect and sometimes to subdue it. For the latter purpose, alcohol is frequently drunk in conjunction with cocaine and amphetamines (Doweiko, 2009; Jung, 2010). Valium may also be used to counter the overstimulating effect of cocaine. This was the combination that was used by TV and film actor Robert Downey Jr. when he had his much-publicized relapse. Four small bags of cocaine and 16 Valium tablets were found in his hotel room, and he later tested positive for both drugs (France & Horn, 2001). A large number of deaths due to heroin overdoses are actually the result of taking alcohol and heroin together

("How Drugs Can Kill," 2011). The most dangerous practice is combining two sedatives, such as alcohol and Valium. Many deaths have occurred as well from liver damage caused by combining alcohol and Tylenol (DHHS, 2000). Alcohol impairs the liver's ability to clear toxins from the blood and can easily lead to an overdose. The combination of cold and flu medications plus Tylenol can lead to liver failure as well. The surprising fact about this popular over-the-counter drug, Tylenol (acetaminophen) is how unaware the public is of its potential dangers. Fortunately, due to an official recognition of this problem, the Federal Drug Administration (FDA) is asking manufacturers of acetaminophen/opioid combination drugs to phase out higher strength versions of the drugs and use no more than 325 milligrams of acetaminophen per tablet or capsule (Washington Drug Letter, 2011).

NIDA's *Infofacts* (2010) states that in the majority of known drug-related deaths, more than one drug was involved. Heroin is the illicit drug most frequently involved in accidental deaths, followed by cocaine.

Denning, Little, and Glickman (2004) describe drug interactions that occur from the byproducts formed by two dangerous drugs in combination. Alcohol and cocaine in combination, for example, combine to create a new substance that may be especially toxic to the liver. Moreover, alcohol is metabolized by enzymes in the liver. If another drug requires the same enzymes, the removal of both is slowed, with possibly dire consequences. Forty percent of persons who took high doses of Tylenol (eight extra-strength tablets—500 milligrams) in a controlled experiment showed signs of liver damage (Johnson, 2006). For the average healthy adult, the recommended maximum dose of acetaminophen over a 24 hour period is four grams (4,000 mg).

THE BRAIN AND ADDICTION

If we can unravel the secrets of the brain, we can understand the forces that drive humans into paths of destructiveness, that is, their cravings, passions, and dreams. Today we may not know all the answers, but for the first time in history, neuroscientists have captured images of the brains of chronic drug users and addicted gamblers in the throes of craving a drug or behavior. And it is this craving that is the root of addiction itself, the craving that sends people back into the dungeon—the gambling den, the bar, the crack house—again and again.

The actions of alcohol and cocaine that cause intoxication, initiate and maintain excessive drug-using behavior, and drive the relentless craving during abstinence occur primarily in the brain. A basic understanding of the effects of drugs like alcohol and cocaine on the mechanisms underlying brain function is essential to develop and improve addiction prevention and treatment strategies. Contemporary research on the brain and how it affects behavior is forthcoming all the time; such research helps clarify the mysteries of addiction. Two aspects of brain research are crucial for our understanding of addiction: First is the adaptation factor—how the brain adapts to and compensates for the abnormal signals generated by the drug. The second aspect, one we know far less about, concerns uniqueness in the brains of potentially addicted persons. Before coming to the innate differences in the way the brains of heavy drug users respond to drugs or to images of drug paraphernalia (i.e., the genetic component), let us summarize what scientists know about the workings of the brain itself with regard to addiction.

THE BRAIN

The brain and the spinal cord together make up the central nervous system (CNS) (see Figure 3.2). The brain and spinal cord are hollow structures filled with cerebrospinal fluid (CSF). Alcohol, as a drug affecting the central nervous system, belongs in a class with the barbiturates, minor tranquilizers, and general anesthetics—all depressants. Whereas at low levels of alcohol ingestion an excitement phase may set in, including uninhibited and erratic emotional expression, later a gradual dullness and stupor may occur. The effect of the alcohol on motor activity is seen in slurred speech, unsteady gait, and clumsiness. Alcohol tangibly impairs higher-level functioning—thinking, remembering, and making judgments. Before considering some of the grave neurological consequences of long-term alcohol and other drug misuse, let us consider how alcohol affects the brain at the cellular and biochemical levels, which directly affect the emotions.

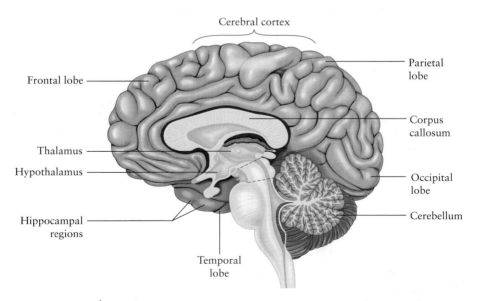

FIGURE 3.2 | SCHEMATIC DRAWING OF THE HUMAN BRAIN, SHOWING REGIONS VULNERABLE TO ALCOHOLISM-RELATED ABNORMALITIES

Source: NIAAA. *Alcohol Alert*, October 2004, no. 63, p. 4. *Alcohol's Damaging Effects on the Brain.* Available at http://pubs.niaaa.nih.gov/publications/aa63/aa63.htm.

Each nerve cell of the brain is separated from its neighbor by a narrow gap called a *synapse*. Nerve cells communicate with one another by way of chemical messengers called *neurotransmitters;* most commonly, however, drugs disrupt neurotransmitter functions because they happen to resemble the chemical structure of the brain's own neurotransmitters (Miller et al., 2011). Neurotransmitters underlie every thought and emotion as well as memory and learning. A good half dozen of some 50 are known to play a role in addiction. Figure 3.3 illustrates the neuron cell membrane.

Cocaine, like alcohol, brings about marked changes in brain chemistry. Accumulated evidence indicates that cocaine's chief biological activity is in preventing the reuptake (reabsorption) of the neurochemical transmitter

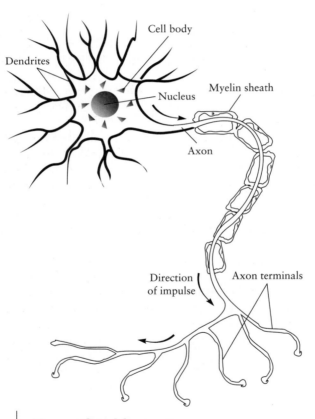

FIGURE 3.3 | Neuron Cell Membrane

Structural features of a neuron: This drawing depicts the major components of neuronal structure, including the cell body, nucleus, and dendritic trees. At the axon terminal, the synapse links the neuron to another neuron.

Source: NIDA. 2007a. *Mind over Matter: Teacher's Guide.* Available from http://teens.drugabuse.gov/mom/tg_nerves.php.

dopamine (NIDA, 2010). Drug-addicted laboratory rats will ignore food and sex, and tolerate electric shocks for the opportunity to ingest cocaine. A depletion of dopamine following cocaine use probably accounts for cocaine binges, tolerance, craving, and the obsessive behavior of cocaine users. The brain cuts back on the oversupply of dopamine, which is why increasing doses of cocaine are needed to keep the user feeling normal (Ginsberg, Nackerud, & Larrison, 2004). And as researchers and the general public are increasingly aware, nicotine behaves remarkably like cocaine, causing a surge of dopamine in the brain. Dopamine is the "feel-good" neurotransmitter; too little dopamine is implicated in the tremors of Parkinson's disease, and too much causes the bizarre thoughts of schizophrenia. A drug-generated surge in dopamine is what triggers a drug user's high.

Serotonin is another neurotransmitter highly influenced by alcohol and other drug use. Serotonin is involved in sleep and sensory experiences. It has received a great deal of attention from researchers and the popular press. Decreased levels of this neurotransmitter have been linked to behaviors associated with intoxicated states, depression, anxiety, poor impulse control, aggressiveness, and suicidal behavior. Middle-aged and older men with a combination of alcohol dependence and mood disorders are at particularly high risk of suicide (Sher, 2006).

As Figure 3.4 shows, cocaine blocks the reuptake of certain chemicals by neurons in the brain. It is these nerve cells that release the neurotransmitters. Laboratory research with monkeys shows that those with lower availability of dopamine receptors were especially responsive to cocaine's reinforcing effects; possibly serotonin was involved as well (Whitten, 2009). The good news is that for some of them, their brains recovered in less than a year. Further research is needed to reveal the exact effect of the different neurotransmitters, dopamine, serotonin, and others.

The discovery through brain imaging and genetics of the role that serotonin plays in addiction and also in mental disorders, in conjunction with simultaneous discoveries of drugs that reduce drug cravings in rats and monkeys, has opened up a whole world of medical possibilities. We now know that nicotine, for example, sends a rush to the brain's "pleasure center," where cocaine and amphetamines do their work (Linden, 2011). Continued smoking, like other drug use, actually changes the brain, and measurable cognitive deficits occur following years of chronic use (Gould, 2010). The more we can learn about these cognitive processes, the closer we will come to finding effective treatments.

Cocaine, like alcohol, opens the neurotransmitter floodgates. Dopamine, serotonin (which governs our sense of well-being), and gamma-aminobutyric acid (GABA) (which, when released, regulates anxiety and has a soporific effect) are all involved in producing a high (Linden, 2011). Increasingly, research is focusing on the connection between GABA receptor genes and alcohol, which enhances GABA activity (Hasin, Hatzenbuehler, & Waxman, 2006). The search for a genetic predisposition to alcoholism has led researchers to see a

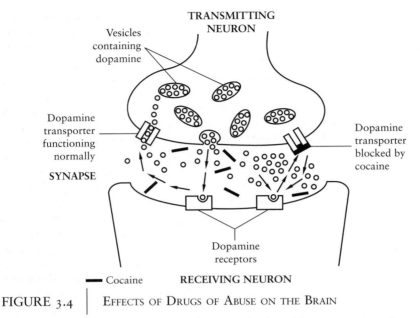

FIGURE 3.4 | EFFECTS OF DRUGS OF ABUSE ON THE BRAIN

In the normal communication process, dopamine is released by a neuron into the synapse, where it can bind with dopamine receptors on neighboring neurons. Normally, dopamine is then recycled back into the transmitting neuron by a specialized protein called the dopamine transporter. If cocaine is present, it attaches to the dopamine transporter and blocks the normal recycling process, resulting in a build-up of dopamine in the synapse that contributes to the pleasurable effects of cocaine.

When cocaine enters the brain, it blocks the dopamine transporter from pumping dopamine back into the transmitting neuron, flooding the synapse with dopamine. This intensifies and prolongs the stimulation of receiving neurons in the brain's pleasure circuits, causing a cocaine "high."

Source: NIDA. 2007b. *Mind over Matter: Teacher's Guide.* Retrieved from http://teens.drugabuse.gov/mom/tg_effects.php#.

strong relationship between alcoholism and receptor GABA, A2 receptor genes on chromosome 4. We can anticipate much more attention to this neurotransmitter in the future.

Through the use of sophisticated technology such as functional magnetic resonance imaging (fMRI), scientists can observe the dynamic changes that occur in the brain as an individual takes a drug. Researchers are now recording the brain changes that occur as a person experiences the rush, or high, and later, the craving for cocaine. They can even identify parts of the brain, the pleasure circuits, that become active when a cocaine addict sees stimuli such as drug paraphernalia that trigger the craving for the drug. The memories of drug use are so enduring and so powerful that even seeing a bare arm beneath a rolled-up sleeve can reawaken the cue-induced craving (Linden, 2011). The situation is similar to Pavlov's dog salivating when it heard the ringing of a bell associated with food. Relapse occurs, as every Alcoholics Anonymous (AA) member knows, from visiting the old haunts from drinking days (As AA members say, "Slips occur in slippery places"). Now there is scientific proof for this folk wisdom about the importance of avoiding people, places, and things associated with past drug use. Figure 3.5 is a diagram of the reward pathway in the brain.

Relapse might also reflect the brain changes described by Volkow (2010b). Recall that to produce a high, a drug such as cocaine keeps the transporters of dopamine from clearing the synapse of the dopamine following the release. Cocaine, for example, blocks the removal of dopamine from the synapse, resulting in an accumulation of dopamine and feelings of euphoria. As Begley (2001) explains the impact of the blocking of the receptor: "When all the seats on this so-called transporter molecule are occupied by cocaine," she says, "there is no room for dopamine, which therefore hangs around and keeps the pleasure circuit firing" (p. 42). This firing releases dopamine into the synapse. The neurotransmitter in turn must attach itself to receptors on the next cell to fire some more. Repeated activation enhances the high. Repeated activation also leads to cell adaptation over time. Drugs, therefore, don't have the same effect as they did before. This is called tolerance (see Linden, 2011). With the same dosage, the drug user cannot achieve that original high because his or her brain has changed.

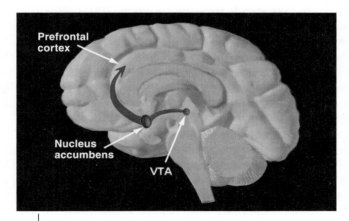

FIGURE 3.5 | THE REWARD PATHWAY

One pathway important to understanding the effects of drugs on the brain is the reward pathway, which consists of several parts of the brain highlighted in this diagram: the ventral tegmental area (VTA), the nucleus accumbens, and the prefrontal cortex. When the brain is activated by a rewarding stimulus (e.g., food, water, sex), information travels from the VTA to the nucleus accumbens and then up to the prefrontal cortex.

Source: The National Institute on Drug Abuse (NIDA). Retrieved from http://www.drugabuse.gov/pubs/teaching/Teaching2/largegifs/slide11.gif.

An inmate from Oklahoma State Penitentiary (OSP) describes how, even after years of sobriety, craving can rear its ugly head:

> One thing I observed was the force of psychological addiction. OSP is a maximum security prison, but drugs are as plentiful as blackberries in the spring; however, there are inevitable interruptions, meaning that nobody here can become physically addicted. I lived with one man—the first person I ever saw use a needle—who bought heroin when it was available. He was exceptionally bright and his family was wealthy. He and I would read from dawn to dusk and sometimes not say 20 words to one another, although we were locked in a cell the size of a bathroom for 24 hours a day. He was refined, considerate, gracious, and fairly laid back, the kind of cellmate one does not stumble on often. After 2 months, he received word that some heroin was available. For hours before it arrived, he was a changed man, pacing frantically, jumping up every few minutes to look out the door, noticeably agitated. His anxiety consumed him ... and amazed me. When it arrived, he was in obvious haste to use it and did not slow down until the needle came out of his arm. I associated all those manifestations with physical addiction. I subsequently saw others who would lie, steal, and risk their life for marijuana. I don't doubt that you know all about this phenomenon, but I had no idea psychological addiction was so intense, especially in sporadic users. I'm addicted to chocolate, and I assumed it was something like that. It's not. (personal communication; November 11, 2003)

Current theories of addiction rely heavily on neurobiological evidence showing connections between addiction-related behaviors and neural structures and functions (Nestler, 2005). Addiction is a brain disease, as Volkow (2010b) suggests. These brain changes are neural adaptations to brain functioning under the influence of the drug (Whitten, 2005). When the use is discontinued, the system experiences a breakdown of sorts.

In *Memoirs of an Addicted Brain,* neuroscientist Marc Lewis (2011), who was also addicted to a number of drugs—from LSD to heroin—before he became a scientist, provides a personal documentation of the cycle of craving from his own personal experiences. The answer to the riddle of addiction—to drugs, sex, love, and cigarettes—he contends, lies in the structure and function of the human brain.

Almost all drugs of abuse are believed to induce two kinds of changes in brain structure and function. These are the loss of motivation—to achieve, engage in fun activities, and so forth—and the storing of emotional memories of the high (Johnson, 2004). Even though the initial drug taking is a voluntary act, Volkow explains, once neurochemical changes have occurred with prolonged use, the compulsion to return to drug taking or drinking is no longer voluntary. An addicted brain is therefore different from a nonaddicted brain. As some researchers indicate, however, the notion of brain injury is more accurate than the notion of brain disease in describing the course of events involving changes in the brain due to substance misuse. It can be argued that the brain of the addict is not so much diseased as injured by exposure to self-administered toxins. As with other injuries, healing can occur when the source of the injury has been eliminated.

The discovery that different parts of the human brain are activated during cocaine *rush* versus cocaine *craving* may be useful in the development of medications for reducing the craving that makes relapse almost a matter of course (Linden, 2011). Particular regions of the brain can be associated with levels of feeling because cocaine-addicted volunteers can now, with new technology, rate their rush experiences and their cravings associated with cues. Cues such as the smell of marijuana or cigarette smoke and pictures of drugs such as meth or cocaine trigger this memory. The fact that memory sites are involved in connection with the cues is consistent with drug users' reports of strong feelings associated with drug use and their intense response to what researchers term their "feeling memories" (Whitten, 2005). Such memories of intense pleasure can last a lifetime (Johnson, 2004). Cues related to the drug evoke the memories and involve serious risk of relapse.

The craving that can preoccupy an addict's mind and very being involves the irresistible urge to get another rush. The memory of past euphoria, coupled with dopamine deficit related to long-term use, means the addict seeks out drugs not to feel low. Due to neuronal damage caused by extensive drug use, the individual can no longer feel pleasure normally. Traditionally, it was thought that the reason some people continue to drink and use was to ward off withdrawal symptoms. However, study of various drugs of addiction reveals this is not the case. Cocaine produces no physical withdrawal symptoms, but it is recognizably more addictive than heroin. The drive to return to drug use, therefore, must be associated with memory as well as with changes in brain chemistry. Even mere anticipation of receiving cocaine has been shown, in rat studies, to lead to a surge in dopamine in the brain (Phillips, Stuber, Heien, Wrightman, & Carelli, 2003). Hyman (2005) has introduced an "extreme memory" theory to explain the potential of craving. The idea behind this theory is that the human brain, for survival purposes, evolved to respond to essentials such as food, water, or sex. The reward is release of dopamine. Long-term memories are laid down through conditioning. Drugs usurp the system to the extent that the brain overlearns the urge to repeat the experience. Addiction can thus be viewed as a malfunction of the normal human craving for excitement. This new model opens the way to search for medical solutions to breaking the memories of the pleasure of the drug.

Researchers can diminish the euphoric effects of alcohol and other drugs in addicted persons by giving them drugs that increase the availability of serotonin. Such medications reduce craving because the addiction is to the rush, the euphoria, and not to the substance itself. Later in this chapter, we will see how medications such as ondansetron, which acts on serotonin, can help some persons in recovery by reducing their craving for drugs. Following a year or two of recovery, the brain, as far as we know, replenishes itself (Whitten, 2009). Perhaps this is why long-term treatment has been found more successful than short-term treatment. Those who remain in treatment for at least a year and/or receive intensive after-care follow-up programming are considerably more likely than those who received short-term treatment to remain clean (Doweiko, 2009).

What do the brain studies show about male–female differences in neuro-logical damage caused by drug use? Only in recent years have brain studies devoted attention to alcohol-related brain damage in women. Results of brain imaging studies show that thinking and memory abilities are markedly affected in alcoholic women and that brain shrinkage is more pronounced in women than in men with similar drinking histories (Doweiko, 2009). Research on cocaine's effects on male and female brains, on the other hand, seems to indicate that women process cocaine cues differently from men (Whitten, 2004). As reported by Whitten, an experiment measured the blood flow in the brains of cocaine users as they listened to a script about cocaine. In both the women and men, the pleasure centers of the brain were activated. During this craving period, however, the brain research showed that part of the emotional response to the craving in women was inhibited. The signifi-cance of this difference requires further study; the findings could have impor-tant treatment implications because craving is a key factor in relapse.

A Nonsubstance Addiction: Gambling

Research findings on the neurobiology of pathological gambling are still in the promising, but early, stage of development. In general, biochemical, neuroim-aging, genetic research and treatment research suggest a strong neurobiologi-cal link between gambling and substance use addiction (Grant, Brewer, & Potenza, 2006; Potenza, 2008). Given the substantial co-occurrence of these disorders, it only makes sense that there are linkages on many levels.

THE BRAIN Abnormalities in the brain function of pathological gamblers are similar to those observed in other addictions. Specifically, decreased levels of serotonin and alterations in the dopamine and opioid system functioning in the brain may explain the exaggerated craving state and the greater difficulty pathological gamblers have in controlling urges to gamble (Potenza, 2008). Medications that affect these areas of brain functioning, such as SSRIs (selective serotonin reuptake inhibitors), bupropion, lithium, and naltrexone have been found to be helpful in reducing symptoms (Ravindran, da Silva, Ravindran, Richter, & Rector, 2009).

Other intriguing brain research has found that dopamine transmission is most active where the reward is uncertain, that is, the *anticipation* of a reward may be the strongest trigger for a dopamine rush (Fiorillo, 2004). Because the results of gambling are always uncertain, the dopamine activity may continue to reinforce gambling behavior regardless of whether a person wins or loses. This may explain why near misses are so thrilling: Watching the slot machine numbers drop after you've already pulled two sevens will get the dopamine surging no matter what the outcome. Your brain wants you to be "in action," that is, in a position to anticipate and get the dopamine rush, regardless of whether you are winning or losing.

We depend on our brain to evaluate situations and tell us, "*Don't Do It!!*" when our choices will inevitably result in high risk consequences. However, the executive functioning of the prefrontal cortex part of the brain of a compulsive gambler has a broad range of deficits in controlling impulses, and it seems to say, *"Do It Anyway!!"* (Grant, Brewer, & Potenza, 2006). For example, a recent study found that pathological gamblers, when compared with controls, showed specific deficits on measures of planning and decision making (Ledgerwood, Orr, Kaploun, Milosevic, Frisch, Rupcich, & Lundahl, 2011). In her interviews of women recovering from compulsive gambling, Davis (2009) found a common core of flawed cognitive rationalizations that allowed the women to continue gambling in spite of heavy consequences. Here is a sample of how some of the women successfully overruled any executive functioning that would tell them that continuing to gamble would be a disaster:

"This will be the last time."

"Just a few hundred and then I'll leave."

"I can't pay that bill anyway, so I might as well risk it."

"Everybody else has a life, all I have is work, work, work. I deserve a break."'

Although research has established that a number of things are different in the brains of compulsive gamblers, they also emphasize that we do not yet understand which comes first—the addiction or the brain differences (Grant et al., 2006). Furthermore, most of the brain research has been done with male gamblers, raising concerns about the generalizability to women (Potenza, 2008).

GENES Similar to substance use disorders, genetic factors play a substantial role in gambling addiction. In a study of the Vietnam Era Twin Registry sample of male twins, researchers estimated that 62% of the variance for pathological gambling could be attributed to familial factors (Shah, Eisen, Xian, & Potenza, 2005). A more recent investigation of 2,889 twin pairs from the Australia Twin Registry, of which 57% were women, revealed for the first time that genes are as important in the etiology of pathological gambling in women as they are in men; an estimated 49.2% of the variance could be attributed to familial factors in women (Slutske, Zhu, et al., 2010). In addition to the direct contribution of family genes to gambling addiction, it is also clear from consistent studies that pathological gamblers are more likely to have higher rates of first-degree relatives with substance use disorders (Shah, Potenza, & Eisen, 2004). Thus, such an unlucky person can share a genetic vulnerability to both problems, further highlighting the shared association between the two disorders.

Withdrawal Withdrawal symptoms have been fully dramatized in movies and are well documented in the substance abuse field, but are not as widely known with gambling addiction. However, just like people with substance use disorders, many compulsive gamblers experience a wide range of withdrawal symptoms when they stop or attempt to stop gambling. Although restlessness and irritability are the two common symptoms associated with withdrawal, there has been consistent documentation of physiological symptoms attributable to gambling withdrawal. In a study of 222 Gamblers Anonymous members, Rosenthal and Lesieur (1992) found that 90% reported restlessness and irritability when they quit, and 65% reported at least one withdrawal symptom such as insomnia, headaches, stomach upset, and so on. In a more recent study in the St. Louis, Missouri, area of gamblers who met the criteria for disordered gambling, researchers found that nearly 25% experienced restlessness and irritability upon attempting to quit or control gambling (Cunningham-Williams, Gattis, Dore, Shi, & Spitznagel, 2009). In addition, almost 40% of the sample experienced other symptoms such as disappointment in self, guilt, anger, loss of control, and depression or hopelessness.

Withdrawal symptoms from gambling are aggravated by other realities, such as crushing debt, a brain that is "out of whack," and the estrangement of family and friends. Withdrawal effects listed by the women in the Internet survey done by Davis (2009) include extreme night sweats, rapid heart rate, anxiety, a general ill-at-ease feeling, extreme boredom, guilt, depression, mood swings, weight gain, weakened leg muscles, and the increase of other addictive behaviors. Stepping through the door to recovery can be a little like stepping into some special version of hell, at least initially. Withdrawal pain may explain, in part, the high rate of relapse. In addition, the compulsive gambler has one other unique reality that haunts him or her during withdrawal: Gambling is the only addiction that offers both escape from symptoms *and* the chance of winning enough money to solve your debt problems by engaging in the behavior. Gambling is the source of the pain, but gambling also can appear to the suffering gambler as the only way out.

Although science is uncovering so many mysteries of the neurobiology of addiction, one question left unanswered is why some people are so highly susceptible to the lure of addictive practices while so many others can just "take it or leave it." These differences in people probably, at least in part, have something to do with genetic makeup.

The Role of Genes in Addiction

About 40–60% of the risk of alcohol use disorders is explained by genes and the rest through gene–environment associations, according to Schuckit (2009). By environment, Schuckit is referring to such things as peer pressure and levels of stress. We have always known about the social and other environmental factors in addiction; we have only more recently come to learn about the factor of genes. Genetic understandings are important, according to Schuckit, to identify children who might be at risk of alcohol use disorders.

In testimony before the House Subcommittee on Labor, Health and Human Services, and Education, T. R. Insel (2005), the director of the National Institute on Mental Health, submitted the following information:

> Mental and substance abuse disorders are inherently intertwined with co-occurring diagnoses of substance abuse and mental disorders. ... Substance use

disorders are especially prevalent in individuals with schizophrenia (47%), bipolar disorder (45%), anxiety (25%), and major depression (24%). (p. 2)

As many as 80% of alcohol-dependent people are regular smokers, a co-occurrence that could reflect either use of the second drug to deal with effects of the first or overlapping genetic predispositions (Schuckit, 2009). The first study to examine the human genetic makeup (or genome) for regions that involve both alcohol dependence and smoking has identified genes and regions of genes that may be involved in both alcohol and other drugs and nicotine dependence. This research suggests that some overlap may exist between genes that code for sensitivity to alcohol and those that influence sensitivity to nicotine (NIAAA, 2007). Bipolar (manic-depressive) disorder, for example, has a close association with chemical dependence.

In their earlier review of the literature, Brady and Sinha (2005) found that estimates ranged between 45 and 86% of men and women with substance use disorders who also had at least one co-occurring psychiatric disorder, and the risk relationship appeared to be reciprocal. This finding of dual disorders in the same individual suggests an underlying biological vulnerability for a number of disabilities. This vulnerability is interactive in that it involves a biological predisposition to overreact to stress in combination with a high-risk, nonprotective, stressful environment (Brady & Sinha, 2005; Johnson, 2004). Brady and Sinha's model is based in part on animal studies showing that early life trauma and chronic stress result in long-term changes in stress responses. Such changes can alter the dopamine system and can increase susceptibility to stress, leading in turn to the altering substances.

Johnson (2004) points to the role of serotonin in the addiction process. Decreased levels of this neurotransmitter have been linked to behaviors associated with intoxicated states, depression, anxiety, poor impulse control, aggressiveness, and suicidal behavior. The usual search for whether the mental disorder or the addiction came first may thus be futile. Similarly, a specific vulnerability may not be to alcohol misuse but, rather, to problems with a number of substances. A brain susceptibility to addiction itself may prevail.

Addiction, as we know and as the *DSM-5* will make clear, exists along a continuum. A gene that relates to risk taking and impulsiveness, similarly, is found to vary along a continuum from healthy behavior to extremely high risk taking, with people who use heroin having the gene for extreme novelty-seeking behavior (Russo, 2007). The new research gives scientific support to longstanding claims that alcoholism and other addictions are intergenerational.

That there appears to be a genetic tendency for persons in recovery to be likely to use an array of different mood-altering substances is revealed in the following description provided by an anonymous wife of an AA member (shared with van Wormer in correspondence of November, 2008):

> At most AA meetings candy, cakes, doughnuts, etc. will be available in large quantities. This appears to be the norm; the addict gives up one substance, but the psychological attribute that allowed addiction to one also carries over to other substances.

My father-in-law, when trying to stop drinking, would become obsessed with ice cream and frozen yogurt. He lived in the country, but would travel to town at least three times a day to eat his ice cream, shakes, sundaes.

My husband has been in recovery for 10 years. His father, grandmother, grandfather, mother, uncles, aunts, all are alcoholics.

Why does alcoholism seem to run in families? Is alcohol behavior learned or inherited? The search for genetic links began in earnest in the early 1970s with adoption studies in Scandinavia. The aim of these studies was to separate environmental from hereditary determinants. Goodwin (1976) sought an answer by interviewing 133 Danish men who had been adopted as small children. Health records were used to substantiate the interviews. The findings are striking: The biological sons of alcoholic men were four times as likely to have alcohol problems as the children without this heritage. This result has helped put to rest the popular assumption that alcoholic drinking is a learned behavior.

The best known of the Scandinavian studies is the research conducted by Cloninger and colleagues in Sweden. Sweden was chosen, as Denmark was before, because of the availability of thorough government records on every citizen. This research helped clarify the role of environment as well as heredity in the development of alcoholism.

Cloninger Sigvardsson and colleague's (1989) study of 259 male adoptees with alcoholic biological fathers (of a total of 862 male adoptees) found that a somewhat larger proportion of the adoptees with alcoholic fathers were registered with Swedish authorities for alcohol-related problems than were adoptees with nonalcoholic fathers. Alcohol misuse in the adoptive parents, however, was not a determinant of alcohol misuse in the sons. The adopted men were subdivided according to their frequency and severity of registered misuse. Herein lies the major significance of the study: It determined that there is more than one kind of alcoholism.

Cloninger's first category of alcoholism—the Type 1s, who made up around 75% of the total—develop the illness gradually over time. This form of alcoholism is also known as milieu-limited alcoholism because of the environmental influence; low socioeconomic status of the adoptive father seemed to be the key influence. Men in this group tend to have personality traits that make them susceptible to anxiety. In response to the antianxiety effects of alcohol, they rapidly become drug tolerant and dependent and have difficulty terminating drinking binges once they have started. The individual prone to this type of alcoholism avoids situations involving harm or risk and seeks approval from others. Guilt feelings are associated with the drinking and its consequences.

The Type 2 variety of alcoholism, on the other hand, is characterized by a tendency toward risk taking. Type 2 is also called male-limited alcoholism because males dominate this category. Personality traits that distinguish this type of drinker are early and sudden development of alcoholism, hyperactivity, antisocial personality traits, and a history of fights while drinking. More recent research conducted by Langbehn, Cadoret, Caspers, Troughton, and Yucuis (2003) reported an increased risk for drug use and dependence among adoptees whose biological parents had a lifetime history of both anti-social personality disorders and substance misuse. Type 2 alcoholism is highly hereditary, passing from father to son, and is associated with low levels of serotonin and dopamine in the brain. Cloninger recognizes that Types 1 and 2 are not completely discrete and that there is much overlap between categories.

A school counselor from Oshkosh, Wisconsin, describes the characteristics of two of her family members:

> Oh my goodness, the Type 1 characteristics personify my father completely. He is prone to severe anxiety and turns to alcohol due to its antianxiety effects. He has never, to my knowledge, attempted to stop drinking. Rather, he turns to alcohol whenever trouble arises. For instance, recently we had to call the ambulance because my mother collapsed. While I turned to prayer, I saw him reach for the bottle, his whole hand shaking. We were both very upset over the situation; however, we turned to different sources for comfort. Further, he avoids situations involving any harm or risk and is very conscious of what others think of him. He is the type of father who doesn't like it when his children do an activity together, such as go on vacation, because his "eggs are all in one basket." He doesn't hunt and has many fears of succumbing to harm. I have not noticed any guilt feelings, but we don't have heart-to-heart conversations, either!
>
> Although I did not know it at the time, my ex-husband was definitely a Type 2 alcoholic. He started drinking at an early age and developed a high tolerance for alcohol. He could be described as hyperactive. He had difficulty sitting still and flitted from one activity to another. He definitely had an antisocial personality and frequently got into fights while drinking. His pattern was quite predictable; however, I didn't even recognize it as alcoholism at the time. He would get dressed up to go out for the evening. This would consist of visiting several bars. He would *never* just have a couple of drinks. He always drank rapidly and heavily until he achieved intoxication. He would start to act silly and sometimes speak loudly, and would frequently end up fighting with someone. He had a quick temper to begin with, and drinking made it much worse. (personal communication; November 8, 1999)

Further scientific validation for the Type 1–Type 2 theory is experimentation with a multiauthored study led by Bankole Johnson, MD, on the effects of ondansetron, a medication most often used to treat nausea and vomiting in cancer patients receiving chemotherapy. This drug, which appears to work by acting on serotonin, was found, in a highly empirical, randomized study, to have little or no effect on the Type 1, or late-onset, variety of alcoholism. It was effective in reducing consumption in patients of the early-onset variety, however. These results led the researchers to conclude that ondansetron may ameliorate an inherited abnormality in that alcoholic subtype (Johnson et al., 2000). Personal e-mail correspondence with Bankole Johnson of September 13, 2000, confirms that this drug was effective with a small sample of Type 2 females as well. Now more recently, a report has come from the National

Institutes of Health (2011) that Johnson and his colleagues have extended their research with ondansetron. Again it was determined that the effects of this drug were more pronounced with individuals who had certain gene variants that are associated with severe forms of the disease. Subjects who lacked the gene showed no improvement when given this drug. Elsewhere, the NIAAA (2003) reports a correlation between pain sensitivity and Type 2 alcoholism. According to this study, people who drink alcoholically tend to perceive stimuli strongly, as do children of alcoholics. Drinking may be one way to adapt to the sensitivity.

Based on his genetic research, Schuckit (2009) reports that variations in genes for enzymes that metabolize alcohol are generally associated with a lower risk of alcohol use disorders because they increase sensitivity to alcohol. Gene forms associated with impulsivity and sensation-seeking, on the other hand, contribute to vulnerability to both drug use and alcohol use disorders perhaps through impaired judgment and difficulty learning from mistakes. These risk-takers and people who have low responsiveness (or low sensitivity) to alcohol are more likely to drink more on each occasion to get the desired effect, which increases their risk of alcohol use disorders.

Rodent studies provide further evidence for genetic factors in alcoholism. Studies from the University of North Carolina involving rat as well as human subjects reveal that strong sweet cravings are associated with alcoholism. It is not the sweet cravings alone but these cravings in combination with certain personality traits such as a tendency toward risk-taking or conversely, harm avoidance (Kampov-Polevoy, Eick, et al., 2004).

Twin studies compare behaviors in identical and nonidentical twins or likenesses in twins who were separated at birth. Research shows that about half of alcoholism vulnerability has a genetic basis. When one in a pair of identical twins develops alcoholism (or is a smoker), the likelihood that the other twin has the same problem is between 40% and 60% (Hasin et al., 2006).

Finding the genes involved in addiction vulnerability is thus a high priority for scientific research. In both animal experiments and research on humans, low sensitivity to alcohol-induced sedation is associated with higher alcohol consumption levels, as the NIAAA (2003) report on hereditary factors indicates. By identifying the proteins these genes encode and the mechanisms that determine the animal's response to alcohol, scientists can pursue the development of pharmaceuticals that short-circuit these genetically defined processes.

Genetic differences in personality factors may indirectly render some individuals more vulnerable than others to drug dependence. People who compulsively seek novelty, the adventure seekers, also tend to experiment with drugs more than persons who are cautious by nature and prefer routine. The same dopamine system, in fact, is apparently activated both by drugs and by risk-taking adventures such as parachuting. Research on disordered gambling shows that gambling disorders run in families (Linden, 2011). Relatives of compulsive gamblers disproportionately have substance use problems and personality and mental disorders.

It has long been known that introverts, who are subject to a strong reaction to stimuli and concomitant anxiety, are inclined to get sleepy under the influence of alcohol, whereas extroverts are inclined to feel more stimulated and ready for action. Variously called introverted, shy, or harm avoidant, individuals who react strongly to stress are prime candidates for misuse of alcohol and tranquilizing drugs. Monkey research offers some evidence that future drinking may be predicted by responses to stress during infancy.

Genetic factors have been shown to be prominent in some monkeys that were separated from their mothers at birth and that had high cortical concentration in their blood, which indicated a high level of sensitivity. In adulthood, these more sensitive monkeys drank more alcohol than did other monkeys that had endured the same degree of stress (NIAAA, 2000). Now, for the first time, according to Carey (2009), researchers have direct evidence that the same system is at work in humans. In a comparison study of the brains of people who committed suicide and who had had been abused in childhood with brains of others who committed suicide and who had not suffered abuse, researchers found evidence of genetic alterations that made the former group more susceptible to stress. Together, such studies confirm a nature–nurture interconnectedness.

Now researchers are finding that mice lacking a particular enzyme (PKCe) are far less likely to consume alcohol than those with this enzyme. Mice lacking PKCe react strongly to a limited amount of alcohol and to tranquilizers (benzodiazepines); the absence of this enzyme enhances the effect of alcohol and other depressants on a molecule receptor involved in the transmission of feelings of relaxation and sedation. The findings from this study support the emerging concept that increased sensitivity to intoxication reduces the likelihood that one will drink heavily. If these results are confirmed in humans, they may provide a means to help identify high risk youth for targeted intervention programs (Merkl, 2010).

Genetic differences in people can also inhibit the risk of addiction. Many Asians, for example, as we have seen, suffer rapid metabolism of alcohol to the poison acetaldehyde. This leads to greater buildup of this toxic product in the bloodstream, which produces flushing and palpitations. Marc Schuckit (2000) includes Israelis and the Maori peoples of New Zealand along with Asians as groups that experience negative reactions to alcohol consumption. All three groups have a lower rate of alcoholism than other ethnic populations, at least in part because of this genetic anomaly.

Another "defective" gene sometimes found in humans prevents nicotine addiction. Men with this genetic mutation are unlikely to become addicted to cigarettes and are likely to be able to quit smoking easily, according to recent research (Schuckit, 2009). Conversely, it is thought that persons with certain genetic variations can tolerate more nicotine without feeling sick and therefore, they smoke more and are highly inclined to become addicted (American

Psychological Association, 2009). Common genes likely play a part in the strong link between nicotine and ethanol intake in the same individuals.

According to the theory of evolution, members of a species develop traits that are best adapted to their environment, with the result that survival rates are higher in offspring that have those traits. Writing in the best-selling *Genome,* Ridley (2000) provides a striking example of genetic adaptability to the environment by ethnic groups isolated for long periods. The ability to regularly drink alcohol without developing dependence, which most people have in countries where water was unsanitary, resulted from thousands of years of selection of people who could drink. Nomadic persons in Australia and North America, however, who lived where water was safe, did not require alcohol and developed no resistance to its effects. Such changes that do occur through adaptation, however, have developed through a long evolutionary process (Ginsberg et al., 2004).

Differences in brain chemistry may predispose some people to become users not only of depressants such as alcohol but also of stimulants. In this case, those with lower levels of dopamine D2 receptors in their brains are more inclined than others to like the effect of stimulants (Giordano & Blum, 2010). In food- and drug-addicted individuals, dopamine deficiency is usually due to an association with the dopamine D2 receptor gene A1 allele. In such individuals craving for substances that will increase dopamine availability at the brain's reward site is common. Repeated episodes of substance use can result in reduced dopamine receptivity. Meanwhile, researchers are opening many new avenues of research into common factors in genetic vulnerability (differences in the sequence of DNA among individuals) to addiction through their scanning of the human genome to identify genes linked to substance misuse. Studies currently underway are helping to identify how the variations in relevant genes contribute to differences in addiction vulnerability and in the development of medications to normalize brain functions.

Recall the research from NIAAA (2007) that smoking reduces one's sensitivity to alcohol. Although the gateway theory that one drug leads to another has been largely discounted, these research findings give some credence to the notion that the effect of smoking may increase the tolerance for drinking, and tolerance, as we know, is associated with alcohol dependence. For persons wishing to curb their drinking consumption, smoking cessation might be the place to start.

The overlap between smoking in people of all ages and attention deficit hyperactivity disorder (ADHD) is widely noted in the literature (Modesto-Lowe, Danforth, et al., 2010). It is easy to understand the appeal addictive substances have for individuals with short attention spans and/or hyperactivity, the defining characteristics of ADHD. The self-medication factor is also pronounced in drug use by people with ADHD because it improves their level of concentration. Typically, the individual with hyperactivity is driven to drive himself or herself excessively; to spend money, also excessively; and to engage in risk taking such as experimentation with drugs. Adolescents who self-report ADHD tend to smoke at an earlier age of onset and to smoke a higher quantity of cigarettes than adolescent smokers who do not have these characteristics.

In conclusion, there is no one genetic marker by which scientists or physicians could determine who will become alcohol dependent. As with other genetic disorders, as Schuckit (2009) cautions, it is likely that a variety of genetic characteristics, in combination with key environmental factors, contribute to the risk of addiction.

MEDICAL CONSEQUENCES OF SUBSTANCE MISUSE

Alcohol misuse costs the United States a staggering $185 billion a year, more than all illegal drugs combined. These costs were attributed to lost productivity, healthcare expenditures, motor vehicle accidents, and crime (NIAAA, 2009). American businesses lose an estimated $134 billion a year in lost productivity, on-the-job accidents, compensation claims, and absenteeism from alcohol misuse alone (Brink, 2004). Yet, insurance coverage for substance abuse treatment far from meets the need.

Because alcohol is water soluble, the body absorbs alcohol directly into the bloodstream. Alcohol's molecules easily travel across the blood–brain barrier and affect brain functioning almost immediately. Alcohol can even cross the placental barrier and affect fetal development in a way that no other drug can. Over the years, medical scientists have documented the effects of alcohol on the body's organs and its role on the development of a variety of psychological problems, including brain structure and functioning, liver cirrhosis, cardiovascular diseases, and fetal alcohol syndrome (McNeece & DiNitto, 2005). In contrast, research on the long-term effects of some of the newer drugs is in its infancy.

Alcohol misuse can be an indirect cause of death such as by a heart attack. The World Health Organization (WHO) (2010), in its first global report on substance use determined that:

- Many more people suffer from alcohol use disorders compared to drug use disorders, and both types are more common in men than women.
- Alcohol causes the highest demand for treatment of substance use disorders in most world regions except the Americas, where treatment demand is mainly for cocaine use disorders.
- Every year alcohol kills 35 people per every 100,000, and illicit drugs kill four people per every 100,000 people.

The leading cause of preventable death worldwide, however, is tobacco use, which kills nearly 5 million people each year (WHO, 2011c). An estimated 80% of these premature deaths occur in persons living in low- and middle-income countries.

Because many of the estimated deaths associated with alcohol intoxication are due to injuries sustained in accidents, suicides, drownings, and homicides, much of the loss of life is of young people, that is, people in their prime who would have had many years ahead of them. The number of deaths tied to illicit drug use is estimated to be far lower than those attributed to alcohol. Another interesting fact about mortality statistics, as reported by Sherer (2006) in the *Psychiatric Times,* is that substance-related fatalities are occurring in an older age group than those in previous decades. In this section, we focus on that part of the body uniquely affected by substance (and especially alcohol) misuse—the brain.

Brain Impairment

Alcohol contributes to brain damage both directly and indirectly. Damage may occur in the form of a brain shrinking from the toxic effects of the alcohol itself, or as a result of damage to the nervous system because of nutritional deficits associated with alcoholism. Wernicke's syndrome and Korsakoff's psychosis are thought to derive from a lack of thiamine, or vitamin B_1 (NIAAA, 2004). Some researchers, however, believe the effect of alcohol per se is involved, whether directly or indirectly, from poor general health status or from severe liver disease.

Heavy drinking affects the cardiovascular system. Three or more drinks per day increase both blood pressure and low-density lipoprotein (LDL) cholesterol, and also enhance the risk of cardiomyopathy.

Wernicke's syndrome is characterized by paralysis of normal eye movements, mental confusion, and problems with walking and balance. This syndrome, according to Osher (2000), affects several sections of the brain—the midbrain and third and fourth ventricles.

Korsakoff's psychosis results from damage to areas of the brain important to memory function. Wernicke's syndrome is often associated with *peripheral neuropathy,* or damage to the peripheral nerves. Fifteen percent of those with alcohol dependence develop peripheral neuropathy associated with numbness and decreases in vibration and position sense, especially in the legs (Schuckit, 2009). Numbness in one's lower legs is the consequence.

Numbness that does not disappear with vitamin therapy indicates that damage to the nervous system is permanent and irreversible. Approximately 80–90% of people with Wernicke's encephalopathy also develop Korsakoff's (NIAAA, 2004).

Korsakoff's psychosis, sometimes called Wernicke–Korsakoff's syndrome and popularly known as wet brain, is a long-term result of brain damage. Patients with this disease experience much confusion and severe short-term memory deficits. They may not retain information. *Confabulation* is a unique characteristic that involves fantasizing to fill in the gaps of memory. Although the "tall tales" seem to be ridiculous fabrications or downright lies, there appears to be no "method in this madness" other than an inability to distinguish fact from fiction. Although individuals with this affliction can become paranoid on occasion, they generally have a carefree unconcern about the

FIGURE 3.6 | REDUCED BRAIN MASS IN ALCOHOLICS

Images displayed in the coronal orientation from MRI and DTI studies of a 61-year-old
healthy man (upper images) and a 60-year-old alcoholic man (lower images). The
high-resolution MRI slices are at the same locations as the fractional anisotropy images
of the DTI panels. Note on the MRI the thinner corpus callosum displaced upward by
enlarged ventricles and, on the DTI, less well-delineated white matter tracts in the
alcoholic man compared with the healthy man.

Source: NIAAA, 2004. *Using Magnetic Resonance Imaging and Diffusion Tensor Imaging to Assess Brain
Damage in Alcoholics.* Images by Margaret Rosenbloom, Edith V. Sullivan, and Adolf Pfefferbaum. Retrieved
from http://pubs.niaaa.nih.gov/publications/arh27-2/146-152.htm.

present or future. Figure 3.6 presents photographs of a normal cross-section
of the brain and one that is severely damaged by alcohol misuse.

Research shows a correlation between alcoholism and a poor sense of
smell. Even in recovery, people have been shown to experience deficiencies in
prefrontal cognitive abilities, and these abilities are correlated with a defective
sense of smell (Rupp, Fleischhacker, et al., 2006). These findings on the significance of smell were based on extensive testing of 32 alcohol-dependent
patients and 30 healthy comparison subjects and provide further support to
the hypothesis that the frontal lobes are especially vulnerable to alcohol-
related damage.

Oliver Sacks (1985), neurologist and author of *Awakenings* and *The Man
Who Mistook His Wife for a Hat,* provides rich case histories of persons with

neurological disorders. The latter provides portraits of two individuals with Korsakoff's psychosis. Mr. Thompson, an ex-grocer with severe Korsakoff's, was institutionalized for his memory problems. Sacks describes the working of Mr. Thompson's mind: "Deprived of continuity, of a quiet, continuous, inner narrative, he is driven to a sort of irrational frenzy—hence his ceaseless tales, his confabulations, his mythomania [abnormal tendency to lie]" (p. 111). Lack of feelings is a key characteristic of this condition. This man had become desouled, according to Sacks. Typically, such patients fail to realize the tragedy of the situation or the distress of their loved ones in dealing with them. (van Wormer's father suffered from Korsakoff's psychosis for the last two decades or so of his life.)

Use of the popular drug Ecstasy also may cause long-term impairment. Brain scans of heavy Ecstasy users provide evidence of neuron damage associated with an inability to use serotonin (Doweiko, 2009). Similarly, after heavy methamphetamine use, the impact is seen in memory and motor coordination. A review of the brain research on marijuana users with regard to the long-term impact of use on neurocognitive abilities revealed that although marijuana is associated with short-term memory and learning problems, the damage is not permanent (Grant, Gonzalez, Carey, Natarajan, & Wolfson, 2003).

LIVER DAMAGE

Because the liver metabolizes alcohol ahead of anything else, alcohol misuse's toll to the body is enormous. Chronic exposure to alcohol may result in liver damage; some individuals are more susceptible than others. The first manifestation of alcohol-related liver problems is the development of a fatty liver. Although the symptoms are not obvious, this condition can easily be detected through blood tests (Doweiko, 2009).

About one in three heavy drinkers eventually develops scars in the liver associated with cirrhosis, a disease in which liver cells are destroyed and the organ no longer is able to process nutrients in food. *Alcoholic hepatitis* (not the same as general hepatitis, which has a different etiology) can be considered the second stage of alcoholic liver disease. This highly dangerous condition is characterized by liver swelling, jaundice, and fever. Many persons with liver disease take on a yellow skin color, which comes from excessive amounts of bile that circulate in the bloodstream. With abstinence, this condition can be reversed. If the condition is not reversed, *cirrhosis* of the liver can occur. About 10% of all people who have been diagnosed with alcoholism go on to develop cirrhosis (Zetterman, 2010). With the progression of this disease, all of the liver's functions are compromised, including, first and foremost, the immune system.

As more tissue of the liver is damaged over time, the liver is no longer able to effectively remove toxins from the blood. Blood pressure builds up within the vessels, and increasing pressure is put on the heart (Doweiko, 2009). People with serious drinking problems who smoke more than one pack of cigarettes per day have three times the risk of cirrhosis as do hard drinkers who do not smoke (NIAAA, 2005). The scarred liver, unable to handle the usual blood flow, moreover, causes the blood to seek alternative routes to the heart. A tremendous pressure builds up in alternative vessels. When bulging veins emerge on the surface of the esophagus, the potentially fatal condition called *esophageal varices* occurs (Doweiko, 2009). Spidery veins may appear on the face and chest, and hemorrhoids may develop. The patient may die from hemorrhage. Edema, which is fluid accumulation throughout the body, is another serious consequence of cirrhosis. Large amounts of fluid can collect until the abdomen is shockingly distended, a condition known as ascites.

Treatment of alcoholic cirrhosis consists of total abstinence from alcohol and careful attention to diet. For terminally ill patients, a liver transplant provides the only possibility of survival. A summary of empirical research results of liver transplantation reveals that survival rates for persons who lost their liver function through drinking are as good as those for patients who did not have drinking problems (NIAAA, 2005). However popular opposition continues to providing replacement for people who destroyed their livers through drinking.

Because chronic heavy drinking is the primary cause of cirrhosis, the World Health Organization (2004) presents annual mortality rates by country for death due to cirrhosis. The rates provide researchers with the most reliable estimates of a nation's alcoholism rates. Some interesting examples of cirrhosis of the liver mortality rates per 100,000 are Greece 3.8, Ireland 3.94, Sweden 3.97, United States 7.47, Cuba 7.6, Costa Rica 7.8, and Hungary 45.79. There is speculation that the extremely high cirrhosis of the liver rate in Hungary, as in other European countries, is related to the poor quality of the alcohol consumed (Szcs, Sarvary, McKee, & Adany, 2005). Interestingly, as a study of these rates will show, high alcohol consumption in a population does not always mean a high rate of disease. A key factor in alcohol-related disease is how much alcohol is consumed at any one time. The reason is illustrated by examining the state of Wisconsin, where consumption seems to be spread fairly evenly across the population (Wisconsin is a state of extremely high alcohol consumption and a relatively low rate of cirrhosis of the liver) (CDC, 2010a). Alcoholism is not associated with liver disease alone, but also with malnutrition, as so many of the calories are consumed in the form of alcohol. Infections are another major problem, especially for persons with liver problems. Because alcohol interferes with the function of white blood cells, heavy drinkers are highly susceptible to colds and pneumonia. Poor nutrition, in itself, influences all aspects of immunity.

Skin diseases such as psoriasis may cover the entire body. Additionally, digestive abnormalities and chronic diarrhea contribute to overall susceptibility to disease. The pancreas is another trouble spot for heavy users of alcohol. A major organ of the body, the pancreas, secretes digestive enzymes and insulin, that help break down food into its small, basic chemical components for the absorption in the intestines. When the pancreas is swollen from chronic alcohol abuse, digestion becomes very difficult. *Pancreatitis,* often caused by alcohol-induced inflammation, is an extremely painful and dangerous condition.

THE HEART

Although moderate drinking generally decreases the risk for cardiovascular disease, heavy drinking over long periods will likely have the opposite effect (WHO, 2004). Chronic alcohol use results in the suppression of normal red blood cell formation and can harm the cardiovascular system. Such heavy drinking can also cause the heart to become enlarged and lose some of its ability to contract

The highly addictive substance, nicotine, is incontrovertibly implicated in the genesis of cardiovascular disease (Perkinson, 2012). Nicotine is both water- and fat-soluble; thus, it accumulates throughout the organs of the body. One of the effects of nicotine, according to the American Heart Association, is that it causes constriction of the blood vessels. Nicotine increases blood pressure and heart rate, causing smokers to breathe faster and less deeply. Smoking leads to inadequate blood supply due to the effects of carbon monoxide discharged from tobacco smoke, so the heart needs to work faster for the body to maintain an adequate supply of oxygen (Doweiko, 2009). Because of the propensity for persons to continue to smoke during recovery from alcoholism, the leading cause of death for persons in recovery is tobacco-related illness (NIAAA, 2007).

Cocaine is the drug most closely associated in the public mind with heart problems and heart attacks. Although this occurs rarely, cocaine-related deaths may occur on first use and are often a result of cardiac arrest or seizures followed by respiratory arrest. More common is a disturbance in heart rhythm, detected as an irregular heartbeat. The risk comes not in occasional use of small amounts but after tolerance has developed and increased dosage leads to toxicity. The deaths that do result are commonly due to the synergistic effect of cocaine and alcohol together (NIDA, 2010).

THE GENITOURINARY TRACT

In both sexes, problems with urination may result from excessive alcohol use. Indirect interference in the filtration process and the elimination of the waste produced by the kidney seem to be the problem (Kinney, 2011). When *kidney failure* follows, the trouble is not in the kidneys themselves but in a circulating toxic factor resulting from the associated liver disease.

Effects on the *reproductive system* are widely known to accompany heavy alcohol use. The few clinical studies of alcoholic women suggest ovulation and menstrual difficulties are caused by alcohol-induced hormonal imbalance (Doweiko, 2009). In men, impotence, low testosterone levels, low sperm count, and testicular atrophy are widely reported. Breast enlargement has been observed in alcoholic men, as has an absence of body hair on the chest and arms accompanied by a lower rate of baldness.

Inasmuch as intoxication lowers inhibitions and caution may be "thrown to the wind," the risks of both AIDS contraction and unwanted pregnancy multiply. Perhaps the most tragic consequences of substance use in one generation are seen in the birth defects of the next generation. *Fetal alcohol syndrome* (FAS) is now recognized as a leading known cause of mental retardation. Medical reports confirm that the fetus takes in alcohol from the mother's blood. Whereas classical fetal alcohol syndrome may be readily identified by physical characteristics in the child—smaller upper lip, flat nose, and small head—milder defects, classified as *fetal alcohol effects* (FAE), are properly diagnosed only rarely. Figure 3.7 shows the discriminating features characteristic of children with FAS.

Although the percentage of hard-drinking mothers who have spontaneous abortions or babies with FAS is not known, it is known that habitual or even occasional drinking by an expectant mother can endanger the health of her fetus. The effect on neurological development occurs in the earliest stage of pregnancy (Thomas, Warren, & Hewitt, 2010). This means that by the time

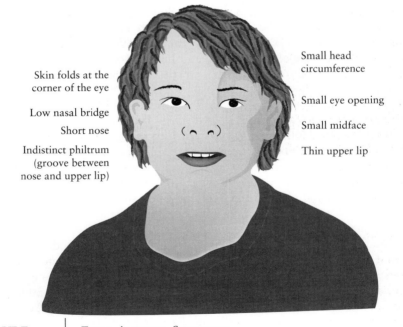

Skin folds at the corner of the eye

Low nasal bridge

Short nose

Indistinct philtrum (groove between nose and upper lip)

Small head circumference

Small eye opening

Small midface

Thin upper lip

FIGURE 3.7 | FETAL ALCOHOL SYNDROME

Facial features characteristic of fetal alcohol syndrome (FAS).

Source: NIAAA. *Alcohol Alert*, October 2004, no. 63, p. 5. http://www.niaaa.nih.gov/Publications/AlcoholAlerts/Documents/aa63.pdf.

a fertile woman confirms her pregnancy, the damage may already be done. In countries such as South Africa, where among certain farm workers high liquor consumption during pregnancy is common, and in Russia where heavy drinking of vodka is common, the FAS rate is extremely high.

A large dose of alcohol given to a pregnant mouse experimentally produces severe abnormalities in the developing fetus. The eye damage, stunted brain, and facial deformities that result are reminiscent of human babies with FAS (Anthony, Vinci-Booher, et al., 2010).

The role of intoxication on male sperm and its impact on the conceived child has only recently been studied. Sperm susceptibility to environmental damage, such as pesticides, of course has been known for years; recent studies link male smoking to the birth of underweight infants. Rodent experiments reveal learning difficulties in offspring of morphine-exposed fathers. Data on cocaine's ability to bind to sperm ("Cocaine May Piggyback," 1991; Taleff & Babcock, 2006) indicate the need for further studies on the long-unrecognized impact of male intoxication on development of the fetus. In a review of studies on the impact of alcohol consumption in male rats on their offspring, Abel (2004) and the U.S. Department of Health and Human Services (2000) concluded that damaged sperm may indeed have an impact on the development of the unborn child.

Longitudinal studies indicate that FAS and FAE exist on a continuum of cognitive-behavioral defects. School-age children born of heavily drinking mothers are found to be highly distractible in their learning operations. Hyperactivity, subnormal intelligence, and mood problems are found to persist over time. Long-term treatment for high-risk pregnant women is one of the greatest unmet needs of alcoholism prevention efforts today. Help for adults who suffer the effects of FAS is also hard to find.

Diagnosis of FAS and FAE has always been difficult. Through magnetic resonance imaging (MRI), we can now compare brain structures in normal adolescents with those exposed in utero to the effects of maternal heavy drinking. Imaging studies have demonstrated structural abnormalities in some brain regions but not in others. Although such research is in its infancy, what we do know is that prenatal alcohol exposure can cause specific irreversible damage and that such brain damage may be present even in the absence of identifiable facial characteristics. Although too expensive for regular use, this technology offers much promise for the future detection of fetal alcohol syndrome in children and adults and clarification of which areas of the brain are most affected. A news report from Canada indicates that a simple test that tracks eye movements can accurately diagnose fetal alcohol syndrome (Ubelacker, 2005).

What is the effect of crack cocaine use on unborn children? Are "crack babies" the hopeless cases that earlier media reports made them out to be? In fact, as experts inform us, alcohol and nicotine pose greater dangers to unborn babies than does crack cocaine (Okie, 2009). Fortunately, infants exposed to crack cocaine often outgrow their health problems, especially when placed in a nurturing environment. The same is not true for alcohol-exposed babies, however. A recent study of orphaned children from Russia and other countries in Eastern Europe who were adopted in Sweden revealed that around half of them had an alcohol-related neurodevelopmental disorder of some sort, most often the most severe form, fetal alcohol syndrome (Landgren, Svensson, et al., 2010). Tobacco use by pregnant women often itself is associated with sudden infant deaths and later respiratory problems in offspring as well as behavioral problems in adolescence (Doweiko, 2009). And research shows that prenatal exposure to tobacco makes it more likely that the offspring will smoke themselves. It is not yet known if this is true for drugs such as cocaine (Okie, 2009).

Opiates, like alcohol, cross the placental barrier in pregnant women; babies born to mothers who have used heroin thus have withdrawal symptoms, and some die as a result. In the Midwest, an increasing number of methamphetamine-addicted babies are being born. Because meth has more long-lasting effects than cocaine, experts fear the impact of prenatal exposure could be more long lasting (Lippert, 2000).

BIOLOGICALLY BASED INTERVENTIONS

We have seen in our review of the empirical research how, through prolonged drug exposure, ongoing damage to the brain creates a situation of high drug tolerance and relentless craving. A major emphasis of neurobiological research today is on finding ways to restore normal brain functioning and treat what Volkow (2010b) describes as a brain disease. Just as individuals with schizophrenia require medical treatments to normalize their behavior, we need to contemplate similar treatment for persons whose brain states have been altered artificially through drugs. Far from being a threat to traditional therapy, medical interventions should help clients rebound sooner and, accordingly, be more amenable to treatment.

Although the psychological and social components of the illness must be attended to, as long as the "brain is screaming for booze," as Knapp (1997) puts it, "no number of revelations about underlying causes is going to counter that call" (p. 129). In recent years, the development of medications to treat substance dependence has ushered in a new era of treatment and attitudes toward treatment. Until 1995, when naltrexone obtained government approval, the only medical treatment approved for alcoholism in the United States was Antabuse (disulfiram). Antabuse simply keeps people from drinking because, when combined with alcohol, this drug will provoke intense vomiting. The bulk of the early research in the field of substance abuse treatment focused on reducing withdrawal pain and risk. Today, pharmacological researchers are conducting clinical trials with medications, singly and in combination, designed to help people manage alcohol and drug cravings and avoid relapse. The search is on for new and more effective medications appropriate for populations not previously included in clinical trials: adolescents, women, and older adults with various addictions and mental disorders.

One of the most promising recent research developments related to the biology of the brain comes ironically from the cognitive school—behavioral therapies.

BEHAVIORAL THERAPIES

According to research, which is still preliminary, behavioral therapies geared toward helping individuals who have problems stemming from low levels of serotonin or dopamine available in the brain can actually alter these levels of the brain's natural opiates through deliberate changes in thought processes. We begin this section, however, with behavioral therapy of a different sort, the controversial treatment that is derived straight from classical conditioning.

CHEMICAL AVERSION THERAPY

The treatment intervention known as aversion treatment is based on Pavlov's classical conditioning in the form of noxious drugs that produce nausea when paired with alcohol. After four sessions of intense vomiting, patients begin to gag at the mere sight of alcohol. This form of treatment became familiar to van Wormer while she was working in Washington State counseling graduates of the Schick Shadel Hospital program. Described on its website as having the "#1 success rate for addiction treatment" (2011), Schick Shadel is a licensed medical facility that qualifies for insurance reimbursement by the major insurance companies. The website (http://www.schickshadel.com) includes the smiling faces of ex-clients and current staff.

The oldest behavioral conditioning approach to alcoholism, aversion therapy was popular before the advent of AA. In fact, as Nan Robertson (1988, p. 184) informs us, Bill W., before he cofounded AA, was treated unsuccessfully in a "purge and puke" program. This type of therapy is based on Skinner's operant conditioning principles: If drinking alcohol leads to rewarding consequences, it is likely to continue; if it leads to punishment, it is likely to be discontinued. For effective results, the punishment must be closely connected to the act. A hangover the day after or bankruptcy a year later is too far removed from the stimulus to yield to aversion therapy.

Treatment relies on nausea-inducing drugs (for example, emetine) given in conjunction with alcohol. When this is repeated over time, the alcohol itself, ideally, will elicit nausea. The pairing of the alcohol with the emetic causes the nausea to create the desired association of the experience of vomiting with the drinking. Although there have been unlicensed treatment centers that have used various forms of aversion therapy, only one licensed treatment facility survives, and that is the Schick Shadel Hospital in Seattle, Washington. Schick Shadel is a reputable treatment center, purportedly with a high success rate. Serious precautions are taken at this clinic to screen clients with health problems that could put them at risk from painful procedures. For clients with heart conditions or high blood pressure or for bulimic patients (with their damaged vomiting reflexes), shock treatments are substituted for the emetine. Pregnant women are excluded from these treatments.

A full description of Schick Shadel treatment and its philosophy can be obtained on its website. Treatment today, as compared with 10 or so years ago, is no longer only for alcoholism but for problems concerning crystal meth, cocaine, and nicotine addiction. Reports in the late 1970s of high death rates among elderly clients caused several of these types of treatment centers to close their doors. Although the treatment is more carefully provided today, the infliction of pain, nausea, sickness, and electric shock to condition aversion to alcohol raises some ethical concerns. Moreover, it is aesthetically unappealing. Nevertheless, chemical aversion therapy consistently has been shown to be highly effective for alcoholism treatment (Hester & Miller, 2003).

COVERT SENSITIZATION

Another variety of aversion therapy that has been shown effective involves instructing clients to imagine physical discomfort in association with drinking. Imagining the sensation of throwing up while drinking can bring positive results. The advantages over aversive conditioning are obvious: Because the client does not actually experience nausea or shock, there are no medical dangers (Fisher & Harrison, 2008). Covert sensitization and imagining are easy for clients to learn and apply when they think they might be using again; these techniques can be tailored for individual use (Stevens & Smith, 2004).

CHANGING BRAIN CHEMISTRY

The bad news about heavy intoxicants, as we learned earlier in this chapter, is the neurological brain injury that can result. The good news, as modern research shows us, is that some of the brain degeneration can be reversed through therapy. Clinical studies suggest that exercising the brain likely brings about regrowth in the frontal cortex. Improvement in this part of the brain enhances one's chances of recovery. Additionally, thiamine therapy seems to increase treatment effects inasmuch as depletion of this vitamin is thought to be implicated in brain dysfunction associated with alcoholism.

Begley (2007) reveals how modern science has refuted earlier dogma—the doctrine of the unchanging human brain. In place of this dogma has come the realization that the adult brain retains impressive powers of *neuroplasticity*, or "the ability to change its structure and function in response to experience" (p. 74). Jeffrey Schwartz (1997), the author of *Brain Lock* and the coauthor of *The Mind and the Brain* (Schwartz & Begley, 2003), revealed this phenomenon earlier, namely, that psychological counseling can alter brain chemistry and possibly restore more normal functioning. In an experiment described by Schwartz, clients suffering from obsessive-compulsive disorder were guided to substitute healthy for unhealthy thoughts every time an obsessive urge came over them. After 10 weeks of behavioral instruction, neuroimaging revealed observable changes in brain chemistry; these changes were observed in the part of the brain thought to be affected by this disorder. More recently, when being interviewed by Begley (2007), Schwartz called his cognitive-behavioral therapy a form of "self-directed neuroplasticity" and concluded that "the mind can change the brain" (p. 77).

The implications of these findings are profound. Just as mental and physical practice of the piano paves the way for mastery as the brain strengthens connections among neurons for this function, so the individual can learn cognitive techniques in therapy with results that are physiological as well as psychological. Given the knowledge that the brain has the ability to rewire itself through cognitive exercises, counselors can feel confident that their teaching of exercises geared toward changing the client's unhealthy "self-talk" (see Chapter 8) are empirically valid. And lest we be skeptical of these claims, we can contemplate the more familiar phenomenon of brain recovery as revealed in experimentation with stroke victims who learn to redirect activities to undamaged areas of the brain and in people with obsessive-compulsive disorder who learn thinking exercises to get their compulsions under control.

Further support is lent to the notion that brain structure and function can be altered by cognitions in studies of the impact of trauma on the brain. Particular hormones secreted in times of severe stress can alter neurochemistry sufficiently to effect long-term changes in neurons and brain systems. PET scans of eight children reared in Romanian orphanages until their adoption showed such abnormalities, as Harriette Johnson (2004) indicates.

The technological revolution in neurological research is providing documentation for theories that previously were based only on behavioral observation. Although more has been learned in the past few years than in several previous decades, we are just on the brink of understanding addiction and the roots of addiction in the brain.

PHARMACEUTICAL INTERVENTIONS

If drug dependence is considered less a matter of will than of brain chemistry, then the development of medications to prevent the lows or block the highs is inevitable. The growing awareness of serotonin's central role in mood and compulsive behavior has been paralleled by a boom in the introduction of drugs that target serotonin levels. Selective serotonin reuptake inhibitors (SSRIs), such as fluoxetine (Prozac), sertraline hydrochloride (Zoloft), and paroxetine (Paxil), are prescribed to treat a wide range of disorders, such as binge drinking and eating, obsessive-compulsive disorder, autism, panic attacks, schizophrenia, and uncontrolled aggression. But these now familiar medications are just the beginning.

Biochemical problems call for biochemical solutions, or so it is argued. The findings from brain research have laid the groundwork for a series of dozens of clinical trials of various prescriptions to be funded by the two major research funding organizations: NIAAA and NIDA. The Substance Abuse and Mental Health Services Administration (SAMHSA) has produced *TIP 49*, which is a whole manual with one chapter each devoted to one of the new medications that have been approved for use by the Food and Drug Administration for treating alcohol use disorders. Only four of the most widely used prescription drugs are discussed—acamprosate, disulfiram (Antabuse), oral naltrexone, and extended-release injectable naltrexone, but more knowledge will be added to the website at http://www.kap.samhsa.gov as it becomes available. In response to this contemporary approach to rely on medication management, even many of the mainstream treatment centers, such as Hazelden in Minnesota, are conducting research on the effectiveness of medications that act on the brain as an aid in recovery.

Still, as *TIP 49* suggests:

> Pharmacotherapy for alcohol use disorders (AUDs) is underused both in specialized substance abuse treatment programs and in office-based medical practice. The consensus panel acknowledges that much resistance to pharmacotherapy exists—from third-party payers, some clinicians, some individuals participating in self-help groups who view medications as substituting a pill for self-empowerment and self-responsibility, and some patients and their families. (p. 45)

Pharmacotherapy may be underused as the SAMHSA manual suggests. But there is no doubt this is the wave of the future. Attitudes have definitely changed, and treatment providers are increasingly regarding medications as useful adjuncts to counseling and other psychosocial interventions (Van Pelt, 2009). We are now in the midst of a major paradigm shift in the acceptance by substance abuse treatment providers of taking a medication orally (or a shot or wearing a patch) to curb excessive appetites and bingeing, something that would have been unthinkable one or two decades ago. Today, virtually all substance-use federal funding seems to be geared toward medical as opposed to psychotherapeutic treatments. Although healthcare providers, in this time of tight fiscal constraints, are in search of effective but brief interventions, pharmaceutical companies have a strong economic stake in producing and marketing products to meet the growing treatment demand.

The identification of genes that encode subunits of receptors for neurotransmitters such as dopamine, GABA, serotonin, and others paves the way for the identification of people at risk for both depression and alcoholism because both conditions often co-occur in the same individual. Such identification of risk-associated genes also paves the way for specialized medication development (Li, 2004).

ALCOHOLISM

Several types of medications are used to help prevent relapse. Psychoactive drugs act upon certain neurotransmitters. Some drugs, such as morphine, bind the receptor site and enhance the effect of the neurotransmitter, whereas certain antipsychotic drugs block the effect of dopamine. The SSRI antidepressants (e.g., Zoloft and Prozac), block the neurotransmitters from reuptake, thus allowing the chemical more time and influence at the receptor site. People who are depressed, as all counselors know, lose their incentive to stay sober. Keeping their spirits up, especially early in treatment, is vital. Lest too much faith be put in these antidepressants, readers should refer to a provocative article in the *Journal of the American Medical Association* by Fournier, DeRebeis, and colleagues (2010). In their examination of data from empirically based research on the effectiveness of antidepressants, the authors reached this jarring conclusion: "Antidepressant medications represent the best established treatment for major depressive disorder, but there is little evidence that they have a specific pharmacological effect relative to pill placebo for patients with less severe depression" (p. 47). A seven-page article in *Newsweek* by science writer Sharon Begley (2010) entitled "The Depressing News about Antidepressants" referred to this and related research. We should keep in mind, as Begley notes, that antidepressants produced profits of $9.6 billion in 2008, and that the drug companies have a major influence on research and on those who prescribe the medication.

Naltrexone is the drug approved by the Federal Drug Administration in 1995 to reduce craving in people addicted to heroin. This medication is in a separate class from the antidepressants and from the addictive antianxiety drugs such as Valium and Librium. It is also in a separate class from the antidepressants such as Prozac. Those drugs are classified as agonists. Agonists are drugs that can mimic the effects of a natural neurotransmitter to produce a high (Miller et al., 2011). Naltrexone, in contrast, is an anti-agonist. Such drugs work by blocking alcohol–brain interactions that produce a high. Naltrexone is an abstinence-enhancing drug. Basically, the fun is removed from the drinking, so patients taking these drugs lose their desire to partake. Remember the brain studies that showed how visual cues associated with drugs of choice produced conditioned responses in the brain? Well, naltrexone has been shown to block the chemical changes in the brain elicited by the environmental cues (smell of alcohol, sight of foaming beer, etc.).

In studies with alcohol-drinking rats, naltrexone was shown to decrease the amount of alcohol-induced dopamine (DHHS, 2000). In research on humans, it is found that patients with intense alcohol cravings during treatment may experience greater medication benefit than patients with low levels of alcohol craving (SAMHSA, 2009). The effectiveness of this drug apparently is limited to persons who drink to get a high, and for them it does not prevent an initial slip but reduces the amount of alcohol that is consumed (Doweiko, 2009). Because naltrexone targets the opiates in the brain, it reduces the reinforcing effects of alcohol and curbs cravings for both opioids and alcohol (SAMHSA).

The aim of the researchers and the pharmaceutical companies, no doubt, is to come up with a menu of medications for alcoholism similar to the variety of depression treatments available. As yet, however, these discoveries, like genetic research, are in their infancy, and most doctors consider alcoholism largely a behavioral problem. Results from an NIAAA-funded study found that naltrexone and treatment by means of 20 sessions of behavioral counseling are equally effective options for alcohol dependence when delivered with medical management (monitoring to encourage drug compliance). This 3-year COMBINE (Combining Medications and Behavioral Interventions for Alcoholism) study provided 16 weeks of treatment for 1,300 recently abstinent patients and then assessed the patients for clinical outcome. In the carefully controlled study, patients received naltrexone, acamprosate, both of these medications together, or placebo pills. Another four groups received counseling of various sorts in addition to the medications. The results, as reported in the *Journal of the American Medical Association* by Anton, O'Malley, and 17 colleagues (2006), showed that acamprosate had no significant effect on drinking and that naltrexone was effective in its own right even in the absence of counseling. Despite these disappointing results, European research has found acamprosate to be effective, and it is one of the most widely used medications to prevent relapse on that side of the Atlantic (SAMHSA, 2009). The efficacy of this drug, however, according to Miller and colleagues (2011) seems doubtful.

A more recent U.S. investigation that covered 3 years of combination treatments did find significant cost savings in regard to healthcare, prevention of arrest, and accidents when people with drinking problems received medical management and a combination of acamprosate and naltrexone (Zarkin, Bray, Aldridge, et al., 2010). These findings indirectly revealed the benefit of providing counseling along with the medicine. Around 800 patients participated in the study.

A major problem with naltrexone is that most people with alcohol and substance use disorders simply stop taking it (Doweiko, 2009; Miller et al., 2011). Another major drawback is the person has to be drug free before taking it. A new option that may help with the first problem, and that has been found to be effective with binge drinkers, is the extended release, injectable form of naltrexone, called Vivitrol (Vimont, 2011; Wasserman, 2006). Vivitrol, which is injected once a month, suppresses alcohol dependence by binding to opioid receptors in the brain. This drug blocks the neurotransmitters associated with alcohol dependence. Vivitrol is too expensive to be of practical use at the present time (Doweiko, 2009). One serious drawback with these types of drugs, in any case, is the low motivation of people to use them. After all, these antagonist drugs block the pleasure of drug taking, something many drug users may have no interest in doing.

To prevent homelessness and protect drug users who live on the streets, treatment providers need to be able to offer them a choice: Would they like to be treated with harm reduction strategies that help people with addiction problems cut down? Or would they prefer an addiction substitute such as methadone? Or would they prefer to be rendered immune to the drug's euphoric properties with a blocker medication such as naltrexone?

In our earlier review of the research led by Cloninger, which delineated Type 1 (late onset) and the more severe Type 2 (early onset) forms of alcoholism, we discussed a medication that was effective with only the early onset variety of the illness. This was the drug ondansetron. The study found ondansetron to have few side effects, and it can be given to people who are still drinking, which precludes the need for detoxification. This drug appears to block serotonin receptors in the brain, thus decreasing the craving for alcohol.

It is often said that people who have been seriously addicted to alcohol can never learn to drink moderately. Indeed, without the help of a medication that apparently normalizes their brain, they probably cannot handle alcohol. One would think if the brain could be normalized, then maybe even the seriously addicted drinker would know when, as the Norwegians say, "to put the cork back on the bottle" (Halvorsen, 2011, p. 268). They could then handle the alcohol before the alcohol handles them.

One direction for future clinical trials involves the mixing of two prescribed medications, such as ondansetron and naltrexone. The implications of the discovery of the differing effects of medication on different types of alcoholism are dramatic, not only for the future treatment of addiction but for what it says about the biological basis of alcohol dependence in general. Successful medication trials such as the ondansetron study targeting alcoholic subtypes and cocaine users, mark the dawn of a new day in the substance use treatment field. As it gets easier to determine people's genotypes, the door will be opened to tailoring addiction treatment with drugs such as ondansetron based on an individual's genes (Roan, 2011a).

One more medication discovery that provides hope for people with alcohol and other drug use disorders is a GABA-enhancing drug. (Recall from the discussion earlier in the chapter that the neurotransmitter GABA is an inhibitor that keeps our highs from overwhelming us.) This drug, topiramate (Topamax), is used to control epilepsy. For years, patients with epilepsy have reported that it helps them fight food cravings and lose weight. Now it is showing promise in early studies with alcoholism (Roan, 2011a) as well as gambling and eating disorders (Ehrenfeld, 2005). It has an advantage in that it can be started early, even with a person who is still drinking (Miller et al., 2011). Being able to apply one drug to different addictions is another major advantage. This ability makes sense because the same pleasure centers and pathways in the brain are activated by many different substances and behaviors. This finding is consistent with a major contention of this book, as stated in Chapter 1, that the disease is not alcoholism or an eating disorder but rather the tendency toward addiction itself.

NICOTINE TREATMENT

Nicotine takes a terrible toll on American health. People with brain receptor types more prone to addiction could be helped with intensive prevention efforts. For addictive types, breaking the smoking habit is reportedly as difficult as ending heroin addiction. In fact, the urge to light up a cigarette is practically irresistible for the 50 million or so who are still puffing. Those who would or could quit more easily have already done so.

Effective approaches for smoking cessation generally involve some form of nicotine substitute. Unlike other pharmacotherapy trials and treatment, these do not typically include a behavioral counseling component (Miller et al., 2011). The one exception would be the inpatient nicotine cessation program at the Mayo Clinic.

In recent years, nicotine chewing gum, skin patches, inhalers, nasal sprays, and antidepressant medications such as bupropion (Zyban) have helped to quell cravings for tobacco's addictive ingredient. Smoking-cessation classes that draw on mild aversion exercises such as requiring participants to chew the cigarette are waning in popularity now that medications are of proven effectiveness. Zyban and Wellbutrin are both brand names for bupro-prion, an antidepressant that is thought to work through blocking dopamine reuptake and targeting the nicotine receptor (O'Malley & Kosten, 2006). Zyban works differently from nicotine-replacement therapies, which help the smoker maintain his or her level of nicotine while breaking the habit. This medication is taken 1 or 2 weeks prior to the quit date as well as after to reduce the urge to smoke.

Chantix is the brand name for varenicline, another promising medication, although perhaps not as promising as the ads would have us believe. According to an article in *Medical News Today* (2009), this drug has the potential to be at least as effective as naltrexone in reducing drinking and smoking. Unlike naltrexone, this drug is not metabolized by the liver and may be safe to use by persons with impaired liver function. It works by making the patient produce more dopamine, which is supposed to lower the cravings. This drug can be considered a partial nicotine agonist to block nicotine receptors but still allow for a high (Miller et al., 2011). Gonzales and colleagues (2006) reported a success rate that was about one and a half times that of Zyban in keeping people off cigarettes for one year. One problem with the study, published in the *Journal of the American Medical Association,* was that it was funded by Pfizer, the makers of Chantix. This fact was not disclosed until after the study was published. In any case, the Food and Drug Administration approved this drug based on the reported effectiveness.

Naltrexone, which can be used for a wide variety of addictions, also has been found to help with smoking cessation, even in moderate smokers. Turning chain smokers into moderate smokers carries significant health benefits and can make quitting ultimately easier. King, Cao, and colleagues (2009) studied medical tests that were run on 78 nonalcoholic smokers enrolled in a clinical trial of naltrexone. Results showed that this drug reduced the frequency of heavy drinking in the participants as well as improved smoking cessation rates of the heavy drinkers and others in the study.

A benefit of Zyban and nicotine gum or the patch is that weight gain is significantly less when smokers use these products compared to a placebo group. The drug rimonabant (Accomplia) has been found especially effective in preventing weight gain in obese smokers who have quit (Filozof, Fernandez, & Fernandez-Cruz, 2004).

Nicotine maintenance products, such as gum, skin patches, and nasal sprays, help smokers wean themselves from cigarettes. Nicotine elevates mood and sharpens concentration, which explains why people with a history of depression, attention-deficit disorder, or schizophrenia are likely to smoke and get seriously hooked. Although nicotine gum is intended to be used only for several months, researchers are finding that in a small minority of ex-smokers, nicotine gum is chewed for years and years as the only way they can stop themselves from inhaling nicotine. One problem with nicotine gum apart from the unpleasant taste is that it takes several hours for the full effect to kick in. This is true of the patch as well. The spray, however, helps reduce cigarette cravings up to three times faster and thus is more effective overall (Peeples, 2010).

NIDA-supported research has played a major role in providing crucial insights into the neurobiological aspects of nicotine addiction; these understandings in turn have paved the way for pharmaceutical advances in treatment. Treating nicotine addiction as a medical problem helps remove the stigma attached to a person's difficulty in giving up smoking. In short, a medical understanding takes some of the blame off smokers and places it on the tobacco companies. This recognition of the similarity of nicotine addiction to other forms of chronic addiction, moreover, has brought about a major shift in thinking for the chemical dependence treatment field. The shift has evolved from clients smoking with staff in their therapy sessions, to smoking only in special areas, to having their smoking addiction treated as a drug dependence like any other.

Although inpatient treatment has been available for some time for people with alcohol and other drug disorders, chronic smokers, whose habits may be just as life threatening, have been denied this privilege. According to the Mayo Clinic (2011) website, its Nicotine Dependence Center offers the most up-to-date treatment approaches for outpatients, individuals who are hospitalized, and those who participate in the 8-day residential program. The clinic is also a research center that conducts clinical trials of drugs to help people lose their urge to smoke. Treatment at the Mayo Nicotine Dependence Center consists of the use of medications to relieve withdrawal, individual and group counseling, stress management, exercise sessions, and family work. More than 45,000 people have received services from this program, according to the website. The cost is increasingly covered by insurance.

For alcoholic smokers, it is better to quit both addictions at once, according to research in continuing experiments with humans such as that conducted at the University of California at San Francisco (Meyerhoff et al., 2006). Using fMRIs to scan the brains of 25 subjects diagnosed with alcoholism, around half of whom smoked, researchers found that after the subjects quit drinking, brain function and health improved only for those who did not smoke. Both chronic alcoholism and smoking are associated with cortical gray matter loss, which is a risk factor in cognitive decline. These findings point to the importance of smoking cessation early in substance abuse treatment to enhance sobriety (including sober thinking.) For clients taking Chantix, what works best is to take this drug for several weeks before actually quitting smoking in order to enhance treatment success (Roan, 2011b). This recommendation is based on research in England where successful results were obtained with a sample of smokers trying to quit.

ANTIDOTES FOR COCAINE AND METHAMPHETAMINE

A pharmaceutical strategy to medical treatment for cocaine addiction is to develop a drug that blocks production of dopamine produced in conjunction with cocaine use. Gamma vinyl-GABA (GVG), a drug used for years in Europe and Canada to treat epilepsy, has shown effectiveness in small clinical trials conducted in Mexico (Brodie, Case, et al., 2009). GVG, which blocks the addiction-related effects of cocaine, was found to help people with cocaine and alcohol use disorders maintain abstinence, and there were no side effects.

The blood pressure drug propranolol might help reduce cravings for cocaine in humans. Animal studies in which rats that were injected with cocaine to the point of addiction showed that their cocaine-seeking behavior was reduced under the influence of this beta blocker (Otis & Mueller, 2011).

MEDICATION FOR HEROIN USERS

When Hurricane Katrina struck, a story that got largely overlooked in the news was the suffering of former illicit drug users who had been treated at a methadone clinic and were now forced to leave the city, and their methadone treatment. Methadone is a synthetic form of heroin that is legally provided for persons with heroin addiction to keep them stabilized and from having withdrawal symptoms. Methadone is a highly addictive medication, however, so without it, these migrants from New Orleans faced a harrowing withdrawal (Keilman, 2005). Those who were lucky found their way to the Baton Rouge Treatment Center, where there were long lines of people waiting for the medication. There were reports of people desperate to get fixes looting pharmacies of morphine and other prescription painkillers or buying them on the street.

For the nation's 1 million people struggling with heroin addiction, the primary remedy is methadone (McCaffrey, cited in *Addiction Treatment Forum,* 2006). Sadly, however, as former drug czar General McCaffrey asserts, only about one in eight persons with heroin addiction participate in methadone programs. Long waiting lists are common; in Seattle, for example, drug users may wait one year for treatment. In rural areas, methadone clinics are practically nonexistent. The state of Iowa, for example, has only three such clinics to serve the whole state. Policymakers and even many substance abuse providers reject methadone maintenance in the belief that use of methadone substitutes one addiction for another. Physicians, moreover, have been severely restricted in their authority to dispense this medication.

In Europe, methadone maintenance (and in Britain, heroin maintenance) is the preferred treatment for heroin addiction, where it has been used with some success, especially in reducing the number of AIDS cases. Methadone works by occupying the opiate receptors of the brain that are involved in heroin craving. Given orally, and requiring daily visits to a clinic, methadone gives users a mild high that does not interfere with their ability to work or function. Because tolerance to this drug remains steady, patients can be maintained indefinitely on a fixed amount. Because methadone reduces the harm (risk of heroin overdose, criminal activity to support the habit, contracting AIDS through use of dirty needles), methadone therapy is a mainstay of harm reduction treatment. Still, methadone maintenance is not a panacea. Only about half of heroin patients who attend methadone maintenance clinics are able to stay off heroin. And if they quit methadone, about 80% will relapse over the next few years (Marion, 2005).

Although methadone maintenance is considered an overall success in its lifesaving and crime-reducing aspects, many habitual heroin users seem resistant to methadone treatment. Researchers in one study, as reported on the Join Together (2000) website, discovered that the clients who failed the program were likely to have a genetic variation making these people highly addictive and less amenable than others to standardized forms of treatment. Interestingly, this gene—DRD2 (dopamine D2 receptor gene)—has been implicated in more virulent forms of alcoholism, smoking, and compulsive eating as well. A more recent British study from the University of Bristol also found that the dopamine receptor gene was strongly associated with alcohol consumption and the high that some people derive from drugs such as alcohol (*Science Daily,* 2005).

Another reason for treatment failure no doubt relates to the failure of many methadone maintenance treatment programs to prescribe adequate daily doses of methadone. Persons unresponsive to treatment in an experimental study in Switzerland, for example, all did well when levels of the drug were raised well above the usual 100-milligram level ("MMT & Beyond," 2001). Over the years, street heroin has gotten purer in quality and lower in price. Consequently, there is a greater need for higher doses of methadone today than are currently considered adequate by previous standards.

A development that may seem somewhat surprising is the use of methadone in the criminal justice system. New York, Baltimore, and Seattle are a few of the cities that provide access to methadone (or another synthetic opioid) for people in their jails who are addicted to heroin.

Marion (2005) compares methadone treatment of the 1970s with the situation 35 years later. For a start, today's patients are much different from former patients: They tend to be polydrug users, not just addicted to heroin, and there are both a higher percentage of youths and older adults obtaining treatment today. The HIV and hepatitis C epidemics have taken their toll in recent years. Regarding treatment, methadone maintenance, as Marion observes, is far more pragmatic today than formerly; in fact, the treatment is going mainstream. Treatment needs are tailored to each individual, and it is no longer assumed that methadone use is only short-term or that patients must be pushed into being drug free within a certain time frame. Today, the methadone dosage is individualized to take into account differences in metabolism and the effects of interaction with concurrent medications. No longer must every patient report every day for treatment; those in good standing can fill prescriptions at the pharmacy. In short, unless another better drug comes to take its place, methadone is here to stay.

Advocates and policymakers need to know what the costs and benefits are of particular drug treatment programming. A report in *Health Economics* (Zarkin, Dunlap, Hicks, & Mamo, 2005) looked at the lifetime costs and benefits of methadone maintenance for heroin users. Their study included such variables as heroin use, criminal behavior, employment, and healthcare utilization and showed that every dollar spent on methadone treatment yielded $38 in related economic benefits.

One drug possibly better than the synthetic methadone for controlled treatment is heroin itself. The Canadian cities of Vancouver, Toronto, and Montreal have adopted a prescription heroin trial of around 500 hard-core drug users, half of whom will get daily doses of heroin and half of whom will get methadone (Armstrong, 2005). Although similar treatment programs have been set up in Europe, this experiment is unique in North America.

Encouraging results were obtained in an empirically based study published in the British medical journal *Lancet*. Researchers found that heroin users had three times the success rate (measured as not taking illicit heroin) when treated with supervised heroin injection rather than with oral methadone (Strang, Metrebian, et al., 2010). The subjects in this study were 127 chronic heroin users who continued to inject street heroin on a regular basis, despite ongoing treatment with oral methadone. They were randomly placed in groups to receive injectable methadone, injectable heroin, or optimized oral methadone treatment.

A new development of a different sort took place in the United States when legislation was passed in 2002 to allow physicians who take qualifying training classes to prescribe anti-opiate medications from their offices (Rosier, 2010). The advantage of these drugs over methadone is that they are safer on measures of overdose risks such as respiratory depression (O'Malley & Kosten, 2006). Buprenorphine is the first of a new generation of prescription drugs that is changing the landscape of addiction treatment. The new treatments parallel discoveries about the neurobiological nature of addiction and allow for drug dependence and relapse to be treated in a manner similar to diabetes, hypertension, or any other chronic disease. The drug buprenorphine acts like extra mild methadone at low doses. Unlike other opioids, including heroin, other narcotic painkillers, and methadone, buprenorphine has a "ceiling effect" that substantially reduces the likelihood of death through overdose (Rosier, 2010). Buprenorphine, moreover, is less addictive than the other opioids.

Unlike naltrexone, buprenorphine is a narcotic, the only controlled substance approved by the Food and Drug Administration for the treatment of opioid addiction that can be prescribed in a doctor's office. Casadonte (2004), a physician who treats heroin-addicted veterans at the New York Harbor Healthcare System medical center, describes how use of buprenorphine has totally changed his treatment program. Previously, methadone was provided; patients took this in a liquid form so that they could be watched swallowing the drug. Buprenorphine, in contrast, is taken in pill or lozenge form and weekly rather than daily. Patients not using other drugs can get a prescription for home use. In hopes of keeping this opiate from being diverted onto the streets, the amount of the drug prescribed is carefully monitored. However, under the brand name Suboxone, this drug has become the most common one smuggled into prison because it can be slipped in very easily.

Buprenorphine (Suboxone), allows opioid-dependent patients to bypass specialized methadone clinics and receive treatment in the privacy of a nonstigmatized setting. The advantages of office treatment are many; a new clientele is already developing as patients who became addicted to prescription medication feel more comfortable receiving treatment from their regular doctor rather than in a specialized addiction clinic. A major drawback of this development is that buprenorphine is expensive, and insurance coverage is minimal (Rosier, 2010).

Rapid detox and vaccines are two other developments discussed in the treatment literature. Persons addicted to heroin are known to have a dreadful time coming off the drug. In Spain, Israel, and Australia, a form of rapid detox is being used in some places. Doctors are using massive injections of naltrexone to speed people addicted to opioid drugs through the harrowing process of withdrawal. Instead of shaking, sweating, and retching for 10 days, the patients are placed under heavy sedation for a rapid detox. Research in the United States has shown mixed results. Whereas media reports uniformly touted the success of the rapid detox technique as used in Australia and elsewhere, later research reported that the use of anesthesia proved to be dangerous in itself, leaving patients with serious side effects when they gained consciousness (Abadinsky, 2011). Its high expense is another disadvantage of this form of treatment for detox.

A whole different approach to tackling the addiction problem is with immunization. New vaccines are being developed against addiction and relapse. According to a news headline in the *Washington Post*, "Vaccine against Heroin Works—at Least on Rats" (Brown, 2011), the vaccine described in this article stimulates the immune system to make antibodies against addictive compounds. The antibodies prevent these compounds from entering the brain, where they would exert their euphoric and addictive effects. Since the original lab experiments of a heroin vaccine were published in 1974, scientists have developed vaccines against nicotine, cocaine, and amphetamines. Now researchers are making some headway in vaccinating laboratory rats against the effects of heroin. Although both nicotine and cocaine vaccines have gone as far as human tests, none has been licensed for commercial use.

MEDICATION FOR EATING DISORDERS

Why do compulsive eaters feel such intense cravings for chocolates and other sweets (or potato chips)? Perhaps they have some of the same abnormal brain chemistry seen in persons with alcohol and drug use disorders. Researchers at the University of Pittsburgh Medical Center (2005), building on genetic studies showing gene alterations in some individuals with anorexia nervosa, examined PET scans of 10 women in recovery from anorexia and 12 normal subjects. They found significant differences in the activity of brain dopamine receptors in the two groups of women. The difference was in increased receptor binding; this relates to harm avoidance and reward seeking and may help explain why women with anorexia exhibit exaggerated worry and concern. Significantly, as the medical center's report points out, people who are obese and substance users exhibit reduced binding of these dopamine receptors.

Eating is a survival behavior that must be pleasurable to sustain the species. The same primitive reward system in the brain is central to the development of both excessive eating and chemical addiction. The high rate of comorbidity between eating and other disorders, as discussed in Chapter 9, bears out the interconnectedness in these addictive and compulsive tendencies.

Chemical addiction and eating disorders share many clinical features. The commonalties are not limited to behavioral observations but involve an array of neurotransmitter abnormalities. Dopamine is involved in both. Thus, it stands to reason that teasing out dopamine's effects could lead to new drugs for the millions of people with binge eating disorders. Researchers are excited about a pill called rimonabant (Accomplia) that has been shown in animal studies to fight relapse in drug users. In humans, it helps in weight loss as well as smoking cessation (Join Together, 2006). Acomplia is an experimental drug developed by a French pharmaceutical firm primarily as a diet pill, but the drug works differently than most diet pills in that it blocks the brain's reward system ("Accomplia: Diet Pill," 2008). One side effect—depression—is worrisome, however.

Drugs in the serotonin reuptake class (such as Prozac, Luvox, and Paxil) have been found to produce significantly better outcomes in patients with binge eating problems and bulimia than those given a placebo (Capasso, Petrella, & Milano, 2009). Study results summarized by Brewerton (2004) indicate that cognitive therapy focusing on challenging rigid thought patterns and healthy expression of feelings in combination with medication is more effective than the use of medication alone. What is not known at this point is whether a deficit in receptors in the brain cells of seriously obese people is a cause or a result of the obesity. Future studies should make the connection clear.

Results in the use of pharmacological agents for anorexia in producing weight gain have been disappointing. Only when patients are on the mend do selective serotonin reuptake inhibitors (SSRIs) help with weight recovery. The reason, as Brewerton (2004) suggests, is because in a body depleted of amino acids due to starvation, the serotonin enhancing drugs cannot take effect. Olanzapine (Zypresa), an antipsychotic medication, however, is being given to adolescents with purported promising results.

Help for Behavioral Addictions

Little is written about the use of prescription medication for the behavioral addictions, such as compulsive gambling and shopping. Given the interrelatedness of these addictions and drug addictions, however, it stands to reason that similar medication would work for both drug-seeking and money-related behavior.

Donald Black and his colleagues at the University of Iowa Medical School seemed to have some success in prescribing fluvoxamine (Luvox) for compulsive shoppers. However, later tests that used a placebo showed that the psychological effect of taking a medication produced the favorable result (see Chapter 5). In subsequent research from the University of Iowa, Kuzma and Black (2006) cautioned against reliance on medication to control the shoppers' behavior and recommended a cognitive approach. Such an approach would be directed at faulty thinking patterns, such as an overemphasis on clothes or fashion, and the development of self-protective behaviors, such as canceling credit cards and shopping only with an understanding friend or relative.

For compulsive gamblers and kleptomaniacs (persons who compulsively steal), naltrexone has been used successfully in experiments to curb their destructive behavior. The focus at the Brown Medical School is on using drugs to block the receptors in the brain that register the pleasurable high (Grant, 2005). A Mayo Clinic report (2006) confirms this finding. The clinic's recommendation is for an SSRI for compulsive gamblers with bipolar disorder and naltrexone for others. More research is needed, however. Other techniques used to help kleptomaniacs are anti-depression drugs, shock treatments, and therapy in which the patient is instructed to hold his or her breath or think of vomiting when experiencing the urge to steal.

Can medication that enhances the neurotransmitters actually cause addiction to a behavior? Although it seems unlikely, recent reports seem to indicate that dopamine-enhancing drugs prescribed for Parkinson's disease possibly lead some people into compulsive gambling and overwhelming sexual urges. According to Vedantan (2006) of the *Washington Post*, anecdotal reports of case after case of strange obsessive behavior associated with these drugs have led some pharmaceutical companies to issue warnings about these possible side effects (see Chapter 5).

How do motivational theorists and counselors feel about the use of all these medicinal supplements to treatment? Pharmacotherapy is a topic that has been rarely addressed in the motivational literature until now. Miller and colleagues (2011) in their new book on treating addiction discuss several of the new medications and research findings concerning their effectiveness. Pharmacotherapy, as these researchers point out, can serve as a motivator for change. The addition of medication to behavioral treatment helps reduce the stigma for people receiving treatment as it reinforces the medical nature of the illness; it increases clients' optimism that they are getting better, that they are being given treatment directed at what they might want to see as the source of the problem.

HOLISTIC APPROACHES

Other remedies directed toward the physical side of drug use are more natural, holistic approaches. These include various herbal remedies, acupuncture, massage, hypnosis, and biofeedback. Herbal medicines are regulated as dietary supplements rather than as drugs, so they can make no specific claims to treat a disease. Because plants cannot be patented, there is little financial incentive for private companies to fund clinical trials for research on treatment effectiveness. Sometimes studies are funded by drug companies such as Pfizer, the makers of Zoloft and others, with vested interests in proving a rival herbal remedy has no benefits (Spinella, 2005). This happened in research on St. John's wort, a popular herbal remedy for depression.

A quick look at the popular literature on herbal remedies reveals that one day's wonder drug is the next day's despair. Until scientific testing is conducted, the truth is hard to ascertain. For example, an article in *Nature* (Aldous, 2005) describes a Vietnamese concoction, Heantos, that contains a mixture of 13 herbs that reportedly makes drug cravings disappear. Used in Vietnam for people addicted to opium, the drug is consumed for 4 days in half-quart doses. The United Nations Development Program and the Norwegian government are funding a scientific study into its effectiveness.

Three recent clinical studies, two about cocaine addiction and one about compulsive gambling, examine the role of a simple amino acid in normalizing brain chemistry of persons with addiction. This substance is N-acetylcysteine (NAC). Taken by mouth, NAC has been shown to increase concentrations of the neurotransmitter glutamate in the regions of the brain (the nucleus accumbens) that, when low in glutamate, are associated with addictive behavior and cravings (Kane, 2008).

Kudzu, the plant imported from Korea to Alabama and grown out of control to the distress of farmers and foresters, has been found to help heavy drinkers cut down on their consumption (Lukas, Penetar, Berko, et al., 2005). A compound extracted from the kudzu weed has been used in China for treatment of alcoholism. Animal studies in the United States were promising.

An experiment on men and women who were heavy drinkers by Lukas and colleagues (2005) showed that when under the influence of this substance, they consumed less because they apparently were feeling the effects of the alcohol more readily. A synthetic form of kudzu, which builds up acetaldehyde in the body and makes people feel uncomfortable if they drink, is thought to have potential as a future remedy (Anderson, 2009).

Ibogaine is a drug derived from a West African shrub. This drug has potent, long-lasting hallucinogenic effects that typically last from 24 to 36 hours (Spinella, 2005). Ibogaine is used by treatment providers in Canada, Mexico, and elsewhere to combat the effects of withdrawal (Pulkkinenen, 2011). Proponents contend that people can kick their addictions during days-long treatments with the controversial drug; it is also used in religious practices in Africa. The anti-addictive effects of ibogaine were originally reported by heroin users who, after experimenting with this hallucinogen, found they no longer craved heroin. Animal research, according to Spinella, has shown that the drug reduces cocaine use in mice. But, according to Walters (2008), pharmaceutical companies do not want to see Ibogaine on the market because it is not profitable. Hevesi (2010), however, reports that a number of deaths have been associated with its use in opioid withdrawal. Recently, in a sting operation, a doctor from Bellingham, Washington, was arrested along with a substance abuse counselor for his role in providing this treatment. Ibogaine is illegal in the United States and cannot legally be prescribed. According to a news article by Pulkkinenen (2011), the doctor had reportedly supplied the drug to over 400 patients.

St. John's wort, considered nature's own Prozac, is widely prescribed in Germany for depression and sleeping problems, and it is sold in most American health food stores. St. John's wort has been shown in multiple clinical studies to alleviate depression in human subjects. Like pharmaceutical products, it takes about two weeks to work (Spinella, 2005). In a randomized trial on its effectiveness for smoking cessation, however, Mayo Clinic medical researchers found the herb did no better than a placebo in promoting smoking abstinence.

The goal of holistic therapies is to restore the body to its naturally healthy state. Holistic philosophy, as Apostolides (1996) suggests, overlaps with the harm reduction approach to addiction in its focus on treating the entire person, often with psychotherapy as well as medical remedies. In the major U.S. cities, harm reduction centers now offer programs that include acupuncture, massage therapy, yoga, and substance misuse counseling.

Acupuncture consists of stimulating certain points on or near the surface of the body by inserting needles. Practiced in China for more than 5,000 years, its use in the treatment of narcotic addiction goes back only several decades (Reuben, Chen, Blum, et al., 2005; Han & Cui, 2011). The discovery of the effectiveness of acupuncture in enhancing opium withdrawal came about serendipitously when acupuncture was performed on an opium-addicted patient for the purposes of performing surgery. It was discovered that all the patient's withdrawal symptoms disappeared. This treatment was then successfully used with others in China. Rat experiments have shown good effects in reducing cravings for alcohol and various other drugs. In humans more research is needed to determine if acupuncture works well in reducing cravings for alcohol or nicotine, but successful treatments in reducing the desire to take addictive substances were reported earlier by Reuben and colleagues (2005) and NIDA (2000). More study is needed, as Han and Cui argue, because there is great potential here.

Massage therapy has achieved impressive results in tests on people dealing with anorexia, bulimia, smoking, and other addictions (Apostolides, 1996). The neurological response to body contact and to the loosening of tight muscles releases tension and helps clients "reconnect physically and center themselves emotionally" (p. 37). Similarly, yoga helps people get in tune with their physical processes, including muscular exertion—holding certain positions—and breathing.

Simple exercise is effective in reducing tension and in elevating mood because, with continuous activity, the body produces endorphins the natural way. Exercise has been found to decrease symptoms of depression. Animal studies of exercise show that such physical activity stimulates the secretion of the natural opiates and serotonin in the brain (Haga, 2004). In humans, exercise probably also works by distracting people from their worries and having a calming effect. Unfortunately, treatment centers often overlook the curative powers of activities such as swimming, hiking, and biking.

Heavy drinking and other drug misuse can cause hypoglycemia, or low blood sugar, as well; the craving for sugar is a consequence. Vitamin C sometimes is used by nutrition therapists to modify the withdrawal symptoms related to detoxification (Apostolides, 1996; "Alternative Medicines," 2011). Replenishing nutrients that have been depleted through chemical misuse and faulty diets, accordingly, is an important component of recovery. Drinking large quantities of alcohol, for example, depletes the body of thiamine and other vitamins (Doweiko, 2009). Nutrients such as niacin, amino acids, and magnesium are given to alleviate problems caused by low levels of glucose in the brain. In early recovery, sleeping in a nondrugged state can present major problems. Drinking a glass of milk or a herbal tea, such as Sleepy Bear, can be immensely helpful.

Melatonin is an over-the-counter drug taken in pill form that induces a natural sleep and has few side effects. The hormone melatonin is one that is depleted in chronic alcoholism as in the aging process. In laboratory experiments with selectively bred alcohol-preferring rats, Dennis Rasmussen (2011), a researcher at the University of Washington School of Medicine, successfully demonstrated that when given melatonin, rats have a decreased desire to consume alcohol. The grant was funded by the National Institutes of Health. Depletion of this hormone is known to occur through the aging process and also as a result of chronic alcoholism. This investigation demonstrated the ability of melatonin to reverse changes in brain and neuroendocrine systems. The changes that melatonin reverses have been suggested to contribute to relapse. Rasmussen's research also demonstrated that melatonin decreases alcohol self-administration in these alcohol-preferring rats. Because melatonin tablets are available at most grocery stores and are inexpensive, these research have promising implications for relapse prevention in humans.

Pet therapy is recommended by Haga (2004) for stress reduction, providing touch, and building self-esteem, especially for children. Clients suffering from PTSD often bond with animals for valuable companionship. The physical act of taking care of an animal helps pull people out of depression.

Hypnosis is another remedy that helps people gain control over their urges to use, in this case through the use of suggestion. While in a trance, patients may be told to view their drug of choice with distaste (Murphy, 2004). Treatments usually last for 30 minutes, and only a few sessions are required. From a more positive stance, people can rehearse coping with urges to use until they develop the capacity to do so while in a nontrancelike state.

Like hypnosis and acupuncture, biofeedback is administered by persons with specialized training. The aim of biofeedback is brainwave training to reduce stress. And like hypnosis, biofeedback (also called brainwave training) is a "mind over matter" phenomenon in which the individual, through training, learns to attain a deep level of relaxation for the purpose of helping maintain sobriety (Doweiko, 2009). The way this method works is that electroencephalograph (EEG) measures of anxiety levels are obtained so that the individual can monitor his or her response in conjunction with the feedback. After pretraining, individuals receive alpha-theta brainwave training. This process helps individuals gain more control over their feelings for the development of a greater sense of self-efficacy.

Thomas Keefe (2011) recommends meditation as a strategy in helping clients maintain control as they deal with stress. Meditation can both prevent maladaptive coping with stress through substance use and help treat problems once they have developed. This process of learning to induce a state of relaxation is especially helpful to people who suffer from high anxiety and extreme overreactions to stress. Norwegian psychiatrist Halvorsen (2011) believes that meditation in the Buddhist tradition is a method to help us accept both the light and darkness within us, to get in touch with the here and now of existence. This approach is helpful to people in recovery, and as Halvorsen informs us, it is a method used in many Twelve-Step treatment programs.

SUMMARY AND CONCLUSION

For direct practice in the addiction field, the helping professional requires advanced knowledge of the physiology of chemical addiction, including the basic characteristics and organic effects of each of the popular sedative and stimulant drugs. To work with clients, a biological understanding of the nature of addiction, and especially of the kind of relentless craving that accompanies drug use, is essential. (Recovering professionals have an experiential knowledge of such urges that puts them on the same wavelength as their clients; all counselors and educators can benefit, however, from an awareness of the brain changes that make addiction what it is.) Brain imaging has brought about unprecedented breakthroughs in our knowledge. Virtually all psychoactive drugs, as we now know, affect a single pathway deep within the brain and activate the limbic reward system in various ways. The new techniques that enable researchers to view these workings within the limbic system also make it possible to observe changes in the brain caused by prolonged use of harmful chemicals. Previously, those alterations could only be inferred. Scientists can now experience addiction secondhand as an image on a screen; in so doing, they have hit upon some elements in human nature that defy logic. In a real sense, they have brought us face to face with some of our most primitive, pleasure-seeking drives, which may or may not spell addiction.

We are all creatures of biology and of our genes. If we succumb to getting hooked on toxic substances, the physiological damage to the brain, liver, heart, or unborn child can be severe. In focusing on the *bio* portion of the biopsychosocial model of addiction, this chapter has described the most commonly used drugs of choice. Divided into four basic categories—depressants, stimulants, hallucinogens, and cannabis—the drugs of choice were discussed in terms of their chemical properties and metabolism. Then we proceeded to move into more uncharted territory by addressing the imponderables: Is addiction a brain disease? How are the brains of addicted people different from those of others? Why are some individuals more susceptible to becoming hooked on psychoactive substances than others?

The genetic factor was revealed in research on mice bred to prefer alcohol to water and in studies of children of alcoholic parents. Many of those children displayed a high tolerance for alcohol, which paradoxically is correlated with the later development of alcoholism. Since the mid-1990s, research has offered new understandings both as to why addiction runs in families and also about the precise nature of the damage that psychoactive substances do to the body, most interestingly to the brain. The addicted brain, as we now realize, is significantly different from the normally functioning brain. Through long-term drug misuse, the depletion of the brain's natural opiates creates a condition ripe for the kind of relentless craving that is known to all "who have been there." Compounding the problem of molecular alterations in the brain (experienced as a general malaise) is the fact that each time a neurotransmitter such as dopamine floods a synapse through the introduction of a powerful drug like crack or meth into the body, circuits that trigger pleasure are indelibly imprinted in the brain. So when the smells, sights, and sounds associated with the memory are experienced, these feeling memories are aroused as well. So palpable, in fact, are these feeling memories that researchers can detect differences in the brains of an individual who is in a state of craving.

Solutions, to be true solutions, must be directed at the source of the problem. And if we agree with the teachings of the National Institute on Drug Abuse that addiction is a brain disease, it makes sense to seek solutions that are medical. Hence the focus today by the national institutes tends to be almost exclusively on medical research. And the use of medications to quell the biological urges to relapse is today revolutionizing the field of addiction treatment. The shibboleths of the profession are changing from the old absolutes mandating abstinence from all mood-altering substances to a much greater acceptance of the use of nicotine patches and antidepressants. Because one of the leading causes of relapse is depression, medications that help replenish the brain with the natural opiates should be an effective adjunct to relapse prevention. Naltrexone and buprenorphine, drugs in a different category from the dopamine and serotonin-boosting medications, function by blocking cravings for substances like alcohol and heroin. Because people who struggle with chemical addictions seem to have an underlying vulnerability to a number of compulsive behaviors, including compulsive gambling and eating disorders, medication geared toward normalizing brain functioning might reap benefits in these related areas as well.

There are two major risks as we move in this direction. The first is that much of the personal therapy that we see in the field of substance abuse counseling will be replaced with a prescription for a bottle of pills. The second is that the medication prescribed will be only of the expensive variety and of more benefit to the pharmaceutical companies than to the individuals in need of care.

Every bit as important in terms of biologically based advances are the new understandings of a phenomenon that is called *neuroplasticity*. Neuroplasticity takes place when biochemical abnormalities associated with a mental or substance use disorder are reversed through cognitive work. For people in treatment for addiction problems and others in recovery, cognitive work—learning to replace unhealthy thoughts with healthy ones—shows great promise in repairing much of the brain injury that has been done by heavy substance use, or, for that matter, from trauma. This is one of the most promising messages to come out of current research, as stated in the title of Sharon Begley's (2007) book—*Change Your Mind, Change Your Brain*.

As is always the case with new technologies, there is a cultural lag between discovery and treatment. Addiction professionals will want to follow developments in pharmacology and at the same time keep up with research so that they can evaluate the claims of effectiveness of the various drugs and other interventions being marketed. And they will want to advocate for continued funding for therapy at the personal level to help motivate people toward change and to work with them on issues of relationships, stress management, communication patterns, and the like. In the next chapter, we explore treatment issues relevant to gender and sexuality.

REFERENCES

Abadinsky, H. (2011). *Drug use and abuse: A comprehensive introduction* (7th ed.). Belmont, CA: Wadsworth.

Abel, E. (2004). Paternal contribution to fetal alcohol syndrome. *Addiction Biology*, 9(2), 127–133.

Accomplia: Diet Pill Fights Addiction Too. (2008, May 27). *About.com.Alcoholism*. Retrieved from http://alcoholism.about

Addiction Treatment Forum. (2006, Spring). Atlanta conference focuses on criminal justice system. *AT Forum*, 15(2), 2–4.

Ahlm, K., Hassler, S., Sjölander, P., & Eriksson, A. (2010). Unnatural deaths in reindeer-herding Sami families in Sweden: 1961–2001. *International Journal of Circimpolars Health*, 69(2), 129–137.

Alcoholics Anonymous World Services (AAWS). (1976/1939). *Alcoholics anonymous*. New York: Author.

Allday, E. (2010, December 25). More research supports moderate drinking. *San Francisco Chronicle*, p. A1.

"Alternative Medicines for Alcoholism and Drug Addiction." (2011). *Discovery Fit and Health*. Retrieved from http://health.hostuffworks.com

American Lung Association. (2011). *General smoking facts*. Retrieved from http://www.lungusa.org

American Psychiatric Association (APA). (2000). *Diagnostic and statistical manual of mental disorders, text revision* (4th ed.). Washington, DC: Author.

American Psychological Association. (2009, March 6). *Studies underscore genetic involvement in nicotine addiction and aggressive hostility*. Retrieved from http://www.apa.org

Anderson, L. (2009, November 16). Kudzu compound could help alcoholics quit drinking. *USA Today*. Retrieved from http://www.usatoday.com

Anthony, B., Vinci-Booher, S., Wetherill, L., Ward R., Goodlett C., & Zhou F. (2010). Alcohol-induced facial dysmorphology in C57BL/6 mouse models of fetal alcohol spectrum disorder. *Alcohol*, 44(7), 659–671.

Anton, R. F., O'Malley, S. S., Ciraulo, D. A., Cisler, R. A., Couper, D., Donovan, D. M., et al., for the COMBINE Study Research Group. (2006). Combined pharmacotherapies and behavioral interventions for alcohol dependence: The COMBINE Study. *Journal of the American Medical Association*, 295(17), 2003–2017.

Apostolides, M. (1996, September/October). How to quit the holistic way. *Psychology Today*, pp. 35–43, 68–70.

Arif, A. A., & Rohrer, J. E. (2005). Patterns of alcohol drinking and its association with obesity: Data from the third National Health and Nutrition Examination Survey, 1988–1994. *BMC (Biomed Central) Public Health*, 5, 126. Retrieved from http://www.jointogether.org

Armstrong, J. (2005, January 31). Is free heroin just a quick fix? *Globe and Mail*, p. A1.

Australian Medical Association. (2009, June 22). *Information paper: Alcohol use and harms in Australia*. Retrieved from http://ama.com.au/node/4762

Begley, S. (2001, February 12). How it all starts in your brain. *Newsweek*, pp. 40–43.

Begley, S. (2007). *Train your mind, change your brain*. New York: Ballantine Books.

Begley, S. (2010, February 8). The depressing news about antidepressants. *Newsweek*, pp. 34–41.

Bhattacharya, S. (2003). Alcoholic blackouts may lead to heavier drinking. *Alcoholism: Clinical and Experimental Research, 27,* 628.

Brady, K., & Sinha, R. (2005). Co-occurring mental and substance use disorders: The effects of chronic stress. *American Journal of Psychiatry, 162,* 1483–1493.

Brewerton, T. D. (2004, May). Pharmacotherapy for patients with eating disorders. *Psychiatric Times, 21*(6). Retrieved from http://psychiatrictimes.com

Brink, S. (2004). The price of booze. *U.S. News & World Report,* pp. 48–50.

Brodie, J. D., Case, B. G., Figueroa, E., Dewey, S. L., Robinson, J. A., Wanderling, J. A., & Laska, E. M. (2009). Randomized, double-blind, placebo-controlled trial of vigabatrin for the treatment of cocaine dependence in Mexican parolees. *American Journal of Psychiatry, 166*(11), 1269–1277.

Brown, D. (2011, July 25). Vaccine against heroin works, at least in rats. *Washington Post.* Retrieved from http://washingtonpost.com

Canadian Centre on Substance Abuse. (2006, March). Assessing the high costs of substance abuse. *Acting News, 16*(1), 1, 4.

Capasso, A., Petrella, C., & Milano, W. (2009). Pharmacological profile of SSRIs and SNRIs in the treatment of eating disorders. *Current Clinical Pharmacology, 4*(1), 78–83.

Carey, B. (2009, February 24). After abuse, changes in the brain. *New York Times,* p. D5.

Casadonte, P. (2004, August). Community treatment programs take up buprenorphine. *Science and Practice Perspectives,* pp. 24–29.

Center for Substance Abuse Research. (2004). *Rohypnol.* Retrieved from http://www.cesar.umd.edu

Centers for Disease Control and Prevention (CDC). (2010a). *Deaths: Final data for 2007.* Atlanta, GA: Department of Health and Human Services. Retrieved from http://www.cdc.gov

Centers for Disease Control and Prevention (CDC). (2010b). *Fact sheet: Alcohol use and health.* Atlanta, GA: Department of Health and Human Service. Retrieved from http://www.cdc.gov

Centers for Disease Control and Prevention (CDC). (2011). *Resources for entertainment education: Drowning.* Atlanta, GA: Department of Health and Human Service.

"Cigarette Tax Unbalances Profits." (2009, April 9). *Prague Post.* Retrieved from http://snus-news.blogspot.com

Clements, K., & Schumacher, J. (2010). Perceptual biases in social cognition as potential moderators of the relationship between alcohol and intimate partner violence: A review." *Aggression and Violent Behavior, 15*(5), 357–368.

Cloninger, C. R., Sigvardsson, S., Gilligan, S., van Knorring, A., Reich, T., & Bohman, M. (1989). Genetic heterogeneity and the classification of alcoholism. *Advances in Alcohol and Substance Abuse, 7,* 3–16.

Collier, C. (2010, October 6). A kandi-coated world. *Fort Worth Weekly.* Retrieved from http://www.fwweekly.com

Cunningham-Williams, R., Gattis, M., Dore, P., Shi, P., & Spitznagel, E. (2009). Towards DSM-V: Considering other withdrawal-like symptoms of pathological gambling disorder. *International Journal of Methods in Psychiatric Research, 18*(1), 13–22.

DanceSafe. (2010). *Promoting health and safety within the rave and nightclub community.* Retrieved from http://www.dancesafe.org

Davis, D. R. (2009). *Taking back your life: Women and problem gambling*. Center City, MN: Hazelden.

Dell, C. (2005, November 7–9). *What the data tell us about volatile solvent abuse in Canada*. Invited paper presentation by the National Institute of Drug Abuse. Retrieved from www.drugabuse.gov

Denning, P., Little, J., & Glickman, A. (2004). *Over the influence: The harm reduction guide for managing drugs and alcohol*. New York: Guilford Press.

Desmon, S. (2011, January 3). Study of hallucinogen salvia shows intense, novel effects. *The Johns Hopkins Gazette*. Retrieved from http://gazette.jhu.edu

Doweiko, H. E. (2009). *Concepts of chemical dependency* (8th ed.). Belmont, CA: Brooks/Cole.

Drug Abuse Warning Network. (2011, June 16). *Trends in emergency department visits for drug-related suicide attempts. The DAWN report*. Retrieved from http://www.oas.samhsa.gov

Drummon, K. (2010, September 2). Vets get ecstasy to treat their PTSD. *Wired*. Retrieved from http://www.wired.com

Durazzo, T. C., Gazdzinski, S., Banys, P., & Meyerhoff, D. J. (December 2004). Cigarette smoking exacerbates chronic alcohol-induced brain damage: A preliminary metabolite imaging study. *Alcoholism: Clinical and Experimental Research*, 28(12), 1849–1860.

Editor, Counselor Magazine. (2010, August). From the editor. *Counselor: The Magazine for Addiction Professionals*, 11(4). Retrieved from http://www.counselormagazine.com

Ehrenfeld, T. (2005, June 13). New hope for addicts? *Newsweek*, p. 68.

Encyclopaedia Britannica. (2006). Alcohol and drug consumption. Macropaedia (15th ed., pp. 195–223). Chicago: Encyclopaedia Britannica.

Encyclopedia of Drugs and Addictive Substances. (2011). *Nicotine: Overview*. Retrieved from http://www.enotes.com

Eriksson, A., & Fotina, S. (2010, Spring). *Alcohol tax in Sweden: Should it be reduced?* Research paper from the University of Gothenberg School of Business, Economics and Law. Retrieved from http://gul.gu.se/public/pp/public_courses/course44889/published/

Fiorillo, C. D. (2004). The uncertain nature of dopamine. *Molecular Psychiatry*, 9(2), 122–123.

Filozof, C., Fernandez, P., & Fernandez-Cruz, A. (2004). Smoking cessation and weight gain. *Obesity Review*, 5(2), 95–103.

Fisher, G., & Harrison, T. C. (2008). *Substance abuse: Information for school counselors, social workers, therapists, and counselors* (4th ed.). Boston: Allyn & Bacon.

Fisher, M. S. (2009). Substance abuse and aggression. *Alcohol, Tobacco and Other Drugs: Section Connection*, 1, 1, 3.

Fournier, J. R., Hollon, S., Dimidijan, S., Amsterdam, J., Shelton, R., & Fawcett, J. (2010). Antidepressant drug effects and depression severity: A patient-level meta-analysis. *Journal of the American Medical Association*, 303(1), 47–53.

France, D., & Horn, J. (2001, February 12). Robert Downey, Jr. takes one day at a time. *Newsweek*, pp. 52–54.

Friend, J., Langhinrichsen-Rohling, J., & Eichold, B. (2011). Same-day substance use in men and women charged with felony domestic violence offenses. *Criminal Justice and Behavior*, 38(6), 619–633.

Frosch, D. (2011, July 19). Marijuana may be studied for combat disorder. *New York Times*, p. A15.

Giordano, J., & Blum, K. (2010, October). Probing the mysteries of recovery through nutrigenomics and holistic medicine. *Counselor: The Magazine for Addiction Counselors*, 11(5). Retrieved from http://www.counselormagazine.com

Ginsberg, L., Nackerud, L., & Larrison, C. (2004). *Human biology for social workers: Development, ecology, genetics, and health*. Boston: Allyn & Bacon.

Gmel, G., Bissery, A., Gammeter, R., Givel, J., Calmes, J., Yersin, B., et al. (2006, March). Alcohol-attributable injuries in admissions to a Swiss emergency room. *Alcoholism: Clinical and Experimental Research*, 30(3), 501–509.

Gonzales, D., Rennard, S. I., Nides, M., Oncken, C., Azoulay, S., Billing, C., et al. (2006). Varenicline, an alpha4beta2 nicotinic acetylcholine receptor partial agonist. *Journal of the American Medical Association*, 296, 47–55.

Goodenough, A. (2011, March 28). States battling meth makers look to ingredients. *New York Times*, p. A19.

Goodenough, A., & Zezima, K. (2010, July 24). Drivers on prescription drugs are hard to convict. *New York Times*, p. A1.

Goodenough, A., & Zezima, K. (2011, June 15). Drug is harder to abuse, but users persevere. *New York Times*, p. A21.

Goodwin, D. (1976). *Is alcoholism hereditary?* New York: Oxford University Press.

Gordh, A. S., & Söderpalm, B. (2011). Healthy subjects with a family history of alcoholism show increased stimulative subjective effects of alcohol. *Alcoholism: Clinical and Experimental Research*, 35(8): 1426–1434.

Gould, T. (2010). Addiction and cognition. *Addiction Science and Clinical Practice*, 5(2), 5–14.

Grant, J. E. (2005). Outcome study of kleptomania patients treated with naltrexone. *Clinical Neuropharmacology*, 28(1), 11–14.

Grant, J., Brewer, J., & Potenza, M. (2006). The neurobiology of substance and behavioral addictions. *CNS Spectrums*, 11(12), 924–930.

Grant, I., Gonzalez, R., Carey, C., Natarajan, L., & Wolfson, T. (2003). Non-acute (residual) neurocognitive effects of cannabis use: A meta-analysis study. *Journal of the International Neuropsychological Society*, 9, 679–689.

Greenberg, R. (2006, April 30). Reefer madness redux [Letter to the editor]. *Des Moines Sunday Register*, p. 20P.

Haas, B. (2011, April 30). China smoking ban may have little effect. *Los Angeles Times*. Retrieved from http://www.latimes.com

Haga, J. (2004). Multiple routes to quality of life. In H.Johnson, *Psyche and synapse behavior, thinking, and addiction for non-scientists* (pp. 299–315). Greenfield, MA: Deerfield Valley.

Halvorsen, J. S. (2011). AA (Anonyme Alkoholikere), 12-trinns programmet og rusbehandling (246-272). In K.Lossius (Ed.), *Håndbok I rusbehandling: Til pasienterr med moderat til alvorlig rusmiddelavhengighet*. Oslo, Norway: Gyldendal Norsk Forlag.

Han, J.-S., & Cui, C. (2011). Acupuncture. In *Lowinson and Ruiz's Substance abuse: A comprehensive textbook* (pp. 466–476). Philadelphia: Lippincott Williams and Wilkins.

Harris, G. (2004). What all social workers should know about MDMA (Ecstasy). *Journal of Social Work Practice in the Addictions*, 4(1), 23–37.

Hasin, D., Hatzenbuehler, M., & Waxman, R. (2006). Genetics of substance use disorders. In W.Miller & K.Carroll (Eds.), *Rethinking substance abuse: What the science shows and what we should do about it* (pp. 61–77). New York: Guilford Press.

Hester, R., & Miller, W. R. (2003). *Handbook of alcoholism treatment approaches* (3rd ed.). Boston: Allyn & Bacon.

Hevesi, D. (2010, February 18). Howard Lotsof, 66; Saw drug cure in a plant. *New York Times*, p. B13.

Hensrud, D. (2010, November 5). *What does research say about coffee and health?* Mayo Clinic. Retrieved from http://www.mayoclinic.com

Highfield, R. (2011, January 11). Much advice about the effects of drinking proves to be false. *Washington Post*. Retrieved from http://www.washingtonpost.com

Hoeffel, J. (2011, July 9). U.S. decrees that marijuana has no accepted medical use. *Los Angeles Times*. Retrieved from http://www.latimes.com

Holahan, C. J., Schutte, K. K., Brennan, P. L., Holahan, C. K., Moos, B. S., & Moos, R. H. (2010). Late-life alcohol consumption and 20-year mortality. *Alcoholism: Clinical and Experimental Research*, 34, 1961–1971.

"How Drugs Can Kill." (2011). *Genetic Science Learning Center, University of Utah*. Retrieved from http://learn.genetics.utah.edu

Hurt, R. D. (2010, November 5). *Quit smoking*. Mayo Clinic. Retrieved from http://www.mayoclinic.com

Hyman, S. E. (2005). Addiction: A disease of learning and memory. *American Journal of Psychology*, 162, 1414–1422.

Insel, T. R. (2005, April 27). Testimony before the House Subcommittee on Labor-HHS-Education Appropriations. Washington, DC: U.S. Congress.

Johnson, B. A., Roache, J. D., Javors, M. A., DiClemente, C., Cloninger, C., Prihoda, T., et al. (2000). Ondansetron for reduction of drinking among biologically predisposed alcoholic patients: A randomized controlled trial. *Journal of the American Medical Association*, 284(8), 963–971.

Johnson, C. (2006, July 5). High Tylenol doses linked to liver woes. *Washington Post*. Retrieved from http://www.washingtonpost.com/wp-dyn

Johnson, H. C. (2004). *Psyche and synapse expanding worlds: The role of neurobiology in emotions, behavior, thinking, and addiction for non-scientists* (2nd ed.). Greenfield, MA: Deerfield Valley.

Join Together. (2006). Accomplia shows promise as anti-craving drug. *Join Together Online*. Retrieved from http://www.jointogether.org/news/headlines

Join Together Staff. (2011, July 18). "Bath salts" have dangerous and long-lasting effects, doctors say. *Join Together*. Retrieved from http://drugfree.org

Jung, J. (2010). *Alcohol, other drugs, and behavior: Psychological research perspectives*. Thousand Oaks, CA: SAGE.

Kampov-Polevoy, A. B., Eick, C., Boland, G., Khalitov, E., & Crews, F. T. (2004). Sweet liking, novelty seeking, and gender predict alcoholic status. *Alcohol Clinical and Experimental Research*, 28(9), 1291–1298.

Kane, E. (2008, January 14). NAC as a natural treatment for cocaine addiction? *Natural News*. Retrieved from http://www.naturalnews.com

Kaufman, M. (2006, May 26). Study finds no cancer-marijuana connection. *Washington Post*, p. AO3.

Keefe, T. (2011). Meditation and social work practice. In F.Turner (Ed.), *Social work Treatment: Interlocking theoretical approaches* (pp. 293–314). New York: Oxford University Press.

Keilman, J. (2005, September 9). Storm chaos cuts help for addicts. *Chicago Tribune*, pp. 1, 4.

Kerlikowske, G. (2011, January 6). Quoted in Office of National Drug Control Policy press release. New data reveal doubling of emergency department visits involving pharmaceutical abuse. Retrieved from http://www.whitehousedrug.gov

Kershaw, S., & Cathcart, R. (2009, July 19). Marijuana is gateway drug for two debates. *New York Times*, p. ST1.

Kilen, M. (2009, July 19). Life after meth. *Des Moines Register*, pp. 1E, 2E.

King, L. (2004). An overview of cannabis potency in Europe. The European Monitoring Centre for Drugs and Drug Addiction. Lisbon, Portugal.

King, A., Cao, D., Vanier, C., & Wilcox, T. (2009). Naltrexone decreases heavy drinking rates in smoking cessation treatment: An exploratory study. *Alcoholism: Clinical and Experimental Research*, 33(6), 1044–1050.

Kinney, J. (2011). *Loosening the grip: A handbook of alcohol information* (10th ed.). Boston: McGraw Hill.

Knapp, C. (1997). *Drinking: A love story*. New York: Delta.

Kuzma, J., & Black, D. W. (2006). Compulsive shopping: When spending begins to consume the consumer. *Current Psychiatry Online*, 5(7). Retrieved from http://www.currentpsychiatry.com

Landgren, M., Svensson, L., Strömland. K., & Andersson G. M. (2010). Prenatal alcohol exposure and neurodevelopmental disorders in children adopted from eastern Europe. *Pediatrics*, 125(5), 1178–1185.

Langbehn, D. R., Cadoret, R. J., Caspers, K., Troughton, E., & Yucuis, R. (2003). Genetic and environmental risk factors for the onset of drug use and problems in adoptees. *Drug Alcohol Dependency*, 64(2), 151–167.

Lê, A. D., Li, Z., Funk, D., Li, T., & Shaham, Y. (2006). Increased vulnerability to nicotine self-administration and relapse in alcohol-naive offspring of rats selectively bred for high alcohol intake. *Journal of Neuroscience* 26, 1872–1879.

Lee, D. (2001, January 1). About that hangover. *Courier-Journal* (Louisville, KY), p. 1E.

Lee, Y. (2006). House allows federal prosecution of medical marijuana users. *All Headline News*. Retrieved from http://www.allheadlinenews.com/articles

Lewis, M. (2011). *Memoirs of an addicted brain: A neuroscientist examines his former life on drugs*. Toronto: Random House of Canada.

Li, T.-K. (2004, April). Neuroscience research and therapeutic targets. National Institute on Alcohol Abuse and Alcoholism. *Alcohol Alert*, 61, 1–4.

Linden, D. (2011). *Compass of pleasure*. New York: Penguin.

Lippert, J. (2000, June 23). Meth infants called the new "crack babies." *Des Moines Register*. Retrieved from http://www.geocities.com/joanlippert/methinfants.html

Lukas, S., Penetar, D., Berko, J., Vicens, L., Palmer, C., Mallya, G., et al. (2005). An extract of the Chinese herbal root kudzu reduces alcohol drinking by heavy drinkers in a naturalistic setting. *Alcoholism: Clinical and Epidemiological Research*, 29(5), 756–762.

Maisto, S., Galizio. M., & Connors, G. (2010). *Drug use and abuse*. Belmont, CA: Wadsworth.

Marion, I. J. (2005). Methadone treatment at forty. *Science and Practice Perspective*, 3(1), 25–33.

Martin, Fr. J. (1972). *Chalk talk on alcohol* [Revised. video]. Aberdeen, MD: Kelly Productions.

Mayo Clinic. (2006, April 6). Compulsive gambling. *Health Library*. Special to CNN. Retrieved from http://www.cnn.com/health/library

Mayo Clinic. (2011). *Nicotine dependence center*. Retrieved from http://www.mayoclinic.org

McCarthy, C. (2000, July 23). Life sentences, no time off for innocence. *Sun* (Baltimore), p. 1A.

McCourt, M. (2000). *Singing my him song*. New York: HarperCollins.

McNeece, C. A., & DiNitto, D. M. (2005). *Chemical dependency: A systems approach* (3rd ed.). Boston: Allyn & Bacon.

Medical News Today. (2009, March 3). *One drug may help people both lay down the drink and put out the cigarette*. Retrieved from http://www.medicalnewstoday.com

Merkl, L. (2010, November 1). *Professor's goal is to develop alcoholism drug*. Texas Medical Center. Retrieved from http://www.texasmedicalcenter.org

Meyerhoff, D. J., Tizabi, Y., Staley, J. K., Durazzo, T. C., Glass, J. M., & Nixon, S. J. (2006). Smoking comorbidity in alcoholism. *Alcohol Clinical Experimental Research*, 30(2), 253–264.

Miller, W. R., Forcehimes, A., & Zweben, A. (2011). *Treating addiction: A guide for professionals*. New York: Guilford Press.

Murphy, K. (2004, February 2). There's entrancing news about hypnosis. *Business Week*, p. 88.

Naqvi, N., Rudrauf, D., Damasio, H., & Bechara, A. (2007, January). Damage to the insula disrupts addiction to cigarette smoking. *Science*, 315, 531–534.

National Cancer Institute. (2003). *Smokeless tobacco: Health and after effects*. Retrieved from http://cancercontrol.cancer.gov

National Cancer Institute. (2011). *Laboratory/animal/preclinical studies*. National Institutes of Health. Retrieved from http://www.cancer.gov

National Center on Addiction and Substance Abuse (CASA). (2003). *Underage drinkers more likely to drink excessively as adults*. Retrieved from http://www.casacolumbia.org

National Center on Addiction and Substance Abuse (CASA). (2006). *Women under the influence*. Baltimore: Johns Hopkins University Press.

National Highway Traffic Safety Administration. (2007). *Appendix*. Retrieved from http://www.nhtsa.dot.gov.

National Institute on Alcohol Abuse and Alcoholism (NIAAA). (2000). Stress hormone linked to increased alcohol consumption in animal model. *NIH News Advisory*, pp. 1–2.

National Institute on Alcohol Abuse and Alcoholism (NIAAA). (2003). The genetics of alcoholism. *Alcohol Alert*, 60, 1–3.

National Institute on Alcohol Abuse and Alcoholism (NIAAA). (2004). Alcohol's damaging effects on the brain. *Alcohol Alert*, 63. Retrieved from http://pubs.niaaa.nih.gov/publications

National Institute on Alcohol Abuse and Alcoholism (NIAAA). (2005, January). Alcoholic liver disease. *Alcohol Alert*, 64. NIAAA: Rockville, MD. Retrieved from http://pubs.niaaa.nih.gov/publications/aa64/aa64.htm

National Institute on Alcohol and Alcoholism (NIAAA). (2007). *Alcohol and tobacco.* Alcohol Alert. Retrieved from http://pubs.niaaa.nih.gov/publications

National Institute on Alcohol Abuse and Alcoholism (NIAAA). (2009). *NIAAA five year strategic plan: FY 09-14: Alcohol across the lifespan.* National Institute of Health. Retrieved from www.niaaa.nih.gov/publications

National Institute on Alcohol Abuse and Alcoholism (NIAAA). (2010a). *A snapshot of high-risk college drinking consequences.* Retrieved from http://www.collegedrinkingprevention.gov

National Institute on Alcohol and Alcoholism (NIAAA). (2010b). Surveillance Report #89. *Trends in alcohol-related morbidity among short-stay community hospital discharges.* Arlington, VA: U.S. Department of Health and Human Services.

National Institute on Drug Abuse (NIDA). (2000, August 13). Study finds acupuncture shows promise for treating cocaine addiction. *NIDA News Release,* pp. 1–2.

National Institute on Drug Abuse (NIDA). (2002). Methamphetamine abuse and addiction. *NIDA Research Report Series.* Retrieved from http://nida.nih.gov

National Institute on Drug Abuse (NIDA). (2007a). *Mind over matter: Teacher's guide.* Nerve cell. Retrieved from http://teens.drugabuse.gov/mom/tg_nerves.asp

National Institute on Drug Abuse (NIDA). (2007b). *Mind over matter: Teacher's guide.* Effects of drugs of abuse. Retrieved from http://www.drugabuse.gov/NIDA_Notes/NNVol13N2/Brain.html

National Institute on Drug Abuse (NIDA). (2010). Science-based facts on drug abuse and addiction. *NIDA Infofacts.* Retrieved from http://www.nida.nih.gov/infofacts/infofactsindex.html

National Institutes of Health (NIH). (2011, January 19). *NIH News.* Gene variants predict treatment success. Bethesda, MD: National Institute on Alcohol and Alcohol Abuse.

Neale, T. (2008, October 29). CHEST: Combat troops in Iraq take to tobacco at high rate. *Medpage Today.* Retrieved from http://www.medpagetoday.com

Nestler, E. (2005). The neurobiology of cocaine addiction. *Science and Practice Perspectives,* 3(1), 4–12.

Northwestern Law Center on Wrongful Convictions. (2002). *The exonerated: Gary Gauger.* Retrieved from www.law.com

Okie, S. (2009, January 26). The epidemic that wasn't. *New York Times,* p. D1.

O'Malley, S. S., & Kosten, T. (2006). Pharmacotherapy of addictive disorders. In W. R.Miller & K. M.Carroll (Eds.), *Rethinking substance abuse: What the science shows and what we should do about it* (pp. 240–256). New York: Guilford Press.

Otis, J., & Mueller, D. (2011). Inhibition of β-adrenergic receptors induces a persistent deficit in retrieval of a cocaine-associated memory providing protection against reinstatement. *Neuropsychopharmacology* 36, 1912–1920.

Parker, R. (2011, April 3). Methamphetamine's changing face: Drug cooks exploit loopholes, enforcement money dwindles. *Kalamazoo Gazette.* Retrieved from http://www.mlive.com/news/kalamazoo

Parnell, S., West, J., & Chen, W. (2006). Nicotine decreases blood alcohol concentrations in adult rats: A phenomenon potentially related to gastric function. *Alcoholism: Clinical and Experimental Research,* 30(7), 1413.

Paynter, B. (2011, June 20–26). The drug is fake, the high is real. *Bloomberg Business Week,* pp. 57–64.

Peele, S. (1999, October). Bottle battle. *Reason,* 31(5), 52–55.

Pérez-Peña, R. (2011, July 17). Marijuana for patients remains off-limits. *New York Times*, p. A13.

Peeples, L. (2010, June 10). *Nicotine mouth spray quickly curbs cravings.* Reuters. Retrieved from http://www.reuters.com

Perkinson, R. (2012). *Chemical dependency counseling: A practical guide* (4th ed.). Thousand Oaks, CA: SAGE.

Philip Morris' spin on dying draws fire. (2001, August 9). *Waterloo–Cedar Falls Courier*, p. A6.

Phillips, P, Stuber, G., Heien, M., Wrightman, R., & Carelli, R. (2003). Subsecond dopamine release promotes cocaine seeking. *Nature, 422*, 614–618.

Potenza, M. (2008). The neurobiology of pathological gambling and drug addiction: An overview and new findings. *Philosophical Transactions of the Royal Society Biological Sciences, 363*, 3181–3189.

Pulkkinenen, L. (2011, July 21). Feds link Bellingham doctor to illegal drug via "shaman." *Seattle Post Intelligencer*. Retrieved from http://www.seattlepi.com

Raloff, J. (2003, March 8). When drinking helps. *Science News*, pp. 155–156.

Rasmussen, D. (2011). *Neuroendocrine therapy of alcohol abuse.* Department of Psychiatry, University of Washington School of Medicine. Dennis Rasmussen: bio. Retrieved from http://www.psychiatry.org

Ravindran, A., da Silva, T., Ravindran, L., Richter, M., & Rector, N. (2009). Obsessive-compulsive spectrum disorders: A review of evidence-based treatments. *Canadian Journal of Psychiatry, 54*(5), 331–343.

Reding, N. (2009). *Methland: The death and life of an American small town.* New York: Bloomsburg USA.

Reuben, C., Chen, T. J., Blum, S. H., Braverman, E., Miller, J., Waite, R., et al. (2005, December). Acupuncture and auriculotherapy: Valuable treatment modalities for addiction. *Townsend Letter for Doctors and Patients, 1269*, 81–85.

Ridley, M. (2000). *Genome: Autobiography of a species in 23 chapters.* New York: Harper Perennial.

"Ritalin and Cocaine: The Connection and the Controversy." (2011). *Genetic Science Learning Center, University of Utah*. Retrieved from http://learn.genetics.utah

Roan, S. (2011a, January 21). Alcohol use curbed by anti-nausea medication. *Los Angeles Times*. Retrieved from http://www.latimes.com

Roan, S. (2011b, April 25). Starting Chantix earlier may help smokers quit. *Los Angeles Times*. Retrieved from http://www.latimes.com

Robertson, N. (1988). *Getting better: Inside Alcoholics Anonymous.* New York: William Morrow.

Room, R., Fischer, B., Hall, W., Lenton, S., & Reuter, P. (2010). *Cannabis policy: Moving beyond stalemate.* New York: Oxford University Press.

Rosier, M. (2010, August). Pharmacotherapy treatment options for opioid use disorders. *Counselor: Magazine for Addiction Professionals, 11*(4). Retrieved from http://www.counselormagazine.com

Rupp, C. I., Fleischhacker, W., Drexler, A., Hausmann, A., Hinterhuber, H., & Kurz, M. (2006). Olfactory deficits in alcoholism: Association with impaired executive function. *Chemical Senses, 31*, A34.

Russo, F. (2007, January 18). How to change a personality. *Time*, p. 100.

Sacks, O. (1985). *The man who mistook his wife for a hat and other clinical tales.* New York: Harper & Row.

Schuckit, M. A. (2000). Genetics of the risk for alcoholism. *American Journal on Addictions*, 9, 103–112.

Schuckit, M. (2009). Alcohol-use disorders. *Lancet*, 373, 492–501.

Schwartz, J. (1997). *Brain lock: Free yourself from obsessive compulsive behavior*. New York: HarperCollins.

Schwartz, J. M., & Begley, S. (2003). *The mind and the brain: Neuroplasticity and the power of mental force*. New York: Regan Books.

Science Daily. (2005, April 4). Genes for alcohol consumption identified. University of Bristol. Retrieved from http://www.sciencedaily.com/releases/2005

Shah, K. R., Eisen, S. A., Xian H., & Potenza, M. N. (2005). Genetic studies of pathological gambling: a review of methodology and analyses of data from the Vietnam Era Twin (VET) Registry. *Journal of Gambling Studies*, 21, 177–201.

Shah, K. R., Potenza, M. N., & Eisen, S. A. (2004). Biological basis for pathological gambling. In J. E.Grant & M. N.Potenza (Eds.), *Pathological gambling: A clinical guide to treatment* (pp.127–142). Washington, DC: American Psychiatric Publishing.

Shapiro, L. (1996, January 22). To your health? *Newsweek*, pp. 52–54.

Sharman, C. (2005). The problem with drinking. *Perspectives in Health: Pan American Health Organization*, 10(1). Retrieved from http://www.paho.org

Sher, L. (2006). Alcohol consumption and suicide. *QJM: Monthly Journal of the Association of Physicians*, 99(1), 57–62.

Sherer, R. (2006, April). Drug abuse hitting middle-aged more than genXers. *Psychiatric Times*, 23(4). Retrieved from http://www.psychiatrictimes.com

Shorter Oxford English Dictionary. (2007). New York: Oxford University Press.

Slutske, W. S., Zhu, G., Meier, M. H., & Martin, N. G. (2010). Genetic and environmental influences on disordered gambling in men and women. *Archives of General Psychiatry*, 67(6), 624–630.

Smith, S. (2007, January 18). Cigarettes packing more nicotine and puffs, researchers say. *International Herald Tribune*. Retrieved from http://www.iht.com

"Spice" traps troops. (2011, April 25). *Honolulu: Star Advertiser*. Retrieved from http://www.staradvertiser.com

Spinella, M. (2005). *Concise handbook of psychoactive herbs*. New York: Haworth Herbal Press.

Stevens, P., & Smith, R. L. (2004). *Substance abuse counseling: Theory and practice* (3rd ed.). Upper Saddle River, NJ: Prentice Hall.

Stewart, P., & Sitaramiah, G. (1997, November 13). America's heartland grapples with rise of dangerous drug. *Christian Science Monitor*, pp. 1, 18.

Strang, J., Metrebian, N., Lintzeris, N., Potts, L., Carnwath, T., Mayet, S. et al. (2010). Supervised injectable heroin or injectable methadone versus optimized oral methadone as treatment for chronic heroin addicts in England after persistent failure in orthodox treatment (RIOTT): A randomized trial. *Lancet*, 375, 1885–1895.

"Struggling with alcohol? Better quit smoking too." (2008, October 27). *Health News*. Retrieved from http://news.health.com

Substance Abuse and Mental Health Services Administration. SAMHSA brings buprenorphine to the field. *SAMHSA News*, 12(2), 1–9.

Substance Abuse and Mental Health Services Administration (SAMHSA). (2009). *Incorporating alcohol pharmacotherapies into medical practice: A treatment improvement protocol: TIP 49*. Rockville, MD: SAMHSA.

Szcs, S., Sarvary, A., McKee, M., & Adany, R. (2005). Could the high level of cirrhosis in Central and Eastern Europe be due partly to the quality of alcohol consumed? An exploratory investigation. *Addiction*, 100(4), 536–542.

Taleff, M., & Babcock, M. (2006, June). What about Dad? *Counselor, The Magazine for Addiction Professionals*, 7(3), 72–73.

Thomas, E. (2003, October 20). "I am addicted to prescription pain medication." *Newsweek*, pp. 42–46.

Thomas, J. D., Warren, K. R., & Hewitt, B. G. (2010). Fetal alcohol spectrum disorders: From research to policy. *Alcohol Research and Health*, 33(1/2), 118–126.

Tierney, J. (2010, April 11). Hallucinogens have doctors tuning in again. *New York Times*, p. A1.

Twain, M. (1876). *Adventures of Tom Sawyer*. New York: Harper.

Ubelacker, S. (2005, November 12). New eye test can identify fetal alcohol syndrome. *Globe and Mail*, p. A6.

University of Pittsburgh Medical Center. (2005, July 7). *Specific regions of brain implicated in anorexia nervosa*. Retrieved from http://www.upmc.com/Communications/NewsBureau/

U.S. Department of Health and Human Services (DHHS). (2000). *Tenth special report to the U.S. Congress: Alcohol and health*. Washington, DC: U.S. Government Printing Office.

Van Pelt, J. (2009, May/June). New form of medication for alcohol dependence shows promise. *Social Work Today*, 22–25.

Vedantan, S. (2006, March 19). Lawsuits claim dopamine drugs cause obsessive behavior. *Washington Post*, p. A01.

Vimont, C. (2011). Vivitro slowly makes its way into opioid dependence treatment. *Join Together*. Retrieved from http://www.drugfree.org/join-together

Volkow, N. D. (2005). MDMA (Ecstasy) abuse. From the director. *NIDA Research Reports*. Retrieved from http://www.drugabuse.gov/ResearchReports/MDMA/

Volkow, N. (2009). *Tobacco addictions: Letter from the director*. Retrieved from http://www.nida.nih.gov

Volkow, N. (2010a). *Cocaine: Abuse and addiction, Letter from the director*. National Institute on Drug Abuse. Retrieved from http://www.nida.nih.gov

Volkow, N. (2010b, August). *The science of addiction: Drugs, brains, and behavior*. Washington, DC: NIDA.

Volkow, N. (2011). Message from the Director on "Bath Salts"—Emerging and dangerous products. National Institute on Drug Abuse. Retrieved from http://www.drugabuse.gov

Walters, S. (2008). Ibogaine: Nature's cure for drug addiction. *Natural News*. Retrieved from http://www.naturalnews.com

Washington Drug Letter (2011, January 17). FDA phasing out acetaminophen in high doses in combo drugs. Federal Drug Administration. *FDA News*, 43(3). Retrieved from fdanews.com

Wasserman, B. (2006, April 16). FDA approves Vivitrol for alcoholism. *Drug News*. Retrieved from http://www.foodconsumer.org/777/8

Weiss, R. (2005, January 3–9). Easing fear of the greatest unknown. *Washington Post*, National Weekly Edition, p. 35.

Welsh, I. (1996). *Trainspotting*. Scranton, PA: Norton.

White, A. M. (2004, July). *What happened? Alcohol, memory, blackouts, and the brain*. NIAAA: Rockville, MD.

Whitten, L. (2004). Men and women process cocaine cues differently. National Institute on Drug Abuse (NIDA). *NIDA Notes, 19*(4). Retrieved from http://www.niaaa.nih.gov

Whitten, L. (2005). A single cocaine "binge" can establish long-term cue-induced drug seeking in rats. *NIDA Notes, 19*(6). Retrieved from http://www.drugabuse.gov? NIDA

Whitten, L. (2009). Low dopamine receptor availability may promote cocaine addiction. *NIDA Research Findings, 22*(3), 5–7.

World Health Organization (WHO). (2004). *Global status report on alcohol 2004.* Geneva, Switzerland: WHO. Retrieved from http://www.who.int

World Health Organization (WHO). (2010). *ATLAS 2010: First global report on substance use disorders launched.* Retrieved from http://www.who.int

World Health Organization (WHO). (2011a). *Global status report on alcohol: 2011.* 4. Geneva, Switzerland: WHO.

World Health Organization (WHO). (2011b). *Lexicon of alcohol and drug terms.* Retrieved from http://www.who.int/substance_abuse/terminology/who_lexicon/en/

World Health Organization (WHO). (2011c). WHO report on the global tobacco epidemic: 2011. Retrieved from http://www.who.int/tobacco

"Wrinkles are traced to tobacco." (2001, March 23). *Des Moines Register*, p. 4A.

Zarkin, G. A., Dunlap, L. N., Hicks, K., & Mamo, D. (2005). Benefits and costs of methadone treatment: Results from a lifetime simulation model. *Health Economics, 14*(11), 1133–1150.

Zarkin, G. A., Bray, J. W., Aldridge, A., Mills, M., Cisler, R. A., Couper, D., et al. (2010). The effect of alcohol treatment on social costs of alcohol dependence: Results from the COMBINE study. *Medical Care, 48*(5), 396–401.

Zetterman, R. (2010). Alcoholic liver disease. *Medscape Today News.* Retrieved from http://www.medscape.com

Zuger, A. (2011, June 14). A general in the drug war. *New York Times*, p. D1.

GENDER AND SEXUAL ORIENTATION DIFFERENCES

They treat women alcoholics different than men. It's like "How dare you, how could you! You have children!" Like it's okay for a man, but we're worse.

—A woman in treatment (from Lafave, Desportes, & McBride, 2009, p. 63)

INTRODUCTION

Since the early 1980s, a great deal of energy, resources, and research, along with many women's voices, have changed the way we look at traditional drug and alcohol treatment programming. In 1984, with the federal requirement that 5% of each block grant to states be set aside for new or expanded alcohol and drug abuse services for women, a wide array of special services began to appear. Within another 4 years, the war on drugs and the national press obsession with "crack babies" helped inspire Congress to double the federal set-aside to target programs for pregnant women and women with dependent children. Grants became available to fund demonstration programs for women-only groups and treatment programs; for more supportive and less confrontational approaches; for programs with enhanced services such as parenting, skill development, and prevocational training; and for programs that incorporated prenatal and postnatal care, or at least child care while the woman was in treatment sessions. In 1993, the National Institutes of Health (NIH) mandated that enough women had to be included in clinical trials that gender differences could be tested. By 2004, the Center for Substance Abuse Treatment (CSAT) and the Center for Mental Health Services (2004) had funded over 100 grantees specifically targeting services for women (SAMHSA, 2005a). Results from these and other studies are incorporated into a CSAT (2009) Treatment Improvement Protocol (TIP 51) on *Substance Abuse Treatment: Addressing the Specific Needs of Women*, which can be downloaded free at http://www.samhsa.gov. Although SAMHSA has established practice standards of gender-sensitive treatment, some researchers have questioned the robustness of previous research findings, noting they come primarily from cross-sectional, descriptive, quasi-experimental, and observational studies (Greefield et al, 2007; Plant, 2008). In addition, male-specific treatment that considers men's experience of gender is in its infancy (*Alcoholism Drug Abuse Weekly*, 2009).

During this same time frame, the voices of gay men and lesbians also began to be heard. The connection between injected drugs, the gay population, and the acquired immune deficiency syndrome AIDS epidemic added pressure for federal funders to pay attention to gay males as a special population. An indication of the change is the National Institute on Drug Abuse (NIDA) 5-year epidemiological study launched in 1991, which surveyed 1,067 respondents, of which 53% were gay men and 47% were lesbians.

Similarly, women have become more visible in treatment and research on problem gambling. Historically, gambling was the province of men, but the unprecedented growth of casino gambling in the last 30 years has changed that reality. Go to any casino and you will see as many women as men sitting at the slot machines and video poker outlets. Gambling has been "sanitized" into "gaming" and has become much more attractive and accessible to women (Davis, 2009). Research and treatment protocols are catching up to this phenomenon, with some programming beginning to occur around the special needs of women problem gamblers (Piquette-Tomel, Norman, Dwyer, & McCaslin, 2008).

Although legislative and research changes signal an enormous shift in what has been heterosexual male–dominated addiction research and treatment programs, the actual changing of treatment options for women, gay men, and lesbian women is still an ongoing effort. Researchers and practitioners continue to identify gender differences in biology, genetics, paths to dependence, responses to various treatment options, relapse, and social contexts, which suggest different prevention and treatment programs for men and women. A rich array of treatment approaches is being developed that far surpasses the beginning focus on simple gender differences (Greenfield & Grella, 2009). However, these findings are still not widely applied to practice settings; when they have been, the research findings on the outcomes of specialized programs for women have produced mixed results. Few studies have addressed outcomes in male-only interventions. There is also no consensus as to whether gay men and lesbians should be treated separately from heterosexual clients or separately from each other. The next step is further development of research measures and projects to conduct empirically robust research on treatment effectiveness for these diverse populations (Greenfield & Grella, 2009).

This chapter focuses first on gender differences and then on sexual orientation differences that may affect a person's ability to resist addiction, seek and find treatment, and maintain recovery. Programs designed to enhance the ability of women, gay men, and lesbians to succeed in their recovery are described. Controversies that surround these developments are discussed, and research findings are offered to practitioners.

GENDER DIFFERENCES

Before we lump people into gender categories to illustrate their differences, it is important to remember that all women are not alike, and of course, neither are all men. Scientists and researchers who adhere to a "developmental" approach to addiction stress the interplay of sociocultural, psychological, and neurobiological processes that influence each individual a little bit differently depending on the person's age, gender, and ethnic group and on the cultural influences on each person's age cohort (U.S. Secretary of Health and Human Services, 2000).

Murphy and Rosenbaum (1997) argue that gender, race, and class are more important in shaping how people develop drug problems with illicit drugs than the drug itself. Thus, as described in their classic study, Becky, a White, middle-class young woman interviewed in their NIDA-sponsored research project, had more options for controlling her cocaine use than Monique, a young Black woman living in a poor inner-city neighborhood. Becky used cocaine within the protected context that is afforded the middle class. She had a job and resources to buy her own powder cocaine, the privacy to use it without being hassled by police, and thus could maintain a "nondeviant" identity. When her period of heavy use became an unsatisfying experience that threatened other life goals that she had every opportunity to attain, she could rely on the resources of the middle class (school, family, job connections) to help her quit using. On the other hand, Monique was introduced to "crack," a more dangerous form of cocaine that was readily available in her neighborhood, quickly resorted to trading sexual favors for her drug as the only currency available, was frequently arrested on the streets, and became homeless and totally impoverished, with few resources to deal with her predicament. Becky went to Hawaii with her father to make a break from cocaine use; Monique went to jail.

The protective power of race and class extends to only some women and men, and no one would claim it prevents addiction. However, it can condition and influence how a person uses drugs, alcohol, and gambling and mediate the consequences of that use or misuse. Cultural differences around the world regarding the acceptance of alcohol for each gender and the extent to which sex roles are strictly defined appear to influence the wide variation in alcoholism. According to the Global Status Report on Alcohol (WHO, 2004), the male–female ratio of heavy episodic drinking was: Canada, 28:11, France, 27.9:9.7, Germany, 42:13, Italy, 13:12, Mexico, 46:5, Russia, 15:3, United Kingdom, 24:9. One can see by examining these ratios that heavy drinking is more a male than a female characteristic and that the gender gap in some nations, such as Mexico, is extremely large.

GENDER DIFFERENCES IN PREVALENCE

Gender alone does make a difference in the prevalence of addictive behavior and treatment needs (CSAT, 2009). The Substance Abuse and Mental Health Services Administration (SAMHSA) conducts a yearly survey, called the National Household Survey on Drug Use and Health (NHSDUH), to estimate the use of drugs, alcohol, and tobacco; dependence; and treatment occurring within the United States (SAMHSA, 2010a). Data from the 2009 survey indicate that males 12 years or older were more likely to report current illicit drug use than females (10.8% vs. 6.6%, respectively), almost twice as likely to use marijuana as females (8.6% vs. 4.8%), and almost twice as likely to use cocaine (0.9% vs. 0.4%). Adult males and females had the same rates for the nonmedical use of tranquilizers (0.8% for both) and methamphetamines (0.2%) (Figure 4.1). Among youth, age 12–17, males had higher rates for current use of illicit drugs (10.6% vs. 9.4%). Maleyouth were also more likely to report current alcohol use (57.6% vs. 46.5%). More males than females reported current alcohol use (28.5% vs. 25.8%), binge drinking (20.5% vs. 15.5%), and heavy drinking 7.0% vs. 3.7%) (Figure 4.2).

In terms of substance dependence or abuse, the rates for males aged 12 or older (11.9%) were about twice as high as for females (6.1%) in 2009 and the 5 years preceding (Figure 4.2). Among youth aged 12 to 17, however, the rate

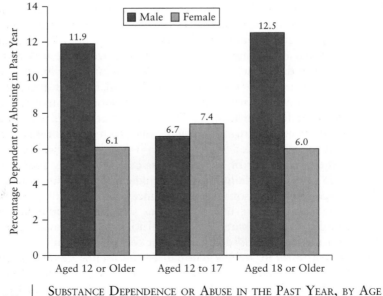

FIGURE 4.1 | SUBSTANCE DEPENDENCE OR ABUSE IN THE PAST YEAR, BY AGE AND GENDER: 2009

Source: SAMSHA (2010). Results from the 2009 National Survey on Drug Use and Health.

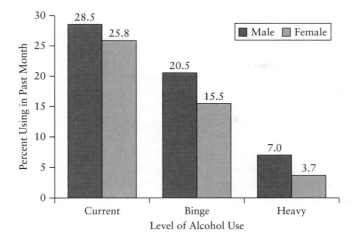

FIGURE 4.2 | CURRENT, BINGE, AND HEAVY ALCOHOL USE AMONG PERSONS AGED 12 TO 20, BY GENDER: 2009

Source: SAMSHA (2010). Results from the 2009 National Survey on Drug Use and Health.

of substance dependence or abuse among males was similar to the rate among females (6.7% males vs. 7.4% females). As has been noted, this may be "an equality women don't want" (Davis & DiNitto, 2005, p. 503). Some would argue that women have always been drinking and using drugs more than shows up in research studies but that poor methodology, indifference, and sex-role stereotyping have kept the numbers lower.

Compulsive gambling surveys consistently report that men are much more likely to be pathological or problem gamblers than are women. Analyses from the 2001 National Epidemiologic Survey on Alcohol and Related Conditions indicate that the lifetime prevalence for *Diagnostic and Statistical Manual of Mental Disorders, Text Revision (DSM–IV–TR)*–diagnosed pathological gambling for males was 0.64% compared to 0.23% for females. Problem gambling (subclinical) lifetime rates were about twice as high for males (6.79%) than for females (3.26%). The authors also found that women were more likely to have a later onset of gambling problems than men, have a life-time diagnoses of mood and anxiety disorders, and report gambling to relieve depressed mood (Blanco, Hasin, Petry, Stinson, & Grant, 2006). For youth (ages 14–22), 30% of the females surveyed report gambling in an average month compared to 57% of males (Annenberg Public Policy Center, 2005).

Most of the state problem gambling helplines report that the percentage of women seeking help with gambling problems has been increasing. In New Jersey, calls about women problem gamblers have doubled since 1990. In California, of the more than 4,400 calls in 2006, the gambler's gender was 57.4% male and 42.6% female (California Help-Line Survey, 2006). A Man-itoba, Canada, study found that 43% of the helpline calls were from women about their own gambling (Heater & Patton, 2006). In Nevada, 44% of the helpline calls were from women concerning their own problems (Nevada Council on Problem Gambling, 2004). Research from Arizona based on a population sample found the male–female ratio of gamblers was about even for persons who gambled in the past month. (Volberg, 2005). An interesting finding from this study is that 67.8% of females with gambling problems were late onset, whereas the majority of the males developed these problems at a young age.

Since 1965, men have been smoking less (a drop of 46%), and women have been smoking a little bit less (a drop of 35%). Consequently, the gender gap in smoking rates has narrowed. In 2005, 35.8% of adult males used a tobacco product compared to 23.4% of adult women, and in 2009, the rate dropped again to 33.5% for males and 22.2% for females. In the younger age group (12–17), the males smoking rate was only slightly higher (9.2%) compared to females (8.6%) (SAMHSA, 2006, 2010a).

SOCIOCULTURAL GENDER DIFFERENCES

In the recent past (and even today), women identified as alcoholics, drug addicts, or compulsive gamblers were considered especially deviant and promiscuous. Substance misuse among females is more highly stigmatized than among males and can be a serious barrier to getting help (Brady & Ashley, 2005; CSAT, 2009). We can consider women who are addicted a discredited social group who suffer from a "double whammy" because they are both addicted and female. It seems reasonable to expect that women addicted to alcohol, drugs, or gambling would internalize these sociocultural forces. In interviews with women recovering from compulsive gambling, Davis (2009, p. 9) found that many expressed a great deal of shame and regret over their inability to carry on the roles that society expects females to performwhile in the midst of their gambling problems. When asked what they regret the most, many noted the impact on their families:

- "Gambling robbed me of my soul, values, and I caused my family to worry about me."
- "I caused my family so much mental anguish, especially my son."
- "I lost me, and I lost so much time with my children."

To what extent does the "shame factor" affect a woman's path to addiction or her ability to get help and recover? It may be part of the larger environment of women's struggle for economic and political equality. The basic premise of CSAT's (2009) Treatment Improvement Protocol called *Addressing the Specific Needs of Women* is that women are biopsychosocially unique in ways that influence substance use and substance abuse treatment. The core principles for gender responsive treatment include:

- Acknowledging the importance as well as the role of the socioeconomic issues and differences among women.
- Promoting cultural competence specific to women.

- Recognizing the role as well as the significance of relationships in women's lives.
- Addressing women's unique health concerns.
- Endorsing a developmental perspective.
- Attending to the relevance and influence of various caregiver roles that women often assume throughout the course of their lives.
- Recognizing that ascribed roles and gender expectations across cultures affect societal attitudes toward women who abuse substances.
- Adopting a trauma-informed perspective.
- Using a strength-based model for women's treatment.
- Incorporating an integrated and multidisciplinary approach to women's treatment.
- Maintaining a gender responsive treatment environment across settings.

Women as a group are oppressed in many ways in the dominant culture of the United States. More women than men are poor, and many women continue to be paid less than men in similar positions. Indirect discrimination exists not just with treatment centers but also with employment and educational organizations that do not provide a way for them to meet their child-rearing responsibilities. Cultural stereotypes still cast women as dependent on men, illogical, emotionally unstable, and incapable of many tasks that require leadership, math skills, or mechanical skills (Abramovitz, 1997). Women are far more likely than men to be subjected to violence and murder by a person with whom they have an intimate relationship. These factors affect all women, but a woman who is trying to get help for an addiction may be particularly affected by her lack of money and resources, less tolerance and less support from partner and family, the lack of treatment available for women with children, and the role expectations that are attached to being female. For example, in a qualitative study on relapse among women, Sun (2007) found that the women's struggle with sobriety was related to gender role expectations that hampered their ability to express negative emotions, and to let go of unhealthy relationships and establish new healthy relationships. Ironically, the use of alcohol and drugs can function as a means of connecting with a more assertive self. A woman interviewed in another qualitative study (Rivaux, Sohn, Armour, & Bell, 2008, p. 965) expressed:

> The positive thing I gained from [using drugs] is that I became me again. I found a part of my spirit, a part of me that my husband had ... knocked down for so many years. And it was like I blossomed into who I really was again ... the me I lost.

Another woman in this study described how alcohol gave her a voice: "[Drinking] let me speak up and say what is on my mind" (p. 965). The challenge for maintaining recovery becomes helping clients find a way to express themselves without resorting to their addictive behavior.

Studies of clients who enter treatment support the reality that often women are more dependent on welfare and/or disability payments, while men have more skilled jobs. Overall women have less education and lower rates of employment than men, and women are more likely to lack employment skills. Women are twice as likely to have children in their households and to report greater concerns about issues related to children, although both men and women were concerned about the effect of drug treatment on the custody of their children (Brady & Ashley, 2005; Wong, Badger, Sigman, & Higgins, 2002). Women problem gamblers are significantly more likely than men to report financial difficulties (even though both groups had many difficulties) and have less annual income to deal with these problems, according to a study of callers to a gambling helpline (Potenza et al., 2001).

Using a feminist methodology and analysis to look at environmental factors affecting women gamblers, Brown and Coventry (1997) launched a community-based research project in Victoria, Australia, called Queen of Hearts. The findings suggest that women compulsive gamblers may be the victims of social stereotypes and the economic and gender limitations imposed on women. Even the definitions of gambling problems that focus on individual "pathology" instead of including a sociocultural framework "have serious stigmatizing effects, such as discouraging gamblers from seeking assistance, inviting moral and legalistic judgments, and invoking the label of 'deviant'" (p. 9).

PARTNER RELATIONSHIPS

Significant relationships play a powerful role in the initiation, pattern of use, and continuation of substance abuse for women (CSAT, 2009). Women who are substance dependent are more likely than their male counterparts to have a substance dependent spouse or partner (SAMHSA, 2005a). Having a male partner who is drinking or using drugs has consistently been found to be a predisposing factor (some would say the greatest factor) in a woman's addiction (Brady & Ashley, 2005; Westermeyer & Boedicker, 2000). When a woman tries to change her situation by seeking help or treatment, partners may prevent them (Tuten & Jones, 2004). Even when a woman finally gets to treatment, she is less likely to complete it if her male partner is using drugs (Jones, Tuten, & O'Grady, 2011). Laudet, Magura, Furst, and Kumar (1999) found that men who were active crack/cocaine users were able to give only passive and inconsistent support to their partners in treatment. Reasons included the men's own active use, their desire to maintain the relationship status quo where the man has the dominant role, their preoccupation with working on their own recovery, their disagreement with abstinence as a necessity, and their desire to avoid the stigma attached to their female partner as an addict. In contrast, men report that they are influenced positively by a spouse or partner to enter treatment or that they enter because of the criminal justice system (Grella & Joshi, 1999). Recovery often comes with relationship costs for women (Rivaux et al., 2008).

To counteract this problem, a unique treatment program for male partners who are also drug-dependent was designed to improve the treatment outcomes of their female pregnant partners (Jones, Tuten, & O'Grady, 2011).

In this program, the men targeted for intervention were heroin users who had no initial interest in seeking treatment, but their pregnant partners were involved in a methadone maintenance program. The men were randomly selected for the program and were encouraged to participate through a six-session Motivational Enhancement intervention, followed by a contingency-based voucher incentive program that rewarded drug abstinence. They could choose either detoxification and aftercare support, or methadone mainte-nance. Couple's counseling and a men's educational support group were pro-vided in addition to the substance abuse treatment. Results indicated that, compared to the control group, the men showed positive outcomes including increased treatment retention, decreased heroin use, and increased social sup-port for their pregnant partners. Although this was a small pilot study ($n = 62$), it does demonstrate that drug-using partners can be attracted to treatment and that such a program can have a positive effect on a female partner's abil-ity to sustain treatment—a hopeful beginning.

BEING A MOM AND A CARETAKER   In addition to the lack of familial support and the likelihood their spouse or partner is also abusing substances, women are less likely to enter treatment for many other reasons: (1) the obligation of child rearing, (2) the unavailability of treatment slots for women with chil-dren or pregnant women, (3) barriers such as transportation and lack of child care, and (4) treatment programs not designed to meet these and other special needs of women clients. A shocking example of the unavailability of treatment to parents in the U.S. child welfare system is the estimate by the Child Welfare League of America that 67% of parents involved in the system needed drug or alcohol treatment, yet services were available to only 31% (Young, Gardner, & Dennis, 1998). It is well recognized in the treatment field that many women do not participate in treatment because they are unable to obtain quality child care or because they fear being required to relinquish their children (CASA, 2006).

Paradoxically, gambling is a way for some women to rebel against care-taking duties and traditional feminine obligations. An addiction therapist (female) who works full-time with problem gamblers explores this idea:

> Almost every female client I have seen states that gambling is in some manner a way of her "letting go of her obligations"; "rebelling"; "doing what I want, finally, after taking care of everyone else all my life." Many of my clients have experienced abusive relationships and lasting loneliness. Several are grandmothers, many are divorced, and a few are young and with partners. The crux of this rebellion seems to be the end result of feeling emotionally and physically responsible to others first and themselves last. When the pressure cap finally blows, and the woman says, "Screw you, world, watch me do what I want!" she finds herself "asserting" her autonomy in a casino or bingo game, etc. (Anonymous, 2003, p. 2)

CRIME AND PUNISHMENT FOR WOMEN WITH CHILDREN   Addiction and the use of illicit drugs bring women into the criminal and civil justice system in a way unique to their gender. The criminalization of women who use illicit drugs during pregnancy and the termination of their parental rights has no male counterpart. Although state appellate courts have consistently found that criminal prosecutions of pregnant women for the effects of their drug use on their unborn child is not permissible, that does not prevent local prosecutors who want to punish women for their drug use from continuing to bring charges of criminal child endangerment and even attempted homicide, and under child abuse statues (Stone-Manista, 2009). During 2007 and 2008, eight women in one Alabama jurisdiction alone were prosecuted for drug use during pregnancy. South Carolina remains the only state where using drugs or being addicted to drugs during pregnancy is still criminalized, despite appellate court decisions. (Harris & Paltrow, 2007).

Many women have lost custody of their children to child welfare agencies due to drug or alcohol use. Substance abuse has been indicated in at least 60% of the homes for which child maltreatment has been found to occur (National Clearinghouse on Child Abuse and Neglect Information, 2003). Child protection statutes of 47 states, the District of Columbia, Guam, and the U.S Virgin Islands address the issue of substance abuse by parents. Twelve states and the District of Columbia include prenatal exposure to drugs in the definition of child abuse or neglect (Young, Gardner, Otero, Dennis, Chang, Earle, & Amatetti, 2009). Consequently, these children can be removed from the mother when the child is born (Harris & Paltrow, 2007).

Another law that impacts mothers with substance abuse problems is the Federal Adoption and Safe Families Act (ASFA, Public Law 105-89, 1997). ASFA was created to counteract "foster care drift," the long time periods young children would languish in the foster care system waiting for parents to be able to provide a safe home for them. ASFA requires that parents who have come to the attention of child welfare agencies for child abuse or neglect have a limited time to comply with reunification requirements (usually around 12 months), which include demonstrating and maintaining abstinence from their addiction, or they face permanent termination of their parental rights (CSAT, 2010). Demanding abstinence from someone with a chronic, relapsing condition like addiction can cause serious problems. Obtaining treatment and maintaining abstinence can be a much more lengthy process than the timelines for ASFA. Consequently, parents have to become engaged in treatment as soon as possible. Historically, a lack of coordination, collaboration, and treatment options has hindered the ability of child welfare, substance abuse treatment, and family/dependency court systems to support these families and engage them in treatment in a timely manner. Based on National Survey on Drug Use and Health reports, in 2005, only 6% of the pregnant women aged 15–44 who were classified as needing treatment for alcohol and/or drug problems actually received treatment. Only 17% of treatment facilities have a specific program for pregnant and postpartum women (Young et al., 2009).

In an effort to remedy the time-crunch of the ASFA regulations, several states developed demonstration projects that co-located substance abuse specialists within the child welfare office or dependency court to assist in engaging clients with substance abuse problems with treatment. A review of seven projects indicated some success (CSAT, 2010). Although evaluation methods were not uniformly in place across projects, the Delaware site reported that in 2005, 24% of the parents working with a substance abuse counselor completed a treatment program, and an Illinois dependency court reported a rate of 22% in 2004 plus increased rates of reunification and shorter lengths of stay in foster care.

Other promising approaches include recovery coaches and family drug courts. In an Illinois project (Ryan et al., 2008), recovery coaches were assigned to the experimental group of pregnant and addicted mothers who were also in substance abuse treatment. The addition of recovery coaches significantly improved the chances of the baby being born substance-free (85% compared to the 79% of mothers who received only treatment). In Sacramento, California, a family drug court (the STARS program) was developed to assist parents over a 2-year program, who were involved with the child welfare system and who had substance abuse disorders. Of the parents who graduated from the program, 70.9% were reunified with their children (Boles & Young, 2007). Clearly, more innovations and intervention outcome studies are needed to ensure that fragile parents have effective resources to deal with their substance abuse problems in a timely fashion.

Although illicit drug use is not limited to any class or race of women, women of color are significantly more likely to be penalized by arrest or the attention of child welfare agencies (Stone-Manista, 2009). While illicit drug use is the focus of most prosecutions and child welfare investigations, alcohol has been extensively documented to cause the most severe birth defects and that cigarette smoking is highly correlated with low birth weight and prematurity, yet these problems are overlooked The prevalence rates of fetal alcohol syndrome (FAS) are estimated at 0.2–1.5 cases per 1,000 live births, and other prenatal conditions, such as alcohol-related neurodevelopmental disorders and alcohol-related birth defects, are believed to occur about three times as often as FAS (Young et al., 2009). In 2006 and 2007, an estimated 11.6% of pregnant women aged 15–44 reported using alcohol in the past month (SAMHSA, 2008). However, the primary targets of prosecution from the legal and child welfare systems are poor women of color using cocaine or crack. The result of such racist and oppressive policies has not been less drug use; rather, it has deterred especially at-risk poor women from sharing important information with their healthcare providers and from seeking prenatal care at all (Lester, Andreozz, & Applah, 2004).

In summary, women continue to be singled out for blame related to using drugs during pregnancy. Social services are not seen as a support, but rather as a threat (Goddard, 2009). Blame is placed on individual women rather than acknowledging the larger issues of poverty, lack of treatment for pregnant women, and lack of supportive (rather than punitive) healthcare. A hopeful sign is that in 2009, SAMHSA awarded $14.7 million over 3 years in grants to support residential treatment programs for pregnant and postpartum women in need of services for substance use disorders (U.S. Federal News Service, 2009).

JAIL AND PRISON   The rising number of women incarcerated in jails and prisons is another step toward equality that women do not want. Largely because of the impact of the U.S. war on drugs and mandatory sentencing, the female prisoner population in the United States nearly doubled from 1995 to 2005 (Bureau of Justice Statistics (BJS), 2006). Women offenders, especially in the younger age brackets, are being arrested at increasingly high rates for drug offenses, and women of color are experiencing the greatest overall increase in criminal justice supervision, including parole and imprisonment. African Americans and Hispanics/Latinas account for nearly two-thirds of incarcerated women (CSAT, 2010).

Most incarcerated women are serving time for crimes, especially in the federal prison system, that involved drugs. Around 72% of women confined in the federal prison system were convicted of a drug violation (BJS, 2000). Drunk-driving arrests are rapidly rising for women and declining for men, although men's arrests still outnumber women's by 4:1. Women's arrests for driving while intoxicated (DWI) were almost 30% higher in 2007 than in 1998, while men's arrests declined 7.5% (Compton & Benning, 2009). Keep in mind that other crimes for which women are sentenced, including property crime and crimes against public order, also might be alcohol and/or drug related.

Karberg and James (2005) gathered data based on interviews conducted in over 400 jails. Substance misuse emerged as a primary cause of and contributor to crime for both men and women residing in jail at the time of the study. The breakdown by gender for substance dependence and abuse revealed that approximately 68% of female jail inmates met the criteria for substance dependence, a rate that was similar to that of men. Convicted female jail inmates had a higher rate of previous drug use (61%) compared to a male sample of inmates (54%). In Iowa, and increasingly in other states, methamphetamine (meth) is listed as the drug of choice among female but not male inmates. Illegal drugs were implicated more than alcohol in women's crimes; for men, the pattern was reversed. In addition to higher drug use and dependence than men, incarcerated women also have higher rates of medical disorders and psychiatric disorders, histories of sexual violence and other forms of abuse, as well as custody and parenting issues (Binswanger et al., 2010; CSAT, 2010). In response to these differences, many have advocated for women-sensitive treatment during incarceration and after release.

A survey from the National Association of Counties showed that over one-third of drug and alcohol–dependent inmates had received treatment while incarcerated or on probation or parole (Zernike, 2005). Treatment as defined in the survey included attendance at self-help groups such as Alcoholics Anonymous (AA) or Narcotics Anonymous (NA). Female inmates in this category reported more treatment involvement than men, and Whites reported more treatment than persons of other races. Less than 10% of drug-involved inmates had received specialized treatment since entering jail. Federal prisons offer the highest percentage of substance abuse treatment, and local jails provide the least (van Wormer & Bartollas, 2007).

Community-based options such as drug courts have empirical support, but few studies have examined how effective this model is specifically with women. Drug courts offer a combination of treatment services, judicial monitoring, probation supervision, and a nonadversarial team-work approach to support the successful rehabilitation and recovery of the participants (Drug Courts Program Office, 2004). One study compared moderate to high-risk drug court women participants to women probationers in a 2-year follow-up and found drug court participants significantly less likely to recidivate (Shaffer, Hartman, & Listwan, 2009).

Jail, prison, or drug court may be the first place anyone has offered treatment or talked to women about the abuse they have experienced. As told by two women in recovery from drug addiction interviewed by Hirsch (1999):

> I started using alcohol and pills when I was thirteen. I was raped when I was twelve, my father was an alcoholic, my mother was using pills. He used to beat her up all the time—it was pretty crazy. No, no one helped me. The [drug and alcohol treatment program in jail] is the first place anyone talked about it.
>
> [In jail] they had all different kind of classes—about being raped in the street, about being raped in your family. I needed both those classes. This is my first time in treatment. I couldn't get Medical Assistance, so I couldn't get treatment. Now I'm court-stipulated, so I can get treatment. (p. 2)

VIOLENCE AND TRAUMA Violence against women is an area where the influence of sociocultural attitudes has been well documented. Widely cited in the literature is the work of Kantor and Straus (1989), who discovered in an analysis of data from a national family violence survey that the strongest predictor of family violence is cultural approval of violence, and this factor is even more significant than the level of alcohol abuse. In the United States, we "approve" of violence through advertisements featuring malnourished women in stiletto heels and chains, films that show scenes of women being slapped or raped, ineffective laws and law enforcement, and the lack of a viable well-resourced support system for women seeking help. Yodanis (2004) documented, in a cross-cultural test of feminist theory attributing the extent of violence against women to cultural attitudes, that in nations where women's status is low (as measured in terms of levels of occupational equality), the rate of wife and partner violence is higher than in nations where women have a higher level of equality.

When boys and girls become young men and women, the perpetrators of violence differ depending on gender. Stephanie Covington (2008) describes the typical patterns:

> In adolescence, boys are at risk if they are gay, young men of color, or gang members. Their risk is from people who dislike or hate them. For a young woman, the risk is in her relationships, from the person(s) to whom she is saying, "I love you." For an adult man, the risk for abuse comes from being in combat or being a victim of crime. His risk is from "the enemy" or from a stranger. For an adult woman, the primary risk is again in her relationship with the person to whom she says, "I love you." Clinically, it is very possible that this may account

for the increase in mental health problems for women. In short, it is more confusing and distressing to have the person who is supposed to love and care for you
do harm to you than it is to be harmed by someone who dislikes you or is a
stranger. (p. 380)

The Centers for Disease Control and Prevention's (CDC) National Center
for Injury Prevention and Control estimates that nearly 5.3 million domestic
violence incidents happen each year among women 18 years and older, resulting in 2 million injuries and 1,300 deaths (CDC, 2006). Women with a history of intimate partner violence are more likely to display behaviors that
present further health risks (e.g., substance abuse, alcoholism, suicide
attempts). Studies show that the more severe the violence, the stronger its relationship to negative health behaviors by victims, such as engaging in high-risk
sexual behavior, having multiple sex partners, and trading sex for food,
money, or other items.

The use of alcohol and drugs has consistently been found to be a major
factor in intimate-partner violence (BJS, 2003). In several studies, the significant correlation between the use of alcohol and intimate-partner violence
against women holds after controlling for sociodemographic variables, hostility, and marital satisfaction. It holds across all ethnic groups and social classes
(Leonard, 1993). A descriptive study of the types of violence against women
and the associated use of alcohol and illicit drugs by the perpetrator revealed
that physical abuse was significantly higher for women with perpetrators who
used drugs only compared with perpetrators who used alcohol only (Willson
et al., 2000). According to a large data analysis by the National Center on
Addiction and Substance Abuse at Columbia University (CASA, 2006), 70%
of drug-addicted, low-income pregnant women in methadone maintenance
have been beaten—86% by their husbands or partners. Women who use
cocaine are at high risk for being murdered. In New York City, from 1990
to 1992, the number of fatal injuries following cocaine use was higher
than the number of deaths from AIDS, cancer, or heart disease for young
Black and Hispanic women ages 15–24. Alcoholic women do not escape
either; in one study of spousal abuse, alcoholic women were found to be
nine times more likely to be slapped by their husband, five times more likely
to be kicked or hit, five times more likely to be beaten, and four times more
likely to have their lives threatened than were nonalcoholic women.

In the following, we read the words of a North Carolina woman:

> I married an alcoholic. I married him because I thought he was the only guy who
> would ever show me any attention. In those seven years, I put up with mental
> abuse, physical abuse, and somewhat sexual abuse. The way that alcohol and mar-
> ijuana played a role in my marriage—that was the only way of getting along with
> him. He was mean as a snake. He run me down onto the ground and start beating
> me. To relax, I drank, I smoked pot and go into my own little dream world. That's
> what the marijuana did, was put you in a dream state, where you would forget all
> the pain and all the anger and all the abuse and get high. Until the next morning,
> and then it started all over again. (Smith & Chescheir, 1995, p. 32)

In addition to domestic violence (which some feminists prefer to call household terrorism), women are far more likely than men to be subjected to sexual violence (as children or adults). The National Crime Victimization Survey reports that in 2004, there were 209,880 victims of rape, attempted rape, or sexual assault (BJS, 2004). Since 1993, although the rate of these crimes has fallen by a dramatic 64%, women are still the primary victims (90% vs. 10%). Most (67%) of these assaults were committed by someone who is known to the victim.

There is a growing body of research that supports the relationship between childhood sexual abuse and subsequent substance abuse in women (Brady & Ashley, 2005; Downs & Miller, 2002; Neumann, Houskamp, Pollock, & Briere, 1996; Wilsnack, Vogeltanz, Klassen, & Harris, 1997). In addition, the experience of childhood sexual and physical abuse is linked to a greater risk of sexually transmitted diseases (STDs) (El-Bassel et al., 1998), unintended pregnancy (Kenney, Reinholtz, & Angelini, 1997), and prostitution in women (Widom, Ireland, & Glynn, 1995). Men who experience sexual abuse are likelier than nonabused men to use drugs and engage in risky sexual behavior (Holmes & Slap, 1998; Pierre, Shrier, Emans, & DuRant, 1998).

An empirically based study that examined the history of abuse and violence in over 1,000 meth users (Cohen et al., 2003) provides validation to media claims that meth leads to violent behavior. In the research on men and women in treatment for meth addiction, the reported violence was extensive, with 80% of women reporting partner violence. Experiences of early life violence were commonly recounted as well. Men also experienced violence, more commonly from friends and acquaintances.

Compared to male substance misusers, females have a disproportionately high rate of multiple victimization. Chesney-Lind and Pasko (2004) map out the pathway that sometimes leads a girl, desperate to escape the sexual and physical abuse at home, to run away; seek solace in drugs and the company of drug users, gang members, and the like; and survive on the streets through prostitution. This pattern is highlighted in inner-city females for whom prostitution may serve as a means of survival in circumstances of extreme economic hardship. Belknap (2001) and Enos (2001) similarly stress the role of poverty and sexual and physical abuse in women who assist men in the commission of crimes.

Trauma can also be related to war and military service. A participant in a recent study on women veterans says, "I went from childhood abuse to husband abuse, and then from husband abuse to military abuse" (Hamilton, Poza, & Washington, 2011, p. 206). Using focus groups with 29 homeless veterans, the authors distinguished five precipitating experiences that initiated the pathways toward homelessness for women veterans: (1) childhood adversity; (2) trauma and/or substance abuse during military service; (3) post-military abuse; (4) post-military mental health, substance abuse, and/or medical problems; and (5) unemployment. This "web of vulnerability" is another indication that treatment solutions must be trauma-informed and holistic in nature.

The use of alcohol and drugs by women is linked to all forms of trauma, not just sexual or physical violence (SAMHSA, 2005a). The high rate of co-occurrence of substance use and a history of personal violence has treatment implications. First, for women who have been and are involved in violent relationships, treatment that relies on confrontational approaches, such as is common in therapeutic communities, can trigger the same kind of powerlessness as the original trauma. Also, treatment that is too narrowly specialized and at different agencies—substance abuse treatment here and counseling for victims of domestic violence there—can confuse an individual. The different models underlying the treatment approaches at the various agencies may not be in harmony (Hiebert-Murphy & Woytkiw, 2000).

There is emerging evidence that addressing substance use and trauma in an integrated way may have better results than providing the treatment under specialized umbrellas. For example, in a classic randomized trial, Cohen and Hien (2006) compared the effectiveness of (1) a cognitive approach that addressed both posttraumatic stress disorder (PTSD) and substance abuse and (2) a cognitive relapse prevention approach that focused on emotional triggers to standard community care. They found that participants (low-income women from an urban setting) in the two treatment groups significantly reduced their substance use and PTSD symptom severity compared to the standard community care group, whose PTSD symptoms actually got worse.

PSYCHOLOGICAL DIFFERENCES BY GENDER

The field of modern psychology focuses primarily on the vulnerabilities and dysfunctions of normal mind processes and only lately is looking at resilience factors and strengths of the mind. The question of precisely how environment and biology affect the mind and addictive processes is still being answered. Maybe men really are from Mars and women from Venus! It seems reasonable that sociocultural gender differences (in economics, victimization, support systems, etc.), as discussed earlier, would be reflected differently in the minds of men and women. For example, researchers studying the effects of trauma propose that a lifetime of traumatic abuse, characteristic of many women who are addicted, causes low self-esteem and self-disgust that presses these women into situations of further abuse (Downs & Miller, 2002).

In addition to low self-esteem, another indication of psychological distress that is more problematic for women is a higher rate of co-occurring disorders. In 2002, an estimated 2 million adult women reported both a serious mental illness and a substance use disorder during the past year (SAMHSA, 2005). A review of recent research indicates that women with a substance use disorder have more major depressions, anxiety disorders, panic disorders, bipolar affective disorders, psychosexual disorders, eating disorders, PTSD, and phobias than men with a substance use disorder (SAMHSA, 2005). In general, these differences are consistent with the differences in psychiatric disorders in the general population. However, there is a unique effect of depression on substance users; that is, depression is associated with relapse, especially in women (Schutte, Seable, & Moos, 1997). Findings from a federal study of services for women found that one-third of the sample of women in publicly funded treatment had co-occurring mental health and substance abuse problems (Newmann & Sallmann, 2004). Compared to the other women, 95% of the group with co-occurring problems also reported physical or sexual abuse, over half were separated from their children against their will, and the majority reported incarceration experiences.

Gender differences in the prevalence of co-occurring disorders become even more pronounced in jail and prison populations. In a study conducted on men and women admitted to a prison substance abuse program, women were significantly more likely than men to report lifetime psychiatric disorders in all categories except anti-social personality disorder. Women were twice to three times more likely to report major depression; PTSD; borderline personality disorder or any affective, anxiety, or psychotic disorder; and 18 times more likely to report an eating disorder. These differences were adjusted for race, marital status, and employment status (Zlotnick, Clarke, Friedmann, Roberts, Sacks, & Melnick, 2008). Similar results were reported in a study of jail inmates, where a higher rate of drug dependency in women was also found (Binswanger et al., 2010)

Men and women tend to smoke cigarettes to relieve different psychological states. "Males respond more to nicotine's rewarding effects than do females, especially the dopamine-mediated euphoric effects," according to Dr. Neil Grunberg, professor of medical psychology, clinical psychology, and neuroscience at Uniformed Services University of the Health Sciences, Bethesda, Maryland ("New Study," 2000). Men attempt to relieve boredom and fatigue or increase arousal and concentration by smoking; women attempt to control their weight and to decrease stress, anger, and other negative feelings. Although nicotine helps to decrease appetite and control weight in both genders, it has stronger effects on women. Women also have more difficulty in stopping smoking than men and do not respond well to confrontational approaches in smoking cessation programs.

Gambling as psychological "pain medication" is a common theme in the stories of many women who are compulsive gamblers. As one woman explained, "For me, sitting for hours at slot machines was the ultimate drug of escape" (Davis, 2009, p. 16). Women have reported seeking a temporary escape from painful events and situations as the reason they started gambling seriously. These included such situations as the death of family members, divorce, anxiety, depression, problems with adult children and grandchildren, retirement, problems with teenage children, and debt and money problem (Davis, 2009).

The following story illustrates how using gambling as an escape from trouble worked for "Alice":

> Upon retirement, I found myself faced with the dilemma of what do I do now? I tried volunteering, cooking, gardening, reading, and so on, but nothing quite satisfied nor completed me the way my career had. That is, until I rediscovered the casino ... I had tasted the bittersweet gambling scene occasionally in the years

prior to my retirement. Nothing serious, really, just a fun little afternoon adventure. However, with time on my hands and money to spare, gambling soon became routine. I'd awake in the morning, get my chores for the day taken care of and head out to the casino "Where The Fun Never Ends!" I rarely won anything. It wasn't necessary. Winning money was a secondary benefit. I was there to escape. Escape boredom, responsibility, life, problems, people, and obligations. And guess what? It worked! I had a new reason to live! This was the most fun I had ever had, and the most destructive. Once in a while a little angel would tap me on the shoulder and ask, "What in the heck are you doing?" Denial is a very powerful defense mechanism. I didn't have a problem. I never smoked, drank much, nor did drugs. I had great parents, raised terrific kids, and paid my bills on time. This couldn't be happening to me! For God's sake, I'm a Catholic! Well, guess what? When it came to addiction, none of that mattered. (p. 62)

In earlier days of problem gambling treatment, women like Alice were characterized as escape gamblers, whereas men were likely to be designated by the more manly term *action gamblers*. Escape gamblers were thought to become compulsive in their gambling in a span of 6 months to 3 years, and play "luck" games such as bingo, slots, and video poker. They start playing as a recreation but quickly move into using gambling to escape from problems (Arizona Council on Compulsive Gambling, 2000; Lesieur & Blume, 1991). The lure of the escape is characterized by changing the feeling of stress or psychological discomfort into feeling "hypnotized," "in a trance," "having tunnel vision where nothing else mattered," or even "out of body."

In contrast, action gamblers tend to begin early in life, have a long-term problem (10–30 years), focus on "skill" games such as poker, horses, and sports, and seek action as well as escape. A gender comparison of a large treatment sample in Australia (Crisp et al., 2000) revealed from the assessment data that women were 1.5 times more likely to gamble as a way of escaping from other problems than men. Females reported average debts of less than half what was owed by the male gamblers. Women were far more likely to report using electronic gambling machines than men (91.1% vs. 61.4%) and more likely to play bingo (4.8% vs. 1.0%).

Although the descriptions of action and escape gamblers appear intuitively attractive, with the advent of widespread availability of casino gambling, those distinctions are no longer as applicable. There could even be a patronizing edge of the dominant culture in designating women as preferring "nonskill" gambling games and consequently not living up to the popular culture's idea of "real" gambling. Discounting out-of-control gambling behavior because it involves games like bingo only adds to the difficulties of these women in recognizing their own problems and getting help. In addition, there is growing evidence that men are participating more and more in what we have called the escape gambler profile. In 1999, 49% of the men who called the Arizona Council on Compulsive Gambling Hotline identified themselves as escape gamblers. The council makes an interesting point: "The accessibility of casino-type gambling is now affecting men who had no previous history of gambling or compulsive gambling in the same way it affects women. Perhaps the least previously identified and least understood compulsive gambler of all was the male 'escape gambler'" (Arizona Council on Compulsive Gambling, 2000, p. 2).

BIOLOGICAL DIFFERENCES BY GENDER

Earlier research on the pharmacology, genetics, and biological impact of alcohol and drugs was done primarily with males, under the assumption that the findings would apply equally to women. Not true. Beginning in the 1970s and 1980s, we began to realize that women and men differ in their biological response to alcohol, tobacco, and other drugs in ways that have important treatment implications. The results from the *2005 Alcohol and Drug Services Study* (SAMHSA, 2006), confirmed in the CSAT Treatment Improvement Protocol for Women (2009), make clear that, compared to men, women tend to:

1. Have a much shorter interval between regular use, onset of drinking-related problems, and entry into treatment. In spite of fewer years of use, once they enter treatment their symptom severity is generally equivalent to males.
2. Even with fewer years of use, average more medical consequences. Women experience a higher rate of physiological impairment earlier in their drinking careers, such as cirrhosis, hepatitis, brain damage, and cardiac problems. The consequences associated with heavy drinking may be accelerated or "telescoped" in women. For example, the female liver appears more vulnerable to the damage from alcohol; consequently, more alcohol-dependent women die from cirrhosis than alcohol-dependent men.
3. Become intoxicated after drinking smaller quantities of alcohol because the alcohol concentration in the blood is higher for women than men after drinking the same amounts of alcohol. Women have more fat and lower body water content than men of comparable size, and because alcohol is diluted through body water, a woman drinking the same as a man of the same size will have a higher blood alcohol level. Also, women may have diminished activity of alcohol dehydrogenase, an enzyme involved in the metabolism of alcohol in the stomach, and a fluctuation in gonadal hormone levels during the menstrual cycle.
4. Have much poorer overall physical health, mental health, overall impairment, and higher mortality rates from alcohol misuse. CASA (2006) found that physical problems (e.g., cirrhosis, hypertension, and brain damage from alcohol; lung cancer, emphysema, and chronic bronchitis from smoking) develop in women more rapidly and at lower rates than men.

Chronic heavy drinking is associated with negative effects on the sexual functions of both men and women. Men report loss of sexual interest, difficulty achieving erections, impotence, and premature ejaculation (National Institute of Alcohol Abuse and Alcoholism (NIAAA), 1993). Although many women and men attest to the disinhibiting qualities of alcohol, in reality alcohol acts as a depressant on physiological arousal. Women alcoholics persist in expecting greater sexual desire and enjoyment after drinking while at the same time reporting a variety of sexual dysfunctions, such as inhibition of ovulation, infertility, and depressed orgasm (Blume, 1997; CASA, 2006). In early sobriety, women have reported avoidance of sex, but a study of recovering alcoholic women who had a regular sexual partner showed significant improvement in sexual desire, arousal, and the ability to achieve orgasm as abstinence continued (Apter-Marsh, 1984).

Smoking affects the reproductive functions of women. In young women, smoking increases the risk of menstrual irregularity and pain (CASA, 2006). Older women smokers are subject to a reduction in estrogen levels and earlier menopause. Because of the link between smoking and cancer and heart disease, women now account for 39% of all smoking-related deaths in the United States. Despite knowing these facts, girls and women often refuse to quit out of fear of weight gain.

The female propensity to weight obsession is also evident in eating disorders. *Feminist Perspectives on Eating Disorders,* edited by Fallon, Katzman, and Wooley (1994), is an invaluable resource for analyzing the role of gender in the etiology and treatment of eating disorders. Overeaters Anonymous (OA), the popular self-help group that has been immensely helpful to some women, is not spared from criticism in this biting and thought-provoking collection.

Some effects of illicit drugs vary with gender. Marijuana is reported to enhance the sexual feelings of both men and women, but regular use in men may result in lower testosterone levels, affect sperm production and fertility, and cause erectile difficulties. In women, potential adverse affects include menstrual abnormalities, abnormal ova, and prolonged childbirth (Hubbard, Franco, & Onaivi, 1999).

In the Drug Abuse Treatment Outcome Study (DATOS) of men and women entering drug treatment (including methadone treatment), women reported greater proportions of health-related issues (Wechsberg, Craddock, & Hubbard, 1998). For women, the rate of respiratory problems was the highest, followed by the rates of gynecological problems and then STDs. For men, respiratory problems also had the highest rate, followed by heart problems and then digestive problems. However, women have higher rates in all three of the top problem areas for men..

Two of three AIDS cases in American women are associated with drug abuse (CASA, 2006). Because of the strong connection between AIDS and IV drug use, it is important to note that an HIV-infected woman with half the amount of virus in the bloodstream as an infected man will develop AIDS as quickly. Women are in general also diagnosed later in the course of AIDS and have poorer access to treatment.

Are there gender differences in the inheritance of alcoholism? Geneticists measure heritability by looking at studies of adoptions, twins, and genetic markers (such as the D2 dopamine receptor). Examining all this evidence to date, McGue and Slutske (1996) conclude that an inherited component of alcoholism exists among men, but there is not unequivocal support for the existence of a heritable component to alcoholism among women. Still, CASA

(2006), in its summary of research on women's substance use, brings our attention to research on physical reactions to certain substances. Women with a family history of alcoholism tend to have a higher level of tolerance for alcohol than women without such a history. Other research found that women with such a history tend to produce more saliva when exposed to alcohol than women without such a history. Both reactions are risk factors for alcoholism. Genetics undoubtedly plays a role in the susceptibility to alcohol abuse and dependence in women and men, although there is some evidence that women may be more susceptible to environmental factors.

TREATMENT IMPLICATIONS

Women-only programs and special programs for pregnant and postpartum women have been advocated by clinicians and researchers for years. Greenfield & Grella (2009) cite three compelling reasons: (1) the high prevalence of trauma and history of violence among women with addiction problems (much of which was perpetrated by men); (2) the high prevalence of co-occurring disorders, especially mood, anxiety, and eating disorders; and (3) the central role that caretaking and relationships with children, partners, and others play in women's addiction and recovery. All of these well-researched issues impact a woman's chances for attaining and maintaining recovery from her addiction.

During the 1980s and 1990s, federal grants were aimed at developing treatment programs for drug-abusing pregnant women and their children, such as the Pregnant and Postpartum Women and Their Infants (PPWI) initiative that awarded 147 grants in 37 states. SAMHSA, through the Center for Substance Abuse Treatment (CSAT) and the Center for Mental Health Services (CMHS), continues this focus today by funding comprehensive residential substance abuse treatment for pregnant, postpartum, and/or parenting women and their children. More than 100 grantees targeting women had been funded by CSAT as of June 2004, and a 5-year initiative to study women with co-occurring disorders and a history of violence has been launched (SAMHSA, 2005a). As the result of these efforts, the National Survey of Substance Abuse Treatment Services found that by 2005, 41% of substance abuse treatment facilities that accepted women as clients provided special programs or groups for women (Figure 4.3). The most common types of special services for women were individual therapy and group therapy. Child care was provided by only 18% of the programs offering special programs for women, and residential beds for client's children were provided by only 9%.

Other components of women-focused programs can include (1) addressing some of the barriers to treatment that many women experience, such as lack of transportation, child care, and treatment availability; (2) changing program goals and processes to accommodate women's needs for more support, less confrontation, job skill training, and parenting skills; and (3) embracing an empowerment model of change. Many of these programs use female staff members so that women clients may feel more comfortable telling their

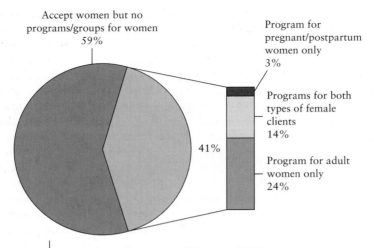

Accept women but no
programs/groups for women
59%

Program for
pregnant/postpartum
women only
3%

Programs for both
types of female
clients
14%

41%

Program for adult
women only
24%

FIGURE 4.3 | FACILITIES ACCEPTING WOMEN: 2005

Source: 2005 SAMHSA National Survey of Substance Abuse Treatment Services.

stories. Particular treatment issues relevant to women include attention to their feelings of shame and stigma and the need to heal from the impact of trauma (SAMHSA, 2005b). Substance use recovery and trauma recovery should occur together, and a sense of safety must be ensured so that women will feel free to reveal personal issues. A woman's perception of social and emotional support has also been found to be associated with treatment completion (Lewandowski & Hill, 2009). The authors noted that such simple things as the staff being perceived as helpful during the intake interview was predictive of treatment completion for women.

An example of a program that has many attributes of women-sensitive programming is A Woman's Place, established in the mid-1980s to offer substance abuse treatment for women (LaFave, Desportes, & McBride, 2009; LaFave & Echols, 1999). Although the program began by using the traditional Twelve-Step Minnesota Model with strict guidelines for compliance, homework, and attendance at AA, program staff became frustrated and disillusioned with their lack of success and the inconsistency between the values of compliance and empowerment for women. LaFave & Echols (1999) note that compliance is not an attribute of the mutual-help program of Alcoholics Anonymous, which is based on voluntary participation and suggestions only; however, compliance is an element of the Twelve-Step–based Minnesota Model in treatment programs. In 1993, A Woman's Place embraced different change models that emphasize choice, not compliance, such as solution-focused therapy and motivational interviewing (see Chapter 8; Berg & Shafer, 2004; Miller et al., 2011). All aspects of the program were affected by this change. Women who were court ordered or came voluntarily to treatment are asked at the orientation session to choose which services they think they

ITEM CHARGED

Patron: Kassandra Lynn Marsala
Patron Barcode:

Patron Group: Undergraduate

Due Date: 2/12/2016 07:00 PM
Title: Treatment of child abuse : common ground for mental health, medical, and legal practitioners / edited by Robert M. Reece.
Author:
Call Number: WA320 T784 2000
Enumeration:
Chronology:
Copy: 1
Item Barcode:

This patron has permission to remove these items from the library

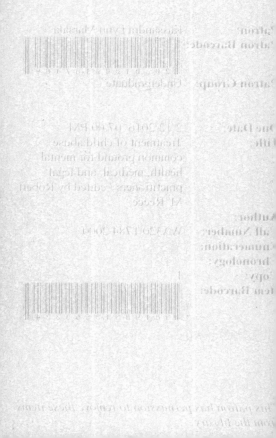

would like. If a woman is not concerned about her substance use, she is asked whether there are any other goals she would like to address and whether she is choosing to comply with the referral source. The menu of services includes day treatment, substance abuse groups once a week, a women's issues group, individual counseling, couples and family counseling, and case management services, including transportation. In contrast to a traditional Twelve-Step treatment model, the operating premise of this program is that, when offered choices, women will ultimately choose directions that help them function better.

Using the solution-focused approach, any period of sobriety or cutting down on alcohol or other drug use is celebrated, and the woman is questioned closely on how she was able to do this. For clients who are uncertain about the changes they want to make, motivational interviewing techniques help explore the meaning of the problem for them and make a decision about their motivation to change. According to the authors, preliminary quantitative and qualitative evaluations of the program suggest that using these approaches "has a favorable impact on participants' life functioning in a number of domains, and that participants feel that the program has benefited them in a variety of ways" (LaFave & Echols, 1999, p. 350).

In a subsequent evaluation, A Woman's Place (LaFave, Desportes, & McBride, 2009) participants were measured pre- and post-treatment to assess their perceptions of their strengths and current functioning in several areas of life skills, including recovery. Scores improved significantly in all areas (life skills, finance, leisure, relationships, living arrangements, health, internal resources and recovery) except the area of occupation/education. Interviews with representative participants revealed the importance of choice in this program. As one woman expressed: "Once upon a time you had to have those AA papers. Now it's not mandatory. It's up to you ... They can't tell you 'don't go out and go to the liquor store.' If you want to leave here and go to a liquor store, it's your choice, but you're not hurting them, you're hurting yourself "(LaFave et al., 2009, p. 58).

A qualitative study of group therapy for women problem gamblers (Piquette-Tomei, Norman, Dwyer, & McCaslin, 2008) found that there were several components of the program that made it particularly attractive for them as women: (1) accessibility (group occurred in the evening, (2) safety in discussing personal topics ("with men, I do not feel as comfortable; I am not so sure I could talk about problems," "older male gamblers seemed to monopolize time and want to ask women for their numbers"), (3) all women of various ages ("we are looking at it [problem gambling] from a woman's point of view") (p. 5).

The first and only (to date) gambling-specific residential treatment center for women in the United States is Hulan's Hope, which opened May 1, 2011 in Scottsdale, Arizona (see hulenshope.com). Named for Don Hulan, longtime executive director and co-founder of the Arizona Council on Problem Gambling, Hulan's Hope includes a wide array of programming for women including individual and group therapy with a focus on healing historical trauma and broken relationships, three women's Gamblers Anonymous meetings a week in nearby Phoenix, spiritual counseling, programming on nutrition, a health facility, and financial counseling. The program is recommended as a minimum 30-day residential stay, with an optional 60–90 days. Davis discussed the development of this unique program with Rick Benson, Certified Gambling Counselor-II, Executive Director of Algamus Recovery Services, who is also a consultant to Hulun's Hope. Benson noted that the majority of treatment available to problem gamblers is developed as an add-on to established substance abuse treatment, and he strongly advocated the need for gambling-specific services. "It's very unlikely that you will convince a gambling addict in early abstinence that they have anything in common with a heroin addict with tracks up their arms or a meth addict with rotten teeth," he says (personal communication; September 1, 2011).

The implications of gender differences are in the earliest stage of establishing a reliable and valid base of information for treatment programming. In a review of 280 research articles from 1975 to 2005, 40% of the studies were published since 2000, and only about 12% of the studies were randomized clinical trials (Greenfield et al., 2007). This is understandable because to meet the emerging needs of women, programs were developed as pilot projects or demonstrations and were not in a stage of development to produce more rigorous research or to develop manuals that can be used to replicate treatment protocols. However, there is evidence to suggest certain findings on treatment entry, retention, and outcomes that do have implications for treatment development:

1. *Women are less likely than men to enter treatment over their lifetime* (Greenfield et al., 2007). This finding needs to be put in the context that many men *and* women are not getting the treatment they need in a specialty facility (inpatient, outpatient or mental health center). In 2009, only 11.2% of persons aged 12 and older who needed treatment for an illicit drug or alcohol problem actually received treatment at a specialty facility (SAMHSA, 2010a). The issues discussed earlier, such as the economic disadvantages of women compared to men, lower educational attainment, less social support (especially from intimate partners), more caretaking responsibilities, and fear of losing custody of their children, have an influence on treatment entry (Tuchman, 2010). The clear implication is that treatment needs to include services (such as child care, involvement of the intimate partner, perinatal services) that could enhance access for many women.

2. *Gender is not a significant predictor of retention, completion, or outcome* (Greenfield et al., 2007; CSAT, 2010). Men and women appear to benefit equally well (in some cases women do better) once treatment is begun. However, some researchers suggest it is no longer adequate to measure treatment effectiveness by gender alone. There is a need to investigate more closely the characteristics that vary by gender and that negatively affect treatment retention and outcomes. Subgroups of women are impacted by co-occurring disorders; a history of victimization, violence

and abuse; low socioeconomic status, dependent children, and racial discrimination—all of which can negatively affect treatment outcome.

3. *Gender-specific programming enhances treatment entry, retention, and outcome among certain subgroups of women with substance abuse disorders* (Greenfield at al., 2007).

Early outcome research on specialized women's programs had mixed results (Gerolamo, 2004). Some studies suggested better treatment outcomes in specialized women's programs or women's groups within mixed-gender programs (Brown, Melchior, Waite-O'Brien, & Hub, 2002; CASA, 2006), and others suggested no difference (Copeland, Hall, Didcott, & Biggs, 1993; Harshman, 2000). Project MATCH, the NIAAA-funded major research study, found no gender-related differences in the outcomes of the three treatment approaches used in individual sessions with a large sample of male and female clients (Project MATCH Research Group, 1997). Studies that focused on matching patient–therapist gender also found no difference in treatment retention (Sterling, Gottheil, Weinstein, & Serota, 1998) or outcome (Atkinson & Schein, 1996; Corrigan, 1995). ·

However, several qualitative studies (Davis, 1997; Kauffman, Dore, & Nelson-Zlupko, 1995; Nelson-Zlupko, Dore, Kauffman, & Kaltenback, 1996; Sowers, Ellis, Washington, & Currant, 2002; La Fave, Desportes, & McBride, 2009; LaFave & Echols, 1999; Piquette-Tomei, Norman, Dwyerr, & McCaslin, 2008) that have included interviews with recovering women participating in all-women's groups or programs told a different story. In the Nelson-Zlupko and colleagues study (1996, p. 57), the female participants "overwhelmingly" felt that their needs were different from those of men, and when they were in mixed-gender groups, these needs were either "silenced or minimized." All of the women in this study had attended at least two other treatment programs, with an average of four treatment experiences per person. These women affirmed previous research that being paired with a female counselor was not important; what they saw as critical to their success was respect from the counselor, no matter the gender.

There is a smaller body of quantitative research that confirms the effectiveness of treatment programming for women. In a review of 37 studies of substance abuse treatment programs for women that occurred between 1980 and 2000, 36 studies reported improved treatment outcomes. In the seven studies that were randomized trials, all showed positive results such as increased birthweight for pregnant outpatient methadone clinic patients, decreased alcohol use for women in alcohol treatment, reduction of risky injection behaviors, and decreased drug use and increased program retention for cocaine-dependent mothers (SAMHSA, 2005b).

Research that has focused on other outcomes, such as service provision and eliminating barriers to treatment, have found that specialized women's programs were more likely to provide services that meet typical women's needs, such as parenting training, empowerment, nutrition, child care, and transportation, and less likely to deny access to women with special needs, such as pregnancy and mental problems (CASA, 2006; Grella et al., 1999; Prendergast, Wellisch, & Falkin, 1995). Through qualitative interviews of women in treatment, Nelson-Zlupko and colleagues (1996) found another disturbing barrier to mixed-gender patient–therapist treatment: Sexual harassment of female clients by male counselors was spontaneously reported by over half of the study's participants, even though they were never asked about this in the interview.

Some critics would argue that traditional abstinence-only treatment for both genders produces discouraging results and that a different treatment model for both men and women is needed. Citing studies that indicate poor treatment outcome (e.g., 52–75% of men and women in outpatient treatment drop out by the fourth session [Siegal, Rapp, Fisher, Cole, & Wagner, 1993] and between 40 and 60% that do complete treatment are not abstinent after 1 year (Hubbard, 1997), LaFave and Echols (1999) argue for increasing the flexibility of substance abuse treatment for all populations. Although their article argues for a choice-driven model for women as practiced in A Woman's Place, they join Calamari, Cox, and Roth (1996) in advocating for a treatment model for men "that promotes hope; recognizes incremental changes, such as an increase in number of days of sobriety; and allows men to identify, express, and process their affective experiences" (p. 347).

In her study on the outcome of treatment for Irish alcoholic women, Corrigan (1995) found that at 1-year follow-up, the majority (71%) had drunk at some point since treatment; however, 43% had not been drinking for 6 or more months. She concludes that "the assumption that treatment programs should insist on total abstinence as the only acceptable treatment goal is particularly questionable in view of the fact that at follow-up only half of the women surveyed are in fact abstinent" (p. 52).

Although definitive research in effective intervention programs for women is in the early stages of development (Romero, Donohue, & Allen [2010, p. 287] have called it "deplorably lacking"), progress is occurring. At the very least, a convergence of findings has made clear that providing specialized women's treatment for subgroups of women with conditions that predictably affect their ability to recover from their addictions (such as co-occurring disorders, historical trauma, low socioeconomic status) has been demonstrated to enhance treatment entry, retention, and outcomes (Greenfield et al., 2007). Future research agendas need to include Stage I (initial) trials of new therapeutic interventions and Stage II randomized controlled trials of a particular substance abuse treatment approach in single-gender male, single-gender female, and mixed-gender groups. A notable effort in that direction is the Women's Recovery Group Study, a Stage I trial to develop a manual-based 12-session women's recovery group and to pilot test this new treatment in a randomized controlled trial against a standard mixed-gender group therapy control group. Pilot test results indicate that women who received the women's recovery programming demonstrated significantly greater reductions in drug and alcohol use over the long-term 6-month follow-up period (Greenfield, Trucco, McHugh, Lincoln, & Gallup, 2007).

SUBSTANCE ABUSE COUNSELING AND SEXUAL ORIENTATION

Heterosexism and *homophobia* are words that describe the prejudice against lesbian, gay, bisexual, and transgender people. *Homophobia* refers to fear of homosexuality, often of one's own tendencies in that direction; these tendencies may be displaced onto gays and lesbians. *Heterosexism,* the counterpart to racism and sexism, is prejudice against sexual minorities. It includes stereotyping and a belief in myths. Among the myths pertaining to lesbians are: They hate men, and they turned lesbian after a bad experience with a man; lesbianism can be "corrected" with female hormonal treatment; lesbians would prefer to be heterosexual; in partnerships, one woman plays the part of the man; and lesbians have a high rate of AIDS. In fact, lesbians, like heterosexuals, are a heterogeneous lot; their sex-role behavior ranges from very feminine to very masculine. Some lesbians believe their identity is a preference or choice; others believe it is an innate tendency to be sexually and emotionally attracted to women. Among the categories of gay males, heterosexual males, heterosexual women, and lesbians, lesbians have the lowest rate of AIDS (National Women's Law Center, 2004). Although HIV transmission is considered rare, sexual minority women who are drug injectors have high rates of transmission (Anderson, 2009).

Pervasive myths pertaining to gay males are: Homosexuality is a choice; gay males are attracted to children and are at risk of molesting them; and gay males are effeminate. In fact, the overwhelming majority of gay males believe their gayness is an innate characteristic that is often recognized in early to middle childhood. Accordingly, they prefer the term *sexual orientation* to *sexual preference*. There is no evidence to support the claim that homosexuals are any more apt to be child molesters than are heterosexuals (American Psychological Association, 2004). In sex-role behavior and mannerisms, gay males range from effeminate to very masculine. Many gay men, however, have traits in common with women. In childhood, for example, their play was often less rough than that of other children, and they were often ridiculed in school for being "sissies" or "different" (CSAT, 2001).

Counselors need to be aware of the numerous myths our society generates so that they can establish rapport with gay and lesbian clients. The best way to build trust is to demonstrate openness about non-normative living arrangements and sexuality. Use gay-friendly intake forms (including terms such as *partner* and *significant other*), display pamphlets that cater to a variety of ethnically and sexually diverse groups (e.g., gay AA meeting listings), and use inclusive language in interviews and lectures (referring to "spouse or partner" rather than just "spouse").

Despite societal barriers to being gay, lesbian, bisexual, or (most of all) transgendered in our society, there is no reason to assume that such clients need to work on any areas other than the services they came to receive. The focus of their treatment, therefore, should be no different from that of any other client. The challenge, however, is to provide a gay- and lesbian-friendly environment when many of the heterosexual clients and some counselors are homophobic or heterosexist.

RISKS FACTORS FOR SUBSTANCE USE

Family victimization—which is commonly experienced by gay, lesbian, and transgender youth—is a risk factor for suicide attempts (Anderson, 2009). Ryan, Huebner, and colleagues (2009), in a survey of 224 white and Latino lesbian, gay, and bisexual young adults found that family rejection in adolescence was a key factor in self-destructive behavior, then and later. The young people were over eight times more likely to report having attempted suicide than were their heterosexual peers. Rates of depression, illicit drug use, and unprotected sex were also high. This study is consistent with earlier studies that show a high suicide rate among gay youth.

We have filtered out from the literature on gays, lesbians, bisexuals, and trangendered persons the following risk factors to their health. These are risks that are uniquely associated with persons dealing with their minority sexuality and with implications for addictive behavior. We found the major risk factors were:

- Having a sense of shame about his or her sexual identity.
- A lack of family support that prevents disclosure of one's sexual identification.
- Membership in a fundamentalist religious group.
- Spending time in gay bars.
- Being rejected by one's peers.
- Heterosexism in one's school or work place.
- Using addictive substances to cope with stress.
- A rate of smoking that is significantly higher than that of straight people.

There are several reasons that alcohol and tobacco use among lesbians is high. First is the role of the gay bar and women's bars as a key gathering place for coming-out and closeted lesbians. Second is the heavy substance use among more mature members of this community who function as role models. Third is the interactive relationship among stress attached to living what is regarded as a deviant lifestyle, relationship strain in the absence of public role models, and problems related to internalized homophobia, especially among lesbian youth. Fourth, the fact that fewer lesbians than heterosexual women are taking care of children gives them more freedom to party and socialize in gay bars than persons persons with parenting roles (van Wormer, 2011). (However, some lesbians have children from a previous marriage, and more and more lesbians are arranging to have their children through the use of donors.) And finally, the intensive marketing to gays and lesbians by tobacco and alcohol companies, as reported by the American Lung Association (2010), is probably responsible at least in part for the high rate of smoking in this population. An extensive review of the literature revealed that lesbians and gay males have up to two times the rate of smoking of straight people, and bisexuals have the highest rates of all. Reasons for the high rates are attributed to the stigma of being a sexual minority and use of smoking as a bonding activity. Higher rates are correlated with a sense of rejection by society. As is universally true, people who feel good about themselves take care of themselves, but people who do not are inclined to jeopardize their health through the use of mood-altering substances.

LESBIANS AND SUBSTANCE MISUSE

For the most part, lesbians and bisexual women face the same health issues as heterosexual women, but the risks of self-harm and depression may be higher among those who are not open about their sexual orientation and who lack social support (Mravcak, 2006). Although the data are somewhat contradictory, chemical dependence is also a major concern within this group. Because of a serious lack of empirically based national data, however, the exact incidence of substance use among lesbians is unknown. Studies focusing on women's alcohol and other drug use rarely consider sexual orientation as a variable, and studies on lesbian behavior rarely encompass addiction rates. The most commonly cited figure for alcohol-related problems in lesbians is one out of three. More recent studies have shown, however, that heavy drinking is equally high among youth of all sexual orientations. The difference that shows up is in the amount of illicit drugs and tobacco consumed. Many of the earlier studies exaggerated the use of alcohol among lesbians (as they did with gay males) because they drew their samples from gay bars (Senreich & Vairo, 2004).

Due to the unique needs of this special population and the need for lesbians, like other women, to deal with issues related to victimization and sexuality in a safe and understanding environment, a lesbian-affirming treatment atmosphere is essential. Unfortunately, substance abuse providers tend to hold traditional attitudes toward women's sex roles and to lack training in gay–lesbian dynamics (Anderson, 2009; Shelton, 2011). A feminist, nonheterosexist model is appropriate to empower lesbians to make the personal adjustments (in thinking and behavior) necessary for recovery. For lesbian alcoholics in need of inpatient treatment, referral to a lesbian-friendly treatment center, such as the PRIDE Institute in Eden Prairie, Minnesota, or the Gables Recovery Home in Rochester, Minnesota, is appropriate. The former provides special attention to PTSD issues for gays and lesbians related to the HIV/AIDS crisis, and the latter is a woman-centered treatment center that relies on a Twelve-Step–based philosophy and provides treatment for eating disorders. The expense of residential treatment, however, may be prohibitive for a client who lacks generous insurance coverage for inpatient treatment. A growing trend throughout the United States is the proliferation of healthcare clinics catering to lesbians, such as the Audre Lorde Lesbian Health Clinic of Los Angeles. Some of the clinics offer sperm banks for lesbians wishing to parent children. This positive development has received its impetus from the awareness of the general indifference toward lesbians by medical professionals in traditional practice.

Gay and lesbian self-help groups such as Gay and Lesbian AA are widely available, even in small cities across the United States. Since the 1980s, as VanGelder and Brandt (1996) indicate, heavy alcohol consumption lost ground within the lesbian community. Suddenly, according to these authors, there was a stronger AA crowd than a drinking crowd; lesbians attending the annual October Women's Weekend had a choice of seven Twelve-Step meetings per day.

Gay Males and Substance Misuse

Young nonmasculine men thrown into a jail cell, cross-dressers, youths considered to be gay or gender inappropriate in their behavior—these are examples of males who are prone to be physically attacked and possibly even killed. The scapegoating of gay males, even more pronounced than that of lesbians, creates a major health risk, physically and mentally, for the survivors and victims of this terrifying kind of abuse.

Sometimes, society's hatred is turned within. The highest percentage of teenagers who actually attempt or commit suicide are those struggling with sexual orientation issues (Jackson, 2004). Shernoff (2006), in his study of male barebacking (or anal sex without a condom with strange men), relates this practice to internalized homophobia. Such self-hatred "can contribute to an unconscious sense that a gay man is unimportant and undervalued, thus increasing his sense that he is expendable" (p. 106). Senreich and Vair (2004) attribute such self-destructive behavior to survivor guilt in gay males who have seen their friends die as they live on. Barebacking also is associated, as Shernoff further suggests, with the wide-spread use in the gay community of "party drugs" such as Ecstasy and crystal meth. Shelton (2011) agrees that meth use is often a factor in barebacking. For men who come to the attention of therapists, both Shernoff and Shelton recommend a harm reduction approach to help individuals refrain from self-destructive behaviors and reduce the risks to themselves and others.

Bullied children are prone to self-hatred, and boys who are considered to be gender-inappropriate or sissies are especially vulnerable to attacks on the playground. As such, then or later, they are apt to engage in health risk behaviors, sexually or otherwise. When gay youth are pushed out of their homes because of having an "unacceptable lifestyle," as their parents claim, they may act in self-destructive ways and even court death. In a real sense, therefore, prejudice kills. The compelling 2009 TV drama *Prayers for Bobby* (produced by Lifetime TV) tells the true story about a devoutly religious homemaker and mother of a gay son whose continuous preaching that God could cure him of his "sin" drove him to suicide. Eventually, the mother resolved her religious crisis through getting counseling from a gay-friendly church. Today, she is a crusader for human rights. The film is unique in containing extensive educational dialogue concerning certain passages in the Bible forbidding homosexuality that are attended to, while other passages forbidding the mixing of fibers in your clothes, or the requirement to stone disobedient children and adulterers are passed over.

Eisenberg and Resnick (2006) found that for adolescents of all sexual orientations, connectedness to one's family is the primary factor that prevents suicide attempts. Their survey was conducted on over 22,000 Minnesota youths; of this number over 2,200 respondents reported some same-gender sexual experience. Of these, 29% of the gay males reported having attempted suicide, which was over twice as many as heterosexual males, and 52% of the lesbians reported suicide attempts compared to less than half as many heterosexuals. Protective factors for all the youth were family ties, adult caring, and school safety.

Heavy use of alcohol and other drugs has long been noted as a problem in the gay community. Although obtaining a random sample of gay men is extremely difficult, all the research that has been done confirms a high incidence of alcohol and other substance use; estimates range from 20 to 35% (Burroughs, 2003; SAMHSA, 2010b). Compared to lesbians, gay males are more likely to have multiple partners; sex and intimacy are more often split off in this group (Shelton, 2011). Gay bars and clubs are central to the social fabric of gay life; cocaine, methamphetamines, and other dangerous drugs are readily available in after-hours clubs frequented by gay men (Burroughs, 2003). A glance at the ads in gay and lesbian magazines reveals a marketing blitz of hard liquor advertising that is far from subtle in its message.

The three groups with the highest rates of HIV/AIDS are low-income heterosexuals (2%), IV drug users (9%), and gay and bisexual men (19%) (DeVera, 2011). These results are from a national study of 30,000 individuals in 21 cities. Young black men who have sex with men have the highest rate. Approximately 4 to 5% of heterosexual drug injectors are HIV positive. About 40% of men who have sex with men and shoot crystal meth are HIV positive, according to a study by Clay (1997). Clay discovered, in interviews with meth users in Washington State, that crystal meth was used as a powerful sexual facilitator, a means of overcoming sexual fears and reservations. When people are influenced by such strong chemicals, safe-sex practices, needless to say, are thrown to the wayside.

Unique to this population, compared to heterosexual men, is that heavy alcohol consumption and associated problems continue across the life span rather than diminish with age. One possible explanation is that gay men do not "settle down" as readily as heterosexual men, and they are freer to spend more time drinking. Another factor relating to their substance use is the tendency of sexual minorities to use mind-altering chemicals to break down their sexual inhibitions; such inhibitions or hang-ups are related to sexuality that is out of step with societal norms (Shelton, 2011). One of the most pressing challenges for gay male substance users, according to Anderson (2009), is the need to separate sexual activity from substance use. In substance abuse treatment, one of the biggest risks to sobriety for gays and lesbians entails the need to learn how to initiate same-sex encounters without the aid of alcohol as a "social lubricant." This problem plagues many heterosexuals as well.

Transgendered Individuals

A publication from the Center for Substance Abuse Treatment (2001), *A Provider's Introduction to Substance Abuse Treatment for Lesbian, Gay, Bisexual, and Transgender Individuals,* which is available free of charge from the Substance Abuse and Mental Health Services Administration (SAMHSA), offers a comprehensive discussion of multiple issues related to working with transgendered individuals. As defined in this document, *transgendered* individuals are those who conform to the gender-role expectations of the opposite sex or those who may clearly identify their gender as the opposite of their biological sex. In common usage, *transgender* usually refers to people in the transsexual group, which may include people contemplating or preparing for sexual reassignment surgery—called preoperative—or who have under-gone sexual reassignment surgery—called postoperative. A transgendered person may be sexually attracted to males, females, or both. *Transvestites* cross-dress—that is, wear clothes usually worn by people of the opposite biological sex. They do not, however, identify themselves as having a gender identity different from their biological sex or gender role (SAMHSA, 2001). Table 4.1 presents a list of do's and don'ts related to work with this population.

Of all the sexual minorities, transgendered persons, whether their change is from male to female or female to male, are the most subject to violent assault and employment discrimination. The American Psychiatric Association (APA) (2000) classifies a condition termed "gender identity disorder" as a mental disorder in the *DSM–IV–TR*. This is hardly a positive development.

In contrast to the treatment of transgendered persons in modern society, many American Indian tribes honor them as two-spirited and carved out a special place in society for them (Anderson, 2009). *Berdache,* as this custom was named by outside observers, in effect, constituted a separate gender (CSAT, 2001).

Little research has been done on this population with regard to substance use. As stated by CSAT, one fact that has been revealed in research is an extremely high prevalence of HIV/AIDS in transgendered women who were born with male genitalia.

Bisexuality

Many studies indicate that women tend to be more bisexual by nature (flexible in terms of attraction to either gender) than men, who are more exclusively heterosexual or homosexual (CSAT, 2001; van Wormer et al., 2000). A major point for therapists to know is that a bisexual orientation is a separate identity in itself that is often refuted by both the heterosexual majority and by many gay men and lesbians. A complicating factor is that due to the strident heterosexism within the African American community, many people of color define themselves as bisexual even if they focus exclusively on people of the same sex (CSAT, 2001). African American and Latino American gays and lesbians face potential racial prejudice coupled with a lack

TABLE 4.1	DO'S AND DON'TS ABOUT WORKING WITH TRANSGENDER AND TRANSVESTITE CLIENTS

- Use the proper pronouns based on *their self-identity* when talking to and about transgender individuals.

- Get clinical supervision if you have issues about working with transgender individuals.

- Allow transgender clients to continue the use of hormones when they are prescribed. Advocate that the trans-gender client using "street" hormones get immediate medical care and legally prescribed hormones.

- Require training on transgender issues for all staff.

- Find out the sexual orientation of all clients.

- Allow transgender clients to use bath-rooms and showers based on their gender self-identity and gender role.

- Require all clients and staff to create and maintain a safe environment for all transgender clients. Post a non-discrimination policy in the waiting room that explicitly includes sexual orientation and gender identity.

- Don't call someone who identifies himself as a female *he* or *him* or call someone who identifies herself as male *she* or *her.*

- Don't project your transphobia onto the transgender client or share transphobic comments with other staff or clients.

- Never make the transgender client choose between hormones and treatment and recovery.

- Don't make the transgender client educate the staff.

- Don't assume transgender women or men are gay.

- Don't make transgender individuals living as females use male facilities or transgender individuals living as males use female facilities.

- Never allow staff or clients to make transphobic comments or put transgender clients at risk for physical or sexual abuse or harassment.

Source: CSAT (2001).

of full acceptance by their home communities and religious denominations. As Morales, Sheafor, and Scott (2010) suggest, members of minority groups within the United States tend to have close ties to their communities and to maintain a residence nearby. Viewing their racial and ethnic heritage as primary, they frequently live as heterosexuals and may identify as bisexuals. Because their communities tend to be religiously and culturally traditional, coming out may not be a practical option.

TREATMENT ISSUES

Gay and lesbian alcoholics and other substance users most often find themselves in predominantly heterosexual treatment centers. A recent survey of

U.S. treatment centers by SAMHSA (2010b) found that privately run treatment facilities, particularly for-profit facilities, are twice as likely to offer special gay and lesbian programs as federal government–run facilities. The number of facilities offering such specialized treatment is small (7% of privately run for-profit treatment programs and 2.6% of federal facilities). And fewer than 6% of state government-run programs and private nonprofit programs offer specialized services. This means sexual minorities are most likely to receive treatment in groups surrounded by heterosexuals. Because of the homophobia present in the typical treatment group, few gays and lesbians will want to take the risk of disclosing their sexual orientation when they feel like outsiders in such a group. This is why substance abuse programming should make every effort to be more inclusive.

To encourage private sharing in individual sessions, the counselor will find it helpful to display literature about gay and lesbian AA meetings, a Safe Place symbol (placed on a pink triangle), or a rainbow sticker on the office door. Counselors should not post the commonly seen slogan "I'm straight but not narrow," which many gays and lesbians construe as a subtle proclamation of the counselor's heterosexuality. To meet the needs of sexual diversity, every large agency should make a point of having one or more openly gay or lesbian counselors on the staff.

In helping gay men come to terms with their sexuality and problems related to their self-image, a strengths approach is essential. Strategies of gay-positive counseling are described by Crisp (2006). Use of a gay-affirmative model is crucial to affirm a lesbian, gay, or bisexual identity as positive and to validate same-sex relationships (Crisp, 2006).

Treatment issues that concern all clients but that have special relevance to sexual minorities include determining the client's comfort level with his or her sexual orientation; respecting gays' and lesbians' heightened need for privacy and confidentiality; recognizing special health risks that pertain to sexual practices among intoxicated gay males; addressing domestic violence issues (note that terms such as *wife beating* are inadvertently heterosexist); dealing with child custody issues; and working with the family of origin regarding acceptance of their gay and lesbian children.

The organization Parents, Families, and Friends of Lesbians and Gays (PFLAG) is both a self-help and an advocacy group. Membership is open to gays and lesbians as well as to concerned members of the community. (For an in-depth description of the functioning of this remarkable group, see van Wormer [2011].) Substance abuse treatment centers can call on PFLAG at any time to present a panel, usually of the parents of gays and lesbians, who, in telling their personal stories, help dispel myths pertaining to homosexuality. Speakers from this group can also enlighten members of the treatment community about the significance of the coming-out process, which substance abuse practitioners might have the opportunity to assist clients in undergoing (information can be found at http://community.pflag.org).

Most sexual minorities in treatment are in heterosexual-dominated programs. Addiction specialist Philip McCabe (interviewed by Jackson, 2004) states that the programs may range from gay avoidant to gay tolerant to gay sensitive to gay affirming. Pride Institute, a 36-bed facility in Eden Prairie, Minnesota, near Minneapolis, is a gay-specialized treatment center. This treatment center figures prominently in *Dry: A Memoir*, the amusing but informative autobiography of Augusten Burroughs (2003). Burroughs, a gay man who downed a liter of Dewar's scotch each night, was forced into treatment by his employer, an advertising company. When given the choice of treatment centers, he choose what he names in his biography, not very subtly, "Proud Institute ... the gay rehab center in Minnesota." At the thought of spending a month at this center, Burroughs thinks, "A rehab hospital run by fags will be hip. Plus there's the possibility of good music and sex" (p. 23).

Later, he describes his experience in more down-to-earth terms: "It was like emotion, emotion, emotion half of the day. And facts, facts, facts the other half. It was like *Jerry Springer* meets medical school" (p. 116). *Dry* shows both the uniqueness of the male gay experience, especially in terms of issues related to guilt and grief, and that the treatment, alcohol craving, turbulent journey from denial to acceptance, haunting memories from childhood, and obsessive relationships are the issues faced by every alcoholic who endures treatment.

As described on its website (http://pride-institute.com), we learn that PRIDE's unique program addresses issues such as internalized homophobia, low self-esteem, coming out to family and friends, same-sex sexuality, early-childhood sexual abuse, and safe-sex practices, in addition to addictions education and treatment. Other gay, lesbian, bisexual, and transgender specialized treatment centers are Pacifica Treatment Centers, a residential center in Vancouver, Canada; Alternatives, Inc. in Los Angeles; and the branch of PRIDE Institute in Florida. These gay-affirming programs can be expected to have openly gay staff; a mission statement that includes gay, lesbian, bisexual, transgender sensitivity; and sensitivity training for the staff. Alternatives, Inc. announces on their website that the clinic specializes in treatment of crystal meth abusers and treatment counseling for grief and loss related to HIV/AIDS.

Most metropolitan communities have gay-affirming outreach center programs. Harm reduction treatment programs on the West Coast, for example, help clients reduce the harm to themselves in other areas as well as substance misuse.

A FOCUS ON SPIRITUALITY

A source of major comfort to many people—the church—is so often a source of despair to one group of people—sexual minorities. Most of these people, unlike other minority groups, grew up worshiping in religious environments in which the message was hostile to the very essence of what they would become. And sadly, most have internalized the church's negative teachings on homosexuality. A major cause of suicide among youth dealing with gender issues, as we have seen, is the sense of rejection by fundamentalist churches. Anderson (2009) refers to what she terms "religious-based trauma" (p. 144). This is the condition involving pain and psychological wounds related to a feeling of rejection by one's religious group. An important part of the treatment plan, according to Anderson, is to assess if religious-based trauma is present and to help clients resolve issues they are dealing with. When organized religion is important to clients, they can be referred to a gay-affirmative religious group. In their survey of California gays and lesbians, Ryan, Russell, and colleagues (2010) confirmed the importance of family acceptance as a protective factor against depression, substance use, and suicidal behavior in early adulthood. An interesting finding, in addition, was that participants who reported childhood religious affiliation also reported lower family acceptance compared to participants who were without a religious affiliation in their backgrounds.

Resolution may consist of futile attempts to deny one's sexuality while embracing church doctrine; finding a gay-friendly church, synagogue, or mosque; or finding spiritual nourishment outside orthodox channels. Achieving a high level of spiritual well-being was found in research on a sample of gays and lesbians to be a significant predictor of their psychological development (Tan, 2005).

Senreich and Vairo (2006) suggest that a Twelve-Step program can help gays and lesbians in treatment get in touch with their spiritual needs. Moreover, spirituality, as distinguished from organized religion, can help people deal with grief issues related to the AIDS pandemic. Referral to a gay AA meeting may be appropriate in this regard. But as Senreich and Vairo warn, such referral should be done with some care because of the sexual cruising that sometimes takes place in these settings. As with heterosexual addicts and alcoholics, the temptation to get romantically involved during the earliest period of recovery can be overwhelming and can elicit emotions for which one is ill prepared. On the other hand, since it is often hard for gays and lesbians with substance-related problems to imagine a social life outside the gay bar, a specialized AA or NA meeting or a gay-friendly religious group may provide just the kind of sober support system that is essential to recovery.

SUMMARY AND CONCLUSION

Vulnerability, victimization, and substance misuse are the themes that emerged in this chapter on gender and sex orientation differences. Although there is considerable within-group variability, gender differences in biology, genetics, paths to dependence, responses to various treatment options, relapse triggers, and social contexts continue to be identified by research studies and practitioners. Women entering treatment often have lower economic status, less support from their male counterparts, more need for parenting and vocational skills, quicker and more severe physiological damage, more sexual and physical abuse in their backgrounds, and more need for transportation and child care than men. Such differences suggest the desirability of gender-specific prevention and treatment approaches for subgroups of women with these characteristics, and indeed, many new programs have developed since the infusion of female-specific federal funding in the mid-1980s. Research on the outcomes of women who receive treatment programming that includes child care services, prenatal services, women-only treatment, and mental health services is positive. These outcomes are not measured in terms of abstinence only; rather, the focus is on decreased substance use, increased treatment retention, improved birth outcomes, higher self-esteem, lower depression, and HIV risk reduction. Given the consistently poor results when narrowly measuring success as abstinence only, some critics are calling for new models for both men and women that would incorporate more choice and less coercion.

Lesbians, gays, bisexuals, and transgender people have horrendous problems with discrimination and hate crimes. Their invisibility is one difficulty making problematic the pursuit of their rights, including the right to gay-affirmative or at least gay-sensitive treatment. Yet paramount is their need for whole-person counseling that takes into account identities, relationships, and resiliencies. In recognition of this, specialized resources are being set up nationwide, albeit only in the major cities.

References

Abramovitz, M. (1997). *Regulating the lives of women: Social welfare policy from colonial times to the present* (Rev. ed.). Boston: South End Press.

Alcoholism Drug Abuse Weekly. (2009). Biological, societal factors compel field to consider more gender-responsive care. *Alcoholism Drug Abuse Weekly, 21*(22), 1–6.

American Lung Association, (2010). *Smoking out a deadly threat: Tobacco use in the LGBT community.* Washington, DC: American Lung Association.

American Psychiatric Association (APA). (2000). *The diagnostic and statistical manual of mental disorders, text revision (DSM-IV-TR).* Washington, DC: Author.

American Psychological Association, (2004, July 28). *Sexual orientation, parents, and children: Policy statement.* Retrieved Sept 10, 2002 from http://www.apa.org/about/governance/council/policy/parenting.aspx

Anderson, S. (2009). *Substance use disorders in lesbian, gay, bisexual, and transgender clients: Assessment and treatment.* New York: Columbia University Press.

Annenberg Public Policy Center. (2005). Card playing trend in young people continues. *University of Pennsylvania.* Retrieved January 2007 from http://www.annenbergpublicpolicycenter.org/Downloads/Adolescent_Risk/Gambling/Gambling Release20050928.pdf.

Anonymous. (2003). Reflections on problem gambling therapy with female clients. *eGambling*, *8*(May). Retrieved Feb. 7, 2009 from http://www.camh.net/egam-bling/issue8/first_person/index.html

Apter-Marsh, M. (1984). The sexual behavior of alcoholic women while drinking and during sobriety. *Alcoholism Treatment Quarterly*, *1*(3), 35–48.

Arizona Council on Compulsive Gambling. (2000). *Escape vs. action*. Retrieved from http://www.azccg.org

Atkinson, D. R., & Schein, S. (1986). Similarity in counseling. *Counseling Psychologist*, *14*, 319–354.

Belknap, J. (2001). *The invisible woman: Gender, crime, and justice*. Belmont, CA: Wadsworth.

Benson, R. (2011). Personal communication, September 1, 2011.

Berg, I. K., & Shafer, K. C. (2004). Working with mandated substance abusers: The language of solutions. In S. L. Straussner (Ed.), *Clinical work with substance-abusing clients* (2nd ed., pp. 82–102). New York: Guilford Press.

Binswanger, I., Merrill, J., Krueger, P., White, M., Booth, R., & Elmore, J. (2010). Gender differences in chronic medical, psychiatric, and substance-dependence disorders among jail inmates. *American Journal of Public Health*, *100*(3), 476–482.

Blanco, C., Hasin, D., Petry, N., Stinson, F., & Grant, B. (2006). Sex differences in subclinical and DSM IV pathological gambling: Results from the National Epidemiologic Survey on Alcohol and Related Conditions. *Psychological Medicine*, *36*(7), 943–953.

Blume, S. (1997). Women: Clinical aspects. In J.Lowinson, P.Ruiz, R. B.Millman, & J. G. Langrod (Eds.), *Substance abuse: A comprehensive textbook* (pp. 645–653). Baltimore: Williams & Wilkins.

Boles, S., & Young, N. (2007). *Sacramento County Drug Dependency Court: The first four years*. Irvine, CA: Children and Family Futures.

Brady, T. M., & Ashley, O. S. (Eds.). (2005). Women in substance abuse treatment: Results from the alcohol and drug services study (DHHS Publication No. SMA 04-3968). Rockville, MD: Substance Abuse and Mental Health Services Administration.

Brown, S., & Coventry, L. (1997). *Queen of hearts*. Victoria, Australia: Financial and Consumer Rights Council.

Brown, V. B., Melchior, L. A., Waite-O'Brien, N., & Huba, G. J. (2002). Effects of women-sensitive long-term residential treatment on psychological function of diverse populations of women. *Journal of Substance Abuse Treatment*, *23*, 133–144.

Bureau of Justice Statistics (BJS). (2000). *Women offenders*. Washington, DC: U.S. Department of Justice.

Bureau of Justice Statistics (BJS). (2003). *Intimate partner violence: 1993–2001*. Washington, DC: U.S. Department of Justice.

Bureau of Justice Statistics (BJS). (2004). *National Crime Victimization Survey, Criminal Victimization: 2003*. Retrieved Sept 24, 2011, from http://bjs.ojp.usdoj.gov/content/pub/pdf/cv03.pdf.

Bureau of Justice Statistics (BJS). (2006). *Prison and jail inmates at midyear 2005*. Washington, DC: U.S. Department of Justice.

Burroughs, A. (2003). *Dry: A memoir*. New York: St. Martin's Press.

Calamari, J., Cox, W., & Roth, J. (1996). Group treatment for men with alcohol problems. In M.Andronico (Ed.), *Men in groups: Insights, interventions, and psychoeducational work* (pp. 305–321). Washington, DC: American Psychological Association.

Center for Substance Abuse Treatment (CSAT). (2001). *A provider's introduction to substance abuse treatment for lesbian, gay, bisexual, and transgender individuals.* Rockville, MD: SAMHSA.

Center for Substance Abuse Treatment (CSAT). (2009). *Substance abuse treatment: Addressing the specific needs of women.* Treatment Improvement Protocol (TIP) Series 51. HHS Publication No. (SMA) 09-4426. Rockville, MD: Substance Abuse and Mental Health Services Administration.

Center for Substance Abuse Treatment (CSAT). (2010) *Substance abuse specialists in child welfare agencies and dependency courts considerations for program designers and evaluators.* HHS Pub. No. (SMA) 10-4557 Rockville, MD: Substance Abuse and Mental Health Services Administration.

Centers for Disease Control and Prevention (CDC). (2006). *Intimate partner violence: Fact sheet.* National Center for Injury Prevention and Control. Retrieved October 2006 from http://www.cdc.gov/ncipc

Chesney-Lind, M., & Pasko, L. (2004). *The female offender: Girls, women, and crime* (2nd ed.). Thousand Oaks, CA: Sage.

Clay, C. (1997, Spring). Bisexual crystal injectors in Seattle. *Harm Reduction*, pp. 18–19.

Cohen, J., Dickow, A., Horner, K., Zweben, J., Balabis, J., Vandersloot, D., et al. (2003). Abuse and violence history of men and women in treatment for methamphetamine dependence. *American Journal on Addictions*, 12(5), 377–385.

Cohen, L., & Hienk, D. (2006). Treatment outcomes for women with substance abuse and PTSD who have experienced complex trauma. *Psychiatric Services*, 57(1), 100–106.

Compton, R. & Benning, A. (2009). *Results of the 2007 national roadside survey of alcohol and drug use by drivers.* National Highway Traffic Safety Administration (NHTSA). Retrieved August 2011 from http://www.nhtsa.gov

Copeland, J., Hall, W., Didcott, P., & Biggs, V. (1993). A comparison of a specialist women's alcohol and other drug treatment service with two traditional mixed-sex services: Client characteristics and treatment outcome. *Drug and Alcohol Dependence*, 32, 81–92.

Corrigan, E. (1995). Outcome of treatment for Irish alcoholic women. *Irish Journal of Psychological Medicine*, 12(2), 48–52.

Covington, S. (2008). Women and addiction: A trauma-informed approach. *Journal of Psychoactive Drugs*, Supplement 5, p. 377–385.

Crisp, B., Thomas, S., Jackson, A., Thomason, N., Smith, S., Borrell, J., et al. (2000). Sex differences in the treatment needs and outcomes of problem gamblers. *Research on Social Work Practice*, 10(2), 229–242.

Crisp, C. (2006). The Gay Affirmative Practice scale (GAP): A new measure for assessing cultural competence with gay and lesbian clients. *Social Work*, 51(2), 106–113.

Davis, D. (1997). Women healing from alcoholism: A qualitative study. *Contemporary Drug Problems*, 24, 147–177.

Davis, D., & DiNitto, D. (2005). Gender and the use of drugs and alcohol: Fact, fiction, and unanswered questions. In C. A.McNeece & D.DiNitto, *Chemical dependency: A systems approach* (3rd ed., pp. 503–545). Boston: Allyn & Bacon.

Davis, D. (2009). *Taking back your life: Women and problem gambling.* Center City, MN: Hazelden.

DeVera, K. (2011, August 17). CDC announces efforts to eliminate HIV infections among high-risk groups. *Health News.* Retrieved from http://www.healthnews.com

Downs, W. R., & Miller, B. B. (2002). Treating dual problems of partner violence and substance abuse. In C.Wekerle & A.Wall (Eds.), *The violence and addiction equation: Theoretical and clinical issues in substance abuse and relationship violence* (pp. 254–274). London: Brunner/Routledge, Hove.

Drug Courts Program Office, Office of Justice Programs. (2004). *Defining drug courts: The key components.* Washington, DC: U.S. Department of Justice.

Eisenberg, M., & Resnick, M. (2006). Suicidality among gay, lesbian, and bisexual youth: The role of protective factors. *Journal of Adolescent Health, 39*(5), 662–668.

El-Bassel, N., Gilbert, L., Krishnan, S., Schilling, R. F., Gaeta, T., Purpura, S., et al. (1998). Partner violence and sexual HIV-risk behaviors among women in an inner-city emergency department. *Violence and Victims, 13*(4), 1–17.

Enos, S. (2001). *Mothering from the inside: Parenting in a women's prison.* Albany: State University of New York Press.

Fallon, P., Katzman, M. A., & Wooley, S. C. (Eds.). (1994). *Feminist perspectives on eating disorders.* New York: Guilford Press.

Gerolamo, A. (2004). State of the science: Women and the nonpharmacological treatment of substance abuse. *Journal of the American Psychiatric Nurses Association, 10*(4), 181–189.

Goddard, K. (2009). Pregnancy and its effects on opiate and alcohol use. *Drugs and Alcohol Today, 9*(4), 18–21.

Greenfield, S., Brooks, A., Gordon, S., Green, C., Kropp, F., McHugh, R., Lincoln, M., Hien, D. & Miele, G. (2007). Substance abuse treatment entry, retention, and outcome in women: A review of the literature. *Drug and Alcohol Dependence, 86,* 1–21.

Greenfield, S., & Grella, C. (2009). What is "women-focused" treatment for substance use disorders? *Psychiatric Services, 60*(7), 880–882.

Greenfield, S., Trucco, E., McHugh, R., Lincoln, M., & Gallop, R. (2007). The Women's Recovery Group Study: a Stage I trial of women-focused group therapy for substance use disorders versus mixed-gender group drug counseling. *Drug Alcohol Dependence, 90*(1), 39–47.

Grella, C., & Joshi, V. (1999). Gender differences in drug treatment careers among clients in the National Drug Abuse Treatment Outcome Study. *American Journal of Drug and Alcohol Abuse, 25*(3), 385–406.

Grella, C. E., Polinsky, M. L., Hser, Y., & Perry, S. M. (1999). Characteristics of women-only and mixed-gender drug abuse treatment programs. *Journal of Substance Abuse Treatment, 17*(1/2), 37–44.

Hamilton, A., Poza, I., Washington, D. (2011). "Homelessness and trauma go hand-in-hand": Pathways to homelessness among women veterans. *Women's Health Issues, 21*(4Suppl), S203–209.

Harris, L., & Paltrow, L. (2007). The status of pregnant women and fetuses in U.S. criminal law. *Journal of the American Medical Association, 289*(13), 1697–1699.

Harshman, W. L. (2000). A comparison of a gender-specific and traditional model of substance abuse treatment within the therapeutic community on treatment success (Doctoral dissertation, Wayne State University, 2000). *Dissertation Abstracts International, 61*(1-A), 97.

Heater, J., & Patton, D. (2006). Gender differences in problem gambling behavior from help-line callers. *Journal of Gambling Issues, 16*, 1–5.

Hiebert-Murphy, D., & Woytkiw, L. (2000). A model for working with women dealing with child sexual abuse and addictions: The Laurel Centre, Winnipeg, Manitoba, Canada. *Journal of Substance Abuse Treatment, 18*, 387–394.

Hirsch, A. (1999). Some days are harder than hard: Welfare reform and women with drug conviction in Pennsylvania. *Center for Law and Social Policy.* Retrieved from http://www.clasp.org/publications/some_days_are_harder_than_hard.pdf

Holmes, W. C., & Slap, G. B. (1998). Sexual abuse of boys: Definition, prevalence, correlates, sequelae, and management. *Journal of the American Medical Association, 280*(21), 1855–1862.

Hubbard, J. R., Franco, S. E., & Onaivi, E. (1999). Marijuana: Medical implications. *American Family Physician.* Retrieved from http://www.aafp.org/afp/991201ap/2583.html

Hubbard, R. L. (1997). Evaluation and outcome of treatment. In J. H.Lowinson, P. Ruiz, R. B.Millman, & J. G.Langrod (Eds.), *Substance abuse: A comprehensive textbook* (pp. 499–512). Baltimore: Williams & Wilkins.

Jackson, K. (2004, May/June). What's sex got to do with it? Addiction in the GLBT community. *Social Work Today*, p. 15.

Jones, H., Tuten, M., & O'Grady, K. (2011). Treating the partners of opioid-dependent pregnant patients: Feasibility and efficacy. *American Journal of Drug and Alcohol Abuse, 37*, 170–178.

Kantor, G., & Strauss, M. (1989). Substance abuse as a precipitant of wife abuse victimizations. *American Journal of Drug and Alcohol Abuse, 15*(2), 173–189.

Karberg, J., & James, D. (2005). *Substance dependence, abuse, and treatment of jail inmates: 2002.* Washington, DC: U.S. Department of Justice.

Kauffman, E., Dore, M. M., & Nelson-Zlupko, L. (1995). The role of women's therapy groups in the treatment of chemical dependence. *American Journal of Orthopsychiatry, 65*(3), 355–363.

Kenney, J. W., Reinholtz, C., & Angelini, P. J. (1997). Ethnic differences in childhood pregnancy and adolescent sexual abuse and teenage pregnancy. *Journal of Adolescent Health, 21*, 3–10.

LaFave, L. M., & Echols, L. D. (1999). An argument for choice: An alternative women's treatment program. *Journal of Substance Abuse Treatment, 16*(4), 345–352.

LaFave, L., Desportes, L., & McBride, C. (2009). Treatment outcomes and perceived benefits: A qualitative and quantitative assessment of a women's substance abuse treatment program. *Women and Therapy, 32*, 51–68.

Laudet, A., Magura, S., Furst, R., & Kumar, N. (1999). Male partners of substance-abusing women in treatment: An exploratory study. *American Journal of Drug and Alcohol Abuse, 25*(4), 607–627.

Leonard, K. E. (1993). Drinking patterns and intoxication in marital violence: Review, critique, and future directions for research. In S. E.Martin (Ed.), *Alcohol and interpersonal violence: Fostering multidisciplinary perspectives* (NIH Publication No. 93-3496, NIH Research Monograph 24, pp. 281–290). Washington, DC: National Institutes of Health.

Lesieur, H., & Blume, S. (1991). When Lady Luck loses: Women and compulsive gambling. In N.Van Den Bergh (Ed.), *Feminist perspectives on addictions* (pp. 181–197). New York: Springer.

Lester, B., Andreozzi, L. & Appiah, L. (2004). Substance use during pregnancy: Time for policy to catch up with research. *Harm Reduction Journal, 1*(5). Retrieved September 1, 2011 from http://www.harmreductionjournal.com/content/1/1/5

Lewandowski, C., & Hill, T. (2009). The impact of emotional and material social support on women's drug treatment completion. *Health and Social Work, 34*(3), 213–221.

McGue, M., & Slutske, W. (1996). The inheritance of alcoholism in women. In J. M. Howard, S. E. Martin, P. D. Mail, M. E. Hilton, & E. D.Taylor (Eds.), *Women and alcohol: Issues for prevention research* (Research Monograph No. 32, pp. 65–92). Bethesda, MD: National Institutes of Health.

Miller, B., Downs, W., & Gondoli, D. (1989). Spousal violence among alcoholic women as compared to a random household sample of women. *Journal of Studies on Alcohol, 50,* 533–540.

Miller, B. A., Downs, W. R., & Testa, M. (1993). Interrelationships between victimization experiences and women's alcohol use. *Journal of Studies on Alcohol,* Suppl. 2, 109–117.

Miller, W., Forcehimes, A., Zweben, A., & McClellan, A. (2011). *Treating addiction: A guide for professionals.* New York: Guilford Press.

Miller, W. R., & Rollnick, S. (2002). *Motivational interviewing: Preparing people to change addictive behavior* (2nd ed.). New York: Guilford Press.

Morales, A., Sheafor, B., & Scott, M. (2010). *Social work: A profession of many faces* (12th ed.). Boston: Allyn & Bacon.

Mravcak, S. S. (2006). Primary care for lesbian, bisexual women. *American Family Physician, 74*(2), 287–288.

Murphy, S., & Rosenbaum, M. (1997). Two women who used cocaine too much. In C.Reinarman & H.Levine (Eds.), *Crack in America: Demon drugs and social justice* (pp. 98–112). Berkeley: University of California Press.

National Center on Addiction and Substance Abuse (CASA). (2006). *Women under the influence.* Baltimore: Johns Hopkins University Press.

National Clearinghouse on Child Abuse and Neglect Information. (2003). *Substance abuse and child maltreatment.* Retrieved Sept 22, 2011 from http://centerforchildwelfare.fmhi.usf.edu/kb/subsabse/substance%20abuse%20and%20child%20maltreatment.pdf

National Institute on Alcohol Abuse and Alcoholism (NIAAA). (1993). *Eighth Special Report to the U.S. Congress on Alcohol and Health.* Rockville, MD: Author.

National Women's Law Center. (2004). *Making the grade on women's health: A national and state-by-state report card.* Washington, DC: Author

Nelson-Zlupko, L., Dore, M. M., Kauffman, E., & Kaltenback, K. (1996). Women in recovery: Their perceptions of treatment effectiveness. *Journal of Substance Abuse Treatment, 13*(1), 51–59.

Neumann, D. A., Houskamp, B. M., Pollock, V. E., & Briere, J. (1996). The long-term sequelae of childhood sexual abuse in women: A meta-analytic review. *Child Maltreatment: Journal of the Professional Society on the Abuse of Children, 1,* 6–16.

Neumann, J. P., & Sallmann, J. (2004). Women, trauma histories, and co-occurring disorders: Assessing the scope of the problem. *Social Service Review, 78*(3), 466–500.

Nevada Council on Problem Gambling. (2004). *Annual Report.* Las Vegas, NV. Retrieved October 2006 from http://www.nevadacouncil.org/2004AnnualReport. pdf

New study highlights gender's impact on addiction. (2000). *American Medical News, 43*(7), 30.

Pierre, N., Shrier, L. A., Emans, S. J., & DuRant, R. H. (1998). Adolescent males involved in pregnancy: Association of forced sexual contact and risk behaviors. *Journal of Adolescent Health, 23*(6), 364–369.

Piquette-Tomei, N., Norman, E., Dwyer, S. & McCaslin, E. (2008). Group therapy for women problem gamblers: A space of their own. *Journal of Gambling Issues, 22,* 1–9.

Plant, M. (2008). The role of alcohol is women's lives: A review of issues and responses. *Journal of Substance Use, 13,* 155–191.

Potenza, M., Steinberg, M., McLaughlin, S., Wu, R., Rounsaville, B., & O'Malley, S. (2001). Gender-related differences in the characteristics of problem gamblers using a gambling helpline. *American Journal of Psychiatry, 158*(9), 1500–1505.

Prendergast, M. L., Wellisch, J., & Falkin, G. P. (1995). Assessment of services for substance-abusing women offenders in community and correctional settings. *Prison Journal, 75,* 240–256.

Project MATCH Research Group. (1997). Matching alcoholism treatment to client heterogeneity: Project MATCH Posttreatment drinking outcomes. *Journal of Studies on Alcohol, 58,* 7–29.

Rivaux, S., Sohn, S., Armour, M., & Bell, H. (2008). Women's early recovery: Managing the dilemma of substance abuse and intimate partner relationships. *Journal of Drug Issues, 38*(4), 957–979.

Romero, V., Donohue, B., & Allen, D. (2010). Treatment of concurrent substance dependence, child neglect and domestic violence: A single case examination involving family behavior therapy. *Journal of Family Violence, 25,* 287–295.

Ryan, J., Chois, S., Hong, J., Hernandez, P., & Larrison, C. (2008). Recovery coaches and substance exposure at birth. *Child Abuse and Neglect, 32*(11), 1072–1079.

Ryan, C., Huebner, D., Rafael M., Diaz, R., & Sanchez, J. (2009). Family rejection as a predictor of negative health outcomes in white and Latino lesbian, gay, and bisexual young adults. *Pediatrics, 123,* 346–352.

Ryan, C., Russell, S., Huebner, D., Diaz, R., & Sanchez, J. (2010). Family acceptance in adolescence and the health of LGBT young adults. *Journal of the International Society of Psychiatric Mental Health Nursing, 23*(4), 205–213.

Schutte, K. K., Seable, J. H., & Moos, R. H. (1997). Gender differences in the relations between depressive symptoms and drinking behavior among problem drinkers: A three-wave study. *Journal of Consulting Clinical Psychology, 65,* 392–404.

Senreich, E., & Vairo, E. (2006). Treatment of gay and lesbian substance abusers. In S. L.Straussner (Ed.), *Clinical work with substance-abusing clients* (pp. 392–423). New York: Guilford Press.

Shafer, D., Hartman, J., & Listwan, S. (2009). Drug abusing women in the community: The impact of drug court involvement on recidivism. *Journal of Drug Issues, 39*(4), 803–827.

Shelton, M. (2011). *Gay men and substance abuse: A basic guide for addicts and those who care for them.* Center City, MN: Hazelden.

Shernoff, M. (2006). Condomless sex: Gay men, barebacking, and harm reduction. *Social Work, 51*(2), 106–113.

Smith, P. H., & Chescheir, N. (1995). *Battered substance-abusing women: A vulnerable and underserved population in North Carolina.* (Final report submitted to North Carolina Governor's Institute for Alcohol and Substance Abuse, Raleigh. North Carolina Governor's Institute for Alcohol and Substance Abuse), as quoted in CASA (1996), p. 32.

Sowers, K. M., Ellis, R. A., Washington, T. S., & Currant, M. (2002). Optimizing treatment effects for substance abusing women with children: An evaluation of the Susan B. Anthony Center. *Research on Social Work Practice, 12*(1), 143–158.

Sterling, R. C., Gottheil, E., Weinstein, S. P., & Serota, R. (1998). Therapist/patient race and sex matching: Treatment retention and 9-month follow-up outcome. *Addiction, 93*(7), 1043–1050.

Stone-Manista, K. (2009). Protecting pregnant women: A guide to successfully challenging criminal child abuse prosecutions of pregnant drug addicts. *Journal of Criminal Law and Criminology, 99*(3), 823–856.

Substance Abuse and Mental Health Services Administration (SAMHSA). (2001). A provider's introduction to substance abuse treatment for lesbian, gay, bisexual, and transgender individuals. Rockville, MD: Author.

Substance Abuse and Mental Health Services Administration (SAMHSA). (2005a). Substance abuse treatment for persons with co-occurring disorders. Treatment Improvement Protocol (TIP) Series, No. 42 (DHHS Publication No. SMA 05-3992). Rockville, MD: Author.

Substance Abuse and Mental Health Services Administration (SAMHSA). (2005b). *Women in substance abuse treatment: Results from the Alcohol and Drug Services Study.* Office of Applied Studies. Retrieved October 7, 2006 from http://oas.samhsa.gov/WomenTX/WomenTX.htm

Substance Abuse and Mental Health Services Administration (SAMHSA). (2006). *Results from the 2005 National Survey on Drug Use and Health: National Findings.* Retrieved February 2007 from http://oas.samhsa.gov/NSDUH/2K5NSDUH/2K5results.htm

Substance Abuse and Mental Health Services Administration (SAMHSA). (2008). Office of Applied Studies. *The NSDUH Report: Alcohol use among pregnant women and recent mothers: 2002 to 2007.* Rockville, MD.

Substance Abuse and Mental Health Services Administration (SAMHSA). (2010a). *Results from the 2009 National Survey on Drug Use and Health: Volume I. Summary of National Findings* (Office of Applied Studies, NSDUH Series H-38A, HHS Publication No. SMA 10-4586 Findings). Rockville, MD.

Substance Abuse and Mental Health Services Administration (SAMHSA). (2010b). *Substance abuse treatment programs for gays and lesbians.* Washington, DC: Office of Applied Studies.

Sun, A. (2007). Relapse among substance-abusing women: Components and processes. *Substance Use and Misuse, 42*(1), 1–21.

Tan, P. (2005). The importance of spirituality among gay and lesbian individuals. *Journal of Homosexuality, 49*(2), 135–145.

Tuchman, E. (2010). Women and addiction: The importance of gender issues in substance abuse research. *Addictive Diseases, 29*, 127–138.

Tuten, M., Jones, H., Tran, G., & Svikis, D. (2004). Partner violence impacts the psychosocial and psychiatric status of pregnant, drug-dependent women. *Addictive Behaviors, 29*(5), 1029–1034.

U.S. Federal News Service. (Oct 6, 2009). *SAMHSA awards $14.7 million in grants for the residential treatment of pregnant, postpartum women with substance abuse problems.* Washington, DC: Dolan Company.

U.S. Secretary of Health and Human Services. (2000). *Tenth special report to the U.S. Congress on alcohol and health.* Rockville, MD: National Institute on Alcohol Abuse and Alcoholism.

VanGelder, L., & Brandt, P. R. (1996). *The girl next door: Into the heart of lesbian America.* New York: Simon & Schuster.

van Wormer, K., Wells, J., & Boes, M. (2000). *Social work with lesbians, gays, and bisexuals: A strengths perspective.* Boston: Allyn & Bacon.

van Wormer, K., & Bartollas, C. (2007) *Women and the criminal justice system* (2nd ed.). Boston: Allyn & Bacon.

van Wormer, K. (2011). *Human behavior and the social environment, micro level: Individuals and families.* New York: Oxford University Press.

Volberg, R. (2005). *Gambling and problem gambling in Arizona: Report to the Arizona Lottery.* Retrieved October 2006 from http://www.problemgambling.az.gov

Wechsberg, W., Craddock, S., & Hubbard, R. (1998). How are women who enter substance abuse treatment different than men? A gender comparison from the Drug Abuse Treatment Outcome Study. *Drugs and Society, 13*(1/2), 97–115.

Westermeyer, J., & Boedicker, A. (2000). Course, severity and treatment of substance abuse among women versus men. *American Journal of Drug and Alcohol Abuse, 26*(4), 523–535.

Widom, C., Ireland, T., & Glynn, P. (1995). Alcohol abuse in abused and neglected children follow-up: Are they at increased risk? *Journal of Studies on Alcohol, 56*, 207–217.

Willson, P., McFarlane, J., Malecha, A., Watson, K., Lemmey, D., Schultz, P., et al. (2000). Severity of violence against women by intimate partners and associated use of alcohol and/or illicit drugs by the perpetrator. *Journal of Interpersonal Violence, 15*(9), 996–1008.

Wong, C. J., Badger, G. J., Sigmon, S. C., & Higgins, S. T. (2002). Examining possible gender differences among cocaine-dependent outpatients. *Experimental and Clinical Psychopharmacology, 10*, 216–323.

World Health Organization (WHO). (2004). *Global status report on alcohol.* Retrieved October 2006 from http://www.who.int/substance_abuse/publications

Yodanis, C. (2004). Gender inequality, violence: A cross-national test of the feminist theory of violence against women. *Journal of Interpersonal Violence, 19*(6), 655–675.

Young, N., Gardner, S., & Dennis, K. (1998). *Responding to alcohol and other drug problems in child welfare: Weaving together practice and policy.* Washington, DC: Child Welfare Press.

Young, N., Gardner, S., Otero, C., Dennis, K., Chang, R., Earle, K. & Amatetti, S. (2009). *Substance-exposed infants: State responses to the problem*. HHS Pub No. (SMA) 09-4369. Rockville, MD: SAMHSA.

Zernike, K. (2005, July 6). Officials across U.S. describe drug woes. *New York Times*. Retrieved from http://www.nytimes.com

Zlotnick, C., Clarke, J., Friedmann, P., Roberts, M., Sacks, S., & Melnick, G. (2008). Gender differences in comorbid disorders among offenders in prison substance abuse treatment programs. *Behavioral Sciences and the Law*, 26, 403–412.

GAMBLING, EATING DISORDERS, SHOPPING, AND OTHER BEHAVIORAL ADDICTIONS

CHAPTER 5

"It became my sex; it became my lover; it became my mother."
—Davis, 2009, p. 45

The addictions we discuss in this chapter, rarely covered in books on substance misuse, are not what you think of as your ordinary addictions, and only one involves a substance—food. What these addictions share is that they all involve everyday legal activities: eating, shopping, sexual activity, gambling, and surfing the Internet. What these behavioral or pleasure-related addictions have in common with the substance dependencies is that they are compulsive and obsessive, and they involve euphoria that is not induced artificially by a drug. Like all addictions, the ones we discuss in this chapter have strong biological, psychological, and social components.

Nora Volkow, the director of the National Institute of Drug Abuse and one of the country's leading addiction researchers, believes that low levels of dopamine receptors in the brain, whether caused by a high degree of stress or due to genetic susceptibility, may explain why some can drink or use a drug without getting addicted while others apparently cannot. Science shows, as Volkow (2007) asserts, that everyone has the potential to be addicted to something, and that all addictions, whether to drugs, alcohol, tobacco, sex, gambling, or even food, are more alike than was previously thought. And although we may

255

think that being addicted to food is not as bad as being addicted to heroin, researchers are teaching us that we had better think about this again.

"Are addictions to video games, gambling, or shopping really like drug or alcohol addiction in terms of brain function?" asks David Linden (2011), the author of *The Compass of Pleasure* (p. 126). "At the biological level," he responds, "there is now reason to believe that a broad definition of addiction— one that encompasses drugs, sex, food, gambling, video games, and some other compulsions—is valid" (p. 127).

For helping professionals working in the substance abuse treatment field, an understanding of these other addictive behaviors commonly found in clients receiving treatment for another disorder is essential. For example, the person who engages in alcohol bingeing might engage in compulsive overeating as well, and in recovery from drug misuse, the client may become a workaholic or, worse, develop an addiction to shopping and spending. "Everything we learn about one type of addiction," notes Volkow (2006), "has the potential to teach us something about the others" (p. 77).

"I get addicted to everything I touch." How often this comment is heard in substance abuse treatment circles! Yet the dynamics of this phenomenon, the tendency of some individuals to take everything to extremes, have not been properly understood or even acknowledged by scientists until now. Today, there is mounting evidence that all addiction—chemical or otherwise—arises from the same neurobiological processes located deep inside the brain and not in the cerebral cortex, which is the rational, thinking part of the brain. Recent research shows, for example, that compulsive gambling may hijack the reward and pleasure pathways of the brain in somewhat the same way that psychoactive drugs do (Linden, 2011). Recently, reports of tanning addiction have hit the news. The out-of-control drives of people to constantly sunbathe or to visit tanning booths have been shown to meet the same criteria for addiction or dependence as does drug dependence and to have a neurological basis (Brody, 2010). Van Wormer had earlier observed unhealthy tanning booth patterns among alcoholic clients at a treatment center in Norway that had its own tanning room. (The effects of excessive tanning could be easily observed in the fair-complexioned Norwegians.)

In his book on attention-deficit disorder, *Scattered,* Gabor Maté (1999) anticipated what we now know about the nature of addiction from science:

> Less obvious (than alcoholic lurches) but no less physiological are the effects on the brain of self-stimulating behaviors. The gambler and the sexaholic, the compulsive shopper, and the man or woman who insists on skiing uncharted glaciers are all looking for the same hit of dopamine and endorphins that the ingestion of substances gives the drug addict. Whatever gets you through the night. (p. 298)

Some individuals, because of a genetic predisposition or trauma early in life, are especially vulnerable neurologically to the disorganizing effects of substance misuse. They have a tendency to suffer a loss of control when exposed to addictive products and experiences of all sorts. The cumulative effect of traumatic stress, as Morgan (2009) explains, has been found in scientific research to have a lasting effect on brain structure, function, and long-term responses to additional stress. These individuals seem to have less resistance to addiction than do others. The source of the addiction may be a mood-altering substance; a love relationship; or a thrilling pastime, such as betting on horses; or all three. Based on our theory of vulnerability, we would predict that medication for any one of these "maladies" should alleviate the other problems as well. This, in fact, is the case. Drugs that reduce the craving to drink, for example, might make an individual more laid back in other areas.

One way to study the effects of genetic and personality characteristics on the later development of addiction problems is to study children across the life span. Slutske, Caspi, Moffitt, and Poulton (2005) designed such a study that included about 1,000 children born in the 1970s. One purpose of the study was to determine which kind of temperaments were most likely to lead to addictions. The results showed that the children who later became compulsive gamblers, alcoholics, and other addicts had personalities characterized by negativity, nervousness, anger, and a tendency to worry and feel victimized. Another significant trait—impulsiveness combined with thrill seeking—was also part of the mix. Add to that the availability of drugs or casinos, and we could say that "nature takes its course."

Keeping in mind that the biology and psychology of addiction are so often inseparable, we can see further that the particular form the addiction takes may be a matter of chance or availability; that is, whether the addiction is to a substance such as heroin or to a behavior such as gambling, the pattern is more or less the same. Psychologically, this pattern entails all the mind games that the addict engages in to continue the mad pursuit (e.g., inappropriate sex or betting on cards). Socially (i.e., how the addiction impacts family, peers, and colleagues), the consequences are relatively comparable as well. Could anyone argue that the parents of a child with anorexia don't suffer as much as the parents of a child using drugs?

In this chapter, we consider both the commonalities and uniquenesses of numerous varieties of addiction: gambling addiction, eating disorders, shopping addiction, sex addiction, as well as compulsive use of the social networks, including Facebook, the newest "kid on the block." A basic assumption of this chapter, as of this book, is that the most effective therapeutic practices for these kinds of addictions, as for addiction in general, are cognitive-based approaches with an emphasis on motivation. The fundamentals of cognitive therapy, including the thinking and feeling work and the use of positive self-talk that are described in the final portion of this chapter, are principles as relevant to working with people with drug use disorders as with individuals out of control with eating, gambling, or sex. The cognitive interventions presented in this chapter are not viewed as a separate treatment modality but rather as strategies that transcend all the basic modalities. All therapy and counseling are about helping people take control of their lives, learning how to cope, and learning how to survive. All therapy is psychological in this sense. In this chapter, what we do is single it out and define the tools therapists need to help clients modify, and thereby moderate, unhealthy thought patterns (e.g., "I'm going to fast for a week"; "I'm going to gamble for big stakes to get back what I lost."). Management of anger and stress, reframing of one's definition of self, and the therapeutic use of humor are among the other topics covered. In contrast to much of the cognitive work that counselors are engaged in today, especially in working with offenders and addicts, our approach is consistent with the strengths and empowerment perspective.

DISORDERED OR COMPULSIVE GAMBLING

Gambling, like drinking, is at once a harmless social activity and a highly addictive behavior. Every year in North America and throughout the world, chronic, compulsive gambling shatters the lives of millions. Fortunately, many learn the hard way to finally let go of the overwhelming urge to play the stakes. There is a lot we can learn from a recovering gambling addict, such as from this university student who shared his story in a personal interview with van Wormer:

> I am a compulsive gambler. I haven't gambled, though, for 4 years. When I reached my eighteenth birthday, I went to a small Indian reservation near Sioux City, Iowa. I think I was addicted the first time I went there to gamble. I'm addicted to just about everything—addicted to drugs, cigarettes, but alcohol didn't cause me any problems. My father was a compulsive gambler before me.
>
> Gambling for me was euphoric; something clicked. You get sucked in. I'd go at 6:00 at night, go straight to the slot machines, and be there until four in the morning. Family members would come to get me and take me home sometimes at two in the morning. We had lots of arguments. Over the years that I gambled I lost from $12,000 to $15,000 altogether. The biggest jackpot I ever won was $500. At the beautiful casino in Mystic Lake, Minnesota, I'd walk in with cigarettes in hand and go straight to the slot machines with my $20 bills. I didn't go to have fun; I went to win.

When a casino moves into the area, residents and tourists go for enjoyment and most have a good time. Win or lose, they leave when they plan to. For others like Bill Lee (2005), the author of *Born to Lose* who became utterly bankrupt and was led to the brink of suicide, and who, like the student mentioned previously was finally able to break the pattern of self-destruction, gambling is a high-risk activity.

It was a big event when a casino—the Isle—a replica of the extravagant casino in Biloxi, Mississippi, came to Waterloo, Iowa. From the start, the casino donated considerable sums of money to local museums and charities. When, after 10 years, the governor tried to raise the casino's taxes, the owners threatened to withdraw their donations to local causes, the outcry was considerable, and the governor eventually retreated. According to a news report from that time:

> [The governor's plan] would endanger an industry he claimed contributes roughly $1 billion to the Iowa economy. The industry said the casinos employ about 10,000 people and give about $50 million in charitable donations annually. (Duffelmeyer, 2011, p. 1)

About that time, a statewide referendum gave overwhelming support to the casinos. The casino not only brought a lot of directly related jobs to the community but also jobs for gambling addictions counselors. A new Gamblers Anonymous (GA) meeting joined the other self-help groups at the local hospital. And there were many calls to 1-800-Bets-Off, the Iowa hotline for people in need of help for their gambling. Among the personal stories that emerged from the Waterloo community of gambling addiction were these: (1) a couple in their seventies who had gone through all their 401(k) retirement, two homes, two cars, and their relationships with their children, and the worse it got, the more they felt they had to keep going back to gamble to pay their bills; (2) a developmentally disabled man who won $40,000 on the slot machines, but who one year later had a much larger credit card debt; and (3) an ex-prisoner who returned to the community for addiction treatment after he had served time for embezzlement from his employer and stealing checks from his family members in order to pay his gambling debts.

Now that some form of gambling has become legal in every state except two (Utah and Hawaii) and with hundreds of casinos operating across the states, we are familiar with catastrophic situations such as these and even more likely, the winning stories from others—they put in $5 and got back $100. On the whole, "gaming" (the preferred term of the gambling industry) has become a socially acceptable and accessible form of recreation throughout the country for both men and women. According to the National Council on Problem Gambling (2011), 60% of Americans indicate in surveys that they gambled in the past year. Two million (1%) U.S. adults are estimated to meet criteria for pathological gambling in a given year, and another 2–3% would be considered problem gamblers.

In *High Stakes: The Cost of America's Gambling Addiction,* investigative reporter Sam Skolnik (2011) explores the business angle of the gaming industry. Drawing on data from state budgets, political campaigns, casino industry economics, as well as addiction treatment sources, Skolnik convincingly makes the case that the economic costs of this $92 billion industry are enormous.

Business administration professor and noted economist John Kindt agrees. For every dollar of revenue generated for the state by gambling, the costs to taxpayers are $3 or more, he states. In his words:

> According to research, the social costs of increased access to casinos and convenience gambling include an increase in personal and professional bankruptcies, up anywhere from 18 to 42 percent, as well as an increase in crime by at least 10 percent. In high gambling areas, people buy at least 10 percent less food and 20 percent less durable goods. So, the real question is, why should taxpayers subsidize social problems? (Ciciora, 2011, p. 1)

Casino owners generally insist that they do not want to attract problem gamblers to their facilities, but only people to engage in recreational gambling. Yet according to empirically based research from Canada, most of the money wagered in Alberta comes out of the pockets of a tiny group of players: 6% of gamblers in Alberta account for 75% of gambling expenditures (Kleiss, 2011). Researchers at the Alberta Gaming Research Institute estimate that gambling contributes to 10–20% of bankruptcies, around 3,000 cases of separation and divorce, and to a huge number of suicides and attempted suicides each year. A harm reduction strategy recommended by these researchers is for gambling cards to be issued with limits. This strategy is used in Norway to effectively control gambling losses.

The *Diagnostic and Statistical Manual of Mental Disorders, Fifth Edition (DSM-5)*, to be published in 2013, is reclassifying pathological gambling which was listed as an impulse-control disorder to an addiction-related disorder. The term pathological gambling will now be called a gambling disorder (American Psychiatric Association [APA], 2011). The criteria for gambling disorder are:

Persistent and recurrent maladaptive gambling behavior as indicated by five (or more) of the following:

1. is preoccupied with gambling (e.g., preoccupied with reliving past gambling experiences, handicapping or planning the next venture, or thinking of ways to get money with which to gamble
2. needs to gamble with increasing amounts of money in order to achieve the desired excitement
3. has repeated unsuccessful efforts to control, cut back, or stop gambling
4. is restless or irritable when attempting to cut down or stop gambling
5. gambles as a way of escaping from problems or of relieving a dysphoric mood (e.g., feelings of helplessness, guilt, anxiety, depression)
6. after losing money gambling, often returns another day to get even ("chasing" one's losses)
7. lies to family members, therapist, or others to conceal the extent of involvement with gambling
8. has jeopardized or lost a significant relationship, job, or educational or career opportunity because of gambling
9. relies on other to provide money to relieve a desperate financial situation caused by gambling (available at http://www.dsm5.org)

The symptoms of this addiction, as certified gambling counselor Jim Thompson indicates (personal communication, 2011), are interwoven with those of all mood-altering substance disorders. The loss of control, the family disintegration, the increased tolerance—the features and the tragedies of one addiction are the features and tragedies of the other.

Unfortunately, despite recognition of this disordered gambling as an addiction, state revenues to finance treatment for people who need help with gambling problems have been reduced considerably as states wrestle to control their budgets (Berzon, 2011). Reductions in New York and Nevada have been the most severe. As a result, only a fraction of the estimated 2.6 million people with such problems receive treatment through state-funded programs.

To understand why some people have so little resistance to the lure of gambling, while most others have no problems with it all, researchers have begun focusing on the biology of gambling addiction and how a situation of risk punctuated by occasional rewards can have such a powerful attraction to many individuals, dulling, in effect, the rational portion of the mind. Researchers are studying human and lower order animal behavior in the laboratory and are looking at the reward center, the pleasure circuit in the brain. What they are finding is that, as with other addictions, dopamine plays a large role in determining susceptibility of some individuals, while for most people the dopamine just makes the games of chance a controllable attraction. Linden (2011) sums up the research. "We know," he writes, "that blunted dopamine function in the human pleasure circuit has been found in both drug addicts and food addicts" (p. 142). In persons with gambling addiction, as Linden further states, the pleasure regions of their brains are less activated by winning than are those of members of the nonaddicted control group. In experiments using video games, however, an increased level of activation of the dopamine pleasure circuit was noted in men but not in women. Such research helps us understand what clinical evidence shows—that some people get really excited when they indulge in these fast-action games, and that such individuals are susceptible to becoming addicted.

Knowledge of the biological drives helps explain some of the irrational behavior that accompanies gambling. Periodically newspaper stories describe heart-wrenching situations in which parents leave their infants in the car while they "pop in" someplace to gamble and the infants are either rescued when the police are called or found dead. The following news headlines describe other regrettable situations:

> "Gambling addiction derails lives" (Petroski, 2009)
> "Gambling and workplace embezzlement on the rise" (Delaughter, 2010)
> "Man strangles wife over $20K gambling debt" (Solomon, 2011)

Problem gambling is a category generally used in research studies to indicate that the person has developed some family, work, or financial problems because of gambling but hasn't met all the criteria of a full-blown addiction. This term is also applied to adolescents, regardless of their scores on various assessment instruments because of a reluctance to label them "pathological" while in the midst of fluctuating and experimental behavior patterns. In the future, fortunately, the term "pathological" will no longer be used (Skolnik, 2011). Many times, the general term *problem gamblers* is used inclusively to indicate both problem gamblers and those who are addicted.

Perhaps even more than with other addictions, gambling strikes at families, places of employment, and friends. As compulsive gamblers begin to lose and lose big, forever chasing that original high of an early win, they sell or pawn possessions, plead for loans from all around them, and steal the rest. Embezzlement is a big problem among addicted gamblers, often as an act of desperation. Where gambling is widely available, gambling problems are often experienced by older community members. A New Jersey poll, for example, found that 23% of older persons who gambled had gambling disorders (Fairleigh Dickinson University, 2006).

Michael Burke, who practiced law for 25 years in Michigan, shared his story with a reporter from the *Detroit Free Press,* telling of how he went from being nominated as citizen of the year for his community service work to stealing money from his clients' trust accounts (Newman, 2008). In recovery from alcoholism, he actively attended AA meetings. "The difference between gambling and drinking," he said, "is that gambling is a very easy addiction to hide. ... When I sat in front of that slot machine, it was my vodka. It was my medication. ... When I was away from the slot machine, I was terrified" (p. 3). Burke ended up serving time in prison; today he spends his time speaking to community organizations, social workers, and anyone else who will listen about the grip of gambling addiction.

DEMOGRPAPHIC FACTORS

Research shows that Native Americans, when compared to non-Native populations, are four to six times more likely to have a diagnosable gambling addiction problem (Momper & Dennis, 2010). In a comparison of Native American and Latino military veterans in the Southwest, Westermeyer (2005) found the rate of gambling addiction of Native American veterans at 9–10% was more than double that of Latino veterans. His explanation was that where gambling is widely available as on reservations, a higher percentage of the population will develop problems. Female veterans had the same rate as male veterans, an unexpected finding.

In a national survey conducted by Welte and colleagues (2011), the researchers found that Whites and Blacks had a low rate of gambling involvement but that Blacks had a high rate of gambling problems when they did gamble. More Native Americans gambled than did any other group, and they had the most gambling problems. Asians were least likely to be involved in gambling, but Asians who did engage in gambling often developed serious problems.

Casinos actively target some racial and ethnic groups, especially Chinese Americans who have strong gambling traditions. Skolnik (2011) provides extensive documentation of how shuttle vans and buses stream daily into Chinatowns all over the United States for transport to casinos, and the casinos advertise actively in Chinese American communities. Another group of people that the gambling establishments are increasingly looking to for profits are women.

GENDER DIFFERENCES

Spouse and child abuse often occur in homes in which there are serious gambling problems. Women are often the victims in these situations. Muelleman, DenOtter, Wadman, Tran, and Anderson (2002) interviewed 61 women who were treated in an Omaha emergency room for partner violence. Disproportionately high numbers of these women compared to other female patients in the emergency room reported gambling problems in their partners. The combination of drinking and gambling was even more closely associated with problem gambling.

Epidemiological surveys consistently report that men are much more likely to be pathological or problem gamblers than are women (Petry, Stinson, & Grant, 2005). Approximately one-third of persons addicted to gambling are female. In treatment programs, females are underrepresented; they are only 2–4% of the population of GA (APA, 2000). But the research also shows that men and women gamble at almost the same rate in areas where slot machines or video poker machines are located in the community, such as in stores and restaurants (Davis, 2009).

Most of the state problem gambling helplines, however, report that the percentage of women seeking help with gambling problems has been increasing. As early as 1993, an Alberta, Canada, study concluded that women are the gender group most likely to experience gambling problems in the future as more of them engage in this pastime. Research shows that the rates of women who developed problems with gambling increased rapidly after 1990 (Davis, 2009).

In contrast to women, who are inclined to gamble as an escape mechanism, even to the point of feeling "hypnotized" or in a "trance" (personal communication, September 2000), men are more likely to be characterized as "action" gamblers; that is, gambling for men begins early in life; can be a long-term problem for 10 to 30 years; focuses on "skill" games, such as poker, horses, and sports; and provides action as well as escape (Arizona Council on Compulsive Gambling, 2000). Another motivation for women to gamble compulsively may be the social stereotypes and economic limitations that are still imposed on many of them. Female gamblers coming into treatment after "losing it all" on slot machines often report they took up gambling as an escape from unhappy lives (Beaucar, 1999). Results from an online survey of over 250 women in recovery from compulsive gambling reveal that many women reported getting started with gambling because of a sense of boredom. The majority of respondents to the survey reported severe family problems in their backgrounds or emptiness in their lives (Davis & Avery, 2004).

In a poster session at the conference of the American Society of Addiction Medicine, Silvia Martins reported the results of her comparative study of 78 men and 78 women in treatment in Brazil for gambling problems. She found that men more often than women had substance-related problems, an earlier onset of gambling, and involvement in Gamblers Anonymous. Significantly more women had made a suicide attempt and were seriously depressed than were the men (Evans, 2004).

An innovative program to counsel women with gambling problems is conducted at the Coffee Creek Correctional Facility in Oregon. An Oregon survey found that 20–30% of the female inmates have gambling problems and that 86% of the problem gamblers admitted to crimes, including prostitution, to pay off debts. Before their release, the women with gambling problems are provided with an intervention by a team of certified problem gambling counselors. Treatment includes weekly 90-minute group sessions (Oregon Department of Corrections, 2004).

CO-OCCURRENCE OF OTHER PROBLEMS

In their review of recent empirically based literature, Bellegarde and Potenza (2010) found a correlation between substance use disorders and disordered gambling, also that persons with antisocial personality, mood disorders, and other psychiatric disorders had disproportionately high rates of gambling problems. Schizophrenia has also been shown to render some individuals vulnerable to gambling addiction. Desai and Potenza (2009), in their inter-views with a sample of 337 patients diagnosed with and in outpatient treat-ment for schizophrenia/schizoaffective disorder, found that these patients may be at a particularly high risk for gambling disorders. Although 46% did not gamble, and around a third were recreational gamblers, over 9% were classified as problem gamblers, and almost 10% as having serious addiction problems. This is compared to around 1% of the total population that have a serious gambling disorder. Desai and Potenza explain the high susceptibility of persons with a schizophrenia-related disorder to gambling addiction as due to the cognitive disturbances and lack of impulse control which characterizes both disorders. We also know that nicotine addiction is common to both schizophrenia and gambling disorders.

Pietrzak and Petry (2005) evaluated 237 clients with gambling addiction problems who were in an outpatient substance abuse treatment program. They found that over 16% met the diagnosable criteria for antisocial person-ality disorder. They also found that within this subgroup, the clients were pre-dominantly male and had more severe drug problems than did other clients. Similarly, a study of over 2,000 Canadian high school students found that youth with gambling problems reported more negative life events than other students and had less mature coping styles in dealing with problems (Bergevin, Gupta, Derevensky, & Kaufman, 2006).

According to the National Council on Problem Gambling, the suicide rate for persons with gambling disorders is higher than for persons with any other addictive disorder (National Gambling Impact Study Commission, 1999). At a minimum, shame, guilt, and remorse are constant companions related to huge losses, making it even more difficult for a problem gambler to seek help (see Davis, 2009).

TREATMENT PROVISIONS

Because most health insurers and managed care providers do not reimburse for addictive gambling treatment, and because persons with gambling problems are often in no position to provide payment themselves, treatment provisions are sparse (Robb, 2005). State helplines now operate in only 35 of the 48 states that have some form of legalized gambling. About half of these states support some type of treatment with public funding, but the level of funding is minis-cule compared to the amount of income the states receive from gambling enter-prises. In 2006, less than $36 million a year was spent by the government and gambling industry for education and treatment of gambling problems (Peterson, 2006). This is out of the $20 billion or so in tax revenues states col-lected from gambling in the same year. Given this state of affairs and the reluc-tance of compulsive gamblers to seek out specialized help for the problem, it is important that helping professionals become knowledgeable about compulsive gambling and screen for this as well as other addictions in their clientele.

The addiction/disease model is the conceptual basis for using treatment methods established in substance abuse treatment centers and slightly modifying them for persons with gambling disorders. Because many of the *DSM* criteria for addiction are indicative of physiological dependence, treatment professionals must rely on strategies to treat other addictive disorders, including the prescription for abstinence. Treatment centers for persons with gambling problems commonly refer clients to the Twelve-Step group Gamblers Anonymous (GA) for additional help. Of the GA Twenty Questions (based on the *DSM* criteria), most compulsive gamblers will answer yes to at least seven (GA, 1999). As is customary in Twelve-Step groups, the final "diagnosis" is left up to the person to decide for himself or herself. Members of the group acknowledge their state of being powerless over their urges to gamble. When one has reached that point, abstinence from all gambling is deemed a necessary goal.

The GA program acknowledges Alcoholics Anonymous (AA) as a guide and foundation and utilizes the same Twelve Steps of recovery and the same organizational principles. The only requirement for membership is "a desire to stop gambling" (GA, 2000, p. 2). GA is run entirely by recovering compulsive gamblers who volunteer their time to be sponsors, chair meetings, arrange for meeting places, secure GA literature, and respond to requests for help day and night. GA meetings can be found by calling the state problem gambling helpline, looking in the yellow pages of the phone book for a local contact number, or accessing the Gamblers Anonymous International Service Office online at http://gamblersanonymous.org/. For family members, Gam-Anon can be extremely helpful; information and listings are available at this same site.

Even normal people sometimes register increased blood flow to the same region of the brain affected by cocaine use, according to a widely publicized study from Massachusetts General Hospital (Wen, 2001). What differentiates these normal euphoric states from those in compulsive gamblers is probably a matter of intensity or the contrast between this high and the person's normal state of mind. The anticipation of winning triggers a dopamine rush (Johnson, 2004). The impulsive part of the brain then drives the behaviors as judgment is put to sleep. Curiously, as has been widely reported in the media, patients with Parkinson's disease who were medicated with dopamine-boosting drugs developed many addictions, including to food, sex, and gambling (Ubelacker, 2005). The reason for this unexpected reaction that occurs in a minority of patients is attributed to a mania-like state that is sometimes induced by the medications and associated with high-risk–taking behavior. Problems with gambling and spending have also developed with ropinirole (Requip), the widely advertised medicine prescribed for people with restless legs syndrome.

Box 5.1 presents the portrait of a compulsive gambler, the tale of a highly respected African American youth worker who ended up losing control over his gambling bets.

The addiction/disease model is bolstered by research indicating that dopamine and serotonin brain functions are altered in persons with gambling addiction (APA, 2000). Consistent with the disease model, experiments with medications such as serotonin reuptake inhibitors to treat compulsive gamblers are currently under way. A promising area of research involves the use

| Box 5.1 | REFLECTIONS OF A MALE COMPULSIVE GAMBLER |

Gambling is a source of entertainment for many people in the world today. With the increase in casino outlets, as well as the influx of offshore gambling available through the Internet, Americans can bet on practically anything imaginable. For many of these people, gambling does not present a serious problem (to borrow a phrase from the Iowa lottery advertisements). However, for a small percentage statistically, gambling can become a serious addiction. I, myself, fall into this category. For nearly 5 years, I was addicted to sports betting. Although I have not related this story to anyone previous to now, I hope that it will shed some light on the subject of compulsive gambling.

In Omaha, I worked with behaviorally impaired adolescent boys. In this field, the support staff is dominated by males who usually have a background that includes, at some level, participation in competitive sports. Such men are supposedly more equipped to deal with the rough nature of the clients involved. It was in this environment that I was first introduced to the world of sports gambling. The circumstances were that a colleague would pick up a bookie sheet (a form containing a list of all of the available games that could be bet on during a particular day) and bring it to work. Initially, I only looked at college and professional football games that were played on the weekends. This, however, did not produce the winnings I imagined. My gambling eventually became daily, if not twice daily. I went from betting on weekend games to daily gambling on basketball, baseball, and hockey contests, and as this happened over a period of 5 years, I lost thousands and thousands of dollars and numerous other possessions. Before it was over, I nearly lost my family.

In the beginning, my wife had participated in the "fun" of gambling. The very occasional wins were encouraging and euphoric. As I began to delve deeper into the gambling, however, she bored of the losses and began to see less pleasure in the hobby. In fact, she encouraged me to get out of the practice. But by then the compulsion for me was too great.

As I began to spend a large portion of my salary on gambling, this created a strain on the marriage. My wife is a certified teacher and makes a considerable amount of money working with students who are emotionally and behaviorally impaired in a private educational setting. In one year, according to our tax returns, we earned nearly $50,000, and yet we had to file bankruptcy not once, but twice! The bank account just could not keep up with the mounting losses.

My ambition in life became the same as other compulsive gamblers, to get my money back. I was always going to win big. Be persistent—that's the thought pattern of a compulsive gambler.

Located in the heart of the Black neighborhood, these bookie joints are packed with people; one would be hard pressed to find a larger crowd at any of the local churches in the area. There is a distinct culture among the gamblers who socialize while discussing the odds. What's the hot pick of the day? Who's guaranteed to lose? And so forth. There isn't a Caucasian in sight. If one does appear, there is hushed silence until the stranger is identified as a regular or knows someone present. The staff of about six or seven (two remain behind a counter while the others mingle in the crowd) write tickets and collect the money. In the particular neighborhood I frequented, there is no credit issued when you place a bet. The fee is paid up front; this eliminates the need for henchmen to go collecting on outstanding bets. After placing the bet, my favorite thing to do would be to watch the game.

For the casual gambler, the win or loss would put an end to the matter for the day. However, for the compulsive gambler, this is just the beginning. As soon as the outcome was determined—win or lose—I would be racing out of the door to place my afternoon bet. If I lost, I was going to get it back. If I won, I was going to make more money to make up for past losses. It was an endless cycle. The excitement of the game was my driving force. Often after losing in the afternoon games on the weekend, I would rush off to the bookie joint with the intention of betting on the night games. If the place was closed, I would be extremely upset that I had arrived late. Dejected, I would return home to consider my losses and to plot for the next day's picks. It was very difficult to suppress my emotional roller coaster from my wife and children. My mood swings were apparent. As things began to collapse around me, I sought help from the local Gamblers Anonymous group. After a short period of sobriety, though, I returned to gambling. Gambling had simply become a part of my life that I couldn't avoid. It was entrenched in my social contacts and easily accessible, making it very difficult for me to stop. For me, a geographical relocation was the answer.

Living in Omaha had become increasingly difficult. The embarrassment that accompanies the life of a compulsive gambler, although at times nonexistent to the gambler, is always apparent to their family. Evictions, repossessions, cut-off utilities, collection agencies, and the daily concern of paying the bills are real to the family. My wife was advocating for a "new life," one she believed could exist without gambling. She was also at a point in her career that she needed a change, and she began to explore graduate programs. I, myself, had not completed a bachelor's degree, earning only 40 credits in my many attempts at college, and I began to contemplate seriously a return to school.

It is frequently said in Alcoholics Anonymous that a geographical relocation is not a cure. As one adolescent treatment counselor once said, "A drunk in South Dakota can as easily be a drunk in Iowa." This is probably true for all addictions. However, in my case, the geographical relocation was my answer for a cure. I have not gambled in 4 years, have completed my BA in History, and am one semester away from my MA in sports psychology. My relationship with my wife has improved dramatically, and I now have time to spend with my kids. I can watch sports without feeling the need to bet on who will win—with the exception of an occasional $1 bet with my 11-year-old son.

Personal communication; July 27, 2000. The author, due to the nature of his work, wishes to remain anonymous.

of naltrexone hydrochloride (Naltrexone), an opioid antagonist that has been used to block the excitement of addictive drugs such as alcohol, cocaine, and heroin. In tightly controlled studies, Naltrexone has been found to mitigate the frequent and intense cravings experienced by compulsive gamblers who are receiving treatment (Grant & Kim, 2002). Drugs such as lithium carbonate (Lithium), used to treat concurrent bipolar disorder, have also been found to decrease compulsive gambling (Rogers & Goodwin, 2005).

INTERNET GAMBLING

A look at the prevalence studies of the upcoming generation, the first generation brought up with sanctioned gaming, indicates that adolescents are at particular risk of developing problems with gambling. About 1 in 20 youths are considered to be addicted to Internet gambling (*Christian Science Monitor,* 2006). National surveys on gambling in youth are scarce. One exception is the NIAAA-funded research conducted by Welte, Barnes, and colleagues (2011) at the Research Institute on Addictions. In their national telephone survey of thousands of respondents, the goal of which was to determine the prevalence of gambling activities across the lifespan, the investigators found that the diagnosable rate for the 14–17-year-old age group was low. On the basis of standard *DSM IV* criteria, the pathological gambling rate was only 1.7%, but it rose to 3.4% for young adults age 18–19. On the basis of gambling frequency, however, the rates were considerably higher. Over the past year, 18% of youths age 16–18 gambled over 52 times. Interestingly, these youths are practically all male; women get their start much later, according to Welte and colleagues. Another key finding was that the lower the socioeconomic class, the higher the rate of gambling. Because age restrictions are in place at casinos, one would think that much of this youthful gambling activity takes place on the Internet. Video games involving gambling are especially appealing to young males.

Internet gambling is the fastest growing segment of the gambling market. Today, 2.5 million Americans of all ages play online poker and bet $30 million annually (Vardi, 2010). To enhance the ability of prosecutors to go after the online gaming industry, Congress passed the Unlawful Internet Gambling Enforcement Act, which was signed into law in October 2006 but did not come into full effect until 2010 (Vardi, 2010). This law prohibits the use of credit cards and bank transfers by U.S. citizens in transactions for unlawful gambling. The passage of the law was surprising, as argued in an earlier editorial in the *Christian Science Monitor* (2006), because of the millions of dollars paid in campaign donations to political candidates for federal office by the casino and gambling industry. Despite the law, the lure of lottery and other gambling industry revenues for state governments has led to laxity in enforcement of laws against youth gambling at all levels of law enforcement.

The new forms of gambling such as video lottery terminals in community settings, Internet gambling, and community casinos take a huge toll socially because of the negative impact such compulsive behavior has on relationships, not even considering the money involved. In its power to captivate and hook the player, video poker is said to be the "crack cocaine of gambling." A large majority of people in treatment for gambling disorders are heavy video poker players (Robb, 2005). A Canadian national survey found the prevalence of gambling problems, which average 2% nationally, was higher in regions of the country with video lottery terminals (Cox, Yu, Afifi, & Ladouceur, 2005).

A special attraction to women, according to an article in *Time* magazine, is betting on the Internet. Doing so, women who are new to gambling can find online teaching tools (Russo, 2005). They also can disguise their gender and take notes on plays. At Empire Poker.com, women have gone from 3% of players 3 years ago to 20% today. In addition, many women are now playing on all-female sites.

MOTIVATIONAL AND COGNITIVE THERAPY

It is important to remember that with gambling, the main source of information about the behavior is self-reporting by the gamblers themselves. There is no urine drug screen or even the typical patterns of withdrawal symptoms that might confirm recent use or severity of the problem. Many sources in the literature focus on the gambler's seemingly amazing ability to cover his or her tracks and to deceive close friends and relatives for a long time. And if there is a relapse, it might not be apparent right away.

Actually, that the counselor would need to take the client's word that he or she is improving, is one of several reasons that the motivational enhancement model with its focus on trust in conjunction with a strengths perspective with its principle of "suspension of disbelief" (Saleebey, 2009) is a perfect fit for treatment of gambling addiction. And as Hodgins and Diskin (2008) indicate, on the same point, motivational interviewing is the gambling addiction counselor's treatment of choice because of the client's sense of urgency to straighten out his or her finances and relationships, and because natural recovery from this form of addiction so often happens with individuals who have really suffered from their gambling problems. The promotion of self-recovery should therefore be highly effective with this population, as Hodgins and Diskin suggest.

"I'm wondering how gambling activities or the gambling of someone in your family may play into what we've been discussing. Could I ask you a few questions?" This is one of the exploratory-type questions that might be asked in a typical counseling session. Drawing on principles from a solution-focused rather than problem-focused approach, the therapist would assist the client in defining his or her own conception of the situation and goals for change. Specific techniques to find out what is important to the client might involve asking for exceptions to the bad decisions made recently and about times when he or she successfully coped with difficulties in life. Strengths and past successes in dealing with problems of living would be highlighted instead of deficits or pathology. Among the sample questions a motivational therapist might ask are:

- What are good things about your gambling? What are some of the negatives?
- (following a brief assessment) Did someone else say anything about your gambling?

- Would you like to see your score for gambling addiction compared to others to see the norms?
- What would be the benefits if your gambling stayed the same? What would be the benefits of making a change? (adapted loosely from Hodgins and Diskin, 2008, p. 124)

Hodgins and Diskin describe their own preliminary research into treatment effectiveness. Using media sources, they recruited a sample of around 80 people who had concerns about their gambling. Respondents were divided into two groups—one to receive the complete motivational intervention, and a second to receive only a brief intervention based on a workbook. When the participants were interviewed 24 months later, 54% from the longer-term treatment group reported they were abstinent compared to 25% from the control group. Significantly, the most severely addicted individuals benefited a great deal more from the extensive motivational intervention than they did from the workbook session; the low severity participants, however, did just as well with the brief treatment intervention.

In contrast to a traditional model based on breaking denial, a perspective based on strengths is especially relevant when working with clients such as compulsive gamblers who, typically, are plagued with guilt feelings, having thrown so much of their and others' earnings away. If they do not feel intimidated and defensive by a confrontational therapist, they likely will welcome the opportunity to talk openly and honestly. To the extent that there is resistance, a motivational interviewing model or a solution-focused therapy model interprets this as a natural product of a confrontational environment, which serves only to bring forth attitudes of resistance (see Lee, 2011; Miller, Forcehimes, & Zweben, 2011). Interviewing strategies that engage the person in formulating his or her own goals for change and be congruent with the client's process of change are preferred. The therapeutic alliance is crucial; the strengths-oriented therapist works in collaboration with the client in selecting and working on goals, even if these goals don't initially include giving up gambling. The motivational therapist, moreover, joins allies in the community who can offer family, legal, and/or spiritual support to help the individual cease from further compulsive and high-risk behavior.

Programs for youth founded on a harm reduction approach inform youth of the risks associated with gambling and help them develop the critical thinking skills needed to remain in control of the situation. Harm reduction programs need to identify and work with at-risk youth, including communities and/or schools where gambling problems proliferate (Messerlian, Derevensky, & Gupta, 2005). Given that age of onset is a significant risk factor, the availability of gambling activities needs to be drastically restricted. Parents must be educated about marketing ploys that are used to appeal to youth, and they must monitor their children's Internet activity.

FURTHER WORK IN THE COGNITIVE AREA

In this section, we focus on interventions directed at the cognitive distortions that are associated with problem gambling, distortions that get the individuals who are playing the slots and casting their bets, for example, to keep investing more and more in a clearly losing enterprise. The strengths-based therapist will strive to reinforce the client's movement in a direction of positive but more realistic thinking while helping the client to eliminate counterproductive and superstitious beliefs. We get a glimpse of the thinking process associated with the act of gambling as expressed by one individual:

> The lady on the other side of me swears, and I glance at her machine just in time to see that she'd "missed" the white 7's by one. "They look like they're ready to come," I say. "Just teasing me," she replies. (anonymous contribution, GA website, 2000)

This excerpt illustrates two cognitive distortions common among compulsive gamblers: giving the slot machine human qualities and misunderstanding the nature of randomness.

In fact, problem gamblers, as sociologist Bo Bernhard tells us, "have unique cognitive distortions" whereby the cause of their problems is also the cure of their problems. Unlike substance misusers, gamblers are notorious for "chasing their losses" or doubling their bets from one day to the next. "By asking the right questions, clinicians can strengthen their safety nets and start catching problem gamblers" (quoted by Robb, 2005, p. 22).

Cognitive interventions are based on the premises that thoughts influence emotions and behaviors and that distorted and maladaptive thoughts can be brought to awareness and changed, resulting in behavior change. Especially relevant to gambling, cognitive therapies emphasize the development of irrational cognitive schemas in response to early and repeated wins. These include illusions of control, biased thinking, the attribution of human qualities to gambling devices, and erroneous beliefs about the nature of randomness (Blaszczynski, 2000; Turner, 2000).

The most common errors include a false belief concerning the phenomenon of randomness, the extent to which outcomes could be predicted ("I've put so much money into this machine, it's bound to hit!"), and personification of the gambling machines or dice (giving them human qualities, as in "Come on baby!"). Gender comparisons in one small study of 20 revealed that women were more likely than men to personify slot machines (Delfabbro & Winefield, 2000). Other common distortions include (a) *the illusion of control,* such as believing that conditions such as the choice of a dealer or a certain table, choosing a favorite slot machine, and walking into a casino through a certain entrance will enhance success; (b) *flexible attributions,* such as transforming losses into near wins, predicting a loss after it has happened by identifying "fluke" events that contribute to the loss; (c) *the availability bias*, where a person judges an event's probability based on the sounds of winning around him or memories of highly publicized winners; and (d) *the fixation on absolute frequency*, where the gambler measures the absolute frequency of wins (they remember how many times they win but not the relative frequency in that they lose more than they win) (Davis, 2009, p. 115).

The role of the therapist in cognitive therapy is to help clients identify the irrational thoughts that influence them to continue to gamble, bring those thoughts to conscious awareness, monitor them, and replace them with rational and more adaptive thoughts (Davis, 2009).

Here are several questions that can serve to aid professional counselors in identifying gambling problems once clients are willing to proceed (derived from the criteria for diagnosis of pathological gambling from the *DSM–TR–IV*) (APA, 2000).

1. Have you ever borrowed money to gamble or cover lost money?
2. Have you ever thought you might have a gambling problem or been told that you might?
3. Have you ever been untruthful about the extent of your gambling or hidden it from others?
4. Have you ever tried to stop or cut back on how much or how often you gamble?

Answering yes to any of these questions suggests a problem and indicates that further exploration of the issue would be useful.

From a harm reduction perspective, here are several practical suggestions that may help the individual with gambling problems avoid further problems:

1. Carry the minimum amount of money needed for that day.
2. Turn personal checks and credit cards over to the care of someone else.
3. Require an additional signature to withdraw money from a bank.
4. Voluntarily request to be banned from frequented casinos and card rooms.
5. Avoid the company of other gamblers.
6. Avoid going to places where gambling is allowed.

As noted by Blanco and colleagues (2000), "After more than 10,000 years of the existence of the disorder, the field of pathological gambling research and treatment is still in its infancy" (p. 406). The bulk of the research has been done on male, not female, problem gamblers. Nevertheless, women with gambling problems (sometimes reported in the news in cases of embezzlement) are becoming more visible to the general public, and research studies have begun to focus on women and report gender differences that should be of interest to practitioners.

Policies of harm reduction for the community would minimize accessibility, disallow drinking at casinos, produce ads on TV about the risks of gambling addiction, and provide for treatment at little or no cost. All levels of government have a responsibility to develop policies and regulations to restrict the most addictive forms of gambling—those that carry high social costs, such as video gambling machines.

The opposite of harm reduction is seen in strategies used by gambling establishments to get people to relinquish their money. Because casinos depend on enticing new gamblers to spend large sums of money, and approximately 30–40% of their revenues come from persons with addiction problems, casino executives use marketing techniques based on principles of psychology. As described in an article in the *U.S. News & World Report,* slot machines are designed so that players push buttons; this speeds up the process and leaves little time to think. To manipulate bettors, casino owners offer free drinks, use fake money such as chips so that there is less reluctance to bet, use artificial lighting to mask the passage of time, have an absence of clocks, and even crowd slot machines to make it seem like there is a multitude of winners (Clark, 2005). A more subtle strategy is to design the slot machine so that gamblers think they have suffered near misses. Another favorite technique is to inflate the patron's win ratio during the free introduction games. It is well known that if a first-time player loses, he or she probably won't come back. But if the player wins some money, the thrill is often fantastic, and he or she might forever after be "chasing that first high." As with any addiction, the cues set off the brain's juices and the craving intensifies.

The casino industry hires psychologists as consultants to help them boost their winnings while keeping customers coming back. The "near misses" strategy comes straight from brain research conducted by psychologists. This research, as summarized by Linden (2011), reveals that the pleasure circuit of the brain is significantly activated by near misses on a video slot machine. Subjects indicated a strong willingness to continue to play when they had experienced the near misses. Manufacturers of video slot machines, as Linden states, are well aware of this effect, and some have programmed their devices accordingly.

Some researchers have noted that casinos have jingling bells and whining sirens that sound when there is a significant win. These sounds then become associated with the high of gambling. People get conditioned to the sound of bells, smell of cigarette smoke, and the glamour and glitz of the casino (Robb, 2005). People fast become addicted to the sensations of gambling just as the state becomes addicted to the enormous revenues generated.

CANADIAN RESEARCH

To determine scientifically the proportion of revenue derived from problem as opposed to recreational gamblers, Canadian social scientists Williams and Wood (2004) paid a random sample of gamblers to fill out a diary of their gambling practices—wins, losses, and which gambling devices they used. These researchers found that, on average, 35% of Ontario gambling revenue came from mild and severe problem gamblers (as determined by analysis of the diary entries) and that males, Native populations, low-income persons, and single people were disproportionately represented. With gaming machines, the addiction rate is much higher; 62% of the revenue from this fast-paced equipment is derived from problem gamblers. Citing research that shows that casinos breed crime in the areas surrounding their location, Williams and Wood concluded that the social costs well outweighed the benefits.

An excellent source of information, *Casino State: Legalized Gambling in Canada*, edited by Cosgrave and Klassen (2009), presents an overview of the economics of gambling in Canada while summarizing basic facts gleaned from this anthology. A unique aspect of Canadian gambling is that, in contrast to Australia, the United States, and the United Kingdom, legal gambling in Canada is totally under government control. The government not only takes on the roles of regulator and tax collector, but provides the development and marketing as well. In his review of this book, Taylor (2011) makes a strong recommendation that Canada convene a national commission to review the consequences of its two-decade explosion in gambling. These two features of Canadian gambling—government ownership and lack of comprehensive government review—present a ripe opportunity for academic research, Taylor notes.

Facts as revealed in *Casino State* are that: more than 40,000 Canadians are employed in the gambling industry; between 3 and 6% of government revenues are now derived from gambling; 4.8% of the gamblers in Ontario account for 36% of revenues, and 80% of the patrons at the Windsor (Ontario) Casino, which is located across the border from Detroit, are American, so much of the social costs are incurred on the U.S. side of the border. The links between crime and gambling are seen in the documented associations of this form of entertainment with fraud, domestic disputes, and suicide. Illegal gambling has flourished as well as this pastime has become more socially acceptable.

Does putting benefits and costs under the same governmental roof generate a conflict of interest? This question is asked rhetorically by Taylor (2011). We can end this discussion by asking the same thing about arrangements by U.S. state governments. We can take into consideration connections between the casino industry and politicians, city mayors, and even directors of charity organizations who have become dependent on these sources of revenue.

In summary, there is a need for more research on gambling disorders, including which individuals are susceptible and which practices by the casinos and other gambling businesses are harmful to the public. More extensive research is also needed on racial/ethnic and gender differences in susceptibility to disordered gambling. Research is also needed on the impact of gambling availability to the community. Such research would draw comparisons of impacts on communities with gambling establishments versus comparable communities without them. Chhabra, Lutz, and Gonnerman (2005) conducted such a study for the Iowa legislative council. Their research showed that crime rates were higher in casino than control counties. There was also an association between gambling availability and rate of bankruptcy.

EATING DISORDERS

"Addicted to Starvation" (Gura, 2008)
  "Heroin vs. Häagen-Dazs: What Food Addiction Looks Like in the Brain" (Szalavitz, 2011)
    "Risk for Alcoholism Linked to Risk for Obesity" (*Science Daily*, 2010)

So state the headlines in *Scientific American, Time* Magazine and *Science Daily* respectively. Although researchers have known for several years that a person's chances of developing an eating disorder depend partly on genetics, it is only in recent years that science has given some credence to earlier anecdotal reports. Much of the new research is being funded by NIAAA and NIDA. So today, researchers are probing the brains of women with anorexia, and their work is painting a picture of anorexia as a multifaceted brain disorder (Gura, 2008), one with a strong hereditary component (Grucza, Krueger, et al., 2010).

Research findings from two earlier studies identified several core traits that appeared to be linked to genes associated with anorexia and bulimia. The first study (Bulik et al., 2005) identified concern over mistakes (perfectionism), early age of menstruation, and food-related obsessions that were linked to bulimia. Anxiety and obsessiveness were more closely linked to anorexia. The second of the two articles (Bacanu et al., 2005) linked behavioral characteristics to genetic information. The bulimia cohort showed more linkage with their identified characteristics and certain chromosomes than did the anorexic cohort. One of the chromosomes is also linked to obesity. Anorexia was linked, as predicted, with the obsessiveness trait. The significance of these papers is in revealing genetic differences between these two eating disorders. In her review of the recent research on women who were in recovery from anorexia, Gura (2008) described findings that indicated these women, when compared to normal women, responded with blunted affect to sweet tastes and to games involving winning prizes. These traits coincide with high anxiety and perfectionism. Genes, according to Gura, are part but not all of the story. Female hormones that come into play following puberty apparently have something to do with the development of anorexia, as do personal experiences. Moreover, extreme dieting can put young athletes at risk of what Gura calls a dangerous addiction to undereating. There is a great deal more we need to know, however, about the biology of this and other eating disorders. The research is in its infancy. Compulsive overeating is a little easier to understand than is a behavior such as deliberate self-starvation. Far more people suffer from compulsive bingeing on food (in the absence of bulimia) than from anorexia and bulimia combined (Mellace, 2010). To help us learn more about the neurology of compulsive overeating, Gearhardt, Yokum, and colleagues (2011) devised an experimental situation to measure brain responses to images of food and to eating food that most would find delicious. The study included 48 normal and addiction-prone women as determined by *DSM* criteria. The scientists found that when viewing images of ice cream, the women who had three or more symptoms of food addiction—for example, frequently worrying about overeating, eating to the point of feeling sick, and having difficulty functioning due to attempts to control overeating or overeating itself—showed more brain activity in the amygdala and other regions involved with pleasure and craving than did women who had one or no such symptoms. The significance of this finding is that these are the same regions of the brain that light up in drug addicts who are shown images of drug paraphernalia or drugs.

When the addiction-prone women actually were consuming a milkshake that was given to them, their response was rather blunted; it was the *anticipation* of the taste or of the eating that evoked the strong response. Food cravings, therefore, could be expected to be high, and viewing advertisements for sweet and high-fat food would act as a trigger to generate such cravings. Such hyper-palatable foods, as Grucza and colleagues (2010) suggest, appeal to people with addictive tendencies

In their research that analyzed sets of data on alcoholism, Grucza and his team found that women with alcoholism in their family backgrounds were 49% more likely than other women to be obese. This shows a possible link between substance misuse and eating disorders, One problem with his research, however, is that obese people do not necessarily have eating disorders, and many with eating disorders are of normal weight.

The National Center on Addiction and Substance Abuse (CASA) at Columbia University (2003) in its report *Food for Thought* presented the first comprehensive examination of the link between substance abuse and eating. Researchers found that about half of individuals with eating disorders misuse alcohol or other drugs, compared to 9% of the general population. At the same time, up to 35% of substance misusers have eating disorders, compared to 3% of the population. The risk factors for substance misuse and eating disorders are relatively the same and include common brain chemistry, the impact of stress and trauma, and susceptibility to messages from advertising and entertainment media.

More recent research also confirmed the link between eating and substance use disorders (SAMHSA, 2011). Gadalla and Piran (2007), for example, found that women with either a substance use disorder or an eating disorder were more than four times as likely to develop the *other* disorder as were women who had neither disorder. And Piran and Robinson (2006) found that as eating disorders became more severe, the number of different substances used increased. Severe binge eating disorder was consistently associated with alcohol use, and attempts to lose weight by purging (with or without binge eating) were associated with the stimulant/amphetamine and sleeping pill misuse.

The environment can exacerbate any latent addictive tendencies that exist. Some girls and women are especially influenced by advertisements, according to the CASA (2003) report. Women's magazines contain more than 10 times the ads and articles related to losing weight than do men's magazines. The average female model appearing in these magazines is 5 feet, 11 inches tall and weighs 117 pounds, which is far thinner than the average woman.

Other findings of interest from the CASA report are

- Middle school girls (10–14-year-olds) who diet more than once a week are nearly four times more likely than other girls to become smokers.
- Girls with eating disorder symptoms are almost four times more likely to use inhalants and cocaine.
- Hispanic girls are slightly more likely than Caucasian girls and significantly more likely than African American girls to report having fasted for 24 hours or more and having vomited or taken laxatives to lose weight.
- As many as 1 million men and boys suffer from eating disorders; gay and bisexual males are at increased risk of such disorders (p. 2).

Anorexia nervosa is characterized by a refusal to maintain a minimally normal body weight, even to the extent of self-starvation. One of the most perplexing aspects of anorexia is that its victims continue to think they are fat despite ribs and other bones showing through their skin. Bulimia, in contrast, is characterized by repeated episodes of binge eating followed by vomiting, abusing laxatives or diuretics, taking enemas, or exercising obsessively to get rid of the food or burn the calories (NIMH, 2011). Some anorexics binge and then purge to maintain their low weight. Family, friends, and physicians often have difficulty detecting bulimia in someone they know because the person's body weight may be normal. Dentists may detect telltale tooth enamel damage in bulimics who regularly vomit.

As with anorexia, bulimia typically begins in adolescence. More than 90% of these two eating disorders occurs in females. A surprise finding with regard to bulimia in men is that when it does exist, its medical consequences are severe and its occurrence is related to low levels of the male hormone testosterone ("Anorexia, Bulimia, Found More Dangerous in Men," 2000). A more recent study, for the first time using nationally representative data (extracted from national mental health survey data) on eating disorders, found that 0.9% of women and 0.3% of men said they had had or were still suffering from anorexia nervosa, whereas for bulimia, the figures were 1.5% of women and 0.5% of men. The prevalence of binge eating disorder is 3.5% of women and 2.0% of men (Hudson, Hiripi, Pope, & Kessler, 2007).

SAMHSA (2011) provides a breakdown from recent research on the co-occurrence of eating and other mental health disorders. Bulimia had the highest rate of this co-occurrence across the board. Binge eating came next with a co-occurrence of 65% for anxiety disorders, 46% for mood disorders, and 43% with impulse disorders (e.g., ADHD).

DSM DIAGNOSES

The *Diagnostic and Statistical Manual of Mental Disorders, Text Revision* (*DSM–IV–TR*) (APA, 2000) describes three diagnostic categories for eating disorders: anorexia nervosa, bulimia nervosa, and eating disorder not otherwise specified. Mental health professionals have criticized the exclusion of compulsive eating or binge eating as a standard disorder. This form of eating disorder is the one most clearly related to other substance use disorders. When we talk of food addiction, we are talking of this kind of out-of-control bingeing. Binge eating can lead to morbid obesity and therefore is life threatening as well as a cause of much personal stigmatizing, ridicule, and grief. Most people who request treatment for eating disorders have problems with compulsive overeating. Yet the fact that this disorder is included in the *DSM-IV-TR* only as a possible symptom of other behavioral health disorders means that it is not taken seriously and that the risks are not seen as profound (Mellace, 2010). This diagnosis also means that insurance reimbursement has not been forthcoming.

Fortunately, these days are coming to an end. The *DSM-5* is being revamped to finally include binge-eating disorder as a recognized mental disorder, as a stand-alone diagnosis. Additional proposed changes are that the new *DSM* will have a broader definition for anorexia and eliminate the weight requirement and the absence-of-menstruation as a criterion for anorexia nervosa. SAMHSA (2011) provides the following list of the new criteria, which is adapted from the *DSM-5* website at http://www.dsm5.org:

Proposed *DSM-5* Diagnostic Criteria for Binge Eating Disorder

A. Recurrent episodes of binge eating. An episode of binge eating is characterized by both of the following:
    1. Eating, in a discrete period of time (for example, within any 2-hour period), an amount of food that is definitely larger than most people would eat in a similar period of time under similar circumstances
    2. A sense of lack of control over eating during the episode (for example, a feeling that one cannot stop eating or control what or how much one is eating)
B. The binge eating episodes are associated with three (or more) of the following:
    1. Eating much more rapidly than normal
    2. Eating until feeling uncomfortably full
    3. Eating large amounts of food when not feeling physically hungry
    4. Eating alone because of being embarrassed by how much one is eating
    5. Feeling disgusted with oneself, depressed, or very guilty afterwards
C. Marked distress regarding binge eating is present.
D. The binge eating occurs, on average, at least once a week for three months.
E. The binge eating is not associated with the recurrent use of inappropriate compensatory behavior (for example, purging) and does not occur exclusively during the course of Anorexia Nervosa, Bulimia Nervosa, or Avoidant/ Restrictive Food Intake Disorder. (p. 4)

ANOREXIA NERVOSA

The *DSM–IV–TR* (APA, 2000) includes in its diagnostic criteria for anorexia the following description that will also be included in the new *DSM-5*: physical signs and symptoms, many of which are attributable to starvation: cold intolerance, lethargy, constipation, and the appearance of lanugo, or fine body hair. Mortality from anorexia is over 10%, with death most commonly resulting from starvation, suicide, or electrolyte imbalance. The average lifetime duration for anorexia is only 1.7 years (Hudson et al., 2007).

People with eating disorders share certain personality traits: low self-esteem, clinical depression (which often runs in their families), and an inability to handle stress (NIMH, 2011). The high anxiety and social phobias associated with anorexia most commonly begin in early childhood before the onset of an eating disorder. This was the conclusion of an extensive study of more than 500 persons with eating disorders conducted by Kaye, Bulik, Thornton, Barbarich, and Masters (2004). Perfectionism is pronounced among people with anorexia, as is a likelihood of athletic involvement (especially gymnastics and ballet). An empirical study by Ringham and colleagues (2006) based on assessments of dozens of ballet dancers found that 83% had eating disorders. Binge eating and purging were common; the study participants' profiles were similar to a comparison group of women with eating disorders. The following description found in *Dancing on My Grave,* by prominent ballerina Gelsey Kirkland (1986), is typical of the body obsession that afflicts many ballet dancers:

> I sat in bed at night and thumbed through fashion magazines, memorizing faces and figures. This began as a game I played to beat insomnia. I wanted to be a gorgeous someone, anyone other than who I was. I clung irrationally to the idea that my body had been the cause of all my problems. I prayed for a perfect body. Please, God, make me into the doll that everyone wants me to be. I stared at pictures of models and imagined that I might wake up in the morning as one of them. I wanted to free myself from the weight of artistic choice.... Starvation and poisoning (from cocaine) were not excesses, but measures taken to stay within the norm, both professionally and aesthetically. (pp. 205–209)

A social work major shares this account:

> When I got down to 70 pounds, I could not do most of the activities that I did before. I knew that I had a problem. My physical appearance was frightening. I was a human skeleton. The color of my face was gone. My hair was falling out. It took a lot of energy for me to do anything. I knew that I had to eat but I just could not eat. I was afraid to eat. If I ate, I thought something bad might happen to me. I knew if I did not eat something bad might happen. I was stuck and I did not know what to do. I told my friend's mother what I was doing. We had a long talk. I was afraid to go to my mother about my problem. My friend's mother told me if I get any worse she will tell my mother. I began to eat again gradually but I became very nauseous but I still ate because I knew that I had to. I ate small portions and little things at first. I am not cured completely of this disorder. When I become stressed, nervous, or

mad, I cannot eat. I try, but nothing seems to go down. I can finally talk to my mother about my disorder but not very well. She still does not understand why I did what I did. I do not understand entirely why I did what I did. I know what I did had to do with major emotional and internal problems with people that I have been dealing with from my childhood and adolescence. (personal communication, December 2004)

Note the theme of compulsive ritualism in these personal descriptions. The connection between anorexia and obsessive-compulsive disorder (OCD) is more than coincidental; it is real (see Kaye, Bulik, et al., 2004). Before reviewing the research findings on this connection, let us examine the psychiatric criteria provided by the APA (2000). Under the heading OCD, obsessions and compulsions are defined separately; the person with OCD may have obsessions, compulsions, or both. *Obsessions* are defined as recurrent and persistent thoughts or urges that are experienced as intrusive and that cause marked anxiety or distress. *Compulsions* are the repetitive behaviors (compulsive hand washing, checking, etc.) often associated in the public mind with OCD. These rituals may be associated unrealistically with some dreaded event. Scientists, according to Johnson (2004), have found biochemical similarities between people with eating disorders and OCD. The similarities relate to abnormal serotonin levels. NIMH researchers have found that many patients with bulimia have OCD as severe as patients with a primary diagnosis of OCD. A genetic trait is likely a key factor in the development of eating disorders, according to psychiatric research at the University of Iowa (Gura, 2008; Kaye et al., 2004). Interestingly, OCD, like anorexia, often begins in adolescence.

The problem of severe hoarding has received much attention in the media and has been overdramatized on TV programs (Van Pelt, 2011). Originally classified by the *DSM* as a symptom of OCD, researchers now see this compulsive behavior as a separate disorder. See the section on shopping and spending addiction later on in this chapter.

The Mind and the Brain (Schwartz and Begley, 2003) and *Train Your Mind, Train Your Brain* (Begley, 2007) describe Schwartz's clinical research and treatment approach with obsessive-compulsive, "brain-locked" patients. Such patients are typically overwhelmed by insistent, repetitive urges to wash their hands of feared germs or ward off uncomfortable feelings of danger by persistently checking stoves and lights. As explained by Schwartz and Begley, OCD can be considered brain lock because four key structures of the brain become locked together, and messages from the front part of the brain get stuck there, in the locked region. This leads to a maddening repetition of unwanted thoughts. Schwartz's Relabel, Reattribute, Refocus, Revalue (4Rs) approach to treating OCD is a cognitive approach that relies on constant self-talk; this method differs dramatically from a sometimes disturbing behavioral exposure approach in which the client is exposed to the source of the fear (e.g., snakes). Central to the 4Rs method is the theme of *neuroplasticity*. This theme asserts that the human brain's neurons have the ability to form new brain connections, stimulate new pathways through the cortex, and assume new roles and functions. Brain scans reveal marked improvement in brain functioning through cognitive exercises that are performed by patients with OCD.

The form that the obsession takes—the relentless intrusiveness—is universal in persons with OCD, according to Begley (2007), but the content of the obsessions varies with the individual and culture. The fact that eating disorders occur primarily in cultures or subcultures that value thinness and in which there is exposure to media images of Barbie doll–shaped bodies attests to the significance of culture in determining the expression of a mental disorder. Thus, mothers concerned about their own weight typically will transmit the cultural prescription to their daughters. Writing in the journal *Pediatrics,* Davison and Birch (2001), however, reported that girls who were constantly dieting said it was their father's opinion that was goading them on.

Research by Feldman and Meyer (2007) found in a fairly large sample of lesbians and bisexual males no evidence of anorexia but that the rates for other eating disorders were about the same as those of heterosexual women. The most striking finding was that approximately 15% of the gay and bisexual males had at least some of the symptoms of eating disorders, mostly those that involved binge eating. An earlier study on the subject found that for anorexia in men, homosexuality is a risk factor due to a stress on slimness in the gay community (CASA, 2003). Sometimes when anorexia is the primary disorder, it is accompanied by uncontrollable bingeing that follows the period of starvation. Brandi Halverson shares her story:

> I have suffered from both anorexia and bulimia for the last 10 years. It took many forms: from limiting calories to about 700–1,000 a day; to bingeing and purging; to bingeing and exercising; to bingeing and restricting. My symptoms have occurred on and off over the last 10 years, but most recently, I have had bulimia to such a degree that I sought inpatient hospitalization for it.
>
> While my eating disorder began in junior high at about age 14, I lived in denial of its gravity until much later and after many years of suffering alone. I, like many who struggle with eating disorders, am very good at hiding it and denying it, not only to others, but to myself. I would tell myself I was okay. But no matter what I looked like, or what behavior I chose, I was still suffering. This is an important thing about people with eating disorders—what the person looks like on the outside does not give a clear idea of how much the person is suffering on the inside.
>
> Over and over again I have thought about what might have caused my eating disorder. I don't know anyone else in my family who has or had an eating disorder, so I couldn't conclude "it ran in the family." I guess to some degree it was a combination of things. I felt pressure from society (primarily in the form of media) to be thin. I lacked self-esteem, didn't know how to handle stress or express my emotions and feelings, had a terrible drive for perfection, and desperately feared failure. (personal communication; May 1, 2006)

The form of anorexia to which the writer is referring is sometimes called the binge–purge anorexia. In contrast to bulimia, this disorder is characterized by severe underweight.

A frightening development is occurring on the Internet, where some 500 websites that deal with anorexia are often pro-ana (*ana* is short for anorexia) and pro-mia (*mia* is short for bulimia). Girls share tips for losing weight on these sites and provide a positive image of these disorders that is enticing (Van Pelt, 2009). Research on girls who view these websites as compared to a control group shows that the viewers had lower social self-esteem and negative affect.

Extreme dieting has become a way of life for young women in much of Asia. In Hong Kong, for example, women try to keep their weight under 100 pounds regardless of their height (Chu, 2010). In Asian countries, many women want to stay skinny without exercising to avoid become muscular, which is considered a masculine trait. In Hong Kong, more than 100 patients were hospitalized for eating disorders over the past 10 years. In Korea, thinness for women is so important that women's career opportunities depend on her weight; being overweight is associated with laziness, according to Chu. Compared to the U.S., obesity in Korea and China is not much of a problem, but the extreme obsession with thinness is.

BULIMIA NERVOSA

NIMH (2011) lists the following symptoms of bulimia nervosa:

- Recurrent episodes of binge eating, characterized by eating an excessive amount of food within a discrete period of time and by a sense of lack of control over eating during the episode
- Recurrent inappropriate compensatory behavior in order to prevent weight gain, such as self-induced vomiting or misuse of laxatives, diuretics, enemas, or other medications (purging); fasting; or excessive exercise
- The binge-eating and purging cycle happens anywhere from several times a week to many times a day (p. 4)

Many physical conditions result from the purging aspect of the illness, including electrolyte imbalances, gastrointestinal problems, and oral and tooth-related problems.

Other symptoms include:

- Chronically inflamed and sore throat
- Swollen glands in the neck and below the jaw
- Worn tooth enamel and increasingly sensitive and decaying teeth as a result of exposure to stomach acids
- Gastroesophageal reflux disorder (GERD)
- Intestinal distress and irritation from laxative abuse
- Severe dehydration from purging of fluids (p. 4)

Women who develop bulimia may have a history of weight gain or come from a family in which overweight is a problem. In terms of personality, these women usually are extraverted, have voracious appetites, and experience episodes of binge eating. Unlike anorexia, which is not necessarily a chronic illness, the average lifetime duration for bulimia and binge-eating disorder is more than 8 years (Hudson et al., 2007). In her fascinating book *Wasted: A Memoir of Anorexia and Bulimia,* Hornbacher (1998), who suffered from both problems, differentiates bulimia from anorexia:

> Bulimia, of course, gives in to the temptations of the flesh, while anorexia is anointed, is a complete removal of the bearer from the material realm. Bulimia hearkens back to the hedonistic Roman days of pleasure and feast, anorexia to the medieval age of bodily mortification and voluntary famine. (p. 153)

Because of the considerable co-occurrence of bulimia and substance use disorders (especially alcoholism and cocaine addiction), substance abuse counselors should always assess for eating disorders in their clients and clients' family members. Whether it is cutting a line of cocaine or a slab of cake, the symptomology of eating disorders and substance misuse is strikingly similar. Both disorders are long-term, chronically relapsing, and life threatening.

In common with women who have substance use disorders, women diagnosed with bulimia are several times more likely to have been sexually abused as children than women who do not suffer from this disorder. Sanci, Olsson, and colleagues (2008) found a close association between a background of early childhood sexual abuse and later development of bulimia. Perhaps because compulsive eating stimulates a rise in the levels of mood enhancers in the brain, food can serve as a drug to curb the feelings of shame, self-disgust, and depression that often accompany compulsive eating problems. This urge to binge may explain why sexual abuse is more predictive of bulimic than of anorexic symptoms. Gerke, Mazzeo, and Kliewer (2006) found that depression was a mediating factor in the incidence of bulimia in girls who had been emotionally abused in childhood.

COMPULSIVE OVEREATERS

And what about those individuals who binge eat but do not throw up? Compulsive overeating, in the absence of bulimia, is a grave health risk because persons with this disorder sometimes gain hundreds of pounds. As mentioned previously, surveys show binge eating to be the most prevalent eating disorder.

Binge-eating disorder is characterized by NIMH (2011) as recurrent binge-eating episodes during which "a person loses control over his or her eating" (p. 3). Unlike bulimia, binge-eating episodes are not followed by purging, excessive exercise, or fasting. People with binge-eating disorder, therefore, are often overweight. They also are inclined to experience guilt, shame, and/or distress about the binge eating, which can lead to more binge eating. People with this disorder often have coexisting psychological illnesses including anxiety, depression, and personality disorders. Treatment options for binge eating disorder, according to the NIMH website, are similar to those used to treat bulimia. Fluoxetine (Prozac) and other antidepressants may reduce binge-eating episodes and help alleviate depression in some patients.

From the British medical journal *Lancet* ("Scientists Find Link," 2001) came a groundbreaking study on the neurological characteristics of morbidly obese people. A lack of dopamine receptors in the brains of morbidly obese people has been documented through the use of PET scans. The greater the weight of the person, the lower his or her level of receptors. Later brain research has confirmed this finding (Wang, Volkow, Thanos, & Fowler, 2004; Linden, 2011).

An interesting case history is provided by Spencer (2006) in an article in the *Wall Street Journal*. The case is of Patty Worrells, a compulsive overeater who would binge on cookies and ice cream at 3 A.M. Her weight shot up to 265 pounds. She found her solution in gastric-bypass surgery and her weight dropped 134 pounds. A new craving consumed her, however—drinking 15 to 20 shots of tequila at a time. "I drank the way I ate," she said (p. 3). Part of the reason she took to alcohol so quickly is that bypass surgery enables the alcohol to pass more rapidly into the patient's system. Alcoholism also ran in her family, so the tendency was there. Paradoxically, Worrells worked as a director of a substance abuse clinic. Finally, she got help through attending Twelve-Step meetings. What this case history shows, according to the article, is the probability of a neurological and psychological basis for compulsive eating that is similar to other addictions. At the Betty Ford Center, around 25% of alcoholics switch to a new addictive drug or behavior after treatment. And roughly 20% of gastric-bypass surgery patients acquire new addictive behaviors.

Because it is directly linked with severe obesity and other damaging health problems, compulsive overeating is a major public health concern. Fortunately, now that the *DSM-5* is recognizing binge eating disorder as a separate mental disorder, and the risks of morbid obesity have become much more widely publicized, we can expect the federal government to do more in terms of data gathering and the funding of treatment and prevention research efforts in the future.

Treatment Interventions

Although more research is needed on the subject, most reports in the literature indicate that a combination of pharmaceutical and cognitive interventions is the preferred treatment for disordered eating. Selective serotonin-enhancing antidepressants have been found helpful for bulimia (Vastag, 2001). Ondansetron (Zofran), a drug normally given to cancer patients and others to prevent nausea and vomiting, also works for bulimia. A recent report in the *Journal of the American Medical Association* concerned research on the topic of medication versus psychotherapy in cases of bulimia. The review of all the major databases of empirically based comparative research showed that cognitive behavioral therapy (CBT) was more effective than antidepressant medications in reducing the average number of binge eating episodes for most individuals. The research also showed that patients receiving CBT were more likely to go into remission from purging and demonstrate improvements in associated eating disorder pathology than were patients treated with antidepressants alone (Mitka, 2011). The research on combination treatments of CBT plus medication failed to meet the standard of empirically based research as determined by the authors of the study, so no definitive conclusions could be drawn.

For patients with anorexia, the risk of dying is 18 times that of others of similar age in the general population (NIMH, 2011). For hospitalized patients, the major focus is weight restoration. Once weight is restored to a level that is no longer life threatening, much of the patient's depression lifts and thinking becomes more rational.

Some research suggests that the use of medications, such as antidepressants, antipsychotics, or mood stabilizers, may be modestly effective in treating patients with anorexia by helping to resolve mood and anxiety symptoms that often co-exist with anorexia (NIMH, 2011). No medication has been shown to be effective during the critical first phase of restoring a patient to healthy weight, probably because of the effect of starvation on the body and brain. It stands to reason, however, because of the close connection between OCD and anorexia, that the same drug would be effective for both. Anorexia, unlike the addictions, is not about getting high or dulling the senses. Anorexia has more in common with compulsive, ritualistic behavior based on a delusion; it is related more to avoidance of pain than to pleasure. Probably for this reason, Johnson (2004) recommends medical management as a useful adjunct to cognitive-behavioral treatment of anorexia. The favored treatment for eating disorders is multimodal intervention; this includes, in addition to medication to reduce the obsessiveness, education on the basics of good nutrition, consciousness raising concerning media images and unhealthy thinking, and intensive psychotherapy in cases of a history of early childhood sexual abuse. The most promising results can be expected from interventions that are empirically tested as the field of treating eating disorders moves rapidly forward. Multidisciplinary team approaches including physicians, nutritionists, and social workers are considered essential when treating these complex disorders (Pomeroy & Browning, 2008). A focus on symptom management is not enough; attention must also be paid to the underlying etiology or biopsychosocial factors that accompany this disorder.

Research indicates the efficacy of various types of group work with individuals who have eating disorders (NIMH, 2011). The effectiveness of group treatment for women who have eating problems stems from the tremendous sharing and support that come from a positive collective experience. Women's relationships become more open through the process of mutual decision making and feedback. Women can develop a sense of self in relation to others in a group setting. When a woman begins to build trust and empathy with others, she also may begin to look at herself differently as she learns to value herself for who she is rather than to judge herself in terms of her body size.

The primary challenge in eating disorders treatment compared to other substance abuse treatment is that unlike alcohol and cocaine, food is required for life and so treatment protocols that involve a commitment to abstinence

Box 5.2	In Treatment for Bulimia: Two Contrasting Programs

The first of the two programs I will be discussing is Iowa City's Eating Disorder Program. This program is a cognitive-behavioral–based program, which is among the top ways to treat eating disorders. This program is highly structured—every single day was the same, with every hour from 7 A.M. to 10 P.M. filled. The patients have no control over what they eat, or how much. Diet is taken care of by a nutritionist based on what the patient weighs.

The group sessions that I attended were cognitively based, providing an exploration of the patients' core beliefs, schemas, cognitive distortions, how the distortions might have been acquired, and rational ways to perceive disturbing situations. Patients met with a psychiatrist and other doctors every day to discuss any concerns or effects of medication that might have been prescribed. Patients were required to keep daily journals, to map out the day including downtime, and to report events that were anxiety provoking. The program was built on a level system; one could progress upward based on cooperative behavior, improvement in thinking, and normalization of weight. The eating disorder patients were on the same wing as the mood disorder track and we did not relate well to each other. Iowa City's program is entirely focused only on the eating disorder and "fixing" the coping mechanisms. The counselors do not address issues that may have provoked needing the coping mechanisms in the first place. In fact, when the doctors were confronted with a patient who had already done work in the area of sexual abuse treatment and wanted to do more within the context of eating disorder treatment, they told her to focus only on the eating disorder and not to talk about the other issues, even in a group setting. This is

(successful with alcohol and cocaine) do not apply. Individuals with eating problems must learn moderation. As many cigarette smokers are aware, it is often easier to give up a substance altogether than to practice moderation. A second factor affecting recovery evaluation and outcomes is the difficulty in defining or detecting a relapse of abnormal eating patterns. The binge–purge cycle, in fact, can go on for years undetected by family members as well as practitioners. Third, as every adolescent girl or woman knows, society rewards slimness far more than it rewards moderation.

Cognitive-behavioral therapy is the treatment of choice in addressing the complex interplay of irrational thoughts that plague persons with eating disorders (NIMH, 2001). The focus in this type of therapy is on the beliefs that power the distorted thoughts and the behavior based on those thoughts. Women's pursuit of the cultural stereotype of feminine beauty is characterized by thoughts such as "If I am fat, then I am ugly, and if I am ugly, I am unlovable," and "Because I have eaten three cookies, I might as well eat the whole box." These self-defeating thoughts and the resultant actions serve to sabotage women's lives and perpetuate the eating disorder.

like saying that the patient needed to forget about what caused the disorder in the first place, or at least heavily contributed. The approach in Iowa is strictly cognitive, in a limited sense of the term.

Because I needed to work on past issues, I was sent from there to a program at Two Rivers Psychiatric Hospital in Kansas City, Missouri, and specifically to their trauma-based program. Eating disorders there are classified as related to trauma disorders, such as childhood sexual abuse, rape, or domestic violence. These experiences are highly correlated to eating disorders and the development of other addictive problems. This program's primary focus is to stabilize behavior by teaching different healthy coping skills, providing a safe environment for healing and growth, and promoting improvements in balanced living.

This program also provided groups, including anger management, body awareness, cognitive therapy, crafts, contours drawing, and psychodrama. This program, like that of Iowa City, provides a psychiatrist who comes every day to discuss individual concerns and medication. Each patient also has a therapist who he or she meets with daily for an hour. This time provides the opportunity to discuss any personal questions or issues with group counselors on the unit and go a little more in depth with the complex issues concerning the past.

Two Rivers' treatment model is much more effective for the treatment of an individual with a dual diagnosis of an eating disorder and a history of sexual trauma. Iowa City's eating disorders program is nationally acclaimed for their treatment of such disorders, so when I found that they had no support for, or even acknowledgment of, sexual trauma given the high correlation between the two, I was both surprised and upset.

Anonymous (Personal communication; October 14, 2004).

The skilled cognitive-behavioral therapist will selectively address issues of weight phobia, distorted perceptions of the body, fear of loss of control about eating and weight, and negative self-perceptions. Cognitive-behavioral treatment is generally focused on the present, serving to identify the immediate behavioral consequences of irrational beliefs (Fossati et al., 2004).

Affective (feeling) work is critical in the treatment of persons with eating disorders. Inability to cope with early painful experiences such as rape, incest, an alcoholic family, and transitions from childhood to adolescence or from adolescence to adulthood are common underlying dynamics.

Because these persons may lack experience in identifying and expressing a broad range of feelings, counseling sessions initially may be oriented toward the examination of affective states, with counselors modeling appropriate affect for given situations and practicing healthy modes of expression.

Family therapy, particularly for the adolescent girl, is an important first step in educating the family as a whole to the apparently strange behaviors of individuals with eating disorders. Parents need to be encouraged to set clear boundaries about appropriate behaviors, such as insisting on some financial contribution to the household grocery bill from a daughter who regularly binges on "family" food. Family members also need a forum in which they can express the feelings of frustration, confusion, and mistrust that accompany life with a person who has an eating disorder, as well as a place to begin to explore the familial issues that encourage the dysfunctional eating.

For clients who are overweight, strict dieting is discouraged because for many people, food deprivation sets the stage for a starvation–binge-eating cycle. In addition, counting calories reinforces food and eating obsessiveness. Used alone or with other treatments, cognitive-behavioral therapy results in significant reductions in behavior associated with disordered eating (Fossati et al., 2004). Such therapy principally addresses irrational thought patterns, such as distorted body image, low self-esteem, perfectionism, and preoccupation with the body and with gaining weight.

A student in van Wormer's addiction course whose bulimia was out of control went to one treatment center with a strong cognitive base and then was transferred to another clinic for intensive trauma work. In Box 5.2, the student compares and contrasts the two treatment experiences.

A controversial cognitive-based "love-them-back-to-health" approach was taken by Peggy Claude-Pierre, a woman with no training who became a celebrity following extensive television coverage of her work in saving the lives of starving anorexics. Overwhelmingly positive media coverage earned Claude-Pierre's clinic a worldwide reputation before allegations of force-feeding and patients being held against their will ultimately led to the British Columbia clinic losing its license (McLintock, 2002). TV coverage touted a miracle cure of loving anorexic children into normal eating patterns. Medical supervision was not provided due to Claude-Pierre's belief that she had the secret formula for saving these girls' lives. Although the television broadcasts focused on the seeming miracle cures with this approach, this form of cultlike and non-medically based treatment is ill advised.

When reputable professionals, using evidence-based techniques, train patients to control rigid thought patterns, including identifying and handling feelings and assertiveness, there can be lifelong benefits. The insights and tools acquired for dealing with an eating disorder can empower a person to overcome a variety of challenges and obstacles in day-to-day life. Johnson (2004) recommends dialectical behavior therapy, an approach that is similar to motivational interviewing because it starts with acceptance of the client where the client is. This approach can be used in conjunction with medication for maximum results.

Nicole, age 20, described her battle overcoming bulimia:

> I weighed 160 pounds in college and got into exercising so I could wear cute shorts. It was normal dieting at the beginning; I got my weight down to 120. The social pressures were enormous, so many compliments, "What are you doing to look so good?" I ate it up.... In reality, I was a mess, addicted to laxatives, surviving on apples and graham crackers. After taking 10 laxatives, I landed in the hospital and from there into counseling. Social workers and a dietician worked with me and my family.

In family counseling we explored family secrets; we were a "perfect" family. Rules were set for us—not talking about food. I learned about underlying factors in my behavior—my feelings, the "voice in my head."

Later I joined a support group. An educator showed us magazine clippings and explained how distorted our images are. We made lists: Ten things to do instead of bingeing. My list said: "Go for a walk, call a friend or my sister, pray." I deal with my problem every single day. (personal communication; February 7, 1997)

Gradually, most adolescents with an eating disorder mature out of it, but nobody knows why. Perhaps the recovery is related to the maturity of the brain and the stabilizing of hormones. Still, there is no cure for this disorder. As Hornbacher (1998) describes her state of recovery in her memoir, aptly entitled *Wasted,* "It is not a sudden leap from sick to well. It is a slow, strange meander from sick to mostly well" (p. 284).

Sometimes, however, in middle age, the old imposter returns. In Philadelphia, the Renfrew Center Foundation reported a jump in admission of women older than 35 (Newsome, 2005). To meet the need, the center has set up an outpatient recovery group for over-30s. These women deal with issues related to family responsibilities and aging. The health risks of eating disorders to mature women, such as bone fractures, demand specialized attention as well.

Because a similar problem in men—based on obsession over the way their bodies look—has been largely ignored, male-oriented treatments are scarce (Holm, 2006). Although some men with eating disorders have a kind of fat phobia and become emaciated, it is the impetus to have a muscular build that creates the greatest risk for men in terms of compulsive dieting. Boys who think they are too small are at a greater risk for using steroids or other dangerous drugs to increase muscle mass (NIMH, 2011). Bodybuilders seeking physical perfection may watch every ounce of food they eat, gorge on protein, weigh themselves throughout the day, and devote hours every day to lifting weights. *Muscle dysmorphia* is the psychiatric term for this disorder. Sufferers commonly take steroids (see Chapter 6). The good news, according to Holm (2006) is that antidepressants in conjunction with counseling can control this behavior. The bad news is that only a few will seek help, and for those who do, treatment centers for males are hard to find.

Overeaters Anonymous (OA) is the self-help group for individuals who seek group support for eating problems. The beauty of OA is that it is ubiquitous in the United States, is free, can be attended as needed, and is open to all who desire to stop eating compulsively. Founded by a woman who was attending a GA meeting in 1958 with a friend when the similarity between her problem with compulsive overeating and the attenders' problems with gambling were remarkably similar. This history is described on the OA website (http://www.oa.org). We also learn on this website that today OA, a Twelve-Step program, now has approximately 6,500 meeting groups in more than 75 countries throughout the world, for a membership of over 54,000. There are also online group meetings. OA members do not all have one specific and common substance or attribute that causes cravings. Because individual members have cravings for different kinds of foods or eating behaviors, each member has to develop his or her own plan of eating. OA uses the concept of abstinence from compulsive eating rather than sobriety. Therefore, a plan of eating ideally would eliminate those foods and/or eating behaviors that cause cravings. Members admit they're powerless over overeating. As stated on the website, "We believe we have a threefold illness—physical, emotional, and spiritual."

A semihumorous encounter with OA is given by Malachy McCourt (2000). Refusing to deal with his alcoholism problem, McCourt decided to do something about his weight problem. After getting poor results with earlier diets, he tried a number of fad diets, among them the protein diet and the grapefruit diet. Weight Watchers costs money, so he decided to go to OA:

> I sat with a group made up almost entirely of women, of every age, and heard horrendous stories of anorexia, bulimia, starvation, bingeing, and other stuff I never knew went on in this prosperous society.... People talked about "stuffing down feelings with food."
>
> [Following a month of meetings, McCourt came to the realization that his problem was alcohol.] So I stopped drinking, just like that—suddenly, precipitately, and perhaps foolishly, but being a man of extremes, it seemed the right thing to do. (pp. 175–176)

SHOPPING OR SPENDING ADDICTION

Compulsive buying disorder is the term used by the foremost medical authority on spending addiction, Donald Black, MD (2007). Characteristics of this disorder are a preoccupation with shopping, prepurchase tension followed by a sense of relief upon making the purchase, associated mood and anxiety disorders, and a family history of similar problems. The lifetime prevalence for this disorder, according to Black, is 5.8% of the U.S. population; the condition affects predominantly women. Koran, Faber, and colleagues (2006) in their survey of over 2,500 persons, on the other hand, found that compulsive spending afflicts men and women at about the same rate. And psychologist April Benson (2008), the author of *To Buy or Not to Buy* agrees that as many men as women can be considered what she calls overshoppers. Because we tend to associate shopping with women, she argues, it is probable that fewer men come forward and admit they have a problem. In addition, there is a difference in the items that men and women with this disorder buy, with men spending much more on fewer purchases, such as cars, boats, and machinery, while women are drawn more to buy items of clothing and household purchases. This means women may spend more time shopping and buying, but the key factor is how much money is spent on products that are not needed.

Binge buyers, according to Koran and colleagues, often end up in financial bankruptcy—and they are suffering from a disease similar to alcoholism.

Certainly the losses and the heartaches can be as great. And there is evidence that the same pleasure circuits of the brain are affected as well. In an article titled "Inside the Shopping Brain," scientist Sharon Begley (2008) describes how when a person sees something desirable, the brain's pleasure-anticipating center, called the nuclear accumbens, turns on. The power of the attraction determines whether you buy. Depending on personality traits, many succumb to sales appeals and buy irrationally. If people feel sad, they might be especially vulnerable to buying what they do not need.

Shopping addiction and spending addiction derive from the same urge to get something for nothing, to drive a hard bargain, and to splurge. They both involve impulsive buying. The consequences of unpaid bills and wrecked families are the same as well. The problem is not the shopping, of course; it is the buying of merchandise that one does not need or even later want that causes a momentary euphoria or high. Svoboda (2010) differentiates three types of compulsive shoppers: emotional shopaholics who shop to banish feelings of low self-esteem or depression, bipolar shopaholics who go on wild spending sprees while in a manic state, and obsessive shopaholics who keep buying replacement items to feel that their possessions are perfect or that they have the perfect set.

Compulsive shopping has long been considered a disorder of impulse control, but it is more than that. Although compulsive shoppers may obsess about material possessions such as clothes, shopping addiction, at its core, is not about materialism or attachment to what consumers buy but rather about a lack of control over buying itself. That this disorder is often devastating in its consequences is revealed in Avis Cardella's 2010 memoir *Spent*. When her mother died, she comforted herself with extravagant shopping sprees. Finally, she was pushed to the brink of financial bankruptcy. Her book chronicles this descent into indebtedness but also her self-education into compulsive spending as a mental disorder, one related to emotional deprivations in childhood. From today's standpoint of self-awareness, Cardella describes her earlier state of mind:

> I was silly enough to believe that buying the right shoes to wear with that Prada dress would cause a chain reaction of events that could change the course of my life.... The only thing that made me feel worse about myself was more shopping. The only thing that made me feel better about myself was more shopping. (p. 160)

The following self-description from a woman who shops uncontrollably and who is also "an exercise freak" and compulsive dieter, is typical:

> I have a disorder in relation to shopping for clothes through mail-order catalogs. I have had it for a good 10 years but it probably started before that. I spend a lot of time every day thinking about, listing, planning for clothes that will go together if I order them and the costs involved and the time spent ordering, looking at the items over and over, etc. I have so many clothes now; I could probably go over a year and never wear the same thing twice. My common sense tells me that I have all I will ever need. My will to say no and not give in doesn't always

work. I went 8 months last year without buying a thing. Then after my mom died, I got depressed and gave in and started buying all over again. This is kind of like alcoholics who can be sober for a period of time and something happens in their lives to drive them to drink again or becomes the excuse they use to drink again. It is the same for me as a shopaholic—I even worked with a company to figure out payments for the credit cards I have with mail-order companies to get them all paid off in 2 years. I was able to stick to the schedule for a while but am floundering again. I finally reached a point where I closed accounts as I paid each one off, and I wrote the mail preference service to have my name taken off mail-order lists. I hope I can be successful, but this is how I see obsessive-compulsive disorder. I have it. Thank God I don't drink, because with my family history I would probably be the all-or-nothing type. (personal communication, January 1999)

Common to both these personal stories is the theme of grief and the drift into compulsive shopping and buying of clothes to relieve emotional distress. Mental health professionals say compulsive shoppers feel euphoric as they buy and spend. The drug-like high following a purchase can lead to kleptomania, particularly if money has run out (O'Leary, 2000). The index of the *DSM–IV–TR* does not include shopping dependence or any other listing for shopping. It does list kleptomania, which it defines as the stealing of items not needed, an act associated with a buildup of tension beforehand and gratification or relief afterward. Kleptomania, according to this source (APA, 2000), "may be associated with compulsive buying" (p. 667). This is not the usual form of shoplifting and is characteristic of only around 5% of the U.S. population. Shopping addiction, or compulsive buying, is not the usual form of shopping, either. As stated on the *DSM-5* website, the diagnosis of kleptomania will remain in the fifth edition as an impulse control disorder, but compulsive buying will not be added as a diagnosable behavioral addiction. As with all commonly occurring addictions, marketers play into people's irrational tendencies to get them to spend their money on unnecessary activities and products. Benson (2008) describes the role of commercialism in the development of this disorder: "We're immersed cradle to grave in buy-messages that, with greater and greater psychological satisfaction, misleadingly associate products we don't need with feeling-states we deeply desire" (p. 3). Consumers with compulsive-buying tendencies often prefer shopping online because the Internet enables them to avoid social interactions and to purchase items with little notice, according to an expert quoted in the *Wall Street Journal* (Dodes, 2008). The same article quotes Benson, who deplores marketing strategies such as a video sales pitch that urges women to "go mental in the shoe department" and states that buying a pair of Christian Louboutin boots is "the best way for relieving holiday tension" (p. A1).

Luvox is the serotonin-enhancing drug previously prescribed by Dr. Black in the course of his experimental research in the department of psychiatry at the University of Iowa. Initially, he reported success in helping compulsive buyers become able to pass through a store without making a purchase or while buying only what they need. Later, when a placebo pill was used, however, the results showed that success was achieved at high levels both with the medication and with the placebo. Black attributed the success to the placebo effect of taking a pill as well as to the behavioral therapy that accompanied the medication. More research is currently under way. Promising results have been found in controlled studies with the antidepressant and serotonin enhancer citalopram (Celexa) (Black, 2007; Stanford School of Medicine, 2003). Because medication is effective in treating this disorder, it may be possible that it has a neurobiological aspect. A further finding—that compulsive shoppers are likely to have more than one psychiatric disorder, and their close relatives are likely to suffer from depression and drug use disorders—also indicates that this disorder has a biological component (Black, 2007).

Although shopping addiction generally does not qualify as a legal defense, one news story reported that a woman who was facing up to 18 months in prison for the theft of $250,000 from her employer to finance her shopping addiction was sentenced to probation. The federal judge ruled that the defendant suffered from diminished mental capacity due to her shopping addiction (O'Connor, 2001).

Treatment recommendations provided by Black (2007) are that people with buying compulsions consider getting marriage counseling, getting financial counseling, and attending Debtors Anonymous (DA) groups. Practical suggestions are that to resist temptation, people get rid of their credit cards and checkbooks, always shop with another person, and find a meaningful leisure time activity.

Debtors Anonymous (DA) groups are being established all over the United States. DA members, like those in AA, first admit they have a problem and then try to fight it by devising a budget they can live with and a realistic repayment plan. According to the DA website,

> Members share their experiences in recovery from compulsive indebtedness on a one-to-one basis, and introduce the newcomer to DA's Twelve Steps of personal recovery.... Today numerous DA members come to us from court programs and counseling services, some arrive voluntarily; others do not.... Our primary purpose is to stay solvent. (Debtors Anonymous, "Information for Helping Professionals," 2011)

Practical tips, described on the website, are to have only one or no credit cards, to shop with cash only, to avoid shopping or buying online, and to exercise when there is an urge to shop. Related to compulsive buying is hoarding, or the refusal to throw anything away. We discussed this phenomenon briefly in relation to OCD because DSM IV classified hoarding as a related disturbance.

HOARDING

Typically, persons with problematic hoarding have basements and rooms in their houses that can look like flea markets or garbage dumps, in its extreme manifestation. This compulsion, which is hard for some to understand, can reach the point where it is impossible for its sufferers to move around in their living space; friends and family members are deeply troubled at this behavior. The A&E TV hit series *Hoarders* has excited public interest in this condition. On the program, the climax generally involves clearing the house or apartment of most of the accumulated items. But experts on hoarding say that quick forced cleanouts often do more harm than good (Webley, 2010). Today across the United States task forces have formed to help deal with an issue that sometimes becomes a public health problem for the community. These groups work with local agencies, including the police and mental health departments, to deal with hoarding therapeutically. Counseling is provided to persons with this compulsion to help motivate them to let go of most of the articles and to participate in the clean-up effort. Expectations are that in the new edition of the DSM—*DSM-5*—the American Psychiatric Association will list hoarding as a separate disorder from OCD. Family therapy and cognitive behavior therapy (CBT) are the interventions recommended for this condition.

LOST IN CYBERSPACE

In a speech given before a course on addiction treatment, a student described her struggles with her 16-year-old son.

> My son is a video game addict. He is hooked on *Call of Duty*, a violent, bloody warfare game. This is one of the most addictive games; it's lifelike and graphic. At first I liked it when he started playing because he was staying at home. A few months later, his teacher told me he had not turned in one assignment; he was failing every class. (His sister's fiancé is hooked on the same game.) My son's girlfriend finally broke up with him because he didn't pay any attention to her. He wouldn't eat or sleep. He can play 10 hours in a row. I took the game away from him until he gets his grades up. (talk given in van Wormer's addiction treatment class; June 29, 2011)

The digital age has sparked increasing debate about the impact of the new technologies—on youths, on families, on marriages. California imposed a ban on selling or renting to minors video games that depict killing, raping, and maiming images of human beings. This law was challenged and made it all the way to the U.S. Supreme Court. In the interests of freedom of speech for children, the court struck the law down. The decision likened the videos to the gruesome stories in Grimm's Fairy Tales. The $25 billion video game industry hailed the ruling as a green light for creative freedom (Morain, 2011).

Perhaps in no country has the teen Internet addiction problem been so great as in South Korea. In a country in which broadband is ubiquitously available, the average high school student plays video games for 23 hours each week ("Addicted? Really?" 2011). The South Korean government estimates that around 210,000 children need treatment for Internet addiction. To meet this need, the government has opened more than 100 clinics for Internet addiction and sponsored an Internet "rescue camp" to remove children from the new technologies. Psychiatrists have received training to help children who are addicted to the Internet (Si-Young, 2006). The Chinese government, coping with a similar problem, takes a different approach; addicted children and adolescents are sent to highly punitive militaristic boot camps ("Addicted? Really?" 2011).

The media today are full of accounts of a new, technology-generated disorder variously called computer addiction, pathological Internet use, or online obsession. There is even a special website for people who fear they are "caught in the net": NetAddictionRecovery.com. The Internet's omnipresent offer of escape from reality, its accessibility, and the opportunity for anonymity can lure otherwise ordinary people to compulsive use (Kershaw, 2005; Turkle, 2011). According to *Internet Addiction* (Young & de Abreu, 2011), typical warning signs of this form of addiction are preoccupation with the Internet; spending increasing amounts of time online; failed attempts to control this compulsion; jeopardized relationships; lying about time spent on the computer, and use as a form of escape from personal problems. How do these heavy Internet users spend their time? Clinical research conducted by the psychologists associated with this website reveals that these users spend their time mainly in chat rooms (a practice that often leads to cyberaffairs) and in playing multiuser dungeon games. The cure offered on one website—HealthyPlace.com—is online therapy at their "Virtual Clinic"!

According to surveys, approximately 8% of web users develop serious problems with their pastime (Stanford School of Medicine, 2006). Online activity is a fairly acceptable way of shifting consciousness: Some users enter a fantasy world where they "bare their souls" to strangers; often, they use fictitious names. Among employers, a concern is that workers are using their office computers to enter chat rooms and pornography sites and to trade stocks. Internet activity at the workplace is increasingly being monitored, often with embarrassing results. Around 30% of companies have terminated employees for inappropriate Internet use, as reported by the Stanford School of Medicine (2006). Consider, for example, this news story:

> **White Plains, New York** (AP)—A man who was fired by IBM for visiting an adult chat room at work is suing the company for $5 million, claiming he is an Internet addict who deserves treatment and sympathy rather than dismissal.
>
> James Pacenza, 58, of Montgomery, says he visits chat rooms to treat traumatic stress incurred in 1969 when he saw his best friend killed during an Army patrol in Vietnam.
>
> In papers filed in federal court in White Plains, Pacenza said the stress caused him to become "a sex addict, and with the development of the Internet, an Internet addict." He claimed protection under the Americans with Disabilities Act. ("Man sues IBM over firing," CNN, 2007).

ARE FACEBOOK AND TEXTING ADDICTIVE?

Excessive texting and social networking among high school students are reaching the point that many of them are working so hard to be perceived as popular that these activities are taking over their lives. Researchers at Case Western Reserve University who surveyed 4,000 Ohio students found that one-fifth of them sent at least 120 text messages a day, one-tenth were on social networks such as Facebook for three hours or more, and 4% did both (Rabin, 2010). The more extreme the time devoted to texting, the more likely the students were involved in high-risk activities such as binge drinking and other drug use. In their book *Internet Addiction*, Young and de Abreu (2011) discuss working with patients who come to therapy and have Internet addiction problems, including obsessive use of social networking technologies. Although Facebook provides a wonderful outlet for individuals who are shy and who otherwise might retreat from communication and making friendships, there is also the risk that they will rely on pseudo-intimate bonds rather than engaging in more well-rounded relationships. Therapists need to monitor these patients' use of the new technologies and help them keep their usage under control. Young and de Abreu see the United States trailing behind countries like Germany that include Internet and media addiction education along with drug and alcohol programming and Spain, which has set up training conferences on healthy Internet use.

Here are some harm reduction strategies for people whose Internet use is out of control: Set a kitchen timer and force yourself to log off when it rings, visit only sites needed for work or for information and don't detour, and cut back mailing list memberships.

Drawing on William Miller's motivational interviewing therapy, Young and de Abreu (2011) provide treatment guidelines to help clients get in touch with the functions that the computer serves for them, that is, the feelings that are attached to this heavy usage. Six common elements of effective therapy described by Miller, Forcehimes, and Zweben (2011) can be incorporated into motivational work with people who need to break away from Internet addiction. These key elements that comprise the acronym FRAMES as adapted to this form of addiction are

F: Feedback to the client of personally relevant information about his or her use of time on the computer and related devices and its consequences.

R: An emphasis on the client's personal responsibility for change—that it is up to the individual to decide and choose what, if anything, to change.

A: Clear advice from the provider recommending behavior change.

M: A menu of options from which to choose, if the client should decide to pursue change.

E: An empathic counseling style that is respectful and supportive, that includes listening to the client's own concerns and perspective.

S: Encouragement of self-efficacy, that the client could be successful in changing. (p. 148)

SEX ADDICTION

When former President Bill Clinton was battling allegations of multiple sexual transgressions, there was speculation that he might be the victim of sex addiction (Hamilton, 2003). Among the arguments put forward were that Clinton was prone to lying, he had an insatiable need to be loved, he grew up in an alcoholic and violent household, he learned to use sex as an escape, and he would risk all for reckless sexual intrigues. No less an addiction expert than Stanton Peele (2011), however, states emphatically that Bill Clinton's behavior does not meet the criteria for a true addiction, nor does the behavior of former New York Representative Anthony Weiner, for the same reason: Both men were able to function normally and successfully carry out their jobs. Their behavior was not all-consuming in their lives.

Other politicians and celebrities, perhaps, would qualify for a diagnosis of addiction. Champion golf player Tiger Woods, for example, was admitted to a treatment center that specialized in sex addiction after he admitted infidelities when at least a dozen women came forward to claim they had had sex with him. Cloud (2011) includes Tiger Woods, actor Charlie Sheen, and Italian Prime Minister Silvio Berlusconi as examples of men whose sexual behavior is likely addictive.

Despite the press and popular book accounts, there is no consensus that sex addiction is a bona fide disorder at all; sex addiction is not recognized by the American Medical Association or its Canadian counterpart, not even as an impulse disorder. Most clinicians, however, agree there is such a thing as pathological sexuality (Miller, 2005). But questions remain about whether this condition should be classified as an impulse-control disorder or as an addictive behavior. For *DSM-5*, plans are underway to introduce hypersexual disorder, which would include problematic, compulsive pornography use (Hilton & Watts, 2011). Criteria for this disorder are spending so much time pursuing intercourse or masturbation as to interfere with one's job or other important activities. Hypersexual disorder will not be considered an addiction because of the lack of available empirical data that could provide a basis for such a diagnosis. In any case, treatment for sex addiction is available at the Promises Treatment Center in Malibu, California; the Sexual Recovery Institute in Los Angeles; and Genesis House Addiction Treatment Center in Palm Beach, Florida. Now that legitimacy has been provided to sex addiction and due to publicity surrounding high profile cases, requests for sex addiction treatment, as Cloud (2011) informs us, are overwhelming addiction treatment centers.

Defining elements of this disorder are secrecy and an escalation that often result in diminished judgment and self-control (Carnes, 2001). Sex addiction takes many forms. Carnes lists the range from obsessions with pornography and masturbation to the more dangerous forms of voyeurism, Cybersex, affairs, sex with strangers, and incest and rape.

Today, there is a sharp escalation of Cybersex, which is sexual experiences that one obtains transmitted via the Internet. According to Claudia Black (2009), an estimated 70% of people in treatment for sex addiction report having problematic online sexual involvement. In the minds of members of Sex Addicts Anonymous, there is no doubt that having "out of bounds" sex is an addiction. Sex addicts in this group may request to have sponsors help them monitor their behavior. Sobriety is defined as remaining "in the bounds." There are thousands of adherents to this self-help movement and over 790 Sex Addicts Anonymous groups established worldwide (Sex Addicts Anonymous, 2007).

The gender breakdown of sex addiction is unclear; it is generally conceived as a predominantly male problem. According to an article in the *Journal of Addictions Nursing,* sex addiction in women is increasingly recognized as a problem, although much of it is misconstrued as normal but sexually provocative behavior (Cyndi, 2004). A pattern of early childhood sexual abuse typically is found in the backgrounds of women who behave in this way. Women who compulsively act out sexually in a compulsive manner are at high risk of contracting diseases and suffering violent victimization.

For both women and men, high-risk behavior typically progresses into riskier behavior. The addictive act, once it has begun, invariably fuels the problem with guilt, shame, lowered self-esteem, and isolation (Miller, 2005). These feelings in turn can lead to seeking a dangerous sexual situation, the thrill of which produces an intense adrenaline rush. The neurobiology of the anticipation of sex for these individuals parallels that of cocaine in its relationship to dopamine (Landau et al., 2008). Who the partner is makes little difference.

Therapists and other experts say the problem usually has its origins in childhood, often in homes plagued by addiction, violence, rigid authoritarianism by the parents, and sexual abuse of the child (Carnes, 2005). Central to this disorder is the inability of the individual to adequately bond or form attachments in intimate relationships. Its origin, as Landau, Garrett, and Webb (2008) suggest, is rooted in attachment disorders in early childhood development.

Treatment consists of psychotherapy, group counseling, prescription medication in some cases, and referral to a self-help group. Therapists need to be knowledgeable about Cybersex, which can involve pornographic sites and chat rooms. What can family members do about the problem? Often embarrassment keeps them from discussing the situation they face when a loved one is consumed with viewing pornographic films or engaging in high-risk sex with strangers. Sometimes the situation comes to light after the husband is fired from his job for viewing pornography on the Internet at work.

Landau and colleagues (2008) have developed a motivational interviewing protocol to help these families. Motivational therapy works well in such situations because it draws on family resilience, and its nonconfrontational nature is helpful to families dealing with the shame of addictive sex. ARISE (A Relational Intervention Sequence for Engagement) is an intervention that trains families to develop motivational strategies to convince reluctant family members to enter therapy for their addiction. This intervention is described in more detail in Chapter 10 on family treatment.

COGNITIVE THERAPY AND THE STRENGTHS PERSPECTIVE

Distortions in thinking are common in all addictions, but they play a special role in the addictions discussed in this chapter. Persons with gambling disorders, as we saw earlier, suffer from denial, superstitions, overconfidence when they are feeling high, and/or an unrealistic sense of power or fate. Anorexics have the delusion that they are fat in conjunction with a phobia about being fat. Compulsive Internet users retreat into a fantasy world, and sex addicts and compulsive spenders keep having lapses in judgment. Common to all these addictions is the tendency toward extreme and immoderate behavior.

As far as the biological side of addiction is concerned, medication may provide a boost and be immensely helpful during the first stages of sobriety. And as for the social aspects, one's social world certainly plays a role in sustaining (or controlling) high-risk behavior. But in the final analysis, the psychological component is primary. The client, in conjuring up his or her inner resources, can channel biological impulses of a destructive sort in productive directions while controlling the social environment through the selection of friends and activities conducive to health.

Although cognitive-behavioral therapy (CBT) can be considered a specialized modality, such as the CBT strategies used in Project MATCH, a formulation that taught specific social skills and stress management techniques (Project MATCH Research Group, 1997), the *cognitive approach,* as the term is used here, is much broader. The focus of clients' thought patterns is characteristic of all the treatment modalities except for aversion treatment. The success of AA, OA, GA, and similar groups is due in part to the help they provide people in clearing up their "stinking thinking," in replacing thoughts conducive to harmful, addictive behavior with healthy, calming slogans, such as "one day at a time" or, as the Norwegians say, paradoxically, "Hurry slowly."

The method known as rational recovery (RR) is built almost exclusively on cognitive work. As Jack Trimpey (personal communication, November 30, 2000) describes it, "Rational recovery is purely a program of planned, permanent abstinence." Trimpey, an alcoholic who disliked AA, originally based RR on rational-emotive behavior therapy (REBT) but then developed an online course for self-development. RR, therefore, no longer holds meetings but offers a for-profit crash course on its website (Volpicelli & Szalavitz, 2000).

Motivational interviewing (MI) is a strategy designed to mobilize a person's own motivation and resources for change (Miller & Rollnick, 2002). MI can be differentiated from other cognitive strategies in that its techniques are derived from principles of social psychology related to getting people to change their behavior. Argumentation and confrontation are avoided in favor of a focus on "building up" rather than "tearing down." Motivational interviewing is both cognitively based and client centered at once. In contrast to MI, rational-emotive behavior therapy (REBT), formulated by Albert Ellis, is adversarial in tone. (The guidebook *Rational-Emotive Therapy with Alcoholics and Substance Abusers* [Ellis, McInerney, Di Giuseppe, & Yeager, 1989] contains one highly useful chapter on unhealthy relationships. See also *Overcoming Destructive Beliefs, Feelings, and Behaviors* [Ellis, 2001].) Like CBT, of which it is a part, REBT concentrates on peoples' current beliefs, attitudes, and statements (van Wormer, 2010). Homework assignments are given, following assessment of the individual's thought patterns, to promote client awareness. Compared with harm reduction strategies, the REBT model is more authoritative; the therapist, in the role of educator, teaches the client what is wrong with his or her thinking. There is no "rolling with resistance" (the theme of motivational enhancement therapy) here in which the therapist avoids confrontation. Much more negative than Ellis's model are the cognitive principles presented by Yochelson and Samenow (1976) and Samenow (1984). Unfortunately, these theories and techniques, which are geared toward criminal thinking and manipulations, are commonly used in correctional addictions programming. In such programming, offenders are required to focus on their wrong-doings, with the goal of instilling self-disgust and a desire to reform their errant ways (see van Wormer, 2010).

Collaboration and choice are hallmarks of MI. Cognitive therapy, as Volpicelli and Szalavitz (2000) indicate, is often used in conjunction with motivational enhancement to help people unlearn what their addictive lifestyle has taught them. As with REBT, the focus is on thoughts (cognitions) and the addictive behaviors associated with them. The motivational therapist's style in MI is demonstrably different from Samenow's therapy style, however, with its emphasis on criminal thinking and harsh confrontation. Instead of telling the client what is wrong, the MI therapist gets the client to achieve insights into his or her problems and to tell the therapist what is wrong (e.g., about continuing to gamble). Then together as a team, the therapist and client collaborate to identify, assess, and plan for situations that may be problematic. These situations include negative emotional states, interpersonal conflict and stress, and social pressures. Having a balanced lifestyle and avoiding excess are emphasized throughout.

How to Elicit Strengths

Self-defeating thoughts are intertwined with low feelings and a sense of fatalism. The leading cause of relapse is depression of this sort: "Who cares? I might as well go back to what I was doing before."

The starting point for behavior change is a collaborative analysis of the thinking and feeling realm. Developed by Aaron Beck in the 1970s, cognitive therapy is based on the theory that the way a person thinks determines how he or she feels and behaves (see Beck, 1991). Underlying most of the problems for which people seek counseling—depression, addiction, anger, violence—is an intensity of feeling or emotional pain. The challenge for the social worker is to help the client separate the feelings from the thoughts and the thoughts from the actions as a first step toward alleviating the pain. The cognitive approach, so often used to break addicts' defenses, such as denial, can be much more effectively directed toward promoting motivation while at the same time building a sense of self-worth and awareness of inner strengths and capabilities.

McQuaide and Ehrenreich (1997) have devised a useful 38-item strengths questionnaire that the client can fill out together with the counselor. The complete questionnaire is provided in their article "Assessing Client Strengths"

(p. 209). Among the agree–disagree items in this clinical instrument are the following: I am a creative person; I have an accurate view of my strengths and weaknesses; I think about my mistakes and learn from them; I have techniques I use to calm myself down when I'm upset. This thoughtful and positive questionnaire can provide a wealth of valuable information.

Anderson, Cowger, and Snively (2009) similarly provide guidelines to help social workers assess individual strengths and resilient capacities through attentive listening to people's personal narratives. Individuals' identities are shaped, they suggest, by the sense they make of their own life stories. The role of the social worker thus becomes to draw out positives embedded in the story. This can be done through asking questions, such as, Is there anything about yourself that you feel you were born with that has helped you in your life? What kinds of things have you done to help others? Anderson and colleagues (2009) have developed sample questions to facilitate the assessment process for situations of oppression. The example provided is an assessment of a woman who has experienced domestic violence. Among questions that might be asked are these: In what ways did you try to reduce the violence? How did you manage to protect other family members from the violence? Are there ways you resisted being socially isolated? (p. 190). The goal of the therapist in assessing oppressive situations is to look for signs of resilience as individuals reveal instances of survival skills that they acquired through the hardship. At the same time, an effort is made to help individuals come to terms with oppressive experiences and to discover ways that oppression could be further resisted. When counselors think from a strengths-based perspective, appropriate questions will emerge naturally. Building on client strengths may require looking at a client's problems from a different angle. The strengths assessment process itself, as Rapp and Goscha (2012) suggest, is often experienced by clients as a unique experience because they are not used to thinking of their talents and dreams.

We have come up with questions that could be asked to elicit statements in the desired direction. These are: Can you tell about a time when you successfully handled a problem that confronted you? Where did you find the strength to deal with those challenges? How have your family members helped you get through this situation? How have you managed to cope up to this point? What do other people like about you? What have you learned from your situation?

Participating in this kind of a process is highly motivating as the client recalls past successes long forgotten. Helping clients see the well part of themselves is a way to reinforce their wellness.

Miller and Rollnick (2002) recommend pretreatment testing such as addictions inventories not only for screening purposes but as a foundation for motivational counseling. Test results can be helpful in mobilizing the client toward committing to change. Results can be presented with a prefatory comment, as the authors recommend (p. 150), that emphasizes freedom of choice: "I don't know what you will make of this result, but...." Scare tactic tones are avoided. Finding the positive in test results gives a boost to an approach centered on uncovering client strengths. A cautionary reminder: The role of "expert" should be underplayed; the client and helper *collaborate* on figuring things out (Saleebey, 2009). Clients are usually the experts on their own situation; *they* are the ones who have been there, after all.

SELF-TALK AND POSITIVE REFRAMING

Through learning positive "self-talk" and cognitive restructuring, clients can be actively helped to replace unhealthy thought processes with healthy and productive ones. In leading a client to awareness of his or her own resources and the possibility of utilizing them, the strengths perspective joins the cognitive approach. Self-defeating patterns of behavior, we need to remember, are often associated with criminality as well as addictive behavior. In turn, the resulting legal and social problems compound the original negativism and even fatalism.

One way out of this maze of destruction is through collaborative work with a therapist to help eliminate illogical and/or self-defeating thought patterns. Positive self-talk is taught by the counselor's juxtaposition of the client's defeatist cognition—"I might as well quit"—with more encouraging pronouncements—"I can do it; I've done it before!" The client can be trained to say, "Stop!" when the old ideas appear and then to very deliberately substitute new formulations for them. Often, the client may have been previously unaware of the destructive nature of the thoughts that were going through his or her head as well as of their emotionally draining power. The underlying premise of this approach is the belief that people's cognitions (or the way they view the world) and their motivation to improve their life circumstances are intertwined.

Sometimes, as in the case of a younger woman suffering from bulimia, the self-destructive behavior and low self-esteem are rooted in the past as an outgrowth of early sexual trauma. This abuse often does not end in childhood but continues as a damaging feature of adult experiences. Theorists writing about motivational interviewing and cognitive therapy nevertheless focus only on "the here and now." The Twelve-Step program, similarly, and even the emphasis on sharing your "experience, strength, and hope," presents a largely present-oriented focus. That you can't change the past and that what happened in the past is just an excuse for bad behavior are the themes of most modern-day approaches, including many in social work.

The cognitive approach can be reformulated, however, to incorporate the past, to help women and men come to terms with their lives, and to see themselves as survivors rather than victims of their childhood. "Start where the client is" is a theme of social work. If the client's problems (and low self-esteem) are rooted in the past, that is the place to begin. The unconscious mind knows neither past nor present; sometimes, to go forward, you have to trace your steps backward and find out where you took a wrong turn. The cognitive techniques of restructuring our view of the past are essential to self-acceptance. The cognitive framework is ideally suited for this task.

The repetitive nature of information provided to clients in the early stage of recovery serves to reinforce learning and memory. New members of Twelve-Step groups are continually restructuring self-defeating beliefs through slogans such as "Easy does it" and "Let go and let God." When the thinking gets a little frantic or the "old tapes" start playing again, the universally known Serenity Prayer may be said: "God grant me the serenity to accept the things I cannot change, the courage to change the things I can, and the wisdom to know the difference."

FEELING WORK

Treatment centers often have clients list losses related to their addictive behaviors. Sometimes, they have to add up the costs in dollars as well. Such exercises, however, only reinforce the negative feelings of loss, compounded now with public shame as these consequences are shared in a group. Compulsive gamblers and spenders have problem enough with self-flagellation; there is no need to accentuate these negative thoughts. It would be better to provide information concerning how slot machine owners bilk their customers or how marketers of products seduce unwitting buyers. Information concerning the brain and addiction can help the client overwhelmed with the consequences of his of her behavior make sense of things. Being with others in a supportive group can emphasize the awareness that good people can make foolish choices.

ANGER MANAGEMENT   Male gamblers who have "lost it all" may be consumed with anger, and they may displace this anger on their family members. Their female counterparts may be unaware of the anger, which has become internalized, and be overcome with depression or guilt. Among addicts in recovery, anger may cause problems both when it is suppressed and when it is manifested (e.g., periodic explosions of rage). Sometimes, anger at one object (e.g., the judicial system) is displaced onto another (e.g., the counselor or correctional officer).

Knowledge of feelings and the thought processes connected with these feelings ("I hate my mother," "I hate myself") helps clients work toward change. Helpful guidelines that clients can use to help get in touch with their feelings are to: identify the feeling, possibly using a list of possible feeling states; define the visceral or inner body response associated with that feeling; listen to the self-talk and note extremes in thinking and words such as *never, can't, always,* and *everybody.* Once the facts of the matter have been identified, the next step is to take some deep breaths and repeat healthy self-talk out loud three times. For example, "I used drugs to escape from problems. I now have learned solid coping skills and I have been clean for two years. My children are proud of me. My life is not ruined." After this healthy self-talk, the client can see how angry, jealous, or semi-hysterical feelings change.

Sometimes, anger that surfaces is a cover for another deeper emotion, such as a feeling of betrayal or even insecurity. An intriguing question to ask the perpetually angry client is, "If you weren't feeling anger, what would you be feeling?" The answer may be a revelation to the client as well as to the therapist.

Some women who have difficulty labeling or expressing anger become compulsive housecleaners, energizing themselves in the endless war on dust and dirt. Such individuals need coaching to help them learn to absorb the angry feeling without fear and to mobilize that energy in a positive direction. Assertiveness training can help people get their needs met. Persons who have difficulty containing their anger should work on the de-escalating techniques of anger management.

Anger management training teaches the origins of anger, what triggers extreme anger and why, and that there is nothing wrong with having stormy feelings (Tavris & Aronson, 2007). Learning to express anger verbally and calmly—for example, to say, "When you do ... I feel insulted (or rejected, or annoyed)"—instead of lashing out physically or with cursing is the kind of training that can be offered in groups. Group members enhance their self-esteem as they take more responsibility for themselves and learn to channel the energy that goes into outbursts of anger into more productive and rewarding directions.

One anger management program with a lot of promise is described by Demaree and Harrison (2003) as an outgrowth of ongoing neurological research that examined the link between hostility and brain chemistry. Hostile people might have deficits on the right side of the cerebrum and an inability to control negative emotions or simply a lack of awareness of physiological changes that occur when they are angry. Teaching people to be more self-aware of bodily cues, such as a racing heart, can help them to protect themselves from chronic anger.

Venting anger inappropriately not only might get the client in trouble but also might actually increase his or her level of hostility. This is what psychological research has always shown (American Psychological Association, 2006; Tavris &Aronson, 2007). Repression is bad, but the unhealthy release of anger (e.g., beating the dog) is bad as well. A healthier response would be to pet the dog. Bushman (2002) recommends petting the dog as one method of deferring anger. His conclusion that trying to release one's anger through an aggressive act is derived from his experimental research on a large sample of students in an anger-inducing situation. Students who vented their anger on a punching bag demonstrated an escalation of aggression compared to a control group who did not vent their anger. Table 5.1 lists healthy ways to deal with anger.

STRESS MANAGEMENT Stress is considered a major precipitant of relapse (Koob, 2006). This is understandable because stress hormones interfere with sleep and create a heightened alertness; the heart and breathing rates increase, and blood pressure rises (Johnson, 2004). The perpetual nervousness that plagues many individuals with addiction problems can be reduced through cognitive therapy techniques. Worrying, anxiety-provoking self-talk ("My kids will hate me; my parents will never forgive me") can be replaced with new ways of thinking ("I'll do my best to explain things; they'll be happy to see how much healthier I am now that I'm sober").

TABLE 5.1 | DEALING WITH ANGER

Goal	Means of Achievement
Learn to control angry outbursts	Use "time-outs"
Reduce feelings of anger	Find healthy outlets for feelings of anger, for example, exercise
Lessen periods of angry thoughts	Use healthy self-talk to replace angry thoughts
End violent, angry outbursts	Learn to verbalize the reasons for anger; join an anger management group
When appropriate, feel the anger	Explore the history of how you were socialized to express or suppress anger; assertiveness training

Some common therapeutic goals pertaining to fear and anxiety are learning to handle fears, managing to face fears calmly, identifying what one is truly afraid of, and being emotionally prepared for likely outcomes. Imagining the worst possible thing that can happen is often helpful. For clients who have phobias, or irrational fears, the origins of the phobias should be traced. Behavioral treatment provides for exposure to the feared source (e.g., a snake) in slow steps until the panic response is extinguished.

Teaching the development of adaptive coping skills to stress is a vital part of relapse prevention (Wallace (2005). Such training is based on the identification of high-risk situations where negative emotions are strong. Skills training is a method that can increase the client's sense of control in a threatening situation. Research has verified the effectiveness of such training, which often consists of rehearsal and role-play (Wallace, 2005).

Through reducing the use of stimulants, such as coffee and tea, physical anxiety can be reduced greatly. A serving of warm milk at any time can produce a quieting effect. When adrenaline is high, brisk exercise aids in using up the excess energy and enhancing relaxation. The usefulness of physical exercise as a treatment intervention has been verified in empirical studies with animals and humans (Johnson, 2004). For persons with co-occurring disorders, exercise has been shown highly effective, yet it is used too rarely. Results indicate significantly reduced levels of both anxiety and depression by virtue of the physical training provided.

Perfectionism is almost always a part of the compulsiveness found in pathological dieting; it also may play into the relentless drive to strike it rich through gambling or day trading on the Internet. The perfectionism itself is not a side effect of these disorders but a personality trait that puts people at risk for these problems and for substance misuse as well ("Persistent Perfectionists," 1996).

ALL-OR-NOTHING THINKING An all-or-nothing mode of thinking causes people to get trapped in their destructive behavior. "I can't quit until I hit the jackpot" is typical of this line of thought. An anonymous graduate student (in personal communication with van Wormer of January, 2010) describes this phenomenon:

> People who are all-or-nothing thinkers need to be the best at things or they are not worth trying. An example of a situation involving several all-or-nothing thinkers could be found within a casino. I have gone with people to the casino who had the attitude that they were either going to win big or lose all of their money. An interesting thing about one such person is, even if he gets $100 ahead in the casino, he still does not stop. This does not seem to be big enough of a win for these people, who end up staying until they lose all that they had just won.

Some people with weight disorders also have all-or-nothing thinking. They may feel that if they cannot have the perfect figure, then why even try to diet or exercise.

Examples of illogical beliefs, in a checklist that can be used effectively in group sessions, include the following:

- All-or-nothing thinking
- Jumping to negative conclusions
- Overgeneralizing about others
- Making "mountains out of molehills"
- Putting down members of your own group (e.g., other women)
- Self-blaming
- "I can't live without" a certain person
- I must be perfect
- Everyone must like me
- If things do not go according to plan, it is a catastrophe
- I never forgive or forget a wrong
- People are either all good or all bad
- Victims of crime have themselves to blame

Sometimes, the simple act of realizing that one's present thinking is irrational brings about a major improvement in this area. In talking to a counselor who is nonjudgmental and enthusiastic about analyzing thought processes we all share, clients will begin to question and challenge many of their long-held assumptions and find they can change the way they feel (e.g., depressed, anxious, guilty) by being more accepting of themselves and of others.

USE OF HUMOR One of the best ways to conquer the kind of catastrophizing and fatalistic thinking that leads to dangerous forms of escape (from indulgence in addictive behavior to suicide) is through the use of humor. Humor provides perspective on the human condition and on one's personality quirks in a healthy way. In many treatment centers, unfortunately, clowning and laughing are pathologized and off limits. An episode in the movie 28 Days effectively captures this tradition. After Gwen, the young woman sentenced to

28-day rehab, cracks a joke, a counselor asks her, "Do you always use humor to deflect things when you're uncomfortable?"

In recognition of the contribution it makes to group bonding and enjoyment, the typical AA meeting uses humor quite a bit. Here are a few examples collected by van Wormer over the years:

- A man attending an AA meeting said he was like Dr. Jekyll and Mr. Hyde when drunk. "Too bad you sobered up the wrong one," a member called out.
- A good Irish joke is, "Last week I drank only twice, once for three days, once for four."
- There is even a group for paranoid people. It's called Paranoids Anonymous—PA. The only problem is if you call the number in the phonebook, they won't tell you where they are.

EXERCISES FOR FEELING WORK IN THE GROUP

Consistent with the principles of strengths-based MI as described in this chapter are the following exercises. Such exercises can be used to provide structure for a therapy group. The focus of these activities is on allowing deep feelings to arise spontaneously in a warm, supportive group setting.

1. Art Therapy
    Purposes: To reveal feelings that may not be expressed. May bring out perfectionism as a secondary function.

    Have clients draw their world during the time before they came to treatment, during treatment, and after treatment. Clients are told they can draw stick-people; there's no need for talent. This exercise, seriously undertaken, gives an indication of future hopes and fears. Those who, because of lack of confidence or anxiety, resist this exercise can have someone else draw what they describe in words.

2. Turning Points
    Purpose: To promote critical thinking about one's life and reinforce change from a life of crime.

    Have participants as a homework assignment write about or prepare to tell about a turning point in their lives. At the next session, they will share their revelations.

3. Faces
    Purpose: To elicit discussion of feelings.

    Use a sheet of faces with diverse expressions on them. Simple cartoon faces, including duck faces, are effective. This exercise works with non-readers and equally well with men and women. Give the following instructions: "Choose the face that shows how you feel today and also one that shows how you felt earlier in the week. Each of you will share your selection with the group."

4. Grief and Loss

   Purpose: To reveal underlying feelings of grief and guilt over loss.
   On a sheet of paper have clients:
   a. Identify a significant loss. (This can be a person, a job, or some other loss.)
   b. Describe the support you have received for the loss and what you have learned from this experience.

5. Quiz Cards

   Purposes: To share in the group; to elicit a wide range of responses. This exercise has the possibility of eliciting some fairly deep feelings and is not advisable to use with persons who are in a state of depression.
   Examples:
   When I think of my mother ___
   When I remember my father ___
   Eating, spending money, cocaine, heroin, etc. was for me ___
   Sobriety is ___
   As a child, I was lucky I had ___
   Love is ___
   I feel proud of myself for ___

6. Dream Analysis

   Purpose: To help clients get in touch with a part of themselves they may have little awareness of.

   Give an ongoing homework assignment for participants to record their dreams on paper immediately after they have them. Then have those who can remember them share their dreams in the group as members look for meanings. Themes to look for are fears, anxieties, anger, forgiveness, attempts to communicate with loved ones, sobriety issues, and return of repressed memories. This often-untapped resource of recalling dream content can speak to group members, often in unexpected ways. Dream content can provide counselor and group members with clues about the individual's readiness to make changes. (Native Americans are often skilled at remembering and learning from their dreams.)

7. Assertiveness

   Purpose: Clients in treatment, when asked to set a goal for themselves, often say they would like to be more assertive or to work on assertiveness. Assertiveness training is geared toward persons who come across as aggressive when they do not intend to and persons who need to learn to speak up for themselves to have their interests met. Assertive behavior involves expressing preferences without undue anxiety in a manner that will be well received by others. Alternatives to aggressive reactions include calming self-talk, making polite requests, and reframing situations so that they do not overwhelm the individual (Gambrill, 2006). The University of Texas Counseling and Mental Health Center provides assertiveness workshop and stress management guidelines for use by professionals at http://www.cmhc.utexas.edu/stress.html. These materials are free of charge.

SUMMARY AND CONCLUSION

In vulnerable individuals, mass media and corporate marketing influences create situations ripe for problems with overeating or self-starvation, buying products never used or needed, and games turned into nightmares. In this chapter, as in others, we looked at the biological, psychological, and social factors related to the addictions in question: eating disorders; gambling, shopping, sex, and Internet addiction; and others. Research using new brain imaging techniques indicates that gambling may share the same addictive process and have similar effects as those produced by psychoactive drugs. New medications are being developed to target the dopamine and serotonin levels in the brain to quell addictive urges.

We chose to include this chapter in the biological section of the book because of new discoveries in brain research that pertain not only to the impact of mood-altering chemicals on the body but the biological impact of the act of getting high itself. We are talking about endorphins produced when a person feels high and the process by which some people get hooked on the high while others can reach a state of satiation of their hungers and go on. Food and sex addiction are the two addictions discussed in this chapter that are obviously biologically based because the eating and sex drives are directly related to survival of the species. And yet, as Linden (2011), the author of *The Compass of Pleasure*, which is a book about the role of brain chemicals and the pleasure center of the brain in addiction, suggests, there is now reason to believe that a broad definition of addiction is valid, that there are some factors in brain chemistry that for some individuals will turn their drives for pleasure into pathology.

The knowledge presented in this chapter is not only biologically-based, but strongly psychological, both in its origins as well as in its treatment. Thinking and feeling, as cognitive theory tells us, are intertwined. Cognitively based therapy, accordingly, has been effective in helping people cope with their problems and stresses and, somewhat remarkably, if the reports from studies on obsessive-compulsive disorder are accurate, to promote recovery of the brain as well. "Change your mind, change your brain" is the title of one of the sources that informed this chapter (Begley, 2007). Although usually geared toward thinking and feeling patterns related to the disorder at hand, cognitive therapy is also suitable for helping clients deal with past issues. From the vantage point of today, clients can begin to view themselves as survivors rather than as victims of their lives. From a strengths perspective, a counselor can help clients reframe their life stories to identify strengths and survival skills that were all but taken for granted until then. In so doing, they might let go of some of the anger they have felt for family members as well.

Speaking of stories, in this chapter, we heard from a self-starved ballerina, a bulimic student whose desperate practices landed her in the hospital, an overweight Irishman who gave OA and later AA a try, and a youth counselor who unwittingly got in "over his head" with compulsive betting. What these narrators all had in common, apart from their addictive behavior, was that they eventually got the help they needed for a new start in life. Some of the techniques they might have learned in treatment were presented here: stress management, anger management, and ways to deal with powerful feelings and somehow get beyond them. As we move into the next chapter of the book, we will see how many of these same interventions described here can be adapted to serve the needs of clients with various addictive problems across the life span—from adolescence through old age.

REFERENCES

"Addicted? Really?" (2011, March 12). *Economist*, p. 9.

American Psychiatric Association (APA). (2000). *Diagnostic and statistical manual of mental disorders, text revision* (4th ed.). Washington, DC: Author.

American Psychiatric Association (APA). (2011). *Diagnostic and statistical manual of mental disorders* (DSM)-5 development. Washington, DC: Author. Retrieved from http://www.dsm5.org

American Psychological Association. (2006). *Controlling anger before it controls you*. Retrieved March 2006 from http://www.apa.org/pubinfo

Anderson, K., Cowger, C. D., & Snively, C. (2009). Assessing strengths: Identifying acts of resistance to violence and oppression. In D. Saleebey (Ed.), The strengths perspective in social work practice (5th ed., pp. 181–200). Boston: Pearson.

Anorexia, bulimia, found more dangerous in men. (2000, June 7). *Chicago Tribune*, evening update, p. 7.

Arizona Council on Compulsive Gambling. (2000). Retrieved from http://www.azccg.org

Bacanu, S. A., Bulik, C., Klump, K., Fichter, M., Halmi, K., Keel, P., et al. (2005). Linkage analysis of anorexia and bulimia nervosa cohorts using selected behavioral phenotypes as quantitative traits or covariates. American Journal of Medical Genetics, 139(1), 61–68.

Beaucar, K. O. (1999, October). When games turn into nightmares. NASW News, p. 3.

Beck, A. (1991). Cognitive therapy: A 30-year retrospective. American Psychologist, 46(4), 368–375.

Begley, S. (2007). *Train your mind, change your brain*. New York: Ballantine Books.

Begley, S. (2008, December 6). Inside the shopping brain. Newsweek. Retrieved from http://www.newsweek.com/2008/12/06/inside-the-shopping-brain.html

Bellegarde, J., & Potenza, M. (2010). Neurobiology of pathological gambling. In D.Ross, H. Kincaid, D. Spurett, & P. Collins (Eds.), What is addiction? (pp. 27–51). Cambridge, MA: Massachusetts Institute of Technology Press.

Benson, A. (2008). *To buy or not to buy: Why we overshop and how to stop*. Boston: Trumpeter Books.

Bergevin, T., Gupta, R., Derevensky, J., & Kaufman, F. (2006). *Adolescent gambling: Understanding the role of stress and coping. Journal of Gambling Studies*, 22(2), 195–208.

Berzon, A. (2011, April 30). Cash off table for gambling addicts. Wall Street Journal. Retrieved from http://online.wsj.com

Black, C. (2009). *Deceived: Facing sexual betrayal, lies, and secrets*. Center City, MN: Hazelden.

Black, D. W. (2007). A review of compulsive buying disorder. World Psychiatry, 6, 14–18.

Blaszczynski, A. (2000, March). Pathways to pathological gambling: Identifying typologies. E-Gambling: Electronic Journal of Gambling Issues, 1. Retrieved from http://www.camh.net/egambling/issue1/feature

Brody, J. (2010, June 21). When tanning turns into an addiction. New York Times, p. D7.

Bulik, C., Bacanu, S. A., Klump, K., Fichter, M., Halmi, K., Keel, P., et al. (2005). Selection of eating disorders phenotypes for linkage analysis. American Journal of Medical Genetics, 139(1), 81–87.

Bushman, B. (2002). Does venting anger feed or extinguish the flame? Catharsis, rumination, distraction, anger, and aggressive responding. Personality and Social Psychological Bulletin, 28, 724–731.

Cardella, A. (2010). *Spent: Memoirs of a shopping addict.* New York: Little, Brown & Co.

Carnes, P. (2001). *Out of the shadows: Understanding sexual addiction.* Center City, MN: Hazelden.

Carnes, P. (2005). *Facing the shadow: Starting sexual and relationship recovery.* Carefree, AZ: Gentle Path Press.

Chhabra, D., Lutz, G., & Gonnerman, M. (2005). *Socioeconomic impact of gambling on Iowans: Final report.* Des Moines: Iowa Legislative Council.

Christian Science Monitor (2006, August 1). *Tempting the temptation of Web casinos,* p. 8.

Chu, K. (2010, March 30). Extreme dieting spreads in Asia. USA Today. Retrieved from http://www.usatoday.com

Ciciora, P. (2011, January 5). A minute with business and legal policy expert John Kindt. Chicago: University of Illinois. News Bureau. Retrieved from http://illinois.edu

Clark, K. (2005, May 23). *Against the odds. U.S. News & World Report,* pp. 47–54.

Cloud, J. (2011, February 18). *The truth about sex addiction. Time,* pp.42–50.

Cosgrave, J., & Klassen, T. (2009). *Casino state: Legalized gambling in Canada.* Toronto: University of Toronto Press.

Cyndi, R. (2004). Sex addiction and women: A nursing issue. *Journal of Addictions Nursing,* 15(2), 53–62.

Davis, D. R., & Avery, L. (2004). Women who have taken their lives back from compulsive gambling. Results from an online survey. *Journal of Social Work Practice in the Addictions,* 4(1), 61–80.

Davis, D. R. (2009). *Taking back your life: Women and problem gambling.* Center City, MN: Hazelden.

Davison, K. K., & Birch, L. L. (2001). Weight status, parent reaction, and self-concept in five-year-old girls. Pediatrics, 107(1), 46–53.

Debtors Anonymous (2011). Information for Helping Professionals. (2011). Retrieved from http://www.debtorsanonymous.org/professionals.htm

Delaughter, G. (2010, June 28). *Gambling and workplace embezzlement on the rise.* Houston, TX: Public Radio News, KUHF-FM.

Delfabbro, P., & Winefield, A. (2000). Predictors of irrational thinking in regular slot machine gamblers. Journal of Psychology, 134(2), 117–128.

Demaree, H. A., & Harrison, D. W. (2003). Physiological and neuropsychological correlates of hostility. In P. K. Lehman, C. Dula, & J. Finney (Eds.), Introductory psychology recitation reader (pp. 27–37). Boston: McGraw-Hill.

Desai, R.A., & Potenza, M.N. (2009). A cross-sectional study of problem and pathological gambling in patients with schizophrenia/schizoaffective disorder. *Journal of Clinical Psychiatry,* 70(9), 1250–1257.

Dodes, R. (2008, December 15). This year, more than ever, it's tough to be a compulsive shopper. *Wall Street Journal,* p. A1.

Duffelmeyer, A. (2011, February 3). Industry says tax jump would close some casinos. *Times-Republican*. Retrieved from http://www.timesrepublican.com

Ellis, A. (2001). *Overcoming destructive beliefs, feelings, and behaviors: New directions for rational emotive behavior therapy*. Essex, UK: Prometheus Books.

Ellis, A., McInerney, J. F., DiGiuseppe, R., & Yeager, R. J. (1989). *Rational-emotive therapy with alcoholics and substance abusers*. New York: Pergamon Press.

Evans, J. (2004, October 1). Pathological gambling differs in females, teens. *Family Practice News, 34*(19), 39–40.

Fairleigh Dickinson University. (2006). *New Jersey seniors gamble away. Public mind poll*. Retrieved February 2007 from http://publicmind.fdu.edu/gamble

Feldman, M. B., & Meyer, I. H. (2007). Eating disorders in diverse lesbian, gay, and bisexual populations. *International Journal of Eating Disorders, 40*, 218–226.

Fossati, M., Amati, F., Painot, D., Reiner, M., Haenni, C., & Golay, A. (2004). Cognitive-behavioral therapy with simultaneous nutritional and physical activity education in obese patients with binge eating disorder. *Eating and Weight Disorder, 9*(2), 134–138.

Gadalla, T., & Piran, N. (2007). Co-occurrence of eating disorders and alcohol use disorders in women: A meta analysis. *Archives of Women's Mental Health, 10*, 133–140.

Gamblers Anonymous (GA). (1999). *Sharing recovery through Gamblers Anonymous*. Los Angeles: Author.

Gamblers Anonymous (GA). (2000). *Gamblers Anonymous: A new beginning* (4th ed.). Los Angeles: Author.

Gambrill, E. (2006). *Social work practice: A critical thinker's guide* (2nd ed.). New York: Oxford University Press.

Gearhardt, A., Yokum S., Orr, P., Stice E,, Corbin, W., & Brownell, K. (2011). *Neural correlates of food addiction. Archives of General Psychiatry,68*(8) 808–816. .

Gerke, C., Mazzeo, S., & Kliewer, W. (2006, October 30). The role of depression and dissociation in the relationship between childhood trauma and bulimic symptoms among ethnically diverse female undergraduates. *Child Abuse and Neglect, 10*, 1161–1172.

Grant, J. E., & Kim, S. W. (2002). Effectiveness of pharmacotherapy for pathological gambling: A chart review. *Annals of Clinical Psychiatry, 14*(3), 155–161.

Grucza R., Krueger, R., Racette, S., Norberg, K., Hipp, P., & Bierut, L. (2010). The emerging link between alcoholism risk and obesity in the United States. *Archives of General Psychiatry, 67*(12), 1301–1308.

Gura, T. (2008, June/July). Addicted to starvation. *Scientific American Mind*, pp. 61–67.

Hamilton, N. (2003). *Bill Clinton: An American journey, great expectations*. New York: Random House.

Hilton, D., & Watts, C. (2011, February 26). Pornography addiction: A neuroscience perspective. *Surgical Neurology International, 2*, 19.

Hodgins, D., & Diskin, K. (2008). Motivational interviewing in the treatment of problem and pathological gambling. In H. Arkowitz, H. Wesha, W. R. Miller, & S. Rollnick (Eds.), *Motivational interviewing in the treatment of psychological problems* (pp. 225–248). New York: Guilford Press.

Holm, K. (2006, July 30). Dying to be thin. *Courier, Waterloo–Cedar Falls*, pp. A1, A7.

Hornbacher, M. (1998). *Wasted: A memoir of anorexia and bulimia*. New York: Harper Flamingo.

Hudson, J. I., Hiripi, E., Pope, H., & Kessler, R. C. (2007). The prevalence and correlates of eating disorders in the national comorbidity survey replication. *Biological Psychiatry, 61*(3), 348–358.

Johnson, H. C. (2004). *Psyche and synapse explaining worlds: The role of neurobiology in emotions, behavior, thinking, and addiction for non-scientists* (2nd ed.). Greenfield, MA: Deerfield Valley.

Kaye, W., Bulik, C., Thornton, L., Barbarich, N., & Masters, K. (2004). Comorbidity of anxiety disorders with anorexia and bulimia nervosa. *American Journal of Psychiatry*, *161*, 2215–2221.

Kershaw, S. (2005, December 1). Hooked on the web. *New York Times*. Retrieved September 2006 from http://www.nytimes.com/2005/12/01/fashion

Kirkland, G. (1986). *Dancing on my grave*. New York: Jove Books.

Kleiss, K. (2011, April 30). Charities can't win for losing. *Edmonton Journal*. Retrieved from http://www.edmontonjournal.com

Koob, G. (2006). The neurobiology of addiction. In W. R. Miller & K. Carroll (Eds.), Rethinking substance abuse (pp. 25–45), New York: Guilford Press.

Koran, L., Faber, R., Aboujaoude, E., Large, M., & Serpe, R. (2006). Estimated prevalence of compulsive buying behavior in the United States. *American Journal of Psychiatry*, *163*(10), 1806–1812.

Landau, J., Garrett, J., & Webb, R. (2008). Assisting a concerned person to motivate someone experiencing cybersex into treatment. *Journal of Marital and Family Therapy*, *34*(4), 498–511.

Lee, B. (2005). *Born to lose: Memoir of a compulsive gambler*. Center City, MN: Hazelden.

Lee, M. Y. (2011). *Solution-focused theory*. In F. Turner (Ed.), *Social work treatment: Interlocking theoretical approaches* (pp.460–476). New York: Oxford University Press.

Linden, D. J. (2011). *The compass of pleasure*. New York: Viking.

Man sues IBM over firing, says he's an Internet addict. (2007, February 18). *CNN*. Retrieved February 2007 from http://www.cnn.com/2007/LAW.

Maté, G. (1999). *Scattered: How attention deficit disorder originates and what you can do about it*. New York: Plume.

McCourt, M. (2000). *Singing my him song*. New York: HarperCollins.

McQuaide, S., & Ehrenreich, J. H. (1997, March/April). Assessing client strengths. *Families in Society*, pp. 201–212.

Mellace, J. (2010). Eating disorders not otherwise specified. *Social Work Today*, *10*(4), 14–17.

Messerlian, C., Derevensky, J., & Gupta, R. (2005). Youth gambling patterns: A public health perspective. *Health Promotion International*, *20*(1), 69–79.

Miller, G. (2005). *Learning the language of addiction counseling* (2nd ed.). New York: Wiley.

Miller, W. R., & Rollnick, S. (2002). *Motivating interviewing: Preparing people to change addictive behavior* (2nd ed.). New York: Guilford Press.

Miller, W. R., Forcehimes, A., & Zweben, A. (2011). *Treating addiction: A guide for professionals*. New York: Guilford.

Mitka, M. (2011). Report weighs options for bulimia nervosa treatment. *Journal of the American Medical Association*, *302*(8), 836–837.

Momper, S., & Dennis, M. (2010). American Indian women report on the community impact of a tribal casino. *Race and Social Problems*, *2*, 59–68.

Morain, M. (2011, July 1). Ruling on violent content draws fire. *Des Moines Register*, p. 1E.

Morgan, O. J. (2009). Thoughts on the interaction of trauma, addiction, and spirituality. *Journal of Addictions and Offender Counseling*, *30*(1), 5–16.

Muelleman, R., DenOtter, T., Wadman, M. C., Tran, T. P., & Anderson, J. (2002). Problem gambling in the partner of the emergency department patient. *Journal of Emergency Medicine, 23*(3), 307–312.

National Center on Addiction and Substance Abuse (CASA). (2003). *Food for thought: Substance abuse and eating disorders.* New York: Columbia University.

National Gambling Impact Study Commission. (1999, June 18). *Report of the commission.* Washington, DC: U.S. Government Printing Office.

National Institute of Mental Health (NIMH). (2011). *Eating disorders.* National Institutes of Health. Retrieved from http://www.nimh.nih.gov

Newman, H. (2008, June 7). Addiction to gambling among seniors is on rise. *Detroit Free Press.* Retrieved from http://www.poststar.com

Newsome, M. (2005, September). Not just for kids. *Time*, p. W12.

O'Connor, M. (2001, May 24). Judge buys shopaholic defense in embezzling. Retrieved from http://www.chicagotribune.com

O'Leary, S. (2000, November 23). Shopping addiction: Out-of-control spending can ruin lives and families. Retrieved from http://healthsurfing.com/health/2000/11/23/?p=1

Oregon Department of Corrections. (2004, June 14). CCCF (Coffee Creek Correctional Facility) helps inmate with gambling problem. Retrieved from http://egov.oregon.gov/DOC

Peele, S. (2011, June 19). Why Anthony Weiner is not a sex addict (nor Bill Clinton). *Psychology Today.* Retrieved from http://www.psychologytoday.com

"Persistent perfectionists". (1996, May/June). *Psychology Today, 29*(3), 11.

Petry, N., Stinson, F., & Grant, B. (2005). Comorbidity of DSM–IV pathological gambling and other psychiatric disorders: Results from the national epidemiologic survey on alcohol and related conditions. *Journal of Clinical Psychiatry, 66,* 564–574.

Pietrzak, R., & Petry, N. (2005). Antisocial personality disorder is associated with increased severity of gambling, medical, drug, and psychiatric problems. *Addiction, 100*(8), 1183–1193.

Petroski, W. (2009, April 19). Gambling addiction derails lives. *Des Moines Register,* p. 7A.

Piran, N., & Robinson, S. R. (2006). The association between disordered eating and substance use and abuse in women: A community-based investigation. *Women and Health, 44*(1), 1–20.

Pomeroy, E., & Browning, P.Y. (2008). *Eating disorders.* In *NASW Encyclopedia of social work* (20th ed., pp. 93–97). New York: Oxford University Press.

Project MATCH Research Group. (1997). Matching alcoholism treatments to client heterogeneity: Project MATCH post treatment drinking outcomes. *Journal of Studies on Alcohol, 58,* 7–29.

Rabin, R. (2010, November 9). Behavior: Too much texting is linked to other problems. *New York Times*, p. D6.

Rapp, C. A., & Goscha, R. (2006). *The strengths model: Case management with people with psychiatric disabilities* (2nd ed.). New York: Oxford University Press.

Ringham, R., Klump, K., Kaye, W., Stone, D., Libman, S., Stowe, S., et al. (2006). Eating disorder symptomatology among ballet dancers. *International Journal of Eating Disorders, 39*(6), 503–508.

Risk for alcoholism linked to risk for obesity. (2010, December 31). *Science Daily.* Retrieved from http://www.sciencedaily.com

Robb, M. (2005, November/December). Gambling USA: What every social worker should know. *Social Work Today,* pp. 18–22.

Rogers, R., & Goodwin, G. (2005). Lithium may reduce gambling severity in pathological gamblers with bipolar disorder. *Evidence-Based Mental Health*, *8*, 80.

Russo, F. (2005, October 31). Ante up, ladies: As poker mania grips the nation, more women are mastering the game. *Time*, *166*(18), W6.

Saleebey, D. (2009). Introduction: Power in the people. In D. Saleebey (Ed.), *The strengths perspective in social work practice* (4th ed., pp. 1–23). Boston: Pearson.

Samenow, S. E. (1984). *Inside the criminal mind*. New York: Times Books.

Sanci, L., Olsson C., Reid, S., Carlin, J., & Patton, G. (2008). Childhood sexual abuse and eating disorders in females. *Archives of Pediatrics and Adolescent Medicine*, *162*, 261–267.

Schwartz, J. M., & Begley, S. (2003). *The mind and the brain: Neuroplasticity and the power of mental force*. New York: Regan Books.

Sex Addicts Anonymous. (2007). *Sex Addicts Anonymous (SAA) home page*. Retrieved February 2007 from http://saa-recovery.org

Si-Young, H. (2006, September 15). Korea: Internet addicts to receive counseling. *Korea Herald*. Retrieved September 2006 from http://www.asiamedia.vcla.edu/article

Skolnik, S. (2011). *High stakes: The rising cost of America's gambling addiction*. Boston: Beacon Press.

Slutske, W., Caspi, A., Moffitt, T., & Poulton, R. (2005). Personality and problem gambling. *Archives of General Psychiatry*, *62*, 769–775.

Solomon, B. (2011, January 18). Man strangles wife over $20K gambling debt. Online Poker.net. Retrieved from http://www.onlinepoker.net

Spencer, J. (2006, July 18). The new science of addiction. *Wall Street Journal*, pp. D1, D2.

Stanford School of Medicine. (2003, July16). News release. Antidepressant helps alleviate compulsive shopping disorder, Stanford researchers find. News Release. Retrieved February 2007 from http://med.stanford.edu/news_releases/2003/july/shopping.html

Stanford School of Medicine. (2006, October 17). Internet addiction: Stanford study seeks to define whether it's a problem. News Release. Retrieved from http://med-news.stanford.edu/releases/2006/october/internet.html.

Substance Abuse and Mental Health Services Administration (SAMHSA) (2011). *Knowledge Application Program. Clients with substance use and eating disorders*. Rockville MD: Department of Health and Human Services.

Svoboda, E. (2010, September/October). Shopaholic. *Psychology Today*, 30–31.

Szalavitz, M. (2011, April 4). Heroin vs. Häagen-Dazs: What food addiction looks like in the brain. *Time*: Healthland. Retrieved from http://healthland.time.com

Tavris, C., & Aronson, E. (2007). *Mistakes were made (but not by me)*. Orlando, FL: A Harvest Book.

Taylor, J. (2011). *Casino state: Legalized gambling in Canada. Journal of Gambling Issues*, *25*, 136–139.

Turkle, S. (2011). *Alone together: Why we expect more from technology and less from each other*. New York: Basic Books.

Turner, N. (2002, June 17). Randomness, does it matter? *E-Gambling: Electronic Journal of Gambling Issues*, *2*. Centre for Addiction and Mental Health. Retrieved from http://www.austgamingcouncil.org.au/images/pdf/eLibrary/779.pdf

Ubelacker, S. (2005, July 11). Parkinson's medication linked to compulsive gambling, sex. *Globe and Mail*. Retrieved September 2006 from http://www.theglobeandmail.com

Van Pelt, J. (2009). Eating disorders on the web. *Social Work Today*, *9*(5), 20–25.

Van Pelt, J. (2011). Treating people who hoard. *Social Work Today, 11*(3), 14–28.

van Wormer, K. (2010). *Working with female offenders: A gender-sensitive approach.* Hoboken, NJ: Wiley & Sons.

van Wormer, K. (2011). *Human behavior and the social environment, micro level: Individuals and families* (2nd ed.) New York: Oxford University Press.

Vardi, N. (2010, June 1). Legal deadline ups the ante for online poker. *Forbes.* Retrieved from http://www.msnbc.msn.com

Vastag, B. (2001). What's the connection? No easy answers for people with eating disorders and drug abuse. *Journal of the American Medical Association, 285*(8), 1006–1008.

Volkow, N. (2006, December 24). Quoted in article by P. Wingert, "Nora Volkow: A passionate advocate for addicts of all kinds." *Newsweek,* p.77.

Volkow, N. (2007, July 10). No, really, this is your brain on drugs. *National Public Radio: Fresh Air.* Interview with Nora Volkow. Retrieved from http://www.npr.org/templates/story/story.php?storyId=11847222

Volpicelli, J., & Szalavitz, M. (2000). *Recovery options: The complete guide.* New York: Wiley.

Wallace, B. C. (2005). *Making mandated addictions treatment work.* Lanham, MD: Jason Aronson.

Wang, G.-J., Volkow, N., Thanos, P., & Fowler, J. (2004). Similarity between obesity and drug addiction as assessed by neurofunctional imaging. *Journal of Addictive Diseases, 23*(3), 39–53.

Webley, K. (2010, July 19). Cleaning house: How community task forces are dealing with hoarding, one pile of junk at a time. *Time,* pp. 43–44.

Welte, J., Barnes, G., Tidwell, M.-C., & Hoffman, J. (2010). *Gambling and problem gambling across the lifespan. Journal of Gambling Studies, 27*(1), 49–61.

Wen, P. (2001, May 24). An addictive thrill. *Boston Globe,* pp. A1, A21.

Westermeyer, J. (2005). Gambling in American Indian and Hispanic veterans. *American Journal of Public Health, 95*(5), 860–866.

Williams, R., & Wood, R. (2004, June 23). The demographics of Ontario gaming revenue. Paper prepared for the Ontario Problem Gambling Centre. Retrieved February 2007 from http://www.gamblingresearch.org/

Yochelson, S., & Samenow, S. (1976). *The criminal personality* (Vol. 1). New York: Jason Aronson.

Young, K. S., & de Abreu, C. (Eds.) (2011). *Internet addiction: A handbook and guide to evaluation and treatment.* Hoboken, NJ: Wiley.

THE PSYCHOLOGY
OF ADDICTION

PART | 3

The four chapters that make up this central part of the book take us into the heart of therapy itself, which gets at the thinking side of addiction and concomitantly at the feelings that emerge during the working stage of substance abuse treatment.

Chapter 6, Addiction across the Life Span, was placed in the psychological part of the book because it draws on the developmental stages of life and relates the role of drugs to these life stages. For this discussion, we draw on the work of ego psychologist Erik Erikson and family development theorist Jacqueline Wallen.

Assessment, a major function of the treatment process, determines which questions to ask in order to obtain the necessary information to guide the treatment effort. A basic argument of Chapter 7 is that specialized, culturally sensitive instruments are necessary to guide work with specific populations, for example, for older adults who developed addiction problems late in life, and persons with co-occurring disorders.

Probably the most important chapter in the book is Chapter 8, which describes and illustrates strengths-based treatment interventions. Motivational interviewing, solutions-focused treatment, cognitive-behavioral approaches—all are found here in this comprehensive discussion.

The study of mental illness links biology with psychology, the brain and the mind. Chapter 9 delves into the complex area of the treatment of persons who have co-occurring disorders (or both a substance use and a mental health disorder). We have included mental disorders in this book on addictions because of the frequent overlap among multiple disorders. Harm reduction therapists and other substance abuse counselors need to be alert to psychological problems, especially those of a serious nature, that can interfere with treatment and recovery. There is no easy way to assess the relative impact of drug misuse on mental conditions. Another major difficulty is the drug interaction between psychotropic medications and the alcohol and other drugs that the client might be taking.

In the past, clients who had a combination of substance misuse and mental health problems were often treated for one diagnosis to the neglect of the other. Alternatively, persons with dual and multiple diagnoses were shuttled back and forth between systems of care. Today, mental health agencies are apt to have substance abuse specialists on the staff, and chemical dependence treatment centers are anxiously recruiting counselors with expertise in mental illness. The central argument of this chapter is the call for integrated treatment of such persons at one central location.

ADDICTION ACROSS THE LIFE SPAN

All the world's a stage,
And all the men and women merely players,
Each have their exits and their entrances;
And one man in his time plays many parts,
His acts being seven ages.

—William Shakespeare, *As You Like It*. I (139)

The life span or life course perspective on addiction and addictive behavior addresses conceptual and analytical issues related to alcohol and drug use and provides an organizing framework for the chapter. For the purpose of organization, we have divided the chapter into three sections to explore addictive behaviors of teens and young adults, alcohol and other drug use in middle age, and similar patterns among older adults. Because society and the media are much more concerned with the habits and destructive behavior of the young than of the old, a vast literature exists on alcohol and other drug use and binge drinking by this population. Policies to curb substance misuse, similarly, focus almost entirely on social control of the young. Since the beginning of time, the older generation has been preoccupied with ways to control the sexual and other pleasure-driven appetites of the young. Although this emphasis on risk-taking behaviors by teens and college-age youth is reflected in this chapter, attention also is devoted to problems in the so-called baby boom generation of social experiences as well as longitudinal to addictive behavior that is found during the final stage of life.

THE STAGES OF GROWTH AND DEVELOPMENT

The behavioral problems associated with alcohol and other drugs emerge, in most people, during late adolescence and early adulthood (Agrawal, Sartor, Lynskey, et al., 2009). Identifying and understanding the course of those problems, accordingly, require a developmental perspective. Many of the risk factors can already be spotted in early childhood by children's parents, teachers, and counselors, even as early as preschool.

Erik Erikson (1963) constructed a model of psychosocial development consisting of eight stages. His model, like other models of growth and development across the life span, focused on how an individual's personality interacts with biological and social systems to affect behavior. From birth to old age, in this conceptualization, life consists of a chronological series of age-related developmental stages and tasks that need to be completed. For the practitioner, knowledge of psychological milestones normally negotiated, such as during adolescence and young adulthood, is important for the overall assessment of behavior and functioning (Zastrow & Kirst-Ashman, 2010).

In Erikson's terminology, at each critical juncture of life, an individual must resolve a crisis relevant to that developmental stage before moving to the next one. Often, as Jacqueline Wallen (1993), the author of *Addiction in Human Development,* contends, behaviors that seem "symptomatic" are in fact coping strategies that enable the individual to survive hardships during childhood.

Four stages that concern us in this chapter are Stage 5: identity versus role confusion (12–17 years); Stage 6: intimacy versus isolation (young adulthood); Stage 7: generativity versus stagnation; and Stage 8: ego integrity versus despair (older adulthood). As substance abuse counselors are aware, when life crises are resolved through consistent use of chemicals, the resolution of crises is put on hold, and the level of maturity does not match the chronological age. In conjunction with the damage done to the drug-exposed brain, the individual who develops alcohol and other drug problems experiences regression rather than progression.

A planned intervention, as we discuss in Chapter 10, is a technique for persuading an alcoholic or addict to accept treatment. In this process, family members and friends express their concern and caring for an individual in need of help. Following developmental theory, as Wallen indicates, interventions with older persons must proceed differently from interventions with youth. In particular, they must be conducted much more slowly. Awareness of the special needs of older adults and of their difficulty in making changes is important for the therapist. Sensitivity to age-stage differences in recovery also enhances the treatment effort.

The transition between childhood and adulthood is associated with a variety of challenges as youth struggle to acquire the behavioral skills necessary for later independent living. Certain features of the adolescent brain may predispose a youngster to behave in ways that place him or her at particular risk for trying alcohol or other drugs. Many teenagers engage in foolish, high-risk behavior that seems incongruous with their values and their physical maturity. But the brain lags behind. We now know this thanks to the powerful new imaging technology. Scientists can actually see what changes happen in the brain with age, and they are finding that a spectacular growth of synaptic connections between brain cells occurs in late adolescence. This process is not complete until the mid-twenties (Winters & Arria, 2011). Adults used to explain teens' impulsive behavior in terms of raging hormones; but once scientists were able to map where and when the brain changes were happening, our understanding about teenage behavior and why teens often don't seem to be able to "just say no" has advanced significantly. The function of the growth spurt is thought to be the enhancement of the learning capacity of the brain as excess synapses that are not stimulated by experience (e.g., by learning to play an instrument or speak a foreign language) are pruned and others strengthened.

Two types of research across the life span reveal facts about the impact of drug use during certain periods (e.g., early childhood) and the impact of key life events (e.g., marriage, gainful employment, health crises) on one's cessation of drug use (Hser, Longshore, & Anglin, 2007). The first type of research consists of as well as social experiences longitudinal studies, which follow the same cohort from youth to a more mature age, and the second type are interviews of mature people in recovery who recall turning points or crises that led to their decision to get clean and sober. Only recently has attention to such extended follow-up studies been evident in the literature. The life course perspective, as Hser and colleagues indicate, allows for the identification of critical events and other factors, such as personal relationships, that contribute to the persistence of substance use or change during the life span. Biological factors come into play, as we saw in Chapter 3 and will see here. From a developmental standpoint, Hser and colleagues found in their research analysis of hospital and jail records of long-term drug users the existence of age-related trends associated with each drug of choice. Marijuana and methamphetamine use declined significantly as the cohort aged, cocaine use increased only up to the mid-30s, and heroin use increased steadily across the life span. This pathways-to-change model is useful as we study facts about the onset of alcohol and drug use and its desistance or persistence over time and as we consider risk and protective factors that predict the development of substance use and other addiction problems.

A key starting point in our study of addiction across the life cycle is the period of adolescence. Adolescence is a time of rapid learning and skill development thanks to the neuroplasticity of the adolescent brain. But the same neuroplasticity that facilitates learning also renders it particularly vulnerable to high-risk behavior, including experimentation with harmful substances and related brain damage (Monti et al., 2005; Winters & Arria, 2011). The way the brain develops during adolescence may help explain why youth sometimes make decisions that seem to be risky. Brain development research also shows that the maturing brain may be particularly vulnerable to the acute effects of drugs, and that drug use during adolescence may significantly increase a young person's risk for developing a substance use disorder later in life (Winters & Arria, 2011). Significantly, a number of adult mental disorders, such as schizophrenia and bipolar disorders, have their onset in adolescence and are probably related to developmental brain changes. Such mental health disorders are highly correlated with heavy alcohol and other drug use. Because the development of substance use disorders is especially damaging to the maturing brain, prevention of heavy alcohol and other substance use during this vulnerable period is essential.

The prefrontal cortex, the part of the brain linked to judgment, novelty seeking, and self-awareness, is the region that does not reach full maturity until well after age 20. This fact probably explains why many teens lack the skills to resist peer pressure and why many engage in "daredevil" activity. When hormone changes, peer pressure, and the need for autonomy are added to the equation, the end result can be volatile.

TEENAGE DRINKING AND USING

Before delving into the facts and statistics concerning teen substance use, we draw from the theoretical model of Erik Erikson (1963) who labeled each basic stage of life as a challenge that had to be overcome and in adolescence the challenge was to develop a healthy identity.

IDENTITY VERSUS ROLE CONFUSION

During adolescence, the childhood imitation of adult roles (e.g., playing house) is replaced by experimentation and struggle for a meaningful identity. The risk during this period, every parent's nightmare, is that the adolescent will experiment with drugs and drunkenness and socialize with antisocial peers. The individual who is able to resolve the demands of this period will have a sense of who he or she is and which adult roles to value (Wallen, 1993).

Identity comes as we internalize others' responses to our person and come to see ourselves as others see us. During the turbulence of adolescence, when the growing child pursues his or her identity independently of parents, peer group influence is at its strongest. According to a national survey by the Substance Abuse and Mental Health Services Administration (SAMHSA) (2001), peer drug use and peer attitude are two of the strongest predictors of marijuana use. The odds of youth aged 12 to 17 using marijuana were found to be 39 times higher for those whose close friends used marijuana than for those who did not. At the same time, when the peer group held strong anti-drug attitudes, drug use by the youth was uncommon. Parental attitudes were also influential but less so than peer group attitudes. Use of tobacco and alcohol were other risk factors for marijuana use. In a later empirically based study, Duan, Chou, Andreeva, and Pentz (2009) confirmed these findings; peer influence was especially potent during the middle school years.

As Carol Gilligan (1982, 2002) notes, Erikson's conceptualization for young life stages is male-oriented and showed a lack of sensitivity or concern for the developmental issues of girls. Moral development in girls, as Gilligan (1982) pointed out, is about self-sacrifice and accepting responsibility. In her more recent work, *The Birth of Pleasure*, Gilligan likens the gender conformity pressures on masculinity that intensify for boys around the age of 5, with the pressures placed on girls to be attractive and so forth as they enter adolescence. The loss of freedom is the same in both instances. As we consider drinking and drug use patterns of adolescents, let us be cognizant of sex-role differences; we can also see how the stress on a girl to merge her identity with others, such as a peer group or boyfriend, can be problematic in many instances.

EXTENT OF DRUG USE: EUROPE AND THE UNITED STATES

A study of drug use that the European Public Health Alliance (2005) conducted indicates that illicit drug use in the age range of 15 to 34 was 22% in the United States and less than half that amount in European Union countries. Only the Czech Republic had a higher percentage of citizens in this age group using illicit drugs than is found in the United States.

Alcohol use and binge drinking, however, are more prevalent in Europe than the United States. We can compare the 2007 figures from national surveys conducted on both sides of the Atlantic. The statistics show that 22% of European 15- and 16-year-olds smoked over the past month compared to 14% of tenth grade Americans (Hibell, Guttormsson, Ahlstrom, et al., 2009; Johnston, O'Malley, Bachman, & Schulenberg, 2008). The prevalence of drunkenness among 15- and 16-year-olds is highest in the Western countries of Denmark, Ireland, and the United Kingdom and lowest in the Mediterranean countries of Cypress, Greece, Portugal, Romania, and Turkey (Hibell et al., 2009). Peele (2007; 2008), in his analysis of European data, concludes that regular drinking is inversely related to binge drinking. Ireland is a case in point of a country, unlike Italy and France, in which people are unlikely to drink daily but in which intoxication is common. People in southern Europe regard alcohol, especially wine, as intimately related to food. At the more northerly latitudes, in contrast, alcohol is seen more as a drug. It is hard to change cultural attitudes that are deeply engrained; nevertheless, the Mediterranean pattern of drinking is clearly the one toward which we should aspire. In his book, *Addiction Proof Your Child*, Peele (2007) suggests that harm reduction approaches would be of value in reversing problems caused by excessive drinking. Children might do better to learn to drink moderately at the dinner table with their parents instead of being socialized into drinking through wild drinking rituals with their peers. University of North Carolina researchers Foley, Altman, Durant, and Wolfson (2004) studied the impact of parents' behavior regarding alcohol. They found that kids whose parents supplied them with alcohol were likely to binge, but that parents who actually drank with their children were about one-third less likely to report they had engaged in heavy drinking over the past month than were others in the survey. Drinking with one's parents, the researchers concluded, appears to have a protective effect.

THE EXTENT OF SUBSTANCE USE IN THE UNITED STATES

The use of illicit drugs by U.S. school children is greater than that of Europeans (Hibell et al., 2009). Because the most recent European figures available are for 2007, we can draw on comparable figures from the earlier American 2007 *Monitoring the Future* report (Johnston, 2008). Tables from the European survey, which are provided for 15- and 16-year-olds only, show that 7% of the European students used an illicit drug other than marijuana over the past year, and that 19% used marijuana. The comparative figures from the United States for tenth graders are 13 and 35.6%.

More recent figures are available for the United States, so we can look at the results from the National Survey on Drug Use and Health. This is not a school-based survey but one based on household interviews; the survey involved over 67,000 participants and was administered by the U.S. Department of Health and Human Services (SAMHSA, 2010a). The statistics that emerged show that in 2009, 10% of 12- to 17-year-olds reported some illicit drug use in the past month. The breakdown for current use for these youths in the survey was: 7.3% used marijuana, 3.1% used prescription drugs for nonmedical purposes, 1% used inhalants, 5% used Ecstasy, 4% used hallucinogens, and 3% used cocaine. These figures represent significant increases in prescription pill use and in Ecstasy but a decline since 2002 in other illicit drug use.

For the 16- to 17-year-old group, past month illicit drug use was considerably higher, as one would expect, at 16.7%. Fourteen percent of this was use of marijuana. Of all the age groups, the young adult group—the 18 to 25 age range—had the heaviest illicit drug use. Over the past month of the survey, 21.2% reported that they used illicit drugs, which was an increase from 2002. The breakdown for current use of these young adults is 18.1% used marijuana in the past month, 6.3% used prescription-type drugs nonmedically, 1.8% used hallucinogens, and 1.4% used cocaine. The fact that stands out the most in these figures is the high rate of experimentation with prescription medication.

Tobacco use, according to the national household survey (SAMHSA, 2010a) was 11.6% in the 12- to 17-year-old group. In 2009, rates of alcohol use were: 3.5% among persons aged 12 and 13; 13.0% of persons aged 14 or 15; 26.3% of 16- or 17-year-olds; 49.7% of those aged 18–20; and 70.2% of 21- to 25-year-olds.

Around 17% of 16- and 17-year-olds reported that they engaged in binge drinking (consumed five or more drinks on one occasion) at least once in the past month; this number jumped to 34.7% for the 18–20 age group. White youth topped the list, and the male rate was somewhat higher than the female rate. Such drinking to get drunk is most common in the Midwest and West. The rate peaks for all youth at age 21, when almost half reported regular binge drinking.

Teens who drink to get drunk on a regular basis are inclined to have other drug involvement as well. A national survey of teen attitudes by the National Center on Addiction and Substance Abuse at Columbia University (CASA) (2009) showed that compared to teens who have never tried alcohol, teens who get drunk monthly are

- 18 times likelier to have tried marijuana
- Four times likelier to be able to get marijuana in an hour
- Almost four times likelier to know someone their age who abuses prescription drugs
- More than three times likelier to have friends who use marijuana
- More than twice as likely to know someone their age who uses methamphetamines (meth), Ecstasy, or other drugs such as cocaine, heroin or LSD (p. 2)

The household survey (SAMHSA, 2010a) provides the following breakdown by race and ethnicity. Among persons aged 12 to 20, past month alcohol use rates in 2009 were 16.1% among Asians; 20.4% among blacks; 22.0% among American Indians or Alaska Natives; 25.1% among Hispanics; 27.5% among those reporting two or more races; and 30.4% among whites. The rates of current illicit drug use for major racial and ethnic groups is not broken down by age, but we can draw some conclusions from the figures for all people over age 12 in the household survey. Current illicit drug use in this population showed the lowest rate in 2009 occurring among Asians at 3.7%. Rates were 18.3% for American Indians or Alaska Natives, 14.3% for persons reporting two or more races, 9.6% for Blacks, 8.8% for Whites, and 7.9% for Hispanics.

In school surveys, the results for race and ethnicity are somewhat different. African Americans reported the lowest rates of drinking and getting drunk, and Hispanic rates were lower than those of Whites in the higher grades (Johnston, O'Malley, Bachman, & Schulenberg, 2011). This discrepancy between the household and school surveys reflects significantly higher African and Latino Americans dropout rates. What about drug use rates in younger age groups? Among eighth graders, Hispanics have significantly higher drug use rates than Whites, and Blacks have a somewhat higher rate; a reversal occurs by 12th grade.

The finding of a significantly high rate of substance use for adolescents of mixed races in the household survey deserves further investigation. Choi, Harachi, Gilmore, and Catalano (2006) studied 2,000 middle school students in Seattle. The multiracial adolescents had extremely high rates of smoking and drinking as well as high rates of fighting and carrying guns. Researchers explained the findings in terms of lack of positive ethnic identity for these teens. As they indicate, however, the majority of multiracial youth did not have behavioral problems.

According to the 2010 annual survey of high school students, the use of most illicit drugs including cigarettes (illegal for those under age 18) has decreased significantly over the years. Use of alcohol, however, which is the most life-threatening drug in relation to car crashes, accidental deaths, and violence, continues to be widespread. In Canada, similarly, there is a great deal of concern about the problem of binge drinking. According to a recent survey, over a third of students in grades 7–12 have engaged in binge drinking over the past year, and 11.3% have used illicit drugs (Health Canada, 2010).

Hospital records tell us a lot about the extent of the problem. We can get relevant data on emergency room visits from SAMHSA's Drug Abuse Warning Network (SAMHSA, 2011a) According to their statistics, there were 188,981 alcohol-related emergency room visits made to U.S. hospitals in 2008 by youths aged 12 to 20. Seventy percent of the incidents involved alcohol alone, while the rest involved alcohol and other drugs. Around a third of the other drugs were pharmaceutical drugs such as oxycodone (OxyContin), and the rest were illicit drugs, mainly marijuana.

Prescription drug misuse, according to a report by the White House Office of the National Drug Control Policy (ONDCP) (2011), is the nation's fastest growing drug problem. The death toll from overdoses is in the tens of thousands, and many of the victims are teens (Centers for Disease and Prevention Control (CDC), 2011b). This mortality epidemic in drug-related deaths derives in part from the increased availability of such powerful painkillers such as oxycodone and hydrocodone. The majority of people who gain access to the prescription pain relievers for nonmedical use get them from friends or relatives. In light of the risks involved in the misuse of these drugs, the ONDCP has launched a comprehensive plan to raise awareness of the extent of the problem and to provide education on strategies for the prevention of this medication getting into the wrong hands.

The personal toll of alcohol misuse by school age children is seen in motor vehicle accidents, the commission of violent crime, physical and sexual victimization, burns, drownings, suicide attempts, and fetal alcohol syndrome. The economic toll is estimated in billions of dollars per year. Other intriguing facts revealed by the National Council on Alcoholism and Drug Dependence (2008) include the following:

- Approximately 10% of 9- to 10-year-olds have started drinking, and nearly one-third of youth begin drinking before age 13.
- Persons reporting first use of alcohol before age 15 are more than five times as likely to report past-year alcohol dependence or abuse than persons who first started drinking past age 21.
- Long-term heavy drinking can cause alterations in the structure and function of the developing brain, which continues to mature into the mid- to late-twenties, and may have consequences reaching far beyond adolescence. (pp. 1–2)

The toll from tobacco use is more long-term. The vast majority of persons who begin smoking during adolescence are addicted to nicotine by age 20, according to a recent report from the Centers for Diseases Control and Prevention (CDC) (2011a). Also contained in the report were the following facts: factors associated with smoking include low socioeconomic status, low academic achievement, high-risk sexual behavior, and use of alcohol and other drugs. The highest rates of youth as with adult smoking were among American Indians and Alaskan Natives, particularly by females. In comparison, youth smoking among black females has consistently been lower and has declined during past years.

THE BUSINESS SIDE OF YOUTH ADDICTION

Although media attention focuses on drugs such as Ecstasy and the government spends billions on the controversial war on drugs, little attention is directed toward misuse of the teen drug of choice—alcohol. During the 1980s, the drinking age was raised to 21 in every state. Fewer kids drank after that, but those who do drink today often consume huge amounts at one time (Rivera, 2000). "The booze business is big business," according to a TV news special on *Rivera Live*. Based on alcohol consumption statistics, youth under 21 consume $10 billion worth of alcohol; advertisers beam the message that it is cool to drink. Latino youth are a special target; in fact, they are exposed to the most advertising per capita of any ethnic group (CAMY, 2005).

From 2001 to 2009, Anheuser-Busch, the largest beer company in America, spent almost $2 billion advertising their products (CAMY, 2010). Then under pressure from critics, this company spent 1% of their total advertising budget on promoting responsible drinking. Congress has been lax in passing legislation to control the alcohol industry. Because the beer and liquor companies are the most aggressive and well-funded lobbies in Washington, D.C. the government's political focus and media campaigns have been on the kind of drugs that cannot be legally marketed.

In 2003, the Federal Trade Commission announced that an agreement had been reached that alcohol companies would not advertise on TV programs in which the audiences were more than 30% children. Despite this development, the advertising situation has grown considerably worse. According to a research analysis from the Center on Alcohol Marketing and Youth (CAMY) (2010) at the Johns Hopkins Bloomberg School of Public Health, youth exposure to alcohol advertising on U.S. television increased 71% between 2001 and 2009. This was far more than the exposure of older age groups. Researchers attribute this increase to the rapid expansion of household accessibility to cable TV and the growth of distilled spirits advertising on that medium.

The extent of this exposure is of no small significance because of the strong association between exposure to alcohol marketing and youth drinking behavior. This relationship has been consistently documented in youth surveys. As reviewed on the CAMY (2010) website, middle school surveys show that children in this age group (more so than older youth) are favorably disposed to ads that use animals and people characters. They are also heavily influenced by brand name products shown in the ads. In response to research concerning this susceptibility and the harm associated with the barrage of alcohol ads that are being beamed worldwide, the World Health Organization (2010) issued a strong recommendation for a serious reduction by the member countries in alcohol marketing content by the entertainment media.

At the time of this writing, however, thanks to extensive lobbying by youth advocacy and prevention groups, a landmark bill directed at youth alcohol misuse that was signed into law in 2006 is awaiting reauthorization by Congress (Lautenberg, 2011). This is the Sober Truth on Prevention (STOP) Underage Drinking Act, which will continue to promote a media campaign similar to the anti-drug campaign and provide grant funding for communities to set up prevention programming. The STOP Act was sponsored by many influential groups such as Mothers Against Drunk Driving, the American Medical Association, and the Center for Alcohol Marketing to Youth. According to testimony provided in favor of the bill, alcohol kills six times more young people than all other illegal drugs combined, yet the government spends 25 times more annually to combat illegal drug use than to curb alcohol misuse.

Youth gambling is another problem that has been pushed to the background because of the government's (in this case, the states') vested interest in the gaming enterprise. Legalized gambling is now a source of revenue that is deeply embedded in state politics. Children are exposed to gambling on the Internet, and ads for gambling casinos on TV and on billboards. In addition, many (as revealed in surveys) have played video poker, slot machines, and the lottery. More alarming to researchers is new evidence showing that children get addicted to gambling at a much higher rate than adults; perhaps this is related to the younger brain's immaturity.

Research from Canada, the United States, the United Kingdom, Norway, and Australia reveal the extent of the problem. Findings are that 63–82% of teenagers (12- to 17-year-olds) gamble each year, 4–7% of teens exhibit serious patterns of disordered gambling, and 10–15% are at risk for either developing or returning to a serious gambling problem (Monaghan, Derevensky, & Sklar, 2008). There is increasing evidence to suggest that minors are engaging in gambling and developing more gambling-related problems than any other age cohort. Kids who gamble often steal money from family members, shoplift, and consider suicide. Because this is the first generation of children to be saturated with gambling possibilities and to grow up surrounded by casinos and other forms of legalized gambling, research studies of the impact on children is in its infancy. Fortunately, extensive research is being conducted at McGill University at the International Centre for Youth Gambling Problems in Montreal. One of their school surveys revealed that psychosocial difficulties associated with problem gambling include poor family and social support, heavy substance use, parental gambling, and being male (Hardoon, Gupta, & Derevensky, 2004).

The tobacco industry is heavily invested in creating a climate conducive to the grooming of new smokers from the younger generations. Given the fact that 80% of adult smokers in the United States began lighting up before age 18, tobacco companies have a vested interest in maintaining the smoking rate of youth (Lavelle, 2000). Van Wormer had her students collect examples of magazine ads for tobacco products. One student submitted the following description:

> Before beginning this assignment, I asked my boys for suggestions on which magazines I should look through for alcohol and tobacco advertisements. To my surprise, they guided me to their *Field and Stream* magazines. I looked through their latest issue. To my surprise, the magazine was loaded with ads. I had let the boys order this magazine when their school was doing their latest fundraiser. I thought this would be a good educational subscription that the boys would enjoy. I had never looked through them and was shocked at how many ads were included for tobacco products.
>
> The tobacco ads were all for smokeless tobacco. Red Seal said, "25% more tobacco got my attention. Quality won me over. Get more of a good thing. Red

Seal—The real deal." It included a picture of two fishermen on their boat holding up the can of chew. Timber Wolf's motto was "Leader of the pack." Copenhagen pictured a handsome cowboy impressing a pretty cowgirl … Other ads were for Jack Daniel's Whiskey and Miller Light Beer. (personal communication, September 2004)

A clever, roundabout way to get youths to discontinue their unhealthy habits is to get them involved in strenuous but exciting athletic programs. In an examination of the value of this strategy, Terry-McElrath and O'Malley (2011) analyzed data on almost 12,000 high school graduates. They found that participation in high school sports, athletics, or other types of exercising related to significantly lower tobacco and illicit drug use in early adulthood. For teens involved in team sports, however, drinking rates were higher than the others. The authors speculate that peer pressure to drink after a game and the close tie between sports and alcohol advertising are explanatory factors.

PSYCHOLOGICAL RISK FACTORS

Because people drink and use drugs for different reasons, and because there is no one addictive personality type, it is difficult to predict from early childhood characteristics which children will later develop an alcohol or drug use disorder. Longitudinal studies that follow children through to adulthood offer the best evidence of traits that can be seen, using hindsight, to have been a forerunner of addiction problems. Feldstein and Miller (2006) conducted an extensive review of empirically based research, including longitudinal studies, and found that certain personality traits and experiences were highly correlated with later substance misuse. These are poor family relationships, a diagnosis of attention deficit hyperactivity disorder (ADHD), low academic achievement, and the personality traits of susceptibility to peer group influence, impulsiveness, a quickness to get angry, and sensation-seeking tendencies.

In his assessment of twin studies in Europe and North America, Rose (2005) concluded that although hereditary factors are important, the age of initiation, which is environmentally determined, is equally influential in the development of alcoholism. Such influences are family drinking patterns, the availability of alcohol, and peer group habits. Although further research is needed, it seems reasonable to assume, as Rose suggests, that children at elevated risk for alcoholism may decrease that risk by remaining abstinent throughout adolescence.

Parents are primary role models for their children; their drinking and drug-using behavior are positively associated with adolescent patterns of substance use (CASA, 2009). On the positive side, parental support and communication about proper and improper drinking behaviors correlate with fewer problems among adolescents.

Child abuse and other traumas are serious risk factors for later adolescence and adulthood drinking. In their review of the research. Ryan, Marsh, Testa, and Louderman (2006) report that between 70 and 78% of foster home placements result from parental alcohol and drug misuse. Tragically, according to this report, most parents who need treatment don't receive it, and much of the treatment is not appropriate for these predominately female parents. Ryan and colleagues describe an exemplary Illinois child welfare program that integrates substance abuse and child welfare services. Family reunification was more successfully achieved in the integrated model than in a comparison group of families.

Regarding trauma among adults in treatment, the literature consistently reports a strong link between childhood abuse and the later development of alcoholism and other drug problems (Downs, Capshew, & Rindels, 2004; CASA, 2006). Early initiation of smoking in girls, similarly, has been shown to be strongly correlated with early childhood abuse (Jun, Rich-Edwards, Boynton-Jarrett, et al., 2008). How do we explain the early sexual abuse and later alcoholism link? We cannot conclude the relationship is necessarily causal because other variables, such as parental substance use, may have an influence. Yet to identify youth at risk for substance abuse, we need to help them deal with life events that may be of a traumatic nature. The explanation explored by Goeders (2003)—the self-medication hypothesis—is the one provided throughout the literature: The drug use functions to ameliorate feelings of depression and poor self-esteem that accompany childhood abuse.

The following case history is provided from van Wormer's personal files from her counseling at a treatment center in 1985 in Longview, Washington:

> A client I once had (I'll call her Mary) seemed as cold as ice. Her mother, also in treatment as a result of a court-ordered referral, told me that Mary had once been a sweet and affectionate little girl. But at age 11, "when her father started messing with her," she began to change. When Mary initially told about her father's activities, her mother did not believe her. For years Mary was thought to be a liar. Then one day the mother discovered the truth. By then, the daughter, overwhelmed by the original feelings, plus the anger at her mother and, perhaps, at her own helplessness, had built up her own wall of defenses. Now a mother herself, Mary was verbally abusive and suspicious. Although Mary learned to control her drinking as a practical matter (her mother did not), she never learned to trust or to love. Unable to love herself, she could not reach out to others. Her extremely low self-esteem is characteristic of both alcoholic women and incest survivors; perhaps this connection occurs because of the overlap between these two categories.

What is the meaning of all this? If childhood sexual abuse can be considered a factor in the later development of alcoholism, there must be some intervening variable resulting from the abuse and leading to the drinking later in life. Our hunch is that the combination of a general sense of shame and self-disgust prevails but that specific events (and feelings associated with them) may be repressed to make survival possible. The child survives, but the adult may appear emotionally stunted; there is little resilience for ordinary life crisis. There is no "talking things out" or "laughing it off." The discovery of alcohol, often in the teenager years, may seem to offer relief.

This theory linking early trauma and a later inability to cope with psychological stress is entirely consistent with recent neurological evidence of brain chemistry changes that result from early trauma. Because of these changes, the former victim's stress response is weakened; this fact sets the stage for future psychological problems, especially under conditions of repeated stress (Basham & Miehls, 2004). Adults who have been traumatized as children retain their immature responses (fight-or-flight reactions) to stress. This memory becomes a "body memory," as Basham and Miehls explain. When childhood trauma occurs with the accompanying brain chemistry, the stage is set for future psychological problems, especially under repeated conditions of stress. In a controlled laboratory study, survivors of childhood trauma have been shown to react strongly to deliberately stress-inducing situations compared to a control group that did not suffer trauma in childhood (Yahuda & LaDoux, 2008).

The mechanisms responsible for the relationship between childhood trauma and adolescent alcohol use disorders are relatively unexplored. Probable explanations are the use of alcohol for emotional pain relief, dulling bad feelings about the self, and drinking to subdue feelings of anxiety related to the abuse. We know from animal studies that stress and alcohol consumption levels are highly correlated (Goeders, 2003). Presumably, the physiological response to stress—increased heart and pulse rates, for example—is being subdued through self-medication with alcohol.

As Albert Ellis said long ago, it is not the event itself but our perception of the event that is important (1965). There is evidence that sensitivity (defined as an exaggerated response to stimuli, which is perceived as stress) is an inborn trait (Aron, 1996) and that it is correlated with alcoholism (see Chapter 4). Researchers have postulated that the presumed increase in anxiety and stress during adolescence contributes to the frequent initiation into drug use observed at this time. Experiments have shown that juvenile mice exhibit a greater overall hormonal response to stress than both younger and older animals (Bava & Tapert, 2010). Compared to mature rodents, those of adolescent age exhibit a heightened response to alcohol and to other drugs as well. Research findings on the adolescent's perception of the events as stressful reveal that the perception of stress is a more important predictor of alcoholism than the absolute number of such events (Romeo, 2010). The need for further research into the effects of stress on the development of alcohol problems in humans is clearly indicated.

The link between trauma and stress is further confirmed in a remarkable study on child abuse presented in the *Journal of the American Medical Association*, as reported by Sternberg (2000). It is touted as the first human study to find persistent changes in stress reactivity in adult survivors of early trauma. A comparative study of 49 healthy women revealed detectable biochemical abnormalities in those who had been severely abused in childhood. In a laboratory situation, women survivors were four times more likely than other women to develop excessive stress responses to mild stimuli. Those who were abused and now have anxiety disorder or depression are six times more likely than other women to suffer an abnormal stress response.

Psychiatric Disorders

Boys with attention-deficit hyperactivity disorder (ADHD) have been found to have significantly higher rates of substance misuse than boys without ADHD

(Childress, 2006). Studies of adult cocaine abusers have found that many of them had undiagnosed ADHD as children (Stocker, 2000). Substance use disorders and ADHD are strongly correlated, and both are believed to have a hereditary component. Recent research from the University of Finland in which parents and classroom teachers assessed 1,545 adolescents for ADHD symptoms at age 11–12 years and again several years later came up with an unexpected finding: at ages 17 and 18, the existence of symptoms of ADHD in girls proved to be a stronger predictor of substance use involvement than it was for the boys (reported by Nauert, 2011).

Much concern exists related to the use of stimulant medication, such as methylphenidate (Ritalin) to help children reach their potential in school, and whether use of this drug is associated with the later development of substance use disorders. Currently, little evidence exists to support this notion; most research, in fact, suggests that stimulant treatment serves as a protective factor for substance use (Looby, 2008). (For a strengths-based description of ADHD as a personality characteristic rather than a disorder, see van Wormer, 2011).

Other psychiatric disorders, such as anxiety and depression, correlate highly with substance misuse among youth. Depression, a key risk factor for substance abuse, tends to be higher in girls than in boys (Office of National Drug Control Policy, 2006). Suicidal behavior correlates highly with alcohol misuse in teens as well (CASA, 2006).

SPECIAL RISKS FOR GIRLS

More girls are being arrested and jailed for drug abuse, assault, and loitering than ever before. One reason for the increase in arrests is an expansion of the definition of domestic violence to include girls assaulting their parents (see van Wormer, 2010). A lack of services aimed at helping troubled girls is another reason cited in the report for girls being the fastest growing segment of the juvenile justice population.

In a large Chicago sample of female adolescents, girls who had been physically or sexually assaulted were found to be twice as likely as girls who were not victimized to engage in violent crime (Molnar, Browne, Cerda, & Buka, 2005). Victimization may lead girls into delinquency indirectly through their alcohol and other drug involvement or through causing them to run away from home. As runaways, girls may engage in panhandling, petty theft, prostitution, and drug use. Early intervention in the lives of victimized children is crucial to protect them from a path of self-destructiveness.

Related to childhood victimization, self-mutilation which usually takes the form of cutting oneself is a common problem known to practitioners who work with troubled teens. Within the peer group or in institutions, this behavior has a contagious element. Research on this problem is scarce. Ross and Heath (2002), who studied self-mutilation in an urban high school and reviewed clinical files from elsewhere, found that 13.9% of high school students had mutilated themselves at least once. Teens (the ratio of girls to boys is about two to one) engaged in this behavior, according to Ross and Heath, to relieve anger in conjunction with anxiety by turning it inward. The most popular forms of self-mutilation were cutting the skin, hitting oneself, and pinching. Some researchers look to neurological factors, such as endorphins released by the body, that reinforce self-mutilations (Kluger, 2005).

A special report from the Office of National Drug Control Policy (2006) entitled "Girls and Drugs" reminds us that girls are closing the gap with boys in usage of marijuana, alcohol, and cigarettes, and they exceed boys' misuse of prescription medications. Use of alcohol and other drugs places girls at high risk of having unprotected sex, sometimes with multiple partners. It is estimated that girls who binge drink are up to 63% more likely than others to become teen mothers.

According to the CASA (2009) survey on teen attitudes, compared to teens who have never tried alcohol, those who get drunk at least once a month are

- Twice as likely to know a girl who was forced to do something sexual she didn't want to do
- Nearly four times likelier to know a boy who uses drugs or alcohol before having sexual intercourse

"The message for parents is loud and clear," according to the report: "If your teen is drinking, the odds are your teen is getting drunk. And teens who get drunk are much likelier to try marijuana and hang out with friends who are abusing prescription drugs and illegal drugs like cocaine and heroin" (p. 2).

Prevention efforts are vitally needed to help young women cope with the stresses of adolescence, many of which are related to dating pressures, sexuality, concerns over weight, and issues of self-esteem and body image. Unlike boys, who often use illegal substances for a sense of excitement, teenage girls use alcohol and other drugs as an escape or as a result of peer pressure.

For girls, dissatisfaction with and attempts to control body weight play an important role in promoting eating disorders and substance use (CASA, 2006). Media-generated weight obsession is a major problem among girls of European American ethnicity. Not only does this obsession lead to major problems with eating, such as anorexia and bulimia (as discussed in Chapter 5), but many Whites are resorting to another high-risk behavior—cigarette smoking—for the purpose of weight control. Teenage girls who diet frequently also seem more likely to smoke.

Drawing on the CASA research and other empirically based studies in the literature, health training professional Adrienne Ressler (2008) discusses the link between eating disorders and substance use. Research shows that approximately 35% of alcohol or illicit drug users have eating disorders compared with 3% of the general population. Girls who binge and purge are more likely than those with anorexia to engage in substance abuse. These findings show the need for treatment providers to screen for the presence of eating disorders in connection with their standard substance use screenings.

Much of the initiation of cigarette smoking by girls is attributable to attempts to lose weight. The statistics on cigarette smoking reveal that

23.4% of females smoke, and among adolescents aged 12–17, the numbers of girls who smoke (10.8%) is about the same as the number as boys (10.7%) who do so (SAMHSA, 2006).

About one-third as many Black female adolescents as White female adolescents smoke, according to a national household survey of teens aged 12–17 (CDC, 2006). So striking are the racial differences in female smoking that some years ago the CDC commissioned a study that involved talking with 1,000 adolescents in 150 focus groups. Findings were that some White adolescents equated smoking with empowerment and sexual equality; White girls appeared to buy into advertising images of smokers as attractive and competent, and above all slim.

Special Risks for Boys

The biggest threats to life and health for adolescent boys are alcohol-related accidents. Surveys show that males 12- to 20-years-old often engage in binge drinking. Such heavy drinking by males is highly associated with motor vehicle accidents, sexual assaults, and other violence.

The male counterpart to anorexia in females is muscle dysmorphia, a newly identified psychiatric disorder. A male with this condition, which is characterized by a body obsession, could be so preoccupied with his body that he might spend all day in the gym or weigh himself throughout the day. Although studies are filling the psychiatric literature, the *DSM–IV–TR* (*Diagnostic and Statistical Manual of Mental Disorders, Text Revision*, American Psychiatric Association (APA), 2000) discusses body dysmorphic disorder only briefly and in a gender-neutral manner. (This is in sharp contrast to its extensive treatment of anorexia.)

According to a recent report by the National Association of School Psychologists, steroids that are used are smuggled in from other countries or diverted from pharmacies (Gober, Klein, Berger, Vindigni, & McCabe, 2006). The extent to which obsessive bodybuilding is a major problem for young males is revealed in the popularity of anabolic steroids, which are human-made substances related to male sex hormones. When used in combination with exercise, training, and high protein diets, anabolic steroids can promote muscle building, improve endurance, and decrease recovery time between workouts (Gober et al., 2006). *Anabolic* refers to building muscles. These drugs are legally available by prescription to treat conditions related to testosterone deficiencies. According to a nationwide survey, 2.5% of all male high school seniors reported using steroids compared to only 0.3% of girls (Johnston et al., 2010). The good news from this survey is that in the younger age groups, steroid use has tapered off.

Pressures from coaches, parents, and peers to gain muscle weight and strength are implicated as factors that entice athletes and weightlifters to take steroids. Media images of the ideal physique for a man and articles on strengthening muscles are appealing to adolescent boys whose bodies are rapidly changing. According to a nationwide annual school survey conducted by the

University of Michigan, annual prevalence rates were 0.7%, 1.3%, and 2.5% for boys in grades 8, 10, and 12, compared with 0.3%, 0.5%, and 0.3% for girls (colleagues, 2011). In the words of a former steroid user:

> Any bodybuilder would be on steroids. Ventura (governor of Minnesota) in his wrestling days took that.... The drugs are transported to this university from a big guy who brings them in from Mexico.... I was lifting weights and hit a plateau. I'm goal oriented. Some guys said, "You should get on the juice. One time won't hurt; the results are great. I take an injectable steroid from Mexico."
>
> I'm 6 feet tall, had a 48-inch coat size. Taking eight shots once a week, after 2 months I took a 56-inch coat size. I had to buy all new clothes. I never was comfortable. I could feel my kidneys hurt; my blood pressure rose; I couldn't breathe. A lot of my friends stacked—took a lot all in a row. I was really in a bad mood for 2 months straight. The drug is not physically addictive but psychologically addictive. Here we were sticking needles in each others' butts. You have to switch cheeks, and it hurts. All the things I thought wouldn't happen to me did happen: balding (see, my hair never grew back), weight gain, water retention, sleeping problems. I blew a disc in my back from the weight. My chin got big. Before, I was a happy-go-lucky guy. But steroids change you; you get aggressive and people back off. On juice you start to like that. I remember a guy who hit a kid who hit on his girlfriend. He left him lying unconscious in the snow. (personal communication; February 20, 2001)

Health hazards of misusing anabolic steroids include risk for heart attacks and strokes, liver problems if taken orally, and undesirable body changes, such as breast development and shrinking testicles, stunted growth, and acne (DHHS, 2000). Personality changes associated with the use of this drug are frightening. Rapid mood swings, irritability, and aggression are typical side effects (Gober et al., 2006). During withdrawal, antidepressants may be required to alleviate depression. That steroids may be physically addictive is indicated by experiments that showed for the first time that rats will self-administer drinks laced with testosterone ("Rats Get Hooked," 1999). Like other addictive drugs, testosterone and its synthetic counterparts may activate pleasure pathways in the brain, according to the scientists who conducted this study.

Aggression in young boys is generally considered a predictor of later problems including getting into trouble with substance use. A longitudinal study from the University of Montreal (2010) that followed boys through the high school grades found that the risk of substance use increases substantially if the boys also affiliate with deviant and misbehaving friends. But in cases where parents provided close supervision of their aggressive children, the boys tended to make friends with more conventional children and to therefore to stay out of trouble later.

Extensive news coverage of the impact of clergy sexual abuse on boys has been highlighted in news reports internationally over the past decade. One might speculate that a high percentage of the victims and survivors would have used alcohol or other drugs as a coping mechanism. We can predict the likelihood of this outcome based on the literature on the impact of early male-on-male child molestation of boys as well as from anecdotal reports from experienced substance abuse counselors. Schraufnagel, Davis, George, and Norris (2010) examined questionnaires on sexual behavior that were filled out by 56 men who reported that they had been sexually victimized in early childhood. As adults they engaged in much high-risk sexual activity. The researchers speculated that heavy alcohol use was the link between the sexual victimization and the later risky sexual behavior.

An earlier study by Sherman (2003) specifically examined the impact of priest abuse on young boys in their care. Twenty-three of the 26 men who engaged in psychiatric interviews reported that they had engaged or were engaging in misuse of alcohol or drugs. Because there was no indication that the men had come from heavy drinking families, the drinking appears to have been an attempt to handle emotional pain and trauma. The fact that many of the boys had been given wine, often communion wine, just before the sexual encounter may have exacerbated the inclination to engage in heavy drinking. Another significant finding in the study was that men who remembered having been subjected to anal penetration were liable to experience much higher levels of depression and substance abuse than those who had no memory of it.

BINGE DRINKING IN YOUNG ADULTS

An 18-year-old University of Colorado freshman underwent a Chi Psi fraternity initiation with 26 other pledges. They were urged as a group to drink 10 gallons of hard liquor and wine in 30 minutes as part of initiation. When the student, Gordie, became unconscious, the fraternity brothers did not call the police until it was too late, as they feared getting into trouble for underage drinking (Fisher, 2009).

In October 2010, nine students from Central Washington University were hospitalized with high blood alcohol levels after drinking Four Loko, an alcoholic caffeinated drink. The previous month, 23 students from Ramapo College in New Jersey were hospitalized for the same reason (Associated Press, 2010). How did we get to this situation?

In the 1980s, in an attempt to curtail drunken driving by youth, the U.S. government imposed (through funding directives) a nationwide minimum drinking age of 21. Gradually all states complied in order to get highway funding. Thus, we had a new form of prohibition—prohibition of drinking on the basis of age. Harsh total abstinence campaigns were conducted on college campuses, and as with many laws, there were unintended negative consequences.

Drinking consumption levels went down on college campuses, for faculty as well as students. But new cultural norms of extreme drinking developed over time. In response to the problems, many in connection with football games and fraternity parties, college administrators and campus substance abuse counselors called for tighter enforcement of the "underage" drinking laws. Advocacy organizations such as Mothers Against Drunk Driving

(MADD) and government-funded organizations such as National Association of Alcoholism and Alcohol Abuse (NIAAA) have taken strong public stands on behalf of the age-21 drinking laws. But as drinking surveys reveal and everybody knows, these laws are not obeyed. "Party till you puke" is a sign occasionally posted in University of Northern Iowa dorms to announce a pending raucous event. On this Midwestern campus, one's 21st birthday is often celebrated by being taken by friends from bar to bar for unlimited free drinks. This initiation into adulthood has led to hospital trips for some individuals with low tolerance. Rutledge, Park, and Sher (2008) investigated drinking on one's 21st birthday in surveys of a large sample of college seniors at an unidentified Midwestern university. Four out of five of the students drank to celebrate their maturity. Of those who drank, around half of the men had a blood alcohol concentration (BAC) of .26, whereas 35% of the women were estimated to have reached this level. Researchers made these calculations based on the quantity of the drinks that were consumed. Thus, many of the students were severely intoxicated. We need to keep in mind, however, that these findings can be generalized only to campuses in a part of the country with notoriously high binge drinking rates.

For statistics that show the extent of the problem, we can consult the National Survey on Drug Use and Health (SAMHSA, 2011d), which conducted a national household survey in 2010. In the survey, young adults aged 18 to 22 who were enrolled full time in college indicated regular heavy involvement in alcohol use. Among full-time college students in 2010, 63.3% were current drinkers, 42.1% of the total number were binge drinkers (drank four–five drinks at a time over the last month of the survey), and 15.6% were heavy drinkers (drank four–five drinks at a time five or more times in the last month) (p. 33). These rates were higher than those for young people of the same age who did not attend college; however, the rates for illicit drug use were similar for all young adults in the society. For college students, the rate for current illicit drug use was 22%, of which was mostly for marijuana, and 5% engaged in nonmedical use of prescription medications.

Among college students, about half of all alcohol consumed is consumed by those under age 21 (CAMY, 2005). Awareness of student alcohol-related deaths, vandalism, and sexual assault has contributed to a certain revulsion against drinking excesses that have been widely publicized. According to a recent College Alcohol Survey, which surveys the same 330 colleges every 3 years, the number of required health education courses that stress alcohol awareness have decreased while social control strategies, such as drug testing of college athletes, have increased. Colleges reported that alcohol was involved in 52% of acquaintance rapes in 2009, compared with 42% in 1994. Fifty-eight percent of cases of violent behavior involved alcohol in 2009, versus 48% in 1994 (Ashburn & Lipka, 2011). In the Midwest, for example, at the University of Iowa, a comprehensive alcohol prevention program that is used on over 500 other campuses has shown excellent results (Fabiano, 2011). Dangerous drinking behavior declined significantly from 2009 to 2011. The university, however, still has one of the highest binge drinking rates in the nation.

Fraternities are also working to improve their members' behavior and clean up their ribald partying image. Fraternity involvement in community service activities is increasingly common, and whole fraternities are enrolling in brief online education courses that include issues such as hazing, property destruction, and sexual assault (see GreekLifeEdu, 2011).

In light of the magnitude of the campus drinking situation, the National Institute on Alcohol Abuse and Alcoholism (NIAAA) (2010) developed a website on this subject at http://www.collegedrinkingprevention.gov. On this website, under the heading "Snapshot of Drinking Consequences," the following facts were provided revealing the injury and death toll due to motor vehicle accidents and drownings related to heavy drinking by college students annually:

- **Death:** 1,825 college students between the ages of 18 and 24 die from alcohol-related unintentional injuries, including motor vehicle crash.
- **Injury:** 599,000 students between the ages of 18 and 24 are unintentionally injured under the influence of alcohol (Hingson et al., 2009).
- **Assault:** 696,000 students between the ages of 18 and 24 are assaulted by another student who has been drinking (Hingson et al., 2009).
- **Sexual Abuse:** 97,000 students between the ages of 18 and 24 are victims of alcohol-related sexual assault or date rape (Hingson et al., 2009).
- **Unsafe Sex:** 400,000 students between the ages of 18 and 24 had unprotected sex, and more than 100,000 students between the ages of 18 and 24 report having been too intoxicated to know if they consented to having sex (Hingson et al., 2002).

In addition, nearly one in four college students report academic difficulties related to their drinking (see more facts on the harm caused by heavy drinking at http://www.collegedrinkingprevention.gov/StatsSummaries/snapshot.aspx).

Among the recommendations provided in the NIAAA report are implement college screening and counseling programs based on motivational enhancement interventions, educate parents concerning risks of excessive drinking, increase taxes on alcohol, control drinking at sports events, work toward the elimination of "happy hours" at local bars, and offer safe ride programs. These strategies are consistent with a harm reduction approach. The NIAAA's recommendation to provide greater enforcement of the legal drinking age of 21 and zero tolerance laws, however, is not consistent with the harm reduction approach. In the words of the report: "The minimum legal drinking age law is the most well-studied alcohol control policy. Compared to other programs aimed at youth in general, increasing the legal age for purchase and consumption of alcohol has been the most successful effort to date in reducing underage drinking and alcohol-related problems" (p. 2).

The major claim in support of this argument by NIAAA spokespersons and as presented on the Mothers Against Drunk Driving (MADD) (2011) website is the saving of thousands of lives since the passage of the age-21 drinking laws. Indeed, as referenced on the MADD website and available on the website of the National Highway Traffic Safety Administration (nd) are graphs showing that between 1982 and 1998, there were 61% fewer drinking drivers involved in fatal crashes under age 21 and a 56% decrease among 21- to 24-year-olds. A case could be made that because the reduction in fatal crashes was almost as high in the over-21 age group, forces were at work other than the restrictive drinking laws that were passed in many states starting in 1984. New seat belt regulations, stricter drinking and driving laws, and law enforcement policies went into force during this same time period. Many young people also started relying upon designated drivers to escort them home from the parties.

A movement to consider lowering the drinking age was given a major boost in 2008, when 128 university presidents and chancellors produced a proposal that legislators reconsider the national drinking age (Levy, 2008). According to the Amethyst website (http://www.amethystinitiative.org), the present count of signers is 136. The name Amethyst was adopted for this proposal by the university leaders in reference to Greek mythology in which Bacchus, the god of wine, poured wine over a stone turning it into a puple gem; this Amethyst gem was considered an antidote against drunkenness. The Amethyst Initiative, as the document is called, basically argues that the present laws are not working, that total abstinence as the only legal option has not resulted in significant constructive behavioral change among our students, and that European and Canadian data show an even greater decline in traffic accidents during the same period as occurred where the age-21 drinking laws were in effect. In addition, the proponents of the Amethyst Initiative argue that

- Adults under age 21 are deemed capable of voting, signing contracts, serving on juries, and enlisting in the military, but are told they are not mature enough to have a beer.
- By choosing to use fake IDs, students make ethical compromises that erode respect for the law.

From a harm reduction perspective, we endorse the following strategies: legislation to restrict policies that encourage heavy drinking such as happy hours and 21 for 21 birthday specials along with tight restrictions on the marketing of alcoholic products in college newspapers and at sports events. Bans on alcohol ads in school newspapers are controversial, however. When the state of Virginia tried to prevent college newspapers from accepting such ads, a U.S. District Court judge ruled this ban was a violation of students' First Amendment rights. A higher court, however, overruled this decision, and the U.S. Supreme Court ruled against hearing the case (Moxley, 2010).

From an educational standpoint, the key is to teach students, starting in high school, to feel free to choose not to drink or to drink in a responsible way. The goal would be to thereby to change the culture of campus drinking. The starting point for such a change is to revoke the age-21 drinking laws and consider lowering the drinking age to 16 instead of the traditional 18 so that youths will have some time to establish sensible drinking patterns and get used to drinking moderately in public under adult supervision as well as in the home before they reach college age.. Unfortunately, the heavy episodic drinking that occurs on many college campuses has evolved into a rite of passage, so this culture will perhaps take a whole generation to change.

As Barrett Seaman (2005), author of *Binge*, argues, tighter enforcement of the minimum drinking age of 21 is not the solution; it is part of the problem. Seaman notes that a sea change in campus culture began with the new laws. This change was marked by a shift in drinking from beer to hard liquor, "consumed not in large social settings, since that is now illegal, but furtively and dangerously in students' residences" (p. 80). In his interviews with college officials around the country, Seaman learned that they thought the law impeded their efforts to monitor students' drinking because to do so would be to encourage them to break the law.

American students who have lived in another country, as on a student exchange, have discovered a different drinking culture altogether. Melissa Hoekstra, a school counselor, describes her experience as a 16-year-old exchange student in Argentina:

> It was a wonderful experience, and one thing I learned was the United States is going about handling the alcohol situation the wrong way. In Argentina there was no drinking age. We did not have milk for supper; we had wine or beer. I believe that the norm in Argentina is to drink to be social, not to get drunk. I believe that there should be no drinking age law and that, instead, we should emphasize teaching moderation. (personal communication; April 5, 2000)

P. L. shares his memories of growing up in the United States, where he got such a rush from secretly drinking to get drunk with friends, and in Greece:

> The Greek guys that I went to school with would go out with me to eat, and normally they would have a drink or two and stop because that was the social norm for their culture, and I would have to have at least a six pack or my friends from Iowa would, too. The social norm I believe for the United States is that you don't drink on a daily basis unless you are an alcoholic, whereas the Europeans do drink on a more regular basis so they can control better the amount of liquor they ingest. As Americans we drink fewer times than the Europeans, but it is a norm for us to go out when we get the chance to drink and just get drunk; then normally, we feel that we are okay to drive ourselves home. When I would sit at the bar when I drank heavily, you would see maybe a handful of people who were sober to drive home, and everyone else would be drunk. My Greek friends knew that they either limited their intake or they would have a designated driver to accompany them. Americans who don't drink every day but who binge drink when they get the chance are at a greater risk to become alcoholics as they move from an Epsilon to Gamma.[Jellinek's patterns of drinking—see Chapter 2]. They start to think that they need to have alcohol around to have fun, and they, like myself, progressed to the Gamma where I got my body thinking I needed it to survive. (personal communication; August 8, 2005)

In recognition of these facts and in light of high-profile cases in the media of campus rioting and students dying of overdoses, a number of U.S. colleges are changing their approach to on-campus drinking (Join Together, 2005). Messages of moderation are replacing messages of not drinking. In fact,

Anheuser-Busch has committed hundreds of thousands of dollars to six colleges for social norms campaigns. An example of such a message—displayed on T-shirts and posters—is: "'A' students average no more than three drinks when they party, while 'C' students average five." Unfortunately, the empirical evidence on the efficacy of the social norms approach is mixed, and rigorous research such as that conducted by Kacapyr and Choudhury (2006) at Ithaca College have found it likely to be ineffective as students' perceptions of the typical amount of alcohol consumption does not figure into their decisions about how much to drink.

Another new strategy is to notify parents when their underage children get into trouble because of their drinking. A more controversial measure, which affects recovering drug addicts, is Congress's decision to deny financial aid to college students who have been convicted of drug offenses. Students from underprivileged and minority backgrounds have been hit especially hard by this law. Fortunately, the 1998 law was toned down in 2006 so that now it applies only to college students arrested for drug-related crime while they were recipients of student aid (Martindale, 2010). Criticism of the harsher law still applies to this law in that its enforcement affects minority and low-income groups disproportionately and overlooks serious crimes such as physical and sexual assault.

Colleges have been slower to restrict enticing beer ads from campus newspapers and happy hour traditions at bars (e.g., two drinks for the price of one). Restrictions of this sort would be consistent with harm reduction. In fact, colleges accept millions from the beer industry, especially in their sport sponsorships. According to an article in the *Boston Globe*, we as a society remain hypocritical regarding alcohol abuse by college students in continuing to let top beer companies target them with advertising, and the National Collegiate Athletic Association is one of the worst violators (Jackson, 2010). During the 2009 Division 1 basketball tournament telecasts, for example, Anheuser-Busch and Miller were the fifth and sixth top advertisers. Despite their claims to the contrary, the alcohol industry makes an estimated $22.5 billion by selling to underage drinkers and especially to heavy drinking consumers (Foster, Vaughan, Foster, & Califano, 2006).

A recent marketing scheme drew the attention of the Boston mayor when he passed a display of Nike T-shirts that combined slogans of "Just Do It" "Get High" with pictures of pill bottles (Heslam, 2011). In response to the mayor's complaint, a Nike spokesperson said the T-shirts "are part of an action sports campaign featuring marquee athletes using commonly used and accepted expressions for performance" (p. 1). We have to keep in mind that harm reduction policies have a tough time competing with marketers of the harmful products that are the focus of our interventions. One of the most popular interventions used on college campuses today is the Brief Alcohol Screening and Intervention of College Students (BASICS).

Designed for 18- to 24-year-old students, BASICS is an instructive manual designed to assist colleges in helping young adults reduce their alcohol consumption and decrease the behavioral and health risks associated with heavy drinking. The program is not designed for the alcohol-addicted student but rather the student who already drinks heavily but has no addiction problems. The goal, from a harm reduction focus, is to help motivate students to reduce the risks to themselves and others. Useful reproducible handouts and assessment forms are included in BASICS manual. Research has confirmed the effectiveness of this approach. Grossberg, Brown, and Fleming (2004) found that even years later, such brief interventions of young adults had a significant effect in reducing incidents of alcohol-related accidents as compared to a control group that did not receive the intervention.

The DrinkWise program was developed in Canada and especially designed for students with moderate alcohol problems. The focus is on choice. Students are directed to conduct a self-evaluation (available to the public at the Centre for Addiction and Mental Health at http://notes.camh.net/efeed. nsf/feedback) to assess their likelihood of developing alcohol problems.

Other countries, such as New Zealand and the United Kingdom, have looked toward harm reduction strategies. The New Zealand Parliament has introduced the Alcohol Reform Bill and vacillated on the issue of raising the drinking age in hopes of curbing college drinking problems (Johnston & Davison, 2011). In the United Kingdom, where binge drinking is the highest in all of Western Europe (two-fifths of young men drink heavily on a regular basis), a surprising harm reduction strategy was to remove requirements that bars close at any particular time. The aim was to stagger the exit of intoxicated youth from the bars (Carvel, 2006). This policy has not been successful, however, in that binge drinking has even gotten worse. The latest plan is to tax the pubs to help pay for the extra police, street cleaners and cover the cost of treating alcohol-related health problems (European Alcohol Policy Alliance, 2011).

Long-term studies concerning alcohol and other drug use offer encouraging news. Most individuals mature out of wild drinking in early adulthood. Bachman, O'Malley, Johnston, and Schulenberg's (2002) analysis of data gathered annually on more than 33,000 young adults reveals how they change over time. Drinking is heaviest among singles and those who are divorced. College students who live in dorms or share apartments have the highest binge rates. Yet, they typically settle down to moderate drinking a few years later. The one exception to the trend toward moderation, as these researchers point out, concerns cigarettes. Here, the reverse of what happens with the decline in heavy drinking over time takes place. The majority of men and women who smoked a half a pack or more daily in high school are still smoking by age 32. Because of the well-recognized addictiveness of nicotine, prevention efforts are far more effective than treatment long after the addiction has set in.

PREVENTION OF SUBSTANCE MISUSE IN TEENS

A modern view of addiction holds that for children and youth it is a developmental disease (Addiction Technology Transfer Center (ATTC), 2004). This view recognizes the significance of timing—at what stage of development the use of addictive substances began. The beginning of drug and alcohol use in childhood and youth has a significant impact because of the brain changes that occur in adolescence. This probably explains why the rate of drug and alcohol dependence in adulthood is significantly higher among those who started using at an early age compared to late starters. Animal studies confirm the significance of early-life drug experience. Researchers using rats have showed that juvenile rats exposed to amphetamines were more sensitized to the drug when it was reintroduced in maturity, opening the door to addiction (Avital & Richter-Levin, 2005). This rat study also revealed that exposure to extreme stress early in life is associated with a reduced ability to handle stress at a later stage. Other studies have shown that subjects low in self-esteem are more vulnerable to stress (Gorman, 2007). In fact, differences have been found in the memory area of the brain on scans of people who test low on measures of self-esteem. These findings suggest that it is harder for such individuals to turn off the stress response. Some people have extreme overreactions to stress, and others get so overwhelmed they fail to seek rational ways to reduce the stress. Experiments with mice bear this out; if the escape route is blocked while a mouse is given an electrical shock accompanied by the sound of a bell, and later the escape path is open, the animals simply freeze at the sound of the tone, even when they earlier knew how to avoid the shock. Behavioral scientists use the term *learned helplessness* for the same phenomenon. One could speculate from these findings that youth who experience extreme and chronic stress might be highly vulnerable to depression and later behaviors that are self-destructive.

Knowledge of the developmental progression of substance use is important because it has implications for the focus and timing of treatment interventions (Botvin and Griffin, 2011). Such an understanding is also crucial in terms of knowing facts about both the progression of the addiction from alcohol and other drug experimentation to psychological and physiological dependence. Many youth experiment with substances out of curiosity and to conform to peer group norms, and many have little or no interest in going down that path again. Others, however, will go to almost any length to achieve a state of altered consciousness. The important thing is to keep as many kids as possible from starting to risk their futures through chemical misuse in the first place or from embarking on an unhealthy acquaintanceship with alcohol. We are talking about prevention.

Adolescent alcohol misuse is more likely to kill young people than all illegal drugs combined (NIAAA, 2003). Yet, in 2006 research showed that the federal government spent 25 times more on preventing illicit drug use than on preventing misuse of alcohol (White, 2008). The focus has remained on illicit drug use, yet the funding for the anti-drug advertising has been greatly reduced as has funding for all substance use prevention programming in the schools (Feliz, 2011). A redesigned Above the Influence campaign—with a broader focus on those substances most often abused by teens, including marijuana, alcohol and prescription drugs—was launched in June 2010. To what extent the new ads will reduce the use of these drugs remains to be seen. Random drug testing is another strategy that has been generously funded by the government and that has been criticized for its failure to achieve its objectives. As described by Rosenbaum (2004), who has written a book on the subject:

> Random drug testing alienates students. Students must be observed (by a teacher or other adult) as they urinate to be sure the sample is their own. The collection of a specimen is a humiliating violation of privacy, especially embarrassing for an adolescent. Testing can have the unanticipated effect of keeping students from participating in after-school, extracurricular programs—activities that would fill their time during the peak teenage drug-using hours of 3–6 P.M.
>
> A student in Tulia, Texas, summed it up: "I know lots of kids who don't want to get into sports ... because they don't want to get drug tested. That's one of the reasons I'm not into any [activity]. I'm on medication, so I would always test positive, and then they would have to ask me about my medication, and I would be embarrassed. And what if I'm on my period? I would be too embarrassed." (p. 1)

According to anecdotal reports and the legal guide from the National Work-rights Institute (2010), however, the test takers are absolutely not to physically observe the person while he or she is in the process of providing the sample. Lawsuits have been settled in favor of students whose rights were violated.

Early intervention is essential to stem the tide of high-risk experimentation with alcohol, tobacco, and other drugs. Because zero-tolerance policies of officials, teachers, and parents drive drinking underground and encourage other high-risk behaviors, realistic and proven-effective measures may make the difference between life and death. Harm reduction strategies start where young people are at on a personal level, working with them rather than against them. At the societal level, strategies for youth include strict drinking and driving laws, high taxes on alcoholic beverages, and restrictions on marketing practices.

Harm reduction principles apply at various levels, ranging from community-based educational programs to individual guidance. Some methods of reducing harm are indirect—for example, reducing the size of schools and classes to create a more personal learning environment. Unlike law enforcement strategies that focus on reducing the supply side of drugs, harm reduction strategies are geared to reducing the demand for drugs in the first place. This form of prevention, sometimes termed primary prevention, includes interventions to reduce primary risk factors, such as child abuse, as well as early prevention education and treatment programs. The aims of all these efforts are to help children get through adolescence relatively unscathed and to prevent experimentation with substances whose use carries the potential for personal destructiveness down the road. Many of the developmental changes that are necessary prerequisites for healthy adulthood increase an adolescent's risk of smoking, drinking heavily, or using drugs. Due to adolescents' unique developmental issues, differences in priorities, and susceptibility to peer influence, they must be approached differently from adults.

The public health approach to preventing harm is multidimensional and ideally operates across systems. Knowledge of the developmental progression of substance use is important for the focus and timing of preventive interventions. Knowledge of the typical pathways that lead to the reckless use of substances is also instrumental in alleviating or treating underlying psychological problems that can increase the risks for harmful experimentation. Prevention of early childhood abuse and trauma is key to preventing the development of the kind of substance misuse that relates to affect—use of chemicals to counteract low feelings resulting from early childhood trauma. Social policy initiatives must include a coordination of services to protect children from the earliest age onward. Parenting courses, periodic public health nurse visits to all homes where there are babies, and a well-funded child welfare system to ensure the safety of children as the first priority are among the initiatives sorely needed. In the United Kingdom, the government has introduced harm reduction strategies based on a coordination of efforts across national and local bodies, including education, health, and prevention services to reduce the demand for drugs. Produced by the British Department of Health, the *Guidance on the Consumption of Alcohol by Children and Young People* (Donaldson, 2009) consists of two major sections. The first discusses the extent of the alcohol problem among school children, for example, the fact that since 1990 the consumption rate of alcohol by children aged 11 to 15 has doubled. The second section offers general guidelines for care professionals (social workers, teachers, psychologists, etc.) who work with children. In a nutshell, the report recommends against any drinking by children under age 15, and drinking for youths aged 15 to 17 should always be with the guidance of a parent or caretaker or in an otherwise-supervised environment. The drinking should never exceed recommended adult daily limits and on consumption should usually be below such levels. For our purposes, primary prevention efforts can be divided into eight general strategies:

1. Child protection aimed at the cycle of violence and substance misuse
2. School-based prevention programs directed toward social influences prompting youth to smoke
3. Information dissemination approaches focusing on the immediate consequences of smoking (e.g., bad breath, breathing problems)
4. Mass media campaigns showing the negative side of alcohol, tobacco, and other drug misuse
5. Social resistance and personal competence skills approaches (e.g., anxiety management skills, assertiveness training)
6. Campaigns to reduce or eliminate TV beer ads, student newspaper local bar ads, and national beer ads
7. Advocacy for hiring more school counselors and social workers to work with high-risk students (e.g., bullies, victims, children who suffer from mental disorders, children of alcoholics and addicts)
8. The creation of small schools to reduce the sense of alienation and provide a personalized learning environment

An underlying assumption of this prevention model is that an all-out effort should be made to keep youth from ever starting to smoke; this effort should be bolstered by community and media support. (Research from the National Center on Addiction and Substance Abuse at Columbia University [CASA] reveals that teens who smoke cigarettes are 14 times likelier than non-smokers to try marijuana and have friends who smoke marijuana.) Because many families can enjoy moderate drinking while condemning intoxication and because cultural traditions come into play here, our second major assumption is this: Moderate drinking and abstinence should be presented by health education classes as equally acceptable choices. Because practically all youth will at least sample alcohol, a focus on safe and unsafe practices associated with its use is the only practical course.

Expecting youngsters not to drink until they reach 21 and then suddenly to become responsible drinkers is unrealistic. Information based on ideology rather than fact, furthermore, will be given little credibility by teens. The whole strategy of demonizing alcohol for youth and reserving its pleasures for adults over a certain age merely increases its attractiveness A behavior disorders teacher from rural Iowa draws a link between the words *prohibit* and *defiance*:

> When another person tells me what to do and leaves no room for alternative or choice, I become offended. The same applies to our youth and consumption. Choices provide my students with a sense of integrity and responsibility for their actions. When I present my behaviorally challenged students with alternatives, defiant behavior decreases. Part of the reason we have such a high rate of illegal consumption during adolescence is because no choice is allowed. If we taught our youth to drink moderately and allowed them to think for themselves, defiant behavior would decrease. Currently, the right to consume is celebrated on an individual's 21st birthday. Is this the positive alternative we want to provide our youth for the abstinent use of alcohol: a drunken celebration? Why not teach our youth to drink moderately, if at all? After all, our society seems to welcome moderate consumption in the social arena. In my behavior disorder classroom, I am constantly providing choices of socially appropriate behavior. Isn't the moderate consumption of alcohol socially appropriate? If not, then maybe we as adults are living a double standard! It's my belief that the Prohibition movement has caused us to become negligent in imparting healthy social values. Our youth deserve better! (personal communication; March 5, 2000)

Special mention should be made of the advantage of small schools over larger ones. The results of a national longitudinal study of 72,000 junior high and high school students found that when the number of students exceeded 1,000, students become isolated (Fletcher, 2002). The sense of connectedness that a child feels to the small school community means that he or she is less likely to engage in high-risk behavior. Some large urban school systems are developing learning communities within the megaschools in hopes of creating a more intimate learning environment. A positive development that is benefiting children in some urban areas stems from a decision by the Bill and Melinda Gates Foundation to contribute millions of dollars to finance the creation of small schools across the United States. Such a policy can be considered a form of harm reduction.

Given the high rates of pregnancy, sexually transmitted diseases, growing rates of HIV infection, and risk of lethal overdose among teens, especially among marginalized teens, harm reduction holds the maximum potential of protection. In their book chapter on school-based prevention, Botvin and Griffin (2011) describe personality factors associated with substance use, for example, impulsiveness, low self-esteem, mood disorders, and high anxiety. Using drugs to escape emotional pain, youth in this category are bent on self-medication. Their problem is getting through today; therefore, messages about long-term damage are apt to have little impact. Fear-arousing messages, paradoxically, are apt to attract the risktakers among them. To reach high-risk students early and to keep them from resorting to using drugs to cope with their feelings, these authors recommend a form of psychological insulation through competence enhancement programming provided in the school system to help all children better cope with the life challenges they will face later without resorting to substance use. One helpful resource relevant to prevention and available in most communities free of charge is the self-help group for children of alcoholics, Alateen, the children's equivalent of Al-Anon, which addresses the needs of families and friends of alcoholics. Supervised by an adult, often a recovering adult, Alateen is a support group where the children of alcoholics can learn that they are not alone and not at fault. Attention given to expressing one's feelings can do much to stem the intergenerational cycle of addiction.

Research on school-based prevention effectiveness surveyed by Botvin and Griffin (2011) points to social life skills training, either alone or in combination with other approaches, as having the most effective impact on substance use behavior. These approaches, as Botvin and Griffin indicate, utilize well-tested behavioral intervention techniques; they also provide preparation for dealing with strong feelings without resorting to the use of alcohol and other drugs. The coping mechanisms acquired here should be invaluable in later life as well.

The war on drugs is exacting a double toll on some children. First, it takes their parents away and subjects them to the tragedy of premature separation. Second, the stigma of having a parent incarcerated weighs heavily upon a growing child. Facts as summarized in a comprehensive report, *Children on the Outside*, by Allard and Greene (2011) are compelling. Parental imprisonment is associated with

- Three times the odds that children will engage in antisocial or delinquent behavior (violence or drug abuse)
- Negative outcomes as children and adults (school failure and unemployment)
- Twice the odds of developing serious mental health problems (p. i)

As the report also informs us, racial disparity behind bars is reflected among the children of incarcerated parents, with black children 7.5 times more likely than white children to have a parent in prison. To protect these innocent victims from punishment for crimes they did not commit, rehabilitation of parents whose offenses were substance use-related, is vital. Otherwise, it will be the same story, generation after generation.

Youth who get into trouble with drugs and who are sent to juvenile facilities have high rates of recidivism (Noble & Reed, 2000). Yet, increasing numbers of youth are being dealt with harshly in juvenile court for minor crimes and tried as adults for major crimes. The drug court movement—an innovative and carefully orchestrated development—provides mandatory alcohol and drug treatment and a continuum of community services to ensure compliance with its 2-year program. Education, vocational experiences, and life skills training are provided.

More than 300 juvenile drug courts provide intensive case management to youth who would otherwise reside in correctional residential institutions (Butts & Roman, 2004). Treatment strategies are geared to a person's maturity level—that is, to his or her readiness to address the substance use problem. Another innovative approach is a recovery school that high school students can attend straight from chemical dependency treatment. As of 2011, the Association of Recovery Schools has 22 member high schools in nine states (Vimont, 2011). Helping students in recovery make the transition back into student life is the underlying purpose of the program. The most unique and student-centered of these schools is the PEASE Academy (Peers Enjoying Sober Education) in Minneapolis (Riestenberg, 2005). Communication and learning are done through restorative circles in which students share their feelings, progress in maintaining sobriety, and show concern for each other. The circles make use of a talking stick passed from speaker to speaker. Staff are trained in the principles of restorative justice in which the focus is on truth telling, relationships, and healing. (See Chapter 10, Box 10.2 for a firsthand description of a recovery school from the point of view of a family member whose brother graduated from such a school in Minneapolis.)

MOTIVATIONAL ENHANCEMENT STRATEGIES

Ideally suited for work with troubled and rebellious substance misusers, the harm reduction model meets the youth where the youth is and is disarmingly nonthreatening. There is no moralizing tone here and no forcing kids to self-disclose negative facts about themselves and label themselves as alcoholics or addicts. A certain amount of ambivalence is expected and deemed healthy. In every stage of the stages-of-change model, originally formulated by Prochaska and DiClemente (1992)— precontemplation through maintenance or relapse—resolving ambivalence is a central theme. Helping people make decisions that will benefit their lives is the overriding goal of motivational enhancement therapy. Table 6.1 presents typical client statements at each stage of the stages-of-change continuum.

Through a close therapeutic relationship, the counselor can help a person develop a commitment to change. Motivational theory maintains that if the

TABLE 6.1 | STAGE-SPECIFIC MOTIVATIONAL STATEMENTS

Stages of Change	Adolescent Comments
Precontemplation	My parents can't tell me what to do; I still use and I don't see the harm in it—do you?
Contemplation	I'm on top of the world when I'm high, but then when I come down, I'm really down. It was better before I got started on these things.
Preparation	I'm feeling good about setting a date to quit, but who knows?
Action	Staying clean may be healthy, but it sure makes for a dull life. Maybe I'll check out one of these groups.
Maintenance	It's been a few months; I'm not there yet but I'm hanging out with some new friends.

therapist can get the client to do something, *anything*, to get better, this client will have a chance at success. This is a basic principle of social psychology. Such tasks pinpointed by Miller, Forcehimes, and Zweben (2011) as predictors of recovery are going to AA meetings, coming to treatment sessions, completing homework assignments, and taking medication (even a placebo pill). The question then becomes: How can I help my clients do something to take action on their own behalf? A related principle of social psychology is that in defending a position aloud, as in a debate, we become committed to it. One would predict, according to motivational enhancement theory, that if the therapist elicits defensive statements from the client, the client would become more committed to the status quo and less willing to change. For this reason, as Miller and colleagues explain, confrontational approaches tend to be ineffective. Research has shown that people are more likely to grow and change in a positive direction on their own than if they get caught up in a battle of wills.

The effectiveness of motivational strategies in eliciting change in even the most recalcitrant of people (see Chapter 1) is worthy of closer analysis. Actually, the effectiveness of this model of person-centered counseling should come as no surprise because each of the basic principles is derived from strategies that have been shown effective in social psychology laboratory situations. The overall technique of eliciting self-motivating statements by the client is perhaps the most basic of these scientific insights. We have filtered from one of the most popular books on social psychology—*The Social Animal* by Elliot Aronson (2004)—the basic principles of persuasion. The ones that most closely parallel the principles of motivational enhancement are these:

- If we're encouraged to state a position, we become motivated to defend that position. (p. 85)
- When individuals commit themselves in a small way, the likelihood that they will commit themselves further is increased. The behavior needs to be justified so that attitudes are changed. (p. 158)

- People with high self-esteem are more likely to resist the temptation to commit immoral acts. (p. 186)
- A person can become committed to a situation by making a decision and then working hard to attain a goal. (p. 186)
- Dissonance theory predicts that people will change their attitudes to bring them in line with the evidence. (p. 189)
- Changing one's attitudes to justify one's behavior can initiate healthy thinking patterns and behavior that are persistent over time. (p. 193)
- People desire dissonance-reducing behavior. (p. 198)

Keep these teachings in mind in your study of motivational strategies and compare them with less scientific attempts to get people to break their bad habits and self-destructive behavior. Some typical counselor pitfalls are discussed by Miller and Rollnick (2002) in the guidance they provide in the art and science of motivational enhancement. In this series, the don'ts are as revealing as the do's. According to this therapy team, the don'ts, or traps for therapists to avoid, are

- A premature focus, such as on one's addictive behavior
- The confrontational/denial round between therapist and client
- The labeling trap—forcing the individual to accept a label such as alcoholic or addict
- The blaming trap, a fallacy that is especially pronounced in couples counseling
- The question/answer habit, which is characterized by asking several questions in a row and reliance on closed yes-or-no responses, which exchange paves the way for the expert trap
- The expert trap, whereby the client is put down (the opposite of a collaborative exchange of information)

These precautions relate exceptionally well to work with teens, as does the motivational theorists' handling of client resistance. Miller and Rollnick (2002) are uncomfortable with the concept of *resistance;* their preference is to think of clients as simply cautious in trusting the therapist. They view resistance as a part of the client's ambivalence. To establish this trust and to elicit in the client the desired statements such as "I think I do have a problem," the skilled therapist relies on open and multifaceted questions, reflective listening, and purposeful summarizing of the client's story. Key to this process is reframing the client's story in the direction of decision making. A format such as "I sense that you are saying, on the one hand, that smoking means a lot to you and, on the other hand, that you are beginning to have some health concerns about the damage that the smoking is causing you or may cause you in the future" provides helpful feedback to the reluctant client by reflecting back to him or her what is heard.

Following the formulation set forth by Miller and Rollnick (2002) and Wallen (1993), major tasks for the adolescent's counselor at each stage of decision making directly parallel the client's state of mind. At the *precontemplation* stage, goals are to establish rapport, to ask rather than to tell, and to build trust. Eliciting the young person's definition of the situation, the counselor reinforces discrepancies between the client's and others' perceptions of the problem. During the *contemplation* stage, while helping to tip the decision toward reduced drug and/or alcohol use, the counselor emphasizes the client's freedom of choice. "No one can make this decision for you" is a typical way to phrase this sentiment. Information is presented in a neutral, "take-it-or-leave-it" manner. Typical questions are: "What do you get out of drinking?" "What is the down side?" and (to elicit strengths) "What makes your (sister) believe in your ability to do this?" At the *preparation* for change and *action* stages, questions such as "What do you think will work for you?" help guide the youth forward without pushing too far or too fast. When there is resistance, as there inevitably will be with young substance misusers, Miller and Rollnick advise rolling with the resistance instead of fighting it. Use of reflective summarizing statements is helpful, for example, "Let's see if I've got this right. You have a concern that I'm trying to get you to give up smoking and drinking all at once. We do seem to be moving along too fast. Why don't we look at some things people have done in this situation, some of the options you might want to consider?" Central to this whole treatment strategy is the belief that clients are amenable to change and that timing is crucial in persuading clients to take the steps that will free them from drug-related harm.

On the college campus, the most promising type of intervention to address high-risk alcohol use (and ultimately reduce harm) appears to be a brief intervention with motivational interviewing. In Britain, New Zealand, and Canada, such brief sessions that promoted reflection on substance use and the personal consequences have been shown in randomized controlled trials of high-risk students to reduce drinking and drug use significantly (Poulin, 2006).

GENDER-SPECIFIC PROGRAMMING FOR GIRLS

Equality does not mean sameness; recognition of male–female developmental differences is important in shaping approaches that will tap into the interests and strengths of each gender. As Belknap and Holsinger (2006) inform us, programs for boys are more successful when they offer ways to advance within a structured environment, whereas programs for girls do better when they focus on relationships and assertiveness within relationships. Gender-responsive policy provides effective interventions that address intersecting issues of substance use, trauma, mental health, and economic oppression (Bloom, Owen, & Covington, 2004).

The empirically validated strategies that are used for the control of juvenile delinquents, according to Hubbard and Matthews (2008), were developed on white male samples, and they place the sole responsibility for the criminal activity on the individual and ignore macro-level factors such as poverty, sexism, and racism, not to mention mental health issues. For working with girls, gender-responsive theorists support therapeutic approaches that are based on a relational model and provide treatment for past victimization. Hubbard and

Matthews call for an integrated approach that is research-based and that directs cognitive strategies toward girls' "self-debasing distortions" (p. 249) and internalized victimization. To meet girls' special needs, these researchers recommend a focus on career development, vocational training, relationship issues, life skills, assertiveness, and empowering activities.

Special attention to girls' unique biology and body image concerns is essential as well, for these are often major female concerns. In recognizing girls' special needs, so often ignored in male-oriented treatment programs, we recommend the establishment of girls' group treatment homes. Such homes would provide gender-specific programming focused on healthy relationships, a female-centered school curriculum, caring mentors to provide encouragement in setting realistic educational goals, and special services for young women who are pregnant or already parents. Individual and group counseling for survivors of sexual abuse trauma would be provided as well; these matters cannot be properly addressed in mixed settings or in gender-neutral programs.

In Waterloo, Iowa, group homes that were once co-ed now specialize in the care of teenage girls, many of whom are already mothers. A system of nurturant foster care has been established in Waterloo, Iowa, in conjunction with Quakerdale, one of the few youth residential facilities in the state that accepts pregnant teens. "Partnering with families ... restoring hope" is the theme of this program that places pregnant teens in trouble with the law in the residential facility. Following their release, teens have the option of moving into foster care with their babies (Hemenway-Forbes, 2001). Other programs focus on the development of girls' special talents in the areas of arts and crafts. The thinking here is that success in one area can be generalized to other areas and help girls develop effective living strategies and abandon problematic behavior patterns. Central to all these program innovations is the theme of personal empowerment. In a program that is empowering, the client is aided to build a positive self-identity and find strength in her own voice and pride in her cultural heritage.

Learning life skills and the importance of family can flow naturally and spontaneously through involvement in mutual-aid or support groups focused on a common, all-absorbing task. From a strengths perspective, the hallmark of the effective group leader is enthusiasm and unshakable confidence in the young women's latent talents and abilities. The leader's or social worker's role, as Gutiérrez and Suarez (1999) state, should be that of consultant and facilitator rather than instructor, so as not to reinforce the sense of powerlessness that these victimized and addicted girls need to overcome. Small groups, according to these authors, have special relevance for empowerment practice with Latinas because it is in keeping with the Latinas' history of working with one another to provide mutual aid. African American culture is similarly oriented more toward family and community systems than toward individual achievement.

Zahn (2007) stresses the importance of providing discussions of and information about gender, sexuality, and health and information on how to establish nonabusive relationships with romantic partners, including attention to the selection of male peer friendships. In conjunction with the special treatment needs of girls who have gotten into trouble, Sherri Rice and colleagues (2003) developed a statewide gender-specific plan for Nevada, one that could apply to any state. According to their definition, gender-specific programs empower young women; acknowledge and address female offenders' core needs such as victimization and abuse issues, substance use, mental health disorders and chronic academic failure; and are family- and community-oriented.

The importance of such gender-specific programming for the participants is that gaining competence in one area—writing poetry, drawing, parenting—can lead to skills in performing other adult roles valued by society. The socially empowering group, even within the confines of the stark juvenile justice setting, can be individually transformative, the more so among women who have been removed from and punished by society, estranged from loved ones, and forced into lockstep with institutional demands. The actively working, fun-loving group can thus represent a strange and powerful anomaly, given where it is and the personal history of its members. Such a group can serve as a bridge to the cultural and social milieu of the larger society. Above all, reintegration of the juvenile offender into society is the one thing the present correctional apparatus is the most tragically, shamefully, ill prepared to do. The negative labeling and punitive response to girls in trouble with the law puts them at more risk of further drug misuse in the future, often by way of self-destructive relationships. The widespread use of a model geared to break convicts of criminal thought patterns is consistent with the present politically conservative climate and entirely inappropriate for work with girls and women (Pollack, 2004). What is needed today is a paradigm shift from society's current retributive justice response to the healing model of gender-based restorative justice. In restorative justice, the focus is on restoring individual family networks; healing, not punishment, is emphasized (see van Wormer & Besthorn, 2011).

ADDICTION PROBLEMS IN MIDDLE ADULTHOOD

Erik Erikson (1950/1963) in *Childhood and Society* understandably did not focus on middle age. But he did briefly describe this period in life as the stage of generativity versus stagnation. Mature people need to feel they are needed and that they have made a contribution to others, which is what generativity is all about. The task of middle age is to leave something behind for future generations and begin to resolve ambivalent feelings about mortality. In his developmental model, in contrast to Freud, who believed that people do not change their personalities after age 50, Erikson maintained that change occurs throughout life, and this can mean personality change.

The fact is that with recovery, long-time users of addictive substances do demonstrate personality change as they begin to discover forms of pleasure not related to the use of chemicals and they begin to reach out to their loved ones in new ways. And personality change, at least to some degree, often emerges in people whose addictive behavior is of recent origin—the 40-year-old woman who develops a heroin addiction, for example, following use of opiates prescribed by her doctor for short-term pain control, or the 35-year-old man who becomes a compulsive gambler.

In his biography, *The Night of the Gun*, New York Times reporter David Carr (2008) chronicles his drinking relapse following 14 years of sobriety. In his words:

> It was a daylight waterfall of regret known to all addicts. It can't get worse, but it does. When the bottom arrives, the cold fact of it all, it is always a surprise. (p. 8)

And later in the book:

> When I was in the midst of an off-and-on jag with booze, I would have given anything to go to bed like a normal person and get up and go to work with no consideration of the dosage the night before or the shakes that inevitably arrived the following morning. (p. 380)

So, yes, in the middle course of life, whether from drug induced or psychological forces, one can feel on the inside and/or seem on the outside to be very different from the person he or she was before. And the mature person, unlike the young teen, often has responsibilities, including a family to care for.

Although the addiction literature devotes little attention to the middle period of life in contrast to the extensive writings on alcohol and other drug use among adolescents or even prescription drug problems in old age, there is an increasing awareness of issues pertinent to the baby boomers, to use the terminology popular in the press. Some interest is being invoked relevant to national survey statistics showing the prevalence of alcohol and other drug use in our society beyond the young adult years. Another area of media and general public interest concerns addictive behavior by veterans returning from war, many of whom are middle-aged men and women. We will consider facts pertaining to both these topics in the section, starting with the statistics.

Prevalence of Substance Use

First, we note that most heavy drinking and drug-taking youths reduce their intake considerably as they age and take on mature responsibilities. And even for those who have problems with addiction, natural recovery or self-change is the normal course. According to a research investigation by Day and Best (2007) of national survey statistics on substance use, of the millions who had ever used addictive substances, such as heroin, only a small percentage were still using. The highest rates of alcohol and illicit drug consumption, as we know, occur among young people in their 20s. This effect is generalizable, as Day and Best suggest, cross-culturally. And, as they further suggest in their literature review of multiple longitudinal studies, the large majority of persons spent some time in treatment for substance use disorders recovered on their own without treatment. Natural recovery is found to be related to an awareness of negative consequences, the development of substitute dependencies, and the joining of new social groups including religious and self-help groups. What is the message of these findings? Day and Best reach two conclusions: (1) clinicians have likely overstated the difficulty of overcoming addiction due to their experiences only with treatment populations, and (2) the context in which substance use occurs is an integral part of addiction and recovery. They refer to the famous example of veterans returning from the war in Vietnam addicted to heroin and their rapid recovery upon returning to life as normal. We will return to veterans in a moment, but now will delve more into the statistics of substance use in the adult age group.

According to the National Survey on Drug Use and Health (SAMHSA, 2011d),

- Among adults aged 26 or older, 6.6% were current illicit drug users in 2010.
- In this age group, 4.5% used marijuana, and 2.2% used prescription drugs nonmedically. Less than 1% used cocaine (0.5%), hallucinogens (0.2%), heroin (0.1%), and inhalants (0.1%).
- Among pregnant women aged 15 to 44, an estimated 10.8% reported current alcohol use, and 3.7% reported binge drinking; These rates were significantly lower than the rates for nonpregnant women in the same age group (54.7 and 24.6, respectively).
- About one in six pregnant women aged 15 to 44 had smoked cigarettes in the past month.
- A higher percentage of unemployed adults aged 18 or older were classified with dependence or abuse (15.7%) than were full-time employed adults (8.9%) or part-time employed adults (10.9%).

In a specialized report for SAMHSA titled *An Examination of Trends in Illicit Drug Use among Adults Aged 50 to 59*, Han, Gfroerer, & Colliver (2009) found that illicit drug use rates doubled in the age group between 2002 and 2007. During this time, rates among all other age groups stayed the same or declined. That this is a reflection of a relatively high rate of drug use among members of one particular cohort (the baby boom cohort) is revealed in further statistical analysis. Han and colleagues followed this cohort—people born between 1968 and 1962—and their substance use rates across time and found the rates were consistently high compared to other age groups. Another relevant point is that when asked when they initiated the illicit drug use, only 3% did so after age 50. There is some concern about this continued heavy use in the baby boom cohort when they get into their 70s and beyond.

Biological factors to consider are that drugs have more severe effects on the body as people age; one's metabolism is slower and there is a lower body water content, which means the drug can remain in the system longer. We would be remiss to minimize the impact of heavy drinking and drug use at this time of life. According to an article in the *Psychiatric Times* by Sherer (2006), government data on death rates in major U.S. cities show that most substance-related deaths occurred in the 35 to 54 age group. An analysis of emergency room visits reaffirms the point that people in this age group account for a high percentage of drug-related emergencies. The fact that long-term drug users use more potent drugs over time is one factor; the damage caused to the body organs by heavy alcohol use is another. Facts such as these emphasize the importance of early and effective interventions with young people, including public health policies geared toward the prevention of harmful substance use practices.

Increased Risk Among Combat Veterans

The media have focused on high suicide rates of returning veterans from the Iraq and Afghanistan wars; little attention was paid to the issue of substance use until 2008. Consider the following headlines from popular and academic media that appeared after 2008:

"U.S. Navy Culture and Workplace Leads to Heavy Drinking, Study Suggests" (*Science Daily*, 2009)

"Substance Use by Soldiers Who Abuse Their Spouses" (Martin, Gibbs et al., *Violence Against Women*, 2010)

"Alcohol Abuse Weighs on Army" (Zoroya, *USA Today*, 2010)

"As a Brigade Returns Safe, Some Meet New Enemies" (Williams, *New York Times*, 2010)

Among veterans of the wars in Iraq and Afghanistan who received care from the Department of Veterans Affairs between 2001 and 2005, nearly one-third were diagnosed with mental health and/or psychosocial problems, and one-fifth were diagnosed with a substance use disorder (SAMHSA, 2007). In an analysis of survey data from the National Survey on Drug Use and Health, the 2007 SAMHSA investigation focused on the minority of respondents who were veterans and combined data over a 3-year period for a larger sample. They found that although the highest number of soldiers diagnosed with post-traumatic stress disorder (PTSD) and substance use disorders are in the 18 to 25 age range, over 11% were aged 26 to 54. This means that psychologists, social workers, and others in the counseling professions can expect to be working with veterans of the recent wars for years to come.

Domestic violence counselors who provide batterer intervention treatment can expect, as well, that many of their treatment group members may have substance use problems stemming from engagement in combat. In their examination of data on over 7,000 soldier spouse abuse offenders, Martin, Gibbs, and colleagues (2010) found that 25% had used addictive substances during their abusive episodes. Some of these offenders were women.

Readers will recall from previous discussions the link between extreme stress and the use of substances as a coping mechanism. Members of the military, as most would agree, are subject to very high levels of stress. So it will come as no surprise that a survey conducted across all branches of the military found that almost half of the respondents had engaged in binge drinking during the past 30 days (Schmickle, 2009). The drinking events typically took place on military bases before and after deployments. Think of this fact as you consider the tragic, possibly substance-related events that took place at Fort Bliss, Texas. A *New York Times* article describes a situation where more of the returning soldiers were killed at home after their return than had been killed in Iraq. Substance use was rampant among members of the Fourth Brigade; the record included suicide, murder, assault, and drunken driving in addition to drug use (Williams, 2010).

TREATMENT IMPLICATIONS

For war veterans and mental health professionals alike, the challenges ahead are formidable as increasing numbers of combat troops return home. We should remember too the tremendous numbers of civilian contractors who also have been exposed to horrific situations in Afghanistan and Iraq and who will have received less medical and psychological help than the veterans. Most of these returning troops and others will successfully reintegrate to their communities; many will attend college. But clinicians will inevitably be working with the war veterans who have sustained brain and other physical injuries, and men and women seeking treatment for PTSD. The (Department of Veterans Affairs) VA has determined that 15% of female veterans have been victims of military sexual trauma at the hands of their fellow soldiers (Robb, 2009). In the course of treatment, mental health workers should assess for substance use, as heavy drinking and drug misuse are closely correlated with these other disorders. In a speech before a group of Virginia counselors, Larry Ashley (quoted by Heinatz, 2008), a veteran of the Vietnam War and an addiction specialist, warned the members of the audience:

> Most civilian counselors aren't trained in combat trauma, and there are some unique challenges in working with military veterans who have faced combat.... War veterans give out the trauma, by the very nature of what they do, and receive the trauma. Let's get real. In combat, your job is to kill. Knowing you've inflicted trauma, or killed someone, can be just as damaging as facing a life-threatening event. (p. 1)

The Department of Defense is channeling billions of dollars into flagship programs that partner with the National Institute of Drug Abuse (NIDA), SAMHSA, and other disease-related organizations to recognize, treat, and prevent substance use disorders (Robb, 2009). One can anticipate the hiring of many social workers and addiction specialists to meet the burgeoning treatment needs. One exemplary program that is geared to confront the military's culture of binge drinking is offered by the Minnesota National Guard. The Beyond the Yellow Ribbon program provides sessions at several intervals through the first year of deployment to help returning soldiers reintegrate with their communities, to educate them and their families to prevent substance use problems from arising, and to recognize and deal with them if they do (Schmickle, 2009).

While the military is attending to the treatment side of substance use disorders, little attention is paid to certain policies and practices that encourage the initiation of addictive behavior in the first place. For example, a program integrating smoking cessation with PTSD treatment has been expanded at VA medical centers around the country; a response to high smoking rates among combat veterans and especially among PTSD patients (Join Together Staff, 2011). At the same time, the military, according to an investigation by reporter Sally Herships (2011), sells millions of dollars of cigarettes, cigars, and chewing tobacco at prices lower than the law allows. Chewing tobacco is especially popular with marines. In interviews, service personnel said that tobacco helped reduce their stress.

In a speech on the campus of the University of Northern Iowa, a veteran who had served in the air force for 11.5 years, Joe Liddle, described the encouragement of heavy drinking and smoking by his branch of the military:

> The military stressors are great. Being separated from your family is one thing; I was separated for four and a half years. People die at home when you are gone. In the barracks, there is a free flow of alcohol. The bosses who served in Vietnam drank heavily at the Airmen's Club. There you get steaks and alcohol. According to the chain of command, each one from the top rank down bought a round of drinks. Moving in these circles is tied to promotion. The tradition is that minor infractions are acceptable if they are related to drinking.
>
> As far as cigarettes are concerned, when they were $15 a carton, we could get them for $3, no tax. Military clubs sell liquor cheap. Beer can be purchased in soda machines. (April 8, 2011)

Today, Liddle is attending graduate school on the GI bill and working with veterans in Des Moines, Iowa. He hopes to get the word out on the need for drastic policy changes to practices that actually promote rather than deter addiction. He did not mention this in his speech, but the best form of harm reduction, of course, would be the prevention of war.

As mentioned previously, the government is funding campaigns to reduce drinking and other drug problems by military personnel. As one army veteran, who wishes to remain anonymous in this book, stated in a speech of June 29, 2011 at the University of Northern Iowa:

> I was deployed to Iraq as a medic and served for 11 years. I witnessed big changes from a drinking culture in which toasts to fallen comrades led to heavy consumption. But soldiers, in my experience, never tolerated anyone to be intoxicated when they were on the battlefield. You have to be completely alert at all times. Anyway, the changes came after 9/11. Today the Army Substance Abuse Program (ASAP) operates a zero tolerance policy for underage drinking and any illegal drug use.

In fact, the Army Substance Abuse Program (ASAP) (2011) has produced a 284-page handbook available online at http://acsap.army.mil/prevention/UPLHandbook.pdf. The Air Force has launched a campaign as well against underage drinking and to promote responsible drinking by active-duty Air Force members. Successful pilot programs have developed intervention activities in selected towns with a high percentage of active-duty personnel (Spera, Franklin, Uekawa, et al., 2010).

ADDICTION PROBLEMS AMONG OLDER ADULTS

Moving to the other end of the spectrum from adolescence and middle age, we come to the final stage of life. The challenge at this stage, according to Erikson (1963), is to achieve ego integrity rather than despair. Ego integrity is defined as the ultimate form of identity integration; people who attain this attribute, suggests Erikson, enjoy a sense of peace and pride in their contribution and accomplishments. Others fail to cope satisfactorily, however; retirement, widowhood, and the accumulation of losses can lead to loneliness and depression.

Persons aged 65 and older constitute about 13% of the U.S. population; they are the fastest growing age cohort (U.S. Census Bureau, 2011). Few realize the true extent of substance abuse by this older segment of the population because these older adults are often retired and more likely to drink and use drugs (prescription medication) at home than in public. Alcohol-related consequences of heavy drinking, moreover, are often confused by health care professionals and family members with medical or psychiatric conditions. The diagnosis and treatment of alcohol problems are likely to become increasingly important as this segment of the population grows.

PREVALENCE OF SUBSTANCE USE

The latest SAMHSA (2011b) short report, *Illicit Drug Use among Older Adults*, shows that an estimated 4.8 million adults aged 50 or older (5.2%) used an illicit drug in the past year. Keep in mind that this number is no higher than it is because it includes large numbers in their eighties and over who have a low rate of this kind of activity. In fact, 8% of men aged 50 to 59 had used marijuana in the past year (as opposed to 3.9% of women in this age group). The SAMHSA report also shows that marijuana use was more common than misuse of prescription drugs among males over age 50, but among females the rates of marijuana use and prescription drug misuse were similar.

Substance use at any age is associated with health problems, but as people get older, age-related physiological changes make them more vulnerable to the harmful effects of drug taking.

A SAMHSA (2011d) report gives a breakdown for all ages of alcohol and other drug use. From this report, we learn that marijuana use was more common than nonmedical use of prescription drugs for adults aged 50 to 59, and that among those aged 65 and older, nonmedical use of prescription drugs was more common than marijuana. Other relevant facts about older substance users are these:

- The rate of binge drinking among persons aged 65 or older was 7.6%, and the rate of heavy drinking was 1.6% in this age group.

- Among adults aged 50 to 59, the rate of current illicit drug use increased from 2.7% to 5.8% between 2002 and 2010.

These patterns and trends have something to do with members of the baby boom cohort, whose rates of illicit drug use have over time been higher than those of previous cohorts. Drug-related suicide attempts among older women have increased significantly; the drugs used in these attempts were often those used to treat anxiety and insomnia, along with pain relieving narcotics (SAMHSA, 2011c). Today, the Administration on Aging is working with SAMHSA to meet the challenge of substance misuse in this age group.

In contrast to the young, older adults tend to drink smaller amounts at one time, misuse drugs prescribed by doctors (licit as opposed to illicit drugs), experience a hidden alcohol problem, and drink in connection with a number of late-life stresses, including bereavement from the loss of family and friends and loss of occupational roles through retirement (DHHS, 2005). The rate of smoking is 9.1% by older men and women, with a somewhat lower rate for women than for men (SAMHSA, 2011d). Around 38.2% of those over age 65 are regular consumers of alcohol, about half as many as among those in the younger age group. Whites are more likely to drink than members of minority groups. Unlike young adults, who seek out drugs for recreational use, the elderly may be seeking a therapeutic effect, such as pain relief.

Surveys of various age groups suggest that older adults consume less alcohol and have fewer alcohol-related problems than younger persons. As might be expected, this segment of the population consumes a large percentage of all prescription medication; in fact, older adults consume almost a third of these medications (Benshoff, Harrawood, & Darwin, 2003). Of great concern to health professionals is the large number of elderly using a variety of prescription medications without proper physician supervision. Prescription drug misuse is estimated to affect almost 4% of older adults in the 50–59 age range and a significantly smaller percentage of those over 60 (SAMHSA, 2011b). Addiction to benzodiazepines, such as diazepam (Valium) and alprazolam (Xanax), is quite common in this age group.

In contrast to studies of the general population, surveys conducted in healthcare settings have found a substantial prevalence of signs of alcohol problems—6–11% of those admitted to hospitals, 20% in psychiatric wards, 14% in emergency rooms, and 49% of those admitted to nursing homes (DHHS, 2005). The extremely high prevalence of alcohol problems in nursing home admissions may reflect a trend toward using nursing homes for short-term alcoholism rehabilitation stays, according to the report. Stringfellow (2011) writes that skilled nursing facilities may be reluctant to offer accommodations to persons who are actively using, citing increased risk and liability to their other residents, yet we can expect to see an increase in referrals as an increasing number of older members of the aging population may develop health complications due to heavy alcohol use as well as due to the aging process itself. At the same time, as Stringfellow suggests, senior living providers are ill equipped to offer substance abuse treatment and want to cater to active older adult lifestyles. Some assisted living facilities are even offering happy hours and cocktail parties on a regular basis. Stringfellow believes this will present unique challenges for residents with a history of substance use. From a harm reduction standpoint, however, such drinking opportunities could be carefully monitored as to quantity of consumption without ill effects, as happens in many of the comparable British establishments. The key is to make the alcohol available only for a limited time but on a daily basis.

To gauge the extent of the substance use problem in a local Iowa nursing home, Marcia Walker, at the request of van Wormer, interviewed a social worker who worked there. In the words of the social worker:

> The rule in the retirement community is that anything that says, "Keep out of reach of children" has to be locked up in the med room. That includes medicines, scissors, cigarettes, alcohol, some soaps, some deodorants, etc. If residents are smokers, they must go outside independently without the help of staff to smoke. The nursing home tries to put these people on medication to stop smoking. Of course, they must have a doctor's order for this.
>
> The retirement center uses the patch and a prescription for Wellbutrin [bupropion] for the purpose of helping a resident stop smoking. Staff are not allowed to provide cigarettes or alcohol to residents. Residents can use alcohol anywhere in the facility; but those that do must have a doctor's order to use it. The doctor usually gives the order of one drink per day or one beer every two days. The alcohol must be locked up in the med room. The retirement center doesn't have a big problem with this. With residents who have been alcoholics all their lives, usually when they enter a retirement home, they don't have much family support. Those family relationships have been broken by the time the alcoholic gets to the nursing home. (Personal communication, June 2006)

And as Walker later commented:

> So, how widespread is the problem? The social worker says there is no problem now; but as the younger generation gets older and enters the retirement community, she thinks there will be a bigger problem with drug usage since the younger people experiment with it now.

Investigators have distinguished two types of alcoholism in older adults: early onset and late onset. The early-onset variety is characteristic of persons who began to have drinking problems early in life and have carried them into old age. Those who have been drinking heavily their whole lives are more apt than others to be dually or multiply diagnosed and to have a family history of alcoholism (Ruffin & Kaye, 2004). Women who come into treatment are more likely to have started drinking late in life than are the men. Approximately two-thirds of elderly alcoholics are of the early-onset variety (Kinney, 2011). Research shows that early-onset subjects were likely to have changed residence related to their unstable lifestyles, to have been intoxicated more often, and to have experienced more severe levels of depression and anxiety. A large group of early-onset but now abstinent male alcoholics reside in nursing homes and suffer from Korsakoff's syndrome and other alcohol-related neurological problems (Shibusawa, 2006). For both groups, depression, loneliness, and lack of social support were the most frequently reported antecedents to readmission drinking behavior. In contrast to the long-term drinkers, late-onset subjects were more likely to remain in treatment.

In van Wormer's experience, the late-onset group had close family ties. Initially, these clients were overcome with the stigma of the alcoholism diagnosis; after a life of sobriety, a tainted self-image in old age (such as following a DWI [driving while intoxicated] arrest) was an unexpected blow. For these well-motivated but sensitive clients, an empathic therapeutic environment is essential.

One reason for finding a lower rate of alcoholism among the general population of older adults undoubtedly is related to the high mortality rate among heavy alcohol consumers and smokers. The statistics also reflect that a disproportionate number of the elderly are women. And elderly women, due to sex-role expectations from their youth, are apt to drink little if at all (Benshoff et al., 2003). If they do drink to any great extent, they are careful to keep this fact hidden.

TREATMENT FOR DRUG MISUSE

Older Americans comprise fewer than 13% of the population but receive between 25 and 30% of all prescriptions and account for more than half of the hospitalizations resulting from drug reactions. About 17% of older adults experience problems with abuse of alcohol or misuse of prescription drugs, and 20% of the mental health problems experienced by those over 55 are not part of the normal aging process, according to *SAMHSA* (2006). With these facts in mind and to caution older adults about the risks associated with pain medication, SAMHSA and the Food and Drug Administration (FDA) have launched an information campaign for older adults called Do the Right Dose.

According to a SAMHSA (2010a) report on substance abuse treatment of older adults, one of every eight persons seeking help for substance use in 2008 were aged 50 and over. And their share of treatment admissions doubled between 1992 and 2008, an increase that was far beyond their increase in the population. One demographic change that may be linked to this increase is the higher percentage of treatment admissions who were unmarried and who had no significant source of income.

According to the SAMHSA report, alcohol was the primary substance of misuse among the older treatment population, and then heroin followed by cocaine. The number reporting heroin as their drug of choice has risen substantially over the last 20 years. Among clients who were late initiators of drug use, 25% had problems with prescription medications, which was a huge increase from 1992. This problem was also more common among older adults over age 75.

In spite of the increased recognition in recent years that substance misuse is a growing problem among the older generation, many researchers believe that the numbers are grossly underestimated. Few older adults with drinking problems are getting the help they need. Reasons contributing to their neglect, as delineated by Beechem (2002), are

- Older adults with substance use problems tend to avoid substance abuse services.
- They are rarely referred from court services for drug-induced criminal activity.
- The problem of misdiagnosis, mentioned previously, exists.
- Friends and relatives can be indulgent or neglectful.
- Established criteria for classifying alcohol problems among the aged are inadequate or irrelevant.
- So much of their time is spent alone.

BIOLOGICAL CONSIDERATIONS

One reason drinking inventories are inadequate as diagnostic tools for older adults is that their bodies metabolize alcohol differently. Any psychoactive drug is likely to have a more pronounced effect on an elderly person than on someone younger. A decline in body fluid and an increase in the proportion of body fat make for a greater effect of any alcohol that is consumed. The slower metabolism, lower body mass, and decrease in an enzyme called alcohol dehydrogenase that accompany aging drive down the tolerance of older adults (Hauser, 2005). The high tolerance that younger people who drink heavily seem to enjoy gives way with long-term use and age, and tolerance reversal is characteristic. As Father Martin (1972) once phrased it in his memorable videotape *Chalk Talks on Alcohol*, "You get drunk quicker and it ain't worth it." (Virtually all the standard drinking inventories include high tolerance as a criterion of alcohol dependence.)

Compared to younger persons, older drinkers are more prone to addiction due to their more frequent use of medications, especially of depressants, blood pressure medication, and painkillers, and due as well to the high prevalence of depression and anxiety disorders in this age group. Death due to the synergistic effect of drug interactions is higher among the elderly than among any other group, including adolescents (Beechem, 2002).

Other medical complications associated with long-term alcohol misuse include:

- Problems in the gastrointestinal system—ulcers, pancreatitis, cirrhosis of the liver
- Hip fractures related to decrease in bone density and falls while intoxicated
- Injuries in car crashes
- Alcohol–medication interactions that decrease the effectiveness of prescription medications
- A likelihood of suicide associated with depressive disorders
- Brain damage in the cerebellum affecting balance and in the frontal lobes affecting functioning

- The incidence of pneumonia, pulmonary disease, heart disease, and lung cancer is extremely high because the majority of older adults with alcohol problems smoke

SOCIAL RISK FACTORS

Aging in our society is equated with obsolescence and physical decay—witness all the magazine and TV ads highlighting products to disguise the aging process. In a future-oriented society, those with a claim on the past may find themselves considered passé. Stresses in old age are related to the accumulation of losses—loss of family members and friends; loss of meaningful activities (including work); loss of identity as a teacher, truck driver, construction worker, and so forth; and loss of health. In Erikson's terms, in the absence of integrity, there is despair.

Psychological factors related to loss and unresolved grief contribute to drug and alcohol problems among older adults. The isolation and withdrawal associated with substance misuse reduce one's inclination to socialize and lead an active life. Family members may avoid or reject heavy-drinking individuals out of embarrassment and/or accumulated anger over previous episodes. In the belief that older family members are unlikely to change, relatives rarely bring them in or commit them to treatment. They often come to treatment because of arrests for drinking and driving. Once in treatment, their recovery prospects, especially for late-onset drinkers, are good (Benshoff et al., 2003).

TREATMENT INTERVENTIONS

Whether to treat older patients in age-segregated settings or with the regular substance abuse treatment population is an unanswered question in the research literature. Kathleen Farkas (2006) convincingly makes the case for senior programs. Based on her experience, Farkas has found that older adults bond with each other because, like the young, they share similar problems. In mixed groups, the issues of the young may be horrifying to older clients; prostitution among heroin addicts is one such example, and the use of strong language is another. In age-specific programs, which are slower paced and use treatment techniques adapted for older clients, such clients feel more comfortable and are more likely to remain in treatment longer. Many treatment centers do not have the luxury of separate programming. Van Wormer found that many clients thoroughly enjoyed the mix of ages in her therapy groups: Older clients seemed to benefit from giving advice and sharing their stories with younger group members. They also seemed to like getting personally involved in hearing of the intrigues and relationship crises of others in the group. One drawback was the general lack of patience toward those occasional group members who were hard of hearing. The chiding of participants to speak up had a dampening effect on group interaction.

Excellent results are reported from the Elder Care Program at Odyssey House, a residential program in New York City for those over age 55

(Jones, 2005; Springfellow, 2011). The clients in this treatment center sit in circles and share stories of their past and present struggles with alcohol and prescription medication. Sometimes substance use followed a too-early retirement or death of a loved one. The recovery rate is significantly higher in this than in younger age groups. Residents speak of spending quality time with their grandchildren and wanting to now take care of their health. Fewer than 20% of licensed substance abuse treatment centers offer programs specifically geared for persons of this age.

The *Substance Abuse Relapse Prevention for Older Adults: A Group Treatment Approach* (Center for Substance Abuse Treatment (CSAT), 2005) recommends incorporating seven features into treatment of older alcohol misusers:

1. Emphasis on age-specific rather than mixed-age treatment
2. Use of supportive, nonconfrontational approaches that build self-esteem
3. Focus on cognitive-behavioral approaches to address negative emotional states such as depression, loneliness, and feelings of loss
4. Development of skills for improving social support
5. Recruitment of counselors trained and motivated to work with older adults
6. Capacity to provide referrals to medical, mental health, and aging services
7. Appropriate pace and content for older adults (p. 13)

Additional tips provided by this government source are to provide a clear statement of the goal and purpose of each session; to make use of simultaneous visual and oral presentation of material, enlarged print, nonglaring light, reduction of background noise; to keep group sessions short (55 minutes maximum); and to begin each session with a review of previous material.

In her work with older female clients, van Wormer found them remarkably receptive to treatment, grateful for the opportunity to come to group, and as often as not, seeing the crisis that brought them through the treatment doors as a blessing. When two older female graduates of the program requested diplomas to put on their walls, the receptionist obligingly rushed out to have some made up. (Such a request had never been made before.) In working with such older women, one can expect that feelings of guilt and shame about drinking will emerge. In consideration of this fact and in light of her personal experience in working with older women with substance use problems, Cohen (2000) recommends approaching an older woman about her drinking in an atmosphere of privacy and respect for her personal history. In addition, Cohen suggests that counselors recognize the stigma that the words *alcoholism* and *alcoholic* might hold for her. Terms such as *drinking* and *drinking problems* can be used instead. A focus on health and a healthy lifestyle is usually well received.

Hanson and Gutheil (2004) detail the use of motivational strategies with older adults who have drinking and other drug problems. These strategies are especially useful in healthcare centers, social service agencies, nursing homes, and other establishments that are likely places of first contact with members of the older population who have substance use problems. Brief interventions can be provided while using the client's concerns as a focal point to facilitate discussion. To build motivation for sustained change, feedback must be personalized but also raise the client's awareness of the extent of the problem. Involving the client's family can help increase the success of motivational counseling. Because many older individuals are sensitive to the stigma of alcohol misuse, motivation strategies provided in nonstigmatized agencies such as healthcare facilities work best (American Association for Geriatric Psychiatry, 2003).

Beechem (2002, Chapter 8) delineates common pitfalls for the counselor who provides substance abuse treatment to an older clientele: (a) *ageism* and stereotyping of which the counselor may be unaware (use of derogatory off-the-cuff remarks such as "this dates me" sends a message that old is bad); (b) *countertransference*, the unconscious process in which older individuals trigger feelings in the helper about his or her parents and grandparents that interfere with therapy; (c) *avoidance and denial* of the addiction problems in assessment; and (d) *expressing sympathy* rather than empathy, which compounds the clients' self-pity and helplessness.

Contemporary barriers to healthcare stemming from managed healthcare restrictions and federal and state cutbacks take a heavy toll on persons of advanced age with substance use problems that need treatment. Whereas Medicare, the healthcare provision for people over age 65, traditionally covered 12 days of inpatient alcohol treatment, many states, under pressure from managed care companies, are eliminating this coverage. In view of the large number of physical and cognitive problems among polydrug using older adults, including lengthy withdrawals, coverage of at least 12 days of inpatient treatment is an extremely important option.

Health Canada (2007) states that "since even low levels of alcohol consumption in seniors can have deleterious effects, any reduction in drinking behaviour will likely be beneficial" (p. 46). Similarly, a reduction in the excessive use of prescription medication will contribute to improved personal health and functioning. For many older people with short-term substance use problems, brief interventions are all that are needed to help them discontinue their drug use. Harm reduction approaches also need to address misuse of prescription medications by finding ways to increase compliance with prescription or over-the-counter medications. Health Canada cites under their examples of best practices a harm reduction program described by Graham and Brett (1994). Funded by a grant from the city of Ottawa, Canada, the project, Lifestyle Enrichment for Senior Adults, was designed to reach senior apartment residents suspected of having problems with alcohol and psychoactive medication. Participants learned of the project through news stories, hospital referrals, or friends. This client-centered program was conducted in the tradition of Carl Rogers, a tradition high on empathy and warmth and low on confrontation. Unique to this program was the acceptance given to persons who had little or no desire to quit drinking or using drugs and would have been excluded from conventional, abstinence-based programs. By focusing on the harm associated with the substance use rather than solely on the use itself, both counselor and client could consider a broad range of solutions (e.g., delaying drinking until the evening). To reduce the stigma of slips and relapses, the focal point was on personal issues rather than substance use. For example, a person who had begun using drugs or alcohol following the death of a spouse might, in developing a rapport with the counselor or group, find solace through dealing with repressed feelings related to unresolved grief and/or in joining a local bereavement support group.

In their in-depth interviews with participants and graduates of the Lifestyle Enrichment for Senior Adults program, Graham and Brett found the clients' dependence problems were of two varieties. Either these problems were related to a mental disorder and were longstanding in nature, or more often, the addiction problems had evolved out of loneliness and isolation. Program participants improved their health-seeking behaviors considerably as a result of the treatment interventions and personal attention received. Social events were an active and popular component of this program; group meetings served as aftercare insurance against relapse.

Many older problem drinkers in harm reduction and conventional programs decide abstinence is their best course. Some of the most active members of Alcoholics Anonymous are retired individuals who derive great personal satisfaction in helping newly sober younger alcoholics. AA's use of storytelling is attractive to older people, who often have spellbinding stories from years past. Most cities have meetings specifically for older AA members. Attendees often derive great satisfaction from the camaraderie and interactive ritualism of such mutual-support groups.

PREVENTION OF RELAPSE

Relapse, or a "lapse" as it is commonly called by harm reduction model proponents, does not mean, in AA parlance, "one drink, one drunk." Nor does it refer to a failed drug test that shows one is "dirty" if one smokes a single marijuana cigarette over a month's time. A relapse is not a one-time slip or setback but rather a process. A client's return to harmful use can be interpreted as a temporary lapse in the path to changing addictive behavior. At the thinking level, relapse is seen as leading back from the action stage to the contemplation or precontemplation level (Daisy, Thomas, & Worley, 2002). By helping clients appreciate that changing addictive behavior is a learning process, lapses can be reframed as valuable learning opportunities rather than indications of personal failure (Witkiewitz, 2005). This reframing is crucial to keep the lapses from leading to a full relapse. Once a client is overwhelmed with guilt and conflict, his or her sense of failure can easily become a self-fulfilling prophecy. Specific strategies to prevent a lapse from turning into a full-blown relapse, as adapted from guidelines offered by Witkiewitz and Marlatt (2007, p. 12), are

- Stop, look, and listen. Clients can be taught in advance that a lapse is a warning signal that they are in danger and need to retire to a quiet place to review these strategies.

- Keep calm; avoid feelings of guilt and self-blame.
- Renew commitment; after a lapse, the most important thing to deal with is motivation.
- Review the situation leading up to the lapse.
- Make an immediate plan for recovery, such as getting rid of the pills or alcohol or leaving the high-risk situation.
- Dealing with the abstinence violation effect. Teach clients not to view the cause of the lapse as a personal failure.... but instead ask them to pay attention to the environmental and psychological factors in the high risk situation.
- Draw on the support network for help.

Broadly speaking, interventions for relapse management can be thought of as efforts to minimize the harm associated with a return to unhealthy practices following a period of abstinence or controlled use.

The return to addictive patterns following treatment more often than not is associated with negative emotions, such as anger, anxiety, depression, and boredom, and a desire to suppress those strong emotions. Clients can be taught to avoid or to prepare themselves to handle unrealistic expectations, environmental cues, or triggers such as the smell of alcohol; both positive and negative emotional states; and sexual triggers. Achieving a balanced satisfying lifestyle is an essential part of reducing the potential for relapse (Washton & Zweben, 2006). A favorite saying in substance abuse treatment is HALT! Don't get too

Hungry

Angry

Lonely

Tired

Triggers such as peer pressure and work-related problems are common among younger alcoholics, but elderly alcoholics are more apt to be influenced by late-life situations (Beechem, 2002). Depression, loneliness, and unresolved loss-grief issues are negative emotions that may be associated with the use of a chemical to dull the senses, if not to get high. In extreme cases, such low feelings combined with drug use can be a precursor to suicide.

Especially for young people, the setting of an unrealistic goal, such as never drinking again, can be counterproductive. If the treatment goal is total abstinence, then any transgressions may be viewed negatively, which may actually lead to an increase in the problematic behavior (Witkiewitz, 2005).

The learning of critical thinking skills is a key factor in maintaining recovery following treatment. Valtonen, Sogren, and Cameron-Padmore (2006) conducted research in rehabilitation facilities in Trinidad. Their focus was on coping styles in handling stress. They found that only a minority of the clients had acquired mature problem-solving skills or knew how to draw strength from social support systems to deal with grief and loss, for example. As research such as that of Valtonen and colleagues indicates, one focus of therapy practice must be directed to counterproductive responses learned early in life that have to be unlearned to help insulate the person from relapse.

Beechem offers a cognitively based three-stage approach to relapse prevention geared toward high-risk situations for older adults. In stage one, high-risk situations are spelled out. Although a standardized checklist of typical risks may be provided, the client's personal list is derived through collaboration and discussion. Typical risks that may be listed are watching old family movies, returning home from a family reunion or funeral, suffering sleep loss, harping on one's regrets in life ("If only I had …"), and hanging around bars.

In stage two, clients are helped to monitor the antecedents of drinking urges. Together with the counselor, a plan for continuous self-monitoring of negative thoughts and deeds is drawn up. Evolving from homework assignments is a clear sense of the client's strengths, support systems, and capabilities. Through prompting, as the older client reviews his or her life crises and blessings, the counselor can help the client appreciate his or her coping style, strengths, and purpose in life (professional and/or personal triumphs). Stage three stresses the self-management and self-efficacy that are keys to sober living.

Central to this three-stage approach of high-risk prevention is the notion that clients are consumers and that their concerns and needs are paramount. Forcing them to conform their thinking to standard belief systems that have worked for some (e.g., to have to say, "My sobriety comes first") is less effective than helping an individual elicit his or her own insights. Many clients have a spiritual life or did at one time. Helping the client tap into his or her spirituality can provide a source of strength and comfort. Other persons with substance misuse problems might be of a more secular bent; a group such as Rational Recovery or Women for Sobriety might suit their particular needs. In the words of harm reduction theorists Denning, Little, and Glickman (2004), "*You* are the expert. You know better than anyone what works and doesn't work. You are the one with the power to choose what's best for you" (p. 16).

Loss and Grief

Death of a loved one is a constant fact of life for persons who survive into old age; loss and grief are therefore inevitable at this stage of life. Most people grieve and go on. Unresolved grief and depression, however, sometimes are associated with excessive drinking and use of prescription pills for anxiety or depression. For older adults with substance use issues, recovery means learning to grieve effectively without using substances to ease the pain (Willis, 2008).

As alcoholics share their life histories in treatment, the link between grief and loss and other feelings such as guilt and anger becomes apparent. In long-term alcoholics, an early loss that was deeply troubling and even traumatizing may have played a role in the later use of chemicals as a form of relief. Guilt feelings connected to the early childhood loss are now compounded by the addictive behavior.

Among widows and widowers, many of whom never had a drinking problem, unhealthy guilt feelings may arise in connection with a dying family member. Three types of guilt typically found in family members of the terminally ill are survivor guilt, a sense of helplessness, and ambivalence guilt. Interestingly, these same unhealthy responses are often seen in the families of alcoholics, torn as they are by feelings of helplessness and responsibility.

Survivor guilt occurs when one person is spared death or a calamity while another or others are not. The one who is spared may go into a depression marked by obsessive thoughts. The "why me?" syndrome of the victim has its counterpart in the "why not me?" reaction of the survivor. The survivor, such as the person who lived through Hiroshima or a plane crash, may feel a need to justify his or her own survival. Underneath, there may be a feeling of unworthiness.

Parents who have lost children, children who have lost parents, and surviving spouses and partners all can experience their own version of survivor guilt. For parents who survive their children, their failure to carry out the most fundamental task of protection arouses a special overwhelming despair. Sometimes, the elderly outlive a middle-aged son or daughter.

When a family member is terminally ill, the partner or spouse invariably will feel a sense of personal failure, for the caregiver is unable to do what he or she believes should be done—namely, to heal the one who is suffering and make the pain go away. Parents of ill children, for example, are apt to suffer much emotional pain in their inability to take their child's illness away. This is the second type of guilt—*guilt due to helplessness*. The dying person's dependence on drugs for relief may further contribute to the survivor's sense of helplessness and frustration, especially when the drugs fail to bring the relief desired. Futile attempts to get the dying patient to eat can also be problematic.

Ambivalence guilt is present as the caregiver begins to resent this role. Loss of a partially loved spouse is sometimes more difficult than loss of a beloved spouse. As one older woman in this situation once said to van Wormer, "Sometimes I wish this whole thing would end. Do you think I'm terrible?" Loss due to suicide compounds the guilt, which is often accompanied by a sense of shame (Jackson, 2004).

Some individuals grieving over suicide are so overcome that they themselves are at risk for suicide and/or substance misuse. Jackson likens the strong grief reaction of family members who lose a loved one to suicide to the reaction of the family members of a woman who was addicted to heroin, was homeless, and died in the street of an overdose. She sees a similarity also in both situations in the feelings of shame brought out in the family members. People blame each other in an event of this sort.

Persons who work with older clients with addiction problems would do well to explore the dynamics of grieving and the relationship between negative feelings and the use of substances to quell them. Therapy groups for older clients can delve into bereavement issues as they arise. In helping group members understand the emotional impact of death and dying and to accept any alien feelings for what they are—an integral part of the grieving process—the practitioner can help them cope better.

The ability to come to terms with loss and grief, and thereby to transcend them, is a major factor in the alcoholic's successful recovery.

SPIRITUAL HEALING

Many early psychologists, Jung (1933) and Maslow (1950/1971) the most renowned among them, have written of the essence of experience that goes beyond the "natural" realm into a higher level of consciousness. Today, however, spirituality is a resource that is often overlooked in the literature, especially in the literature on empowerment practice and harm reduction. And yet, if they seek to draw on the strengths of clients and of their community, how can practitioners disregard a force that traditionally has offered marginalized people the greatest support of all?

"Spiritual well-being," as defined by Canda and Furman (2010), "is a quality of developing and being oriented toward ultimate or sacred concerns that alleviates personal and collective suffering" (p. 93). Erikson, as Canda and Furman note, suggested that people in late adulthood often review their lives with increased interest and concern as the reality of their own mortality beckons.. Most people have a heightened sense of spirituality at this stage, which they may or may not have experienced before, as they seek the meaning of their own life. Thanks to lobbying by Canda and others, religion was added by the Council on Social Work Education (CSWE) in 1995 to key characteristics of diversity to be covered in the social work curriculum, and, more recently, spiritual development was recognized by CSWE as a central aspect of human behavior. To start where the client is and to approach the client developmentally across the life cycle, we need to assess for the possibility that the client has a sense of the meaning of life, including a religious faith that he or she can draw on. Religious faith can be a help or a hindrance, but often a sense of faith and/or membership in a worship community can be appreciated by the therapist as sources of strength. Sheridan (2004) describes the healing power of nature that her students discovered in their work with women in residential treatment. Her goal, paralleling that of Besthorn (2003), is to enable clients to become more aware of the spiritual dimension of their experience with the natural world. Van Wormer learned in Norway from her alcoholic clients of the Higher-Power-As-Nature—that the sense of oneness with nature can have a marvelous unifying effect on people and provide a sense of meaning and comfort. The cultural ethos of Norwegians is reminiscent of that of North America's First Nations Peoples (see van Wormer & Besthorn, 2011).

Attention not only to the biopsychosocial but also to the spiritual dimension has special relevance to the field of substance abuse treatment because of the strong spirituality component of AA. The Twelfth Step (which begins, "Having had a spiritual awakening as the result of these steps ...") sums up this focus, which entails a move away from a self-centered view of the world to one that places the individual in relation to a larger universe. Spirituality is of special relevance to addictions treatment not only because of AA's stress but also in its own right. The heavy load of guilt feelings that recovering people often carry explains the desire that many persons in recovery have for reconciliation and renewal, even forgiveness. Some who once derived great satisfaction from membership in a religious organization may seek a return to that type of involvement. Older adults in treatment for alcohol or other drug problems often have spiritual needs related to their stage of life, perhaps to their growing familiarity with the prospect of death. In the face of despair associated with earthly losses, spirituality can bolster one's courage in taking risks to pursue personal change and perhaps get involved in a formal association or reading group.

Religious writers in this field often conceive of alcoholism as a spiritual illness, a condition seen as resulting from a spiritual void in one's life and from a search for a connection. And yet they noted, as did Father James Royce (1989), based on his observations from the 1980s, that an overwhelming majority of alcoholism treatment clients complained that their spiritual needs were not met in standard treatment programs. *Spirituality* is a word not generally associated with harm reduction enthusiasts. Happily, as Orzech (2006) indicates, there is a keen recognition today of how spiritual and religious factors affect the quality of one's recovery. People who attend Twelve-Step groups are more likely than others to get in tune with their spiritual side. Early results of research funded by NIAAA single out spirituality as a boon to sustained recovery (Orzech, 2006). More recent results have been encouraging as well. For example, to test the hypothesis that religious and spiritual growth in recovery would enhance sobriety, Robinson, Krentzman, Webb, and Brower (2011) conducted an empirically based longitudinal study of recovering alcoholics that controlled for AA membership. They found significant changes in a 6-month period that included an increase in spiritual or religious beliefs and practices, daily spiritual experiences, attitudes of forgiveness, and sense of purpose in life. Increases in private spiritual and religious practices and forgiveness of self were the strongest predictors of improvements in drinking outcomes.

What about harm reduction advocates? An earlier view was voiced by Patt Denning (2000), who boldly stated in the introduction to her book on practicing harm reduction psychotherapy that her increasing resistance to Twelve-Step–based interventions, "particularly the emphasis on powerlessness and spirituality," led her to seek out an alternative model (p. xvi).

More recently, one of the best known of the harm reduction researchers, Alan Marlatt, took a step in the other direction. He introduced a treatment approach for prison inmates in Washington State that is rooted in Buddhist meditation. Clients meditate long hours for 10 days in a row. When compared to a control group, the inmates used significantly less tobacco and heroin upon release (reported by Orzech, 2004).

If we conceptualize recovery as a kind of journey, we can see it as a path leading from isolation to meaning, as the achievement, in the final analysis, of serenity and spiritual health. Grief work can help people who want to pursue it to move beyond self-blame into a realm of higher consciousness. Recovery itself can be conceptualized as a grieving process. Letting go and grieving, as Maria Carroll (1999) suggests, are integral to the human and spiritual journey.

Carroll (1987, 1999) conceptualizes the spiritual journey in terms of breaking the bonds to earthly attachments and achieving a mastery of oneself through strengthened virtues. For the recovering alcoholic, one earthly attachment is to the substance alcohol. Only when the bond to their addiction is broken can alcoholics move to higher things and embark on "a journey home." To Carroll, the journey home entails constructing a personal reality, becoming disillusioned with this reality, letting the ego-self disintegrate, surrendering, reframing the old reality, and then allowing a new reality to develop as the transformed state. Through *surrendering* to the reality of the present, the recovering alcoholic moves through a spiritual awakening process toward wholeness and a larger humanity. Drawing on her exploratory and in-depth research on spirituality and recovering alcoholics, Carroll (1993) suggests that the Twelve Steps can offer a guide toward increasing self-knowledge, giving to others, and reaching a higher state of consciousness. Other ways of achieving spiritual well-being and belongingness include religious faith and a sense of harmony with nature and the universe.

For the person with serious alcohol problems, merely being well does not provide enough protection to withstand future temptations of alcohol and/or some other addiction. Mantell (1983) believes that to ensure sobriety, such individuals must achieve a level that is "weller than well." Spiritual well-being is considered by Cowley (1993) to be the epitome of health. It may come from a sense of unity with the cosmos or from a personal closeness to God or to nature. The experience of wholeness and integration is not dependent on religious belief or affiliation. Fulfillment of the spiritual dimension is important in providing a sense of meaning in life.

Studies on addiction recovery indicate that approaches to heightened spiritual awareness markedly increase a sense of purpose in life (O'Connell, 1999). A growing body of research indicates, moreover, as O'Connell reports, that spiritual practices such as prayer, contemplation, yoga, Zen, and transcendental meditation have a measurable effect on physiological processes in the brain. The fact that spiritual contemplation can be registered in terms of brain activity (actually inactivity in one region of the brain) gives the experience a neuroscientific reality. Recent advances in neuroscience help explain why some people experience ineffable, transcendent events to be as real as their normal range of sensory impressions (Begley, 2007). O'Connell's recommendation is that the client's attitude toward and sense of spirituality be routinely assessed in the recovery process. There is a growing recognition among providers of culturally specific programs such as those for African Americans and North American Native populations that spiritual beliefs offer a great resource. Clients from other ethnic groups as well can benefit from tapping into this often overlooked resource. Spiritual beliefs have special meaning to persons who have reached the time of life when they are inclined to review the past, that is, look back over the years and reflect on the turning points. Wrestling with issues of mortality and immortality, people in late adulthood are prone to ponder the meaning of their lives and of life itself.

In the words of theologian Karen Armstrong (1993), "Human beings cannot endure emptiness and desolation; they will fill the vacuum by creating a new focus of meaning" (p. 399). Without imposing their own religious and spiritual beliefs on their clients, professionals in this field should help clients in their search for spiritual truth. All clients should have access to spiritual literature and the possibility of consultation with a spiritual mentor.

SUMMARY AND CONCLUSION

The first and the last, the new and the old—this chapter has focused on the major psychological growth tasks and pitfalls confronting youth and people in their middle and later years. Although problems with drinking and drug use occur across the life span, we have chosen to focus primarily on the first and last stages of life because of the special vulnerabilities accruing to these transitional stages. If we were following the lives of particular clients in treatment for one of the substance use disorders, we could see that unresolved crises and bad habits from the earlier period of life have come to a head at a later stage. Adolescent addicts require intensive treatment stays because of attitude, whereas the elderly require a lengthy recovery period because of biology. Although the young have little or no sense of their mortality, the old may be much too absorbed with this same issue.

Two prevalent myths in society are that the young will not listen and the old will not learn. According to this logic, there would be little point in treatment for either of these groups. In fact, cost-effectiveness research reveals just the opposite: Prevention and treatment at each level of maturity can be highly effective when geared toward the special concerns of the clients in that age group. Each stage of life carries its own reward for sobriety and its own treatment needs. As a basic principle of effective leadership and counseling states: Lead a person only as far as he or she is likely to follow. The focus is set by the client, not the counselor, and so is the rhythm of therapy.

REFERENCES

Addiction Technology Transfer Center (ATTC). (2004). Adolescents. *ATTC Networker*, 6(2), 1–2.

Agrawal, A., Sartor, C. E., Lynskey, M. T., Grant, J. D., Pergadia, M. L., Grucza, R., Bucholz, K. K., Nelson, E. C., Madden, P. A., Martin, N. G., & Heath, A. C. (2009). Evidence for an interaction between age at first drink and genetic influences on DSM-IV alcohol dependence symptoms. *Alcoholism: Clinical and Experimental Research*, 33(12), 2047–2056.

Allard, P., & Greene, J. (2011). *Children on the outside: Voicing the pain and human costs of parental incarceration*. Brooklyn, NY: Justice Strategies. Research report can be downloaded at: www.justicestrategies.org

American Association for Geriatric Psychiatry. (2003). Alcohol misuse in late life: Treatment issues. *Annual Meeting: Symposia highlights*. Retrieved February 2007 from http://www.cmecorner.com/macmcm/AAGP/aagp2003_08.htm

American Psychiatric Association (APA). (2000). *Diagnostic and statistical manual of mental disorders, text revision* (4th ed.). Washington, DC: Author.

Armstrong, K. (1993). *A history of God: The 4,000-year quest of Judaism, Christianity, and Islam*. New York: Ballantine Books.

Aron, E. (1996). *The highly sensitive person: How to thrive when the world overwhelms you*. New York: Broadway Books.

Aronson, E. (2004). *The social animal*. New York: Worth Publishers.

Ashburn, E., & Lipka, S. (2011, April 3). Conference notebook: Battle against alcohol abuse lags, but drinking doesn't. *Chronicle of Higher Education*. Retrieved from http://chronicle.com

Associated Press. (2010, October 25). Washington: High-alcohol drink sickened students. *New York Times*, p. A13.

Avital, A., & Richter-Levin, G. (2005). Exposure to juvenile stress exacerbates the behavioural consequences of exposure to stress in the adult rat. *International Journal of Neuropsychopharmacology*, 8(2), 163–173.

Bachman, J. G., O'Malley, P. M., Johnston, L., & Schulenberg, J. E. (2002). *The decline of substance use in young adulthood: Changes in social activities, roles, and beliefs*. Mahwah, NJ: Erlbaum.

Basham, K., & Miehls, D. (2004). *Transforming the legacy: Couple therapy with survivors of childhood trauma*. New York: Columbia University Press.

Bava, S., & Tapert, S. F. (2010). Adolescent brain development and the risk for alcohol and other drug problems. *Neuropsychologist Review, 20*(4), 398–413.

Beechem, M. (2002). *Elderly alcoholism: Intervention strategies.* Springfield, IL: Charles C Thomas.

Begley, S. (2007). Train your mind: Change your brain. New York: Random House.

Belknap, J., & Holsinger, K. (2006). The gendered nature of risk factors for delinquency. *Feminist Criminology, 1*(1), 48–71.

Benshoff, J. J., Harrawood, L., & Darwin, S. (2003). Substance abuse and the elderly: Unique issues and concerns. *Journal of Rehabilitation, 69*(9), 43–48.

Besthorn, F. H. (2003, February). *Eco-spiritual helping and group process: Earth-based perspectives for social work practice.* Presentation at the annual meeting of the Council on Social Work Education, Atlanta, GA.

Bloom, B., Owen, B., & Covington, S. (2004). Women offenders and the gendered effects of public policy. *Review of Policy Research, 21*(1), 31–48.

Botvin, G. J., & Griffin, K. (2011). School-based programs. In P. Ruiz and E. Strain (Eds.), *Lowinson and Ruiz's substance abuse: A comprehensive textbook* (5th ed., pp. 742–753). Philadelphia: Lippincott, Williams & Wilkins.

Butts, J., & Roman, J. (2004). *Juvenile drug courts and teen substance abuse.* Washington, DC: Urban Institute Press.

Canda, E. R., & Furman, L. (2010). *Spiritual diversity in social work practice: The heart of healing.* New York: Oxford University Press.

Carr, D. (2008). *The night of the gun: A reporter investigates the darkest story of his life, his own.* New York: Simon & Schuster.

Carroll, M. M. (1987). Alcoholism as an attachment and a gift on a spiritual journey. *Journal of Consciousness and Change, 10*(2), 45–48.

Carroll, M. M. (1993). *Spiritual growth of recovering alcoholic adult children of alcoholics.* Unpublished doctoral dissertation, University of Maryland, Baltimore.

Carroll, M. M. (1999). Spirituality and alcoholism: Self-actualization and faith stage. *Journal of Ministry in Addiction and Recovery, 6*(1), 67–84.

Carvel, J. (2006, November 29). Britain's binge drinkers begin to sober up. *Guardian.* Retrieved December 1, 2006, from http://society.guardian.co.uk

Center on Alcohol Marketing and Youth (CAMY). (2005, November 26). Alcohol industry's marketing overexposes Hispanic teens. *Join Together Online.* Retrieved September 2006 from http://www.jointogether.org/sa/news

Center on Alcohol Marketing and Youth (CAMY). (2010, December 15). *Youth exposure to alcohol advertising on TV: 2001–2009.* Baltimore, MD: Johns Hopkins Bloomberg School of Public Health. Retrieved from http:www.camy.org

Center for Substance Abuse Treatment (CSAT). (2005). *Substance abuse relapse prevention for older adults: A group treatment approach.* Rockville, MD: U.S. Department of Health and Human Services.

Centers for Disease Control and Prevention (CDC). (2006). Racial/ethnic differences among youths in cigarette smoking. *Mortality and Morbidity Weekly Report, 55*(47), 1275–1277.

Centers for Disease Control and Prevention (CDC). (2011a, January 14). Health disparities and inequalities report. *Morbidity and Mortality Weekly Report, Supplement, 60.* Washington, DC: Department of Health and Human Services.

Centers for Disease Control and Prevention (CDC). (2011b, February 18). *Prescription drug overdoses: An American epidemic.* Retrieved from http://www.cdc.gov

Childress, A. R. (2006). What can human brain imaging tell us about vulnerability to addiction and to relapse? In W. R. Miller & K. M. Carroll (Eds.), *Rethinking substance abuse: What the science shows, and what we should do about it* (pp. 46–60). New York: Guilford Press.

Cohen, M. (2000). *Counseling addicted women: A practical guide.* Thousand Oaks, CA: Sage.

Cowley, A. D. (1993). Transpersonal social work: A theory for the 1990s. *Social Work, 38,* 527–534.

Daisy, F., Thomas, L. R., & Worley, C. (2002). Alcohol use and harm reduction within the Native community. In G. A. Marlatt (Ed.), *Harm reduction: Pragmatic strategies for managing high-risk behaviors* (pp. 327–352). New York: Guilford Press.

Day, E., & Best, D. (2007). Natural history of substance-related problems. *Psychiatry, 6*(1), 12–15.

Denning, P. (2000). *Practicing harm reduction psychotherapy.* New York: Guilford Press.

Denning, P., Little, J., Glickman, A. (2004). *Over the influence: The harm reduction guide for managing drugs and alcohol.* New York: Guilford Press.

Downs, W. R., Capshew, T., & Rindels, B. (2004). Relationships between adult men's alcohol problems and their childhood experiences of parental violence and psychological aggression. *Journal of Studies on Alcohol, 65*(3), 336–345.

Duan, L., Chou, C-P., Andreeva, V., & Pentz, M.A. (2009). Trajectories of peer social influences as long-term predictors of drug use from early through late adolescence. *Journal of Youth and Adolescence, 38*(3), 454–465.

Ellis, A. (1965). Commentary in *Three approaches to psychotherapy.* Montreal, Canada: Peerless Film Processing.

Erikson, E. (1950/1963). *Children and society.* New York: Norton.

European Alcohol Policy Alliance (2011, August 29). UK—Drinkers in bars in towns and cities could pay extra. *EuroCare.* Retrieved from http://notes.camh.net/efeed.nsf/feedback

European Public Health Alliance. (2005). *European Monitoring Centre for Drugs and Drug Addiction.* Retrieved from http://ar2005.emcdda.europa.eu

Fabiano, J. (2011, June 23). UI officials attribute binge drinking dip to 21-ordinance. *Daily Iowan.* Retrieved from http://www.dailyiowan.com/2011/06/23/Metro/23838.html

Farkas, K. J. (2006). Alcohol abuse in later life. In S. L. Straussner (Ed.), *Clinical work with substance abusers* (pp. 330–346). New York: Guilford Press.

Feldstein, S., & Miller, W. R. (2006). Substance use and risk-taking among adolescents. *Journal of Mental Health, 15*(6), 633–643.

Feliz, J. (2011, January 12). Survey: Exposure to anti-drug messages among teens drops dramatically by two-thirds as drug use goes up. *The Partnership at Drugfree.Org.* Retrieved from http://www.drugfree.org

Fisher, M. (2009). Underage drinking: The stories of Gordie and Mark. *Section Connection. Alcohol, Tobacco and Other Drugs, 2,* 1–2.

Fletcher, M. (2002, April 12). Connectedness called key to student behavior. *Washington Post,* p. A03.

Foley, K. L., Altman, D., Durant, R. H., & Wolfson, M. (2004). Adults' approval and adolescents' alcohol use. *Journal of Adolescent Health, 35*(4), 7–26.

Gilligan, C. (1982). *In a different voice: Psychological theory and women's development*. Cambridge, MA: Harvard University Press.

Gilligan, C. (2002). *The birth of pleasure*. New York: Knopf.

Gober, S., Klein, M., Berger, T., Vindigni, C., & McCabe, P. (2006). Steroids in adolescence: The cost of achieving a physical ideal. *National Association of School Psychologists (NASP) Communiqué, 34*(7). Retrieved from http:www.nasponline.org

Goeders, N. (2003). The impact of stress on addiction. *European Neuropsychopharmacology, 13*, 435–441.

Gorman, C. (2007, January 29). Lessons for handling stress. *Time*, pp. 84–85.

Graham, K., & Brett, P. J. (1994, March 7–10). *A harm reduction approach to treating older adults: The clients speak*. Paper presented at the fifth International Conference on the Reduction of Drug-Related Harm. Toronto, Canada.

Grossberg, P. M., Brown, D. D., & Fleming, M. F. (2004). Brief physician advice for high-risk drinking among young adults. *Annals of Family Medicine, 2*(5), 474–480.

Gutiérrez, L., & Suarez, Z. (1999). Empowerment with Latinas. In L. Gutiérrez & E. A. Lewis (Eds.), *Empowerment of women of color* (pp. 167–186). New York: Columbia University Press.

Han, B., Gfroerer, J., & Colliver, J. (2009, August). *An examination of trends in illicit drug use among adults aged 50 to 59 in the United States*. Retrieved from http://www.oas.samhsa.gov

Hanson, M., & Gutheil, I. (2004). Motivational strategies with alcohol-involved older adults: Implications for social work practice. *Social Work, 49*(3), 364–372.

Hardoon, K. K., Gupta, R., & Derevensky, J. (2004). Psychosocial variables associated with adolescent gambling: A model for problem gambling. *Psychology of Addictive Behaviors, 18*(2), 170–179.

Hauser, C. (2005, December 16). As baby boomers approach 60, experts see upsurge in aging addicts. *New York Times*, p. C14.

Health Canada. (2007, March 7). *Best practices: Treatment and rehabilitation for seniors with substance use problems*. Retrieved from www.hc-sc.gc.ca

Health Canada. (2010, August, 20). *Summary of results of the 2008–2009 youth smoking survey*. Retrieved from www.hc-sc.gc.ca

Heinatz, S. (2008). Combat trauma can fuel addictions, experts say. *Newport News: Daily Press*. Retrieved from http://articles.dailypress.com/2008-03-31/news/0803300144_1_veterans-affairs-war-veterans-combat-trauma

Hemenway-Forbes, M. (2001, April 30). Comfort in love. *Waterloo–Cedar Falls Courier*, p. B4.

Herships, S. (2011, June 1). Military underprices tobacco more than law allows. *Marketplace*. Retrieved from http://marketplace.publicradio.org

Heslam, J. (2011, June 21). Mayor Thomas M. Menino blasts Nike over dopey t-shirts. *Boston Herald*. Retrieved from http://www.bostonherald.com

Hibell, B., Guttormsson, U., Ahlstrom, S., & Balakireva, O., Bjarnason, T., et al. (2009). *The 2007 ESPAD (European School Survey Project on Alcohol and Other Drugs): Substance use among students in 35 countries*. Retrieved from http://www.epad.org

Hser, Y-I., Longshore, D., & Anglin, M. D. (2007). The life course perspective on drug use: A conceptual framework for understanding drug use trajectories. *Evaluation Review, 31,* 515–547.

Hubbard, D., & Matthews, B. (2008). Reconciling the differences between the "gender-responsive" and "what works" literature to improve services for girls. *Crime and Delinquency, 54,* 225–258.

Jackson, D.Z. (2010, November 20). Targeting youth to start drinking. *Boston Globe.* Retrieved from http://articles.boston.com

Jackson, K. (2004, May/June). In the shadow of suicide. *Social Work Today,* pp. 38–40.

Johnston, L. D., O'Malley, P. M., Bachman, J. G., & Schulenberg, J. E. (2008). *Monitoring the Future: National survey results on substance abuse, 1975–2007.* Washington, DC: U.S. Department of Health and Human Services.

Johnston, L. D., O'Malley, P. M., Bachman, J. G., & Schulenberg, J. E. (2011). *Monitoring the Future: Demographic subgroup trends for various licit and illicit drugs, 1975–2010* (Monitoring for the Occasional Paper No. 74). Washington, DC: U.S. Department of Health and Human Services.

Johnston, M., & Davison, I. (2010, June 10). Shocking world of our student drunks. *New Zealand Herald.* Retrieved from www.NZherald.co.nz

Join Together Staff. (2005). Colleges curtail campus alcohol marketing. *Join Together Online.* Retrieved from http://www.drugfree.org/jointogether.org

Join Together Staff. (2011, May 10). Veterans' program integrating smoking cessation with PTSD treatment expands. Retrieved from http://www.drugfree.org/jointogether

Jones, C. (2005, January 21). Senior drug addicts increasing. *USA Today,* p. 3A.

Jung, C. G. (1933). *Modern man in search of a soul.* New York: Harcourt Brace & World.

Kacapyr, E., & Choudhury, S. (2006). The determinants of alcohol consumption among college students. *New York Economic Review, 37,* 3–19.

Kinney, J. (2011). *Loosening the grip: A handbook of alcohol information* (10th ed.). Boston: McGraw Hill.

Kluger, J. (2005, May 16). The cruelest cut. *Time,* pp. 48–50.

Lautenberg, F. (2011, April 15). *Press release: Sen. Lautenberg, Rep. Roybal-Allard introduce bill to reauthorize programs that prevent underage drinking.* Retrieved from http://lautenberg.senate.gov/newsroom/record.cfm?id=332523&

Lavelle, M. (2000, February 7). Teen tobacco wars. *U.S. News & World Report,* pp. 14–16.

Looby, A. (2008). Childhood attention deficit hyperactivity disorder and the development of substance use disorders: valid concern or exaggeration? *Addictive Behavior, 33*(3), 451–463.

Mantell, M. (1983). Student and employee assistance programs: A model for secondary prevention. *Labor–Management Alcoholism Journal, 12,* 113–124.

Martin, Fr. J. (1972). *Chalk talks on alcohol,* revised. Video. Aberdeen, MD: Kelly Productions.

Martin, S. L., Gibbs, D., Johnson, R., Sullivan, K., Clinton-Sherrod, M., Walters, J., & Rentz, E. (2010). Substance use by soldiers who abuse their spouses. *Violence against Women, 16*(11), 1295–1310.

Martindale, G. (2010, December 11). Drug convictions: How they affect your financial aid. *College and University Blog*. Retrieved from http://www.state university.com

Maslow, A. (1950/1971). *The farther reaches of human nature*. New York: Viking Press.

Miller, W. R., & Rollnick, S. (2002). *Motivational interviewing: Preparing people to change addictive behavior* (2nd ed.). New York: Guilford Press.

Miller, W. R., Forcehimes, A., & Zweben, A. (2011). *Treating addiction: A guide for professionals*. New York: Guilford.

Molnar, Browne, Cerda, & Buka. (2005). Violent behavior by girls reporting violent victimization. *Archives of Pediatrics and Adolescent Medicine, 158*(8), 731–739.

Monaghan, S., Derevensky, J., & Sklar, A. (2008). Impact of gambling advertisements and marketing on children and adolescents: Policy recommendations to minimise harm. *Journal of Gambling Issues, 22,* 252–274.

Monti, P. M., Miranda, R., Jr., Nixon, K., Sher, K. J., Swartzwelder, H. S., Tapert, S. F., et al. (February 2005). Adolescence: Booze, brains, and behavior. Proceedings of symposium at the 2004 RSA meeting. *Alcoholism: Clinical and Experimental Research, 29*(2), 207–220.

Mothers Against Drunk Driving (MADD). (2011). History of the 21 minimum drinking age: History speaks for itself. Retrieved from http://www.madd.org/underage-drinking/why21/history.html

Moxley, T. (2010, November 29). Supreme Court won't hear college newspapers' suit against state ban on alcohol advertising. *Roanoke Times*. Retrieved from http://www.roanoke.com

National Center on Addiction and Substance Abuse at Columbia University (CASA). (2006, August). *National survey of American attitudes on substance abuse XI: Teens and parents*. Retrieved from http://www.casacolumbia.org

National Center on Addiction and Substance Abuse at Columbia University (CASA). (2009). National survey of American attitudes on substance abuse XIV: Teens and parents. Retrieved from http://www.casacolumbia.org

National Council on Alcoholism and Drug Dependence. (2008). *Facts about underage drinking*. Retrieved from http://www.ncadd.org/pubs/UnderAgeDrinking-FactSheet.pdf

National Highway Traffic Safety Administration. (nd). *What happened?* Retrieved from http://www.nhtsa.gov/people/injury/research/feweryoungdrivers/iii__what_happened.htm

National Institute on Alcohol Abuse and Alcoholism (NIAAA). (2003, April). Underage drinking: A major public health challenge. *Alcohol Alert, 59,* 1–4.

National Institute on Alcohol Abuse and Alcoholism (NIAAA). (2010, July 1). A snapshot of annual college drinking consequences. Retrieved from http://www.college-drinkingprevention.gov/StatsSummaries/snapshot.aspx

National Workrights Institute (2010). Public employee drug testing: A legal guide. Princeton, NJ: National Workrights Institute. Retrieved from http://workrights.us

Nauert, R. (2011, June 13). Substance abuse risk greater for girls with ADHD than boys. *PsychCentral*. Retrieved from http://psychcentral.com

Noble, M. C., & Reed, C. (2000, January). Kentucky drug courts. *Bench & Bar, 64*(1), 6–10.

O'Connell, D. F. (1999, December 13). Spirituality's importance in recovery cannot be denied. *Alcoholism and Drug Abuse Weekly, 11*(47), 5.

Office of National Drug Control Policy. (2006, February 9). *Girls and drugs.* Retrieved August 2006 from http://www.mediacampaign.org/pdf/girls_and_drugs.pdf

Orzech, D. (2004, May/June). Meditation: The less traveled road to recovery. *Social Work Today*, pp. 32–35.

Orzech, D. (2006, March/April). Soul survivors. *Social Work Today*, pp. 36–39.

Peele, S. (2006). Reducing harms from youth drinking. *Journal of Alcohol and Drug Education, 50*(4), 67–81.

Peele, S. (2007). Addiction proof your child: A realistic approach to preventing drug, alcohol, and other dependencies. New York: Three Rivers Press.

Pollack, S. (2004). Anti-oppressive social work practice with women in prison: Discursive reconstructions and alternative practices. *British Journal of Social Work, 34*, 693–707.

Poulin, C. (2006, August). Harm reduction policies and programs for youth. *Canadian Centre on Substance Abuse.* Retrieved August 2006 from http://www.ccsa.ca

Prochaska, J., & DiClemente, C. (1992). In search of how people change: Applications to addictive behaviors. *American Psychologist, 47*, 1102–1114.

Ressler, A. (2008). Eating disorders and substance abuse. *Social Work Today, 8* (4), 30.

Riestenberg, W. (2005, July 19). PEASE Academy: The restorative recovery school. International Institute for Restorative Practices. *E Forum.* Retrieved June 2006 from http://www.iirp.org

Rivera, G. (2000, July 14). Smashed: Kids and alcohol. *Geraldo Rivera Reports*, NBC TV. Retrieved February 2007 from http://tvnews.vanderbilt.edu/tvn-openweb-request.pl

Robb, M. (2009, September/October). Stars and stripes....and substance abuse: Military interventions. *Social Work Today, 9*(5), 11–15.

Robinson, E. A., Krentzman, A. R., Webb, J. R., & Brower, K. J. (2011). Six-month changes in spirituality and religiousness in alcoholics predict drinking outcomes at nine months. *Journal of Studies on Alcohol and Drugs, 72*(4), 660–668.

Romeo, R. D. (2010). Adolescence: A central event in shaping stress reactivity. *Developmental Psychobiology, 52*(3), 244–253.

Rose, R. J. (2005). Prenatal programming of behavior: A twin-study perspective. *Neuroscience and Biobehavioral Reviews, 29*, 321–327.

Rosenbaum, M. (2004, March 18). Con: Merits, pitfalls of student drug testing. *Fresno Bee* (California). Retrieved May 2004 from http://www.fresnobee.com

Ross, S., & Heath, N. (2002). A study in the frequency of self-mutilation in a community sample of adolescents. *Journal of Youth and Adolescence, 31*(1), 67–78.

Royce, J. E. (1989). *Alcohol problems and alcoholism: A comprehensive survey* (Rev. ed.). New York: Free Press.

Ruffin, L., & Kaye, L. W. (2004, May/June). Alcohol and aging. *Social Work Today*, pp. 24–27.

Rutledge, P., Park, A., & Sher, K. J. (2008). 21st birthday drinking: Extremely extreme. *Journal of Consulting and Clinical Psychology, 76*, 511–516.

Ryan, J. P., Marsh, L., Testa, M., & Louderman, R. (2006). Integrating substance abuse and treatment and child welfare services. *Social Work Research*, *30*(2), 95–108.

Schmickle, S. (2009, February 12). U. of M. study details military's culture of binge and underage drinking. Retrieved from http://www.minnpost.com

Schraufnagel, T., Davis, K. C., George, W. H., & Norris, J. (2010). Childhood sexual abuse in males and subsequent risky sexual behavior: A potential alcohol-use pathway. *Child Abuse and Neglect*, *34*(5), 369–378.

Seaman, B. (2005, August 29). How bingeing became the new college sport. *Time*, p. 80.

Sherer, R. (2006, April 1). Drug abuse hitting middle-aged more than gen-Xers. *Psychiatric Times*, *23*(4). Retrieved from http://www.psychiatrictimes.com

Sheridan, M. (2004). Earth as source of spirit. *Spirituality and Social Work Forum*, *10*, 14–15.

Sherman, C. (2003). Years after sexual abuse by priests, psychic sequelai remain for men. *Clinical Psychiatry News*, 60–61.

Shibusawa, T. (2006). Older adults with substance abuse problems. In B. Berkman & S. D'Ambruoso (Eds.) *The Oxford handbook of social work in health and aging* (pp.141–148). New York: Oxford University Press.

Spera, C., Franklin, K., Uekawa, K., Kunz, J., Szoc, R., Thomas, R., & Cambridge, M. (2010). Reducing drinking among junior enlisted Air Force members in five communities: Early findings of the EUDL program's influence on self-reported drinking behaviors. *Journal of Studies on Alcohol and Drugs*, *71*(3), 373–383.

Stringfellow, A. (2011, June 10). *Happy hour in assisted living? Substance abuse among seniors on the rise*. Retrieved from http://www.seniorhomes.com

Sternberg, S. (2000, August 2). Abuse can damage girls' brain chemistry. *USA Today*, p. 10D.

Stocker, S. (2000). Medications reduce incidence of substance abuse among ADHD patients. *NIDA Notes*, *14*(4), 1–4.

Substance Abuse and Mental Health Services Administration (SAMHSA). (2006, May/June). SAMHSA, FDA launch campaign for older adults. *SAMHSA News*, *13*(3), 7.

Substance Abuse and Mental Health Services Administration (SAMHSA). (2007). *Serious psychological distress and substance abuse disorders among veterans: National Survey on Drug Use and Health*. Rockville, MD: Office of Applied Studies.

Substance Abuse and Mental Health Services Administation. (SAMHSA). (2010a). Results from the 2010 National Survey on Drug Use and Health: Detailed tables. Retrieved from www.oas.samhsa.gov.

Substance Abuse and Mental Health Services Administration (SAMHSA). (2010b, June 17). *The TEDS Report: Changing Substance Abuse Patterns among Older Admissions: 1992 and 2008*. Rockville, MD: Office of Applied Studies.

Substance Abuse and Mental Health Services Administration (SAMHSA). (2011a, January 13). *Emergency department visits involving underage alcohol use in combination with other drugs*. Rockville, MD: Office of Applied Studies.

Substance Abuse and Mental Health Services Administration (SAMHSA). (2011b, September 1) *Illicit drug use among older adults*. Rockville, MD: Office of Applied Studies.

Substance Abuse and Mental Health Services Administration (SAMHSA) (2011c, May, 18). New study shows 49 percent rise in emergency department visits. Retrieved from http://www.samhsa.gov

Substance Abuse and Mental Health Services Administration (SAMHSA). (2011d). *Results from the 2010 National Survey on Drug Use and Health: Volume I. Summary of National Findings*. Rockville, MD: Office of Applied Studies.

Terry-McElrath, Y., & O'Malley, P. (2011). Substance use and exercise participation among young adults: Parallel trajectories in a national cohort-sequential study. *Addiction, 106*.

University of Montreal. (2010, August 17). Heavy drug-use among bad boys curbed by parental monitoring and peers. *Science News*. Retrieved from http://www.sciencedaily.com

U.S. Census Bureau. (2011). *State and county quick facts*. Retrieved from http://quickfacts.census.gov/qfd/states/00000.html

U.S. Department of Health and Human Services (DHHS). (2000). *Anabolic steroid abuse: Research report* (pp. 1–8). Washington, DC: National Institutes of Health.

U.S. Department of Health and Human Services (DHHS). (2005). *65+ in the United States: Current population reports*. Washington, DC: National Institutes of Health.

Valtonen, K., Sogren, M., & CameronPadmore, L. (2006). Coping styles in persons recovering from substance abuse. *British Journal of Social Work, 36*(1), 57–73.

van Wormer, K. (2010). *Working with female offenders: A gender-sensitive approach*. Hoboken, NJ: Wiley.

van Wormer, K. (2011). *Human behavior and the social environment, micro level: Individuals and families* (2nd ed.). New York: Oxford University Press.

van Wormer, K., & Besthorn, F. H. (2011). *Human behavior and the social environment, macro level: Groups, communities, and organizations* (2nd ed.). New York: Oxford University Press.

Wallen, J. (1993). *Addiction in human development: Developmental perspective on addiction and recovery*. New York: Haworth.

Washton, A., & Zweben, J. (2006). *Treating alcohol and drug problems in psychotherapy practice: Doing what works*. New York: Guilford Press.

White, D.W. (2008). Report of the Massachusetts Bar Association drug policy task force. The failure of the war on drugs. Retrieved from www.massbar.org

White House Office of the National Drug Control Policy (ONDCP). (2011). *Epidemic: Responding to America's prescription drug abuse crisis*. Washington, DC: Author.

Williams, T. (2010, July 14). As a brigade returns safe, some meet new enemies. *New York Times*, p. A4.

Willis, A. (2008). Aging under the influence. *Social Work Today, 8*(5), 10–11.

Winters, K. C., & Amelia, A. (2011). Adolescent brain development and drugs. *Prevention Researcher, 18*(2), 21–25.

Witkiewitz, K. (2005). Defining relapse from a harm reduction perspective. *Journal of Evidence-Based Social Work, 2*(1/2), 191–206.

Witkiewitz, K., & Marlatt, G. A. (2007). Overview of relapse prevention. In K. Witkiewitz and G. A. Marlatt (Eds.), *Therapist's guide to evidence-based relapse prevention* (pp. 3–18). Burlington, MA: Academic Press.

World Health Organization. (2010). *Global strategy to reduce the harmful use of alcohol.* Retrieved from http://apps.who.int/gb/ebwha/pdf_files/WHA63/A63_13-en.pdf.

Zahn, M. (2007). The causes of girls' delinquency and their program implications. *Family Court Review, 45*(3), 456–465.

Zastrow, C., & Kirst-Ashman, K. (2010). *Understanding human behavior and the social environment* (8th ed.). Belmont, CA: Brooks/Cole.

SCREENING AND ASSESSMENT

CHAPTER **7**

INTRODUCTION

The process of screening and assessment is changing as the addiction field moves steadily in the direction of client-centered, strength-based practices. In the traditional framework, screening and assessment has been the centerpiece of the initial point of client contact, where clients may spend a great deal of time filling out various assessment instruments or being interviewed by designated intake workers. This arrangement serves three purposes: it "qualifies" the client with an appropriate problem so that it is clear the client is in the right place, it allows the agency or treatment program to get reimbursed based on the client having an appropriate diagnosis, and it quickly furnishes information to the counselor who will eventually be assigned to work with the person. There are, however, unintended consequences to such an arrangement (Miller, Forcehimes, Zweben & McClellan, 2011).

Asking a lot of questions initially can set up an expectation that the agency (counselor) is the expert on the client's condition, and given enough information, can come up with the right answer to fix the problem. Spending a lot of time on filling out assessments can delay the important business of building a trusting relationship between the client and the counselor. The delay can be especially critical if the client is not 100% motivated to be "helped." A more strength-based approach is to find ways to integrate screening and assessment into the ongoing process of treatment and keep it centered on how exactly this information will be useful to identifying and achieving goals that reflect what the client wants. Some clients who have serious trauma history or are currently struggling to maintain survival status cannot tolerate formal questioning. The Harm Reduction Therapy Center in San Francisco, which typically works with homeless and seriously marginalized clients, conducts their formal assessments over long periods of time (Little & Franskoviak, 2010). They call this "assessment as treatment," where the therapist continually observes and inquires about the client's experience as the relationship builds, offering recommendations only when the clients have given their permission to do so.

Using assessment tools with persons who are part of ethnic minority groups or who do not use English as a first language requires additional cautions. Measurement error can occur because not many instruments have been normed on clients of color (Blume & Lovato, 2010). When the only instruments available are those developed from the majority culture (often white college students), then care must be taken in interpreting the results. In addition, the clients may have a different cultural worldview than the Western definitions of the particular addiction. Among Native Americans, for example, peyote use may be considered a ritualized experience, not a destructive practice associated with loss of control. Questions on assessment forms concerning hallucinations need to take into account cultural practices of some persons where participants go to great lengths to induce hallucinations for spiritual purposes. When clients and therapists speak different first languages, translation problems and misunderstandings are rampant, whether through written forms or with personal translators. As an example, the English word *craving* is not easily translated into Spanish, nor is the concept easily understood (Blume, Morera, & de la Cruz, 2005). In Norway, in van Wormer's experience, the term *powerless* (as in "powerless over alcohol") was most commonly translated with the word *hjelpeløs* or "helpless" in English.

With these cautions in mind, there are many screening and assessment tools in the addiction field that can be helpful and effective, ranging from one question screens that can be incorporated into any intake process to more complex instruments that require training and scoring. The function of screening and assessment will vary, depending on the context and environment of the first meeting with the client. Does it take place in the emergency room after a person has come in with injuries from a motor vehicle accident? Is it a meeting with a client who comes to his family doctor for an annual check-up? Does the assessment take place in prison, or a homeless shelter, or an outpatient treatment program for problem gamblers or alcohol or drug users? This chapter will describe several common screens and assessment tools for alcohol, drug, and gambling problems and their use in various settings. We will also suggest a toolbox of screening and assessment types of questions that can be helpful in building a relationship with the client, increasing motivation for change, assessing client strengths, and finding supports available to help clients through the change process.

SCREENING INSTRUMENTS AND STRATEGIES

Screening instruments are tools (one question or a short series of questions) that can quickly help detect the possibility of a problem with substance use, gambling, or whatever disorder is of interest. Screens are usually the first step in the assessment process: they cast a wide, more imprecise net than assessment tools, so sometimes people show up "positive" on a screen, when in fact they have no problem at all, or they are "negative" on a screen when they actually do have a problem. The examples that follow are screens that are short, simple, easy to work into the intake process in any setting and context, and have a reasonable chance of screening accurately. Because of the stigma that surrounds addiction, or even the possibility of having these kinds of problems, it is a good idea to let people know that the screening questions are routine and asked of all clients. It is also helpful to first ask, "Do you sometimes drink?" or "Do you sometimes gamble?" or "Do you sometimes use drugs of any kind?" as a prescreening question to rule out people who never engage in any of these behaviors.

The Lie/Bet questionnaire (Johnson, Hamer, Nora, Tan, Eistenstein, & Englehart, 1988) is valid and reliable for ruling out pathological gambling behaviors, that is, these two questions differentiate between pathological and nonproblem gambling and tell the clinician if further assessment is warranted. If the client answers "yes" to one or both questions, further assessment is needed. The Lie/Bet questions are:

1. Have you ever felt the need to bet more and more money?
2. Have you ever had to lie to people important to you about how much you gambled?

A "yes" answer to either of these questions also calls for a follow-up open-ended question like "Tell me more about that ..." to further understand the client's experience.

A simple one-question screen for men or women to rule out alcohol problems is recommended to clinicians by the National Institute on Alcohol Abuse and Alcoholism (NIAAA) (2005). A study by Williams and Vinson (2001) found that this one question identified 86% of individuals who had an alcohol use disorder. In this screen, one or more heavy drinking days indicates the client is an at-risk drinker, and further assessment is warranted. One standard drink is equivalent to 12 ounces of beer, 5 ounces of wine, or 1.5 ounces of 80-proof spirits.

(For men): "How many times in the past year have you had five or more drinks in a day?"

(For women): "How many times in the past year have you had four or more drinks in a day?"

With a slight change, the same question can be used with good results for ruling out illicit drug or prescription drug problems (Smith, Schmidt, Allensworth-Davis, & Suitz, 2010). The question becomes

"How many times in the past year have you used an illegal drug or used a prescription medication for nonmedical reasons?"

These simple screening questions are especially helpful in primary care settings or other helping contexts (family agencies, vocational rehabilitation, child welfare, etc.) where the presenting problem is something other than problematic substance use or problem gambling. Davis recently conducted a local training with child welfare workers on problem gamblers and found that there is no gambling screen in the state-wide intake protocol. However, as the participants in the workshop pointed out, there are cases coming to their attention where problem gambling is the primary cause behind child neglect. Utilizing a simple screen could help pinpoint the problem in a timely manner.

Slightly more complicated and longer screens have also proven helpful and are still simple enough to carry around in the clinician's head in acronym form. The CAGE, developed by Ewing (1984) for screening alcohol problems, is probably the most familiar. A later version changed the wording to include drug problems (Brown, Leonard, Saunders, & Papasouliotis, 1998). If the client answers "yes" to two or more questions, then further assessment is warranted:

C   Have you ever felt you ought to **cut** down on your drinking or drug use?

A   Have people **annoyed** you by criticizing your drinking or drug use?

G   Have you ever felt bad or **guilty** about your drinking or drug use?

E   Have you ever had a drink or used drugs first think in the morning to steady your nerves or get rid of a hangover?

According to Bradley and colleagues (1998), the CAGE and TWEAK were the optimal screening tests for identification of alcohol problems in women. However, effectiveness varied by ethnicity. For Black obstetric patients and for White women, questionnaires that asked about tolerance for alcohol (e.g., TWEAK) were more sensitive. For use with mixed populations, therefore, the researchers recommend TWEAK. Again, an answer of "yes" to two or more of these indicates a problem:

T   Tolerance: How many drinks can you hold? (6 or more drinks indicates tolerance) or How many drinks does it take before you begin to feel the first effect of the alcohol? (3 or more drinks indicates tolerance)

W   Worried: Have close friends or relatives worried or complained about your drinking in the past year?

E   Eye openers: Do you sometimes take a drink in the morning when you first get up?

A   Amnesia: Has a friend or family member ever told you about things you said or did while you were drinking that you could not remember?

K   Kut down: Do you sometimes feel the need to cut down on your drinking?

The Alcohol Use Disorders Identification Test (AUDIT), developed by the World Health Organization (Babor, Higgins-Biddle, Saunders, & Monteiro, 2001) is the only screening test designed and validated for international use in a wide variety of populations, cultures, and languages. It is brief, rapid, and flexible, and it can be used in many contexts: primary care health clinics, emergency rooms, outpatient clinics, jails and prisons, and other human service agencies. The AUDIT is comprised of ten items that cover amount and frequency of drinking, alcohol dependence symptoms, personal problems, and social problems (e.g., "Have you or someone else been injured because of your drinking?"). The scoring is designed to discriminate between different levels of risk—hazardous, harmful, and possible dependence—so it can be used as a prevention tool to help clients assess their current status and the road ahead if things do not change. The AUDIT can be given to the client as a questionnaire to fill out, or it can be used as interview questions. It takes approximately 2 minutes to complete the AUDIT. Both versions can be downloaded for free on the website http://whqlibdoc.who.int/hq/2001/who_msd_msb_01.6a.pdf. This helpful website also provides complete scoring and interpretation instructions (which are not complicated), as well as a wealth of suggestions on how to introduce the screen and use the results in a client-centered, strength-based manner.

There are a number of Internet-based screening tools available through a simple Google search of "Alcohol Screens," or whatever behavior you are focusing on. One good example, "About my drinking," has been developed by Hazelden using the AUDIT as the basis for the screen (http://www.about-mydrinking.org). Depending on how one answers the questions, the interpretation will rate your risk of alcohol-related harm and discuss possible physical consequences, prevention strategies, and reasons for seeking further assistance if indicated. As a counselor, taking this test is an easy way to be introduced to the usefulness of the AUDIT.

ASSESSMENT TOOLS

According to the Center for Substance Abuse Treatment (CSAT) (2005), assessment is the "process for defining the nature of the problem and developing specific treatment recommendations for addressing the problem" (p. 68). There are all kinds of ways to do that, ranging from simply telling the client you are "interested in what brought them in to see you and what they want to get out of your time together," to using formal assessment tools to get a deeper picture of the client's readiness to change, problem areas, their severity, and the client's strengths and "recovery capital." As Miller and his colleagues (2011) remind us, "neither screening nor diagnosis, however, provides much information about what is actually happening in a particular person's life and substance use, why problems are emerging, and what treatment options would be most appropriate to try" (p. 71). That kind of information develops through the careful effort of building a trusting relationship with the client. As a working relationship is built, there are assessment tools that can be helpful in pinpointing the uniqueness of the person's experience.

| Box 7.1 | GAMBLERS ANONYMOUS TWENTY QUESTIONS |

1. Did you ever lose time from work or school due to gambling?
2. Has gambling ever made your home life unhappy?
3. Did gambling affect your reputation?
4. Have you ever felt remorse after gambling?
5. Did you ever gamble to get money with which to pay debts or otherwise solve financial difficulties?
6. Did gambling cause a decrease in your ambition or efficiency?
7. After losing did you feel you must return as soon as possible and win back your losses?
8. After a win did you have a strong urge to return and win more?
9. Did you often gamble until your last dollar was gone?
10. Did you ever borrow to finance your gambling?
11. Have you ever sold anything to finance gambling?
12. Were you reluctant to use "gambling money" for normal expenditures?
13. Did gambling make you careless of the welfare of yourself or your family?
14. Did you ever gamble longer than was planned?
15. Have you ever gambled to escape worry or trouble?
16. Have you ever committed, or considered committing, an illegal act to finance gambling?
17. Did gambling cause you to have difficulty in sleeping?
18. Do arguments, disappointments or frustrations create within you an urge to gamble?
19. Did you ever have an urge to celebrate any good fortune by a few hours of gambling?
20. Have you ever considered self-destruction or suicide as a result of your gambling?

Source: Reprinted from the official Gamblers Anonymous Web site, www.gamblers anonymous.org, with permission.

Many times clients figure out for themselves they have a problem with substance use or gambling. Perhaps they attended a Gamblers Anonymous (GA) meeting, and chimed in with the rest of the group to answer GA Twenty Questions, which are usually read aloud at every meeting. In GA, as in other Twelve-Step groups, it does not matter how many signs you have of the problem, or whether an expert has diagnosed you with the problem. The real problem is to figure out for yourself if you want to quit gambling. The GA Twenty Questions help people figure that out (see Box 7.1) by raising their awareness of the consequences of continuing to gamble. According to GA, most compulsive gamblers will answer "yes" to at least seven of the questions. Self-described compulsive gamblers, not treatment providers or researchers, developed these questions in the 1950s. However, two researchers (Ursua & Uribelarrea, 1998) tested the Spanish version of the GA Twenty Questions and found it to have high reliability and validity in discriminating between problem gamblers and social gamblers. They recommend it "as good as the best clinical and diagnostic instruments proposed at present" (p. 11).

A more recent psychometric study by Toneatto (2008), using the English version, confirmed high reliability and a high correlation with the *DSM-IV-R* as well as the South Oaks Gambling Screen.

A good start to finding out the nature and severity of substance use problems is to ask the client some open-ended questions about what he or she has been using, how he or she is using the substance, how often, and what have been the costs and benefits of the use. If you want to cover all the possibilities, there are many instruments available. The Addiction Research Institute, Center for Social Work Research, at the University of Texas at Austin, maintains an extensive website that will help you access the instruments and documentation from various sources: http://www.utexas.edu/research/cswr/nida/instrumentListing.html. This listing includes all the alcohol and drug instruments from the National Institute of Alcohol and Alcohol Abuse; the Center on Alcoholism, Substance Abuse, and Addictions; and the Institute for Behavioral Research at Texas Christian University. To help narrow down your many choices, Miller and colleagues (2011) recommend the following structured assessments: the Addiction Severity Index (ASI), the Alcohol Dependence Scale, the Drinker Inventory of Consequences (Drinc), the Inventory of Drug Use Consequences (InDUC), and the Severity of Alcohol Dependence Questionnaire (SADQ).

Here is an example of two instruments that are available free by download on the Internet. The Drinker Inventory of Consequences (Drinc) (Forcehimes, Tonigan, Miller, Kenna, & Baer, 2007), originally designed for Project MATCH, is a 50-item questionnaire that covers physical, social, intrapersonal, impulse control, and interpersonal problem areas. Psychometric testing suggests it is reliable, valid, and can be clinically useful. Sample questions include some potential positives from drinking ("How often has drinking helped me to relax?"), and mostly negative possibilities ("How often has my ability to be a good parent been harmed by my drinking"). The Drinc is in the public domain and can be downloaded free at http://casaa.unm.edu/inst/DrInC-2R.pdf. The Inventory of Drug Use Consequences (InDUC) (Tonigan & Miller, 2002) has the same purpose and format only changed to assess drug consequences. It is also in the public domain and can be downloaded free at http://casaa.unm.edu/inst/InDuc-2L.pdf.

The Substance Abuse Screening Inventory (SASSI) (Miller & Lazowski, 1999) is a somewhat different approach to assessment instruments. Known by some as the stealth assessment, most of the true/false items on one side of the form do not inquire directly about alcohol or drug use. Items such as "I am often resentful," and "I like to obey the law" can indicate whether the respondent fits the profile of a chemically dependent person in areas such as defensiveness, willingness to acknowledge problematic behavior, depressed affect, likelihood of legal problems, and so on. The reverse side of the form inquires directly about alcohol and drug use. The use of less obvious measures at the beginning of the form is designed to minimize client defensiveness. However, ethical conduct does require that the client be told exactly why he or she is being asked to complete the instrument (McNeece & DiNitto, 2005).

ASSESSING LEVELS OF CARE

There are several systems for assessing the appropriate level of care for a person with substance use problems. The American Society of Addiction Medicine's Patient Placement Criteria (ASAM PPC-2R) is one of the most widely recognized systems in the majority of states for guiding addiction treatment matching (CSAT, 2005). The ASAM system outlines treatment as a continuum within which there are five levels of care:

1. Level 0.5: Early Intervention
2. Level I: Outpatient Treatment
3. Level II: Intensive Outpatient/Partial Hospitalization Treatment
4. Level III: Residential/Inpatient Treatment
5. Level IV: Medically Managed Intensive Inpatient Treatment.

Each level of care includes several layers of intensity. For example, Level III.1 refers to "Clinically Managed Low-Intensity Residential Treatment," and Level III.7 refers to "Medically Monitored Inpatient Detoxification." Clients are evaluated using the following dimensions to decide which level of care is optimal: (1) acute intoxication or withdrawal potential; (2) biomedical conditions and complications; (3) emotional, behavioral, or cognitive conditions and complications; (4) readiness to change; (5) relapse, continued use, or continued problem potential; and (6) recovery/living environment. An example of using these criteria will be presented in the next section on co-occurring disorders (COD).

A different classification system, developed by the consensus panel for TIP 42 (CSAT, 2005) on Co-occurring Disorders is to divide levels of care into basic, intermediate, advanced, or fully integrated, which describe the capability of programs to offer needed services for persons with COD. A *basic* program provides treatment for one disorder, but screens for the other disorder; an *intermediate* level focuses primarily on one disorder but also addresses some specific needs of the other (e.g., a counselor could provide motivational interviewing regarding substance use while holding medication management groups for psychiatric patients); an *advanced* level provides services for both disorders using an integrated perspective (e.g., adding interventions such as mutual self-help and relapse prevention groups to a mental health setting); and a *fully integrated* program is essentially a one-stop shop that actively provides treatment for both disorders by the same clinicians who are trained in psychopathology, assessment, and treatment strategies for both mental and substance use disorders, and the funding streams are fully integrated.

ASSESSMENT OF PERSONS WITH CO-OCCURRING DISORDERS (COD)

Integrated assessment is critical to understanding the interactions between mental illness and substance misuse. Substance misuse worsens the outcome of severe mental illness, and vice versa. Co-occurring mental health and substance use issues are so common with individuals who present for any kind of treatment, it is considered the norm, not the exception (Miller et al., 2011). In clinic samples, 40–50% of individuals presenting in mental health settings have a co-occurring substance use diagnosis, and 60–80% of individuals presenting in a substance use facility have a co-occurring mental illness diagnosis (Meuser, Drake, Turner, & McGovern, 2006). Chapter 9 presents the background on the social issues and preferred treatment options for people with COD; this section will focus on specific screening and assessment instruments.

When a client presents with potential COD, it may overwhelm the counselor because of the number of needs, the complexities in sorting out treatment options, and the disarray of most clients' lives who find themselves in that situation. There are times practitioners will find themselves not knowing how to proceed. These are the times that the Center for Substance Abuse Treatment (2005) reminds us that "empathy and hope are the most valuable components of your work with a client. When in doubt about how to manage a client with COD, stay connected, be empathic and hopeful, and work with the client and the treatment team to try to figure out the best approach over time" (p. 67).

Working "over time" is a key component in the screening and assessment phase of clients with COD. The difficulties of sorting out whether mental health symptoms are independent or dependent on the use of substances may be revealed only over weeks and months of contact with the client. Chapter 8 discusses more about these complications in the section titled "The perils of differential diagnosis." In this section we will confine ourselves to screening and assessment tools that will help answer "yes" or "no" to the general question, "Does the substance abuse (or mental health) client show signs of a possible mental health (or substance abuse problem)?"

There are certain prerequisites that are essential before a counselor can embark on screening and assessment for COD:

1. Be familiar with the diagnostic criteria for common mental disorders (CSAT, 2005). In these times, when eligibility for many services depends on the client meeting certain *DSM-IV* criteria, it is critical for all practitioners in the helping professions to at least have a copy of the *Quick Reference Guide to the DSM-IV-TR* (APA, 2000). This is an easy to utilize desk copy that is about five pounds lighter than the complete *DSM-IV-R* and extremely helpful in finding plenty of details and criteria for each mental health diagnosis. For Internet enthusiasts, any diagnosis can be found through a Google search, but the options can be bewildering. A recent search of "schizophrenia" came up with 21,100,000 results.

2. Be familiar with the names and indications of common psychiatric medications and the potential interactions that many occur (Denning, 2004). The names and drugs are always changing, so it is best to use an Internet source to keep up with the latest psychotropic medications that are used. An excellent reference, updated yearly, is *Psychotherapeutic Medications 2011: What Every Counselor Should Know* (Addiction Technology

Transfer Center Network, 2011) found at http://www.nattc.org/regcenters/index_midamerica.asp. This booklet contains information on generic and brand names, their purpose, usual dose and frequency, side effects, potential for abuse and dependence, emergency conditions, and cautions. This site also provides your own web-based current desktop reference where you can get the same information by plugging in the particular drug you are looking for in the search on http://www.findrxinformation. org.

3. Understand the policies of your particular agency or helping context on the procedures for gathering information. For example, CSAT (2005) recommends that every effort be made to contact all parties, including family, probation officers, and treatment professionals who have worked with the person. However, practitioners at the Harm Reduction Therapy Center in San Francisco gather information from family and significant others only if the client wishes to do so, and then only with the client present (Little & Franskoviak, 2010).

4. Do not be afraid that you do not have all the answers (CSAT, 2005). That is why we have supervisors! Identify at least one person who is a good source for possibilities and a sounding board for frustrations.

5. Know your community resources, in terms of who provides what in the ASAM levels of care, and what level of programming is available for people with COD. It is especially important to know the options available for housing (and what the rules are regarding abstinence), medication and medical assistance, substance abuse and gambling treatment (and potential waiting lists), and other resources that could increase the client's recovery capital (friends, churches, hobby groups, drop-in centers with activities, food pantries, etc.). Mueser and colleagues (2006) point out several areas that may need assessment: housing, case management needs for severe mental illness, supported employment, family psycho education, social skills training, training of clients for illness management, and pharmacological treatment. Assessment needs to include both the strengths and limitations the client has in each area.

There is no single instrument that is the "gold standard" for COD assessment (CSAT, 2005). The common substance abuse screening tools mentioned previously are used with individuals with COD, including the CAGE and the AUDIT. In addition, the Simple Screening Instrument for Substance Abuse (SSI-SA) was developed by a consensus panel of experts for CSAT in 1994, using existing alcohol and drug screening tools. It is widely used either as an interview or self-administered, and it is one of the most common screening instruments used in correctional settings (CSAT, 2005). The SSI-SA is in the public domain, can be accessed in TIP 42 (CSAT 2005), and is reproduced in its entirety in Box 7.2. Of the 16 items, questions 1 and 15 are not scored, so the included scores range from 0 to 14. A score of 4 or more is the cut-off point that indicates a further full assessment is needed. A score of 2–3 indicates minimal risk.

| Box 7.2 | SIMPLE SCREENING INSTRUMENT FOR SUBSTANCE ABUSE (SSI-SA) SELF-ADMINISTERED FORM |

Directions: The questions that follow are about your use of alcohol and other drugs. Your answers will be kept private. Mark the response that best fits for you. Answer the questions in terms of your experiences in the past 6 months.

During the last 6 months ...

1. Have you used alcohol or other drugs? (such as wine, beer hard liquor, pot, coke, heroin or other opioids, uppers, downers, hallucinogens, or inhalants? (Yes   No)

2. Have you felt that you use too much alcohol or other drugs? (Yes   No)

3. Have you tried to cut down or quit drinking or using alcohol or other drugs? (Yes   No)

4. Have you gone to anyone for help because of your drinking or drug use? (Such as Alcoholics Anonymous, Narcotic Anonymous, Cocaine Anonymous, counselors, or a treatment program?) (Yes   No)

5. Have you had any health problems? For example, have you:
   __Had blackouts or other periods of memory loss?
   __Injured your head after drinking or using drugs?
   __Had convulsions, delirium tremens ("DTs")?
   __Had hepatitis or other liver problems?
   __Felt sick, shaky, or depressed when you stopped?
   __Felt "coke bug" or a crawling feeling under the skin after you stopped using drugs?
   __Been injured after drinking or using?
   __Used needles to shoot drugs?

6. Has drinking or other drug use caused problems between you and your family or friends? (Yes   No)

7. Has your drinking or other drug use caused problems at school or at work? (Yes   No)

8. Have you been arrested or had other legal problems? (Such as bouncing bad checks, driving while intoxicated, theft, or drug possession?) (Yes   No)

9. Have you lost your temper or gotten into arguments or fight while drinking or using other drugs? (Yes   No)

10. Are you needing to drink or use drugs more and more to get the effect you want? (Yes   No)

(continued)

| Box 7.2 | SIMPLE SCREENING INSTRUMENT FOR SUBSTANCE ABUSE (SSI-SA) SELF-ADMINISTERED FORM *(continued)* |

11. Do you spend a lot of time thinking about or trying to get alcohol or other drugs? (Yes   No)

12. When drinking or using drugs, are you more likely to do something you wouldn't normally do, such as break rules, break the law, sell things that are important to you, or have unprotected sex with someone? (Yes   No)

13. Do you feel bad or guilty about your drinking or drug use? (Yes   No)

The next questions are about your lifetime experiences.

14. Have you ever had a drinking or other drug problem? (Yes   No)

15. Have any of your family members ever had a drinking or drug problem? (Yes   No)

16. Do you feel that you have a drinking or drug problem now? (Yes   No)

Source: CSAT, 2005, p. 509–510.

Similarly, the Mental Health Screening Form-III (MHSF-III) is designed to screen for present or past symptoms of most of the main mental disorders (Carroll & McGinley, 2001). The authors have described it as a "rough screening device" because it asks only one question for each disorder, and if the client misunderstands the question or does not remember, the screen would produce a false negative (p. 31). Nevertheless, CSAT (2005) recommends it as an initial screen to be used in substance abuse or other settings to help identify clients who may have mental health problems. The screen is in the public domain and can be found on numerous websites that include scoring directions, such as http://www.fadaa.org/servicrds/events/2004_FIS/NMSF3ProjectReturn.pdf. The MHSF-III has 18 questions, such as "Have you ever felt that people had something against you, without them necessarily saying so, or that someone or some group may be trying to influence your thoughts or behavior? Have you ever been depressed for weeks at a time, lost interest or pleasure in most activities, had trouble concentrating and making decisions, or thought about killing yourself?" The authors recommend the screen be given in interview format so that follow-up questions can be asked about any "yes" answers, such as "When did that happen?" "How long did it last?" and "Did that happen before, during, or after your use of (substance)?" It also includes a question about gambling: "Have you ever lost considerable sums of money through gambling or had problems at work, in school, with your family and friends because of gambling?"

A client who has COD problems could be assessed as fitting any one of the ASAM levels, depending on how the client is evaluated in the different

Box 7.3	JANE B.

The client is a 28-year-old single Caucasian female with a diagnosis of paranoid schizophrenia, alcohol dependence, crack cocaine dependence, and a history of multiple episodes of sexual victimization. Jane B. is homeless (living in a shelter), actively psychotic, and refuses to admit to a drug or alcohol problem. She has made frequent visits to the local emergency room for both mental health and medical complaints, but she refuses any follow-up treatment. Her main requests are for money and food, not treatment. Jane has been offered involvement in a housing program that does not require treatment engagement or sobriety but has refused due to paranoia regarding working with staff to help her in this setting. Jane B. refuses all medication due to her paranoia, but she does not appear to be acutely dangerous to herself or others.

Source: CSAT, 2005, p. 70.

dimensions. For example, dimension three is the "emotional, behavioral or cognitive conditions and complications" (ASAM, 2001). There are five areas of risk that need evaluation within this dimension: suicide potential and level of lethality, the degree to which the emotional or behavioral factors interfere with recovery, social functioning, the ability for self-care, and a prediction of the patient's likely response to treatment. Consideration of dimension three helps to determine what level would best fit the needs of the individual. For example, a person with co-occurring disorders, "Jane B" is illustrated in Box 7.3 (CSAT, 2005). In this example, because of the severity of her situation, one might leap to the conclusion that Jane needs Level III or IV care. However, a more careful review shows us that although she is psychotic and homeless, she is not suicidal, homicidal, or unable to feed herself and find shelter. Therefore, Jane does not meet criteria for involuntary psychiatric treatment. Level III is not an option because she is completely unmotivated to accept voluntary mental health services, and she is probably too psychotic to participate in treatment at this point. Homelessness alone does not qualify a person for Level III. The ASAM analysis would lead us to recommend starting with Level I.5 intensive mental disorder case management. Of course, recommending this level of treatment does not make it happen. We should anticipate a long period of engagement, using strategies described in the next chapter, to build trust over time. We would hope that, in the months to come, Jane would begin to trust the case management team enough to accept small measures of help that would build over time. Thus, the ASAM criteria can be helpful in adjusting our own expectations to what is real and possible, as well as a system of treatment matching. Because it is a complex multidimensional assessment, the ASAM requires additional training to implement with accuracy. Opportunities for ASAM workshops are available through substance abuse treatment programs, college coursework, and Internet resources.

ELDER SCREENING AND ASSESSMENT

Healthcare providers are advised to include questions about drinking and smoking habits on their health inventory forms, and most of them do. Brief interventions at the doctor's office—advice to quit or cut down—have proven effective. Advice to older patients should include warnings about medical conditions, such as high blood pressure and ulcers, that can be worsened by drinking and the risks of taking over-the-counter and prescription drugs in combination with alcohol.

When clients appear at a treatment center, a thorough assessment of their drinking and drug-using habits is undertaken. As mentioned previously, the standard forms, like diagnoses from the *DSM–IV–TR*, contain several items that are inappropriate for clients of advanced age (e.g., items concerning tolerance and legal and occupational consequences of substance misuse).

People are more likely to develop a gambling problem when they are coping with major life changes or losses than when life is going well. In his review of the research on gambling among older adults, Surface (2009) found that casinos are going to great lengths to reach out to this population by providing scooters, wheelchairs, and even oxygen. For those living in senior centers as well, there are plentiful opportunities to gamble. Inexpensive bus excursions transport older citizens to casinos, even picking people up in low-income neighborhoods who can ill afford to lose their social security checks and other means of support.

Because of the expanded availability of gambling establishments and easy transportation to get there, many older persons are attracted to this life for the excitement and escape from boredom. A study by Levens, Dyer, Zurbitsky, Knott, and Oslin (2005) assessed the prevalence of gambling problems in a sample of over 800 older patients with scheduled primary-care clinic appointments. Just under 70% reported that they gambled at least once a year, and around 11% of them were identified as at-risk gamblers. Risk factors that emerged from the study were the existence of problems with binge drinking, the presence of current posttraumatic stress disorder symptoms, minority race or ethnicity, and being a Veterans Affairs (VA) patient. These findings indicate that substance abuse clinics would do well to assess for gambling problems by including a few simple questions about gambling activities, winnings, and losses in assessment forms.

Two well-known alcohol-screening devices that have been validated for use with older adults are CAGE and the Geriatric MAST. CAGE consists of four simple questions (see Chapter 3). The MAST-G (Michigan Alcoholism Screening Test—Geriatric Version) consists of 24 questions with special relevance to the elderly. Samples are: Does having a drink help you sleep? Did you find your drinking increased after someone close to you died? When you feel lonely, does having a drink help? (CSAT, 2001, pp. 7–8). The Geriatric MAST can be downloaded at http://kap.samhsa.gov/products/tools/keys/pdfs/KK_26.pdf.

DIAGNOSING ADDICTION PROBLEMS

Diagnosis is the process that determines whether a person meets certain predetermined criteria for substance abuse, dependence, or pathological gambling. Because there is no gold standard or physiological test for addiction, the criteria used by most U.S. clinicians to classify these disorders are behavioral standards set by the American Psychiatric Association's (2000) *Diagnostic and Statistical Manual of Mental Disorders (DSM IV-R)*. International clinicians tend to use the *International Classification of Diseases (ICD)* from the World Health Organization (1990). Both of these classification systems have evolved over time, with changes published approximately every 10 years. Changes to the *DSM-5* and *ICD-10* are already proposed and are being reviewed. The new edition of the *DSM* is expected to be released around 2013 (see Chapter 1 for proposed changes and *DSM* criteria). Diagnosis alone does not determine how to proceed with treatment. The *DSM-IV-R* describes the behavioral manifestations of the problem, somewhat like a bird classification system that identifies red beak and blue feathers as the markers of a particular bird without saying how or why they got that way. However, a formal diagnosis, like all classification systems, serves several purposes: (1) it helps clinicians talk to each other, using the same term to mean the same thing; (2) it serves as the basis of eligibility for services and third-party reimbursement; (3) it establishes the seriousness of the situation; and (4) it can sometimes reassure the recipient of the diagnosis that he or she is not alone with the problem. The downside of the *DSM* system is that it is subject to the political influence of the pharmaceutical industry, is deficit-focused, stresses individual deficiencies, and pays little attention to the issues of social injustice and equality that may cause or increase the symptom and problems (Anderson, Cowger, & Snively, 2009). When using the DSM, it is critical to be aware of these potential shortcomings and balance the assessment with strength-based practices.

A formal diagnosis is usually made by a physician, licensed psychologist, or licensed social worker, depending on the rules of the individual state and/or insurance company. The most common approach to diagnosing is through a clinical interview with the client, comparing current symptoms and behaviors to the criteria specified in the *DSM IV-R* (Miller et al., 2011). There are structured diagnostic interviews available that require specialized training, such as the Diagnostic Interview Schedule (DIS) (Aktan, Calkins, Ribisl, Kroliczak, & Kasim, 1997) and the Structured Clinical Interview for DSM (SCID) (First, Spitzer, Gibbon, & Williams, 1997).

ASSESSMENT AND THE STRENGTH PERSPECTIVE

Assessment is much more than a toolbox of screening questions and assessment instruments. We do not want to lose the forest (recovery) for the trees (identifying the deficits). To balance the tilt toward the deficit, we also need to assess client strengths and resources and bring them to the light of day.

A person recovering from addiction needs all the support they can get for the long and lonely process of setting aside the addiction that used to be their best friend and dealing with "the wreckage of the past." One woman in the Davis (2009) study on women who were recovering from problem gambling said, "Professional help helps you to get over the devastation of you going through shame, you going through guilt, you going through humiliation, you going through alienation from your family, your friends, and anybody that cares about you" (p. 128). A significant part of how we help people through such devastation is to build a relationship with them.

A good way to discover a person's strengths and build a relationship is to focus on what is happening in the client's life and what the client wants to be different. This may mean setting aside, for the time being, the need to gather specific intake, screening, and assessment information about the client and the presenting problems. Bill Miller tells the story of making a dramatic change in a treatment program he directed (Miller et al., 2011). Instead of the client's first contact being with a clerk who directed the intake process of forms and questions, he changed the first contact to be with a senior counselor. He directed the counselor to start with this statement: "After a while I'm going to ask you some questions that we need to ask everyone, but right now I just want to know why you're here, what's happening in your life, and what you hope we might be able to do for you" (p. 75). Counselors spent the first part of the session hearing the client's story, and when it came time to fill in the forms, they already knew most of the content. The results were a higher retention rate, and the clients wanted to stay with the person who did their intake. Clearly, a therapeutic relationship with the client had a better chance of building after these changes were made.

A guiding principle of strength-based practice is that clients are in charge of setting their own goals and deciding how to achieve them (Rapp & Lane, 2009). Thus, part of the assessment process is to discover what the goals may be that are important to the client. Focusing attention on what the client wants to see happen as a result of working together with the clinician, as in Miller's example, sets up a partnership that is based on the assumption that people have invaluable information about their experience and lives (Weik, Krieder, & Chamberlain, 2009).

Some strength-based practitioners see assessment as a political activity (Anderson, Cowger, & Snively, 2009). When the assessment process focuses only on deficits, it can reinforce the politically conservative idea that individual deficits are the cause of human problems, not oppressive or mismanaged social systems. In the addiction field, it is common for the public to marginalize "crack mothers" or "gambling addicts" as flawed individuals, instead of looking deeper into the social conditions that generate unequal power, like poverty. When clinicians look at only what has gone wrong in the client's life, they inadvertently reinforce the idea that the person is the problem, instead of the problem being the problem. The authors recommend several guidelines for a strength assessment, based on the understanding that there are multiple constructions of reality for each person, and that problem situations are forever changing. Some examples of their practical suggestions include (p. 186):

- When assessments are written, they should be written in simple English with a minimum of professional nomenclature so that it is clear to all involved. Whenever possible, use direct quotes to describe the problem and solutions.
- Support and validate the story. This requires belief that clients are basically trustworthy.
- Honor self-determination and help clients discover their own points of view, meanings, choices, and vision for the future.
- Move the assessment toward strengths, both intrapersonal (motivation, emotional strengths and ability to think clearly) and interpersonal (family networks, significant others, voluntary organizations, community groups, and public institutions).
- Discover uniqueness—find the unique situation the client is experiencing.
- Reach a mutual agreement on the assessment, stressing the importance of the individual's understanding of the situation and their wants. The person can feel ownership only if the assessment is open and shared.
- Do not get caught up in the labels of a diagnosis. A diagnosis should never "totalize" a person's identity, and is not the only outcome of an assessment.

Specific questions that help to move the assessment toward strengths are imbedded in each of the models discussed in the next chapter. For example, a typical technique in motivational interviewing is to ask about what changes the client has successfully made in the past? What was the change? How did they do it? What barriers did they overcome to make the change? (Miller et al., 2011). A familiar line of questioning to clinicians using the Solution-Focused model is "exception questions," that is, asking about times when the problem is absent or a little less intense, and finding out what is different about those times (Lee, 2010).

A foundation of clinical skills is needed to put strength-based assessment into practice. One of the most essential is the quality of *empathy*. Miller and colleagues (2011) found through a series of research studies that regardless of the intervention model, drinking outcomes were strongly predicted by the extent that the counselor practiced empathic, reflective listening during the treatment process. The more empathy, the more recovery. Using Carl Rogers's definition, empathy is defined as "the ability to listen to your clients and accurately reflect back to them the essence and meaning of what they have said" (p. 50). Empathy requires the additional skill of *reflective listening*. Reflective listening is not just repeating what the client says, but making a responsive statement, based on your experience and what you have heard, as to what the person really meant. For example, a woman who is experiencing problems with gambling may say, "I don't have any money to pay the rent, my food is running out, and I'm about to lose my job..." A reflective response might be, "So you're really at the end of your rope and probably wondering if you should even be here." Other foundation skills essential to strength-based assessment include the ability to ask open-ended questions, affirm the client's experience, and make short summaries as the interview progresses. In motivational interviewing, these are called the OARS skills: open-ended questions, affirmations, reflections, and summaries (Miller et al., 2011).

Finally, a strength-based assessment rests on the elusive quality of *hope*. For some women in the problem gambling study (Davis, 2009), the turning point arrived and recovery began with the tiny kindling of hope by another person: a sense that they were not alone, they were not crazy, and they could, somehow, stop gambling. Hope can be kindled in a professional treatment context or an informal setting. For one woman, her hope began when a psychiatrist told her, "You're not crazy, you just need Gamblers Anonymous!" Finding strengths in the upside-down world of the woman with gambling problems is a testament to hope. In what could be the standard for clinicians everywhere, a counselor of women problem gamblers describes her therapeutic stance as follows:

> The women want good strategies from me, but this is not what I feel they demand most. They seem to want to know that I am there with them, to acknowledge that I see their pain and I am not afraid of them; that I can bear their stories and carry them, and that I will attend to them when they feel unworthy. I feel I am asked to testify to their survival; to help them see what I see: a person, deeply injured, and with great, unbelievable resilience. (Anonymous, 2003)

SUMMARY AND CONCLUSIONS

Many tools are available to help the counselor and the client assess the likelihood of alcohol, drug, or gambling problems. Screening tools, as short as one question, can alert clinicians to the possibility of a problem behavior. More complex assessment tools help define the seriousness of the problem and the consequences of the behavior. A formal diagnosis can qualify the client for particular services and third-party payments. Levels of care classifications assist in treatment matching.

As the addiction field moves steadily in the direction of client-centered, strength-based practice, screening and assessment becomes a more collaborative process that honors clients' meanings of their experience, their goals for the future, and their strengths as well as limitations. The traditional medical model, where the physician tests for symptoms, diagnosis the problem, and prescribes the solution, no longer prevails in the complex, multidimensional world of clients who are oppressed by an addiction. Instead, assessment is treated (1) as part of the engagement process, where the emphasis is on listening deeply to the client and empathically reflecting their words and meanings; (2) as part of the treatment process, where goals are established, maintained, and evaluated within the framework of what the client wants to be different; and (3) as a mechanism for identifying not just problems, but also client strengths and resources to aid in the recovery process. The next chapter will focus in depth on four different models of intervention (harm reduction, motivational interviewing, solution-focused, and cognitive-behavioral) that use different approaches and techniques to further strength-based, effective practices.

REFERENCES

Addiction Technology Transfer Center Network. (2011). *Psychotherapeutic medications, 2011: What every counselor should know.* Retrieved August 10, 2011 from http://www.nattc.org/regcenters/index_midamerica.asp

Aktan, G., Calkins, R., Ribisl, K., Kroliczak, A., & Kasim, R. (1997). Test-retest reliability of psychoactive substance abuse and dependence diagnoses in telephone interviews using a modified Diagnostic Interview Schedule substance abuse module, *American Journal of Drug and Alcohol Abuse, 23,* 229–248.

American Psychiatric Association (APA). (2000). *Diagnostic and statistical manual of mental disorders, text revision* (4th ed.). Washington, DC: Author. Quick Reference.

Anderson, K., Cowger, C., & Snively, C. (2009). Assessing strengths: Identifying acts of resistance to violence and oppression. In D. Saleeby (Ed.) *The strengths perspective in social work practice* (pp. 181–200). Boston: Pearson.

Anonymous. (2003). Reflections on problem gambling therapy with female clients. *eGambling, 8.* Retrieved February 7, 2009 from www.camh.net/egambling/issue8/first_person/index.html

Babor, T., Higgins-Biddle, J., Saunders, J., & Monteiro, M. (2001). *The Alcohol Use Disorders Identification Test: Guidelines for use in primary care* (2nd ed.). Geneva, Switzerland: World Health Organization.

Blume, A., & Lovato, L. (2010). Empowering the disempowered: Harm reduction with racial/ethnic minority clients. *Journal of Clinical Psychology: In Session, 66*(2), 189–200.

Blume, A., Morera, O., & de la Cruz, B. (2005). Assessment of addictive behaviors in ethnic-minority cultures. In D. Donovan & G. A. Marlatt (Eds.), *Assessment of addictive behaviors* (2nd ed., pp. 49–70). New York: Guilford Press.

Bradley, K., Boyd-Wickizer, J., Powell, S., & Burman, M. (1998, July 8). Alcohol screening questionnaires in women: A critical review. *Journal of the American Medical Association, 280*(2), 166–171.

Brown, R., Leonard, T., Saunders, L., & Papasouliotis, O. (1998). The prevalence and detection of substance use disorder among inpatients ages 18–49: An opportunity for prevention. *Preventive Medicine, 27,* 101–110.

Carroll, K., & McGinley, J. (2001). A screening form for identifying mental health problems in alcohol/other drug dependent persons. *Alcoholism Treatment Quarterly, 19*(4), 33–47.

Center for Substance Abuse Treatment (CSAT). (2005). *Substance abuse treatment for persons with co-occurring disorder, Treatment improvement protocol (TIP) Series 42.* DHHS Publication No. (SMA) 05-3992. Rockville, MD: SAMHSA.

Davis, D. (2009). *Taking back your life: Women and problem gambling.* Center City, MN: Hazelden.

Denning, P. (2004). *Practicing harm reduction psychotherapy: An alternative approach to addictions.* New York: Guilford Press.

Ewing, J. (1984). Detecting alcoholism: The CAGE questionnaire. *Journal of the American Medical Association, 252,* 1905–1907.

First, M., Spitzer, R., Gibbon, M., & Williams, J. (1997). *User guide for the Structured Clinical Interview for the DSM-IV Axis I disorders: Clinician version.* Washington, DC: American Psychiatric Press.

Forcehimes, A., Tonigan, J., Miller, W., Kenna, G., & Baer, J. (2007). Psychometrics of the Drinker Inventory of Consequences (DrInC). *Addictive Behaviors, 32,* 1699–1704.

Johnson, E., Hamer, R., Nora, R., Tan, B., Eistenstein, N., & Englehart, C. (1988). The lie/bet questionnaire for screening pathological gamblers. *Psychological Reports, 80,* 80–88.

Lee, M. (2010). Solution-focused theory. In F.Turner (Ed). *Social work treatment: Interlocking theoretical approaches* (pp. 460–485). New York: Oxford University Press.

Little, J., & Franskoviak, P. (2010). So glad you came! Harm reduction therapy in community settings. *Journal of Clinical Psychology: In Session, 66*(2), 175–188.

McNeece, C., & DiNitto, D. (2005). *Chemical dependency: A systems approach.* Boston: Pearson.

Meuser, K., Drake, R., Turner, W., & McGovern, M. (2006). Comorbid substance use disorders and psychiatric disorders. In W. R. Miller & K. M. Carroll (Eds.), *Rethinking substance abuse: What the science show and what we should do about it* (pp.115–133). New York: Guilford Press.

Miller, F., & Lazowski, L. (1999). *The Substance Abuse Subtle Screening Inventory-3 (SASSI) manual.* Springville, IN: SASSI Institute.

Miller, W., Forcehimes, A., Zweben, A., & McClellan, A. (2011). *Treating addiction: A guide for professionals.* New York: Guilford Press.

National Institute on Alcohol Abuse and Alcoholism (NIAAA). (2005). *Helping patients who drink too much: A clinician's guide.* Bethesda, MD: National Institutes of Health.

Rapp, R., & Lane, D. (2009). Implementation of brief strengths-based case management: An evidenced-based intervention for improving linkage with care. In D. Saleeby (Ed.) *The strengths perspective in social work practice* (pp. 146–160). Boston: Pearson.

Smith, P., Schmidt, S., Allensworth-Davies, D., & Saitz, R. (2010). A single question screening test for drug use in primary care. *Archives of Internal Medicine, 170*(13), 1155–1160.

Surface, D. (2009, March/April). High risk recreation problem gambling in older adults. *Social Work Today,* 18–23.

Toneatto, T (2008). Reliability and validity of Gamblers Anonymous 20 Questions. *Journal of Psychopathology and Behavioral Assessment, 30*(1), 71–78.

Tonigan, J. S. & Miller, W. R. (2002). The Inventory of Drug Use Consequences (InDUC): Test-retest stability and sensitivity to detect change. *Psychology of Addictive Behaviors, 16*(2), 165-168.

Ursua, M., & Uribelarrea, L. (1998). 20 Questions of Gamblers Anonymous: A psychometric study with population of Spain. *Journal of Gambling Studies, 14*(1), 3–15.

Weik, A., Kreider, J., & Chamberlain, R. (2009). Key dimensions of the strengths perspective in case management, clinical practice, and community practice. In D. Saleeby (Ed.) *The strengths perspective in social work practice* (pp. 108–121). Boston: Pearson.

Williams, R., & Vinson, D. (2001). Validation of a single screening question for problem drinking. *Journal of Family Practice, 50,* 307–312.

Strengths- and Evidence-Based Helping Strategies

CHAPTER 8

The Rose

Andrea Davis

The queen shouts profanities as I lay her jeweled head and losing
   face upon the green felt table.
My bleeding ulcer twists and turns, flaring up with the extra acid
   from adrenaline.
I bear to admit I have lost everything I thought I won. My back is
   bent, hunching me forward,
The weight is huge, larger than my being. I am kneeling on all
   fours.
Crying that I might never get up.
Maybe I'll just fold beneath the weight, and let it suffocate me. I
   live a life the hue of coal, dark, solid, and cold.
And I am trying to press the precious stone out of it. Looking for
   something to fill the void.
Searching for the beauty within me. Hoping for the knowledge
   that I am loved.
In self-defeat, self-loathing, self-destruction, I am still loved. Life
   calls me on.
Today, tomorrow, forever I hope. And in that hope I feel free.
For the gleam that speckles the inside of my dark cocoon with
   prisms of light
Shows me, I am not just the darkness, my secret life. I am beauty.

Printed with the permission of Andrea Davis.

INTRODUCTION

Practitioners of strengths-based helping strategies fiercely adhere to the hope offered in the preceding poem by Andrea Davis that "I am not just the darkness, my secret life. / I am beauty." Strengths-based practitioners believe that no matter how dismal the circumstances, people have possibilities, resiliencies, and capacities for change and even transformation. They look for and try to nurture the "gleam" that is often hidden by misery, protective strategies, and the failure to achieve goals set by others.

Davis once heard a highly regarded professor in social work state emphatically that ("for your own good") you just have to "write off" anyone who has been in treatment more than five times. An alternative, strengths-based understanding is that addiction is a chronic, relapsing condition that, like other chronic conditions, may require periodic interventions over time (Miller, Forcehimes, & Zweben, 2011). "Don't give up until the miracle happens" is an Alcoholics Anonymous (AA) saying that applies to clinicians as well as clients. This does not mean that you as a counselor must doggedly chase down a client and try to force your agenda for change. It does mean that you continue to focus on strengths rather than liabilities, not because they are "truer," but because it is a more effective way of helping a client find the hope, motivation, and self-efficacy necessary for making changes.

The strengths perspective in social work practice and other helping professions continues to develop conceptually. Strengths-based practice is eloquently defined by Saleebey (2006), as "a versatile practice approach, relying heavily on ingenuity and creativity.... Rather than focusing on problems, your eye turns toward possibility" (p. 1). Saleebey offers a "lexicon of strengths" that also serves as a statement of principles. Key concepts in the strengths lexicon are empowerment of individuals and communities; membership or belongingness; resilience, healing, and wholeness; dialogue and collaboration; and suspension of disbelief in what the client says. The interventions described in this chapter share these characteristics, in particular the emphasis on *choice, providing options, and paying attention to the client's state of readiness for change.*

Choice is the hallmark of a strengths-based intervention. In the substance misuse arena, this means choice about the goals of the helping relationship (harm reduction, including abstinence); informed choice about a variety of treatment contexts (same gender, group, individual, day treatment, outpatient, inpatient, mutual-help groups); and informed choice about treatment methods (cognitive-behavioral, Twelve-Step approach, solution-focused, motivational interviewing, types of nicotine replacement therapy, etc.). The emphasis on choice of treatment, of course, implies that a variety of community resources *are* available to help people alleviate their troubles with substance misuse and that these treatment choices are affordable. Granted, these kinds of choices are an ideal, not a reality, in the United States, but we advocate finding ways to weave a variety of options into existing programs to the fullest extent possible.

People who use illicit drugs or are dependent on alcohol, gambling, purging, and so forth are typically marginalized in their choices about what they need or want to change and how best to accomplish it. This stance is based on the belief that such people are not capable of making a good choice and must be manipulated or coerced into doing the right thing for themselves and concerned others. Granted, it is tempting to play God, particularly with people who may have wreaked havoc on themselves and others. However, in a strengths-based approach, one concedes that it simply does not work. A Canadian research group has discounted claims about the effectiveness of mandated treatment as nonempirical and replete with methodological problems in a review of 850 articles on the topic (Wild, 1999). Inevitably, people seem to find a way to use and misuse alcohol and drugs, gamble, smoke, and so on, even in prison and in treatment centers, if that is their goal.

By honoring choice, a strengths-based practitioner respects the right of the individual to manage his or her own destiny and to take responsibility for his or her own actions. In the field of social work, this is called the value of self-determination, the belief that people have a right to arrange their lives in accordance with their own preferences (National Association of Social Work, 2008). However, the right of clients to pursue their own goals regarding their addiction, take risks or reduce harms, make mistakes, and even harm themselves in the process is not uniformly endorsed by social workers or other clinicians. Many professional social workers justify or simply "go along" with legal and agency interference to these rights because of the "risk clause;" that is, "social workers may limit clients' right to self-determination when in the social workers' professional judgment, clients' actions or potential actions pose a serious, foreseeable, and imminent risk to themselves or others" (NASW, 2008), Standard 1.02.

Chronic alcohol and drug addiction, however, is not in the same crisis category as imminent suicide. It is what the ethicist Reamer (1998) refers to as one of "the more subtle forms of self-harming behavior that pose difficult ethical dilemmas for social workers" (p. 29). He says many practitioners have "instincts to protect vulnerable people from engaging in self-destructive behavior." It is this very instinct, based on good intentions, that may be a barrier for social workers and other practitioners to honor self-determination with persons who are misusing substances or addicted. However, as Miller and colleagues (2011) remind us, "whatever clinicians may do, it is ultimately the client who decides whether, when, and how to change … in that sense, telling clients that they 'can't' or 'must' is not actually accurate" (p. 352).

In strengths-based interventions, we try to keep in mind that alcohol, drug use, and addiction are risky behaviors that have been occurring since ancient times. These behaviors are usually tolerated and "self-determined" in the middle and upper classes. However, if you are economically poor or a member of an oppressed minority group and live in the United States, these same behaviors can make you extremely vulnerable to incarceration. You can lose custody of your children and have limited options for reducing the harm of your addiction. Harm reduction and strengths-based practices would extend the right of choice and self-determination to all economic and racial and ethnic groups.

Providing options is the second tenet of strengths-based approaches. It does not help to have the right to choose without options to choose from. If a treatment center is based solely on the abstinence-only model, there is no choice. In the same way, if a community does not provide low-cost housing or if federal government regulations prohibit publicly financed housing for people with drug-related convictions (see Chapter 13), there is no choice. A strengths-based practitioner may have to go the extra mile to develop an extensive network of referral sources and options. Rapp (2006) examined the impact of strengths-based case management in two different research projects and found that it is imperative that case managers prepare extensive networks of referral sources that include formal service providers, informal networks, program requirements, and natural helpers.

The third basic tenet of strengths-based approaches is to *pay attention to the readiness of the clients and/or client systems to make changes* in the arena they have chosen. No longer are people assumed to be eager for the counselor to tell them what to do and labeled resistant if they are not eagerly compliant. Instead, change is seen as a process on a continuum that moves from a position of unwillingness to even consider making the change to acting on behaviors that will maintain the change. The development by Prochaska and DiClemente (1986) of the transtheoretical change model was instrumental in helping the addiction field consider the implications of the client's readiness for change. Relapse is regarded not as a personal failure but rather as an expected part of the change process.

In this chapter, we describe four strengths-based approaches and the evidence that supports their effectiveness. What these approaches have in common is that they honor the principle of client self-determination, attend to the client's stage of readiness, and focus on the resources and capabilities the client and client's family may use to further their goals. The four approaches are (1) the practices of harm reduction, (2) motivational interviewing, (3) solution-focused interventions, and (4) cognitive behavioral therapy.

In addition, we will include a section on group therapy led by a designated therapist (unlike mutual-help groups), which is the most common form of treatment in both inpatient and outpatient settings today (Miller et al., 2011). The last section of the chapter describes what is still the prevailing system of treatment care commonly available in the United States—detoxification, treatment, and aftercare—and suggests ways to incorporate strength-based and community-based approaches. We realize that the particular intervention models we have chosen (harm reduction, motivational interviewing, solution-focused, and cognitive-behavioral) all contain one essential ingredient: clients are encouraged to choose their own goals for improving their lives. In the United States today, abstinence is the only treatment goal offered by 75% of alcohol and drug treatment providers (Tatarsky & Marlatt, 2010). However, the models we will discuss are being progressively incorporated into traditional treatment. We invite you to consider the evidence available about the effectiveness of these approaches with substance misusers and others struggling with addictive processes, as well as examine the underlying values of the different models and how these matches your own values and beliefs regarding professional helping processes. We are also confident that many aspects of the models we will discuss can be, and are currently, being threaded into an abstinence-only treatment environment.

HARM REDUCTION

On one level, all programs that deal with people who are misusing substances or are addicted, including abstinence-only programs, share the goal of reducing harm caused by the addiction. The term *harm reduction* itself is not precise. It can be used to designate international policies, such as the 1973 World Health Organization's (WHO) recommendation to implement harm reduction policies as a viable alternative to a drug control approach (Ball, 2010). Harm reduction has also been used to characterize practices of various communities to reduce the harm of particular substances and protect the community, such as the rituals and taboos surrounding the use of coca products in Latin America, or even the practice of providing food and shelter to homeless alcoholics in the 18th century. Public health experts tend to characterize harm reduction as pragmatic interventions that have good evidence of public health benefit such as providing clean injecting equipment to intravenous (IV) drug users; agonist maintenance treatment for opioid dependence; education about blood-borne virus risk behavior and ways to reduce it; HIV testing, counseling, and treatment; and even supervised injecting facilities in settings with high risk street injecting (Hall, 2007). Although harm reduction is part of the health and drug policies of most developed and some developing nations, the United States has historically supported an abstinence-only approach to addiction. However, there is some cause for optimism that harm reduction approaches are making headway in the United States. Tatarsky and Marlatt (2010) cite several factors that support the spread of harm reduction: (1) increased support for treatment instead of incarceration; (2) growing public understanding that addiction problems occur in a co-occurring context with social, economic, medical, and mental health problems; (3) increased reliance on evidence-based practices instead of tradition and ideology; and (4) a pledge by the Obama administration to support science over ideology in the treatment of addiction.

In this section, we will limit ourselves to a discussion of specific harm reduction treatment strategies that take place in the context of professional treatment, and refer to practices that aim at reducing drug, alcohol, or gambling related harm without requiring abstinence from the problem behavior itself (Tatarsky & Marlatt, 2010).

Based on a public health model of primary, secondary, and tertiary prevention, harm reduction (at the tertiary level) attempts to alleviate the social, legal, and medical problems associated with unmanaged addiction. In so doing, it tries to limit the harms, such as infectious diseases like HIV, hepatitis, and tuberculosis; violence; criminal activity; and early death, without necessarily attempting to "cure" the addiction (Tatarsky & Marlatt, 2010; Kleining, 2008). Abstinence may be an ideal outcome for many addicted persons, but harm reduction advocates point out we are not 100% effective in convincing people to become abstinent. A review of the literature on treatment options for opioid-dependent patients by Brink and Haasen (2006) concluded that abstinence-only interventions are effective only for a select few: motivated persons with stable living conditions and social support. The Project MATCH Research Group (1997) found that only 19% of the outpatient subjects maintained complete abstinence throughout the 12-month follow-up period; however, there was substantial positive improvement. This same group abstained on average more than 80% of the days posttreatment compared with slightly more than 20% pretreatment. From a harm reduction standpoint, abstinence is viewed as *only one of several means* of improving and is a goal only when the client proposes it as a goal.

Because of myths surrounding harm reduction practices, it may be helpful to start with what harm reduction is not. It is not:

- A conspiracy to seduce alcoholics or addicts into thinking they can use alcohol or drugs moderately, thus prolonging their agony. (Rather, the extent of a person's drug or alcohol use per se is not the focus of harm reduction—use is secondary to the risk of harms *consequent* to use.)
- A potent excuse for an alcoholic, compulsive gambler, or drug addict to continue to use alcohol or drugs or gamble. (Rather, for a person who is in the throes of addiction, the principles of harm reduction are no more potent than "today it is raining" as a reason to use alcohol, drugs, gamble, etc.)
- A foolish, dangerous model designed by academics or people who do not know anything about addiction or do not care about the consequences of not getting people to abstain from their addiction. (Harm reduction practices evolved from the demands of injection drug users for strategies to prevent the spread of HIV.)
- A misguided approach that makes it easier for addicts to keep on being addicted by furnishing shelter, food, clean needles, methadone, and even heroin to people who are addicted. (Most harm reduction programs attend first to the most pressing needs of an individual as a step in the direction of less risky use or, if appropriate, abstinence.)

Harm reduction practices can be understood by looking at how one might treat a person with diabetes. Harm reduction practitioners would not wait until the person was in a diabetic coma and brought into the hospital for treatment. Rather, they would try to educate health providers and other likely contacts about the symptoms of diabetes so that people who are in harm's way can be alerted and given informed choices about different ways to proceed and the cost and benefits of such actions. Resources would be available to assist the persons in finding the right path for them, whether a different diet or insulin shots.

Families and the community at large would be educated about the typical harms of the disease, such as the emotional roller coaster that can result when the problem is ignored. People with diabetes would be encouraged to reduce the various harms of going untreated, and resources would be made available to assist them. Their choices would be respected (even if we do not agree with them), and we would expect them to take responsibility for their choices. Sound familiar? This is the way it actually works in the public health system. The harm reduction model simply applies this approach to addiction.

Reducing Barriers

Harm reduction practitioners reduce barriers that make it less likely that people who are misusing alcohol/drugs or addicted will get help. Typical barriers present in many treatment programs today include program locations inaccessible to or remote from the community they are trying to target, professional staff who may be perceived as knowing little about street culture or survival rules, waiting lists for intake and treatment, financial costs, and a requirement that abstinence be the goal of treatment. For people who are homeless and have mental health problems as well as dealing with survival needs on a daily basis, barriers also include having to sit still in a waiting room, filling out paperwork for intake, or even entering an office with staff with the door closed (Little & Franskoviak, 2010). Providing low threshold services is critical if we want to help people who have a treatment need. In 2009, only 11.2% of people (age 12 or older) who needed treatment for an illicit drug or alcohol problem actually received it (SAMHSA, 2010). An estimated 10% of pathological gamblers identified in prevalence studies will seek treatment (Ladouceur, 2005).

By far the most controversial aspect of providing low threshold services in the United States is promoting access to services without requiring abstinence as a precondition for receiving treatment. Proponents of harm reduction say that a high threshold barrier of abstinence does not distinguish between lighter and heavier use and degrees of harm. Harm reduction is also a "profoundly non-coercive treatment experience" and requiring a preordained goal of abstinence is seen as denying the voice of the consumer (Little & Franskoviak, 2010, p. 181). A substance abuse treatment provider describes it like this to Lee & Petersen (2009): "The challenge has been that once a substance user walks in the door ... red light, red light, this is a problem, you know forget about self-determination because they're not (seen as) capable of self-determination" (p. 623). When consumers know that their ideas about goals will be listened to, they are more likely to enter treatment. For example, a preliminary study of low-threshold gambling treatment found some gamblers can eliminate the harms of their excessive gambling by controlling the amount of money bet and the amount of time spent gambling. The author notes that none of the participants would have been willing to engage in treatment if the requirement had been abstinence (Ladouceur, 2005).

Another way to reduce barriers to treatment is to provide outreach in the community where potential users live. Outreach often involves providing drug education materials telling the user how to reduce the risks associated with using drugs as well as building a relationship and providing referrals for treatment and support services. Examples of pamphlets available in English and Spanish on the Internet from the Harm Reduction Coalition include "Taking Care of Your Veins: Rotate Your Spot!" and "Avoiding Arteries and Nerves When You Want a Vein" (http://www.harmreduction.org).

Increasing accessibility to harm reduction aids is accomplished in a variety of creative ways, some of which may surprise the U.S. reader. For example, in Amsterdam, police stations provide clean syringes on an exchange basis; automated syringe exchange machines are accessible 24 hours a day in many European and Australian cities; in several provinces in Canada, pharmacists are actively involved in syringe exchange programs; in the United Kingdom, Europe, and Australia, methadone is available from general practitioners as well as clinics, and some even distribute through "methadone buses" (Riley et al., 1999). Activities more common in the United States include mobile vans or street workers delivering services to parts of the community where injection drug users live or "hang out." The Harm Reduction Therapy Center (HRTC) in San Francisco operates seven community-based programs in the Tenderloin area, which has the highest concentration of homelessness, mental illness, drug abuse, HIV, and poverty in the city (Little & Franskoviak, 2010). The HRTC approach is defined by flexibility, easy access, and offering as many points of entry as possible. Because the programs are located in public health clinics and drop-in centers, an array of options is available for the consumer to choose how they may access services. Here is how Little and Franskoviak (2010) describe their outreach services:

> We walk around the agencies in which our programs are located, greeting folks, smiling, making eye contact when invited, and stopping to chat when it seems clear that someone has something to say. For some, we may spend months saying hello on the sidewalk outside the drop-in center, or perhaps offering a daily cup of coffee to a person sitting alone in the midst of the agency's drop-in center. For others, outreach might mean asking permission to sit with them as they wait to see the doctor to have an abscess treated, letting them come forward, listening closely to what they want to share, and expressing interest in hearing more, so that treatment becomes a conversation, and not an appointment or a session, with the expectation inherent in those contacts. (Little & Franskoviak, 2010, p. 182)

A goal of harm reduction practitioners in the United States is to make methadone treatment and needle exchange programs more accessible. Although the United States has had institutionalized methadone maintenance programs since the 1960s, the distribution of methadone is confined to specialized clinics, usually in larger cities, subject to strict federal and state regulations that require exacting compliance from clients. Syringe exchange programs in the United States continue to be unfunded by federal dollars and legally harassed in many localities, despite abundant research on the positive results of these programs. Although it still remains controversial in the United States, syringe exchange programs and budgets have continued to grow. The number of programs known to the North American Syringe Exchange Network have increased from 68 in 1994–1995 to 186 in 2007. Public funding from state and local governments has increased from $3.9 million to $14.4 million (Des Jarlais, McKnight, Goldblatt, & Purchase, 2008). A large majority (89%) now permit "secondary" exchange where a person is allowed to exchange for peers who may be absent. Almost all programs provide condoms, alcohol pads, HIV counseling and testing, referrals to substance abuse treatment, and education about HIV, hepatitis A, B, and C, vein care and abscess prevention. A majority also provide food, clothing, and personal hygiene products. Although the availability of syringe exchange programs has increased, there are many areas of the country with no coverage or very little coverage. Nevertheless, the expansion has contributed to substantial reductions in HIV prevalence among IV drug users in the United States. With 33 states reporting, new HIV diagnoses declined by approximately 10% per year from 2001 to 2005, and injecting drug use was the only transmission category that declined over this time period (Des Jarlais et al., 2008). Clearly, the reduction of HIV incidence is an optimistic sign that this low-threshold approach of reaching out to consumers who need help is working. Other strategies that have demonstrated effectiveness in reducing barriers include rapid intake (Dennis, Ingram, Burks, & Rachal, 1994), where people who want to enter treatment are no longer delayed, and lowered financial barriers, such as passing out free coupons for treatment. In a New Jersey study where coupons for free methadone treatment were passed out in the IDU community, 59% redeemed treatment coupons. Nearly 50% of these people had never been in treatment; 58% tested positive for HIV (Bux, Iguchi, Lidz, Baxter, & Platt, 1993). In a random assignment study in Denver that compared free treatment to paying for treatment, 52% of the injecting drug users assigned to free treatment entered treatment compared to 32% for those who had to pay (Booth et al., 1998). In spite of this evidence, lowering financial barriers is not endorsed by professionals who believe that clients "have to pay" to receive positive benefits from programs.

Looking for larger system interventions that would help reduce the barriers for women to get help with gambling problems, Davis (2008, p. 130) elicited suggestions from women gamblers. Their ideas include:

1. Timely access to other supporting services, such as mental health and especially financial counseling. As one woman commented, "People that have screwed up their lives this bad, you know, need to be pointed in directions where people can help them, like consumer credit counseling."
2. Access to female counselors because of the need to disclose problems such as physical, sexual, and emotional abuse.
3. Easily accessible services in downtown areas as well as rural environments where services are co-located with other supportive services to lessen stigmatization and promote referrals.

Other examples of harm reduction strategies that improve access are selling nicotine replacement therapies over the counter instead of requiring a prescription; making clean syringes and methadone available in prisons; supplying free bleach kits for cleaning injecting equipment to prevent hepatitis; providing testing for street drugs at "rave" dances; developing "tolerance zones" or "injection rooms" where drug users can get clean equipment, condoms, medical advice, and attention and even take drugs in a safe environment; and launching various websites to keep consumers informed, such as the Ravesafe organization that started in South Africa in 1993 (http://www.ravesafe.org). Although many of these practices are controversial in the United States and Canada, the overall purpose of improving access to a treatment system that is not yet user friendly (some say built for providers to punish consumers) needs to be respected.

CHOOSING TO REDUCE HARM: WHO CHOOSES?

Diane Riley and colleagues (1999), of the Canadian Centre on Substance Abuse National Working Group on Policy, raise some thought-provoking questions: What drug-related "harms" should be given priority? Is preventing HIV infection more important than eliminating dependence? Abstinence-only proponents tend to view dependence as a top priority, but many harm reduction proponents do not. Success in harm reduction terms is "any reduction in drug-related harm" (Denning, 2000, p. 37). Another critical question is who decides. In abstinence-based treatment, professionals decide the priorities to be addressed, starting with abstinence. In the harm reduction approach, the person/consumer/client decides the priorities to be addressed—that is, what harms to address and in what order. A further complication can occur when harm reduction practices become compulsory, such as the no-smoking bans in public places, wearing seatbelts and helmets for motorcycles, or the recent compulsory vaccination of schoolgirls ordered by the Governor of Texas. As Kleining (2008) suggests, compulsory harm reduction practices force us to evaluate the ethical issue of who decides, who participates in the decision, and what evidence makes us think it would be an effective measure.

Recognizing the importance of choice in finding one's own path, Patt Denning (2000) states that "people have the right to make their own decisions in life.... The fact that they may make treatment choices and life choices that conflict with my professional or personal beliefs does not relieve me of my responsibility to offer them what help I can" (p. 25). Denning is a therapist who lives in San Francisco, where, since September 2000, official city policy has required that all substance abuse and HIV/AIDS treatment providers address how they will provide harm reduction treatment options and that they develop harm reduction guidelines. As a consultant and trainer to many treatment providers, Denning (2000) acknowledges that harm reduction strategies may focus on what the user might see as more pressing problems than drug or alcohol use, such as housing, repairing broken relationships or support systems, jobs, social skills training, and psychiatric symptoms. The goals within the professional helping relationship are based on the rights of individuals to make their own choices. Consequently, cultural, racial, and ethnic differences that may influence goals are not problematic but are looked on as resources and potential supports.

Although reducing the probability of HIV transmission is a common goal among most treatment providers, other "harms" that are the focus of harm reduction strategies include the risks of procuring illegal drugs, such as legal consequences, incarceration, and the loss of custody of children. Larger system harms may include the alarming growth of prisons, the marginalizing of certain groups, such as "crack moms," and the large amount of national resources devoted to interdiction instead of treatment (see Chapter 13 on public policy). The definition of *harms* also varies depending on the type of problem and the co-occurrence of other problems, such as mental disorders, gambling, homelessness, and domestic violence.

For example, people who are homeless and chronically alcoholic are vulnerable to serious difficulties with the police, continual health crises, and deterioration of functioning at all levels. An innovative program in Canada used the principles of harm reduction to design a shelter-based project that provided healthcare, supervision, assistance with daily living tasks, and a maximum of one standard drink of alcohol hourly on demand during waking hours (Podymow, Turnbull, Coyle, Yetisir, & Wells, 2006). Although the study had only 17 participants (mean age 51, mean duration of alcoholism 35 years), the results are encouraging from a harm reduction perspective. The number of emergency room visits and police encounters decreased significantly, hygiene improved, and participants reported less alcohol consumption.

Unfortunately, for a homeless woman with a history of substance misuse who finds a place to live through a social agency, the most immediate harm of using alcohol or drugs may be the risk of homelessness. Kate Fewel, MSW, worked in a downtown women's drop-in center in Spokane, Washington, and case-managed four homeless women (with histories of alcohol/drug misuse and/or domestic violence) in their own apartments through a neighborhood-housing program. She notes the difference between the women she worked with, who are required to maintain abstinence not only from drugs or alcohol but also from abusive relationships, and an alternative model in her same community that practices harm reduction. In her housing model, abstinence is required to encourage the women to focus on the issues that led to their homelessness. However,

> The stress level is higher because they are more immediately accountable (but not over the long run) and they are at risk of losing housing if they break the rules or get caught. In the harm reduction setting, the women may experience relapse, but not at the risk of losing their housing. Because housing is the safety net, their relapses are actually informing them and helping them solidify their foundations of recovery. For example, a woman in my program drank. I had to kick her out. However, I was able to get her in the other program (harm reduction), and even though she continued to relapse a couple of times, in the long run she was able to go to outpatient treatment, resume participation in recovery meetings, and all

the things that can't happen when you are homeless. (personal communication; March 21, 2001)

Women who gamble experience their own particular harms. The Queen of Hearts Australian project (Brown & Coventry, 1997) found that women who were experiencing problems with gambling also experienced stigmatization, loneliness, oppressive role requirements as women with few opportunities to socialize without the company of men, and serious financial and emotional turmoil. Suggestions from the women gamblers for reducing harm on a larger system level include (1) involvement of all the groups associated with gambling (including women gamblers, financial institutions, gaming operators, and government) to work on solutions, instead of leaving it up to the "victims" to cope; (2) establishing alternative recreations for women in neighborhoods; (3) decreasing the accessibility of gaming venues, removing them from shopping centers, strip malls, clubs, and hotels throughout the state; and (4) timely access to other supporting services, such as mental health and especially financial counseling.

Many of the harm reduction strategies used with tobacco addiction are initiated by people on their own, without professional help or intervention. It is estimated that "self-change" or "natural recovery" occurs with 80–90% of all those who stop smoking altogether (U.S. Department of Health and Human Services (DHHS), 1988). Harm reduction strategies to reduce the harmful effects of smoking include over-the counter nicotine patches, lozenges, gum, spray, inhalers, and tablets. In a review of the effectiveness of such strategies, Logan and Marlatt (2010) found dozens of studies document an increase in smoking cessation, even among the difficult to treat homeless population. The recent introduction of electronic cigarettes, devices that deliver vaporized nicotine without combusting tobacco, show promise in expanding options for smokers to achieve substantial health benefits (Cahn & Siegel, 2011).

Harm reduction strategies for alcohol misuse are based on the premise that alcohol use ranges across a continuum, starting with no consequences for use and ending with devastating consequences for use, with many states in between. Harm reductionists emphasize the research evidence that alcohol problems are more likely to be intermittent or discontinuous; are subject to "natural recovery" without formal intervention, just like quitting smoking; and can continue at a stable level for years at a time (Larimer et al., 1998; Sobell, Ellingstad, & Sobell, 2000; Vaillant, 1996). These conclusions are difficult to swallow for professionals who have been trained to see a "progressive, fatal disease state" that never gets better once you have it. As Larimer and colleagues (1998) point out, "the occurrence of even a single case of controlled drinking by an alcoholic challenges the very definition of alcoholism as a disease" (p. 75). Controversy over the research on this subject has been going on since Davies (1962) found seven "normal" drinkers among a treated group of 93 male alcoholics in the United Kingdom. Other research that consistently replicates the finding that moderate drinking is an outcome of treatment for some alcohol-dependent clients (both in moderation treatments and abstinence treatments) has been vilified and even called "fraudulent" by people who adhere to the disease model. The review of the research by Larimer and colleagues led them to conclude

1. A majority of people with drinking problems self-recover with no formal treatment.
2. Over time, rates of abstinence (compared to controlled drinking) tend to increase.
3. A choice of goals tends to result in greater treatment retention and the recruitment of a broader range of problem drinkers.
4. When given a choice, people tend to choose the goal that is most appropriate for the severity of their problems.

Harm reduction strategies for alcohol misuse and dependence primarily involve offering more choice about outcome goals (moderation training as well as abstinence training), brief interventions that focus on advice and increasing motivation to change, and brief assessments that give people the opportunity to assess harm without prescriptions for a particular treatment. In a review of the effectiveness of alcohol-related harm reduction programs, Logan and Marlatt (2010) found that a variety of harm reduction methods are successful. Two programs for college students are examples: the Alcohol Skills Training Program (ASTP), which uses a group setting, and the Brief Alcohol Screening and Intervention for College Students (BASICS), which is an individual approach. Both programs use aspects of brief motivational interviewing techniques, and both reduce drinking amounts and consequences in extensive follow-up studies. Because college students have the highest prevalence of diagnosable alcohol use disorders, it is important to reach this age group with an approach they do not find as judgmental or coercive. Web- or computer-based harm reduction programs are also showing promising results. For example, the Drinker's Check-Up is a computer-based brief intervention that can reduce the quantity and frequency of drinking by 50%, with reductions sustained through 12 months of follow-up (Hester, Squires, & Delaney, 2005). The National Institute of Alcohol Abuse and Alcoholism has also launched an Internet site called Rethinking Drinking (http://rethinkingdrinking.niaaa.nih.gov) that is interactive and provides tools to help people cut back on their drinking (Witkiewitz & Marlatt, 2011).

ATTENDING TO READINESS TO CHANGE

All harm reduction strategies just described are based on a common assumption: people are ultimately capable of making an informed choice in their own best interest. The choices they make depend on their readiness to change, that is, what stage of change they are in. The stages-of-change model, sometimes referred to as the *transtheoretical model* because it relies on several theories of social psychology, was first proposed by Prochaska and DiClemente (1986). It has since been applied and adopted in many addiction treatment and other helping settings around the world.

The stages-of-change model is a circular process that includes five stages in the process of behavior change. A sixth stage, precontemplation, lies outside the wheel because the person in this stage sees no need to change or has no intention of changing behavior at this time. The precontemplator may be defensive or angry when confronted or even questioned about alcohol or drug problems. Once there is a glimmer in the mind of the client that a problem does exist, the person enters the circle and proceeds through each stage several times before finally achieving stable change. The stages are: (1) *precontemplation* (characterized by defensiveness about substance use), (2) *contemplation* (when the person is aware that a problem exists but is ambivalent about making a change or has anxiety about what change will mean), (3) *preparation* (when the person intends to make a change in the near future or has unsuccessfully taken action in the past year), (4) *action* (when the person takes action to change his or her behavior or environment to overcome a problem behavior, such as becoming abstinent or cutting down on drug use), (5) *maintenance* (when the person consolidates gains and works to prevent relapse), and (6) *relapse* (which may occur repeatedly and is considered a normal, inevitable part of the behavior change process) (Miller, Forcehimes, & Zweben, 2011). Most treatment programs and mutual-help organizations such as Alcoholics Anonymous are designed to help people who are in the action stage of change; that is, they already have a "desire to stop drinking" and are ready to take action. Regrettably, a number of studies indicate that most people start at the precontemplation or contemplation stage of change. Consequently, counselors need to know how to work with unmotivated clients who may have been forced into treatment by their families or the legal system.

Many professional counselors also assume that the person is in the action stage of change or *should be in the action stage,* given all the obvious (to the counselor or family) reasons for changing behaviors. When clients are in the precontemplative or contemplative stage, they have been labeled unmotivated, resistant, or in denial. Instead of the counselor's jumping to this conclusion, Miller and colleagues (2011) propose that these problems occur when a counselor is using strategies that do not match up with a client's current stage of readiness to change. They designed the process of motivational interviewing, discussed later in this chapter, to provide a more productive fit between counselor behavior and client reality.

Rapp, Li, Siegal, and DeLiberty (2003) found that there is little relationship between a client's initial motivation at treatment entry and outcomes six months later. Consequently, they recommend that paying attention to the client's immediate concerns using client-centered strengths-based practices is more helpful to treatment retention and success than assigning the label of motivated or unmotivated. Harm reduction practices are designed to help people move through the stages of change at their own pace. Instead of a dualistic framework of either recovery or relapse, harm reduction practice offers a wider path that encompasses and honors all stages in the change process. The application of this model to the families and friends of addicted persons can be helpful in helping families deal with the guilt, pain, and stress involved in their relationship to the addicted person. Denning (2010) describes using harm reduction and stages of change concepts with families because the "the problem is that tough love usually doesn't work...and it feels awful to everyone"(p. 165). As an alternative, she adheres to the principle that change occurs in small steps and over time. She offers the idea of "Not having hope," which means to not allow celebration or feeling relieved when a loved one is doing "good" (not using drugs, going to treatment, going to school, etc.). Instead, she asks families to consider the more practical and realistic idea that today is a good day but that tomorrow may bring the same old problems. In effect, this helps families detach from the cycle of hope and despair that causes so much guilt and pain.

HARM REDUCTION PSYCHOTHERAPY

Harm reduction psychotherapy is a relatively recent term that was first introduced to the literature by Andrew Tatarsky in 1988. Essentially, it is a collection of clinical principles that guide the practitioner on how to view the consumer, how to create the helping relationship, and how to select various interventions (Tatarsky & Marlatt, 2010). The harm reduction psychotherapist may use of variety of the interventions described in the rest of this chapter. For example, the Harm Reduction Therapy Center teams in San Francisco integrate motivational interviewing, cognitive-behavioral skills training (stress reduction, relapse prevention, mindfulness, refusal skills, substance use management), life coaching (money management, nutrition), and nonverbal approaches like drumming (Little & Franskoviak, 2010).

The clinical principles of harm reduction, as defined by Tatarsky & Marlatt (2010), look familiar to a practitioner who adheres to a strength perspective. They are

1. Substance use problems are best understood and addressed in the context of the whole person in his or her social environment.
2. Meet the client as an individual.
3. The client has strengths that can be supported.
4. Challenge stigmatization.
5. Substances are used for adaptive reasons.
6. Drug use falls on a continuum of harmful consequences from relatively safe to imminently life-threatening.
7. Not holding abstinence (or any other preconceived notions) as a precondition of the therapy before really getting to know the individual.
8. Engagement in treatment is the primary goal (accepting the client's definition of the problem as the starting point).
9. Start where the patient is.
10. Look for and mobilize the client's strengths in service of change.
11. Develop a collaborative, empowering relationship with the client.
12. Goals and strategies emerge from the therapeutic process. (Tartarsky & Marlatt, 2011, pp. 120–121).

Underneath this umbrella of clinical principles, the practitioner will no longer operate on a top-down basis of power. Rather, the relationship is formed on a more equal basis of respect for the individuality of the consumer, and an invitation to collaborate on what might be helpful. This is part of the process of "demarginalizing the marginalized," as described by Lee and Petersen (2009). By encouraging nonjudgmental, open conversations about drug use and any other matter of importance to the client, the clinician builds the groundwork for chipping away at the powerlessness that is experienced by most addicted people when they present themselves to professional helpers. It becomes part of our jobs as clinicians to help undo the negative expectations formed by prior experience with treatment or social service agencies (Little & Franskoviak, 2010). This is particularly important with racial and ethnic minority consumers who, in addition to the stigma of substance use problems, have endured overt and covert racism, prejudice, and destructive historical trauma (Blume & Lovato, 2009).

Individual therapy, depending on the harm reduction setting, may take place in a few minutes at the drop-in center or needle exchange or may be a half-hour or longer, once the consumer moves to regular appointments. When this happens, the therapeutic relationship deepens and may focus on other life trauma and its relationship to the drug/alcohol use and other behaviors and relationships. Given the client's multiple problems and the harm reduction principle that clinicians start with where the patient is, many other life issues (housing, family, violence, health) are grist for the therapeutic encounter (Little & Franskoviak, 2010).

The Alcoholics Anonymous adage "progress not perfection" certainly applies to the measurement of success in harm reduction psychotherapy. Any step in the right direction of reducing harm is considered successful, from clean razors for people who engage in cutting/self-harm behaviors to stopping this behavior entirely. In this model, the standard of success is set by the client, not the treatment agency, the court, the probation officer, or someone's mother. When a client cannot or will not meet our ideals for treatment outcome, harm reduction therapy means we keep on offering services, no matter what. The story of Karen from the Harm Reduction Therapy Center in San Francisco (Little & Franskoviak, 2010) illustrates this commitment (Box 8.1).

MOTIVATIONAL INTERVIEWING

> "Happily, once you know what to look for, your clients become your best teachers." (Miller, Forvcehimes, & Zweben, 2011, p. 163)

The development of motivational interviewing (MI) is credited to the relentless, spirited questioning by student interns in Norway of William R. Miller as he demonstrated how he would work with clients in various settings (Miller, 1996). This kind of questioning ("Why have you taken this approach rather than another?") required Miller to "make explicit the approach I had learned from my clients" (p. 835). The result was a beginning conceptual

| Box 8.1 | CASE ILLUSTRATION OF HARM REDUCTION THERAPY |

Karen is a 68-year-old Caucasian native San Franciscan. She suffers from schizophrenia. Most of her life she has been in state hospitals, board and care homes, and acute diversion units. She spent more than 10 years living on the streets in the Tenderloin after running away from a group home; it was here that Karen was introduced to crack and experienced exploitation and abuse as many people took advantage of her kindness and lack of personal boundaries.

Eight months ago, Karen began coming to the Sixth Street Self-help Center, which is only a few doors down from the SRO she calls "home." The center is open from 9 to 5, and Karen is generally the first one in and the last to leave. Because of her paranoia, Karen can't tolerate large crowds and avoids many of the larger agencies where people eat and receive services. When she started coming to the Self-Help Center, she was receiving services through a community mental health agency on the other side of town. Because she frequently presented with lice and bed bugs, she was asked to not participate in the "socialization room" there, and so her main interactions with other people involved hanging out on Sixth Street, which is a haven for drinkers and crack smokers. Most days she comes to the Sixth Street Self-Help Center, attends the drop-in harm reduction group, and checks in briefly with her therapist. It is through this relationship that her therapist is able to work with Karen in small doses.

Karen has made great strides in the last 8 months. Although she still smokes crack, she has remained bug free and her hygiene is good most days. She has made friends since coming to the Center, especially in the harm reduction group. Her case manager from another agency reports that Karen is doing the best she has ever seen in many years of working with her, and contributes this to Karen coming in for treatment. Karen report, "I'm feeling the best I have in 20 years!" (Little & Franskoviak, 2010, pp. 184–185)

model (Miller, 1983) that was followed by years of testing and refinements and that culminated in the text *Motivational Interviewing: Preparing People to Change Addictive Behavior* (Miller & Rollnick, 1991). Since then, MI has been adapted to create motivational enhancement therapy (MET) in Project MATCH (1997), the multisite collaborative trial of three treatments for alcoholism (see Chapter 1). It has also been applied to a wide variety of problem areas, including gambling (Hodgins, Currie, Currie, & Fick, 2009); domestic violence offenders (McMurran, 2009); health such as diet, exercise, and safe sex (Lundahl, Kunz, Brownell, Tollefson, & Burke, 2010); child welfare (Hohman, 1998); medical practice (Knight, McGowan, & Dickens, 2006); low-income, urban, community-based organizations (Carey et al., 2000); HIV risk behavior (Carey et al., 2000); weight loss (Goldberg & Kiernan, 2005); and even breastfeeding (Wilhelm, Flanders Stepans, & Hertzog, 2006).

In the MI framework, as we have seen in previous examples, a person who is exhibiting addictive behaviors is viewed as having a diminished capacity for self-control over time, but this capacity is believed to be retrievable.

Miller (1998, p. 2) notes that even extreme disease-model proponents and programs still rely on the client's "volitional abstinence" to interrupt the destructive behavior. However, in MI terms, retrieving the capacity for self-control is much more than will power or "just saying no." Motivation to change the addictive pattern comes from a combination of complex factors that includes learning, conditioning, emotion, social influences, and biology. The way out of the cycle of addictive behavior for MI proponents involves an internal accounting of suffering and negative consequences associated with the addiction and enough hope that this behavior can change. Thus, the central aim of MI is to "evoke from clients their own motivations for and commitment to change" (Miller et al., 2011, p. 163).

Unfortunately, addiction counselors have been trained in the opposite direction, that is, to somehow get clients to admit they have a problem. Instead of actually helping the client to uncover the reasons they might have for change, confrontation usually invokes a defiant or defensive response. Clients, being human, are likely to respond with all the reasons they do not have a problem. Hearing their own arguments against change, they become more committed to *not changing*. Counselors can then blame the client for being "in denial."

This no-win cycle can be dramatically changed by utilizing MI principles. Although the techniques appear simple, MI is a complex counseling model that takes time and practice to master (Miller et al., 2011). Davis has noticed, in teaching MI to MSW students, that early in the quarter students are enthusiastic about applying certain MI techniques, such as reflection and the decision/balance exercise, but soon realize "they don't know where to go with them." They seem to hit a barrier about mid-term, when they realize they have a much harder job of grappling with their own blind spots. Most commonly, the blind spots are their own assumptions about what the client needs to change, and a lack of skill in listening for the client's "change talk" (hints about the client's own motivations for change). As in all counseling models, practice and a deepening commitment to tune in to the client's perspective helps to sort out these barriers. Miller (1998, p. 6) says this kind of empathic merger with the clients' perspective and lending them a mirror to see themselves differently is "essentially a form of loving."

Motivational interviewing is defined as a "client-centered, directive method for enhancing intrinsic motivation to change by exploring and resolving ambivalence" (Miller & Rollnick, 2002, p. 25). It is directive in terms of the process and techniques of resolving client ambivalence, not directive about the outcome of the counseling. It is client-centered because all the benefits and consequences of making a change are elicited from the client. Motivational interviewing assumes that the *state* of motivation may fluctuate from one time or situation to another and that motivation itself has several different components with distinctly different meanings. There is motivation of *desire* (want to change, wish to change), motivation of *ability* (I can, I could), motivation based on reasons for change (pros and cons), motivation based on need (I've got to quit! I really should quit), and the motivation that signals commitment to change (I will, I guess I will, I might) (Miller et al., 2011). Because of its fluidity and complexity, motivation can be influenced. By providing a safe, nonconfrontational environment, eliciting hope, and helping clients clarify their ambivalence about making a change, counselors can be helpful in "tipping the scales" in favor of readiness to make a positive change. Asking open-ended questions such as the following helps clients evoke their own motivation for change (Miller et al., 2011, p. 164):

"How might you *like* for things to be different?" (Desire)

"If you did decide to quit, how could you do it?" (Ability)

"What reasons might there be for you to make a change?"(Reasons)

"How important is it for you do something about your cocaine use?" (Need)

"What do you think you'll do?" (Commitment)

In addition to these types of questions, MI counselors pay a great deal of attention to eliciting the person's current level of motivation, or stage of change, instead of assuming that the person is ready to jump into action behavior. Scaling questions can be used to do this, such as the following

1. If, on a scale of 1 to 10, 1 is not at all motivated to give up smoking and 10 is 100% motivated to give it up, what number would you give yourself at the moment?
2. If you were to decide to give up smoking now, how confident are you that you would succeed? If, on a scale of 1 to 10, 1 means that you are not at all confident and 10 means that you are 100% confident you could give it up and remain a nonsmoker, what number would you give yourself now?

These questions can help identify a person's stage of change, and the answers can also build motivation or confidence by encouraging the client to identify arguments for change. This is done by asking specific follow-up questions:

1. Why did the person score as he or she did rather than a lower number; for example, "Why did you give yourself a 4 rather than a 1?" The client will then respond with some positive reasons for being motivated or confident, such as, "I know it's bad for my lungs to keep on smoking" or "I think I've finally had enough."
2. What would have to happen for the person to move up the scale to more motivation or confidence? For example, "What does it take for your motivation (or confidence) to move one step higher, from a 5 to a 6?" The client will then respond with strategies that will increase his or her motivation or confidence, such as, "I think I need to get tested for my actual lung damage so far."

These types of questions illustrate how MI techniques can help the client with his or her primary task, that is, to identify and mobilize the client's own values and goals for behavior changes. Unresolved ambivalence can be an obstacle to change, so another task of the clinician is help the client to articulate and resolve that ambivalence. One of the best tools to do that is the decisional balance sheet (Miller & Rollnick, 2002). The counselor simply asks the client to jot down the benefits and costs of continuing the behavior as is ("continuing to gamble as you are gambling now") and follows with a list of the benefits and costs of stopping gambling. An open-ended question to the client, like "What do you make of this?" helps encourage the client to sort out his or her own meanings from the exercise.

Techniques for Enhancing Motivation

Motivational interviewing practitioners rely on the following general principles (Miller & Rollnick, 2002) to enhance a person's motivation to change:

1. *Express empathy.* The MI style is warm, respectful, and accepting. Irrational ideas and ambivalence about change are accepted as a normal part of human experience. The client is seen as "stuck," not pathological.

2. *Develop discrepancy.* Create and amplify the discrepancy between present behavior and important personal goals. Reflective listening and focused feedback can help to highlight discrepancies using the client's own words. For example, "On the one hand, you say it's important to you to get out of debt, but every time you gamble, you lose hundreds of dollars. Tell me about this."

3. *Avoid argumentation.* In contrast to other more traditional approaches that evolved in addiction counseling, MI practitioners do not try to persuade, confront, or argue with clients that they are in deep trouble and would be much better off giving up their addiction. "Breaking through denial" is seen as a tactic that is not just useless but that actually can increase the likelihood of resistance and decrease the likelihood of change. For example, when a person expresses that he or she didn't really want to come to an assessment meeting and wonders "Do you think I'm alcoholic?" the MI counselor would avoid the trap of starting an argument and say something like this: "That's a term that means many things to different people. What matters, really, is that we take a good close look at what's going on here. I'd like to help you get clear on what risk you're facing, and then what, if anything, you want to do about it" (Miller & Rollnick, 2002, p. 146).

4. *Roll with resistance.* Compliance from the client is not a goal. Resistance can be redirected by the simple statement, "It's really up to you." Reluctance and ambivalence are understood to be a natural stage of the change process (contemplation stage). New perspectives are invited, but not imposed. For example, "What you do with this information is entirely up to you."

5. *Support self-efficacy.* If people have no hope for change, then regardless of how serious they perceive the problem, they will not make an effort to change. The counselor can support people's confidence that they can change by removing the false idea that the counselor will change them, by showing them the success of others, and by inviting them to choose from alternative approaches to what they have already tried. A series of relapses or treatment "failures" can be reframed as "getting closer to their goal."

PHASE II. CLOSING THE DEAL

The second phase of motivational interviewing occurs after the client has built a framework of intrinsic motivation for change (Miller & Rollnick, 2002). This is visible because of a decrease in resistance, an increase in change talk, and more questions about how a change might occur. He or she may start to envision life after the change, or experiment with some change actions between sessions. At this point, some key questions are in order that will illicit what the client wants and plans to do. For example, "What changes, if any, are you thinking about making?"

It's important for the clinician to be cautious at this point about underestimating ambivalence and to recognize the likelihood that ambivalence will reoccur. Another caution is to be aware of inserting your own agenda for change, when your client's goals do not correspond with what you have in mind as an ideal outcome. When all goes well and a plan emerges, it is helpful to summarize what has been proposed by the client or write it out in a simple change plan. Sometimes "buyer's remorse" can surface, and the client can show signs of reluctance. Miller and Rollnick (2002) recommend we stick to the same agenda of client self-determination with something like the following:

> If you're not quite ready, then I don't want you to make a commitment yet. This is too important, and you don't have to make up your mind this minute. Go home and think about it, and we can talk about it more next time. (p. 138)

Elaboration on these techniques, as well as blogs from MI developers, manuals, and training materials can be found on the motivational interviewing website at http://www.motivationalinterview.org.

MOTIVATIONAL ENHANCEMENT THERAPY

Motivational enhancement therapy (MET) is simply the addition of providing particular assessment feedback to the regular MI processes of counseling. Personal feedback about where one stands in relation to others in terms of severity of problems is helpful in building motivation for change. In a study with college students, using web-based feedback on the results of the AUDIT screen (see Chapter 7), the researchers found significantly less alcohol use and fewer drinking episodes at follow-up (Palfai, Zisserson, & Saitz, 2011). In the spirit of MI, this is accomplished in an informational, not confrontational, style.

Miller and colleagues (2011) recommend that you share how the assessment findings relate to the norms from the general population, that is, where does the client stand in relation to other people? If your assessment tool is something like the Addiction Severity Index, for example, you could share the different dimensions on the scale such as level of use, severity of problems, and risk factors and how the client's score compares with others. Getting good information on where one stands in the big picture of things can help people come to their own conclusions about the need for change.

Box 8.2	SUMMARIZING FEEDBACK

Mary, would it be okay if I offered a little information to you based on what we've talked about so far? Correct me if I'm wrong about anything. To begin, it sounds like you've noticed an escalating pattern in your cocaine use. This is a source of some concern to you both because of your parents' history of substance misuse and because you've begun to drop away from your old friends. You're spending a lot more time recovering from the use and the financial drain has begun to create some issues with your husband. You've also noticed the high has changed and you're using more to get to that place you want. Finally, you are concerned about your relationship with your kids. You swore that you were going to be a better mom to your kids than your mom was to you, but now you're not so sure how you've done with that. I'm wondering what you make of all this?

Source: http://motivationalinterview.net/clincal/strategies.html.

Another possibility is to offer feedback that is simply a review of what the client has shared with you, including inconsistencies. If you end the summary with "What do you make of all this?" then it becomes the client's job to make meaning of the feedback (see Box 8.2).

RESEARCH ON THE EFFECTIVENESS OF MOTIVATIONAL INTERVIEWING

Motivational interviewing seems to be the new darling of researchers in the addiction field and in broader arenas. More than 200 clinical trials of MI have been published, most reporting significant findings of effectiveness, particularly in the area of addictive behaviors (Miller et al., 2010).

Some of the most interesting findings show support for *very* brief MI interventions. For example, in the problem gambling field, a randomized clinical trial compared two brief MI interventions: (1) a telephone motivational interview prior to a mailed self-help workbook or (2) a telephone motivational interview prior to a mailed self-help workbook with six booster telephone support calls over a 9-month period (Hodgin, Currie, Currie, & Fick, 2009). These two interventions were compared with a 6-week waiting list control group and a workbook-only control group. There were no significant differences in the groups on demographics or gambling histories; pathological gambling criteria was met by 89% of the participants. The results indicated that those participants who received either one of the brief MI interventions gambled significantly less often than either control group. Of interest is that the booster calls made no real difference in outcome; both interventions were positive. Findings such as these are particularly important in the problem gambling field where so few enter formal treatment. In addition, these interventions could be easily adapted for use by telephone help-lines for gamblers, providing a low-cost, time efficient alternative to formal treatment.

There are four meta-analyses in the field of MI: Burke, Arkowitz and Menchola, 2003; Hettema, Steele, and Miller, 2005; Vasilaki, Hosier, and Cox, 2006; and Lundahl, Kunz, Brownell, Tollefson, and Burke, 2010. Burke and colleagues (2003) and Hettema and colleagues (2005) focused on studies across a wide range of behavioral problems; Vasilaki and colleagues (2006) focused on studies of excessive alcohol consumption. The most recent meta-analysis by Lundahl and colleagues (2010) focused on studies where the contribution of the MI effect could be more distinguished. All found sufficient evidence to support MI as a viable and effective treatment method (Lundahl et al., 2010).

Project MATCH (1997) compared motivational enhancement therapy (four sessions) to cognitive-behavioral coping skills therapy (12 sessions) and Twelve-Step facilitation (12 sessions). The focus of MET was to employ motivational interviewing strategies (as described earlier) to produce internal motivation for change, not to guide the client through particular steps to recovery. The results indicated little difference in outcomes by type of treatment, but overall improvements in drinking outcomes were achieved by all. In aftercare, 35% of the subjects reported continued complete abstinence throughout the 12 follow-up months; 65% slipped or relapsed during that period. For the outpatient subjects, 19% maintained complete abstinence throughout the follow-up, 46% had a heavy-drinking period, and the rest "slipped." Outpatient clients low in motivation ultimately did better in MET than in the other types. The complete therapy manual for MET procedures can be obtained for no charge from the website http://motivationalinterviewing.org. Although most research on MI is conducted with adults, there is a growing body of studies that indicate this approach is successful with adolescents, who are typically a difficult population to engage (Feldstein, 2006). McCambridge and Strang (2004) found in their study that adolescent polysubstance abusers who received an MI intervention significantly decreased their use. In another large randomized controlled study of outpatient treatments for adolescents that included motivational enhancement treatment (MET), the authors found that MET was one of the three most cost-effective brief interventions (Dennis et al., 2004).

SOLUTION-FOCUSED THERAPY

The origins of solution-focused therapy (SFT) are found in the work of Milton Erickson (1954), who strongly believed that solving the problem was more important than finding and elaborating on the root "cause" of the problem and that clients had the ability within themselves and/or their social system to bring about change. The development of the solution-focused brief therapy approach began in 1978, when Insoo Kim Berg and Steve deShazer borrowed money and put up their house for collateral to open a small brief therapy office in Milwaukee (see more background information on the Solution

Focused Brief Therapy Association website at http://www.sfbta.org). Since then, what has been called a "different paradigm" is practiced in many different settings all over the world.

This approach treats problem gambling, substance misuse or dependence, and eating disorders using the same assumptions and techniques practiced with any other need or problem that a client may bring to the therapeutic environment. Like feminists and narrative therapists, SFT practitioners do not see the particular addiction as a "unitary disease" that affected everyone alike but rather assist the person to define his or her own conception of the problem and goals for change. In a national sample of 284 alcoholism counselors (members of the National Association of Alcoholism and Drug Abuse Counselors), Osborn (1997) found that 79% of the counselors endorsed solution-focused principles, such as identifying and using client strengths and abilities, client–counselor collaboration throughout the course of treatment, highlighting and promoting already occurring nonproblem behavior, meeting the client's goal(s), and constructing solutions rather than resolving client problems. However, the counselors identified beliefs in different conceptual frameworks: 54% agreed or strongly agreed with a psychosocial concept of alcoholism (social learning theory—alcohol dependence is understood as a continuum), and 45% agreed or strongly agreed with the tenets of a disease concept of alcoholism. These results suggest that a strong adherence to the disease concept by alcoholism counselors may not be as prevalent as some have reported and that, even when it is the dominant framework for some clinicians, it is not incompatible with practicing solution-focused treatment. Since the Osborne study (1997), the SFT model has flourished in many areas of addiction treatment, for example, group therapy (Smock, Trepper, Wetchler, McCollum, Ray, & Pierce, 2008; McCollum, Trepper, & Smock, 2003), inpatient and outpatient settings (deShazer & Isebaert, 2003), rural settings (West, 2010), and culturally diverse treatment settings (Zamarripa, 2009).

Specific techniques to find out what is important to the client might involve the "miracle question," asking for exceptions to the problem, scaling questions, and coping questions. Strengths and past successes in dealing with problems of living would be highlighted instead of deficits or "pathology." The person would be seen more as a valuable resource to form goals and find solutions than as an impaired person with poor judgment. The client's immediate goal would be accepted as a good goal, whether or not it involved quitting the addiction (De Jong & Berg, 2002).

A classic example of solution-focused therapy applied to addiction is the story of "Mr. Glue-Head" (Berg & Miller, 1992, p. 15). The subject is a young man who was ordered to treatment again because of his arrest for "sniffing glue" and public intoxication. He had a long history of arrests and treatment episodes, but nothing had changed. Using a solution-focused approach that emphasized cooperation with the client, the therapist asked what he wanted to accomplish with this referral.

"Elmer" made it very clear that discontinuing glue sniffing was not what he wanted. He only wanted to stop getting arrested. The therapist then wondered whether sniffing glue on the back porch might be an acceptable alternative to getting high on the front porch—a place, the therapist pointed out, where the police could see him easily. He readily agreed to try out the idea as "an experiment" and to return in a week to report his findings.

When Elmer returned the following week, he reported that the police never even bothered to check the back porch, even though they had driven by his home on several occasions. The only time the police had stopped was late one afternoon as he sat relaxing on the front porch, "enjoying the sunset" without the help of sniffing glue. After this experience, Elmer began sitting out on the front porch just for the fun of it. The result, of course, was that he did not get arrested again or referred for any more treatment. Once the arrests and referrals had stopped, Elmer began to curtail his use of inhalants on his own.

According to Berg and Miller (1992), the case example of Mr. Glue Head illustrates several main tenets of the solution-focused approach. The therapist avoided issues that had always been considered problems by the therapist and others but that were not identified as problems by Elmer. Instead, the focus was shifted to a problem that Elmer identified, "not getting arrested." By following Elmer's lead, the therapist avoided perpetuating the past nonsolutions and worked with Elmer on "doing something different."

Solution-focused therapy is based on the assumption that the future can be created and negotiated regardless of the problem. The future "is not a slave of the past events in a person's life; therefore, in spite of past traumatic events, a person can negotiate and implement many useful steps that are likely to lead him/her to a more satisfying life" (Berg, 2001, p. 4). The resources, skills, and knowledge to take such steps can be uncovered through the use of several techniques.

The *miracle question* is a particularly helpful technique in supporting hope that things can be different in spite of many past attempts and failures to change. This question leads the client directly into imagining, describing, creating, and embellishing on a day in the future without the burden of the particular problem that led or required the client to seek help. The question is asked deliberately and dramatically: "*Suppose* that one night, while you are sleeping and the entire house is quiet, a miracle happens. The miracle is that *the problem that brought you here is solved.* However, because you are sleeping, you don't know that the miracle has happened. So, when you wake up tomorrow morning, *what will be different* that will tell you that a miracle has happened and the problem that brought you here is solved?"(DeJong & Berg, 2002, p. 85)

Through persistent questioning about what the person would be doing differently on this new, problem-free day, who would notice the difference, and what effect this would have on the person, a rich picture emerges that can provide momentum for a person to start making changes. Because the different behaviors are already specified in the imagined future (e.g., "I would get up in the morning feeling good, no hangover. I would sit down and eat breakfast with my son. I would be humming as I got him dressed for school.), it is a natural progression to find out what small step the person could take in reality to reach a little bit of the miracle picture.

Because clients are asked to create their own goals, they may not always create goals that center on substance abuse or a decrease in addictive behavior. For example, West (2010) describes using the SFT model in group treatment in a rural setting in Michigan. Members are encouraged to focus on goals for any area of their life that they deem is problematic. For some, the problem is coming to the group in order to "satisfy the court." This goal is honored and respected as a valid and meaningful goal. The author reports that many of these clients end up experiencing the group as meaningful, much to their surprise. When that happens, they are much more likely to be willing to consider treatment in the future. *Scaling questions* are used in a variety of ways to help the client assess level of hope, determination, confidence, sadness, how much change has occurred, and so on, similar to the motivational interviewing scales described earlier. For example, "On a scale of 1 to 10, where 10 stands for the worst upset you have ever felt, how upset are you today? What would it take for you to move up by 1 point? When you move up by 1 point, what would your husband (friend, cat, coworker) notice that would tell him that you are doing a little bit better?"

Coping questions can be used to bring out the survival strategies of people who have been managing somehow in spite of their addictions. This is helpful in building hope and self-efficacy, two key ingredients for change. For example, "You've been through a lot in the last month with your gambling. How in the world have you coped with so much while still holding down a job?" "What else have you managed to do in spite of your addiction?" "How did you do this?"

A "not knowing" stance is fundamental to the SF model. Not knowing means that we do not presume to know the lived experience of the client or the goals that may be important to him or her. It means we must practice deeply listening to what the person says and ask questions that will open the door for their experience to take center stage. Not knowing is a particularly helpful stance when working with people outside one's own cultural context. Zamarripa (2009) finds that it "allows the therapist to remain in the role of learner so that the client becomes the expert of his/her story" (p. 2).

Solution-focused therapy (as well as motivational interviewing) has an unintended consequence of helping counselors feel less burned out, more hopeful, and upbeat. Besides focusing on strengths, these models recognize that if you try to sell something like abstinence to people who are not ready or do not want it, then the counselor will be frustrated most of the time. For example, over a period of several months, a long-term residential and day treatment center in California changed its treatment modality from a more confrontational deficit model that focused primarily on what the person had done wrong to a solution-focused approach focusing on client strengths and on goals that the client wants from treatment (Mott & Gysin, 2003). The surprise benefit to this change was the change in the atmosphere of the agency. The staff became more positive and in a better mood. The change was even noted by child welfare representatives who visited regularly. Their question was, appropriately enough, "What are you doing differently?" (p. 15).

RESEARCH ON THE EFFECTIVENESS OF
SOLUTION-FOCUSED THERAPY

Rigorous research studies on the effectiveness of solution-focused therapy are scarce, but an effort is underway by SFT researchers to remedy this situation. The first meta-analysis of SFT was conducted by Gingerich and Eisengart (2000). They cite 15 controlled outcome studies on solution-focused brief therapy that provide preliminary support for the efficacy of this approach in a broad range of applications, but they caution that more study is needed. Others have found these same studies problematic because of limited research designs, small samples, and the lack of a systematic intervention (Coady, Stalker, & Levene, 2000). Kim (2008) conducted another meta-analysis on 22 studies between 1988 and 2005. Findings indicate that SFT showed small but positive effects on the measured outcomes. However, again he calls for more rigorous research designs with bigger samples. To aid in these efforts, the research committee of the Solution Focused Brief Therapy Association (SFBTA) has developed a treatment manual to offer researchers a standardized method so that replication could more easily occur. This manual can be located on the SFBTA website at http://www.solutionfocused.net/treatment-manual.html. In the meantime, efforts are underway by SFT researchers to add SFT to federal and state registries of evidence-based practices (Kim, Smock, Trepper, McCollum, & Franklin, 2010). To date, SFT has been added to the Office of Juvenile Justice and Delinquency Prevention (OJJDP) evidence-based practice website with a "promising" rating.

Trepper, Dolan, McCollum, and Nelson (2006) note there is enough evidence through clinical trial studies, clinically based, and quasi-experimental studies to conclude that SFT is at least as effective as other current treatment models. For some problems, it is more effective and considerably more cost-effective in achieving positive outcomes.

COGNITIVE-BEHAVIORAL THERAPY

Cognitive-behavioral therapy (CBT) is based on the idea that maladaptive thinking and bad habits are the mechanisms that both cause problems and keep them going. In a sense, problems can be viewed as exaggerated versions of what previously looked like a good idea, but the behavior has now become extremely burdensome. The good news from CBT is that the cycle can be interrupted and problems can be relieved by learning to think and behave differently. In his wonderfully titled self-help book *Sex, Drugs, Gambling and Chocolate: A Workbook for Overcoming Addictions*, Horvath (2004) explains that addiction, in its various gradations, can be viewed as an extreme form of habit, and that overcoming addictions can occur by using the same normal human processes that we use to change other bad habits. Although this is quite different than viewing addiction as a disease with an inevitable progression, CBT strategies are now routinely incorporated into many substance abuse treatment center programs, through contingency contracting, stress reduction and relapse prevention groups, and social skills training.

Cognitive and behavioral frameworks of practice each have distinct histories and areas of emphasis. In the 1950s and 1960s, behavioral therapy was generally looked down upon as naïve and inconsequential by the dominant psychoanalytic establishment, However, the impact of Ivan Pavlov's experimental research on classical conditioning, B. F. Skinner's application of this process to human beings, and the research and writings of Hans Eysenck defining behavior as the application of modern learning theory, propelled behavior therapy to becoming a well accepted part of the current psychotherapeutic establishment (Wilson, 2008).

Cognitive therapy began in the early 1960s as a result of Aaron Beck's research on depression. Instead of finding repressed anger turned inward (the Freudian theory of depression), Beck carefully observed that depressed patients exhibited a negative bias in the way they cognitively processed their environment. Thus, a major departure from prevailing psychoanalytic theory was begun. The application and growth of cognitive therapy was greatly expanded by the work of Albert Ellis (1962). He also rejected his analytic training and instead developed active dialogues with his patients, challenging what he considered their erroneous belief systems. Beck's style developed into a more collaborative, exploratory stance with the client (Beck & Wisharr, 2008).

Although subject to a great deal of debate in the field, it may be helpful to think of the development of these theories and practices as "waves," each building on the other (Hayes, 2004). The first wave could be viewed as the development phase; the second wave as the recognition of the link between dysfunctional cognitions and maladaptive behaviors, evolving into rational-emotive therapy (RET) and cognitive behavioral therapy. The third wave, now upon us, is a repertoire of interventions that build on CBT, but emphasize mindfulness and acceptance instead of change of negative thoughts and sensations. Third wave interventions include such approaches as dialectical behavior therapy (DBT), mindfulness-based cognitive therapy (MBCT), and acceptance and commitment therapy (ACT) (Brown, Gaudiano, & Miller, 2011). Third wave types of interventions are beginning to make an impact in the addition field and can now be seen on the Substance Abuse and Mental Health Services Administration's (SAMHSA) list of evidence-based practices.

There are several tenets of CBT that play a powerful role in the initiation, maintenance, and recovery of addiction (Parrish, 2009). Let us look at how these apply to problem gamblers (Davis, 2009):

1. *Reinforcement*: Reinforcement is the process of shaping behavior by controlling the consequences of the behavior (positive or negative reinforcement). Responses to stimuli that are followed by satisfaction will be strengthened; responses to stimuli that are followed by punishment will

be weakened. The behavior of problem gamblers who play modern casino slot machines has an enhanced opportunity to be "shaped" by three elements of reinforcement: (1) a rapid rate of play (15 games a minute, 900 per hour), (2) an intermittent schedule of reinforcement (just when you think the machine has gone cold, up pops a winner!), and (3) *Winner!!!* Extraordinary visual displays, special sounds and music, the attention of the casino attendants, and the players around you, all combine to reinforce wins immediately. One woman in the Davis (2009) study said the music stayed with her for days, and she had to work hard to "turn off my brain." A recovery strategy to help problem gamblers mitigate the powerful effects of reinforcement is to find meaningful methods of rewarding oneself for periods of abstinence.

2. *Modeling.* Modeling is learning by observing what others do and seeing the costs and benefits of such behavior. Advertising makes good use of modeling by featuring ecstatic, attractive young people winning jackpots and having fun at the casino (when in reality, any visit to a casino will quickly show you rows upon rows of mostly middle age to elderly people sitting in a trance in front of machines). Modeling is also accomplished when someone in your row of machines gets a winning combination, which tells your brain "it can be done." A recovery strategy to help counteract these effects is to offer group treatment (or find a Gamblers Anonymous meeting or a GA sponsor) where the problem gambler can see, through the modeling of people further along in recovery, that there are concrete and attainable benefits in stopping gambling.

3. *Conditioned responding.* Like Pavlov's dog, problem gamblers respond to environmental stimuli or cues elicited internally or through the senses (sight, smell, sound, internal states) that trigger the impulse to gamble. In the Davis study (2009) one woman became conditioned to crowded parking lots, which triggered the impulse to go to an *always crowded casino parking lot* where her gambling sequence could begin. Recovery strategies to counteract this powerful form of learning involve carefully identifying potential triggers and coming up with alternative strategies to diffuse them.

4. *Cognitive factors.* There are a variety of cognitive distortions that impact the initiation, maintenance, and recovery trajectories of people who are addicted. These may involve the belief that one cannot cope with a particular situation without resorting to the addiction, that is, the person lacks a belief in his or her own self-efficacy, or power to effect change (Parrish, 2009). Irrational thinking is a common attribute of problem gamblers (Davis, 2009). The most common thinking error is misunderstanding the meaning of randomness and the extent to which outcomes can be predicted. Many gamblers think, "I've put so much money in the machines, it's bound to hit," when in reality all games of chance are based on randomness that cannot be predicted because each event is independent of the others. Other common thinking errors include the personification of the gambling machines or dice (gently rubbing a slot machine to coax out a win), the illusion of control (following a particular sequence will enhance your chances,

like rubbing the dice before throwing, entering the casino through the same entrance door, wearing your lucky t-shirt), the use of flexible attributions (viewing losses as "near wins"), and fixating on absolute frequency (remembering the times you win, without considering the relative number of losses, as in "I won three jackpots in the last two months!").

CBT strategies that help to straighten out some of the distorted thinking are the "ABC of emotions model" where A stands for an activating event (such as waking up on 11/11/11), B stands for one's interpretation or belief about this event ("this is my lucky day to gamble!"), and C stands for the consequences of such an interpretation (can't pay my rent now after losing at the racetrack all day). By reevaluating the B part and changing the interpretation ("Today is just like any other day, and if I go to the racetrack I'm likely to lose; therefore, I think I'll call my friend Susan") gamblers can begin to change their thinking and the consequences of their thinking (Ladouceur, Sylvain, Boutin, & Doucet, 2002).

The nature of CBT interventions, with their reliance on educational materials and standardized approaches, lends itself to the making of practice manuals for practitioners and self-help manuals for consumers. Both are extremely helpful in learning the basic approaches in CBT. There are a number of CBT manuals readily available that detail how interpersonal and intrapersonal coping skills can be taught in individual or group sessions. Two of these manuals are free of charge by download: (1) the National Institutes of Alcohol Abuse and Alcoholism (NIAAA) offers the *Cognitive-Behavioral Coping Skills Therapy Manual* (Kadden, Carroll, Donovan, Cooney, Monti, Abrams, Litt, & Hester, 1994) based on the Project MATCH protocols available at http://pubs.niaaa.nih.gov/publications/MATCH-Series3/index.htm, and (2) the National Institute of Drug Abuse offers *A Cognitive-Behavioral Approach: Treating Cocaine Addiction* (Carroll, 1998) at http://archives.drugabuse.gov/txmanuals/CBT/CBT1.html Self-help materials range from Horvath's (2004) comprehensive *Sex, Drugs, Gambling and Chocolate: A Workbook for Overcoming Addictions,* to brief (and free) *Your First Step to Change*, developed as a public service project by the Massachusetts Council for Compulsive Gambling, which can be downloaded at http://www.divisionaddictions.org/html/publications/gamtoolkit.pdf.

The structure of CBT sessions commonly begins with an introduction to the CBT approach, why it may be beneficial for the client, and why it is helpful with the particular problem the client is presenting. Here is a sample script recommended by Parrish (2009) that was originally developed by Monti (2002) and colleagues:

> We all have some problems getting along with family, friends, and coworkers; meeting strangers; handling our moods and feelings. Everyone has different strengths and weaknesses in coping skills. Because alcohol (or substance use) is often used to cope with problems, interpersonal difficulties and negative feeling are often triggers for relapse. The triggers include such things as feeling frustrated with someone, being offered a drink (or drugs) at a party, and feeling depressed, angry, sad, lonely, and so on.

An important goal of this treatment is to teach some skills you can use to cope with your high-risk situations. We will focus on ways to handle various difficult interpersonal situations more comfortably and honestly. We will teach you some skills and have you practice these skills while role-playing these high-risk situations. In this way, you will learn to cope with high-risk situations and to prevent problems that could lead to drinking (or substance use). (p. 45)

Usually individual sessions last an hour, and group sessions last 90 minutes. Before moving to the particular focus on the session, the clinician will want to spend 15 minutes or so in supportive therapy, discussing current problems, assessing current needs, and reviewing any homework assignment from the previous session. It is important to ensure that the client views the session as relevant to the problems they are facing right now. Clients should be routinely encouraged to actively engage in the material and provide their own examples throughout the session. For example, "Triggers to use cocaine can occur at any time of day or night. Can you think of any occasions where triggers occur when you don't expect them?"

Clinicians are expected to have a full repertoire of therapeutic skills, such as active listening, reflecting, paraphrasing, summarizing, the ability to "roll with resistance," and an ability to empathize with the client. Following the brief supportive therapy, the clinician introduces the CBT material for that session, beginning with a rationale that makes connections between the skill being introduced and the client's concerns. For example, "You talked a little about how tough it is to see the ads for the casino on TV, especially when you don't expect them, and especially where everyone is smiling and supposedly winning. Today, the skill we will focus on will help you prepare ahead of time some things to do when those ads pop up, so they don't get you so bad. Does that sound like a good idea?" After the introduction of the skill, a role-play scenario is developed so that the client can practice using the skill. Role-plays (behavioral rehearsals, in CBT speak) play a major part in the acquisition of new skills, whether in individual sessions or in a groups. To be effective, role-plays also require that the clinician be prepared to give coaching hints and feedback to the client, and sometimes to do reverse plays so that the client can get a feel of how the skill may be helpful when dealing with others. Each CBT session usually concludes with a preplanned practice exercise (homework) so that the client can practice newly learned skills in the real world and *reinforce* what they have learned. Because homework assignments may give a grown-up client the unpleasant feeling they are suddenly 10 years old again, it is helpful to explain why reinforcement is valuable, help the client envision how they will do the homework, and identify any barriers to completing the assignment.

CBT or some variation can be found in virtually every type of context in the addiction field. In the following sections, we will explore in more depth two types of CBT interventions practiced in a variety of addiction settings: relapse prevention and contingency contracting. In the process, some of the nuts and bolts of CBT practices should become clear.

RELAPSE PREVENTION

> "I couldn't help it. I can resist everything except temptation." (Oscar Wilde, 1893, Lady Windemer's Fan, Act I)

Although every intervention available could be thought of as relapse prevention or the maintenance of improvement (in MI terms), CBT offers specific techniques to help consumers learn how to negotiate the world without resorting to their addiction. In relapse prevention, coping skills are divided into the *interpersonal* kind, which help clients deal with high-risk relapse situations and to develop social support for their recovery, and *intrapersonal* coping skills, which focus on learning how to cope with one's own internal triggers, such as anger, stress, and negative moods (Parrish, 2009). Typical CBT modules that address increasing interpersonal coping skills include such topics as communication skills (including conversation skills); assertiveness skills; giving and receiving positive feedback; listening skills; giving constructive criticism; receiving criticism about drinking, drug use, gambling, and so on; refusal skills; resolving relationship problems; and developing social support networks.

Here is a sample of how a relapse prevention module on refusal skills would work. The interesting thing about this example is that it comes from a computerized module called CBT4CBT (computer based training for cognitive behavioral therapyIn a recent clinical trial, CBT4CBT was compared to standard treatment (weekly, individual, and group counseling of general drug counseling) (Carroll, Ball, Martino, Nich, Babuscio, Nuro, Gordon, Portnoy, & Rounsaville, 2008). The CBT4CBT group members were provided access to the program in a room at the clinic. No previous experience with computers was required. All participants met *DSM-IV* criteria for substance dependence, including alcohol, cocaine, opioids, or marijuana. Here is a summary of what they received from the module on refusal skills (Carroll et al., 2008):

> The key concept of "refusal skills" is introduced through a brief movie of actors using realistic settings in which an individual was offered drugs. Next, after graphics and voiceovers explain the key skill, the "movie" is repeated, this time with a different ending. The same character applies the skills to "change the story" of the outcome of the situation. Additional vignettes are shown to reinforce the skills taught. The consumer can click buttons to see additional examples of the characters demonstrating assertive versus aggressive versus passive responding to the offer of substances of various kinds. An interactive segment follows with a short vignette on how to the skill helped the actor, and how that same skill could be applied to other problems. The module concludes with a summary of key points, then a demonstration of how the actor would complete the homework assignment on refusal skills. The participants were then given a practice assignment and reminder sheet to take with them.
>
> Participants completed six such computerized lessons on a variety of CBT core concepts, such as coping with craving, and problem-solving skills. Results of the study are promising, in that participants using the CBT4CBT program submitted significantly fewer drug-positive urines specimens and tended to have longer periods of abstinence during treatment compared with standard treatment as usual at a community-based clinic. A larger clinical trial of this innovative method is underway. (p. 882)

CONTINGENCY MANAGEMENT

Picture a room of smiling and laughing people, all clapping for the young meth addict who is shakily moving to the front of the room to collect her chip for 30 days clean time in Narcotics Anonymous. Or in a treatment context, imagine the anticipation of a room full of substance abusers of various types who are waiting to see who will draw a big prize from the fishbowl that week. As simple as these interventions sound, 25 years of research confirms that they will increase motivation for staying abstinent, increase attendance in treatment programs, and increase the attainment of specific treatment goals (Petry, 2000). Contingency management, based on the principles of operant conditioning, uses reinforcing and punishing consequences to alter substance use behavior (Witkiewitz & Marlatt, 2011).

In treatment settings, contingency management programs need to be carefully planned to maximize their effect. Nancy Petry, a well-respected researcher in the field, has developed a brief guide on how to implement such programs, available at http://www.bhrm.org/guidelines/petry.pdf. Some of the considerations involve:

1. Deciding what specific behavior you want to reinforce through contingency management. The behavior could be better attendance at group meetings; abstinence from a particular drug, substance, or behavior; the attainment of goals from the individual treatment plan; and so on.
2. Setting up a specific plan to quickly monitor the attainment of that behavior. For example, if urine tests are used, the results must be available quickly, not weeks later. The attainment of treatment goals must be verifiable, that is, if a consumer goal is to research opportunities for attaining a G.E.D., the results of that research must be presented.
3. Deciding what kind of tangible positive rewards are feasible. Some agencies, strapped for cash, use a fishbowl approach that reinforces patients some, but not all of the time. Clients who qualify (e.g., by having clean urines for that week) get to draw for the chance of winning various prizes (mostly small but a few larger ones like a toaster or VCR). Other studies found that providing a dollar a day increased attendance at group therapy.
4. Decide if negative consequences will be employed. The absence of a positive reward is one type of negative consequence. For example, a program may set up reports to a parole officer each time the client produces a negative urine screen (no drug use detected). If the client submits a positive screen, the absence of a positive report becomes a definite negative. In the case of methadone clinics, the removal of take-home dosage privileges is sometimes used as a consequence.

Although cognitive therapy is typically not a direct part of contingency management programs, there are some indirect cognitive benefits to consumers. Increased abstinence leads to a greater sense of self-efficacy in clients who have been struggling in addictive patterns (Litt, Kadden, Kabela-Cormier, & Petry, 2009).

RESEARCH ON CBT EFFECTIVENESS

Behavioral and cognitive-behavioral approaches dominate the federal and professional lists of evidence-based practices in the mental health as well as the addiction field (Kazdin, 2004). While motivational interviewing may be the new darling of researchers, CBT is the matriarch, with decades of effectiveness studies behind it. In the Miller and Wilbourne (2002) comparison of the effectiveness of treatments using different treatment designs, behavioral interventions including community reinforcement, behavioral contracting, skills training, and self-control training rank in the top 20 of all treatment modalities (based on 361 controlled studies). Numerous studies show CBT as the most empirically supported form of group therapy for addictions (Miller, Forcehimes, & Zweben, 2011). In Project MATCH (see Chapter 1), cognitive-behavioral (CBT) skill training was compared to Twelve-Step facilitation (TSF) and motivational enhancement therapy (MET). The clients in the CBT group and TSF group reduced their drinking more quickly than in MET, and in the 3-year follow-up showed statistically equal and substantial benefits compared to the other treatments on outcome measures (Babor & Del Boca, 2003). Numerous meta-analysis of clinical trials of CBT consistently report the effectiveness of this approach in addiction treatment (Magill & Ray, 2009).

GROUP THERAPY

Group therapy is the most popular context of delivering treatment and for good reason. It is cost-effective, helps people learn from other people's experience, and can be particularly beneficial for those who have become isolated from family and significant others while in the throes of addiction. In general, group therapy can be counted on to be just as effective as individual counseling; however, all group therapies are not alike. Surprisingly, the traditional educational group that uses films and lecture to illustrate the nature of addiction, costs, brain-functioning, and so on is the least effective of all. In a study of 48 treatment methods, this type of treatment showed few positive effects and was ranked at the bottom (Miller, Wilborne, & Hettema, 2003). On the other hand, group therapy that teaches coping skills and relapse prevention using cognitive-behavioral approaches ranked highest in effectiveness and continues to provide evidence that it is at least as good if not better than individual behavior therapy (Miller, Forcehimes, & Zweben, 2011).

Some common practical issues must be addressed when a practitioner decides to offer help in a group context. Some of the answers will be guided by the agency context, the nature of the referral, and the type of clients likely to participate in the group. For example, treatment goals of abstinence-only programs may be pre-ordained for clients who are referred from child welfare or the probation department. However, it is up to the practitioner (within the agency context) to decide if abstinence becomes a required group goal and if so, how to work with the inevitability that there will be clients who may not be able or want to embrace this goal. Will clients be allowed to attend group while they struggle with this issue? Will it be acceptable for them to work on other goals that are important to them?

The type and length of group therapy should match the biological readiness of the client to participate. A brain damaged by alcohol and other drugs can take in only so much. As Patt Denning (2000) indicates, heavy alcohol intake or excessive use of tranquilizers is associated with diminished abstract reasoning ability; paranoid thinking may be evident in long-term stimulant users. A client with 6 months of physical recovery and 6 months of practice in social skills and motivational work is clearly better able to work on deeper emotional issues than a man or woman sober for a few days or intermittently sober. When clients have complications from additional mental health problems, such as bipolar disorder, schizophrenia, or depression, the group structure should accommodate their needs. Treatment strategies, in short, cannot exceed the mind's ability to absorb them.

In the early phase of treatment, the primary focus of intervention is to establish a favorable client–therapist relationship as a springboard for building trust and motivation (SAMHSA, 2005). This may take months or even years in a drop-in group setting for people who are homeless and have co-occurring disorders. Once trust is established, the group facilitator is in a position to give advice and, better yet, in a skillful drawing out of helpful comments from group members, to reinforce their insights, which are often quite astute. Group feedback is far more powerful than individual feedback. Group members who may not be ready to assess their own behavior realistically often do well in assessing others' behaviors. In van Wormer's women's therapy group in Washington State, for example, group members, many of whom were involved in destructive, often battering relationships, were quick to realize when another woman was being exploited by her boyfriend.

Other practical issues to grapple with before launching a group are in the area of group norms. For example, what will be the standards about touching or hugging in the group? How will this get decided? What will be the rules about who talks when? Will members be encouraged to comment on what another person talks about, and if so, will they be coached on how to give helpful feedback? Confidentiality is not a group norm; it is an ethical requirement. Group members need to be clearly informed that they may not discuss any personal content outside the group or anything that might reveal the identity of other members. It is also important to let group members know that violence toward others will not be tolerated.

An issue unique to substance abuse groups is how to deal with persons who may show up intoxicated. Most agencies do not allow a person to participate if they are obviously under the influence of alcohol or a drug; however, some harm reduction groups that work with particularly fragile clients will allow a person to stay in the group if he or she is not disruptive to others. A secondary question is who decides? Miller and colleagues (2011) acknowledge that the group leader is the final judge and recommend that in announcing the rules about intoxication to the group, you apologize in advance for false positives.

The following sections provide a description of three types of groups using different therapeutic models that were explored earlier in the chapter. As you will see, the practical issues raised previously are addressed differently, depending on the purpose of the group and the type of client who may be a member of such a group.

AN EXAMPLE OF MOTIVATIONAL INTERVIEWING IN A GROUP SETTING

In this example, the group is a brief intervention to assist college students make a decision about whether it would be a good idea to reduce their alcohol use. All the participants (n = 167) elected to attend the single session rather than be fined and put on disciplinary probation for violation of alcohol policy at the university. Labrie, Pederson, Lamb, and Quinlan (2006) evaluated the results of this single-session group intervention. Each group had 10 to 15 participants and met for 60–90 minutes, led by an MI-trained facilitator. During the session, participants were encouraged to express their frustrations, and the facilitator empathized with their predicament. The students were given information about campus norms regarding alcohol use and the relationship between alcohol use and other consequences such as violence and forced sex. They generated reasons for and against reducing their levels of drinking and discussed specific high-risk situations they might experience. During the discussions, the facilitator maintained a nonjudgmental stance that aided in decreasing resistance. At the end of the group, participants wrote down a behavioral goal of how they would drink in the next 30 days and shared this with the group. During the next 3 months, participants were asked to keep a daily record of their drinking and any related consequences. The authors found significant reductions in levels of drinking, alcohol-related consequences (e.g., not completing homework, fighting, missing class), and judicial recidivism at the end of the 3 months. The heaviest drinkers (males and frequent binge drinkers) achieved the biggest reductions.

AN EXAMPLE OF A HARM REDUCTION DROP IN GROUP: "COME AS YOU ARE"

In this example, the practical issues of group structure, norms, and purpose are addressed differently to meet the needs of consumers in an impoverished area of San Francisco. As described by Little, Hodari, Lavender, and Berg (2008), at any point in time, 50–85% of group members are formally dually diagnosed with serious and persistent mental illnesses, 50% are homeless and living on the streets, and 50% are currently maintaining or pursuing abstinence as a goal. The Sobriety Support Group, the first harm reduction treatment group in the United States, first began in 1994 at the Veteran's Affairs Homeless Center, a drop-in center that provides social work and medical service to homeless veterans. The group has no conditions for group membership; there is no requirement that members have a desire to get clean and sober, that they attend regularly, or even that they participate in the process of the group. Thus, the responsibility for treatment rests solely in the hands of the consumer. The purpose of the group is to welcome consumers into "a bona fide treatment relationship in which they can freely examine their relationship with drugs and begin a process of gradual amelioration of drug-related problems, psychiatric symptoms, and social problems" (Little et al., 2008 p. 168).

To understand what this means, the authors describe an important moment from an early group process that set the tone for this remarkable group:

> A homeless man, heroin and alcohol dependent with paranoid schizophrenia, was persuaded by his social worker to attend the group. His daily ritual was to come into our center, park his shopping cart, and sleep until we closed. He left his cart in his social worker's office, came into the group, sat in our circle, and promptly fell asleep with his head hanging at an awkward angle. The other seven group members looked at me expectantly. Some had been in treatment programs where it was prohibited to sleep in group. What was I to do? I focused on his immediate need—to sleep. If he continued to sleep in this posture, he was going to wake up with a terrible crick in his neck. I stood up, gathered up several jackets, rolled them into a pillow, placed them under his head, then sat back down. The group looked at me incredulously. But since that moment, a caring and gentle culture has prevailed, and many group members have expressed the feeling, "There but for the grace of God go I." Our culture of respect, unquestioning acceptance, and care was thus started with a bang—or a pillow—and truly embodies the welcome to "come as you are." (pp. 168–169)

The spoken content of the group is entirely driven by what the members bring up: About half the time this means talking about drug use and change, and the other half may be about emotional issues, struggles to survive, relationships, and mental health or HIV treatment. There is only one rule in the Sobriety Support Group: As an integral part of the culture of respect, members and the leader must ask permission before offering feedback or comments to another member. Group leaders rely on different therapeutic approaches to guide their own behavior and assist consumers: motivational interviewing and cognitive-behavioral skills training (stress reduction, mindfulness, substance use management, and life coaching) (Little & Franskoviak, 2010). The Harm Reduction Therapy Center, which is the umbrella agency for the Sobriety Support Group, does not conduct formal outcome research to date, but they do maintain record systems that indicate the purpose of the group is being fulfilled. Overall, about 60% of HRTC clients are successfully managing their substance use, 50% no longer present in crisis, 70% have more stable mental health, 60% are taking psychiatric medications, and 60% are more stable in housing (Little & Franskoviak, 2010).

AN EXAMPLE OF A SOLUTION-FOCUSED GROUP

In this example, a solution-focused group was developed for substance abusers who met the American Society of Addiction Medicine (ASAM) criteria for Level 1 (meaning they did not require inpatient treatment but did need outpatient treatment for up to 9 hours per week). The group was designed and implemented as part of a study to compare SFT to a control group that was based on the Hazelden model, a traditional problem-focused psychoeducational program (Smock, Trepper, Wetchler, McCollum, Ray, & Pierce, 2008). The study was focused on the outcomes of depression and interpersonal functioning, not substance abuse. The primary difference between the two groups was that in the SFT group, clients determined their own goals and outcomes for the therapy. Both groups met for 90 minutes each week for 6 weeks. Patients were randomly assigned to either group.

The SFT group was conducted by a therapeutic team, where two co-therapists rotated into the group at different times, and the others, along with a clinical supervisor, sat behind a two-way mirror to assist in developing group themes and feedback. The group leaders followed a solution-focused group treatment manual that prescribed the format of each session to include common SFT techniques, such as the following:

1. Based on the member's introduction at the beginning of each group, a common theme for the session is developed.
2. Group leaders ask a future-oriented question (e.g., "What will be different when the struggle for sobriety is all gone?") and get as many details as possible from the different answers from group members.
3. Group leaders also listen for any exceptions and amplify those exceptions (e.g., "When is the last time you felt that sense of calm? What was happening then?")
4. Group leaders ask scaling questions to determine a client's progress towards his or her goal, asks what that client has done to maintain progress, and how significant others might rate him or her on the progress scale.
5. Group leaders ask how the session theme relates to clients' miracles.
6. Feedback is given to the group on theme work.
7. Clients are invited to assign themselves homework, and homework sheets are passed out.

Results from the study indicated that clients in both the SFT group and the traditional group improved overall, and clients in the SFT group improved significantly more in the within group measures of depression and interpersonal functioning (Smock et al., 2008).

TRADITIONAL TREATMENT AND THE CONTINUUM OF CARE

The treatment system for persons with an alcohol or drug misuse problem is commonly conceptualized as: (1) detoxification, (2) intensive treatment, (3) residential programs, (4) outpatient services, and (5) aftercare services. Although this continuum of care is not available in many rural areas of the

United States, it is usually possible to piece together all of these elements by utilizing programs from other states or metropolitan areas. The American Society of Addiction Medicine's Patient Placement Criteria (ASAM PPC-2R) (ASAM, 2001) envisions treatment as a continuum within which there are five levels of care:

- Level 0.5: Early Intervention
- Level I: Outpatient Treatment
- Level II: Intensive Outpatient/Partial Hospitalization Treatment
- Level III: Residential/Inpatient Treatment
- Level IV: Medically Managed Intensive Inpatient Treatment

ASAM criteria are used to guide addiction treatment matching in a majority of states and have made an impact in every state (CSAT, 2005). Detoxification can occur at any one of these five levels. ASAM (2001) guidelines for deciding the appropriate level of care for detoxification within the five levels of care include these dimensions: (1) acute intoxication or withdrawal potential; (2) biomedical conditions and complications; (3) emotional, behavioral, or cognitive conditions and complications; (4) readiness to change; (5) relapse, continued use, or continued problem potential; and (6) recovery and living environment. The answers to these questions indicate whether a person should be recommended for the least intensive Level I-D: Ambulatory detoxification without extended onsite monitoring, or to the most intensive Level IV-D: Medically managed intensive inpatient detoxification.

The primary purpose of detoxification services is to help the client medically stabilize and reduce or endure withdrawal symptoms that could be fatal without intervention. Commonly referred to as detox centers, these centers may either stand alone in community-based programs or be attached to a hospital-based treatment program. Staff includes physicians and nurses for medical supervision and a variety of professional helpers to attend to other immediate needs and encourage the client to continue utilizing help. Clients in community-based detox centers are often referred by the police, probation or parole officers, and mental health practitioners. These clients are frequently from poverty or homeless situations; many are dually diagnosed. Detox with good medical supervision can be safe and effective on an outpatient basis for most patients (Miller et al., 2011). Although detox programs consistently provide safe withdrawal environments, their effectiveness in reducing drug or alcohol use can be questioned. Based on the Substance Abuse and Mental Health Services Administration's (SAMHSA) Treatment Episode Data Set (TEDS) conducted in 2000, the completion rate for detoxification episodes was 52%, and only 8% were transferred for further treatment (SAMHSA, 2006). Some of the barriers to transitioning to a treatment program include waiting lists, transportation and administrative hurdles, asking clients to make the contact themselves instead of linking them to an appointment for a specific program, and not taking the opportunity to increase their motivation to make changes (Miller et al., 2011).

A strengths-based approach to detoxification services may see this as an opportunity to introduce the client to choices about how to take care of immediate needs such as housing, health concerns (especially screening for hepatitis C, HIV, other sexually transmitted diseases, and nutritional problems), financial assistance, and job-related services. Basic areas of inquiry that are consistent with harm reduction and motivation enhancement practices include finding out what stage of change the person is in, how much insight the person has about the harms and benefits of the use of alcohol/drugs, and what personal strengths and resources (past exceptions to the present troubles, important persons or family that care about the person, survival strategies, and capacities for development) might be helpful (Miller et al., 2011; Denning, 2000; Drake & Meuser, 2000).

In an ideal world, treatment would be a seamless process connected to detox services and aftercare. In the real world, there is usually a long waiting list for treatment programs that are often located in states or metropolitan areas far from the day-to-day lives of the clients, and aftercare services may be pasted together in the local community with whatever resources exist. Many treatment programs currently involve some combination of intensive inpatient services for up to a week, intensive outpatient services or all-day sessions for another week or two, and regular outpatient services several times a week that gradually evolve into aftercare appointments once a month. Based on the TEDS conducted in 2000, the overall hospital inpatient treatment completion rate was 55% compared to a 38% (alcohol) completion rate for long-term residential treatment, 67% (alcohol) for short-term residential treatment, 41% for all intensive outpatient treatment, and 34% for all outpatient treatments (SAMHSA, 2006). Inpatient treatment is still recommended for persons who live under conditions unfavorable to recovery, such as few financial resources, risky environments, or co-occurring disorders (NIAAA, 2000).

Residential services include halfway houses (originally designed to serve alcoholics), therapeutic communities (originally designed to serve drug addicts), and missions. These programs provide a safe environment where people practice living sober with one foot in the community.

Outpatient treatment is primarily group counseling with adjunct individual sessions, offered several times a week for a period of 8 to 12 weeks. Content may include topics similar to those found in inpatient treatment, such as information on the effects of alcohol and drugs, an increasing emphasis on relapse prevention, and in the United States, an introduction to Twelve-Step programs. Given the lack of specificity about treatment modalities and a lack of research, it is difficult to evaluate the effectiveness of group treatment compared to individual treatment or to recommend one modality over another. No single approach has been found clearly superior in the treatment of alcoholism (NIAAA, 2000).

Aftercare is the final formal link between professional help and the client's recovery process, and it usually involves monthly meetings with the service provider. This phase may also involve attendance at a Twelve-Step group or other support system, such as religious counseling, and/or adjunctive services to help with other problems the client may be experiencing in early recovery. More intensive case management services may be provided to persons with coexisting mental disorders, as discussed in Chapter 8. Aftercare programs may also be the mechanism for monitoring progress for mandatory court requirements.

Many strengths-based approaches are already incorporated into the existing treatment system, especially offering support and encouragement to people who may be particularly hopeless about their abilities, tolerating relapses and turning them into learning opportunities, encouraging family and extended family support, and incorporating the clients' needs into formal treatment goals. Further steps in the direction of strengths-based practice would include a serious assessment of the stage of change the client is in when entering treatment and an effort to gear treatment strategies to the needs of that stage, offering an array of change options that include abstinence but are not limited to abstinence, and honoring the ability of the person to make choices that will eventually benefit him or her.

SUMMARY AND CONCLUSION

In this chapter, we have described four strengths-based approaches that honor the principle of client self-determination; focus on the resources, capabilities, and possibilities that the client and client system may be able to use to further client goals; and pay attention to the client's stage of readiness. They are equally viable as individual or group approaches. The practices of harm reduction are well entrenched in addiction treatment outside the United States, but a growing number of practitioners in the United States and Canada are finding reasons to creatively incorporate harm reduction methods in a variety of settings. Motivational interviewing techniques, with a focus on readiness to change and resolving ambivalence, have become well-accepted practices in many areas of addiction treatment. The therapy of solution-focused brief interventions is beginning to be acknowledged as a viable alternative conceptualization that differs from the problem-saturated approach of the medical model. It offers new ways of connecting to a person experiencing problems and helps us appreciate the diverse ways people develop meaning and find new life paths within their cultural, racial, and ethnic influences. Cognitive-behavioral approaches produce significant reductions in addiction problems and related harms and have the added advantage of numerous training manuals and self-help books to guide both practitioner and consumer in helpful practices. We hope the reader will be inspired to follow up on the numerous Internet resources that have been identified throughout the chapter to further investigate the many possibilities offered.

REFERENCES

American Society of Addiction Medicine. (2001). *Patient placement criteria for the treatment of substance-related disorder (PPC-2R)*. Chevy Chase, MD: Author.

Babor, T., & Del Boca, F. (Eds.), (2003). *Treatment matching in alcoholism.* Cambridge, UK: Cambridge University Press.

Beck, A., & Weishaar, M. (2008). Cognitive therapy. In R. Corsini & D. Wedding (Eds.), *Current psychotherapies* (8th ed., pp. 263–292). Belmont, CA:Thomson/Brooks/Cole.

Berg, I. (2001). *What is unique about solution-focused brief therapy?* Retrieved June 15, 2011 from http://www.brief-therapy.org/insoo_essays.htm.

Berg, I., & Miller, S. (1992). *Working with the problem drinker: A solution-focused approach.* New York: Norton.

Blume, A., & Lovato, L. (2009). Empowering the disempowered: Harm reduction with racial/ethnic minority clients. *Journal of Clinical Psychology: In Session,* 66(2), 189–200.

Booth, R. E., Kwiatkowski, C., Iguchi, M. Y., Pinto, F., & John, D. (1998). Facilitating treatment entry among out-of-treatment injection drug users. *Public Health Reports,* 113(1), 116–128.

Brink, W., & Haasen, C. (2006). Evidenced-based treatment of opioid-dependent patients. *Canadian Journal of Psychiatry,* 51(10), 635–646.

Brown, S., & Coventry, L. (1997). *Queen of hearts: The needs of women with gambling problems.* Sydney, Australia: Financial and Consumer Rights Council.

Brown, L., Gaudiano, B., & Miller, I. (2011). Investigating the similarities and differences between practitioners of second and theird wave cognitive-behavioral therapies. *Behavior Modification,* 35(2), 187–200.

Burke, B., Arkowitz, H., & Menchola, M. (2003). The efficacy of motivational interviewing: A meta-analysis of controlled clinical trials. *Journal of Consulting and Clinical Psychology,* 71, 843–861.

Bux, D. A., Iguchi, M. Y., Lidz, V., Baxter, R. C., & Platt, J. J. (1993). Participation in a coupon distribution program for free methadone detoxification. *Hospital Community Psychiatry,* 44, 1066–1072.

Cahn, Z., & Siegel, M. (2011). Electronic cigarettes as a harm reduction strategy for tobacco control: A step forward or a repeat of past mistakes? *Journal of Public Health Policy,* 32(1), 16–31.

Carey, M., Braaten, L., Maisto, S., Gleason, J., Forsyth, A., Durant, L., et al. (2000). Using information, motivational enhancement, and skills training to reduce the risk of HIV infection for low-income urban women: A second randomized clinical trial. *Health Psychology,* 19(1), 3–11.

Carroll, K. (1998). *A cognitive-behavioral approach: Treating cocaine addiction.* NIDA Therapy Manuyals for Drug Addiction, NIH Publication No. 98-4308. Rockville, MD: NIDA.

Carroll, K., Ball, S., Martino, S., Nich, C., Babuscio, T., Nuro, K., Gordon, M., Portnoy, G., & Rounsaville, B. (2008). Computer-assisted delivery of cognitive-behavioral therapy for addictyion: A randomized trial of CBT4CBT. *American Journal of Psychiatry,* 165(7), 881–888.

Coady, N., Stalker, C., & Levene, J. (2000). A closer examination of the empirical support for claims about the effectiveness of solution-focused brief therapy: Stalker et al. respond to Gingerich. *Families in Society,* 81(2), 223–227.

Davies, D. (1962). Normal drinking in recovered alcoholics. *Quarterly Journal of Studies on Alcohol,* 23, 94–104.

Davis, D. (2009). *Taking back your life: Women and problem gambling*. Center City, MN: Hazelden.

De Jong, P., & Berg, I. (2002). *Interviewing for solutions* (2nd ed.). Pacific Grove, CA: Wadsworth.

Denning, P. (2000). *Practicing harm reduction psychotherapy*. New York: Guilford Press.

Denning, P. (2010). Harm reduction therapy with families and friends of people with drug problems. *Journal of Clinical Psychology: In Session, 66*(2), 164–174.

Dennis, M. L., Godley, S. H., Diamond, G., Tims, F. M., Babor, T., Donaldson, J., et al. (2004). The Cannibis Youth Treatment Study: Main findings from two randomized trials. *Journal of Substance Abuse Treatment, 27*(3), 197–213.

Dennis, M. L., Ingram, P. W., Burks, M. E., & Rachal, J. V. (1994). Effectiveness of streamlined admissions to methadone treatment: A simplified time series analysis. *Journal of Psychoactive Drugs, 26,* 207–216.

Des Jarlais, D., McKnight, C., Goldblatt, C., & Purchase, D. (2008). Doing harm reduction better: Syringe exchange in the United States. *Addiction, 104,* 1441–1446.

Drake, R., & Meuser, K. (2000). Psychosocial approaches to dual diagnosis. *Schizophrenia Bulletin, 26*(1), 105–118.

Ellis, A. (1962). *Reason and emotion in psychotherapy*. New York: Lyle Stuart.

Feldstein, S. W. (2006). Motivational interviewing with dually diagnosed adolescents in juvenile justice settings. *Brief Treatment and Crisis Intervention, 6*(3), 218–233.

Gingerich, W., & Eisengart, S. (2000). Solution-focused brief therapy: A review of the outcome research. *Family Process, 39*(4), 477–499.

Goldberg, J., & Kiernan, M. (2005). Innovative techniques to address retention in a behavioral weight-loss trial. *Health Education Research, 20*(4), 439–446.

Hall, W. (2007). What's in a name? *Addiction, 102,* 691–692.

Hayes, S. (2004). Acceptance and commitment therapy, relational frame theory, and the third wave of behavioral and cognitive therapies. *Behavior Therapy, 35,* 639–665.

Hohman, M. (1998). Motivational interviewing: An intervention tool for child welfare case workers working with substance-abusing parents. *Child Welfare, 127*(3), 275–289.

Hester, R., Squires, D., & Delaney, H. (2005). The Drinker's Check-up: 12 month outcomes of a controlled clinical trial of a stand-alone software program for problem drinkers. *Journal of Substance Abuse Treatment, 28*(2), 159–169.

Hettema, J., Steele, J., & Miller, W. (2005). Motivational interviewing. *Annual Review of Clinical Psychology, 1,* 91–111.

Hodgins, D., Currie, S., Currie, G., & Fick, G. (2009). Randomized trial of brief motivational treatment for pathological gamblers: More is not necessarily better. *Journal of Consulting and Clinical Psychology, 77*(5), 950–960.

Horvath, A. (2004). *Sex, drugs, gambling and chocolate: A workbook for overcoming addictions* (2nd ed.). Atascadero, CA: Impact Publishers.

Kadden, R., Carroll, K., Donovan, D., Cooney, N., Monti, P., Abrams, D., Litt, M., & Hester, R. (1994). *Cognitive-behavioral coping skills therapy manual: A clinical research guide for therapists treating individuals with alcohol abuse and dependency*. Project MATCH Monograph Series, Vol. 3. DHHS Publication No. 94-3724.

Kazdin, A. (2004). Psychotherapy for children and adolescents. In M. Lambert (Ed.), *Bergin and Garfield's handbook of psychotherapy and behavior change* (pp. 543–589). Hoboken, NJ: Wiley & Sons.

Kim, J. (2008). Examining the effectiveness of solution-focused brief therapy: A meta-analysis. *Research and Social Work Practice*, 18, 107–116.

Kim, J., Smock, S., Trepper, T., McCollum, E., & Franklin, C. (2010). Is solution-focused brief therapy evidence based? *Families in Society*, 91, 300–306.

Knight, K. M., McGowan, L., & Dickens, C. (2006). A systematic review of motivational interviewing in physical health care settings. *British Journal of Health Psychology*, 11(2), 319–332.

Ladouceur, R., Sylvain, C., Boutin, C., & Doucet, C. (2002). *Understanding and treating the pathological gambler*. New York: Wiley & Sons.

Ladouceur, R. (2005). Controlled gambling for pathological gamblers. *Journal of Gambling Studies*, 21(1), 51–59.

Larimer, M. E., Marlatt, G. A., Baer, J. S., Quigley, L. A., Blume, A. W., & Hawkins, E. H. (1998). Harm reduction for alcohol problems: Expanding access to and acceptability of prevention and treatment services. In G. A. Marlatt (Ed.), *Harm reduction: Pragmatic strategies for managing high-risk behaviors* (pp. 69–121). New York: Guilford Press.

Lee, H., & Petersen, S. (2009). Demarginalizing the marginalized in substance abuse treatment: Stories of homeless, active substance users in an urban harm reduction based drop-in center. *Addiction Research and Theory*, 17(6), 622–636.

Litt, M., Kadden, R., Kabela-Cormier, E., & Petry, N. (2009). Changing network support for drinking: Network Support Project two-year follow-up. *Journal of Consulting and Clinical Psychology*, 77(2), 229–242.

Little, J., Hodari, K., Lavender, J., & Berg, A. (2008). Come as you are: Harm reduction drop-in groups for multi-diagnosed drug users. *Journal of Groups in Addiction and Recovery*, 3(3/4), 161–192.

Little, J., & Franskoviak, P. (2010). So glad you came! Harm reduction therapy in community settings. *Journal of Clinical Psychology: In session*, 66(2), 175–188.

Logan, D., & Marlatt, G. (2010). Harm reduction therapy: A practice-friendly review of research. *Journal of Clinical Psychology: In Session*, 66(2), 201–214.

Lundahl, B., Kunz, C., Brownell, C., Tollefson, D., & Burke, B. (2010). A meta-analysis of motivational interviewing: Twenty-five years of empirical studies. *Research on Social Work Practice*, 20(2), 137–160.

Magill, M., & Ray, L. (2009). Cognitive-behavioral treatment with adult alcohol and illicit drug users: A meta-analysis of randomized controlled trials. *Journal of Studies on Alcohol and Drugs*, 70(4), 516–527.

McCambridge, J., & Strang, J. (2004). The efficacy of single-session motivational interviewing in reducing drug consumption and perceptions of drug-related risk and harm among young people: Results from a multi-site cluster randomized trial. *Addiction*, 99, 39–52.

McCollum, E., Trepper, T., & Smock, S. (2003). Solution focused group therapy for substance abuse: Extending competency-based models. *Journal of Family Psychotherapy*, 14(4), 27–42.

McMurran, M. (2009). Motivational interviewing with offenders: A systematic review. *Legal and Criminological Psychology*, 14(1), 83–100.

Miller, W. (1983). Motivational interviewing with problem drinkers. *Behavioral Psychotherapy*, 11, 147–172.

Miller, W. R. (1996). Motivational interviewing: Research, practice, and puzzles. *Addictive Behaviors*, 21(6), 835–842.

Miller, W. R. (1998). Toward a motivational definition and understanding of addiction. *Motivational Interviewing Newsletter for Trainers*, 5(3), 2–6.

Miller, W., Forcehimes, A., & Zweben, A. (2011). *Treating addiction: A guide for professionals*. New York: Guilford Press.

Miller, W. R., & Rollnick, S. (2002). *Motivational interviewing: Preparing people for change* (2nd ed.). New York: Guilford Press.

Miller, W., & Wilbourne, P. (2002). Mesa Grande: A methodological analysis of clinical trials of treatment for alcohol use disorders. *Addiction*, 97(3), 265–277.

Miller, W., Wilbourne, P., & Hettma, J. (2003). What works? A summary of alcohol treatment outcome research. In R. K. Hester & W. R. Miller (Eds.), *Handbook of alcoholism treatment approaches: Effective alternatives* (3rd ed., pp. 13–63). Boston: Allyn & Bacon.

Monti, P., Kadden, R., Rohsenow, D., Cooney, N., & Abrams, D. (2002). *Treating alcohol dependence: A coping skills training guide* (2nd ed.). New York: Guilford Press.

Mott, S., & Gyson, T. (2003). Post-modern ideas in substance abuse treatment. *Journal of Social Work Practice in the Addictions*, 3(3), 3–19.

National Association of Social Workers (NASW). (2008). *Code of ethics*. Silver Spring, MD: Author.

National Institute on Alcohol Abuse and Alcoholism (NIAAA). (2000). *10th special report to the U.S. Congress on alcohol and health*. Rockville, MD: U.S. Department of Health and Human Services.

Osborne, C. (1997). Does disease matter? Incorporating solution-focused brief therapy in alcoholism treatment. *Journal of Drug and Alcohol Education*, 43(1), 18–30.

Palfai, T., Zisserson, R., & Saitz, R. (2011). Using personalized feedback to reduce alcohol use among hazardous drinking college students: The moderating effect of alcohol-related consequences. *Addictive Behavior* 36(5), 539–542.

Parrish, D. (2009). Cognitive behavioral coping skills therapy for adults. In D. Springer & A. Rubin (Eds.), *Substance abuse treatment for youth and adults* (pp. 209–259). Hoboken, NJ: Wiley.

Petry, N. M., Martin, B., Cooney, J. L., & Kranzler, H. R. (2000). Give them prizes and they will come: Contingency management for the treatment of alcohol dependence. *Journal of Consulting and Clinical Psychology*, 68, 250–257.

Podymow, T., Turnbull, J., Coyle, D., Yetisir, E., & Wells, G. (2006). Shelter-based managed alcohol administration to chronically homeless people addicted to alcohol. *Canadian Medical Association Journal*, 174(1), 45–50.

Prochaska, J., & DiClemente, C. (1986). The transtheoretical approach. In J. C. Norcross (Ed.), *Handbook of eclectic psychotherapy* (pp. 163–200). New York: Brunner/Mazel.

Project MATCH Research Group. (1997). Matching alcoholism treatments to client heterogeneity: Project MATCH posttreatment drinking outcomes. *Journal of Studies on Alcohol*, 58, 7–29.

Rapp, R. C. (2006). Strengths-based case management: Enhancing treatment for persons with substance abuse problems. In D. Saleebey (Ed.), *The strengths perspective in social work practice* (4th ed., pp. 128–147). Boston: Allyn & Bacon.

Rapp, R. C., Li, L., Siegal, H., & DeLiberty, R. (2003). Demographic and clinical correlates of client motivation among substance abusers. *Health and Social Work*, 26(2), 107–115.

Reamer, F. (1998). *Ethical standards in social work*. Washington, DC: NASW Press.

Riley, D., Sawka, E., Conley P., Hewitt, D., Mitic, W., Poulin, C., Room, R., Single, E., & Topp, J. (1999). Harm reduction, concepts and practice: A policy discussion paper. *Substance Use and Misuse*, 34(1), 9–24.

Saleebey, D. (2006). Introduction: Power in the people. In D. Saleebey (Ed.), *The strengths perspective in social work practice* (4th ed., pp. 1–22). Boston: Allyn & Bacon.

Smock, S., Trepper, T., Wetchler, J., McCollum, E., Ray, R., & Pierce, K. (2008). Solution-focused group therapy for Level 1 substance abusers. *Journal of Marital and Family Therapy*, 34(1), 107–120.

Sobell, L. C., Ellingstad, T. P., & Sobell, M. B. (2000). Natural recovery from alcohol and drug problems: Methodological review of the research with suggestions for future directions. *Addiction*, 95, 749–764.

Substance Abuse and Mental Health Services Administration (SAMHSA). (2010). *Results from the 2009 National Survey on Drug Use and Health: Volume I, Summary of National Findings*. Office of Applied Studies, NSDUH Series H-38A, HHS Publication No. SMA 10-4586 Findings. Rockville, MD.

Substance Abuse and Mental Health Services Administration. (SAMHSA). (2006). *The DASIS Report: Discharges from Intensive Outpatient Treatment*, 2000. Office of Applied Studies. Retrieved October 22, 2006 from http://oas.samhsa.gov/2k3/intensiveOutDischarges/intensiveOutDischarges.cfm

Substance Abuse and Mental Health Services Administration (SAMHSA). (2005). *Substance abuse treatment for persons with co-occurring disorders*. Treatment Improvement Protocol (TIP) Series, No. 42. Washington, DC: U.S. Department of Health and Human Services.

Tatarsky, A., & Marlatt, G. (2010). State of the art in harm reduction psychotherapy: An emerging treatment for substance misuse. *Journal of Clinical Psychology: In Session*, 66(2), 117–122.

Trepper, T. S., Dolan, Y., McCollum, E., & Nelson, T. (2006). Steve deShazer and the future of solution-focused therapy. *Journal of Marital and Family Therapy*, 32(2), 133–140.

U.S. Department of Health and Human Services (DHHS). (1988). *The health consequences of smoking: Nicotine addiction, a report of the surgeon general*. Washington, DC: U.S. Government Printing Office.

Vaillant, G. (1996). A long-term follow-up of male alcohol abuse. *Archives of General Psychiatry*, 53, 243–249.

Vasilaki, E., Hosier, S., & Cox, W. (2006). The efficacy of motivational interviewing as a brief intervention for excessive drinking: A meta-analytic review. *Alcohol and Alcoholism*, 41, 328–335.

West, C. (2010). Solution-focused group treatment with publicly funded alcohol/other drug abuse clients in rural settings. *Alcoholism Treatment Quarterly*, 28, 176–183.

Wild, T. C. (1999). Compulsory substance-user treatment and harm reduction: A critical analysis. *Substance Use and Misuse*, 34(1), 83–102.

Witkiewitz, K., & Marlatt, G. (2011). Behavioral therapy across the spectrum. *Alcohol, Research and Health*, 33(4), 313–319.

Wilhelm, S., Flanders Stepans, M., & Hertzog, M. (2006). Motivational interviewing to promote sustained breastfeeding. *Journal of Obstetric, Gynecologic, and Neonatal Nursing*, 35(2), 340–348.

Wilson, G. (2008). Behavior therapy. In R.Corsini & D.Wedding (Eds.), *Current psychotherapies* (8th ed., pp. 223–259). Belmont, CA:Thomson/Brooks/Cole.

Zamarripa, M. (2009). Solution-focused therapy in the South Texas Borderlands. *Journal of Systemic Therapies*, 28(4), 1–11.

9 CHAPTER | SUBSTANCE MISUSE WITH A CO-OCCURRING MENTAL DISORDER OR DISABILITY

I was much too far out all my life
And not waving but drowning.

—Stevie Smith (1983, p. 303)

INTRODUCTION

Mental illness is terrifying when it spirals out of control. Repeated alcohol or drug misuse often brings misery, regret, and dire consequences. When the two are combined, the result can be a double whammy of troubles that worsens each condition (Swann, 2010). This also applies to a person who also has a developmental, physical, or cognitive disability or any other major challenge to living life and uses alcohol, drugs, or gambling in a harmful way. One such person is Robert, who was eventually diagnosed with schizoaffective disorder and alcohol dependence (National Council on Community Behavioral Healthcare, NCCBH, 2011). For a while, Robert was sleeping behind a building in a cardboard box and eating from the trash. He was picked up and taken to the dump and wasn't sure if he was going to the shredder. Homeless for almost 10 years, Robert left home at 14. Before he left, his father beat him severely and locked him in a closet, often for days at a time. He didn't attend school because he had too many bruises. Upon leaving home, he drifted from job to job and started drinking to take away the pain. Eventually, his whole life revolved around alcohol and he ended up homeless, sleeping in the cardboard box.

Getting help when you have multiple needs, like Robert, has never been easy. Professional treatment providers and educators in the mental health, disability, and substance misuse field have often acted as if a person could be divided up into just one area of trouble at a time. Competition around traditionally separate national and state funding streams, turf battles over which disorder is "primary," different attitudes toward treatment methods, and educational deficits for professionals in each field have contributed to this unhelpful stance. In the recent past people like Robert who were diagnosed both bipolar and alcoholic and still drinking could be refused treatment at a mental health facility because they were not abstinent. At the same time, they could be refused treatment at a substance abuse treatment center because of their mental health symptoms or were told to give up antidepressant medication. As one treatment provider put it, "All of us treat dually diagnosed patients, but few of us provide dual diagnosis treatment" (Shulman, 1995, p. 33). Standard practice by most mental health systems in the United States is not evidence-based; the same is true for most substance abuse treatment centers (Biegel et al., 2003). Consequently, emergency rooms have become the dumping ground when mental health and substance abuse problems get out of hand. In 2007, 12 million (12.5%) of emergency room visits by adults in the United States had to do with mental disorders, a substance abuse problem, or both (Owens, Mutter, & Stocks, 2010).

Similarly, persons with physical disabilities or cognitive impairments have generally not been served well by existing treatment and support systems (Handmaker, Packard, & Conforti, 2002). For example, families and professionals in the disability field have tended to overlook substance misuse problems, and treatment facilities and self-help groups often are not accessible for those with mobility problems. Written and other visual materials are designed for people who see and do not have brain trauma or learning needs, and interpreters for the deaf are seldom employed.

Overwhelming evidence showed that the "hardening of the categories" between mental health disabilities and substance abuse was not working. Most research studies indicated that parallel or sequential treatment approaches for dual disorders had annual rates of stable remission of less than 5%. Parallel and sequential treatments in which clients are treated by two agencies for each problem separately have been found ineffective because this approach ignores the interactive and cyclical nature of the two types of disorders. For years, different bureaucracies and philosophical approaches at mental health and substance abuse agencies as well as funding barriers have precluded active collaboration. Traditional approaches protected program boundaries but have been shown ineffective for the care of either psychiatric or substance use disorders (Mueser, Noordsy, Drake, & Fox, 2003).

Something had to give—and did. In the mid-1980s, reforms began developing, catalyzed by 13 federally funded demonstration projects across the country in 1987. By 2004, 35% of the facilities surveyed in the National Survey of Substance Abuse Treatment Services had special programs or groups for clients with co-occurring psychiatric and substance abuse disorders

(Substance Abuse Mental Health Service Administration, SAMHSA, 2004). However, in 2005, among the 5.2 million adults with both serious psychological distress and a substance use disorder, 53% received no treatment at all, 34.3% received only treatment for mental health problems, and 4.1% received only specialty substance use treatment. A mere 8.5% received both treatment for mental health problems and specialty substance use treatment (SAMHSA, 2006b) (Figure 9.1).

Robert, mentioned earlier in the chapter, was one of the lucky ones. A local mental health center got Robert off the street and diagnosed him with schizoaffective disorder and alcohol dependence. Today, thanks to the Mental Health Center of Denver, Robert is living independently with his dog, Buddy, and is working to complete his General Educational Development (GED) certification (NCCBH, 2011). Although the policy surrounding the treatment of persons with both a mental and a substance use disorder is advancing from bifurcation in programming to a "no wrong door" philosophy, we clearly have a way to go to achieve integrated care for all who need it.

The implications from these projects, other pilot programs, recent research findings, and federal legislation have stimulated substantial and dramatic changes in traditional treatment practices and access to treatment. The Mental Health Parity and Addiction Equity Act of 2008 ended discrimination against consumers of mental health and substance abuse treatment services in insurance coverage (SAMHSA, 2008a). In addition, concurrent developments of the consumer and advocacy movement in the mental health field and the

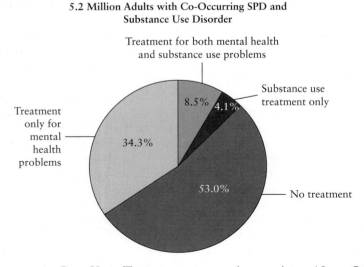

5.2 Million Adults with Co-Occurring SPD and Substance Use Disorder

Treatment for both mental health and substance use problems

Substance use treatment only

8.5%   4.1%

Treatment only for mental health problems

34.3%

53.0%   No treatment

FIGURE 9.1 | Past Year Treatment among Adults Aged 18 or Older with Both Serious Psychological Distress (SPD) and a Substance Use Disorder: 2005

Source: Office of Applied Studies, 2005 National Survey on Drug Use and Health: National Results.
Note: Due to rounding, these percentages do not add to 100%.

independent living movement in the disability field have supported the direction of these positive changes. Some people refer to this as a movement toward a "nonpunitive helping stance."

Traditionally, the most common approach to treating clients with dual or multiple disorders has been to identify one disorder as primary and the other as secondary (Mueser et al., 2003). Social workers often were taught that if they got at the underlying problem (e.g., depression) and treated that disorder, the addiction problems would then go away. Meanwhile, substance abuse counselors generally viewed the mental health disorders as symptoms that would disappear once the substance misuse stopped. One of the major ideological conflicts around which problem was primary receded from view when more advanced technologies taught us more about diseases of the brain. It then became possible to treat clients simultaneously with an integrated approach for all their needs. The introduction of harm reduction techniques and motivational interviewing has been helpful in engaging people who were alienated by traditional assessment and treatment strategies. Abstinence is now considered an appropriate long-term goal for many, instead of a rigid requirement for receiving treatment. Categories variously named *dual diagnosis, coexisting disorders, persons with mental illness and chemical abuse or addiction* (MICAA, indicating an Axis I mental disorder), or *persons with chemical abuse and mental illness* (CAMI, indicating an Axis II personality disorder) are now referred to as *co-occurring disorders* to indicate the presence of both substance abuse/ dependence and serious mental disorders (CSAT, 2005). Funding streams for research and pilot programs are now available. New approaches that emphasize self-determination, client strengths, and harm reduction have shown promising results.

This chapter presents the new body of knowledge that has been developed since the early 1990s to address the needs of persons with coexisting problems. The first part of the chapter presents a brief summary of the prevalence, characteristics, and typical concerns that a person with multiple problems may present. Following a description of the basic mental disorders, we discuss integrative treatment practices for persons who have substance misuse and mental health problems. Next, we address working with persons who misuse substances and have developmental, cognitive, or physical disabilities. Throughout the chapter, we discuss treatment approaches and programs that are evidence-based, and we provide practical tips for working with several types of coexisting disorders.

SUBSTANCE MISUSE AND MENTAL DISORDERS

Prevalence rates of co-occurring disorders depend on what is included in the "serious mental disorders" category. The definition is far from simple. Some clinicians in the substance abuse treatment field note that it is rare to uncover a normal, well-adjusted, average person hiding under a serious addiction because the substance misuse in and of itself takes a heavy psychological and emotional toll (Denning, 2004). Complications in definition occur because the severity of either disorder varies from individual to individual and within individuals over time. To address that challenge, the Quadrants of Care was developed by the National Association of State Alcohol and Drug Abuse Directors (NASADAD) and the National Association of State Mental Health Program Directors (NASMHPD) (Figure 9.2). The four quadrants are: (1) less severe mental disorder/less severe substance disorder, (2) more severe mental disorder/less severe substance disorder, (3) less severe mental disorder/more severe substance disorder, and (4) more severe mental disorder/more severe substance disorder (CSAT, 2005). This classification system is helpful in treatment matching, which will be discussed later in the chapter. People with severe mental illness seem to have a heightened sensitivity to the effects of alcohol or psychoactive drugs. Just a small amount can be their undoing and precipitate hospitalization or other major living problems. Very few persons who are severely mentally ill (less than 5%, according to Drake and Wallach [1993]) can even drink alcohol or use drugs at a moderate level without consequences. Consequently, about 50% of these people choose abstinence, and those who do use are unlikely to sustain heavy use (Drake & Mueser, 2000). For some people who have a biological vulnerability, even low or moderate use of substances could trigger a psychiatric episode (Mueser at al., 2006). Thus, the term *co-occurring disorders* is not a precise, distinctive category. For the purpose of this chapter, it will refer to substance use disorder and mental disorders.

The prevalence of serious mental disorders is so high in the substancing abusing population it can be considered the norm, not the exception (Miller, Forcehimes, & Zweben, 2011). For persons clinically diagnosed with a severe mental illness, coexisting substance misuse is more common than not, especially if the person is young, male, single, less educated, and has a history of substance misuse or conduct disorder or if he or she is homeless or in jail, or presents to an emergency room (Drake & Mueser, 2000). In 2005, 5.2 million adults met the criteria for both serious psychological distress and a substance use disorder. Past year illicit drug use was higher among adults with serious mental illness (26.8%) than adults without it (12.7%). The rate of past month cigarette use in 2005 was 42.8% among adults with serious mental illness compared to a 24.5% rate for adults without it. Combining all categories of substance dependence or abuse (including alcohol), 21.3% (5.2 million) of adults with serious mental illness were dependent on or abused illicit drugs or alcohol; the rate among adults without serious mental illness was 7.7% (14.9 million) (SAMHSA, 2006b).

Similarly, about half of the people who present for substance abuse treatment will have another serious mental disorder (Grant, Dawson, Stinson, Chou, Dufour, & Pickering, 2004). Some of the most common problems are bipolar disorders, generalized anxiety disorders, posttraumatic stress disorder, schizophrenia, schizoaffective disorders, major depression, personality disorders, and pathological gambling (Miller et al., 2011).

Alcohol, cannabis, and cocaine, in that order, are the most commonly used substances by persons with severe mental illness (Mueser et al., 2003).

Persons with coexisting disorders appear to use alcohol and other drugs for the same reasons persons without coexisting disorders use substances—loneliness, anxiety, boredom, and insomnia (Mueser, Drake, & Wallach, 1998; Mueser et al., 2003). Meuser and colleagues (2006) also found that peers influence the drug of choice more than symptoms, and that use persists over time despite varying degrees of symptoms. These findings contradict the popular notion that persons with mental illness use alcohol and other substances to "self-medicate" their symptoms or the side effects of their medication.

Persons who are dually diagnosed with substance misuse and mental disorders can expect more vulnerability than just plain substance misusers in a variety of ways. They are more likely to experience frequent hospitalizations, relapse, depression and suicide, severe housing and financial problems, homelessness, high rates of sexually transmitted diseases (STDs), violence, incarceration, and legal problems. At the same time, they are less likely to comply with their medication regimen (Drake & Mueser, 2000), and medication may be less effective (e.g., nicotine decreases the potency of standard antipsychotic medication) (Goff, Henderson, & Amico, 1992).

The problems of mental illness and substance misuse are particularly severe among poor urban individuals. A homeless, dually diagnosed woman interviewed in the Washington, D.C., Dual Diagnosis Project describes her situation as follows: "Sometimes I do think I'm going to get murdered. I was raped and stuck up before.... I was just spending money on drugs.... People—friends, relatives and mental health staff—just did me in. They did enough torture to put a butcher knife to me and throw me off the bridge" (Quimby, 1995, p. 266).

All too frequently, these extremely vulnerable persons receive no treatment at all or are still shuttled back and forth between the mental health system and the alcohol/drug system. Tom Jackson (2008), writing for the *Washington Post*, chronicled the life and death of Danny Watt, who drowned in 2008 at the age of 21. His parents had refinanced their house three times to put Danny in countless substance abuse treatment centers and mental health facilities beginning at age 16. After his first overdose and subsequent hospitalization, he was diagnosed as bipolar, and later on schizophrenic. He also drank alcohol, used cocaine, shot heroin and meth, and whatever else was available. Danny frequently ended up in jail, and as the problems increased, his parents begged the police to arrest him just to keep him off the streets. Mental health facilities discharged him as soon as he became "stable." "It was always, 'Get him stable, get him out,'" said his father, Bobby Watt. "No long-term plans.... We wanted him in a place where he was locked up with proper medical attention until he became stable. I begged them to put him in a mental hospital. I told them, 'If you put him out on the streets, he'll be dead in a week.'" That was April 3, 2008. Eleven days later, Danny was dead. His story illustrates the black holes created by the deinstitutionalization of the mental health system in the 1960s, the subsequent lack of care for the seriously mentally ill, and the narrow focus of the substance abuse field that has dominated treatment until recently.

THE PERILS OF DIFFERENTIAL DIAGNOSIS

Most professionals in the mental health and substance abuse treatment fields have been trained to believe that an accurate diagnosis is essential for treatment planning. We would like to be able to determine with some certainty whether the specific mental illness is independent of or is dependent on the substance abuse and plan treatment accordingly. Making a differential diagnosis is complicated because many substances have effects during the intoxication or withdrawal phase that mimic psychiatric symptoms. For example, intoxication from alcohol can cause euphoria, and withdrawal can cause anxiety and hallucinations. Intoxication from hallucinogens can cause panic, and withdrawal can cause depression. The diagnosis of a separate mental health disorder (not substance abuse related) is clearest when the mental health symptoms occurred prior to the onset of substance use and if symptoms persist for a month or more after abstinence from the substance use, or if the symptoms are in excess of what would be expected as a result of the substance use (Miller et al., 2011). Diagnosis, under the best of circumstances, is a complex decision (see Box 9.1).

In the real world of co-occurring disorders and people like Danny Watt, described earlier in the chapter, a period of abstinence or even stabilization may not always be possible. Numerous studies have found that the majority

---

Box 9.1	DIAGNOSIS IN A TEAM SETTING

The following narrative, by Catherine Crisp (2005), who at the time of the writing was a clinical social worker on an inpatient psychiatry unit at a large teaching hospital, expresses some of the challenges of diagnosis in a team setting.

On several occasions, our team has had lengthy debates about the diagnosis of a particular client. Is he/she depressed because he/she can't get off drugs? Did the depression precede the drug use? If the depression preceded the drug use, at what point did they start to use drugs and how did that affect their depression? What is their diagnosis? Is it substance-induced mood disorder or is it a major depression with a coexisting substance dependence problem? Is the client's irritability due to (1) a component of their mental illness, (2) the effects of withdrawing from their drug of choice (irritability is particularly common among people who are addicted to crack cocaine), (3) a component of a personality disorder, or (4) just a part of their personality style? Many times, each of the team members has a very different opinion about the diagnosis and the recommended course of treatment. It seems like a miracle when we can all agree. At other times, it is clear that we will not reach a consensus. When this happens, the attending psychiatrist ultimately makes the final call about the diagnosis and treatment that we will provide. Although I am surrounded by people with a clear medical model bias, I feel that my opinions and the bio-psycho-social-spiritual perspective I bring to the team are respected and valued by those I work with. (p. 206) of mentally ill persons do not start out ready and motivated for abstinence-based treatment (Mercer-McFadden, Drake, Brown, & Fox, 1997). Some people start drinking or using drugs at an age earlier than when mental illnesses become apparent. Persons who are homeless are unlikely to have reliable family members available to elaborate on their history. Careful attention to prior inpatient and outpatient records is a good strategy, but it is viable only when those records can be found and made available in a timely manner.

What is most important is to continue to evaluate psychiatric symptoms and their relationship to abstinence *or* ongoing substance abuse over time (CSAT, 2005). In a harm reduction approach where many clients are dealing with co-occurring disorders and survival needs, the cornerstones of "assessment as treatment" are (1) flexibility and (2) a long engagement period building a relationship with the client on the client's terms. Formal assessment is conducted over a long period of time and in fact never stops throughout the course of treatment (Little & Franskoviak, 2010). In the meantime, harm reduction clinicians focus the therapy on any given day to the clients' hierarchy of needs as they define them, whether that be medication assessment, housing, help getting to an appointment, a support group, or a nonjudgmental presence in their lives. Denning (2000) advocates working without a diagnosis or with a partial diagnosis "with a general spirit of courage and risk taking on the part of clinicians" (p. 167). She cites the wasted time in arguing about a correct diagnosis, the need for constant reassessment, and the growing knowledge base in pharmacology and treatment strategies as good reasons to carry on working with a person even though a differential diagnosis may not be readily apparent. Assessment in this framework really becomes part of ongoing treatment.

Many substance-induced symptoms begin to improve within hours or days after substance use has stopped. For example, anxiety symptoms (worry, apprehensive expectations, tension, sweating, hyperarousal, insomnia, irritability, poor concentration) are the most common psychiatric symptoms manifested by substance misusers (CSAT, 1994). However, most of these anxiety symptoms are gone within a few days or weeks of abstinence, in which case little or no treatment is required. Notable exceptions are psychotic symptoms caused by heavy and long-term amphetamine abuse and the dementia (problems with memory, concentration, and problem solving) caused by using substances directly toxic to the brain, most commonly alcohol, inhalants like gasoline, and again amphetamines (CSAT, 2005). If mild to debilitating anxiety continues long after abstinence, it makes sense to assess the person for a coexisting anxiety disorder that may require specific medication and treatment intervention.

The goal over time is an ongoing multidisciplinary assessment that includes the client's perspective. If other disciplines are represented on the team, their specialty areas would also be included. Basic areas of inquiry that are consistent with harm reduction and motivation enhancement practices (Denning, 2004; Drake & Mueser, 2000) include finding out what stage of change the person is in, how much insight the person has about the harms and benefits of her or his use of alcohol/drugs, and what personal strengths and resources may be helpful (past exceptions to the present troubles, important persons or family that care about the person, survival strategies, and capacities for development).

In addition to finding out the details of the person's use of alcohol and drugs (e.g., type, frequency, amount, patterns, expectancies related to use, positive and negative results), it is just as important to find out the details of any prescribed psychiatric medications, both past and present, and the person's particular patterns in taking the medication. This can lead to a discussion of any other attempts the person has made to help himself or herself or alleviate symptoms, such as professional treatment, self-help group participation, and religious or cultural practices. What helped and what did not?

Eventually, it will be important to elicit personal goals in the areas of use of alcohol and drugs; types of supports, resources, and treatments desired to attain this goal and personal goals in the areas of social relationships; fun, recreational activities, hobbies, work, and education; financial or legal circumstances; and spiritual, religious, or cultural practices.

The continuous development of these areas of inquiry over time will help the clinician focus on finding meaningful direction for the person with a coexisting disorder, on validating the person's unique experience, and on mutually discovering strengths that can be brought to bear on the situation at hand.

The Center for Substance Abuse Treatment (CSAT) (2005) offers the following summary of knowledge essential for counselors who plan to work persons who have the combination of substance misuse and psychotic disorders:

- There is no clear pattern of drug choice among clients with schizophrenia. Instead, it is likely that whatever substances happen to be available or in vogue will be the substances used most typically.
- What looks like resistance or denial may in reality be a manifestation of negative symptoms of schizophrenia.
- An accurate understanding of the role of substance use disorders in the client's psychosis requires a multiple-contact, longitudinal assessment.
- Clients with a co-occurring mental disorder involving psychosis have a higher risk for self-destructive and violent behaviors.
- Clients with a co-occurring mental disorder involving psychosis are particularly vulnerable to homelessness, housing instability, victimization, poor nutrition, and inadequate financial resources.
- Both psychotic and substance use disorders tend to be chronic disorders with multiple relapses and remissions, supporting the need for long-term treatment. For clients with co-occurring disorders involving psychosis, a long-term approach is imperative.
- It is important that the program philosophy be based on a multidisciplinary team approach. Ideally, team members should be cross-trained, and there should be representatives from the medical, mental health, and

addiction systems. The overall goals of long-term management should include (1) providing comprehensive and integrated services for both the mental and substance use disorders, and (2) doing so with a long-term focus that addresses biopsychosocial issues in accord with a treatment plan with goals specific to a client's situation. (pp. 231–232)

Prescribing psychiatric medication can be another challenge connected to diagnosis, especially if the medications are psychoactive or potentially addictive. Addiction treatment staff historically avoided the use of any medication. This made sense given the number of patients they saw addicted to prescription drugs and the large number of primary care physicians who were prescribing anti-anxiety medications, many of which (e.g., benzodiazepines) were psycho-active and could be addictive. However, this prohibition has changed as treatment providers have become trained in the appropriate use of nonaddicting psychiatric medications and have come to understand that withholding psychiatric medication can increase relapse. As discussed in Chapter 7, the most current information on medications commonly prescribed in mental health treatment and the effects these drugs may have on the recovery process of an individual who is also misusing alcohol or drugs is the publication "Psychotherapeutic medications 2011: What every counselor should know." It is available from the Mid-America Addiction Technology Transfer Center for free download at http://www.findrxinformation.org. The information is updated annually and addresses generic and trade psychiatric medication names, purpose, usual dose and frequency, potential side effects, emergency conditions, cautions, and common addiction treatment medications. Medication strategies are still in the process of being developed in this complex area.

DISORDERS THAT COMMONLY CO-OCCUR WITH SUBSTANCE MISUSE

This section describes mental disorders that commonly coexist with substance abuse and dependence. The diagnostic labels and brief descriptions are from the *Diagnostic and Statistical Manual of Mental Disorders, Text Revision (DSM–IV–TR)* (APA, 2000). For further description, see the CSAT Treatment Improvement Protocol (TIP 42), called *Substance Abuse Treatment for Persons with Co-occurring Disorders*, downloadable from http://www.samhsa. gov. Although this textbook focuses on the strengths perspective and harm reduction, it is important to include a section based on the classification system of the *DSM–IV–TR*, The purpose is to (1) provide for a means of communicating with other mental health professionals trained to use these categories, (2) use the *DSM-IV-TR* for the resource it provides best (i.e., behavioral descriptions of well-accepted categories), and (3) recognize the reality that many providers cannot exist without payments based on utilizing *DSM-IV-TR* diagnoses. Later in the chapter, we will detail how critical the strengths perspective and harm reduction practices are when actually working with individuals with multiple challenges.

ANXIETY

Anxiety symptoms are experienced by everyone at some time in their lives—cold, clammy hands, tremulous voice, the shakes, panic, shortness of breath, increased heart rate, restlessness, or the almost relentless urge to move about. Anxiety is a normal response to danger. The *DSM–IV–TR* includes panic attacks, agoraphobia, phobias, obsessive-compulsive disorders, posttraumatic stress disorders, as well as generalized anxiety disorders within the classification of anxiety disorders (APA, 2000). However, in persons with alcohol or other drug disorders AOD problems, anxiety and mood disorders are the most common psychiatric symptoms encountered. Addiction itself can be anxiety-producing because of the extreme stress of living and surviving an "addicted life." Many times, such a life can include homelessness, dangerous and illegal activities, physical assaults, acute illness, and extreme isolation from friends and family. The process of recovery also becomes a process of dealing with what Twelve-Step groups call "the wreckage of the past," the nightmares, and the fragility of surviving.

Anxiety disorders can be diagnosed in approximately 25% of alcohol-dependent persons and about 40% of those who are drug-dependent (Grant, Hasin, Stinson, Dawson, Chou, Ruan, & Huang, 2005). Anxiety is sometimes a direct result of ingesting psychoactive drugs, such as stimulants, marijuana, and hallucinogenic drugs. The *DSM–IV* diagnosis substance-induced anxiety disorder is used to describe anxiety symptoms associated with intoxication or withdrawal states. In recovery, anxiety can be the result of acute or prolonged abstinence syndromes, especially from alcohol, sedative depressant drugs, opiates, and long-term cocaine use. Most anxiety symptoms related to AOD misuse clear within 2 to 4 weeks (CSAT, 2005). Anxiety frequently occurs with depression, and the combination puts the person at high suicide risk. When symptoms persist after 30 days of abstinence, the person should be assessed for an independent coexisting anxiety disorder that might interfere with recovery.

POSTTRAUMATIC STRESS DISORDER (PTSD)

It was not until 1980, in response to Vietnam War veterans and the militancy of the antiwar movement, that the American Psychiatric Association (APA) included the diagnosis of posttraumatic stress disorder (PTSD) in the *DSM-IV-TR* in acknowledgment of the symptoms. The feminist movement was influential in this development as well because women had begun to speak out about the impact of rape (van Wormer, 2007). The *DSM–IV–TR* (2000) describes PTSD as the re-experiencing of an extremely traumatic event that the person has experienced or witnessed, accompanied by symptoms of increased arousal (e.g., sleep disturbance, irritability, hypervigilance, difficulty concentrating) and by avoidance of stimuli associated with the trauma and numbing.

According to the National Mental Health Association (NMHA, 2006), 25 to 30% of people exposed to severe trauma, and 5 to 10% of people exposed to moderate trauma, will develop substance use problems. Clients with the dual diagnosis of PTSD and substance misuse have worse outcomes than those with either disorder alone and may internalize a sense of failure when they do not succeed in standard treatment programs that work for others (Navits, 2004). A study of 60 women participants in a prison-based substance abuse treatment program, over half of whom were diagnosed with PTSD, found that the dually diagnosed women had a significantly higher rate of drug relapse upon release than did women with a background of substance misuse only (Kubiak, 2004). Typical sources of the trauma were early childhood sexual abuse and/or later battering and rape experiences. Addiction treatment for clients with PTSD raises several issues. It is important for the counselor to recognize that becoming abstinent from substances does not resolve PTSD, and indeed, some of the symptoms might even become worse at first (CSAT, 2005). Clients may be overwhelmed by a flood of memories that their substance use had kept at bay. Still, integrated treatment is likely to be more successful than substance abuse treatment alone; treatment outcomes for clients with PTSD and substance use disorders typically are worse than for other clients in treatment, even for other clients with other mental disorders (CSAT, 2005). Counselors are recommended to prepare clients with PTSD for this possibility and to consider referral for medications targeting anxiety. If the client is at risk of further harm, developing a plan for increased safety is essential.

PTSD Related to Combat   Among veterans of the wars in Iraq and Afghanistan who received care from the Department of Veterans Affairs, nearly one-third were diagnosed with mental health and/or psychosocial problems, and one-fifth were diagnosed with a substance use problem (Seal, Bertenthal, Miner, Sen, & Marmar, 2007). From 2004 to 2006, approximately 1.5% of veterans 18 or older (395,000 veterans) had co-occurring substance use disorder and serious psychological distress (SAMHSA, 2007). The youngest veterans had the highest rate (8.4%) followed by veterans with family incomes less than $20,000 a year (4.1%). Some veterans of past wars are among the homeless persons who congregate on city streets. According to Veterans Administration (VA) studies, 76% of homeless veterans experienced alcohol, drug, or mental disorders duringthe past month of the survey (CSAT, 2004). PTSD was associated with an increased rate of substance misuse: About one-third of men and women who report PTSD during their lifetime also report drug or alcohol misuse at some point in their lives. Joanna Herrington, an MSW student from the University of Maryland, reports on her experiences and the different way soldiers deal with combat trauma (Box 9.2).

Box 9.2	A VETERAN'S EXPERIENCE
	Joanna Herrington

I have been on two, 1-year tours to Iraq. During those deployments, I observed the impact of trauma on soldiers and how differently they react. One friend developed post traumatic stress disorder (PTSD) and used his traumatic experience as a learning opportunity. Another friend became addicted to alcohol to cope with the trauma resulting from killing a prisoner who was escaping the compound. Another friend lived next to a girl who committed suicide.

During my first deployment, a group of soldiers drove into the city of Baghdad to buy personal supplies for themselves and other members of the platoon. The squad drove over an IED [improvised explosive device] and was attacked by insurgents from a nearby building. All members received minor injuries, except for the driver who, unfortunately, lost his legs. The driver was automatically sent home to mentally and physically recover in a Texas military hospital. The other individuals involved were not sent home and continued their mission in Iraq. The soldier sent home received prosthetic legs and was diagnosed with PTSD but turned his traumatic experience into a learning opportunity by traveling the U.S. and speaking to people about his experience, having PTSD, and comforting other military personnel who were injured in combat.

That same year another friend shot a prisoner who was escaping. All prisoners were informed daily in Arabic and English that if they escape they will be killed. One night, two detainees were escaping from our temporary holding facility in Iraq. My friend ran after the individuals and killed one of them. Later, another military company found and apprehended the second detainee and escorted him back to our facility. I asked my friend how he felt and he said, "I was fine, but now I'm starting to think about his family. Do you think I am a bad person because I killed someone?"

I told him, "No. All the detainees know the rules; it was their fault. You were doing what you were trained to do." We did not have any mental health personnel in our area, but he was given the opportunity to speak with the chaplain. My unit was deployed at the beginning of the war and there were not many mental

An Israeli psychiatrist with extensive relevant experience recommended immediate intervention with a cognitive-behavioral therapy (CBT) and serotonin enhancing drugs. Serotonin enhancing drugs and even tranquilizers (or alcohol) are likely to offset the formation of traumatic memories because they dull the senses and reduce the flow of adrenaline associated with the imprinting of memories. People in Manhattan who experienced the horrors of 9/11 and who were taking psychotropic medications, for example, seemed to cope better in the wake of the attack (Jackson, 2003).

A social work graduate student shared her experience as the third wife of a Vietnam veteran who has a severe case of PTSD. In her words:

C's drinking was once so bad that his daughter had to go into foster care. My husband was on the front lines in Vietnam; he saw the people he killed eye to health professionals available. However, there were chaplains to help individuals cope with difficult experiences. After a few days off and speaking to a chaplain, my friend stayed and finished his mission in Iraq.

When he returned home, he developed an addiction to alcohol, which caused him to struggle with his civilian and military jobs. His drinking affected his relationship with his girlfriend and his son. After a few months home, he entered rehabilitation at a Veterans Affairs hospital to conquer his addiction so he could have a healthy relationship with his 2-year-old son. His son was an inspiration to overcome his desire to drink. Fortunately, the treatment was successful and he is now a good father to his son.

The stories mentioned in the above paragraphs were events that happened in my first trip to Iraq. Only one traumatic event happened in my second tour. A friend woke up to a loud bang and thought we were being attacked. She ran to the hallway and saw a screaming girl with blood on her clothes. The girl's roommate had committed suicide. Three individuals from my platoon lived in the room next door. Even though they did not witness the suicide, it still affected them. She told me that she kept seeing the dead girl in the hallways and had trouble sleeping. Every time she heard a door slam, she thought about the suicide.

My friend spoke with me and other friends but never sought mental health treatment because she believed it was not necessary. She also believed that she would be able to deal with the experience once our company returned home from Iraq. After she filled out an electronic health assessment questionnaire, which was required of all military personnel coming home from a combat zone, the computer suggested [that she] speak with a psychologist when she returned home. However, professional mental health counseling was never sought. A few months later, her symptoms such as trouble sleeping and flashbacks seemed to be diminishing. She coped with the traumatic experience by removing herself from the area where the event occurred.

Every individual reacted to his or her traumatic experience differently. One turned his experience into a motivational story for other veterans. Another used alcohol to cope with the trauma, but overcame his addiction so he could be a better father. Another felt the best treatment for her was returning home to friends and family. Whether it was the removal, the inspiration from a loved one, or using the trauma as a helping tool for others, all of these soldiers survived and are now leading healthy lives.

---

eye. C is 100% disabled with PTSD. He keeps reliving a mission in which he didn't bring his men back. When certain anniversary dates come, he binges and can't stop. It affects the children because out of the blue, Dad's gone crazy again.

C's sleep disturbances are so bad he leaves the TV running for distraction. And then there's his hyperalertness—you do not want to approach him straight on. In a restaurant, his back is to the wall. C has flashbacks, is not present for 3 hours, thinks he is in Vietnam; he almost beat me with a pole. Watching news reports of war on TV or visiting a military base brings it all back ...

The VA sent out a document of the effects of war trauma. The government is working on this, not like it was during the war in Vietnam. The VA is using Ecstasy to bring down the distrust level. C has gone through the PTSD unit at the VA and has been in and out of the hospital. (personal communication, November 2005)

One can see from this wife's description that PTSD isn't just a problem of the individual; like addiction, it affects the whole family. Also, just as the Vietnam veteran's wife reported, the war in Iraq, with the guerrilla warfare, explosions, and feeling that the enemy is everywhere, is a trigger for flashbacks of horrors experienced long ago by many Vietnam veterans. Figures from the VA show a 36% rise since 2003 in the number of Vietnam veterans seeking help for trauma (St. George, 2006). Women of all wars are seeking help due to their exposure to high-risk situations in the danger zones. Other women are seeking counseling for sexual assault, a growing problem for women in the military (Streisand, 2006). The best place for all veterans of either sex to get the help they need is at the local Veteran Centers, which operate without the delays and bureaucratic restrictions of VA. The centers are small and staffed by veterans who help with practical matters concerning veterans as well as deeper issues.

Trauma From Natural Disasters

National disasters, such as Hurricanes Katrina and Rita in 2006, are examples of extremely traumatic events that can elicit PTSD, increased substance use, or

---

Box 9.3	TRAUMA AND RESILIENCE POST-KATRINA AND RITA
	Diane Rae Davis

The car full of Red Cross volunteers driving into New Orleans a few weeks after Katrina became silent when we crossed the only bridge passable to get into the city. Silence, then soft murmurs of disbelief, then tears. We experienced block after block of no people, no dogs or cats, no noise at all. Only an upside-down world of mud, and cars where they shouldn't be, and broken houses, signs, and telephone poles. Being there helped make sense of what people from Louisiana were telling us when they made it to the Red Cross service center in Mississippi, where we had been volunteering as mental health professionals for the past week.

In Mississippi, Rita, or the "hidden hurricane," directly impacted many of the families we saw from the surrounding region. One of the many unreported results of this hurricane was the lack of electricity for 2 to 3 weeks. In rural Mississippi in 100-degree weather, this means one thing: The freezer thawed out. Food that had been carefully and thriftily "laid by" for the winter was spoiled. In the rural poverty that exists in Mississippi, this was disaster, and the Red Cross, FEMA [Federal Emergency Management Agency], and public assistance such as food stamps were not prepared to deal with it. More obvious traumas, such as houses blown away, made whole counties "eligible" for the aid of these formal support systems.

As mental health workers, we worked with immediate problems one might expect in such circumstances, such as panic, depression, and anxiety, with the disaster victims and sometimes the Red Cross volunteers. What was unexpected for me were the stories that revealed incredible strength and resilience in the midst of tragedy. Some people talked about camping out with their family near their devastated house, reading stories to the kids by candlelight, and becoming close as a other mental health problems. People who are displaced from their homes as a result of a natural disaster are especially vulnerable. The National Survey on Drug Use and Health (SAMHSA, 2008) compared mental health and substance use indicators from the year before Katrina and Rita to the year after. Adults aged 18 or older who were displaced from their homes for *2 or more weeks* following the hurricanes had higher past month rates of illicit drug use, marijuana use, and cigarette use and higher past year rates of serious psychological distress, major depressive episode, and unmet need for mental health treatment or counseling in 2006 than those who were not displaced in the affected areas. However, for people who were not displaced from their homes, the rate of past month marijuana use actually went down, and there were no significant differences in illicit drug use, cigarette use, serious psychological distress, or major depressive episodes between the year after and the year before the hurricanes.

Some speculate that even in disasters like this, there is the phenomenon of "post-traumatic growth" that supports a strengths perspective (see Box 9.3).

family in ways that normal modern life did not foster. One woman told me, "I know how to survive this 'cause I grew up poor." Another explained how, while her husband went to find help, she spent one whole day under a bridge up to her knees in water, holding her infant granddaughter, to keep the baby cool enough in the hot, humid weather to survive.

An extraordinary study, funded by NIMH after Katrina and Rita, attests to the phenomenon of "post-traumatic personal growth" that has been noticed in other disasters (Kessler, Galea, Jones, & Parker, 2006). Over a period of years, the study will track the mental health needs of the 1,034 members of the Hurricane Katrina Community Advisory Group, a sample of people who lived in Alabama, Mississippi, and Louisiana who were directly affected by Katrina. The results of the first baseline survey revealed serious mental health problems among 11.3% of respondents compared with 6.1% in a similar sample before the hurricane. Mild to moderate mental illness also nearly doubled, from 9.7 to 19.9%.

However, according to the authors of the study, there are more sides to trauma than just the negative mental health consequences. Instead of an expected suicide increase, they found that thoughts of suicide among people with mental health problems actually decreased. They also found that 88.5% of respondents said that "Their experience with the hurricane helped them develop a deeper sense of meaning or purpose in life" (Kessler et al., 2006, p. 19). The vast majority of respondents (including persons with mental health problems) also said their experiences made them more spiritual or religious. They were highly optimistic about their ability to rebuild their lives, and the hurricane helped them discover inner strengths they did not know they had.

Although the authors of the study (and this author) caution that these resilient qualities may be temporary, and that the survey will hold more weight over time, the initial results do attest to the assumption held throughout this text. Even in the most dire circumstances, it is possible to find a ray of hope.

PATHOLOGICAL (COMPULSIVE) GAMBLING

A clinical diagnosis of pathological gambling is defined in the *DSM–IV–TR* when a person meets five or more of the following criteria: preoccupation with gambling, a need to gamble with increasing amounts of money, making repeated efforts to quit, gambling from stress, lying to conceal activities, and borrowing money to pay debts (APA, 2000). In the newer version (*DSM-5*), pathological gambling will be listed under Behavioral Addictions (see Chapter 1).

CSAT (2005) estimates that the rate of problem gambling among people with substance use disorders is four to five times the rate found in the general population. In an analysis of the 2000–2001 National Epidemiological Study on Alcohol and Related Conditions, Petry, Stinson, and Grant (2005) found that almost three-quarters (73.2%) of pathological gamblers had an alcohol use disorder, 38.1% had a drug use disorder, 60.4% had nicotine dependence, 49.6% had a mood disorder, 41.3% had an anxiety disorder, and 60.8% had a personality disorder. A large majority of the associations between pathological gambling and substance use, mood, anxiety, and personality disorders were overwhelmingly positive and significant ($p < .05$), even after controlling for sociodemographic and socioeconomic characteristics.

Attempted suicide and suicide may be real threats. A study of 114 consecutively admitted patients to a gambling program for veterans found that 40% had made a suicide attempt at some point in their lives. Of these suicide attempters, 73% had a history of substance misuse, but so did 62% of the others. Impulsivity was correlated with suicide risk in these gamblers (Kausch, 2003). According to the National Council on Problem Gambling, the suicide rate for pathological gamblers is higher than for any other addictive disorder (National Gambling Impact Study Commission, 1999).

EATING DISORDERS

Eating disorders are described in the *DSM–IV–TR* as severe disturbances in eating behavior. This category includes anorexia (refusal to maintain a minimally normal body weight) and bulimia (repeated episodes of binge eating followed by compensatory behaviors such as self-induced vomiting, misuse of laxatives, and excessive exercise) (APA, 2000). Stimulant use is widespread to help control weight. Although estimates vary widely, persons with bulimia have more prevalence of substance abuse (between 3 and 49%) than persons with anorexia nervosa (not much different from women in the general population). One study of an inpatient treatment center found that 15% of the women and 1% of the men had an eating disorder (CSAT, 2005). Treatment centers report eating binges and starvation as relapse triggers. Food is also a powerful mood-altering substance on its own and is sometimes used (by bingeing or starving) to enhance the euphoric effect of drugs (see Chapter 6).

Mood Disorders

Mood disorders, which include major depression, dysthymia, mania, hypomania, bipolar disorders, and cyclothymia, are basically abnormal (pathological) highs and lows in mood (APA, 2000). Since all psychoactive substances affect mood, it is not surprising that mood disorders, along with anxiety, are the most common psychiatric diagnoses for persons with an AOD disorder. Among persons with a coexisting AOD disorder, women, Native Americans, patients with HIV, patients on methadone, and the elderly are all at higher risk for depression. Manic symptoms can be induced by a variety of substances, such as stimulants, steroids, and hallucinogens, and can also occur during withdrawal from alcohol. Depressive symptoms can result from acute or chronic drug use and can also be triggered by withdrawal. It is critical to assess whether the person is at imminent risk for suicide or a danger to themselves or others. Symptoms that persist after 30 days of abstinence or 30 days after acute intoxication should be assessed for an independent coexisting mood disorder that might mildly to severely interfere with the recovery process (CSAT, 2005).

Bipolar disorder (formerly called manic-depressive disorder) is characterized by episodes of mania and depression. The mania is extreme; the person is highly talkative and evidences a flight of ideas and engagement in activities that are highly pleasurable, such as spending sprees (CSAT, 2005). The depression is extreme at the other end of the spectrum. In a study of a prison population, 90% of persons diagnosed with bipolar disorder also had substance-related problems. Some persons with this disorder use cocaine to lengthen the euphoric mood state or alcohol to help subdue the mania.

Personality Disorders

Personality disorders—such as borderline, dependent, antisocial, or narcissistic personality and passive-aggressive and obsessive-compulsive—are described in the *DSM–IV–TR* as rigid, maladaptive patterns of deeply ingrained behaviors and thoughts that deviate markedly from the expectations of the individual's culture, are pervasive, and cause great personal distress (APA, 2000). Unfortunately, the diagnosis of a personality disorder has too often been the result of cultural, ethnic, or personal bias. For example, women are most often diagnosed with dependent, histrionic, or borderline personality disorders, and men are most often diagnosed with antisocial personality disorders. The diagnostic criteria for personality disorder is expected to change in the next revision of the *DSM* because of lack of clarity among categories and a concern about what distinguishes normal behavior from pathological behavior (CSAT, 2005). Many persons with AOD disorders do not meet the criteria for antisocial personality once they become abstinent; the "antisocial" behaviors were part of their strategy for maintaining addiction. CSAT (1994) says that it is helpful to conceptualize personality disorder behaviors as "survivor behaviors" because they have helped the person survive serious difficulties. Suicidal behavior or threats of other self-harm must be taken seriously and attended to promptly. Counseling strategies for personality disorders often involve working with (not against) the person to reach his or her own stated goals (provided they are legal) in small, concrete, measurable steps.

THOUGHT DISORDERS

Persons who suffer from thought disorders (e.g., schizophrenia and schizoaffective and delusional disorders) typically experience periods when they cannot distinguish between information from the outside world and information from the inner world of the mind. Almost half of the people who have met criteria for schizophrenia or schizophreniform disorder have also met criteria for an alcohol/drug use disorder (Grant et al., 2005). There can be some confusion over the term *psychotic*, which historically was used in a vague sense to denote mental illness (CSAT, 2005). The narrowest definition of psychotic as used today is restricted to delusions or prominent hallucinations, with the hallucinations occurring in the absence of insight into their pathological nature. A slightly less restrictive definition also would include prominent hallucinations that the individual realizes are hallucinatory experiences. Broader still is a definition that includes other positive symptoms of schizophrenia (i.e., disorganized speech or grossly disorganized or catatonic behavior). The most commonly diagnosed psychosis is *schizophrenia*. About 1% of people develop schizophrenia during their lifetime; it usually develops between the ages of 16 and 30 (Mueser et al., 2003). According to the American Psychiatric Association (2000), to be diagnosed with schizophrenia, a person must experience a decrease in social functioning for at least 6 months and experience two or more of the following symptoms for at least 1 month: delusions, hallucinations, disorganized speech, or grossly disorganized or catatonic behavior. *Paranoid schizophrenia* is a subtype in which the person experiences delusions that he or she is being attacked or about to be attacked. Nobel Prize–winning economist John Nash today is in remission from this form of schizophrenia; his life was portrayed in the award-winning 2001 film *A Beautiful Mind*, directed by Ron Howard and starring Russell Crowe.

Negative symptoms associated with schizophrenia are flattened affect, apathy and low motivation, loss of pleasure, and limited content of speech. This psychosis may cause problems in concentration or in one's ability to relate to or tolerate others. Drug and alcohol use and misuse are likely. For example, the Epidemiologic Catchment Area study reports a lifetime substance misuse in the general population of 17% compared with 48% for persons with schizophrenia. Amphetamines are commonly used as well (CSAT, 2005). As noted earlier, treatment of persons with coexisting disorders requires a highly supportive, long-term commitment and integration of both substance abuse and mental health treatment strategies.

A CONCEPTUAL FRAMEWORK:
THE QUADRANT MODEL

The quadrant model is a way of conceptualizing the variations of co-occurring disorders in order to match treatment to their different needs (McGovern, Clark, & Samnaliev, 2007; CSAT 2005) (Figure 9.2).

In this conceptualization, the categories are divided into severity levels of each disorder:

1. Quadrant 1 is reserved for people who have a low severity of both substance abuse and mental disorders. Because of the low severity of problems, they can be treated in nonspecialist settings, such as a primary healthcare setting, with an emphasis on prevention.
2. Quadrant 2 is comprised of persons with high severity of mental health problems and a low severity of substance abuse problems. These persons would typically be treated in mental health facilities, with the collaboration and consultation of substance abuse professionals, or where service teams are blended into a single team.

Treatment for Patients with Co-occurring Disorders (COD)
Quadrants of Care Model

FIGURE 9.2   TREATMENT FOR PATIENTS WITH CO-OCCURRING DISORDERS (COD) QUADRANTS OF CARE MODEL

Source: Center for Substance Abuse Treatment. Identifying and Helping Patients with Co-Occurring Substance Use and Mental Disorders: A Guide for Primary Care Providers. *Substance Abuse in Brief Fact Sheet*, Fall 2006, Volume 4, Issue 2.

3. Quadrant 3 is reserved for the opposite combination: high severity of substance abuse problems and a low severity of mental health problems. Consequently, these people would typically be treated in substance abuse programs, with the collaboration and consultation of mental health providers, or where services teams are blended into a single team.

4. Quadrant 4 people have both severe substance use and severe mental health problems. These are the people who have historically been bounced between mental health providers, substance abuse providers, jails, and emergency rooms. To correct these historical injustices and failures, an integrated service model has been designed and is now being implemented.

INTEGRATED TREATMENT PRACTICES

One of the most important system changes for a person needing help with coexisting disorders is the development of the integrated treatment program, now the preferred model of the Substance Abuse and Mental Health Services Administration (CSAT, 2005). After 30 years of development and research, integrated treatment has become an evidence-based practice that helps clients acquire skills and supports to manage both illnesses and pursue a better life for themselves (Horsefall, Cleary, Hunt, & Walter, 2009).

Integrated treatment (in contrast to sequential or parallel treatment) provides simultaneous treatment for the mental illness and the substance use disorder. The person no longer has to travel to two different locations to receive and try to reconcile two different messages. Although this may sound like mere common sense from today's vantage point, it required (and still requires in many parts of the country) massive system changes to become a treatment option. This section focuses on integrated treatment programs, but traditional treatment (parallel and sequential) programs can benefit from many aspects of the model as complementary to their programs. In a review of services for persons with co-occurring disorders, Horsefall and colleagues (2009) conclude that regardless of whether services follow integrated or parallel models, they should be well coordinated, take a team approach, be multidisciplinary, have specialist-trained personnel (including 24-hour access), include a range of program types, and provide for long-term follow-up. Many traditional treatment programs are already moving in that direction, becoming less confrontational, more collaborative with other helping systems, and more likely to use treatment stages—all hallmarks of an integrated approach. Other developments, such as the mental health "consumer" movement that underscores the rights of the individual patient (Minkoff, 1996), the adaptation of some self-help groups to clients with co-occurring disorders, and pharmacological advances with fewer side effects, have supported treatment innovation. The emergence of treatment populations with high rates of co-occurring disorders (e.g., people who are homeless, imprisoned, or have HIV/AIDS or PTSD) have also led to new models of service delivery. Additional impetus has come from the parallel development in healthcare reform of the principle "no wrong door"—that is, substance abuse treatment, mental health, and physical health systems have a "responsibility to address the range of client needs wherever and whenever a client presents for care" (CSAT, 2005, p. 12).

Integrated treatment for co-occurring disorders is based on seven practice principles (SAMHSA, 2009):

1. Mental health and substance abuse treatment are integrated to meet the needs of people with co-occurring disorders.
2. Integrated treatment specialists are trained to treat both substance use disorders and serious mental illnesses.
3. Co-occurring disorders are treated in a stage-wise fashion with different services provided at different stages.
4. Motivational interventions are used to treat consumers in all stages, but especially in the "persuasion" stage.
5. Substance abuse counseling, using a cognitive-behavioral approach, is used to treat consumers in the active treatment and relapse prevention stages.
6. Multiple formats for services are available, including individual, group, self-help, and family.
7. Medication services are integrated and coordinated with psychosocial services.

One of the most unique aspects of integrative treatment is that all of these services are available for the lifetime of the consumer. Staying connected to the integrated program is a goal in and of itself. In this respect the integrative treatment system models the care given to any person with a chronic disease (Miller et al., 2011). CSAT (2005) classifies integrated treatment into four levels: (1) basic, which includes treatment for one disorder, screening and consultation for the other; (2) intermediate, which includes treatment for one disorder, but addresses some of the needs of the other, such as continuing psychiatric medication; (3) advanced, which includes providing services for both disorders; and (4) fully integrated, which actively combines treatment for the whole person, including related problems, with fully integrated staff, funding, and policies and procedures. At the crux of a fully integrated treatment program is the designation of one clinician (supported by a treatment team that may include professionals such as physicians, probation officers, AOD and mental health specialists, self-help sponsors, and housing specialists) to provide a seamless and individualized menu of interventions for a specific person over a long period of time. This shift alone requires providers to:

- Acknowledge that their profession doesn't have all the answers.
- Find a home for the integrated program (outpatient mental health programs, separate hospital units, community agencies).
- Change admission criteria to include persons with co-occurring disorders and implement serious cross-training of professional staff.
- Change the target population of the agency.
- Sort out funding streams, state regulations, and legal requirements.
- Create new procedures for confidentiality, data collection, and reimbursement.

- Participate with other providers in developing long-term structural mechanisms (coordinating bodies, letters of agreement, etc.) and planning that will improve the delivery of seamless services to persons with co-occurring disorders.

A new KIT (Knowledge Informing Transformation) series from SAMSHA (2009) tackles the formidable job of retraining frontline staff and helping mental health and substance abuse administrators and program leaders think through and develop the structure of integrated treatment in the community. The KIT series for Integrated Treatment for Co-occurring Disorders can be downloaded or ordered at http://www.samhsa.gov/shin.

Is the transition from separate to integrated treatment worth the effort? Research indicates it is. Mueser, Drake, and Noordsy (1998), for example, found that as the result of integrated treatment practices, stable remission rates went from 5% per year under the traditional system to 10–20% per year. Although this may still seem low, it comes close to the same rate as persons with only substance use disorders. There are also other positive improvements associated with integrated treatment, such as more and better housing, decreased victimization, more satisfaction with life, decreased shame, open expression, and increased socialization, learning, and insight (Drake, Yovetich, Bebout, Harris, & McHugo, 1997; Mueser, Drake, & Noordsy, 1998; Sciacca & Thompson, 1996). Research summarized by Mueser and colleagues (2003) reveals the comprehensive, motivation-based, long-term integrated treatment programs resulted in significantly better substance-related outcomes than those of standard, nonintegrated care. In a review of services for persons with COD, Horesfall and colleagues (2009) conclude the results of the integrative model are encouraging but note that the studies are hampered by small, heterogeneous samples, high attrition rates, short follow-up periods, and unclear description of treatment components. Although it is clear that more controlled studies are needed, SAMHSA (2009) supports integrative treatment as an evidence-based practice that is associated with improvement in psychiatric symptoms and function, decreased hospitalization, increased housing stability, few arrests, and improved quality of life.

STAGE-WISE TREATMENT

There are two important assumptions that set integrated treatment apart from historical mental health and substance abuse treatment in the United States. One major premise is that persons with coexisting disorders are capable of making decisions and taking actions that will help them achieve their goals. A second premise is that "motivation for abstinence must reside *in the patient*, not in the clinician or family" (Mueser, Drake, & Noordsy, 1998, p. 135). Together, these assumptions point the way to a variety of assessment and intervention practices that view persons with coexisting disorders through strengths perspective glasses.

Stage-wise treatment is a successful strategy that is built on the premise that people go through (and continue to recycle through) stages of change. The utility of stage-wise treatment was first demonstrated in the evaluation of the 13 Community Support Program federal demonstration projects between 1987 and 1991 (Mercer-McFadden et al., 1997). Intervention strategies are offered to consumers and geared to whatever stage the person is in. Stages can be determined by finding out how much persons with coexisting disorders are aware of the negative consequences of the substance misuse to them, their motivation to change their substance use, and their goals for living and/or treatment. The model developed by Osher and Kofoed (1989), based on Prochaska and DiClemente's cycle of change (1992) and used in many integrated treatment models, divides the stages into four parts (SAMHSA, 2009):

1. *Engagement*, where there is little or no insight into the consequences of the substance misuse, no plan to change the pattern of use, and no regular contact with treatment staff
2. *Persuasion*, where there is still no motivation to change the substance use but where regular contact is occurring with a case manager or treatment staff, practical assistance and support are accepted, and psychiatric symptoms are stabilizing
3. *Active treatment*, where the person has identified how substance misuse interferes with personal goals, is attempting to reduce or stop use, and is willing to pursue treatment strategies (e.g., self-help and psychoeducational groups, counseling, family therapy, and education) to achieve goals
4. *Relapse prevention*, where the person has been abstinent or has not experienced any negative consequences from substance use for at least 6 months and is willing to work on sustaining a meaningful recovery in all areas of life

As we discuss each stage in more detail, it will be helpful to refer to Box 9.4, Sheryl's Story, as an illustration of the different stages of treatment.

Box 9.4	CASE STUDY: SHERYL'S STORY

Sheryl is a 20-year-old woman with a diagnosis of schizophrenia. Her first contact with the mental health center was through a community outreach worker. Someone from the local shelter had called the mental health center because the staff there was concerned about Sheryl's behavior. She often stayed up half the night yelling back at voices that she said called her names. Even more worrisome, she often spent nights on the street prostituting for cocaine.

The outreach worker met Sheryl in the shelter. She was suspicious, fidgety, distracted, and had difficulty talking coherently. The only goal she could think of was to get her own apartment. The outreach worker said that that was something they could work on and asked Sheryl to come to the mental health center to meet with a psychiatrist. Sheryl refused to come to the mental health center, but she did agree to meet with the outreach worker again. The next day

(continued)

| BOX 9.4 | CASE STUDY: SHERYL'S STORY (*continued*) |

the outreach worker picked Sheryl up and took her out for a cup of coffee and a sandwich. Sheryl reported feeling that she had no one to help her, that she was totally alone. She was angry with her mother, who had hit her and kicked her out when she was 16. Her father refused to talk with her. She did not know where her siblings were. She said she could not trust anyone. The outreach worker began to meet with Sheryl each morning before she left the shelter and gradually introduced her to other treatment team members. An integrated treatment specialist met daily with Sheryl at the shelter, the soup kitchen, or the local coffee shop. Sheryl continued to insist that an apartment was her only goal. After 2 months, the treatment team agreed to help her find an apartment if she would meet with the psychiatrist. The psychiatrist diagnosed Sheryl with schizophrenia, alcohol dependence, and cocaine dependence. He prescribed an antipsychotic medication. The outreach worker brought medications to Sheryl, and she agreed to take them knowing that the treatment team would help her get money and an apartment. Sheryl began to receive Supplemental Security Income benefits and with help from the treatment team, Sheryl got an apartment. Within days, however, it became clear that Sheryl was prostituting and selling drugs in the apartment, and her landlord soon evicted her. When Sheryl landed back in the shelter, the treatment team offered again to help. Sheryl admitted that she had not been taking the medications, and she rejected suggestions about a payee and a group home. She wanted to control her money and to get another apartment. For several weeks, Sheryl's behavior worsened with increasing paranoia, less predictable appearances in the shelter, and more frequent signs of physical abuse. At this point, she was arrested for breaking into her mother's home, stealing money, and assaulting her mother. Because of her psychotic appearance and behavior, she was diverted to a local psychiatric hospital. Treatment team members visited her regularly and worked with the hospital staff. As Sheryl took medications, got rest, and had a few weeks away from cocaine, she became clearer and more personable than the team had ever seen her. She expressed regrets about her life of addiction, prostitution, and victimization. The integrated treatment specialist helped her select a self-help group for women with co-occurring disorders and another group for women with sexual abuse histories; she began to share her fears and anxieties with others. In anticipation of discharge, she agreed to allow the treatment team to become her payee and to live in a supervised apartment. She expressed a strong interest in continuing with the groups.

Having been through the engagement process with several co-occurring disorder consumers such as Sheryl, her integrated treatment specialist knew that she would probably continue to have crises and relapses. But she also knew that she was developing a trusting relationship with her that would encourage Sheryl to continue in treatment and pursue her personal recovery goals.

Source: SAMHSA, 2009.

ENGAGEMENT STAGE

Engagement may be a long-term process in stage-wise treatment. Because persons with coexisting disorders often present with disorganization, confusion, and a past history of unhelpful professional contacts and may live in an environment oppressed by poverty, violence, and ongoing substance misuse, it is understandably difficult for them to engage and remain active in a treatment process. Research on integrated treatment suggests it can be done. In fact, most persons with COD can be engaged in treatment for extended periods of time (beyond a year) (Mueser, Drake, & Noordsy, 1998). New ideas about stages of treatment and the role of the clinician in the engagement process have been critical in making this possible.

The precontemplation stage (when a person does not even recognize the need to change) roughly translates to what is called the engagement phase of integrated treatment. The goal of engagement from a clinician's standpoint is to develop a therapeutic alliance with the person that is built on trust, not to attend to substance misuse. Without a trusting relationship, it is difficult to further any change in behavior other than temporary compliance. The engagement process often requires the following attributes (SAMHSA, 2009): time, patience, an accepting attitude, a persistent approach, and being available when an opportunity appears.

Creative strategies for promoting engagement typically involve outreach, some kind of concrete practical assistance, crisis intervention services, support in building a wider arena of social networks, and efforts to stabilize the psychiatric symptoms (SAMHSA, 2009; Mueser et al., 2003).

Other examples of engagement strategies used in integrated treatment programs include:

- Introducing informal drop-in informational groups at the medication clinic to parallel the lack of structure in actively drug using clients (Handmaker et al., 2002).
- Being available in an area populated by people who are homeless and meeting with them at a local diner, not a clinic; spending months saying hello on the sidewalk outside a drop-in center; offering help for basic needs such as clothes, showers, and food; asking permission to sit with them as they wait to see the doctor to have an abscess treated (Little & Fanskoviak, 2010).
- Helping people learn how to shop, clean apartments, and do laundry (Mueser et al., 2003).
- Providing nonverbal stress management training, such as basic yoga, progressive relaxation techniques, and gentle movement exercises (Brady et al., 1996).
- Providing safety, such as involuntary hospitalization, when a person becomes acutely ill, actively suicidal, or dangerously psychotic (SAMHSA, 2005).
- Assisting homeless persons with non–abstinence-based supportive housing (van Wormer & van Wormer, 2009).

In what ways does the integrated treatment specialist engage Sheryl (Box 9.4)?

PERSUASION STAGE

In the persuasion stage, the consumer has established regular contact with an integrated treatment specialist but may continue to use the same amount of substances, or has reduced substance use for less than 1 month. The persuasion stage may be the most challenging for clinicians trained in traditional substance abuse or mental health practices. As described by Denning (2004), this is when dominant stereotypes, assumptions (e.g., that addicts routinely lie and deny their problems), and expectations about who is in control may enter the potential therapeutic relationship. "The client expects to be controlled and does not want to be, and the therapist expects the client to want to be helped, to be willing to be controlled in some subtle way. When we view an addict as being a problem, or not motivated, or in denial, we are often speaking of this conflict of expectations" (p. 108). Clients are also likely to have their own expectations that they are mistrusted, even scary to the clinician, and feel protective about disclosing anything that might bring on negative consequences.

To break through these barriers, clinicians need to give up the illusion that they are in control. It is critical to rid ourselves of the idea that people with coexisting disorders will change their habits of drug or alcohol use just because it might be "good for them," *even if this is obvious to the clinician and the family*. When a clinician can embrace the fact that, like it or not, motivation for abstinence or cutting down use resides in the consumer, strategies for increasing motivation to formulate goals around substance use can begin. A practical suggestion from Denning (2004) for the beginning stages is to affirm clearly with clients that they have the right to live their own life and that your job as a therapist is to help them find their own goals and make decisions on how to reach them. Then expect to be tested on this assertion.

During the persuasion state, it is not the goal of clinicians to persuade the client to be abstinent, take antipsychotic medication, get into stable housing, reframe their point of view, or attempt to persuade them of anything else (SAMSHA, 2009). The *persuasion* part has to do with opening up opportunities for the consumer to think about their own life goals and whether substance use or mental health symptoms deter them in achieving these goals. Helpful strategies for counselors include expressing empathy, reflective listening, asking exploratory questions about experiences and goals, educating consumers about substance use and mental illness, rolling with resistance, avoiding argumentation, and developing discrepancy between future goals and present behavior. These are the familiar techniques most exemplified by the Motivational Interviewing approach discussed in the preceding chapter (Miller et al., 2011).

For example, at the point where Sheryl had been hospitalized for a few weeks and free of cocaine (See Box 9.4), a decisional balance exercise might be helpful. In this exercise, Sheryl would be asked to identify the "good" things in her life, and the "not so good" things. Some of the good things might include her clearheadness and newfound ability to weigh her options. Some of the "not so good things" might include her loneliness and fear about the future and where she might live. In the course of this exercise, the role that cocaine has played in Sheryl's goal attainment becomes a natural part of the discussion. This exercise lends itself to the consumer setting goals that are meaningful to them, such as attending supportive groups or finding supportive housing.

Motivational interviewing is a particularly helpful strengths-based practice when consumers have not yet accepted that there may be a relationship between the misery they experience and their use of alcohol or drugs (Carey, 1996; Mueser, Drake, & Noordsy, 1998; Sciacca & Thompson, 1996). By helping clients to clarify goals and decide how their substance use interferes with their goals, it is possible to consistently address the important question that all of us ask at decision points: "What's in it for me?"

Goals that may be meaningful for persons with coexisting disorders include getting or holding a job, finding housing, surviving or improving health, avoiding AIDS or death, getting admitted to detox for room and board when hungry or homeless, allowing medications to work, stopping the consequences of AOD use (e.g., increased anxiety, child protective service involvement), and placating family or significant others. The fact that many of these goals result from the consequences of alcohol or drug use is not relevant in the beginning stages. The therapeutic goal is to establish an environment of trust and to provide concrete assistance, not judgment.

Motivational interviewing can also be used effectively in a brief session prior to psychiatric hospital discharge to enhance outpatient treatment entry into a dual diagnosis program. Daley and Zuckoff (1998) report using the MI principles of (1) accepting clients' ambivalence toward change as normal; (2) avoiding confrontation; (3) identifying current needs, wishes, and goals; (4) exploring the risks associated with continued substance use and the probable impact on these goals of offering a menu of change options that may help clients; (5) supporting clients' self-efficacy that positive change can occur; and (6) inviting clients to consider the benefits of keeping their outpatient appointment as a first step. This process contrasts with the more usual directive to follow through with the outpatient appointment. As a result, the initial outpatient show rate almost doubled, from 35 to 67%, for the clients who received a brief MI session.

In a rare ethnographic study of substance abuse among persons with severe mental illness, Alverson, Alverson, and Drake (2000) found that attaining four "positive quality-of-life factors" actually preceded and predicted sobriety among the people in the study. Furthermore, reduction of the factors preceded rather than followed a relapse into substance abuse. These important factors are similar to those for any persons recovering from substance abuse: a meaningful activity (job, hobby, social network), decent and stable housing, a meaningful relationship with someone who accepts them, and a positive, regular relationship with a mental health professional. The fact that, for the clients in this study, achieving these factors came before sobriety underscores the importance of focusing on the needs identified by the client, even when these needs do not include abstinence.

In addition to Motivational Interviewing, other helpful supports for the persuasion stage include support groups (drop-in, women's groups, veteran's groups, self-help groups), basic social skills training, vocational supports, and housing supports. There is some evidence that attending a "dual-diagnosis group" correlates with a favorable outcome, especially when combined with intensive case management (Kelly & Yeterian, 2008; Klein, Cnaan, & White-craft, 1998), but no particular type of group appears more effective than another (Drake & Mueser, 2000). However, "more is better," according to the findings of Laudet and colleagues (2000), where higher levels of support from a greater number of people were linked to less substance use. One such group, called the Good Chemistry Group, is a combination of therapy, psy-choeducation, and peer support. Members are encouraged to have "natural highs" and "good chemistry" by getting involved in fun and healthy activities that do not require using alcohol or drugs (DiNitto & Webb, 2005). Two other groups that model on the Alcoholics Anonymous Twelve-Step approach are Double-Trouble in Recovery (DTR) and Dual Recovery Anonymous (DRA). These groups are modified from the typical AA format to incorporate the issue of mental illness (Step One reads "we admitted we were powerless over our dual illness of chemical dependency and emotional or psychiatric ill-ness—that our lives had become unmanageable"). Although these groups are not widely available, they are expanding. DRA has 345 groups nationwide; DTR has about 200 (Kelly & Yeterian, 2008).

Mutual-help groups such as Alcoholics Anonymous can provide much needed social support for some persons outside the professional arena. How-ever, research also suggests that many clients with major mental illness, espe-cially schizophrenia, will have difficulties participating in these groups (Noordsy, Schwab, Fox, & Drake, 1996). Members may have trouble under-standing severe mental illness and be uncomfortable with some of the behav-ioral manifestations of the illness. Historically, some AA members have refused to consider psychiatric medication as anything other than "drugs" and have urged people who very much need it to discontinue use. For these reasons, a referral to AA or NA should be accompanied by some help in link-ing them to a receptive group in the community.

Other suggestions for increasing the likelihood of a good experience in AA include (1) waiting to refer until the person is in the active treatment stage and wants abstinence, (2) affirming that the person has the absolute right to choose whether to attend and participate, (3) suggesting that he or she can be a "visitor" for a few meetings to observe and politely "pass" the invitation to read or talk during the meeting, (4) giving them the AA-approved brochure "The AA Member—Medications and Other Drugs" that welcomes persons who are taking psychiatric medications (AA, 1984), and (5) introduc-ing the person to an AA member who will take that person to his or her first meeting (Powell, Kurtz, Garvin, & Hill, 1996). Other helpful preparation can include role-playing social interactions in session to prepare the consumer for meeting attendance, and resolving attendance barriers such as transportation and scheduling (Kelly & Yeterian, 2008).

ACTIVE TREATMENT AND RELAPSE PREVENTION

The active treatment stage occurs when the consumer is engaged in treatment and has reduced or abstained from substance use for 1 to 6 months (SAMHSA, 2009). The primary focus of this stage is to manage substance use cravings and mental illness symptoms. Cognitive behavioral interventions are recommended to help the client identify thoughts, emotions, behaviors, and situations that lead to substance use, and to change these patterns using behavioral techniques.

For example, when Sheryl (Box 9.4) reached the stage of active treatment, she may have been asked how her feelings related to victimization led her to want to use cocaine. She might benefit from creating an ABC chart (antecedent, behavior, consequences) using a cognitive-behavioral approach. In this exercise, she would be asked to keep a journal for a week, write down every time she felt she wanted to use cocaine, what she was thinking and feeling, what behaviors might result, and what might be the possible consequences of deciding to use. This helps to reinforce how substance use worsens her problems and also opens the door to practicing new skills to help her maintain her goals. Sheryl also might learn how to cope with her anxieties better by participating in relaxation and mindfulness training with her integrated treatment counselor or in one of the groups she attends. Behavioral techniques could include learning refusal skills, assertiveness skills, relaxation skills; improving conversation skills; and managing mood problems. An important part of a behavioral approach is learning how to reward oneself for attaining small goals, or in some cases, learning how to have fun for the first time without using.

The use of cognitive-behavioral techniques should be informed by the consumer's experience and developed with consumers. To help someone learn to avoid or cope with internal cues and external situations that lead to substance use or the aggravation of mental health symptoms, the counselor needs to know the specific experiences of the person's life regarding withdrawal, craving, triggers to use or triggers for exaggerated mental health symptoms, expectations of use, and what reinforces use for that person.

The relapse prevention stage is a continuation of learning these skills and practicing sobriety. The formal relapse prevention stage is defined as the point at which the consumer is engaged in treatment and has abstained from substance use for 6 months or more (SAMHSA, 2009). Relapse prevention strategies have a dual focus on substance abuse and mental health problems. Common goals for consumers include avoiding substance use, reducing the impact of relapse from both disorders, returning to work, improving social relationship, and getting more involved in recreational activities (SAMHSA, 2009)) For example, a social skills training group may be developed to emphasize problem solving, communication skills, management of psychiatric symptoms, medication compliance, and relapse prevention. Relapse and slips are handled in a nonjudgmental manner. Group members help bring out the circumstances and results of slips to help the person with a new plan. Group members learn to identify triggers and early warning signs of substance use and psychiatric symptoms and at the same time support hope and self-efficacy with each other. Depending on the membership, the group process may need to be adapted to fit the attention span and communication skills of the group.

ASSERTIVE COMMUNITY TREATMENT (ACT)

Assertive community treatment (ACT) has been recognized as a best practice model by the American Psychological Association for serious mental illness (American Psychological Association for the Advancement of Professional Practice, APA/CAPP, 2007). This approach was first developed in the 1970s in response to deinstitutionalization, when thousands of mentally ill persons were discharged from mental institutions and put out into a world that had very few systems in place to help them. The originators of ACT, Drs. Arnold Marx, Leonard Stein, and Mary Ann Test, looked at the way mental health services were delivered and created a new paradigm of care so that people diagnosed with a serious mental illness could become integral members of the community (SAMHSA, 2008). The ACT approach is now implemented across the United States partially or statewide in 47 states. Consumers of the ACT program are the most seriously mentally ill; are likely to have co-occurring problems with substance abuse, physical illness, or disabilities; are likely to have problems in basic functioning, employment, and maintaining a safe living situation; and have a history of high-service needs, such as repeated psychiatric hospitalizations. The ACT model parallels the integrative treatment approach in that it features:

- Team approach: ACT team members with various professional training and general life skills work closely together.
- Small caseload: Teams of 10–12 serve 100 consumers.
- Time unlimited services.
- Shared caseload: A service team acts as a whole to ensure consumers receive what they need to live in the community; ACT team members do not have individual caseloads.

ACT is different from integrated treatment in three ways: (1) services are provided "in vivo," meaning they are delivered to the person in the community rather than requiring the person to come to an agency or treatment center for treatment; (2) ACT teams are available any time of the day or night to keep crises from turning into hospitalizations; and (3) ACT teams include peer support specialists from the community who have personal successful experiences of recovery (Miller et al., 2011; SAMHSA, 2008b).

The use of an ACT team to deliver integrative services has been found to be particularly effective with people who are diagnosed with antisocial personality disorder (Frisman et al., 2009). Consumers in the ACT approach showed a significantly greater reduction in alcohol use and were less likely to go to jail than those who received standard case management treatment. Long-term outcomes for populations with forensic issues who are working with an ACT program in Arkansas show strong results in preventing criminal recidivism and improving mental health, abstinence, and quality of life (Smith, Jennings, & Cimino, 2010).

CASE MANAGEMENT TEAMS

Case management in the integrated treatment model does not mean that a professional expert or team of experts provides services to a "case." Case management in this approach is closer to the independent living model in disability and the consumer movement in mental health, where it is recognized that consumers have the strength and right to manage their own lives (Mackelprang & Salsgiver, 1999). Consequently, although individual team members may be expert in their respective fields, they have also become experts at collaboration with each other and most important, with the person they are trying to help. The purpose of the collaborative case management approach is to offer a menu of supports, services, and opportunities that are in tune with the person's direction rather than prescribing these services for the case.

The Ohio Substance Abuse and Mental Illness Coordinating Center of Excellence provides an integrated model to address the needs of the whole person in the context of community social supports (Biegel et al., 2003). This model utilizes biopsychosocial treatments and educational intervention in programming and provides training across the state; funding is provided by the Ohio Department of Mental Health. This integrated model requires that team members have a basic awareness of addictions and mental health assessment; training interviewing strategies as well have a solid grounding in the biological aspects of co-occurring disorders.

When faced with a list of the overwhelming needs that can be presented by some clients with COD, professionals may be tempted to "fill up the hole" with referral after referral. Sometimes, coercion is used to require the person to participate in what the case manager has decided is in the client's best interest, such as withholding income or other financial support. These practices reinforce the oppressive notion that a person with coexisting disorders cannot make decisions in his or her own best interest.

A staff member may have intense emotional reactions and disagreements about how to be an effective consultant to the person, particularly when there are a variety of unmet needs in the eyes of the professional. Clinicians who are used to working on an appointment schedule using a specific therapeutic process will find themselves needing to be more flexible in their ways of helping (Denning, 2004). For example, tackling a housing problem is more likely to come before therapy, insight, or abstinence. Staff members need time to readjust and redefine their roles in an integrative treatment team. It takes about 1 year of training to solidify a team (Drake & Mueser, 2000), and it may take several years of work to make the necessary system changes. SAMHSA (2009) recommends that the program leaders of integrative case management teams hold weekly group supervision, using case examples and following evidence-based practice principles and procedures. The good news is that it is demonstratively worth the effort. Persons with coexisting disorders can move from being "no one's clients" to becoming "everyone's clients" (Sciacca & Thompson, 1996) and ideally move from being perceived as a client to being viewed as an individual, citizen, and/or consumer.

Working as an integrated team member requires training as well as patience. Currently, the middle-aged substance abuse workforce is poorly trained to meet the challenge of providing integrative treatment (Darcy, Dalphonse, & Winsor, 2010). Many entered the field because of their own recovery, not specialized training. Even those trained with master's degrees were unlikely to receive anything like the integration of coursework necessary to successfully deliver quality service or administration of integrated treatment. Academia is split between mental health counseling programs and separate chemical dependency programs, and state licensing requirements mirror the academic requirements. The graduate level counseling programs at Rhode Island College are one of the few examples of higher education grappling with the complexities of putting together a program to qualify students to be a Certified Co-occurring Disorder Professional (Darcy, Dalphonse, & Winsor, 2010).

HOMELESSNESS

Clients with co-occurring disorders are vulnerable to housing instability and homelessness, as their illnesses often lead to erratic, agitated behaviors that result in eviction by landlords or family (Mueser et al., 2003). According to SAMHSA's treatment data set, more than 175,000 people admitted to substance abuse treatment in 2004 were homeless at the time; the homeless comprised 13% of all admissions, which is an increase from 10% in 2000. Alcohol was the primary substance of abuse (52%), followed by opiates (21%) and cocaine (17%) (SAMHSA, 2006a). Although it is generally thought that the addiction causes the homelessness, it is more likely the case that the stress caused by homelessness and the availability of alcohol and other drugs on the streets causes people to seek relief in alcohol or drugs.

Traditionally, it has been thought that housing should not be provided until people who are homeless got off the drugs and alcohol. According to Padgett, Gulcur, and Tsemberis (2006), however, longitudinal comparative research shows no significant group differences in substance misuse in participants who received the housing first and then got treatment compared to the reverse arrangement. Another consideration is the question of human rights. Is adequate shelter a need or a basic human right? van Wormer and van Wormer (2009) argue that adopting a human rights framework would eliminate the question of who is worthy of housing and effectively challenge state governments to ensure adequate housing for all persons.

A promising development is the provision of housing under the supported housing model. This model seeks to provide a permanent place to live (as opposed to transitional housing) and intensive case management for persons with co-occurring disorders. Thus, in addition to housing, they get help with budgeting, referral to community services, and medication compliance. Donald Linhorst (2006) describes supported housing as empowering in that the residents have some control over their housing and decisions related to their life in that residence. This includes, according to the harm reduction model, a choice of diet, times to sleep and wake up, and the choice of which substances are used in persons' own homes (Mueser et al., 2003). The Housing First approach is an example of supported housing that offers direct access to housing without sobriety requirements as well as consumer choice about which other supportive services they may want to participate in (Pearson, Montgomery, & Locke, 2009).

Pathways to Housing, Inc., of New York City, perhaps the most well-known of the Housing First approach, is an award-winning program that illustrates the effectiveness of supportive housing. Pathways' focus is on clients that no one else wants; they have been homeless for a long time and have a serious mental health problem, most (75%) have a co-occurring substance use disorder, and they have usually failed in other programs. The program is based on the principles that consumers can make competent choices, housing is a basic right of every human being, and recovery is possible. Housing is offered immediately, regardless of whether a person has "earned" that right by completing substance abuse treatment or any other preconditions. Harm reduction practices include honoring client choices about the services they want to use and helping to support their choices through Assertive Community Treatment (ACT) teams that provide individually tailored case management, psychiatric and medical treatment, counseling, supported employment, self-help groups, help with budgeting, help with obtaining benefits, and classes such as art, photography, and writing (Pathways to Housing, 2005). Research on the program indicates much higher rates of housing stability than standard care programs, and clients can remain stable without increasing their substance use. One longitudinal study of this program found that at the end of 5 years, 88% of the Pathway clients remained housed compared to 47% of clients who were housed through a linear residential treatment approach (Tsemberis & Eisenberg, 2000). Another study found that after 48 months, there were no significant group differences in alcohol and drug use when the Pathways clients were compared to standard care programs (Padgett, Gulcur, & Tsemberis, 2006). A recent study of three Housing First programs (including Pathway) found that of the 80 participants tracked over 12 months, 84% remained enrolled in the program for 1 year, indicating housing stability in the hardest-to-serve chronically homeless population (Pearson, Montgomery, & Locke, 2009).

INTEGRATED PHARMACOTHERAPY

The use of medications for both mental health and substance use disorders is a complex issue because of the interactions between alcohol and drugs and some psychiatric medications and because undermedication for psychiatric symptoms may cause a relapse in substance misuse. Ideally, a physician is part of the treatment team, and medication is integrated and closely moni-tored as part of the total integrated approach. Denning (2004) advises that the entire team have expertise in pharmacology and the potential drug inter-actions that may occur, be prepared to provide references to other clinicians, be willing to examine their own biases around medication for substance misu-sers, and engage in frequent discussions about these issues on behalf of each client. For example, it is important to distinguish psychoactive medications (e.g., opioids, stimulants, benzodiazepines, barbiturates, and other sedative-hypnotics), which can cause rapid changes in mood, thought, and behavior, from nonpsychoactive medications (e.g., lithium, antipsychotics, beta-blockers, antidepressants, monoamine oxidase inhibitors, antihistamines, anticonvulsants, and anticholinergics), which normalize thinking processes. Understanding the use of these medications and their typical side-effects will help clinicians work more effectively with consumers who express ambiva-lence about taking psychiatric medications (Miller et al., 2011).

Specific pharmacotherapies for persons with coexisting disorders are still in the beginning stage, and there is a lack of research, especially controlled studies, to guide clinicians. However, the Center for Substance Abuse Treat-ment (CSAT) (2005) offers these guidelines:

- Acute and severe symptoms that occur with such disorders as mania, psy-chotic depression, and schizophrenia require immediate medication.
- If symptoms are not acute, use a step-wise approach of (1) trying no med-ication for less severe problems, such as anxiety or mild depression; (2) adding nonpsychoactive medication if the symptoms do not lessen after detoxification and psychosocial approaches; and (3) adding psychoactive medications if the symptoms do not abate or if they get worse.

In summary, integrated treatment programs, as developed over the past 30 years, have begun to offer more hope to the person with coexisting disorders. Research affirms that when this type of treatment is provided over several years, clients attain higher rates of stable remission as well as improve their quality of life. The integrated approach embraces many strengths-based practices, such as motivational interviewing, harm reduction, and stages of treatment interven-tions. Multidisciplinary teams with a variety of training and philosophical back-grounds have, over time, been able to put aside their differences and learn new approaches to helping people in this vulnerable situation.

SUBSTANCE MISUSE AND DEVELOPMENTAL, PHYSICAL, AND COGNITIVE DISABILITIES

Substance misuse can stand in the way of a person's adequately dealing with an adjustment to a disability as well as aggravate the disability itself. How-ever, until recently, substance misusers who have coexisting developmental, physical, or cognitive disabilities have been largely ignored in treatment set-tings, research, professional training, and public awareness.

The 1990 Americans with Disabilities Act (ADA) helped changes begin by guaranteeing full participation and access to community services and facilities for all people with disabilities. Treatment programs and mental health centers were put on notice that they must adapt their programs to meet the needs of people with coexisting disabilities. The Department of Justice ADA website at www.ada.gov offers technical assistance, mediation, and current information on all aspects of the act. However, findings from a national study suggest that at least 50% of all persons with a coexisting disability are still not being identified as such by the system that provides them with services (Rehabilitation Research and Training Center on Drugs and Disability, 1995). For example, a condition often overlooked is learning disorders, which has been diagnosed in 40–70% of chemically dependent adolescents (Yu, Buka, Fitzmaurice, & McCormick, 2006).

This section focuses on a wide range of disabilities, excluding the mental disorders already covered. Using the principle of the independent living movement that persons with disabilities share more commonality than differences in their experience of living, we discuss common themes around traditional barriers to treatment, the development of new assessment tools, and new treatment practices relevant to persons with substance misuse and a coexisting disability. Because many people in the able culture still view people with disabilities in terms of what they cannot do or should not attempt to do and because helping agencies continue to reflect that bias, a strengths-based approach to practice is particularly important and will be emphasized. Space requirements limit detailed discussion of individual types of disability; we attempt to compensate by using examples from a range of different disabilities.

PREVALENCE AND CHARACTERISTICS

Estimating the prevalence of substance abuse or dependence among persons who have various types of disabilities is difficult because data is not uniformly collected by federal and state agencies, service providers typically underestimate the occurrence, and consumers may be isolated in their own communities. The substance abuse literature has not focused on disability issues. According to West (2002), less than 12% of the substance abuse literature contains any reference to disabilities. From the data that is available, it is clear that persons with disabilities are at greater risk for substance abuse problems than the general population (Ebener & Smedema, 2011). According to an estimate by the U.S. Department of Health and Human Services (2011), persons with disabilities experience substance abuse rates at two to four times that of the general population. Some prevalence rates are much higher. Substance abuse rates approach or exceed 50% for persons with traumatic brain injuries and spinal cord injuries. Conditions such as deafness, arthritis, or multiple sclerosis have shown substance abuse rates of at least double the general population estimates.

DiNitto and Webb's (2005) review of existing research on the prevalence of substance misusers with mental retardation suggests that this population is less likely to use or misuse alcohol and drugs than the general population. However, as they also note, this finding may be the result of such factors as close supervision, reporting bias from institutional settings that prohibit alcohol or drug use, people's unwillingness to report use, or the fact that individuals with mental retardation are a protected class and securing informed consent to participate in research is difficult and time consuming. In its review of the literature on substance misuse, CSAT (2004) concluded that people who qualify for vocational rehabilitation services are two times more likely to use alcohol and other drugs (20%) than the general population (10%).

Wounded war veterans are another group at high risk for substance-related problems. Because of the large number of wounded veterans who survive explosions, the United States can expect to be paying for the war in Iraq for many years to come. One worrisome fact contained in information supplied by the Walter Reed Army Medical Center (Okie, 2005) is that more than 60% of soldiers injured in the war in Iraq have potentially life-altering brain injuries.

According to a news report in *USA Today*, traumatic brain injury is the sort of injury that many soldiers in previous wars never lived long enough to suffer (Zoroya, 2005). The body armor used today keeps people alive. But the shock wave from the bomb explosion can damage brain tissue. Behavioral changes, headaches, and a loss of problem-solving abilities are common. Those who survive head injuries often suffer from emotional problems, including difficulty with memory, as well as high rates of depression, alcohol use, and posttraumatic anxieties. Substance abuse counselors can expect to work with the injured victims of the wars in the Middle East, whether their injuries are to the mind or the body, who have sought relief in drinking or other drug misuse.

The effects of substance abuse on persons with disabilities are many when compared to persons with disabilities who abstain from substance use: decreased employment rates, increased poverty rates, delayed adjustment to acquired disability, higher likelihood of being a victim of crimes, higher likelihood of being involved in accidents, higher likelihood of having a variety of substance use–related health and social problems (West, 2007).

ASSESSING TREATMENT BARRIERS

In spite of the prevalence of substance misuse among people with disabilities and the American with Disabilities Act of 1990 there is much evidence that these persons are less likely to enter or complete treatment. Findings from Krahn and colleagues (2007) indicate that adults with Medicaid disability codes are only half as likely as other Medicaid enrollees to enter treatment during any year. Furthermore, the gap between the disability group and the nondisability group has been increasing over time, in spite of Medicaid expansion and the implementation of managed care.

One of the main barriers is accessibility. In a study that examined broad accessibility issues in a stratified random sample of substance abuse treatment facilities nationwide, West (2007) found an alarming lack of compliance with federally mandated statutes. For example, 20% did not have accessible parking spaces, 20% did not have accessible restroom facilities, 26% did not have accessible showers or baths in residential facilities. Most (84%) did not have anyone on staff that could use American Sign Language (ASL) or signed English, most (94%) could not produce materials in Braille, and 58% of the transportation provided by the treatment center was not wheelchair accessible.

People with learning differences (mental retardation, borderline intelligence, learning disabilities, hyperactivity, and traumatic brain injury) can experience a number of barriers to effective treatment (Campbell, Essex, & Held, 1994). Insight-oriented approaches and the use of complex audiovisual aids and extensive writing assignments may be confusing. The popular modality of group treatment is likely to be too fast-paced or abstract, or to demand behaviors that a person with a brain injury may not be able to sustain. Fellow group participants may have negative stereotypes of persons with learning differences. Programs may need to adapt by using picture books, flash cards, and art therapy techniques. The U.S. Department of Health and Human Services (2011) notes that there are over 5 million students in special education programs in this country, yet there are few substance abuse prevention programs designed to address these students' learning needs.

Other barriers result from a lack of knowledge, experience, and understanding among treatment staff. For example, Hector Del Valle, who has quadriplegia and is a faculty member of the School of Social Work at the University of Central Florida, shared his story at a United Spinal Association's Independence Expo (Drill, 2009, p. 30). "Del Valle began 'using' at age 12 or 13—marijuana, cocaine, and acid—until his senior year in high school. He sustained a C5-6 SCI (spinal cord injury) at age 17, when he was injured in an auto accident. He had been drinking and using drugs, blacked out, and remembers being cut out of the vehicle he had been driving, and waking up in the emergency room. A nurse told him, 'That's what you get for drinking and driving.' Stereotypical beliefs that may be prevalent in the larger culture can find a home in treatment staff. A list provided by CSAT (1998) of commonly held beliefs that pose barriers to treatment includes:

- People with disabilities do not abuse substances.
- People with disabilities should receive exactly the same treatment protocol as everyone else so that they are not singled out as different.
- A person is noncompliant when his or her disability prevents him or her from responding to treatment.
- A person with a disability will make other clients uncomfortable.
- People with disabilities will sue the program regardless of the services offered.
- People with disabilities deserve pity, so they should be allowed more latitude to indulge in substance use.

Communication barriers are particularly prevalent with persons who are deaf and persons with slow or impaired speech, significant respiratory problems, or delays in cognition. Accommodations need to be made by using sign language interpreters, telecommunication devices for the deaf (TDDs), computer terminals and boards, and speech synthesizers.

It is a major premise of the independent living movement that "nonaccess in society resulted from architectural and attitudinal barriers rather than the dysfunction of the individual person with a disability" (Mackelprang & Salsgiver, 1999, p. 51). Architectural barriers include everything from no wheelchair access to a lack of transportation from the bus stop to the program entrance. The critical point is that when the physical, attitudinal, and communication barriers are removed, it becomes possible to establish a productive relationship that has a chance of being helpful to a person with coexisting disabilities.

Arguably, some of the greatest barriers to treatment for disabilities occur in the military, especially among troops who are serving on the battlefield. The goals of treatment, from the military's standpoint, are to provide temporary relief of mental or even physical symptoms to maintain the fighting force. For this purpose, in Iraq, for example, there are more than 200 mental health professionals who counsel soldiers after a tough battle to help them get their emotions under control (Streisand, 2006). Since it is well established that repeated exposure to combat stress is the greatest risk factor for PTSD, this work of the psychiatrists and other mental health experts raises some ethical issues related to their first responsibility, which is to the welfare of the client.

When their term of duty is up, the returning soldiers are assessed for mental health problems, and then again, 3 to 6 months later, they are given a mental health screening. Few of these former soldiers are referred for treatment, however (Streisand, 2006). Yet research has shown that during this time period—several months after departure from a war zone—30% of the former troops will have developed stress-related mental health problems (*USA Today*, 2005). This barrier to treatment is institutional. A more serious barrier, though, is psychological—the reluctance of traumatized soldiers to admit their problems and to seek help in the belief that any such request will jeopardize their military careers. Acknowledgment of a mental disorder, as well, is often viewed, especially by men, as a sign of weakness. Still, unprecedented numbers of veterans who saw combat in Iraq and Afghanistan are seeking treatment at the VA, and many were pushed to take this step by worried and frightened family members. Recently, the Departments of Defense and Veterans Affairs have stepped up efforts to meet the increasing demand.

INTAKE AND SCREENING

As with any other person who might be seeking help, the most important task of assessment is to begin to build trust and credibility with that person. This requires a nonconfrontational, supportive environment that will reduce anxiety, not increase it. If it is already known that the person has a particular disability, accommodations should already be made to eliminate functional barriers. For example, for persons in a wheelchair, the table should be at the right height; for persons who are deaf, a sign language interpreter must be available; for people with traumatic brain injury, questions should be concrete and checks for understanding should be made often. For a thorough discussion of potential accommodations needed, see CSAT (1998).

If a person is willing to seek help with stopping his or her substance misuse or in eliminating the consequences of such use, it is important to find out if there are any functional barriers that may get in the way. It is not necessary to diagnose a disability; that role is reserved for a disabilities expert (e.g., specialized medical services or state vocational rehabilitation programs). It is necessary to find out if any functional adjustments are needed that could help the clinician be a more helpful consultant to this person.

An initial screening for disabilities is practical: It helps identify potential programmatic barriers so that they can be modified. It is important to ask everyone involved in the intake process, "Do you need any accommodations to participate fully in this program?" Screening can also help identify areas where it may be beneficial for the person to link with other services. A basic screening instrument for identifying functional limitations that may pose barriers in treatment can be found in CSAT (1998, p. 21).

TREATMENT PRACTICES

Although there are many barriers to accessing treatment, once involved in treatment, persons with disabilities appear to be as likely to stay in treatment and achieve treatment goals as any other group (Krahn et al., 2007). A number of therapeutic issues need to be addressed to increase the likelihood of treatment success. Treatment plans may feature different elements and concerns and may require more time depending on the disability. A person with coexisting disabilities may have different reasons for wanting to abstain from alcohol or drugs. For example, the fact that alcohol can lower the seizure threshold for persons with traumatic brain injury (TBI) may be a motivation to quit drinking alcohol.

The CSAT 29 recommends that each task written on a treatment contract be accompanied by a list of specific accommodations needed for that task to be accomplished. For example, for persons with memory problems expected to attend group sessions, "Call and remind them that a session is occurring or assist them in creating memory books that include necessary information on group meetings" (CSAT, 1998, p. 49).

Modifications for counseling sessions could include flexibility with the time and length of the session, preparing for sessions by researching the disability, providing specific examples of behaviors and concepts to persons with cognitive disabilities, preparing accessible written materials, and finding alternative media. Behavioral therapy may be preferable to insight-oriented, psychodynamic approaches because it offers small, concrete steps to long-term goals (DiNitto & Webb, 2005).

Helwig and Holicky (1994) suggest specific therapeutic issues that are common to many persons with physical disabilities and particularly trauma-induced disabilities:

> Learning to live in a world designed for able-bodied people who value normality and who shun difference demands the ability to face and solve a never-ending string of problems ... These problems include major changes in almost every aspect of life, including a loss of privacy in areas of self-care; devaluing, enabling, or patronizing social attitudes; loss of control or determination; and incredible stress on one's family and support system. (p. 229)

In addition, grief and loss issues related to the disability and the addiction may be important therapeutic themes.

Motivational interviewing techniques have been found successful with adults who have traumatic brain injury. By helping the person to assess his or her motivation to use alcohol and other drugs, identify and evaluate goals, resolve conflicts among interfering goals, and develop skills for reaching realistic goals, the person is engaged in immediately gratifying activities. Homework activities are designed to be positive, goal-oriented, and immediately measurable on a "goal ladder" that leads to a long-term goal. Results from an evaluation of using this approach with 60 persons with TBI during a 12-week treatment program suggest that motivational interviewing was effective in reducing substance use. At the 1-year follow-up, 40% maintained abstinence, 14% became abstinent, 38% continued using, and 8% began using (Heinemann, 1997).

Slater (2007) notes that there is very little empirical evidence regarding effective substance abuse treatment approaches with regard to people with intellectual disabilities. Many authors discuss the need to practice from a strengths perspective when working with persons who have a disability (CSAT, 1998; Mackelprang & Salsgiver, 1999). If a treatment goal is not met, it is important to look first at whether accommodations were sufficient to support the process instead of immediately blaming the individual for resistance to treatment.

SUMMARY AND CONCLUSION

In the mid-1980s, clinicians were still arguing about which disorder should be treated first: mental illness or substance dependence. Clients were falling through the categorical cracks. Since then, research has demonstrated that it works best when we treat both problems at once in an integrated team approach that coordinates the treatments of both systems. Within the overall context of harm reduction, strengths-based interventions, such as motivational interviewing and stage-wise treatment, are successful strategies that help the clinician stay focused on the client's goals. Professionals who work with persons who have physical disabilities or cognitive impairments are recognizing that substance misuse problems can no longer be overlooked, and substance abuse treatment programs are making innovative accommodations to better serve these populations. The challenge now is for health maintenance organizations and state and federal funding sources to create reimbursement and policy practices that will enhance these developments.

REFERENCES

Alcoholics Anonymous (AA). (1984). *The AA member: Medications and other drugs.* New York: AA World Services.

Alverson, H., Alverson, M., & Drake, R. E. (2000). An ethnographic study of the longitudinal course of substance abuse among people with severe mental illness. *Community Mental Health Journal, 36*(6), 557–569.

American Psychiatric Association (APA). (2000). *Diagnostic and statistical manual of mental disorders, text revision* (4th ed.) (DSM–IV–TR). Washington, DC: Author.

APA/CAPP. (2007). American Psychological Association's Committee for the Advancement of Professional Practice's Task Force on Serious Mental Illness and Severe Emotional Disturbance. *Catalog of clinical training opportunities: Best practices for recovery and improved outcomes for people with serious mental illness.* Retrieved August 20, 2011 from http://www.apa.org/practice/resources/grid/index.aspx

Bearman, D., Claydon, K., Kincheloe, J., & Lodise, C. (1997). Breaking the cycle of dependency: Dual diagnosis and AFDC families. *Journal of Psychoactive Drugs, 29*(4), 359–367.

Biegel, D., Kola, L. A., Ronis, R. J., Boyle, P. E., Reyes, C., Wieder, B., et al. (2003). The Ohio Substance Abuse and Mental Illness Coordinating Center of Excellence: Implementation support for evidence-based practice. *Research on Social Work Practice, 13*(4), 531–545.

Brady, S., Hiam, C. M., Saemann, R., Humbert, L., Fleming, M., & DawkinsBrickhouse, K. (1996). Dual diagnosis: A treatment model for substance abuse and major mental illness. *Community Mental Health Journal, 32*(6), 573–579.

Campbell, J. A., Essex, E. L., & Held, G. (1994). Issues in chemical dependency treatment and aftercare for people with learning differences. *Health and Social Work, 19*(1), 63–70.

Carey, K. B. (1996). Substance use reduction in the context of outpatient psychiatric treatment: A collaborative motivational, harm reduction approach. *Community Mental Health Journal, 32,* 291–306.

Center for Substance Abuse Treatment (CSAT). (1994). *Assessment and treatment of patients with coexisting mental illness and alcohol and other drug abuse.* Treatment Improvement Protocol (TIP) Series, No. 9. U.S. Department of Health and Human Services, Public Health Service. Rockville, MD: Author.

Center for Substance Abuse Treatment (CSAT). (1998). *Substance use disorder treatment for people with physical and cognitive disabilities.* Treatment Improvement Protocol (TIP) Series, No. 29. U.S. Department of Health and Human Services, Public Health Service. Rockville, MD: Author.

Center for Substance Abuse Treatment (CSAT). (2004). *Substance abuse treatment and family therapy.* Treatment Improvement Protocol (TIP) Series, No. 39. U.S. Department of Health and Human Services. Rockville, MD: Author.

Center for Substance Abuse Treatment (CSAT). (2005). *Substance abuse treatment for persons with co-occurring disorders.* Treatment Improvement Protocol (TIP) Series,

No. 42. DHHS Publication No. (SMA) 05-3922. Rockville, MD: Substance Abuse and Mental Health Services Administration.

Crisp, C. L. (2005). Dual diagnosis: Substance abuse and mental health in an inpatient setting. In L. M.Grobman (Ed.), *Days in the lives of social workers: Forty-one professionals tell "real life" stories from social work practice* (3rd ed., pp. 205–210). Harrisburg, PA: White Hat Community.

Daley, D. C., & Zuckoff, A. (1998). Improving compliance with the initial outpatient session among discharged inpatient dual diagnosis clients. *Social Work*, *43*(5), 470–473.

Darcy, M., Dalphonse, L., & Winsor, C. (2010, July). Developing a more skilled co-occurring disorders workforce. *Counselor Magazine*, 1–9.

Denning, P. (2000). *Practicing harm reduction psychotherapy: An alternative approach to addictions*. New York: Guilford Press.

Denning, P. (2004). *Practicing harm reduction psychotherapy: An alternative approach to addictions*. New York: Guilford Press.

DiNitto, D. M., & Webb, D. K. (2005). Compounding the problem: Substance abuse and other disabilities. In C. A. McNeece & D. M. DiNitto, *Chemical dependency: A systems approach* (2nd ed., pp. 423–483). Boston: Allyn & Bacon.

Drake, R. E. (1996). Substance use reduction among patients with severe mental illness. *Community Mental Health Journal*, *32*(3), 311–314.

Drake, R. E., & Mueser, K. T. (2000). Psychosocial approaches to dual diagnosis. *Schizophrenia Bulletin*, *26*(1), 105–118.

Drake, R. E., & Wallach, M. A. (1993). Moderate drinking among people with severe mental illness. *Hospital and Community Psychiatry*, *44*, 780–782.

Drake, R. E., Yovetich, N. A., Bebout, R. R., Harris, M., & McHugo, G. J. (1997). Integrated treatment for dually diagnosed homeless adults. *Journal of Nervous and Mental Disease*, *185*, 298–305.

Drill, H. (2009, November). Are you disabled—and addicted? *Paraplegia News*, 30–31.

Frisman, L., Mueser, K., Covell, N., Lin, H., Crocker, A., Drake, R., & Essock, S. (2009). Use of integrated dual disorder treatment via assertive community treatment versus clinical case management for persons with co-occurring disorders and antisocial personality disorder. *Journal of Nervous and Mental Disease*, *197*(11), 822–828.

Goff, D. C., Henderson, D. C., & Amico, E. (1992). Cigarette smoking in schizophrenia: Relationship to psychopathology and medication side effects. *American Journal of Psychiatry*, *149*, 1189–1194.

Grant, B., Dawson, D., Stinson, F., Chou, S., Dufour, M., & Pickering, R. (2004). The 12-month prevalence and trends in DSM-IV alcohol abuse and dependence: United States, 1991–1992 and 2001–2002. *Drug and Alcohol Dependence*, *74*(3), 223–234.

Grant, B., Hasin, D., Stinson, F., Dawson, D., Chou, S., Ruan, W., & Huang, B. (2005). Co-occurrence of 12-month mood and anxiety disorders and personality disorder in the U.S.: Results from the National Epidemiologic Survey on Alcohol and Related Conditions. *Journal of Psychiatric Research*, *39*(1), 1–9.

Handmaker, N., Packard, M., & Conforti, K. (2002). Motivational interviewing in the treatment of dual disorders. In W. R. Miller & S. Rollnick (Eds.), *Motivational interviewing: Preparing people for change* (pp. 262–276). New York: Guilford Press.

Heinemann, A. W. (1997). Persons with disabilities. In J. Lowinson, P. Ruiz, R. Millman, & J. Langrod (Eds.), *Substance abuse: A comprehensive textbook* (3rd ed., pp. 716–725). Baltimore: Williams & Wilkins.

Helwig, A., & Holicky, R. (1994). Substance abuse in persons with disabilities: Treatment considerations. *Journal of Counseling and Development, 72,* 227–233.

Horsfall, J., Cleary, M., Hunt, G., & Walter, G. (2009). Psychosocial treatments for people with co-occurring severe mental illnesses and substance use disorder (dual diagnosis): A review of empirical evidence. *Harvard Review of Psychiatry, 17*(1), 24–34.

Jackson, K. (2003, June). Trauma and the national psyche. *Social Work Today,* pp. 20–23.

Jackmann, T. (2009, July 28). Dual disorders are rarely treated properly. *Washington Post.* Retrieved August 16, 2011 from http://www.washingtonpost.com/wp-dyn/content/discussion/2009/07/28/DI2009072801297.html

Kausch, O. (2003). Suicide attempts among veterans seeking treatment for pathological gambling. *Journal of Clinical Psychiatry, 64*(9), 1031–1038.

Kelly, J., & Yeterian, J. (2008). Mutual-help groups for dually diagnosed individuals: Rationale, description, and review of the evidence. *Journal of Groups in Addiction and Recovery, 3*(3/4), 217–242.

Kessler, R. C., Galea, S., Jones, R., & Parker, H. A. (2006). Mental illness and suicidality after Hurricane Katrina. *Bulletin of the World Health Organization, 84,* 930–939.

Klein, A., Cnaan, R., & Whitecraft, J. (1998). Significance of peer social support with dually diagnosed clients: Findings from a pilot study. *Research on Social Work Practice, 8*(5), 529–551.

Kowal, J. (2006, July 5). Homeless alcoholics receive a permanent place to live, and drink. *New York Times.* Retrieved September15, 2006 from http://www.nytimes.com/2006/07/05/us/05homeless.htm

Krahn, G., Deck, D., Gabriel, R., & Farrell, N. (2007). A population-based study on substance abuse treatment for adults with disabilities: Access, utilization, and treatment outcomes. *American Journal of Drug and Alcohol Abuse, 33,* 791–798.

Kubiak, S. P. (2004). The effects of PTSD on treatment adherence, drug relapse, and criminal recidivism in a sample of incarcerated men and women. *Research on Social Work Practice, 14*(6), 424–433.

Laudet, A. B., Magura, S., Vogel, H. S., & Knight, E. (2000). Addictions services: Support, mutual aid and recovery from dual diagnosis. *Community Mental Health Journal, 36*(5), 457–476.

Little, J., & Franskoviak, P. (2010). So glad you came! Harm reduction therapy in community settings. *Journal of Clinical Psychology: In Session, 66*(2), 175–188.

Linhorst, D. M. (2006). *Empowering people with severe mental illness.* New York: Oxford University Press.

Mackelprang, R., & Salsgiver, R. (1999). *Disability: A diversity model approach in human service practice.* Pacific Grove, CA: Brooks/Cole.

McGovern, M., Clark, R., & Samnaliev, M. (2007). Co-occurring psychiatric and substance use disorders: A multistate feasibility study of the quadrant model. *Psychiatric Services, 58*(7), 949–954.

Mercer-McFadden, C., Drake, R. E., Brown, N. B., & Fox, R. S. (1997). The community support program demonstrations of services for young adults with severe mental illness and substance use. *Psychiatric Rehabilitation Journal*, 20(3), 13–24.

Minkoff, K. (1996). Discussion of "Substance use reduction in the context of outpatient psychiatric treatment." *Community Mental Health Journal*, 32, 307–310.

Miller, W., Forechimes, A., & Zweben, A. (2011). *Treating addiction: A guide for professionals*. New York: Guillford Press.

Mueser, K. T., Drake, R. E., & Noordsy, D. L. (1998). Integrated mental health and substance abuse disorders. *Journal of Practical Psychiatry and Behavioral Health*, 4, 129–139.

Mueser, K. T., Drake, R. E., & Wallach, M. A. (1998). A review of etiological theories. *Addictive Behaviors*, 23, 717–734.

Mueser, K., Drake, R., Turner, W., & McGovern, M. (2006). Comorbid substance use disorders and psychiatric disorder. In W. R. Miller & K. M. Carroll (Eds.), *Rethinking substance abuse: What the science show, and what we should do about it* (pp. 115–133). New York: Guilford Press.

Mueser, K. T., Noordsy, D. L., Drake, R. E., & Fox, L. (2003). *Integrated treatment for dual disorders: A guide to effective practice*. New York: Guilford Press.

National Council for Community Behavioral Healthcare (NCCBH). (2011). Real stories, real people: Co-occurring disorders. Retrieved August 16, 2011 from www.thenationalcouncil.org.

National Gambling Impact Study Commission. (1999, June 18). *Report of the commission*. Washington, DC: U.S. Government Printing Office.

National Mental Health Association (NMHA). (2006) Hurricane Katrina: NMHA responds. Retrieved September 23, 2006 from http://www.nmha.org/katrina/index.cfm.

Navits, L. M. (2004). Treatment of posttraumatic stress disorder and substance abuse: Clinical guidelines for implementing seeking safety therapy. *Alcoholism Treatment Quarterly*, 22, 43–62.

Nigam, R., Schottenfeld, R., & Kosten, T. (1992). Treatment of dual diagnosis patients: A relapse prevention group approach. *Journal of Substance Abuse Treatment*, 9, 305–309.

Noordsy, D. L., Schwab, B., Fox, L., & Drake, R. E. (1996). The role of self-help programs in the rehabilitation of persons with severe mental illness and substance use disorders. *Community Mental Health Journal*, 32, 71–81.

Office of Applied Studies. (2004). Results from the 2003 National Survey on Drug Use and Health. *National Outcome Measures*. Retrieved September 15 2006 from http://www.oas.samhsa.gov/nhsda.htm

Okie, S. (2005) Traumatic brain injury in the war zone. *New England Journal of Medicine*, 352, 2043–2047.

Orlin, L., O'Neill, M., & Davis, J. (2004). Assessment and intervention with clients who have coexisting psychiatric and substance-related disorders. In S. L. Straussner (Ed.), *Clinical work with substance-abusing clients* (pp. 103–124). New York: Guilford Press.

Osher, F. C., & Kofoed, L. (1989). Treatment of patients with psychiatric and psychoactive substance abuse disorders. *Hospital and Community Psychiatry*, 40, 1025–1030.

Owens, P. L., Mutter, R., & Stocks, C. (2010, July). *Mental health and substance abuse-related emergency department visits among adults: 2007.* HCUP Statistical Brief 92. Agency for Healthcare Research and Quality, Rockville, MD. Retrieved August 16, 2011 from http://www.hcup-us.ahrq.gov/reports/statbriefs/sb92.pdf

Padgett, D. K., Gulcur, L., & Tsemberis, S. (2006). Housing first services for people who are homeless with co-occurring serious mental illness and substance abuse. *Research on Social Work Practice, 16*(1), 74–83.

Pathways to Housing. (2005). 2005 APA gold award: Providing housing first and recovery services for homeless adults with severe mental illness. *Psychiatric Services, 56,* 1303–1305.

Pearson, C., Montgomery, A., & Locke, G. (2009). Housing stability among homeless individuals with serious mental illness participating in Housing First programs. *Journal of Community Psychology, 37*(3), 404–417.

Petry, N., Stinson, F., Grant, B. (2005). Comorbitity of DSM-IV Pathological gambling and other psychiatric disorders: Results from the Epidemiological Survey on Alcohol and Related Conditions. *Journal of Clinical Psychiatry, 66*(5), 564–574.

Phillips, P., & Labrow, J. (2000). Dual diagnosis: Does harm reduction have a role? *International Journal of Drug Policy, 11,* 279–283.

Powell, T. J., Kurtz, L. F., Garvin, C. D., & Hill, E. M. (1996). A model of AA utilization by persons with a dual diagnosis (the co-occurrence of alcoholism and severe mental illness). *Contemporary Drug Problems, 23,* 139–157.

Prochaska, J., & DiClemente, C. (1992). Stages of change in the modification of problem behaviors. In M. Hersen, R. M. Eisler, & P. M. Miller (Eds.), *Progress in behavior modification* (pp. 184–214). Sycamore, IL: Sycamore Press.

Quimby, E. (1995). Homeless clients' perspectives on recovery in the Washington, D.C., Dual Diagnosis Project. *Contemporary Drug Problems, 22*(2), 265–289.

Rehabilitation Research and Training Center on Drugs and Disability. (1995). *National Needs Assessment Survey results summary.* Dayton, OH: Author.

Sciacca, K., & Thompson, C. (1996). Program development and integrated treatment across systems for dual diagnosis: Mental illness, drug addiction, and alcoholism (MIDAA). *Journal of Mental Health Administration, 23*(3), 288–297.

Seal, K., Bertenthal, D., Miner, C., Sen, S., & Marmar, C. (2007). Bringing the war back home: Mental health disorders among 103,788 U.S. veterans returning from Iraq and Afghanistan seen at Department of Veterans Affairs facilities. *Archives of Internal Medicine, 167,* 476–482.

Shavelson, L. (2002). *Hooked: Five addicts challenge our misguided drug rehab system.* New York: New Press.

Shulman, G. (1995, September/October). Reorienting CD treatment for dual diagnosis. *Behavioral Health Management,* pp. 30–33.

Slayter, E. (2007). Substance abuse and mental retardation: Balancing risk management with the "dignity of risk." *Families in Society, 88*(4), 651–659.

Smith, S. (1983). *Collected poems.* New York: New Directions.

Smith, R., Jennings, J., & Cimino, A. (2010). Forensic continuum of care with Assertive Community Treatment (ACT) for persons recovering from co-occurring disabilities: Long-term outcomes. *Psychiatric Rehabilitation Journal, 33*(3), 207–218.

St. George, D. (2006, June 20). Iraq war may add stress for past vets. *Washington Post,* p. A01.

Streisand, B. (2006, October 9). Treating war's toll on the mind. *U.S. News & World Report,* pp. 55–62.

Substance Abuse and Mental Health Services Administration (SAMHSA). (2001). New SAMHSA report shows value of integrating state mental health, substance abuse, and Medicaid data. Retrieved Sept 15, 2000 from http://www.samhsa.gov/news

Substance Abuse and Mental Health Services Administration (SAMHSA). (2004). The DASIS Report: Facilities offering special programs or groups for clients with co-occurring disorders, 2004. Office of Applied Studies. Retrieved February 14, 2007, from http://www.oas.samhsa.gov/2k6/DualTX/DualTX.cfm

Substance Abuse and Mental Health Services Administration (SAMHSA). (2006a). *Homeless admissions to substance abuse treatment: 2004.* The Drug and Alcohol Services Information System (DASIS). Retrieved October 15, 2000 2006 from http://oas.samhsa.gov

Substance Abuse and Mental Health Services Administration (SAMHSA). (2006b). Results from the 2005 NSDUH: National Findings. Office of Applied Studies. Retrieved September 22, 2006 from http://www.oas.samhsa.gov/nsduh/2k5nsduh/2k5results.htm

Substance Abuse and Mental Health Services Administration (SAMHSA). (2008a). Parity: What does the new law mean? SAMHSA News, *16*(6), 1–4. Rockville, MD: Department of Health and Human Services.

Substance Abuse and Mental Health Services Administration (SAMHSA). (2008b). *Assertive Community Treatment.* DHS Publication No. SMA-08-4344. Rockville, MD: Center for Mental Health Services, Substance Abuse and Mental Health Services Administration, U.S. Department of Health and Human Services.

Substance Abuse and Mental Health Services Administration (SAMHSA). (2009). *Integrated treatment for co-occurring disorders: Training frontline staff.* DHHS Pub. No. SMA-08-4366, Rockville, MD: Center for Mental Health Services, Substance Abuse and Mental Health Services Administration, U.S. Department of Health and Human Services.

Substance Abuse and Mental Health Services Administration, Office of Applied Studies. (2007). *The NSDUH Report: Serious psychological distress and substance use disorder among veterans.* Rockville, MD.

Substance Abuse and Mental Health Services Administration, Office of Applied Studies (2008). *The NSDUH Report: Impact of Hurricanes Katrina and Rita on substance abuse and mental health.* Rockville, MD.

Swann, A. (2010). The strong relationship between bipolar and substance-use disorder. *Annals of the New York Academy of Sciences, 1187,* 276–293.

Timko, C., & Moos, R. H. (1998). Outcomes of the treatment climate in psychiatric and substance abuse program. *Journal of Clinical Psychology, 54*(8), 1137–1150.

Tsemberis, S., & Eisenberg, R. (2000). Pathways to Housing: Supported housing for street-dwelling homeless individuals with psychiatric disabilities. *Psychiatric Services, 51,* 487–493.

USA Today. (2005, July 28). Survey: 30% of returning Iraq vets suffer mental ills. *USA Today.* Retrieved September 15, 2006 from http://www.usatoday.com/news/health/2005-07-28-iraq-vets-health_x.htm.

U.S. Department of Health and Human Services (DHHS). (2011). *Substance abuse and disability.* Retrieved August 25, 2011 from www.hhs.gov/od/about/fact_sheets/substanceabuse.html.

van Wormer, K. (2007). *Human behavior and the social environment, micro level: Individuals and families.* New York: Oxford University Press.

van Wormer, R., & van Wormer, K. (2009). Non-abstinence-based supportive housing for persons with co-occurring disorders: A human right perspective. *Journal of Progressive Human Services, 20*, 152–165.

West, S. (2002). *The inclusion of persons with disabilities in research on substance abuse.* Poster session presented at Addictions 2002, September 2002, Eindhoven, Netherlands.

West, S. (2007). The accessibility of substance abuse treatment facilities in the United States for persons with disabilities. *Journal of Substance Abuse Treatment, 33,* 1–5.

Yu, J., Buka, S., Fitzmaurice, G., & McCormick, M. (2006). Treatment outcomes for substance abuse among adolescents with learning disorders. *Journal of Behavioral Health Services and Research, 33*(3), 275–286.

Zoroya, G. (2005, March 3). Key Iraq wound: Brain trauma. *USA Today.* Retrieved Sept 15, 2004 from http://www.usatoday.com/news/nation/2005-03-03-brain trauma-lede_x.htm

Recommended Videos

The following videos have been recommended by the National Association on Alcohol, Drugs and Disability Inc. (NAADD), an organization developed to promote awareness and education about substance abuse among people with coexisting disabilities. More information can be found on their website at www.naadd.org/index.html

An American Sign Language Interpretation of the 12-Step Program
  Availability: Minnesota Chemical Dependency Program for Deaf & Hard of Hearing Individuals, 2450 Riverside Avenue, Minneapolis, MN 55454. (800) 282 3323 (TTY).

Dreams of Denial
  Availability: Minnesota Chemical Dependency Program for Deaf & Hard of Hearing Individuals, 2450 Riverside Avenue, Minneapolis, MN 55454. (800) 282 3323 (TTY).

J.R.'s Story: The Disability of Chemical Dependency
  Availability: AIMS Multi-Media. (800) 367 2467. $49.95. *Follows a young man who is quadriplegic as he struggles with his alcohol and drug addiction (28 minutes).*

PRTA: Living Out Loud
  Availability: Progressive Research & Training for Action, 2809 Telegraph Avenue, Ste. 208, Berkeley, CA 94705. (510) 705 8918; (510) 705 8535 (TTY). *Chronicles a high-risk youth prevention program for teenage girls with disabilities.*

Silent Storm: Disability and Coexisting Substance Abuse
  Availability: United Cerebral Palsy Association of New Jersey, 354 South Broad Street, Trenton, NJ 08909. (609) 392 4004; (609) 392 7044 (TTY). $40.00.

A brief overview of the major issues surrounding alcohol and other drug problems and people with disabilities. Features interviews with NAADD board members and staff (10 minutes).

Understanding a Need ... Alcohol and Other Drug Abuse Prevention for People with Disabilities

Availability: National Clearinghouse on Alcohol and Drug Information, Catalogue #VHS091. (800) 729 6686; (800) 487 4889 (TTY).

An overview of the major issues of people with disabilities and prevention (15 minutes).

THE SOCIAL ASPECTS
OF ADDICTION

Addiction to substances and behaviors begins and ends in the context of social relationships and therefore must be treated in the larger context of the social network. Unlike traditional treatment, typically focused on the individual in a standardized format, strengths-based therapy looks to family and other support systems as a buffer against addiction and as an essential resource in recovery. Strengths-based therapy, moreover, starts where the client is and stays where the client is: in his or her role in the family and community life. The starting point in treatment, therefore, should be with the family in terms of both risks and resiliencies. Accordingly, Chapter 10, the first chapter in this part, describes family dynamics and strategies for engaging the family in treatment. Working with ethnically diverse families is discussed in this chapter and later in Chapter 12 ethnicity, culture, and class issues are addressed relative to addiction patterns.

The task for practitioners who work with these and all other populations is to help people tap into their individual and collective resources. Throughout this part of the book, therefore, attention is paid to family-centered (Chapter 10), ethnic-sensitive (Chapter 12) interventions. Chapter 11 applies the strengths perspective to an appreciation for the role that mutual-help support groups play in recovery. Consistent with the model that is the guiding theme of this book, the focus is on the appreciation, rather than the depreciation, of strategies that work.

Chapter 13, the policy chapter, which stands apart from the others in Part 4, is linked to them by the common thread of a concern with the social side (as opposed to the biological or psychological aspects) of addiction. The chapters that comprise the final portion of this book, in short, relate to social (including cultural and political) factors because these factors relate to treatment. We start with the oldest and most fundamental and enduring of all social institutions—the family.

FAMILY RISKS AND RESILIENCIES

CHAPTER **10**

Mam asks him if he brought any money. He tells her times are hard, jobs are scarce, and she says, Is it coddin' me you are? There's a war on and there's nothing but jobs in England. You drank the money, didn't you? You drank the money, Dad.

—**Frank McCourt (1996, p. 270)**

How we cope, how we see ourselves, how we love—these are the lessons learned at our mother's knee and at our father's. Whether as ghosts or as active participants, our grandparents (often our nurturers) are there as well.

The family is a system composed of members in constant and dynamic interaction with one another. Patterns of interaction get established—who interacts with whom, who talks and who listens, who has the authority, and who is the controlling force behind the scenes. The family has a pattern, a rhythm that is more than the sum of its parts. Any change in the behavior of one of its members affects not only each of the others but the system as a whole. Addiction, therefore, is often defined as an illness not just of the individual but of the entire family. Family, friendships, and intimate relationships often suffer; the impact is seen in high rates of divorce, alienation, and loss of child custody (Miller, Forcehimes, & Zweben, 2011).

Sometimes, the level of suffering is so extreme that the family unit barely functions at all; such was the situation immortalized in *Angela's Ashes,* as expressed in the chapter's opening quote. Children growing up in such families fail to get the nurturing and care they need. The anger in such a family is palpable. Because needs are not met, the webs of addiction and impaired parenting perpetuate themselves across generations.

When a teenager in an otherwise highly functional family gets caught up in the cycle of drug addiction, the impact can be enormous and long-lasting if the addiction continues for years. Cindy Fowler (not her real name) presents a mother's grief over a son's long-term addiction to heroin and cocaine:

> I'm a critical care nurse. The effect on the family has been profound; it has affected all of us. I lost a bunch of weight from the stress. This affected my relationship with my husband. Sam and I were keeping secrets from each other to protect each other instead of supporting each other. We were totally consumed, guilty of rescuing him financially. I lived in a world of what if. In the book *Codependency No More*, I saw myself—all aspects. I needed to let go, not to enable, not to fix. I learned the slogan—the three C's—from Al-Anon: "You didn't cause it, can't control it, can't cure it."
>
> Although David's addiction has been devastating to our family, I don't feel it has torn us apart. I think if anything it has drawn the other children even closer to my husband and myself and to each other. They have been extremely supportive. (personal narrative shared at the University of Northern Iowa on June 29, 2011)

When the parents themselves are involved in the use of illicit drugs, they often get entangled in the criminal justice system, a source of added stress to the children and grandparents. A student at the University of Northern Iowa (in a paper submitted to van Wormer in October 2009) describes the insecurity she faced in her early life:

> I was okay as long as I was with my mother, but my grandmother's house was my safety zone. I lived there when my mother would go off on heroin and begin committing crimes to support her habit—robbing dealers, etcetera. I would be afraid at night wondering if she was okay. I was afraid I would see my mother on television for a crime or even murdered. When she went to prison, I began wetting the bed. I became violent toward my peers and just wanted to be alone.

For every person who suffers from alcohol, cocaine, gambling, and other addictive problems, the lives of at least four other people are consistently altered. Around 12% of children in the United States live with at least one parent who is dependent on or has abused alcohol or an illicit drug, according to a report from the Substance Abuse and Mental Health Services Administration (SAMHSA) (2009). These other individuals—both children and adults— may be in as much pain as their loved one; they also may require help in how to deal with the harms related to the addiction as well as with their own powerful feelings related to the stress. Family counseling, even in only a few sessions, can be invaluable in reducing the significant others' feelings of guilt or confusion. Researchers in England conducted a comparison study of individuals who received both short-term and long-term counseling concerning the addiction of a family member (Copello, Templeton, & Orford, 2009). Both forms of intervention were highly effective in reducing family stress. Family-based interventions, moreover, can be invaluable in preparing the family for changes that are needed to enhance and maintain the addicted relative's recovery. Sometimes, the anger and resentment that significant others harbor need to be addressed before a recovering family member can return to the family setting. Sometimes, of course, the family environment itself is toxic, with all the participants having serious problems with drugs, for example. Here, too, interventions must be directed toward the whole family. To treat the individual in isolation is to ignore the context in which much of that behavior takes place.

From the perspective of this chapter, the family is viewed as a preventive resource—a system of both risk and resilience. Relevant to families in which alcoholic or other addictive behavior is a problem, a determination of both family risks and resiliencies is an important aspect of assessment (Gruber & Taylor, 2006). *Resilience* is more than just the ability of an individual family member to recover; rather, it involves protective factors within the entire family system or the family system dynamics. To know the context within which the addiction operates, an understanding of the systemic and intergenerational nature of addiction is essential.

That addiction is a family illness is a basic assumption of this book. The term *family illness* refers to the fact that the addicted family is malfunctioning. It does not mean that the addiction stems from family dynamics but, rather, that this dysfunction in one or more members affects the family dynamics. The chaos that the afflicted person experiences in the abyss of his or her addiction is replicated in the chaos and unpredictability of family life surrounding the addiction. Similar to other serious illnesses, for example, Alzheimer's, addiction is a source of major stress that reverberates across and within the family system and affects the family's interactions internally as well as interactions with every other system in the community. The emotional and financial resources of the family may be almost entirely depleted by the malfunctioning of one of its family members. Read Box 10.1, which aptly depicts the havoc that methamphetamine addiction wreaks on parents, children, and one Iowa community.

That the family is a natural source of interpersonal influence on the individual is a second basic assumption of this text. As William Miller (2006) tells us:

> It is now abundantly clear from research that an individual's motivation for changing substance abuse can be enhanced by unilateral intervention through concerned significant others ... [U]nilateral family counseling approaches have been successful both in relieving family distress and in engaging a high percentage (usually two-thirds to three-fourths) of substance-abusing loved ones in treatment. Here a professional counselor helps family members to learn strategies for decreasing their loved one's substance use and for initiating treatment. (p. 139)

Because of addiction's stigma, the family therapy field has devoted little effort to addictions-focused treatment and has tended to refer members with drinking and drug problems to specialized services or self-help groups. And because of the difficulty that substance abuse treatment centers face in working with the whole family, combined with third-party reimbursement disincentives to do so, often little more than lip service is given to family members' needs by these treatment centers. Yet for children and partners in the family system, the need to sort out their feelings and learn more about the nature of

Box 10.1	CHILDREN OF ADDICTS
	Colleen Krantz

Zoey Montgomery was 8 years old when she got on her hands and knees to look for a missing television remote under her family's couch and found bags of drugs instead. She knew her mother was the reason the marijuana was there in the room where she and her little brother played.

It's the kind of story that Zoey, now 10, knows only her friend Toddy Svoboda—and other children of addicts—could truly understand.

It was those shared stories of methamphetamine-addicted mothers leaving them for long periods, of caring for themselves too often, too young, and of being sent to live with grandparents when things went badly that led the two Fort Dodge girls to start a support group for children of addicts. They started out planning to call it Kids of Meth Heads, but were soon persuaded by other adults in their lives that it might go off better as Kids Supporting Kids of Addicted Parents.

They've hung fliers around Fort Dodge, which begin: "Do your parents spend more time with their 'friends' than with you? Are your parents taking money from you? Do you feel like you are being dumped?"

It's one more sign of how far meth has infiltrated Iowa, where 760 clandestine labs—a setting where meth is "cooked"—were found in the state last year. The numbers are a significant decline from the previous year—with most of the credit recently being given to a new law that makes it more difficult to obtain pseudoephedrine, a meth ingredient—but the highly addictive drug is a long way from disappearing from the lives of Iowans, including children whose parents are too focused on the drug to pay attention to them.

"It's really become a societal problem," said Dixie Lovain, a child advocate with the Fort Dodge–based Domestic/Sexual Assault Outreach Center. "It's such a problem, but I thought the girls' idea was the neatest thing I'd heard of."

In 2005, more than 1,350 abuse cases involved children who were found to have illegal drugs in their system because of actions of a parent or caregiver, according to the Iowa Department of Human Services. The department found 128 children who were present while a parent or guardian was manufacturing meth.

Statewide data pertaining to the number of children whose parents are addicted to meth is not kept. But last year, nearly half of the 1,605 child welfare cases in a 16-county area in southwest Iowa involved parental meth use, according to a study done by an Iowa Department of Human Services social work administrator.

Zoey and Toddy are hoping other children who have been neglected by parents addicted to meth or another drug show up at the weekly meetings the two girls have begun holding with Lovain, the child advocate.

"We don't want it to be just kids of meth heads," Toddy, 11, said. "But all things like alcohol, other drugs or even gambling."

Toddy's mother, Stephanie Svoboda, who is now in treatment and has been clean for more than two months, would often leave her daughter home alone during the night at age 8 or 9, said Toddy, who is living temporarily with Zoey's grandparents, who are family friends.

"She'd always threaten she was going to kill herself and then would leave for the night," Toddy said. "I couldn't sleep because I'd be worried."

She also remembers having to break up verbal and physical fights between her mother and her mother's boyfriend. "I'd just get in the middle of it and make them stop. I hated it," Toddy remembers. "I'd make them sit down or make one of them leave."

"I was a parent for a long time," Toddy said.

Zoey, who now lives with her father, can relate to Toddy's stories. By the time she was 7, she was not only getting her own breakfast and dinner, but was also often feeding her brother, who is 6 years younger. She also frequently changed her brother's diapers.

She remembers one morning when her mother hadn't returned home from a night of partying and she couldn't wake her stepfather. She had to get on the school bus and felt terrible because her little brother was essentially "alone in that house."

Stephanie Svoboda, 30, said she has been using illegal drugs since she was 18 or 19 and has known for years that she had to kick the habit for her and her daughter's sake.

"Right now, every day is hard for me" because of the continuing temptation that meth represents even after being clean for more than two months, said Svoboda, who attends a Moms off Meth support group while the girls meet.

She thinks the group her daughter and Zoey have started is a "good idea."

The challenge, she said, will be that many parents will view taking their children to such a meeting as a threat because it might be seen as admitting use of illegal drugs.

Zoey's mother, Jody Montgomery, 30, said she is "really proud" of her daughter for helping establish the group. "I am ashamed of what I've done. But it is a disease and it's harder for kids if you don't communicate with them about it," said Montgomery, who is undergoing treatment for her addiction. The group may help her daughter and others to do the talking that's so important.

Zoey said she and Toddy don't hate their mothers, they just hate what they've put them through. "I love her, but she still has to earn back my trust," Zoey said.

The girls will continue sharing stories with each other but hope others will be able to join them. "We talk about our moms a lot and it's better" when someone else understands, Zoey said.

Lovain said, "What impressed me about these girls is not only that they want to do this, but they really, really care."

Source: 'Des Moines Register', April 1, 2006, p. 1A. Reprinted by permission of the Des Moines Register. Article by Colleen Krantz.

the problem that has so consumed them over the years is crucial for the long-term recovery of everyone involved. Too often, also, any family that doesn't match the traditional mold tends to be invisible, and the importance of the extended family as a vital resource goes unrecognized.

Dedicated to the principle that addiction is a family illness, this chapter starts by reviewing the precepts of family systems theory, historical and modern, and then, through drawing on personal testimonials, shows what addiction does to family rules, roles, communication patterns, and above all, to love. As dramatically stated by literary scholar Linda Leonard (1989): "All addictions are killers; each in its own way kills living in the moment, kills creativity, love, and the trusting faith of the inner child" (p. 196). In contrast to traditional family therapy, the family treatment interventions described in this chapter are designed to elicit resilience and healing in family members rather than focusing on the family's presumed role in perpetuating addiction. We have adapted interventions to parallel the readiness of the family for change—a phase approach. The phase approach views treatment needs in terms of the five basic intervals, stretching from precontemplation through the maintenance period. The stages of family needs may or may not correspond directly to the addict's stage of recovery. The chapter concludes with a list of exercises geared toward work with families in **Family Week programming**.

CLASSIC FAMILY SYSTEMS THERAPY

The leading proponents of family systems theory have tended to focus almost exclusively on interpersonal transactions. From the classic systems perspective, a disorder such as mental illness, anorexia, or alcoholism is viewed as stemming from faulty family communication or functioning. Miller and colleagues (2011) refer to this as the disturbed family hypothesis, which was an advance over the disturbed spouse hypothesis that was popular in the 1940s and which pinned the blame for the alcoholism on the woman's unconscious desire to keep her husband in an inebriated state. The solution was psychotherapy for the wife, who it was thought otherwise would sabotage treatment.

The solution was for family systems therapists to work with the whole family because that was where the illness was located—in the family dynamics. Although this viewpoint had its own limitations, we need to understand that the systems model for understanding human behavior developed as an intellectual reaction against simplistic, mechanistic views of individuals whose behavior was viewed in terms of locating the problem in unconscious drives of the wife or of a repression of other basic biological drives by the person who used substances to escape. The systems conceptualization was thus a major advance in knowledge, a conceptual orientation that attempted to explain the problematic behavior of individuals through a dysfunction in interacting components of the system (Andreae, 2011, p. 243). In this tradition, the systems therapist does not do individual therapy, that is, try to fix "the identified patient." Rather, the patient is viewed within the context of the family, where the symptoms or problems presumably evolved (Amodeo & Lopez, 2008; Galanter, Dermatis, Keller, & Trujillo, 2002; Poulin, 2010). Relationships and communication are stressed. The fact that the designated sick person in the family could truly be sick and be the source of the family's stress and malfunctioning is rarely considered. The therapeutic task, according to Poulin (2010), is to "delabel" the identified patient and help family members assume ownership for the roles they play in the problem. The focus is then on roles, relationships, and communication styles in the family.

Much of what we know as family mental illness patterns, systems theory, and therapy today was developed by Bowen in work with families of schizophrenic children. Key concepts concerning the intricacies of family communication, such as double-bind theory and receiving mixed messages, were seen as instrumental in the development of schizophrenia in the child. The presenting problem was seen as serving a function within the family (Thompson, Pomeroy, & Gober, 2005).

Following her work with systems theorist Gregory Bateson, Virginia Satir helped popularize the notion of the role of family interaction in the "development of mental illness in a family member" (quoted by Chase-Marshall, 1976, p. 26). Similarly, alcoholism was conceptualized by Bowen (1978) as a mere symptom of a problem in the larger family or social unit. Alcoholism, like schizophrenia, was not viewed as the problem but as the solution to the problem. Family therapy, divorced from alcoholism treatment, was the sole intervention required; once the family was working as a system, individual problems such as mental illness and alcoholism would evaporate.

The individual with substance use problems is viewed by classical family systems theorists as "the symptom carrier" of the family dysfunction (Bradshaw, 1988). In his or her aberrant behavior, the person who is strung out on drugs, for example, helps maintain the family balance by deflecting attention away from the real problems (Kaufman & Kaufman, 2002). Common to all these systems thinkers is the belief that the key to changing the drinking behavior lies in strengthening interaction patterns among family members. The significance in addiction is in maintaining equilibrium in the family; remove the person who is the scapegoat and another family member will start acting out, goes the thinking.

Missing from traditional family systems models is a grounding in empirical research as well as a confusion of cause and effect—that is, whether unique communication patterns and role-playing in the family were the cause of the disorder (e.g., schizophrenia) or whether dealing with the disorder affected the communication patterns and role-playing. Accordingly, medical needs were often overlooked, and angry responses or guilt feelings in the family clients were aroused.

The literature on eating disorders, likewise, is rife with what we might call systemic determinism or a pathology focus. Minuchin (1974) and Nichols (1984) were only the first of thousands of theorists to place the source of anorexia in tension within the family. Even in the early 1990s, researchers such as Ellis-Ordway (1992), in his article titled "The Impact of Family

Dynamics on Anorexia," echoed the classic formulation. Consistent with this formulation, the parents were targeted and family therapy was the treatment of choice to discover the underlying family problems responsible for the adolescent's symptoms (Woodside & Shekter-Wolfson, 2003). Much criticism came from a feminist perspective, however. Rabinor (1994), for example, decried what amounted to the "mother-blaming" in the eating disorders literature.

Fortunately, attention has shifted today to a recognition of the biochemical component in a number of disorders and behaviors, including disorders related to eating. The role of cultural factors and distorted media images of the "perfect body" in the development of anorexia and bulimia is also widely recognized. Family researchers view the role of families as caught up in a complex and frightening disorder (Woodside & Shekter-Wolfson, 2003). Increasingly, the focus of family counseling is in teaching family members about the biological and cultural nature of the disorder, providing support, and helping them play a positive role in recovery.

Cultural diversity is another issue that has long been overlooked in family therapy. Only in the past few years, as Krestan indicates, has family therapy as a whole dealt with issues of diversity at all. Family counselors from the helping professions would do well to consult *Ethnicity and Family Therapy*, edited by McGoldrick, Giordano, and Garcia-Petro (2005a) to learn how to best approach members of various ethnic and racial backgrounds. In this comprehensive volume, dozens of chapters, each written by experts on a specific ethnicity—for example, Russian Jewish families, Irish families, Czech and Slovak families—provide helpful guidelines for working with each unique population.

Another excellent resource is provided by the Center for Substance Abuse Treatment (CSAT) (2004), a government office under SAMHSA that has produced an extensive protocol for family treatment. The CSAT document contrasts the teachings of family therapy and addiction treatment. Family therapists, as the document notes, tend to conceptualize substance misuse as a symptom and dysfunction in the family that serves a purpose within the family unit. Such assumptions as these cannot be empirically verified. Family therapy focuses on the inner dynamics of the family, but substance abuse treatment is geared toward the client and involves the family only for the purpose of helping the client with the addiction problem. Spirituality is addressed in substance abuse treatment but is relatively ignored in family therapy.

Sadly, the legacy of family blaming still persists in some quarters. For example, Saatcioglu, Erim, and Cakmak (2006) state the following: "(Substance) abuse is a family disease [that] requires joint treatment of family members. Family is an important part of the diagnosis and treatment chain of alcohol and substance abuse. Abuse of alcohol and substance is a response to fluctuations in the family system.... A family often needs as much treatment as the family member who is the abuser of alcohol or a substance" (p. 125). (This article, curiously, was published in a prestigious psychiatric journal.) Saatcioglu and colleagues are correct that joint treatment of family members is highly desirable to ensure recovery of both the alcoholic or addict and family members who have been through their own private hell. Yet, the location of the cause of the substance misuse in the family is reminiscent of the flawed deterministic logic of an earlier day. Instead of family blaming, credit is due to many families that, instead of being dysfunctional, have demonstrated remarkable survival skills while encountering multiple levels of oppression (e.g., racism, heterosexism) in the larger social structure.

To summarize thus far, family therapists tend to overlook the stress imposed on the family when one of its members struggles in the throes of addiction, and substance abuse counselors often focus on the addictive behavior itself outside of the context of family dynamics. According to the CSAT (2004) Treatment Improvement Protocol 39, collaboration by both disciplines is needed for a multidimensional approach. Working out ways for the two disciplines to collaborate will require a broadening of assumptions common in the two fields. Substance abuse counselors can learn from a systems approach the impact that treatment will have on the whole family because when an individual changes, so do family roles and relationships.

Focus on the Family

In the addiction treatment literature if not always in treatment itself, a major focus has been on children of alcoholics, adult children of alcoholics, and rules and role-playing in the chemically dependent family. The family's stages of progression into the illness of alcoholism was first noted and graphically described by Joan Jackson (1954), who published an article on the subject in the *Quarterly Journal of Substance Abuse*. During the 1970s, when the family therapy movement began to gain momentum, the concept of viewing the family as a system led to the notion of alcoholism as a family disease (Brooks & Rice, 1997). Sharon Wegscheider's (1981) groundbreaking writing and films on "the family trap" marked a departure from the earlier atomistic and individualistic approaches of addictions specialists. In her depiction of typical roles that members of the chemically dependent person's family play, Wegscheider (now Wegscheider-Cruse) conceptualized alcoholism in terms of both its physical and social dimensions. Her approach was highly practical in its implications and one with which family members could easily identify.

Popular author and public speaker Claudia Black was influenced by the writings of fellow social worker and systems theorist Virginia Satir. Black's (1981) thought-provoking book *It Will Never Happen to Me!* applied many of the fundamentals of systems theory concepts to family alcoholism treatment. Her "don't talk, don't trust, don't feel" formulation neatly summed up the dynamics in an alcoholic household. In 2002, Black updated her book to include addictions other than alcoholism and issues pertaining to "adult children" as well as younger children.

In 1983, Lawson and Lawson published *Alcoholism and the Family*, which helped integrate family therapy concepts and substance abuse treatment. The view of the family as client was provided in this text. The second edition was published in 1998. Kaufman (1985) similarly provided helpful guidelines for family counseling in his *Substance Abuse and Family Therapy,* and later, Kaufman and Kaufman (2002) further developed the techniques of family therapy in situations of alcohol and other drug use. Wallen's (1993) *Addiction in Human Development* contributed a developmental model to addiction treatment. Because alcoholic families often resist change, as Wallen noted, particular attention must be paid to their life cycle stages as the system adapts to the problem drinking of a family member. Families as well as individuals move through stages of recovery that affect the balance or equilibrium that has evolved through the underfunctioning of one family member. The final stage of recovery, according to Wallen, involves restoring the system to a balance that maintains sobriety.

A student of social work (in a paper submitted to van Wormer on August 8, 2005) describes the trickle-down effect on the family related to his uncle's drinking:

> I have seen this with my old alcoholic uncle because my grandparents would attack his lifestyle, and my aunt would sit down and defend him even though it was making my aunt grow apart from her parents. Then you had my cousins who would have to choose sides. Then my parents would get involved when my aunt or my grandparents would call to discuss the matter. Then if they said the wrong thing, my other aunt would get mad and she would talk bad to her spouse and kids about my parents or the other aunt.

The same writer goes on to describe how his family system changed when his father quit drinking:

> When my father was going through the 12-Step program, his family members all finally came and supported him. Before they would not really want to be around him, yet they knew this was the time that he needed help, so we all rallied around to do whatever it took to keep him sober. And to this day it has worked. That is how a change in a person's behavior has repercussions throughout the whole family.

Formal family treatment often is not necessary thanks to the almost universal presence of self-help groups that have developed to provide support and guidance to families torn apart by the ravages of addiction. Al-Anon, founded in 1951 to serve the families of Alcoholics Anonymous (AA) members, today has groups in more than 70 countries. In its early days, Al-Anon was only for wives, who often were seen as somehow responsible for their partners' drinking. Today, male partners of alcoholics, although a minority, are members of Al-Anon as well. The focus is on group support and establishing independence from the sick patterns associated with addiction. There is no evidence, however, that attendance by a concerned family member at such groups helps motivate his or her loved one to quit drinking or using, or to get treatment (Miller et al., 2011). The reason may become clear in the following description from a visitor to Al-Anon.

Jaclyn Randolph (in personal correspondence with van Wormer or November 13, 2009) shares how her thinking changed regarding her boyfriend's treatment. This change took place, according to her, after only one 30-minute Al-Anon meeting. As she tells us:

> The group focused on one of the Twelve Steps for that day. The one they happened to be on was an eye opener for me. I did not realize it until they came across to one woman who I felt I was a lot alike. She explained about how she had been mean to the man in her life who as an alcoholic. She would threaten him and say things that were not very helpful for the alcoholic. It made me realize I had not been very helpful to my boyfriend. I criticized him, got mad at him when he drank, and threatened to leave if he did not change. For me it was frustrating because he would say he was in control, but his actions never showed that, and I would always point that out. Our last fight had been about his drinking. He said I reminded him of his dad, someone I never wanted to be compared to. He said I made him feel terrible, and when he told me that I felt awful. So later I told him I would work on it. My going to this program caused me to realize that even if he does not admit he is an alcoholic I need to do something for myself. I never really wanted to leave him— I loved him and knew he could be a good guy when he was not drinking. I was willing to accept that, and I knew I was not perfect. When the lady at the Al-Anon meeting said the things she said about her relationship, emotions just flooded for me, and when they came to me I broke down. I was embarrassed, but it was then I realized just how mean I had been. I had been claiming to be there for him but I wasn't really. I was hurting him.
>
> This program only lasted 30 minutes, but those 30 minutes I attended changed my life. (Printed with permission of Jaclyn Randolph)

One of the most significant referrals the addictions counselor can make to family members of alcoholics is to a local Al-Anon group. Clients should be prepared for a kind of ritualistic openness and friendliness that may at first seem intrusive; they should be encouraged to visit several meetings before deciding on whether to join. Self-help groups such as this are particularly appealing to clients who are outgoing and extroverted.

The Twelve Steps used by Al-Anon were modified slightly to pertain to persons who are powerless not over alcohol but over another's use of alcohol. Individual work is directed toward independence and self-awareness. Learning that attempts to shield the alcoholic or addict from the consequences of his or her addiction are futile and counterproductive helps free the family members from the emotionally wearing attempt to control what cannot be controlled. Members are aided in achieving detachment from the active alcoholic or addict. Al-Anon members rave about the close personal bonds that develop from membership in this group. Recognition of one's powerlessness over another's addiction goes a long way toward reducing one's guilt feelings.

Alateen is the organization for children of alcoholic parents. Children are helped to achieve understanding of alcoholism and awareness of severe family problems. Nar-Anon is the comparable group for family members of narcotics users, and Gam-Anon is for the families of compulsive gamblers. Adult Children of Alcoholics (ACOA) is a rapidly growing group for those who grew up in alcoholic homes and who may have many unresolved feelings and issues pertaining to their family life. Members are encouraged to give full vent to their repressed

TABLE 10.1

The following facts were presented on the website of the National Council on Alcoholism and Drug Dependence during Alcohol Awareness Month, April 2010. This press release was set to coincide with the showing of the film *When Love Is Not Enough: The Lois Wilson Story*, which highlighted the life of the co-founder of Al-Anon.

Some basic facts:

- 22.2 million addicted to alcohol and other drugs
- 15.4 million to alcohol alone
- 3.6 million to illicit drugs, no alcohol
- 3.3 million to illicit drugs and alcohol
- $400 billion—annual cost of alcohol and drug problems: productivity, accidents, etc.
- 85,000 annual deaths due to alcohol

Addiction to alcohol and drugs is a family disease:

- 18% of adults (1 in 5) have alcoholism in family
- 38% of adults have 1 relative with alcoholism
- 76 million (4 out of 10) affected by alcoholism
- 10 million married to someone with alcoholism
- 27 million children of alcoholics (COAs); it is estimated that 11 million are under the age of 18
- 13–25% of children of alcoholics develop alcoholism

Hope, Help and Healing:

- Over 20 million individuals, family members and children are in recovery from alcohol/drug addiction
- With education, intervention, treatment, recovery and self-help, children and families affected by alcohol/drug addiction can break the chain of addiction

Source: New York. The National Council on Alcoholism and Drug Dependence (NCADD). (2010, April). Retrieved from http://ncadd.org/NCADD_Alcohol_Awareness_Month_2010.pdf.

feelings. Because emotions may be intense, newly sober alcoholics may be advised to achieve a lengthy sobriety first before joining such an endeavor.

MODERN DEVELOPMENTS

Fortunately, thanks to the influence of the feminist movement and modern biological research concerning the etiology of mental disorders, family systems theory has, to some extent, reconceptualized its teachings. The addiction treatment field, to its credit, never did view the family as the source of pathology; addiction was seen as primary in its own right. It is the cause rather than the symptom of family communication problems. In fact, with the disease model firmly entrenched and the focus on the individual alcoholic, the wonder is that the family was incorporated into treatment programming at all. That the family's needs do get addressed is probably a reflection of the increasingly interdisciplinary nature of the chemically dependent treatment field and the fact that so many practitioners in the field come from alcoholic family backgrounds. Professionals schooled in family counseling techniques, moreover, have brought to addictions work a modified and highly useful understanding of family pain and dynamics. In short, a gradual paradigm shift in thought from family as enemy to family as treatment ally has occurred.

Whereas family therapy as a profession is informed by a systems theory that focuses on internal dynamics of the family, social work draws on systems concepts in a more holistic way, often as part of an ecological perspective. This perspective avoids simplistic explanations about causation and views the person and environment in constant interaction. In its pure form, systems theory and the closely related ecological model view cause and effect as intertwined; relationships are interactive. Causation, like the seasons, is viewed as circular. Combining these basic systems concepts with ecology's model of the person in the environment, an ecosystems perspective provides a useful framework for viewing family dynamics. This approach is especially relevant today because the very concept of what constitutes a family is changing.

In the United States and many industrialized nations, the concept of family has undergone rapid change over the past two generations. During the latter half of the 20th century in the United States, for example, the proportion of married couples with children shrank; such families made up only 24% of all households in 2000. The idea of family has come to signify many familial arrangements, including blended families, divorced single mothers or fathers with children, never married women with children, cohabiting heterosexual partners, and gay or lesbian families (CSAT, 2004). The family, in other words, is a complex ecosystem.

The ecosystems perspective views people as nested in constant interaction with forces in their environment. Individuals are nested in families; families are nested in communities (Germain, 1991). The substance misuser's ecosystem might consist of the family, peers (those in recovery as well as those still using), treatment providers, nonfamily support sources, the workplace, and the legal system (CSAT, 2004). In severely troubled families, family members often are connected not just to each other but also to any of a number of government agencies, such as social services, criminal justice, or child protective services. From this viewpoint, substance misuse is associated interactively with physical problems, mental health problems, and shortcomings in treatment provisions in social services designed to promote physical and mental health. *Interactionism* is the theme—society's neglect in treatment and prevention and failure to reduce the stress to individuals suffering unemployment, the lack of affordable housing, and the like and individuals seeking stress relief in substance use and/or gambling, actions that only compound the stress. Stress and addictive behavior can be seen interactively as phenomena that go round and round and are mutually reinforcing. Clearly, society pays a price in regard to the social problems related to widespread substance misuse and other dysfunctional escape avenues. The economic toll includes a huge drain on people's employability and other elements of productivity as well as on medical and local and state government resources. But, most immediately, the impact of this cycle of stress and self-destructive, escapist behavior is experienced in the home.

FAMILY ADAPTATION TO ADDICTION

Adaptation is a useful way to conceptualize the family's response to a member's destructive and addictive behavior. Adaptation is defined by Germain (1991) in terms of her ecological framework as an active process of self-change, environmental change, or both, not a mere passive adjustment to circumstances. Adaptation flows from and helps alleviate stress caused in the family system by the drinking, gambling, compulsive sexual behavior, and so on. Paralleling individual adaptation to stress by the addict is the awesome set of demands imposed on family members.

The idea of an ecological framework within which substance abuse occurs is consistent with family therapy's focus on understanding human behavior in terms of constant interaction with the people and other systems in a person's life (CSAT, 2004). In this view, family members inevitably adapt to the behavior of one of the members who is underfunctioning in some way, such as from an illness, including a substance use disorder. Typically, the family develops patterns of accommodation and ways of coping with the substance use (e.g., keeping children quiet and out of sight or resorting to social isolation).

Each family has its own peculiar style of adaptation—coping through hiding key resources (money), blaming, covering up for the addictive behavior, joining in the addiction, or becoming extremely touchy with outsiders who criticize. The stress of the addictive pattern (e.g., gambling and winning, gambling and entering a losing streak) has a synergistic, or multiplying, effect throughout the family system and related social networks. The family, awkwardly, may come to serve in a mediating role between the addict and other systems—work, school, larger family. But gradually, as the illness progresses, the bridges between the alcoholic and his or her social world will be broken. The family may then adapt to the social isolation and continual stress of the progressing alcoholism, or members may regroup and form a reconstituted family without the addicted member. A third alternative, of course, is substance abuse treatment for the individual separately and within the context of the family. Treatment considerations would focus on the development of new, nondestructive communication patterns and adaptation to changes associated with recovery.

A teacher whose husband grew up in an alcoholic home comments on Germain's concept of adaptation by the family to illness in an adult member:

> Perhaps my husband and his younger brother are good examples of Germain's premise. Bill was 16 and his brother, Eric, was 7 when their alcoholic father

died. Eric was the younger child. Bill's perception had more years of exposure, while Eric's remained that of a small child's view. Bill grew up to be a man who rarely drinks. Eric not only is an alcoholic, but his behavior when he was an active drinker landed him in prison.

Bill basically hated his father because he saw more abuse and had to shoulder more responsibility because of the alcohol, while Eric did not. Their perceptions influenced the choices they made in living environments. Bill adapted by using the influence as a picture of how not to be. Eric saw that influence as a way to get people to do things for you so you can be "happy." His perception led him to choose similar environments to fill his need for a comfort zone. This environment influenced more abusive drinking and behavior, which ultimately led to his incarceration. (personal communication; May 14, 2001)

As Leo Tolstoy once wrote, "All happy families are alike, but every unhappy family is unhappy in its own way" (1917/1876, p. 1). Individuals within the same family, likewise, adapt differently to the same stress. Consider the following description of life in an alcoholic home as remembered by one high school teacher:

Communication in my family was much like Claudia Black's rules suggest. "Don't talk, don't trust, and don't feel." We were not allowed to talk about the problems of my dad's drinking and mental illness. If I attempted to talk about it, I was just told, "He's sick and can't help it." Communication was so poor that my mom participated in what I consider an unhealthy game to communicate with my dad. She would call one of my older sisters who lived outside the home and, within my dad's earshot, tell her something she wanted my dad to hear. For instance, if she wanted to go to a baby shower, she would tell one of my sisters and hope my father would hear. Then he would ask her what she was talking about. Most of the time he didn't allow her to go anyway, but this was her method of trying. My father was guilty of unhealthy communication as well. He would stop talking to my mother for up to four days at a time if she said or did something he didn't like. He would then communicate sarcastically through me. If I would ask him why the television wasn't working right, he would say, "Ask your mother, she thinks she knows everything." He would tell me adult information while she was in the room. Although he was talking to me, he was really talking to her.

I remember coming home and feeling like I was walking on eggshells every day because I never knew what the mood would be. I spent a lot of time being tense. We were not allowed to discuss our problems with outsiders or bring outsiders into the home. We were not allowed to have any feelings except laughter. If we were hurt, we could laugh but not cry. I was told exactly how to feel, so to this day I have a hard time describing how I actually feel. (personal communication shared with van Wormer, November 2005).

As the addicted person learns to adapt his or her lifestyle to accommodate the tremendous demands of this illness, so the family unit adapts to the stress that has been imposed on its functioning. As various individuals come forward to fill the essential family roles, the integrity of the family is preserved; equilibrium is maintained but at the expense of one or more individual members. If the person with the substance use disorder later recovers, the operating family system will be "thrown out of whack," a crisis will occur, and individual and group adaptation will be required.

In summary, according to ecosystems insights, the individual, whether the family member or the close relative with the addiction problems, is not viewed in isolation but as someone in dynamic interaction with the environment. Attention is paid to the complex ways that individual persons, in terms of the roles they perform, are intertwined with other roles in the family.

WEGSCHEIDER'S ROLE THEORY

Wegscheider (1981) introduced a small clanging mobile (the same device that hangs over a baby's crib) to represent the family interaction pattern; as one piece of the mobile is moved, the whole apparatus moves. Roles that individual family members play reinforce or clash with roles of other members.

Wegscheider, who, like Claudia Black, was inspired by Virginia Satir's role theory, labeled the following roles played in the chemically dependent family: the chemically dependent person, the chief enabler, the hero, the scapegoat, the lost child, and the mascot. These types are based on her and others' observations and they should be regarded as ideal types only; their existence is not scientifically validated. Associated with upwardly mobile middle-class families, the following purported characteristics may or may not apply to other social classes and ethnic groups. (See Chaput [2001] and McGoldrick and colleagues [2005a], for a comparative analysis of styles of family functioning in the presence of substance misuse.) Van Wormer, in her practice in Norway, found that family members readily identified themselves and others in their families with these roles. Many identified with more than one role, saying, for example, "I was a little bit the hero and a little bit the clown growing up." The following descriptions are drawn from van Wormer's Family Week presentation in Norway (see van Wormer [1995] for more details). Our purpose in presenting these roles is not because we believe they represent reality but because the concept of role-playing has been found helpful in engaging people in family systems work. The use of childhood labels is controversial; even the authors of this text disagree about their usefulness in family group programming. But we do agree that Wegscheider-Cruse's conceptualization has helped popularize the idea of family systems work and that this is a positive development. Please regard the descriptions that follow with appropriate skepticism.

THE CHEMICALLY DEPENDENT PERSON This member of the family is gripped by contradictions. Sensitive to the point of touchiness, the chemically dependent person is selfishly preoccupied with the sources of addiction. Often charming and talented, this family member tends to see life events and personalities in terms of black and white, all or nothing. There is a tendency to escape the scene when very high expectations (of relationships, work, studies) are not realized. When a man occupies this role, he is often treated with great fondness by his children. The woman alcoholic or addict is inclined to be either divorced or married to a fellow alcoholic or addict. She is subject to strong criticism for her neglect of motherhood responsibilities.

THE FAMILY MANAGER Because Wegscheider's term *chief enabler* has acquired pejorative connotations, in disregard of the survivorship nature of this role, we prefer the term *family manager*. The individual who occupies this position is often the sober partner of an alcoholic or addict. The role that the family manager assumes is to overfunction to compensate for the partner's under-functioning. As the family sinks along with the alcoholic or addict into near ruin, this individual worries, nags, and struggles to balance the checkbook. His or her denial in the early stages of the partner's addiction may be replaced by a frantic and bitter awareness later on. The person who occupies this position in the family structure suffers from a bad press that relates to the game he or she often ends up playing in conjunction with the games of the alcoholic or addict. Counselors at treatment centers are quick to condemn the sober partner for some of the covering-up devices that make survival as a family possible. If not accorded a great deal of sensitivity, family managers are often plagued by feelings of shame and guilt.

THE HERO Often the firstborn child in the family, this high-achieving and competent individual is constantly seeking approval. The family labels this child as the star—scholar, athletic hero, or performer. Inclined to suffer from low self-esteem, the child in this position tends to feel loved for what he or she does rather than for who he or she is. Accustomed to baby-sitting and caring for younger siblings, this child often grows up to work in the helping professions. Perfectionism is a key risk. Marrying an alcoholic or addict is a risk, according to Wegscheider (1981) and Black (1981, 2002); such a mar-riage recapitulates one's caretaking role from the family of origin.

THE SCAPEGOAT This is the child, often the second born, whom everyone loves to blame. The negative label is applied and seems to stick. The irresponsible behavior that accompanies this role often lands the perpetrator in trouble. According to the typology, early pregnancy is a risk for girls and delinquency for boys; school performance is poor, and early experimentation with drugs and alcohol is common.

THE LOST CHILD This child lives in a fantasy world and is said to be little or no trouble. Although he or she may be lonely, this younger child can entertain him- or herself through endless playing with dolls, watching television, or playing computer games. When family members fight, the lost child has an excellent escape mechanism. To grow into a responsible, mature adult, the boy or girl in this role requires a tremendous amount of help with self-expression and facing problems realistically.

THE MASCOT Forever clowning, the occupier of this role helps provide comic relief for the family unit. Encouraged to be cute and to joke around, the mascot can attract much positive attention while distracting members from serious matters. Often hyperactive, this child has a short attention span, which may be linked in some way to the needs of the family. The means of escape is laughter.

But don't children in all families play roles? This is a commonly asked question when a counselor presents these role descriptions. The answer is yes. All of us play roles in our families, at work, and in therapy groups. When stress is high, the roles tend to become rigid and are used as defense mechanisms (i.e., forms of escape). The children's roles, like that of the family manager, are best conceived as normal responses to an abnormal situation.

The strengths inherent in the roles are rarely mentioned. And yet, the family manager typically has excellent organizational skills and flexibility. This person's capabilities and resourcefulness help the family survive. Angela, the mother described by Frank McCourt in *Angela's Ashes,* resorted to all sorts of compromising behavior in her struggle to keep her children from going hungry as the father squandered the family's money through drinking and lost jobs.

Children who grew up in addict or alcoholic homes often develop coping mechanisms that may be useful later. The hero, for example, learns to assume responsibility early and often becomes a leader in adulthood. The scapegoat, who makes friends easily, may become a business success because of his or her willingness to take risks. The lost child has a great imagination and may write poetry or get involved with the arts. The mascot is often popular and, of course, knows how to use humor in creative and original ways. And as Fisher and Harrison (2008) point out, the roles that children play in the alcoholic home are similar to those played in all dysfunctional or disease-ridden families. And most such children play a combination of roles, not just one.

The term *codependence,* originally used to describe the strain of being a partner to a chemically dependent person, has taken on a life far beyond the intent of the original use of the term. Sometimes, this phenomenon is described as a disease that predated the relationship with a partner who was addicted to alcohol or other drugs. Fisher and Harrison (2009), for example, regard codependence as a useful paradigm to depict the impact of substance dependence on the family. And they view the condition of codependence as a potential problem among substance abuse professionals who themselves have experienced the same pain as their clients.

The use of this concept has been criticized for pathologizing caring functions, particularly those that have traditionally been part of a woman's family role, such as showing empathy and engaging in self-sacrifice (CSAT, 2004). Sandra Anderson (2009), for example, in her book on substance use disorders in lesbian, gay, bisexual, and transgender clients, is highly critical of the way this concept has been used to pathologize characteristics associated with women, and to encourage separation rather than connectedness with one's family of origin. As she also indicates, little scientific inquiry has focused on codependence, so there is no validity to the concept. This fact notwithstanding, the codependency movement has spawned a plethora of books, workbooks, and workshops across the United States, and a huge market in the sale of related products. Whereas early models (influenced by psychoanalytical theory) blamed wives for their husbands' alcoholism, the more recent formulations look to the family for the perpetuation of the illness. The codependence formulation theoretically is a combination of the disturbed spouse and the disturbed family hypothesis (Miller et al., 2011). None of these three hypotheses, as Miller and his colleagues suggest, are supported by research evidence.

In addition, the use of the negative codependency label is inconsistent with the precepts of the strengths perspective. Further, the codependency teachings, from a cross-cultural perspective, are problematic for work with people from cultures that stress intergenerational connectedness and close extended family ties.

As early as 1987, the Hazelden Family Center disassociated itself from use of this codependence "diagnosis":

> The view we take at the Hazelden Family Center is rooted in health promotion, a systems approach to health problems. We believe that each member of the family has an innate power of self-healing, and we try to awaken that power within our clients. Our practices are based on a combination of Al-Anon principles and the family systems theories developed by Murray Bowen, Ph.D. Both de-emphasize the need for a diagnosable sickness, instead requiring a sincere desire to change.
>
> There are many ways to help families return to health, and we respect the philosophical differences that shape various practices in our growing field. Codependency, both as a clinical and popular term, brings some of these differences into focus. (Hazelden Publishing Company, 1987, p. 2)

Interestingly, the book *Codependent No More* by Melody Beattie (1980), which quickly sold over 5 million copies, is published by Hazelden Publishing Company and is on display in the treatment center's bookstore. A 2011 edition of the *Codependent No More Workbook* is now available. As of 2011, a search of the Hazelden bookstore on the website at http://www.hazelden.org lists around 50 books with content pertaining to codependency and 14 books with this term in the title.

The *Diagnostic and Statistical Manual of Mental Disorders, Text Revision* (*DSM–IV–TR*) does not include codependence in its manual of mental disorders, nor is there any indication this term will be included in future editions. This omission was a big issue in the 1980s as chemical dependence professionals sought to have that diagnosis receive official sanction from the medical community and also to open up the possibility for insurance reimbursement for treatment. The notion of codependence as a disease in its own right, characterized by a lack of control and inevitable progression created a rift between substance abuse counselors who included this term in their treatment vocabulary and professionals in the mental health field who favored a more evidence-based approach (Fisher & Harrison, 2008).

Instead of using the pejorative term *codependent*, our suggestion is that a more positive term such as *survivor* or *caring family member* be applied to women (and men) who have done whatever is necessary to protect themselves and their families from the consequences of their partners' drinking, gambling, or drug use. To describe the situation of a family member who is sinking into the abyss of illness along with the loved one, the term *coaddiction* might be applied. Instead of a disturbed family or codependence hypothesis, Miller and colleagues (2011) have introduced the term *stress-coping hypothesis* to depict the family's response to the addiction of one of its members.

Despite the fact that the family members do not have a disease—only the symptoms of struggling against a loved one's addictive behavior—individual and family counseling can be extremely beneficial in the healing process for these caring family members. Work in the area of self-esteem can do much to help resolve powerful feelings accompanying years of abuse and unshared pain.

SOME MODERN TREATMENT MODELS

Work with the whole family is now recognized, at least theoretically, as a vital component in addiction treatment. Research shows that family involvement can help mobilize substance users to enter treatment and have a successful recovery (Landau & Garrett, 2008; Miller, 2006). In her review of the relevant literature, McCrady (2006) concluded that family-involved treatment is associated with higher rates of treatment compliance and retention than is treatment without family involvement. Having a functioning support system is crucial in preventing a lapse into previous problematic behavior. And because family members often develop problems in response to someone else's drinking or other drug use, including early experimentation with psychoactive substances by children, getting the entire family together for counseling should be a standard of addiction prevention. Family sessions offer an opportunity, moreover, to help children in the family understand some of the stresses their non–problem-drinking parent has been under.

The introduction of network therapy is a disease-based approach designed to reinforce social networks. This form of treatment, which involves family members and peers in the client's relapse prevention efforts through the promotion of cohesion teamwork among network members, is a welcome addition to the chemical dependence field (CSAT, 2004; Galanter et al., 2002). Research shows that the children in these families benefit from these interventions that seek to prevent their development of substance use problems.

One highly structured approach that trains family members in how best to deal with the addicted client has shown a 64% success rate in getting loved ones into treatment. As Pies, Fiellin, Miller, and Saitz (2009) point out, this success rate far exceeds that of the more traditional approaches. Called the Community Reinforcement and Family Training Approach (CRAFT), this treatment intervention was created by Robert Meyers. It consists of 12 one-hour sessions in which the therapist teaches families skills needed to help change their interaction style and develop a new way of dealing with the drinker or drug user. The training encourages participants to take care of their personal needs and to provide positive feedback when their loved one is sober. Little (2005) tested the effectiveness of this approach by randomly assigning 130 significant others to CRAFT, the Johnson Institute Intervention, and Al-Anon Facilitation Therapy. The CRAFT program was found to be several times more effective than the other traditional approaches in helping family members feel empowered and getting their alcoholic or addicted relative into treatment. Motivational psychologists, such as Miller and colleagues (2011) strongly endorse this approach, given its proven effectiveness. The CRAFT program, as these researchers indicate, utilizes an approach that is conceptually opposite to Al-Anon in counseling family members that indeed they can have substantial influence on their loved one's substance use and on initiating treatment. In contrast to the teachings of Al-Anon, which is that family members need to focus solely on their own issues, CRAFT teaches specific skills to family members in the belief that they can make a difference. Among the skills taught are the following: reinforcement for reduction in alcohol or drug consumption, encouragement to seek help, scheduling other events during usual substance use periods, and emotional withdrawal when he or she is using.

Our viewpoint is that there is room for both these approaches; which one is best depends on a particular family's needs. The goal of Al-Anon is to help the family members detach emotionally from their chemically dependent spouse or relative for their own peace of mind and personal development. In this regard, attendance at the group's meetings has been shown to be effective. For family members who desire a more proactive approach, a skills-training model might be more beneficial.

Family group counseling is a major contribution borrowed from New Zealand child welfare programming, which originally was based on indigenous forms of treatment. The typical format is for social workers to gather all the relatives together who could be helpful in resolving the difficulty (e.g., child neglect due to heavy alcohol use by the parents). The process is empowering for all concerned because the persons with the biggest stake in effecting individual change are the ones looked to for the solutions. Most often, some sort of kinship care is the result.

In child welfare as in some other areas of social work, there has been a paradigm shift in our notion of family. What were once considered alternative family forms—alternative to the stereotypical White middle-class nuclear family—are now considered all-American. Social workers and counselors who have learned to draw on kinship care with African American families are now widening the net for all families in search of resources and strengths. The very concept of family in turn has been expanded as well. As more single parents are raising children, relationships involving three or more generations are becoming increasingly important to individuals and families; these relationships are diverse in structure and functions, and for many Americans, multigenerational bonds are important ties for well-being and support over the course of their lives (CSAT, 2004).

McGoldrick and colleagues (2005b) bring our attention to the role that cultural differences play in worldview and basic values, and how these differences impinge on the therapy sessions. Even the definition of family differs greatly from culture to culture, as they suggest:

> The dominant American (Anglo) definition focuses on the intact nuclear family, whereas for Italians there is no such thing as the "nuclear" family. To them, family means a strong, tightly knit three- or four-generational family, which also includes godparents and old friends. African American families focus on an even wider network of kin and community. And Asian families include all ancestors, going all the way back to the beginning of time, and all descendants, or at least male ancestors and descendants, reflecting a sense of time that is almost inconceivable to most other Americans.... British American families are likely to feel that they have failed if their children do not move away from the family and become independent, whereas Italians generally believe they have failed if their children do move away. (p. 24)

Family interventions, to be effective, need to be geared toward the family's stage of recovery. This stage may or may not parallel their relative's journey toward the same end. The following technique directs the therapist's attention to the needs of the family as they progress into wellness. Consistent with other chapters in this book, we are drawing on Prochaska and DiClemente's (1992) and DiClemente's (2006) stages-of-change model.

STAGES OF CHANGE AND FAMILY TREATMENT

Research on the effectiveness of family counseling based on the motivational enhancement model is sparse. There is no Project MATCH for gauging the effectiveness of motivational family treatment techniques. Within Project MATCH, however, the success of treatment outcomes was related to the extent to which the client's social network supported sobriety (DHHS, 1999). In a review of the motivational literature, the Center for Substance Abuse Treatment (CSAT, 1999) located several studies with favorable outcomes that involved counseling the spouses of alcoholics from this person-centered perspective. The stages-of-change model has been found helpful for understanding how to enhance families' awareness of the need for help and change in how addictive substances are used in the family.

Thomas and Corcoran's (2001) findings in their review of the empirical literature on family-of-alcoholic interventions are relevant here. Interventions in the studies located were of three types: unilateral interventions that involved the family only without the drinker's direct involvement; marital-partner therapy in which the focus is on improving communication patterns to promote sobriety; and work with the entire family in which all parties work on the problem in question together. A consistent finding in the literature review was that the unilateral approach, especially when reinforcement training was provided, produced a positive outcome in getting the substance using person to commit to treatment and/or behavioral change.

The following typology of family stages of adjustment corresponds in many ways to where the alcoholic or addict is with regard to the continuum toward recovery. Often the substance-using relative lags behind the rest of the family regarding recognition of the problem and progress toward change. Or individual family members may be at a stage that parallels that of the person who is the focus of their concern. There are many variations on this theme, however; sometimes, especially in cases where a woman is making progress in treatment, her partner is continuing to drink and denying her problem or the fact that he (or in the case of lesbians, she) has a problem as well.

Prochaska and DiClemente's stages of change—the transtheoretical model—is featured prominently in this book because of its organizational power and flexibility in describing advances toward change in a positive direction. Such a progression is not conceived of as linear but as a spiraling, sometimes up and sometimes down. There is room in the model for both advances and occasional setbacks. For our discussion of the progression of family members from a position of "nobody in our family has a problem that time won't take care of" to a position of "we are all engaged in recovery work together," we have chosen to draw on the stages of changes as an organizational framework. Adaptation of the transtheoretical model to work with families with addiction problems helps us appreciate the level of ambivalence that family members experience as they grapple with emotions concerning their disappointments and grief. These emotions might not have been shared even among the family members themselves; some of the feelings might have been repressed for years. This adaptation of Prochaska and DiClemente's model can aid practitioners who work with families to have a better understanding of the uneven process of family coping with the reality of addiction, an understanding that can help reduce the blame often placed on family members for taking such a long time to act decisively and who are often given the pejorative label of "enablers" of their addicted relative.

Precontemplation

Under one scenario, unilateral therapy, the family attends treatment sessions to work on their problems and feelings surrounding a loved one who refuses to get help and who is destroying the lives of those around him or her. Even if the strategies are not successful toward the goal of helping the substance user to change, there is some evidence that the sessions help unite the rest of the family and provide benefits in terms of reduced levels of frustration and depression (Thomas & Corcoran, 2001).

If the family unit is in this early stage of adjustment to the illness, a stage characterized by a general lack of awareness of the magnitude of the problem, it is unlikely the family will approach the treatment center for help. Sometimes, however, the family's presence is encouraged as a part of the client's treatment plan. Family members might be urged to attend a family evening–type program, such as when a relative gets into trouble with the law through a driving-while-intoxicated conviction and follow-up assessment or through a child welfare referral.

The rules that the initiated family follows at this stage of recovery are likely to be of the "don't talk, don't trust, don't feel" variety (Black, 2002). Consider what one 9-year-old child in an alcoholic family said to Black when she was encouraged in a counseling session to open up and discuss her father's alcoholism, "When you have a rule in your house for so long, to not talk about Dad's drinking, it's really hard to talk now—even when he is sober" (p. 30). That is the "don't talk" rule. The "don't trust" rule comes about when children lose their sense of safety and when rituals and routines are perpetually broken. "Don't feel" is the end result as children in alcoholic or addict homes get out of touch with feelings they cannot communicate and that do not get validated.

Contact with family members seen at this stage is apt to be short-term and superficial. Sometimes, families attend lectures that present information. Generally, counselors provide a description of family roles along with a discussion of characteristics of the so-called functional family. And what are the characteristics of a functional family? Open communication, respect for individual differences and boundaries, stable routines and rituals, and having fun and a sense of humor are among the qualities generally elicited (from the grouping of family members). Figure 10.1 depicts various family styles of interaction

A. The *enmeshed family.* Spouses are estranged: one child is enmeshed with the father, one with the mother.

B. The *isolated family.* Lack of cohesion and social support. Each member is protected by a wall of defenses.

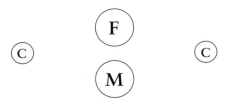

C. The *healthy family.* All are touching, but their boundaries are not overlapping.

FIGURE 10.1 | FAMILY FORMS

Source: van Wormer (1995), p. 207.

that can be shared with the group of family members. Participants will often volunteer to diagram their families of origin and current families in this manner. A discussion of healthy boundaries often ensues.

In working with a family in which there are addictive problems, the therapist might start by helping members identify their family's goals. He or she asks open-ended questions, such as: "What brings you here?" "What would you like to happen in our work together?" "If you could change some things, what would they be?" "Describe a time in the family when things were going well."

An excellent discussion starter at this point is the miracle question used in solution-based counseling, "What if a miracle would happen? What would your family life be like then?" The purpose of this question is to help build incentives to change the problem as family members contemplate a happier family life than the one they have.

According to O'Farrell and Fals-Stewart (2006), motivational interviewing has a place in counseling partners who both have substance-related problems because this approach can help them resolve ambivalence about changing their behavior. Motivational interviewing can be used to help partners discover that their most cherished values are incompatible with the choices they are currently making. It is essential to get both partners to commit to change; otherwise, the relationship is threatened, and the risk of relapse to the partner in recovery is constant.

Typically, assessment of the individual with the problematic behaviors is done at this initial stage of treatment. As required by the court or insurance company, assessment most often is solely of the individual with the diagnosable problem, with family members providing input at a later stage, if at all. In so separating the person engaged in treatment from significant others, however, the opportunity is missed to engage family members in the process. The inclusion of family members from the start offers several advantages. Such inclusion provides a means of observing how family members relate as a unit, a means for discovering strengths in the client's background, and an opportunity to provide education into the biological and psychosocial aspects of addiction. In addition, it is never too early to begin preparing the family for the changes members will need to make in conjunction with the addict's recovery. The first session may close with the assignment of tasks designed to get family members to take some small steps in areas where change is feasible. One such step might be to attend a relevant support group, such as Al-Anon or Nar-Anon; involvement in such a group can be invaluable in helping members maintain their sanity and receive group support.

One message that family members who attend these Twelve-Step groups receive, however, is that they should give up attempts to influence the addictive person's behavior. (Al-Anon's first step is the same as that of the traditional Twelve Steps: that one is powerless over the alcohol, but here it has an indirect meaning because the powerlessness is over another's addiction to this substance.) The more proactive model that we are describing here, in contrast, is consistent with empirical research. Thomas and Corcoran (2001) hold that caring persons may be able to have an influence in getting the drinker or drug user to seek help. When recommending that clients who are family members attend Al-Anon meetings, the counselor might do well to prepare them for the different messages of the diverse approaches of Al-Anon and the family counseling program.

Barber (2002) combines behavioral theory with the harm reduction model and provides extensive instructions for counselors and family members of behaviors to accompany each of the stages of change. A mistake partners make, he suggests, is to behave the same regardless of whether the other partner drinks. "But," he states, "their drinking does matter to you and your behavior should convey this" (p. 71). His recommendations are not to prepare meals, keep them warm, enter into conversations, or watch TV with the drunken partner. "If your partner collapses on the floor or gets sick, leave him or her to sort it out when sober" (p. 73). Then he recommends a loving and nurturing response when the person is not drinking. The message helps the person distinguish acceptable from unacceptable behavior and recognizes that the heavy drinker has good qualities as well.

Contemplation

During the contemplation stage, the family member acknowledges concerns and is considering the possibility of the need for change—for example, in recognizing that the loved one has a serious addiction problem. Psychologically, the shift is from reluctance to acknowledge a problem to anger caused by the suffering related to the drinking, gambling, or other addiction. Many families are ambivalent, however, and waver between "He can't help it" and "She won't do anything" (CSAT, 2004).

The therapist often gets involved when a client requests counseling for help with a marital problem, child custody situations, or behavioral problems in his or her children. Then, in assessing the client's needs and goals, the role of addiction in the family's life becomes apparent. Just as he or she does in working with clients in early stage treatment, the therapist strives to elicit self-motivational statements of insight and ideas about solutions from the family clients. Reinforcement of clients' capabilities and survival skills are vital to help strengthen these persons to take action toward the desired solution. Possible actions that the family members might be willing to consider are to meet with the therapist for several sessions of family counseling to communicate needs and expectations; to work toward getting their loved one to receive help for the addictive behavior, perhaps through attending a self-help group such as AA; and to work on plans for a trial separation. Whether or not the situation improves, family counseling of this sort can be a godsend for the partner and other family members; having a dispassionate but compassionate outsider to talk to can be immensely therapeutic. An Australian study by Oreo and Ozgula (2007) revealed that parents of adult children with substance-related problems have strong grief reactions and that there is a clear need for parents to have their feelings of distress validated and for interventions that promote grief work and facilitate family coping. Although the participation of significant others in treatment has been found to be one of the best predictors of cocaine abstinence, Laudet, Magura, Furst, Kumar, and Whitney (1999) found the male partners of cocaine-using women to be far more difficult to engage in family treatment than the female partners of users. The men's active drug use and their refusal to focus on this fact are among the reasons hypothesized for this finding. However, more recent research from the United Kingdom on male partners of female problem drinkers found that, contrary to expectations, the males did not withdraw from their female partners, but rather were anxious to be actively involved in their treatment (Philpott & Christie, 2008).

While we are on the subject of male partners, consider *Taking Back Your Life: Women and Problem Gambling* by Davis (2009), which describes the particular hardship facing the woman in recovery from compulsive gambling. "There is something about a woman gambling away the family nest egg, pawning the wedding rings, or maxing out credit cards that becomes unforgivable in the eyes of many husbands and partners" (p. 143). There is rejection of the woman by families and friends who do not understand the role that addiction plays in the problem. The pain inflicted upon family members is one of the biggest regrets reported by women in the study. One woman who was quoted in the study compared the grief inflicted upon her family by her gambling with the harm done by her husband's addiction to alcohol. The drinking, she said, did not devastate the family in the way her gambling did. In the end, her family cut her out of their lives.

Gam-Anon is a self-help group for family members of compulsive gamblers. Attendance at the group's meetings can give these families the support they need. Open Gamblers Anonymous meetings—meetings that are open to visitors—can help reduce the amount of blame placed on the person with the gambling problem; persons who attend these meetings can bring family members with them. Fortunately, as Davis indicates, some gambling treatment programs recognize the need for family members to get therapeutic help and offer weekly family groups as a part of the treatment package.

PREPARATION

The theme for this stage of change can be summarized in the sober partner's attitude of "I can't take it any more. I am at the breaking point." Tasks for the counselor during this period are to help family members clarify their goals and strategies for effecting change, offer a list of options and advice if so desired, and steer the family toward social support networks. Boosting the partner's confidence at this stage is tremendously important. The family members can even be taught the principles of motivational interviewing, which they can use themselves to minimize resistance in their loved one.

Typically, one or more family members in this stage begin to look for a solution. The motivational therapist will now introduce treatment or other options that have been successful with other clients. This moves the group into the action stage.

ACTION

At this point, let us assume the whole family is involved in counseling except for the addicted individual. All family participants are bent on seeing change happen. Family sessions at this stage are crucial in building solidarity so that the individual in question will not be able to play one family member off against another. The sessions are crucial also in providing these individuals with the opportunity to ventilate their feelings—grief, rage, despair, and so forth—and to learn about addiction as illness. If the substance-using relative is still unwilling to do anything about the problem, professional interventions may be called for (CSAT, 2004).

If the timing is right, an often effective therapeutic technique that the family members might want to consider engaging in is a formal Intervention (we are capitalizing this term to differentiate it from the standard usage of the word) with their loved one. Associated with the Johnson Institute in Minneapolis, the ritualized Intervention is a process for providing feedback to the person with addiction problems. Key players in the addicted person's life are identified; these may include a spouse, a doctor, a boss (if one's work is in jeopardy), a member of the clergy, and close friends.

In Box 10.2, Carroll Schuety, a counselor who has conducted numerous successful Interventions with Iowa farm families, describes the process. This boxed reading is presented with some reservations, however, in light of harm reduction expert and psychologist G. Alan Marlatt's belief (as expressed to Jackson, 2005) that Interventions shouldn't be performed under any circumstances. His belief is that interventions are confrontational and punishing, and that such strategies increase resistance and denial. Miller (2006) reports that 80% of families find the confrontational meeting unacceptable and refuse to go through with it. Among those who complete an Intervention, however, a high percentage of their family members with addiction problems do enter treatment. The kind of Intervention performed by Carroll Schuety uses a softer touch, with excellent results that are well known in her local area.

Box 10.2 is presented with an additional cautionary note: Interventions can place too much psychological pressure on people who may feel ganged up on; sometimes, the reaction is suicide. This happened in the case of the musician Kurt Cobain, whose tragic death, according to Marlatt, came on the heels of an intervention arranged by his wife. Addictions specialist and social work professor Lala Straussner, cited in the same article by Jackson (2005), concurs. She favors a motivational approach and advises social workers to be mindful that there is more potential for harm than good when an Intervention is performed by someone without specialized training.

The CRAFT approach described in a previous section is an example of a motivational approach. Family members ready to take action would do well with the CRAFT skills training. Connors, Donovan, and DiClemente (2004) advocate a similar strengths-based approach that avoids the conspiracy aspect of the Johnson Institute model of Intervention. Called ARISE (A Relational Intervention Sequence for Engagement), the process begins at home as family

Box 10.2	STEPS TO INTERVENE
	Carroll Schuety, Pathways Treatment Center, Waverly, Iowa

It's 2:30 Saturday morning. A car swerves and rolls up over the curb onto the lawn. The driver stumbles out of the car and staggers into the house. Suddenly, there is a shattering of glass as a lamp crashes to the floor, and cursing echoes throughout the house. The spouse and children lie silently in their beds, not moving a muscle, fearful of provoking further anger in their spouse or parent. They listen for the sounds of heavy breathing as a sign that he or she is asleep so they can feel safe from verbal and/or physical abuse for a few more hours. Society assumes that alcoholism involves and destroys only the drinker and that the family suffers no devastating effects. Many people also believe that the spouse and children must remain passive and helpless as the drinker sinks deeper into the deadly disease of alcoholism. In fact, nothing is further from the truth. Family members can take constructive action to stop the destruction of the drinker and themselves through the process of an intervention.

What is an intervention? It is a method of confronting the drinker for the purpose of getting him or her into treatment. It is a confrontation that causes a family crisis that will bring the drinker to the painful realization that his drinking has caused problems and he cannot continue as he has been. This can be facilitated by a substance abuse counselor. Although if a layperson understands the process, a counselor is not necessary.

The first step in organizing an intervention is to gather two or more persons together who have witnessed the destructive drinking behavior. The people could consist of family members, friends, clergy, coworkers, employers, or a physician. It has been my experience that children who have suffered from the behavior of the drinker are often most effective in forcing the drinker to see himself realistically.

In the second step, each person prepares a detailed written list of specific examples involving alcohol misuse that he or she has personally witnessed. These actual events force the drinker to admit that the concerns are legitimate. Another important aspect of writing the lists and reading them to each other prior to the actual confrontation is that it unites the group. In preparing your list, you should avoid opinions and general statements such as:

"You're always drinking."

"You drink too much."

"You might get fired."

"Your drinking is getting worse."

You should point out instead:

"Last month, I felt scared when you fell down the stairs and broke your foot after you had been drinking."

"Last Thursday, I saw you drinking on the job. I felt concerned because your job performance has been going down in the past few months."

(continued)

Box 10.2	Steps to Intervene *(continued)*
	Carroll Schuety, Pathways Treatment Center, Waverly, Iowa

"I'm feeling scared because in the past year, you've been arrested twice for drunk driving offenses."

"When you attended my school conferences, you were drunk and I felt embarrassed."

It is important to talk about your feelings when you share the situation that you are describing with "I feel" or "I felt" statements. Feeling statements will help reduce the defensiveness of the drinker.

You must, as an Intervention team, agree on a "what if" clause in case the drinker rejects all your options by declaring, "I can do it myself. I'll just stop drinking." If this happens, you must persuade the drinker to make a commitment to enter treatment if his or her own attempt to quit is unsuccessful. It must also be understood that even one drink constitutes failure on his part. Another action that could be taken is to commit the person to treatment through a legal process. The local prosecutor's office or treatment center can usually provide the details.

Source: Printed with permission of Carroll Schuety.

members express their concerns. The ARISE interventionist collaborates with members of the extended family and trains them in the techniques of motivational enhancement. This more gradual approach to motivate an individual to accept help has been found to have better long-term results than the Johnson Institute style of Intervention. Bearing this finding in mind, Landau and Garrett (2008) speculated that the rebellious response and subsequent pattern of relapse noted in the Johnson Intervention group could be avoided by using a method that started with an invitation rather than by surprise or coercion. In extensive interviews with former clients of the Johnson Institute following an Intervention, they found that the clients resented the way they had been forced into treatment, a fact that had caused many to drop out. Interviews with family members who refused to get involved in their loved one's treatment showed that these people disliked the confrontational aspect of the Intervention program. In contrast, investigations of the ARISE programming found that it was a user-friendly, strengths-based, and cost-effective method of engaging family members in treatment. A distinction of this approach from the CRAFT model is that this is a systemic, not a unilateral, approach. In contrast with that of the Johnson Institute, there is no surprise here; the individual with the addiction problems is invited to participate from the start. The researchers attribute the success of this model to the fact that it draws on the connectedness and commitment of concerned members of the extended family to motivate their ailing family member to get professional help.

Bear Landau and Garrett's research findings in mind as you read the following testimonial from a young woman who provided this poignant account of her childhood memory of a formal Intervention of her father:

> When I was around 13, we visited a counselor for a rehearsal. The next week my dad's brothers and sister, close friends who were recovering alcoholics, my mom, my sister, and I gathered at our house on the farm and dad came home. I think he was aware of what was going on and became extremely emotional, crying with his head down at the table. I remember exactly where I was standing, at the end of the table against the wall with my sister, and when it came my turn to read my statement all I could say was, "I want you to go because I love you" and began to sob. I remember going up to my mom and dad's room to get his suitcase and Dad couldn't say a word; he just cried and hugged us and got in the car to go. It is one of the saddest memories I have from childhood. He was gone for 1 month, and about 3 months after he returned we sold our farm and he relapsed, yet to return to treatment about a year later on his own will; he has been sober ever since. I can honestly say I am very proud of him. (personal communication; January 28, 1999).

As mentioned in Chapter 6, an excellent thing for teens with a history of substance use who are in the early stages of recovery is to transfer from their old school to a school that specializes in recovery. For family members, graduation from a recovery school is a powerful event. Read Box 10.3 for a description by the graduate's sister.

MAINTENANCE

More important than the role of family in assessment and treatment is the role of family in early recovery. As the central client's progress toward health and wholeness becomes more and more a reality, the family therapist may take on the role of facilitator to aid in the process of reconciliation. Members of the family may want to come to terms with lifelong feelings of rejection; there may or may not be a desire for forgiveness.

Brown and Lewis (2002) delineate the therapeutic tasks and pitfalls involved in the process of recovery. *The Alcoholic Family in Recovery* draws on the experiences of members of four recovering families to describe the ways recovery has challenged and changed their relationships. Much of this process, as Brown and Lewis demonstrate, is painful.

Transition, as Brown and Lewis explain, is characterized by massive change that affects children and adults at every level. The environment feels unsafe; the family structure, after years of chaos, is not strong enough to handle change. In the counseling session, the therapist addresses family concerns and recovery progress. Individual members may have issues from the past that they want addressed at this time.

Familiar ways of interacting must change if the family is to maintain a healthy emotional balance and support sobriety (CSAT, 2004). As behavioral changes are established in the family, the focus of sessions shifts toward maintenance of change independent of the therapist. Now that the problematic

Box 10.3	MY BROTHER'S GRADUATION, BY ASHLEY HARDER

"We thank God for giving this gift back to us, and pray that He may help us guide them through this new chapter of their lives."

Not the typical start to a high school graduation, but this was no typical high school. To better explain, a little history is necessary. My 18-year-old younger brother, Ryan, is a drug addict who has 20 months of sobriety. Ryan's addiction and recovery has been at the center of my family for the past four years, starting with years of lying, enabling and pleading. Ryan entered his life of recovery on April 23, 2009. After two attempts at inpatient treatment and several relapses, as Ryan puts it, "Something just stuck," and he has not used a chemical to alter his mood or physical state since October 15, 2009. Being a high school sophomore at the start of his recovery, Ryan made the decision, with the strong persuasion of my family, to start at Sobriety High School instead of return to his old high school, where his chances of staying sober around using friends and in a drug-rich environment were slim.

Sobriety High School has two campuses in Minnesota, Arona and Alliance, each serving the northern and southern suburbs of Minneapolis, respectively. The purpose of the school is to provide a sober and recovery-focused education for high school students who struggle with addiction and have made the conscious decision to live a life of sobriety. It functions like a normal school, with all the required classes, but with the addition of "group," an hour set aside each day for peer counseling. It is a concentration of 60 highly emotional and impulsive teenagers, a group that is already a challenge for teachers and parents. Add to that their addictions and emotional struggles that accompany recovery, and you can imagine the courage, patience, and compassion of the staff. Instead of a dean of students, they have a recovery director. Students call teachers by their first names, and there is an obvious personal connection between the staff and their students. Many of the kids would likely have dropped out of high school and never finished without the amazing program offered by Sobriety High School.

Cigarette smoke stung my eyes as I walked through a thick cloud to enter the building, the stale and familiar scent following me inside. A soft buzz floats around the sanctuary in a sober church, called the Recovery Church, where the graduation ceremony is being held. From the hall outside the sanctuary, the piercing notes of a bagpipe render the crowd silent. All eyes turn to the back of the room, as 30 misfit teenagers with crooked caps and floor-length black gowns enter the room behind the bagpipes. If you steal a glance around the room, you can see the tears of joy, pride and painful memories swell in the eyes of parents, family members and the school's staff, who have grown so close to these graduates. You can see each teenager beaming with genuine smiles, many of them feeling for the first time a sense of accomplishment and self-worth.

The average person, unaffected by the pulls of addiction, would be too distracted by the wild hair, tattoos, piercings and dark, heavy makeup to understand the significance of the occasion. This is a group of students who, from the outside, appear to be the stereotypical drug addicts, the kids you would likely avoid at the mall or in the hallways at school. But, for those who know the circumstances surrounding this unique class of 2011, it is easy to look past the tattoos and see the hardworking, caring, funny and sweet kids who got lost in the throes of their addiction to drugs or alcohol.

The ceremony is opened with a prayer, not to the Christian God, but to "God as we understand him," a key principle to the belief system of Alcoholics Anonymous, the twelve step program [that] is embraced by Sobriety High School. Following the prayer, a short documentary is shown, made by the recovery director. The video is a series of short interviews with students, each one telling a similar story of fear, loneliness and hopelessness, only to be turned around into joy, friendship and support by the environment provided to them by Sobriety High School. The graduation is short, but with only 30 grads, 15 from each campus, it is intensely personal. Each student is called up individually to accept the diploma as a quote from the student is shared with the audience. Most students take this opportunity to thank family members and friends for the support and motivation to be sober and finish school. An outsider would likely be confused at the emotion in the room, so thick and heavy you can feel it.

At the moment my brother's name is called, in the blink of an eye I am taken back to the struggles. The desperation felt by my family to get him out of his dangerous lifestyle. The lying on my part to help him cover his tracks, the pleading to get him to come home after days out using. The Intervention stings my memory, the late night phone calls of Ryan begging me between sobs to get him from treatment. The disappointment and hurt accompanying each relapse. But then, slowly, the pride. The memory of each small victory. The joy of watching the compassion and love come back into my brother. The overwhelming need to brag about him to every person I meet. The laughter, as his once stellar sense of humor slowly sneaks its way back into his personality. The new memories we have created, the close bond we have re-established. Suddenly, I am grinning from ear to ear as tears well in my eyes, a combination of sadness and pain for the past, relief for his recovery, happiness for his renewed sense of hope, gratefulness for our relationship, and optimism for his bright future, now filled with potential.

I am struck by the words in the prayer of the pastor, thanking God for returning these people back into our lives. As the family member of an addict, that is exactly what I thank God for every day, for giving me my little brother back. As his recovery director reads the quote from Ryan, it reaffirms to me that the Ryan I grew up with is back, to stay. Instead of a mushy, emotional thank you, my brother simply quoted a comedian that we used to listen to with my Dad, and as tears stream down my cheeks I am overcome with laughter, which is the epitome of my wonderful relationship with my little brother, my best friend.

substance use has decreased and other family interactions have improved, other family problems (e.g., suppressed anger and an adolescent's substance misuse) may need to be addressed. Family sessions at this point can help make the difference between sobriety and failure to change and even between keeping the family together and divorce. The therapist can help the family anticipate stressors and support the client who has completed treatment in avoiding triggers and high-risk events.

A complete "what to do if" contingency plan needs to be set in motion in case of backtracking. Clients are given numbers to call and asked to come up with ideas for what to put in a step-by-step plan for getting the help they need. Harm reduction strategies and solutions to sustain the change in behavior should be explored in treatment aftercare counseling. The couple, moreover, often can benefit from receiving information concerning sexual problems that arise in the absence of alcohol and drug use; if the issue is sexual addiction, the posttreatment counseling needs are tremendous.

Together, family members can benefit greatly with work in the areas of communication, decision making, and discussion of rules and how the rules will be enforced. Now that progress toward recovery is well under way, the stage is set for a shared groping for solutions to problems that may never have been identified without outside help. Ideally, the family therapist is a nonparticipant in the immediate, emotionally charged issues within the family (e.g., who takes responsibility for what and the division of labor). The focus of the therapist is not on the content of the interaction but on the process itself. Through skilled and friendly questioning, the therapist imparts awareness of the form of the interaction: "Have you noticed how whenever the two of you argue, your son leans over backward in his chair until you have to stop him?" "I notice when you cry, Mary, your daughter's eyes start watering up too. Does this suggest a strong closeness of feeling between the two of you?" "Who interrupts whom in this family?"

To handle the all too common situation of the newly sober father's bid to reestablish his role of authority in the family, the therapist (T) might proceed as follows with the father, Bill (B):

T: Bill, I'd like you to stop for a moment and check out what you're doing. You expressed concern that the children don't talk to you more openly. Right?

B: Yes.

T: Let's think about what just happened with Steve. He began to tell you how he felt about those reckless rides in the car and you cut him off with "Not now." Did you notice how he pulled back then? How did you feel, Steve, when your father cut you off in this way?

Instead of excessive emotionalism in family sessions, a calm, intellectual atmosphere should be encouraged. Members are helped to listen to each other. Heavy emotion can be defused. For example, if a mother becomes distraught, other members can be asked what they can do to provide support or how they feel about the outburst. In interviewing with the mother, the focus can be on the thoughts that accompany her feelings.

Emotions may need to be defused when couples shout at each other. A helpful intervention is to interrupt with a loud "Stop!" Each person is then requested to take turns addressing the therapist individually. To reinforce listening, the therapist can ask the nonspeaking partner to reiterate what he or she heard the speaker say.

Conversely, couples who are not connecting emotionally with each other can be asked to look at each other and speak directly to each other, not to the therapist. To encourage engagement in a mutual undertaking or to introduce new forms of communication, homework assignments can be given to strengthen the communication process.

Through the various intervention devices described in this section, the family systems therapist guides a family with a recovering member toward their own process of recovery. As the newly sober member regains responsibility within the family, other members have to adapt accordingly. Acting as a coach or guide, the therapist can help map the course of this adaptation. The entire family must be prepared to accept as a member a sober and somewhat changed person. Every person's role in the family alters in the process of one individual's change.

The following list of rules can be drawn up and passed out to family members. Members read the rules, practice them in sessions, and agree to abide by them at home:

- Attack the behavior, not the person or his or her background. Use a pleasant tone of voice; avoid yelling, hitting, cursing, or name calling. Deal with one issue at a time—don't let your partner counter with, "Well, if you think I'm bad, you ought to see how you come across!" or "When you get a decent job, I'll think about it!"
- No mind reading. Don't say, "You are jealous" or "You're just angry because you…"
- Narrow the problem to a manageable size rather than focusing on vague wholes.
- No accusations and putdowns, such as, "You're just like your father!"
- Don't rehash the past.

WORK WITH FAMILIES IN WHICH THERE ARE CO-OCCURRING DISORDERS

Family psychoeducation programs for mental illness teach families in single family and multifamily group formats about the biological nature of the disease, the role of medications, the risks of drug interactions, and how family members can reinforce compliance with regard to prescription medication. A basic principle of family psychoeducation is improving coordination of all elements of treatment (Moore, 2005).

Mueser, Noordsky, Drake, and Fox (2003) describe the role of motivational interviewing strategies in working with families of persons with co-occurring disorders. Early contacts focus on providing support and expressing empathy. Substance use is not given priority at first unless the family members bring it up themselves. When goals are identified, the steps toward achieving them are identified, prompting family members to explore the possible interference by substance abuse to achieving the goal. During the preparation stage, family work involves helping families overcome their ambivalence about change and instilling the hope that change can be achieved even after many years of frustration.

Family members who have experienced so many defeats and disappointments in caring for and maintaining a close relationship with their children and partners with mental disorders need a tremendous amount of affirmation and reinforcement of self-efficacy. In short, as Mueser and colleagues (2003) suggest, motivational interviewing techniques have wide applicability in working with families in these situations.

IN SITUATIONS OF DOMESTIC VIOLENCE

Intimate partner violence among alcohol and drug misusing couples is alarmingly high (Fals-Stewart & Kennedy, 2005). More often than not, one form of abuse predicts the other form of abuse (Bennett & Williams, 2003). Counselors who work at women's shelters should informally assess women who need their services for substance misuse problems in their families. If the violence is substance related (most often the substance is alcohol, meth, and/or cocaine), treatment should be provided for one or both parties. Any time families are brought in for mental health or relationship counseling, and especially when substance misuse is a factor, it is critical to screen for domestic violence. If there is violence against children or children are endangered, child welfare authorities must be notified. If the wife is being victimized, the husband or partner should be referred to a batterers' group.

Couples in which there is battering should not be referred to conjoint counseling because if the wife reveals secrets about the marriage—for example, some sort of inadequacy in her partner—she is at risk of being beaten when they return home. Even family counseling that includes the children with the mother is a high-risk proposition; an insecure and suspicious husband might question the children to find out what was said at the sessions. Down the line, after the batterer has been successfully treated, some family counseling may be attempted. Safety for all family members, however, must be the first consideration.

Because of the interconnectedness of substance use and violence, close collaboration between substance abuse agencies and women's shelters is essential (van Wormer & Roberts, 2009). Following screening and assessment of populations that come to the attention of service providers, coordinated programming to reduce the risk of harm to oneself or others is the approach that makes the most sense (Bennett & Williams, 2003). Due to their adherence to different, often conflicting models, however, the two types of treatment settings often operate under completely separate auspices with little or no direct contact. Because women's shelter providers operate from a feminist model and substance abuse counselors from a disease concept, collaboration between agencies has been a source of difficulty. The radical feminist model applied by the Duluth Domestic Intervention Project focuses on male power and control within a patriarchal society (interview with project representative Michelle Johnson, February 21, 2006); substance use by the perpetrator is regarded as merely an excuse for the battering. By the same token, substance abuse counselors give priority to the alcoholism or addiction factor in physical aggression to the neglect of cultural factors (e.g., a belief in male privilege or coming from a violent family). This bifurcation of treatment resources is much to the detriment of battered women in need of treatment of a substance-related disorder herself or for her partner, or of women in counseling for substance misuse who are being victimized in the home.

Harm reduction principles would go far to bridge the conceptual gap between the fields of domestic violence intervention and substance abuse counseling. Safety is the first consideration in both instances. Motivational work and the stages-of-change model are especially applicable to batterer education programs to establish rapport and help the batterer take steps toward behavioral change. This model, as adapted for work with batterers, is described in some detail in *Death by Domestic Violence: Preventing the Murders and the Murder-Suicides* by van Wormer and Roberts (2009). For battered women, the parallels between the stages of deciding to leave a violent relationship and deciding to get help for substance-related problems are striking. Most domestic violence interventions are based on empowerment practice and choice of options, in any case. Frasier, Slatt, Kowlwitz, and Glowa (2001) spell out motivational interventions with battered women to help them at the precontemplation stage develop a safety plan on the road to making a final decision about severing or maintaining the relationship. If the woman reaches the contemplation stage, she is asked to draw up a list of pros and cons regarding her decision to stay or leave. The woman is affirmed in her decision-making powers.

A promising development is the interdisciplinary education being provided across the United States that joins staff from substance abuse and domestic violence programming for the purpose of recognizing their common interests. Principles from motivational interviewing are often taught as a mutually relevant model to help men and women in treatment move in new and more productive directions.

CULTURAL CONSIDERATIONS

Chapter 5 of the CSAT protocol Substance Abuse Treatment and Family Therapy provides general guidelines based on the literature for working with multicultural and other specific populations. We draw on much of this information in the following sections. Information contained here is consistent with that provided by McGoldrick and colleagues (2005a).

WORK WITH NATIVE/AMERICAN INDIAN FAMILIES

Over multiple generations, American Indian communities have endured a succession of traumatic events that have enduring consequences for community members (Evans-Campbell, 2008). The Centers for Substance Abuse Treatment (CSAT, 2008) similarly stresses the role of cultural trauma in the backgrounds of American Indians and the need for practitioners to address the cultural pain caused by government policies promoting family breakup in the past by removing the young people from their families of origin. The high rates of substance misuse found in this population today in both the United States and Canada is often attributed to the loss of cultural strengths from the past. Alcohol, for example, is involved in five times more deaths of natives than of non-natives (Bearse, 2008). Rates of personal victimization are more than double that of any other racial group, even when controlled for income.

Although in many tribes large numbers of the membership abstain entirely from drinking and drug use, in some communities, according to the CSAT report, alcohol consumption is the norm, and abstainers may be ostracized. In the words of the report:

> When drinking together is a major family activity, the woman who abstains may, in effect, lose her family. With such high rates of alcohol and drug use, a woman's family and friends are unlikely to offer strong support for recovery. By acknowledging the role and the importance of family and community in either perpetuating the substance use or in providing a nurturing recovery environment, treatment providers must involve family and community members from the outset. (p. 123)

Because of the intergenerational aspect of substance misuse and in light of strong ties to family and community in the tribes represented, family and community-based approaches are strongly recommended. Native Americans, as Bearse (2008) indicates, often have broad definitions of family. Aunts, uncles, and cousins are prominent in family life. Thus, in light of the high rates of alcohol and other drug use found in this population, many more people are affected than is the case within a cultural setting in which the nuclear family is dominant and perhaps relatively isolated. A public health focus is important to address health issues as well, for example, HIV/AIDS and fetal alcohol syndrome. For treatment with Native American women, the CSAT report emphasizes the importance of gender-sensitive treatment services for disease prevention as well as assessment for a history of traumatic events, including sexual and physical abuse. The following guidelines are offered for effective family-focused counseling:

- Acknowledge the importance of family history and extended family members, and as deemed appropriate, involve family members during the course of treatment.
- Explore the woman's beliefs regarding healing and knowledge of cultural practices. Don't assume that a Native American woman follows traditional practices.

- Understand and acknowledge the specific tribe's cultural values, beliefs, and practices, including customs, habits, sex roles, rituals, and communication styles. (p. 121)

Cultural activities play a significant role in Indian tribal life, both in terms of healing and in boosting the self-esteem of tribal members. Typical activities of this sort include sweat lodges, powwows, talking circles, tribal music and crafts, traditional foods, and meetings with medicine people and tribal elders.

WORK WITH AFRICAN AMERICAN FAMILIES

To work effectively with African American families, family therapists must become familiar with the complex interactions, strengths, and problems of extended families. Many extended African American families incorporate various related people into a network that provides emotional and economic support. Often, numerous adults and older children participate in raising younger children, often interchanging family functions and roles (CSAT, 2004). Reciprocity is a key theme in the African American community: The practice of exchanging assistance is an essential part of extended family life. Such reciprocity may take the form of caring for another's child and knowing that the favor will be returned when necessary. Many extended families also take in secondary members, such as cousins, siblings of the parents, elders of the parents, or grandchildren. In other cases, families take in children to whom they are not biologically related.

The Center for Substance Abuse Treatment (CSAT, 2004) advises that the personal connection between family and therapist is the single most important element in working with African American families. Without rapport, treatment techniques are worthless and the family will likely terminate therapy early. Techniques shown to be effective with African Americans will be rendered ineffective if the therapist acts in a bureaucratic manner that is naturally alienating to clients.

WORK WITH LATINO FAMILIES

Keep in mind as we consider establishing a productive working relationship with Latino families that in Latin American countries, the family is generally prioritized above the individual (Tapia, Schwartz, Prado, Lopez, & Pantin, 2006). As a result, family treatment can be successful, but the quality of the relationship that develops in the first session is crucial to engaging families for return visits. The following guidelines for working with Latino families are adapted from CSAT (2004):

- A businesslike approach to treatment will not appeal to Hispanic/Latino families. A personable approach will yield much more effective results.
- Hispanic/Latino family members will be much more forthcoming when the therapist solicits their feelings through subtle and indirect means. Encouraging clients to speak forcefully and directly may have the unintended effect of inhibiting their participation.

- The establishment of behavioral contracts and homework assignments may be an overly task-oriented approach for this population. Scheduling time ahead to resolve intimate issues may also be unacceptable to these clients.
- Extending the disease model to incorporate the impact of a toxic social environment and the effects of oppression as factors contributing to substance dependence is an effective approach. While still holding people with substance use disorders accountable for their actions, this approach helps to frame substance abuse as a communal problem and spur family members into learning more about the effects of oppression.
- Using fundamental spiritual precepts can inspire hope and patience. The endurance of suffering, the practice of forgiveness, and the importance of repentance may be fertile values to use in working with Latino family members. This strategy should be used only when it is in harmony with the spiritual views of the individual family or family member. (p. 122)

WORK WITH ASIAN AND ASIAN AMERICAN FAMILIES

CSAT (2004) provides the following considerations for engaging Asian and Asian American families:

- Family therapists should be careful that therapy does not breach proscribed gender roles or boundaries between generations. The first appointment should be made with the decision maker of the family, who will most likely be the father.
- Asian clients respond best to credible experts who provide specific suggestions for alleviating distress.
- Sensitivity to clients' privacy is just as important at a macro level. Because different Asian American clients may live in the same tight-knit community, therapists should assure them of confidentiality and avoid sharing information regarding one client with another.
- Family therapists should not presume that therapy sessions will move forward on a regular basis. Counselors must choose between making the most of the first or initial sessions and scheduling ongoing regular sessions. Many Asians are unfamiliar with Western treatment models and will adopt a more infrequent, crisis-oriented approach to therapy.
- Clients may feel slighted if the therapist spends limited time with the family without providing a thorough explanation of his or her plan for treatment.
- It may be effective to leverage the family's willingness and arrange a rapid follow-up (sooner than 1 week) to strengthen the budding therapeutic relationship. (p. 126)

WORK WITH APPALACHIAN FAMILIES

The following guidelines are drawn from a research article on holistic work with Appalachian families (Denham, Meyer, Toborg, & Mande, 2004). The purpose of the research was to learn how to best increase motivation of rural Appalachian families to improve their healthcare practices and to reduce risk-taking behaviors within the family, for example, smoking. Because women in this culture are the family health monitors, messages concerning healthy practices must be directed toward them. Based on extensive focus-group work, observers discovered three levels of motivation among the women that ranged from high to low. Messages need to be tailored to each of these groups depending on their readiness for change. Additional guidelines for culturally sensitive disease prevention are these:

- Appalachian women who are motivated and confident need to receive only the relevant information.
- Women who are motivated but lack self-efficacy require support and encouragement to get the task done.
- Unmotivated women require work in the skills area and then the confidence to help their families get the treatment they need.
- Information must be presented in a factual, nonjudgmental way to allow recipients to draw their own conclusions about those facts.

WORK WITH GAY AND LESBIAN FAMILIES

Family can be a sensitive issue for gay and lesbian clients. Therapists must be careful to use the client's definition of family rather than rely on a heterosexual-based model. The following guidelines are adapted from the CSAT (2004) discussion of issues relevant to family work with gays and lesbians.

- The therapist should accept whatever identification an individual chooses for himself or herself, usually partner rather than friend or roommate, for example.
- Family therapists must be careful not to pathologize issues of boundaries and fusion, as many gay or lesbian couples appear to have more permeable boundaries than are commonly seen among heterosexual couples.
- A lesbian may seek support from an ex-partner to help with difficulties with a current partner more often than would typically be seen in a heterosexual female.
- When violence between partners is a treatment issue, safety must be the therapist's main concern.
- Many lesbian and gay clients may be reluctant to include other members of their families of origin in therapy because they fear rejection and further distancing.
- Gays and lesbians should not be encouraged to come out when they are not ready or when the family is not ready. (p. 131)

HEALING

The family chapter in *Social Work with Lesbians, Gays, and Bisexuals* presented the "rename, reframe, and reclaim" model (van Wormer, Wells, & Boes, 2000, pp. 174–175). Because this model is well adapted to the counseling needs of the family in recovery, we have further developed it here to provide a theoretical base for counseling families that contain an alcoholic or other drug addicted member.

RENAME

The particular choices of terminology are up to the family members and relate in part to the treatment model preferred. The clients and their family members, for example, may find that terms such as *recovering alcoholic*, *recovering grateful alcoholic*, and *recovered alcoholic* are positive attributions. The spouse or partner, ideally, will not choose to call himself or herself a codependent, but ultimately, the choice belongs to the client. If the use of the label brings a good result, the therapist would do well not to argue over the nomenclature. Key questions for the therapist to consider are: Are the new truths and realizations derived from treatment having a positive effect on your life? Are these new concepts consistent with a positive self-concept? In the end, perception is what matters.

The challenge to practitioners in a field whose literature and other teachings are guided by a language of damage and defects is to adopt a language that corresponds to concepts of strengths and resilience. The recovery movement, as Selekman (2008) informs us, consistently lists all the negative traits that children who grow up in alcoholic or addict homes are supposed to have. Helping the family members discover how well they have done under trying circumstances, their success in pulling together as a family unit, will go a long way toward reinforcing strengths that otherwise would go unnoticed. Labels like "survivor" and "family manager" should be used whenever appropriate. Indeed, family members should be encouraged to take pride in their resourcefulness because they have survived (with or without their addicted partner or relative) the turmoil of addiction and the stress of treatment, and because they have not only endured but prevailed.

Adopting a language of strengths has important ramifications when the substance misuser in the family is an adolescent. Generally, the use of labels like "alcoholic" and "addict" should be avoided. At a stage of life when they have not yet settled on an identity, the risk in having teens identify themselves as alcoholics and addicts is in creating a self-fulfilling prophecy with negative consequences. Selekman (2008) warns counselors against using the disease model with adolescents; he is referring to forcing young clients to refer to themselves as alcoholics or addicts, labels that they likely will resist using. Referring youth to AA and NA meetings also may present problems because of the customary use of forced labeling in these groups. Sometimes, on the other hand, the addict or alcoholic label is construed as the more positive alternative to something worse, such as when delinquent or criminal behavior can be understood as a part of drug-related addictive behavior. Under these circumstances, a referral to a Twelve-Step program, such as NA, might pave the way toward a more positive self-image and reconciliation with one's family.

From a family systems standpoint, relabeling problem behavior such as compulsive shopping as an addiction as opposed to foolish behavior changes the meaning by casting it in a more compassionate light. Renaming a relapse as a lapse similarly helps it to be seen as a mere setback that is manageable. When dealing with events of the past, the explanation "That was a part of the illness of addiction" helps family members get beyond individual blaming, reduces misunderstandings, and opens the door to more effective communication. These healthier ways of viewing the problematic behavior based on the use of more positive terminology are closely related to reframing.

REFRAME

Positive reframing is a helpful, in fact an essential, technique used by the therapist to instill hope and pride in one's accomplishments. To the seasoned counselor, helping clients reframe their experiences is probably second nature. Take relapse as an example; instead of treating this as a disaster, the counselor typically helps the client see it as a valuable learning experience. This approach is integral to harm reduction; instead of the concept of relapse prevention, relapse management is a more realistic term, one that is recommended by Brad Karoll (2010). From the reframing perspective, clients can be directed toward a more positive view of a situation through deliberate questioning. Looking over the entire addiction experience in retrospect, clients can be asked, "Can you find anything positive that has come out of this experience?" Somewhat amazingly, clients and family members typically say, for instance, that it makes them understand one another better or that they want to help others and their families with similar difficulties to overcome. Therapists and clients should refrain from looking at children who grew up in alcoholic or addict homes through a deficit framework, such as seems to be the norm in addiction treatment circles.

Instead, as Walker and Lee (1998) rightfully tell us, the search should be for evidence of resilience in the families of origin as well as in the current household. Children of alcoholics, as Walker and Lee further indicate, do not necessarily become substance misusers; nor are they doomed to marry addicted persons. The best insurance against such a happenstance is the development of a strong inner drive to achieve and a strong support system for affirmation. Where other practitioners and theorists seek and find defects in adult children of alcoholics ("guessing at what normal is"), for example, the therapist of the strengths-based school will look for resilience—and will probably find it.

To Maria Carroll (1993), reframing one's reality is integral to the healing process. For recovering persons, only when the bond to addiction is broken can they move to higher things and embark on "a journey home." To Carroll, the journey home entails constructing a personal reality, becoming disillusioned with this reality, letting the ego-self disintegrate, surrendering, reframing the old reality, and then allowing a new reality to develop as the transformed state. Through surrendering to the reality of the present, the person in recovery moves through a spiritual awakening toward wholeness and a sense of oneness with humanity. The process is similar for family members, who are embarking on a journey of their own from isolation to intimacy and from refusing to reach out and seek help to a willingness to ask for help when they need it.

RECLAIM

Healing is simply the inner change. It is the sense of peace that may result from therapy work in labeling feelings and controlling them through cognitive techniques, reframing troubling events in one's life, and recognizing how past events influence present feelings, thoughts, and behavior. Reclaiming lost and damaged childhood selves may occur through the joint effort embodied in the treatment relationship.

Healing often involves reclaiming what was lost either through drug addiction or in living in a family consumed with another's addiction. There is so much to reclaim: the fun in life, one's sense of peace and safety, one's spirituality, one's wholeness. Sometimes, to reclaim one's wholeness, the couple bonded by alcohol or other drug use find they have little else in common and can be enabled by the therapist to go their separate ways.

A prominent theme in the literature is that adult children of alcoholics find sources of strength and resilience in the nurturant parts of their cultural community and heritage (Cable, 2000). The emphasis on "we-ness," as Cable indicates, is integral to traditional Native American culture and can be reclaimed through collaboration with natural support systems in treatment. Community healing is often achieved through spiritual rituals and ceremonial gatherings (Bearse, 2008). Communitywide interventions in situation of rampant substance misuse may be conducted through a family circles program to help American Indian families reclaim their cultural identity and pride.

EXERCISES FOR FAMILY GROUPS

1. Family Sculpture
   Purposes: To portray roles in the family; to illustrate how the family works as a system; to help reveal feelings that accompany each role.

   The worker begins by explaining the technique to the family. This is a nonverbal technique that involves physical placement of persons in a symbolic fashion. The "sculptor" moves various family members into particular positions. The exercise begins with everyone standing up.

   Talking is not allowed. A family member volunteers to be the sculptor. The therapist instructs the sculptor to arrange the family members to show who is close to whom and what people do together. The setting reproduced may be the family at home in the evening or on an outing, such as a picnic. Following the sculpture display, participants discuss the meaning of each sculpture and how each felt about the role he or she played.

CASE 10.1	KATHY AND ED

The following case study recaptures van Wormer's yearlong, very up-and-down treatment relationship with "Kathy" and "Ed."

The challenge of treating this angry couple was such that I had to conjure up all my training as a sociologist as well as a social worker. And as is typical with alcoholic clients in treatment, it was not the alcohol that was the focal point of the sessions. No, the focal point was money—fights over money.

This couple is troubled. After 7 stormy years of marriage, they are literally and figuratively tearing each other apart. Ed has spent many nights in jail. "Because of racism," he says. "I never touched her." As I sit facing them both, I notice the racial differences: He is Black; she is White. Physical differences are pronounced also: He is large and muscular; she is small. But as we get into dialogue and emotions run wild, the personality and cultural differences, the seething hatred, are all that count.

Kathy speaks, complains bitterly, and words flow effortlessly while her husband, a laborer, quieter, struggles to get a word in. He is my client; I know and trust him. He has described his wife as a master manipulator, and today, he has brought her in for me to see for myself.

If she hates him so much, how can she love him, I wonder. To help sort out this question, I have each client write on a sheet of paper what is good and what is bad about their marriage. Kathy's negative list is three pages long; on the positive side, she lists only one thing, "great sex." His list is sketchy, but he agrees on the physical attraction.

Money is their biggest source of conflict. I already know Ed is sneaking money for his earlier family. Kathy shouts, "I want every penny accounted for. We have two children to feed! Is he drinking away the money? Where does it go?"

Earlier in his private session, Ed had told me that Kathy clawed herself on the chest with her own fingernails and then called the police. She claimed physical assault. Upon hearing this story, I talked Ed into getting his own place. He did so, but then, according to him, she called up begging him to return. Because of the risk of violence between them, I do not try to sort out the facts. My aim is to state the obvious: They can't live together and can't seem to stay apart. Yet they need to realize that for the children's sake they are better apart and sane than together and fighting.

After a request for them to work on communication, I bring out my Fighting Fair scheme, which lists the rules of communication. This conflict resolution scheme has rules such as no name calling, don't rehash the past, and practice exercises that go "I feel ___ when you ___." The purpose of this exercise is to help clients know their feelings and then to make requests of each other. Kathy, it turns out, is tormented with feelings of jealousy and possessiveness. She is putting all her energy into one failing relationship when her need is for other adult support. She is cut off from her family, who disapprove of her

(continued)

| CASE 10.1 | Kathy and Ed *(continued)* |

interracial marriage and biracial children. The best hope for connection to the wider community for her, therefore, is through active participation in self-help groups. I refer her to a private counselor to help her work on the source of her anger and to realize her need for close personal friends as a support system to help her as a single parent.

Ed, faithfully, sees me once a week for a year; he has had a year of sobriety and is making progress following through on goals. During this time, I explain some of Kathy's behavior in terms of her ethnicity (White Anglo-Saxon Protestant), especially her beliefs about family boundaries and the nuclear family. I reinforce Ed in his strengths and help him arrange visitation with his children.

In the end, Kathy became a local leader in Women for Sobriety, and Ed grew to love his weekly AA support group. Once they developed support systems of their own, they went their separate ways, much healthier apart than they had ever been or would ever be together.

Family sculpture can be effectively used in a Family Week program. Volunteers are asked to play the roles they play in their families or, in another variation, to play a very different role. Various roles, such as the substance user, the family manager, the mother's helper, the rebel, and the athlete, are given to participants. With the help of the therapist as sculptor, each arranges him- or herself in a way that best represents the role. For instance, a mother with alcohol problems may be put high on the chair or seated stooped over the table. The child who fantasizes when things get rough may stand in a corner or watch television. The family manager may extend his or her arm around the mother. All members freeze as for a portrait. Afterward, each person is asked to recapture the feelings of being in the role. The audience and players discuss the meaning of what they saw.

2. Drawing Family Maps
   Purposes: To open discussion about family lines of communication and closeness and to help the family gain insight into where the boundaries are.

   The therapist draws a circle on a chalkboard or flip chart to represent a hypothetical family. For example, an alcoholic mother and daughter could be represented by two circles with boundaries that overlap. Typically, if the mother cries, the daughter cries too. The sober father and the other daughter are also close, but these two, represented by two more circles, are apart from the others. Family members are asked to take turns drawing their families.

3. Family Relapse Prevention Plan

   Purpose: To help family members and the client being treated identify the warning signs of pending relapse.

   A list of warning signs is written by each participant. Signs must be clearly spelled out. Family members discuss these warning signs, such as extreme and obsessive devotion to work. They discuss what these symptoms meant in the past and reach agreement on what to do if they recur. An action plan is drawn up.

4. Genograms, or Family Tree

   Purposes: To provide information on patterns in families; to reveal possible hereditary and cultural themes that have been passed from generation to generation; to reveal similarities and differences across families joined by marriage.

   See http://www.samhsa.gov (TIP 39; Chapter 3) for an illustration of how diagrams can be constructed through the use of symbols. A marital pair is indicated by a line drawn from a square (male) to a circle (female). Divorce is indicated by two slash marks on the line. Words can be used for events, occupations, dates, and ethnic origins.

5. Showing Videos/DVDs

   Have family members arrive early to view a video/DVD portraying family roles. *Soft Is the Heart of a Child* (1979), though somewhat dated, portrays the family roles memorably. (A Spanish version is available at http://www.hazelden.org.) Viewers can be asked to discuss the roles and relate the tape to their own lives. A 1996 version, *Reflections from the Heart of a Child,* also includes the roles but adds a theme of domestic violence. Both films are around 20–30 minutes. The earlier one is simpler and more emotionally powerful; the second contains violence. Family members would also enjoy watching the 2010 Hallmark TV production on the life of the Al-Anon co-founder, *When Love Is Not Enough: The Lois Wilson Story.*

   Another option is to show *End Broken Promises* (1998), which features such commentators as Claudia Black in a discussion on the help adults can provide to children in alcohol- and drug-dependent families. All the videos mentioned are available from the Idaho RADAR Network Center lending library.

   A modern documentary, *Lost Childhood: Growing Up in an Alcoholic Family* (2004), interviews children of alcoholics at a special summer camp and then interviews some of them 15 years later about how the childhood camp experience affected their lives. (Available at a low price from Young Broadcasting of San Francisco at http://gigcat.midhudson.org.)

   Movies can be custom suited to the individual client. An African American survivor of family sex abuse might find a lot of meaning in watching the film adaptation of *I Know Why the Caged Bird Sings;* a southern White survivor might get in touch with her feelings in a viewing of *Bastard Out of Carolina.*

SUMMARY AND CONCLUSION

Family therapy is an exciting dimension of addiction treatment. Family work with alcoholics and other drug misusers is an area especially amenable to the biopsychosocial framework. Systems therapists can utilize a didactic focus to teach biological and physiological factors of substance misuse and the interlinkages among all the addictions. The psychological realm can be addressed through work on the thinking–feeling dyad. The social aspect relates to the systems component. This three-pronged focus can offer a shared assessment of the structure and interaction patterns in the family. Through this multidimensional approach, the therapist can help prepare the family for accepting back a member who, in the words of the old Scottish hymn, "once was lost, but now is found." The therapist can help prepare the family to cope with setbacks and even eventual separation from their substance-using relative. Through the use of various communications exercises or listening skills, workers can help family members deal with feelings of anger, shame, and guilt that have plagued them for a long time.

The family systems approach described in this chapter provides a view of the family as a system of interdependent parts. The commonly used metaphor of a mobile suspended from a ceiling was described: If one part moves, the other parts shift simultaneously. Counselors can use this metaphor as a starting point to educate clients about the boundary concept, the reciprocity of role-playing, and the development and enforcement of rules in the family.

Because addiction did not arise in a social vacuum and the people who developed the addiction problems did not suffer the consequences of addiction alone, attention needs to be directed toward the total social environment. The growth process for the family often requires a period of chaos that precedes the old state's breaking down before the formation of a new state can occur. The family systems paradigm offers addiction treatment a way of conceptualizing addiction as both an interpersonal and an intergenerational phenomenon. Even if the treatment agency lacks a full-fledged family program, individual counselors can usually invite clients to bring their significant others with them to sessions. The family should be regarded as a potentially valuable resource. Unfortunately, the legacy of blaming the family still persists. This potential can be countered by using the "rename, reframe, reclaim" framework introduced in this chapter.

References

Amodeo, M., & Lopez, L. (2008). Alcohol and drug problems: Practice interventions. In the National Association of Social Workers (NASW) (Ed.), *Encyclopedia of social work* (20th ed., vol. 1, pp. 136–141). New York: Oxford University Press.

Anderson, S. (2009). *Substance use disorders in lesbian, gay, bisexual, and transgender clients: Assessment and treatment.* New York: Columbia University Press.

Andreae, D. (2011). General systems theory: Contributions to social work theory and practice In F. Turner (Ed.) *Social work treatment: Interlocking theoretical approaches* (pp. 242–254). New York: Oxford University Press.

Barber, J. G. (2002). *Social work with addictions* (2nd ed.). Hampshire, England: Palgrave Macmillan.

Bearse, M. (2008). Native Americans practice interventions. In the National Association of Social Workers (NASW) (Ed.), *Encyclopedia of social work* (20th ed., vol. 3, pp. 299–308). New York: Oxford University Press.

Beattie, M. (1980). *Codependent no more.* Center City, MN: Hazelden.

Beattie, M. (2011). *Codependent no more workbook.* Center City, MN: Hazelden.

Bennett, L., & Williams, O. (2003). Substance abuse and men who batter. *Violence Against Women, 9*(5), 558–575.

Black, C. (1981). *It will never happen to me!* New York: Ballantine Books.

Black, C. (2002). *It will never happen to me: Growing up with addiction as youngsters, adolescents, adults.* Center City, MN: Hazelden.

Bowen, M. (1978). *Family therapy in clinical practice.* New York: Aronson.

Bradshaw, J. (1988). *Bradshaw on the family: A revolutionary way of self-discovery.* Pompano Beach, FL: Health Communications.

Brooks, C. S., & Rice, K. F. (1997). *Families in recovery: Coming full circle.* Baltimore: Paul H. Brookes.

Brown, S., & Lewis, V. (2002). *The alcoholic family in recovery: A developmental model.* New York: Guilford Press.

Cable, L. C. (2000). Kaleidoscope and epic tales: Diverse narratives of adult children of alcoholics. In J. Krestan (Ed.), *Bridges to recovery* (pp. 45–76). New York: Free Press.

Carroll, M. (1993). *Spiritual growth of recovering alcoholic adult children of alcoholics.* Unpublished doctoral dissertation, University of Maryland, Baltimore.

Center for Substance Abuse Treatment (CSAT). (1999). *Enhancing motivation for change in substance abuse treatment.* Treatment Improvement Protocol (TIP) Series, No. 35. Retrieved September 2006 from http://www.ncbi.nlm.nih.gov/books

Center for Substance Abuse Treatment (CSAT). (2004). *Substance abuse treatment and family therapy.* Treatment Improvement Protocol (TIP) Series, No. 39. Rockville, MD: Substance Abuse and Mental Health Services Administration.

Center for Substance Abuse Treatment (CSAT). (2009). *Substance abuse treatment: Addressing the specific needs of women.* Treatment Improvement Protocol (TIP) Series 51. HHS Publication No. (SMA) 09-4426. Rockville, MD: Substance Abuse and Mental Health Services Administration.

Chaput, L. L. (2001). *Assessment of family functioning in a clinical population of ethnically diverse substance users: Implications for practice.* Unpublished doctoral dissertation, University of Texas, Arlington.

Chase-Marshall, J. (1976, September). Virginia Satir: Everybody's family therapist. *Human Behavior,* pp. 25–31.

Connors, G., Donovan, D., & DiClemente, C. (2004). *Substance abuse treatment and the stages of change.* New York: Guilford Press.

Copello, A., Templeton, L., Orford, J., Velleman, R., Patel, A., Moore, L., & Godfrey, C. (2009). The relative efficacy of two levels of a primary care intervention for family members affected by the addiction problem of a close relative. *Addiction, 104*(1), 49–58.

Davis, D. R. (2009). *Taking back your life: Women and problem gambling.* Center City, MN: Hazelden.

Denham, S., Meyer, M., Toborg, M., & Mande, M. (2004). Providing health education to Appalachia populations. *Holistic Nursing Practice, 18*(6), 293–302.

DiClemente, C. C. (2006). *Addiction and change: How addictions develop and addictive people recover*. New York: Guilford Press.

Ellis-Ordway, N. (1992). The impact of family dynamics on anorexia: A transactional view of treatment. In E. Freeman (Ed.), *The addiction process: Effective social work approaches* (pp. 180–191). New York: Longman.

Evans-Campbell, T. (2008) Historical trauma in American Indian/native Alaska communities: A multilevel framework for exploring impacts on individuals, families, and communities. *Journal of Interpersonal Violence, 23*(3), 316–339.

Fals-Stewart, W., & Kennedy, C. (2005). Addressing intimate partner violence in substance abuse treatment. *Journal of Substance Abuse Treatment, 29*(1), 5–17.

Fisher, G. L., & Harrison, T. C. (2008). *Substance abuse: Information for school counselors, social workers, therapists, and counselors* (4th ed.). Boston: Allyn & Bacon.

Frasier, P., Slatt, L., Kowlwitz, V., & Glowa, P. (2001). Using the stages of change model to counsel victims of intimate partner violence. *Patient Education and Counseling, 43*(2), 211–217. family risks and resiliencies 417

Galanter, M. D., Dermatis, H., Keller, D., & Trujillo, M. (2002). Network therapy for cocaine abuse: Use of family and peer supports. *American Journal of Addictions, 11*(2), 161–166.

Germain, C. (1991). *Human behavior in the social environment: An ecological view*. New York: Columbia University Press.

Gruber, K., & Taylor, M. (2006). A family perspective for substance abuse: Implications from the literature. *Journal of Social Work Practice in the Addictions, 6*(1/2), 1–29.

Hazelden Publishing Company. (1987). Some thoughts on codependency. *Hazelden Professional Update, 5*(3), 2.

Jackson, J. (1954). The adjustment of the family to the crisis of alcoholism. *Quarterly Journal of Substance Abuse, 15*, 562–586.

Jackson, K. (2005, January/February). Do drug and alcohol interventions really work? *Social Work Today*, pp. 28–31.

Karoll, B. (2010). Applying social work approaches, harm reduction, and practice wisdom to better serve those with alcohol and drug use disorders. *Journal of Social Work, 10*(3), 263–281.

Kaufman, E. (1985). *Substance abuse and family therapy*. Orlando, FL: Grune & Stratton.

Kaufman, E., & Kaufman, P. (2002). *Family therapy of drug and alcohol abuse* (2nd ed.). Boston: Allyn & Bacon.

Krestan, J. (2000). Introduction. In J. Krestan (Ed.), *Bridges to recovery: Addiction, family therapy, and multicultural treatment* (pp. 1–12). New York: Free Press.

Landau, J., & Garrett, J. (2008). Invitational intervention: The ARISE model for engaging reluctant substance abusers in treatment. *Alcoholism Treatment Quarterly, 26*(1/2), 147–168.

Laudet, A., Magura, S., Furst, R. T., Kumar, N., & Whitney, S. (1999). Male partners of substance-abusing women in treatment: An exploratory study. *American Journal of Drug and Alcohol Abuse, 25*(4), 607–618.

Lawson, A., & Lawson, G. (1998). *Alcoholism and the family: A guide to treatment and prevention* (2nd ed.). Gaithersburg, MD: Aspen.

Leonard, L. (1989). *Witness to the fire: Creativity and the veil of addiction*. Boston: Shambhala.

Little, L. (2005). Program trains families to address addiction. *Family Practice News*, *35*(22), 43–44.

McCourt, F. (1996). *Angela's ashes: A memoir*. New York: Scribner.

McCrady, B. (2006). Family and other close relationships. In W. R. Miller & K. Carroll (Eds.), *Rethinking substance abuse* (pp. 166–181). New York: Guilford Press.

McGoldrick, M., Giordano, J., & Garcia-Petro, N. (Eds.). (2005a). *Ethnicity and family therapy*. New York: Guilford Press.

McGoldrick, M., Giordano, J., & Garcia-Preto, N. (2005b). Overview: Ethnicity and family therapy. In M. McGoldrick, J. Giordano, & N. Garcia-Preto (Eds.), *Ethnicity and family therapy* (pp. 1–40). New York: Guilford Press.

Miller, W. R. (2006). Motivational factors in addictive behaviors. In W. R.Miller & K. M.Carroll (Eds.), *Rethinking substance abuse: What the science shows* (pp. 134–150). New York: Guilford Press.

Miller, W. R., Forcehimes, A., & Zweben, A. (2011). *Treating addiction: A guide for professionals*. New York: Guilford Press.

Minuchin, S. (1974). *Families and family therapy*. Cambridge, MA: Harvard University Press.

Moore, B. C. (2005). Empirically supported family and peer interventions for dual disorders. *Research on Social Work Practice*, *15*(4), 231–245.

Mueser, K., Noordsy, D., Drake, R., & Fox, L. (2003). *Integrated treatment for dual disorders: A guide to effective practice*. New York: Guilford Press.

Nichols, M. (1984). *Family therapy*. New York: Gardner Press.

O'Farrell, T., & Fals-Stewart, W. (2006). *Behavioral couples therapy for alcoholism and drug abuse*. New York: Guilford Press.

Philpott, H., & Christie, M. (2008). Coping in male partners of female problem drinkers. *Journal of Substance Use*, *13*(3), 193–203.

Poulin, J. (2010). *Strengths-based general practice: A collaborative approach* (3rd ed.). Belmont, CA: Wadsworth.

Prochaska, J. O., & DiClemente, C. C. (1992). Stages of change in the modification of problem behaviors. In M. Hersen, R. M. Eisler, & P. M. Miller (Eds.), *Progress in behavioral modification* (pp. 184–214). Sycamore, IL: Sycamore Press.

Rabinor, J. R. (1994). Mothers, daughters, and eating disorders: Honoring the mother–daughter relationship. In P. Fallon, M. Katzman, & S. Wooley (Eds.), *Feminist perspectives on eating disorders* (pp. 272–286). New York: Guilford Press.

Ries, R., Fiellin, D., Miller, S., & Saitz, R. (2009). *Principles of addiction medicine* (4th ed.). Philadelphia: Lippicott, Williams and Wilkins.

Saatcioglu, O., Erim, R., & Cakmak, D. (2006). Role of family in alcohol and substance abuse. *Psychiatry and Clinical Neurosciences*, *60*(2), 125–133.

Selekman, M. (2008). *Pathways to change: Brief therapy with difficult adolescents*. New York: Guilford.

Substance Abuse and Mental Health Services Administration (SAMHSA). (2009). *Children living with substance-dependent or substance-abusing parents: 2002–2007*. Rockville, MD: Office of Applied Studies.

Tapia, M., Schwartz, S., Prado, G., Lopez, B., & Pantin, H. (2006). Parent-centered intervention: A practical approach for preventing drug abuse in Hispanic adolescents. *Research on Social Work Practice*, *16*(2), 146–165.

Thomas, C., & Corcoran, J. (2001). Empirically based marital and family interventions for alcohol abuse: A review. *Research on Social Work Practice*, *11*(5), 549–575.

Thompson, S., Pomeroy, E., & Gober, K. (2005). Family-based treatment models targeting substance use and high-risk behaviors among adolescents: A review. *Journal of Evidence-Based Social Work*, 2(1/2), 207–233.

Tolstoy, L. (1917). *Anna Karenina*. NewYork: Collier & Son. (Original work published 1876).

U.S. Department of Health and Human Services (DHHS). (1999). *Brief interventions and brief therapies for substance abuse*. Treatment Improvement Protocol (TIP) Series, No. 34. Rockville, MD: U.S. Government Printing Office.

van Wormer, K., & Roberts, A. R. (2009). *Death by domestic violence: Preventing the murders and the murder-suicides*. Westport, CT: Praeger.

van Wormer, K., Wells, J., & Boes, M. (2000). *Social work with lesbians, gays, and bisexuals: A strengths perspective*. Boston: Allyn & Bacon.

Walker, J. P., & Lee, R. E. (1998). Uncovering strengths of children of alcoholic parents. *Contemporary Family Therapy*, 20(4), 521–538.

Wallen, J. (1993). *Addiction in human development: Developmental perspectives on addiction and recovery*. New York: Haworth.

Wegscheider, S. (1981). *Another chance: Hope and health for the alcoholic family*. Palo Alto, CA: Science and Behavior Books.

Wetzel, J. (1991). Universal mental health classification systems: Reclaiming women's experience. *Affilia*, 6(3), 8–31.

Woodside, D., & Shekter-Wolfson, L. (2003). *Families and eating disorders*. Retrieved November 29, 2006, from http://www.nedic.ca

MUTUAL-HELP GROUPS: A STRENGTHS PERSPECTIVE

CHAPTER 11

You will know your full name and address.
You will be able to walk a straight line and pass the sobriety test.
You will lose your fear of police cars.
You will be able to answer the door without looking through the little hole.
You will realize what a mess you've been and thank God or your HP for your Twelve-Step Program.

—"The Twelve Promises for Recovery Beginners" (*Alcohol Self-Help News*, 2007, p. 1).

INTRODUCTION

Although mutual-help groups are typically organized around serious problems, "The Twelve Promises for Recovery Beginners" is a good example of the strengths and humor that abound in such organizations. Newcomers and professionals who visit a Twelve-Step group for the first time are often shocked to hear laughter and fun poking when dire situations are described by a fellow member. Later, they understand that the laughter comes from self-recognition and hope. It is a powerful part of the healing process for both listener and speaker. For example, at an all-women's meeting of Alcoholics Anonymous (AA) with over 50 women attending, a young woman named "Susan," three days out of detox at her first AA meeting, had the following experience:

SUSAN: (very softly) "I just got out of detox ..."

GROUP: (starts to get very quiet, side-conversations stop)

SUSAN: "I don't know who I am ..."

GROUP: (very quiet now)

SUSAN: (crying now) "I'm like a stranger in my own body ... (puts her head down, sobbing) I just want to get fucked-up!"

GROUP: (someone passes her the Kleenex box that has "Crying is healing" written on the outside with purple ink)

SUSAN: "So ... I guess I'll just take it slow ..."

GROUP: (laughter all around, cheers, everyone starts clapping)

SUSAN: (smiles shyly)

GROUP: someone shouts, "Keep breathing!!!" and everybody laughs

There are no easy cures or answers to many of the problems we experience as human beings. With solace, care, and support, we can, as social beings, help each other through difficult experiences that are sometimes excruciatingly painful and can lead to what Gamblers Anonymous (GA) members call incomprehensible de-moralization when faced alone. Since the 1950s, divorce, job relocation, and changing family expectations have undermined the role extended families played in attempting to provide this kind of support. Mutual-help groups (an estimated half-million) have filled in the gap to deal with almost every human problem, including self-care groups for major diseases, recovery groups for addiction and other problems, and advocacy groups for certain circumstances (elderly, mentally ill, etc.). The term *mutual help* is used interchangeably in this chapter with the more popular term *self-help*; however mutual help conveys more of the reciprocity that exists in these organizations. Both terms refer to a group of people who feel they have a common problem and voluntarily get together to do something about it, usually because of a sense of powerlessness in the broader healthcare system (Flora, Raftopoulos, & Pontikes, 2010).

Although social scientists did not pay much attention to the phenomenon of the self-help movement until the 1970s, this did not prevent self-help groups from continuing to multiply and become more diverse in focus. There are now over a million members of self-help organizations run by and for mental health consumers and/or family members (Goldstrom, Campbell, Rogers, Lambert, Blacklow, Henderson, & Manderscheld, 2006), there are over 2 million members of Alcoholics Anonymous (AA, 2011), and an estimated 5 million persons attended a self-help group in the past year because of their use of alcohol or drugs (SAMHSA, 2008). The emergence of mutual-help groups has been critically important in the addiction field, both as an adjunct to professional treatment and as a stand-alone resource. Looking at abstinent rates of persons 12 and older who attended self-help groups, 45.1% abstained from substance use in the past month (SAMHSA, 2008). Online support groups are increasingly common; benefits include accessibility, convenience, and anonymity. In this chapter, we describe the major mutual-help groups that have been helpful to persons who are oppressed by some addiction, focusing on alcohol, drugs, and gambling, We will also report on the development of Recovery Community Centers, which are sanctuaries located in the hearts of various communities to support recovery from any addiction and are staffed primarily by recovering volunteers and their families. To understand the philosophy, purpose, and meeting behaviors of Twelve-Step programs, we focus in depth on Alcoholics Anonymous, the model for Narcotics Anonymous (NA), Overeaters Anonymous (OA), Gamblers Anonymous, and Nicotine Anonymous. To the extent possible, recent research findings that indicate the effectiveness of these groups are cited, although most research activity has been centered on Alcoholics Anonymous.

TWELVE-STEP FACILITATION VERSUS TWELVE-STEP MUTUAL-HELP GROUPS IN THE COMMUNITY

Some harm reductionists and others aligned with strengths perspective practice see AA as the perpetrator of a monolithic disease model that requires abstinence and makes meeting attendance mandatory. This misconception may come from the confusion of Twelve-Step facilitation as practiced in professional treatment programs and the mutual-help Twelve-Step programs as they are practiced in the community. It is critical to understand the difference between the two approaches (Travis, 2010).

The growth and spread of AA principles in professional treatment began in the United States in 1952 when a psychiatrist and a psychologist created a unique program at Wilmer State Hospital in Minnesota. As the program developed over the next 3 years, it featured the integration of professional staff with trained recovering alcoholics and embraced the disease model and the link to Twelve-Step groups, family involvement, abstinence from all addictive drugs, and client and family education on the effects of addiction, individualized treatment plans, and aftercare (Chappel & DuPont, 1999). This new model of treatment, subsequently known as the Minnesota Model, was adopted by Hazelden in 1961 and spread so rapidly that by 1989, 95% of the treatment programs in the United States were basing their programs on the Twelve-Step AA program.

In actuality, the practice of AA in the community differs in fundamental ways from the Twelve-Step facilitation that is practiced in professional treatment centers. AA in the community is not "treatment." It is a spiritually based fellowship that supports the development and maintenance of abstinence for those who want it and offers steps for sobriety and lifelong character development. AA could hardly be more different in its structure than a typical public or private addiction treatment program. AA groups in the community are self-supporting, led by fellow alcoholics, and are free of charge. There is no federal or state funding, no licensing or monitoring by any regulatory agency, no records of attendance, and no case records. In contrast, Twelve-Step facilitation models implemented in treatment programs have paid professionals teach AA assumptions (powerlessness over alcohol, spirituality, Twelve Steps to recovery); require people to admit they are alcoholics, complete the work on the initial steps in a specific time frame, and go to a certain number of AA meetings; charge money for the treatment program; and are monitored by state and federal regulators (Travis, 2010; Fisher & Harrison, 2008).

A fundamental difference between the writings of cofounder Bill Wilson, the philosophy of The Big Book of AA, and professional treatment programs that practice Twelve-Step facilitation is around the issue of compliance. As noted by LaFave and Echols (1999), "Twelve-Step self-help programs stress the voluntary nature of attendance and offer their ideas as suggestions. ... The highly directive nature of Twelve-Step treatment models is, therefore, a departure from the approach used in Twelve-Step self-help programs" (p. 348).

AA and other Twelve-Step groups do a delicate dance of keeping alive the voluntary nature of the mutual-help program, in spite of pressures from treatment centers and probation and parole officers on clients to bring back attendance slips signed by the chairperson of the particular group. As noted on the official AA website, "Proof of attendance at meetings is *not* part of AA's procedure. Each group is autonomous and has the right to choose whether or not to sign court slips. In some areas the attendees report on themselves, at the request of the referring agency, and thus alleviate breaking AA members' anonymity."

Twelve-Step Programs and Harm Reduction

It may surprise some readers that the authors of this text consider Twelve-Step mutual-help organizations such as Alcoholics Anonymous and Narcotics Anonymous to be compatible with a harm reduction philosophy. In addition to the voluntary nature of the programs, there are other principles of Twelve-Step programs as practiced in the community that are consistent with harm reduction practices. A fundamental concept of the AA program is the need for self-assessment as to whether you "qualify" as a member—that is, "have a desire to stop drinking." This is based on the belief that alcoholics want to stop drinking because eventually their own experience and their failure at numerous experiments to control their drinking tell them they can no longer control it once they start. In other words, they have tried and failed at various harm reduction strategies and consequently have reached the stage of actually having a desire to stop drinking. As described in The Big Book of Alcoholics Anonymous (2001):

> Here are some of the methods we have tried: Drinking beer only, limiting the number of drinks, never drinking alone, never drinking in the morning, drinking only at home, never having it in the house, never drinking during business hours,

drinking only at parties, switching from scotch to brandy, drinking only natural wines, agreeing to resign if ever drunk on the job, taking a trip, not taking a trip, etc. (p. 31)

The critical issue is that people finally reach the decision to stop drinking *for themselves,* not because a professional person insisted on it. AA says, "We do not like to pronounce any individual as alcoholic, but you can quickly diagnose yourself. Step over to the nearest barroom and try some controlled drinking" (p. 31).

Other concepts consistent with harm reduction philosophy practiced in Twelve-Step programs in the community are the ideas of limited control; that is, don't drink "one day at a time," rather than "never drink again," and the embracing of human fallibility (the only requirement for membership is "a desire to stop drinking," not "you have to have so much amount of abstinence to stay in this program"). Michael White (2000), codeveloper of the Narrative therapy approach, remarks that:

> AA's responses to persons who turn back to the bottle are generally compassionate rather than judging. This is an antidote to the demoralizing sense of personal failure that is so often occasioned by such U-turns, and keeps the door open on options for persons to try again, and yet again. In response to these U-turns, the AA community just goes on reaching out. This is a reaching out by persons who have "been there," and who have a strong appreciation of the desperation that is experienced in this struggle. (p. 32)

William Miller, noted researcher and developer of Motivational Interviewing (MI), says he was a traditional behaviorist who dismissed AA "without investigation." Over time, he met and worked with several colleagues who introduced the ideas of AA, went to AA meetings, and collaborated on AA research. The more he understood the writings of Bill W., "the more it sounds like Motivational Interviewing ... I have come to a heartfelt appreciation of the breadth and depth of AA, and its untiring ministry to those who continue to suffer." (Miller, Forcehimes, Zweben, & McClellan, 2011, p. 233).

ALCOHOLICS ANONYMOUS

Alcoholics Anonymous had its seventy-fifth anniversary in 2010. It is the prototype for other mutual-help groups that have adopted the Twelve Steps and corresponding traditions. As we explore this organization, it should be understood that the authors do not and cannot speak for Alcoholics Anonymous (AA). (Official AA literature on various topics can be obtained by writing to Alcoholics Anonymous, Box 459, Grand Central Station, New York, NY 10163, or by accessing the website at http://www.aa.org.)

The meaning of Alcoholics Anonymous depends on our worldview in relation to this mutual-help group for alcoholics. For example, Stanton Peele (2010), a champion of harm reduction and personal choice, criticizes AA as "a movement spearheaded by true believers who believe what was good for them is good for everyone" (p. 3). Over half of the addiction professionals in the United

States (67%) that were surveyed worry that patients can get re-traumatized in Twelve-Step programs, and almost 40% are concerned that Twelve-Step programs can lead to pick up, or relapse (Vederhus, Laudet, Kristensen & Clausen, 2010). Social workers have variously described AA as a set of principles developed by alcohol-dependent men (Nelson-Zlupko, 1995; Kauffman & Dore, 1995), "a very successful model for self-help groups" (Borkman, 1989, p. 63), and disempowering to women (Finfgeld, 2002). Some feminists (Kasl, 1992) dismiss it as another White, middle-class male organization that enjoins women to depend on "having a Higher Power, which is usually described as an all-powerful male God" (p. 150) and to follow one journey to recovery "as defined by privileged males" (p. 147). From another feminist perspective, AA is seen as helping to create a culturally feminist environment where women can choose to go to women-only meetings, where they not only bond with each other, but also influence the culture of AA in general (Sanders, 2010). Perhaps the greatest meaning of Alcoholics Anonymous, from the vantage point of the individual person who got sober through AA, is that their lives were saved.

In this section, we address issues related to women and other common criticisms of AA by reframing the meaning of AA from an alternative treatment or service delivery model to an understanding based on metaphor (Davis & Jansen, 1998). Viewing AA in this framework allows us to suggest meanings of key metaphors, or narratives, of the AA program. We describe areas of program strength and potential barriers for clinicians (and consequently, for those persons who consult with us) and review the research findings concerning the efficacy of this program.

A THUMBNAIL SKETCH OF ALCOHOLICS ANONYMOUS

Alcoholics Anonymous is an approach to recovery from alcoholism developed by and for alcoholics around 1935, a time when alcoholism was considered hopeless by the medical profession and a moral failing by most everyone. Bill Wilson and Dr. Bob Smith, both late-stage alcoholics desperate for an alternative, joined together to create anonymous support meetings that borrowed principles from the Oxford Group (a nondenominational Christian movement) and created other principles important to the recovery from alcoholism as they experienced it. Their ideas were eventually written in a book on paper so thick and bulky that the original volume of *Alcoholics Anonymous* (2001) was called "The Big Book," a title affectionately, and perhaps metaphorically, continued by AA members ever since, even though it is now a regular-sized book (E. Kurtz, 1979).

At the heart of the AA program is a group of principles "suggested" for recovery called the Twelve Steps (see Box 11.1). These are specific individual actions, spiritual in nature, and "guides to progress ... not spiritual perfection" (AA, 2001, p. 60). They were painstakingly designed by fellow alcoholics to help a person obtain sobriety and make the spiritual transformation necessary to create a sober life that is worth living. For the developing AA groups to survive and function effectively, a set of principles called the

Box 11.1	THE TWELVE STEPS OF ALCOHOLICS ANONYMOUS

1. We admitted we were powerless over alcohol—that our lives had become unmanageable.
2. Came to believe that a Power greater than ourselves could restore us to sanity.
3. Made a decision to turn our will and our lives over to the care of God as we understood Him.
4. Made a searching and fearless moral inventory of ourselves.
5. Admitted to God, to ourselves and to another human being the exact nature of our wrongs.
6. Were entirely ready to have God remove all these defects of character.
7. Humbly asked Him to remove our shortcomings.
8. Made a list of all persons we had harmed, and became willing to make amends to them all.
9. Made direct amends to such people wherever possible, except when to do so would injure them or others.
10. Continued to take personal inventory and, when we were wrong, promptly admitted it.
11. Sought through prayer and meditation to improve our conscious contact with God, as we understood Him, praying only for knowledge of His will for us and the power to carry that out.
12. Having had a spiritual awakening as the result of these steps, we tried to carry this message to alcoholics, and to practice these principles in all our affairs.

Source: The Twelve Steps are reprinted with permission of Alcoholics Anonymous World Services, Inc. (A.A.W.S.). Permission to reprint the Twelve Steps does not mean that A.A. W.S. has reviewed or approved the contents of this publication, or that A.A.W.S. necessarily agrees with the views expressed herein. A.A. is a program of recovery from alcoholism ONLY- use of the Twelve Steps in connection with programs and activities which are patterned after A.A., but which address other problems, or in any other non-A.A. context, does not imply otherwise.

Twelve Traditions evolved to set forth a working philosophy for this mutual-help community. The Foreword to the second edition of *Alcoholics Anonymous* (1955) explains the Twelve Traditions as they apply to community:

> No alcoholic man or woman could be excluded from our Society. ... Our leaders might serve but never govern. ... Each group was to be autonomous and there was to be no professional class of therapy. ... There were to be no fees or dues. ... There was to be the least possible organization, even in our service centers. ... Our public relations were to be based upon attraction rather than promotion. ... All members ought to be anonymous at the level of press, radio, TV, and films, and in no circumstances should we give endorsements, make alliances, or enter public controversies. (p. vii)

These twelve guidelines for a nonorganization, although not as familiar as the Twelve Steps, have made it possible for a decentralized organization like AA to avoid the temptations of power, money, and bureaucracy that would have brought about the death of the organization (Borkman, 2006). However, it is not suggested guidelines alone have enabled the AA organization to survive. In a fascinating ethnographic study of how AA groups have managed to avoid highly disruptive and combative conduct in meetings, Hoffman (2006) suggests that social control is achieved through various means: (1) highly structured rules of discourse, where "cross-talk" (giving advice or rebutting someone's point) is not allowed; (2) depending on high-status (longer length of sobriety, frequent meeting attendance) members to intervene with newcomers who may not understand the norms of the group; (3) various means of criticism in group meetings, primarily indirect or humorous comments to let people know when they are out of line. An example of the humorous form of social control is as follows: When a chronically late person introduced himself by saying, "My name's Darryl, I'm an alcoholic," the group responded with the expected "Hi Darryl." However, one member responded with "Hi, on-time" (Hoffman, 2006, p. 687). Another effective way AA has of discouraging confrontations is that members are free to attend meetings anywhere else if they do not like what is going on in the particular group, or they can start their own AA meeting. Hoffman (2006) quotes an old AA proverb that "all you need to start your own AA meeting is a resentment and a coffeepot."

As a result of the guidance from the Twelve Traditions and the internal mechanisms of social control, more than 107,000 groups of Alcoholics Anonymous meetings in more than 160 countries have been created and remain stable, with 2,057,672 members throughout the world at last count (AA, 2011). According to a 2007 random survey of 8,000 AA members in the United States and Canada, the average AA member is male (67% vs. 33% female), white (85.1%), and middle-aged (2.3% under 21, 11.3% age 21–30, 16.5% age 31–40, 29.5% age 41–50, 23.6% age 51–60, 12.3% age 61–70, and 5.3% over age 70). Before coming to AA, 63% of the members received some kind of professional treatment or counseling. Alcoholics Anonymous has a stable group of long-time members who come to meetings on a regular basis. According to the survey, 33% of the members have been sober for more than 10 years; 31% are "newbies," that is, sober less than a year. Most AA members have a sponsor (79%), and these people got a sponsor within the first 90 days (AA, 2007).

Attributes of the program important to many counselors include a policy of no dues or fees, its availability in small towns and in medium to large cities, and usually offering an array of culturally diverse options for a variety of groups (e.g., women, veterans, older persons, Native Americans, Hispanics, gay men, lesbians, newcomers). Also, transportation for housebound persons or out-of-town visitors can be arranged through voluntary help from members who are on-call for such circumstances.

Research on Effectiveness

Although beset by methodological problems aggravated by the anonymous, voluntary, self-selection of AA membership, there is evidence to indicate that

AA is an extremely useful approach for some alcoholics trying to stop drink-ing, especially when accompanied by professional treatment. Emrick's (1987) review of surveys and outcome evaluations of AA alone or as an adjunct to professional treatment indicates that about 40–50% of alcoholics who main-tain long-term, active membership in AA will have several years of total absti-nence while involved; and 60–68% will improve, drinking less or not at all during AA participation. More recent studies and reviews of studies have found that participation in AA over time is associated with improved out-comes (Walitzer, Derman, & Barrick, 2009; Bodin, 2006; Moos & Moos, 2006; Kelly, Stout, Zywiak, & Schneider, 2006). Among women who had been incarcerated, weekly or more frequent AA attendance is associated with a reduction of negative drinking consequences and a lower frequency of drink-ing days (Schonbrun, Strong, Anderson, Caviness, Brown, & Stein, 2011). Involvement or active participation in AA practices (e.g., "working the Twelve Steps"), rather than just attendance at AA meetings, was related to positive outcome (Majer, Droege, & Jason, 2010; Gossop et al., 2003). For example, in a 16-year follow-up study, Moos and Moos (2006) found that extended participation in AA throughout the first, second, and third years after treat-ment was associated with better alcohol-related and self-efficacy outcomes.

These positive findings are not without their skeptics. Major criticisms include the large percentage of alcoholics who drop out of AA (according to AA's own survey, 50% after 3 months) (Chappel, 1993; Galaif & Sussman, 1995); contradictory studies that indicate AA works no better than other approaches, including no treatment (Peele, 2011); and findings that indicate no significant relationship between AA attendance and out-comes (McLatchie & Lomp, 1988; Miller, Leckman, Delaney, & Tinkcorn, 1992). In addition, despite years of research, a definitive picture of a person's characteristics that can predict a positive or negative outcome with AA has not emerged. One recent study looked at factors identified with AA member-ship in a sample of people who had at least one year of sobriety (Krentzman, Robinson, Perron, & Cranford, 2011). The findings indicate that higher drinking consequences and more belief in a loving God was predictive of AA membership.

In the meantime, there is adequate (although not perfect) evidence to sug-gest that many alcoholics who become involved in AA will find something they can use to improve their lives on a long-term basis and, consequently, that helping professionals will benefit from more knowledge of this potentially valuable resource. Kurtz and Fisher (2003), in their interviews with 33 indivi-duals actively involved in Twelve-Step fellowships and community activity, demonstrated that through the Twelve-Step fellowship, they developed the skills and confidence to seek out and engage in community service. Similarly, Sanders (2010) found that making connections with other women in AA con-tributed to sobriety. As one woman states: "I also started to develop friend-ships in the groups, especially with women. The women's meetings really 'spoke' to me. I was asked to join a group of recovering women meeting once a week for dinner and friendly conversation. I have been attending this group regularly for 9 years and think this has been one of the reasons for my now 11.5 years of sobriety" (p. 27).

Myths and Metaphors About Alcoholics Anonymous

Alcoholics Anonymous describes itself as a "simple program" that has only one requirement for membership, "a desire to stop drinking," and one primary purpose, "to carry its message to the alcoholic who still suffers" (AA, 2001, p. 562). The apparent single-mindedness of this nonpolitical, self-supporting program masks a remarkably subtle and, in some ways, counter-establishment worldview that challenges dominant cultural expectations regarding hierarchy, power, and models of helping. Because AA is the language of narrative and metaphor, it is easily misunderstood without the context of lived experience and meaning-making of the membership as a whole. What follows is an attempt to increase understanding of the AA program, with an aim of avoiding the pitfalls of what John Wallace (1983) calls the unwary translator of AA, who "may find himself banging away at the concrete rather than flowing with the analogy" (p. 301).

Framing AA as a Narrative Community

Professional service providers, who live with concepts of treatment, clients, and service models, often understand AA as an alternative treatment model. This understanding, according to Rappaport (1993), is limited for gaining insight into what AA means to those who join. For a different understanding, he proposes reframing the meaning of AA (and other mutual-help groups) in terms of a narrative perspective:

> In its simplest form, the narrative approach means understanding life to be experienced as a constructed story. The stories that people tell and are told are powerful forms of communication to both others and one's self. Stories order experience, give coherence and meaning to events, and provide a sense of history and of the future. (p. 240)

The stories are told in community, and these communities have powerful narratives about change, about themselves, and about their members. In this sense, AA can be seen as a "normative structure in social experience" (Rappaport, 1993, p. 246). It is a normative structure because it is more comparable to other voluntary associations of people "living lives," such as religious organizations, professional organizations, political parties, and even families, than it is to a social service agency setting where clients come to receive services from professional helpers. In the narrative framework, people joining AA are not help-seekers in search of treatment, but storytellers who through telling and listening transform their lives. Personal stories become the narratives that define a "caring and sharing community of givers as well as receivers, with hope, and with a sense of their own capacity for positive change" (p. 245).

Consistent with postmodern thought, the narrative perspective embraces the idea that personal reality is itself constructed, as in a life story, and therefore has the capacity to be reconstructed throughout a person's life. In other words, as narrative therapists would say, "people make meaning, meaning is not made for us" (Monk, Winslade, Crocket, & Epston, 1997, p. 33). The AA community provides a safe harbor and a rich tradition of stories useful to reconstruct one's life story from that of a "hopeless alcoholic" to a person with "experience, strength, and hope." Hearing things in the stories of others can offer hope that your own life can change. For example, Smith (1993) cites this woman's experience in her early days in AA:

> A man I met told me that if I didn't think I belonged, I should hang around and I'd hear my story. Then a few weeks later, this girl got up and as she spoke, it started to dawn on me. I was so engrossed ... every word she said I could relate to where I had come from. Here was this woman with seven or eight years in the program telling my story! (p. 696)

Smith (1993) elaborates on the process of individual integration into the "social world" of AA by describing how each step in the process of affiliation (attending meetings, sharing "experience, strength, and hope" in meetings, getting a sponsor, working the Twelve Steps of recovery, doing service work to help other alcoholics) enhances the person's comfort level in forming new relationships with others. It makes it possible for the individual to take some risks and experience small successes, it enhances self-esteem, and it leads to further commitment to the community. Understanding AA in a narrative framework where people tell stories about their lives within a community implies a conceptual shift from a rational (service delivery) model to a metaphorical (spiritual) understanding.

Michael White (2000), codeveloper of narrative therapy, sees the principal metaphor in AA as a "right of passage" and believes that "the originators of Alcoholics Anonymous had great vision, and a profound understanding of the significance of rites of passage" (p. 31). According to White,

> The center of AA is a ritual event that provides for a formalization of the stages of separation and reincorporation and for a marking of the turning points of persons' lives. This is accompanied by the convening of forums that provide the opportunity for persons to give testimony to the decisions they have made to break from excessive alcohol consumption, to the desires and purposes that motivate these decisions, and to tell and retell the stories of their lives before a group of witnesses, many of whom are veterans of such journeys. (p. 31)

The metaphorical level is the framework for the following interpretations of the meanings of AA.

THE METAPHOR OF POWERLESSNESS: "GIVING IN IS THE GREATEST FORM OF CONTROL" The koan in the title (a mental puzzle used by practicing Buddhists as meditation material to further enlightenment) was created by "solution-focused" therapists to assist a practicing Buddhist client translate the first step of AA to something that utilized her Buddhist beliefs (Berg & Miller, 1992). It is also a good example of how the language of AA can be understood as metaphorical. A parallel metaphor more familiar to Christians might be "to gain your life you must first lose it."

Step One of the Twelve Steps of Alcoholics Anonymous, "We admitted we were powerless over alcohol—that our lives had become unmanageable," is the cornerstone of recovery for alcoholics trying to get well through the AA program (AA, 2001). However, from a rational purview, it is also the stumbling block for many professionals who are concerned that AA pushes "powerlessness" on persons who are already powerless in the dominant culture. Wetzel (1991) voices these concerns regarding women: "The Twelve-Step program reinforces one's belief in one's powerlessness and the necessity to relinquish the self to a 'higher power' (something most women have been doing all their lives in a secular sense)" (p. 23).

For the nonaddicted to make sense of Step One, it is helpful to try and stand inside the circle of addiction and look around at the miserable state of affairs most women and men face when they first begin the road to recovery. The lived experience of the alcoholic is like the woman who said, "I was on an endless cycle of 'I'll do better tomorrow' and of course I was always drunk again by 9 o'clock that night" (Davis, 1996, p. 152). A study of recovering alcoholics attending AA (DeSoto, O'Donnell, & DeSoto, 1989) revealed an extremely high rate of psychological distress measured by the Symptom Checklist (SCL-90) in the first 3 months of recovery, comparable to psychiatric inpatients. The authors comment: "With a life situation in disarray, suffering a protracted withdrawal syndrome, and experiencing cognitive deficits, it is a challenge indeed for an alcoholic to abstain from the drug that promises at least temporary relief" (p. 697).

The hard fact of being out of control with the addiction, no matter what you try to do, and having your life in shambles all around you roughly translates to the understanding of powerlessness that is the starting point in the AA program. AA invites people who declare themselves eligible to survey their world and embrace the idea of Step One: "I am powerless *over alcohol,* and my life has become unmanageable" (AA, 2001, p. 59). In other words, Step One says: Face the reality and give up the illusion that you are in control of your use of alcohol. If people have doubts about their status, *The Big Book* suggests that they figure it out for themselves, experientially:

> Step over to the nearest barroom and try some controlled drinking. Try to drink and stop abruptly. Try it more than once. It will not take long for you to decide, if you are honest about it. It may be worth a bad case of the jitters if you get a full knowledge of your condition. (AA, 2001, pp. 31–32)

The organization invites those who have "lost the power of choice in drink" and have "a desire to stop drinking" to join the fellowship (AA, 2001, pp. 24, 562). Accepting the metaphor of powerlessness, thereby accepting individual limitations, goes against the dominant Western cultural message of "pulling yourself up by the bootstraps," independence, competition, and will power. Bateson (1972) suggests that AA provides a paradoxical metaphor much like the title koan at the beginning of this section in that "the experience of defeat not only serves to convince the alcoholic that change is necessary; it *is* the first step in that change ... to be defeated by the bottle and to know it is the first 'spiritual' experience" (p. 313).

The AA notion of powerlessness in the context of such group narratives transforms the competitive stance with others (who have tried to force them to stop drinking) into a complementary relationship with other alcoholics who are in the same boat, in the same meeting, and weaving and sharing similar stories of "experience, strength, and hope. Therefore, powerlessness in this context is a metaphor of connectedness, not isolation. It is a good example of the power of the "narrative community" to transform lives by reauthoring one's alcoholic experience. Stephanie Brown (1994) calls this a "power from within model" instead of a "power over" model (p. 26). An alternative understanding is what Riessman (1985) calls "self-help induced empowerment." He states that "when people join together with others who have similar problems to deal with those problems ... they feel empowered; they are able to control some aspect of their lives. The help is not given to them from the outside, from an expert, a professional, a politician" (p. 2). Looking at AA through these glasses may help explain the findings that greater AA attendance was associated with decreased depression, as well as improvements in alcohol use (Kelly, Stout, Magill, Tonigan, & Pagano, 2010). This is different from the meanings of powerlessness associated with contemporary social and behavioral sciences, such as alienation, anomie, victimization, oppression, discrimination, and poverty (Borkman, 1989). Understanding this alternative meaning of powerlessness is helpful in resisting the temptation to oversimplify and interpret AA language in terms of social science terminology instead of the language of transformation.

THE METAPHOR OF DISEASE: "ALCOHOLISM IS A THREEFOLD DISEASE—MENTAL, PHYSICAL, AND SPIRITUAL."   AA is often criticized for its support and promulgation of the "disease concept" of alcoholism (Peele, 2011), especially by some clinicians who adhere to the "strengths perspective." These two concepts have been presented as competing metaphors wherein the disease concept is negatively described as emphasizing the pathological, not the healthy; where physicians and clinicians assume the expert role; clients are passive and not responsible for their predicament; and recovery goals are designed and directed by treatment staff. On the other side, the strengths perspective is optimistically portrayed as emphasizing wellness and nonhierarchical and collaborative helping relationships, and recovery goals are co-constructed by facilitators and clients (Rapp & Goscha, 2006; Saleebey, 2006).

Although these comparisons may not do justice to either metaphor, the discourse continues to be fueled by current interest in collaborative models of helping (feminist, narrative, solution-focused, motivational interviewing) and perhaps a desire to set these models apart as different from the medical model of helping. Further complications that obscure the issue of alcoholism as disease include a general inability to agree on just what alcoholism is, to have consensus on just what constitutes disease, or to agree on a single theory that adequately describes the etiology of alcoholism (McNeece & DiNitto, 2005). In theory, the AA program leaves the debate to the professionals; it simply treats the controversy of alcoholism as disease as an outside issue, following the principle of the Tenth Tradition of AA, which states, "Alcoholics Anonymous has no opinions on outside issues; hence the AA name ought never to be drawn into public controversy" (AA, 2001, p. 562). Although *The Big Book* of Alcoholics Anonymous, the suggested guide to the program, avoids the term *disease*, it does use the terms *malady*, *illness*, and *allergy* to suggest the hopelessness of the condition of active alcoholism. E. Kurtz's (1979) historical analysis states that Bill Wilson (the cofounder of AA) "always remained wary of referring to alcoholism as a 'disease' because he wished to avoid the medical controversy over the existence or nonexistence of a specific 'disease-entity' " (p. 22). It is somewhat ironic that in many current versions of the controversy, AA is linked firmly to the promulgation of the disease concept. However, as E. Kurtz (1979) suggests, "the Alcoholics Anonymous understanding of alcoholism begs for exploration within the insight that disease can also be metaphor" (p. 200). He reminds us that disease as metaphor has been prevalent throughout history, beginning in antiquity with leprosy as sin, to the Great Plague of decaying Europe, to the "white death" of tuberculosis in the slums of industrial cities, and to the malignancy of cancer in the postmodern era of uncontrolled growth and greed. Alcoholism, or any number of addictions, is perhaps the metaphor for modern-day separation and despair.

Many individual members of AA look upon alcoholism as a threefold disease involving spiritual, mental, and physical factors. This implies a unity of life, a holistic frame familiar to adherents of Native American traditions, Christian creationist philosophy, and Buddhist meditations, among others. Modern isolation and disconnectedness can be understood as arising from a foolish and doomed attempt to separate these unified parts of the whole person. To be fully human (and in the case of the alcoholic, to want to live sober), the physical, mental, and especially spiritual parts must be integrated. AA members attempt to live out this metaphor on a practical level by working on a spiritual program that attends to the physical, mental, and spiritual needs of the alcoholic who still suffers.

THE METAPHORS OF DEPENDENCE, INDEPENDENCE, AND INTERDEPENDENCE   Another major criticism of AA is that it promotes dependence in the alcoholic by providing a substitute addiction or a crutch. In a comparison between the attitudes of addiction professionals in the United States and Norway, both groups viewed dependence on Twelve-Step groups as an obstacle to participation (69% of the U.S. counselors and 64% of the Norwegian counselors) (Vederhus, Laudet, Kristensen, & Clausen, 2010). Inherent in the metaphor of the dominant culture is the notion of do it yourself, or self-reliance. In contrast, the Alcoholics Anonymous approach to extreme dependence (alcoholism) is to embrace the metaphor of connectedness. That is, we as humans are limited and dependent on other humans. Connecting with others through the fellowship of meetings, sponsors, and AA-sponsored events is perceived as a way to help strengthen one's identity, not shrink it. As one woman expressed this feeling, "Connecting with women in the program has also helped me to learn to trust myself and others again" (Sanders, 2010, p. 27). Connecting to others through helping (sponsorship, practice of the twelfth step) has also been associated with better drinking outcomes (Pagano, Krentzman, Onder, Baryak, Murphy, Zywiak, & Stout, 2010). Perhaps the most poignant example of the value of helping others comes from interviews with homeless men in a shelter in Florida. The authors of the study (Rayburn & Wright, 2010) found that the men were taking the twelfth step (practicing the principles in all your affairs) very seriously—they were cleaning the property, helping out in the kitchen, making trips to bring in donations, and trying to find other homeless people to help. The men expressed a strong desire to "do their part, to give instead of take, and to become useful—not sentiments that would be stereotypically associated with homeless alcoholic men" (p. 334).

It may be helpful to note that the same criticisms about creating dependence are also aimed at psychotherapy, welfare assistance, certain religious communities, mothers, and other entities that offer a port in the storm of life. In spite of the dominant cultural suspicion that there must be something wrong with dependence, levels of dependence usually shift naturally as a person becomes more stable. Some AA members suggest that in the early stages of recovery after detoxification , every alcoholic or drug addict needs a healthy substitute dependence and, left to him- or herself, may choose another high-risk behavior, such as gambling, spending, sex, or eating. AA offers a way to begin the development of healthier patterns.

In AA, newcomers may spend entire days in meeting after meeting, and it is routinely suggested that they attend "90 meetings in 90 days." As the length of sobriety and stability increases, participation generally shifts to helping others (making coffee, chairing meetings, sponsoring others). Many old-timers with years of sobriety continue participation to provide sponsorship and support for newcomers and because they depend on AA meetings to help them maintain their spiritual program, not just their sobriety. According to the 2007 AA membership survey, members attended an average of two meetings a week. Independence, in the American sense of doing it alone, is not the goal; instead, the individual (isolated by alcoholism and an array of negative social consequences) is taught in small steps how to depend on others and how to allow others to depend on him or her.

THE REALITIES OF ABSTINENCE: ONE DAY AT A TIME The basic text of *Alcoholics Anonymous* (2001) suggests that "for those who are unable to drink moderately the question is how to stop altogether ... We are assuming, of course, that the reader desires to stop" (p. 34). As discussed earlier, the need for self-assessment, and the belief that underneath it all alcoholics want to stop drinking precisely because their own experience and numerous experiments tell them they can no longer control it once they start, is a fundamental concept of the AA program.

However, abstinence (if it means to never drink again) was considered too unrealistic, too absolute, and perhaps too frightening to the alcoholics who created the AA program. Instead, they developed the idea of limited control—that is, not drinking "one day at a time" instead of forever. According to E. Kurtz (1979), this message serves both to "protect against grandiosity and to affirm the sense of individual worthwhileness so especially important to the drinking alcoholic mired in self-hatred over his failure to achieve absolute control over his drinking" (p. 105). The concept of limited control and the embracing of human fallibility are other examples of how the AA program stands apart from our dominant culture's obsessive drive for perfection. Several AA slogans underscore the concept of limited control: "Progress not perfection," "Easy does it," and "One day at a time." Recovery is seen as an ongoing process, more in tune with the feminist principle of emphasizing process over product, and cooperation over competition. In the addiction field, programs or research that suggest an alcoholic can return to controlled drinking are seen as diametrically opposed to the AA premise of stopping drinking (McNeece & DiNitto, 2005). On one level of meaning, it is not surprising that the idea of teaching an alcoholic controlled drinking strikes the AA member as absurd because in AA the alcoholic is *self-defined* as a person who cannot control her or his drinking. For those who can control it (through whatever means), the message is, "Our hats are off to him" (AA, 2001, p. 31). On another level of meaning, focusing on controlling drinking misses the point. In AA, the alcoholic who has lost control does not just have a bad habit and does not just need to stop drinking. That is only the first step in eliminating an alcoholic lifestyle based on self-centeredness, immaturity, and spiritual bankruptcy (Kurtz, 1979). As discussed earlier, the alcoholic is viewed as having a threefold problem involving mental, spiritual, and physical suffering. In AA, eliminating drinking is only the first step, although it is both necessary and essential to begin the process of recovery.

THE METAPHOR OF HIGHER POWER: "IT'S MY SOUL-SELF" Lamb of God, Ancient Thing, Buddha, Yahweh, Love, Truth, Oneness, the Light, Mother God, Mother Nature, God, the Thursday evening "Insanity to Serenity" AA meeting, the Friday at 7 A.M. "Eye-Openers" meeting: All of these and many other versions may describe an AA member's Higher Power. The encouragement to choose the nature of this power is a freedom that underlies the spiritual nature of the AA program and distinguishes it from an organized religious program. The emphasis is not on what kind of Higher Power is embraced but that the idea of human limitations and "a power greater than ourselves" is accepted. For atheists, Bill Wilson recommended that the Higher Power be the AA group they were attending: "When they come in, most of their AA group is sober, and they are drunk. Therefore, the group is a 'Higher Power.' That's a good enough start, and most of them do progress from there. I know how they feel because I was once that way myself" (Bill W., 1967, p. 226).

For some, the Higher Power is located *within* the self. For example, in Covington (1994), Maureen describes how important it was to let go of the ego on the outside and seek the bigger self inside:

> Developing a sense of self is critical to my well-being .... There is a power in me that's greater than the small self I've been accustomed to; it's larger than the way I've been trained to think about who I am. It's my soul-self. In cooperating with it, I surrender to a part of me that carries wisdom and truth. It brings me back into harmony and balance with myself—that's what spirituality is for me. (p. 35)

Step Two, "Came to believe that a Power greater than ourselves could restore us to sanity," and Step Three, "Made a decision to turn our will and our lives over to the care of God as we understand Him" (AA, 2001, p. 59), are the spiritual cornerstones of the AA program. These two steps suggest that alcoholics connect with the healing energy (grace, Godness) of the world and/ or within themselves and become receptive to spiritual guidance, whether that source be the wisdom of their AA group on staying sober or some other version of a power greater than themselves.

A literal reading of the first three steps has been interpreted by some feminists (Kasl, 1992) as sacrificing and martyring oneself for the sake of others, notably males. However, as Clemmons (1991) notes, the Third Step "does not promote this kind of detrimental repression, but it does suggest that we must be willing to let go of people and situations outside of our control. 'Letting go' halts the alcoholic/addict's efforts to control the uncontrollable and focuses on developing and listening to the true self" (p. 104). That is, power is seen not in relational terms with other people but vis-à-vis the addiction. The power of the alcohol, or the small self as Maureen put it, is let go through the shift of accepting a Higher Power.

AA is fundamentally a spiritual program that promotes the ability of an individual to live a meaningful life (Galanter, 2006). Many clinicians have difficulty with this position; as a counseling profession, we have historically focused rationally on the temporal conditions of our clients and their environment, excluding the spiritual. In addition, Galanter (1999) points out that most psychiatrists (56%) don't believe in God or a Higher Power themselves, in contrast to the 94% of Americans who do. He cites an interesting study on medical students who were treating indigent, hospitalized addicts. The addicts ranked spirituality and belief in God as the most important components of their recovery; the medical students considered these factors the least important. In that mindset, it is easy to construe AA's concept of Higher Power as religion and the metaphor of letting go of those things we cannot change as passive dependence.

STORYTELLING AS METAPHOR: "HI, MY NAME IS JACKIE AND I'M AN ALCOHOLIC"   Many observers of AA fail to grasp the complex and metaphorical meanings of common terms and practices as they are used by AA members (Davis & Jansen, 1998). Wallace (1983) notes that "the extended meanings that characterize the AA language system will continue to elude external observers who remain at literal, concrete levels of analysis and fail to consider the nature of symbolic communication and the purposes it serves in complex social contexts and transactions" (p. 302). For example, it is common practice (but not required) to introduce oneself at AA meetings with your name, followed by "and I'm an alcoholic." This greeting has been interpreted by some critics as a counter-therapeutic reinforcement of a negative label, but as Smith (1993) points out, "It is understood by AA members that the word takes on a different and positive meaning in the context of AA" (p. 702). Using Wallace's (1983) idea of illustrating how a common AA slogan can have various meanings depending on the context, the meaning of the "I'm Joe and I'm an alcoholic" greeting in the context of an AA meeting could be any, all, or none of the following (Davis & Jansen, 1998):

1. I have faced the reality that I am alcohol-dependent and I want to quit drinking. Harm reduction strategies have not worked for me and I cannot control my drinking.
2. I have suffered and caused others to suffer, just like you.
3. I don't buy in to the shame attached to this label by the outside world.
4. Even though I am an alcoholic and my natural state would be to be drinking, I'm sober today and participating in this meeting to help my mental, spiritual, and physical recovery.
5. Even though I'm not drinking today, there is a part of me that is immature and self-centered, spiritually bankrupt, egotistical, superficial—that is, an "alcoholic personality" that sometimes operates in the world in a "drunk mode" or "dry drunk." I claim this part, instead of trying to hide my problems in living under a superficial sheen of perfection.
6. I'm grateful to be an alcoholic because having this condition put me on a spiritual path that I never would have found otherwise.
7. I'm not unique, better than, worse off, or any different from any of the rest of you in this meeting. We are here to confront a common problem and to help each other. (p. 178)

These possibilities are extended meanings that can occur within the context of a particular meeting and that depend on the circumstances and histories of individuals who are introducing themselves. Central to the meanings of AA phrases and language is a redefinition of the experience of being an alcoholic. A practicing alcoholic (one that is currently drinking) may be better understood in AA as practicing a flawed way of life, dominated by self-centeredness, superficiality with others, and spiritual bankruptcy. The personal stories told in AA, "what we used to be like, what happened, and what we are like now" (AA, 2001, p. 58), are vehicles for making sense of the chaos of the typical alcoholic's life by redefining it within this logic. As Marion describes the process in Maracle (1989):

> The more I went to meetings, the more I heard what other people said. I'd come home and think about it. I'd reflect on my own life, far back, up close, when I

started drinking, what happened, how much of my life was related to alcohol, drinking. That's how I began to connect the depression and the drinking. I began to connect information, to put pieces together. I'd really *listen* at meetings. *Hear* what people said. And think about it all. And about me. I got real serious about trying to understand. (p. 154)

Thune's (1977) analysis of AA from a phenomenological perspective argues that it is precisely *because* AA members are taught to reinterpret their alcoholic life story as spiritually bankrupt that they can give meaning to a past filled with degradation and chaos and can have hope for the creation of a different future. Thus, the AA approach to recovery, which aims for a transformed life based on spiritual principles instead of alcoholic strategies, is different from approaching alcoholism as merely a disease or a bad habit to be reformed. The deeply individual piece of transformation, within the context of the narrative community, transcends the dichotomies of self–other and exemplifies the embedded interdependence of these communities.

Whom Does AA Benefit?

Researchers and clinicians would like to know more about who exactly would benefit the most from a Twelve-Step group like AA and who would be least likely to benefit. Unfortunately, there is no definitive answer to this important question. A major goal of Project MATCH was to predict which treatment approach would be more effective, given specific client characteristics. However, only 4 of 21 possible matches of client characteristics to particular treatment approaches were detected, and one of these matches disappeared after 1 year (Fuller & Hiller-Sturmhofel, 1999). An earlier study by Montgomery and colleagues (1995) found that AA attendees, when compared with nonattendees, could not be distinguished by pretreatment patient characteristics and that there was no evidence of an "AA personality." However, there continue to be concerns about whether AA is too culture bound with American, White, heterosexual, male dominance to be of any help to other groups, such as women, homosexuals, and people from different races and cultures. As one of the authors of this text heard from a woman in an open AA meeting in Scotland, "I never thought I could identify with an American male stockbroker! [i.e., Bill W.]."

Women comprise a steadily increasing membership in Alcoholics Anonymous. In 2007, women of all ages made up an estimated 33% of members compared with 30% in 1983 and 22% in 1968 (AA, 2007), and almost 80% of the women attending AA in a recent survey had held a group position of responsibility, such as secretary, treasurer, or literature person (Sanders, 2010). Prominent women, for example, Betty Ford in the 1970s, helped to pave the way for women to overcome some of the shame barriers in seeking help. However, many women in AA continued to react to the predominance of sexist language in *The Big Book*, which remains unchanged since the original edition (1939); "13th stepping" (soliciting more than friendship from vulnerable new members); and the tendency in some groups to be dominated by male chairpersons who call primarily on male members to share their stories. Consequently, in many medium-sized towns and certainly in larger cities, women-only groups have developed to alleviate some of this tension. Over 50% of the women surveyed on why they attended a women-only AA meeting pointed to the following reasons: to learn from other women who have had similar experiences, to socialize with other women in the program, to seek encouragement and support from women in AA, to build closer relationships with women in recovery, to talk about issues that are of more interest to women than men, to discuss intimate issues of recovery in a safe environment, and to help new female members of AA (Sanders, 2010). A Swedish study (Bodin, 2006) suggests that AA does appeal to women and that they participate to a greater degree than men. Women who attended AA reported more affiliation activities, such as calling on an AA member for help, experiencing a spiritual awakening, and reading AA literature.

There are also specialized meetings for a variety of groups, such as veterans, Hispanics, gays, lesbians, elders, and Native Americans. Sometimes, the principles of AA are blended with other cultural traditions to create a more effective approach. For example, the Wellbriety Movement in Native American communities combines the teachings of the medicine wheel with AA's Twelve Steps (Coyhis & Simonelli, 2005). Each step is placed at an appropriate place around the four directions of the medicine wheel: Steps 1 through 3 (honesty, hope, and faith) are grouped in the eastern part of the wheel and so on. However, not all problems can be solved by specialized groups or blending, as demonstrated by the different responses from lesbian women interviewed by Joanne Hall (1996). Some lesbian women felt perfectly comfortable in mainstream AA:

> It's comforting for me to see people from all walks of life who have the same disease as me. It's not just a bunch of dykes, you know? I just need to see that sometimes. (p. 122)
>
> AA is really great. All these people who are not like you are interested in keeping you sober. They call you—and you don't know why they wanna be around you, but they do anyway. I thought it was beautiful that these strangers that I had nothing in common with would call me and cared about me and would sit with me. (p. 123)

Others felt that the inclusion of culturally distinct persons in AA is superficial and that lesbian groups were important for identification:

> The lesbian AA groups are so much more open-minded .... The straight AA groups I find are real traditionally AA. In lesbian meetings other things can come out, like talking about incest, or just about living the life of a lesbian. (p. 123)

Still others rejected lesbian meetings because AA mainstream values lacked prominence in the specialized meetings and because they feared being "engulfed, sexualized, or rejected by women who were 'just like me' when they attended these lesbian meetings" (p. 124).

Some commentators raise concerns that African Americans are less likely to associate with AA because it is culturally bound by middle-class White Americans. A cross-sectional study by Kaskutas, Weisner, Lee, and Humphries (1999) found that African Americans are about twice as likely as Whites to report having attended AA as recommended by their professional treatment but that Whites are more likely to attend AA on their own. Although both groups are equally likely to actively engage in the program, they participated differently: African Americans were more likely to say they felt like a member of AA (64% vs. 54% of Whites) and had a spiritual awakening as a result of AA (38% vs. 37%), whereas Whites were more likely to have had a sponsor (23% vs. 14%) and to have read program literature (77% vs. 67%).

Project MATCH found no significant differences in the rates of AA attendance among African American, Hispanic, and White clients. Hispanic clients reported a higher level of AA involvement (e.g., working the Steps, having a sponsor, celebrating sobriety birthdays) than White clients (Tonigan, Connors, & Miller, 1998).

The spread of AA to over 160 countries and the publication of AA literature in at least eight languages would argue that AA's philosophy is flexible and broad enough that many different kinds of people can find a way to benefit. Because of Tradition Ten, "Alcoholics Anonymous has no opinion on outside issues; hence the AA name ought never be drawn into public controversy" (AA, 2001, p. 562), AA is not involved with any political organizations or social movements that might taint the single purpose of this organization, which is to "carry its message to the alcoholic who still suffers."

GAMBLERS ANONYMOUS

Attending one's first meeting of any mutual-help group can be a daunting experience. "Irene," one of the women interviewed by Davis (2009), was told by her counselor to go to at least five Gamblers Anonymous meetings. Her response was, "Anything anonymous, *excuse me*!" Here's how she describes her first meeting:

> I was so scared. The first meeting you sit there and you get your little packet and you're like, "Shit, what am I doing here!" And you're like, "No way." I mean I had never heard of the Twelve Steps. You know, it was a real eye-opener for me. I couldn't even really talk that first meeting, I was so choked up, I was so sick. It was like a bucket of cold water was dumped on my head. But I think what it was, was reading those Twenty Question, I went, "Ahhh ahhh, yes, yes, yeeesss." (Davis, 2009, p. 85).

Gamblers Anonymous (GA) is a Twelve-Step mutual-help program of men and women "who share their experience, strength, and hope with each other that they may solve their common problem and help others to recover from a gambling problem" (GA, 2000, p. 2). The GA program acknowledges Alcoholics Anonymous (AA) as a guide and foundation and utilizes the same Twelve Steps of recovery and the same organizational principles. The only requirement for membership is "a desire to stop gambling" (p. 2); consequently, abstinence from gambling is a goal.

Like other Twelve-Step groups, GA is run entirely by recovering individuals, in this case compulsive gamblers, who volunteer their time to be sponsors, chair meetings, arrange for meeting places, secure GA literature, and respond to requests for help day and night. GA meetings are available in all 50 states and are accessible online. GA meetings can be found by calling state problem gambling helplines, looking in the yellow pages of the phone book for a local contact number, or accessing the Gamblers Anonymous International Service Office online site (http://gamblersanonymous.org). The number of GA chapters increased from 650 in 1990 to 1,328 in October 1998, which may indicate some impact from the rapid expansion of legalized gambling (National Gambling Impact Study Commission, 1999). There are GA meetings available in many different countries, including the United Kingdom, Japan, Spain, Uganda, Kenya, Israel, and Brazil.

The format for a GA meeting is similar to other Twelve-Step groups; a short reading from the GA literature, a suggested topic, and sharing of thoughts and feelings by the members. The Twenty Questions that Irene referred to earlier in this section are usually read and responded to by the group. They provide a short screen for problem gambling, containing questions such as "Did you ever lose time from work or school to due to gambling?" and "Have you ever gambled to escape worry or trouble?" Tonetto (2008) investigated the psychometric properties of this screen, developed by gamblers in GA in 1958, and found it to be a reliable and valid measure of problem gambling.

Although GA is "probably the most popular intervention for pathological gambling" (Blanco, Ibanez, Saiz-Ruiz, Blanco-Jerez, & Nunes, 2000, p. 402), like its counterpart AA it is not without critics. GA, like AA, is perceived by some as a white, male, middle-class organization that is not user friendly to women. Actually, people who do attend GA appear to have different characteristics than those gamblers who present for treatment with no history of GA attendance. Petry (2003) found in her comparative study of 342 pathological gamblers, where 54% had previously attended GA, that the GA attendees were older; were less likely to be single; had higher incomes, more debts, more years of gambling, higher scores on the South Oaks Gambling Screen, and more family problems, but fewer drug problems. On an encouraging note, GA attendees were more likely to be abstinent after 2 months of treatment.

The historical dominance of men in GA may still be the case in some areas, but it appears the landscape is changing rapidly as more women seek help for gambling problems. For example, according to the Arizona Council on Compulsive Gambling (2000), even though GA started in that state in 1973,

> for the first 18 years, a few women walked through the doors ... and left. By their own admission, the men didn't quite know what to do with them. The women were told they hadn't gambled long enough; they hadn't lost enough to be real gamblers. They didn't play real games. Their tears and their stories were ridiculed. They were "hit" on, "Let's go for coffee ... at my place, baby." They

didn't stay. The men said, "Women just don't seem to have what it takes to stay in recovery." (Arizona Council on Compulsive Gambling, 2000)

The year 1992 marked a change in Arizona, when one woman (Marilyn L.) started a "women preferred" GA meeting in her home. Although the meeting struggled in the beginning, by 1999 there were three women preferred meetings out of the 19 GA meetings in the Phoenix area. The Arizona Council on Compulsive Gambling estimates that women now make up about 40% of GA meeting attendance.

Responses to an online survey of recovering women (Avery & Davis, 2008) support the idea that "times are changing," but a gender barrier can still exist. Some women noted barriers: "When I came into GA in 1991, the men didn't think slot players were real gamblers," and "I'm a woman, so they ignored me the first three months." On the other hand, many of the women responding to the survey felt welcomed: "Although I was the only woman, I felt welcomed," "I did not feel alone," "They understood my problem as no one who is not a compulsive gambler ever will," "When I finally began attending regularly, I felt welcomed in every way ... mostly, I felt that I belonged somewhere."

New GA members who have been longstanding members of AA sometimes have a problem adjusting to differences found in the meeting tone and format. Critics of GA say the program is more focused on solving financial problems than spiritual growth (Davis, 2009). For example, GA has an option of calling together a "pressure relief group" made up of GA members who have been successful in stopping gambling, to meet with a new member to help address their financial problems and their spouses and family members. Some GA groups incorporate the option of crosstalk at meetings to allow members to respond to the content of what another member has shared, and some meetings go on for as long as three hours (Straus, 2006).

How well does GA work? Folk-wisdom among members of GA is that "attending GA ruins your gambling." The small number of research studies available suggests that GA attendance is often associated with increased abstinence (Harvard Mental Health Letter, 2010; Petry, 2005). Like studies of AA, serious methodological problems arise from the voluntary, anonymous, self-selection of GA membership. Petry (2005) found there is no evidence to definitively prove the effectiveness of GA because of the lack of rigor in the methodology of the few studies available (no random assignment). However, her review of the research does suggest that persons who attend GA are more likely to become involved in professional treatment, have a higher rate of abstinence after starting professional treatment, and have a higher rate of long-term abstinence. Clearly, more research, and research that is gender specific, is needed in this area.

OTHER TWELVE-STEP GROUPS

As already mentioned, there are numerous other Twelve-Step groups available to help with every possible addiction. Space requirements preclude describing every one of them. The Twelve Steps and Twelve Traditions of Alcoholics

Anonymous have been translated to deal with many addictive problems. For example, in Narcotics Anonymous (NA), drug terminology is substituted for alcohol; in Cocaine Anonymous (CA), cocaine is substituted for alcohol; in Nicotine Anonymous (NA), nicotine is substituted for alcohol; and so on.

NA was started in the 1950s when polyaddiction became more common and some "pure alcoholics" in AA were uncomfortable when discussion often included more than just alcohol. Today, NA is a multilingual, multicultural organization that has 58,000 weekly meetings and members in 161 countries (NA, 2011). Similarly, Cocaine Anonymous emerged with the increased use of this drug and the differences in lifestyle, drug-seeking behaviors, and consequences of this drug. Other Twelve-Step groups provide support to family members and significant others, such as Families Anonymous, Al-Anon/Alateen, Nar-Anon, and Gam-Anon (see Chapter 10, for more on Al-Anon). The Internet is a bountiful resource on all the various Twelve-Step groups.

OTHER MUTUAL-SUPPORT GROUPS

There are also a variety of other types of mutual-help groups that offer support for addictive behavior that are fundamentally different in philosophy and purpose from Twelve-Step groups. For example, the three groups we briefly describe as examples do not emphasize reliance on a "Higher Power" for recovery and do not expect members to attend for life. However, like AA, substantial empirical support for their effectiveness is lacking, they are self-supporting, and they offer meetings in person and online services at no charge.

Women for Sobriety (WFS)

Women for Sobriety (WFS) (see website at http://www.womenforsobriety.org) was founded by Jean Kirkpatrick, PhD, in 1976 to address the unique issues for women that might be barriers to their recovery, such as lack of self-esteem, depression, and overwhelming feelings of guilt. In their mission statement, WFS states the belief that "addiction began to overcome stress, loneliness, frustration or emotional deprivation in daily life—dependence often resulted" (WFS, 2011). Kirkpatrick sees spirituality as a goal for recovery but stresses that WFS is not a "God-oriented program." She asks, "Do diabetics go to God-oriented meetings for their diabetes?"(Kirkpatrick, 2001, p. 2). Instead, the WFS meetings stress the "New Life" Program of Acceptance, which is based on Thirteen Statements. These include positive self-statements such as "Negative thoughts destroy only myself" and "The past is gone forever." (For a complete list, see http://www.womenforsobriety.org.) WFS recommends that women review these statements each morning, use one of them consciously all day, and review its effects at the end of the day.

Meetings are led by a certified moderator, a person with at least one year of sobriety and certified knowledge about WFS principles. Meetings are open to all women alcoholics and to those with prescription drug problems. According to Becky Feenner, current WFS Director, there are approximately

200 meetings through the United States, Canada, and a few foreign countries. She estimates that 200,000 to 300,000 women have used or are using the WFS program (Fenner, 2011). Two studies by Kaskutas (1994, 1995) support the idea that women attending WFS find support, nurturance, and a safe environment for discussions of women's issues. Another earlier study of 115 women in AA or WFS (Talan, 1982) found no differences between groups on reaction to the groups, length of time attending, or treatment outcome.

SMART RECOVERY

SMART, which stands for Self Management and Recovery Training, is another alternative mutual-help group, started in 1992 as an offshoot of Rational Recovery (see the group's website at http://www.smartrecovery.org). The group's approach is drawn from the principles of cognitive-behavioral therapy and particularly from rational emotive behavior therapy, as developed by Albert Ellis, PhD. Addiction is viewed more as a maladaptive behavior than a disease and could arise from both substance use (e.g., alcohol, nicotine, caffeine, food, illicit drugs, or prescribed medications) and involvement in activities (e.g., gambling, sexual behavior, eating, spending, relationships, or exercise). As stated on their website, "We assume that there are degrees of addictive behavior, and that all individuals to some degree experience it."

SMART Recovery attempts to fill in the gap posed by the following questions, raised by Nick Rajacic (2011, p.1), coordinator of the Keweenaw Area SMART Recovery Program:

> Why can't people be encouraged and motivated to creatively seek their own solutions instead of looking for answers outside of themselves in the form of groups and Higher Powers? Why can't people just be taught effective skills to cope with the problems of living sober in a drug-using culture? Why can't they just be taught the cognitive-behavioral skills of emotional self-management? Why can't they develop new and rewarding lifestyles around interests other than recovery alone?

The program has two primary goals: (1) to help individuals gain independence from addictive behavior (through abstinence) and (2) to teach people how to enhance and maintain motivation to abstain; cope with urges; manage thoughts, feelings, and behavior; and balance momentary and enduring satisfactions. To accomplish this, cognitive-behavioral techniques, communication skills, anger management skills, and stress management techniques are incorporated into the meetings.

Meetings typically include discussions of the primary goals, activating events (urges, life happenings, or any other experiences that might lead to negative consequences), and analysis of the events using a cognitive approach. Personal homework projects are usually assigned to put ideas from the meetings into practice. Current meeting locations are listed, by states and contacts, on the group's website. There are approximately 600 different meetings in the United States and meetings in several other countries including Canada,

Australia, Scotland, Sweden, Iran, and Uzbekistan (SMART, 2011). According to a recent survey of membership, the average member is white (93%), male (57%), middle-aged (68% between age 40 and 60), and well-educated (88% with some college, bachelors, masters, or professional degree). Almost half of the respondents attend face-to-face meetings, and 35% attend online meetings (SMART, 2011).

SMART meeting coordinators are volunteers, trained from literature available at the website, recommended readings, and regular consultation with a volunteer professional advisor who is typically a licensed professional with addiction training and experience. The SMART program has a highly developed online presence, offering a message board, online library, chat room, meetings, voice chats, and special event speakers in the SMART room. As one member attests: "I shall be forever grateful for the encouragement and support I found (on the website) when I was so confused and scared. The message boards and the early morning 'chats' kept me feeling I could do this and that all the physical signs that come from quitting were to be expected" (SMART, 2011).

MODERATION MANAGEMENT (MM)

Moderation Management (MM), as the name implies, is a mutual-help group dedicated to supporting individuals who have a desire to drink alcohol moderately (Kosok, 2006). Drinking problems are viewed as bad habits rather than a disease. MM is not intended for "those who experience significant withdrawal symptoms when they stop drinking, or those with any physical or mental condition, including pregnancy, that could be adversely affected by alcohol, even in moderate amounts. Also this association is not intended for former dependent drinkers who are now abstaining" (http://www.moderation.org). Rather, MM may be viewed as a prevention measure or a harm reduction strategy for persons who wish to drink moderately. Moderation is defined for males as no more than four drinks per day, no more than four drinking days per week, and no more than fourteen standard drinks per week; for females moderation is considered to be no more than three standard drinks per day, no more than four drinking days per week, and no more than nine drinks per week.

MM strategies include a voluntary abstention from alcohol for 30 days, during which the person is asked to examine how drinking has affected his or her life, write down priorities, and take a look at how much, how often, and under what circumstances drinking occurs. Moderate drinking levels are set using the MM guidelines, and the person is encouraged to try cognitive-behavioral techniques found in several recommended texts. MM recommends 6–18 months of weekly meetings, which are devoted to discussion of MM goals and individuals' activities since the last meeting.

MM was under fire in the press and from the National Council on Alcoholism and Drug Dependence (NCADD) because of the tragic experience of MM founder Audrey Kishline (Verhovek, 2000). She pleaded guilty to two counts of vehicular homicide after a binge-drinking episode in March 2000 in which she drove in the wrong lane and caused a collision that killed two people.

Although Kishline had resigned from MM the previous January, stating she had shifted her drinking goal to abstinence and attending AA, many who are abstinence-only proponents took the opportunity to hold up her experience as an example of "denial in action" and "the delusion behind the idea that alcoholics can be taught to drink without harm" (Verhovek, 2000, p. 1). The board of directors of MM countered this by reminding people that Kishline adhered to the basic tenets of MM by shifting her goal to abstinence when she could not maintain moderate drinking. Like many members of AA and other support groups, she relapsed, which should not be blamed on AA or MM but should be seen as a personal tragedy (MM, 2000).

Current face-to-face meetings and chat rooms can be found on the MM website. One of the few studies conducted on MM effectiveness found partial evidence that using the MM website in combination with the resources on ModerateDrinking.com is helpful with problem drinkers (Hester, Delaney, & Campbell, 2011). Kosok (2006) examined questionnaire responses from 272 MM members and determined that the growth of the organization was solely through the Internet. The majority of members are women, middle class, and highly educated; and they do not have severe drinking problems. Because the survey found that only a small minority of members received treatment previously, Kosok concludes that MM offers a viable treatment option that can reach an underserved population who otherwise would not have entered any program.

RECOVERY COMMUNITY CENTERS

The development of Recovery Community Centers is a recent effort spearheaded by the Recovery Management philosophy that healing takes place in the community over the long term and the support of others is critical (see Chapter 1). It is included in this section because of the heavy reliance on volunteers from the local recovery community to "put a face on recovery" and support others in the recovery process (Faces & Voices, 2011). The Recovery Community model challenges the prevailing idea in professional treatment programs that an "expert" is required to diagnose and treat a person's addiction problems. Instead of the typical hierarchical relationship with professionals, the relationship shifts to a "recovery management partnership" that incorporates support relationships in the community (with volunteer recovery coaches) that are natural, reciprocal, and noncommercialized. A basic assumption of the model is that "there is no universally effective professional intervention for severe alcohol or drug AOD problems" (White & Sanders, 2008). Consequently, the professional staff, the community volunteers, and the clients work together to design meaningful helping strategies that will be effective as their lives play out in the community over time.

The states of Connecticut, Vermont, and Massachusetts have pioneered this new development. Funded by state and federal money and private donations, the centers provide services such as telephone support (usually by a volunteer in recovery), family support groups, housing assistance, recovery group meetings, social events, and recovery coaching. Advocacy groups of recovering people are also organized to participate in nonpartisan activities like voter registration and lobbying candidates to support policies and legislation helpful to recovering persons.

Recovery Community Centers make a point that they are a new option on the continuum of supports available to anyone suffering an addiction. They are not treatment agencies, Twelve-Step clubs, or drop-in centers, although elements of these can be found in some form under the Community Center umbrella. The primary purpose is to "build recovery capital and serve as a physical location where the local recovery community's ability to care is organized" (Faces & Voices, 2011, p.1). Does it work? Too early to call, although preliminary data gathered for the Connecticut Recovery Community Center found participants had high rates of abstinence, low recidivism rates, and increased housing stability and employment.

HOW TO SUPPORT CLIENT INVOLVEMENT IN MUTUAL-HELP GROUPS

In spite of the positive findings that mutual-help groups do help many people, some clinicians are reluctant to refer clients. McCartney (2010) recommends facilitating mutual-help participation by attending open mutual-aid group meetings. Readers of this book will then be able to discover their own meanings of the similarities and differences between their professional helping and the help offered by mutual-help groups by putting themselves in a position to experience firsthand the mutual-help community and the hope that it offers to many persons. It appears that getting familiar with Twelve-Step programs through attending a meeting is common among U.S. addiction professionals. In a comparison between Norwegian and U.S. addiction professionals, 89% of the American clinicians had attended a Twelve-Step group meeting, compared to 32% of the Norwegian clinicians (Vederhus et al., 2010).

However, attending one open AA meeting or other self-help group may not be sufficient. The decentralized nature of self-help groups translates into a wide variation in terms of their social structure and characteristics, such as cohesiveness, typical members, and expressiveness. The Center for Substance Abuse Treatment (CSAT) recommends that counselors offer more than one choice about possible groups or types of groups to attend, and that the client should attend several meetings before settling in on a judgment about the groups (CSAT, 2008). Miller and colleagues (2011) remind us that it is not a good idea to pressure or coerce people to attend meetings, and that Twelve-Step groups have always been meant to be a voluntary association. If you are in a medium-sized or large city, you may find an array of options or types of meetings that appeal to groups such as men, women, gay men, lesbians, veterans, elders, smokers, and nonsmokers. As a visitor, you are invited to attend any meeting identified as open. Closed meetings are reserved for those who have a desire to stop the particular behavior the group is organized around.

For information regarding meeting times and schedules (which change frequently), consult the yellow pages of the phone book under "Alcoholism or "Gambling," the classified ads in the local newspaper, or the Internet. In larger towns, call the AA central office in your area (run by volunteers, not paid staff) to get the meeting schedules and advise you about meetings that might be a good match for your client. One of the most effective ways of ensuring that clients try out at least one meeting is to invite them, while still in your office, to talk via telephone to a volunteer who goes to that particular meeting (Miller et al., 2011).

In Twelve-Step groups, visitors and newcomers may be asked to identify themselves by their first names only when they attend an open meeting. As members talk, they identify themselves by their first name only, not their profession, not their family name, and not where they live. The practice of anonymity is considered by many Twelve-Step members to be a spiritual foundation of recovery (AA, 2001). As a respectful visitor, it is critical to honor this tradition.

Online resources are abundant and a good place to start to become familiar with mutual-aid groups in your community. Information on these different groups is available by a key word search at the American Self-Help Clearinghouse site on the Internet. Another resource guide that is updated monthly and lists groups, Internet resources, and recovery stories can be found at http://www.facesandvoicesofrecovery.org.

SUMMARY AND CONCLUSION

Much more could be said to describe the various methods and purposes of mutual help, but the purpose of this chapter was limited to introducing counselors to a way of understanding some of the primary features of several of the main mutual-help organizations. Alcoholics Anonymous, as practiced in the community, is the prototype of Twelve-Step mutual-help organizations such as Narcotics Anonymous and Gamblers Anonymous. This organization is seen as a narrative community where identity transformation takes place through the telling of stories and the identification of personal meanings of metaphors. Spirituality is central to the healing process in Twelve-Step communities.

In contrast, Women for Sobriety, SMART Recovery, and Moderation Management do not require a spiritual orientation. WFS and SMART are both abstinence-based programs; MM is designed to help problem drinkers drink moderately. Recovery Community Centers are inclusive of all methods of recovery from addiction. All of these programs and many more can be accessed through the Internet, and most have online meetings and chat rooms.

At a minimum, the members of these mutual-help programs can offer acceptance on a deep level to persons who have been isolated and shamed by their circumstances and can affirm the hope that one can recover. For these reasons alone, a referral, with some preparation as to how the meetings are conducted, how to find the meetings, and a brief summary of the meeting format, should be considered.

REFERENCES

Alcoholics Anonymous (AA). (1955). *Alcoholics Anonymous: The story of how many thousands of men and women have recovered from alcoholism* (2nd ed.). New York: Alcoholics Anonymous World Services.

Alcoholics Anonymous (AA). (2001). *Alcoholics Anonymous: The story of how many thousands of men and women have recovered from alcoholism* (4th ed.). New York: Alcoholics Anonymous World Services.

Alcoholics Anonymous (AA). (2007). *Alcoholics Anonymous membership survey*. New York: Alcoholics Anonymous World Services. Retrieved July 15, 2011 from http://www.aa.org

Alcoholics Anonymous (AA). (2011). *Estimates of AA groups and members*. Retrieved July 15, 2011 from: http://www.aa.org

Arizona Council on Compulsive Gambling. (2000). *Women and recovery in Arizona: A brief history*. Retrieved August 17, 2011 from http://www.azccg.org

Avery, L., & Davis, D. (2008). Women's recovery from compulsive gambling: Results of an online survey. *Journal of Social Work Practice in the Addictions, 8*(2), 171–191.

Bateson, G. (1972). *Steps to an ecology of mind*. New York: Ballantine Books.

Berg, I., & Miller, S. (1992). *Working with the problem drinker: A solution-focused approach*. New York: Norton.

Bill, W. (1967). *As Bill sees it*. New York: Alcoholics Anonymous World Services.

Blanco, C., Ibanez, A., Saiz-Ruiz, J., Blanco-Jerez, C., & Nunes, E. (2000). Epidemiology, pathophysiology and treatment of pathological gambling. *CNS Drugs, 13*(6), 397–407.

Bodin, M. (2006). Gender aspects of affiliation with Alcoholics Anonymous after treatment. *Contemporary Drug Problems, 33*(1), 123–141.

Borkman, T. (1989, Spring). Alcoholics Anonymous: The stories. *Social Policy*, pp. 58–63.

Borkman, R. (2006). Sharing experience, conveying hope: Egalitarian relations as the essential method of Alcoholics Anonymous. *Nonprofit Management and Leadership, 17*(2), 145–152.

Brown, S. (1994). Alcoholics Anonymous: An interpretation of its spiritual foundation. *Behavioral Health Management, 14*(1), 25–27.

Center for Substance Abuse Treatment (CSAT). (2008). An introduction to mutual support groups for alcohol and drug abuse. *Substance Abuse in Brief Fact Sheet, 5*(1). Rockville, MD: SAMHSA.

Clemmons, P. (1991). Feminists, spirituality, and the Twelve Steps of Alcoholics Anonymous. *Women and Therapy, 11*(2), 97–109.

Coyhis, D., & Simonelli, R. (2005). Rebuilding Native American communities. *Child Welfare, 84*(2), 323–337.

Covington, S. (1994). *A woman's way through the Twelve Steps*. Center City, MN: Hazelden.

Davis, D. (1996). Women healing from alcoholism: A qualitative study. *Contemporary Drug Problems, 24,* 147–177.

Davis, D. (2009). *Taking back your life: Women and problem gambling*. Center City, MN: Hazelden.

Davis, D., & Jansen, G. (1998). Making meaning of Alcoholics Anonymous for social workers: Myths, metaphors and realities. *Social Work, 43*(2), 169–182.

DeSoto, C. B., O'Donnel, W. E., & DeSoto, J. L. (1989). Long-term recovery in alcoholics. *Alcoholism: Clinical and Experimental Research, 13*(5), 693–697. Emrick, C. D. (1987). Alcoholics Anonymous: Affiliation processes and effectiveness as treatment. *Alcoholism: Clinical and Experimental Research, 11*(5), 416–423.

Fenner, Becky, (2011). Personal communication to Diane Davis, 7-23-11. .

Finfgeld, D. (2002). Feminist spirituality and alcohol treatment. *Journal of Holistic Nursing, 20*(2), 113–127.

Fisher, G. L., & Harrison, T. C. (2008). *Substance abuse: Information for school counselors, social workers, therapists, and counselors* (4th ed.). Boston: Allyn & Bacon.

Flora, K., Raftopoulos, A., & Pontikes, T. (2010). A look at the evolution of the self-help movement. *Journal of Groups in Addiction and Recovery, 5,* 214–225.

Fuller, R., & Hiller-Sturmhofel, S. (1999). Alcoholism treatment in the United States: An overview. *Alcohol, Research, and Health, 23*(2), 69–77.

Galaif, E. R., & Sussman, S. (1995). For whom does Alcoholics Anonymous work? *International Journal of the Addictions, 30*(2), 161–184.

Galanter, M. (1999). Research on spirituality and Alcoholics Anonymous. *Alcoholism: Clinical and Experimental Research, 23,* 716–719.

Galanter, M. (2006). Spirituality in Alcoholics Anonymous: A valuable adjunct to psychiatric services. *Psychiatric Services, 57*(3), 307–314.

Gamblers Anonymous (GA). (2000). *Gamblers Anonymous: A new beginning* (4th ed.). Los Angeles: Author.

Goldstrom, I., Campbell, J., Rogers, J., Lambert, D., Blacklow, B., Henderson, M., & Manderscheid, R. (2006). National estimates for mental health mutual support groups, self-help organizations, and consumer operated services. *Administration and Policy in Mental Health and Mental Health Services Research, 33*(1), 92–103.

Gossop, M., Harris, J., Best, D., Man, L., Manning, V., Marshall, J., et al. (2003). Is attendance at Alcoholics Anonymous meetings after inpatient treatment related to improved outcomes? A 6 month follow-up study. *Alcohol and Alcoholism: International Journal of the Medical Council on Alcoholism, 38*(5), 421–426.

Hall, J. (1996). Lesbians' participation in Alcoholics Anonymous: Experiences of social, personal, and political tensions. *Contemporary Drug Problems, 23,* 113–139.

Harvard Mental Health Letter. (2010). Pathological gambling. *Harvard Health Publications, 27*(2), 1–3.

Hester, R., Delaney, H., & Campbell, W. (2011). ModerateDrinking.com and Moderation Management: Outcomes of a randomized clinical trial with non-dependent problem drinkers. *Journal of Consulting and Clinical Psychology, 79*(2), 215–224.

Hoffman, H. (2006). Criticism as deviance and social control ion Alcoholics Anonymous. *Journal of Contemporary Ethnography, 35,* 669–695.

Kaskutas, L. (1994). What do women get out of self-help? Their reasons for attending Women for Sobriety and Alcoholics Anonymous. *Journal of Substance Abuse Treatment, 11,* 185–195.

Kaskutas, L. (1995). *An analysis of "Women for Sobriety."* Unpublished doctoral dissertation, University of California, Berkeley.

Kaskutas, L., Weisner, C., Lee, M., & Humphries, K. (1999). Alcoholics Anonymous affiliation at treatment intake among White and Black Americans. *Journal of Studies on Alcohol, 60*(6), 810–817.

Kasl, C. D. (1992). *Many roads, one journey: Moving beyond the Twelve Steps.* New York: Harper Perennial.

Kelly, J., Stout, R., Magill, M., Tonigan, J., & Pagano, M. (2010). Mechanism of behavior change in Alcoholics Anonymous: Des AA lead to better alcohol use outcomes by reducing depression symptoms? *Addiction, 105,* 626–636.

Kelly, J., Stout, R., Zywiak, W., & Schneider, R. (2006). A 3-year study of addiction mutual-help group participation following intensive outpatient treatment. *Alcoholism: Clinical and Experimental Research, 30*(8), 1381–1392.

Kirkpatrick, J. (2001). *Spirituality.* Retrieved July 6, 2011 from http://www.womenforsobriety.org/ articles

Kosok, A. (2006). The moderation management programme in 2004: What type of drinker seeks controlled drinking? *International Journal of Drug Policy, 17*(4), 295–303.

Kurtz, E. (1979). *Not-God: A history of Alcoholic Anonymous.* Center City, MN: Hazelden.

Kurtz, E. (1982). Why AA works: The intellectual significance of Alcoholics Anonymous. *Journal of Studies on Alcohol, 43,* 38–80.

Kurtz, L. F., & Chambon, A. (1987). Comparison of self-help groups for mental health. *Health and Social Work, 12,* 275–283.

Kurtz, L. F., & Fisher, M. (2003). Participation in community life by AA and NA members. *Contemporary Drug Problems, 30,* 875–904.

LaFave, L., & Echols, L. (1999). An argument for choice: Meeting the needs of chemically dependent women. *Journal of Substance Abuse Treatment, 16*(4), 345–352.

Majer, J., Droege, J., & Jason, L. (2010). A categorical assessment of 12-step involvement in relation to recovery resources. *Journal of Groups in Addiction and Recovery, 5,* 155–167.

Maracle, M. F. (1989). *Beyond abstinence: A study of recovery among women in Alcoholics Anonymous.* Unpublished doctoral dissertation, Washington University, St. Louis, MO.

McLatchie, B. H., & Lomp, K. G. E. (1988). Alcoholics Anonymous affiliation and treatment outcome among a clinical sample of problem drinkers. *American Journal of Drug and Alcohol Abuse, 14,* 309–324.

McNeece, C., & DiNitto, D. (2005). *Chemical dependency: A systems approach* (3rd ed.). Boston: Allyn & Bacon.

Miller, W., Forcehimes, A., Zweben, A., & McClellan, A. (2011). *Treating addiction: A guide for professionals.* New York: Guilford Press.

Miller, W. R., Leckman, A. L., Delaney, H. D., & Tinkcorn, M. (1992). Long-term follow-up of behavioral self-control training. *Journal of Studies on Alcohol, 53,* 249–261.

Monk, G., Winslade, J., Crocket, K., & Epston, D. (1997). *Narrative therapy in practice: The archaeology of hope.* San Francisco: Jossey-Bass.

Montgomery, H. A., Miller, W. R., & Tonigan, J. S. (1995). Does Alcoholics Anonymous involvement predict treatment outcome? *Journal of Substance Abuse Treatment, 12*(4) 241–246.

Moos, R. H., & Moos, B. S. (2006). Participation in treatment and Alcoholics Anonymous: A 16 year follow-up of initially untreated individuals. *Journal of Clinical Psychology*, 62(6), 735–750.

Narcotics Anonymous (NA). (2011). *Facts about NA*. Retrieved July 18, 2010 from http://www.na.org

National Gambling Impact Study Commission. (1999). *Report of the commission*. Washington, DC: U.S. Government Printing Office.

Nelson-Zlupko, L., Kauffman, E., & Dore, M. (1995). Gender differences in drug addiction and treatment: Implications for social work intervention with substance-abusing women. *Social Work*, 40(1), 45–54.

Peele, S. (2010). *AA isn't the best solution: Alternatives for alcoholics*. Retrieved July 18, 2011 from http://www.huffingtonpost.com/stanton-peele/aa-isnt-the-best-solution_b_629004.html

Petry, N. (2003). Patterns and correlates of Gamblers Anonymous attendance in pathological gamblers seeking treatment. *Addictive Behaviors*, 28(6), 1049–1062.

Petry, N. (2005). Gamblers Anonymous and cognitive-behavioral therapies for pathological gamblers. *Journal of Gambling Studies*, 21(1), 27–33.

Rajacic, N. (2011). Nick's story. Retrieved Sept 12, 2011 from http://www.smartrecovery.org/resources/library.

Rapp, C. A., & Goscha, R. (2006). *The strengths model: Case management with people with psychiatric disabilities* (2nd ed.). New York: Oxford University Press.

Rappaport, J. (1993). Narrative studies, personal stories, and identity transformation in the mutual-help context. *Journal of Applied Behavioral Science*, 29(2), 239–256.

Saleebey, D. (Ed.). (2006). *The strengths perspective in social work practice* (4th ed.). Boston: Allyn & Bacon.

Sanders, J. (2010). Acknowledging gender in women-only meetings of Alcoholics Anonymous. *Journal of Groups in Addiction and Recovery*, 5, 17–33.

Schonbrun, Y., Strong, D., Anderson, B., Caviness, C., Brown, R., & Stein, M. (2011). Alcoholics Anonymous and hazardously drinking women returning to the community after incarceration: Predictors of attendance and outcome. *Alcoholism: Clinical and Experimental Research*, 35(3), 532–539.

SMART Recovery. (2011). *Meetings in your area*. Retrieved July 24, 2011 from http://www.smartrecovery.org

Smith, A. R. (1993). The social construction of group dependency in Alcoholics Anonymous. *Journal of Drug Issues*, 23(4), 689–704.

Taber, J., McCormick, R., Russo, A., Adkins, B., & Ramirez, L. (1987). Follow-up of pathological gamblers after treatment. *American Journal of Psychiatry*, 144, 757–761.

Talan, B. (1982). *Power and control: Predictors for the alcoholic woman's choice and effectiveness of treatment*. Unpublished doctoral dissertation, University of Detroit, MI.

Thune, C. (1977). Alcoholism and the archetypal past: A phenomenological perspective on Alcoholics Anonymous. *Journal of Studies on Alcohol*, 38, 75–88.

Tonigan, J. S., Connors, G., & Miller, W. (1998). Special populations in Alcoholics Anonymous. *Alcohol, Health, and Research World*, 22(4), 281–285.

Tonigan, J. S., Connors, G. J., & Miller, W. R. (2003). Participation and involvement in Alcoholics Anonymous. In T. F. Babor & F. K. Del Boca (Eds.), *Treatment matching in alcoholism* (pp. 184–204). Cambridge, England: Cambridge University Press.

Toneatto, T. (2008). Reliability and validity of the Gamblers Anonymous Twenty Questions. *Journal of Psychopathology and Behavioral Assessment, 30*, 71–78.

Travis, T. (2010). *The language of the heart: A cultural history of the recovery movement from Alcoholics Anonymous to Oprah Winfrey.* Chapel Hill: University of North Carolina Press.

Vederhus, J., Laudet, Al., Kristensen, O., & Clausen, T. (2010). Obstacles to 12-step group participation as seen by addiction professionals: Comparing Norway to the United States. *Journal of Substance Abuse Treatment, 39*, 210–217.

Verhovek, S. (2000, July 9). Advocate of moderation for heavy drinkers learns sobering lesson. *New York Times*, pp. 1, 10.

Walitzer, K., Derman, K., & Barrick, C. (2009). Facilitating involvement in alcoholics Anonymous during out-patient treatment: a randomized clinical trial. *Addiction, 104*, 391–401.

Wallace, J. (1983). Ideology, belief and behavior: Alcoholics Anonymous as a social movement. In E.Gottheil, K.Draley, T.Skolada, & H.Waxman (Eds.), *Etiologic aspects of alcohol and drug abuse* (pp. 285–305). Springfield, IL: Charles C. Thomas.

Wetzel, J. W. (1991). Universal mental health classification systems: Reclaiming women's experience. *Affilia, 6*(3), 8–31.

White, M. (2000). *Reflections on narrative practice: Essays and interviews.* Adelaide, South Australia: Dulwich Centre.

White, W., & Sanders, M. (2008). Recovery Management and people of color: Redesigning addiction treatment for historically disempowered communities. *Alcoholism Treatment Quarterly, 26*(3), 365–395.

Women for Sobriety (WFS). (2011). *WFS Facts.* Retrieved July 23, 2011 from http://www.womenforsobriety.org

RACE, ETHNIC, CULTURE, AND CLASS ISSUES

CHAPTER 12

INTRODUCTION

In earlier days of assessment and treatment, alcoholism was explained to treatment clients and the general public through the U-shaped Jellinek curve, which shows inevitable progressive stages, starting with occasional relief drinking, bottoming out with obsessive drinking and loss of control, and finally going up the other side through the stages of recovery. Everyone was predicted to go through the same stages of progressive alcoholism and recovery, in spite of the fact that Jellineck himself described this as only one of the several different types of the "species of alcoholism." (See Chapter 2 for more on Jellineck's study.) Although it may have been comforting to have a feeling of certainty about how alcoholism develops and progresses for everyone, we no longer live in such an uncomplicated world. Professionals now understand that a person's trajectory to addiction problems and road to recovery is not preordained; rather it is mediated by many individual factors and varies widely. Culture, ethnicity, race, and class are four of the important social factors in the biopsychosocial model that impact the course of a person's addiction problems and recovery.

According to the Office of Applied Statistics (OAS) (2009), sociodemographic differences in substance use among and within racial and ethnic subgroups explain, at least in part, the subgroups' different prevalence of substance misuse and differential treatment needs. In their classic ethnographic study on women and cocaine, for example, Murphy and Rosenbaum (1997) note that race and economic class heavily influence geographic location, access to drugs, and a variety of other factors. In the example they use, Monique is poor and black; Becky is middle-class and white. Their different status of race and class influences (1) how potent the available drugs are (crack in poor inner cities versus powdered cocaine in affluent suburbs), (2) the relationship between sex and drugs in the particular social scene (Monique, who had to prostitute for money versus Becky, who had a well-paying job), (3) the ability of a person to maintain a "nondeviant" identity by being able to conceal drug use, (4) the availability of resources to cushion the consequences of using illegal drugs, and (5) the availability of options to leave the drug "scene" and move on to a different way of life (Monique, who went to a homeless shelter versus Becky, who went to Hawaii with her dad). Thus, the combination of racial oppression *and* economic class profoundly influences the context of drug initiation, drug use patterns, and the consequences of drug misuse and addiction.

The Recovery Management model (RM) (see Chapter 1) is a new paradigm for addressing the differences so glaringly apparent in the stories of Becky and Monique. Recovery Management would be particularly helpful for someone like Monique, who had very few, if any, supports for recovery within her family (estranged and fractured) and social networks (fellow crack addicts). The RM model focuses on designing services based on the magnitude of the problem and the amount of "recovery capital" available to individual clients within their communities (White & Saunders, 2008; White & Kelly, 2010). Recovery capital is a concept that identifies strengths and resources within communities that have been overlooked in traditional acute care models. For example, the capacity for patience, compassion, and forgiveness within communities of color is viewed as a resource of hope, not a sign of codependency. The community ecosystem itself is perceived as the source of healing, and thus the RM model seeks to enhance the recovery support of families, kinship networks, mutual-help groups, churches, and tribes. Indigenous healers in the community, such as the medicine man or woman, curandero, minister, shaman, or herbalist as well as relevant cultural rituals and ceremonies are sought out and included with the RM team approach. White and Sanders (2008) advocate for an assertive approach of community outreach because of several possible conditions of marginalized people that make engagement more difficult:

1. Lack of money, skills, and language to negotiate the treatment system.
2. High tolerance for pain and suffering.
3. Illegal status.
4. Negative experiences in other service systems (courts, child welfare, schools).
5. Cultural or religious beliefs that conflict with mainstream treatment centers.
6. Fear of "losing face" or bringing shame on the family by disclosing personal problems.

Another view of why culturally competent services are needed comes from a 31-year-old man with an Indian Hindu background who is struggling with substance abuse. The program he attends, the Bac-in-Black and Asian Cultural Identification of Narcotics in Nottingham (United Kingdom), offers support 24 hours a day to black and minority ethnic addicts, and it is staffed by primarily former addicts who between them speak seven languages. He said, "The support I'm currently receiving goes beyond anything else. When I've been to other services, the approach is very clinical; there's no empathy with an individual or understanding of your culture. There are a lot of complex issues; the responsibility of being the elder son and not living up to it, the cultural shame" (Monk, 2011, p. 2).

In 2004, the City of Philadelphia began a major transformation of its behavioral health care system along the line of Recovery Management (McLaulin, Evans, & White, 2009). One of the fundamental changes of the Philadelphia Model is that services at all levels of care link to communities of recovery (self-help groups, support groups, community centers, recovery homes, recovery ministries, and recovery advocacy organizations).

Harm reduction approaches, stressing client self-determination and empowerment (see Chapter 1) have also been empirically supported as effective with ethnic minority communities (Blume & Lovato, 2010). Attaining small goals over a period of time may make more sense to clients who may have worldviews that differ from the majority culture in terms of the measurement of time, the value of family and community over the individual, the value of patience, and the meaning of health and illness. A harm reduction approach would not impose the abstinence-only model still prevalent in many treatment centers.

Treatment and recovery models aimed at working more effectively with ethnic minority clients, like RM and harm reduction approaches, are just beginning to take hold. However, attending to cultural and ethnic differences is now a focus of all the helping professions. The Council on Social Work Education (CSWE) specifies that the ability to "engage diversity and difference in practice" is one of the ten core competencies required of students in order to maintain an accredited social work program at the baccalaureate or master's level (CSWE, 2008). In the CSWE requirement, diversity includes race, culture, class, and color as well as immigration status, sexual orientation, gender, disability, and age. According to Escobar and Vega (2006), it is significant for psychiatrists that the *Review of Psychiatry* (the traditional text for updating progress in psychiatry) states that it is essential to consider culture in the diagnosis and treatment of culturally diverse individuals. Since 2002, the American Psychological Association has implemented multicultural guidelines for psychologists that include applying culturally appropriate skills in clinical practice (Bogo, Tsang, & Lee, 2011). We should bear in mind that cultural competence is not just a skill set required by the various helping professions but is a in essence, a continual self-evaluating stance by the counselor of his or her own world view and potential biases.

We all agree on the importance of considering racial, ethnic, cultural, and class issues, but it is not always clear what we mean by these words. In simpler times, most people saw the world divided into familiar categories of race: white, black, Asian, and a broad "other" category of Hispanic. However, the whole concept of race has gradually been discredited by many important international bodies because there are no natural distinctions among people rooted in biogenetic differences; that is, race is not a biological category, it is a social category (Escobar & Vega, 2006). To complicate things even further, racial categories lose meaning because of the reality of our multicultural world. On the 2010 U.S. census, 9 million people (2.9% of the population) identified themselves as more than one racial category; and among children, the multiracial population is the fastest growing youth group in the country, having increased 50% since the 2000 census (Saulny, 2011). Another problem is that the concept of race has been used throughout time to oppress, enslave, diminish, and marginalize a particular group of people who have some common physical traits. Unfortunately, we appear to be stuck with the category of race, as long as the federal government continues to use it as the basis for data collection for the U.S. Census, U.S. Office of Management and Budget, and federal agencies such as the Substance Abuse Mental Health Services Administration. Consequently, this chapter will use the prescribed racial classifications of African Americans (blacks), American Indians and Alaska Natives, and Asian Americans and Pacific Islanders as general categories, but we will make every effort to point out the diversity among these groups.

Hispanic American (Latino) will also be a category in this chapter, but it is considered an ethnicity in federal classification systems. An ethnicity may apply to a person of any race (e.g., some people from the Dominican Republic may consider their ethnicity to be Hispanic and their race to be black). Groups are divided into ethnic categories based on a common historical experience (such as the colonial experience of native Hawaiians), language (such as the Nimi'ipuu language spoken by the Nez Perce tribe in Idaho), religion, rituals, ceremonies, and common preferences for music and food. Ethnic categories are fluid within the broader categories of race, not precise, and not recognized as very meaningful outside of the United States (Escobar & Vega, 2006). One can "see" ethnicity in Irish pubs that are full of Gaelic song and beer, in the Native Americans hunched over stick-games at a pow-wow, and in the colorful fiestas of San Antonio: We know it is there; it is just hard to quantify.

The concept of culture is also difficult to pin down. Generally, culture refers to learned values, behaviors, and beliefs that are shared by other group members, including patterns of language, spiritual ideals, and worldviews (Escobar & Vega, 2006; Straussner, 2001). Thus we have hip-hop culture, crackhead culture, GLBTQI culture, and so on. Attitudes about the use and abuse of alcohol, drugs, and gambling are heavily influenced by our own cultural context. For example, superstitions about what brings good luck in gambling vary by culture: some Hispanic communities use Ojovenado, a seed from Mexico, as a lucky charm; gamblers in the Roma (gypsy) tribe wash their hands in chamomile tea before gambling; and the number 4 is considered unlucky in Chinese, Korean, Vietnames, and Japanese cultures (Ontario Resource Group, 2010). Culture can also be a barrier to finding and receiving professional help when faced with problems. As one member of a GLBTQI focus group expressed it:

> It is often hard to speak to professionals about my needs or considerations because I find myself teaching them. You can't expect someone who is learning

about the basics of your very existence to be helpful in providing guidance or suggesting paths to recovery. (SAMHSA, 2009)

Many authors argue that the effects of group membership cannot be separated from the effects of social class, and in fact many so-called attributes of ethnicity or culture are in reality effects of class. For example, close ties and reliance on extended family may be related to the bleak economic future of undereducated and poor individuals on their own. Class, or socioeconomic status (SES), is related to a person's level of education and current employment and income status, but it clearly impacts every aspect of a person's life (see, e.g., McGoldrick, Giordano, & Garcia-Preto, 2005). For example, in the case of gambling, class (low SES) has been found to interact with the trait of impulsivity to increase the risk of gambling onset among youth (Auger, Cantinotti, & O'Loughlin, 2010). Higher adult rates of substance dependence or abuse are associated with lower education (11.6% for those who did not graduate from high school, compared to 7.5% for those who have a college degree), and higher rates are associated with current unemployment (16.6% compared to 9.6% for those who are employed) (SAMHSA, 2009).

As bell hooks (2000) says:

> Class matters. Race and gender can be used as screens to deflect attention away from the harsh realities class politics exposes. Clearly, just when we should all be paying attention to class, using race and gender to understand and explain its new dimensions, society, even our government, says let's talk about race and racial injustice. It is impossible to talk meaningfully about ending racism without talking about class. (p. 7)

Another important variable is the effect of recent immigration by various racial and ethnic groups on substance use practices (CSAT, 2004). Asian and Hispanic immigrants may face major stressors such as crowded, inadequate housing; socioeconomic hardships; not speaking English; and posttraumatic stress resulting from war and life in refugee camps. Additional stressors include separation of families during the immigration process and the inevitable rift between children brought up in the United States and their parents, who may cling to traditional ways. First-generation youth are vulnerable to substance misuse as they attempt to be accepted in the new culture. Many times, as acculturation increases, so do substance use problems. For example, in a narrative study of young Asian Americans in a dance club/rave scene, drug use was viewed by one group of participants as indicative of the degree to which they had grown apart from Asian culture and toward White/American culture (Moloney, Hunt, & Evans, 2008). Lee and Mock (2005) point out that the consequences of immigration may be different even for the same ethnic group. For example, Vietnamese and Cambodian persons who emigrated shortly after the Vietnam war in 1975 were mostly well-educated people who had lived in urban areas; however, the second wave, in the 1980s, frequently included farmers and peasants who were illiterate in their own language, had been in refugee camps for a long period, and had experienced violence and starvation before coming to the United States. Although both groups are from Southeast Asia, their acculturation into and adjustment to the United States were markedly different.

Because of the "wildly heterogeneous" (Closser & Blow, 1993) nature of these various groups in terms of acculturation, economic class, and education, among other important variables, many writers pay lip service to the idea that it is not correct to generalize across cultures. As McGoldrick and colleagues (2005) indicate, however, that without some concept of the cultural norms of a given group, "we would have no compass for our clinical work at all" (p. 13). In the following discussion of Asian/Pacific Islanders, Alaskan/Native Americans, Hispanic Americans, and African Americans, we avoid stereotyping by highlighting the complexity and diversity of each "group" and encouraging the reader to use this information as a launching pad for further investigation of subgroups. We focus on strengths as well as traditional values of the most vulnerable in each group—that is, those who are recent immigrants, are poor, have a history of oppression, and may be undereducated—in an attempt to track influences on the path to drug initiation, drug use patterns, the consequences of drug misuse and addiction, and the resources available for recovery. Although the success of culturally specific treatment programs is still a contested area that needs more research, we will describe several programs that have made progress in this area.

Given the great variability and number of factors that influence a person's cultural pattern within his or her group, we go back to the original question: How can counselors learn to be culturally sensitive and at the same time not stereotype a whole culture or race? The Ontario Resource Group on Gambling, Ethnicity and Culture (2010, p. 11) suggests skills that are helpful for counselors to develop, including:

1. client-driven problem-solving skills;
2. assessment skills that identify the role of socioeconomic disadvantage, racism, homophobia, and ableism in presenting problems;
3. networking skills to learn more about services, resources, and cultures from other service agencies working specifically with ethnocultural groups, and exchange ideas, expertise, and innovative initiatives;
4. advocacy skills to work toward enhancing access to services and culturally competent care and to raise awareness of cultural issues; and
5. interpersonal skills to build rapport with family and other support systems in cross-cultural interactions, being aware of culturally specific power dynamics and levels of hierarchy within families.

In addition, the Ontario Group states that the counselor must be self-aware of biases and values and how these may affect the therapeutic relationship. Mastering these cultural competency skills may be a tall order for counselors trained in acute care models of treatment where the primary focus is on fixing the immediate problem of addiction, not on building community with disenfranchised groups.

Analyzing case studies is a helpful way to practice cultural competency skills. Read the case of "Todd" (Box 12.1) from the Ontario Resource

Box 12.1	# Chinese Immigrant Case Study: In Trouble with Gambling

Todd, a 45-year-old Chinese man, called your agency and asked for help with his gambling problem. He had heard about your agency through another gambler a while ago, but did not call until he had a serious verbal fight with his wife over money natters a couple of days preceding the call.

In 1997, he migrated to Toronto from Hong Kong with his wife, Ann, and his older son, who was 3-years-old at that time. He is a graphic designer and runs a small business from his basement. Todd was the sole breadwinner until the second son was born in 1999, after which his wife found a job at a local hospital. Todd describes himself as an atheist and his wife as a "fervent religious" person. Todd explains that his wife's disapproval of gambling is to a large extent related to her religious beliefs.

He tells you that his gambling became a problem 2 years ago, even though he started gambling when he was in his late 20s. He shares that 2 years ago he accompanied a visiting friend to the casino in Windsor and won $40,000 at a blackjack table. At the table, he suddenly recalled being told by a fortuneteller in Hong Kong that the chance to become rich would come before he turned 50. From that day onward, he continuously thought about going back to the casino. As his wife was against gambling, Todd used every means to sneak behind her back to the closest casino. Since he was self-employed, the most common excuse was that he had appointments in cities close to casinos. In order to maximize the time he could spend gambling, he would speed, and he collected over 20 speeding tickets within a span of 3 months.

When Ann found out about his gambling problem, she was furious. In a heated argument, Todd blamed her for displacing the anger she had toward her own father (who was also a chronic gambler) on him. Attempting to seek a compromise, Todd begged his wife for a "quota" to gamble four times a year. Ann agreed to the proposition, even though she was not fully behind the idea. However, this strategy did not improve their relationship as he found the quota was not enough and continued lying to his wife so that he could gamble as often as possible. The more frequently he went to the casino, the more urges he had. Todd reported that the urges increased particularly when his business took a hit after one of his major clients retired. Gradually, Todd's debt increased to such an extent that he could not contribute to the family the way he used to. Ashamed that he was a disgrace for not being able to financially support his family, he decided to borrow money on his credit card. As the "man of the house," he could not imagine himself relying on a woman for financial support. The more debt he incurred, the more tempted he was to gamble in order to break even.

When Todd attended the first session for assessment, he shared that he wanted to stop gambling, mainly because he was increasingly aware that he had lost control of himself. He described the feeling as "scary." He also felt that he was losing status in the family because his wife was financially more competent than he was. He felt guilty, ashamed and angry with himself.

Source: Ontario Resource Group (2010) p. 32–33.

Group (2010) and ask yourself what areas you would focus on if you were using a culturally competent model of treatment.

What issues come to mind in Todd's situation that may require a culturally competent response? The Ontario Group (2010) recommends that we keep in mind the following as we attempt to help Todd with his goal of stopping gambling:

1. Asking for help took a lot of courage because seeking counseling is still a taboo for many Chinese who feel shame about disclosing problems outside of the family. Consequently, it was important to see Todd the same day he called and explain confidentiality. In reality, Todd told the counselors that he might have changed his mind if this had not happened.

2. It will be important to assess to what extent superstition, and in particular his memory of what the fortuneteller told him about becoming rich, has become part of his core beliefs in viewing life and relationships. What does he believe about luck?

3. Give a clear picture of how counseling works, and Todd's role in the process. To foster empowerment, suggest that he does not have to commit himself to regular sessions. Debunk the myth that you, as the counselor, are going to "fix" him.

4. Explore with Todd how, if, and when he wants to involve his wife and family in the process. In the Chinese culture, individuals are usually seen in the context of the family and community.

5. Give Todd information about problem gambling, stages of change, and impact on relationships and family. It is important to identify problem gambling because of the general perception in the Chinese community that gambling is just a normal pastime.

6. Address the guilt and shame factor as a major trigger for continued gambling. Help him rethink his way of evaluating his worth as a person, father, and husband.

In essence, a culturally competent approach from engagement through treatment is based on building a trustful and respectful relationship with the person and deeply listening to their worldviews. Knowledge of cultural traditions of diverse groups is essential to understand how problems with alcohol and drugs can develop. For example, according to Bromley and Sip (2001), it was not unusual for traditional Cambodians to use herbs, drugs, and alcohol in moderation, when they were available, to treat suffering and stress in Cambodia. Cambodian immigrants suffered a great deal of stress from war, persecution, torture, refugee camps, and all of the problems of adjusting to a completely different culture and language when they finally got to the United States. Alcohol was suddenly much more available and affordable. The authors theorize that "many Cambodian refugees turned to alcohol to 'medicate' themselves from the impact of these horrifying experiences" (p. 329).

Many intervention approaches that are effective when applied to one ethnic or cultural group fail miserably when transplanted into another (NIAAA, 2005). For example, behaviorally oriented methods may be more effective for some groups than for others. And some mainstream programming has been rejected by certain groups such as Native Americans because it did not take into account the cultural needs of the community (Milbrodt, 2002).

Each of these cultural variables can shed a new light on how to help a particular client or family and the particular strengths of the family experience. Unfortunately, because of time constraints on most clinical practices, this kind of careful, individualized, and culturally specific groundwork is likely to be put aside as something nice but impractical. However, we eventually pay the cost in terms of underutilized treatment programs and the failure to meet the needs of many vulnerable groups.

ASIAN AMERICANS AND PACIFIC ISLANDERS

The danger of lumping people into one group is obvious when you consider that in the U.S. Census (2010), "Asian" refers to people having origins in the East Asia, Southeast Asia, or the Indian subcontinent. It includes people who identified themselves as Cambodian, Asian Indian, Chinese, Filipino, Korean, Japanese, Vietnamese, Burmese, Hmong, Pakistani, Thai, or Malaysian. Since the 2000 census, the Asian population had the fastest rate of growth (43%) (U.S. Census, 2010). Native Hawaiian and Other Pacific Islander refers to people having origins in the original persons of Hawaii, Guam, Samoa, or other Pacific Islands and includes persons who identified themselves as Native Hawaiian, Guamanian or Chamorro, Samoan, Other Pacific Islander, Tahitian, Mariana Islander, or Chuukese. Native Hawaiians and Other Pacific Islanders, together with American Indians and Alaska Natives, were more likely to report multiple races (U.S. Census, 2010). Even with all this variety, there are numerous subgroups within each group that may form a distinct ethnic group with different ways of approaching substance use and addiction.

PREVALENCE PATTERNS

Because both education and economic class influence substance use patterns and the availability of resources to alleviate problems, the variability of these factors within the Asian and Pacific Islander group may help explain some of the variability of substance use patterns. Results from the 2009 National Survey on Drug Use and Health indicate that the Asian rate of illicit drug use among persons aged 12 or older (3.7%) and the rate of substance dependence or abuse (3.5%) was the lowest compared to all other racial categories (SAMHSA, 2010). The rate of substance dependence or abuse for Pacific Islanders was 11.0%, and the rate of illicit drug use of Native Hawaiians or other Pacific Islanders was 8.7% (SAMHSA, 2006). In 2003, Asian American, Native Hawaiian, or other Pacific Islander comprised 1.1% of admission to publicly funded substance abuse treatment programs (NIDA, 2006).

The low rate of alcohol and drug misuse for the Asian group may be underreported and inaccurate because of several factors: (1) national database surveys have ignored this group and consistently put Asian/Pacific Islanders in the category of "other," (2) the low treatment rate may be the result of the lack of culturally relevant services, (3) methodological weak-nesses in the research have resulted in an underestimate of the levels of substance misuse and dependence, and (4) there is a belief that alcoholism is rare in this group because of the absence of the enzyme aldehyde dehydrogenase in widely vary-ing percentages of Asians and Pacific Islanders, which can cause flushing and discomfort when alcohol is ingested, although this has proven not to be true uniformly (NIAAA, 2005). Gambling problems have also been poorly reported among Asians, in spite of the fact that there is evidence that high rates of gambling does occur within some of the cultural groups (Oei & Raylu, 2007). A recent study comparing single race and multiple race preva-lence rates found that multiple-race Asians had higher prevalence patterns in alcohol dependence (Native Hawaiians and Filipinos) and illicit drug use (Native Hawaiians, Filipino and Korean) than single-race Caucasians (Sakai, Wang, & Price, 2010).

Although female Native Hawaiians comprise less than 10% of the total state population, they constitute 40% of women in prison in Hawaii. Lee Stein (2001) explains this in terms of violent victimization within the family and harsh sentencing practices related to drug use. Discrimination against Native Hawaiians has also played a role. Stein recommends gender-specific and culturally sensitive treatment programming for this group.

SOCIOCULTURAL FACTORS

In addition to ethnic background, this group varies greatly in educational level and economic status. The most recent median income figures (U.S. Census Bureau, 2009) indicate that single race Asian households have a high median income ($70,069). However, income levels differed greatly by Asian group. For example, for single-race Asian Indians, the median income was $90,528; for single-race Vietnamese-Americans, it was $55,667; and for Native Hawai-ians and Other Pacific Islander it was $57,721. The poverty rate also varied by group, with a rate of 11.8% for single-race Asians, and a higher rate of 16.3% for Native Hawaiian and Other Pacific Islanders, suggesting that some subgroups have a higher than average economic status and other groups are below average.

There are also great differences in education status among this group. Fifty percent of single-race Asians (age 25 and over) have a bachelor's degree or higher level of education, compared with 28% of all Americans. Unfortu-nately, the high level of academic achievement of this group has led to the myth of Asians as the "model minority" without addiction problems. On the other hand, only 15% of Native Hawaiian and Other Pacific Islanders have at least a bachelor's degree (U.S. Census Bureau, 2009). Although there is great variation because of economic class, education, and level of acculturation as to how traditional values are actualized in individual people, several authors have pointed out consistent traditional cultural themes that may pose barriers to getting help through mainstream treatment programs and may even contribute to "culture clash" stress that contribute to a person's own drug use (CSAT, 2004; Maloney, Hunt, & Evans, 2008). For example, a young Chinese American woman describes the pressure she experienced from her Chinese-born parents to keep her struggles to herself and to play the part of an "honorable daughter:"

> If I wasn't so repressed maybe ... if I was able to talk to my parents or have conversations with them about concerns I was having...I wouldn't have to turn to other people...And I think it did contribute to, you know, drug usage. (Maloney, Hunt, & Evans, 2008, p. 389)

On the other hand, these same values provide family support, family resources, and a family commitment to the best interests of the family member who may be suffering consequences from addiction. Counselors will want to understand through a "not knowing" and respectful stance whether the following traditional immigrant Asian values and practices may apply:

- The theme of filial piety (devotion, obligation, duty) dominates traditional Asian culture. That is, the individual within the family is secondary to the interests of the family as a whole. Communications are indirect and based on roles within the family hierarchy. Emotions are not generally shared because doing so might emphasize the individual over the interdependent needs of the family.
- The initial response of the family to substance use or mental health problems may be to ignore it. It may not even be considered a problem as long as the individual continues to meet family responsibilities. Among many Southeast Asians, alcohol is viewed as a substance that has healing properties, and it is culturally acceptable for elderly persons to drink alcohol and smoke marijuana.
- If a problem gets identified and family functioning is threatened, the family risks deep shame and "losing face" in the community. To keep from losing face, families may try to isolate the person with the problem from the community, shame or scold the person, and even reject the person. The extended family may be asked to intervene.
- Seeking outside help is equated to failure. When it does occur, families may have "quick-fix" expectations. The person with the problem is likely to be angry because of the family's "betrayal" and resistant when brought to treatment.

Although traditional parents are practicing in ways that mirror their native countries, their sons and daughters may have acculturated to the point of relying more on their peers and popular culture. Consequently, attempts to rein them in using traditional methods of shaming and hierarchical processes may cause a great deal of family conflict.

Oei & Raylu (2007) suggest that it is helpful for counselors to take a practical, structured approach when working with individuals in traditional families presenting with gambling problems. The authors recommend that treatment programs may be most effective when they provide factual information about gambling problems. It is particularly helpful if the groups include other Asians. Because families are so critical to a person's well-being, family support should be offered using an educational rather than a confrontational approach (CSAT, 2004).

TREATMENT ISSUES

Yu, Clark, Chandra, Dias, and Lai (2009) report that Asians with substance dependence are significantly less likely to receive treatment than Caucasians. The authors attribute underutilization of treatment to cultural and language barriers. The results of their study on two outpatient substance abuse programs in New York City (which serve 22% of all the New York City Asian clients admitted each year) indicate that this does not have to be the case: Both underutilization and treatment effectiveness are improved by offering culturally competent services combined with case management and motivational interviewing. Specifically, the two programs used outreach tactics to reach various parts of the Asian population in all of its rich variety, such as substance abuse screening with culturally sensitive instruments at community events and parades. Brief interventions were available for those deemed at risk, using facts sheets written in their native Asian language about the prevalence and types of drugs likely to be used in their community, as well as information to correct misperceptions about alcohol and drug use and potential cultural barriers to treatment. For clients with a substance abuse problem, full intervention at an outpatient treatment program was provided by culturally competent and professionally trained staff who spoke the language of the client (including Cantonese, Mandarin, Korean, Japanese, Hindi, Urdu, Tagalog, Farsi, and Bengali). Motivational interviewing (MI) techniques (see Chapter 8) were used to elicit the client's experience of the problem and to help the client identify the best pathway to making a positive change. The authors note that MI may be particularly helpful with Asian American clients because of community resistance to seeking treatment from outsiders. In addition, a single point of contact was offered to assist clients access the confusing array of other services (social, health) that could be helpful to their recovery. Results show that in the 2 years of study, approximately 58.6% of the Asian American clients at the two outpatient centers completed more than 50% of their treatment goals (compared to the comparable New York City rate of 29.1%). A positive rate of change, higher than the national average, was noted in the areas of substance use (59.4%), criminal justice (11.9%), and social connectedness (17.5%). It is interesting that in the areas of employment, education, and housing, the rate of change was lower than the national average, which may be attributed to the fact that a high number of clients were already stable in these areas. The authors conclude that the application of culturally sensitive programming is indeed helpful in addressing underutilization and low performance of standard treatment programs.

Compared to other youths, Native Hawaiians report higher rates of drug use, particularly in rural communities in Hawaii, but they have the fewest options for treatment (Rehuher, Hiramatsu, & Helm, 2008). General strategies for helping treatment providers of Asian/Pacific Islanders become more user friendly to this group involve hiring staff who come from and can speak the language of the primary target group, providing cultural training for all staff, incorporating the use of elders and native healers, using familiar healing strategies such as acupuncture, and incorporating culture-specific beliefs and spiritual practices about healing and recovery. For example, a culturally based, women-centered residential treatment program in Hawaii uses Ku¨puna, elders of the Hawaiian Native community who carry wisdom and tradition in extended family, to develop parenting classes, facilitate traditional healing practices, provide child care, and act as counselors and listeners. Ethnographic interviewing of the women who participated in the program revealed positive perceptions about Ku¨puna involvement (Morelli & Fong, 2000). As one participant commented, "We'd sing and start talking about culture, about how the ancient Hawaiians used to live off the land, and spiritual things. If you had burdens or problems for the day or you weren't feeling right, they'd pray on you" (p. 42).

A pilot treatment program in a hospital in Amritsar, India offers insight into a culturally specific program for Indian clients who are substance abusers (Khalsa, Khalsa, Khalsa, & Khalsa, 2008). Amritsar is in the Punjab region of India, which is vulnerable to substance abuse because of significant cultural transition and economic development. The 90-day inpatient program used Kundalini Yoga and meditation as the primary therapeutic modality through classes taught by certified instructors three to four times daily. The purpose of yoga and meditation in treatment is to (1) reduce stress, (2) improve mood, especially depression and anxiety, (3) induce a higher stage of consciousness that might replace the need for a substance induced high, (4) improve clients' ability to prevent destructive behavior before its onset, and (5) improve self-esteem. Additional programming included multifamily group sessions, a vegetarian diet designed to rebuild the body systems, music and dance therapies, spiritual studies and Sikh religious practices, Sat Nam Rasayan (a form of energy medicine/spiritual healing), acupuncture, and education related to addiction and relapse prevention. Evaluation of the program through several psychological self-report questionnaires and qualitative observations showed the clients benefitted substantially from the program. Although the program was small, and it is difficult to determine which components were the most important contributors, the authors of the study suggest that the success of the program was due in part to the incorporation of spiritual and religious practices respected (and in some cases rediscovered) by the clients (Khalsa, Khalsa, Khalsa, & Khalsa, 2008).

Case studies from the Vietnamese community in Queensland, Australia also show the need for culturally appropriate services (Chui, 2008). The featured cases illustrate how gambling in a casino can alleviate social isolation for women with limited English skills. As stated by one of the women, "[Vietnamese people] … can't go to movies because they can't understand … they can't go to clubs or pubs. So what are they supposed to do? Gambling … they don't need to speak good English" (p. 278). The women did not like seeking help for gambling problems outside the family because of the stigma and shame, although seeking help for financial problems and meeting immediate family needs and food vouchers was more acceptable. They preferred Vietnamese social service workers because language was a problem. The offer of practical, tangible assistance appears to be a needed bridge for building a trusting relationship. The author calls for more "listening to the voices" of this marginalized group to develop more sensitive interventions for those who experience addictions (Chui, 2008).

AMERICAN INDIANS AND ALASKAN NATIVES

Although Asian Americans may be misrepresented by the myth of the model minority with few substance use problems, Native Americans and Alaskan Natives have historically been stereotyped in the other direction. On the one hand, the myth of the drunken Indian who is powerless over the White man's spirits still colors the popular culture; on the other hand, there is the politically correct, romantic version of a uniform Indian culture that extols peacefulness, connectedness, and environmental soundness. These contrary beliefs are so widespread that Weaver (2001) cautions that "few people have stopped to critically examine what is actually known and empirically supported" (p. 77). One thing that is supported by facts is that a recovery movement that is sustained by a return to traditional Native culture is alive and well in Native communities today (Coyhis & Simonelli, 2008).

Prevalence Patterns

In the United States in 2010, there were approximately 2.9 million (0.9% of the total population) who classified themselves as American Indian and Alaskan Native (AI/AN), and 2.2 million more who classified themselves as American Indian and Alaska Native in combination with another race (0.7% of the total population) (U.S. Census, 2010). Thus, almost half of the AI/AN population reported themselves as more than one race in the 2010 Census. To complicate things further, there are more than 560 federally recognized tribes in 35 states, and the majority of AI/AN live in various urban communities, not on tribal reservations (Young & Joe, 2009). Today, AI/AN people "can and do live anywhere on a social spectrum that might run from 'traditional' to 'acculturated,' and everything in-between"(Coyhis & Simonelli, 2008, p. 1929). Many authors agree that it is difficult to make an accurate estimate of alcohol and drug misuse within this group because of vast differences among Native populations that are sampled and a historical distrust of researchers (Weaver, 2001), Differences in drinking patterns among various tribes are influenced by the same factors that influence variation among many ethnic or cultural groups; that is, they may be the result of differing cultural guidelines about tolerating deviant behavior, different socioeconomic conditions, different contexts of highly urban to remote rural areas, different levels of acculturation to the dominant society, and/or the extent to which traditional values, language, and ways of life are practiced. For example, one clear difference among AI/AN reservations and communities is that more than half are "dry," meaning that the consumption and sale of alcohol is forbidden (Young & Joe, 2009).

Results from the National Survey on Drug Use and Health (SAMHSA, 2010) indicate that among persons aged 12 or older, the rate of substance dependence or abuse was highest among American Indians or Alaskan Natives (15.5%). The rate of current illicit drug use for this group (18.3%) was also the highest of all the racial categories, but the rate of alcohol use was the lowest (37.1% compared to the highest rate for whites at 56.7%). However, the rate of binge drinking for the adult AI/AN group was 22.2%, compared to a low of 11.1% for Asians and a high of 25% for Hispanics. For those living in poverty, the rate of binge drinking for AI/NA persons jumped to 36.1% (SAMHSA, 2010). In terms of treatment, 18% of AI/AN adults were in need of alcohol or illicit drug treatment in the past year of 2009, higher than the national average of 9.6%, Unfortunately, of those needing treatment, only one in eight (12.6%) received it at a specialty facility, a little higher than the national rate of only 10.4% (SAMHSA, 2010). American Indians and Alaska Natives have the highest rate of current use of a tobacco product of any group at 41.8% (SAMHSA, 2010). Because of the small numbers of the AI/NAyouth, use and abuse patterns are less likely to be included in national surveys. It appears that in general, Native youth follow the patterns of the grown-ups. A notable exception is the rate of current alcohol use: in NA/AN adults, alcohol use was the lowest of all racial and ethnic groups (37.1%), but among NA/AN youth aged 12–17, the rate of 11.9% puts them in the middle of the racial categories (white youths are highest with 16.7%, and Asian youth are lowest with 6.5% (SAMHSA, 2010). The smoking rate for NA/AI youth declined dramatically from 18.9% in 2008 to 11.6% in 2009; however, this rate was still the highest of current smoking for youths aged 12–17 (SAMHSA, 2010), The current rates of illicit drug use for AI/AN youth in the young adult category from age 18 to 25 was higher than the national average for this age group (25.4% vs. 19.7%) (SAMHSA, 2010). SAMHSA (2010) reports a past year rate of 5.5% in the 12–17 age group for the use of inhalants, the highest rate of all youths in this category,

The trend of alcohol, drug, and tobacco use being higher in AI/AN youth than other groups has been generally consistent during the last 30 years, according to researchers from the Tri-Ethnic Center for Prevention Research at Colorado State University (Beauvais, Jumper-Thurman, & Burnside, 2008). Each year these researchers administer anonymous questionnaires to a nationally representative sample of youth attending schools on or near reservations to determine lifetime use of various drugs. Lifetime prevalence measures are general and do not give information on frequency or intensity of use; however, they do provide a solid measure of exposure to drugs across time. Although there is continued concern that AI youth are more at risk for inhalant abuse than non-AI youth, the authors maintain that inhalants are used by Native youths *who are attending school* at the same level as non-AI youth. The focus and energy put into prevention efforts in native communities may have contributed to this result (Beauvais et al., 2008). Drinking-related consequences are higher in Native populations compared to other groups. The Centers for Disease Control and Prevention (CDC) (2008) reported that almost 12% of AI/NA deaths are alcohol-related, more than three times the rate of the general population. Even this high rate is likely an underestimate because of the miscategorization of race on death certificates, and because homicides, suicides, and some diseases for which alcohol is believed to be an important risk factor were not included by the CDC. About half of the deaths were from acute causes, mainly motor vehicle accidents, and the other half came from chronic causes, primarily alcoholic liver disease. The greatest number of alcohol-related deaths occurred in the Northern Plains, the least number occurred in Alaska, 68% were male, and almost 7% were to youth under 20 years of age. One Native American woman working in substance abuse treatment in the Northwest described to Davis (the author) that her reservation was in a state of "perpetual mourning" because of the unremittingly high number of early deaths among people who know each other or are related through extended family. Although there is disagreement about the prevalence of fetal alcohol syndrome (FAS) in the Native population, there is some evidence that it is more prevalent among Native Americans than in the U.S. population as a whole. One survey of the literature found that the average rate of FAS among several higher-risk tribes was between 9 and 10 per 1,000 births, compared to 0.5–2 per 1,000 in the general population (May, Miller, Goodhart, Maestas, Buckley, Trujillo, & Gossage, 2008), Prevalence rates vary from 6 to 30 times greater and reflect the variation among different tribes. High rates have been found among some, such as the FAS rate of one in four children on the Pine Ridge and Rosebud Reservations in South Dakota (Weaver, 2001). There is some encouraging evidence that this highly preventable problem may be turning around in some Native communities. In a study of 22 states, results indicate that AI/NA women who were moderate drinkers before conception were over two times more likely than white women to reduce drinking after becoming pregnant (Tenkku, Morris, Salas, & Xaverius, 2009). The state of Alaska has also documented a 32% drop in the rate of Alaska Native children born with fetal alcohol syndrome, dropping from 20 per 1,000 births to 13.5 per 1,000 births (Shinohara, 2010). More focused and better funded prevention, screening, and treatment programs for Native women in the last several years may be having a positive effect.

GAMBLING PROBLEMS IN THE AI/NA CULTURE

Gambling has ancient roots in the Native American culture. Traditional games served many tribal purposes, such as redistributing wealth, connecting to legends, providing communal entertainment during festivals, and teaching through gambling stories (e.g., tales of the trickster Coyote) (Luna-Firebaugh & Tippeconnic, 2010). Since the Supreme Court ruling of 1987 (*California v.*

Cabazon Band of Mission Indians) and the passage of the 1988 Indian Gaming Regulatory Act, Native American casinos have developed and expanded rapidly, with an estimated revenue of $26.4 billion in 2009 (Boulard, 2011). In 2005, there were 391 casinos located on Indian reservations; half of California's tribes run some kind of gambling operation (Economist, 2007). However, the wealth from the "White Buffalo" of casino gambling is unevenly distributed to the few tribes whose lands are strategically located and are successful in developing casinos.

The dramatically increased number of gambling venues for Native Americans brings an increased opportunity to develop gambling problems. However, the prevalence of gambling problems in the NA/AN group remains largely undefined because national surveys usually combine the small number of NA/AN participants in the catch-all "other" group. Studies that do address this population agree that problem gambling has increased and that Native Americans have the highest incidence of gambling problems compared to other groups (Volberg & Abbott, 1997; Elia & Jacobs, 1993). In a study of gambling and problem gambling in New Mexico, Volberg and Bernhard (2006) found that the prevalence of at-risk, problem and pathological gambling is significantly higher among Native Americans than among non-Natives. An interesting study on mothers who were gambling at a tribal casino on a Great Lakes Indian reservation addressed the question of how gambling is affecting parenting (Momper & Jackson, 2007). Not surprisingly, the authors found that pathological gambling was significantly associated with more frequent gambling, less adequate parenting, and more child behavior problems. However, further analysis indicated that when the women received social support from their families, the negative effects of frequent gambling were moderated. In general, social support, or the lack of it, is an important factor in moderating the effects of an addiction.

SOCIOCULTURAL FACTORS

Socioeconomic and cultural factors are also potent forces in the development of addiction problems, the ability to get and receive help, and the availability of supports for a recovery process. Some researchers and Native treatment programs theorize that the historical trauma suffered by Native persons that suppressed and destroyed Native culture resulted in emotional injury that led to alcoholism and drug abuse (Carvajal & Young, 2009). Consequently, for many Native Americans, recovering from addiction also means recovering *culturally* (Coyhis & Simonelli, 2008).

Historical trauma is the term used by Maria Yellow Horse Brave Heart (2007) to refer to the cumulative cultural, emotional and psychological wounding across generations that results from a people's collective traumatic experiences. Substance misuse, suicide, depression, anxiety, and difficulty expressing emotions are features most frequently associated with historical trauma. As Brave Heart suggests, this response is prevalent in the American Indian and Alaskan Native population. The legacy of the deliberate breakdown of cultural ties, including spirituality, that began in the 1860s is seen as largely responsible for the loss of cultural pride and stability that characterize much of tribal life today. To regain a sense of cultural mastery and empowerment, Brave Heart has developed the Historical Trauma and Unresolved Grief intervention as a psychoeducational intervention for Native groups. Working through memories and emotions in small and large groups, facilitators use a combination of traditional techniques, including prayer, to help participants connect with their Native values.

Another fundamental social problem in the Native community today is poverty. The average poverty rate for American Indians and Alaskan Natives is 27.6%, compared to a national rate of 11.5%. Nearly one-sixth are without health insurance (SAMHSA, 2010). In addition, families have been broken for generations because of the boarding system imposed by the federal government, which had the intent of eliminating Indian culture and replacing it with White culture. Children were separated from their families by hundreds of miles for months from age 6, even for years at a time, and were forbidden to talk in their Native language or participate in any Native practices. More than 100,000 were forced into these Christian schools until the policy ended (Smith, 2006). Members of the Boarding School Healing Project say that the current levels of violence and dysfunction in Native communities are a legacy of human rights abuses perpetrated against past generations.

War, poverty, disease, and displacement have taken a horrendous toll on Native families. For example, in 1900, an influenza epidemic spread throughout Alaska and killed 60% of the Eskimo and Athabascan people, often whole villages. As Lowery (1998) states, "The sense of coherence of an entire people was shattered at the turn of the century. There was no lawfulness, no cultural explanation, no magic, no predictability. The world truly went upside-down" (p. 131).

From this upside-down world, there are some indicators that progress is being made in some Native American communities, beginning with the civil rights and anti-poverty programs of the 1960s and 1970s. Today, Native Americans have a higher percentage of persons whose highest degree is high school graduates (30.5%) than the total population (28.5%) and a higher rate of persons with some college or an associate's degree (33%) than the general population (28.9%) (U.S. Census, 2009). Another 13% have a bachelor's degree or graduate/professional degree. The Wellbriety movement and a simultaneous movement toward the values of traditional Native culture are "vibrantly alive" in many communities (Coyhis & Simonelli, 2008, p. 1927). Another area of growth is in film-making by Native directors. Many recent films have a common theme of preserving the native culture, such as the Canadian First Nation filmmaker Tracey Deer's (Mohawk) documentary *Club Native* (2008). Chris Eyre's (Cheyenne-Arapaho) *Trail of Tears* (2008) was included in the PBS "American Experience" series (Davies, 2009).

In cultural areas, treatment and prevention programs have taken a lead in reinforcing, and in some cases teaching for the first time, traditional Native values by incorporating drumming, sweats, beading, medicine wheel philosophy, and other traditional practices into programming. The strong cultural and spiritual component is intended to help invigorate traditional practices as well as give the individual strength in the recovery process (Chong, Fortier, & Morris, 2009; Sutton & Broken Nose, 2005). Community approaches to substance misuse and prevention are reinforcing traditional values of caregiving and responsibility for those who come after them, as, for example, in fetal alcohol syndrome prevention programming. The Native American Church, which uses peyote as a sacramental food and curative for substance misuse, has between 200,000 and 500,000 members in the United States, Mexico, and Canada (Moreno, 2005). This church practices a fusion of Christianity and traditional Indian religions and is the largest indigenous religion in North America.

SPIRITUAL AND CULTURAL VALUES

It is presumptuous to speak of "Native values" as if they were of one piece, given the differences among individuals and between tribes. However, there are some identifiable cultural values prevalent among many Indian tribes that could impact the path to substance misuse and the path to recovery. Spirituality is often mentioned as a dominant Indian value, manifest in the recognition of the spirit and connectedness in all living things and in the responsibility the Creator gave to Indian people to preserve Mother Earth (Lowery, 1998). However, the idea that the responsibility for one's behavior lies in the hands of family, community, and spiritual forces is contrary to the Western notion that change is a personal responsibility (Dell, Seguin, Hopkins, Tempier, Mehl-Madrona, Dell, Duncan, & Mosier, 2011). The Indian idea calls for a ceremonial and community solution to problems and imbalances; the Western idea leads to a biomedical focus on the individual. Because of the emphasis on spirituality in many Native cultures, addiction is seen as a "crisis of the spirit" and requires "a healing of the spirit, of the mind, and of the body within a larger framework of existence, the extended family network nested within community clan, tribe, and nation" (Lowery, 1998, p. 131).

For example, according to Coyhis and Simonelli (2008), the concept of the Medicine Wheel in Cherokee and many Plains Indian traditional cultures embraces a holistic framework by including four components of the inner circle: spirit, natural environment, body, and mind. The four directions in the circle represent the four winds: East (belonging), South (mastery), West (independence), and North (generosity). In this conception, disharmony, including substance misuse, results when a person is out of balance or out of harmony with the interaction of mind, body, spirit, and natural environment. The Medicine Wheel teaches that there is a "seen" world of the physical and materialistic aspects of life and an "unseen" world of the "heart center." Native people using this framework can access their traditional roots and the unseen world through ceremonies such as the sweat lodge, sun dance, vision quest, smudging, the Hoop ceremony, and others. Both worlds are embraced (the head and the heart), but the "heart-centered processes seem to be the key that opens the lock to recovery and then on to Wellbriety for Native peoples" (Coyhis & Simonelli, 2008, p. 1933).

Wellbriety is a term in Native recovery circles that means becoming clean and sober and then continuing the journey to health and balance in all four directions of the Medicine Wheel and healing the wounds of intergenerational trauma suffered by many Native persons. The Wellbriety Movement began in the mid-1990s, embraces a variety of local tribal traditions and ceremonies as well as the Red Road to Recovery (see Box 12.2), and the merger of the Medicine Wheel teachings with the Twelve-Step program of Alcoholics Anonymous (AA) program, (see Box 12.2) (Coyhis & Simonelli, 2008). Further information on the Red Road to Recovery, with a calendar of events, meetings, women's issues, and meditations among other material, is available on the website http://www.whitebison.org.

Box 12.2	THE RED ROAD TO RECOVERY
	Raymond Slick

In our world we have a lot of problems with drugs and alcohol. I lost two uncles with cirrhosis and have seen some people die.

I want to talk about the Red Road philosophy of life as described in the Indian film *The Red Road to Sobriety*. Walking the Red Road is walking with the Creator, seeking visions for guidance. This is an inner journey: There may be dances, deprivation of food, ingestion of substances. Peyote was used on Turtle Island (North America) as sacrament with prayer and ceremonies. The sweat lodge was for purification. Drinking of alcohol was done in a few tribes but only in controlled ceremonies.

When the Europeans came there was suddenly introduced a new form of spirits that was much more potent, such as rum. The Chief of the Seneca Nation had a vision leading us back from the Black Road of suffering to the good road.

But we did not have instructions for how to cope with what the white man brought—strong drink. And we were not prepared for the loss of culture, the genocide, the wounded spirits. This was the American Holocaust—100 million Indian people died. War, starvation, and European diseases led to a sense of hopelessness, cultural trauma that passes down the generations.

Today we are trying to find what was lost. Elders are our wisdom keepers and help sustain our culture. Our elders teach us to include the concept of life in a circle—there is the physical part, the mental part, the spiritual part. We need to keep all of these aspects of our selves in balance.

I don't share this very much because I made a commitment to hold most of these experiences sacred, but in healing circles that I have had some experiences in, the spiritual bonding is very healing. Sobriety is the traditional way, the Red Road. When people are healed their ancestors are healed.

Source: Raymond Slick, class presentation, University of Northern Iowa, August 28, 2006. Printed with permission of Raymond Slick, Tama, Iowa.

Treatment Issues

Since the mid-1990s, much of the substance abuse treatment provided by the Indian Health Service (HIS) has shifted to local tribal control. However, according to SAMHSA (2009) only 55% of AI/ANs rely on the INS or tribally operated clinics or hospitals, and the rest rely on other public or private facilities. In 2007, there were 335 substance abuse treatment facilities identified by SAMHSA that specifically served the AI/AN population. Although, as noted previously, the majority of the AI/AN population lives in urban areas, only 40% of these treatment centers were in urban settings, while the other 60% were rural. Only 4% provided opioid treatment programs that dispensed methadone or buprenorphine. In terms of cultural competency, 43% of these facilities offered treatment in one or more AI/AN languages, most commonly Lakota, Hopi, or Yupik. The National Survey of Substance Abuse Treatment Services (N-SSATS) collects data from treatment facilities to find out which of nine clinical/therapeutic approaches are used in treatment. In NA/AI facilities, the most common approaches were substance abuse counseling, relapse prevention, and the Twelve-Step approach. Notably missing from the top three were brief intervention, cognitive-behavioral, and motivational interviewing (SAMHSA, 2009). The findings did not report the prevalence or existence of culturally specific programming, except for the language component.

Substance abuse treatment programs accessed by AI/ANs range from a strictly medical model with no regard for culture, to a "melting pot" model that fuses, to varying degrees, traditional Native ceremonies and philosophy with mainstream strategies. There are many examples of the use of traditional cultural and spiritual practices in treatment, including sweats, medicine wheels, drumming, beading, talking circles, and bringing in elders and medicine men to facilitate healing ceremonies. However, as discussed in a conference held in Tucson, Arizona, on the types of culturally relevant interventions that are promising, "a need exists to systematically evaluate the efficacy of these approaches" (Carvaja & Young, 2009). One unresolved issue that has not been addressed by enough systematic study is that not all clients may benefit from these programs. As Sutton and Broken Nose (2005) point out, no single approach works for all Indian subgroups; some may benefit from traditional healing practices, and others from mainstream treatment programs. Some AI/NAs may not be interested in traditional practices or may be from Christian or other traditions that frown on such participation, or they may be from different tribes that have different spiritual practices (Carvajal & Young, 2009). One attempt to resolve this dilemma is the development of an assessment instrument that would help determine whether clients (in this study, female clients) would benefit from participating in traditional spiritual practices as part of their substance abuse treatment program (Chong, Fortier & Morris, 2009).

The development of systematic research on the effectiveness of culturally based interventions has been hampered by researchers' past exploitation of Native communities. Tribal communities are now understandably reluctant to allow access (Carvajal & Young, 2009). Some researchers have been able to build trust with Native communities by carefully respecting their interests and expertise. For example, the TriEthnic Research group at Colorado State University has built and maintained rapport on a national level over the last 30 years by respectfully reporting the data from their surveys in the aggregate; no single tribe is identified as having more problems than others. A group of researchers working with the Suquamish Tribe in Washington state are using a participatory research design where the tribe serves as co-investigator of the evaluation (Thomas, Donovan, Sigo, Austin, Marlatt, and the Suquamish Tribe, 2009). The benefit of collaborating with Native groups for research purposes are many. For example, when researchers used focus groups from the diverse urban Native community in Denver, they discovered that the concept of the Medicine Wheel was important to Northern Plains Indians living in Denver, but considered inappropriate to southwest tribes such as the Navajo who lived in Denver. Consequently, they changed the idea to Circle of Life, to represent the values of harmony and balance in both groups (Moran & Bussey, 2007).

NATIVE AMERICAN CULTURALLY BASED SERVICES

Many ethnographic studies and program evaluations show positive results when traditional cultural practices are combined with standard substance abuse treatment. One such program is the Teen Intervention Project for Cherokee adolescent high school students who were referred by school counselors for substance abuse problems (Lowe, 2006). Every week for 10 weeks, the participants would meet in a talking circle group setting with trained interventionists and share stories and explore topic materials on such subjects as Cherokee traditions of being responsible, being disciplined and being confident; Cherokee traditional activities; and Cherokee family structures and roles, as well as information on substance abuse and relapse prevention topics. Pre-post (90-day) measures indicated substance abuse significantly declined for participants, and self-reliance scores developed from Cherokee values significantly increased.

A quasi-experimental treatment/nonequivalent control group research design was used to evaluate a prevention program in Denver, called the Seventh Generation Program (Moran & Busey, 2006). In planning the project, researchers collaborated with the Indian community to determine cultural themes and values, which also resulted in the name of the project. The Seventh Generation has meaning for Lakotas as a time of healing and also represents placing the child in the center of seven generations, remembering the wisdom of the elders and considering the impact of their actions on future generations. The children met for 13 weeks after school and were exposed to topics such as American Indian values, American Indians and alcohol, and strengthening American Indian identity and enhancing self-esteem. Compared to children who did not receive the intervention, results indicate that the Seventh Generation program was successful in decreasing children's depression and increasing children's locus of control, perceived social support, and protective alcohol beliefs. Harm reduction philosophy that incorporates the stages-of-change model of Prochaska and DiClemente is particularly respectful of the Native view that behavioral change is a circular process that occurs in gradual steps (Daisy, Thomas, & Worley, 1998). Harm reduction methods also support the involvement of the Native substance users and their community in the development of long-term plans that will benefit recovery. The authors point out that the traditional practice of the talking circle aligns well with harm reduction philosophy in that it provides an opportunity for community members to express their feelings and opinions on how alcohol, drugs, and gambling have affected the community; how to manage them; and how the community can respond to problems. Such strategies that honor indigenous traditions of consensus building are needed to help heal the effect of colonialism on Native American and Canadian communities.

We end this section with a story told to researchers by staff working in the Nimkee NupiGawagan Healing Centre in Muncey, Ontario (Dell et al., 2011). It is a beautiful example of how combining traditional Aboriginal medicine and the Western approach of behavioral modification can help a young man in his recovery from solvent abuse:

When John started at the Nimkee NupiGawagan Healing Centre he learned that he had to take part in a spiritual assessment (for lack of a better word) with an Elder. The Elder does a type of reading through which he is able to see negative energy blocks in a person. The Elder can tell from this whether the youth needs certain medicines, for example, or a feast. A lot of youth like to participate in the assessment because it is a time when they can have their name, clan, and colors identified to them. When John arrived at Nimkee it was quickly evident that he used his size to intimidate, control, and bully others, including Elders. In John's assessment, the Elder said he saw a trauma near John's neck, and John responded that he had never tried to commit suicide. The Elder continued to see this energy at John's neck, and John eventually relayed that his father tried to stab him in the neck when he was a young boy. The Elder told John that this block needed to be moved because John could not express himself with his voice, and as a consequence, he was compensating by being physical.

The Elder held a spiritual intervention; he sang traditional healing songs, used his hands to move the energy block, prayed, and used traditional medicines, They included blueberries and unshelled peanuts. The Elder told John that when he felt himself getting angry, he needed to ask the staff for his medicine. Blueberries are a sacred traditional medicine, as they are the first food to be offered by the earth. They will assist John in reconnecting with his internal energy and strength. Shelling peanuts gave John an activity to occupy himself with and time to reflect on his emotions and return to a calmer state of being. The Elder also encouraged John to speak with his counselors each time he finished his medicine. (p. 81)

HISPANICS/LATINOS

The terms *Hispanic* and *Latino* describe a population that includes several subgroups such as Mexican, Puerto Rican, Cuban, South or Central American, Spanish, and in the Census Bureau statistics, "other Spanish culture or origin regardless of race."

PREVALENCE PATTERNS

Hispanics/Latinos, who may be of any race, totaled 16% of the U.S. population in 2010, or 50.5 million persons (U.S. Census Bureau, 2010). However, the numbers do not convey the explosive growth of this population—the increase in the Hispanic/Latino group between 2000 and 2010 accounted for more than half of the growth in the total population of the United States. Although every region in the United States gained in the number of Hispanics, more than three-fourths live in the West or South.

Taken together, the rate of substance dependence or abuse for persons reporting themselves as Hispanic was 10.1% (SAMHSA, 2010). Hispanic subgroups vary significantly in their prevalence of alcohol and drug use and related problems (SAMHSA, 2010). For example, the rate of illicit drug use (marijuana, cocaine, and other drugs) ranged from a high of 13.1% among adults of Spanish origin to a low of 3.9% among those of Dominican origin. Overall, the rate of past month alcohol use and illicit drug use were lower among Hispanics than the national averages. However, admissions to methamphetamine treatment tell a different story. While admissions of white, non-Hispanics were down from 81 to 65% of the treatment population between 1997 and 2007; Hispanic admissions more than doubled in the same time period, from 9 to 21% (SAMHSA, 2009). The overall rate of substance dependence or abuse was 10.1% for Hispanics, compared to a low of 3.5% among Asians and a high of 15.5% for American Indians/Alaska Natives (SAMHSA, 2010). Hispanics who met criteria for dependence or abuse of alcohol or drugs and deemed in need of treatment varied among subcategories (SAMSHA, 2009). The need for alcohol use treatment was highest among Mexicans (9.2%), and the need for illicit drug use treatment was highest among Puerto Ricans (6.1%). Like all races and ethnicities, only a small percentage of those who actually needed treatment received it in a specialty facility (7.7% of those needing alcohol treatment and 15.1% who needed illicit drug use treatment). The most common primary substances of abuse among Hispanics receiving treatment is reported as alcohol (36%), opiates (28%), and marijuana (15%) (Office of Applied Statistics, 2005a).

Cigarette use shows a different pattern, with an overall rate of smoking in the past month of 21.9%, compared to the national rate of 25.4% (SAMSHA, 2006). Again, this varied widely among subgroups, with Puerto Ricans having the highest rate of 28.8% and Central and South Americans at the lowest rate (18.9%). Overall, past month alcohol use, binge drinking, and illicit drug use is lower for Hispanic women than for the national average and is consistently lower among women than men in each Hispanic subgroup (SAMSHA, May 27, 2010; Lipsky & Caetano, 2008). The effect of acculturation on Latina women is more evident than among men regarding drinking patterns. Traditional sanctions against female drinking break down the more educated, employed, and middle class Mexican American women become (Lipsky & Caetano, 2009). However, among all Hispanic adults, those who were not born in the United States and (and thus were presumably less acculturated) had lower rates of alcohol use, binge drinking, and illicit drug use than those who were born in the U.S. (SAMSHA, May 27, 2010).

As with the other groups in this chapter, it is difficult to determine the prevalence of gambling in the Hispanic/Latino population, although it is well established in research studies that the incidence of problem gambling is higher in racial and ethnic minorities than it is among whites in the United States (Momper, 2008), A recent study of national data found that Hispanic persons were more likely to exhibit problem or pathological gambling than whites, and that the Hispanic sample of problem gamblers were also more likely than whites to have mood, anxiety and substance use disorders (Barry, Stefanovics, Desai, & Potenza, 2011). In a survey of problem gambling in New Mexico, respondents who identified themselves as Hispanic had the highest rate of problem gambling (21%) compared to whites (7.5%) (Starling, Blankenship, May, & Woodall, 2008). Casinos currently make gambling more attractive to Hispanic patrons by having buffets, providing music by Latino musicians, providing free bus rides to the casinos, and marketing in Spanish, according to a Minnesota focus group from the Latino community (Northstar Problem Gambling Alliance, 2009). This focus group also mentioned that not enough gambling help lines and other resources are available in Spanish. It appears that prevention and treatment programs could learn something from the recruitment efforts of casinos.

One of the most devastating effects of substance misuse in this population, including injectable drugs, has been the transmission of HIV. The rate of new HIV infections (17%) of Hispanics/Latinos in 2006 was the second highest (blacks were first), and 2.5 times that of the white population (CDC, 2010a). Although the rate for Hispanic women was lower than Hispanic men, it was nearly four times that of white women. The CDC considers this an "HIV epidemic of Hispanic/Latino communities" and has launched a variety of new projects in Spanish to increase HIV-related awareness across the United States, including the Act Against AIDS messages on billboards and radio and TV announcements in major cities (CDC, 2010, p. 2).

SOCIOECONOMIC FACTORS

Education and economic status are improving slightly among Latinos and Latinas, but again, there is wide variation among subgroups. Poverty is still a major risk factor. Hispanic families as a whole have a 23.3% poverty rate, compared to a national rate of 14.2%. However, foreign-born Hispanics who are younger than 18 have the highest rate of all (37.5%) (Pew Hispanic

Center, 2009). Lack of health insurance also contributes to the harshness of living life in poverty. Hispanics have the highest uninsured rates of any group, with 31.3% having no health insurance. When considering just foreign-born Hispanics, the rate jumps to 51.4%. The condition of poverty and no health coverage makes it difficult to avoid harmful social and health-related consequences of drinking and using drugs, and makes persons more vulnerable to social sanctions such as jail, prison, and discrimination. For some Hispanics, poverty has been a part of their family life for centuries.

On the whole, Latinos and Latinas are the most undereducated of all ethno-cultural groups in the United States, with the highest school dropout rates (18.3%). However, the dropout rate is much lower among the second generation of immigrants than among the first (U.S. Department of Education, 2010; Pew Research Report, 2009). Consequently, the rate of high school completion is much lower than average—77.2% compared with 89.7% for all youths. The rate of those who did graduate from high school and enroll in college is only 38.8%, again the lowest rate of all groups. Educational status has a big impact on the attainment of well-paying jobs and stable employment. Again, the median household annual income of Hispanics ($39,923) lagged far behind the annual income of the total population ($50,221). (U.S. Census, 2009b). Given the current problems in the U.S. economy, some immigration experts question whether the children of today's Hispanic immigrants will be able to obtain the upward mobility of earlier European immigrants (Pew Research Report, 2009).

Not only have Hispanics replaced African Americans as the largest and fastest growing minority group in the United States, they may have surpassed them as targets of discrimination. According to the Pew Research Center (2010), more Americans see Hispanics as frequent targets of discrimination (23%) than they do African Americans (18%).

Cultural Factors

In what has been called the Immigrant Paradox, foreign-born immigrant family members have been found to have fewer problems than their U.S.-born children who are moving toward acculturation. Immigrants in the foreign born group are less likely to divorce, have fewer mental problems, have lower rates of incarceration, and their youth are less likely to engage in risky behaviors, such as being involved in a gang (Pew Hispanic Center, 2009). Of the young Hispanics born in the United States, 40% say a family member or friend has been in a gang, compared to 17% of immigrant youths. As one 20-year-old Hispanic explains,

> What's happening with gangs is that as Hispanics are becoming ... teenagers ... they are realizing that they have that gap between how they feel they are (and) how their parents expect them to be ... when they are having family problems ... they don't really feel like they can fit in anywhere ... but gangs say ... "We are your family now." (Pew Hispanic Center, 2009, p. 92)

Higher levels of acculturation are generally associated with higher levels of drug and alcohol use, especially among women (De La Rosa, Holleran,

Rugh, & MacMaster, 2005). Cultural gaps between generations or between the person and the mainstream American culture may lead to acting-out behaviors for young people, which in America often means alcohol and substance use.

Traditional views of family and roles within the family can be protective factors against using alcohol and drugs; at the same time, they make it more difficult to seek help. Protective factors identified in a study of 60 young, low-income, predominantly Mexican American women include a cohesive family of origin, adequate rule-setting by parents, and a strong social support system (Lindenberg et al., 1998). The authors suggest that early identification of both risk *and* resilience factors is important to prevention of substance misuse among high-risk populations.

Latino and Latina traditions sharply differentiate the roles of males and females (Alvarez & Ruiz, 2001; Medina, 2001; Rothe & Ruiz, 2001). Women are expected to be the moral authority of the family and provide family connection and care for children, while men are expected to provide for the family as well as discipline and make decisions in financial matters. Women in traditional families are highly discouraged from using alcohol or drugs because of their critical role in child rearing. Although there is great individual variance, many males relate strongly to the value of *machismo*—that is, being brave, strong, a good provider, and dominant. Identification with these qualities may make it difficult to admit to problems with alcohol or drugs. Kinship (*familismo*) is highly valued, and extended family members commonly participate in child rearing and other activities that support the family. Festive occasions, usually celebrated by the entire extended family, tend to promote excessive drinking among males (CSAT, 2004). The protective factors of traditional families are many and include strong family management, intense supervision, enduring relationships, two-parent homes that often include extended relatives, and negative parental attitudes toward substance abuse (Warner, Krebs, & Fishbein, 2008).

Unfortunately, the stress of immigration, poverty, discrimination, isolation from extended family, and acculturation can cause dramatic effects and strain on the traditional Latino support system. These hardships may contribute to an attitude of fatalism, or the belief that life's problems are inevitable and must be accepted (Alvarez & Ruiz, 2001). Spirituality and religion are important values in traditional families. Spiritualism, or *espiritismo*, can include a belief that negative spirits can have a negative effect on a person's health and well-being. Gallardo and Curry (2009) suggest that when clients adhere to such beliefs, service providers should include a traditional healer, such as a *Curandera*, to rid the person of the afflicting spirit.

Treatment Issues

A recent review of the literature on drug and alcohol treatment programs for Hispanic clients found that few employ cultural responsiveness in their programming (Carvajal & Young, 2009). This is indeed unfortunate because there are many barriers to treatment, including language, lack of trust in the Euro-American model, uninviting environments that do not link to community resources, and providers' limited understanding of cultural strengths and traditions. For example, according to Gallardo and Curry (2009):

> ... in the Euro-American model a client seeking counseling travels to an unfamiliar setting (the counseling office) at a set time and is then expected to readily disclose personal information to a stranger (the counselor) for 1 hour. This can be especially uncomfortable for the Latino client who values *orgullo*, or pride/dignity, and views the disclosure of personal problems to non–family members as losing face or disgracing his or her family. (p. 319)

One of the most difficult barriers, according to these authors, is the mainstream idea of conceptualizing substance abuse as a disease. The disease concept is detrimental because it narrowly focuses on pathologizing individuals and does not take into consideration the social and family contexts, and the environmental stresses with which the Hispanic client is trying to cope.

Although there are large gaps in its widespread adaptation, culturally appropriate assessment and treatment is being developed and put to use in some situations. For example, the language barrier has been addressed by translating assessment instruments into Spanish and by creating new ones that are more culturally responsive. The Alcohol Use Disorder and Associated Disabilities Schedule (AUDADIS), which is a structured diagnostic interview developed for the assessment of substance-related disorders and coexisting disorders, has been translated into Spanish and adapted for the Hispanic culture. Gallardo and Curry (2009) suggest the adaptation of a more holistic framework in assessment and treatment, using Brofenbrenner's ecological/systems model to include assessing the influences of family (micro level), school systems (mezzo level), state and federal legislation, and society (macro level) on the individual. This kind of assessment would help Hispanic clients become aware of the sociopolitical context of their lives and how these influences have impacted their method of coping through substance abuse.

In general, confrontational approaches during assessment should be avoided in order not to offend the person's sense of honor and dignity. Rather, as Gallardo and Curry (2009) suggest, the focus should be on client strengths and already existing knowledge to guide the treatment plan. Goal-setting should be collaborative, congruent with the client's needs, and mindful of the client's family and community resources. Machismo barriers to admitting problems may be reframed by appealing to the Hispanic male's role and responsibility as the head of the family. For example, an Alcoholics Anonymous group in Los Angeles made up primarily of recent immigrants from Central America linked machismo with how AA makes it possible to be a head of family, how "overcoming is manly," and how one needs "to have balls" to stay sober each day (Hoffman, 1994). In a similar fashion, a clinician can reframe a fatalistic attitude toward the problem of substance misuse by commenting, "You are here for a reason. You were meant to be helped" (Alvarez & Ruiz, 2001, p. 124).

Including key figures in the family or extended family in the treatment plan is recommended to bypass potential resistance and maximize the family support system. From a mainstream cultural perspective, a client's dependence on family members may be unusual and even labeled codependence. However, for many Hispanics, particularly women, a focus on individualism may be countertherapeutic and actually reduce the potential support available from family members. Medina (2001) recommends working with the family to "support their strengths and needs and to clarify perceptions, feelings, and behaviors that would help them function as a family unit" (p. 153). An example of family involvement she offers is to develop a contract outlining the family goals and behaviors, which the family signs each week for 6 weeks, modifying as needed.

Tapia, Schwartz, Prado, Lopez, and Pantin (2006) describe *Familias Unidas,* an empirically supported, family-based drug use and HIV prevention intervention for Latino immigrant adolescents and their families that has met with some success. Facilitators have all been of Latino origin. The strategy of this program is to first engage the most powerful member of the family, who is usually the father, and to begin with socializing, perhaps by serving coffee. In *Familias Unidas,* parental isolation is addressed by embedding intervention activities within a parent support group format. Therapists will want to keep in mind that the *respeto* (respect) that Latino parents command from children has a different internal meaning and set of expectations from the more egalitarian notion of respect (CSAT, 2004).

The Latino community has strong cultural prohibitions about women drinking (NIAAA, 2005). As Latinas become acculturated to mainstream U.S. culture, however, these traditions break down and their alcohol consumption significantly increases. Latina women who enter substance abuse treatment, like women in general, may have additional needs beyond just addressing substance use. For example, in one study, Latina women entering substance abuse treatment in Massachusetts tended to be Puerto Rican, undereducated, single heads of household, living in unstable housing situations, with few employment skills and with language difficulties (Amaro et al., 1998). The most common coexisting disorder among this group was depression, and 80.3% reported a history of childhood abuse. The authors of the study suggest that poor Latina mothers with substance abuse problems, like this group in Massachusetts, need case management services in their substance abuse treatment to connect them to GED opportunities, English-language classes, and job skills training, as well as to address mental health problems like depression and the effects of abuse. To address these issues, several larger system funding categories and priorities will need to be changed, including the funding of family-centered rather than just one-on-one approaches

As in the other groups discussed in this chapter, there is little scientific evidence on the extent to which cultural interventions are effective, particularly in the area of which clients would benefit from such interventions (Carvajal & Young, 2009). In addition, evidence-based practices, such as family-based treatment of drug abuse among Hispanic youth, have not yet been tested in community-based service agencies, and there are no randomized studies of treatment efficacy on Hispanic women or girls. There is evidence that low treatment utilization rates by Hispanics can be improved by adopting culturally responsive programming (Amaro & Cortes, 2007). Interesting findings have come from a qualitative study based on in-depth interviews with 15 Latino clinicians who work with clients of mixed ethnicity (Gelman, 2004). The purpose of the research was to define how these counselors tailored their approach for Latino clients and to discover their practice principles. The interviews revealed that these clinicians modified their techniques to relate them to the clients' cultural values and expectations, so their approach, in this sense, was culturally sensitive. Remarkable consistency was found in the responses. In describing their work, the clinicians singled out their focus on relationship, individuality, reality, and flexibility. The specific modifications they made in working with Latino clients included a willingness to accept gifts, being more active and directive, speaking Spanish, and using more self-disclosure and physical contact.

Latino Culturally Based Services

Because of the strong association between HIV/AIDS and substance use, especially among poor, urban Latino communities, a description of an ethnic-centered program is appropriate at this point in the chapter. According to Jennifer Herrera, director of prevention services, AIDS Services of Austin, Texas, who was interviewed by Holleran (2005), two significant facts provide the rationale for this prevention services program.

The first is that Latino men who are out of work, undocumented, and under severe stress sometimes turn to injecting heroin or smoking crack. The second is the extreme dependence of Latino women on their husbands. Confronting their partner for his high-risk behavior might mean loss of family income and security.

The Austin program consists of an extensive outreach program of peer educators from the communities with high rates of HIV/AIDS. The educators, who are trained in delivering effective health education and safe sex kits, stop people on the streets, at day labor sites, and at Laundromats. Women are invited to attend a *platica,* or talk, to learn more about the program. The staff members facilitate the workshop in Spanish and provide Mexican food. Following an icebreaker, the women are asked, "Why don't Latinas access HIV prevention services and testing?" A list is written up that includes such reasons as fear of deportation or lack of child care. The women are then informed about the user-friendly services that are provided by the program. As Herrera sums up their approach, "All of our prevention efforts center around a harm reduction model, understanding that people change their behaviors when they are ready, wanting, and able to change, and that our services must address the clients' changing and diverse needs and not our own agendas" (Holleran, 2005, p. 183).

AFRICAN AMERICANS

The U.S. Census Bureau (2010) reports that persons in the Black or African Americans alone category now comprise 12.6% of the U.S. population. When combined with blacks in combination with other races (1.0%) the total is 13.6%. In the U.S. Census, Black or African American refers to a person having origins in any of the Black racial groups of Africa. Their ancestral home may be in many different parts of the world, including Africa, Central America, South America, or the Caribbean. According to Harris-Hastick (2001), the term *African American* implies a common cultural identification with Africa and mainstream U.S. culture, and some kind of response or adaptation to the racism, poverty, and oppression that exist within the United States. However, English-speaking immigrants from the Caribbean (West Indies, Jamaica, Bahamas, etc.) have a different history of slavery (one associated with their home country, not the United States), tend to maintain close ties to their home country and customs long after immigration, and come from countries where it is common for Blacks to be middle-class, educated professionals in positions of power. Again, one size does not fit all.

Within the United States, there is also much variation in custom and life circumstance, depending on which part of the country is home and whether home is a crowded inner city, an affluent suburb, or a remote rural area. In spite of these many differences, most people of African ancestry in the United States share a common history of slavery, an ongoing fight for civil rights, and the stress of racial oppression that still exists.

Institutional racism exerts a significant impact on the lives and well-being of African Americans. Their average life expectancy remains substantially lower than that of Whites, and their rate of death due to AIDS and homicide exceeds that of any other major group (Hines & Boyd-Franklin, 2005). The disillusionment and frustration generated by poor living conditions and oppression and the belief in a lack of opportunity have resulted in a variety of substance abuse problems and a significantly disproportionate rate of incarceration.

PREVALENCE PATTERNS

In general, African Americans were lower in the rate of substance dependence or abuse (8.8%) than Native Americans (15.5%) but higher than Asian Americans (3.5%) (SAMHSA, 2010). The rate of current illicit drug use (9. 6%) was lower than that of Native Americans but higher than Native Hawaiians or other Pacific Islanders, Whites, and Hispanics. Among early adolescents (ages 12–14), African Americans represented 20.5% of the substance abuse treatment admissions; white early adolescents made up 63.5% of admissions (SAMHSA, May 3, 2011). According to NIDA (2006), African American adults comprised a similar percentage (23.6%) of treatment admissions, which, like the adolescents, is about twice their incidence in the general population. The rate of binge drinking among Black adults is 24.5%, compared to

the national average of 21.7% (SAMHSA, Feb 18, 2010). Tobacco use is estimated at 26.5% of the African American population (SAMHSA, 2010).

Compared with national averages, African American women have significantly lower rates of past month alcohol use (33.6% vs. 48.5%) anda slightly
lower binge drinking rate (14.4% vs. 15.9%), and a slightly higher rate of
past month illicit drug use (6.2% vs. 5.7%). Older African American women
(over 65) have a high abstention rate in the past month (85.6%), compared to
the national average for this age group (68.5%) (SAMHSA, Feb 18, 2010).
African Americans are more likely to die of cirrhosis of the liver, alcohol- or
drug-related homicide, and alcohol-related motor vehicle accidents. The death
rate from alcohol-related diseases is 10% greater for African Americans than
for the general population (Center on Alcohol Marketing and Youth (CAMI),
2006). Liver disease and cirrhosis is the ninth leading cause of death for African Americans (CDC, 2009). The devastationof HIV/AIDS is very visible in
the African American drug-using community (CSAT, 2004). Although African
Americans make up about 13% of the overall population, in 2006 they
accounted for 45% of the new HIV/AIDS cases diagnosed in the United States
(CDC, 2010b). Almost half of the people (46%) currently living with an HIV
infection are Black. The good news is that according to the CDC's Healthy
People 2010 Initiative, African Americans have had the best rate for improving health disparities compared to all the groups.

Since the mid-1980s, a major consequence of illicit drug use for African
American men and women has been incarceration in numbers far greater
than their representation in the population. A Sentencing Project study
(Mauer, 2009) reports that African Americans make up 44% of all prisoners
serving time for drug offenses, although they are only 13% of the population.
In contrast, whites (75% of the population), make up 27% of those imprisoned for drug-related offenses. Some progress in the racial disparity is happening in state prisons. The number of African Americans in state prisons
dropped 21.6% from 1999 to 2005, which could be a result of the decline in
crack cocaine use, the shift in law enforcement efforts toa focus on methamphetamines (used and distributed primarily by whites), and the increased use
of drug courts. Since the report of the Sentencing Project, the Fair Sentencing
Act, which was signed by President Obama in 2010, reduced the federal
differential between sentencing on crack and powder cocaine from 100-1 to
18-1; that is, it corrected the harsh mandatory sentencing that punished a person with five grams of crack with the same sentence as a person with 100
times that amount of powder cocaine. The implementation of this act should
help; however, 13 states still have higher disparities in sentencing between
crack and powder cocaine offenses than the federal law (Porter & Wright,
2011). The bottom line is that disparate sentencing has caused the incarceration of so many African American males, and whole communities have been
decimated (Mauer, 2009).

Blacks have a higher rate of problem gambling than whites, despite the
fact that they are significantly less likely than whites to ever gamble. According to a recent national survey, African Americans have an extremely high

chance of developing a gambling problem, once gambling begins (Kessler, Hwang, LaBrie, Petukhova, Sampson, Winters, & Shaffer, 2008). Characteristics of African American callers who identified themselves as in need of help with their gambling problems were gathered by researchers using data from the Connecticut Gambling Helpline. African American callers were significantly more likely than white callers to be female and less educated, have longer durations of gambling problems, and be less likely to have received mental health treatment. Fewer Blacks reported any professional gambling treatment or Gamblers Anonymous attendance (Barry, Steinberg, Wu, & Potenza, 2008).

SOCIOECONOMIC FACTORS

The African American family poverty rate of 22.4% is the second highest of all the groups discussed in this chapter, barely below the Native American rate of 22.7%, and twice as high as the 10.5% rate for all families in the United States (U.S. Census, 2009). Health insurance coverage is better than for Native Americans and Hispanics, but still, at 18.1%, lower than the national average of uninsured (15.1%). The median household income of $33,463 for African Americans is the lowest of all the groups and much lower than the national average of $50,221 (U.S. Census, 2009). Educational attainment is improving: 18.6% have less than a high school diploma, 31.6% are high school graduates, and almost 50% have attained some college or a bachelor's or professional degree (compared to 57% of the total population).

However, too many African Americans live in poverty and are subjected to a number of social and environmental risk factors, including violence, racism, deteriorating housing, lack of resources, cutbacks in healthcare, and limited positive role models as more middle-class Black professionals move from inner cities to more affluent suburbs, and more Black males are incarcerated. African American women are victimized at an astounding rate: Homicide is a leading cause of death, and aggravated assault and rape rates are high but also highly underreported (West, 2003). A large segment of the young Black male population is removed from the community; in the age group of 20-34, one in nine Black males are in prison or jail (Pew Trusts, 2008). As a result, many children have no access to their fathers. In addition, African Americans have been unduly targeted by alcohol advertising in their communities (NIAAA, 2005). In 2004, African American youth saw 34% more alcohol advertising in national magazines than did youth in general; this involved 42% more advertising for distilled spirits (CAMI, 2006).

In spite of all these risk factors and an economic recession that has hit African Americans hard, the Black community has found some reasons for being more optimistic about the state of Black progress (Pew Research Center, Jan 2010). A majority of Blacks (54%) report that the election of Barack Obama as the first Black president of the United States has improved race relations; and nearly twice as many as in 2008 (39% v. 20%) feel that the "situation of black people in this country" is better than it was five years ago. Still, 43% of African Americans still perceive that there is a lot of anti-black discrimination, and that percentage has not changed since 2001. Blacks rate not enough jobs (79%), and drugs and alcoholism (74%) as the two most important problems facing them today (Pew Research Center, Jan 2010).

CULTURAL FACTORS

There are many strengths and protective factors in the culture of African American families. Traditions have survived from African heritage and have been adapted to survive historical conditions like slavery and current conditions like racial oppression. Spirituality appears to be "the cornerstone of hope" for many in the African American community, "enabling them to survive horrendous adversity" (Wright, 2001, p. 34). Spirituality and the practice of religion has served the African American community as a venue for social action, a way of preserving individual identity, and a means of attaining community solidarity (Krentzman, Farkas, & Townsend, 2010).

Several studies have documented the importance of spirituality and religion as a protective factor from substance abuse and addiction, and an advantage in achieving recovery. For example, researchers re-analyzed Project MATCH data from the 1980s and found that as measures of "purpose in life" (spirituality) increased, Blacks were more likely to achieve sobriety than Whites (Krentzman, Farkas, & Townsend, 2010). Bowie, Ensminger, and Robertson (2006) examined data from a longitudinal cohort of over 1,000 inner-city African American residents who were studied through interviews of mothers and the children as the children matured from age 6 to 32. Findings from this empirically based study revealed that key factors in the development of alcohol problems were being male, having a major depressive disorder, dropping out of school, and not attending church at least monthly. Brome and colleagues (2000) examined the relationship between spirituality and African American women in recovery from substance misuse. They found that women who expressed a high level of spirituality had a more positive self-concept, a more active coping style, more positive attitudes toward parenting, more positive relationships with others, and an empowering coping stance.

Communal orientation and family support are also protective factors in the African American community. Individual identity is often defined through relationship to family and extended family and through mutual aid. Family may include people who are not related by blood but are linked with the family through mutual-help arrangements such as child care. *Umoja*, the first of seven principles developed by Maulana Karenga (1977), states that an obligation of every African American is to maintain unity in the family and community. Children should be seen as a gift from God and provided with life-sustaining environments. Elders are to be respected and addressed by their titles to indicate respect, such as Mr., Mrs., Aunt and Reverend. The seven principles form the backbone of Kwanzaa, a weeklong celebration from December 25 to January 1 that was established to help African

Americans connect to their ancestral roots in Africa. The celebration is based on an African harvest festival, with Swahili symbols for the seven principles, and each night a different principle is celebrated. However, the celebration is not without controversy in the Black community. Some feel it is "more about thumbing black noses at white America than at embracing the lost cause of resuming our Africanness," and others celebrate it as "an African-themed event that can be appreciated by an ethnically diverse community" (*New York Times*, 2008, p. 3).

While movements like Kwanzaa have been created to strengthen the African American culture, aspects of popular culture can have the opposite effect. Pope, Wallhagen, and Davis (2010) explored the social processes involved in the use of illicit drugs in an ethnographic study of Africa American baby boomers. Media images appeared to have considerable influence. As one respondent put it, "*Superfly*, the movie, was, well what they did was popularize drugs. Any time you look up a Black movie, it's always about drugs, you know?" (p. 251). In the music scene, the development of hip-hop culture and rap is primarily associated with the African American community, and people either love it or hate it, usually depending on how old they are. Large majorities of black respondents (71%) in a Pew survey say rap is a bad influence on society; however, young blacks are much less likely to see rap as negative (Pew Research Center, 2007). In response to a recent article on The Grio (an msnbc.com feature), one writer comments, "Rappers glorify the selling of 'rock, bricks, and keys (kilos)' while smoking blunts, and drinking to excess while treating women as throwaway 'bitches and hoes.' White, suburban kids listen to it, and sag their pants, smoke blunts, and call each other nigga. Black inner-city kids LIVE this reality, to a great degree, in an environment of drug addiction, drug sales, crime and misery" (Watkins, 2010).

TREATMENT ISSUES

Treatment barriers for African Americans include biased and even racist counselors, inadequate opportunities or appropriate referrals to treatment, lack of child care while a parent is in treatment, lack of insurance, and being placed on a waiting list for too long (Schmidt & Mulia, 2009). A study that used outreach workers to conduct interviews with injection drug users in New York City (60% Hispanic and 30% African American) found several barriers standing in the way of this population of Blacks and Hispanics going into treatment. The top reasons were (1) family (personal issues, such as wanting to conceal addition from a spouse, being the main breadwinner); (2) the demands of the addiction, or no desire to enter treatment; (3) lack of private insurance/ Medicaid; (4) treatment aversion (fear, bad previous treatment experience); and (5) lack of personal identification or other documents to qualify for services or other benefits("too much of a hassle to get into Medicaid"). The most common suggestions for reducing barriers were to admit applicants without Medicaid or identification, reduce waiting periods, and open up more treatment slots (Appel, Ellison, Jansky, & Oldak, 2004). The suggestion about having treatment available "on demand" is a basic tenet of harm reduction philosophy. The need for available and accessible treatment is big, given the fact that only 24.2% of black adults in need of illicit drug treatment in the past year received it at a specialty facility (SAMHSA, Feb 18, 2010).

When African Americans do receive treatment, they are more likely than other groups to enter public programs through legal and court channels (Polcin & Beattie, 2007). Nationally, only about one-third of substance abuse treatment programs offer specialty services for African Americans and Latinos combined. As with the other culturally sensitive programs discussed in this chapter, there has not been rigorous research to prove these programs' effectiveness. Generally speaking, rigorous research involves a randomized controlled study using a culturally specific treatment regimen guided by manuals (Schmidt et al., 2009). However, as Polcin and Beattie (2007) point out, there is some evidence that culturally appropriate programs may increase providers' ability to engage and retain clients in treatment. This ability may also increase client satisfaction.

An unexpected finding in a research project on racial disparities in methadone maintenance clinics helps explain how cultural competency can make a positive difference (Howard, Barrett, & Holmes, 2009). The researchers were investigating results that indicate African Americans heroin addicts still receive lower dosages of methadone than white clients. The recommended dose for maintenance is 60 milligrams per dose (mg/d), but in 2000, 35.5% of African Americans continued to receive less than the recommended levels, and there is evidence this rate got even lower in 2005. Possible explanations from people in the field for this continued disparity included poor staffing, uneducated and biased staff, staff using dosage as a means of social control, and even a conspiracy of genocide against African Americans. The researchers asked this question: Does cultural competency in methadone clinics affect dosage levels? They grouped 123 methadone treatment facilities into programs that were culturally competent or not, based on their adherence to the cultural competency standards of (1) recruiting and retaining African American staff, (2) immersion in the African American culture, (3) training, (4) interpreter services, (5) culturally competent health promotion, (6) use of community health workers, (7) inclusion of family members, and (8) administrative and organizational accommodation. They also surveyed the clinics for the type, number, and availability of support services, such as family services, financial counseling, child care assistance, legal services, HIV prevention, family planning, parenting education, and so on. The results indicate that among the non-–culturally competent clinics, a racial difference exists; that is, African American addicts are more likely to receive dosages of 40 milligrams or less than their white counterparts in the same clinic. The interesting finding, however, is that among culturally competent clinics, there was no racial difference in dosage levels. The authors suggest that the culturally competent clinics, which also offered more support services, were treating the whole person, not just the heroin addiction. They were also addressing poverty, homelessness, unemployment, and other types of stress common to African American heroin addicts.

Transference–countertransference issues related to gender and the reality of the dominance of White culture occur frequently. For example, a Black male immigrant from the Caribbean who is used to having male authority in the family may be more likely to accept a White than an African American female counselor. Black Caribbean women may respond to a male counselor (authority figure) with passivity or anger, regardless of race (Harris-Hastick, 2001). In the course of treatment, African Americans may get in touch with repressed rage toward the racism and oppression they have experienced all their lives (Wright, 2001). bell hooks (1993) connects the struggle of people to recover from the suffering and wounds caused by political oppression and exploitation with the effort to break with addictive behavior. David Goodson, a youth shelter worker and himself an ex-convict, speaking before a social work class, explains the struggle to recover well (cited in van Wormer, 2001):

> I deal with a lot of cultural pain. The same issues come up again and again, and the issue of race always comes up, the issue of Who I am. Who am I as a black man? In a lecture I heard recently the speaker said the only thing that keeps people clean is the fear of dying of an overdose. But in my work we have to go beyond that and acquire a love for life, a love for yourself, a love for your family, and so on. Sometimes we preach a message of *running from* rather than a message of salvation. My point is we have to go beyond fear to the positive. As African Americans we have to view this [drug use] as self-destructive behavior due to cultural self-hatred. (p. 79)

Because of the devastation from illegal drug activity, drug-related HIV, crack houses, and the co-occurring violence and family dislocation from incarceration, many African American communities are not at all in favor of harm reduction practices, such as needle exchange. As Imani Woods (1998) notes,

> People look at me like I'm crazy when I go to the black community to explain harm reduction. I am accused of supporting a policy that makes peace with genocide. How can one talk about "reducing harm" to a people under siege? Harm reduction is seen as settling, giving up, accepting failure, and bargaining with the devil. (p. 301)

However, according to Woods, harm reduction practices are of value to this community because they encourage a more nonjudgmental attitude toward users instead of vilification and stigmatization. The more this change in attitude occurs, the better chance the drug user has to build new attitudes that will help him or her diminish or stop drug use, such as looking squarely at his or her drug lifestyle and the consequences, developing a more positive feeling of worth as a Black person, and finding alternative models of living. A change in attitudes and moderation of use can lead to a greater likelihood of employment and access to treatment. For harm reduction to succeed in the African American community, Woods advocates that it be presented, particularly to churchgoers, as a useful step toward eradication and that these efforts incorporate African American characteristics. These may include the use of oral communication, telling stories, a call-and-response type of presentation instead of the expert speaker and passive audience type of presentation, a working knowledge of African American culture and the complexities involved, and a respect for Black priorities.

BLACK CULTURALLY BASED SERVICES

Focus groups in the Toronto, Ontario area point out that Black immigrant groups from Somalia face multiple barriers in accessing education and treatment services for gambling problems. Not only is there a likelihood of premigration trauma and numerous language and economic problems, but the shame factor is likely to weigh heavily because gambling is forbidden in Islam and prohibited by the Somali culture, According to the Ontario Resource Group (2010), young men in the Somalian community are more accepting of gambling than older adults. Common games include *turub* (a type of poker) usually played in social clubs, lotteries, bingo, and casino games. Somali immigrants are likely to seek spiritual counseling at the mosque, or an ethno-specific community agency. Factors to consider when working with Somali immigrants with gambling (or addiction) problems include the need for an interpreter, previous trauma from the devastation in Somalia, cultural ideas around luck, help with employment, ESL classes, debt management, and how to involve the family in the treatment process (Ontario Resource Group, 2010).

Moving south to Waterloo, Iowa, we discover an African American–focused prevention program combined with a gender-specific program that is administered by Pathways Behavioral Services, a substance abuse treatment center. The philosophy is to instill pride in children from high risk backgrounds and to provide cultural enrichment. Groups of ten children are tracked from the third grade through the end of the fifth grade. This program is described by Felicia Carter, the facilitator of the group:

> The Stop and Think program is research based and funded through grants; the goal is to teach children to learn appropriate skills for getting along with others, solving problems, and resolving conflict, so acting out is no longer their only option. This will help children rise above their surroundings and be productive citizens. This is a prevention measure to prevent or offset the age of them experimenting with drugs. We provide programming after school on Tuesdays and Thursdays and expose the children to cultural events they might not, for whatever reason, get to attend. I took them to my church for service once because I wanted them to know that I believe in something that is bigger than me.
>
> All the children are African American. The original group is now in the fifth grade. We go to the theatre, and I want to raise money to take them to Atlanta to visit the Martin Luther King monument and learn more about how slavery began. We begin teaching them our African history starting from the 1400s to the 1500s about how our ancestors were traded for guns. I want them to take pride in our heritage. The curriculum for girls is Self-Esteem Through Culture Leads to Academic Excellence (SETCLAE), facilitated by Jawanza Kunjufu. Another program she facilitates for African American teen girls is I'm a Girl Empowered and Strong (IMAGES). This program is designed to enhance

self-esteem and promote awareness of Who am I? Where am I going? How do I get there? This is a 13-week program that is held during the summer. (personal communication, November 2, 2006)

Felicia Carter describes herself as a highly spiritual person, which provides her with a sense of calling for this work. Washington and Moxley (2003) similarly discuss the role of spirituality in their counseling of African American women in inpatient treatment for substance misuse problems. In treatment, they found prayer and religious involvement were conducive to increased feelings of self-esteem, to enhanced healing, and to meeting the individuals' spirituality needs. Practitioners who eliminate prayer from the helping process, as Washington and Moxley suggest, may only weaken their efforts to engage in culturally sensitive practice.

On the prevention side, another program, Strengthening Families, focuses on improving family relationships, parenting skills, and increasing the social and life skills of youth from high risk families (including parents with substance abuse problems). Recognized as a model program by SAMHSA and NIDA and endorsed as effective by the Office of Juvenile Justice and Delinquency Prevention, the program has developed several versions to meet the needs of diverse families (SAMHSA Model Programs, 2006).

SUMMARY AND CONCLUSION

In this chapter, we support the fact that all addicts are not alike by exploring differences among Asian/Pacific Islanders, African Americans, Native American/Alaskan Natives, and Hispanics/Latinos. Although there is great variation because of economic class, education, level of acculturation, and gender as to how traditional values are actualized in individual people, there is considerable agreement that taking into consideration and respecting racial and ethnic values are critical parts of engaging and maintaining persons in the recovery process.

Strengths-based practices that focus on assessing what the person wants and the skills, resiliencies, and resources available within the person and the community are well suited to working with clients from different cultures. Instead of defining a medical diagnosis as the problem and a one-size-fits-all intervention as the solution, a strengths-based approach gathers information from the standpoint of the clients' view of their situation and helps plan alternatives within the clients' cultural framework (Rapp, 2006). Harm reduction practices support helping an individual or a family develop an array of choices that fits their unique circumstances.

Developing cultural competence requires a commitment to learn much more about different cultures than could be presented in this chapter. Numerous resources are accessible on the Internet, and a good place to start are the Substance Abuse Resource Guides put out by SAMHSA (https://ncadistore. samhsa.gov/catalog) on Asian and Pacific Islanders, American Indians and Native Alaskans, Hispanics/Latinos, and African Americans. For example, the *Asian and Pacific Islander Americans Resource Guide* includes descriptions of videotapes available in English subtitled in various languages, such as Korean, Khmer, and Tagalog, and several that are in Chinese, Vietnamese, Cambodian, and other languages. In addition, the guide features abstracts from a variety of government publications and research journals that deal with cultural competence and ethnic differences; a list of groups, youth councils, and organizations around the United States that deal with specific ethnic groups; and a list of Internet resource sites.

Putting cultural competence into practice requires a commitment to slow down and take time to ask a variety of questions from a not knowing, nonexpert position. It requires acknowledgment that, as counselors, we are just in the margins of the page that represents the richness and complexity of our clients' lives. We may visit, but we do not live there. Even to visit, it is necessary to become aware of our own "biases, racism, internalized oppression, power dynamics, and classism" so that we do not perpetrate these problems on others (Wright, 2001, p. 44).

REFERENCES

Alvarez, L., & Ruiz, P. (2001). Substance abuse in the Mexican American population. In L. A. Straussner (Ed.), *Ethnocultural factors in substance abuse treatment* (pp. 111–136). New York: Guilford Press.

Amaro, H., Nieves, R., Johannes, S., & Cabeza, N. (1998). Substance abuse treatment: Critical issues and challenges in the treatment of Latina women. *Hispanic Journal of Behavioral Sciences, 21*(3), 266–282.

Amaro, H. & Cortes, D. (2007). *Drug abuse among Hispanics: A brief evidence-based guide for providers.* U.S, Department of Health and Human Services, Substance Abuse and Merntal Health Services Administration. Retrieved July 10, 2011 from www.nhsn.med.miami.edu/documents/drug_abuse_and_hispanics.pdf

Appel, P., Ellison, A., Jansky, H., & Oldak, R. (2004). *American Journal of Drug and Alcohol Abuse, 30*(1), 129–153.

Auger, N., Lo, E., Cantinotti, M., & O'Loughlin, J. (2010). Impulsivity and socio-economic status interact to increase the risk of gambling onset among youth. *Addiction, 105*(12), 2176–2183.

Barry, D., Steinberg, M., Wu, R., & Potenza, M. (2008). Characteristics of Black and White callers to a gambling helpline. *Psychiatric Services, 59*(11), 1347–1350.

Barry, D., Stefanovics, E., Desai, R., & Potenza, M. (2011). Gambling problem severity and psychiatric disorders among Hispanic and white adults: Findings from a nationally representative sample. *Journal of Psychiatric Research, 45*(3), 404–411.

Beauvais, F., Jumper-Thurman, P., & Burnside, M. (2008). The changing patterns of drug use among American Indian students over the past thirty years. *American Indian and Alaska Native Mental Health Research, 15*(2), 15–24.

Blume, A., & Lovato, L. (2010). Empowering the disempowered: Harm reduction with racial/ethnic minority clients. *Journal of Clinical Psychology, 66*(2), 189–200.

Bogo, M., Tsang, A., & Lee, E. (2011). Cross-cultural clinical social work practice. In J. R. Brandell (Ed.), *Theory and practice in clinical social work* (2nd ed., pp. 693–715). Thousand Oaks, CA: Sage.

Boulard, G. (April 14, 2011). A winning bet. *Diverse Issues in Higher Education, 28*(5).

Bowie, J., Ensminger, M., & Robertson, J. (2006). Alcohol-use problems in young Black adults: Effects of religiosity, social resources, and mental health. *Journal of Studies on Alcohol, 67*(1), 44–54.

Brave Heart, M. Y. H. (2007). Historical trauma and substance abuse. *Alcohol, Tobacco and Other Drugs, Section Connection, 2*, 1–5.

Bromley, M., & Sip, S. (2001). *Substance abuse treatment issues with Cambodian Americans.* In L. A. Straussner (Ed.), *Ethnocultural factors in substance abuse treatment* (pp. 321–344). New York: Guilford Press.

Canino, G., Bravo, M., Ramirez, R., Febo, V., Rubio-Stipec M., Fernandez, R., et al. (1999). The Spanish Alcohol Use Disorder and Associated Disabilities Interview Schedule (AUDADIS): Reliability and concordance with clinical diagnoses in a Hispanic population. *Journal of Studies on Alcohol, 60*(6), 790–799.

Carvajal, S., & Young, R. (2009). Culturally based substance abuse treatment for American Indians/Alaska Natives and Latinos. *Journal of Ethnicity in Substance Abuse, 8*(3), 207–222.

Center on Alcohol Marketing and Youth (CAMI). (2006). *African-American youth and alcohol advertising.* Retrieved September 2006 from http://camy.org/factsheets

Center on Substance Abuse Treatment (CSAT). (2004). *Substance abuse treatment and family therapy.* Substance Abuse and Mental Health Services Administration. Treatment Improvement Protocol (TIP) Series, No. 39. Retrieved February 2007 from http://www.ncbi.nlm.nih.gov/books/bv.fcgi?rid=hstat5.chapter.70382

Centers for Disease Control and Prevention (CDC). (2008, August 29). Alcohol-Attributable death and years of potential life lost among American Indians and Alaska Natives, United States: 2001–2005. *Morbidity and Mortality Weekly Report.* Retrieved July 5, 2011 from http://www.cdc.gov/mmwr/preview/mmwrhtml/mm5734a3.htm

Centers for Disease Control and Prevention (CDC). (2009). *Health in the United States.* Retrieved July 12, 2011 from http://www.cdc.gov/nchs/data/hus/hus09.pdf#028

Centers for Disease Control and Prevention (CDC). (2010a). HIV among Hispanics/Latinos. Retrieved July 8, 2011 from http://www.cdc.gov/hiv/hispanics/resources/factsheets/pdf/hispanic.pdf

Centers for Disease Control and Prevention (CDC). (2010b). *HIV among African Americans.* Retrieved July 12, 2011 from http://cdc.gov/hiv/topics/aa/pdf/aa.pdf

Chui, W. H. (2008) True stories: Migrant Vietnamese women with problem gambling in Brisbane, Queensland. *Journal of Social Work Practice in the Addictions, 8*(2), 276–280.

Chong, J., Fortier, Y., & Morris, T. (2009). Cultural practices and spiritual development for women in a Native American alcohol and drug treatment program. *Journal of Ethnicity in Substance Abuse, 8*(3), 261–282.

Coyhis, D., & Simonelli, R. (2008). The Native American healing experience. *Substance Use and Misuse, 43*, 1927–1949.

Council on Social Work Education (CSWE), (2008). *Educational Policy and Accreditation Standards.* Council on Social Work Education, Inc. Retrieved June 26, 2011 from http://www.cswe.org/File.aspx?id=13780

Daisy, F., Thomas, L., & Worley, C. (1998). Alcohol uses and harm reduction within the Native community. In G. A. Marlatt (Ed.), *Harm reduction: Pragmatic strategies for managing high-risk behaviors* (pp. 327–350). New York: Guilford Press.

Davies, L, (2009). Resistance and celebration. *Afterimage, 36*(6, 3–4).

Dell, C., Seguin, M., Hopkins, C., Tempier, R., Mehl-Madrona, L., Dell, D., Duncan, R., & Mosier, K. (2011). From benzos to berries: Treatment offered at an Aboriginal youth solvent abuse treatment centre relays the importance of culture. *Canadian Journal of Psychiatry, 56*(2), 75–83.

De La Rosa, M., Holleran, M., Rugh, D., & MacMaster, S. (2005). Substance abuse among U.S. Latinos: A review of the literature. In M. De La Rosa, L. Holleran, & S. L. Straussner (Eds.), *Substance abusing Latinos: Current research on epidemiology, prevention and treatment* (pp. 1–20). Binghamton, NY: Haworth.

Economist (4/14/2007). The last shall be first, 383 (8524). Retrieved Sept 22, 2011 from: http://www.economist.com/node/9006591.

Elia, C., & Jacobs, D. (1993). The incidence of pathological gambling among Native Americans treated for alcohol dependence. *Substance Use and Misuse, 28*(7), 659–666.

Escobar, J. I. & Vega, W. A. (2006). Cultural issues and psychiatric diagnosis: Providing a general background for considering substance use diagnoses. *Addiction, 101*(Suppl.1), 40–47.

Freese, T., Obert, J., Dickow, A., Cohen, J., & Lord, R. (2000). Methamphetamine abuse: Issues for special populations. *Journal of Psychoactive Drugs, 32*(2), 177–182.

Gallardo, M., & Curry, S. (2009). Shifting perspectives: Culturally responsive interventions with Latino substance abusers. *Journal of Ethnicity in Substance Abuse, 8*(3), 314–329.

Garrett, M., & Carroll, J. (2000). Mending the broken circle: Treatment of substance dependence among Native Americans. *Journal of Counseling and Development, 78*(4), 379–388.

Gelman, C. R. (2004). Empirically based principles for culturally competent practice with Latinos. *Journal of Ethnic and Cultural Diversity in Social Work, 13*(1), 83–108.

Harris-Hastick, E. (2001). Substance abuse issues among English-speaking Caribbean people of African ancestry. In L. A. Straussner (Ed.), *Ethnocultural factors in substance abuse treatment* (pp. 52–74). New York: Guilford Press.

Hines, P. M., & Boyd-Franklin, N. (2005). African American families. In M. McGoldrick, J. Giordano, & N. Garcia-Preto (Eds.), *Ethnicity and family therapy* (3rd ed., pp. 87–100). New York: Guilford Press.

Hoffman, F. (1994). Cultural adaptations of Alcoholics Anonymous to serve Hispanic populations. *International Journal of Addictions, 29*(4), 445–460.

Holleran, L. (2005). HIV/AIDS prevention with Latino/a substance abusers: An interview with Jennifer Herrera. *Journal of Social Work Practice in the Addictions, 5*(1/2), 175–183.

hooks, b. (1993). *Sisters of the yam: Black women and self-recovery.* Boston: South End Press.

hooks, b. (2000). *Where we stand: Class matters.* New York: Routledge.

Howard, D., Barrett, N., & Holmes, D. (2009). Can cultural competency speak to the race disparities in methadone dosage levels? *Review of Black Political Economy, 37*, 7–23.

Ja, D., & Aoki, B. (1993). Substance abuse treatment: Cultural barriers in the Asian American community. *Journal of Psychoactive Drugs, 25*(1), 61–71.

Jones-Webb, R. (1998). Drinking patterns and problems among African Americans: Recent findings. *Alcohol Health and Research World, 22*(4), 260–265.

Khalsa, S., Khalsa, G., Kalsa, H., & Khalsa, M. (2008). *Journal of Ethnicity in Substance Abuse, 7*(1), 67–79.

Karenga, M. (1977). *Kwanzaa: Origin, concepts, practice.* Inglewood, CA: Kawaida.

Kessler, R., Hwang, R., LaBrie, R., Petukhova, M., Sampson, N., Winters, K., & Shaffer, H. (2008). DSM IV Pathological gambling in the National Comorbidity Survey Replication. *Psychological Medicine, 38,* 1351–1360.

Krentzman, A., Farkas, K., & Townsend, A. (2010). Spirituality, religiousness, and alcoholism treatment outcomes: A comparison between black and white participants. *Alcoholism Treatment Quarterly, 28,* 128–150.

Lee, E., & Mock, M. M. (2005). Asian families: An overview. In M. McGoldrick, J. Giordano, & N. Garcia-Preto (Eds.), *Ethnicity and family therapy* (3rd ed., pp. 269–282). New York: Guilford Press.

Lindenberg, C., Solorzano, R., Krantz, M., Galvis, C., Baroni, G., & Strickland, O. (1998). Risk and resilience: Building protective factors. An intervention for preventing substance abuse and sexual risk-taking and for promoting strength and protection among young, low-income Hispanic women. *American Journal of Maternal Child Nursing, 23*(2), 99–104.

Lipsky, S., & Caetano, R. (2009). Epidemiology of substance abuse among Latinos. *Journal of Ethnicity in Substance Abuse, 8*(3), 242–260.

Lowe, J. (2006). Teen Intervention Project–Cherokee (TIP-C). *Pediatric Nursing, 32*(5), 495–500.

Lowery, C. (1998). American Indian perspectives on addiction and recovery. *Health and Social Work, 23*(2), 127–135.

Luna-Firebaugh, E., & Fox, M. (2010). The sharing tradition: Indian gambling in stories and modern life. *Wicazo Sa Review, 25*(1), 75–86.

Mauer. M. (2009). *The Sentencing Project: The changing racial dynamics of the War on Drugs.* Retrieved July 12, 2011 from http://sentencingproject.org

May, P., Miller, J., Goodhart, K., Maestas, O., Buckley, D., Trujillo, P., & Gossage, J. (2008). Enhanced case management to prevent fetal alcohol spectrum disorders in northern plains communities. *Maternal Child Health Journal, 12,* 747–759.

May, P. (1996). Overview of alcohol abuse epidemiology for American Indian populations. In G. Sandefur, R. Rindfuss, & B. Cohen (Eds.), *Changing numbers, changing needs: American Indian demography and public health* (pp. 235–261). Washington, DC: National Academy Press.

McLaulin, J., Evans, A., White, W. (2009). *The role of addiction medicine in the transformation of an urban behavioral health care system.* Unpublished manuscript. Retrieved June 27, 2011 from http://www.dbhids.org/assets/Forms–Documents/transormation/BillWhite/2009AddictionMedicineArticle.pdf. Moloney, M., Hunt, G., & Evans, K. (2008). Asian American identity and drug consumption: From acculturation to normalization. *Journal of Ethnicity in Substance Abuse, 7*(4), 376–403.

McGoldrick, M., Giordano, J., & Garcia-Preto, N. (2005). Overview: Ethnicity and family therapy. In M. McGoldrick, J. Giordano, & N. Garcia-Preto (Eds.), *Ethnicity and family therapy* (3rd ed., pp. 1–40). New York: Guilford Press.

Medina, C. (2001). Toward an understanding of Puerto Rican ethnicity and substance abuse. In L. A. Straussner (Ed.), *Ethnocultural factors in substance abuse treatment* (pp. 137–163). New York: Guilford Press.

Mercado, M. (2000). The invisible family: Counseling Asian American substance abusers and their families. *Family Journal, 8*(3), 267–272.

Milbrodt, T. (2002). Breaking the cycle of alcohol problems among Native Americans: Culturally sensitive treatment in the Lakota community. *Alcoholism Treatment Quarterly, 20*(1), 19–44.

Momper, S., & Jackson, A. (2007). Maternal gambling, parenting, and child behavioral functioning in Native American families. *Social Work, 11*(4), 199–208.

Monk, D. (2011, June 23). Addicts in treatment fear isolation as they lose haven. *Nottingham Evening Post*, Nottingham (UK), p. 2.

Moran, J., & Bussey, M. (2007). Results of an alcohol prevention program with urban American Indian youth. *Child and Adolescent Social Work Journal, 24*(1), 1–21.

Morelli, P., & Fong, R. (2000). The role of Hawaiian elders in substance abuse treatment among Asian/Pacific Islander women. *Journal of Family Social Work, 4*(4), 33–44.

Moreno, S. (2005, September 18). A rare and unusual harvest. *Washington Post*, p. A03.

Murphy, S., & Rosenbaum, M. (1997). Two women who used cocaine too much: Class, race, gender, crack, and coke. In C. Reinarman & H. Levine (Eds.), *Crack in America: Demon drugs and social justice* (pp. 98–112). Berkeley: University of California Press.

New York Times, City Room Blog (2008, December 26). *After 40 years, Kwanzaa spreads its roots.* Retrieved July 13, 2011 from http://cityroom.blogs.nytimes.com

National Institute on Drug Abuse (NIDA). (2006). NIDA InfoFacts: Treatment trends. Retrieved September 22, 2006, from http://www.nida.nih.gov/Infofacts/treatmenttrends.html

Oei, T. P, & Raylu, N. (2007). *Gambling and problem gambling among the Chinese.* Brisbane, Australia: Behavioural Research and Therapy Centre, University of Queensland.

Office of Applied Studies. (2009). *Results from the 2009 national survey on drug use and health.* Substance Abuse and Mental Health Service Administration. Retrieved June 27, 2011 from http:/www.oas.samhsa.gov/NSDUH/2K9NSDUH/2K9Results.htm#2.7

Ontario Resource Group on Gambling, Ethnicity and Culture (March 2010). A guide for counselors working with problem gambling clients from ethno-cultural communities. Retrieved June 27, 2011 from http://www.problemgambling.ca/EN/Documents/GuideforCounsellorsWorkingWithProblemGamblingClientsfromEthno_culturalCommunities.pdf

Pew Research Center. (2007). Blacks see growing values gap between poor and middle class. Retrieved July 12, 2011 from http://pewsocialtrends.org

Pew Hispanic Center. (2009). *Statistical portrait of Hispanics in the U.S.: 2009.* Retrieved July 10, 2011 from http://pewhispanic.org/files/factsheets/factsheet.php?FactsheetID=70. Pew Charitable Trusts (2008). One in 100: Behind bars in America, 2008. Retrieved Sept 22, 2011 from http://www.pewtrusts.org/uploadedFiles/8015PCTS_Prison08_Final_2-1-1_FORWEB.pdf. Pew Research Report. (2009).

Between two worlds: How young Latinos come of age in America. Retrieved July 10, 2011 from http://pewhispanic.org/reports/report.php?ReportID=117

Pew Research Center (Jan 2010). Blacks upbeat about Black progress. Retrieved July 12, 2011 from http://pewsocialtrends.org

Polcin, D. L., & Beattie, M. (2007). Relationship and institutional pressure to enter treatment: Differences by demographics, problem severity, and motivation. *Journal of Studies on Alcohol and Drugs, 68*, 428–436.

Polinsky, M., Hser, Y., & Grella, C. (1998). Consideration of special populations in the drug treatment system of a large metropolitan area. *Journal of Behavioral Health Services and Research, 25*(1), 7–21.

Pope, R., Wallhagen, M., & Davis, H. (2010). The social determinants of substance abuse in African American baby boomers: Effects of family, media images, and environment. *Journal of Transcultural Nursing, 21*(3), 246–256.

Porter, N., & Wright, V. (2011). *Cracked Justice*. Retrieved July 12, 2011 from http://www.sentencingproject.org/doc/publications/dp_CrackedJusticeMar2011.pdf

Randolph, W., Stroup-Benham, C., Black, S., & Markides, K. (1998). Alcohol use among Cuban-Americans, Mexican-Americans, and Puerto Ricans. *Alcohol Health and Research World, 22*(4), 265–270.

Rapp, R. C. (2006). Strengths-based case management: Enhancing treatment for persons with substance abuse problems. In D. Saleebey (Ed.), *The strengths perspective in social work practice* (4th ed., pp. 128–147). Boston: Allyn & Bacon.

Rehuher, D., Hiramatsu, T., & Helm, S. (2008). Evidence-based youth drug prevention: A critique with implications for practice-based contextually relevant prevention in Hawai'i. *Hawai'i Journal of Public Health, 1*, 52–61.

Rothe, E., & Ruiz, P. (2001). Substance abuse among Cuban Americans. In L. A. Straussner (Ed.), *Ethnocultural factors in substance abuse treatment* (pp. 97–110). New York: Guilford Press.

Sakai, J., Ho, P., Shore, J., Risk, N., & Price, R. (2005). Asians in the United States: Substance dependence and use of substance-dependence treatment. *Journal of Substance Abuse Treatment, 29*(2), 75–84.

Sakai, J., Wang, C., & Price, R. (2010). Substance use and dependence among Native Hawaiians, Other Pacific Islanders and Asian ethnic groups in the United States: Contrasting multiple- and single-race prevalence rates from a national survey. *Journal of Ethnicity in ance Abuse, 9*(3), l73–185.

Saulny, S. (2011, March 24). *Census data presents rise in multiracial population of youths*. New York Times. Retrieved June 29, 2011 from http://www.nytimes.com/2011/03/25/us/25race.html

Schmidft, L., & Mulia, N. (2009). *Racial/ethnic disparities in AOD treatment*. Robert Wood Johnson Foundation's Substance Abuse Policy Research Program. Retrieved July 12, 2011 from http://saprp.org/knowledgeassets/knowledge_detail.cfm?KAID=11

Shinohara, R. (2010, February 20). Fetal alcohol syndrome rate in Alaska is declining. *Anchorage Daily News*. Retrieved July 5, 2011 from http://www.adn.com/2010/02/19/11/1148098/fas-rate-among-natives-declining.html

Smith, A. (2006). Soul wound: The legacy of Native American schools. *Amnesty Magazine*. Retrieved December 3, 2006 from http://www.amnestyusa.org/amnestynow/soulwound.html

Starling, R., Blankenship, J., May, P., & Woodall, G. (2009). Problem gambling in New Mexico: 1996–1998. *International Journal of Mental Health and Addiction,* 7, 138–148.

Stein, L. Y. (2001). The psychosocial needs of Hawaiian women incarcerated for drug-related crimes. *Journal of Social Work in the Addictions,* 1(4), 47–70.

Substance Abuse and Mental Health Services Administration (SAMHSA). (2009). GLBTQI mental health: Recommendations for policies and services. UPenn Collaborative on Community Integration and National Alliance on Mental Illness. Retrieved June 30, 2011 from http://www.nami.org/Template.cfm?Section=Multicultural_Support1&-Template=/ContentManagement/ContentDisplay.cfm&ContentID=83077

Substance Abuse and Mental Health Services Administration (SAMHSA). (2010). *Results from the 2009 National Survey on drug use and health: Volume I. Summary of National Findings* (Office of Applied Studies, NSDUH Series H-38A, HHS Publication No., SMA 10-4586Findings). Rockville, MD.

Substance Abuse and Mental Health Services Administration (SAMHSA). (2010). *The NSDUH Report: Substance use among Black adults.* Rockville, MD.

Substance Abuse and Mental Health Services Administration, Center for Behavioral Health Statistics and Quality. (2011). *The TEDS Report: Substance abuse treatment admissions aged 12 to 14.* Rockville, MD.

Substance Abuse and Mental Health Services Administration, Office of Applied Studies. (2006). *Results from the 2005 National Survey on drug use and health: National findings.* Retrieved September 22, 2006 from http://www.oas.samhsa.gov/NSDUH/2k5NSDUH/2k5results.htm

Substance Abuse and Mental Health Services Administration, Office of Applied Studies (2009). *The N-SSATS Report: Substance abuse treatment facilities serving American Indians and Alaska Natives.* Rockville, MD.

Substance Abuse and Mental Health Services Administration, Office of Applied Studies (2009). *The NSDUH Report: Substance use treatment need and receipt among Hispanics.* Rockville, MD.

Substance Abuse and Mental Health Services Administration, Office of Applied Studies (2009). *The TEDS Report: Trends in methamphetamine admissions to treatment: 1997–2007.* Rockville, MD.

Substance Abuse and Mental Health Services Administration, Office of Applied Studies (2010). *The NSDUH Report: Substance use among American Indian or Alaska Native Adults.* Rockville, MD.

Substance Abuse and Mental Health Services Administration, Office of Applied Studies (2010). *The NSDUH Report: Adolescent inhalant use and selected respiratory conditions.* Rockville, MD.

Substance Abuse and Mental Health Services Administration, Office of Applied Studies (2010). *The NSDUH Report: Substance use among Hispanic Adults.* Rockville, MD.

Substance Abuse and Mental Health Services Administration (SAMHSA) Model Programs (2006). *Strengthening Families Program.* Retrieved September 22, 2006 from http://www.strengtheningfamiliesprogram.org/docs/StrengthFPsamhsa.pdf.

Sutton, C. E., & Broken Nose, M. A. (2005). American Indian families: An overview. In M. McGoldrick, J. Giordano, & N. Garcia-Preto (Eds.), *Ethnicity and family therapy* (3rd ed., pp. 43–54). New York: Guilford Press.

Tapia, M., Schwartz, S., Prado, G., Lopez, B., & Pantin, H. (2006). Parent-centered intervention: A practical approach for preventing drug abuse in Hispanic adolescents. *Research on Social Work Practice,* 16(2), 146–165.

Taylor, J., & Jackson, B. (1990). Factors affecting alcohol consumption in Black women: Part II. *International Journal of the Addictions, 25*(12), 1415–1427.

Tenkku, L., Morris, D., Salas, J., & Xaverius, P. (2009). Racial disparities in pregnancy-related drinking reduction. *Maternal Child Health Journal, 13,* 604–613.

Thomas, L., Donovan, D., Sigo, R., Austin, L., & Marlatt, G. (2009). The community pulling together: A tribal community–university partnership project to reduce substance abuse and promote good health in a reservation tribal community. *Journal of Ethnicity and Substance Abuse, 8*(3), 283–300.

U.S. Census Bureau. (2009a). 2009 Community survey, selected population profile: Hispanic or Latino. Retrieved July 10, 2011
 from http://factfinder2.census.gov

U.S. Census Bureau. (2009b). Facts for Features: 2008 American Community Survey. Retrieved June 29, 2011 from http://factfinder2.census.gov

U.S. Census Bureau. (2010). *Overview of race and Hispanic origin: 2010 Census Briefs.* U.S. Department of Commerce, Economics and Statistics Administration. Retrieved June 29, 2011 from http://www.census.gov/prod/cen2010/briefs/c2010br-02.pdf

U.S. Department of Education, National Center for Education Statistics. (2010). *Fast facts.* Retrieved July 10, 2011 from http://nces.ed.gov/fastfacts/display.asp?id=16

Volberg, R., & Abbott, M. (1997). Gambling and problem gambling among Indigenous peoples. *Substance Use and Misuse, 32*(11), 1525–1538.

Volberg, R., & Bernhard, B. (2006). The 2006 study of gambling and problem gambling in New Mexico: Report to the Responsible Gaming Association of New Mexico. Retrieved July 8, 2011 from https://rganm.com/wp-content/uploads/2011/03/RGA-2006-STUDY.pdf

Warner, T., Krebs, C., & Fishbein, D. (2008). Perceiving the risk of substance use: The roles of nativity, acculturation, and family support among Hispanic children. *Journal of Drug Issues, 38*(1), 119–147.

Washington, O. G., & Moxley, D. P. (2003). Group interventions with low-income African American women recovering from chemical dependency. *Health and Social Work, 28*(2), 146–156.

Watkins, B. (2010). Why hip-hop culture is hooked on drugs. Grio, MSNBC.com. Retrieved July 12, 2011 from http://www.thegrio.com/entertainment/why-hip-hop-culture-is-hooked-on-drugs.php

Weaver, H. (2001). Native Americans and substance abuse. In S. L. Straussner (Ed.), *Ethnocultural factors in substance abuse treatment* (pp. 97–110). New York: Guilford Press.

White, W., & Kelly, J. (2010). Introduction: The theory, science, and practice of recovery management. In J. Kelly and W. White (Eds.), *Addiction recovery management: Theory, research and practice* (pp. 1–8). New York: Humana Press.

White, W., & Sanders, M. (2008). Recovery management and people of color: Redesigning addiction treatment for historically disempowered communities. *Alcoholism Treatment Quarterly, 26*(3), 365–395.

Woods, I. (1998). Bringing harm reduction to the Black community. In G. A. Marlatt (Ed.), *Harm reduction: Pragmatic strategies for managing high-risk behaviors* (pp. 301–326). New York: Guilford Press.

Wright, E. (2001). Substance abuse in African American communities. In L. A. Straussner (Ed.), *Ethnocultural factors in substance abuse treatment* (pp. 31–51). New York: Guilford Press.

Young, R., & Joe, J. (2009). Some thoughts about the epidemiology of alcohol and drug use among American Indian/Alaska Native populations. *Journal of Ethnicity in Substance Abuse, 8*(3), 223–241.

Yu, J., Clark, L., Chandra, L., Dias, A., & Lai, T. (2009). Reducing cultural barriers to substance abuse treatment among Asian Americans: A case study in New York City. *Journal of Substance Abuse Treatment, 37*(4), 398–406.

PUBLIC POLICY

CHAPTER **13**

Treatment programs and practices are driven not only by clinical needs, but also by social policies

—Shulamith Lala Ashenberg Straussner and Richard Isralowitz, 2008

The impact of public policies on the availability of resources; treatment methods; the extent to which addicts are penalized, jailed, and punished; and the shaping of public opinion has been emphasized throughout this text. In this chapter, we highlight several current social policies that affect one of the most important public health and social issues facing the United States, that is, how to deal effectively and compassionately with persons who are struggling with addiction and the consequences of addiction.

The authors take the position that the social context of drug use has helped create our drug problems. Instead of harm reduction, standard U.S. policies have often had the effect of "harm induction" in that they have only made things worse, rarely better. A criminal justice approach consistently has been applied to what is essentially a public health problem. Elsewhere other approaches have been applied with a greater degree of success. For example, in Britain and the Netherlands, many heroin addicts under medical supervision have been able to function successfully in their work and lead normal lives. In contrast, America's war on drugs and its zero tolerance policies can claim little success.

There are many alternatives to current policies that would be more compassionate, have more support from scientific evidence, and actually address the problems related to addiction. For example, we could simply have more treatment available, like the city of Baltimore. According to the *Washington Post,* the number of drug-overdose deaths in that city is at the lowest level since the 1990s because the funding for treatment in publicly supported clinics was tripled (Brown, 2006). With a drug epidemic that affects as many as one in six Baltimore residents, the city has continued to fight back. As of 2011 Baltimore had residential and outpatient drug treatment slots to meet the needs of around 5,000 people and expanded methadone programs for many others. Still, a *Baltimore Sun* editorial calls for a stronger prevention emphasis to get at the root causes of addiction ("Rethinking Addiction," 2011). The editors single out the high rates of poverty, unemployment, and homelessness, as well as the density of liquor stores as social factors that need to be addressed. Earlier drug policy experts at the University of Maryland–Baltimore and Baltimore's Abell Foundation in Baltimore looked into heroin maintenance programs as a strategy shown to reduce crime and to get people who are addicted to heroin into treatment (Brewington, 2009).

Across the nation, where many of the same factors are present, unlike in Baltimore, treatment options are scarce. We learn from national statistics that in 2009 the number of persons aged 12 or older needing treatment for a substance-related problem was 23.5 million (9.3% of the population). Of these, 2.6 million (11.2% of those who needed treatment) received treatment at a specialty facility. Thus, there were 20.9 million persons in the United States who needed treatment for an illicit drug or alcohol use problem but did not receive treatment at a specialty substance abuse facility in the year preceding the study (National Survey on Drug Use and Health, 2010). In this chapter, we discuss many other alternatives to the current state of affairs, starting with the need to disengage from the polarized debate of "legalization versus criminalization," and find a middle way to move forward toward decriminalization. In addition, we review recent welfare reforms that impact people with alcohol or drug problems, we review the results of the war on drugs policies, and we briefly address the current lack of social policy and research funding in the area of compulsive gambling.

WELFARE REFORM

Recent welfare reforms are having direct and indirect effects on poor people who have alcohol or drug problems. Federal guidelines for Temporary Assistance for Needy Families (TANF) encourage states to deny cash assistance or food stamps to applicants with recent drug felony convictions (NASW, 2009). This legislation applies to males and females, but single mothers and women who go to public assistance prenatal clinics, and who predominate in the welfare system, carry the brunt. A number of states have passed legislation requiring applicants for TANF to pass a drug test. Florida and Arizona are among them; in Oklahoma, plans are underway but a legal challenge is expected from the American Civil Liberties Union (*Oklahoman* Editorial, 2011). Previous studies have indicated that welfare recipients are no more likely to have substance use problems than other members of the population. The trend to deprive some people of welfare benefits is probably related to the economic crisis that began in 2008 and was associated with increasing unemployment, and a huge increase in applications for welfare aid.

The Personal Responsibility and Work Opportunity Act passed by the Clinton administration in 1996 converted the financing of public aid from an entitlement to a system of block grants that shifts many financial incentives and risks from the federal government to the states and, in effect, to the recipients themselves. Since 1996 it has become clear that the time limit of benefits and the work requirement may reduce the number of low-income Americans with substance use problems who will receive even temporary financial aid (Chatterji & Meara, 2010). The prevalence of substance use among TANF recipients is estimated at around 20 percent (Mesch & Pollack, 2005). This means that many of these people, mostly women, could have benefited from treatment for their substance use problems. Yet the work policies that were enacted limited the states' ability to count treatment for substance use or mental health disorders toward the work requirements (Chatterji & Meara, 2010). A temporary but promising demonstration project, CASAWORKS (The National Center on **Addiction** and **Substance Abuse** at Columbia Universityfor Families, found that intensive wraparound services in housing assistance, mental health treatment, medical treatment, and specialized substance abuse treatment for women led to significant decreases in substance use and increases in employment (Metsch & Pollack, 2005).

Changes in other welfare programs that affect women and men equally include the 1997 removal of coverage for all disabilities that were due exclusively to alcohol or drug addiction from eligibility for federal Supplemental Security Income (SSI) and the work requirements associated with TANF. In their analysis of data on former SSI recipients with drug dependency problems, economists Chatterji and Meara (2010) found that the arrest rates for these individuals increased significantly. They also found that although during the low unemployment levels of the 1990s and the boom in the service industry, many former TANF recipients were able to find work. However, following the economic recession of 2008, this would no longer be the case. Changes in the welfare benefits along with a deep and long recession, as these researchers suggest, signal a new era under which vulnerable, low-skilled individuals with substance use disorders increasingly have fewer sources of support. Clearly, treatment services will be even less accessible because of these new economic barriers.

New policies are needed to counteract the effects of diminished coverage for general health and treatment. Extending Medicaid eligibility to former SSI recipients or simply introducing a program of government-funded universal health care would improve treatment access considerably.

POLICIES PERTAINING TO THE TREATMENT PROFESSION

The substance abuse counseling profession, like any of the helping professions, is largely defined in terms of national laws, local and national fiscal reimbursement policies, and the availability of adequate healthcare resources.

Specific laws protecting consumers' rights (e.g., the right to privacy) also have a bearing on how a profession operates. For addiction services providers, legislative mandates provide treatment for certain populations (e.g., offenders on suspended prison sentences) but not for others. Such mandates shape the nature of addictions work in terms of the clientele served as well as the types of services rendered (e.g., total abstinence from alcohol and other drugs may be required for probationers).

MANAGED CARE

Historically, addiction treatment has been marginalized rather than integrated with the rest of the healthcare system. Today, due to rapidly rising costs of general healthcare in the United States—costs related to the demand for expensive new technologies and the aging of the population—there is a strong impetus to cut costs in other directions. Working Americans who typically get their healthcare coverage from their place of work are being moved over from traditional health insurance to managed care plans. The purpose of managed care is not to manage care but to manage costs. Severe limits have been placed on mental health services and substance abuse treatment under these plans regarding the range of services offered (Olmstead & Sindelar, 2005).

In its emphasis on cost containment, managed care has tended to place increasingly restrictive policies on inpatient detoxification treatment, limiting financial coverage for psychotherapeutic addiction treatment to only brief outpatient visits, and an emphasis on psychiatric medication instead of, rather than in addition to, individual therapy ("Managed Care Takes Toll," 1999; Harris, 2011). Managed care is not only a phenomenon in the private sector but a major force in Medicaid health reform proposals as well. Yet as data from national statewide studies show, every $1 of treatment saves at least $12 in other medical and social costs (CASA, 2009).

At the same time that many private, for-profit treatment centers, especially residential units, are closing their doors, there is a tremendous demand for services for people with co-occurring disorders. Yet even though need has increased because of the nation's economic distress and troops returning home from war, two-thirds of states have actually cut mental health care in the last three years, according to a report released by the National Alliance on Mental Illness (NAMI) (2011).

New treatment programming models emphasize case management as well as networking with vocational rehabilitation services, family services, and probation and parole departments. One promising development, similar to the drug court movement, is the mental health court movement (SAMHSA, 2009). Mental health courts are designed to help persons with mental illness who get into trouble with the law stay out of jail by diverting them into treatment. Today there are hundreds of such courts, as described in Chapter 8. Intensive supervision, mental health counseling, medication management, and substance abuse counseling, if needed, are provided.

The days of independent alcoholism treatment centers staffed by licensed alcoholism counselors are over. The "new" addictions therapist must be highly versatile and knowledgeable concerning the major mental disorders as well as the currently popular drugs of misuse and the treatment of persons with dual diagnoses. A strong background in psychology, mental health counseling, or clinical social work is recommended.

Federal funding for addiction treatment has fallen well below the need; the bulk of the money is diverted into the war on drugs, with billions put into military operations in Latin America alone. Across the states, however, the trends are more rational and cost saving; state after state is moving to fund community-based programs for youth and other prevention services. Earlier California, before the state faced a huge economic crisis, passed legislation sending all first-time drug offenders into intensive treatment. Some of the money, as in Iowa and Nebraska, comes from the national tobacco settlement funds and is appropriately being funneled into treatment.

The Law and Ethical Codes

Respect for client confidence is not only an important aspect of the practitioners' code of ethics but is also strictly regulated under federal law pertaining specifically to "alcohol and drug abuse patient records." The law pertaining to alcohol and drug abuse treatment is unique. Rules set forth in federal regulations, entitled "Confidentiality of Alcohol and Drug Abuse Patient Records" (2011), apply to all agencies that provide alcoholism and drug abuse treatment or prevention. The rules are far more stringent than for any other category of treatment (Barsky, 2010). The general rule is no disclosure without the patient's consent. Even with consent, information that is harmful to the patient may not be released. Generally, a court subpoena can be honored only with the client's or former client's consent. Violation of the federal law and regulations by a practice or program is a crime. Exceptions to confidentiality restrictions are suspected child abuse or neglect, medical emergencies, information about a crime committed by a patient or about any threat to commit such a crime, and life-threatening situations.

Involuntary commitment proceedings are fraught with ethical and legal dilemmas. The purpose of the proceedings is to send an individual, for his or her "own good," to a jail-like facility for "treatment." This is usually a life-and-death situation, with the individual in question at risk of harming himself or herself, or others. The first step for the counselor involved in such proceedings is to obtain the facts. Providing information to those outside the treatment program or requests for information from other sources generally require the client's written permission (Barsky, 2010). Such an authorization states the name of the agency, type of information requested, how the information will be used, the agency requesting the information, the date of the request, and the date on which the release expires (usually 6 months later). Requests should be obtained, ordinarily, from lawyers, all family members who may be involved with the client, and relevant agencies with which the client is in communication. Legal complications occur when the client, under proper legal advice, refuses to sign the Consent-for-Release-of-Information form. It becomes impossible under these circumstances to contact family members as witnesses or for input. Should the patient be committed based on medical evidence alone, further restrictions apply regarding communication with the state treatment facility. Treatment and hospital records may not be released to the treatment center, nor may the name of the patient be revealed before his or her arrival.

One legal issue of particular concern to addictions practitioners working with offenders was a ruling in the Seventh Circuit Court of Appeals in Wisconsin (*Kerr v. Farrey,* 1996). A prisoner's (Kerr's) First Amendment rights were violated, according to this ruling, because he was coerced into attending a Narcotics Anonymous (NA) program. Had Kerr not attended, he would have been transferred to a medium-security prison. Because the NA program was ruled to be religious, not secular, Kerr had a right to refuse treatment. Other court rulings at the U.S. district court level have enforced the same principle of separation of church and state. Significantly, as Alexander (2000) indicates, the lack of availability of treatment options is the key factor. If a prison offers options such as Self Management and Recovery Training (SMART) recovery and Women for Sobriety, in addition to Alcoholics Anonymous (AA) or NA attendance, the prisoners' rights are not violated.

Related to the legal constraints on a profession are ethical considerations. Most professions have a code of ethics to protect clients' rights and to discipline members of the profession if they violate those rights. For substance abuse counselors, each state has its own code of ethics. Typical provisions are practicing nondiscriminatory behavior with clients on the basis of race, color, gender, sexual orientation, age, disability, and so on; continuing professional and educational growth; not exploiting clients sexually or financially; and agreeing to report professional misconduct of colleagues, such as violations of client confidentiality. The Association for Addiction Professionals (NAADAC) includes these principles and also directs professionals to present treatment options to clients and inform them of research about the effectiveness of various treatments (see the NAADAC code of ethics at www.naadac. org/certification/185). This latter requirement is consistent with the position advocated in this book that different approaches work better with different people and the belief in client self-determination.

Laura Kaplan (2005) brings our attention to the issue of dual or multiple relationships in a field like addictions in which the employment of consumers as providers is commonplace. Dual relationships occur with the multiple roles consumer-providers take when the provider and client share relationships outside the professional arena. In the substance abuse field, a personal relationship might precede a previous nonprofessional relationship. This may occur among former "drinking buddies" or, less threateningly, fellow AA members. In both cases, the sharing of intimacies in meetings can be problematic for both parties in outside-of-meeting professional roles. Dual relationships may be further problematic because of concerns with risks of, or actual exploitation of, the client and because the professional's judgment may be impaired. Central to these issues is the perception of power differentials in the professional–client relationship in light of the client's inherent vulnerability. Kaplan's recommendation is for open discourse at the agencies on these matters and greater standardization among professional codes of ethics. Counselors should be alert to potential and actual conflicts of interest, inform clients of this, and consult colleagues and supervisors when questions about boundaries between client and professional arise.

THE WAR ON DRUGS

In 1999, the then "drug czar" General Barry McCaffrey made a striking admission. "We have a failed social policy," he said, "and it has to be reevaluated" (Egan, 1999, p. A1). That was a bold statement in its time. Another bold stand was taken in 2007 when the U.S. Conference of Mayors adopted a resolution stating that due to the failure of the drug war, they were calling for a harm reduction–oriented approach to drug policy (Curley, 2007). Recently, the Global Commission on Drug Policy (2011) led by several former presidents of countries in Latin America, issued a carefully documented report that called for an end to drug prohibition. The international war on drugs has backfired, according to the commission; the crackdown has only driven rates of drug use up and created a black market run by murderous cartels. In light of the bloodbath that has resulted in Central America, the commission's report urges a rethinking of zero tolerance policies and a legalization of substances such as cannabis. The nations of Portugal and Australia are singled out for their policies of decriminalization of the use and possession of at least some drugs, policies that have achieved favorable results.

In agreement with the Global Commission's report, former President Jimmy Carter (2011) wrote an opinion piece for the *New York Times*. Entitled, "Call Off the Global Drug War," Carter's editorial recalls that in his presidency in the 1970s, his administration was moving toward decriminalization of possession of small quantities of marijuana. A focus was placed on treatment rather than punishment. But in the 1980s, after he left office, these policies were reversed in a war on drugs that included a futile effort to control drug imports from foreign countries. Since that time, as Carter further stated, the incarceration rates have skyrocketed, the number of people serving time for nonviolent drug offenses having increased more than twelve times since 1980.

The American people are generally in agreement with Carter's observations. According to recent polls, around three of four Americans said we are losing the war on drugs (Angus Reid Public Opinion, 2010; Polling Report, 2011). A slight majority of persons polled favor legalization of marijuana. In Mexico, where over 43,000 people have been killed since the Mexican president declared a war on drug traffickers, tens of thousands took to the streets in Mexico City to protest the horrible killings among rival gang members and demand an end to the drug war (Ellingwood & Bennett, 2011; Malkin, 2011).

The failures of the present punitive government policies include social and legal injustice on a wide scale, racial oppression, wasted resources spent in a futile attempt to reduce the availability of drugs, and the relentless spread of misinformation and propaganda to the American public. In spite of the negative assessments, the war on drugs goes on. Although other programs have been cut or trimmed, the White House has stated that the total national drug control budget for 2012 is expected to reach $26.2 billion ("White House Says the War Is Working," 2011).

There is still some hope for some middle ground here between the side that pushes for full legalization and the side that pushes for continuation and even escalation of the war on drugs. For example, in spite of White House Drug Policy Director Gil Kerlikowske's statement that legalization would be a profound mistake and lead to more harmful consequences (cited in Ellingwood & Bennett, 2011), the proposed 2012 budget contains a request to significantly increase spending on drug prevention programs coupled with a 17.6% decrease for the international part of the war on drugs (Office of the National Drug Control Policy, 2011). And in a more recent statement, Drug Policy Director Kerlikowske states, "I know we cannot arrest our way out of the drug problem. ... The days of treating drug use as exclusively a law enforcement only issue are long gone" (p. 1).

What is the war on drugs? The essential features of the war were developed about two decades ago under the leadership of President Ronald Reagan, although President Nixon first used the term. Under Reagan, the Office of National Drug Control Policy was created, the director of which has become commonly known as the drug czar (Straussner & Isralowitz, 2008). The focus then, as now, was on the supply side of drugs more than on the demand. Under President Bush (Sr.) strict sentencing laws were passed, laws that were designed to remove any judicial discretion and to force federal judges to give mandatory sentences for particular levels of crime. These guidelines were then followed by all 50 U.S. states. Included in these laws were the following stipulations: (1) mandatory minimum sentences and the criminalization of everything that has to do with marijuana, cocaine, heroin, methamphetamines, or other drugs that have been designated illegal; (2) the presumption that abstinence is the only right relationship to those drugs; (3) support for the strategy of international interdiction practices, such as eradicating poppy fields in South America and increasing border surveillance to diminish the supply of drugs in the United States; and (4) using various practices of enforcement such as drug testing, wiretapping, and forfeiture of property. Despite a significant drop in crime over past decades, the prison industry has ballooned into a $40-billion-a-year industry as a concomitant of the punitive and costly war on drugs (Spencer, 2006).

In late 2007, in a landmark decision, the Supreme Court ruled that the mandatory minimum sentences should not be mandatory at all, but merely advisory. Another progressive development occurred in the same month when the agency that sets guidelines for federal prison sentencing voted to lighten punishments retroactively for inmates who were serving draconian sentences for crack cocaine (Stout, 2007). This decision means that many inmates will be released earlier than planned. A personal story that emerged at the hearing before the body that sets the guidelines was reported in this *New York Times* account:

> Iralee Johnson of Orange, N.J., and the 16-year-old granddaughter she is raising, Secoya Jenkins, attended the hearing in the hope that the commission would give a break to Secoya's mother, Nerika. She was convicted of conspiring to distribute crack in Philadelphia and has been in prison more than a decade.
>
> Ms. Johnson blamed her daughter's fall on "bad company" and said she had "learned her lesson," after serving nearly 11 years. Her relatives said she was a first-time nonviolent offender who had just earned an associate college degree. (Stout, 2007, p. A30)

Although these basic policies are still in effect, a philosophical shift has begun to occur in the federal government in its perceptions of drug offender sanctions, as legal scholar Geneva Brown (2010) indicates. Change came in the form of the passage by Congress of the Fair Sentencing Act of 2010. Signed by President Obama, the new law reduced the 100-to-1 sentencing disparity for crack versus powder cocaine to 18-to-1. The act also reduced the mandatory minimum sentence for possession of 10 grams from 10 years to 5 years and removed the mandatory minimum sentence for simple possession of crack cocaine. Although the penalty for using or dealing crack cocaine is still out of proportion to the penalty for involvement with the more expensive powder variety, the new more lenient laws were welcome news in many circles.

MANDATORY SENTENCING

The Bureau of Justice Statistics (2000) report on women offenders provides evidence of racism and classism ingrained in the system. While nearly two-thirds of women under probation supervision are White, nearly two-thirds of those confined in local jails and prisons are minority. And the overwhelming majority of the women sentenced to prison for drug law violations are poor. Women of color have been disproportionately affected by the mandatory minimum sentencing laws. These laws were passed by Congress in 1986 and signed by the president in the urgent rush to capitalize on the much publicized death of college basketball star Len Bias, who died from an overdose of cocaine (powder form) (Sterling & Stewart, 2006). Federal judges were thus required to sentence drug offenders to a certain number of years in prison without parole, often a minimum of 5 years and up to life. The harshest sentences were reserved for crimes related to crack cocaine, the drug associated with inner-city drug use and violence. These laws were geared toward dealers, but they also applied to anyone involved in a "drug conspiracy."

The gendered nature of drug conspiracy laws is highly discriminatory and a clear example of a failed and unjust war on drugs (Gaskins, 2004). As a result of these laws, women saw a significantly faster prison growth rate than men between the years 1995 to 2005 (BJS, 2006) before the increases tapered off, except for White women convicted of meth use, as mentioned previously. To get the big picture of the effect of mandatory minimum sentences, it is helpful to review current figures. According to the U.S. Department of Justice (2006), over 56% of inmates in federal prison are serving time for drug-related crime. The demographic breakdown is given as 92% male, 53.9% Black, 33% Hispanic, and 25.9% noncitizen.

The growth of the prison industry since the federal mandatory guidelines have been in effect has been explosive. In 1986, when federal mandatory minimum sentences were enacted, the Bureau of Prisons budget was $700 million (Office of Management and Budget, 2006). The 2011 budget was increased by $528 million from the year before to a total of $6.8 billion. (Johnson, 2010).

Although their rate of imprisonment has slowed in recent years, the women's prisons are desperately overcrowded from the rapid increase in women's rate of convictions for drug-related crime and for conspiracy crimes when their lives were connected to male drug dealers and users. Between 1977 and 2004, women's rate of increase was twice the male rate (Frost, Greene, & Pranis, 2006). Drug offenses account for around one-third of women confined in state prisons and a majority in federal prisons.

Since 1987, the number of women in federal prison on drug charges has quadrupled. More than 70% of all women inmates were caring for minor children, and many are pregnant when they enter prison, but judges are not allowed to take this into consideration when sentencing (Frost et al., 2006). Gender-neutral policies prevent judges from looking at either the context of the crime or the consequences in their sentencing of women in trouble with the law. The harsh impact on the children is not considered either. Research shows that children whose mothers are incarcerated typically suffer a host of behavioral problems (Gaskins, 2004). According to a legal issue brief by Brown (2010), incarcerated African American women are often single mothers and heads of household before they become offenders. Upon their mothers' incarceration, their children may become displaced and languish in foster care, awaiting their parents' release from prison or, alternatively, become permanently severed from their families.

In *Orange Is the New Black: My Year in a Woman's Prison*, Piper Kerman (2011) describes how the criminal conspiracy laws work and how years after she played a role in transporting drugs from Europe to the United States, she was turned in by the drug dealers so that they could reduce their own sentences. Then in consultation with her lawyer (and she does have a privately hired attorney) she learned about the mandatory minimum sentences and how she had to plead guilty in order to serve a 1- or 2-year sentence or risk serving years and years. As a blond, blue-eyed graduate of Smith College, Kerman was certainly the exceptional inmate. She describes how she stood out as different, and how privileged she was upon her release to return to a stable housing situation, in contrast to other ex-convicts who would most likely face more challenges than they could meet.

Michelle Alexander's (2010) new book, *The New Jim Crow: Mass Incarceration in the Age of Colorblindness* has been widely cited in the popular media, and Alexander has been actively engaged in speaking tours. Drawing on government data, she discusses in passionate terms the social control aspects of sentencing practices that create a situation in which one in nine black men aged 20 to 35 are behind bars. And for large numbers of children, their parents are absent.

Common to both these best-selling books is their depiction of the human side of the statistics, the personal as well as racial dimension of the laws and how the laws are carried out. In addition, they also present the utter futility of incarcerating people whose basic problem is a substance use and possibly mental health problem.

Every year between 1995 and 2005, the total number of women in custody of the federal system expanded by 7.4%; the rate for the entire decade was 72% (BJS, 2006). In 1996 alone approximately 61,000 women were convicted of felony drug offenses in state and federal courts in the United States. Of those women, 43% were convicted of drug possession, not sales.

Between 2000 and 2009, some interesting changes took place. The incarceration figures for males stayed relatively constant over this period, and there was a small increase in the numbers of women sent to prison (BJS, 2010). But a significant increase in the number of white women incarcerated is balanced by a significant decrease in the numbers of imprisoned African American women. In fact, the increase for white women is around 30% for these 9 years. The reason for the discrepancy is the decline in cocaine (crack) convictions and the increase in convictions for meth use. Meth use is disproportionately the drug of choice for whites.

CIVIL ASSET FORFEITURES

A little-known feature of the war on drugs is the practice of law enforcement's taking the money and property of persons "involved" in a drug crime without the owners' being convicted, indicted, or even arrested for a particular crime. An article in the British journal the *Economist* expresses amazement at this strange American practice ("A Truck in the Dock," 2010). In most states, as discussed in the article, the police can seize property under "civil asset forfeiture" laws. This can include cars and boats that will be auctioned off, raising money that then goes toward the budget of the same police department, a clear conflict of interest. An owner can usually challenge a seizure by arguing that he or she did not know his or her property was being used for criminal purposes. But in 38 out of 50 states, the burden of proof is on him or her to prove his or her innocence.

The Civil Asset Forfeiture Reform Act of 2000 (HR 1658), which was designed to restrict the law and give protections, actually made things worse. The new law expanded government forfeiture laws to include approximately 200 felonies and violations, making more property subject to government forfeiture, even after the statute of limitations has passed for criminal prosecution

(Striker, 2003). As before, the level of evidence required is at a lower standard than that for a conviction of a crime, only a "preponderance of evidence" is needed for federal agencies and police to seize property. Under this law, informants are awarded 25–50% of the value of the seized property. The Patriot Act, passed in 2001 and renewed in 2006, has drawn on the expanded forfeiture act to extend the seizure of property associated in any way with suspected crime from suspected terrorists.

Although it seems incredible in the United States that a person's money and property can be seized on the presumption of guilt instead of innocence, federal and state law enforcement agencies are doing just that and are keeping most of the proceeds. Because of the abuses that have occurred with this kind of police power, several states have initiated reforms that toughen legal standards for forfeiture, require a criminal conviction before seizure, and send the forfeited property to other budget categories, such as education rather than law enforcement. In 2002, for example, the New Mexico Drug Policy Project supported successful reform legislation that requires a criminal conviction and proof that the property was used in or is the fruit of criminal activity before it can be seized and forfeited. Oregon, similarly, enacted legislation that requires a conviction before forfeiture and prevents law enforcement from using the proceeds.

When assets of suspected drug dealers are seized, the whole family and other uninvolved persons may suffer grievous loss. Even when the charges are dismissed, the results can be devastating.

DRUG-FREE ZONES

Drug-free zones were originally designed to protect children from drug trafficking by creating safe harbors in places they might gather. Penalties for drug offenses that occur within designated areas increased dramatically. In 1984, an amended version of the 1970 Comprehensive Drug Abuse, Prevention and Control Act provided federal penalties of twice the maximum punishment for drug offenses committed within 1,000 feet of a school, college, or playground or within 100 feet of a youth center, swimming pool, or video arcade. By 2000, every state had adopted some version of a drug-free zone law. Although no state had done an evaluation of the effectiveness or impact of this policy, the increase of harsh sentences on Black and Hispanic citizens began to spark debate about the fairness of such laws and whether drug-free zones actually protected children.

In March 2006, the Justice Policy Institute issued a stunning report called "Disparity by Design: How Drug-Free Zone Laws Impact Racial Disparity and Fail to Protect Youth" (Greene, Pranis, & Ziedenberg, 2006). The report found no evidence that drug-free zone laws protect children (in Massachusetts, fewer than 1% of the drug-free zone cases involved drug sales to youth; in New Jersey, students were involved in only 2% of cases). The laws have primarily been applied to adult-to-adult transactions, and instead of declining, drug arrests in the zones have risen steadily.

A major concern is the disproportionate sentences meted out to racial and ethnic minorities , who are more likely to live within the zones in urban areas. The Justice Policy Institute report also raises the question of whether the drug-free zones are now used primarily to pressure defendants to plead guilty and accept a plea bargain rather than risk the higher sentence of a drug-free-zone law if the case goes to trial.

Although initially many policymakers took these concerns seriously, a recent search as of October, 2011 of arrests in drug-free zones shows evidence of a large numbers of persons charged with drug transactions in these designated areas. The controversy has arisen in Boston with the introduction of a proposal to shrink the school zone area, however, opposition remains strong (Lavoie, 2011). In Pennsylvania reform is gaining momentum to cancel these laws, which are judged to be ineffective in addressing the problem of selling drugs to minors and to be racist in regard to the neighborhoods where the drug-free zones are located (Beck, 2011). Ideally, other states will follow their lead to eliminate the unintended consequences of this policy of "good intentions."

THE PUNISHMENT OF PREGNANT DRUG ADDICTS

The prosecution of women who are pregnant and addicted and the removal of children from their care and custody are other repressive side effects of the war on drugs. The interplay of race, class, and gender is also at its most pronounced in the prosecution of drug-addicted mothers. Under the rationale of protecting the fetus, drug-addicted mothers, who are often poor and women of color are being taken to court. The women who have become the primary targets of government control are the ones who are the least likely to be able to defend themselves. and the least able to conform to the White middle-class standard of motherhood.

Since the mid-1980s, more than 240 women in 35 states have been criminally prosecuted for using substances thought to be harmful to their unborn child during pregnancy (Paltrow, 2004). A well-publicized study by Chasnoff, Burns, Schnoll, and Burns (1985) of cocaine-exposed infants made dire predictions about long-term negative effects on the children's developmental progress. At the same time, the media's publicizing of information about "crack houses," the degradation of women who resorted to sex in exchange for crack, and "crack babies" encouraged judgmental attitudes by the general public against mothers who used drugs. Extremely punitive laws were passed to punish women for their addictive behavior (Szalavitz, 2011).

Harris and Paltrow (2007), writing in the *Journal of the American Medical Association* state that "poverty and its concomitants—poor nutrition and inadequate health care—are now known to overshadow many of the effects popularly attributed to cocaine exposure" (p. 1698). Crack babies are more accurately described as poverty babies, who suffer from the mother's risk factors of substandard environmental conditions and poor healthcare as well as other factors, including prenatal exposure to tobacco, marijuana, or alcohol.

Despite the fact that the earlier media hype over crack babies was never found to be scientifically tenable, it got embodied into law due to a landmark case, *Whitner v. South Carolina,* which became law in 1997 (Sagatun-Edwards, 2003). The case upheld the prosecution of an African American woman who had ingested crack cocaine during the third trimester of her pregnancy. After the baby was found to have cocaine in his bloodstream, the mother was prosecuted under child abuse and endangerment statutes. In a later case, *Ferguson v. City of Charleston,* the U.S. Supreme Court decided that performing a diagnostic test (urine drug screen) on a pregnant mother for the purpose of criminal investigation without her consent is an unreasonable search and is thus unconstitutional (Harris & Paltrow, 2007). Civil laws are not affected by the ruling, however, and in some states, drug use during pregnancy is considered child neglect and can result in the removal of the child when born.

Women's rights campaigners are concerned about new developments that criminalize drug use during pregnancy in a new way with the introduction of fetal homicide laws. At least 38 of the 50 states have introduced such laws that were intended to protect pregnant women and their unborn children from violent attacks by third parties—usually abusive male partners—but are increasingly being turned by prosecutors against the women themselves (Pilkington, 2011). In Alabama at least 40 cases have been brought under the state's "chemical endangerment" law. In one case, for example, a woman who gave birth to a child with Down Syndrome was charged under this law when it was discovered she had used illicit drugs when pregnant. She was charged under a statute that was designed to protect children whose parents were cooking methamphetamine in the home. Consequently, many women have lost custody of their children because some states now consider child neglect to include prenatal exposure to controlled substances. Since drug testing occurs only in publicly funded healthcare facilities, such laws, needless to say, fall chiefly on poor and minority women. There has been no comparable effort to use a newborn's toxicology screen to check for the role of sperm (damaged by drug use) in causing birth defects (van Wormer & Bartollas, 2010).

Attorney Lynn Paltrow (2004), who specializes in laws that punish pregnant women for potential harm to the fetus, brings our attention to the significance of a law passed and signed by President Bush in 2004—the Unborn Victims of Violence Act. This law, which was aimed at abortion, makes it a crime to cause harm to a "child in utero." More than 30 states have similar laws on the books. Paradoxically, as Paltrow indicates, this federal law does not make it a federal crime to physically attack pregnant women, yet homicide is one of the major causes of death to pregnant women.

The media hyperbole that played into the crackdown on mothers who used crack while pregnant is now being directed toward meth and the mothers associated with this illicit drug. In response to the barrage of stories that appeared in the media concerning an epidemic of birth defects caused by meth use in pregnant women, over 90 leading doctors, scientists, and treatment specialists released a public letter calling on the media to stop the use of terms such as *meth babies* and to consult experts to obtain factual information about the actual effects of prenatal exposure to particular drugs (Lewis, 2005). The use of such terms as "crack baby," they state, harms the children to which they are applied, lowers expectations for their academic success, and is without scientific basis. The suggestion that treatment will not work for people dependent on meth, particularly mothers, also lacks any scientific basis, according to the letter.

"Woman sentenced for drunken breast-feeding" is a headline in the Associated Press (2009) from North Dakota. This woman was arrested by police who answered a domestic disturbance call at her home and found her feeding her baby while drunk.

Both pregnancy and drug "epidemics" are issues ripe for government exploitation and a way of diverting the people's attention away from the major, structural problems onto issues of individual "morality." Drug wars (whether they involve inner-city Blacks and Latinos associated with crack cocaine or poor rural Whites involved in meth production) today make excellent scapegoats, and the international war on drugs can be justified on the basis of images of people strung out on drugs. The increase in the prison population and huge expenditures on the prison industrial complex take billions of dollars that otherwise could be spent on housing, healthcare, and substance abuse treatment on demand.

In summary, women continue to be singled out for blame for using drugs during pregnancy, as they were in the late 19th and early 20th centuries. It appears easier to blame individual women than to acknowledge that the problem of substance use for women has been aggravated by the increase in poverty, homelessness, substandard education, and lack of healthcare and treatment options since the 1980s.

The unfortunate consequence of legal threats to pregnant women has been to deter some women from seeking prenatal care at all. In addition, policies intended to respond to the concerns about drug use during pregnancy do not work to protect the health of women or the babies they are carrying (Paltrow, 2006; Szalavitz, 2011). (In Norway, compulsory but compassionate drug treatment of pregnant substance using mothers is provided until the time of delivery in homelike facilities [Helsedepartementet, 2004]). Perhaps the key issue here is not about punishing drug use in pregnant women but about addressing women's basic social and health needs, which exist with or without pregnancy and do not end with delivery of the baby.

Systems of Payment and Insurance Coverage

As indicated previously, most of the women incarcerated in the United States are serving time for drug-related crimes, and most of them have histories of serious long-term substance abuse problems in conjunction with mental health concerns. The latter is related to the fact that prisons have become the dumping grounds for persons with mental illness. Not surprisingly, a review of the literature suggests that most women who are released from jail or prison are likely to return to the same difficult conditions that played into their legal problems in the first place (Kerman, 2011; Richie, 2004). When unaccustomed child care responsibilities for children who have their own serious problems and resentments are thrust upon them, the challenges can be tremendous. The lack of financial resources only makes the situation more difficult.

Relapse and recidivism risks are major public health problems that echo the original risks that were the cause of grief to the women and their families in the first place. We are referring to the lack of treatment availability for women (and the men in their lives) due to the lack of nationalized healthcare in this country. The majority of the women who were arrested due to drug abuse violations and studied in the government's Arrestee Drug Abuse Monitoring (ADAM) annual report (Taylor, Newton, & Brownstein, 2003) did not have healthcare coverage.

As noted in Chapter 4, women entering treatment, especially women from highly family-oriented cultures, do better with treatment that is comprehensive, involves children, is family focused, and lasts long enough to engage the participant in skills or language training when appropriate. The system of payment and reimbursement from state and federal funding sources does not support any of these goals. Cutbacks in funding for health and social services have been dismantling the minimal infrastructure that existed to care for people with drug problems or, better yet, to prevent them in the first place (Miller & Carroll, 2006). Major funding obstacles include reimbursement rates that do not cover costs of care or of effective co-ordination of funding streams, especially between mental health and substance abuse services. Reimbursement schedules, moreover, are geared to individuals, not families. And federal drug policy, as we know, continues to emphasize costly law enforcement and incarceration.

The 2010 passage of healthcare reform means that millions of Americans will have insurance coverage for addiction treatment as part of their basic benefit package, assuming that the healthcare reform passes the legal hurdles that have been placed in its path. According to SAMHSA (2011), the Affordable Care Act will provide healthcare coverage to millions of Americans who are now uninsured and give them access to prevention programming, early intervention, and treatment of mental and substance use disorders.

Harm reduction strategies should be more widely used in the future, given the Obama administration's emphasis on prevention. Harm reduction policies could be far more effectively instituted than they are at present in one-stop health and social service settings such as exist in Western Europe rather than in the type of specialized treatment clinics set up in the United States, each with different and competing funding sources. A serious consequence of such specialized services, as Miller and Carroll (2006) suggest, has been "continued stigmatization and an unwarranted mystique that has overemphasized the importance of acute treatment" (p. 303). The diseases of addiction can be managed as other chronic health problems are, with a focus on prevention rather than treatment when people are already seriously impaired.

HARM REDUCTION

Although harm reduction continues to be one of the more controversial issues in the substance abuse treatment arena, it is widely recognized in general areas of public health—in the reliance on designated drivers, the mandating of labels issuing warnings on tobacco and all kinds of other potentially harmful products, immunizations, nicotine replacement therapy, and safe havens (anonymous drop-off places for unwanted infants)...the list is endless. Harm reduction exemplifies the social work value base and our professional commitment to social justice and human rights (Abbott, 2003). As advocated by Brocato and Wagner (2003), this approach is built around social work's values of respect for human dignity, social justice, and client self-determination. It also relates to commitments by all the helping professions to identify the best empirically based practices at the micro- and macro-levels and advocates for these rather than traditional punitive approaches that have been shown ineffective or downright harmful (Miller & Carroll, 2006). The need, as expressed by Ann Abbott (2003), is for a multifaceted approach that encompasses primary, secondary, and tertiary care; a coupling of research and practice; and a marriage of prevention and intervention.

There is an emphasis today on the importance of teaching students of social work and related professions about the effectiveness of harm reduction strategies and how they actually work. At Southern Illinois University at Carbondale, for example, Professor Elisabeth Reichert leads a group of social work students twice yearly for 10-day tours in Germany and Switzerland to observe harm reduction programs in action (Gates, 2011). One of the places on the tour is Stiftung Suchthilfe, a harm reduction agency in the city of Saint Gallen, Switzerland. This treatment center offers treatment services for people with chemical dependency, including a medical-grade heroin distribution center.

Although social work and the harm reduction approach are more highly integrated in Canada and Europe than in the United States, we have seen some promising developments in recent years. The National Association of Social Workers (NASW) (2009), for instance, in its policy statement handbook, endorses a comprehensive public health approach for the prevention of alcohol, tobacco, and other drug problems. It has also endorsed harm reduction interventions for persons affected by such problems.

Syringe or needle exchange to prevent the spread of HIV/AIDS virus is one of the best-known public health prevention programs in the United States. It is estimated that 20–34% of people who have contracted HIV/AIDS or hepatitis C in the United States acquired these diseases through sharing contaminated syringes and other drug injection equipment (CDC, 2010; Drug Policy Alliance, 2007). Among women and children, 75% of new AIDS cases can be directly or indirectly attributed to injection drug use. Women who become infected with HIV can transmit the virus to their babies before or during birth or through breastfeeding. African Americans and Hispanics are disproportionately impacted.

According to empirically available research compiled by the Centers for Disease Control and Prevention (CDC) (2010), one of the most effective strategies for reducing the transmission of HIV and other blood-borne infections is ensuring that injection drug users have access to sterile syringes. In recent years, the U.S. has seen a significant decline (80%) in the number of injection-related transmitted HIV incidence. Today, 35 states and 60 countries operate needle exchanges (Lee, 2011). These exchanges, which often provide counseling and other services, are essential to community public health, a fact that was recognized much earlier in European countries.

Another popular form of harm reduction is the use of methadone maintenance to keep heroin users stabilized and to reduce the crime rate, as people can use methadone as a substitute drug (see Chapter 3). The World Health Organization (WHO, 2009a) has endorsed the use of methadone and buprenorphine (Suboxone) as the preferred treatments because they are of proven effectiveness over detoxification alone and because they can be used in a supervised fashion in both inpatient and outpatient settings. The WHO does not recommend heroin maintenance because research studies have been too limited. In the United States, buprenorphine has an advantage over methadone in that it can be prescribed in a doctor's office. Some countries, such as England, Canada, and Switzerland, have established heroin prescription programs where users can stabilize or decrease the use of heroin, hold legitimate employment, and live normal lives without the threat of contracting a disease such as AIDS (Pycroft, 2010).

THE MIDDLE ROAD

There are those who would describe the controversies surrounding the war on drugs as an argument between legalization and criminalization. Legalization would entail treating a substance, such as marijuana, the same as tobacco—regulating it, taxing it, and marketing it. Decriminalization would entail allowing people to use the drug without any penalties being imposed, but the drug would not be sold at grocery stores and other public places. When Portugal decriminalized the personal use of all drugs, including heroin and cocaine, the foreign media "set alarm bells ringing" ("Treating, Not Punishing," 2009, p. 43). Because drug possession is still illegal, users of these drugs could be stopped by police, have the drugs confiscated, and be sent to appear before a commission to be questioned, but no punishments are handed out. Researchers at the Cato Institute, an American think tank, studied the effects of the decriminalization in Portugal and found positive results: Drug trafficking and other crimes were significantly reduced, as were deaths from drug overdose.

The Portuguese drug policy's emphasis is on the health aspect of drug use. Officials believe that by removing fears of prosecution, the policy has encouraged people who desire it to enter treatment. Statistics on persons requesting treatment bear this out. Research that has examined Vancouver, Canada's, safe injection site similarly shows that a harm reduction approach reduces behaviors that lead to deadly infections such as HIV and hepatitis C. Harm reduction also reduces public disorder by getting intravenous (IV) drug use off the streets (Picard, 2011). Decriminalization and harm reduction are clearly pragmatic approaches. However, even though Canadian policies are conservative compared to those of the Netherlands, where "coffee shops" also sell joints of marijuana, they are unlikely to receive a warm reception anytime soon in the United States.

In contrast to the moralistic approach to drug abuse and a heavy reliance on law enforcement, the harm reduction model views addiction as an adaptive response to a wide range of variables that influence behavior (Sowers & Rowe, 2009). Recently, the American Society of Addiction Medicine (2011), the largest professional society of doctors dedicated to treating and preventing addiction, released a new definition of addiction, calling it a brain disorder rather than a behavioral problem. This was in response to scientific findings that the brain adapts to the presence of addictive substances and changes following long-term exposure to drugs. A loss of control over the substance is a defining characteristic. From a harm reduction perspective, the challenge is to help people break the addiction cycle and to avoid negative consequences related to their behavior. This finding is endorsed by the WHO (World Health Organization) (2009b):

> WHO strongly supports harm reduction as an evidence-based approach to HIV prevention, treatment and care for drug users. WHO advocates for universal access to a comprehensive harm reduction package of interventions for drug injectors which include needle and syringe programmes, drug dependence treatment—in particular opioid substitution therapy—as well as risk reduction counseling, HIV counseling and testing and, HIV care and treatment. (p. 1)

The comprehensive report "Shoveling Up" from the National Center on Addiction and Substance Abuse at Columbia University (CASA) (2009) provides another strong call for change in the direction of a sustainable national policy. As CASA founder and leader Joseph A. Califano Jr. stated upon release of the report:

> Under any circumstances spending more than 95 percent of taxpayer dollars on the consequences of tobacco, alcohol and other drug abuse and addiction and less than two percent to relieve individuals and taxpayers of this burden would be considered a reckless misallocation of public funds. In these economic times, such upsidedown-cake public policy is unconscionable. (p. 1)

The facts revealed in this report constitute a searing indictment of governmental policies at every level. This comprehensive report on state spending considered all the costs of substance use and addiction in 16 budget categories and found that of every dollar the states spent on dealing with substance use and addiction, 96 cents went to "shoveling up the wreckage," and only 4 cents were used to prevent and treat it.

One encouraging development is that the federal Medicaid program started to pay for screening and brief intervention in January 2007. New codes for treatment reimbursement have been added to Medicaid and Medicare to encourage doctors and public health programs to address alcohol and other drug disorders; private sector facilities, however, are not affected (Curley, 2006).

An extensive national survey found that nearly three out of four Americans agree that health insurance should cover the cost of addiction treatment (Hazelden, 2009). With the passage of the U.S. Mental Health Parity Law, signed into law by the Obama administration, insurance plans that offer both physical and mental health benefits must treat the two similarly (SAMHSA, 2010). The law applies to Medicaid managed care plans as well as to other insurance plans, but not to employers with fewer than 50 employees. The passage of health care reform in 2010 is a major step forward, assuming it clears the legal and political challenges ahead related to right wing opposition. The Affordable Health Care Act of 2010 should lead to noticeable changes in public substance abuse treatment services by increasing funding, expanding the variety of treatment provision, and promoting integration of treatment into the mainstream of general health care (Buck, 2011). The reliance on managed care, however, seriously restricts residential treatment.

While social policy change in a progressive direction has been tediously slow at the federal level, there are many exciting initiatives at the state and local levels. Most are geared to the provision of treatment in lieu of incarceration for drug misusers. The introduction of the drug court system is the most conspicuous of these initiatives. It is crucial for social workers and other practitioners in this and related fields to engage in policy analysis to influence legislation through lobbying at the state and local levels. For up-to-date facts that should be of interest to policymakers seeking cost-effective alternatives to incarceration, visit "Making Drug Policy at the State Level" at www.drugstrategies.org/criticalchoices

Clearly, the war on drugs has not brought the desired result in stemming the flow of illicit drugs. There is no correlation between the harshness of drug laws in a nation and the incidence of drug taking; in fact, citizens living under regimes of prohibition such as in the United States take more drugs than citizens living in more liberal countries such as the Netherlands or Norway (*Economist*, 2009). Likewise, the incarceration of large numbers of people for drug-related offenses has shown little benefit. Fortunately, the tide seems to be turning, and a new consensus is building for treatment of addiction as a public health rather than a criminal justice problem. The social work profession's endorsement of harm reduction strategies is a welcome, pragmatic approach to substance abuse and dependency.

POLICIES RELATED TO GAMBLING

Although the economic recession resulted in declines in gambling revenues in the United States between 2008 and 2010, the gambling industry has overall proven to be near recession-proof. Revenues are expected to increase from $57.2 billion in 2009 to $63.3 billion by 2014 (PriceWaterhouseCooper, 2011). Part of the way some casinos are able to weather the recession is to market to new niche demographics. Instead of focusing on elders, for example, casinos in Southern California are aggressively targeting Hispanics. New programming includes bilingual dealers for blackjack, inviting signs printed in Spanish, and concerts featuring popular Spanish-speaking entertainers. It is working. "People in Vegas would kill for our numbers," touts one casino manager after remaking the casino with a Spanish flair (Medina, 2011, p. A1).

As a result of new marketing and the persistent urge of Americans to gamble, the gambling industry has quickly become one of the biggest and politically most powerful special interests in the country. Forty-eight states have some form of legal gambling, but only 26 appropriate money for treatment, according to an in-depth study by the Community News-paper Holdings, Inc. (CNHI) news service (Jewell, 2006). Only $35.5 million of the total earnings are spent by government and industry in treatment and educational programming. Usually, the money allocated is a percentage of the state earnings.

What is the social cost of the explosion of gambling in this country? Economist Earl Grinois (2004), in his book *Gambling in America*, estimates that addicted gamblers cost the United States between $32.4 billion to $53.8 billion a years in costs such as lost work time, burglaries, embezzlement, related gambling crimes, spousal abuse, child neglect, foreclosures, suicides, bankruptcies, and so on. While the National Problem Gambling Council (2011) estimates the cost to be much lower ($7 billion), the cost is still staggering.

Because the costs of problem gambling were beginning to dawn on the American public, Congress created the National Gambling Impact Study Commission (NGISC) in 1996 to study the impact of gambling in the United States and recommend ways to regulate it. According to Common Cause (2000), the gambling industry so feared supervision, regulation, and potential new taxes that it more than doubled its campaign contributions, to $5.4 million, in political action committee (PAC) and soft money contributions to both parties in 1995 and 1996. It was also successful in watering down the powers of the commission and stacking it with the appointment of several progambling people. Nevertheless, the NGISC Report (1999) has been instrumental in alerting many to the lack of policies and regulation, which impacts on those people who may become or already are addicted to gambling.

A national helpline now operates along with state helplines in most of the states that have some type of legalized gambling. About half of these states, as mentioned earlier, support some type of treatment with public funding, but the level of funding is miniscule compared to income the state receives from gambling enterprises. For example, in Minnesota in 2006, 2% of the state's income from gambling went into educational and treatment allocations, compared to ½ of 1% in Iowa and 1% in Oregon.

A policy recommendation of the National Gambling Impact Study Commission (1999) was that states mandate private and public insurers and managed care providers to "identify successful treatment programs, educate participants about pathological gambling and treatment options, and cover the appropriate programs under their plans" (p. 34). In addition, the commission urged that state and tribal governments use a proportion of their gambling revenue to fund problem gambling–specific research, prevention, education, and treatment programs.

Other important recommendations by the NGISC included restricting all gambling to those who are at least 21 years of age (many states allow lottery tickets to be sold to 18-year-olds), removing slot machines from neighborhood stores, banning betting on collegiate and amateur athletic events, banning aggressive advertising that targets impoverished neighborhoods and youth, prohibiting Internet gambling and passing legislation stating that any credit card debts incurred while gambling on the Internet are unrecoverable, and banning credit card cash advance machines from the immediate area where gambling takes place.

Three changes in national policy recommended by the NGISC had the potential to greatly impact the dismal state of affairs: (1) add gambling to the National Household Survey on Drug Abuse and any other appropriate national surveys on mental health; (2) initiate and fund research by the National Institutes of Health, SAMHSA, or any other appropriate federal agency; and (3) require that all state and tribal governments cooperate fully in any research undertaken by the states to fulfill these recommended policies.

Unfortunately, most of these policies were never implemented. New efforts to minimize the damage of problem gambling through coordinated public health policy have been developed and are recommended by the National Council on Problem Gambling (NCPG). One of these efforts is to strengthen the Prohibition of Internet Gaming, Internet Poker Regulation and UIEGA Enforcement Act (largely unenforced and currently ineffectual) by (NCPG, 2011a):

1. Expanding the scope of the bill to include prevention, public awareness, and treatment.
2. Increasing the annual revenue to $15 million to help states cope with the social costs of problem gambling.
3. Allocating these funds to the Substance Abuse and Mental Health Services Administration (SAMHSA) to distribute through competitive grants for problem gambling prevention, research, and treatment.
4. Requiring operators to provide appropriate access to de-identified data on player behavior for research purposes.

These recommendations are also embodied as main provisions in the Comprehensive Problem Gambling Act (HR 2334) that is a bipartisan bill currently sponsored by 73 representatives in the House and 5 senators (NCPG, 20011b). One of the selling points for this bill is that for every dollar spent on gambling addiction services, taxpayers save more than $2.00 in social costs (NCPG, 2011b).

A further development that may help move these legislative efforts forward is the inclusion of pathological gambling in the "behavioral addictions" category of the new DSM-V. Hopefully, this will improve access to treatment through expanded health insurance coverage. Other potential advantages include an increased awareness of problem gambling among mental health providers, the consideration of gambling abuse, and the likelihood that research and funding efforts will become more available (Petry, 2006).

SOME POSITIVE STEPS TOWARD HARM REDUCTION

Since we published the last edition of this book, some positive strides have been made toward harm reduction. Among them are the following:

- Enhanced understanding of addiction as a brain disorder rather than a behavior problem (ASAM, 2011). A major theoretical breakthrough has occurred in the NIAAA's (2011) recognition that many persons with alcohol addiction can become moderate drinkers at a later stage and the advocacy of a public health approach to addiction.
- A growing number of states are renouncing some of the long prison sentences that have been a hallmark of the war on drugs and are focusing instead on treatment (Koppel & Fields, 2011).
- University counseling programs now focus more on harm reduction through a motivational enhancement focus, instead of a traditional total abstinence model (Higher Education Center, 2009).
- A significant increase in housing-first programs that do not require alcohol and other drug abstinence for residents (Vengerowsky, 2011).
- The Department of Health and Human Services has selected nine graphic and repulsive images to be placed on cigarette packs to deter smoking (Wilson, 2011).
- Passage of a law to repeal the needle exchange funding ban and to allow for federal funding of needle exchange was a major breakthrough toward AIDS prevention efforts (Egelko, 2009).
- Passage of a new law reducing the disparity in penalties for the use of crack and powder cocaine and the Supreme Court ruling that mandatory minimum sentencing laws were guidelines and not mandatory (Stout, 2007).
- Administration officials are promoting the use of drug courts, mental health courts, and veterans' courts, where judges can sentence offenders to treatment and other terms as alternatives to jail time (SAMHSA, 2009).
- The White House is working to expand reentry programs that aim to reduce recidivism rates by assisting the nearly 750,000 drug offenders released from prison each year to transition more easily back into communities (Ellingwood & Bennett, 2011).

SUMMARY AND CONCLUSION

At the public policy level, we have looked beyond the problems of the individual person to the bigger picture of how our society cares for its members who may be vulnerable to the consequences of addiction at one time or another in their lives. We ask these questions: As a society, what do we do for the poor and addicted? How do we care for women and other minorities who may be quadruple-oppressed by also being poor, addicted, and HIV positive?

Positive policies, such as funding drug courts; spending public money on prevention and treatment; building safety nets of healthcare, job, and educational opportunities; and supporting harm reduction policies such as methadone maintenance and syringe exchanges are under way. However, the impact of criminalization, mandated minimum sentences, civil forfeiture, and punishment of pregnant and addicted women means we still have a long way to go before harm reduction policies become the norm rather than the exception.

We are at a crossroads in this country in terms of public policy. We can go forward with a reasoned, compassionate approach that is "user friendly" to those who want to change their relationship to an addiction, or we can continue to punish and shame them in an effort to make them give it up. We can make accurate information available to the public that may prevent addiction to gambling, or we can pretend that gambling has no addictive qualities and merely provides needed money to states in lieu of taxes. In each area of public policy we have discussed, there is a choice to be made. We agree with social work educators Straussner and Isralowitz (2008) that the harm reduction movement, which is "well established in Europe, Canada, and Australia, appears to be growing rapidly in the United States, although how well it will be incorporated within traditional AOD (alcohol and other drug) treatment facilities remains to be seen.

REFERENCES

A truck in the dock. (2010, May 27). *Economist*. Retrieved from http://www.economist.com

Abbott, A. A. (2003). Meeting the challenges of substance misuse: Making inroads one step at a time. *Health and Social Work, 28*(2), 83–88.

Alexander, R. (2000). *Counseling, treatment and intervention: Methods with juvenile and adult offenders*. Belmont, CA: Wadsworth.

Alexander, M. (2010). *The new Jim Crow: Mass incarceration in the age of color-blindness*. New York: The New Press.

American Society of Addiction Medicine (ASAM). (2011, April 12). Public policy statement: Definition of addiction. Chevy Chase, MD: ASAM.

Angus Reid Public Opinion. (2010, July 21). Americans decry war on drugs, blame Mexico for allowing cartels to grow. Retrieved from http://www.visioncritical.com

Associated Press. (2009). Woman sentenced for drunken breast-feeding. MSNBC TV. Retrieved from http:www.msnbc.msn.com

Barsky, A. (2010). *Ethics and values in social work: An integrated approach for a comprehensive curriculum*. New York: Oxford University Press.

Beck, B. (2011, August 24). Sentencing reform gains momentum in Pennsylvania. *U.S. Politics Today*. Retrieved from http://uspolitics.einnews.com

Brewington, K. (2009, February 8). Foundation finds support for clinical heroin programs. *Baltimore Sun*. Retrieved from www.baltimoresun.com

Brocato, J., & Wagner, E. (2003). Harm reduction: A social work practice model and social justice agenda. *Health and Social Work, 28*(2), 117–125.

Brown, D. (2006, June 9). Drug-related deaths hit 10-year low in Baltimore. *Washington Post*, p. A10.

Brown, G. (2010, November). *The intersectionality of race, gender, and reentry: Challenges for African-American women*. American Constitution Society for Law and Society: Washington, DC.

Buck, J. (2011, November 8). The looming expansion and transformation of public substance abuse treatment under the Affordable Care Act. *Health Affairs, 30*(8), 1402–1410.

Bureau of Justice Statistics (BJS). (2000). *Women offenders*. Washington, DC: U.S. Department of Justice.

Bureau of Justice Statistics (BJS). (2005). *Substance dependence, abuse, and treatment of jail inmates*. Washington, DC: U.S. Department of Justice.

Bureau of Justice Statistics (BJS). (2006, May). *Prison and jail inmates at midyear 2005*. U.S. Department of Justice. Washington, DC: Office of Justice Programs.

Bureau of Justice Statistics (BJS). (2010, June). *Prison inmates at midyear 2009*. Washington, DC: Office of Justice Programs.

Carter, J. (2011, June 16). Call off the global drug war. *New York Times*, p. A35.

Centers for Disease Control and Prevention (CDC). (2010, November 19). Syringe exchange programs: United States. *Morbidity and Mortality Weekly Report*. Retrieved from http://www.cdc.gov

Chasnoff, I., Burns, W., Schnoll, S., & Burns, K. (1985). Cocaine use in pregnancy. *New England Journal of Medicine, 313*, 666–669.

Chatterji, P., & Meara, E. (2010). Consequences of eliminating federal disability benefits for substance abusers. *Journal of Health Economics, 29*(2), 226–240.

Common Cause. (2000). *Paying the price: How tobacco, gun, gambling, and alcohol interests block common sense solutions to some of the nation's most urgent problems*. Retrieved from http://www.commoncause.org/publications/campaign_finance.htm

Confidentiality of Alcohol and Drug Abuse Patient Records. (2011, August 25). Part 2. Title 42—Public health. Electronic code of federal regulations. Retrieved from http://ecfr.gpoaccess.gov

Curley, B. (2006, October 5). Medicaid will pay for addiction screening: Advocates seek AMA action too. *Join Together Online*. Retrieved from http:// www.join-together.org

Curley, B. (2007, July 18). U.S. mayors declare drug war a failure. *Join Together Online*. Retrieved from http://www.jointogether.org

Drug Policy Alliance. (2007). *Sterile syringe access*. Retrieved from http://www.drug-policy.org/

Egan, T. (1999, February 28). War on crack retreats, still taking prisoners. *New York Times*, p. A1.

Egelko, B. (2009, December 18). U.S. repeals funding ban for needle exchanges. *San Francisco Chronicle*. Retrieved from http://articles.sfgate.com

Ellingwood, K., & Bennett, B. (2011, June 1). High-profile panel urges non-criminal approach to world drug policy. *Los Angeles Times*. Retrieved from http://www.latimes.com

Federation of American Scientists. (1997, September 2). *Press conference: Drug experts call for "Third Way"—neither drug war nor legalization*. Retrieved from http://www.fas.org/drugs/drugspr.htm

Frost, N., Greene, J., & Pranis, K. (2006). *Hard hit: The growth in the imprisonment of women, 1977–2004*. Institute on Women and Criminal Justice. Retrieved October 2006 from http://www.wpaonline.org/institute/hardhit

Gaskins, S. (2004). "Women of circumstance": The effects of mandatory minimum sentencing on women minimally involved in drug crimes. *American Criminal Law Review, 41*(4), 1533–1554.

Gates, T. (2011, Summer). Social work students learn about harm reduction in Switzerland. *New Social Worker Online.* Retrieved from http://www.socialworker.com

Global Commission on Drug Policy. (2011, June). *War on drugs: Report of the global commission on drug policy.* Retrieved from www.globalcommissionondrugs.org

Greene, J., Pranis, K., & Ziedenberg, J. (2006). Disparity by design: How drug-free zone laws impact racial disparity—and fail to protect youth. Justice Policy Institute Report. Retrieved September 30, 2006, from http://www.justicepolicy.org/reports/SchoolZonesReport06.pdf

Grinois, E. (2004). *Gambling in America.* Cambridge, UK: Cambridge University Press.

Harris, G. (2011, March 5). Talk doesn't pay, so psychiatry turns instead to drug therapy. *New York Times,* p. A1.

Harris, L., & Paltrow, L. (2007). The status of pregnant women and fetuses in US criminal law. *Journal of American Medical Association, 289*(13), 1697–1699.

Hazelden. (2009, February 2). *Survey finds Americans want change to support substance abuse treatment. Press release.* Center City, MN: Hazelden.

Helsedepartementet (Health Department). (2004, July). Bedre behandlingstilbud til rusmiddelmisbrukere [Better treatment offer for substance misusers]. Retrieved from http://narkoman.net/doc/russtrategidokument.pdf

Higher Education Center. (2009). Models of exemplary, effective, and promising alcohol or other drug abuse prevention programs on college campuses grant program. Washington, DC: U.S. Department of Education.

Jewell, D. (2006, May 18). Gambling begets millions of neglected addicts. Community Newspaper Holdings, Inc. (CNHI) News Service. *MacAlester News-Capital* (Southeast Oklahoma). Retrieved October 2006 from http://www.mcalesternews.com/homepage

Johnson, K. (2010, February 4). 2011 Federal budget gives $528 million. *USA Today.* Retrieved from http://www.usatoday.com

Kaplan, L. E. (2005). Dual relationships: The challenges for social workers in recovery. *Journal of Social Work Practice in the Addictions, 5*(3), 73–90.

Kerr v. Farrey, 95 F. 3rd 472 (7th Cir. 1996).

Kerlikowske, G. (2011, September 8). *Statement from White House drug policy director Kerlikowske on the results of the 2010 national survey on drug use and health.* Washington, DC: Office of National Drug Control Policy.

Kerman, P. (2011). *Orange is the new black: My year in a women's prison.* New York: Random House.

Koppel, N., & Fields, G. (2011, March 5). States rethink drug laws. *Wall Street Journal,* p. A3.

Lavoie, D. (2011, January 28). Proposal to shrink drug-free school zone draws ire. *Boston Globe.* Retrieved from www.boston.com

Lee, K. (2011, August 22). Denver groups must apply by Friday to be needle-exchange sites. *Denver Post.* Retrieved from http://www.denverpost.com

Lewis, D. (2005, July 27). *Top medical doctors, scientists and specialists urge major media outlets not to create "meth baby" myth.* Public letter reprinted by National Advocates for Pregnant Women. Retrieved from http://www.advocatesfor-pregnantwomen.org

Malkin, E. (2011, May 9). Tens of thousands march in Mexico. *New York Times*, p. A8.

Managed care takes a toll on substance-abuse treatment. (1999, July 15). Retrieved from http://www.jointogether.org.

Medina, J. (2011, August 29). Casino town puts its money on Hispanic market. *New York Times*, p. A1.

Metsch, L., & Pollack, H. (2005). Welfare reform and substance abuse. *Milbank Quarterly*, *83*(1), 65–99.

Miller, W. R., & Carroll, K. M. (2006). Drawing the science together: Ten principles, ten recommendations. In W. R.Miller & K. M.Carroll (Eds.), *Rethinking substance abuse: What the science shows* (pp. 293–312). New York: Guilford Press.

National Alliance on Mental Illness (NAMI). (2011, March 9). *State mental health cuts are a national crisis*. Retrieved from http://www.nami.org

National Association of Alcohol Abuse and Alcoholism (NIAAA) (2011, February). Alcoholism isn't what it used to be. *NIAAA Spectrum*. Retrieved from http://www.spectrum.niaaa.nih.gov/features/alcoholism.aspx

National Association of Social Workers (NASW). (2009). Alcohol, tobacco and other drugs. *Social work speaks: NASW policy statements* (pp. 29–37). Washington, DC: NASW Press.

National Center on Addiction and Substance Abuse at Columbia University (CASA). (2009). *Shoveling up II: The impact on federal, state, and local budgets*. New York: CASA.

National Council on Problem Gambling (NCPG). (2011a). *Strengthen online poker bill problem gambling provisions*. Retrieved from http://www.ncpgambling.org

National Council on Problem Gambling (NCPG). (2011b). *Fight gambling addiction*. Retrieved from http://www.ncpgambling.org

National Gambling Impact Study Commission. (1999, June 18). *Report of the commission*. Washington, DC: U.S. Government Printing Office.

National Survey on Drug Use and Health. (2010). *National findings*. SAMHSA, Office of Applied Studies. Retrieved from http://www.oas.samhsa.gov

Office of Management and Budget. (2006). *Meeting presidential goals*. Retrieved October 2006 from http://www.whitehouse.gov/omb/budget

Office of National Drug Control Policy. (2011). *National drug control budget: FY 2012 Funding highlights*. Washington, DC: Executive Office of the President.

Oklahoman Editorial. (2011, August 11). Oklahoman lawmaker's idea to drug test welfare recipients may face legal hurdles. *Oklahoman*. Retrieved from http://newsok.com

Olmstead, T., & Sindelar, J. (2005). Does the impact of managed care on substance abuse treatment services vary by provider profit status? *Health Services Research*, *40*, 1862–1882.

Paltrow, L. M. (2004, April 5). The pregnancy police. *AlterNet*. Retrieved from http://www.alternet.org

Paltrow, L. M. (2006, July 17). *Blaming pregnant women*. Tom Paine, Common Sense, Institute for America's Future. Retrieved from http://www.tompaine.com

Petry, N. (2006). Should the scope of addictive behaviors be broadened to include pathological gambling? *Addiction*, *10*(Suppl. 1), 152–160.

Picard, A. (2011, April 17). Vancouver's safe injection site cuts overdose deaths. *Globe and Mail*. Retrieved from http://www.theglobeandmail.com

Pilkington, E. (2011, June 29). Outcry in America as pregnant women who lose babies face murder charges. The Guardian. Retrieved from www.guardian.co.uk

Polling Report. (2011). *Illegal drugs.* Retrieved from http://www.pollingreport.com

PriceWaterhouseCooper. (2011). Playing to win. Retrieved from www.pwc.com/e&m

Pycroft, A. (2010). *Understanding and working with substance misusers.* London: SAGE.

Rethinking addiction: Expanding treatment isn't enough. (2011, July 16). *Baltimore Sun.* Retrieved from http://www.baltimoresun.com

Richie, B. E. (2004). Challenges incarcerated women face as they return to their communities. In M.Chesney-Lind & L.Pasko (Eds.), *Girls, women, and crime: Selected readings* (pp. 231–245). Thousand Oaks, CA: Sage.

Sagatun-Edwards, I. (2003). The legal response to substance abuse during pregnancy. In R.Muraskin (Ed.), *It's a crime: Women and justice* (2nd ed., pp. 129–151). Upper Saddle River, NJ: Prentice Hall.

Schilling, R., Dornig, K., & Lungren, L. (2006). Treatment of heroin dependence: Effectiveness, costs, and benefits of methadone maintenance. *Research on Social Work Practice, 16*(1), 48–56.

Sowers, K., & Rowe, W. (2009). International perspectives on social work practice. In A. R.Roberts (Ed.), *Social workers' desk reference* (2nd ed., pp. 863–868). New York: Oxford University Press.

Spencer, N. (2006, June 5). U.S. prison population continues to soar in 2005. *World Socialist website.* Retrieved October 2006 from http://www.wsws.org/articles/2006/jun2006/pris_j05_html.

Sterling, E., & Stewart, J. (2006, June 24). Undo this legacy of Len Bias's death. *Washington Post*, p. A21.

Stout, D., (2007, December12). Retroactively, panel reduces drug sentences. *New York Times*, p. A30.

Straussner, S. L. A., & Isralowitz, R. (2008). Alcohol and drug problems. In T. Mizrahi & L. E.Davis (Eds), *Encyclopedia of Social Work* (pp. 121–130). New York: Oxford University Press.

Striker, R. (2003, September 26). New federal civil forfeiture laws: Creating an army of informants. *Friends of Liberty.* Retrieved November 30, 2006, from http://www.sianews.com

Substance Abuse and Mental Health Services Administration (SAMHSA). (2006). *Drug Addiction Treatment Act of 2000 (DATA).* Retrieved from http://buprenorphine.samhsa.gov/fulllaw.html.

Substance Abuse and Mental Health Services Administration (SAMHSA). (2009). Treatment as an alternative to jail for people with mental illness. *SAMHSA News, 17*(2), 1–4.

Substance Abuse and Mental Health Services Administration (SAMHSA). (2010). Parity: Landmark legislation takes effect. *SAMHSA News, 18*(1), 1–2.

Szalavitz, M. (2011, April 11). Are Oxycontin babies this decade's crack babies? Time Healthland. *Time.* Retrieved from www.healthland.time.com

Taylor, B., Newton, P., & Brownstein, H. (2003). Drug use among adult female arrestees. *ADAM (Arrestee Drug Abuse Monitoring) 2000 Annual Report.* Washington, DC: U.S. Department of Justice.

Treating, not punishing. (2009, August 29). *Economist*, pp. 43–44.

U.S. Department of Justice. (2006, August). *Federal criminal justice trends: 2003.* Office of Justice Programs. Retrieved from http://www.ojp.usdoj.gov

van Wormer, K., & Bartollas, C. (2010)). *Women and the criminal justice system* (3rd ed.). Boston: Pearson.

Vengerowsky, K. (2011, April 6). Homeless addicts get help without getting clean, sober. *USA Today*, p. 3A.

White House says the war is working—The drug war. (2011, June 2). *Los Angeles Times*. Retrieved from http://latimesblogs.latimes.com

Wilson, D. (2011, June 22). U.S. releases graphic images to deter smokers. *New York Times*, p. B1.

World Health Organization (WHO). (2009a). *Guidelines for the psychosocially assisted pharmacological treatment of opioid dependence*. Geneva, Switzerland: Author.

World Health Organization (WHO), (2009b). *Injecting drug use and prisons*. Geneva, Switzerland: Author.

EPILOGUE:
PROVIDING OPTIONS

Writing a book is a journey; there are the things one expects to find all mapped out and researched, and there are the unexpected discoveries along the way. In scholarly terms, there are the truths one plans to include and the truths that seem to emerge on their own accord from the process.

The major task in writing this book was to present an understanding of addiction, one of the most fascinating and baffling of human conditions, and an understanding that would encompass truths from biology, psychology, and sociology. The major challenge, one that never left us, was somehow to make sense of addiction. Addictive behavior (that insatiable thirst for something), by its very nature, of course makes no sense: What sense is there in a woman so hooked on winning at video poker that she won't take a break to use the toilet? What sense does it make when a father in Thailand sells his daughter into prostitution to get money for another fix of heroin or a previous leader of our country risks the presidency for a moment's gratification?

REVELATIONS

A major theme that emerged in this writing was the importance of motivation. How do you get people who have problems caused by chemicals they have learned to use to get a high (or to escape a low) to come in the door and say, "I'd like to talk about my drug use" or, more generally, "I need someone to talk to"? Programs built on abstinence-only models, the use of forced self-labeling, and urinalysis monitoring have their place, but such forms of treatment are hardly inviting. So the questions become not which of the treatments available (forget for the moment that only one may be available) is best, but how far and how fast will people go toward recovery? And how long will they maintain their progress when treatment is done?

Offering a warm, hospitable environment for treatment is critical. Being able to move to the rhythm set by the client/consumer, not by some faraway bureaucrat (from the insurance company or court), is critical as well. Here is where the theory known as motivational enhancement comes in. For each of the populations studied in this book—alcoholics; drug addicts; persons with eating disorders; compulsive gamblers, shoppers, and the like; addicts with mental disorders; the young and the old; African Americans, Latinos, and European Americans; straight and gay; and even families in need of help—we presented interventions geared toward the group's stages of change. Such interventions were timed, a sort of phase approach, to meet clients where they were rather than where we'd like them to be.

Central to motivationally based treatment, and to the strengths perspective of which it can be considered a part, is the element of choice. In this tradition, practitioners do not encourage clients to rely on the practitioner's expertise. Instead, through dialogue, they help clients discern the pros and cons (for their families and themselves) of any particular course of action. In addiction treatment, choice entails presenting options—for example, trying to find a compatible self-help group such as AA or Al-Anon (GA or OA), giving a Twelve-Step group a chance, linking up with a faith-based group if the client is inclined in a religious direction, attending a moderation management group to control the impulse to binge, or, alternatively, attending no group at all and perhaps choosing individual counseling periodically to work on reducing the harm. Several U.S. district courts, as mentioned in Chapter 13, have confirmed the legal right of criminal justice offenders to have an option to participate in a Twelve-Step group. Other clients should have this privilege as well. There is no "one size fits all" in treatment.

In summary, the imperative of providing options for enhancing client motivation was one of the truths that emerged in writing this book. Other truths emerged as well, some from research (e.g., the impact of craving as seen in brain imaging) and some through the creative process itself, the blending of science and art.

Delving into history, we gained a perspective on the present-day U.S. war on drugs, a "war" so clearly rooted in our puritanical past. We learned from a historical perspective how much the support for the legal prohibition of drugs has been associated with fear of a given drug's effect on a specific minority group, whether of opium on the Chinese or marijuana on the Mexicans or crack cocaine on African Americans. The combination of wild media reports and politics has resulted in highly punitive legislation in each case. The projection of blame on foreign nations as a source of supply has been another political trend with historical roots.

A further revelation that emerged from our study of the history of treatment was just how formidable an advance was the introduction of the disease model. Within the context of American moralism and the work ethic, the spread of respect for the work of AA ensued, coupled with a belief that alcoholism was a disease. The shift from a label of the "bad" to the "mad," which has so often been belittled, was, on the whole, a positive development. Now treatment replaced punishment as the standard response. (Today, in many cases, the treatment *is* the punishment.) Respect for alcoholics and other drug addicts in recovery, for men and women who so often have assumed leadership roles in their communities, was an outgrowth of the alcoholism as a disease movement. Economic aspects of the movement did not go unnoticed; critics rightly ridiculed the hypocrisy of a society marketing harmful drugs such as tobacco and hard liquor and then marketing the treatment for those who succumbed to the grip of addiction. The *diseasing* of society—women who love too much, men who love too little, the credo that abstinence is the only cure for indulgence—was countered by a resurgence of a new form of *moralism*. The factor behind substance misuse is irresponsibility—so goes the explanation popularized in the 1990s.

Arguably, this opposing dogma reflects the maelstrom within North American society itself concerning the use of alcohol and other drugs. Although alcohol consumption is promoted vigorously by advertisers, it is simultaneously restricted through harsh legislation, especially concerning persons under the age of 21. Lacking is a focus on health and moderation. The criminalization of other drug use has led to a war on drugs, fought both militarily, to wipe out the supply side of drugs, and on the home front, through mass incarcerations. Each of the two battling ideologies, both influential today, though with different audiences, describes a small part of the whole. Their sole common ground is in their narrowness and in their contempt for proponents of the opposite camp. Both extreme positions promote doctrine to the neglect of the *individual,* the human being described eloquently by Dennis Wrong (1976) as "that plausible creature whose wagging tongue so often hides the despair in his heart" (p. 112). In this case, the forgotten individual is the alcoholic or addict. Somewhere between overdiseasing the society and blaming addicts for their addictive behavior lies a middle way. Somewhere between criminalization and legalization of harmful drug use there is a middle way (as described in Chapter 13) as well.

COMMENT

Increasingly, at the start of our new century, there is a realization that a single model of addiction and treatment does not fit all, even for offenders within the criminal justice system. There are varieties in treatment needs among males depending on their personality characteristics and the character of their addiction, and there are the special needs of women of childbearing age, of older men and women, and of gays and lesbians. Culturally specific programs

for treatment effectiveness with various racial, religious, and ethnic populations are essential. Common to all these approaches is the realization that instead of trying to eliminate illegal drugs through fighting a war on drugs that
is played out as a war on drug users, we can focus on limiting the damage
that some people do to themselves and to society through this drug misuse.

Harm reduction services provide individualized treatment and strengthen
community action. Harm reduction initiatives, in contrast to the "zero tolerance" approach, include policies such as needle exchange (which has been
shown to reduce the spread of AIDS), methadone maintenance to enable addicts to live fairly normal lives, and therapy grounded in motivational enhancement principles to help clients move at their own pace from levels of
heavy alcohol and other drug consumption to ever-decreasing levels of drug
use. Harm reduction concentrates on achievable goals based on client self-
determination; interventions are timed to relate to where the client is in his
or her readiness to change. Interventions ideally are also timed to relate to
the stages of recovery—biological, psychological, social, and spiritual.

LOOKING BACK

The three opening chapters of the book were conceived as a prologue to the
more detailed discussion that followed. Chapter 1, The Nature of Addiction,
took us right into the pain and sorrow associated with substance misuse and
dependence in contrast to the miracle that is recovery. Chapter 2, Historical
Perspectives, could have been subtitled When Will We Ever Learn? Here society's futile attempts to control the flow of drugs and people's bad habits
were chronicled. The presentation of the strengths perspective, a conceptualization borrowed from social work, showed how a focus on people's strengths
is a viable, indeed essential, element in addiction treatment.

Consistent with the biopsychosocial framework of addiction treatment,
the core material of this text is organized into three major parts; each part
corresponds to one key component in addiction, with ramifications for treatment. The *biological* component (Part II) focused on exciting new research.
Chapter 3 explored the biochemical basis of tolerance, withdrawal, craving,
and the memory factor in addiction. As science learns more and more about
the key role of the brain in addiction and can demonstrate through magnetic
resonance imaging how the addicted brain is different from the nonaddicted
brain, there is fresh hope for new treatments. A description of such pharmaceutical remedies was the subject of the latter part of this chapter.

Also included in the biological portion of the book were the following
two chapters on gender issues and, next, on behavioral disorders. Biological
aspects of addiction related to gender as well as issues pertinent to sexual orientation and gender-specific interventions were major themes of Chapter 4.
Half of this chapter dealt with sexual orientation and substance misuse issues.
Cognitive work was the theme of Chapter 5 on behavioral addictions, including disordered gambling, spending addiction, eating disorders, hoarding, and

spending addiction. Motivational enhancement strategies were shown to have a special relevance to the treatment of these disorders.

The *psychology* of addiction is the second major division of this text. Under the rubric of psychology—Part III of the book—first addiction and its treatment across the life span were viewed (Chapter 6). Special attention was paid in this chapter to risks specific to adolescence, addictive behavior in the middle years, and the importance of grief work, spiritual healing, and relapse prevention strategies for work with older adults.

New to this edition were Chapter 7, devoted exclusively to assessment, with an emphasis on eliciting strengths, and Chapter 8, the intervention chapter. Strategies for group therapy, along with recommended exercises directed toward early-stage recovery, were provided in this chapter. For work with persons with co-occurring disorders, the case was made in Chapter 9 for integrated treatment (as opposed to separate treatment for mental disability and for addiction).

The *social aspects* of addiction made up the concluding portion of this book, Part IV. Chapter 10 explored family risks and resiliencies. The focus was on how addiction affects the lives of the addict's loved ones (sometimes to the point that the love flies out the window). Innovations of this chapter, and of this book, were the adaptation of the stages-of-change model to family recovery and the "rename, reframe, reclaim" framework for strengths-based treatment.

Chapter 11 described the various self-help groups. Here the questions considered were: What are the strengths of Twelve-Step treatment? How have Twelve-Step groups helped people? What are some alternative mutual-help groups? Strengths-based approaches, similarly, were directed toward the cultural- and ethnic-sensitive interventions described in Chapter 12.

Addiction Treatment: A Strengths Perspective concluded with a survey of public policy. This time, harm reduction was viewed in policy terms rather than practice terms. Chapter 13 described governmental policies affecting treatment provision and funding as well. Far from a narrow or radical ideology, harm reduction is simply realistic and is about saving lives. Broad in focus, harm reduction, as we saw in earlier chapters, helps clients make healthy choices; joining a Twelve-Step total-abstinence group is one such option.

The unique feature of this book, we think, is not the presentation of content in neat biopsychosocial divisions (a challenge in itself) or the inclusion of eating disorders, compulsive gambling, and Internet use along with the chemical addictions. No, the uniqueness is that our application of the principles of the strengths perspective was directed to treatment modalities at all and then that it was directed toward the strong points in various treatments that are often viewed as in opposition to one another. Consistent with this perspective, we extend our appreciation to the vibrant field of addictions and to the many dedicated workers who have passed this way. The large number of recovering alcoholics and other addicts in society, some of whom are professionals in the field themselves, is testimony to the quality of that work. The field is changing rapidly, professionally and economically. But what now is, is not necessarily better than what was.

REFERENCE

Wrong, D. (1976). The oversocialized conception of man in modern sociology. In L. Coser & B. Rosenberg (Eds.), *Sociology theory* (pp. 104–113). New York: Macmillan.

APPENDIX: RESOURCES

ADVOCACY/ASSOCIATIONS/COALITIONS

Addiction Treatment Forum (hundreds of updated websites and journals listed here): http://www.atforum.com

American Association for the Treatment of Opioid Dependence: http://www.aatod.org

American Society of Addiction Medicine: http://www.asam.org

Coalition Against Present Drug Policy: http://www.november.org

Drug Policy Alliance: http://www.drugpolicy.org

Harm Reduction Coalition: http://www.harmreduction.org

Housing First: http://www.desc.org/index

Mothers Against Drunk Driving: http://www.madd.org

Motivational Interviewing (resources for clinicians): http://www.motivationalinterviewing.org

National Association of Alcoholism and Drug Abuse Counselors: http://www.naadac.org

National Association of Drug Court Professionals: http://www.nadcp.org

National Association of Social Workers, ATOD section: http://www.naswdc.org (see section on ATOD)

National Drug Court Institute: http://www.ndci.org

Restorative Justice: http://www.restorativejustice.org

CENTERS/INSTITUTES/COUNCILS

American Council for Drug Education: http://www.acde.org

The Beckley Foundation: www.beckleyfoundation.org

Center for Education and Drug Abuse Research: http://www.pitt.edu/~cedar

Child Welfare League of America: http://www.cwla.org

Drug Strategies, "Making Drug Policy at the State Level": http://www.drugstrategies.org

Hazelden Foundation: http://www.hazelden.org

Moderation Management: http://www.moderation.org

National Center on Addiction and Substance Abuse at Columbia University: http://www.casacolumbia.org

Pride Institute (treatment for gays and lesbians): http://www.pride-institute.com

National Council on Alcoholism and Drug Dependence: http://www.ncadd.org

Rational Recovery: http://www.rational.org

Redfern Clinic: http://www.redfernclinic.com

Self-Management and Recovery Training: http://www.smartrecovery.org

FEDERAL GOVERNMENT

Centers for Application of Prevention Technologies: http://captus.samhsa.gov

Drug and Crime Statistics: http://www.ojp.usdoj.gov

National Clearinghouse for Alcohol and Drug Information: http://www.higheredcenter.org/resources/national-clearinghouse-alcohol-and-drug-information-ncadi

National Council on Alcohol and Drug Dependence: http://www.ncadd.org

National Institute on Alcohol Abuse and Alcoholism: http://www.niaaa.nih.gov

National Institute on Drug Abuse: http://www.nida.nih.gov

National Institute of Justice: http://www.ojp.usdoj.gov/nij

National Institute of Mental Health: http://www.nimh.nih.gov

National Women's Health Resource Center: http://www.healthywomen.org

Office of National Drug Control Policy: http://www.whitehousedrugpolicy.gov

Substance Abuse and Mental Health Services Administration: http://www.samhsa.gov

Substance Abuse Treatment Facility Locator: http://dasis3.samhsa.gov

INTERNATIONAL

(Canadian) Centre for Addiction and Mental Health: http://www.camh.net

Canadian Centre on Substance Abuse: http://www.ccsa.ca

International Harm Reduction Association: http://www.ihra.net

World Health Organization: www.who.org.int/substance_abuse/en

PREVENTION

Center for Substance Abuse Treatment: http://www.samhsa.gov/about/csat.aspx

Drug and Alcohol Treatment and Prevention Global Network: http://www.drugnet.net

Help for smokers: http://www.quitnet.org

Tobacco Information and Prevention Source: http://www.cdc.gov/tobacco

RESEARCH

Addiction Treatment Forum: http://www.atforum.com

American Indian Health Resources: http://www.ldb.org/vl/geo/america/indi_hn.htm

Dual Diagnosis Website: http://users.erols.com/ksciacca/

Effectiveness Bank Alert: http://findings.org.uk/free_search.htm

HelpGuide (gambling addiction): http://www.helpguide.org/mental/gambling_addiction.htm

Information for Practice: http://www.nyu.edu/socialwork/ip

Information on eating disorders, teen substance abuse, and gambling: http://www.addictions.net

Internet Addiction and Online Addiction: http://psychcentral.com/netaddiction

National Association of Lesbian and Gay Addiction Professionals: http://www.nalgap.org/PDF/Resources/LGBT.pdf

The National Center on Addiction and Substance Abuse at Columbia University: http://www.casacolumbia.org

The Partnership at Drugfree.org (provides an e-mail alert service for weekly research): http://www.drugfree.org

Racial and Ethnic Groups, Reports and Data: http://oas.samhsa.gov/race.htm

Social Work Curriculum on Alcohol Use Disorders: http://pubs.niaaa.nih.gov/publications/social/main.html

Spanish Language Materials: http://oas.samhsa.gov/Spanish.cfm

Web of Addictions: http://www.well.com/user/woa

SELF-HELP

Adult Children of Alcoholics World Service Organization: http://www.adultchildren.org

Alcoholics Anonymous: http://www.aa.org

Al-Anon Family Groups: http://www.al-anon.alateen.org/

Children of Alcoholics Foundation: http://www.coaf.org

Cocaine Anonymous: www.ca.org; www.cocaineanonymous.com

Families of compulsive gamblers: http://www.gam-anon.org

Families of drug addicts: http://nar-anon.org/naranongroups.htm

Gamblers Anonymous: http://www.gamblersanonymous.org

Methadone Anonymous: http://www.methadone-anonymous.org

Methamphetamine group: http://www.crystalmeth.or

Narcotics Anonymous: http://www.na.org

National Organization on Fetal Alcohol Syndrome: http://www.nofas.or

SMART Recovery: http://www.smartrecovery.org

Students Against Destructive Decisions (also Students Against Drunk Driving): http://www.saddonline.com

Women for Sobriety: http://www.womenforsobriety.org

INDEX